1,001

BEST
HOT AND
SPICY
RECIPES

Delicious, Easy-to-Make
Recipes from Around the Globe

DAVE DEWITT

**SURREY
BOOKS**

CHICAGO

Surrey Books is an imprint of Agate Publishing, Inc.

Printed in the United States of America

Library of Congress Cataloging-in-Publication Data

DeWitt, Dave.
  1,001 best hot and spicy recipes : delicious, easy-to-make recipes from around the globe / Dave DeWitt.
      p. cm.
  Summary: "Hot and spicy recipes, from appetizers to desserts, for the home cook"—Provided by publisher.
  Includes index.
  ISBN-13: 978-1-57284-113-0 (pbk.)
  ISBN-10: 1-57284-113-3 (pbk.)
  1. Cookbooks. 2. Cooking (Spices) 3. Quick and easy cooking. I. Title.
  II. Title: One thousand one best hot and spicy recipes. III. Title:
  One thousand and one best hot and spicy recipes.
  TX714.D494 2010
  641.5'55—dc22 2010027933

14 13 12 11 10   10 9 8 7 6 5 4 3 2 1

Agate and Surrey books are available in bulk at discount prices. For more information, go to agatepublishing.com.

Selected Books by Dave DeWitt

The Fiery Cuisines (1984), with Nancy Gerlach
The Whole Chile Pepper Book (1990), with Nancy Gerlach
The Pepper Garden (1993), with Paul W. Bosland
A World of Curries (1994), with Arthur Pais
The Habanero Cookbook (1995), with Nancy Gerlach
The Hot Sauce Bible (1996), with Chuck Evans
Hot & Spicy Caribbean (1996), with Mary Jane Wilan and Melissa
  T. Stock
Great Bowls of Fire (1997), with W. C. Longacre
The Chile Pepper Encyclopedia (1999)
Barbecue Inferno (2001), with Nancy Gerlach
The Spicy Food Lover's Bible (2005), with Nancy Gerlach
Da Vinci's Kitchen (2006)
Cuisines of the Southwest (2007)
The Complete Chile Pepper Book (2009), with Paul W. Bosland
Thomas Jefferson and the Founding Foodies (2010)

DEDICATION

This book is for all the chileheads who have supported and encouraged me all these years by buying my books, reading and subscribing to the magazines I've edited, visiting the SuperSite, coming to the Fiery Foods & Barbecue Show, and sharing their houses and kitchens when Mary Jane and I visit.

ACKNOWLEDGMENTS

Thanks to the cooks who contributed recipes to this collection: Peter Aiken, Michael Baim, Peggy Barnes, Chel Beeson, Deborah Berlin, Lula Bertrán, Thomas Brown, Ellen Burr, Cindy Castillo, Pat Chapman, Michelle Cox, Suzy Dayton, Jeanette DeAnda, Jasmine DeLuisa, Alois Dogue, Rebecca Chastenet de Gry, Jeff Corydon, Robert Dixon, Binh Duong, Rudolfo de Garay, Tim Fex, Stella Fong, Winifred Galarza, Kathy Gallantine, Linda Gant, Nancy and Jeff Gerlach, Janet Go, John Gray, Jeff Gustie, Antonio Heras-Duran, Sharon Hudgins, Shirley Jordan, David Karp, Mary Kinnunen, Judy Knapp, Arnold Krochmal, W. C. Longacre, Leyla Loued-Khenissime, Tita Libin, Donald and Sue Louie, Linda Lynton, Daryl Malloy, Neil and Sandy Mann, André Niederhauser, Rosemary Ann Ogilvie, Jim Peyton, Rosa Rajkovic, Judith Ritter, Loretta Salazar, Todd Sanson, Chris Schlesinger, Devagi Shanmugan, Bud Spillar, Richard Sterling, Mike Stines, Melissa T. Stock, Foo Swasdee, David Tucker, Mary Jane Wilan, Charles Wiley, Martin Yan, and Gloria Zimmerman.

CONTENTS

PREFACE
The Pods That Devoured Me

For the past three decades, my life and career have been consumed by chile peppers and fiery foods. That's why I'm called "The Pope of Peppers" in the media. I've edited two magazines on the subject, Chile Pepper from 1987 to 1996 and Fiery Foods & BBQ from 1997 to 2008. I publish the huge Fiery Foods & Barbecue SuperSite (www.fiery-foods.com), which includes hundreds of articles and thousands of recipes that has been online since 1996. With various coauthors—especially Nancy Gerlach and my wife, Mary Jane Wilan—I have written more than thirty books featuring chile peppers, on subjects ranging from gardening, to health aspects, to food history, to cooking. This is number thirty-seven.

This book is composed of the best dishes from my collection of chile pepper–laden recipes from around the world that I collected on site, from freelance contributors to the magazines and the SuperSite, from coauthors, and by researching the authentic, obscure, and out-of-print cookbooks from all over the world that I collected for my library. That library now resides in Special Collections at the New Mexico State University Library, in an archive that I endowed, along with my chile pepper–related papers, clippings, manuscripts, photographs, and digital material.

In some chapters in this book, the recipes are grouped by type of dish; in the others, they are organized to reflect the order of chile peppers' spread around the globe: South and Central America, Mexico, the Caribbean, the United States, Europe, the Mediterranean and Middle East, Africa, the Indian Subcontinent, and Asia and the Pacific. There is little doubt that this book is the largest and most comprehensive cookbook ever published on this subject. I certainly hope it heats up your life!

INTRODUCTION
Chile Peppers, Commercial Products, and Substitutions

There are literally thousands of varieties of chile peppers grown around the world, but only a few dozen are commonly used for cooking, and all those used in the recipes in this book have substitutions. The heat of any chile depends on two factors: its genetic makeup and the environment in which it's grown—the soil, the nutrients applied to the plant, the weather, and the amount of water. I believe that both factors contribute equally to the heat level. Often, chiles that are stressed from a lack of water or extreme environmental temperatures have a higher heat level than they otherwise would.

Generally speaking, the smaller the pod, the hotter the chile. The one exception is the habanero, which is larger and hotter than the smaller hot chiles called bird peppers—the piquins, chiltepins, and the smaller Asian and African varieties.

Fresh Pods

Available from the garden or the market, fresh peppers are increasing in popularity as they become more commonly available. The most ubiquitous peppers are, of course, the familiar bells, which have no heat unless they are a variety called "Mexi-Bell," which has a mild bite. The poblano, similar in size to a bell, is a Mexican pepper with moderate to mild heat which is often stuffed with cheese and baked.

The most readily available hot peppers in the produce sections of supermarkets these days are jalapeños, serranos, habaneros, and yellow wax peppers. Jalapeños and serranos—either green or fresh red—have similar uses. They are often floated whole in soups or stews to provide a little extra bite and removed before serving. The serranos—smaller, thinner, and hotter than jalapeños—are the classic chiles of the Mexican pico de gallo fresh salsas. Habaneros (they are not spelled "habañero") and their relatives in the same species are the world's hottest peppers, lantern-shaped orange or red devils that have a unique, fruity aroma in addition to their powerful punch. Use them with caution. Generally speaking, any of the small fresh peppers may be substituted for one another; however, they are not an acceptable substitute for poblanos or New Mexican varieties. The yellow wax peppers are usually mild and are often stuffed or chopped for use in salsas and salads.

Several varieties of the long, green New Mexican chiles are available fresh in the Southwest and occasionally in other locations. The "NuMex 6-4" variety is the most common and is available from August through early November. Its hotter cousin, "Sandia," is usually not seen in the green, or immature, form. The mildest New Mexican variety is the "Anaheim," a California variety that is available most of the year. Occasionally, New Mexican chiles are identified by their original grower (such as "Barker") or by a regional appellation ("Chimayo," "Hatch," or "Luna County"), which further confuses the issue. I should point out that Hatch is not a chile variety, and not enough chiles are grown in the vicinity of that little town to supply all the roadside vendors that call their chiles by that name. The Hatch chile is a marketing myth, and vendors in that town regularly import them from other locations and call them "Hatch."

All of the long green chiles must be roasted and peeled before they can be used in a recipe. Blistering or roasting the chile is the process of heating the chile over flames to the point that the tough, transparent skin separates from the meat of the chile so it can be removed. The method is quite simple. While working with the chiles, be sure to wear rubber or latex gloves to protect yourself from the capsaicin (the chemical that gives chiles their heat) that can burn your hands and any other part of your body that you touch. Before roasting, cut a small slit close to the stem in each chile so that the steam can escape. The chiles can then be placed on a baking sheet and put directly under the broiler or on a screen on the top of the stove.

My favorite method is to place the pods on a charcoal grill about 5 to 6 inches from the coals. Blisters will soon indicate that the skin is separating, but be sure that the chiles are blistered all over, or they will not peel properly. Immediately wrap the roasted chiles in damp towels or place them in a plastic bag for ten to fifteen minutes—this steams them and loosens the skins. For crisper, less tender chiles, plunge them into ice water to stop the cooking process.

Green chile is a low-acid fruit, and for that reason I do not recommend home canning. It can be done, but only with a pressure canner and only by carefully following all the manufacturer's specific instructions. I find freezing to be a much easier and more flavor-retaining method of preservation.

After roasting the chiles, freeze them in the form in which you plan to use them—whole, in strips, or chopped. If you are storing them in strips or chopped, peel the pods first. If they are to be frozen whole (rather than chopped), the pods should be roasted, but they do not have to be peeled first. In fact, they are easier to peel after they have been frozen. A handy way to put up chopped or diced chiles is to freeze them in plastic ice cube trays with sections. When they're completely frozen, they can be popped out of the trays and stored in a bag in the freezer. When making a soup or a stew, just drop in a cube! This eliminates the need to hack apart a large slab of frozen chiles when you just need a couple of ounces. Do not buy canned chiles except for chipotles in adobo sauce. The canned green chiles are not spicy, and the packers use steam or a lye bath to remove the skins, which results in an off taste.

The smaller chiles—habaneros, serranos, and jalapeños—can be frozen without processing. Wash the chiles, dry them, arrange them in a single layer on a cookie sheet, and freeze. After they are frozen solid, double-bag them in freezer bags with the air forced out. Their texture holds up surprisingly well in the freezer.

Substitutions for fresh chiles include hot sauces and dried pods of a similar size that have been soaked in water to rehydrate them. You will have to experiment to discover precisely how much hot sauce to use as a substitute because of varying heat levels, but a rule of thumb is that a teaspoon or two of habanero hot sauce will substitute for one whole pod.

Dried Pods

As is true of fresh peppers, the smaller the chile, the hotter it will be. The large dried peppers, such as ancho (a dried poblano) and the New Mexican varieties, are mild enough to be the principal ingredients of sauces. However, when a lot of these chiles are concentrated in a sauce, they become a food rather than a spice, and the resulting heat level can be surprisingly high. (The same is true when the larger peppers are in their green, immature form.) The smaller varieties, such as piquin, are too hot for this purpose and are generally used as a spice in cooking, especially in stir-frying. All dried peppers can be ground into powders (see the next section).

Four main large peppers are used as the base for sauces: ancho, pasilla, New Mexican, and guajillo (a smaller ancestor of the New Mexican chiles). The ancho is a wide, dark pepper with a raisiny aroma. It is the only pepper that is commonly stuffed in its dried form (the pod is softened in water first). The pasilla is a long, thin, dark pepper that also has a raisiny or nutty aroma. Along with the ancho, it commonly appears in Mexican mole sauces.

The red New Mexican chiles are commonly hung in long strings, or ristras, until they are ready to be used in cooking. Then, they are most often rehydrated and combined with onions, garlic, oil, spices, and water to make the classic New Mexican red chile sauce, a common topping for enchiladas in the Southwest. The guajillos, a shorter and hotter version of the New Mexican chiles, are commonly used in sauces in northern Mexico.

Another favorite dried chile pepper is the chipotle, a smoke-dried red jalapeño that has a fiery, smoky flavor. It is available loose in its dried form or canned in adobo sauce. The latter is easier to use because it's already rehydrated. To rehydrate the dried chipotles, simply soak them in hot water for an hour or more. If you can't find chipotles, substitute a hot red chile powder with a little liquid smoke. It's not perfect, but it will work.

There are a bewildering number of small, hot pods, ranging in size from that of a little fingernail (the chiltepin) to the six-inch, skinny-but-hot cayenne. Other varieties include piquin, Thai, santaka, de arbol, mirasol, and tabasco. These chiles appear in stir-fry dishes, are floated in soups or stews, or are used to add heat to sauces that are too mild. They can be freely substituted for one another in most worldwide recipes.

Chile Powders

All chiles can be dried and ground into powder—and most are, including the habanero. Crushed chiles with some of the seeds are called quebrado. Coarse powders are referred to as caribe, while the finer powders are termed molido. The milder powders, such as New Mexican, can also be used as the base for sauces, but the hotter powders, such as cayenne and piquin, are used when heat is needed more than flavor. In my home, I actually have more powders available than the whole pods because the powders are concentrated and take up less storage space. I store them in small, airtight bottles. The fresher the powders, the better they taste, so don't grind up too many pods. Use an electric spice mill, and be sure to wear a painter's mask to protect your nose and throat from the pungent powder. The colors of the powders vary from a bright, electric red-orange (chiltepins), to light green (dried jalapeños), to a dark brown that verges on black (ancho). I love to experiment by changing the powders called for in recipes.

Other Chile Products

A vast number of foods and condiments now contain chile peppers. Quite a few of these products are handy for cooks who love all things hot and spicy. Look for chile-infused vinegars, oils, mustards, catsup, cheeses, pickles, hot sauces, salad dressings, jams and jellies, soups, pastas, potato and corn chips, curry powders and pastes, nuts, and even candies.

Killing the Burn

If you use too much chile in a recipe and the result is unbearably hot, the only thing you can do is dilute the dish by adding more of all the non-chile ingredients. This is not always possible, especially with grilled meats. In that case, all that you can do is rinse off the rub or coating covering the meat and place it back on the grill for a few minutes. If you get burned out from food that is too spicy, forget the false remedies, such as sugar, bread, water, tea, or beer. The liquids, mostly water-based, are not miscible with the capsaicin in chiles that causes the discomfort. The only thing that truly works is dairy products—the thicker the better. A protein called casein in dairy products strips the capsaicin molecules from the receptors in the mouth and tongue, so use heavy cream, sour cream, yogurt, or ice cream to kill the burn.

More Information

For detailed information on chile varieties and how to identify them, grow them, and preserve them, see my book with Dr. Paul Bosland, *The Complete Chile Pepper Book* (Timber Press, 2009) and the Fiery Foods & Barbecue SuperSite at www.Fiery-Foods.com.

ONE

Kitchen Essentials: Chile Pastes, Spice Mixes, Chutneys, Oils, Vinegars, Rubs, Butters, and Stocks

- - - - - - - - - - - - - - -

Here are the basic recipes you will need not only to make a lot of the other recipes in this book, but also to prepare many of the recipes you will encounter in your ongoing exploration of the world of chile peppers and fiery foods. The recipes here are grouped by their geographical origin.

Aji Molido

Yield: About 1 cup (236 mL)   Heat Scale: Hot

This South American paste can be used as a substitute whenever fresh chiles are called for. It will keep for two weeks or more in the refrigerator; for longer storage, increase the vinegar and reduce the olive oil. For a red paste, substitute 15 dried red New Mexican chiles, soaked in water and drained. For a green paste, substitute 10 green New Mexican chiles, roasted, peeled, and chopped. For a much hotter paste, add 5 habanero chiles. All chiles should have the stems and seeds removed.

20 fresh yellow aji chiles (or substitute yellow wax hot peppers or jalapeños), stems and seeds removed, chopped
¼ cup (59 mL) olive oil
1 clove garlic, peeled and minced
2 tablespoons (30 mL) distilled white vinegar
1 teaspoon (5 mL) salt

1. Combine all ingredients in a bowl. Transfer the mixture to food processor in batches and purée to a fine paste.

Achiote Oil

Yield: 1 cup (236 mL)   Heat Scale: Medium

This oil is used to add color and flavor to dishes. Use it in place of vegetable oil in the dishes in this book. Look for annatto (achiote) seeds that are a bright-reddish color; seeds that are brownish in color are old and have probably lost much of their flavor.

1 cup (236 mL) best-quality olive oil or high-quality vegetable oil
½ cup (118 mL) annatto (achiote) seeds, crushed
1 dried malagueta chile (or substitute piquin or Japanese)
1 bay leaf (optional)

1. Combine the oil, annatto seeds, red chile, and bay leaf (if using) in a nonreactive heavy saucepan and allow the mixture to steep for 40 minutes, stirring occasionally.
2. Bring the mixture to a low and gentle boil over medium heat, stirring constantly. Remove the saucepan from the heat and allow the mixture to cool thoroughly.
3. Strain the oil through a very fine sieve. Pour the strained oil into a bottle and cap tightly. Refrigerated and tightly capped, this oil will remain usable up to six months.

Farofa de Malagueta
(Brazilian Chile Condiment)

Yield: 3 cups (708 mL)   Heat Scale: Medium

Farofas are Brazilian condiments made with manioc flour, which is available at Latin markets. They are commonly sprinkled over the top of Brazilian meals such as bifes. Farofieros, those cooks who specialize in the preparation of farofas, have been known to make eighty or more variations. Warning: Palm oil is high in saturated fat.

¼ cup (59 mL) palm oil (or substitute vegetable oil with 3 teaspoons paprika added)
1 cup (236 mL) chopped onion
2 hard-boiled eggs, chopped
1 teaspoon (5 mL) minced fresh or pickled malagueta chile, or substitute piquin (dry chiles can be used if soaked in water first)
2 cups (473 mL) manioc flour or dried bread crumbs

1. Heat the palm oil in a frying pan over high heat and fry the onions until golden brown.
2. Add the hard-boiled eggs and sauté the mixture for 1 minute.
3. Add the chiles and manioc flour and cook, stirring constantly, until the mixture turns golden.

Chiltepines en Escabeche
(Pickled Chiltepins)

Yield: 1 pint (473 mL)   Heat Scale: Extremely Hot

In the states of Sonora and Sinaloa, fresh green and red chiltepins are preserved in vinegar and salt. Used as a condiment, they are popped into the mouth when eating any food—except, perhaps, flan. Since fresh chiltepins are available in the United States only in Arizona and Texas, adventurous cooks and gardeners must grow their own. The tiny chiles are preserved in three layers in a sterilized 1-pint (473 mL) jar. (Note: This recipe requires advance preparation.)

2 cups (473 mL) fresh red and/or green chiltepins
3 cloves garlic, peeled
1 tablespoon (15 mL) salt
3 tablespoons (45 mL) apple cider vinegar

1. Fill the jar one-third full of chiltepins. Add 1 clove garlic, 1 teaspoon (5 mL) salt, and 1 tablespoon (15 mL) apple cider vinegar.
2. Repeat this process twice more, and fill the jar to within ½ inch (1 cm) of the top with water.
3. Seal the jar and allow it to sit for 15 to 30 days.

Chipotles Adobados
(Chipotle Chiles in Adobo Sauce)

Yield: About 1½ quarts (1.4 L)   Heat Scale: Hot

Here's a pickled chile recipe from Tlaxcala. These sweet-hot pickled chiles can be the basis of a sauce of their own if they're further puréed, or they can be served as a condiment with enchiladas and other main dishes.

½ pound (224 g) dried chipotle chiles, stems removed
1 quart (.95 L) distilled white vinegar
1 head garlic, peeled and crushed
½ cup (118 mL) piloncillo, or ½ cup (118 mL) packed brown sugar
1 cup (236 mL) roasted and peeled green chile, such as poblano or
New Mexican
2 medium tomatoes, chopped
6 black peppercorns
3 bay leaves
1 teaspoon (5 mL) ground cumin
Salt, to taste

1. Soak the chipotles in water until they rehydrate, at least an hour, then drain.
2. In a saucepan, combine half the vinegar, half the garlic, and the brown sugar. Cook this mixture over low heat for about 20 minutes, then add the chipotles.
3. In another pan, combine the green chile, tomato, remaining garlic, peppercorns, bay leaves, cumin, remaining vinegar, and salt to taste. Cook over medium heat for about 30 minutes, covered. Add the chipotle chile mixture, stir well, and store in sterilized jars.

Salpicón de Yucatán
(Yucatecan Vegetarian Radish Relish)

Yield: ½ cup (118 mL)   Heat Scale: Medium

Nancy and Jeff Gerlach often wrote about this relish from their favorite region in Mexico, the Yucatán Peninsula, where they retired to a house on the beach. Nancy notes, "The first time we were served this relish of 'little pieces' we were surprised by the use of radishes, which added not only flavor, but an interesting texture to the salsa. For variety, add some diced tomatoes or avocados." Serve this relish over seafood.

2 habanero chiles, stems and seeds removed, diced (or substitute
4 jalapeño or 4 serrano chiles)
1 large red onion, peeled and diced
8 to 10 radishes, thickly sliced
3 tablespoons (45 mL) lime juice (fresh preferred)
3 tablespoons (45 mL) chopped fresh cilantro

1. Combine all the ingredients, except the cilantro, in a bowl.
2. Allow to sit for an hour to blend the flavors. Toss with the cilantro and serve.

Recado Rojo
(Red Seasoning Paste)

Yield: ½ cup (118 mL)   Heat Scale: Mild

Here is a classic Yucatán seasoning paste from Nancy and Jeff Gerlach, who note, "This is the most popular of all the different recados, and it is very typical of Yucatán. It is used to add both flavor and color to foods, and is most commonly used for pibils, or stewed pork dishes. The red color comes from the annatto seeds, which also add a unique flavor to this tasty paste. Available commercially as achiote paste, Recado Rojo is far better when prepared at home."

4 tablespoons (60 mL) ground annatto (achiote) seeds
1 tablespoon (15 mL) mild red chile powder
1 tablespoon (15 mL) dried oregano (Mexican preferred)
10 whole black peppercorns
½ teaspoon (2.5 mL) salt
1 (1-inch [2.5 cm]) cinnamon stick
4 whole cloves
2 whole allspice berries
½ teaspoon (2.5 mL) cumin seeds
3 cloves garlic, peeled and chopped
3 tablespoons (45 mL) distilled white vinegar

1. Place the annatto seeds, chile powder, oregano, peppercorns, salt, cinnamon, cloves, allspice, and cumin in a spice or coffee grinder and process to a fine powder. Add the remaining ingredients and grind to a thick paste, adding a little water if the mixture is too thick.
2. Allow to sit for an hour or overnight to blend the flavors.

West Indian Masala

Yield: About ½ cup (118 mL)

Heat Scale: Medium, with the habanero powder

This spice blend is superior to commercial masalas because the freshly ground seeds have not oxidized and lost their flavor. Generally speaking, when turmeric is added to masala, it becomes curry powder. Adding habanero powder makes it hot masala, which is used in Caribbean curries.

6 tablespoons (90 mL) coriander seeds
1 teaspoon (5 mL) fenugreek seeds
2 teaspoons (10 mL) fennel seeds
1 teaspoon (5 mL) mustard seeds
1½ teaspoons (7.5 mL) cumin seeds
2 teaspoons (10 mL) turmeric (optional)
½ teaspoon (2.5 mL) habanero powder (optional)

1. Toast all the seeds in a dry skillet over high heat, stirring well, until they begin to pop. Lower the heat and cook for an additional 5 minutes, taking care not to burn the seeds. Set aside to cool.
2. Once the seeds are completely cool, grind them finely in a spice mill or with a mortar and pestle. If you wish to make a curry powder, add the turmeric and mix well. Add the habanero powder for a hotter masala.

Colombo Curry Paste

Yield: ½ cup (118 mL)   Heat Scale: Hot

This fiery-hot curry blend from Martinique and Guadeloupe is named after Colombo, the capital of Sri Lanka, which is appropriate considering the heat levels of the curries from that island. The pepper of choice, shaped like the behind of Mrs. Jacques, is recommended because of its unique, fruity aroma. Habaneros are the perfect substitute.

1½ tablespoons (22 mL) turmeric
1½ tablespoons (22 mL) coriander seeds
1½ tablespoons (22 mL) mustard seeds
1½ tablespoons (22 mL) black peppercorns
1½ tablespoons (22 mL) cumin seeds
3 cloves garlic, peeled and crushed
1 (1-inch [2.5 cm]) piece fresh ginger, peeled and grated
2 Le Derriere de Madame Jacques peppers (or habaneros), stems and seeds removed, minced

1. In a spice mill, combine the turmeric, coriander seeds, mustard seeds, black peppercorns, and cumin seeds. Grind the mixture into a coarse powder.
2. Transfer this powder to a bowl and add the garlic, ginger, and chiles. Mix well, adding water as needed to achieve a medium paste.
3. Let sit for at least an hour to blend the flavors.

Jamaican Jerk Dry Rub
Yield: About ½ cup (118 mL)   Heat Scale: Hot

Jamaican jerk barbecue is a fine art. When I visited a jerk center in Ocho Rios, the jerkmaster told me that the secret was in the spices—the rub that gives the pork and chicken such an intense, spicy-hot flavor. Most Jamaican jerk cooks use a dry rub, but on occasion, especially for fish or poultry, the rub is transformed into a paste or marinade by adding vegetable oil. This rub also can be sprinkled over steamed or grilled vegetables.

2 tablespoons (30 mL) onion powder
1 tablespoon (15 mL) ground allspice
1 tablespoon (15 mL) ground thyme
2 teaspoons (10 mL) ground cinnamon
2 teaspoons (10 mL) ground cloves
2 teaspoons (10 mL) brown sugar
2 teaspoons (10 mL) habanero powder
1 teaspoon (5 mL) freshly ground black pepper
1 teaspoon (5 mL) garlic powder
1 teaspoon (5 mL) ground coriander
½ teaspoon (2.5 mL) ground nutmeg
½ teaspoon (2.5 mL) salt

1. Combine all the ingredients in a bowl and mix well. Store any unused rub in a sealed container in the freezer.

North Coast Jerk Marinade
Yield: 2–3 cups (500–708 mL)   Heat Scale: Hot

Variations on Jamaican jerk sauces and marinades range from the early, simple pastes of three or four ingredients to the more modern and rather complicated concoctions with as many twenty-one spices, herbs, and vegetables. By varying the amount of vegetable oil and lime juice, the cook can change the consistency from a paste to a sauce. Traditionally, jerk marinade is used with pork, chicken, or fish.

¼ cup (59 mL) whole Jamaican pimento berries (or ⅛ cup [30 mL] ground allspice)
3 Scotch bonnet chiles (or habaneros), stems and seeds removed, chopped
10 green onions, trimmed and chopped
½ cup (118 mL) chopped onion
4 cloves garlic, peeled and chopped
4 bay leaves, crushed
1 (3-inch [7.5 cm]) piece ginger, peeled and chopped
⅓ cup (79 mL) fresh thyme
1 teaspoon (5 mL) freshly ground nutmeg
1 teaspoon (5 mL) freshly ground cinnamon
1 teaspoon (5 mL) salt (or more, to taste)
1 tablespoon (15 mL) freshly ground black pepper
¼ cup (59 mL) vegetable oil
¼ cup (59 mL) lime juice

1. Roast the pimento berries in a dry skillet over high heat until they are aromatic, about 2 minutes. Remove them from the heat and crush them to a powder in a mortar or spice mill.

2. Add the pimento powder and the remaining ingredients to a food processor and blend with enough water to make a paste or sauce. Transfer to a jar and store in the refrigerator, where it will keep for a month or more.

Trinidad Herb Seasoning Paste

Yield: 2–3 cups (500–708 mL)   Heat Scale: Medium

This seasoning paste and marinade enlivens otherwise bland grilled lamb, pork chops, or chicken. Try it as a basting sauce for grilled vegetables, such as eggplant and zucchini. To marinate 1½ pounds (682 g) meat, combine 3 tablespoons (45 mL) of this seasoning mixture with ½ teaspoon (2.5 mL) soy sauce, freshly ground black pepper to taste, ½ cup (118 mL) chopped tomatoes, and 1 teaspoon (5 mL) Worcestershire sauce and marinate the meat overnight or at least 2 to 3 hours. Some of the measurements are authentically vague, so get your bunches together.

½ Congo pepper (or habanero), stems and seeds removed, chopped
3 bunches chives or green onions, coarsely chopped
1 bunch parsley, coarsely chopped
½ bunch celery leaves, coarsely chopped
1 cup (236 mL) garlic cloves, peeled
1 leaf Spanish thyme (or substitute 2 teaspoons [10 mL] fresh thyme and ½ teaspoon [2.5 mL] fresh Greek oregano)
½ cup (118 mL) distilled white vinegar
1 tablespoon (15 mL) salt, or less to taste
1 tablespoon (15 mL) ground ginger
1 tablespoon (15 mL) fresh or dried thyme

1. Combine all the ingredients in a food processor and blend thoroughly, adding water as necessary to make a medium paste.

Bonney Bajan Seasoning

Yield: ¾ cup (177 mL)   Heat Scale: Hot

There are an astounding number of variations on seasoning, which is similar to the seasoning pastes found in Trinidad. All contain herbs and chiles—and myriad other ingredients. They are added to soups and stews and used as a marinade and basting sauce for grilled meats.

1 bunch green onions, coarsely chopped (about 1½ cups [354 mL])
3 tablespoons (45 mL) fresh lime juice
¼ cup (59 mL) coarsely chopped fresh parsley
1 tablespoon (15 mL) fresh thyme
1 tablespoon (15 mL) fresh marjoram
1 tablespoon (15 mL) fresh chives
2 cloves garlic, peeled
1 Bonney Bajan pepper (or habanero), seeds and stem removed, halved
1 teaspoon (5 mL) paprika
¼ teaspoon (1.25 mL) ground cloves
⅛ teaspoon (.6 mL) salt

1. Combine all the ingredients in a food processor and pulse, adding water as needed until you achieve the desired consistency. Use immediately or store in the refrigerator for up to a week.

Jamaican Green Mango Chutney

Yield: About 4 cups (.95 L)   Heat Scale: Medium

Here is how they make chutney in Kingston. This style is far less sweet than other chutneys from around the world. Serve it with Jamaican Curry Goat. It keeps for a couple of weeks in the refrigerator.

6 medium green mangos, peeled, pits removed, chopped fine
2 cups (473 mL) malt vinegar
½ cup (118 mL) sugar
¼ cup (59 mL) seedless raisins
¼ cup (59 mL) finely chopped ginger root
1 teaspoon (5 mL) finely chopped garlic
2 teaspoons (10 mL) minced Scotch bonnet chile (or habanero)
1 teaspoon (5 mL) ground allspice
½ cup (118 mL) tamarind sauce
1 tablespoon (15 mL) salt

1. Place the mangos and vinegar in a large sauce pan. Bring to a boil over high heat and cook briskly for 10 minutes, stirring occasionally.
2. Stir in the sugar, raisins, ginger, garlic, chiles, allspice, tamarind sauce, and salt. Reduce the heat to low and simmer uncovered for about 45 minutes or until the mango is tender, stirring occasionally.
3. Remove the pan from the heat. Serve the chutney as is or puree it into a smooth sauce.

Mango Kucheela

Yield: 2 cups (473 mL)   Heat Scale: Hot

This chutney-like Trinidadian relish is commonly served with the street food called doubles and with curried dishes of all types, as well as with Pelau. Ripe mangos are never used in kucheela.

2 cups (473 mL) grated meat of green mangos
4 cloves garlic, peeled and minced
2 Congo peppers (or habaneros), stems and seeds removed, minced
2 teaspoons (10 mL) mild curry powder
½ cup (118 mL) mustard oil (or substitute vegetable oil), or more for texture

1. Preheat the oven to 250°F (120°C).
2. Squeeze as much juice as possible out of the grated mango meat, then spread it on a cookie sheet. Bake for 2 hours, or until the meat has dried out.
3. Combine all the ingredients and mix well. Store in sterilized jars in the refrigerator.

Memphis Rib Rub

Yield: About ⅔ cup (158 mL)   Heat Scale: Medium

This rub is great for smoking any cut of pork—ribs, chops, steaks, or even a roast. It has its origins in one of the barbecue centers of America: Memphis, Tennessee, home of the Memphis in May barbecue cook-off. You can also use rubs on grilled meats, so the next time you grill pork or lamb chops, try this recipe.

¼ cup (59 mL) paprika
2 tablespoons (30 mL) garlic salt
1 tablespoon (15 mL) freshly ground black pepper
2 tablespoons (30 mL) brown sugar
1 tablespoon (15 mL) onion powder
1 tablespoon (15 mL) dried oregano
1 tablespoon (15 mL) dry mustard
1½ teaspoons (7.5 mL) ground cayenne

1. Combine all the ingredients in a bowl and mix well. Store any unused rub in a sealed container in the freezer.

Kansas City Dry Rub

Yield: ⅔ cup (158 mL)   Heat Scale: Medium

From another center of the barbecue universe comes one of the dry rubs that made the Kansas City Royal cook-off such a highly competitive event. Try this rub on turkey or chicken.

2 tablespoons (30 mL) brown sugar
2 tablespoons (30 mL) ground paprika
1 tablespoon (15 mL) white sugar
1 tablespoon (15 mL) garlic salt
1 tablespoon (15 mL) celery salt
1 tablespoon (15 mL) commercial chili powder
2 teaspoons (10 mL) freshly ground black pepper
1 teaspoon (5 mL) ground cayenne
½ teaspoon (2.5 mL) dry mustard

1. Combine all the ingredients in a bowl and mix well. Store any unused rub in a sealed container in the freezer.

Genuine, Authentic, South-of-the-Border Chile Rub

Yield: About ⅔ cup (158 mL)   Heat Scale: Hot

Yeah, right. Okay, this is my spin on Mexican flavorings that would work on goat—as in cabrito, pit-roasted goat. Can't find goat at Albertsons, Trader Joe's, or Winn-Dixie? Then use this rub for grilling or smoking beef, pork, or lamb.

3 tablespoons (45 mL) ground ancho chile
2 teaspoons (10 mL) ground chile de arbol
2 teaspoons (10 mL) ground chipotle chile
2 teaspoons (10 mL) dried oregano (Mexican preferred)
2 teaspoons (10 mL) onion salt
1 teaspoon (5 mL) ground cumin
1 teaspoon (5 mL) powdered garlic

1. Combine all the ingredients in a bowl and mix well. Store any unused rub in a sealed container in the freezer.

Ragin' Cajun Rub

Yield: 2½ tablespoons (37 mL)   Heat Scale: Medium

Here's a concentrated rub with origins in Louisiana, where it seems that every home cook has his or her own secret spice mixture for grilled foods. This rub works well with fish and especially shrimp. Sprinkle it on the seafood and marinate at room temperature for about an hour. This rub is also good on chicken before it's grilled.

1 tablespoon (15 mL) paprika
2 teaspoons (10 mL) ground cayenne
2 teaspoons (10 mL) garlic powder
1 teaspoon (5 mL) freshly ground black pepper
1 teaspoon (5 mL) dried thyme
1 teaspoon (5 mL) dried oregano
1 teaspoon (5 mL) onion powder
1 teaspoon (5 mL) salt
1 bay leaf, center stem removed, crushed
½ teaspoon (2.5 mL) ground allspice
¼ teaspoon (1.25 mL) ground white pepper

1. Combine all the ingredients in a spice grinder and process until finely ground. Store any unused rub in a sealed container in the freezer.

Cajun Spices

Yield: About 1 cup (236 mL)   Heat Scale: Hot

Cajun spice mixes are some of the most popular seasonings in the United States, and not just in Louisiana. The Caucasian French-speaking residents, or Cajuns, of the Acadiana parishes in southern Louisiana are known for their robust, spicy dishes, such as jambalaya and étouffée. Use this mix as a seasoning in gumbos, or as a lagniappe, a Cajun-French word meaning "a little something extra," on salads or vegetables.

3 tablespoons (45 mL) garlic salt
3 tablespoons (45 mL) freshly ground black pepper
2 tablespoons (30 mL) ground cayenne
2 tablespoons (30 mL) ground white pepper
2 tablespoons (30 mL) onion powder
1 tablespoon (15 mL) ground paprika
1 tablespoon (15 mL) dried parsley leaves
2 teaspoons (10 mL) dried oregano
2 teaspoons (10 mL) ground thyme
½ teaspoon (2.5 mL) mace

1. Combine all the ingredients in a bowl and stir to blend. Store the mixture in an airtight container.

Crab-Boil Spices

Yield: ½ cup (118 mL)   Heat Scale: Mild

Crab-boil mixtures contain herbs and spices and are used to season the water in which shrimp, crawfish, and crabs are boiled. Commercial mixes, such as Old Bay and Zatarain's, are available, but this mixture is so easy to prepare, why not make your own signature blend?

¼ cup (59 mL) commercial pickling spices
2 tablespoons (30 mL) yellow mustard seeds
2 tablespoons (30 mL) whole black peppercorns
1 tablespoon (15 mL) salt
1 tablespoon (15 mL) celery seeds
1 tablespoon (15 mL) onion flakes
6 piquin chiles
2 teaspoons (10 mL) ground ginger
4 bay leaves
2 teaspoons (10 mL) dried oregano
1 teaspoon (5 mL) dry mustard

1. Place all the ingredients in a blender or food processor and pulse to a coarse powder. Store the mixture in an airtight container.

Creole Mustard

Yield: ½ cup (118 mL)   Heat Scale: Medium

This mustard, a specialty of Louisiana's German Creoles, is a traditional flavoring in the cuisine of New Orleans and a must in the preparation of remoulade sauce. A sharp and slightly sweet mustard with a complex flavor, this will definitely clean out the sinuses. Quick and easy to prepare, it's a good accompaniment to shrimp, ham, fish, or poultry and an important flavor ingredient in many Cajun and Creole dishes. (Note: This recipe requires advance preparation.)

¼ cup (59 mL) yellow mustard powder
1 tablespoon (15 mL) all-purpose flour
1 tablespoon (15 mL) store-bought or homemade Dijon-style mustard
3 tablespoons (45 mL) white wine vinegar
2 teaspoons (10 mL) grated horseradish
1 clove garlic, peeled and minced
1 teaspoon (5 mL) sugar
½ teaspoon (2.5 mL) dried thyme
½ teaspoon (2.5 mL) paprika
½ teaspoon (2.5 mL) ground white pepper
¼ teaspoon (1.25 mL) salt
½ cup (118 mL) water

1. Combine all the ingredients in a saucepan and mix well. Bring to a simmer over medium heat and cook for 2 minutes. Add more water if the mustard gets too thick.

2. Remove the pan from the heat and allow the mustard to cool.
3. Spoon the mustard into a sterilized jar and refrigerate for 1 week before using.

Cracked Black Peppercorn Mustard

Yield: ½ cup (118 mL)   Heat Scale: Medium

This is a quick, easy-to-prepare mustard with a distinctive peppercorn flavor. Its assertive flavor is excellent on dark breads and with smoked meats, and it makes a perfect coating for steaks or burgers before grilling. Add a little of this mustard to beef gravy for an added flavor dimension.

¼ cup (59 mL) whole yellow mustard seeds
¼ cup (59 mL) champagne vinegar
2 tablespoons (30 mL) coarsely cracked black peppercorns
1 teaspoon (5 mL) garlic powder
½ teaspoon (2.5 mL) salt

1. Place the mustard seeds in a spice mill or coffee grinder and process until finely ground.
2. Combine the ground mustard seeds and vinegar in a bowl and stir to mix. Allow the mixture to sit for 15 minutes.
3. Place the mustard-vinegar mixture and the remaining ingredients in a blender or food processor and process until smooth, adding hot water as needed.
4. Spoon the mustard into a sterilized jar, cover, and refrigerate for 1 week before using.

Picante Chile Catsup

Yield: 1 quart (.95 L)   Heat Scale: Medium

Use this fiery version in place of regular catsup to spice up sandwiches, meatloaf, hot dogs, and hamburgers. It also tastes great in salad dressings and on french fries. If you wish, you may freeze the catsup after puréeing it. Check in a canning guide for water bath instructions.

6 pounds (2.72 kg) tomatoes, peeled, seeded, and chopped
2 stalks celery, chopped
1 large onion, peeled and chopped
4 jalapeño or serrano chiles, stems and seeds removed, chopped
(or substitute 2 habanero chiles)
1 red bell pepper, stem and seeds removed, chopped
1 cup (236 mL) brown sugar
1½ cups (352 mL) apple cider vinegar
2 teaspoons (10 mL) dry mustard
1 teaspoon (5 mL) ground cinnamon
½ teaspoon (2.5 mL) ground cloves
¼ teaspoon (1.25 mL) ground allspice
1–2 teaspoons (5–10 mL) salt

1. In a pan over low heat, cook the tomatoes for 15 minutes, then drain off the juice. Add the celery, onion, chiles, and bell pepper and simmer for 1 hour.
2. Add the sugar, vinegar, and spices and simmer for an additional hour. Remove from the heat and purée until smooth.
3. Pour the catsup into sterilized jars and process the jars in a water bath.

Rosemary Chile Vinegar

Yield: 1 quart (.95 L)   Heat Scale: Varies

This is my favorite vinegar. Recommended chiles include serranos and habaneros, but it can also be made with dried pasillas for a raisiny flavor. (Note: This recipe requires advance preparation.)

2 tablespoons (30 mL) minced fresh, small, hot chiles
1 cup (236 mL) fresh rosemary leaves
3 cloves garlic, peeled
1 quart (.95 L) distilled white vinegar

1. Divide the chiles, rosemary, and garlic among several jars and cover with the vinegar. Place the jars in a cool, dark place and leave undisturbed for three to four weeks.
2. Strain out the solids and pour the vinegar into clean, sterilized bottles. Label the bottles clearly.

Oregano-Garlic Green Chile Vinegar

Yield: 1 quart (.95 L)   Heat Scale: Mild

The combination of oregano and garlic imparts an Italian flavor to this vinegar, which I keep on the mild side so that the heat doesn't mask the flavor of the garlic. (Note: This recipe requires advance preparation.)

1 cup (236 mL) fresh oregano leaves
10 cloves garlic, peeled
2 fresh green chiles such as serrano or Thai, halved lengthwise
1 quart (.95 L) distilled white vinegar

1. In a large jar, cover the oregano, garlic, and chiles with the vinegar. Store in a cool, dark place and leave undisturbed for 3 to 4 weeks.
2. Strain out the solids and transfer the vinegar to clean, sterilized jars.

Basic Chile Oil

Yield: 4 cups (.95 L)   Heat Scale: Hot

Bottles of chile oil decorated with ribbons and tiny papier-mâché chiles make nice gifts for anyone who likes to cook. Include your favorite recipe with each gift bottle. Never use fresh chiles, as the oil will not preserve them and botulism may develop. (Note: This recipe requires advance preparation.)

4 cups (.95 L) vegetable oil (peanut preferred)
1 cup (236 mL) small dried red chiles, such as piquins

1. In a pan, heat the oil to 350°F (180°C). Remove the pan from the heat and add the chiles.
2. Cover the pan and let stand for 12 to 24 hours (the longer it steeps, the hotter the oil). Strain the oil into clean, sterilized jars or bottles.
3. Tie a few dried chiles to the jars as decorations.

Yugoslavian Tomato-Pepper Relish

Yield: About 2 cups (473 mL)   Heat Scale: Medium

"This relish is a popular accompaniment to grilled meats in the country," wrote Marge Peterson in Chile Pepper *magazine when I was the editor, "especially in the winter when fresh vegetables are not so plentiful. Serve with meats such as pan-fried pork chops or as you would serve any hot relish. If garlic-flavored salad oil is not readily at hand, soak a clove of garlic in ½ cup (118 mL) vegetable oil overnight." In the winter, canned tomatoes are much better than the useless fresh ones found in supermarkets. (Note: This recipe requires advance preparation.)*

4 dried red New Mexican chiles, seeds and stem removed
2 (16-ounce [454 g]) cans crushed tomatoes
2 tablespoons (30 mL) garlic-flavored vegetable oil
4 tablespoons (60 mL) minced onions
¼ teaspoon (1.25 mL) sugar
Ground cayenne, to taste
Salt, to taste

1. Combine the chiles and tomatoes (including the liquid) in a large bowl and refrigerate overnight.
2. Drain and reserve the liquid. Remove the chiles and purée them until smooth.
3. In a frying pan, heat the garlic oil over medium heat. and Add the onions and sauté until soft, about 5 minutes. Add the tomatoes, chile purée, tomato liquid, and sugar. Cook until the sauce is very thick, stirring occasionally. Season to taste with ground cayenne and salt.

Ajvar
(Eggplant-Chile Relish)

Yield: 5–6 cups (11.8–14.2 L) Heat Scale: Medium

From the former Yugoslavia comes a relish made with chiles and eggplants. Sharon Hudgins, one of my favorite writers, collected this recipe before the war there. She noted, "Fresh ajvar is always made during the late summer and early autumn, just after the pepper harvest—when many households also can or bottle their own ajvar for use throughout the year. Serve as an appetizer to spread on thick slices of country-style white bread or flat pita bread, or use as a side dish to accompany grilled or roasted meats."

8 to 12 fresh red New Mexico chiles
4 medium eggplants
½–¾ cup (125–177 mL) olive oil or corn oil, divided
1 large onion, minced
3 large cloves garlic, peeled and finely chopped
1–2 tablespoons (15–30 mL) lemon juice (or 1 tablespoon [15 mL] red wine vinegar)
Salt, to taste
Freshly ground black pepper, to taste
Chopped fresh parsley, for garnish

1. Roast the chiles and eggplants over charcoal or a gas flame—or bake them in an oven preheated to 475°F (250°C)—until the skins are blistered and black. Place the roasted vegetables in a paper bag and let them steam in their own heat for 10 minutes. Peel off and discard the burnt skins along with the stems and seeds. Mash the peppers and eggplant pulp together to form a homogenous mass—completely smooth or slightly chunky, as desired. You can do this in a food processor.
2. Heat 3 tablespoons (45 mL) of the oil in a large skillet over medium heat. Add the onion and sauté until very soft. Add the garlic and cook 2 minutes longer. Remove from the heat and stir in the pepper-eggplant pulp, mixing well. Slowly drizzle the remaining oil into the mixture, stirring constantly to incorporate it. Add the lemon juice or vinegar and the salt and pepper, to taste. Transfer to a serving bowl and garnish with the parsley.

Classic British Mustard Spread

Yield: About 1¼ cups (295 mL) Heat Scale: Medium

Another hot condiment that predates chile peppers in Europe, this mustard concoction goes well with beef and ham. Feel free to add a little ground cayenne to fire it up a bit.

1 tablespoon (15 mL) unsalted butter
1 tablespoon (15 mL) all-purpose flour
1¼ cups (295 mL) rich beef stock
1 tablespoon (15 mL) prepared horseradish
1 tablespoon (15 mL) hot English mustard, coarse or smooth, or more to taste
½ teaspoon (2.5 mL) salt
Freshly ground black pepper, to taste

1. Melt the butter in a small saucepan over low heat. Add the flour and stir to make a roux. Cook the roux for 2 to 3 minutes, stirring constantly. Remove from the heat and stir in the beef stock. Add the horseradish, mustard, salt, and pepper to taste.

2. Return the pan to the stove and bring to a boil, stirring constantly. Cook for 2 to 3 minutes until quite thickened. Serve immediately.

Dijon-Style Mustard

Yield: 1½ cups (354 mL)   Heat Scale: Medium

The term Dijon moutarde *is strictly controlled by French law. It can only be used on mixtures that contain black and/or brown mustard seeds, and these seeds must be mixed with wine, wine vinegar, or verjuice—the juice of unripe grapes. Any product made with the milder white mustard seeds may be labeled condiment, but never* moutarde. *This is a wonderful mustard to use as a base for adding other ingredients, such as fruits and various herbs. The long aging period changes the flavor from sharp to smooth and mellow. The proportions of ingredients used in the French moutarde are also a closely guarded secret, but this recipe is the closest I've come to the real McCoy. (Note: This recipe requires advance preparation.)*

¾ cup (177 mL) mustard powder
¼ cup (59 mL) cold water
1 cup (236 mL) champagne vinegar
1 cup (236 mL) dry white wine
½ cup (118 mL) minced onions
2 tablespoons (30 mL) minced shallots
2 tablespoons (30 mL) minced garlic
2 bay leaves
20 black peppercorns
10 juniper berries
½ teaspoon (2.5 mL) dried tarragon
¼ teaspoon (1.25 mL) dried thyme
3 tablespoons (45 mL) lemon juice (fresh preferred)
2 teaspoons (10 mL) salt
2 teaspoons (10 mL) sugar

1. In a bowl, combine the mustard powder with the cold water. Stir to form a paste.

2. In a saucepan, combine the vinegar, wine, onion, shallots, garlic, bay leaves, peppercorns, juniper berries, tarragon, and thyme. Bring the mixture to a simmer over medium heat, and cook until it is reduced by two-thirds. Strain the mixture into a bowl, cover, and chill.

3. When the vinegar reduction is cool, stir it into the mustard paste. Add the lemon juice, salt, and sugar and stir to combine. Let the mixture stand for 30 minutes.

4. Transfer the mustard to a saucepan and simmer over low heat for 15 minutes. Remove the pan from the heat and allow it to cool.

5. Spoon the mustard into a sterilized jar and seal. Store the mustard in a dark, cool place for 3 weeks before using.

North African Tabil

Yield: ¼ cup (59 mL)   Heat Scale: Hot

This simple, strong-tasting curry mix is specific to and very popular in Tunisia. It's made with either fresh ingredients or their dried, ground equivalents. Besides referring to the mix itself, the word "tabil" means coriander, and this mix uses a large amount. Tabil is sprinkled over grilled meats and poultry, in stuffings and stews, and on vegetables. It can be made as hot or as mild as you like by adjusting the amount of chile, but the Tunisians like their's hot.

¼ cup (59 mL) coriander seeds
1 tablespoon (15 mL) caraway seeds
2 teaspoons (10 mL) ground red chile, either New Mexican or cayenne
2 teaspoons (10 mL) garlic powder

1. Place all the ingredients in a spice mill or coffee grinder and process to a fine powder.
Store the mixture in an airtight container.

Baharat
(Saudi Mixed Spices)

Yield: ⅓–½ cup (80–120 mL)   Heat Scale: Mild

Baharat means "spice" in Arabic and is derived from the word "bahar," "pepper," so the definition of this recipe is "mixed spice with black pepper." Used to flavor dishes throughout the Gulf states and Iraq, baharat varies to fit individual tastes, but all the variations use black pepper as a dominant spice. It's traditionally used to flavor kibbeh, a ground lamb and bulgur wheat dish, meat stuffings, tomatoes, sauces, soups, and stews.

2 tablespoons (30 mL) freshly ground black pepper
2 tablespoons (30 mL) ground coriander
2 tablespoons (30 mL) ground paprika
1½ tablespoons (22 mL) ground nutmeg
1½ tablespoons (22 mL) curry powder
1½ tablespoons (22 mL) ground dried limes (optional)
1½ teaspoons (7.5 mL) ground cloves
1½ teaspoons (7.5 mL) ground cumin
¾ teaspoon (3.75 mL) ground cardamom

1. Combine all the ingredients in a bowl and stir to blend.
Store the mixture in an airtight container.

Dukkah
(Egyptian Spice Mixture)

Yield: 1 cup (236 mL)   Heat Scale: Mild

Dukkah is a staple in Egyptian households. This blend of spices, seeds, and toasted nuts or chickpeas originated in Egypt, but its popularity has spread throughout the Middle East and even "down under" to Australia and New Zealand. It gets its name from the Arabic word for "pound," since the mixture is crushed or pounded to a coarse, rather than fine, powder. The roots of this dish stretch back to the Bedouin tribes that traveled the deserts in the area. When they would gather at night, they'd roast spices, nuts, and seeds over their campfires, pound them into a coarse powder, and make a meal by dipping hunks of bread into olive oil and then the dukkah. These days, Egyptian street vendors sell small paper cones filled with their unique dukkah blend, along with strips of pita bread. Customers dip the bread into the vendor's bowl of olive oil and then their dukkah. Enjoyed for breakfast and as a snack or an appetizer, dukkah is also a very versatile seasoning that can be used as a topping on salads and vegetables, as a coating for poultry and fish, and as a tasty addition to bread.

½ cup (118 mL) hazelnuts
¼ cup (59 mL) coriander seeds
3 tablespoons (45 mL) sesame seeds
2 tablespoons (30 mL) cumin seeds
1 tablespoon (15 mL) black peppercorns
1 teaspoon (5 mL) fennel seeds
1 teaspoon (5 mL) dried mint leaves
Salt, to taste

1. Heat a heavy skillet over high heat. Add the hazelnuts and dry-roast them until slightly browned and fragrant, being careful that they don't burn. Remove from the heat and cool completely. Repeat the procedure with each of the seeds and the peppercorns. Allow each ingredient to cool completely.
2. Place the nuts and seeds, along with the mint and salt, into a mortar and pound until the mixture is crushed to a coarse powder. Or pulse in a food processor to a coarse consistency; do not allow the mixture to become a paste. Store in an airtight container.

Moroccan Charmoula

Yield: ⅓–½ cup (79–118 mL)   Heat Scale: Mild

Charmoula has been referred to as an all-purpose spicy cilantro pesto. Traditionally served with seafood, it can be used as a marinade or as a fresh sauce on top of baked, grilled, or even poached fish. Don't limit yourself, though, as it's also tasty with chicken or on steamed vegetables. Charmoula is used throughout Morocco, and although the blend of spices and herbs may vary, it always contains cilantro, garlic, olive oil, and lemon.

1 cup lightly packed cilantro (leaves and stems)
5 cloves garlic, peeled and chopped
3 tablespoons (15 mL) chopped parsley (flat leaf preferred)
3 tablespoons (15 mL) lemon juice (fresh preferred)
Zest of 1 lemon
2 teaspoons (10 mL) ground paprika
1 teaspoon (5 mL) ground coriander
1 teaspoon (5 mL) cumin seeds
1 teaspoon (5 mL) ground cayenne
½ teaspoon (2.5 mL) freshly ground black pepper
2 tablespoons (30 mL) apple cider vinegar
¼–⅓ cup (59–79 mL) olive oil

1. Place all the ingredients except the vinegar and oil in a blender or food processor and pulse to coarsely chop. With the motor running slowly, add the vinegar and enough of the oil to make a thick paste.
2. Allow the sauce to sit for 20 to 30 minutes to blend the flavors. The sauce will keep for up to 1 month in the refrigerator.

Zhoug
(Hot Herb Paste from Yemen)

Yield: 1½ cups (354 mL)   Heat Scale: Medium to hot

Yemenites often live to be more than 100 years of age, and that feat could be the result of the daily consumption of zhoug, a chile condiment that is served with meat, fish, and poultry—and just about anything else. The Yemenite Jews in Israel call this paste "shatta" and love it with lamb kebabs.

8 red serrano or jalapeño chiles, stems and seeds removed, chopped
1 cup (236 mL) chopped cilantro
½ cup (118 mL) chopped fresh parsley
2 tablespoons (30 mL) chopped garlic
2 teaspoons (10 mL) ground cumin
1 teaspoon (5 mL) salt
½–¾ cup (125–177 mL) olive oil

1. Place all the ingredients in a blender with enough oil to purée to a smooth paste.

Israeli Sabra Dip

Yield: About 1 cup (236 mL)   Heat Scale: Medium

According to Pat Chapman, the British spicy-food expert who gave me this recipe, sabra is an Israeli colloquialism for people born in the new Israel. This dip forms an important part of the mezzeh table and is served with celery, cucumber, carrots, mushrooms, and hot pita bread for dipping.

1 large ripe avocado, peeled and pitted
2 serrano or jalapeño chiles, stems and seeds removed, halved
1 onion, chopped
3 tablespoons (45 mL) lemon juice
1½ cups (354 mL) cottage or cream cheese
Milk as needed
Salt, to taste

1. In a blender, combine the avocado, pepper and onion and chop coarsely.
2. Add the lemon juice, cottage or cream cheese, and milk as needed and continue to blend until lumpy.
3. Taste for seasoning and add salt as needed.

Hilbeh
(Hot Fenugreek Dip)

Yield: About 1½ cups (354 mL)   Heat Scale: Hot

This Yemeni hot dip has quite a bit of fenugreek in it and tends to be bitter. Pat Chapman, who gave me the recipe, noted, "This dip is rather an acquired taste and is not for the faint-hearted." He recommends soaking the fenugreek seeds in water to remove some of their bitterness. This dip is used with bread, and it is also spread over the Yemeni khouhz bread before it is baked.

¼ cup (59 mL) olive oil
6 cloves garlic, peeled and chopped
1 cup (236 mL) chopped onion
2 tablespoons (30 mL) fenugreek seeds, soaked in ½ cup (118 mL) water for 12 hours
⅛ teaspoon (.7 mL) ground cinnamon
⅛ teaspoon (.7 mL) ground coriander
⅛ teaspoon (.7 mL) ground cloves
⅛ teaspoon (.7 mL) ground cumin
⅛ teaspoon (.7 mL) ground paprika
⅛ teaspoon (.7 mL) freshly ground black pepper
1 cup (236 mL) chopped cilantro
4 canned plum tomatoes
3 tablespoons (45 mL) lemon juice
5 serrano or jalapeño chiles, stems and seeds removed, chopped

1. In a saucepan, heat the oil over medium heat. Add the garlic and sauté for 1 minute. Add the onion and sauté for 3 minutes, stirring constantly.

2. Drain the fenugreek seeds, add them to the saucepan, and cook for 3 more minutes. Add the ground spices and cilantro and cook for 3 more minutes, stirring occasionally. Remove from the heat and transfer to a food processor or blender.

3. Add the remaining ingredients and pulse to a purée.

Harissa Sauce

Yield: 1½ cups (354 mL) Heat Scale: Medium

This sauce is thought to be of Tunisian origin but is found throughout North Africa. It is used to flavor couscous and grilled dishes such as brochettes and as a relish with salads. The sauce reflects the region's love of spicy combinations, all with a definite cumin taste. Cover this sauce with a thin film of olive oil and it will keep for up to a couple of months in the refrigerator.

10 dried whole red New Mexican chiles, stems and seeds removed
2 tablespoons (15 mL) olive oil
5 cloves garlic
1 teaspoon (5 mL) ground cumin
1 teaspoon (5 mL) ground cinnamon
1 teaspoon (5 mL) ground coriander
1 teaspoon (5 mL) ground caraway

1. Cover the chiles with hot water and let them sit for 15 minutes or until they soften.

2. Reserving the soaking water, transfer the chiles to a blender. Add the remaining ingredients and purée until smooth, adding the reserved soaking water as needed to thin the mixture. The sauce should have the consistency of a thick paste.

South African Cape Curry Powder

Yield: ¼ cup (59 mL) Heat Scale: Medium

This curry powder reflects the influence of the Malaysian slaves brought to South Africa by the Dutch and the indentured Indian laborers who worked on the sugar plantations in the 1800s. Some curry mixtures contain as few as three ingredients, while others, such as this one, have a more complex mix of spices. Use this in any dish calling for a curry powder.

2 teaspoons (10 mL) coriander seeds
1 teaspoon (5 mL) black mustard seeds
1 teaspoon (5 mL) black peppercorns
½ teaspoon (2.5 mL) fenugreek seeds
½ teaspoon (2.5 mL) fennel seeds
6 whole cloves
3 bird chiles, stems and seeds removed (or substitute piquins or santakas)
1 teaspoon (5 mL) ground ginger
1 teaspoon (5 mL) ground turmeric
1 teaspoon (5 mL) ground cardamom
¼ teaspoon (1.25 mL) ground cumin

1. Heat a heavy skillet over high heat. Add the coriander, mustard, black peppercorns, fenugreek, fennel, and cloves and dry-roast until the seeds darken and become fragrant, taking care that they don't burn. Remove the skillet from the heat and allow the ingredients to cool completely, then place them in a spice mill or coffee grinder, along with the chiles, and process to a fine powder.
2. Transfer the mixture to a bowl, add the remaining ingredients, and stir to blend. Store the mixture in an airtight container.

Niter Kebbeh
(Ethiopian Curried Spiced Butter)
Yield: About 2 cups (473 mL)   Heat Scale: Mild

An essential ingredient in many traditional Ethiopian dishes, niter kebbeh is a bright orange clarified butter. It's similar to Indian ghee, but this version has a rich aroma and taste. Clarified butter can be cooked at higher temperatures than regular butter because it doesn't contain any of the milk solids that burn. This type of butter is the secret to making a good omelet. Niter kebbeh will solidify in the refrigerator but reliquify at room temperature. Be sure to strain out all of the solids so the butter does not become rancid.

4 whole cloves
1 (1-inch [2.5 cm]) cinnamon stick
¾ teaspoon (3.75 mL) cardamom seeds
½ teaspoon (2.5 mL) fenugreek seeds
2 pounds (1.1 kg) unsalted butter
¼ cup (59 mL) chopped onion
2 tablespoons (30 mL) chopped garlic
1 tablespoon (15 mL) grated ginger
1½ teaspoons (7.5 mL) ground turmeric
¼ teaspoon (1.25 mL) freshly grated nutmeg

1. Heat a heavy skillet over high heat. Add the cloves, cinnamon, cardamom, and fenugreek and dry-roast until the seeds darken and become fragrant, being careful that they don't burn. Remove the skillet from the heat and allow the mixture to cool.
2. Melt the butter in a heavy saucepan over low heat, but do not let it brown. Increase the heat and bring the butter to a boil, stirring frequently. Skim off the foam that forms.
3. Add the remaining ingredients, including the toasted spice mixture, to the pan. Reduce the heat to low and simmer the butter, uncovered, for 45 minutes. Do not stir.
4. When the milk solids at the bottom of the pan are a golden brown, strain the transparent butter through a linen towel into a bowl until no solids remain. Store the butter in the refrigerator or at room temperature for up to 3 months.

Komkommer-Sambal
(Capetown Cucumber Sambal)

Yield: 1½ cups (354 mL)   Heat Scale: Medium

Despite the chiles in this recipe, it's referred to as a "cool" sambal in South Africa, probably because cucumbers are considered a cool and refreshing vegetable. This condiment is typically served with hot curries. Substitute carrots and you have wortel-sambal; apples, and you have appel-sambal.

5 small, sweet cucumbers, peeled and grated
2 tablespoons (10 mL) salt
2 serrano or jalapeño chiles, stems and seeds removed, minced
2 cloves garlic, peeled and minced
1 teaspoon (5 mL) distilled white vinegar

1. Place the cucumbers in a bowl, sprinkle them with the salt, mix well, and let stand for 15 minutes.
2. Squeeze out all the liquid from the cucumber through cloth or paper towels.
3. Combine the cucumbers with the remaining ingredients and mix well. Let stand for 15 minutes to blend the flavors, then serve.

Variation
Fresh red chiles are visually appealing in this condiment.

Teemateem Beqarya
(Fresh Tomato and Green Chile Relish)

Yield: 6 servings   Heat Scale: Medium

The unique feature of this Ethiopian relish is that it is hot and spicy and served chilled, so your taste buds get a double thrill. This recipe is very similar to a Southwestern salsa; however, instead of tortilla chips, injera bread is served with this relish. (Note: This recipe requires advance preparation.)

¾ cup (177 mL) chopped roasted and peeled green New Mexican chiles
3 cups (708 mL) peeled chopped tomatoes
3 tablespoons (45 mL) vegetable oil
⅓ cup (79 mL) chopped red onions
Salt, to taste
1½ tablespoons (22 mL) fresh lemon or lime juice
¼ teaspoon (1.25 mL) freshly ground black pepper

1. In a medium ceramic bowl, combine all the ingredients and toss them together. Cover and marinate at room temperature for 1 hour.
2. Refrigerate the mixture for 2 hours, then serve.

Apple-Raisin Blatjang
Yield: 2–3 quarts (1.9–2.85 L)   Heat Scale: Mild

Feel free to add some spices, such as coriander, to this South African chutney-like condiment if you wish. The apples can be mashed or puréed to make a smoother sauce. Serve at room temperature with curries.

3 pounds (1.5 kg) apples, peeled, cored, and chopped
½ pound (224 g) raisins, chopped
1½ quarts (1.7 L) wine vinegar
1 cup (236 mL) sugar
1 tablespoon (15 mL) salt
2 fresh small green chiles, such as serrano, stems and seeds removed, chopped
1 clove garlic, peeled and chopped
2 tablespoons (30 mL) minced fresh ginger

1. Combine all the ingredients in a large pot and simmer, uncovered, until thick, about 2 hours, stirring occasionally.
2. Spoon into sterilized jars and seal while hot.

Cape Malay Green Mango Atjar
Yield: About 3 pints (1.4 L)   Heat Scale: Medium

The important thing to remember about this "pickle" is to be certain that the mangos are always covered with the oil mixture. If you remove any fruit, be sure the remainder is covered with the atjar mixture to prevent spoilage. (Note: This recipe requires advance preparation.)

1 gallon (3.8 L) water
4 tablespoons (60 mL) salt
5–6 pounds (2.3–2.8 kg) green mangos
2 cups (473 mL) vegetable oil
5 jalapeño chiles, stems and seeds removed, chopped
2 cloves garlic, peeled and crushed
2 tablespoons (30 mL) curry paste
1 teaspoon (5 mL) turmeric
1 teaspoon (5 mL) ground fenugreek

1. Combine the water and salt in a large pot or bowl and stir until the salt is dissolved.
2. Peel the mangos, cut the meat from the pits, and dice it. Add the mango flesh to the water, making sure that it is completely covered. Set aside to marinate mangos for 2 days.
3. In a large saucepan, combine the oil, chiles, garlic, curry paste, turmeric, and fenugreek. Slowly bring the oil mixture to a boil and cook for 5 minutes.

4. Drain the mango meat and dry it with paper towels. Divide the mangos among sterilized jars and pour enough boiling oil into each jar to cover the mango meat completely. Seal the jars and process in a boiling water bath for 20 minutes. Let the atjar age for at least a week before serving.

Berbere
(Ethiopian Chile Paste)
Yield: About 1 cup (236 mL)   Heat Scale: Hot

Originally used as the sauce for kifto, fresh raw meat dishes, berbere is now used as both an ingredient and a condiment in Ethiopian cooking. Like harissa from North Africa, it is essentially a curry-like paste with an abundance of small, hot red chiles. Serve sparingly as a condiment with grilled meats and poultry or add it to soups and stews. This paste will keep for a couple of months refrigerated, and many cooks thin it with water or vinegar to make it pourable.

1 teaspoon (5 mL) ground cardamom
2 teaspoons (10 mL) cumin seeds
½ teaspoon (2.5 mL) coriander seeds
¼ teaspoon (1.25 mL) ground cinnamon
½ teaspoon (2.5 mL) black peppercorns
½ teaspoon (2.5 mL) fenugreek seeds
1 small onion, peeled and coarsely chopped
4 cloves garlic, peeled
1 cup (236 mL) water
14 dried piquin chiles, stems removed
1 tablespoon (15 mL) ground cayenne
2 tablespoons (30 mL) ground paprika
½ teaspoon (2.5 mL) ground ginger
¼ teaspoon (1.25 mL) ground allspice
¼ teaspoon (1.25 mL) ground nutmeg
¼ teaspoon (1.25 mL) ground cloves
3 tablespoons (45 mL) dry red wine
3 tablespoons (45 mL) vegetable oil

1. Heat a skillet over high heat. Add the cardamom, cumin, coriander, cinnamon, peppercorns, and fenugreek and toast, shaking constantly, for a couple of minutes, until they start to release their aroma. Remove the skillet from the heat and allow the spices to cool. In a mortar or spice mill, grind the spices to a powder.
2. Combine the onions, garlic, and ½ cup (118 mL) of the water in a blender or food processor and purée until smooth. Add the roasted spice powder, piquins, ground cayenne, paprika, ginger, allspice, nutmeg, and cloves and continue to blend. Slowly add the remaining ½ cup (118 mL) water, the wine, and the oil and blend until smooth.
3. Transfer the mixture to a saucepan. Simmer for 15 minutes to blend the flavors and thicken the sauce to a paste.

Sambhar Powder

Yield: ¼ cup (59 mL)   Heat Scale: Hot

Sambhar curry powder is fundamental to South Indian Brahmin vegetarian cook-
ing. Brahmin curries are known for their crunchy, nutty taste, which they get from
the dals (dried legumes such as lentils, peas, or chickpeas) that are used in curry
powders and as a thickener in curries. To retain the desired nutty flavor, don't soak
the dals before using. Sambhar powders are widely used to flavor pulses (dried beans,
peas, and lentils), braised and stewed vegetables, and sauces. If I'm making a large
amount of this powder, I roast each spice separately, but for a small amount I roast
them all together.

1 tablespoon (15 mL) coriander seeds
2 teaspoons (10 mL) cumin seeds
1 (2-inch [5 cm]) cinnamon stick
1 teaspoon (5 mL) brown mustard seeds
½ teaspoon (2.5 mL) black peppercorns
½ teaspoon (2.5 mL) fenugreek seeds
1 teaspoon (5 mL) ground turmeric
6 to 8 small dried red chiles, such as piquins, stems and seeds removed
1 tablespoon (15 mL) channa dal (yellow split peas)
2 teaspoons (10 mL) toor dal (pigeon peas)

1. Heat a heavy skillet over high heat. Add the coriander, cumin, cinnamon, mustard, peppercorns, and fenugreek, and dry-roast until the seeds
darken and become fragrant, being careful that they don't burn. Add the
turmeric and roast for an additional minute. Remove the mixture from the
skillet and cool completely.
2. Lower the heat to medium. Add the chiles and toast for 2 to 3 minutes.
Remove the chiles from the skillet and let them cool.
3. Add both dals to the skillet and roast them until they darken, stirring
frequently to prevent burning, about 3 to 4 minutes. Remove the skillet
from the heat and allow to cool completely.
4. When all the ingredients are cool, place them in a spice mill or coffee
grinder and process to a powder. Store the mixture in an airtight container.

Hurry Curry

Yield: About 1½ cups (354 mL)   Heat Scale: Hot

There are scores of curry powders on the market today. Purists may frown on them, but they are indeed useful for making curries in a hurry. Even in India, curry powders have become an integral part of middle-class family life. The following curry powder, called bafat, is from southwestern India. It can be used in meat, fish, or vegetable dishes. It can even be used the same day for two completely different dishes, each with its own unique flavor.

⅓ cup (79 mL) coriander seeds
¼ cup (59 mL) cumin seeds
2 tablespoons (30 mL) mustard seeds
2 tablespoons (30 mL) peppercorns
2 tablespoons (30 mL) whole cloves
1 tablespoon (15 mL) fenugreek seeds
2 tablespoons (30 mL) ground cardamom
2 tablespoons (30 mL) ground cinnamon
2 tablespoons (30 mL) ground turmeric
¼ cup (59 mL) freshly ground hot red chile powder

1. Preheat the oven to 200°F (100°C).
2. Spread the whole spices on a cookie sheet and bake for 15 minutes, taking care that they do not burn. Remove them from the oven and set aside to cool.
3. Grind the cooled spices in a spice mill in small batches. Transfer them to a bowl. Add the ground spices and mix well. Store the curry powder in an airtight container.

Hot Madras Curry Paste

Yield: About 2 cups (473 mL)   Heat Scale: Hot

This recipe is from England's "King of Curries," Pat Chapman, who says it's his standard recipe for a curry paste. Use it in place of commercial curry pastes or powders.

4 tablespoons (60 mL) ground coriander
4 tablespoons (60 mL) ground red chile, such as cayenne
4 teaspoons (20 mL) ground cumin
4 teaspoons (20 mL) garam masala (an Indian spice mix available in Asian markets)
1 tablespoon (15 mL) ground turmeric
1½ teaspoons (7.5 mL) ground fenugreek seeds
1½ teaspoons (7.5 mL) ground fennel seeds
1¼ teaspoons (1.25 mL) ground ginger
1¼ teaspoons (1.25 mL) dry yellow mustard
½ cup (118 mL) distilled white vinegar
1 cup (236 mL) water
⅔ cup (158 mL) corn oil

1. In a bowl, mix the ground spices together. Add the vinegar and water and mix into a paste. Let stand for 15 minutes.
2. In a large pan, heat the oil over high heat. Add the paste (careful of the sputtering), lower the heat, and stir-fry for 5 to 10 minutes. As the liquid reduces, the paste will begin to make a regular bubbling noise (hard to describe, but it goes *chup-chup-chup*) if you don't stir, and it will splatter. This is your audible cue that it is ready. To tell whether the spices are cooked, take the pan off the stove and let stand for 3 to 4 minutes. If the oil floats to the top, the spices are cooked. If not, add a little more oil and repeat.
3. Bottle the paste in sterilized jars. Then heat up a little more oil and top off the paste by pouring in enough oil to cover. Seal the jars and store. Properly cooked, it will last indefinitely.

Green Masala Paste

Yield: About 2 cups (473 mL)   Heat Scale: Medium

This recipe is also from Pat Chapman, who wrote to me: "This curry paste is green in color because of its use of coriander leaves [cilantro] and mint. You can buy it factory made, but it does not have the delicious fresh taste of this recipe. You will come across green masala paste in the Indian home where it is used to enhance curry dishes and impart a subtle flavour that can be obtained in no other way." (Note: This recipe requires advance preparation.)

1 teaspoon (5 mL) fenugreek seeds
6 cloves garlic, peeled and chopped
2 tablespoons (10 mL) finely chopped fresh ginger
¾ cup (177 mL) fresh mint leaves
¾ cup (177 mL) fresh cilantro
1 teaspoon (5 mL) salt
1 tablespoon (15 mL) turmeric
2 teaspoons (10 mL) ground red chile, such as cayenne
½ teaspoon (2.5 mL) ground cloves
1 teaspoon (5 mL) ground cardamom seeds
½ cup (118 mL) distilled white vinegar
½ cup (118 mL) vegetable oil
¼ cup (59 mL) sesame oil

1. Soak the fenugreek seeds in water overnight. They will swell and acquire a jelly-like coating. Strain the fenugreek and discard the water.
2. Combine the soaked fenugreek, garlic, ginger, mint, cilantro, salt, turmeric, chile powder, cloves, and cardamom in a blender or food processor and purée.
3. Add the vinegar and enough water to make a creamy paste.
4. In a wok, heat the oils over high heat. Add the paste. It will splatter a bit, so be careful. Stir constantly to prevent the paste from sticking until the water content is cooked out, about 5 minutes. As the liquid reduces,

the paste will begin to make a regular bubbling noise (hard to describe, but it goes *chup-chup-chup*) if you don't stir, and it will splatter. This is your audible cue that it is ready. To tell whether the spices are cooked, take the wok off the stove and let stand for 3 to 4 minutes. If the oil floats to the top, the spices are cooked. If not, add a little more oil and repeat.

5. Bottle the paste in sterilized jars. Then heat up a little more oil and top off the paste by pouring in enough oil to cover. Seal the jars and store.

Sri Lankan Dark Curry Paste

Yield: About 1 cup (236 mL)   Heat Scale: Hot

Some Sri Lankan curries are quite dark—almost black—because the various seeds that are used are toasted or roasted to a dark brown color. They are also quite hot, as is this basic southern paste that can be used whenever curry paste or powder is called for.

2 dried red New Mexican chiles, stems and seeds removed
10 small, hot dried red chiles, such as piquins, stems and seeds removed
1 tablespoon (15 mL) uncooked rice
1 tablespoon (15 mL) fresh, grated coconut or shredded, unsweetened coconut
2 tablespoons (30 mL) coriander seeds
1 tablespoon (15 mL) cumin seeds
1 tablespoon (15 mL) fennel seeds
1 teaspoon (5 mL) cardamom seeds
1 teaspoon (5 mL) fenugreek seeds
1 (2-inch [5 cm]) cinnamon stick
1 teaspoon (5 mL) dark brown mustard seeds
6 whole cloves
5 curry leaves (optional)
½ cup (118 mL) distilled white vinegar
½ cup (118 mL) vegetable oil

1. Preheat the oven to 350°F (180°C).

2. Roast the chiles on a cookie sheet for 5 to 10 minutes, until they turn very dark. Remove the pan from the oven and allow the chiles to cool.

3. In a dry skillet, roast the rice, coconut, coriander, cumin, fennel, cardamom, fenugreek, cinnamon, and mustard over medium heat, stirring often, for 5 minutes or until everything turns dark brown, almost black.

4. Combine the roasted chiles, roasted spices, cloves, and curry leaves in a spice mill and blend to a fine powder.

5. In a bowl, combine the powder with the vinegar and enough water to make a creamy paste. Heat the vegetable oil in a wok or skillet over medium heat. Add the paste and cook for about 5 minutes.

Andhra Pradesh Ripe Red Chile Chutney
Yield: 2–3 cups (500–708 mL)   Heat Scale: Varies

This recipe was collected in India by contributor Linda Lynton, who noted: "This chutney will last a year under tropical Indian conditions, so it could well last longer in cooler climates."

2 pounds (1.1 kg) red chiles (New Mexican variety for a mild chutney, red jalapeños for a hot chutney), stems removed
1 tablespoon (15 mL) salt
¾ cup (177 mL) tamarind paste (available in Asian markets)
1 teaspoon (5 mL) ground turmeric
1 cup (236 mL) sesame oil
¼ cup (59 mL) fenugreek seeds, roasted and ground to a powder

1. In a food processor, combine the chiles, salt, and tamarind paste and process to a coarse purée. Store the mixture in an airtight, sterile jar in the refrigerator for 2 to 3 days.
2. Heat the sesame oil. Add the fenugreek powder and stir well. Pour the mixture over the chiles in the jar and mix thoroughly. The chutney is ready to eat with curries.

Fresh Mango-Apple Chutney
Yield: About 6 cups (1.4 L)   Heat Scale: Medium

Here is an Indian chutney made in the manner of a salsa, but with very different flavorings. Feel free to experiment with other fruits. Serve this chutney at room temperature with a fiery hot lamb vindaloo. Store the remainder in jars in the refrigerator, where, if tightly sealed, they will keep for a couple of weeks.

3 mangos, peeled, pitted, and chopped fine
3 cups (708 mL) chopped apples
½ cup (118 mL) raisins
½ cup (118 mL) currants
2 cups (473 mL) distilled white vinegar
½ cup (118 mL) sugar
½ cup (118 mL) brown sugar
1 onion, peeled and chopped fine
3 cloves garlic, peeled and minced
½ teaspoon (2.5 mL) salt
3 serrano or jalapeño chiles, stems and seeds removed, minced
1 (2-inch [5 cm]) piece ginger, peeled and grated
1 teaspoon (5 mL) ground cinnamon
1 teaspoon (5 mL) ground allspice
1 teaspoon (5 mL) mustard seeds

1. Combine all the ingredients in a large bowl and mix well, adding water if necessary to adjust the consistency to your liking. Allow to sit for at least 2 hours to blend the flavors, stirring twice.

Kabul Tomato-Nut Chutney

Yield: 1 cup (236 mL)   Heat Scale: Hot

This chutney originated in Kabul, Afghanistan, but it is found in many homes and restaurants in neighboring Pakistan, too. Saffron essence is a concentrated flavor and can be purchased online or from a gourmet food shop. Use fresh rose petals from your garden, or buy them freeze-dried.

1 tablespoon (15 mL) tamarind pulp (or 2 teaspoons [10 mL] lime juice)
½ cup (118 mL) warm water
3 large tomatoes, sliced
¼ cup (59 mL) raw cashews
¼ cup (59 mL) raw almonds
¼ cup (59 mL) raw walnuts
6 green chiles, such as serranos, stems removed
1 teaspoon (5 mL) sugar (optional)
1 teaspoon (5 mL) salt
½ teaspoon (2.5 mL) ground coriander
½ teaspoon (2.5 mL) ground cumin
¼ teaspoon (1.25 mL) ground cloves
¼ teaspoon (1.25 mL) ground nutmeg
½ teaspoon (2.5 mL) saffron essence
½ cup (118 mL) rose petals

1. Soak the tamarind pulp in the warm water for 10 minutes. Strain the pulp and reserve the liquid.
2. In a food processor or blender, purée the tomatoes and nuts. Add the tamarind water, chiles, sugar, salt, and ground spices and continue processing for 5 minutes.
3. Add the saffron essence and rose petals and continue processing for 2 minutes.

Banana-Date Chutney

Yield: 4–6 cups (.95 L–1.4 L)   Heat Scale: Mild

In addition to being accompaniments to curries, chutneys such as this one from South India can be scooped up with a piece of flat bread or even mixed into rice. Chutneys are also great as a dip for rolls, crackers, or vegetables.

6 ripe bananas
½ cup (118 mL) dates, seeds removed
½ cup (118 mL) raisins
1 cup (236 mL) water
2 tablespoons (30 mL) sugar
2 tablespoons (30 mL) ground ginger
1 tablespoon (15 mL) freshly ground black pepper
1 teaspoon (5 mL) hot red chile powder
1 tablespoon (15 mL) ground coriander
¼ cup (59 mL) slivered almonds
¼ cup (59 mL) crushed cashews
¼ cup (59 mL) chopped walnuts
1 green chile, such as serrano, stem removed, minced
Salt, to taste

1. In a food processor or blender, purée the bananas, dates, and raisins.
2. In a saucepan, combine the water and sugar. Bring to a boil over medium heat and boil for 1 minute. Add the ground spices. As the sugar water thickens, add the nuts and green chile and simmer for 1 minute. Add the date mixture and simmer for 5 minutes. Remove from the heat and serve hot or cold. This chutney can be refrigerated for several weeks.

Coconut-Chile Chutney

Yield: 4–6 cups (.95–1.4 L)   Heat Scale: Mild

This chutney from the southwest coast of India can be served as a dip with fried plantains.

1 tablespoon (15 mL) tamarind pulp (or 2 teaspoons [10 mL] lime juice)
½ cup (118 mL) water
½ cup (118 mL) warm water
2 cups (473 mL) shredded coconut
1 (1-inch [2.5 cm]) piece ginger, peeled
8 green chiles, such as serranos, stems removed and halved
4 cloves garlic, peeled
½ cup (118 mL) cilantro
6 large green mangos
1 teaspoon (5 mL) cumin seeds
1 teaspoon (5 mL) fenugreek seeds
4 tablespoons (60 mL) olive or vegetable oil
½ teaspoon (2.5 mL) mustard seeds
1 teaspoon (5 mL) red chile powder
1 teaspoon (5 mL) ground turmeric
¼ cup (59 mL) curry leaves (optional)
½ cup (118 mL) cilantro leaves
Salt, to taste

1. Soak the tamarind pulp, if using, in the warm water for 10 minutes, then strain the pulp and reserve the liquid.
2. In a food processor or blender, grind the coconut, ginger, chiles, garlic, and cilantro into a fine paste. Add the tamarind water. Set aside.
3. Peel the mangos and discard the pits. In a blender or food processor, grind the mango flesh, cumin, and fenugreek into a smooth paste. Set aside.
4. Heat the oil in a large skillet over medium heat for 2 minutes. Reduce the heat and add the mustard seeds. When the seeds begin to pop, add the reserved mango paste, chile powder, turmeric, and coconut-tamarind paste. Add a little water, mix well, and cook over low heat for 10 minutes, stirring occasionally.
5. Remove from the heat and add the curry leaves, cilantro, and salt. Transfer to a jar. This will keep in the refrigerator for at least three months.

Qibe
(Ethiopian Curried Butter)

Yield: ½ cup (118 mL)   Heat Scale: Mild

A staple in Ethiopian cuisine, this butter is used often in recipes and on the native bread, injera. There is no heat to this butter, but you may add some hot chile powder if you wish.

½ pound (224 g) butter
2 teaspoons (10 mL) grated ginger root
1 clove garlic, minced
¼ cup (59 mL) chopped red onion
¼ teaspoon (1.25 mL) fenugreek seeds
¼ teaspoon (1.25 mL) ground cumin
¼ teaspoon (1.25 mL) dried basil or ½ teaspoon (2.5 mL) fresh basil
1 to 8 teaspoons ground cardamom
¼ teaspoon (1.25 mL) dried oregano or ½ teaspoon (2.5 mL) fresh oregano
1 pinch turmeric

1. Melt the butter in a medium saucepan over low heat, stirring constantly. Skim the foam off the top as it cooks, until there is no more foam.
2. Add the ginger root, garlic, onion, and spices and simmer, stirring, for 15 minutes.
3. Remove the saucepan from heat and let stand until all the spices settle. Strain through cheesecloth into a container. Cover and store in a cool place. Qibe does not need to be refrigerated.

Nam Prik Num
(Thai Red Chile–Tomato Dip)

Yield: About 2 cups (473 mL)   Heat Scale: Medium

Here is another sauce that is served in Thailand as a dip for raw vegetables or as a condiment for grilled or roasted meats—but this one traditionally has a slightly burned flavor. To make this sauce milder, substitute fresh red New Mexican chiles for the jalapeños. It will keep, covered and refrigerated, for about a week.

3 fresh red jalapeño chiles, stems removed
3 shallots, peeled and halved
5 cloves garlic, peeled
2 ripe tomatoes
1½ tablespoons (22.5 mL) freshly minced cilantro
1 tablespoon (15 mL) prepared fish sauce
1 tablespoon (15 mL) fresh lime juice

1. Heat a skillet over high heat until very hot. Add the chiles and roast, turning occasionally, until the skins blacken. Transfer the chiles to a bowl.
2. Add the shallots and garlic to the skillet and roast, stirring occasionally, for 5 minutes. Transfer them to a bowl.

3. Add the tomatoes to the skillet and roast, turning occasionally, until the skins are blackened. Transfer them to a bowl and set aside until they are cool enough to handle. Cut the tomatoes into quarters.
4. Combine the chiles (skins on), shallots, garlic, and tomatoes (skins on) in a food processor and pulse to coarsely chop. Transfer this mixture to a bowl. Add the cilantro, fish sauce, and lime juice and mix well.

Gaeng Ped
(Red Curry Paste)

Yield: About 1 cup (236 mL)   Heat Scale: Hot

This paste is, of course, a primary ingredient in many Thai curries. Traditionally, it is patiently pounded by hand with a heavy mortar and pestle, but a food processor does the job quickly and efficiently. It will keep in the refrigerator for about a month.

5 New Mexican dried red chiles, stems and seeds removed
10 small dried red chiles, such as piquins, stems and seeds removed
2 teaspoons (10 mL) ground cumin
2 teaspoons (10 mL) ground coriander
2 small onions
1 teaspoon (5 mL) black peppercorns
½ cup fresh cilantro
¼ cup (59 mL) fresh basil or mint leaves
1 teaspoon (5 mL) salt
3 (2-inch [5 cm]) stalks lemongrass, bulb included
1 (1-inch [2.5 cm]) piece galangal, peeled
1 tablespoon (15 mL) chopped garlic
1 tablespoon (15 mL) shrimp paste
1 tablespoon (15 mL) corn or peanut oil
1 tablespoon (15 mL) lime zest
¼ cup (59 mL) water

1. Soak all the chiles in water for 20 minutes to soften, then drain.
2. In a dry skillet, roast the coriander and cumin seeds over high heat for about 2 minutes. Set aside to cool. When the seeds are cool, grind them to a fine powder in a spice mill.
3. Combine the soaked chiles, the ground seeds, and all the remaining ingredients in a food processor or blender and purée into a fine paste. Store in a tightly sealed jar in the refrigerator.

Gaeng Kiow Wan
(Green Curry Paste)
Yield: About 1¼ cups (295 mL)   Heat Scale: Hot

This standard Thai green curry paste can be used in many ways. Add it to soups or stews, or use it as a marinade for grilled meats. Marinate a dozen shrimp in this paste and stir-fry them quickly in olive oil. The result is an instant lunch or dinner.

1 tablespoon (15 mL) coriander seeds
1 tablespoon (15 mL) cumin seeds
6 whole peppercorns
3 stalks lemongrass, bulb included, chopped
½ cup (118 mL) cilantro
1 (2-inch [5 cm]) piece galangal or ginger, peeled
1 teaspoon (5 mL) lime zest
8 cloves garlic, peeled
4 shallots, peeled and coarsely chopped
12 green chiles, such as serranos, stems and seeds removed, halved
¼ cup (59 mL) water
1 teaspoon (5 mL) salt
1 teaspoon (5 mL) shrimp paste

1. In a dry skillet, roast the coriander and cumin seeds over high heat for about 2 minutes. Set aside to cool. When the seeds are cool, grind them to a fine powder in a spice mill.
2. Combine the ground spices with all the remaining ingredients in a food processor or blender and purée until a fine paste forms.
3. Pour the paste into an airtight jar and refrigerate. It will keep in the refrigerator for about a month.

Gaeng Mussaman
(Muslim Curry Paste)

Yield: About 1¼ cups (295 mL)   Heat Scale: Hot

This is a relatively recent curry paste for Thailand—it is only about 250 years old! Food historians say that Muslim traders from India introduced this curry to King Rama I, and the royal cooks perfected it. Initially, the story goes, the cooks were not keen on using cinnamon, but once they tasted their preparation, they fell in love with the new curry.

12 dried red chiles, such as Thai or piquins, stems and seeds removed
1 cup (236 mL) warm water
2 tablespoons (30 mL) cumin seeds
1 teaspoon (5 mL) coriander seeds
1 teaspoon (5 mL) black peppercorns
1 teaspoon (5 mL) whole cloves
1 teaspoon (5 mL) ground cinnamon
1 teaspoon (5 mL) ground mace
1 teaspoon (5 mL) ground nutmeg
1 teaspoon (5 mL) ground cardamom
3 stalks fresh lemongrass, bulb included
1 (2-inch [5 cm]) piece galangal or ginger, peeled
2 teaspoons (10 mL) salt
6 shallots, peeled and finely chopped
1 tablespoon (15 mL) shrimp paste

1. Soak the chiles in the warm water for 20 minutes, then drain and set aside.
2. Meanwhile, in a dry skillet, roast the cumin, coriander, peppercorns, and cloves over high heat for 2 minutes, then transfer the spices to a bowl to cool. Add the cinnamon, mace, nutmeg, and cardamom to the pan and roast for 1 minute, then remove from the heat. When the whole spices are cool, grind them in a spice mill, and then combine them with the roasted ground spices. Set aside.
3. In a food processor or blender, combine the spices with the remaining ingredients and purée into a fine paste.
4. Transfer the paste to a clean, airtight jar and refrigerate. It will keep for about one month in the refrigerator.

Sambal Badjak
(Pirate's Chile and Nut Relish)
Yield: About 2 cups (473 mL)   Heat Scale: Hot

Badjak is one of the most commonly served Indonesian sambals. It is usually made with candlenuts, which are hard to find in North America. I recommend substituting macadamia nuts or cashews. Serve this sambal with grilled meats.

7 fresh red serrano or jalapeño chiles, stems and seeds removed, chopped
1 tablespoon (15 mL) shrimp paste
1 medium onion, peeled and chopped
4 cloves garlic, peeled and chopped
½ cup (118 mL) chopped macadamia nuts
Salt, to taste
1 tablespoon (15 mL) brown sugar
½ cup (118 mL) water
½ cup (118 mL) coconut milk
3 tablespoons (45 mL) vegetable oil

1. Combine the chiles, shrimp paste, onion, garlic, and nuts in a food processor and purée to a coarse paste. Transfer to a bowl and add the salt, brown sugar, water, and coconut milk. Mix well.
2. In a skillet, heat the oil over medium heat. Add the chile mixture. Sauté the mixture for 20 minutes, stirring constantly.

Sambal Matah
(Hot Shallot and Lemongrass Sambal)
Yield: About 2 cups (473 mL)   Heat Scale: Hot

Here is a Balinese sambal that features lemongrass and "bird's eye" chiles—those tiny but incredibly fiery pods known as chiltepins in Mexico and the United States. It can be served on the side to add heat to any Asian dish, particularly those with rice, fish, or chicken.

10 shallots, peeled and diced
4 cloves garlic, peeled and minced
10 fresh chiltepin, piquin, or Thai chiles, stems removed, minced with the seeds (or substitute 5 fresh red serranos)
4 kaffir lime leaves, minced as finely as possible (available in Asian markets)
1 teaspoon (5 mL) shrimp paste
4 (2-inch [5 cm]) stalks lemongrass, minced
½ teaspoon (2.5 mL) salt
¼ teaspoon (1.25 mL) crushed black peppercorns
2 tablespoons (30 mL) lime juice
⅓ cup (79 mL) peanut oil

1. Combine all ingredients in a bowl, stir well, and allow to sit for 1 hour at room temperature to blend the flavors.

Sambal Timun
(Pineapple, Cucumber, and Chile Condiment)

Yield: About 2 cups (473 mL)   Heat Scale: Medium

This typical relish from Singapore includes Malaysian fruit and Chinese dried shrimp. Serve this Asian "salsa" with rice and curry dishes or any dish where sour, sweet, and hot flavors are desired.

4 fresh serrano or jalapeño chiles, stems and seeds removed, chopped
½ cup (118 mL) dried shrimp
¼ cup (59 mL) lime juice (fresh preferred)
¼ cup (59 mL) distilled white vinegar
1 tablespoon (15 mL) sugar
1 cucumber, peeled and diced
½ cup (118 mL) diced pineapple chunks (fresh preferred)
4 green onions, chopped, including a little of the green
Salt, to taste

1. Combine the chiles, shrimp, lime juice, vinegar, and sugar in a blender and purée until smooth.
2. Toss the remaining ingredients with the dressing and let sit for 2 to 3 hours to blend the flavors before serving.

Petjili Nanas
(Sweet-Hot Indonesian Pineapple Relish)

Yield: 6 servings   Heat Scale: Medium

Sweet relishes are called petjili in Indonesia, but the word "sweet" doesn't exclude chiles—it incorporates them. This relish is perfect to serve as an accompaniment to curries.

1 tablespoon (15 mL) vegetable oil
1 small onion, peeled and chopped
3 red serrano or jalapeño chiles, stems and seeds removed, chopped
1 whole pineapple, peeled, cored, and chopped
1 teaspoon (5 mL) ground cinnamon
2 tablespoons (30 mL) brown sugar
Salt, to taste

1. In a wok, heat the oil over high heat. Add the onion and chiles and stir-fry for 2 minutes. Add the remaining ingredients and stir-fry for 10 minutes.

Variation
To make petjili mangaa, replace the pineapple with 2 cups (473 mL) chopped mangos.

Chinese Chile Oil
Yield: 1 cup (236 mL)   Heat Scale: Extremely Hot

Use this fired-up oil to replace vegetable oils, such as corn oil, in dressings or when frying. It can also be used as a base for dipping sauces. Since capsaicin is miscible with oil (it does not mix with water), the heat of the chiles is really intensified.

1 cup (236 mL) small dried red chiles, such as Thai or santaka, stems removed
1 cup (236 mL) peanut oil
Freshly ground black pepper, to taste (optional)

1. Combine all the ingredients in a small saucepan and cook over high heat until the oil begins to boil. Cook for 5 minutes, taking care that the chiles do not burn. Remove the pan from the heat and allow the mixture to sit for about 4 hours.
2. Strain the peppers and transfer the oil to a bottle. Store in a dark place.

Ginger Plum Sauce Mustard
Yield: 1 cup (236 mL)   Heat Scale: Medium

This Chinese mustard is sweet and hot, with a crisp, sharp, distinctive flavor. The sweetness comes from the ginger, the plum sauce, and even the vinegar, if Chinese black vinegar is used. Found in Asian markets, this vinegar has a distinctive, fruity, salty, complex, nonacidic taste. This mustard is very easy to prepare and makes a great dipping sauce for Asian appetizers or a glaze for ham or duck. (Note: This recipe requires advance preparation.)

¼ cup (59 mL) brown mustard seeds
½ cup (118 mL) yellow mustard powder
2 tablespoons (30 mL) Chinese vegetarian black vinegar (available in Asian markets, or substitute rice or distilled white vinegar)
3 tablespoons (45 mL) Chinese plum sauce (available in Asian markets)
⅓ cup (79 mL) grated ginger
1 tablespoon (15 mL) brown sugar
1 teaspoon (5 mL) finely minced garlic

1. Place the mustard seeds in a spice mill or coffee grinder and process to a powder.
2. In a bowl, combine the mustards and add the vinegar, plum sauce, and ¼ cup (59 mL) water. Stir to form a paste. Add the ginger, sugar, and garlic and mix well.
3. Spoon the mustard into a sterilized jar and refrigerate for 1 week before using.

Shichimi Togarashi (Japanese Seven-Flavor Spice)

Yield: ¼–⅓ cup (59–79 mL)   Heat Scale: Hot

This favorite Japanese seasoning sometimes goes by the name of seven-flavor spice, or just togarashi. Named for the togarashi chile, it's a mixture of seven spices, with the chile being the most important ingredient. Sometimes more than seven spices are used, but even then it's called by the same name. This is a very hot seasoning with a definite citrus flavor, commonly used to spice udon noodles, soups, and yakitoris. It's used as a seasoning and added to finished dishes as a condiment.

3–4 tablespoons (45–60 mL) crushed togarashi chile (or substitute takanot-sume, santaka, or piquin chiles)
1 tablespoon (15 mL) dried orange or tangerine peel
2 teaspoons (10 mL) white sesame seeds
2 teaspoons (10 mL) black sesame seeds
1 teaspoon (5 mL) Sichuan (sansho or fagara) pepper (available by mail order, or substitute equal amounts of anise and allspice)
1 teaspoon (5 mL) shredded nori (available in Asian markets)
½ teaspoon (2.5 mL) ground ginger

1. Place all the ingredients in a spice mill or coffee grinder and process to a coarse powder. Store the mixture in an airtight container.

Kimchi

Yield: About 4 cups (.95 L)   Heat Scale: Medium

Here is a classic Korean condiment that traditionally takes months to make because it is fermented in clay pots. Mine takes only 3 or 4 days. Serve kimchi as an accompaniment to stir-fried Asian dishes and to grilled or broiled meats. (Note: This recipe requires advance preparation.)

1 head Chinese cabbage, coarsely chopped
1 tablespoon (15 mL) salt
5 green or fresh red New Mexican chiles, roasted and peeled, stems and seeds removed, chopped fine
2 tablespoons (30 mL) grated fresh ginger
6 green onions, chopped (including the greens)
1 clove garlic, peeled and minced

1. In a large mixing bowl, sprinkle the cabbage with the salt, cover, and let stand for 1 hour. Rinse well with cold water and drain. Return the cabbage to the bowl.
2. Add the remaining ingredients, stir well, and add water to cover. Allow the mixture to pickle in the refrigerator for 3 or 4 days.
3. To serve, drain off the water and warm to room temperature.

Fijian Coconut Chutney

Yield: About 2½ cups (591 mL)   Heat Scale: Medium

Here is the classic chutney that is served with Fiji's curries. It can also be used as a side dish for various rice recipes. It will last in the refrigerator for a couple of weeks.

2 cups (473 mL) freshly grated coconut
1 cup (236 mL) chopped fresh cilantro leaves
3 tablespoons (45 mL) lemon juice
1 tablespoon (15 mL) minced fresh ginger
1 green chile, such as serrano or jalapeño, seeds and stem removed, minced
Salt, to taste

1. In a bowl, combine all the ingredients and mix well. Allow to sit, covered, in the refrigerator for at least 1 hour to blend the flavors.

Classic White Sauce

Yield: 2 quarts (1.9 L)

This mock béchamel is for use in the soups in Chapter 7. It is not hot and spicy in this form, but you can add chile powder or a hot sauce to taste if you wish. To make sure you don't scorch this sauce, you can also use a double boiler. You may wish to add 1 teaspoon (5 mL) sugar to give the illusion of richness—it's only 17 calories. This sauce will last for a week in the refrigerator. To reheat, use low heat or a double boiler.

½ pound (224 g) butter
1¼ cup (59 mL) all-purpose flour
6 cups (1.4 L) scalded milk
¼ teaspoon (1.25 mL) white pepper
¼ teaspoon (1.25 mL) salt
⅛ teaspoon (.6 mL) freshly ground nutmeg

1. In a pan over low heat, melt the butter. Add the flour and stir with a whisk to make a roux; do not brown.
2. Slowly blend in the milk, stirring with a whisk briskly until there are no lumps.
3. Add the pepper, salt, and nutmeg and mix well.

Basic Beef Stock

Yield: 6 quarts (5.7 L)

Use this stock as a base of some of the soups in Chapter 7. The time you invest in this aromatic procedure will pay off big. Dogs will hang around your kitchen and will not run off. This stock will keep for about a week in the refrigerator, and it will keep in the freezer for months. The yield will depend on how much reduction occurs during the cooking. Some cooks have been known to work with a stock for 100 hours, constantly adding water and reducing. Here, I have used a minimum time. The stock is not hot and spicy in this form, but you can add chile powder or a hot sauce to taste if you wish.

¼ pound (113 g) butter, melted
1½ pounds (681 g) stew beef
3 marrow bones
½ cup (118 mL) red wine
1 tablespoon (15 mL) salt
1 bunch parsley
2 small carrots, peeled if desired, quartered
½ teaspoon (2.5 mL) dried thyme
1½ tablespoons (22.5 mL) black peppercorns
2 medium onions, peeled and quartered
¼ teaspoon (1.25 mL) cloves
2 small leeks, cut in ½-inch (1 cm) rounds
3 large bay leaves
2 ribs celery, with leaves, plus the heart
1 turnip, peeled if desired, quartered (optional)
2 gallons (7.6 L) water

1. Preheat the oven to 375°F (190°C)
2. Pour the butter into a shallow glass baking dish. Place the meat and bones on top of the butter and pour the wine over all. Cover with foil and bake for 30 minutes. Transfer the contents of the dish (including all the scrapings) to a stockpot.
3. Add the remaining ingredients and bring to a rolling boil. Reduce the heat, skim any foam off the top, and simmer, uncovered, for 2 hours. Remove from the heat and strain through cheesecloth. Refrigerate or freeze the stock and skim the fat off the top.

Classic Chicken Stock

Yield: About 1 gallon (3.8 L)

This classic stock from the French school is the base of some of the soups in Chapter 7. It may be reduced further to intensify the flavor. It freezes very well. If you've been buying bouillon in cubes or cans, do yourself a favor, reduce your sodium intake, and make this stock from scratch. Breaking the chicken bones releases marrow and adds flavor. It is not hot and spicy in this form, but you can add chile powder or a hot sauce to taste if you wish. Save the shredded chicken for chicken salad or an enchilada filling.

1(4–5 pound [1.8–2.3 kg]) roasting hen (free-range if possible)
1 gallon (3.8 L)
1½ teaspoons (7.5 mL) salt
4 whole bay leaves
1 medium onion, peeled and halved
4 cloves garlic, peeled
1 bunch parsley, washed
1½ teaspoons (7.5 mL) black peppercorns
1 large carrot, halved lengthwise
1 celery stalk, including leaves

1. Set the hen on a cutting board. With the flat side of a cleaver, press down on the breast until you hear the bone break. Turn the hen on its side and, with the dull side of the cleaver, hit the drumstick once at the midpoint with enough force to crack the bone. Do the same to the wing. Turn the hen on its other side and repeat. Turn the hen breast down and strike the backbone perpendicularly twice, each about a third of the way in from either side, to crack the back.
2. In a large stockpot, combine the water, salt, bay leaves, onion, garlic, parsley, peppercorns, carrot, and celery and bring to a rolling boil. Add the chicken and boil, uncovered, for 1 to 1½ hours, adding more water as needed to keep the chicken covered. Skim off any foam that rises.
3. To test the chicken for doneness, pull on one of the legs. It should separate without force at the joint, and there should not be any visible blood. Do not overcook the chicken.
4. Remove the chicken from the stock and reserve it for another use. Strain the stock and reserve it. For a clearer stock, line the strainer with cheesecloth. Chill the stock in the freezer until the fat congeals and remove the fat with a spoon.

Traditional European Fish Stock

Yield: About 2 quarts (1.9 L)

This is the base of some of the soups in Chapter 7. It is a basic recipe, so don't be afraid to embellish it. Add any frozen seafood trimmings (such as shrimp shells) or any frozen fish from that fishing trip three years ago that you don't want to serve as an entrée. Feel free to add fresh herbs from your garden. Rich fish, such as salmon, make a better stock. This keeps in the refrigerator for about a week and freezes well. The difference between this and court bouillon is that the latter is used for poaching rather than as a base for soups. It is not hot and spicy in this form, but you can add chile powder or a hot sauce to taste if you wish.

2 tablespoons (30 mL) butter
2 pounds (1.1 kg) fish trimmings, such as bones, skin, meat, heads, and tails (not entrails)
3 quarts (2.85 L) water
¼ cup (59 mL) whole parsley, firmly packed
2 medium onions, peeled and quartered
4 large bay leaves
6 large cloves garlic, peeled
2 tablespoons (30 mL) black peppercorns, bruised
1 large leek, white part only, cut into ¼-inch (.5 cm) rounds
3 large celery ribs with heart and leaves, chopped
3 small carrots, peeled if desired, cut into ½-inch (1 cm) rings
2 teaspoons (10 mL) salt

1. In a large, heavy pot, melt the butter over medium heat. Add the fish trimmings and sauté for 3 minutes.
2. Add the water and bring to a boil. Add the remaining ingredients. Reduce the heat and simmer, uncovered, for 1 hour.
3. Remove from the heat and strain through cheesecloth.

Wonton Soup Broth

Yield: 3½ quarts (3.44 L)

This broth is a key ingredient for the wonton soups in this book. Chileheads requiring more pungency than the wontons will provide can add five or six whole chile pods (such as santaka or piquin). Remove the chiles before serving.

3½ quarts (3.44 L) Classic Chicken Stock (page 46)
2 teaspoons (10 mL) ground ginger
1 teaspoon (5 mL) five-spice powder
2 teaspoons (10 mL) sugar
1 tablespoon (15 mL) hoisin sauce
2 tablespoons (30 mL) Chinese rice wine
1 cup (236 mL) chopped green onions, cut diagonally into ⅛-inch (250 mm) lengths

1. In a large pot, heat the stock over high heat. Add the ginger, five-spice powder, sugar, and hoisin sauce. Bring to a boil, then reduce the heat to medium. Add the rice wine and cook for 5 minutes.

Super-Rich Vegetable Stock

Yield: About 10 cups (2.36 L)   Heat Scale: Varies

This stock is used as a base for some of the other recipes in this cookbook, but it's good enough to serve as a first course consommé. Baking or caramelizing the vegetables before adding the water adds an additional richness to the stock. If you wish, adding a 1–2 inch (2.5–5 cm) piece of kombu seaweed will further deepen the flavor. This stock will keep for 2 days, covered, in the refrigerator. It can also be frozen, divided into 2- or 3-cup (500 or 708 mL) freezer containers. The jalapeños are optional for making the stock spicy.

4 onions, unpeeled, cut into eighths
3 large ribs celery, cut into fourths
2 leeks (white part only)
1 head garlic
4 carrots, cut into 2-inch (5 cm) pieces
1½ cups (354 mL) dry white wine
2 tablespoons (30 mL) high-quality olive oil
3 green onions, cut into 1-inch (2.5 cm) pieces
⅓ cup (79 mL) chopped parsley, stems included
¼ cup (59 mL) chopped fresh basil or 2 tablespoons (30 mL) dried basil
1 teaspoon (5 mL) dried marjoram
½ cup (118 mL) chopped button mushrooms
½ cup (118 mL) chopped celery leaves
1 zucchini, peeled and sliced
3 cups (708 mL) coarsely chopped tomatoes
3 jalapeño chiles, stems and seeds removed, chopped (optional)
3 quarts (2.85 L) cold water
5 whole black peppercorns

1. Preheat the oven to 350°F (180°C).
2. Place the onions, celery ribs, leeks, garlic, and carrots in a shallow baking pan and pour the wine over the top. Bake uncovered for 1½ hours.
3. In a large pan, heat the oil over high heat. Add the baked vegetables and the green onions and sauté for 5 minutes, stirring occasionally. Add the parsley, basil, marjoram, mushrooms, celery leaves, zucchini, tomatoes, and chiles, if using, and sauté for 5 minutes, stirring occasionally
4. Add the cold water and peppercorns and bring the mixture to a boil. Lower the heat to a simmer, cover, and cook for 2 hours. Uncover and simmer for another 30 minutes. Strain the stock through a fine strainer lined with cheesecloth or a coffee filter and salt to taste.

TWO

Classic Hot Sauces and Salsas

- - - - - - - - - - - - - - -

Many people believe that hot sauces and salsas are somehow unique to the Western Hemisphere. This is simply not true. As chile peppers spread around the world, innovative cooks in the chile-infiltrated regions immediately began to make sauces that would replace the more expensive spicy ingredients, such as black pepper, with chiles. This chapter is organized by region of the world.

Salsa de Aji
(Ecuadorean Fresh Chile Sauce)
Yield: 1–2 cups (250–473 mL)   Heat Scale: Medium

This basic but classic Latin American salsa recipe was collected in Ecuador. Although the recipe calls for the use of an electric blender, one can follow the traditional method instead and use a mortar and pestle. Ecuadorians are very fond of putting beans in their salsa. The most popular beans are lupini, which are large white beans about the size of lima beans. Just add the cooked beans directly to the salsa. Use this salsa as a dip for chips or as a topping for grilled meats.

2 large tomatoes, seeds removed, finely chopped
1 medium onion, peeled and finely chopped
1 tablespoon (15 mL) chopped fresh cilantro
4 large, fresh aji chiles, stems and seeds removed, chopped (or substitute yellow wax hot or jalapeño chiles)
½ cup (118 mL) water
Salt, to taste

1. In a bowl, combine the tomatoes, onion, and cilantro.
2. Place the chiles, water, and 3 tablespoons (45 mL) of the tomato and onion mixture in a blender or processor and purée until smooth.
3. Add the chile purée to the remaining tomato mixture and mix well. Add salt to taste.

Salsa Picante de Peru
(Peruvian Hot Salsa)
Yield: ¾ cup (177 mL)   Heat Scale: Medium to Hot

This recipe is traditionally served with anticuchos (grilled beef heart) and corn on the cob, but it's a great accompaniment for any grilled meat.

3 fresh aji chiles, stems and seeds removed, minced (or substitute red serranos or jalapeños)
½ medium onion, minced
2 green onions, greens included, minced
4 cloves garlic, peeled and crushed
2 tablespoons (30 mL) vegetable oil
2 tablespoons (30 mL) red wine vinegar

1. Combine all the ingredients in a bowl and let sit for at least an hour to blend the flavors.

Pebre
(Chilean Hot Salsa)

Yield: 1½ cups (354 mL)   Heat Scale: Hot

Here is the classic hot sauce of Chile, one that is served with grilled or roasted meats. The type of chiles used varies considerably, depending on availability and the cook's preference.

2 tablespoons (30 mL) olive oil
1 tablespoon (15 mL) red wine vinegar
⅓ cup (79 mL) water
3 fresh yellow or red rocoto chiles, stems and seeds removed, minced
(or substitute 3 jalapeños or 1 habanero)
2 cloves garlic, peeled and minced
½ cup (118 mL) minced onion
½ cup (118 mL) minced cilantro
1 teaspoon (5 mL) minced fresh oregano
Salt, to taste

1. Combine the olive oil, vinegar, and water in a bowl and beat with a whisk. Add the remaining ingredients, mix well, and let stand for 2 hours to blend the flavors.

Miguel's Peruvian Aji Sauce

Yield: ¾ cup (177 mL)   Heat Scale: Hot

I grow a lot of Peruvian aji chiles in my garden every year, and I always put aside a large bag of them to take to Miguel, a computer wizard friend from Peru. On my second or third trip to Miguel's (it was a bumper harvest of chiles), he was having a late lunch with this aji sauce over his rice.

½ cup (118 mL) olive oil
4 or more fresh aji chiles, stems and seeds removed, minced (or substitute jalapeños)
2 cloves garlic, peeled and minced
¼ teaspoon (1.25 mL) salt
¼ teaspoon (1.25 mL) freshly ground black pepper
1 tablespoon (15 mL) fresh lime juice

1. In a small skillet, heat the oil over high heat. Add the chiles and garlic, lower the heat, and stir constantly to avoid burning the garlic.
2. Add the remaining ingredients and stir. Simmer for 10 minutes and then serve warm over rice or pasta.

Ocopa Sauce, Arequepa-Style

Yield: About 2½ cups (591 mL)   Heat Scale: Medium

From Arequipa, Peru, one of the hottest (chile-wise) cities in Latin America, comes this unusual, delicious sauce that is traditionally served over boiled and sliced potatoes garnished with lettuce, olives, and hardboiled egg slices. Try it over fried fish as well.

8 dried yellow aji chiles, stems and seeds removed, soaked in water to soften and puréed (or substitute 6 dried red New Mexican chiles)
3 soda crackers, crushed
¼ cup (59 mL) walnuts, ground in a spice mill
½ cup (118 mL) grated Monterey Jack cheese
¼ cup (59 mL) vegetable oil
¼ cup (59 mL) crushed onion
1 clove garlic, peeled and mashed
2 hard-boiled eggs, minced
12 medium shrimp, cooked, peeled, and mashed
Milk as needed
Salt, to taste
Freshly ground black pepper, to taste

1. In a large bowl, combine the chiles, crackers, walnuts, cheese, vegetable oil, onion, garlic, eggs, and shrimp and mix well to make a thick paste. Drizzle in milk as needed and use a potato masher to transform the paste into a thick sauce. Add salt and pepper to taste.

Salsa de Mani
(Hot and Spicy Peanut Sauce)

Yield: 2 cups (473 mL)   Heat Scale: Medium

This sauce is commonly served over potatoes in Ecuador. The amount of chile in the recipe can be adjusted to be mild or wild, as you wish. This side dish would add spice to any meat or seafood dish for a truly exotic dinner.

½ cup (118 mL) peanuts
¼ cup (59 mL) cream
¼ cup (59 mL) milk
⅓ cup (79 mL) peanut oil
¼ teaspoon (1.25 mL) salt
¼ teaspoon (1.25 mL) freshly ground black pepper
1½ teaspoons (7.5 mL) aji chile powder (or substitute piquin or cayenne)
1 small onion, peeled and quartered
½ cup (118 mL) grated goat cheese or crumbled feta cheese

1. Place all of the ingredients in a blender or food processor and blend on high speed for a few seconds, or until smooth.
2. Transfer the mixture to a saucepan and cook over low heat for 5 minutes, stirring constantly. Do not boil. Serve the sauce over hot cooked potatoes.

Môlho Malagueta
(Malagueta Sauce)

Yield: Enough to fill 1 (708 mL) wine bottle   Heat Scale: Hot

Here is a basic Brazilian hot sauce featuring malagueta chiles. It is simple and powerful, and it can be added to any recipe (except desserts) to spice it up. You'll need an empty 708 mL wine bottle, washed in boiling water and dried, with its cork, to make this sauce. (Note: This recipe requires advance preparation.)

1 cup (236 mL) fresh or dried malagueta chiles (or substitute tabascos or piquins), stems removed, left whole
708 mL wine bottle
1 cup (236 mL) distilled white vinegar
1¼ cups (295 mL) olive oil, or enough to fill the wine bottle

1. Place the chiles in the wine bottle. Add the vinegar and olive oil and stopper the bottle securely.
2. Place the bottle in the refrigerator and let the chiles steep for at least 2 weeks, shaking the bottle whenever you think about it. Shake well before using.

Môlho de Pimenta e Limao
(Hot Pepper Sauce with Lime)

Yield: ¾ cup (177 mL)   Heat Scale: Hot

This hot sauce from Pernambuco is commonly served in a small dish at Brazilian meals to spice up such dishes as feijoada and seafood stews. It features the malagueta pepper, that close relative of the tabasco pepper.

6 fresh malagueta chiles (or substitute piquins), stems and seeds removed, minced
1 clove garlic, peeled and minced
1 medium onion, peeled and minced
½ teaspoon (2.5 mL) salt
½ cup (118 mL) lemon or lime juice

1. Combine all the ingredients and allow to sit at room temperature for 2 hours to blend all the flavors.

Variation

Make a paste by puréeing the peppers, garlic, onion, and salt in a blender. Add the lemon or lime juice and stir well.

Môlho de Acaraj
(Chile-Shrimp Sauce)

Yield: About ¾ cup (177 mL)   Heat Scale: Hot

This Brazilian sauce is traditionally served over black-eyed pea fritters (acaraj, called accra in the West Indies), but it can also be spread over other bland foods, such as potatoes. It has an intense shrimp flavor and high heat. It is traditionally made with dende, palm oil, but I have substituted an oil with less saturated fat.

6 large shrimp, cooked, shelled, deveined, and mashed
1 onion, peeled and minced
5 fresh malagueta chiles, stems and seeds removed, minced (or substitute tabascos, Thais, or piquins)
½ teaspoon (2.5 mL) salt
3 tablespoons (45 mL) vegetable oil, or more if needed

1. With a mortar and pestle, crush together the shrimps, onion, chiles, and salt to make a paste.
2. In a sauté pan, heat the oil over high heat. Add the paste and sauté for 10 minutes, stirring constantly.

Variation
Add 1 teaspoon (5 mL) minced cilantro and ½ teaspoon (2.5 mL) ground ginger to the paste.

Belizean Habanero Sauce

Yield: 1 cup (236 mL)   Heat Scale: Extremely Hot

To preserve the distinctive flavor of the habaneros, don't cook them with the sauce but add them afterwards. This sauce will keep for weeks in the refrigerator. Use it to spice up eggs, sandwiches, soups, and seafood. This was the original, classic habanero sauce that countless commercial products have imitated.

1 tablespoon (15 mL) vegetable oil
1 small onion, peeled and chopped
½ cup (118 mL) chopped carrots
1 cup (236 mL) water
3 fresh habanero chiles, stems and seeds removed, minced
¼ cup (59 mL) lime juice

1. In a saucepan, heat the oil over high heat. Add the onion and sauté until soft. Add the carrots and water. Bring to a boil, reduce the heat, and simmer until the carrots are soft, about 12 minutes. Allow the mixture to cool at room temperature.
2. Add the habaneros and lime juice to the carrot mixture. Transfer the mixture to a blender and purée until smooth.

Pickapeppa Hot Sauce

Yield: 1½ cups (354 mL) Heat Scale: Medium

This is not the commercial sauce from Jamaica, but rather a specialty from Georgetown, Guyana. It is served over seafood or used to spice up gravies and salad dressings. (Note: This recipe requires advance preparation.)

12 dried bird peppers (chiltepins), stems and seeds removed, crushed (or substitute piquins or Thai chiles)
½ teaspoon (2.5 mL) dried mustard
3 tablespoons (45 mL) soy sauce
3 tablespoons (45 mL) lime juice
¼ cup (59 mL) catsup
1 teaspoon (5 mL) salt
2 teaspoons (10 mL) brown sugar
1 cup (236 mL) dry sherry

1. Combine all ingredients in a bottle and refrigerate for at least a week to blend the flavors. Shake at least once a day.

Chimichurri
(Hot Vinegar-Parsley Sauce)

Yield: 1½ cups (354 mL) Heat Scale: Medium

There is a minor debate about whether or not this Argentinian sauce should contain chile peppers. As usual, there is no real answer because cooks tend to add them or not, according to taste. This sauce is served with broiled, roasted, or grilled meat and poultry.

¼ cup (59 mL) olive oil
1 cup (236 mL) red wine vinegar
2 tablespoons (30 mL) aji chile powder (or substitute ground red New Mexican chile)
4 cloves garlic, peeled and minced
1 teaspoon (5 mL) crushed black peppercorns
1 teaspoon (5 mL) dried oregano
1 bay leaf, crushed
¼ cup (59 mL) minced curly parsley (or substitute Italian parsley)
Salt, to taste

1. In a bowl, combine the olive oil and vinegar and whip with a whisk.
2. Stir in the remaining ingredients, mix thoroughly, and allow to sit for 2 hours to blend the flavors.

Môlho de Churrasco
(Brazilian Barbecue Sauce)
Yield: 4 cups (.95 L)   Heat Scale: Medium

Brazilian barbecues are justly famous, and this sauce can be used for basting during the slow cooking process. Feel free to use it for American-style barbecues as well.

8 dried malagueta chiles, stems and seeds removed, crushed (or substitute piquin or Thai chiles)
3 cups (708 mL) distilled white vinegar
1 teaspoon (5 mL) salt
1 tablespoon (15 mL) sugar
2 cloves garlic, peeled and crushed
1 small onion, peeled and minced
2 tablespoons (30 mL) minced Italian parsley
1 teaspoon (5 mL) crushed dried rosemary
2 teaspoons (10 mL) minced fresh basil leaves
2 teaspoons (10 mL) minced fresh thyme leaves
2 teaspoons (10 mL) minced fresh marjoram or oregano leaves

1. Combine all the ingredients in a glass jar, cover, and shake well. Let stand for at least two hours to blend the flavors. Refrigerate until ready to use.

Salsa Criolla
(Creole Barbecue Sauce)
Yield: About 3 cups (708 mL)   Heat Scale: Medium

Of the many variations on this Creole sauce from Argentina, this is my favorite. It is served with grilled, roasted, or barbecued meats, especially matambre.

2 tablespoons (30 mL) ground aji chile (or substitute ground red New Mexican chile)
2 teaspoons (10 mL) dry yellow mustard
⅓ cup (79 mL) red wine vinegar
½ cup (118 mL) olive oil
2 cloves garlic, peeled and minced
2 onions, peeled and minced
3 ripe tomatoes, chopped fine
2 tablespoons (30 mL) minced Italian parsley
Salt, to taste

1. Combine the chile powder and the mustard with enough of the vinegar to make a paste. Add the remaining vinegar and the olive oil and beat with a whisk. Add the remaining ingredients, stir well, and allow to sit for 2 hours to blend the flavors.

Variation
Add 1 bell pepper and 1 jalapeño, both seeded and minced.

Guasacaca
(Barbecue Sauce from Venezuela)

Yield: About 4 cups (.95 L) Heat Scale: Medium

This is by far the most unusual barbecue sauce in Latin America. Because it contains fresh avocados, it must be used immediately and cannot be stored. Use it to marinate and/or baste grilled or barbecued shrimp, beef slices, or chicken.

1 cup (236 mL) minced onion
2 cloves garlic, peeled and minced
1 habanero chile, seeds and stem removed, minced (or substitute 2 jalapeños)
1 large, ripe avocado, peeled and pitted
2 cups (473 mL) ripe tomatoes, peeled and chopped
1 cup (236 mL) olive oil
¼ cup (59 mL) red wine vinegar (or substitute lime juice)
1 teaspoon (5 mL) prepared mustard
2 tablespoons (30 mL) minced parsley (Italian preferred)
Salt, to taste

1. With a mortar and pestle, mash the onion, garlic, chile, avocado, and tomatoes into a paste (this may need to be done in batches). Add the remaining ingredients and blend well with a fork.

The Earliest Mole Sauce

Yield: 2 cups (473 mL) Heat Scale: Medium

Why wouldn't the cooks of the prehistoric, ash-covered village of Cerén in El Salvador have developed sauces to serve over meats and vegetables? After all, there is evidence that curry mixtures were in existence thousands of years ago in what is now India, and I have to assume that Native Americans experimented with all available ingredients. Perhaps this mole sauce was served over stewed duck meat, as ducks were one of the domesticated meat sources of the Cerén villagers.

3 tablespoons (45 mL) pumpkin or squash seeds (pepitas)
4 tomatillos, husks removed
1 tomato, roasted in a hot, dry skillet and peeled
½ teaspoon (2.5 mL) chile seeds, from dried chile pods
1 corn tortilla, torn into pieces
2 tablespoons (30 mL) ground red chile, such as New Mexican, guajillo, or Chimayó
1 teaspoon (5 mL) annatto (achiote) seeds (or substitute achiote paste)
3 tablespoons (45 mL) vegetable oil
2½ cups (591 mL) chicken broth
1 ounce (28 g) Mexican chocolate (or substitute bittersweet chocolate)

1. Heat a heavy skillet over high heat. Add the pumpkin seeds and dry-roast until they start to pop. Shake the skillet and continue cooking and shaking until the seeds turn golden, about 3 to 5 minutes. Take care that they don't darken. Remove the seeds from the pan to cool completely. When the seeds are cool, place them in a spice mill or coffee grinder and process to a fine powder.

2. Put the pumpkin seeds, tomatillos, tomato, chile seeds, tortilla, chile powder, and annatto seeds in a blender or food processor and process, adding just enough broth to form a paste.

3. Reheat the skillet over medium heat. Add the oil, and when it's hot, add the paste. Fry the paste, stirring constantly, until fragrant, about 4 minutes.

4. Whisk in the remaining chicken broth and the chocolate. Cook, stirring constantly, until the sauce thickens to the desired consistency. If the sauce becomes too thick, thin with broth or water.

Salsa Casera
(Homemade Chiltepin Sauce)
Yield: 2 cups (473 mL)   Heat Scale: Extremely Hot

This diabolically hot sauce is also called pasta de chiltepin (chiltepin paste). It is used in soups and stews and to fire up machaca, eggs, tacos, tostadas, and beans. This is the exact recipe prepared in the home of my friend, Josefina Durán, in Cumpas, Sonora. (Note: This recipe requires advance preparation.)

2 cups (473 mL) chiltepins (or other small, hot chiles)
8 cloves garlic, peeled
1 teaspoon (5 mL) salt
1 teaspoon (5 mL) Mexican oregano
1 teaspoon (5 mL) coriander seed
1 cup (236 mL) water
1 cup (236 mL) apple cider vinegar

1. Combine all the ingredients in a blender and purée on high for 3 to 4 minutes. Refrigerate for 1 day to blend the flavors. This sauce keeps indefinitely in the refrigerator.

Salsa Chile de Arbol
(Chile de Arbol Sauce)

Yield: About 2 ¼ cup (59 mL)   Heat Scale: Hot

This is the sauce commonly bottled in liquor bottles and sold in the mercados and at roadside stands in central and northern Mexico. It is sprinkled over nearly any snack food, from tacos to tostadas.

30 chiles de arbol, stems and seeds removed
1 tablespoon (15 mL) sesame seeds
1 tablespoon (15 mL) pepitas (pumpkin seeds)
¼ teaspoon (1.25 mL) ground cumin
¼ teaspoon (1.25 mL) ground allspice
⅛ teaspoon (.6 mL) ground cloves
3 cloves garlic, peeled
1 cup (236 mL) apple cider vinegar
¾ cup (177 mL) water

1. Soak the chiles in water to cover until softened, about a half hour. Drain and set aside.
2. In a skillet, toast the sesame seeds and pepitas over high heat until they pop and turn brown. Combine the seeds with the drained chiles and the remaining ingredients and purée for about 3 minutes. Strain the mixture through a sieve and transfer to a bottle. It will keep for months in the refrigerator.

Xnipec
(Dog's Nose Salsa)

Yield: 1½ cups (354 mL)   Heat Scale: Extremely Hot

This classic Yucatecan salsa is definitely wild. Xnipec, pronounced "SCHNEE-peck," is Mayan for "dog's nose." Serve it—carefully—with grilled poultry or fish.

1 onion, peeled and diced (red or purple preferred)
Juice of 4 limes
4 habanero chiles, stems and seeds removed, diced
1 tomato, diced
2 tablespoons (30 mL) minced cilantro
Salt, to taste

1. Soak the diced onion in the lime juice for at least 30 minutes. Add the chiles, tomato, and cilantro and mix. Add salt to taste and add a little water if desired.

Salsa de Mole Poblano
(Classic Mole Poblano Sauce)

Yield: 2 cups (473 mL)   Heat Scale: Medium

This subtle blend of chocolate and chile is from Puebla, where it is known as the "National Dish of Mexico" when it is served over turkey. This sauce adds life to any kind of poultry, from roasted game hens to a simple grilled chicken breast. It is also excellent as a sauce over chicken enchiladas.

4 dried pasilla chiles, stems and seeds removed
4 dried red guajillo or New Mexican chiles, stems and seeds removed
1 medium onion, peeled and chopped
2 cloves garlic, peeled and chopped
2 medium tomatoes, peeled, seeds removed, and chopped
2 tablespoons (30 mL) sesame seeds, divided
½ cup (118 mL) almonds
½ corn tortilla, torn into pieces
¼ cup (59 mL) raisins
¼ teaspoon (1.25 mL) ground cloves
¼ teaspoon (1.25 mL) ground cinnamon
¼ teaspoon (1.25 mL) ground coriander
3 tablespoons (45 mL) shortening or vegetable oil
1 cup (236 mL) chicken broth
1 ounce (28 g) bitter chocolate, or more to taste

1. In a bowl, combine the chiles, onion, garlic, tomatoes, 1 tablespoon (15 mL) of the sesame seeds, almonds, tortilla, raisins, cloves, cinnamon, and coriander. Purée this mixture in batches in a blender until smooth.
2. In a skillet over high heat, melt the shortening. Add the purée and sauté for 10 minutes, stirring frequently. Add the chicken broth and chocolate and cook over a very low heat for 45 minutes. The sauce should be very thick. Sprinkle the remaining sesame seeds over the finished dish as a garnish.

Pipián Rojo
(Red Pipián Sauce)

Yield: About 2 cups (473 mL)   Heat Scale: Medium

The chiles, tomatoes, and squash seeds make this a very New World dish, as squash has been a staple of the Mexican diet since it was domesticated millennia ago. Typically, cooked chicken or turkey is added to this sauce from southern Mexico.

1½ cups (354 mL) ripe tomatoes, chopped
½ cup (118 mL) tomatillos, chopped
1 pasilla chile, stem and seeds removed
1 guajillo chile, stem and seeds removed (or substitute dried red New Mexican)
¾ cup (177 mL) water
¼ cup (59 mL) lime juice
½ cup (118 mL) sesame seeds
1 tablespoon (15 mL) pepitas (squash or pumpkin seeds)
1 (1-inch [2.5 cm]) cinnamon stick, broken up
2 teaspoons (10 mL) crushed hot red New Mexican chile
½ cup (118 mL) French bread, cubed
¼ teaspoon (1.25 mL) annatto (achiote) seeds
2 cups (473 mL) chicken broth
1 tablespoon (15 mL) all-purpose flour

1. In a saucepan, combine the tomatoes, tomatillos, and fresh chiles in the water and lime juice. Cook over medium heat for 10 minutes.
2. Toast the sesame seeds, pepitas, cinnamon stick, and crushed chile in a dry skillet over low heat for about 10 minutes.
3. In a food processor or blender, process the toasted ingredients. Add the cooked tomato mixture, stirring to achieve a smooth paste. Add the bread, achiote, chicken broth, and flour, and process until smooth. Return the sauce to the stove and heat through.

Salsa de Chipotle
(Chipotle Chile Sauce)

Yield: About 2½ cups (591 mL)   Heat Scale: Hot

From Tlaxcala comes a wonderful sauce that uses chipotles, or any type of smoked chile. Most commonly, chipotles are smoked red jalapeños. This table sauce is served at room temperature to spice up any main dish, including meats and poultry.

10 dried chipotle chiles
4 mulato chiles (or substitute anchos)
½ onion, chopped
10 cloves garlic, peeled
2 tablespoons (30 mL) olive oil
1 tablespoon (15 mL) sesame seeds
10 black peppercorns
10 cumin seeds
½ cinnamon stick
1 teaspoon (5 mL) Mexican oregano
½ teaspoon (2.5 mL) salt
¼ cup (59 mL) vegetable oil
½ cup (118 mL) distilled white vinegar
1 cup (236 mL) water

1. Soak the chiles in hot water until softened, about 1 hour. Drain. Remove the stems and seeds.
2. In a food processor or blender, combine the soaked chiles, onion, garlic, olive oil, sesame seeds, peppercorns, cumin seeds, cinnamon stick, Mexican oregano, and salt and process to a paste.
3. In a saucepan, heat the vegetable oil over medium heat. Fry the paste, stirring constantly, until it is aromatic, about 5 minutes. Add the vinegar and water, remove from the heat, and stir well.

Trinidadian Bird Pepper Sherry

Yield: 1 cup (236 mL)   Heat Scale: Hot

This recipe, which I found in a 1940s Trinidadian cookbook, is probably one of the earliest methods of preserving peppers in the tropics. It is also called "pepper wine." The sherry, which gradually picks up heat from the bird peppers, is sprinkled into soups and stews and makes them quite exotic. The peppers can be either fresh or dried. (Note: This recipe requires advance preparation.)

20 bird peppers (chiltepins or piquins), stems removed
1 cup (236 mL) dry sherry

1. Add the peppers to the sherry and allow to steep for several days. Keep in a jar in the refrigerator.

Pique de Vinagre y Aji es Bravos
(Bird Pepper Vinegar Pique)

Yield: 1 cup (236 mL)   Heat Scale: Hot

Here is a classic pique recipe from Puerto Rico. As usual, the longer the chiles steep, the hotter the sauce will be. It should be stored in a bottle with a sprinkler cap so the amount of sauce can be controlled as it is sprinkled over grilled fish or poultry, or even into salads. Note: This recipe requires advance preparation.

1 cup (236 mL) apple cider vinegar
10 to 20 bird peppers (chiltepins), or any small, hot chile, fresh or dried
4 cloves garlic, peeled and halved
10 whole peppercorns
⅛ teaspoon (.6 mL) salt
1 sprig fresh oregano, cilantro, or mint (optional)

1. Combine all the ingredients in a glass jar and allow to steep in the refrigerator for at least 24 hours to blend the flavors.

Puerto Rican Sofrito

Yield: About 2 cups (473 mL)   Heat Scale: Medium

Here is an unusual sauce that is almost a stew. In Puerto Rico, some cooks depend on only bell peppers for the capsicum flavor; others add some rocotillo chiles, as I do if I can find them. Otherwise, I use a fourth the amount of habaneros. Serve this sauce over a rice or black bean dish.

½ pound (224 g) salt pork, diced
2 tablespoons (30 mL) annatto (achiote) seeds
4 onions, peeled and finely chopped
1 clove garlic, peeled and chopped
2 green bell peppers, stems and seeds removed, chopped
4 rocotillo chiles, stems and seeds removed, chopped (or substitute
1 habanero)
½ pound (224 g) ham, diced
3 large tomatoes, peeled and chopped (about 2 cups [473 mL])
1 tablespoon (15 mL) minced cilantro
1 tablespoon (15 mL) minced fresh oregano leaves
Salt, to taste
Freshly ground black pepper, to taste

1. In a large skillet, fry the salt pork over medium heat, stirring occasionally, until all the fat is released and the pieces are crisp and brown. Remove the pork and reserve. Add the annatto seeds to the pan and cook, stirring occasionally, for 5 minutes. Remove the skillet from the heat, strain out and discard the seeds, and return the fat to the skillet.

2. Add the onions, garlic, bell peppers, and rocotillo chiles and sauté over medium heat until the onion is tender, about 5 minutes. Add the remaining ingredients and simmer over low heat, uncovered, for 30 minutes, stirring occasionally.
3. This sauce may be canned in sterilized jars or kept in the refrigerator for about 5 days.

Tomato Rundown Sauce
Yield: 2–3 cups (500–708 mL)   Heat Scale: Mild

In Jamaica, this sauce is served over a wide variety of fish and even lobster. It is wonderful served over pasta. The term "rundown" ("oildown" in Barbados and Trinidad) refers to cooking vegetables in coconut milk until most of the milk is absorbed, leaving a light oil.

Meat from 2 coconuts, grated (about 4 cups [.95 L])
4 cups (.95 L) warm water
1 small onion, peeled and chopped
¼ cup (59 mL) chopped bell pepper
¼ cup (59 mL) chopped green onions
1 clove garlic, peeled and minced
2 sprigs fresh thyme
1 Scotch bonnet chile, left whole, or more to taste (or substitute habanero)
⅛ cup (30 mL) tomato paste
Salt, to taste
Freshly ground black pepper, to taste

1. In a blender or food processor, combine the grated coconut meat and water and purée as smooth as possible. Remove and strain, reserving the milk (use the "trash" for candy or pies).
2. In a large pot, bring the coconut milk to a boil over high heat. Cook for about 30 minutes or until the oil begins to separate. Add the onion, bell pepper, green onions, garlic, thyme, and Scotch bonnet. Reduce the heat to medium and cook for about 20 minutes.
3. Add the tomato paste and salt and pepper and cook for 5 minutes longer. Remove the Scotch bonnet. Transfer the sauce to a blender or food processor and purée until smooth. The sauce should be creamy, with a heavy consistency and a light pink color.

Moko Jumbie Papaya Pepper Sauce

Yield: 3–4 cups (750–950 mL)   Heat Scale: Hot

Named after the zombie-like stilt character that prowls around during Carnival celebrations, this sauce features two ingredients common to Trinidadian commercial sauces: papaya and mustard. The sauce can be used as a condiment or as a marinade for meat, poultry, or fish.

1 small, green papaya, unpeeled
2 quarts (1.9 L) water
5 Congo peppers or habaneros, stems and seeds removed, chopped
1 large onion, peeled and chopped fine
2 cloves garlic, peeled and minced
4 tablespoons (60 mL) dry yellow mustard
1 tablespoon (15 mL) salt, or less to taste
3 cups (708 mL) distilled white vinegar (or 1½ cups [354 mL] vinegar mixed with 1½ cups [354 mL] water)
½ teaspoon (2.5 mL) ground turmeric
1 teaspoon (5 mL) commercial curry paste

1. In a large pot, boil the papaya in the water pot for 10 minutes. Remove the papaya and let it cool. Peel the papaya, remove the seeds, and chop the flesh into 1-inch (2.5 cm) cubes.
2. Combine the papaya with the remaining ingredients in a sauce pan. Bring to a boil, reduce the heat, and simmer for 20 minutes.
3. Remove the mixture from the heat and let cool. Purée it in a food processor and transfer it to a bottle. The sauce will last for weeks in the refrigerator.

Asher Sauce

Yield: 2½ cups (591 mL)   Heat Scale: Hot

Island legend holds that the name of this sauce is a corruption of "Limes Ashore!", the phrase called out by British sailors who found limes growing on the Virgin Islands. The limes, originally planted by the Spanish, would save them from scurvy. I guess the bird peppers would save them from bland food. Add this sauce to seafood chowders or grilled fish. (Note: This recipe requires advance preparation.)

15 limes (Key limes preferred)
1 cup (236 mL) salt
10 whole bird peppers such as piquins or chiltepins (or 2 habaneros), halved
3 cups (708 mL) water
½ cup (118 mL) distilled white vinegar
½ cup (118 mL) sugar
2 cardamom pods
1 tablespoon (15 mL) whole cloves
5 allspice berries
¼ teaspoon (1.25 mL) freshly ground black pepper
4 cloves garlic, peeled and sliced
1 bunch green onions, white part only, chopped

1. Quarter the limes, but do not cut all the way through. Open up each lime and rub the inner surfaces with salt. Place the limes on cutting boards, cover them with cheesecloth, and set them in the sun for about a week. Protect them from rain. The limes will shrink and their skins will turn brown.

2. Rinse the limes to remove as much salt as possible. Place the limes in a large pan, cover with water, and add the remaining ingredients. Bring to a boil, reduce the heat, and simmer, uncovered, for 1 hour. Cool and strain the sauce. It will keep for several weeks in the refrigerator.

Saba Scotch Bonnet Sauce

Yield: About 2 cups (473 mL)   Heat Scale: Hot

From the Netherlands Antilles island of Saba comes this simple, steeped hot sauce that graces seafood dishes or simple rice. Malt vinegar, made from malted barley, is the secret ingredient. Because of the vinegar, this sauce can be kept for a month or so in the refrigerator.

1 Scotch bonnet chile (or habanero), stem and seeds removed, minced
¼ cup (59 mL) finely chopped onion
1 clove garlic, peeled and minced
½ cup (118 mL) malt vinegar
½ cup (118 mL) water
½ teaspoon (2.5 mL) salt
¼ cup (59 mL) olive oil

1. Place the chile, onion, and garlic in a small bowl and mix well. Combine the vinegar, water, and salt in a saucepan and bring to a strong boil. Pour the boiling mixture over the chile mixture, stirring. Add the oil and stir well.

Remoulade Sauce
Yield: 1 cup (236 mL)   Heat Scale: Medium

This is a classic Louisiana recipe with French roots. It's traditionally made with mayonnaise, but my version is more heart-healthy. This sauce is great with shrimp, over sliced tomatoes, with pasta, over vegetables and cold meats, in chicken or potato salad, or as an ingredient in deviled eggs.

½ cup (118 mL) Creole mustard, store-bought or homemade
¼ cup (59 mL) catsup
¼ cup (59 mL) apple cider vinegar
2 tablespoons (30 mL) grated horseradish (or substitute prepared horseradish)
1 teaspoon (5 mL) Worcestershire sauce
1 teaspoon (5 mL) garlic powder
¾ teaspoon (3.75 mL) ground paprika
1 teaspoon (5 mL) Louisiana-style hot sauce (or substitute ground cayenne)
⅔ cup (158 mL) olive oil
¼ cup (59 mL) chopped green onions
2 tablespoons (30 mL) chopped celery
1 tablespoon (15 mL) minced capers
1 tablespoon (15 mL) chopped fresh parsley
¼ teaspoon (1.25 mL) ground white pepper
Salt, to taste

1. Combine the mustard, catsup, vinegar, horseradish, Worcestershire sauce, garlic powder, paprika, and hot sauce in a bowl and whisk to combine.
2. Slowly add the oil while continuing to whisk to emulsify the sauce.
3. Fold in the remaining ingredients. Taste and adjust the seasonings as needed.
4. Allow the sauce to sit for an hour to blend the flavors.

Homemade Tabasco®-Style Sauce

Yield: 2 cups (473 mL)   Heat Scale: Hot

The United States has become one of the world's largest producers of hot sauces, and the flagship of the hot sauce fleet is Tabasco®, which is exported all over the world from Avery Island, Louisiana. Because the chiles in mash form are not aged in oak barrels for three years, this recipe will be only a rough approximation of the famous McIlhenny product. You will have to grow your own tabascos or substitute dried ones that have been rehydrated. Other small, hot, fresh red chiles can also be substituted for the tabascos. (Note: This recipe requires advance preparation.)

1 pound fresh red tabasco chiles, chopped
2 cups (473 mL) distilled white vinegar
2 teaspoons (10 mL) salt

1. In a saucepan, combine the chiles and vinegar. Place the pan over high heat. Stir in the salt and simmer for 5 minutes. Remove from the heat, let cool, and transfer to a blender. Purée until smooth.
2. Transfer the mixture to a glass jar. Allow to steep for 2 weeks in the refrigerator.
3. Strain the sauce, and adjust the consistency by adding more vinegar if necessary.

Keeping "Pace®" with Picante Sauces

Yield: About 4 cups (.95 L)   Heat Scale: Medium

Although most commercial salsas and picante sauces are made from similar ingredients, their flavors differ because of the spices, cooking techniques, and proportion of ingredients used in each recipe. Perhaps this home-cooked version outdoes the original of the best-selling American salsa—you tell me. It is important to use only Mexican oregano, as Mediterranean oregano will make this taste like a pasta sauce.

6–8 ripe red tomatoes (about 4 pounds [2.2 kg]), peeled, seeded, and chopped fine
2 onions, peeled and chopped
3 cloves garlic, peeled and minced
1 cup (236 mL) apple cider vinegar
2 teaspoons (10 mL) Mexican oregano
1 tablespoon (15 mL) tomato paste
Salt, to taste
6 jalapeño chiles, stems and seeds removed, chopped

1. In a large saucepan or Dutch oven, combine the tomatoes, onions, garlic, vinegar, oregano, tomato paste, and salt. Bring to a boil, reduce the heat to medium, and cook for 15 minutes to thicken the sauce.
2. Add the jalapeños and continue cooking for 15 more minutes. Remove from the heat, cool to room temperature, and serve with chips.

Pico de Gallo Salsa

Yield: 3 cups (708 mL)   Heat Scale: Medium

This universal salsa, also known as salsa fria, salsa cruda, salsa fresca, salsa Mexicana, and salsa picante, is served all over the Southwest and often shows up with nontraditional ingredients such as canned tomatoes or bell peppers or spices such as oregano. Here is the most authentic version. Remember that all the ingredients should be as fresh as possible, and the vegetables must be hand-chopped. Never, never use a blender or food processor. Pico de gallo ("rooster's beak," for its sharpness) is best when the tomatoes come from the garden rather than the supermarket. It can be used as a dip for chips or for spicing up fajitas and other Southwestern specialties. (Note: This recipe requires advance preparation and will keep for only a day or two in the refrigerator.)

4 serrano or jalapeño chiles, stems and seeds removed, chopped fine
(or more for a hotter salsa)
2 large, ripe tomatoes, finely chopped
1 medium onion, peeled and finely chopped
¼ cup (59 mL) minced fresh cilantro
2 tablespoons (30 mL) distilled white vinegar
2 tablespoons (30 mL) vegetable oil

1. Combine all the ingredients in a large bowl, mix well, and let the salsa sit, covered, for at least an hour to blend the flavors.

Serrano Salsa with Mangos and Tomatillos

Yield: 4 servings   Heat Scale: Medium

Not all Southwest salsas are tomato-based. This one uses tomatillos, the small "husk tomatoes" that are grown mostly in Mexico but are available fresh or canned in many U.S. supermarkets. The natural sweetness of the mango blends perfectly with the tartness of the tomatillos. (Note: This recipe requires advance preparation.)

6 red serrano chiles, stems and seeds removed, minced
1 clove garlic, peeled and minced
2 tablespoons (30 mL) chopped green onions, including the greens
1 mango, peeled, pitted, and coarsely chopped
10 tomatillos, husks removed, chopped
½ cup (118 mL) chopped fresh cilantro
Juice of 1 lime
2 tablespoons (30 mL) olive oil

1. Combine all the ingredients in a bowl and allow to sit for at least three hours—preferably overnight—to blend the flavors.

Salsa de Jalapeño o Serrano Asado
(Roasted Jalapeño or Serrano Salsa)

Yield: 2 to 4 servings   Heat Scale: Medium

The simplicity of this salsa, imported from northern Mexico and popular in Texas, is deceiving, for it is one of the best all-around table sauces. The charred tomatoes and chiles have a robust flavor, and you can control the texture. Some cooks char onion slices on the grill and add them to this salsa.

2 large tomatoes
2 jalapeño or serrano chiles, stems removed
½ teaspoon (2.5 mL) salt, or to taste

1. Grill the tomatoes and chiles by placing them 3 to 6 inches (7.5 to 15 cm) above the flames. Turn them often. When they're ready, they should be soft and the skins should be charred.
2. In a blender, pulse the tomatoes and chiles for 30 seconds to the desired consistency. Add salt to taste. The texture should be smooth and the sauce should be flecked with tiny bits of the charred chile and tomato skins, which add an interesting flavor.

Texas Green Sauce

Yield: 4 cups (.95 L)   Heat Scale: Medium

When you order "green sauce" in Texas, this is what you will be served. It differs from New Mexico's green sauce in that the color is derived from tomatillos rather than from green chiles. This sauce can be used as a dipping sauce, with enchiladas, or as a topping for grilled poultry or fish.

3 pounds (1.5 kg) tomatillos, husked
1 bunch green onions
1 small bunch cilantro
1 tablespoon (15 mL) minced garlic in oil
2 teaspoons (10 mL) sugar
2 teaspoons (10 mL) lime juice
1 tablespoon (15 mL) chicken stock base dissolved in 2 tablespoons (30 mL) water
6 serrano chiles, stems removed

1. Roast the tomatillos in a roasting pan under the broiler until they are brown and squishy. Turn them over with a pair of tongs and repeat the process. Transfer the roasted tomatillos, including all the liquid released during the roasting process, to a food processor. Add the remaining ingredients and purée.
2. Transfer the mixture to a saucepan and simmer for 10 minutes before serving or incorporating into another recipe.

New Mexico Red Chile Sauce

Yield: About 3 cups (708 mL)   Heat Scale: Medium

This basic sauce can be used in any recipe calling for a red sauce, either traditional Mexican or New Southwestern versions of beans, tacos, tamales, and enchiladas.

10 to 12 dried red New Mexican chiles
1 large onion, peeled and chopped
3 cloves garlic, peeled and chopped
3 cups (708 mL) water

1. Preheat the oven to 250°F (120°C).
2. Place the chiles on a baking pan and bake for about 10 to 15 minutes or until the chiles smell like they are toasted, taking care not to let them burn. Remove the stems and seeds and crumble the chiles into a saucepan.
3. Add the remaining ingredients and bring to a boil. Reduce the heat and simmer for 20 to 30 minutes.
4. Purée the mixture in a blender until smooth and strain if necessary. If the sauce is too thin, return it to the stove and simmer until it is reduced to the desired consistency.

Variations

Spices such as cumin, coriander, and Mexican oregano may be added to taste. Some versions of this sauce call for the onion and garlic to be sautéed in lard—or vegetable oil, these days—before the chiles and water are added.

Classic New Mexico Green Chile Sauce

Yield: About 2 cups (473 mL)   Heat Scale: Medium

This all-purpose sauce recipe is from the southern part of New Mexico, where green chile is the one of the state's top food crops and is used more commonly than the red form. It is a great topping for enchiladas and is often served over scrambled eggs.

1 small onion, peeled and chopped
2 cloves garlic, peeled and minced (optional)
2 tablespoons (30 mL) vegetable oil
6 green New Mexican chiles, roasted, peeled, stems and seeds removed, chopped
½ teaspoon (2.5 mL) ground cumin
2 cups (473 mL) chicken broth or water

1. In a sauté pan, heat the oil over medium heat. Add the onion and garlic and sauté until soft.
2. Add the chiles, cumin, and broth or water and simmer for 30 minutes. The sauce may be puréed in a blender to the desired consistency.

Variations

To thicken the sauce, make a roux by sautéing 1 tablespoon (15 mL) flour in 1 tablespoon (15 mL) vegetable oil, taking care not to let it burn. Slowly stir the roux into the sauce and cook to the desired thickness. Coriander and Mexican oregano may be added to taste. For extra heat, add more New Mexican chiles or a serrano or two.

Dave's Fresh Red Chile Sauce

Yield: About 3 cups (708 mL)   Heat Scale: Mild to Medium

This method of making chile sauce differs from others using fresh New Mexican chiles because these chiles aren't roasted and peeled first. Because of the high sugar content of fresh red chiles, this sauce is sweeter than most. I harvested some chiles from Dave's garden one late summer day, made a batch of this sauce, and ate every drop as a soup! It makes a tasty enchilada sauce, too.

¼ cup (59 mL) vegetable oil
8 fresh red New Mexican chiles, stems and seeds removed, chopped, or more to taste
1 large onion, peeled and chopped
3 cloves garlic, peeled
4 cups (.95 L) water
¼ teaspoon (1.25 mL) ground cumin
1 tablespoon (15 mL) minced fresh cilantro
½ teaspoon (2.5 mL) Mexican oregano leaves
Salt, to taste

1. In a large saucepan, heat the oil over medium heat. Add the chiles, onion, and garlic and sauté until the onion is soft, about 7 minutes.
2. Add the remaining ingredients and bring to a boil. Reduce the heat and simmer for 1 hour, uncovered.
3. In a blender, purée the sauce in batches. Return it to the saucepan and cook until it thickens to the desired consistency. Add salt to taste.

Chipotle BBQ Sauce

Yield: About 4 cups (.95 L)   Heat Scale: Medium

The smoked red jalapeño, known as the chipotle chile, has gained such popularity that there are even a couple of cookbooks devoted to it! It works particularly well with barbecuing and grilling, both of which have considerable associations with smoke.

3 dried chipotle chiles
1 cup (236 mL) very hot water
1½ tablespoons (22.5 mL) vegetable oil
1 medium onion, peeled and chopped fine
2 cloves garlic, peeled and minced
2 red bell peppers, quartered, stems and seeds removed
2 onions, peeled and sliced thickly
3 tomatoes, halved
2 cups (473 mL) catsup
¼ cup (59 mL) Worcestershire sauce
¼ cup (59 mL) red wine vinegar
¼ cup (59 mL) brown sugar

1. In a bowl, combine the chipotle chiles with the water and soak for 1 hour or longer to soften. Chop the chipotles finely.
2. In a medium saucepan, heat the oil over medium heat. Add the chopped onion and sauté until translucent. Add the garlic and sauté for 2 minutes.
3. Place the bell peppers, sliced onions, and tomatoes on the grill over a medium fire and grill until they are soft and slightly blackened. Remove and allow to cool. Peel and chop the vegetables.
4. In a large sauce pan over medium heat, combine all the ingredients. Bring the mixture to a low boil, reduce the heat, and simmer for 20 minutes. Let the mixture cool and purée in a blender or food processor until smooth. You can thin the mixture with water if you desire.

Louisiana Barbecue Sauce

Yield: 3 cups (708 mL)   Heat Scale: Medium

This is my version of a recipe that originally appeared in Mary Land's Louisiana Cookery (1954). I have spiced it up a bit—okay, more than a bit—and added a few other spices. This sauce is served with grilled seafood and chicken, but if you wanted to sneak it onto some steamed shrimp or crawdads, I wouldn't turn you in to the food police. It will keep in the refrigerator for a week and freezes nicely.

¼ cup (59 mL) diced onion
1 tablespoon (15 mL) vegetable oil
1 clove garlic, peeled and minced
1 (15½-ounce [434 g]) can diced tomatoes, drained
⅓ cup (79 mL) honey
2 tablespoons (30 mL) distilled white vinegar
3 bay leaves
2 tablespoons (30 mL) Louisiana-style hot sauce, or more to taste
2 teaspoons (10 mL) dry mustard
½ teaspoon (2.5 mL) dried thyme
1½ teaspoons (7.5 mL) freshly ground black pepper
Salt, to taste

1. In a skillet, heat the oil over medium heat. Add the onion and sauté until soft, 5 to 7 minutes. Add the garlic and sauté for 2 minutes more.
2. Transfer the onion and garlic mixture to a saucepan, add the remaining ingredients, and bring to a boil. Reduce the heat to low and simmer, uncovered, for 1 hour. Remove the bay leaves, transfer the mixture to a blender or food processor, and process until just blended.

Deep, Way Deep in the Heart of Texas Barbecue Sauce

Yield: 2 cups (473 mL)   Heat Scale: Medium

Until recently, New Mexican chiles were rarely used in Texas cooking. But as the popularity of chili con carne cook-off contests increased, cooks began experimenting with chiles other than just piquins and jalapeños. Here is one result of this broadening of the chile pepper experience.

4 dried red New Mexican chiles, stems and seeds removed
4 small dried red chiles, such as piquins or chiltepins
2 cups (473 mL) water
2 tablespoons (30 mL) vegetable oil
1 large onion, peeled and chopped
4 cloves garlic, peeled and chopped
1½ cups (354 mL) catsup
12 ounces (336 mL) beer (Shiner Bock preferred)
¼ cup (59 mL) brown sugar
3 tablespoons (45 mL) apple cider vinegar
2 tablespoons (30 mL) Worcestershire sauce
2 teaspoons (10 mL) dry mustard
1 teaspoon (5 mL) freshly ground black pepper

1. In a pan, simmer the chiles in the water for 15 minutes or until softened. Purée the chiles and water to make a smooth sauce. Strain the sauce.
2. In a separate saucepan, heat the oil over medium heat. Add the onions and garlic and sauté until soft, 5 to 7 minutes. Add the puréed chiles and the remaining ingredients and bring to a boil. Reduce the heat and simmer for 1 hour.
3. In a blender, purée the sauce until smooth. If the sauce is not thick enough, return it to the heat and continue to simmer until the desired consistency is achieved.

Kansas City–Style Barbecue Sauce
Yield:1½ cups (354 mL)   Heat Scale: Medium

Here is the way sauce is made for the famous American Royal cook-off in Kansas City—or at least this is my take on the subject. It is truly a finishing sauce and should not be used as a marinade or a basting sauce, as it might burn. Of course, spread it liberally over ribs just off the grill and serve plenty on the side.

1 tablespoon (15 mL) vegetable oil
1 small onion, peeled and chopped
2 cloves garlic, peeled and minced
1 cup (236 mL) catsup
⅓ cup (79 mL) molasses
¼ cup (59 mL) distilled white vinegar
2 tablespoons (30 mL) commercial chili powder
2 teaspoons (10 mL) dry mustard
1 teaspoon (5 mL) celery salt
1 teaspoon (5 mL) paprika
1 teaspoon (5 mL) ground cayenne
½ teaspoon (2.5 mL) freshly ground black pepper
¼ cup (59 mL) water, or more if needed

1. In a pan, heat the oil over medium heat. Add the onion and garlic and sauté until the onions are soft, 5 to 7 minutes.
2. Add the remaining ingredients and simmer for 30 minutes, until thickened.

North Carolina Barbecue Sauce

Yield: 2 cups (473 mL)   Heat Scale: Medium

This is the thin, vinegar sauce in the tradition of eastern North Carolina.
For a rough idea of the western sauce, add 1 cup (236 mL) catsup,
1 teaspoon (5 mL) Worcestershire sauce, and ½ teaspoon (2.5 mL) cinnamon to this
recipe. This is served over sliced or pulled smoked pork.

2 cups (473 mL) apple cider vinegar
¼ cup (59 mL) brown sugar
1 tablespoon (15 mL) crushed red chile pepper
2 teaspoons (10 mL) salt, or to taste
1½ teaspoons (7.5 mL) ground cayenne
1 teaspoon (5 mL) freshly ground black pepper
1 teaspoon (5 mL) ground white pepper

1. Combine all the ingredients in a large bowl, mix well, and let stand for
a couple hours to blend the flavors.

South Carolina Mustard Barbecue Sauce

Yield: 1¾ cups (413 mL)   Heat Scale: Mild

In South Carolina, mustard is a dominant ingredient in barbecue rather than just
an incidental spice. But vinegar makes its appearance here as well, plus some hot
sauce. As in North Carolina, the sauce is primarily used over smoked pork. But you
could also serve this over grilled pork chops.

¾ cup (177 mL) yellow mustard
¼ cup (59 mL) apple cider vinegar
½ cup (118 mL) sugar
1½ tablespoons (22.5 mL) butter
2 teaspoons (10 mL) salt, or to taste
2 teaspoons (10 mL) Worcestershire sauce
1¼ teaspoons (6.25 mL) freshly ground black pepper
2 teaspoons (10 mL) Louisana-style hot sauce, or more to taste

1. Combine all the ingredients in a saucepan, stirring to blend, and simmer over a low heat for 30 minutes.
2. Let stand at room temperature for 1 hour before using.

Memphis-Style Finishing Sauce

Yield: 2½ cups (591 mL)   Heat Scale: Mild

This is the sauce that is traditionally served over smoked ribs in Memphis and other parts of Tennessee. Some cooks add prepared yellow mustard to the recipe. It can be converted into a basting sauce by adding more beer and a little more vinegar. Add more hot sauce to taste, or substitute ground red chile or cayenne.

1 cup (236 mL) tomato sauce (freshly made preferred)
1 cup (236 mL) red wine vinegar
2 teaspoons (10 mL) Louisiana-style hot sauce
1 tablespoon (15 mL) butter
½ teaspoon (2.5 mL) freshly ground black pepper
½ teaspoon (2.5 mL) salt
½ cup (118 mL) light beer

1. Place all the ingredients in a saucepan and bring to a boil, stirring constantly. Reduce the heat and simmer, uncovered, for 15 minutes.
2. Remove from the heat and serve warm over smoked meats.

Canary Islands Mojo Picón

Yield: 1¼ cup (295 mL)   Heat Scale: Medium

Here is the favorite hot sauce of the Canary Islands, where it is commonly served over papas arrugadas, new potatoes boiled in their skins in sea water. It is also sprinkled over grilled or crispy fried fish.

3 cloves garlic, peeled
1 piquin chile (or substitute any small, hot dried chile)
1 teaspoon (5 mL) hot paprika (or substitute ground mild red
New Mexican chile)
1 teaspoon (5 mL) cumin seed
1 cup (236 mL) red wine vinegar
¼ cup (59 mL) olive oil
Salt, to taste
Freshly ground black pepper, to taste
2 teaspoons (10 mL) chopped Italian parsley

1. In a mortar or blender, grind the garlic, chile, paprika, and cumin seed together, adding a little water or vinegar to facilitate the process.
2. Combine the vinegar and oil in a jar, shake well, and add the ground mixture to it. Mix well and add the salt, pepper, and parsley. Shake well before serving.

Variation

Replace the parsley with freshly minced cilantro and you have mojo picón de cilantro.

Môlho de Piri-Piri
(Portuguese Hot Sauce)

Yield: 1¾ cups (413 mL)   Heat Scale: Hot

Early in the sixteenth century, chiles were brought from Portuguese Brazil to the Portuguese colony of Angola. These small, piquin-like chiles (which were probably Brazilian malaguetas) were called piri-piri ("pepper-pepper") and became an integral part of the local cuisine. The sauce made from them was transferred back to Portugual, where it is a staple on dining tables, served with seafood, soups, and stews. Since the piri-piri chiles are rarely available, use chiles de arbol, cayenne chiles, chile piquins, or chiltepins. (Note: This recipe requires advance preparation.)

½ cup (118 mL) chopped dried red chiles, stems and seeds removed
1 cup (236 mL) olive oil
¼ cup (59 mL) apple cider vinegar
1 teaspoon (5 mL) salt

1. Combine all the ingredients in a jar. Cover, shake well, and store at room temperature for 24 hours. Shake well before each use. To make a smooth sauce, blend this mixture in a food processor and thin slightly with water or cider vinegar.

Salsa Colorada
(Spanish Red Sauce)

Yield: About 3 cups (708 mL)   Heat Scale: Medium

Here is a standard Spanish hot sauce that would probably be prepared with the small, hot guindilla ("little cherry") chiles. Serve this tasty sauce over steamed vegetables, roasted meats, or fish prepared by any method.

3 tomatoes
1 head garlic
3 piquin, Thai, or de arbol chiles, stems removed, crushed
2 hard-boiled egg yolks
12 almonds, peeled and toasted
¾ cup (177 mL) olive oil
¼ cup (59 mL) red wine vinegar
Salt, to taste

1. Preheat the oven to 350°F (180°C).
2. Roast the unpeeled tomatoes and garlic on a baking pan until the tomatoes are very soft, about 15 minutes. Remove the pan from the oven and let cool. When the tomatoes and garlic are cool enough to handle, peel them. Place the tomatoes and garlic cloves in a food processor or blender, add the crushed chiles, and pulse until coarsely puréed. Add the egg yolks and almonds and pulse several times, until the almonds are broken up. Purée again, gradually adding the oil and vinegar, until a smooth sauce is formed. Add salt to taste, and keep warm over low heat until serving.

Creamy Horseradish Sauce

Yield: ⅔ cup (158 mL)   Heat Scale: Medium

Horseradish is a classic condiment that's served with roast meats—beef in particular—and cooked or raw vegetables. Since horseradish is very volatile (the active ingredient is isothiocyanate) and loses its flavor and aroma quickly, this simple sauce should be made just before serving time. For an added hit of chile heat, I sometimes add ground habanero chile.

⅔ cup (158 mL) sour cream
¼ cup (59 mL) fresh or prepared horseradish
2 green onions, finely chopped
1 teaspoon (5 mL) distilled white vinegar
1 teaspoon (5 mL) sugar
¾ teaspoon (3.75 mL) chopped fresh dill weed

1. Combine all the ingredients in a bowl and beat until well mixed. Allow the mixture to sit for 15 to 20 minutes to blend the flavors.

Rouille
(Hot Sauce for Fish Stew)

Yield: About 1 cup (236 mL)   Heat Scale: Medium

The famous food writer M. F. K. Fisher described this sauce as follows: "A peppery concoction suited to the taste of bouillabaisse, served separately from the soup to be ladled in at the discretion of the individual diner."

2 small green bell peppers, seeded and cut in small squares
2 small, hot dried chiles, such as piquin or Thai, crushed
1 cup (236 mL) water
2 pimientos, drained and dried (optional)
4 cloves garlic, peeled and coarsely chopped
6 tablespoons (90 mL) olive oil
1–3 teaspoons (5–15 mL) fine dry bread crumbs
Salt, to taste

1. In a saucepan, combine the bell peppers, dried chiles, and water. Simmer until the bell peppers are soft, then drain the peppers and pat dry.
2. Place the peppers, pimientos (if using), and garlic in a mixing bowl or mortar and mash them together until a smooth paste forms. Slowly beat in the olive oil and bread crumbs until the mixture becomes just too thick to pour. (Or, purée the peppers, pimientos, and garlic in a blender while adding the olive oil and bread crumbs.) Add salt to taste.

Espelette Piperade

Yield: About 2½ cups (591 mL)   Heat Scale: Medium

The most famous chile in France is piment d'Espelette, or the Espelette pepper, which has become a cultural and culinary icon in the French part of Basque country. At first, the Espelette farmers formed cooperative enterprises to protect their interests, and eventually they applied to the National Institute for Trade Name Origins for an Appellation d'Origine Controlee (AOC). On December 1, 1999, an AOC was granted to Espelette peppers and products, giving it the same protection as more famous culinary names, such as Champagne sparkling wine. Only ten villages are allowed to use the name "Espelette": Espelette, Ainhoa, Cambo les Bains, Halsou, Itsassou, Jatsou, Laressore, St. Pee sur Nivelle, Souraide, and Ustarritz. The total growing area is about 3,000 acres. Piperade is a colorful pepper sauce that is only spicy when made in the Basque region. This simple but delicious sauce is often served at the Celebration of the Peppers in the village of Espelette. Serve it over boiled potatoes and green beans.

½ cup (118 mL) olive oil, divided
4 medium onions, peeled and chopped
3 cloves garlic, peeled
4 green bell peppers, stems and seeds removed, chopped
2 red bell peppers, stems and seeds removed, chopped
4 large tomatoes, peeled and chopped
3 tablespoons (45 mL) ground Espelette, or more to taste (or substitute hot paprika or New Mexico red chile powder)
1 pinch dried thyme
Salt, to taste
Freshly ground black pepper, to taste

1. Heat ¼ cup (59 mL) olive oil in a large sauté pan over medium heat. Add the onions and garlic and sauté for 5 minutes, stirring occasionally. Add the bell peppers and cook for 10 minutes. Add the tomatoes and Espelette powder and cook for 20 minutes, stirring occasionally. Add the thyme, salt, and pepper and transfer to a bowl. For a smooth sauce, purée this mixture in small batches in a blender or food processor.

Harrisburg

4007 Jonestown Rd. at Rt. 83

717-652-6800

Weekdays 8am-7pm
Sat. 8am-5pm
Sun. 9am-4pm

PENNSYLVANIA
DEPARTMENT
OF
TRANSPORTATION

**OFFICIAL
INSPECTION
STATION**

No Hidden Fees!
No shop fees.
No environmental fees.
No disposal fees.

New Store!
Hummelstown

1900 Kaylor Road

717-566-8525

Weekdays 8am-7pm
Sat. 8am-7pm

Continuing Automotive Service Education

ASE CERTIFIED
TRAINING PROVIDER

No Appointment Necessary! • centralpa.jiffylube.com

Jiffy Lube, the Jiffy Lube design mark and Jiffy Lube Signature Service®
are registered trademarks of Jiffy Lube International, Inc. © 2013 Jiffy Lube International, Inc.

641051 7783

$ **8** OFF

Valid at participating stores.
Not valid with any other offer for same service.
Must present coupon at time of service.

Jiffy Lube
Signature
Service®
Oil Change

ZF3BW2
Expires: 6/22/13

jiffylube®

Romesco Sauce
Yield: ⅓–½ cup (79–118 mL)   Heat Scale: Medium

Romesco is a classic Spanish sauce that is served with a wide variety of dishes, including the famous tortilla Española from the Tarragona region. This Catalan sauce combines almonds with two of the most popular horticultural imports from the New World—chiles and tomatoes. The sauce gets its name from the romesco chile, but these are not readily available outside Spain. A combination of ancho and New Mexican chiles approximates the flavor.

1 ancho chile, stem and seeds removed
2 dried red New Mexican chiles, stems and seeds removed
½ cup (118 mL) toasted almonds
5 cloves garlic, unpeeled
2 tomatoes, unpeeled
½ cup (118 mL) red wine vinegar
⅓ cup (79 mL) extra-virgin olive oil, preferably Spanish
Salt, to taste
Freshly ground black pepper, to taste

1. Preheat the oven to 200°F (100°C).
2. Place the chiles, almonds, garlic, and tomatoes on a baking pan and roast until the nuts are toasted, the chiles are fragrant, and the skins of the tomatoes and garlic are blistered. The nuts will take about 5 minutes, the tomatoes about 20, and the chiles somewhere in between. Check frequently to be sure nothing burns. When everything is done roasting, allow the ingredients to cool.
3. Place the almonds in a spice mill or coffee grinder and process to a powder.
4. Place the chiles in a bowl, cover with them hot water, and allow them to steep for 15 minutes to soften. Drain the chiles and discard the water.
5. Remove the skins from the tomatoes and garlic.
6. Put the almonds, chiles, tomatoes, garlic, and vinegar in a blender or food processor and purée to a smooth paste, adding a little oil if necessary.
7. Transfer the paste to a bowl and slowly whisk in the oil, 1 teaspoon (5 mL) at a time, until half of the oil is absorbed. Gradually add the remaining oil. Season with the salt and pepper. Allow the sauce to sit for an hour or two to blend the flavors.

Salsa Pimentón

Yield: About 1½ cups (354 mL)   Heat Scale: Medium

*The hotbed of chiles in Spain is the valley of La Vera, where the pimientos (chiles)
are grown and smoked to make the famous spice pimentón de la Vera. The majority of the pimentón goes to sausage factories, where it is used to spice up, flavor,
and brighten up the famous Spanish chorizo. But it is also packed in tins for
the consumer market. There are three varieties of pimentón—sweet (dulce), hot
(picante), and bittersweet (agridulce). The hot type is used in winter soups, chorizo,
and Galician pulpo, or octopus. The octopus is boiled and sliced, then sprinkled with
olive oil, salt, and hot pimentón powder. Interestingly, there are recipes for chorizo
and potato stews that utilize all three of the types of pimentón. Serve this sauce over
grilled seafood and chicken.*

1 tablespoon (15 mL) olive oil
6 cloves garlic, peeled and minced
1 medium red onion, peeled and chopped
3 tablespoons (45 mL) hot pimento, divided
Salt, to taste
Freshly ground black pepper, to taste
2 tablespoons (30 mL) chopped fresh Italian parsley
2 medium tomatoes, chopped
2 red bell peppers, roasted, peeled, seeded, and chopped
½ cup (118 mL) minced green olives

1. In a saucepan, heat the oil over medium heat. Add the garlic, onion,
and 1 tablespoon (15 mL) of the pimentón and sauté for about 2 minutes.
Add the black pepper, parsley, and tomatoes and bell peppers and cook
until the mixture thickens, about 5 minutes. Remove from the heat and
transfer to a blender or food processor. Add the remaining pimentón and
the olives and purée. Transfer the sauce back to the pan and keep warm.

Puttanesca Sauce

Yield: About 3 cups (708 mL)   Heat Scale: Mild

The origins of this sauce are obscured in legend and lore. In Italian, salsa puttanesca literally means "harlot's sauce" and was thought to be a favorite meal of prostitutes because it was nourishing—and quick to make. Another source implies that it was a favorite sauce of married ladies who were having an affair; they would come home late and make this rich sauce, which smelled as though it had been cooking all day. Serve it over your favorite pasta or spread it on Italian bread, top with Parmesan cheese, and broil for a hearty sandwich.

2 tablespoons (30 mL) olive oil
2 garlic cloves, peeled and minced
¼ cup (59 mL) minced onion
1 tablespoon (15 mL) capers, chopped
6 ripe tomatoes, peeled, seeded, and coarsely chopped
3 tablespoons (45 mL) tomato paste
½ cup (118 mL) chopped black olives
2 tablespoons (30 mL) minced fresh basil or 1 tablespoon (15 mL) dried
3 tablespoons (45 mL) chopped Italian parsley
1 tablespoon (15 mL) crushed red New Mexican chile
1 cup (236 mL) beef or chicken stock
Salt, to taste
Freshly ground black pepper, to taste

1. In a large, heavy skillet, heat the oil over medium heat. Add the garlic, onion, and capers and sauté for 2 minutes. Add the chopped tomatoes and sauté for 1 minute. Stir in the tomato paste, olives, basil, parsley, and chile and bring to a boil. Turn the heat to low, add ½ cup (118 mL) of the stock, and stir. Cover and simmer 15 minutes. Stir and add more stock if the mixture starts getting too thick. Simmer, uncovered, for another 15 minutes. The mixture should be slightly thick and chunky.

Salsa all'Arrabiata
(Enraged Sauce)

Yield: 3 cups (708 mL)   Heat Scale: Mild

This recipe is from Giuliano Bugialli, as profiled by Nancy Gerlach, who met him in Rome. She commented: "This in an all-purpose sauce that can be used on a variety of pastas. To really 'enrage' the sauce, replace the crushed New Mexican chile with chiltepins or piquin chiles."

3 pounds (1.36 kg) fresh Roma or plum tomatoes, cut in half (or substitute 1 [16-ounce (454 g)]) can peeled Italian tomatoes
3 tablespoons (45 mL) olive oil
2 teaspoons (10 mL) crushed red New Mexican chile
3 large cloves garlic, peeled and minced
½ teaspoon (2.5 mL) sugar
Freshly ground black pepper, to taste
Salt, to taste
2 tablespoons (30 mL) chopped fresh basil or oregano

1. If using fresh tomatoes, preheat the oven to 400°F (200°C). Place the cut tomatoes side down on a cookie pan and bake for 10 minutes or until they are soft.
2. Purée the tomatoes in a blender or food processor, transfer them to a saucepan, and bring to a simmer over high heat.
3. In a large skillet, heat the oil over medium heat. Add the chile and garlic and sauté until the garlic is soft, about 10 minutes.
4. Add the chile mixture and sugar to the simmering tomatoes. Season with the black pepper and salt and continue to simmer until the sauce thickens.
5. Remove from the heat and stir in the fresh herbs.

Salsa Amatriciana
(Spicy Amatrice Sauce)

Yield: About 6 cups   Heat Scale: Varies

From the Sabine town of Amatrice comes this simple but great pasta sauce. Traditionally, it is served over bucatini, a spaghetti-like pasta that is hollow, like a straw. It is then sprinkled with grated pecorino romano.

½ cup (118 mL) olive oil
1 pound (454 g) pancetta or smoked bacon, chopped
2 onions, peeled and minced
2 cloves garlic, peeled and minced
3 dried small, hot red chiles, such as santaka, Thai, or piquin, crushed into a coarse powder
2 (28-ounce [784 g]) cans Italian plum tomatoes, drained, 1 cup (236 mL) juice reserved
Ground cayenne, to taste
Salt, to taste
Freshly ground black pepper, to taste

1. In a large saucepan, heat the oil over medium heat. Add the pancetta and cook until browned, about 20 minutes. Stir occasionally to brown the pancetta evenly. Remove with a slotted spoon and drain on paper towels. Remove and discard all but ½ cup (118 mL) of the remaining fat.
2. Add the onions and sauté until golden, about 15 minutes. Add the garlic and crushed chiles and sauté for 2 minutes. Add the tomatoes and mash them with a spoon. Increase the heat, add the reserved tomato juice and the pancetta, and boil until thickened, 5 to 7 minutes.
3. Taste for heat and seasonings and adjust with cayenne, salt, and pepper.

Salsa Fra Diavolo
(Running with the Devil Sauce)
Yield: About 2 cups (473 mL)   Heat Scale: Mild

"Running with the devil sauce" is my rough translation of salsa fra diavolo, a pasta sauce redolent with fresh herbs. It can be spread over crusty bread, sprinkled with cheese, and baked. If cooked until quite thick, it makes a great pizza sauce, too.

⅓ cup (79 mL) olive oil
½ large green bell pepper, seeded and chopped
2 cloves garlic, peeled and minced
½ small onion, minced
2 tablespoons (30 mL) chopped fresh parsley
4 large tomatoes, peeled, seeded, and chopped
3 tablespoons (45 mL) tomato paste
1 teaspoon (5 mL) crushed red New Mexican chile
2 teaspoons (10 mL) minced fresh oregano
1 teaspoon (5 mL) minced fresh thyme
Salt, to taste

1. Heat the oil in a large, heavy saucepan over medium heat. Add the bell pepper, garlic, and onion and sauté until the onion softens, 5 to 8 minutes. Lower the heat, stir in the parsley, and simmer for 1 minute. Add the remaining ingredients and simmer over a very low heat for about 45 minutes, stirring occasionally.

Hungarian Hot Paprika Sauce
Yield: 1 cup (236 mL) Heat Scale: Medium

Although paprika is used more often in stews than in sauces, this sauce was designed as a condiment for fish. Traditionally, it is served over fried fillets of river fish.

2 tablespoons (30 mL) butter
2 tablespoons (30 mL) all-purpose flour
½ teaspoon (2.5 mL) salt
⅛ teaspoon (.6 mL) freshly ground black pepper
1 cup (236 mL) whole milk
1 teaspoon (5 mL) minced onion
2–3 teaspoons (10–15 mL) hot paprika
1 pinch nutmeg

1. In a saucepan, melt the butter over medium heat. Add the flour, salt, and pepper and stir constantly until it starts to bubble. Gradually add the milk and stir constantly until the mixture is smooth. Bring the mixture to a boil and continue to stir for 1 to 2 minutes. Add the onion, paprika, and nutmeg to the mixture, stir well for 30 seconds, and serve.

Adzhiga Salsa
Yield: About 2 cups (473 mL) Heat Scale: Medium

The ingredients of this specialty from Russia are similar to the traditional Mexican pico de gallo salsa, except that celery replaces tomatoes and dill is added. Georgians spread it thickly onto a piece of lavash (Georgian bread) and wolf it down no matter how many chiles are added to it. (Note: This recipe requires advance preparation, as the adzhiga tastes better when it's served 1 to 3 days after making.)

10 cloves garlic, peeled
2 celery stalks, leaves included, chopped
5 red or green serrano or jalapeño chiles, stems and seeds removed, chopped
2 red bell peppers, stems and seeds removed, chopped
2 cups (473 mL) chopped fresh dill
1½ cups (354 mL) coarsely chopped cilantro
½ cup (118 mL) red wine vinegar
¼ teaspoon (1.25 mL) salt

1. Combine the garlic, celery, chiles, bell peppers, dill, and cilantro in a food processor. Pulse gently until a coarse paste forms. Transfer the mixture to a bowl and stir in the vinegar and salt. Cover and let stand overnight.

Satsivi Sauce

Yield: About 3 cups (708 mL)   Heat Scale: Medium

---

*This classic Russian hot sauce is unusual because walnuts are added. It is tradition-
ally served with poached chicken or fish dishes, and the stock used is determined
accordingly. It can also be served over steamed vegetables.*

¼ cup (59 mL) unsalted butter
1 onion, peeled and minced
1 tablespoon (15 mL) all-purpose flour
2 cups (473 mL) rich chicken stock, divided
3 serrano or jalapeño chiles, stems and seeds removed, minced
1 cup (236 mL) finely ground walnuts
1 tablespoon (15 mL) lemon juice
3 cloves garlic, peeled and minced
¼ cup (59 mL) minced cilantro
1 scant pinch tarragon
1 scant pinch oregano
1 scant pinch basil
1 scant pinch thyme

1. In a large saucepan, melt the butter over medium heat. Add the onions
and sauté until soft, about 10 minutes. Add the flour and stir to incorporate. Add 1 cup (236 mL) of the stock and bring to a boil, stirring constantly. Add the remaining stock and the remaining ingredients. Bring to
a second boil and immediately remove from the heat. Stir well and allow
the sauce to cool to room temperature before serving. If it is too thick, add
a little more stock.

Zhug
(Yemenite Hot Sauce)

Yield: 1½–2 cups (375–473 mL)   Heat Scale: Hot

Popular with the Yemenite Jews in Israel and the Middle East, this hot sauce starts with a paste of garlic and peppers, whatever spices the cook chooses, and cilantro and/or parsley. There are two versions: this green one and a red one that uses red sweet and hot peppers. Tomatoes are sometimes added to tone down the sauce, which can be quite spicy. This quick and easy sauce can be used as a table condiment or as a sauce for grilled fish or meat or for eggs, or it can be added to soups and stews just before serving. It goes especially well with lamb kebabs.

8 serrano chiles, stems removed (or substitute jalapeño chiles)
6 cloves garlic, peeled and coarsely chopped
1½ teaspoons (7.5 mL) caraway seeds
1 teaspoon (5 mL) cumin seeds
1 teaspoon (5 mL) ground cardamom
1 teaspoon (5 mL) freshly ground black pepper
½ teaspoon (2.5 mL) ground cloves
1 tablespoon (15 mL) lemon juice (fresh preferred)
1 cup (236 mL) chopped fresh cilantro
½ cup (118 mL) chopped fresh parsley
½–¾ cup olive oil (125–177 mL)
Salt, to taste

1. Place the chiles, garlic, caraway, cumin, cardamom, pepper, cloves, and lemon juice in a blender or food processor and purée to a smooth paste, adding some of the oil if necessary.
2. Add the cilantro and parsley. While the machine is running slowly, add the oil until a soupy sauce forms. Season with the salt.

West African Pili Pili Sauce

Yield: 2 cups (473 mL)   Heat Scale: Hot

Pili pili, often called piri-piri, is served as a table condiment in West Africa, where it heats up grilled meat, poultry, shrimp, and fish. Nearly any green chile can be used to make this sauce. Some recipes call for the addition of tomatoes or tomato sauce.

1 pound (454 g) serrano or jalapeño chiles, stems and seeds removed, coarsely chopped
1 medium onion, peeled and chopped
1 clove garlic, peeled
Juice of 1 lemon

1. Place all the ingredients in a food processor. Blend into a paste, gradually adding water until the desired consistency is achieved. Store in a jar in the refrigerator, where it will keep for many weeks.

Palaver Sauce

Yield: 2 cups (473 mL)   Heat Scale: Medium

From Sierra Leone, here is one of the more unusual hot sauces I encountered. Besides palm oil, it is characterized by greens such as cassava and sweet potato leaves; spinach makes an adequate substitute. Some versions of this dish are more of a stew than a sauce, but this one is designed to be served over rice. (Warning: Palm oil is high in saturated fat.)

1 cup (236 mL) red palm oil (found in Asian markets, or substitute peanut oil)
½ cup (118 mL) minced lean beef
1 onion, peeled and chopped
3 jalapeño chiles, stems and seeds removed, minced
2 cups (473 mL) shredded spinach
½ cup (118 mL) smoked fish, such as kippers

1. In a large skillet, heat the palm oil over high heat. Add the beef and fry until just brown. Remove the beef from the skillet and set aside.
2. Add the onion and jalapeño to the skillet and cook until soft, about 8 to 10 minutes. Add the spinach and stir-fry for 2 minutes. Return the beef to the skillet, crumble in the fish, and cook for 5 minutes over medium heat, stirring constantly. Add more palm oil if the mixture is too thick.

Sauce Gombo

Yield: About 2 cups (473 mL)   Heat Scale: Hot

Gombo means okra in West Africa, and that vegetable is the primary thickening agent of this simple sauce from Ghana. The sauce can be served like a soup or poured over potatoes, plantains, or other starchy tubers.

1 pound (454 g) fresh okra, sliced into rounds
1 cup (236 mL) water
1 teaspoon (5 mL) ground hot chile, such as cayenne
½ teaspoon (2.5 mL) salt
1 tomato, coarsely chopped

1. Combine all the ingredients in a saucepan and cook over medium heat for 8 to 10 minutes, or until the okra is tender. Serve the sauce as is or purée it in a blender for a smoother texture.

Ata Dindin
(Nigerian Fried Red Pepper Sauce)

Yield: 1½ cups (354 mL)   Heat Scale: Medium

Ata is the Yoruba word for chile pepper, and Nigerian chiles range from the tiny ata wewe to the large ata funfun. This sauce is served as a relish or dip with many West African dishes, particularly grilled meats.

10 dried red New Mexican chiles, stems and seeds removed, soaked in hot water for 1 hour
½ cup (118 mL) peanut oil
1 onion, peeled and chopped
1 (8-ounce [226 mL]) can tomato sauce
1 teaspoon (5 mL) salt

1. Remove the chiles from the water and purée them in a blender or food processor.
2. Heat the oil in a skillet over medium heat. Add the onion, puréed chiles, tomato sauce, and salt. Fry for 1 to 2 minutes, stirring constantly.

Variation
Add 1 chopped bell pepper.

L'Exotic Sauce Dynamite

Yield: 2 cups (473 mL)   Heat Scale: Hot

Here is a typical Madagascar-style sauce that was served at the Restaurant L'Exotic in Montreal. The sauce accompanied most of the entrées at L'Exotic. It can also be added to soups or stews to spice them up.

12 bird's eye chiles (chiltepins or piquins), crushed
3 tablespoons (45 mL) freshly ground ginger root
3 tablespoons (45 mL) freshly ground garlic
1 medium onion, peeled and diced
¼ cup (59 mL) tomato paste
1 cup (236 mL) distilled white vinegar
2 teaspoons (10 mL) salt
1 cup (236 mL) water
1 tablespoon (15 mL) chopped fresh thyme

1. Combine all the ingredients in a saucepan. Bring to a boil, then reduce heat and simmer for 15 minutes. Remove from the heat, cool, and purée in a blender.
2. Transfer the sauce to a small jar. It keeps for up to a year in the refrigerator.

Tsuma Nzole Kalu's Special Sauce

Yield: About 1 cup (236 mL)   Heat Scale: Medium

This recipe was collected for me in Mombasa, Kenya, by Richard Sterling, who wrote, "The barbecue master at the Big Bite Restaurant in Mombasa is Tsuma Nzole Kalu. He concocted this recipe for hot sauce and gave it its name. Serve it over grilled or barbecued meats and poultry."

4 fresh pili pili chiles or red jalapeños, stems and seeds removed
¼ teaspoon (1.25 mL) coriander seeds
¼ teaspoon (1.25 mL) cardamom seeds
1 teaspoon (5 mL) cumin seeds
1 teaspoon (5 mL) black peppercorns
2 whole cloves
1 cinnamon stick
½ teaspoon (2.5 mL) salt
Juice of 1 Ukwaju Kenyan lemon or 1 lime

1. Combine the chiles, spices, and salt in a mortar and pound to a thick paste. Transfer to a jar and add the lemon or lime juice and enough water to make the mixture easily pourable. Shake well and set aside for a few hours to let the flavors marry.

Ugandan Groundnut Sauce

Yield: About 2 cups (473 mL)   Heat Scale: Medium

Variations on this hot sauce appear all over Africa, with the key ingredient being peanuts in any form. Here, peanut butter works well—and it's the cook's choice whether to use smooth or crunchy! Ladle it over fried chicken or fish.

½ pound (224 g) dried fish, such as salt cod, coarsely chopped
4½ cups (1 L) water, divided
2 onions, peeled and chopped
2 teaspoons (10 mL) peanut oil
4 tomatoes, chopped
1 teaspoon (5 mL) curry powder, or to taste
2 teaspoons (10 mL) ground cayenne
1 cup (236 mL) peanut butter
Salt, to taste

1. Soak the dried fish in 2 cups (473 mL) of the water until it softens. Drain and pat dry.
2. In a large skillet, heat the oil over medium heat. Add the onions and fry until brown, about 5 minutes. Add the tomatoes and cook, uncovered, for 5 minutes. Add the fish, curry, cayenne, remaining water, peanut butter, and salt. Simmer, uncovered, for 45 minutes, or until the sauce thickens to the desired consistency.

Rougail
(Réunionaise Salsa)

Yield: ½ cup (118 mL)   Heat Scale: Extremely Hot

Few people have ever heard of the Mascarenes, and these islands are more known by their individual names: Réunion, Mauritius, and Ródrigues. They are a departe-ment of France and lie hundred of miles east of Madagascar, hundreds of miles away from each other. Although they vary greatly in geography, culture, and religion, they have one great thing in common: a love of chile peppers. On all three islands, chiles of every size and heat level are lovingly grown and added to cuisines that can generically be called Creole. Rebecca Chastenet de Gry, one of my writers, collected this recipe for me on Réunion Island. She wrote, "Alter the heat in this extremely hot salsa by changing the chiles used. Traditionally the smaller piquin or bird's eye chiles are the types preferred, but milder ones, such as red serranos, can be used." Serve it—easy does it—over clams, other shellfish, or grilled fish fillets.

½ cup (118 mL) small fresh hot red chiles, such as piquin,
stems and seeds removed
1½ teaspoons (7.5 mL) salt
4 cloves garlic, peeled
1 tablespoon (15 mL) chopped fresh cilantro
2 tablespoons (30 mL) sliced ginger
¼ cup (59 mL) vegetable oil
3 tablespoons (45 mL) distilled white vinegar

1. Place the chiles, salt, garlic, and cilantro in a blender and process until the mixture is combined but still chunky.
2. Combine the chile mixture with the remaining ingredients and mix well. Allow the salsa to sit for a couple of hours to blend the flavors.

Mazavaroo

Yield: 1¼ cups   Heat Scale: Hot

The neighboring island of Mauritius in the Mascarenes has a harissa-like sauce called mazavaroo that is usually served on sandwiches. This recipe for it was given to one of my writers, Leyla Loued-Khenissime, by Virjanan Jeenea, the sous-chef at the Oberoi Hotel in Mauritius. Leyla writes: "I was happy to see that his recipe is simple compared to others I have run into. I tried it four different ways: with fresh bird's eye peppers and again with fresh Thai dragon peppers, then adding shrimp paste to one and ginger to the other. The best result I obtained was by following the Oberoi recipe with the bird's eye peppers, although it still lacks that smoky fantasia found in the jar I initially bought. Below is the Oberoi's adapted version."

⅓ cup (79 mL) vegetable oil
1 teaspoon (5 mL) sliced garlic
½ cup (118 mL) fresh red chiles (preferably pili-pili or bird's eye peppers)
½ teaspoon (2.5 mL) salt
1 lemon, peeled

1. Heat a saucepan over medium heat and add the oil. Add the garlic and chile peppers. Sauté for 15 minutes, being careful not to burn the garlic. Remove the pan from heat. Combine the garlic and peppers with the salt and the lemon in a blender and puree.

Piment Limón (Citrus Hot Sauce)

Yield: 6 cups   Heat Scale: Hot

Here is my version of the classic hot sauce of Ródrigues Island in the Mascarenes. It is very thick, so feel free to thin it with more water. You'd think this sauce might be sour, but it's not—the sugar in the red chiles seems to temper the tart lemons. Any fresh red chiles can be used, and you can adjust the heat level to your liking. The yield is high here, but the color is so beautiful that you should put the excess in decorative bottles as gifts for your friends. It will keep for several weeks in the refrigerator. Serve it over fish or other seafood.

6 cups (1.4 L) water
10 lemons, peeled, thickly sliced, seeds removed (or substitute limes for a different color)
8 to 10 red jalapeños, stems and seeds removed, halved
¼ cup (59 mL) vegetable oil

1. Place the water in a large pot and bring to a boil. Add the lemon slices and boil for 20 minutes. Strain, reserving the water.
2. Place the jalapeños in a blender and add the oil. Purée to a thick paste. Add the lemon slices, a few at a time, along with 3 cups (708 mL) of the reserved water, ½ cup (118 mL) at a time. (You may have to do this in batches if you don't have a large blender.) Purée to a thick sauce. Pour into bottles and label.

Himalayan Chile Sauce

Yield: About 3 cups (708 mL)   Heat Scale: Hot

From one of my far-flung writers, Linda Lynton, this recipe is a basic sauce from northern India and Nepal. She noted: "Although this specific recipe was given to me by a Patna housewife, some peasants originating from a remote Himalayan village in Central Nepal and housewives from an equally remote village in North Bihar gave us the same recipe." Use it as a topping for chicken, fish, or vegetables.

1 pound (454 g) fresh green chiles, such as serranos or jalapeños, stems and seeds removed
4 small potatoes, peeled and boiled until tender
½ cup (118 mL) distilled white vinegar
1 teaspoon (5 mL) salt

1. Combine all the ingredients in batches in a blender and process to a fine purée, adding water as needed to achieve the desired consistency.

Transplanted Sriracha Sauce

Yield: 3–4 cups   Heat Scale: Hot

A table condiment similar in appearance to catsup—but much more pungent—sriracha sauce is named after a seaside town in Thailand. Increasingly popular, this sauce is found on the tables of Thai and Vietnamese restaurants all over North America. Fresh red chiles are the key to the flavor of this recipe.

1 pound (454 g) fresh red serrano, cayenne, Thai, or chile de arbol chiles, stems removed
2½ cups (591 mL) rice vinegar (or substitute distilled white vinegar)
¼ cup (59 mL) sugar
1 tablespoon (15 mL) salt

1. Place the chiles and vinegar in a saucepan and bring to a boil. Turn off the heat, add the sugar and salt, and stir until dissolved. Place the saucepan contents in a food processor or blender and purée to a smooth, thin-paste consistency. Add additional rice vinegar if the mixture is too thick. Allow the mixture to steep for several hours, transfer it to glass containers, and refrigerate. The consistency should be slightly thinner than catsup. Or, strain the sauce through a sieve and discard the solids for a smooth, seedless consistency.

Ngapi Ye
(Hot Burmese Anchovy Sauce)

Yield: ¾ cup (177 mL)   Heat Scale: Medium

This highly aromatic Burmese sauce is commonly used to heat up Southeast Asian curries. Shrimp or prawn paste may be substituted for the fermented dried fish if you can't find it at the Asian market. In a pinch, use canned anchovy fillets.

2 cups (473 mL) fermented dried fish or anchovies
½ cup (118 mL) water
¼ cup (59 mL) shrimp powder (available in Asian markets)
1 teaspoon (5 mL) ground cayenne
2 tablespoons (30 mL) lime juice
6 cloves garlic, peeled and minced

1. In a saucepan, bring the fish and water to a boil. Reduce the heat, simmer for 5 minutes, and mash the fish. Remove the pan from the heat and let the mixture cool. Add the remaining ingredients and stir well.

Balachaung
(Burmese Seasoning Sauce)

Yield: About 3 cups (708 mL)   Heat Scale: Mild

This recipe is from Richard Sterling, author of Dining with Headhunters, *who commented: "Side dishes, tidbits, and condiments are common on the Burmese table, regardless of the meal's abundance or complexity. And for simple meals, as the riverboat's cook demonstrated, a little bit of strongly-flavored accompaniment can go a long way to stretch a bowl of plain rice. This fits the bill."*

1 red chile, such as serrano, stem removed, chopped
2 teaspoons (10 mL) salt
1 teaspoon (5 mL) dried shrimp paste (or Malayan blacan)
½ cup (118 mL) distilled white vinegar
20 cloves garlic
2 cups (473 mL) peanut oil
4 onions, peeled and thinly sliced
8 ounces (224 g) coarse shrimp powder (dried shrimp coarsely ground in a mortar)

1. Combine the chile, salt, shrimp paste, and vinegar and set aside.
2. Place the garlic cloves on a cutting board and strike them firmly with the flat side of a knife blade to loosen their skins. Peel and slice the cloves.
3. Heat the oil in a skillet over medium heat. Fry the onion and garlic separately, for about 10 minutes each, then remove each with a slotted spoon and set aside to cool. Pour off all but 1 cup (236 mL) of the oil. Add the shrimp powder and fry for 5 minutes. Return the onion and garlic mixture and stir-fry until crisp. Remove from the heat and let cool completely.
4. Combine the two mixtures and serve over rice.

Nam Prik
(Thai Pepper Water Sauce)

Yield: ½ cup (118 mL)   Heat Scale: Medium

From one of my writers, Peter Aiken, who paddled to the peppers in his kayak, here is a standard, basic Thai chile sauce. He comments, "I use prik khee nu, or 'mouse dropping' chiles grown by Thai friends." Serve it to brighten up steamed rice, vegetables, and especially fish dishes.

2 cloves garlic, peeled and sliced
3 fresh, small Thai chiles (or substitute fresh chiltepins or piquins), stems removed, minced with the seeds
4 tablespoons lime juice
¼ cup (59 mL) prepared fish sauce
2 cilantro leaves, chopped

1. Combine all the ingredients. Use immediately. Seal and refrigerate any remaining sauce.

Nam Prik Kai Gem
(Nam Prik Egg Sauce)

Yield: ½ cup (118 mL)   Heat Scale: Hot

Nam prik literally means "pepper water," and that is a good description of this varia-
tion. Similar to nuoc cham, many, many varieties are found in Thailand. Serve this
sauce with raw vegetables as a salad; with soup, rice, or curries; or as a table sauce to
add heat to any dish.

8 to 10 fresh serrano or jalapeño chiles, stems and seeds removed, chopped
4 cloves garlic, peeled
4 green onions, white parts only, or shallots, chopped
4 hard-boiled egg yolks
1 tablespoon (15 mL) prepared fish sauce
2 teaspoons (10 mL) sugar
3 tablespoons (45 mL) lime juice

1. Place all the ingredients in a blender and purée to a smooth sauce. Add
more lime juice if necessary.

Nuoc Cham
(Vietnamese Dipping Sauce)

Yield: ½ cup (118 mL)   Heat Scale: Medium

Richard Sterling collected this recipe in Hanoi. He notes: "No Vietnamese table is
complete without a dish of nuoc cham for dipping and drizzling over the dishes. It is
as ubiquitous as rice."

1 or 2 cloves garlic, peeled
1 fresh red chile, such as serrano or jalapeño, stem and seeds removed
2 teaspoons (10 mL) sugar
¼ fresh lime
2 tablespoons (30 mL) prepared nam pla fish sauce
2½ tablespoons (37.5 mL) water

1. With a mortar and pestle, pound the garlic, chile, and sugar into
a paste. Squeeze the lime juice in. With a paring knife, remove the pulp
from the lime and pound it into the paste. Add the water and fish sauce
and mix well.

Variations

For a real thrill, try this with an habanero! To make the traditional Vietnamese sauce for roast beef, nuac cham tuong gung, omit the lime juice
and add 2 tablespoons (30 mL) minced fresh ginger.

Lemongrass Curry Sauce

Yield: 4 cups (.95 L) Heat Scale: Mild

Richard Sterling collected this recipe in Cambodia, where, he said, "There are as many curries as there are cooks. But all true Khmer curries have five constants: lemongrass, garlic, galangal, and coconut milk; the fifth constant is the cooking technique, dictated by the texture of lemongrass and the consistency of coconut milk. This is my personal all-purpose four-cup curry which is based on extensive observation and many trials. To prepare one portion, pour ½ cup [118 mL] of this curry sauce into a shallow vessel or a wok. Add ½ cup [118 mL] of meat or vegetables, bring to a medium boil and cook to desired degree. Try it with frog legs, as the Cambodians do."

⅓ cup (79 mL) sliced lemongrass
4 cloves garlic, peeled
1 teaspoon (5 mL) dried galangal
1 teaspoon (5 mL) ground turmeric
1 jalapeño chile, seeds and stem removed
3 shallots, peeled
3 kaffir lime leaves (available in Asian markets)
1 pinch salt or shrimp paste
3½ cups (827 mL) coconut milk (made by soaking 4 cups [.95 L] grated coconut in 1 quart [.95 L] of water for an hour, then straining it)

1. In a food processor, purée together the lemongrass, garlic, galangal, turmeric, jalapeños, and shallots.
2. Bring the coconut milk to a boil in a saucepan and add the puréed ingredients, lime leaves, and salt or shrimp paste. Boil gently, stirring constantly, for about 5 minutes. Reduce the heat to low and simmer, stirring often, for about 30 minutes, or until the lime leaves are tender and the sauce is creamy. Remove the leaves before serving.

Jaew Bong
(Laotian Garlic-Shallot Hot Sauce)

Yield: About ½ cup (118 mL) Heat Scale: Medium to Hot

Although jaew bong translates as "pickled sauce," that phrase is a misnomer as there is no vinegar in the recipe at all. Like many Southeast Asian sauces, this one is used as a table condiment to add heat to meat and rice dishes.

3 dried red New Mexican chiles, stems removed
2 small, hot, dried red chiles, such as Thai or piquin, stems removed
2 heads garlic, separated into cloves, unpeeled
2 shallots, unpeeled
1 tablespoon (15 mL) minced fresh ginger
¼ teaspoon (1.25 mL) salt
1 tablespoon (15 mL) prepared fish sauce (nam pla)

1. Place the chiles on a broiler pan and place under a gas broiler, about 3 to 4 inches (7.5 to 10 cm) from the flame. Turn frequently and roast until brittle, about 2 minutes. Remove from the heat and let cool. Crumble the chiles, removing as many seeds as possible, and set aside. (This can also be done in a sauté pan over high gas or electric heat.)
2. Place the garlic cloves on a broiler pan and place under the broiler, about 3 to 4 inches (7.5 to 10 cm) from the flame. Roast for about 5 minutes, or until the skins are lightly charred. Remove from the heat and let cool. Repeat the process with the shallots.
3. Peel the garlic and shallots and coarsely chop them together. Add the crumbled chiles, ginger, salt, and fish sauce and transfer to a blender. Purée to a coarse paste. Remove and add enough warm water to make a thinner paste.

Gado Gado
(Spicy Indonesian Peanut Sauce)
Yield: 1 cup (236 mL)   Heat Scale: Hot

This sauce is served over grilled meats, such as sates, or as a sauce for cooked vegetables. You can tone down the spiciness by decreasing the Transplanted Sriracha Sauce, but why bother?

1 tablespoon (15 mL) peanut oil
1 cup (236 mL) sliced onions
1 tablespoon (15 mL) minced garlic
¼ cup (59 mL) crunchy peanut butter
¼ teaspoon (1.25 mL) shrimp paste
1 teaspoon (5 mL) tamarind paste, dissolved in 2 tablespoons (30 mL) boiling water
¼ cup (59 mL) lime juice
2 tablespoons (30 mL) Transplanted Sriracha Sauce (page 94)
2 tablespoons (30 mL) prepared fish sauce (nam pla)
1 tablespoon (15 mL) soy sauce

1. Heat the oil in a skillet over medium-high heat. Add the onions and garlic and stir-fry until the onions are golden, about five minutes.
2. Add the peanut butter, shrimp paste, dissolved tamarind paste, and lime juice. Bring the mixture to a boil, stirring constantly to blend well, and immediately remove from heat.
3. Add the Transplanted Sriracha Sauce, fish sauce, and soy sauce. Stir well.

Katjang Saos
(Indonesian Peanut-Chile Sauce)

Yield: 2½ cups (591 mL)   Heat Scale: Varies

Hot and spicy peanut sauce is a standard condiment in Indonesia. This sauce is used not only with sates but as a base for unusual curries and as a dipping sauce. It is traditionally prepared by pounding peanuts into a paste before using. I have simplified the recipe by substituting crunchy peanut butter.

4 green onions, white part only, chopped
4 cloves garlic, peeled and minced
1 teaspoon (5 mL) minced fresh ginger
1 (3-inch [7.5 cm]) stalk lemongrass, minced
1 tablespoon (15 mL) peanut oil
1½ cups (354 mL) chicken stock
3 tablespoons (45 mL) crushed red chile, such as santaka (hot) or New Mexican (mild) or substitute Transplanted Sriracha Sauce (page 94)
1 tablespoon (15 mL) soy sauce
2 teaspoons (10 mL) dark brown sugar
¼ teaspoon (1.25 mL) ground cumin
1 tablespoon (15 mL) lime juice
1 teaspoon (5 mL) prepared prawn paste (blacan)
1 teaspoon (5 mL) tamarind paste
2 cups (473 mL) crunchy peanut butter
Salt, to taste

1. Sauté the onion, garlic, ginger, and lemongrass in the oil over medium heat for 3 to 4 minutes until the onion is soft and transparent but not browned.
2. Add the chicken stock and bring to a boil. Reduce the heat and stir in the remaining ingredients. Simmer the sauce, uncovered, for 10 to 15 minutes, until thickened.

Lot Mein See
(Hot Sichuan Bean Sauce)

Yield: 2 cups (473 mL)   Heat Scale: Hot

This sauce comes from Deborah Berlin, who notes, "This enticing hot and pungent sauce fires up stir-fry dishes and gives a gourmet twist to old and new recipes." Use it as a dip for tempura vegetables or egg rolls. It will last for 2 to 3 weeks in the refrigerator.

1 (15¼-ounce [423 g]) can red beans
½ cup (118 mL) water, divided
½ teaspoon (2.5 mL) cornstarch
¼ teaspoon (1.25 mL) distilled white vinegar
1 tablespoon (15 mL) vegetable oil
6 fresh or dried small, hot red chiles, such as piquin or santaka, stems and seeds removed, crushed
1 clove garlic, peeled and minced
⅛ teaspoon (.6 mL) salt

1. Drain the beans and purée them in a blender. Set aside.
2. Mix together 1 tablespoon (15 mL) of the water with the cornstarch and vinegar and set aside.
3. In a saucepan, heat the oil over medium heat. Add the chiles and garlic and sauté until the garlic is browned. Add the cornstarch mixture, puréed beans, salt, and remaining water and stir well. Simmer, covered, for 20 minutes. Uncover and simmer an additional 20 minutes to thicken.

Chinese Chile and Garlic Sauce

Yield: About 3 cups (708 mL)   Heat Scale: Hot

From Pat Chapman comes this "archetypal chile sauce," which every Chinese restaurant produces on demand. "Most don't actually make it," he says, because "time is too pressing, and there are many proprietary brands available." This recipe makes enough to bottle, and Pat says it can be kept indefinitely in the refrigerator. (Note: This recipe requires advance preparation.)

1 pound (454 g) fresh red chiles, such as jalapeños or serranos, stems and seeds removed, halved lengthwise
1 cup (236 mL) Chinese white rice vinegar
1 teaspoon (5 mL) salt
1 tablespoon (15 mL) garlic powder
2 teaspoons (10 mL) sugar
2 teaspoons (10 mL) cornstarch

1. In a jar or large bowl, combine the chiles, vinegar, and salt and marinate overnight.
2. The following day, place the chile mixture in a food processor and pulse into a fine purée.
3. Add the garlic powder, sugar, cornstarch, and enough water to produce a pourable consistency. Pulse briefly to mix.
4. Pour the sauce into bottles and refrigerate.

Sichuan Chile Sauce

Yield: About 1¼ cup (295 mL)   Heat Scale: Hot

Here is a classic chile sauce from one of the hottest regions—foodwise—in China. Use it to perk up stir-frys.

2 tablespoons (30 mL) vegetable oil
4 cloves garlic, peeled and finely chopped
1 (1-inch [2.5 cm]) piece fresh ginger, peeled and finely chopped
1 small onion, peeled and finely chopped
6 fresh red chiles, such as jalapeños, stems and seeds removed, finely chopped
¼ cup (59 mL) Chinese red rice vinegar
1 tablespoon (15 mL) sugar
2 tablespoons (30 mL) catsup
2 tablespoons (30 mL) Chinese yellow rice wine
2 teaspoons (10 mL) salt

1. In a wok or frying pan, heat the oil over high heat. Add the garlic and ginger and stir-fry for 30 seconds. Add the onion and stir-fry for another minute.
2. Add the chiles and the vinegar and simmer for 10 minutes, adding water if it gets too dry.
3. Add the sugar, catsup, rice wine, and salt and simmer for 5 more minutes.
4. Remove from the heat and allow to cool. Transfer the mixture to a food processor or blender and process to a fine purée, adding water as necessary to achieve the desired consistency. Transfer the sauce to bottles and refrigerate.

Yang Yeum Kanjang
(Spicy Sesame-Soy Dipping Sauce)

Yield: About ½ cup (118 mL)   Heat Scale: Hot

Perfect for dipping potstickers, this Korean sauce is redolent not only with chile, but with the aroma and flavor of sesame. It can also be used to top stir-fry dishes.

½ teaspoon (2.5 mL) sesame oil
½ cup (118 mL) soy sauce
½ teaspoon (2.5 mL) toasted sesame seeds, crushed
1 green onion, white part only, thinly sliced
1 tablespoon (15 mL) gochu garu, Korean chile paste, or hot red chile powder
½ teaspoon (2.5 mL) sugar
⅛ teaspoon (.6 mL) white pepper

1. Combine all ingredients in a jar and shake well. Store in the refrigerator, where it will last for weeks.

Finadene

Yield: 1 cup (236 mL) Heat Scale: Medium to Hot

This simple sauce from Guam was collected by Janet Go, who comments, "Originally, finadene was made by grating the meat from three or four coconuts, adding a little water, and squeezing the meat through a piece of cheesecloth to produce a thick coconut milk. The milk was boiled, ten finely crumbled hot chiles were added and, when the milk curdled, it was beaten, poured into containers, and refrigerated. This produced a thick, red-hot gravy called finadene. This is today's simpler, less fiery finadene." Serve the sauce over grilled meats and seafood.

1 medium onion, peeled and sliced
½ cup (118 mL) soy sauce
4 to 6 fresh red chiles, such as jalapeños or serranos, stems and seeds removed, minced
½ cup (118 mL) vinegar or lemon juice

1. In a bowl, combine the onions, soy sauce, and chiles. Stir in the vinegar a little at a time, according to taste. The sauce can be stored in a covered jar, refrigerated, indefinitely.

Hawaiian Chile Water

Yield: 2 cups (473 mL) Heat Scale: Hot

Hawaiian chiles are difficult to find, even in Hawaii. There are no commercial growing operations and the ones grown in backyards are often eaten by birds. Substitute fresh piquins, bird's eye, or the small Thai prik khee nu chiles.

2 cups (473 mL) water
¼ cup (59 mL) whole fresh red Hawaiian chiles, stems removed
1 teaspoon (5 mL) kosher salt
4 cloves garlic, peeled

1. In a pot, bring the water to a boil. Remove from the heat and add the rest of the ingredients. Transfer to a blender and purée until smooth. Pour the sauce into a bottle and store it in the refrigerator.

THREE

Dangerous Drinks and Snacks

- - - - - - - - - - - - - - - -

The concept of adding chile peppers to alcoholic and nonalcoholic beverages is not new. Pertsovka, the Russian vodka with chile peppers, dates back more than 50 years, and the spicy Bloody Mary drink originated in 1920 or 1939, depending upon which story you believe. But these drinks are recent compared with those of the Aztecs, who were adding chile peppers to their hot chocolate millennia ago. I seriously doubt that this practice will ever fade away because more and more people are becoming habituated to chile peppers in all the foods they eat.

Tequila Enchilado
(Chilied Tequila)

Yield: 1.06 quarts (1 L)   Heat Scale: Medium

This recipe is a variation on spiced vodkas but with Mexican spices. It can be used in any drink recipe requiring tequila or downed straight. (Note: This recipe requires advance preparation.)

1.06 quarts (1 L) white tequila
10 coriander seeds
10 chiltepins or piquins
10 black peppercorns
2 sprigs cilantro
2 long lime peels
2 tablespoons (30 mL) salt
1 teaspoon (5 mL) chile piquin powder
½ lime

1. Open the bottle of tequila and add the coriander seeds, chiltepins, peppercorns, cilantro, and lime peels. Close the bottle and refrigerate for at least 4 hours and preferably overnight.
2. Combine the salt and chile piquin powder in a shallow bowl.
3. To serve, pass the lime over the rims of shot glasses, dip the glasses in the salt mixture, and pour in the chilled and chilied tequila.

Sangrita de Chapala
(Chapala's Little Bloody Drink)

Yield: About 3 cups (708 mL)   Heat Scale: Medium

This particular version of sangrita, or "little bloody drink," comes from Chapala, Mexico, where the bartenders have not succumbed to the temptation of adding tomato juice to this concoction, as the norteamericanos do. The bloody color comes from the grenadine, so this is truly a sweet heat drink that is also salty. Some people take a sip of tequila after each swallow of sangrita, while others make a cocktail of one part tequila to four parts sangrita.

2 cups (473 mL) orange juice
¾ cup (177 mL) grenadine syrup
2 teaspoons (10 mL) Mexican hot sauce of your choice (or substitute any habanero hot sauce)
1 tablespoon (15 mL) salt

1. Combine all the ingredients in a jar, shake well, and chill.

The Great Montezuma Hot Chocolate Drink

Yield: 2 servings   Heat Scale: Mild

My friend Richard Sterling developed this recipe, which is his version of how the Spaniards transformed Montezuma's favorite spicy beverage with the addition of alcohol. He commented: "Salud! Drink to the Old World and the New."

12 ounces (350 mL) prepared hot chocolate (not too sweet)
2 tablespoons (30 mL) honey
½ teaspoon (2.5 mL) vanilla extract
2 jiggers (88 mL) chile pepper vodka (pages 105 and 106))
2 tablespoons (30 mL) heavy cream
Ground cayenne and cinnamon sticks for garnish
Grated chocolate and dried red chiles, halved lengthwise, for garnish (optional)

1. Combine the hot chocolate, honey, vanilla, and vodka in a small pitcher. Divide between two long-stemmed glasses or Irish coffee glasses. Float the cream on the tops of the two drinks. Dust each with a pinch of ground cayenne and garnish with cinnamon sticks, or dust with grated chocolate and fix dried red chiles to the edge of each glass.

Bloody Maria

Yield: 1 serving   Heat Scale: Medium

Think this drink is just a Bloody Mary with tequila instead of vodka? Well, almost.

2 ounces (60 mL) tequila
3 ounces (90 mL) tomato juice
¼ ounce (7 mL) lime juice
1 dash Worcestershire sauce
1 dash celery salt
1 dash freshly ground black pepper
1 dash salt
1½ teaspoons (7.5 mL) bottled chipotle hot sauce or habanero hot sauce
1 lime slice for garnish

1. Combine all the ingredients in a small pitcher and pour over ice in a glass. Garnish with a slice of lime and serve.

Chiltepin Pepper Vodka

Yield: 1.06 quarts (1 L)   Heat Scale: Medium to Hot

The Russians are the true inventors of pepper vodka, and they usually flavor their vodka with cayenne. Any small fresh or dried chile pepper that will fit in the bottle will work. Be sure to taste it often and to remove the chiles when it reaches the desired heat—the longer the chiles are left in, the hotter the vodka will get. Serve over ice or in tomato juice for an instant Bloody Mary. (Note: This recipe requires advance preparation.)

4 to 6 dried chiltepin or piquin chiles, left whole
1.06 quarts (1 L) vodka

1. Place the chiles in the vodka and let them steep for a week or more. Periodically taste the vodka and remove the chiles when it is hot enough.

Another Chile-Flavored Vodka

Yield: About 1.06 quarts (1 L)
Heat Scale: Varies, but is best served with medium heat

When I write "flavored," I mean it, as I have chosen the chiles that impart the most distinct flavors. The raisiny flavor of the pasilla melds with the apricot overtones of the habanero and the earthiness of the New Mexican chile to create a finely tuned, fiery sipping vodka. Of course, use an excellent vodka such as Stolichnaya or Absolut. (Note: This recipe requires advance preparation.)

1.06 quarts (1 L) vodka
1 pasilla chile, stem and seeds removed, cut into thin strips
½ dried red New Mexican chile, stem and seeds removed, cut in fourths
¼ habanero chile, stem and seeds removed, left whole

1. Open the bottle of vodka and drink some of it to make room for the chiles. Add the chiles and recap. Let sit for at least 3 days to generate some heat. The vodka will get progressively hotter as time passes. As you drink the vodka, replace it with more fresh vodka, and the process will go on for some time.

Southwestern Sangrita with Three Juices

Yield: About 1 quart (.95 L)   Heat Scale: Medium

Serve this northern version of the Mexican drink in a salt-rimmed glass as a chaser to straight tequila. Sip the tequila, then the sangrita, then suck on a lime slice. Repeat the procedure as often as you dare. Or, mix the tequila into the sangrita.

3 green New Mexican chiles, roasted, peeled, stems and seeds removed, chopped
3 cups (708 mL) tomato juice
1 cup (236 mL) orange juice
¼ cup (59 mL) lime juice
2 tablespoons (30 mL) chopped onions
1 teaspoon (5 mL) sugar
Salt, to taste

1. Place all the ingredients in a blender and purée until smooth. Chill before serving.

Hot Tequila, Frozen Margarita

Yield: 4 servings   Heat Scale: Mild

This nontraditional margarita is a favorite with chileheads at Hot Luck dinners.

1 lime wedge
Salt as needed
½ cup (118 mL) fresh lime juice
1½ cups (354 mL) Tabasco® tequila
¼ cup (59 mL) cointreau or triple sec
Crushed ice as needed
4 lime slices for garnish

1. Prepare 4 long-stemmed goblets by rubbing the rims with the lime wedge. Fill a saucer with salt, dip the goblet rims in it, and place the goblets in the freezer for at least 30 minutes.
2. Place the lime juice, tequila, and cointreau or triple sec in a blender. Add enough crushed ice to half fill the blender, then process. Taste and adjust the flavor by adding cointreau or triple sec to make it sweeter, lime juice to make it more tart, tequila to increase the heat level, or ice to decrease the heat level. Pour into the frosted goblets and garnish each serving with a slice of lime.

Jalapeño Margarita

Yield: 1 serving   Heat Scale: Medium

This is certainly a unique capsicum cocktail. (Note: This recipe requires advance preparation.)

1¼ ounces (37 mL) tequila
¾ ounce (22 mL) triple sec
2 ounces (60 mL) Hot and Sour Mix (recipe follows)
1½ ounces (44 mL) lime juice
1 dash Tabasco® Green Jalapeño Pepper Sauce
1 lime slice for garnish
1 whole jalapeño for garnish

1. Place all the ingredients, except the lime slice and whole jalapeño, in a blender and blend to mix. Pour over ice in a glass and garnish with the lime slice and whole jalapeño. To make a frozen margarita, add 1 cup ice (236 mL) to the blender with other ingredients.

Hot and Sour Mix
4 large jalapeños, stems and seeds removed, diced
1 quart (.95 L) sour mix
Add the jalapeños to the sour mix and let steep for at least 24 hours.

"Red Ass" Bloody Mary Mix

Yield: 1 quart   Heat Scale: Hot

So named because it was served to visitors of chili con carne cook-offs by the Red Ass Chili Team, this mix will spice up your morning and may help with that hangover from the night before. Omit the habanero unless you like it extremely hot. I've heard this mix is also good without alcohol, but I've never tried it that way.

1 jalapeño chile, stem and seeds removed
1 habanero chile, stem and seeds removed
6 tablespoons (90 mL) Worcestershire sauce
¼ cup (59 mL) A-1 sauce
2 tablespoons (30 mL) chopped fresh cilantro
1 tablespoon (15 mL) prepared horseradish
1 tablespoon (15 mL) garlic salt
1 teaspoon (5 mL) freshly ground black pepper
¼ teaspoon (1.25 mL) dried oregano
Juice of ½ lemon
1 cup (236 mL) orange juice
1 quart (.95 L) tomato juice
Vodka or tequila, to taste
Salt, to taste
Mild chile powder, to taste
Lemon or lime slices for garnish

1. Place the chiles, Worcestershire sauce, A-1 sauce, cilantro, horseradish, garlic salt, pepper, and oregano in a blender and process until smooth. Stir in the juices and chill.
2. To serve, combine the salt and chile powder on a plate. Wet the rim of the serving glasses with a lime slice and rub each glass upside down on the chile mixture. Pour 1½ ounces (42 mL) liquor in each glass. Add ice to each glass, fill with bloody Mary mix, stir well, garnish with a lime slice, and serve.

Ancho Chile and Rum-Mulled Citrus Cider

Yield: 6 to 8 servings   Heat Scale: Mild

To "mull" a beverage is to heat it with other ingredients to impart their flavor. I mulled over several formulas before choosing this one with its pungent punch.

2 quarts (1.9 L) apple cider
1 tablespoon (15 mL) finely ground ancho or pasilla chile
1 lemon, sliced very thin
½ orange, sliced very thin
2 teaspoons (10 mL) lemon juice
4 (3-inch [7.5 cm]) cinnamon sticks
2 tablespoons (30 mL) whole cloves
2 cups (473 mL) dark rum

1. Combine all the ingredients in a large saucepan and cook over medium-low heat, but do not bring to a boil. Reduce the heat to low and simmer for 15 minutes. Strain the mixture through a sieve, pour into mugs, and serve warm.

Chile-Infused Cranberry Cider
Yield: 4 to 6 servings   Heat Scale: Medium

Here's another mulled cider that contains two chiles, the mild ancho and the super-hot habanero. The ancho adds raisiny overtones while the habanero supplies an additional fruity heat. Serve this cider in large mugs around a roaring fire in the winter.

1 quart (.95 L) apple cider
1 ancho chile, stem and seeds removed, cut into thin strips
2 cups (473 mL) cranberry juice cocktail
1 teaspoon (5 mL) whole cloves
1 (3-inch [7.5 cm]) cinnamon stick
½ habanero chile, stem and seeds removed, left whole
Ground nutmeg or allspice for garnish

1. Combine the cider, ancho chile strips, and cranberry juice cocktail in a large bowl and let sit for 30 minutes.
2. Transfer the mixture to a large saucepan. Add the cloves, cinnamon stick, and habanero chile and bring to a boil. Reduce the heat and simmer, uncovered, for 10 minutes.
3. Remove from the heat, strain, and pour into mugs. Sprinkle some ground nutmeg or allspice over each mug.

Fresh Peach and Chile Daiquiris
Yield: 4 servings   Heat Scale: Medium

For some reason, habanero chiles work particularly well with fruits. These daiquiris will delight chileheads, who will probably suggest adding more habanero to the blender! For a nonalcoholic version of this drink, substitute pineapple juice for the rum and decrease the sugar to 3 tablespoons (45 mL).

2 cups (473 mL) fresh peach slices
¼ cup (59 mL) freshly squeezed lime juice
½ teaspoon (2.5 mL) minced fresh habanero chile
1 cup (236 mL) dark rum
⅓ cup (79 mL) sugar
1 cup (236 mL) crushed ice
Mint sprigs for garnish

1. In a blender, combine the peaches, lime juice, and chile and purée. Add the rum, sugar, and crushed ice and purée until smooth. Pour into stemmed glasses and garnish with mint sprigs.

Mango Lassi with Ghost Chile
Yield: 4 servings   Heat Scale: Medium

This refreshing drink originated in India, where it is often served for dessert after a meal of fiery hot curries. I have, of course, spiced up a drink designed as a cool-down with the hottest chile in the world, the bhut jolokia, or ghost chile. Fruits such as strawberries, peaches, or pineapples may be added to or substituted for the mangos.

2 cups (473 mL) plain yogurt
2 cups (473 mL) buttermilk (or substitute milk)
2 ripe mangos, peeled and pitted
Juice of 1 lemon
2 teaspoons (10 mL) sugar
¼ of a fresh bhut jolokia chile, seeds removed, minced (or substitute 1 habanero)

1. Place all the ingredients in a blender and process until smooth. Serve in dessert glasses over ice, or freeze until slushy and then serve.

Coco Loco
Yield: 8–10 servings   Heat Scale: Mild

This slightly crazy, alcohol-charged tropical drink is perfect for a Hot Luck party. Remember to serve only one of these per guest per hour.

½ cup (118 mL) chile pepper vodka (pages 105 and 106)
¼ cup (59 mL) white rum
¼ cup (59 mL) brandy
¼ cup (59 mL) gin
¼ cup (59 mL) tequila
1 cup (236 mL) orange juice
½ cup (118 mL) pineapple juice
1 cup (236 mL) evaporated milk
2 ounces (56 mL) sweetened coconut cream or syrup
⅛ cup (30 mL) grenadine syrup
Crushed ice as needed
Grated coconut for garnish
Orange slices for garnish

1. Combine all the ingredients except the crushed ice and garnishes in a blender and blend until frothy. Serve over crushed ice in champagne glasses. Sprinkle the coconut over each drink and garnish with the orange slices.

Poblano Pepper Rings
Yield: 4 to 6 servings   Heat Scale: Mild

Since poblanos make some of the tastiest chiles rellenos, it makes sense that they fry up deliciously. Why not dip these rings in guacamole?

1 cup (236 mL) all-purpose flour
1 teaspoon (5 mL) salt
1 teaspoon (5 mL) freshly ground black pepper
½ teaspoon (2.5 mL) ground cayenne
3 cups (708 mL) vegetable oil
3 poblano chiles, roasted, peeled, stems and seeds removed, cut into ¼-inch (.5 cm) rings
1 cup (236 mL) buttermilk

1. In a bowl, combine the flour, salt, pepper, and cayenne and mix well. Transfer the mixture to a plate.
2. In a large pan, heat the oil over high heat until it just begins to smoke, then lower the heat slightly. Dip 4 of the poblano rings in the flour and shake off any excess. Dip them in the buttermilk, then dip them in the flour again. Drop them into the hot oil and fry them until lightly browned. Transfer them to paper towels to drain. Repeat with the rest of the rings. Serve warm.

Devilish Dills
Yield: Varies   Heat Scale: Medium

These are the pickles I put up with some of the cucumber bounty from my garden. I may vary the spices I add, but I never change the proportions of the acid (vinegar) or salt in the recipe. If you have fresh grape leaves, add a couple to the jar. They will help keep your pickles crisp. (Note: This recipe requires advance preparation.)

5 cups (1.2 L) water
3½ cups (826 mL) 5–6% distilled white vinegar
3 tablespoons (45 mL) pickling salt
Fresh grape leaves for the jar (optional)
Small cucumbers, blossom ends removed
Per 1-quart (.95 L) jar:
12 black peppercorns
4 sprigs fresh dill or 2 teaspoons (10 mL) dill seed
3 cloves garlic, peeled
4 dried red chiles, such as piquin, cayenne, or chiltepins

1. In a large pan, combine the water and vinegar with the pickling salt and cook over medium heat until the salt dissolves. Allow the brine to cool and add the cucumbers. Brine the cucumbers overnight, weighing them down with a plate to keep them submerged. Drain the cucumbers, reserving the liquid, and dry.

2. Place the grape leaves, if using, in the bottoms of sterilized jars and add the seasonings. Pack the pickles in the jars.
3. In a saucepan, bring the reserved pickling solution to a boil. Pour the solution over the cucumbers and run a knife along the sides of the jars to release any air bubbles. Seal the jars.
4. Process the jarred pickles in a simmering water bath (180°F [80°C]) for 10 minutes. Remove the jars from the water and let sit for 24 hours. Test the lids to see if they are sealed and store in a cool, dark, dry place.
5. Let stand for 4 to 6 weeks before using.

Spicy Asian Ginger Pickles
Yield: 4 servings   Heat Scale: Medium

This very simple pickle recipe can be prepared in just a matter of minutes. The sweetness of the ginger complements the cool taste of the cucumber. The chile heat keeps the pickles from becoming too sweet. Be sure to marinate the pickles for at least an hour to blend the flavors.

1 large cucumber, chopped
⅓ cup (79 mL) rice vinegar
1 tablespoon (15 mL) chile oil
1 tablespoon (15 mL) grated ginger
2 teaspoons (10 mL) soy sauce
2 teaspoons (10 mL) sugar
Chopped fresh cilantro for garnish

1. Place the cucumber chunks in a nonreactive bowl. In a separate bowl, whisk the remaining ingredients together until combined. Pour this mixture over the pickles and let them marinate for 1 hour.
2. To serve, drain and garnish with the cilantro.

Sichuan Pickles
Yield: 4–6 servings   Heat Scale: Medium

Hot and slightly sweet, these Sichuan pickles complement Asian meals and grilled meats. They are quick and easy to make and can be stored in the refrigerator for up to 4 days.

2 large cucumbers, cut lengthwise into ½-inch (1 cm) strips
1 tablespoon (15 mL) salt
1 tablespoon (15 mL) crushed red chile
3 tablespoons (45 mL) sesame oil
¼ cup (59 mL) rice vinegar
2 tablespoons (30 mL) sugar

1. In a bowl, sprinkle the cucumber slices with the salt and let them sit for 2 hours. Drain any excess water from the cucumber slices and place them in a nonmetallic bowl. Sprinkle the crushed chile over the slices.

2. In a pan, heat the oil, vinegar, and sugar over medium heat and cook, stirring, until the sugar dissolves. Pour the mixture over the slices and refrigerate for 4 hours. Drain before serving.

Hot Shot Olives

Yield: 3 cups (708 mL)   Heat Scale: Mild

These olives keep for several months in the refrigerator. They can be used as an appetizer or as a spicy addition to salads. Try them chopped and mixed with cream cheese and a little mayo as a tangy stuffing for celery or hard-boiled eggs. You can also incorporate them (chopped or sliced) into any dip recipe to liven it up. (Note: This recipe requires advance preparation.)

1¼ pounds (567 g) jarred kalamata olives
3 cloves garlic, peeled and thinly sliced
1½ teaspoons (7.5 mL) dried rosemary, crushed in a mortar and pestle
1 tablespoon (15 mL) ground red New Mexican chile
2 tablespoons (30 mL) balsamic vinegar
1½ cups (354 mL) olive oil

1. Drain the olives thoroughly and set them aside on paper towels. Mix the remaining ingredients together in a bowl and whisk thoroughly.
2. Place ⅓ of the olives in a 1-quart (1 L) jar and cover them with ⅓ of the whisked mixture. Repeat with the remaining olives and mixture until both are used up.
3. Allow the olives to stand at room temperature for 24 hours. Shake the jar well and place it in the refrigerator for two weeks, shaking the jar daily.

Spicy Hot Gigantic Garlic

Yield: 8 servings   Heat Scale: Mild

What I'm talking about here is elephant garlic, which is very large but quite mild. This snack is easy, fast, and tasty.

8 heads elephant garlic
¼ cup (59 mL) butter
2 teaspoons (10 mL) ground red New Mexican chile
4 sprigs fresh rosemary, crushed
8 (12-inch [30 cm]) flour tortillas, cut into wedges

1. Peel the outer skin from the garlic, leaving each head intact. Place the heads on a double thickness of foil. Place the butter in a large, nonmetallic coffee cup and microwave it in 15-second increments until it is melted. Remove the butter from the microwave and stir in the red chile powder and rosemary. Brush the garlic with the butter mixture, then fold up the garlic in the foil and seal. Cook the garlic on the grill over a medium-high flame, turning occasionally, for about 45 minutes. Serve one whole head of garlic per person. Instruct your guests to squeeze the cooked garlic onto the tops of the tortilla wedges.

Chile-Cumin Crackers

Yield: 3 dozen   Heat Scale: Mild

These zesty crackers can be served hot or cold. They can even be made two or three days ahead and kept in an airtight container. They are good to serve as a snack or with a salad for a luncheon.

¾ cup (177 mL) butter, softened
1 cup (236 mL) shredded sharp cheddar
2 teaspoons (10 mL) ground red New Mexican chile
¼ cup (59 mL) minced onion
1½ teaspoons (7.5 mL) ground cumin
2 cups (473 mL) sifted all-purpose flour

1. In a bowl, cream the butter and cheese together thoroughly. Add the chile powder, onion, and cumin and mix. Add the flour gradually, blending well. Form into rolls about 1½ inches (3.5 cm) in diameter. Wrap in waxed paper or foil and chill for several hours or overnight.
2. Preheat the oven to 400°F (200°C). Lightly grease a baking sheet.
3. Remove the dough from the paper or foil. Using a chilled, sharp knife, slice each roll into ¼-inch (.5 cm) slices and arrange them on the prepared baking sheet. Bake them for about 10 minutes or until lightly browned. Remove the crackers from the baking sheet with a spatula and serve immediately or transfer them to a wire rack to cool thoroughly, then store them in an airtight container.

Peppered Walnuts

Yield: 5 cups   Heat Scale: Medium

Hot nuts are quite the rage these days, with commercial brands of hot and spicy pistachios, pecans, and peanuts now available. I add my two cents' worth with this recipe for walnuts.

1 tablespoon (15 mL) safflower oil
1 teaspoon (5 mL) freshly ground black pepper
1 teaspoon (5 mL) ground cayenne
½ teaspoon (2.5 mL) dried thyme, crumbled
2 egg whites
2 teaspoons (10 mL) soy sauce
1 teaspoon (5 mL) Louisiana-style hot sauce
1 teaspoon (5 mL) salt
5 cups (1.2 L) shelled and halved walnuts

1. Place a rack in the upper third of the oven and preheat the oven to 375°F (190°C). Coat a large baking pan with the oil.
2. In a small bowl, mix together the black pepper, cayenne, and thyme.
3. In a separate bowl, beat the egg whites until foamy, then whisk in the soy sauce, hot sauce, and salt. Add the nuts and toss to coat. Add the pepper mixture and toss to coat.

4. Pour the walnuts onto the prepared baking pan, spreading evenly. Bake for 4 minutes, then stir the nuts to break up any clumps. Bake for about 6 more minutes or until golden brown, watching closely to prevent burning. Remove the pan from the oven and pour the nuts into a bowl. Cool to room temperature before serving.

Chile-Spiced Popcorn

Yield: 8 servings   Heat Scale: Mild

This totally addictive snack is a great diversion when watching horror movies on TV. It also goes well with beer when watching football.

½ teaspoon (2.5 mL) ground cumin
½ teaspoon (2.5 mL) ground hot New Mexican chile
¼ teaspoon (1.25 mL) salt
1 dash ground cinnamon
12 cups popped popcorn
Nonstick cooking spray as needed

1. Preheat the oven to 200°F (100°C).
2. In a small bowl, stir together the cumin, chile powder, salt, and cinnamon.
3. Spread the popped popcorn in an even layer in a large, shallow baking pan. Lightly coat the popcorn with the nonstick cooking spray. Sprinkle the spice mixture evenly over the popcorn, then toss to coat.
4. Bake for 10 minutes.

Variation
To make an Indian-flavored popcorn, replace the spices with ½ teaspoon (2.5 mL) curry powder, ½ teaspoon (2.5 mL) garam masala, ¼ teaspoon (1.25 mL) ground turmeric, and ¼ teaspoon (1.25 mL) ground black pepper.

Brilliant Bayou Pumpkin Seed Snack

Yield: 4 servings   Heat Scale: Medium

Neighbors stop by unexpectedly? Don't panic. You can whip up this fun snack in less time than it takes to polish off a beer or two. Of course, the trick is to have these ingredients on hand at all times. This is easily accomplished, as pumpkin seeds last practically forever when kept in an airtight bag or jar in a cool, dry place.

1 egg white
2 teaspoons (10 mL) commercial Cajun seasoning powder
1 teaspoon (5 mL) safflower oil
8 ounces (224 g) shelled, unsalted pumpkin seeds
1 teaspoon (5 mL) salt
8 ounces (224 g) low-fat cream cheese, softened
Fancy crackers for serving
Ground cayenne, to taste

1. Preheat the oven to 350°F (180°C).
2. In a medium bowl, whisk together the egg white, Cajun seasoning, and safflower oil. Add the pumpkin seeds and stir to coat. Spread the seeds on a nonstick baking sheet and sprinkle with the salt. Bake the seeds for 15 minutes, stirring every 5 minutes. Remove the seeds from the oven and let sit for 5 minutes. Place them in the refrigerator if you need them to cool down quickly.
3. Place the softened brick of low-fat cream cheese in a medium mixing bowl. Stir the seeds into the cream cheese, then transfer the mixture to a small, attractive serving dish. Place the dish on a platter and arrange the crackers around the dish.

Sweet Potato Chips Dusted with Chimayo Red Chile

Yield: 4–6 servings   Heat Scale: Medium

This snack is a hot twist on party chips. I have had great success in substituting sweet potatoes for potatoes in many recipes.

2 large sweet potatoes, peeled and cut into ⅛-inch (.25 cm) slices
Vegetable oil for deep-frying
1 tablespoon (15 mL) hot ground red New Mexican chile

1. Heat the vegetable oil to 350°F (180°C) in a deep skillet.
2. Divide the potatoes into 6 portions. Fry each batch, turning once, for 1 minute or until they are golden. With a slotted spoon, transfer the chips to a paper towel to drain and cool. Continue until all the potato chips are fried and cooled.
3. Place the red chile powder in a medium-sized plastic freezer bag. Again working in batches, place the chips in the bag and seal. Shake the bag gently to dust the chips with the powder. After each batch is dusted, transfer them to a napkin-lined basket and serve.

Hot Garlic Potato Chips

Yield: 4–6 servings   Heat Scale: Medium

Of course you can buy spicy potato chips in the supermarket, but have you ever read the ingredients of some of them? These are much better.

4 medium potatoes, peeled, rinsed, and dried
1 tablespoon (15 mL) New Mexico hot red chile powder
1 teaspoon (5 mL) garlic salt
Peanut oil for deep-frying

1. In a small bowl, combine the chile powder and garlic salt and mix well.
2. Using a mandoline, slice the potatoes as thinly as possible.
3. Heat the oil in a large pan or deep fryer. In small batches, fry the potato slices until they are golden brown. Remove them with a slotted spoon and drain them on paper towels. When all the potatoes have drained, sprinkle them with the spice mixture.

Fiery Baked Tortilla Chips

Yield: 3–4 servings   Heat Scale: Medium

I bake rather than fry these chips, which reduces the fat content to practically nothing. Use them as is or with the spicy dip or salsa of your choice.

Nonstick cooking spray as needed
4 (6-inch [15 cm]) corn tortillas, each cut into 6 wedges
½ teaspoon (2.5 mL) brown sugar
¼ teaspoon (1.25 mL) garlic powder
¼ teaspoon (1.25 mL) onion powder
¼ teaspoon (1.25 mL) ground cumin
½ teaspoon (2.5 mL) paprika
½ teaspoon (2.5 mL) ground cayenne

1. Preheat the oven to 375°F (190°C). Spray a baking sheet with the nonstick cooking spray.
2. In a small bowl, mix the spices together. Arrange the tortilla wedges on the prepared baking sheet and spray them lightly. Sprinkle them with the spice mixture. Bake for about 10 minutes, until the wedges are crisp. Let cool and serve.

Habanero Sauce Party Mix

Yield: About 15 servings   Heat Scale: Medium

Looking for a snack to perk up those lagging party guests? This one will wake them up!

¼ cup (59 mL) melted butter
1 tablespoon (15 mL) Worcestershire sauce
2 teaspoons (10 mL) habanero hot sauce
1 teaspoon (5 mL) commercial seasoning salt
8 cups (1.9 L) mixed Chex® brand cereals (corn, rice, and wheat)
1 cup (236 mL) mixed nuts
1 cup (236 mL) mini pretzels
1 cup (236 mL) bite-size cheese crackers

1. Preheat the oven to 250°F (120°C).
2. Combine the butter, Worcestershire sauce, habanero sauce, and seasoning salt in a small bowl and mix well. Place the cereals, nuts, pretzels, and cheese crackers into a large freezer bag and pour the butter mixture over them. Seal the bag securely and shake it until all pieces are evenly coated. Pour the contents of the bag onto a baking sheet and bake for 45 minutes, stirring every 15 minutes. Let cool and serve.

Arizona Beef Jerky

Yield: About 1 pound (454 g)   Heat Scale: Hot

Preserving meat by drying it has always been popular throughout the Southwest, where the hot, dry weather speeds up the process. Jerky, or carne seca, can be eaten as a snack or can be used in burritos and enchiladas. This process can also be done in a food dehydrator.

2 pounds (1.1 kg) extra-lean beef sirloin or flank steak
4 cloves garlic, peeled and halved
2 tablespoons (30 mL) lime juice
4 tablespoons (60 mL) ground red New Mexican chile
1 teaspoon (5 mL) ground cumin
Coarse salt, to taste
Freshly ground black pepper, to taste

1. Preheat the oven to 150°F (60°C).
2. Rub the beef with the garlic cloves. Cut the meat across the grain in slices ⅛-inch (.25 cm) thick and 1-inch (2.5 cm) wide. If you are having difficulty, partially freeze the meat before cutting.
3. Combine the remaining ingredients and rub the beef strips with the mixture.
4. Place the strips on a rack over a drip pan in the oven. Bake for 6 to 8 hours or until the meat is very dry, turning a couple of times during the cooking process. Leaving the oven door slightly ajar will speed up the drying process.

Pakoras Shikarbadi Style

Yield: 6 servings   Heat Scale: Mild

These pakoras are some of the easiest Indian snacks to make. I collected this recipe at the Shikarbadi Hunting Lodge outside of Udaipur. You can use any vegetable you like, but I recommend softer vegetables such as peppers, eggplant, onions, and thinly sliced potatoes.

2 cups (473 mL) gram (chickpea) flour
1 teaspoon (5 mL) red chile powder
½ teaspoon (2.5 mL) salt
½ teaspoon (2.5 mL) turmeric
½ teaspoon (2.5 mL) baking powder
Peanut oil for frying
¾ cup (177 mL) thinly sliced green chiles (such as serranos)
¾ cup (177 mL) thinly sliced onions
¾ cup (177 mL) thinly sliced eggplant
¾ cup (177 mL) thinly sliced potatoes

1. In a bowl, combine the gram flour, chile powder, salt, turmeric, and baking powder and mix well. Add water as needed and mix well until the batter has a creamy consistency. In a deep pan, heat the oil over high heat until water splatters when sprinkled on it.

2. Dip the vegetables in the batter, drop them in the oil a few at a time, and cook them until they are golden brown. Serve them in bowls with the vegetables all mixed together.

Curry Puffs

Yield: 4 to 6 servings   Heat Scale: Medium

Invented by the colonial British, these pastries are a favorite teatime snack in Singapore and Malaysia.

1 (17.3-ounce [484 g]) package frozen prepared puff pastry
2 tablespoons (30 mL) vegetable oil
1 medium onion, peeled and finely chopped
2 tablespoons (30 mL) finely chopped ginger root
2 tablespoons (30 mL) curry powder
1½ cups (354 mL) minced chicken or beef
3–4 serrano chiles, stems and seeds removed, finely chopped
1 medium tomato, chopped
½ teaspoon (2.5 mL) salt
1 large potato, peeled, boiled, and finely diced
2 tablespoons (30 mL) milk
1 egg, lightly beaten with 1 tablespoon (15 mL) milk

1. Preheat the oven to 425°F (220°C).
2. Allow the puff pastry to thaw to room temperature.
3. In a wok, heat the oil over high heat. Add the onion and ginger and stir-fry for 1 minute or until softened. Mix the curry powder with enough water to make a paste and add the mixture to the onion. Stir-fry for an additional minute. Add the meat and continue frying until the meat browns. Add the chiles and tomato, and sprinkle with the salt.
4. Cover the wok and simmer for 10 minutes, stirring occasionally. Add water, a tablespoon at a time, if the mixture becomes dry. Add the potato and cook for another minute or so. Allow to cool.
5. Roll out the pastry to about ⅛-inch (.25 cm) thick and cut into circles 3½ inches (8 cm) in diameter. Brush the edges with the milk, add 1 tablespoon (15 mL) of the curry filling, fold the edges closed, and crimp decoratively with a fork. Brush the pastries with the egg-milk wash.
6. Bake on an ungreased cookie sheet for 12 to 15 minutes or until the curry puffs are golden brown and puffed. Serve warm.

Spicy BBQ-Flavored Beef Jerky
Yield: 6–8 servings   Heat Scale: Medium

You will need an electric food dehydrator to make this recipe, but that handy kitchen device can be used to dry fruits and vegetables as well. (Note: This recipe requires advance preparation.)

2 pounds (1.1 kg) sirloin steak
½ teaspoon (2.5 mL) salt
½ teaspoon (2.5 mL) freshly ground black pepper
1 tablespoon (15 mL) commercial barbecue or grilling rub
1 tablespoon (15 mL) hot ground New Mexican chile

1. Place the steak on a plate and put it in the freezer for about 45 minutes to make it easier to slice.
2. In a bowl, mix together the remaining ingredients.
3. Remove the steak from the freezer and sprinkle the spices over it, then rub them into the meat. Slice the steak across the grain into strips about ¼-inch (.5 cm) thick. Place the strips on the dehydrator racks so they are not touching and set the temperature to low. Dehydrate the strips for about 18 hours, or until they bend but do not snap.

Biltong
(South African Dried Meat)
Yield: About 4 servings   Heat Scale: Mild

This marinated jerky makes a great snack for watching rugby matches! (Note: This recipe requires advance preparation.)

1 tablespoon (15 mL) salt
¼ cup (59 mL) brown sugar
¼ cup (59 mL) Worcestershire sauce
¼ cup (59 mL) soy sauce
½ teaspoon (2.5 mL) freshly ground black pepper
1 tablespoon (15 mL) hot ground New Mexican chile
1 pound (454 g) beef or game flank steak, sliced across the grain into thin strips

1. In a bowl, combine the salt, brown sugar, Worcestershire sauce, soy sauce, pepper, and chile powder. Add the steak strips, mix well, cover, and refrigerate overnight.
2. Remove the strips from the refrigerator and drain on paper towels. Place the strips on the dehydrator racks so they are not touching, and set the temperature to low. Dehydrate the strips for about 18 hours, or until they bend but do not snap.

FOUR

Bold Breakfasts: Eggs, Pancakes, Breads, Jams, and Jellies

I lead off this chapter with my favorite Sunday morning breakfast here in the Great Southwest. It's a three-part affair that's bound to satisfy the most devoted chilehead. After that, the recipes are grouped according to categories.

Scrambled Eggs with Pork Chorizo

Yield: 2 servings   Heat Scale: Medium

This traditional Mexican sausage is often scrambled with eggs or served with Huevos Rancheros (page 125) for breakfast. Unlike other sausages, it is usually not placed in a casing but rather served loose or formed into patties. Only a small amount of chorizo is used in this recipe, so divide the rest into small portions and freeze it. Top the scrambled eggs with New Mexico Red Chile Sauce (page 71). Serve this with Red Homefries for Breakfast and Refried Beans of Choice (recipes follow). (Note: This recipe requires advance preparation.)

1 clove garlic, peeled
½ cup (118 mL) ground red New Mexican chile
½ teaspoon (2.5 mL) freshly ground black pepper
¼ teaspoon (1.25 mL) ground cloves
¼ teaspoon (1.25 mL) ground cinnamon
¼ teaspoon (1.25 mL) ground cumin
½ teaspoon (2.5 mL) salt
1 teaspoon (5 mL) dried oregano
½ cup (118 mL) vinegar
2 pounds (1.1 kg) ground pork
3 large eggs, lightly beaten with 2 tablespoons (30 mL) half-and-half

1. To make the chorizo, combine all the ingredients except the pork, eggs, and half-and-half in a blender and purée. Knead this mixture into the pork until it is thoroughly combined. Place the pork mixture in a bowl, cover, and refrigerate for 24 hours. To cook, crumble ¾ cup (177 mL) of the chorizo in a skillet and fry over medium-high heat until well browned. Drain it on paper towels and return it to the skillet. Add the eggs and fry, stirring constantly, until the eggs are set. Serve immediately.

Red Home Fries for Breakfast

Yield: 4 servings   Heat Scale: Mild

For years, I've been trying to duplicate the home fries served since the early 1960s at Monroe's Restaurant in Albuquerque. This version is the closest I've come to it. Don't let the bacon fat or lard worry you—this is a very special exception to all the rules, and you don't need that much of it. Serve topped with New Mexico Red Chile Sauce (page 71).

8 small red potatoes
2 teaspoons (10 mL) New Mexico red chile powder
Bacon fat (preferred) or lard as needed

1. Place the potatoes in a large pot and add water to cover. Bring to a boil and cook until the potatoes are easily pierced by a fork, but not too soft, about 10 minutes. Drain the potatoes and return to the pot. Using a hand potato masher, crush the potatoes but do not turn them into mush.

2. Heat a comal, griddle, or cast iron skillet over medium-high heat. Add about 2 tablespoons (30 mL) of the bacon fat or lard and distribute it evenly over the bottom of the pan. Add the potatoes and fry until the bottoms are browned. Using a large spatula, turn the potatoes and fry until the other side is browned.

Papas con Chile Colorado (Breakfast Potatoes with Red Chile)

Yield: 4 servings   Heat Scale: Medium

Although the word "colorado" here refers to the red color of the chile rather than the state of the same name, this dish is commonly prepared there—and all over the Southwest. Serve these red chile potatoes in place of hash-browned potatoes for a terrific Southwestern breakfast.

2 tablespoons (30 mL) butter
½ cup (118 mL) chopped onions
1 clove garlic, peeled and minced
2 tablespoons (30 mL) crushed red New Mexican chile, seeds included
2 large potatoes, peeled and diced
1 tablespoon (15 mL) grated Parmesan cheese

1. Preheat the oven to 350°F (180°C).
2. In a sauté pan, melt the butter over medium heat. Add the onions and garlic and sauté until soft, then add the chile. Add the potatoes and toss.
3. Transfer the potatoes to a shallow pan. Add a little water and bake until the potatoes are done, about 45 minutes.
4. Sprinkle the cheese over the top of the potatoes and serve.

Refried Beans of Choice

Yield: 4–6 servings   Heat Scale: Mild

I'm not so fond of pinto beans and prefer to use black beans, but hey—the choice is yours. Be sure to soak the beans overnight and change the water before you cook them. Again, bacon fat or lard is the preferred fat for frying, but if the food police have brainwashed you, use vegetable oil. "Refried" is a misnomer, since the beans are only fried once, but I'm not going to quibble and call them "Recooked Beans." (Note: This recipe requires advance preparation.)

2 cups (473 mL) dried black or pinto beans, sorted and rinsed clean
¼ cup (59 mL) chopped serrano or jalapeño chiles, stems and seeds removed
Bacon fat, lard, or vegetable oil as needed for frying

1. Cover the beans with water and soak overnight. Drain the beans.
2. Transfer the beans to a large pot and add fresh water to cover. Bring to a boil, reduce the heat, and simmer, covered, until the beans are done,

about 2 to 2½ hours. Add the chiles during the last 30 minutes of cooking. Drain the beans completely.

3. In a large skillet, use a large fork to mash the beans as completely as possible. Move the beans to one side of the skillet and add about 2 table-spoons (30 mL) of the cooking fat of your choice. Fry the beans in the fat over medium-high heat, stirring occasionally, for about 5 minutes.

Huevos Uxmal
(Uxmal-Style Eggs)

Yield: 6 servings   Heat Scale: Medium

All the flavors of Yucatán are present in this dish. The cilantro, habanero chiles, and epazote all come together here, and the diner has a choice of green or red sauce or both over the poached eggs. Cook the sauces first, so that they are ready when the eggs are done.

For the Green Sauce:
1 teaspoon (5 mL) vegetable oil
4 epazote leaves, chopped
10 tomatillos or 8 green tomatoes, coarsely chopped
¾–1 cup (177–mL) water
1 habanero chile, stems and seeds removed, halved
4 tablespoons (60 mL) coarsely chopped cilantro
½ teaspoon (2.5 mL) salt
1 green bell pepper, roasted, peeled, stem and seeds removed, quartered
2 teaspoons (10 mL) coarsely chopped epazote

1. In a small skillet, heat the oil over medium heat. Add the epazote and tomatillos and sauté for 1 minute or until the tomatillos are softened. Al-low the mixture to cool for a few minutes, then place it in a blender with the water, habanero, cilantro, salt, bell pepper, and chopped epazote and purée. Return this mixture to the skillet and keep it warm.

For the Red Sauce:
1 teaspoon (5 mL) vegetable oil
8 tomatoes, roasted, peeled, and quartered
½ cup (118 mL) coarsely chopped onion
¼ cup (59 mL) coarsely chopped cilantro
½ teaspoon (2.5 mL) salt
1 habanero chile, stem and seeds removed, halved
2 tablespoons (30 mL) chopped cilantro

1. In a small skillet, heat the oil over medium heat. Add the tomatoes, onion, cilantro, salt, and chile and sauté for 1 minute. Allow the mixture to cool slightly and then pour it into a blender and purée. Return this mix-ture to the saucepan, add the chopped cilantro, and keep the sauce warm.

For the Eggs:
12 fresh eggs, poached in molds or in a large skillet with 2 tablespoons (30 mL) vinegar added to the water

1. Place 2 poached eggs on a warm plate and serve with the red and or green sauce (or both) over them.

Huevos Motuleños
(Motuleño Eggs)

Yield: 5 servings   Heat Scale: Medium

The city of Motul near Mérida is where this recipe originated. This is Yucatán's version of huevos rancheros. The chiltomate is a very traditional Yucatecan tomato sauce; some cooks say that the tomatoes should just be grilled and never fried, and still others maintain that frying brings out additional flavor. In addition to breakfast, serve this as an accompaniment to spicy grilled fish for a big, luscious, Yucatán-style dinner.

2 tablespoons (30 mL) corn oil
1 cup (236 mL) chopped onion
1 clove garlic, peeled and minced
3 tomatoes, grilled, peeled, chopped
1 habanero chile, stem and seeds removed, minced
½ teaspoon (2.5 mL) salt
¼ teaspoon (1.25 mL) freshly ground black pepper
¼ cup (59 mL) chicken stock or water (if needed)
10 corn tortillas, cut into eighths, fried, drained, and coarsely crushed by hand (or substitute 3 cups [708 mL] coarsely crushed packaged corn tortilla chips)
3 cups (708 mL) warm refried black beans, thinned with 3 tablespoons (45 mL) water
10 fried eggs
1 cup (236 mL) chopped boiled ham
1½ cups (354 mL) cooked peas
1½ cups (354 mL) crumbled queso blanco (or substitute crumbled goat cheese or feta)
Sliced bananas for garnish (optional)

1. In a medium-sized skillet, heat the oil over medium heat. Add the onion and sauté for 1 minute. Add the garlic, tomatoes, habanero chile, salt, and pepper and simmer for 5 minutes, adding the chicken stock if the mixture gets too thick.
2. While this mixture is simmering, arrange the tortilla chips on a warm platter and cover them with the hot refried beans.
3. Top the beans with the fried eggs, ham, and peas, and cover everything with the simmering tomato sauce. Sprinkle the cheese over the top, garnish with the banana slices, if desired, and serve.

Huevos Rancheros of the Great Southwest

The recipes may vary from place to place, but the bottom line with ranch-style eggs is that they are delicious for a hearty breakfast or a brunch served with refried beans and hash-browned potatoes.

Tex-Mex Version

Yield: 4 servings   Heat Scale: Medium

4 jalapeño chiles, stems and seeds removed, chopped
1 small onion, peeled and chopped
2 tablespoons (30 mL) vegetable oil
2 medium tomatoes, chopped
4 corn tortillas
Vegetable oil for frying
8 eggs
½ cup (118 mL) grated Monterey Jack cheese for garnish

1. Sauté the jalapeños and onions in the oil over medium heat until soft, about 7 minutes. Add the tomatoes and cook down to a thick sauce.
2. In a sauté pan, heat 2 inches (5 cm) of oil over high heat. Fry each tortilla in the oil for a few seconds on each side until soft, then remove and drain on paper towels.
3. Fry each egg to the desired doneness.
4. To serve, place the sauce on each tortilla and gently slip the eggs on top of the sauce. Garnish with the grated cheese and serve.

New Mexican Version

Yield: 4 servings   Heat Scale: Medium

2 cups (473 mL) Classic Green (page 71) or Red Chile Sauce (page 71)
8 eggs
4 corn tortillas
Vegetable oil for frying
1 medium tomato, chopped, for garnish
½ cup (118 mL) grated cheddar

1. In a frying pan, heat the chile sauce over medium-high heat.
2. Crack the eggs into the sauce, cover the pan with a lid, and poach the eggs to the desired consistency.
3. Heat 2 inches (5 cm) of oil in a sauté pan. Fry each tortilla in the oil for a few seconds on each side until soft, then remove and drain on paper towels.
4. To serve, slip the eggs with the sauce onto the tortillas, add the grated cheddar, garnish with the tomatoes, and serve.

Southern California Version

Yield: 4 servings   Heat Scale: Mild

¼ cup (59 mL) chopped onion
1 clove garlic, peeled and chopped
1 tablespoon (15 mL) vegetable oil
1 cup (236 mL) chopped tomatoes
3 green New Mexican chiles, roasted, peeled, stems and seeds removed, chopped
4 corn tortillas
Vegetable oil for frying
8 eggs
1 cup (236 mL) refried beans
½ cup (118 mL) grated cheddar for garnish
Chopped black olives for garnish
Sour cream for garnish

1. In a sauté pan, heat the oil over medium heat. Add the onions and garlic and sauté until soft. Add the tomatoes and chiles and simmer until the sauce thickens.
2. Heat 2 inches (5 cm) of oil in a sauté pan. Fry each tortilla in the oil for a few seconds on each side, until soft, then remove and drain on paper towels.
3. Fry the eggs, sunny-side up, to the desired consistency.
4. To assemble, spread the beans on each tortilla, place some sauce on each, and top with the eggs. Garnish with the grated cheddar, chopped olives, and a dollop of sour cream, and serve.

Nippy Nopalitos Huevos Rancheros

Yield: 6 servings

Heat Scale: Medium (depending on the heat of the green chile and the salsa)

Outside of the Southwest, cactus is thought of as a nuisance to be avoided. Here, however, it is a symbol of the desert and a source of food. In early spring, the young pads of the prickly pear cactus are harvested, despined, and used in many dishes. The taste is pleasant, similar to that of green beans. The cactus pads, called nopalitos, are available in Latin markets and by mail order.

6 (8-inch [20 cm]) flour tortillas
12 eggs, poached or fried
2½ cups (591 mL) shredded sharp cheddar
1 (16-ounce [454 g]) jar nopalitos, rinsed and drained
2 cups (473 mL) chopped tomatoes
1 cup (236 mL) chopped green New Mexican chile
1½ cups (354 mL) salsa (use a recipe from Chapter 2 or your favorite store-bought salsa), at room temperature

1. Preheat the oven to 350°F (180°C).
2. Place the tortillas directly on an oven rack and back them for 3 to 5 minutes. Remove them from the oven and place them on cookie sheets.
3. Sprinkle the cheese, nopalitos, tomatoes, and green chile over the tortillas. Bake them until the cheese just starts to melt. Top each tortilla with 2 warm eggs, spoon the salsa on top, and serve immediately.

Migas

Yield: 1 serving   Heat Scale: Varies depending on the heat of the salsa

This simple but delicious egg dish hails from Texas and is particularly loved in Austin. It can be made with any fresh or cooked salsa. In Texas, it would likely be made with Pico de Gallo Salsa (page 69).

Vegetable oil for frying
2 corn tortillas, cut into eighths
2 eggs, beaten
½ cup (118 mL) salsa of your choice
4 tablespoons (60 mL) grated Monterey Jack cheese

1. In a sauté pan, heat ½ inch (1 cm) oil over medium-high heat. Add the tortilla pieces and fry until crisp. Remove the tortillas and drain off all but 2 teaspoons (10 mL) of the oil.
2. Return the tortilla pieces to the pan. Add the eggs, stir, and cook over low heat until the eggs are set. Add the salsa or sauce and stir until heated through.
3. Sprinkle the cheese over the top and serve.

Quiche Macho-Style

Yield: 4–6 servings   Heat Scale: Medium

"Real" men will certainly eat this hot quiche! Serve with one of the breads in this chapter and a cup of strong coffee. Okay, okay, make that a chilled Mexican beer.

1 10-inch (25 cm) pastry shell
6 green New Mexican chiles, roasted, peeled, stems and seeds removed, chopped
1 cup (236 mL) grated Swiss cheese
¼ cup (59 mL) sliced black olives
2 eggs
2 egg yolks
1½ cups (354 mL) heavy cream or milk, scalded and cooled
1 cup (236 mL) cooked whole kernel corn
2 tablespoons (30 mL) finely chopped green onions
Salt, to taste

1. Preheat the oven to 350°F (180°C).
2. Line the bottom of the pastry shell with the chopped green chile. Top with the cheese and olives.

3. Combine the eggs and egg yolks with the cream or milk and beat well. Mix in the corn, green onions, and salt. Pour this mixture into the pastry shell.
4. Bake for 30 to 40 minutes or until the custard has set.

Southwestern Chile-Corn Quiche

Yield: 6 servings   Heat Scale: Medium

The interesting cheese crust with minced chiles sets the scene for the filling of this Southwestern-style quiche. Serve it with fresh fruit and yogurt for a wonderful breakfast.

2 cups (473 mL) fine cheese-cracker crumbs
3 tablespoons (45 mL) melted butter, divided
3 tablespoons (45 mL) canola oil, divided
1 serrano chile, stem and seeds removed, minced
½ cup (118 mL) minced onion
2 tablespoons (30 mL) all-purpose flour
½ teaspoon (2.5 mL) salt
⅛ teaspoon (.6 mL) celery seed
⅛ teaspoon (.6 mL) freshly ground white pepper
1¼ cups (295 mL) low-fat milk
2 eggs, beaten
¾ cup (177 mL) diced green New Mexican chiles
1 cup (236 mL) diced zucchini
2 cups (473 mL) cooked fresh corn, or 1 (17-ounce [482 g]) can whole kernel corn, drained

1. Preheat the oven to 400°F (200°C).
2. In a bowl, mix the cracker crumbs with 2 tablespoons (30 mL) of the butter, 2 tablespoons (30 mL) of the canola oil, and the serrano chile. Set aside ½ cup (118 mL) for the topping. Press the remaining crumbs firmly into a 9-inch (22.5 cm) glass pie pan.
3. In a small saucepan, melt the remaining butter, with the remaining canola oil over low heat. Add the onion and sauté for 30 seconds. Sprinkle the flour over the onion. Add the salt, celery seed, and white pepper and stir until the mixture is blended, about 20 to 30 seconds. Add the milk and stir with a wire whisk constantly until the mixture starts to thicken.
4. Add ¼ cup (59 mL) of the milk mixture to the beaten eggs and whisk together. Add this mixture to the milk mixture in the saucepan in a steady, slow drizzle, whisking constantly. Remove the pan from the heat.
5. Stir in the green chiles, zucchini, and corn. Slowly and carefully pour this mixture into the prepared pie shell. Sprinkle the top with the reserved cheese crumbs.
6. Bake for 15 to 20 minutes. Remove the quiche from the oven and allow it to stand for 5 minutes.
7. Cut the quiche into 6 pieces and serve.

Pancho Villa Omelette

Yield: 2 servings   Heat Scale: Mild

I try to be good and cut down on eggs, but on weekends I cheat with this great brunch dish. It tends to change according to what's available in the refrigerator, but the basic green chile and low-fat cream cheese are the two constants. I like to serve it topped with a spicy catsup and some home-fried potatoes.

2 tablespoons (30 mL) butter
3 eggs
3 tablespoons (45 mL) water
¼ cup (59 mL) low-fat cream cheese, softened
½ cup (118 mL) chopped New Mexico green chile

1. In a small skillet, melt the butter over medium-high heat. Whisk the eggs and water briskly and carefully pour this mixture into the sizzling butter. Reduce the heat to low and, using a fork, lift the edges of the omelette to allow the uncooked egg to run underneath. When most of the uncooked egg mixture is off of the top, dot the softened cream cheese over it and follow with the green chiles.
2. Carefully fold one half of the omelette over onto the other half, allowing some of the uncooked mixture to ooze out and cook. Cut the omelette in half, again allowing anything uncooked to run out and cook. Serve immediately.

Spicy Rustic Frittata with Potato Crust

Yield: 4 to 6 servings   Heat Scale: Medium

A frittata is an Italian omelette that has the filling mixed with the eggs instead of being folded inside. It is cooked slowly. The ingredients for this recipe are staples that most of us have in our kitchens. (Note: If the potatoes haven't been rinsed thoroughly in cold water, the result will be a gooey, sticky mess in your skillet.)

1 egg
2 egg whites
¼ teaspoon (1.25 mL) salt, divided
Freshly ground black pepper, to taste
3½ tablespoons (52.5 mL) canola oil, divided
2 medium potatoes, grated, rinsed three times, and squeezed dry
1 cup (236 mL) sliced mushrooms
2 cloves garlic, peeled and minced
½ teaspoon (2.5 mL) dried thyme or 1½ teaspoons (7.5 mL) fresh thyme
3 green onions, chopped
2 jalapeño chiles, stems and seeds removed, minced
1 small red bell pepper, stem and seeds removed, diced
½ cup (118 mL) frozen corn kernels, thawed and rinsed
1 teaspoon (5 mL) fresh lemon juice
2 tablespoons (30 mL) grated Parmesan cheese
1 cup (236 mL) grated Monterey Jack cheese
2–3 tablespoons chopped cilantro for garnish

1. In a bowl, whisk together the egg, egg whites, ⅛ teaspoon (.6 mL) of the salt, a grinding of black pepper, and ½ tablespoon (7.5 mL) of the canola oil. Set aside.

2. Heat 2 tablespoons (30 mL) of the remaining canola oil in a large non-stick skillet over medium-high heat. Add the squeezed-dry potatoes to the hot oil and cook until they are crisp and browned, about 7 to 10 minutes, stirring as needed.

3. In another nonstick skillet, heat the remaining 1 tablespoon (15 mL) canola oil. Add the mushrooms, garlic, thyme, green onions, jalapeño chile, and bell pepper. Sauté for 2 to 3 minutes, then add the corn, the remaining salt, and the lemon juice. Cook the mixture, stirring, until the vegetables are tender and all of the liquid has evaporated, about 5 minutes. Stir in the Parmesan cheese.

4. Reduce the heat under the potatoes to low and pour in the egg mixture. Cook until it begins to set, about 1 minute. Spread the vegetable mixture evenly over the set eggs. Sprinkle the Jack cheese evenly over the top and cover tightly. Cook just until the cheese melts and the eggs are firm. Slide the cooked frittata onto a warm serving plate, garnish with the cilantro, and cut it into wedges. Serve immediately.

Avocado-Feta Frittata

Yield: 2 servings   Heat Scale: Medium

My second spicy frittata is quite different, and if you're an avocado fan, you won't want to miss this dish. Serve it with any of the breads and jams in this chapter.

½ large ripe avocado, cut into 1-inch (2.5 cm) dice
1 tomato, chopped
1 teaspoon (5 mL) lime juice
1 pinch salt
1 ounce (28 g) feta cheese, crumbled
¼ teaspoon (1.25 mL) rosemary
4 black olives, minced
4 fresh mushrooms, washed and sliced
3 eggs (or the equivalent amount of egg substitute)
1 teaspoon (5 mL) ground cayenne
1½ teaspoons (7.5 mL) olive oil

1. Preheat the broiler.

2. Combine the avocado, tomato, lime juice, and salt. Add the feta, rosemary, olives, and mushrooms and stir gently. In another bowl, whisk together the eggs and ground cayenne.

3. In an oven-safe skillet, warm the oil over medium-high heat. When the oil is bubbling but not smoking, add the eggs. Cook the eggs briefly, stirring once, until the bottom is set and the top is still runny. Remove the skillet from the heat and spread the feta-avocado mixture evenly over the eggs. Place the skillet under the broiler until the frittata is set and the edges are golden brown, 5 to 10 minutes.

Tortilla Española con Salsa Romesco
(Spanish Tortilla with Romesco Sauce)

Yield: 6 servings   Heat Scale: Mild

This traditional tapa is nothing like a Mexican tortilla, and it makes a tasty break-
fast dish. A Spanish tortilla is a large, thick, omelette-like cake made with potatoes
and eggs and served at room temperature. Romesco sauce is an all-purpose Spanish
sauce that is served with a wide variety of dishes. From the Tarragona region, this
Catalan sauce combines two of the most popular horticultural imports from the New
World—chiles and tomatoes. The sauce gets its name from the romesco chiles that
are traditionally used but are not readily available outside of Spain. The combina-
tion of ancho and New Mexican chiles approximates the taste.

3 pounds (1.36 kg; approximately 10) medium potatoes, peeled and sliced
into ⅛-inch-thick slices
⅓ cup (79 mL) olive oil (Spanish virgin olive oil preferred)
1 medium onion, peeled and thinly sliced
6 eggs, beaten
¼ teaspoon (1.25 mL) salt
Romesco Sauce (page 81)

1. Preheat the oven to 350°F (180°C).
2. In a small roasting pan, toss the potatoes with the oil. Cover and bake
for 20 minutes.
3. Uncover the pan and spread the onion slices evenly over the potatoes.
Cover and bake for an additional 10 minutes, or until the potatoes are just
done. Remove the pan and pour off the oil, reserving it. Cool the potatoes
to room temperature.
4. Season the eggs with the salt. Gently fold the potato and onion mixture
into the eggs and mix carefully.
5. Heat a nonstick sauté pan over high heat. Add a few tablespoons
(30–45 mL) of the reserved oil. When it's hot, carefully add the egg
mixture. Cook for a minute, gently shaking the pan so the eggs don't stick.
Reduce the heat to the lowest temperature and cook for 15 to 20 minutes,
or until the mixture is firm.
6. Place a plate face-down over the sauté pan and flip the tortilla onto the
plate. (Do this over your sink.) Reheat the skillet over high heat and carefully slide the tortilla back into the pan. Reduce the heat to low and cook
the other side until it's done, about 8 minutes. When the tortilla feels firm
to the touch, it's done.
7. Cool the tortilla to room temperature and slice it into wedges. When
you are ready to serve the tortilla, spoon some of the romesco sauce onto
each plate and place a wedge on top.

Rosemary Chipotle Crêpes

Yield: 8 crêpes (depending on the size of the crêpe pan)
Heat Scale: Medium

*This fragrant, smoky, and elegant dish turns any brunch into something special.
Serve the crêpes with a salad from Chapter 6 and a soup from Chapter 7.*

2 teaspoons (10 mL) butter, plus more if needed
1 egg
1 chipotle chile in adobo sauce, puréed
¼ teaspoon (1.25 mL) salt
⅛ teaspoon (.6 mL) pepper
¾ cup (177 mL) milk, plus more if needed
½ cup (118 mL) all-purpose flour
1 teaspoon (5 mL) rosemary

1. Melt the butter. Pour it into a bowl and add the egg, chipotle, salt, pepper, and milk. Add the flour to the batter slowly, whisking continually. Add the rosemary, and add more butter or milk, if needed, until you have achieved the consistency of heavy cream. Let the batter sit for 20 minutes.
2. Heat a small nonstick crêpe pan over medium heat. Lightly coat the pan with a nonstick cooking spray. Pour 3 tablespoons of the batter into the pan, tilting the pan in all directions so that the batter covers the bottom evenly. When the edges of the crêpe look dry and begin to slightly turn up, after about 30 seconds, turn the crêpe gently. Repeat with the remaining batter. As you finish the crêpes, stack them between sheets of waxed paper.

Bombay Curried Eggs Stuffed in Crepes

Yield: 6–7 servings   Heat Scale: Medium

Curried eggs make an unusual and exotic filling for crêpes. Serve these for breakfast or brunch. Once the crêpes and the sauce are made, it is a simple matter to put the two together for a dish that is exotic, elegant, easy, and ecstasy on the taste buds. Please note that crêpes are a little tricky to prepare and that sometimes the very first crêpe falls apart.

For the Crêpes:
4 eggs (or substitute 2 eggs and Eggbeaters equal to 2 additional eggs)
¼ teaspoon (1.25 mL) salt
2 cups (473 mL) all-purpose flour
2¼ cups (532 mL) low-fat milk
4 tablespoons (60 mL) melted butter, divided

1. In a bowl, combine the eggs and salt. Gradually add the flour and the milk, beating the mixture with a whisk. Beat in 2 tablespoons (30 mL) of the melted butter. Refrigerate the batter for 1 hour.
2. Heat a small sauté pan and use a brush to coat the bottom and sides with a thin coat of the remaining melted butter.

3. Remove the batter from the refrigerator and whisk it briskly. Add about ¼ cup (59 mL) of the batter to the sauté pan, swirling the pan to coat the bottom. Allow the crêpe to cook for 30 seconds, then carefully flip it over with a spatula and cook for another 30 seconds. Remove the cooked crêpe to a plate and cover it with a sheet of waxed paper. Repeat this process until all the batter is used up, stacking the finished crêpes between sheets of wax paper. You'll need 12 to 14 crepes for this recipe; wrap and freeze the remainder for future use.

For the filling:
2 tablespoons (30 mL) butter
2 tablespoons (30 mL) olive oil
1½ teaspoons (7.5 mL) Hurry Curry (page 29)
1 teaspoon (5 mL) grated fresh ginger
¼ teaspoon (1.25 mL) salt
1 clove garlic, peeled and minced
½ cup (118 mL) minced onion
⅛ teaspoon (.6 mL) grated lemon zest
½ cup (118 mL) golden raisins or currants
¾ cup (177 mL) chopped apple
1 teaspoon (5 mL) (or more) of your favorite habanero hot sauce, or 1 teaspoon (5 mL) chopped habanero chile
3 tablespoons (45 mL) chutney (Major Grey's Mango Chutney preferred)
3 tablespoons (45 mL) all-purpose flour
1 cup (236 mL) Super-Rich Vegetable Stock (page 48)
1 cup (236 mL) light cream
5 hard-cooked eggs, shelled and diced
¼ cup (59 mL) toasted coconut

1. In a medium skillet, melt the butter over low heat, then add the olive oil. Add the Hurry Curry, ginger, salt, garlic, onion, lemon zest, raisins or currants, apple, habanero hot sauce or fresh habanero, and chutney. Sauté over low heat for 2 minutes, stirring occasionally.
2. Sprinkle the flour over the mixture in the skillet and stir to combine. Add the vegetable stock and the light cream, whisking and then stirring the mixture as it thickens. Stir in the diced eggs.
3. Preheat the oven to 325°F (165°C). Oil a glass baking dish.
4. Place ¼ cup (59 mL) filling on a crêpe and roll it up. Transfer the filled crêpe to the prepared dish, seam-side down. Repeat with the remaining crêpes. Bake for 10 minutes. Sprinkle the cooked crêpes with the toasted coconut and serve immediately.

Hot-Sauced Shad Roe with Green Chile and Cheese Eggs

Yield: 4 servings   Heat Scale: Medium

You can actually use any fish roe in this recipe, so ask your local fishmonger what is available. If you're in Richmond, Virginia, in April, you'll find this breakfast shad dish in restaurants. Of course, you won't find the green chile eggs, as we do that here in New Mexico. This recipe will not win any awards from the food police.

4 shad roes
¼ cup (59 mL) bacon drippings, melted
1 tablespoon (15 mL) butter
6 eggs, beaten with a little milk
¼ cup (59 mL) chopped green chile
¼ cup (59 mL) grated pepper jack cheese
Hot sauce of your choice

1. In a skillet, combine the shad roes and the bacon drippings and fry over medium-high heat for about 10 minutes, turning several times. When the roes are half done, melt the butter in another skillet. Add the eggs and scramble with a fork. When the eggs are nearly done, add the green chile and cheese. To serve, sprinkle the roes with your favorite hot sauce and place next to the eggs.

Southwest Breakfast Burritos

Yield: 4 servings   Heat Scale: Medium

This all-purpose filling is used here to make a breakfast meal wrapped in a warm flour tortilla, but it is also great in taco shells. In fact, the eggs taste great all by themselves.

8 ounces (224 g) chorizo
½ cup (118 mL) chopped onion
1 clove garlic, peeled and chopped
6 eggs, beaten
1 tablespoon (15 mL) crushed dried red New Mexican chile
¼ teaspoon (1.25 mL) ground cumin
1 cup (236 mL) grated cheddar or Monterey Jack cheese
1 small tomato, cored and diced
1 small avocado, peeled, pitted, and diced
4 (12-inch [30 cm]) flour tortillas
Chopped fresh cilantro for garnish

1. In a skillet over medium heat, cook the chorizo for about 10 minutes, stirring occasionally to break up and clumps. Remove the chorizo from the skillet and transfer it to a paper towel to drain. Pour off all but 2 teaspoons (10 mL) of the accumulated oil. Return the pan to medium heat.

2. Add the onion and garlic to the pan and sauté until they are soft, about 5 minutes. Stir in the eggs, chile, and cumin. Scramble until the eggs are firm and cooked through. Remove the pan from the heat and stir in the cheese, tomato, and avocado.

3. Divide the eggs evenly among the 4 tortillas and top the filling with the cilantro. Roll the tortillas burrito-style and serve.

Prime Beef and Vegetable Chile Hash

Yield: 4–6 servings   Heat Scale: Medium

This breakfast dish is a meal in itself when each serving is topped with a poached egg. Have your favorite bottled hot sauce handy if the hash is not hot enough for you. If you would like an accompaniment, try a fruit salad with mangoes, bananas, peaches, and pineapple.

4 medium potatoes, peeled and diced
½ pound (224 g) leftover prime rib meat, diced
¼ pound (567 g) bacon, diced
1 onion, peeled and chopped
1 red bell pepper, stem and seeds removed, diced
1 yellow bell pepper, stem and seeds removed, diced
½ cup (118 mL) chopped roasted and peeled New Mexican green chile
Salt to taste
Freshly ground black pepper to taste
3 tablespoons (45 mL) minced Italian parsley for garnish
4–6 eggs, poached (optional)

1. In a large pot, boil the potatoes in salted water until tender, about 8 minutes. Drain the potatoes and transfer them to a large bowl. Add the prime rib meat.

2. In a skillet over medium heat, cook the bacon for 5 minutes, stirring often. Add the onion and both bell peppers and cook, stirring often, for 5 more minutes. With a slotted spoon, transfer this mixture to the bowl with the potatoes and meat. Add the green chile, salt, and pepper and mix well.

3. Remove and discard all but 3 tablespoons (45 mL) of the bacon fat from the skillet. Add the hash mixture and cook over medium heat for about 5 minutes. Do not stir it, but take care that it does not burn. Turn the hash with a spatula and cook for 5 more minutes. Transfer the hash to serving plates, garnish it with the parsley, and top it with poached eggs, if desired.

Southwestern Asparagus Strata with Green Chile

Yield: 6–8 servings   Heat Scale: Medium

Serve this great breakfast entrée when you can find fresh asparagus. A strata is an egg-and-bread-based pudding enhanced with vegetables, spices, or herbs. The classic mix is 6 eggs to 3½ cups (826 mL) milk; you can use low-fat milk if you prefer. Buy day-old French bread from a good bakery for this recipe.

1 pound (454 g) day-old French bread, cut into 1½-inch (3.5 cm) cubes
3½ cups (826 mL) milk
6 eggs
½ teaspoon (2.5 mL) freshly ground white pepper
½ teaspoon (2.5 mL) salt
1 pound (454 g) fresh asparagus, cleaned and sliced into 2 inch (5 cm) pieces
2 tablespoons (30 mL) butter
½ pound (224 g) button mushrooms, sliced
½ cup (118 mL) minced sweet onion
1 cup (236 mL) chopped green New Mexican chile, excess water blotted out
2 teaspoons (10 mL) chopped fresh chives
2½ cups (591 mL) mixed shredded Jarlsberg, Gruyere, and Swiss cheeses
2 tablespoons (30 mL) grated Parmesan cheese

1. Preheat the broiler. Place an oven rack about 4 inches (10 cm) under the broiler. Lightly grease a shallow 3- or 4-quart (3 or 4 L) oven-proof casserole or a 9 × 13–inch (22.5 × 32.5 cm) glass baking dish

2. Arrange the bread cubes on a cookie sheet and toast them under the broiler, stirring occasionally, until they are golden brown. Take care not to burn them. Place the cubes in a large bowl. Turn the oven heat to 325°F (165°C).

3. In a separate bowl, beat together the milk, eggs, white pepper, and salt. Pour 1½ cups (354 mL) of this mixture over the bread cubes. Toss the cubes to coat them thoroughly. Set aside the remaining milk-egg mixture.

4. Steam the asparagus for 3 minutes. Rinse it under cold water, drain, and set aside.

5. In a skillet, melt the butter over medium heat. Add the mushrooms and onion and sauté until the onion softens. Use a slotted spoon to transfer this mixture to a small bowl.

6. Add the green chile and chives to the mushroom mixture and mix well.

7. Layer ⅓ of the soaked bread cubes in the bottom of the prepared casserole. Top this mixture with ½ of the asparagus, then ½ of the mushroom mixture. Sprinkle with ½ of the cheeses. Repeat the next layer with half of the remaining bread cubes and the remaining asparagus, mushroom-chile mixture, and cheese. Top with the remaining bread cubes and pour the reserved milk-egg mixture over the top.

8. Bake the strata for 45 minutes. Cover with aluminum foil if it starts to brown too quickly.

Chipotle Chilaquiles

Yield: 2–4 servings   Heat Scale: Medium

Ah, the wonderful, smoky-hot flavor of the chipotle comes through in this Southwestern breakfast classic. It can be baked or microwaved—either way it takes only a few minutes to prepare.

2 tomatoes, chopped
4 chipotles in adobo, chopped
2 cloves garlic, peeled and chopped
½ onion, chopped
½ cup (118 mL) chicken stock
Vegetable oil for frying tortillas
6 corn tortillas, each cut into 8 wedges
4 eggs, beaten
1 cup (236 mL) grated Monterey Jack or cheddar cheese
Chopped cilantro for garnish

1. Preheat the oven to 300°F (150°C), if baking.
2. Combine the tomatoes, chipotles, garlic, onion, and stock in a blender and purée to make a sauce. Transfer the mixture to a saucepan and bring it to a boil. Reduce the heat and simmer for 15 minutes or until the sauce is thickened.
3. Heat 1 inch (2.5 cm) of oil in a skillet. Fry the tortilla wedges for a few seconds on each side, until soft. Drain the wedges on paper towels.
4. Add the sauce to the beaten eggs.
5. Line the bottom of a small casserole dish with tortilla wedges, then add ⅓ of the sauce mixture, and top with ⅓ of the cheese. Repeat twice more, until all the ingredients are used.
6. Bake the casserole in the preheated oven for 15 minutes, or microwave on high for about 5 minutes.
7. Garnish with the cilantro and serve.

Blue Corn Piñon Pancakes with Orange-Spiced Honey

Yield: 12 (4-inch [10 cm]) pancakes   Heat Scale: Medium

Here's one of my favorite breakfast dishes. The blue corn gives these pancakes are a refreshing change from the ordinary.

For the Orange-Spiced Honey:
½ cup (118 mL) honey
¼ cup (59 mL) orange juice
1 teaspoon (5 mL) grated orange peel
½ teaspoon (2.5 mL) habanero powder (or other hot chile powder)

1. Place the honey in a saucepan over medium-low heat and cook until heated through. Stir in the remaining ingredients and keep the mixture warm.

For the Pancakes:
1 cup (236 mL) blue corn flour
½ cup (118 mL) all-purpose flour
3 tablespoons (45 mL) sugar
1¾ teaspoons (8.75 mL) double-acting baking powder
1 large egg, beaten
1 cup (236 mL) buttermilk
3 tablespoons (45 mL) melted butter
3 tablespoons (45 mL) roasted piñon nuts

1. Sift together the flours, sugar, and baking powder into a bowl. In a separate bowl, combine the egg, buttermilk, and melted butter and beat well. Quickly mix the liquids and nuts into the dry batter, being careful not to overbeat the mixture—lumps are okay.
2. Cook the pancakes on a hot griddle over medium-high heat, turning only once, until they are browned and done.
3. Drizzle the pancakes with the warm honey and serve.

Saltfish and Ackee

Yield: 4 servings   Heat Scale: Medium

This interesting recipe is known as the national dish of Jamaica. Traditionally served at breakfast, ackee have a texture similar to scrambled eggs. If you are lucky enough to find fresh ackee, make sure you choose a ripe one, which will be split open revealing the white flesh of the fruit. Choose ackee that are completely open, with the black seed and yellow fruit clearly visible in the scarlet pod. This is important, as unripe ackee contain a highly toxic substance. Although theoretically forbidden for import into North America, ackee can occasionally be found in Latin or Caribbean markets.

2 dozen ackee in pods
½ pound (224 g) salt cod
2 tablespoons (30 mL) butter
¼ cup (59 mL) oil
2 onions, peeled and sliced
1 sprig thyme
½ Scotch bonnet chile (or habanero), stem and seeds removed, minced
1 small tomato, chopped (optional)
Freshly ground black pepper, to taste

1. Remove the ackee from the pods. Discard the seeds and the pink membrane found in the cleft of each fruit. Wash them and put them to boil in a large pot of water with the saltfish. As soon as the ackee are tender, pour the contents of the pot into a large sieve, discarding the water. Separate the ackee from the fish. Run cold water over the fish until they are cool enough that you can remove the bones and skin comfortably, then flake it and set it aside.
2. In a frying pan, heat the butter and oil over medium heat. Add the onions, thyme, chile, and tomato, if using. Stir for a few minutes, then add the flaked fish. Stir for a few more minutes, then add the drained ackee, stirring carefully so as not to crush them. Add a little more oil if necessary and sprinkle with plenty of freshly ground black pepper.
Roasted breadfruit or fried plantains make excellent accompaniments to this famous dish.

New Mexican Spoonbread

Yield: 6 servings   Heat Scale: Mild

This Southwestern spoonbread combines creamed corn and corn meal. Green New Mexican chiles provide the heat, and cheddar cheese flavors the dish even more.

1 (16-ounce [454 g]) can cream-style corn (S & W brand preferred)
¾ cup (177 mL) low-fat milk
⅓ cup (79 mL) melted butter
1½ cups (354 mL) cornmeal
2 eggs, lightly beaten
½ teaspoon (2.5 mL) baking soda
1 teaspoon (5 mL) baking powder
½ teaspoon (2.5 mL) salt (optional, or just add more green chile)
1 teaspoon (5 mL) sugar
½ cup (118 mL) chopped green New Mexican chile
1½ cups (354 mL) grated sharp cheddar cheese

1. Preheat the oven to 400°F (200°C). Grease a 9-inch (22.5 cm) square baking pan.
2. Combine all of the ingredients except the chile and cheese. Pour half of the batter into the prepared pan, then sprinkle the batter with half the green chiles and half the cheese. Add the remaining batter and top with the remaining chile and cheese. Bake for 45 minutes.

Ancho-Piquin Spoonbread

Yield: 4–6 servings   Heat Scale: Medium

My second spoonbread combines anchos (for their raisiny flavor) and piquins (for their heat). This spicy spoonbread is an ideal breakfast bread when combined with one of the spicy fruit jams in this chapter.

2 tablespoons (30 mL) vegetable oil
¼ cup (59 mL) diced green bell pepper
1 small onion, peeled and minced
2 pounds (1.1 kg) tomatoes, peeled and diced, liquid retained (or substitute
1 28-ounce (754 g) can diced tomatoes
1 cup (236 mL) cornmeal
1 egg
2 teaspoons (10 mL) ancho chile powder
½ teaspoon (2.5 mL) piquin chile powder
½ teaspoon (2.5 mL) baking soda
½ teaspoon (2.5 mL) salt
1 cup (236 mL) shredded Monterey Jack cheese
Milk as needed

1. Preheat the oven to 350°F (180°C). Grease a 1½-quart (1.5 L) casserole.
2. Heat the oil over low heat in a skillet. Add the green bell pepper and onion and sauté for 2 minutes. Add the tomatoes and sauté for

10 minutes. Transfer to a bowl and mix in the cornmeal, egg, chile powders, baking soda, salt, and cheese. Mix thoroughly. If the mixture seems extremely thick, add milk, 1 tablespoon (15 mL) at a time, until it is thick but pourable.

3. Pour the batter into the prepared casserole. Bake for 1 hour or until firm. Serve hot.

Chipotle Spoonbread

Yield: 6 servings   Heat Scale: Hot

My final spoonbread features chipotle chiles, those smoky-hot jalapeños that come canned in adobo sauce. The heat level can be adjusted downward, if desired. Dried chipotles soaked in water for 60 minutes before puréeing can be substituted for the canned.

2½ cups (591 mL) low-fat milk, divided
1 cup (236 mL) yellow cornmeal
3 eggs
2 teaspoons (10 mL) sugar
½ teaspoon (2.5 mL) salt
4 tablespoons (60 mL) melted butter
1 teaspoon (5 mL) thyme or marjoram
1 teaspoon (5 mL) baking powder
3 chipotle chiles in adobo, drained and puréed
½ cup (118 mL) grated jalapeño cheese

1. Preheat the oven to 400°F (200°C). Grease a 1½-quart (1.5 L) baking dish or casserole.

2. In a saucepan, heat 2 cups (473 mL) of the milk to simmering and stir in the cornmeal. When the mixture is thickened, remove it from the heat.

3. In a bowl, beat the eggs well. Mix in the remaining ½ cup (118 mL) milk, sugar, salt, and melted butter. Combine this mixture with the hot cornmeal mixture. Stir in the thyme or marjoram, baking powder, and puréed chipotles. Mix thoroughly. Pour the batter into the prepared baking dish or casserole. Bake for 45 minutes or until the spoonbread is firm and lightly browned. Spoon onto plates and serve at once.

Jalapeño-Cheddar Blue Cornbread

Yield: 6 servings   Heat Scale: Medium

Once you taste this, you'll never again think of cornbread as bland. Adjust the heat upward by doubling the jalapeños and serve this with one of the egg dishes in this chapter. If blue cornmeal is not available, substitute the yellow variety.

1 cup (236 mL) coarse blue cornmeal
1 cup (236 mL) all-purpose flour
2 teaspoons (10 mL) sugar
1 teaspoon (5 mL) baking soda
1 teaspoon (5 mL) baking powder
1 teaspoon (5 mL) salt
¼ teaspoon (1.25 mL) garlic powder
1½ cups (354 mL) buttermilk
¼ cup (59 mL) finely chopped jalapeño chiles, stems and seeds removed
1 cup (236 mL) minced onions
2 eggs, beaten
1 cup (236 mL) grated cheddar

1. Preheat the oven to 350°F (180°C). Grease a 9-inch (22.5 cm) square baking pan.
2. In a bowl, combine all the dry ingredients.
3. In a saucepan over medium heat, heat the buttermilk with the jalapeños and onions for 3 minutes, then allow the mixture to cool.
4. In a bowl, combine the eggs and cheese.
5. Add the buttermilk mixture and the egg mixture to the dry ingredients and blend until smooth.
6. Pour the batter into the prepared pan and bake for 40 to 50 minutes or until the cornbread is browned and firm.

Blue Corn Chile Bacon Muffins

Yield: 12–15 muffins   Heat Scale: Medium

These muffins need not be served for breakfast only. They complement almost any chile dish, barbecue, or Tex-Mex meal.

1 cup (236 mL) all-purpose flour
¾ cup (177 mL) blue cornmeal
⅓ cup (79 mL) sugar
1 tablespoon (15 mL) baking powder
¾ teaspoon (3.75 mL) salt
1 cup (236 mL) milk
1 egg, beaten
2 tablespoons (30 mL) melted butter
3 strips crisply cooked bacon, crumbled
2 jalapeños, stems and seeds removed, chopped

1. Preheat the oven to 400°F (200°C). Lightly grease a muffin pan.
2. In a bowl, combine all the dry ingredients.
3. In a separate bowl, combine the milk, egg, butter, bacon, and jalapeños. Add this mixture to the dry ingredients and stir to mix.
4. Spoon the batter into the prepared muffin pan and bake for 15 to 20 minutes.

Strawberry-Ancho Blue Corn Muffins

Yield: 12–15 muffins   Heat Scale: Medium

Sure, these muffins are great for breakfast, served with fresh mangos dusted with red chile powder or even a granola cereal, but they can also be served as dessert with ice cream or sorbet.

1 cup (236 mL) all-purpose flour
¾ cup (177 mL) blue cornmeal
⅓ cup (79 mL) sugar
1 tablespoon (15 mL) baking powder
¾ teaspoon (3.75 mL) salt
2 teaspoons (10 mL) ancho chile powder
1 cup (236 mL) finely chopped strawberries
1 cup (236 mL) milk
1 egg, beaten
2 tablespoons (30 mL) melted butter

1. Preheat the oven to 425°F (220°C). Lightly grease a muffin pan.
2. Sift all the dry ingredients together in a bowl. In a separate bowl, combine the strawberries, milk, egg, and butter. Add the dry ingredients to the wet ingredients and mix well.
3. Pour the batter into the prepared muffin pan, filling each cup about half full. Bake for 15 to 20 minutes.

Banana-Pasilla Macadamia Nut Muffins

Yield: 12 muffins   Heat Scale: Medium

Believe it or not, the macadamia nut tree was first grown only for ornamental purposes. Thankfully, someone experimented with the nuts and discovered their butter-like, slightly sweet nature. This bread is so rich you won't need to butter it. In addition to breakfast, I like to serve it as a late night snack with hot tea.

1½ cups (354 mL) unbleached all-purpose flour
1½ teaspoons (7.5 mL) baking soda
¼ teaspoon (1.25 mL) salt
⅛ teaspoon (.6 mL) ground nutmeg
⅛ teaspoon (.6 mL) ground ginger
1¼ cups (295 mL) mashed ripe bananas (about 3 large)
1 tablespoon (15 mL) grated lemon peel
2 teaspoons (10 mL) pasilla chile powder or paste
½ cup (118 mL) sugar
¼ cup (59 mL) firmly packed dark brown sugar
½ cup (118 mL) butter, softened
¼ cup (59 mL) milk
1 large egg
1 cup (236 mL) chopped unsalted, toasted macadamia nuts

1. Preheat the oven to 350°degree (180°C). Grease two 6-cup muffin pans.
2. Sift the flour, baking soda, salt, nutmeg, and ginger into a large bowl. In a separate bowl, combine the bananas, lemon peel, pasilla powder or paste, both sugars, butter, milk, and eggs. Combine the wet mixture with the dry ingredients. Fold in half the nuts.
3. Divide the batter equally among the prepared muffin cups. Sprinkle the tops of the muffins with the remaining macadamia nuts. Bake for about 25 minutes or until the muffins are golden brown and a toothpick inserted into the center of one comes out clean. Transfer the muffins to a wire rack to cool.

Chile-Dusted Cheese Bolillos

Yield: 6–8 servings   Heat Scale: Mild

I first tasted the heavenly bolillo rolls in Ciudad Juárez, where they are stuffed with ham and avocados for tortas. Here is my spiced-up version.

2 cups (473 mL) very warm water
2¼ teaspoons (11.25 mL) dry yeast
1 tablespoon (15 mL) sugar
2 teaspoons (10 mL) salt
5½ cups (1.3 L) sifted all-purpose flour, divided
1 cup (236 mL) grated cheddar
1 tablespoon (15 mL) cumin seeds
Shortening as needed
1 egg white, unbeaten
1 tablespoon (15 mL) ground red New Mexican chile

1. Preheat the oven to 375°F (190°C). Lightly grease a baking sheet.
2. In a bowl, sprinkle the yeast over the water and stir until dissolved. Let sit for 5 minutes.
3. Add the sugar, salt, and 3 cups (708 mL) of the flour and beat until smooth and shiny. Add the cheese and cumin seeds. Stir in 2 cups (473 mL) of the remaining flour and mix well. Sprinkle the remaining flour on a board and knead the dough, adding more flour if necessary, until it is smooth and shiny, about 5 to 7 minutes. Shape the dough into a ball.
4. Grease a bowl lightly with shortening and press the top of the ball of dough into the bowl, then turn the dough over to coat with the shortening. Cover with a warm, damp towel. Place the bowl in a warm place and allow the dough to rise until doubled in size, about 2 hours.
5. Punch down the dough and let it rest for 5 minutes. Rub a little shortening on your hands and divide the dough into 6 equal portions. Shape each portion into a 6-inch (15 cm) long oblong roll and place them on the prepared baking pan. Make two horizontal indentations on each roll. Bake for 30 minutes or until lightly browned.
6. Brush the rolls with the egg white, sprinkle the chile powder over them, and return them to the oven for 2 minutes. Remove the rolls from the oven and cool them on a wire rack.

Heavenly Green Chile Pineapple-Banana Bread

Yield: 1 loaf   Heat Scale: Medium

This bread is heavenly because it's light as air in texture and calories. It's delicious toasted and covered with a light application of a chile honey.

⅔ cup (158 mL) whole-wheat flour
1 teaspoon (5 mL) baking soda
½ teaspoon (2.5 mL) salt
½ cup (118 mL) softened butter
1 cup (236 mL) sugar
2 eggs
1 teaspoon (5 mL) pure vanilla extract
1 cup (236 mL) mashed banana
½ cup (118 mL) pineapple chunks
½ cup (118 mL) chopped green New Mexican chile
¼ cup (59 mL) low-fat milk
1 tablespoon (15 mL) lemon juice
½ cup (118 mL) chopped walnuts

1. Preheat the oven to 350°F (180°C). Grease a loaf pan.
2. In a small mixing bowl, combine the flour, baking soda, and salt. In a large bowl, beat the butter, sugar, eggs, and vanilla with an electric mixer until fluffy. Slowly add the flour mixture and beat lightly with the mixer. Add the banana, pineapple chunks, chiles, and milk and mix lightly. Add the lemon juice and walnuts and mix for 30 seconds. Pour the batter into the prepared loaf pan.
3. Bake for 1 hour, making sure not to overcook.

Yogurt Scones with Red Chile Honey

Yield: 12 scones

Heat Scale: Varies, although the red chile honey will definitely add a little zip!

Here is a perfect breakfast or teatime treat—cut the calories and add some heat! Red chile honey has become quite popular in New Mexico and other parts of the Southwest.

2⅔ cups (631 mL) unbleached all-purpose flour
1 tablespoon (15 mL) sugar
1 teaspoon (5 mL) baking powder
6 tablespoons (90 mL) chilled butter, cut into small pieces
1 egg
1 egg, separated
1 cup (236 mL) plain low-fat yogurt
1 tablespoon (15 mL) water
1 cup (236 mL) pure honey
1 tablespoon (15 mL) ground red New Mexican chile (or a hotter chile, to taste)

1. Preheat the oven to 400°F (200°C). Grease a baking sheet
2. Combine the flour, sugar, and baking soda in a large bowl. Using a pastry blender or two knives, cut the butter into the dry mixture until it resembles coarse meal. In a separate bowl, mix together the whole egg and the yolk of the separated egg and stir this mixture into the batter. Blend in the yogurt.
3. Turn mixture out onto a lightly floured surface. Knead briefly until the dough sticks together. Roll out to a thickness of 1 inch (2.5 cm). Cut with a 2-inch (5 cm) biscuit cutter (a coyote-shaped cutter works well). Gather together the leftover dough; reroll, and cut additional scones. Place all the cut dough on the prepared baking sheet.
4. Mix the egg white from the separated egg with the water. Brush the top of each scone with the glaze. Bake for about 14 minutes or until golden brown.
5. Meanwhile, in a bowl, mix the red chile powder into the honey until all the chile is evenly distributed. Serve immediately with the freshly baked scones.

Pineapple-Lemon-Apple Preserves with Habanero

Yield: 3 cups (708 mL)   Heat Scale: Hot

Serve these preserves with any of the breads in this chapter or with hot croissants and strong, rich coffee. They can also be served, warmed slightly, over vanilla ice cream.

2½ cups (591 mL) coarsely chopped pineapple (about 1 small pineapple)
1½ cups (354 mL) peeled apples, coarsely chopped
1 habanero chile, stem and seeds, chopped fine
½ cup (118 mL) sliced quartered lemon
3 cups (708 mL) sugar
3 tablespoons (45 mL) brandy or cognac

1. Place the pineapple, apples, and habanero in a large pot and cook over low heat for 10 minutes, stirring occasionally. Meanwhile, bring a small pot of water to a high boil, turn off the heat, and add the lemon. Let sit for 5 minutes, then drain. Add the blanched lemon and the sugar to the pineapple and apple mixture. Cook for 1½ hours, skimming as necessary.
2. Pour the preserves into 3 sterilized half-pint (473 mL) jars and add 1 tablespoon (15 mL) brandy or cognac to each jar. Allow to cool before serving.

Baked and Spiced Raspberry Preserves

Yield: About 3 cups (708 mL)   Heat Scale: Mild

The simple technique of baking the raspberries was inspired by Elizabeth David, one of the finest food writers of the last century. "This is by far the best raspberry jam I have ever tasted," she wrote. "It preserves almost intact the fresh flavour of the fruit, and will keep for a year." I, of course, add red chile powder to spice it up.

3 cups (708 mL) fresh raspberries
2 cups (473 mL) sugar
2 teaspoons (10 mL) ground red New Mexican chile

1. Preheat the oven to 350°F (180°C).
2. Place the raspberries and sugar in separate oven-proof bowls and bake them for 25 minutes.
3. Combine the raspberries, sugar, and chile powder in a bowl and mix well with a spoon. Transfer the mixture to sterilized jars and seal.

Sweltering Pickled Jalapeño Jam

Yield: 3½ pints (1.7 L)   Heat Scale: Medium

Here is a freezer jam that is sweet but spicy hot and easy because there's no cooking and no processing. It's important to chop the chiles finely; if the pieces are too large, they will float on top of jam. You can use a food processor, pulsing to chop, but do not purée. Serve this with bread, scones, or muffins.

1¼ cups (295 mL) pickled jalapeño chiles, drained, stems and seeds removed, finely chopped
1⅓ cups (315 mL) apple juice
4 cups (.95 L) sugar
3 ounces (54 g) liquid pectin
2 tablespoons (30 mL) distilled white vinegar

1. Combine the chiles and apple juice in a large bowl. Stir in the sugar but do not whip. Let stand for 10 minutes, stirring occasionally. In another bowl, combine the liquid pectin and vinegar, then stir it into the chile-sugar mixture. Stir constantly until the sugar is completely dissolved, about 15 minutes.
2. Pour the jam into sterilized jars, leaving ½ inch of head space. Cap and let sit at room temperature for 24 hours. The jam will be soft and thin. Store it in the refrigerator if you plan to use it within 3 weeks; place in the freezer for longer storage.

Red Chile Blueberry Jam

Yield: About 7 cups (1.7 L)   Heat Scale: Mild

Fresh blueberries make a terrific jam, and the red chile powder spices it up just enough. Try this on scones or any other bread. It's also great on waffles.

1½ quarts (1.4 L) fresh blueberries, washed
2 tablespoons (30 mL) fresh lemon juice
1 (¾-ounce [21 g]) packet powdered pectin
4 cups (.95 L) sugar
2 tablespoons (30 mL) ground red New Mexican chile

1. Add the blueberries to a large sauce pan. Crush them with a wooden spoon and add the lemon juice and powdered pectin. Mix well and place the pan over high heat. Bring the mixture to a hard boil and cook for 1 minute. Stir in the sugar and chile powder. Return to a full boil and cook for 1 minute, stirring constantly. Remove from the heat, stir, and skim off any foam with a large spoon.
2. Let sit for about 5 minutes to cool and pour into hot, sterilized jars. Seal immediately.

Jumpin' Red Serrano Marmalade

Yield: 4 cups (.95 L)   Heat Scale: Medium

This marmalade is similar to a relish with its chunks of red and green bell peppers and raisins, spiced just right with cinnamon, cloves, and allspice. As a change from just spreading it on toast or muffins, try it alongside an entrée. It's delicious with pork chops, roast beef, and poultry.

4 medium oranges
3 quarts (2.85 L) plus 1 cup (236 mL) water, divided
1 (3-inch [7.5 cm]) cinnamon stick, broken into pieces
1 teaspoon (5 mL) whole cloves
1 teaspoon (5 mL) whole allspice
1 medium lemon, thinly sliced, then chopped
2 green bell peppers, stems and seeds removed, finely chopped
2 red bell peppers, stems and seeds removed, finely chopped
3 cups (708 mL) sugar
1 cup (236 mL) golden raisins
¼ cup (59 mL) chopped red serrano chiles

1. Peel the oranges, removing most of the white pith from the peel. Cut the peel into very thin strips. Place the peel in a saucepan with 1½ quarts (1.4 L) of the water, bring to a boil, and cook for 5 minutes. Drain and repeat with another 1½ quarts (1.4 L) water.
2. Remove the seeds and membranes from the orange pulp and chop it, then place it in a heavy saucepan. Tie the cinnamon, cloves, and allspice in a square of cheesecloth and add it to the saucepan along with the cooked orange peel, lemon, bell peppers, sugar, raisins, and the remaining 1 cup (236 mL) water. Cook over low heat until the sugar dissolves, about 5 minutes, stirring frequently.
3. Bring to a boil and cook for 5 minutes. Cover and let stand at room temperature for 1 hour to blend the flavors. Return to a rolling boil and cook 10 minutes, stirring occasionally. Add the serranos and cook, stirring frequently, until the marmalade has thickened, about 20 minutes. Remove and discard the cheesecloth bag.
4. Spoon the marmalade into hot, sterilized jars, leaving ¼-inch (.5 cm) space at the top. Wipe the rims with a clean towel, cover with 2-part canning jar lids, and process in a boiling water bath. Allow to cool before serving.

Bittersweet Orange-Habanero Marmalade

Yield: About 3 pints (1.4 L)   Heat Scale: Medium

Legend holds that this classic preserve originated when a cask of Seville oranges was lost at sea and washed up on the coast of Dundee, Scotland. Sea water had leaked into the barrel, partially pickling the oranges. The thrifty Scots, not wishing to waste the precious fruit, decided to preserve it with Scotch whisky. The only thing they forgot was the red habanero chile.

6 bitter oranges
2 quarts (1.9 L) water
1 red habanero chile, stem and seeds removed
2 lemons, juiced
8 cups (1.9 L) sugar
4 tablespoons (60 mL) Scotch whisky

1. Preheat the oven to its lowest setting.
2. Cut the oranges into quarters. Remove the seeds and tie them in a piece of cheesecloth.
3. Scrape the pulp from the peel and shred the peel coarsely. Put the cheesecloth bag and the shredded peel in a saucepan and cover with the water. Boil, covered, over medium heat for 1 hour. Remove the bag of seeds.
4. Meanwhile, put the sugar in a cake pan and bake it for 15 minutes. In a blender or food processor, purée the orange pulp and habanero, then add it, with the lemon juice and sugar, to the pan of shredded peel. Stir over low heat until the sugar has dissolved, then increase the heat slightly and bring to a boil. Boil for about 45 minutes, without stirring, until the marmalade sets.
5. Remove the pan from the heat and stir in the whisky immediately. Bottle in sterile preserving jars while still hot. Seal tightly.

Five-Citrus, Two-Chile Marmalade

Yield: About 4 quarts (3.8 L)   Heat Scale: Medium

I love the flavor of roasted and peeled New Mexican chile, and when paired with jalapeños, it makes a wonderful marmalade. Any combination of citrus fruit can be used in this recipe, as long as the total weight of the raw fruit is approximately half that of the sugar. (Note: This recipe requires advance preparation.)

2 grapefruits
2 lemons
2 limes
2 bitter oranges
2 tangerines
4 quarts (3.8 L) water
½ cup (118 mL) roasted, peeled, and finely chopped green New Mexican chile
2 red jalapeño chiles, stems and seeds removed, minced
12 cups (2.83 L) sugar

1. With a potato peeler, peel the rinds from the fruits in thin strips. Cut the peeled fruit into quarters and remove and reserve the seeds. Peel off the pith and combine it with the seeds, cores, connective tissue, and the skin covering the grapefruit segments in a cheesecloth bag.
2. Place the rinds, pulp, and cheesecloth bag in a large bowl and add the water. Cover and let sit for at least 24 hours.
3. Transfer the contents of the bowl to a large pan. Bring to a boil and simmer over very low heat until the rinds are very soft, about 2 hours.
4. Remove and discard the cheesecloth bag. Bring the liquid to a boil. Add the chiles and sugar, and remove the pan from the heat. Stir with a wooden spoon until the sugar has dissolved. Return the pan to the heat and boil rapidly, without stirring, until the marmalade sets, about 45 minutes.
5. Remove the pan from the heat and let it stand 15 minutes. Bottle the marmalade in sterile preserving jars and seal.

Red and Green Holiday Jelly

Yield: 6 cups   Heat Scale: Hot

From Nancy Gerlach comes a jelly that reflects the color of the season. "You can add some crushed red chile if you want more heat or red color," she notes. "In addition to breakfast, serve this jelly as a canapé with cream cheese and crackers or as an accompaniment to beef, lamb, or pork."

¾ cup (177 mL) chopped green bell pepper
1 cup (236 mL) chopped red bell pepper
¾ cup (177 mL) finely chopped jalapeño chiles
1½ cups (354 mL) apple cider vinegar
6½ cups (1.53 L) white sugar
1 (6-ounce [168 g]) bottle liquid pectin

1. Place the bell peppers in a blender and pulse, being careful not to grind them too fine. Combine the ground peppers, chopped chiles, vinegar, and sugar in a large pan and bring to a fast boil.
2. Pour in the pectin. Return the mixture to a fast boil and boil for 1 minute, stirring constantly. Remove from the heat, let sit for a minute, and skim off the foam. Pour into sterilized jars and seal.

Red Jalapeño–Mango Jelly

Yield: 3 pints (1.4 L) Heat Scale: Hot

Another great jelly from Nancy Gerlach calls for mangos, but apricots, dried peaches, or nectarines work equally well. "Any fresh green chile can also be substituted depending on your heat preference," she notes. "Serranos will make it hotter; roasted and peeled New Mexican chiles will tame it down."

½ cup (118 mL) red jalapeño chiles, stems and seeds removed
1 large red bell pepper, stem and seeds removed
2 cups (473 mL) apple cider vinegar
1½ cups (354 mL) chopped dried mangos
6 cups (1.4 L) sugar
1 (3-ounce [84 g]) jar liquid pectin
3–4 drops red food coloring (optional)

1. Place the chiles, bell pepper, and vinegar in a blender. Pulse until coarsely ground, with some small chunks remaining.
2. Combine the mangos, sugar, and chile mixture in a large saucepan. Bring to a rapid boil and cook for 5 minutes. Remove from the heat and skim off any foam that forms.
3. Allow the mixture to cool for 2 minutes, then mix in the pectin and food coloring, if using.
4. Pour into sterilized jars, seal, and let cool.

Pineapple-Datil Jelly

Yield: 3 pints (1.4 L) Heat Scale: Hot

This interesting sweet/sour jelly recipe was handed down by the family of Mrs. Leonard Shugart of St. Augustine, Florida. It was first published in Chile Pepper *magazine, in the early days when I was the editor.*

1 cup (236 mL) chopped datil peppers (or substitute 2 chopped habaneros and enough chopped red bell pepper to make a cup)
2 cups (473 mL) cranberry juice
1 (16-ounce [454 g]) can crushed pineapple with juice
1 tablespoon (15 mL) lemon juice, fresh or bottled
2 (1.75-ounce [49 g]) packages commercial pectin, such as Sure-Jel
3 cups (708 mL) sugar

1. Combine the peppers, cranberry juice, pineapple, and lemon juice in a blender or food processor and purée until smooth. Transfer the mixture to a large pot and add the pectin according to the package directions. Bring to a boil. Add the sugar and bring to a rolling boil. Do not stir. Boil for 1 minute. Skim off the foam. Fill sterilized glass jars and seal.

Habanero-Carrot Pepper Jelly

Yield: 20 ounces (570 g)   Heat Scale: Extremely Hot

This fiery jelly stunned the tasters at the Pig and Pepper Harvest Festival in Carlisle, Massachusetts. Robert Dixon, who lives and cooks in Winchester, Massachusetts, was the engineer of this devilish dish of sweet heat, and I thank him for this recipe.

¾ cup (177 mL) apple cider vinegar
3¼ cups (767 mL) sugar
½ cup (118 mL) grated carrot
¼ cup (59 mL) red bell pepper, finely chopped
6 habanero chiles, stems and seeds removed, minced
1 (3-ounce [84 g]) pouch liquid pectin

1. Combine the vinegar and sugar in a saucepan and cook over high heat, stirring, until the sugar dissolves. Mix in the carrot and red bell pepper. Bring to a boil and cook for 5 minutes. Add the habanero and boil for an additional 5 minutes.
2. Remove the pan from the heat, add the pectin, and return to a boil. Cook for 1 minute, stirring constantly. Skim off any foam and bottle in sterilized 4-ounce (112 g) jelly jars.

FIVE

Appealing Peppered Appetizers

- -

Call them appetizers, starters, hors d'oeuvres, antojitos, tapas, or zakuski (as they're known in Russia). Any way you say it, these tasty tidbits are designed to get the meal off to the right start. I've arranged these recipes by region so that the cook can take a tour of the world's spiciest beginnings.

Torrejas de Maiz Tierno
(Fresh Corn Fritters)
Yield: About 2 dozen (2-inch [5 cm]) fritters   Heat Scale: Mild

These Colombian corn fritters are a wonderful accompaniment to any seafood dish.
Try serving them with Pickapeppa Hot Sauce (page 55) to really add an authentic
Latin American flavor.

3 cups (708 mL) fresh sweet corn, with its liquid
¼ cup (59 mL) all-purpose flour
2 tablespoons (30 mL) light brown sugar
½ teaspoon (2.5 mL) salt
1 teaspoon (5 mL) habanero hot sauce
1 large egg, lightly beaten
2 tablespoons (30 mL) grated cheddar
¼ cup (59 mL) vegetable oil

1. Gently but thoroughly combine the corn and its liquid with the flour,
sugar, salt, and hot sauce. Blend in the egg and cheese. Stir the batter well.
2. In a skillet, heat the oil to 265°F (130°C) and drop in the batter by the
teaspoonful. Fry until golden brown on all sides. Drain on paper towels
and serve very hot.

Spicy Salbutes
Yield: 4–6 servings   Heat Scale: Varies

These fried, puffed-up tortillas are common throughout the Yucatán Peninsula.
Although they are usually served as an appetizer, I ate three of them sprinkled with
liberal doses of a habanero hot sauce as a lunch entrée during our trip to Ambergris
Caye, Belize. This recipe comes from Nancy Gerlach.

2 cups (473 mL) masa harina
2 tablespoons (30 mL) all-purpose flour
½ teaspoon (2.5 mL) baking powder
½ teaspoon (2.5 mL) salt
¾ cup (177 mL) water, or more if necessary
Vegetable oil for frying
2 chicken breasts, poached, skin removed, shredded
1 small onion, peeled and chopped fine
2 tablespoons (30 mL) chopped cilantro
Belizean habanero sauce or your favorite bottled habanero sauce, to taste

1. Combine the masa, flour, baking powder, and salt. Add enough of
the water to make a soft dough. Knead well and let the dough rest for
15 minutes.
2. Pinch off small amounts of the dough and roll each into a ball. With
a rolling pin, roll the balls into small tortillas about 3 inches (7.5 cm) in

diameter. Fry the tortillas on a hot, dry griddle on both sides until the dough is dry but not brown.

3. Heat the oil in a skillet. Add the tortillas and fry them for a minute or until both sides are brown and crisp. The tortillas should immediately puff up in the oil. Carefully remove them from the oil and drain them on paper towels.

4. Top the fried tortillas with the chicken, onions, and cilantro and sprinkle them with habanero sauce.

Nacatamales (Nicaraguan Tamales)

Yield: 20–30 servings   Heat Scale: Medium

This appetizer requires considerable advance preparation. However, the combination of eclectic ingredients makes it well worth the extra time. If you can locate banana leaves, use them, as they really capture the authentic flavor of the dish. If not, corn husks will work fine. This recipe makes enough nacatamales to serve at a large party.

3 cups (708 mL) white cornmeal
1 quart (.95 L) boiling water
6 tablespoons (90 mL) butter
1 tablespoon (15 mL) salt, divided
2 large eggs, beaten well
4 cups (.95 L) diced lean beef
3 cups (708 mL) diced lean pork
3 cups (708 mL) diced raw chicken
2 cups (473 mL) cold water
3 small cloves garlic, peeled and minced or mashed
2 cups (473 mL) drained canned chick peas, coarsely chopped
⅓ cup (79 mL) olive oil
3 cups (708 mL) coarsely chopped ripe tomatoes
1 cup (236 mL) coarsely chopped green bell pepper
3 cups (708 mL) coarsely chopped onion
1 tablespoon (15 mL) ground cayenne
½ cup (118 mL) finely chopped fresh parsley
4 tablespoons (60 mL) apple cider vinegar
2 teaspoons (10 mL) sugar
3 teaspoons capers, coarsely chopped (optional)
¾ cup (177 mL) halved seedless raisins
¾ cup (177 mL) pimiento-stuffed green olives, thinly sliced
⅓ cup (79 mL) crumbled fried bacon
2 cups (473 mL) corn kernels, cooked
1 cup (236 mL) tiny green peas, drained
⅓ cup (79 mL) diced pimientos (or substitute cooked red bell pepper)
20–30 (6 × 6–inch [15 × 15 cm]) banana leaves (or substitute corn husks)

1. Combine the cornmeal with enough cold water to make a paste, then stir this paste into the saucepan containing the rapidly boiling water. Add the butter and 2 teaspoons (10 mL) of the salt. Remove the pan from the heat and stir in the eggs until a smooth dough results. Set aside.

2. In a large saucepan combine the beef, pork, chicken, cold water, garlic, and chickpeas. Bring to a rapid boil, then reduce the heat and cook, stirring occasionally, about 45 minutes or until the meats are tender. Drain well.

3. In a large skillet with a lid, heat the oil over medium heat. Add the tomatoes, green bell pepper, onion, cayenne, parsley, the remaining 1 teaspoon (5 mL) salt, the vinegar, the sugar, and the cooked meats. Cover and cook over low heat for 15 minutes, stirring occasionally. Remove from the heat and gently stir in the capers, raisins, olives, bacon, corn, peas, and pimientos.

4. Blanch the banana leaves in boiling water and drain. Spread about 4 tablespoons (60 mL) of the dough mixture on the center of a banana leaf and pat out the dough into a thin layer. Place 2–3 tablespoons (30–45 mL) of the meat-vegetable mixture on one edge of the flattened dough, and roll the dough up carefully and tightly, sealing the edges as thoroughly as possible with a little warm water or more dough, if needed. Fold the banana leaf around the nacatamale and tie it securely with kitchen string or a thin strip of banana leaf. Repeat with the remaining dough, meat mixture, and banana leaves. Place the nacatamales in a large pot and add salted water to cover. Simmer over very low heat, covered, for about 1 hour. Serve the nacatamales in their banana-leaf packets, hot or at room temperature.

Empanadas del Pampas
(Turnovers from the Plains)

Yield: 10 empanadas   Heat Scale: Medium

Empanadas, or meat-filled turnovers, are very popular throughout Latin America, where they are most often eaten as a snack or an appetizer. This recipe was collected in Argentina.

For the Crust:
1⅔ cups (394 mL) all-purpose flour
⅛ teaspoon (.6 mL) salt
½ cup (118 mL) butter
⅓ cup (79 mL) milk

1. Sift together the flour and salt into a bowl. Using your fingers or two forks, work the butter into the dry mixture. Add the milk and mix just until the dough comes together and can be formed easily into a ball. Refrigerate for at least an hour.

For the Filling:
1 pound ground beef
2 tablespoons (30 mL) vegetable oil (olive preferred)
1 large onion, peeled and finely chopped
1 red bell pepper, stem and seeds removed, finely chopped
2 fresh aji chiles, stems and seeds removed, minced, or substitute yellow wax hot peppers or jalapeños
10 to 12 green olives, finely chopped
2 tablespoons (30 mL) raisins
1 tablespoon (15 mL) ground mild paprika
1 tablespoon (15 mL) chopped fresh parsley (or substitute 1½ teaspoons [7.5 mL] dried)
1 medium potato, peeled, boiled, and finely chopped
2 hard-boiled eggs, finely chopped
Salt, to taste
Freshly ground black pepper, to taste
1 egg, beaten
1 tablespoon (15 mL) milk

1. Sauté the beef in a skillet over medium heat until well done, stirring frequently with a fork to keep the meat broken up. In a separate skillet, heat the oil over medium heat. Add the onion, bell pepper, and chiles and sauté until the onions are golden brown, about 5 minutes. Combine the cooked beef, sautéed vegetables, olives, raisins, paprika, parsley, potato, eggs, salt, and pepper in a large bowl and mix well.
2. Preheat the oven to 400°F (200°C).
3. Remove the dough from the refrigerator and divide it in two equal portions. Roll the dough out to a thickness of ⅛ inch (.25 cm) and cut into circles 7 inches (17.5 cm) in diameter. Spoon about 1 tablespoon (15 mL) of the filling onto one half of a dough circle, leaving room to fold the

empanada in half and seal. Press the edges with the tip of a fork and cut a
1-inch slice in the top. Repeat with the remaining dough circles and filling. Place the empanadas on an ungreased baking pan.
4. Bake for 10 minutes. Reduce the heat to 350°F (180°C), and continue
baking until the crust turns light brown. Combine the egg and milk.
Brush the tops of the empanadas with the glaze and bake for an additional 5 minutes.

Skewered Spiced Sirloin

Yield: 6 servings   Heat Scale: Medium

*The Argentine cowboys, or gauchos, are very proud of their beef, but not so proud
that they won't borrow a recipe from neighboring Peru. This recipe is their version of
anticuchos, but it is prepared with a better cut of meat. It is wise to soak the skewers
in water for 30 minutes before using, which will prevent them from catching fire
during grilling. Serve the kebabs with a salad from Chapter 6 and a robust red wine.
(Note: This recipe requires advance preparation.)*

2 pounds (1.1 kg) sirloin, cut in 1½ inch (3.5 cm) cubes
1 cup (236 mL) distilled white vinegar
2 cloves garlic, peeled and crushed
3 dried aji chiles, crushed (or substitute New Mexican)
1 teaspoon (5 mL) cumin seeds, crushed
1 teaspoon (5 mL) salt
Freshly ground black pepper, to taste
1 tablespoon (15 mL) chopped cilantro
1 teaspoon (5 mL) Louisiana-style hot sauce
2 tablespoons (30 mL) tomato sauce
2 tablespoons (30 mL) vegetable oil
1 teaspoon (5 mL) Worcestershire sauce

1. Place the sirloin in a bowl. Mix together the vinegar, garlic, chiles,
cumin, salt, pepper to taste, and cilantro. Pour this marinade over the
sirloin cubes. If it does not completely cover the meat, add more vinegar.
Cover and refrigerate overnight. Remove the sirloin and reserve ¾ cup
(177 mL) of the marinade.
2. Combine the hot sauce, tomato sauce, vegetable oil, Worcestershire
sauce, black pepper to taste, and the reserved marinade.
3. Thread the meat onto bamboo or wooden skewers and brush it with the
sauce. Cook over hot coals or a gas grill for about 4 to 6 minutes, depending on the heat of the fire, turning frequently and brushing with the sauce.

Aros de Jalapeño con Queso de Chorizo
(Jalapeño Rings with Chorizo Cream Cheese)

Yield: 4 servings   Heat Scale: Medium

My friend Lula Betrán, from Mexico City, credits the invention of this recipe to her husband, Alberto. "He likes onion rings," she told me. "One day while eating them he said, 'Why don't you do this with chiles?'"

2 cups (473 mL) water
4 large jalapeños, roasted, peeled, stems and seeds removed,
sliced into rings
3 tablespoons (45 mL) distilled white vinegar
½ cup (118 mL) all-purpose flour
½ teaspoon (2.5 mL) baking powder
½ teaspoon (2.5 mL) salt
½ cup (118 mL) milk
Vegetable oil for deep frying
½ cup (118 mL) fried chorizo sausage
½ cup (118 mL) cream cheese

1. Preheat the oven to 200°F (100°C).
2. Bring the water to a boil in a large saucepan. Add the jalapeño rings and vinegar and cook for 5 minutes. Remove from the heat and let cool. Drain the rings and pat them dry.
3. Combine the flour, baking powder, salt, and milk in a bowl to make a batter. Dip the rings into the batter and fry in hot oil over high heat until they are crisp and brown, about 5 minutes. Drain on paper towels.
4. In a bowl, combine the chorizo and cream cheese to make a paste. Fill the rings with the paste, warm them in the oven for 5 to 10 minutes, and serve hot.

Chileajo
(Garlic Chile)
Yield: 4–6 servings   Heat Scale: Medium

This dish is the Mexican version of antipasto. I prefer the vegetables lightly steamed, but they may also be served raw. I collected this recipe in Oaxaca, which is known for its fantastic moles and beautiful pottery as well as its use of exotic flavorful chiles, such as the chilcoxtle and guajillo.

1¼ cups (295 mL) thinly sliced potato rounds
½ cup (118 mL) cubed carrots
½ cup (118 mL) chopped green beans
½ cup (118 mL) peas
4 chilcoxtle chiles, stems and seeds removed, rehydrated in hot water and minced (or substitute pasillas)
2 guajillo chiles, stems and seeds removed, rehydrated in hot water and minced (or substitute New Mexican)
1 head of garlic, cloves separated and peeled
Mexican oregano, to taste
1 cup (236 mL) distilled white vinegar
Salt, to taste
8 ounces asadero cheese, grated (or substitute mozzarella)
1 onion, peeled and sliced

1. Steam the potatoes, carrots, green beans, and peas to the desired consistency, then chill them in the refrigerator.
2. Rinse the chiles in hot water and place them in a bowl with the garlic, oregano, vinegar, and salt.
3. Remove the vegetables from the refrigerator and arrange the potatoes, carrots, green beans, and peas in the center of a platter, then pour the chile mixture over the vegetables. Place the cheese and onion around the edges of the dish, sprinkle the oregano over the top, and serve.

Chiles a la Norita
(Stuffed Ancho Chiles)
Yield: 4–6 servings   Heat Scale: Medium

Ancho chiles make some of the best stuffed appetizers that can be found. However, be careful to choose anchos that are fairly fresh. Look for chiles that are still flexible and that have a strong aroma that can be detected through their packaging.

For the Salsa:
¼ cup (59 mL) vegetable cil
2 onions, peeled and finely chopped
2 green tomatoes, finely chopped
½ cup (118 mL) water
¼ teaspoon (1.25 mL) Mexican oregano
2 tablespoons (30 mL) chopped cilantro

1. Heat the oil in a saucepan over high heat. Add the onion and fry until soft. Add the tomatoes, water, oregano, and cilantro. Cook until the tomatoes are done, then set aside.

For the Stuffed Chiles:
4 cups (.95 L) water
6 large ancho chiles, stems and seeds removed
13 ounces (364 g) aged cheese, such as romano, sliced into 6 equal pieces
5 tablespoons (75 mL) butter
⅓ cup (79 mL) vegetable oil
6 tortillas
6 eggs, scrambled
1 head lettuce, shredded or chopped
1 avocado, peeled, pitted, and sliced
7 ounces (196 g) cheddar, grated

1. Bring the water to a boil in a large sauce pan over high heat. Add the chiles and boil for 2 minutes to rehydrate them. Drain the chiles and carefully pat them dry on paper towels.
2. Fill each chile with a slice of cheese and set aside.
3. In a large skillet, melt the butter over medium heat, then add the oil and turn the heat to high. Add the chiles to the skillet and fry them until they are browned. Remove the chiles from the oil, drain them on a paper towel, and transfer them to a platter.
4. Briefly dip the tortillas in the oil and place them on a separate plate. Place one chile on top of each tortilla, then top each with a spoonful of salsa and egg.
5. Decorate the plates with the lettuce, avocado slices, and shredded cheese.

Chile con Queso Estilo Sonora
(Sonoran-Style Chile with Cheese)
Yield: 4–6 servings   Heat Scale: Medium

Who could ask for a more perfect combination than chile and cheese? This recipe is a specialty of the Sonora area, which has millions of acres of agricultural land along the coastal plains. Serve this with tortilla strips or chips for dipping.

2 tablespoons (30 mL) butter
1 medium onion, peeled and chopped
2 tomatoes, chopped
4 cloves garlic, peeled and finely chopped
5 poblano chiles, roasted, peeled, stems and seeds removed, chopped
3 jalapeño chiles, stems and seeds removed, minced
¾ cup (177 mL) milk
Salt, to taste
Freshly ground black pepper, to taste
1 cup (236 mL) grated Chihuahua cheese or mild cheddar
2 tablespoons (30 mL) chopped cilantro

1. Melt the butter in a skillet over medium heat. Add the onion, tomatoes, and garlic and sauté until the onions are translucent. Add the chiles, milk, and salt and pepper. Let this mixture cook for a few minutes so that the flavors blend, then add the cheese, stirring well.
2. Remove the skillet from the heat and transfer the mixture to a glass bowl. Garnish with the cilantro.

Pescadillos
(Fish Tacos)
Yield: 12 tacos   Heat Scale: Medium

One of the best appetizer treats you will ever taste are fresh fish tacos as prepared in Yucatán.

¾ cup (177 mL) vegetable oil, divided
1 large onion, peeled and finely chopped
2 pounds (1.1 kg) large tomatoes, blanched and chopped
5 serrano chiles, stems and seeds removed, finely chopped
2½ pounds (1.1 kg) marlin, cut into chunks (or substitute your favorite fish)
Chopped cilantro, to taste
1 teaspoon (5 mL) oregano
Salt, to taste
Freshly ground black pepper, to taste
12 corn tortillas
½ cup (118 mL) vegetable oil
1 lemon, cut into wedges

1. In a skillet, heat ¼ cup (59 mL) of the oil over medium heat. Add the onion, tomatoes, and chiles and sauté until soft. Add the marlin, cilantro, oregano, salt, and pepper. Cook until the fish flakes, then set aside.
2. Wrap the tortillas in plastic wrap and microwave them on high for 10 seconds. Stuff them with the fish mixture.
3. In a separate skillet, heat the remaining oil over high heat. Fry the stuffed tortillas until they are light brown or the desired texture. Squeeze the lemons over the fish in each taco and serve.

Jamaican Patties

Yield: 10 (6-inch [15 cm]) patties   Heat Scale: Mild

This recipe for Jamaica's favorite fast food comes from Peggy Barnes, who wrote for me about her island culinary adventures. She suggests that this recipe may be simplified by using dough from the dairy case. For more heat, split the patties in half after they are done baking, and serve them with a habanero-based sauce to spoon inside.

½ pound (224 g) ground pork
½ pound (224 g) ground beef
1 teaspoon (5 mL) ground red New Mexican chile
1 teaspoon (5 mL) paprika
¼ cup (59 mL) minced celery
½ cup (118 mL) minced onion
¼ cup (59 mL) minced green onion tops
¼ cup (59 mL) diced red bell pepper
2 cloves garlic, peeled and crushed
1 teaspoon (5 mL) seasoned salt
1 teaspoon (5 mL) dried thyme
2 tablespoons (30 mL) soy sauce
½ cup (118 mL) dry bread crumbs
1 tablespoon (15 mL) all-purpose flour
2 (16.3-ounce [456 g]) cans grand-size refrigerator biscuits
1 egg yolk, beaten with 1 tablespoon (15 mL) milk

1. In a large skillet over medium-high heat, brown the pork and beef. Drain off any excess fat. Add the ground chile and paprika. Cook, stirring, for 1 minute. Add the celery, onion, green onions, bell pepper, garlic, seasoned salt, thyme, and soy sauce and cook until the celery is tender, about 5 minutes. Add the bread crumbs and flour and combine thoroughly. Remove the pan from the heat and let cool.
2. Preheat the oven to 375°F (190°C). On a floured surface, roll out the biscuits to 6-inch (15 cm) circles and place 2–3 heaping tablespoons (40–60 mL) of filling in the center of one circle. Moisten the edges with water and fold the dough over to form a crescent. Crimp the edges with a fork and brush the crust with the egg-milk mixture. Repeat with the remaining dough and filling. Place the patties on a baking sheet and bake for 30 minutes or until they are golden brown.

Feroce d'Avocat
(Savage Avocado Appetizer)
Yield: 4 servings   Heat Scale: Hot

Feroce d'Avocat is the French name for this hot crab appetizer that is popular in Martinique. The avocado, sometimes referred to as an alligator pear, adds a rich flavor to the crab meat.

8 ounces (224 g) fresh or canned crab meat
1 tablespoon (15 mL) distilled white vinegar
Juice of 1 lime
2 tablespoons (30 mL) vegetable oil
2 cloves garlic, peeled and finely chopped
4 shallots, peeled and finely chopped
4 green onions, chopped
1 habanero chile, stem and seeds removed, minced
4 avocados, peeled, pitted, and diced
1 cup (236 mL) manioc flour (also known as tapioca or cassava meal)
Lettuce or spinach leaves for serving
Extra lime juice for serving

1. Drain the crab, pat it dry, and place it in a bowl. Add the vinegar, lime juice, oil, garlic, shallots, green onions, and chile. Mash the avocado with the manioc flour, add this to the crab mixture, and blend to form a thick paste.
2. Spoon the paste onto lettuce or spinach on individual serving dishes, or roll into balls and arrange on a plate. Sprinkle with lime juice just before serving.

Tropical "Guacamole" with Fruit
Yield: 6–8 servings   Heat Scale: Medium

The only similarity between this French Caribbean "guacamole" and its Mexican cousin is the green color. This sweet, hot combination of fruits, coconut, and avocado is an unusual way to bring a bit of the Caribbean to a barbecue or luncheon.

½ pound (224 g) Hawaiian or Portuguese sweet bread
(also called Easter bread)
2 tablespoons (30 mL) sweetened dried coconut
1 small firm-ripe papaya (about 1 pound [454 g])
1 medium ripe mango
1 large firm-ripe avocado
2 tablespoons (30 mL) lime juice
1 teaspoon (5 mL) sugar
¼ teaspoon (1.25 mL) crushed dried habanero chile

1. Preheat the oven to 300°F (150°C).
2. Cut the bread into ¼-inch (.5 cm) thick slices, then cut the slices diagonally into triangles. Arrange the triangles in a single layer in a 10 × 15–inch (25 × 37.5 cm) baking pan. Bake until lightly browned, about 10 minutes, turning the slices over halfway through baking. Transfer to wire racks to cool. If you are preparing the bread ahead of time, wrap it airtight and store it at room temperature for up to a day.
3. In a frying pan, toast the coconut over medium-high heat, stirring constantly, until golden brown, about 3 minutes. Remove the coconut from the pan and set aside.
4. Cut the papaya in half lengthwise. Discard the seeds and peel, leaving halves intact. From 1 half, cut 2 lengthwise slices about ¼-inch (.5 cm) thick. Dice the remaining papaya and set the fruit aside. Repeat with the mango.
5. Cut the avocado in half lengthwise. Discard the pit and peel, leaving the halves intact. From 1 half, cut 2 lengthwise slices, about ¼-inch (.5 cm) thick. Chop the remaining avocado and combine it with the lime juice, sugar, and habanero.
6. On a serving platter, arrange the avocado mixture and diced papaya-mango mixture side by side in separate mounds. Fan the reserved avocado slices next to the diced papaya and mango and the reserved papaya and mango slices next to the avocado mixture. Sprinkle all with the coconut. Guests can spread the guacamole and fruit mixture on the bread slices.

Spicy Lamb Carnitas

Yield: 6 servings   Heat Scale: Mild

Serve these "little pieces of meat" with toothpicks and several of the salsas from Chapter 2 for dipping. These carnitas can also be grilled.

1 tablespoon (15 mL) ground red New Mexican chile
3 cloves garlic, peeled and minced
¼ cup (59 mL) minced onions
2 teaspoons (10 mL) finely chopped fresh cilantro
1 teaspoon (5 mL) dried oregano
1 teaspoon (5 mL) freshly ground black pepper
1 teaspoon (5 mL) ground cumin
½ teaspoon (2.5 mL) salt
1 pound (454 g) boneless lamb, cut into 1–1½-inch (2.5–3.5 cm) cubes

1. Preheat the oven to 250°F (120°C).
2. Combine all the ingredients except the lamb, in a bowl and mix well. Rub the meat cubes with the mixture. Allow the meat to sit, at room temperature, for an hour or more to marinate.
3. Place the meat on a rack over a pan to catch the drippings. Bake the meat for an hour or until the meat is crisp on the outside but tender on the inside.

Quesadillas with Goat Cheese

Yield: 24 wedges   Heat Scale: Medium

These tortas are excellent when served as an appetizer, or they can replace sandwiches for a real Southwestern lunch.

6 (8-inch [20 cm]) flour tortillas
8 ounces (224 g) goat cheese, crumbled or sliced
6 green New Mexican chiles, roasted, peeled, stems and seeds removed, cut into strips
1 cup (236 mL) nopales (cactus pad) strips
1 small avocado, peeled, pitted, and diced
½ cup (118 mL) chopped onions
1 tablespoon (15 mL) chopped fresh herbs, such as cilantro, oregano, or basil
Ground red New Mexican chile, to taste

1. On half of a tortilla, layer some of the cheese, chiles, nopales, avocado, onions, and herbs. Moisten the edges, fold the tortilla over, and press to seal. Repeat with the remaining tortillas and filling ingredients.
2. Toast the tortillas on each side on a hot griddle over medium-high heat until the cheese melts. Dust with the ground red chile.
Cut each quesadilla into 4 wedges and serve.

Variation
4 ounces (112 g) feta and ¼ cup (59 mL) ricotta cheese may be substituted for the goat cheese.

El Paso Nachos

Yield: 6–8 servings   Heat Scale: Medium

This appetizer has become so popular that you don't have to travel to Texas to enjoy it, although nachos served outside the Southwest may bear little resemblance to the real thing. Try making your own tostadas or corn chips from slightly stale corn tortillas for a more authentic, tasty dish.

1 dozen corn tortillas, cut into wedges
Vegetable oil for frying
¾ cup (177 mL) refried beans
½ pound (224 g) grated sharp cheddar
½ cup (118 mL) sour cream
8 jalapeño chiles, stems and seeds removed, sliced in thin rings

1. Preheat the broiler.
2. In a large skillet, heat 1½ inches (3.5 cm) of oil to 350°F (180°C). Add the tortillas and fry until crispy. Remove the chips from the oil and drain on paper towels.

3. Arrange the tortillas on a baking sheet or an ovenproof plate. Place a small amount of beans on each chip and top with the grated cheese. Heat the plate under the broiler until the cheese melts. Alternatively, microwave the plate for 3–4 minutes.
4. Top with the sour cream and jalapeño slices and serve immediately.

Freshly Fried Nachos with Chile con Queso Asadero

Yield: 6–8 servings   Heat Scale: Medium

Here is a California version of the Tex-Mex favorite—nachos—with, of all things, green olives.

1 dozen corn tortillas, cut into wedges
Vegetable oil for frying
1 cup (236 mL) finely diced tomatoes
1–1½ cups (250–354 mL) grated asadero cheese
¼ cup (59 mL) sliced jalapeño chiles
¼ cup (59 mL) sliced pimiento-stuffed green olives

1. Preheat the broiler.
2. Fry the tortillas in 1½-inches (3.75 cm) oil, at 350°F (180°C), until crispy. Remove the chips from the oil and drain them on paper towels.
3. Arrange the tortillas on a pan or oven-proof plate. Top with the tomatoes, cheese, chiles, and olives. Heat the pan under the broiler until the cheese melts or microwave the plate for 3 to 4 minutes.

Variation
Substitute pepper jack or provolone cheese for the asadero.

Marinated Rajas

Yield: 10 servings   Heat Scale: Mild to Medium

Rajas, or strips of green chile, are commonly cooked with other vegetables. But New Mexican chile has such a great taste that the rajas can stand alone. Serve these tasty appetizers with toothpicks. (Note: This recipe requires advance preparation.)

5 green New Mexican chiles, roasted, peeled, stems and seeds removed, cut into strips
¼ cup (59 mL) olive oil
¼ cup (59 mL) red wine vinegar
1 clove garlic, peeled and finely chopped

1. Combine all the ingredients and marinate in the refrigerator overnight.

Jicama Slices with a Choice of Peppers
Yield: 6–8 servings   Heat Scale: Mild to Medium

The heat of this appetizer will depend on the type of chile powder selected for dipping. Don't limit yourself to jicama—try slices of other fruits and vegetables as well.

1–1½ pounds (454–680 g) jicama, peeled
⅓ cup (79 mL) fresh lime juice
½ cup (118 mL) salt
1 tablespoon (15 mL) ground chiles de arbol
1 tablespoon (15 mL) ground pasilla chile
1 tablespoon (15 mL) ground red New Mexican chile

1. Cut the jicama into sticks ½ inch (1 cm) wide and 3–4 inches (7.5–10 cm) long. Pour the lime juice over the sticks, making sure that they are well coated.
2. Divide the salt into thirds and mix each type of chile powder in each part of the salt.
3. To serve, arrange the sticks on a plate with the three chile salts. Guests will dip the sticks into their choice of chile salts.

Three Versions of Southwestern Guacamole

The combination of avocados and chile to form a versatile salsa is commonplace throughout the Southwest and, these days, around the world. Here are the three best versions. Serve them as a dip with chips, over greens as a salad dressing, with roasted meats or poultry as a dipping sauce, or as a garnish over enchiladas, tostadas, or tacos.

New Mexico Version
Yield: 2 cups (473 mL)   Heat Scale: Mild

3 green New Mexican chiles, roasted, peeled, stems and seeds removed, chopped fine
1 tomato, chopped fine
3 medium avocados, pitted, peeled, and mashed
1 medium onion, peeled and chopped fine
1 teaspoon (5 mL) lemon juice
¼ teaspoon (1.25 mL) garlic powder
¼ teaspoon (1.25 mL) ground cumin
Salt, to taste

1. Combine all the ingredients in a bowl and mix well.

Texas Version

Yield: 2 cups (473 mL)   Heat Scale: Medium

3 jalapeño or serrano chiles, stems and seeds removed, chopped fine
3 medium avocados, pitted, peeled, and mashed
1 medium onion, peeled and chopped fine
¼ teaspoon (1.25 mL) garlic salt
Juice of 1 lemon
Salt, to taste

1. Combine all the ingredients in a bowl and mix well.

California Version

Yield: 2 cups (473 mL)   Heat Scale: Mild

2 green Anaheim chiles, roasted, peeled, stems and seeds removed,
chopped
3 medium avocados, pitted, peeled, and mashed
⅓ cup (79 mL) sour cream
1 small tomato, diced
1 small onion, peeled and minced
1 clove garlic, peeled and minced
2 teaspoons (10 mL) lemon juice
Salt, to taste

1. Combine all the ingredients and mix well.

Green Chile Tortilla Pinwheels

Yield: 48–60 rounds   Heat Scale: Mild

*This is an all-purpose filling that works well on crackers and finger sandwiches. Thin
with milk or light cream to make a super dip for chips or vegetable crudities.*

½ cup (118 mL) chopped roasted green New Mexican chiles
1 (3-ounce [84 g]) package low-fat cream cheese, softened
2 tablespoons (30 mL) milk or cream
¼ teaspoon (1.25 mL) garlic salt
2 teaspoons (10 mL) chopped cilantro
3–4 flour tortillas

1. Preheat the oven to 300°F (150°C).
2. Combine all the ingredients except the tortillas in a bowl and mix well.
3. Wrap the tortillas in a damp towel and place them in the oven to soften. Spread the cream cheese mixture on the tortillas and roll each tortilla as you would a jelly roll. Slice each roll into ½-inch (1 cm) thick rounds.

California Meatballs with Wine-Chile Sauce

Yield: 35–40 meatballs   Heat Scale: Mild

No hors d'oeuvres table would be complete without some type of cocktail meatballs. These are more like albóndigas, or Latin American meatballs, than those of Swedish origin. Serve hot with toothpicks.

For the Meatballs:
8 serrano or jalapeño chiles, stems and seeds removed, chopped
1 pound (454 g) ground beef
1 small onion, peeled and chopped
½ cup (118 mL) fresh bread crumbs
2 eggs, beaten
35–40 pimiento-stuffed green olives
Vegetable oil for frying

1. In a bowl, combine all the ingredients except the olives. Shape some of the meat mixture around each olive to make a ball.
2. Sauté the meatballs in the oil over medium heat, in small batches, until browned. Add more oil if necessary. Remove the meatballs from the oil and drain on paper towels.

For the Sauce:
1 small onion, peeled and chopped
2 cloves garlic, peeled and chopped
2 tablespoons (30 mL) vegetable oil
2 tablespoons (30 mL) ground red New Mexican chile
1 cup (236 mL) beef bouillon
1 cup (236 mL) red wine
2 tablespoons (30 mL) cornstarch
2 tablespoons (30 mL) water

1. In a pan, heat the oil over medium heat. Add the onion and garlic and sauté until soft, about 7 minutes. Add the chile and cook for an additional minute. Transfer the onion mixture to a blender, add the bouillon, and purée until smooth.
2. Deglaze the pan with the wine. Add the onion purée and simmer until heated. Add more bouillon, if needed, to make a sauce.
3. Pour the sauce over the meatballs, cover, and simmer for 15 to 20 minutes to cook the meatballs. Remove the meatballs from the sauce.
4. Combine the cornstarch and water in a cup and stir well with a fork. Bring the sauce to a boil and slowly stir in the cornstarch to slightly thicken the sauce. Pour the sauce over the meatballs and serve hot.

Jalapeño Cherry Bombs

Yield: 24 bombs   Heat Scale: Medium to Hot

These little explosions of flavor make perfect appetizers for chilehead guests.

24 jalapeño chiles
8 ounces (224 g) Monterey Jack or cheddar cheese, sliced
All-purpose flour for dredging
2 eggs, beaten
Vegetable oil for frying

1. Slit each chile pod and remove the seeds with a small spoon or knife. Stuff the peppers with pieces of cheese. If necessary, insert toothpicks to hold the chiles together.
2. Dip each stuffed chile in the flour, then the egg, then the flour again. Heat the oil to 350°F (180°C) and fry the chiles until they are golden brown. Drain on paper towels and serve.

Fiesta Bean Dip

Yield: 3–3½ cups (750–836 mL)   Heat Scale: Medium

Pinto beans get their name from the Spanish word for "spot," which refers to the mottled colors of the bean. One of the most popular of the New World beans, they are used in a wide variety of dishes throughout the Southwest. This dip goes well with corn or tortilla chips and can also be used as a burrito filling or on a tostada.

3 cups (708 mL) cooked mashed pinto beans
6 green New Mexican chiles, roasted, peeled, stems and seeds removed, chopped
2 small tomatoes, peeled and chopped
1 small onion, peeled and chopped
½ teaspoon (2.5 mL) garlic powder
1 cup (236 mL) grated cheddar or Monterey Jack cheese

1. In a saucepan, heat the beans over medium-high heat until they are very hot, about 8 minutes. Add all the other ingredients and stir until the cheese melts. Add water, if necessary, to thin to the desired consistency for dipping.

Queso Flameado with Poblano Strips

Yield: 6 servings   Heat Scale: Mild

This appetizer is so quick and easy to prepare that you can wait until your guests arrive to start it. It is from the northern states of Mexico but is often served in the Southwest.

2 poblano chiles, roasted, peeled, stems and seeds removed, cut into strips
2 tablespoons (30 mL) butter or olive oil
2 cups (473 mL) grated queso blanco, Monterey Jack, or cheddar cheese
Corn tortillas or tostadas for dipping

1. Preheat the oven to 300°F (150°C).
2. In a sauté pan, heat the oil over medium-high heat. Add the poblano strips and sauté until they are soft, about 10 minutes. In a small casserole dish, layer half the cheese, then half the poblano strips, then the remaining cheese. Cover and bake for about 5 minutes, until the cheese has melted. Uncover, add the remaining strips, and bake for 2 more minutes.
3. Remove the dish from the oven and serve with the tortillas or tostadas to dip out the cheese and strips.

Roasted Poblanos Stuffed with Mushroom-Walnut Pesto

Yield: 8 servings   Heat Scale: Medium

This appetizer is fairly rich and extremely tasty. The mushroom pesto may also be served as a paté with crackers or chips.

8 medium poblano chiles, roasted, peeled, seeds removed but stems left on
4 cups (.95 L) fresh basil leaves
½ cup (118 mL) olive oil
4 tablespoons (60 mL) piñons or pine nuts
4 tablespoons (60 mL) chopped walnuts
16 medium fresh mushrooms, quartered
4 cloves garlic, peeled
1 teaspoon (5 mL) salt
4 ounces (112 g) low-fat cream cheese, softened
⅔ cup (158 mL) freshly grated Parmesan cheese

1. Preheat the oven to 400°F (200°C). Oil a baking dish.
2. Arrange the poblanos in the prepared dish and set aside.
3. In a food processor, combine the basil, oil, nuts, mushrooms, garlic, and salt and purée until smooth. Transfer to a mixing bowl and stir in the cream cheese and Parmesan cheese. Mix well.
4. Fill the poblanos with the pesto and refrigerate for at least 1 hour. Bake for 6 to 8 minutes or until completely heated through.

Two-Chile Quesadilla Ecstasy

Yield: 6 appetizer servings   Heat Scale: Hot

Trust us, these are not the usual, bland quesadillas you have been subjected to in the past. When my wife, Mary Jane, taught high school in Albuquerque, the cafeteria served basic quesadillas with American cheese and green chile for breakfast. They were good, gooey, and satisfying, but they lacked pizzazz—just the kind I've added to these quesadillas. The addition of sliced jalapeños makes this quite a spicy appetizer. They can be served in small wedges as an appetizer or cut in large slices and served as a main course with a big salad and a luscious dessert.

3 (10-inch [25 cm]) flour tortillas
5 green New Mexico chiles, roasted, peeled, stems and seeds removed, chopped; or use 2 (4-ounce [114 g]) cans chopped green chile, thoroughly drained and rinsed
1½ cups (354 mL) shredded sharp cheddar
2 cups (473 mL) shredded queso blanco or Monterey Jack cheese
¾ cup (177 mL) sun-dried tomatoes, cut into slivers
1 teaspoon (5 mL) hot sauce (preferably one without a lot of vinegar)
¼ cup (59 mL) sliced jalapeño or serrano chiles (fresh preferred)
10 to 15 mushrooms, sliced and lightly sautéed in butter
¼ cup (59 mL) chopped cilantro
Sprigs of cilantro for garnish

1. Preheat the oven to 400°F (200°C).
2. Place one of the tortillas on a small baking sheet and spread half of the green chiles over it. Sprinkle half of the cheddar and half of the queso blanco over the chile. Then add half the sun-dried tomatoes, half the hot sauce, half the jalapeños, half the mushrooms, and half the chopped cilantro.
3. Place the second tortilla over the first one and repeat the process. Cover with the third tortilla.
4. Bake for 7 to 9 minutes, until the quesadilla is heated through and the cheese is melted. Slice the quesadilla with a very sharp serrated knife or a very sharp pizza cutter. Serve garnished with the fresh cilantro.

Hotsy Hummus
Yield: 2 cups (473 mL)   Heat Scale: Mild

Hummus (houmous) is a traditional Middle Eastern dish; however, I have added an interesting Southwestern twist to this version—the chipotle chile in adobo sauce, which transforms it from a bland concoction of chickpeas to a wonderful, smoky, spicy dip with lots of bite. I have tried numerous chiles with hummus and have found that the chipotle adds just the right element. Serve it with toasted pita bread quarters or Chile-Cumin Crackers (page 114).

⅓ cup (79 mL) fresh lemon juice
3 tablespoons (45 mL) olive oil or chile-infused oil (page 16)
¼ cup (59 mL) whole sesame seeds
4 cloves garlic, peeled
¼ teaspoon (1.25 mL) freshly ground black pepper
2 sprigs fresh cilantro
2 cups (473 mL) canned chickpeas, drained and
rinsed (or 2 cups [473 mL] cooked chickpeas)
1 chipotle chile in adobo sauce

1. In a blender, combine the lemon juice, olive oil, sesame seeds, garlic, black pepper, and cilantro and blend until the mixture is thick and smooth.
2. Add ⅓ of the chickpeas and the chipotle pepper and process until just smooth. Then add the remaining chickpeas and blend again until just smooth.
3. Pour the mixture into a serving bowl and refrigerate for at least 2 hours. About 30 minutes before serving, remove the bowl from the refrigerator, and bring the mixture almost to room temperature.

Snow Peas Stuffed with Goat Cheese Chipotle Sauce
Yield: About 40 appetizers   Heat Scale: Medium

Here is another appetizer that uses the chipotle chile. This one is attractive and tempting with its smoky-hot, creamy filling.

1 pound (454 g) snow peas (about 40), stems removed
½ cup (118 mL) low-fat cream cheese, softened
½ cup (118 mL) goat cheese, crumbled
2 chipotle chiles in adobo sauce
Fresh greens for garnish

1. Rinse and drain the snow peas in a colander. Slice each pea lengthwise along the seam, creating a pocket. Set aside.
2. In a food processor, purée the cream cheese, goat cheese, and chipotles. Transfer this mixture to a pastry bag and use it to fill each snow pea pocket. Arrange the filled peas on a platter garnished with greens.

Cheese-Stuffed Peppers
(Korozottel Toltott Paprika)

Yield: 8 stuffed peppers   Heat Scale: Mild

From my European correspondent, Sharon Hudgins, come these delightful stuffed peppers. She comments, "I first ate these peppers at a Hungarian beer hall in Keszthely on Lake Balaton. In Hungary, the cheese stuffing is often made from Liptói cheese, a soft curd cheese produced from sheep's or goats' milk. The best substitute in the U.S. is a mixture of feta cheese, ricotta cheese, and sour cream." Increase the heat by garnishing with hot paprika. Serve the peppers whole (1 per person) for a cold appetizer, or 2 per person for a luncheon main dish.

8 banana peppers, each about 5 inches (12.5 cm) long
(or substitute yellow wax hot)
1 pound (454 g) ricotta cheese
½ pound (224 g) feta cheese
2–4 tablespoons (30–60 mL) thick sour cream
½ medium onion, finely chopped
¼ cup (59 mL) finely chopped chives
Hot paprika for garnish

1. Carefully slice the top stem end off each pepper. Use a small spoon to scoop out the seeds and veins, keeping each pepper pod intact. Wash and dry the peppers and set them in the refrigerator to chill.
2. Press the ricotta cheese through a sieve into a large bowl. Crumble the feta cheese and press it through the sieve into the same bowl. Stir until the cheeses are well combined. Stir in the sour cream (using only enough to moisten the mixture slightly), then add the chopped onion and chives. Mix well.
3. Spoon the mixture into the pepper pods (being careful not to split or tear the pods). Fill each pod completely with cheese. (Use the handle of a large wooden spoon to press the cheese mixture into all the spaces in the pods.) Place the peppers in a single layer on a large plate, cover loosely with plastic wrap, and refrigerate for at least 2 hours. Just before serving, garnish the exposed cheese (at the end of each pepper) with a sprinkling of hot paprika.

Gravlax with Spicy Mustard Sauce

Yield: 12 or more servings   Heat Scale: Mild

This Swedish dish takes 2 days to make, but it's well worth the effort. After curing, the gravlax is sliced as thinly as possible and served on black bread with a little of the mustard sauce spread over it. (Note: This recipe requires advance preparation.)

¼ cup (59 mL) plus 2 tablespoons (30 mL) sugar
⅓ cup (79 mL) kosher salt
2 teaspoons (10 mL) freshly ground black pepper
2 small bunches dill, coarsely chopped
½ bunch chervil, chopped
1 bunch Italian parsley, chopped
1 bunch lemon balm, chopped
2 tablespoons (30 mL) prepared hot mustard (with chiles)
1 tablespoon (15 mL) dry mustard
2 tablespoons (30 mL) white vinegar
4 tablespoons (60 mL) canola oil
2 tablespoons (30 mL) freshly chopped dill
2 salmon fillets, about 1½ pounds (680 g) each

1. In a bowl, combine ¼ cup (59 mL) of the sugar, the salt, and the pepper. In a separate bowl, combine the dill, chervil, parsley, and lemon balm. In a third bowl, combine the prepared mustard, dry mustard, remaining sugar, vinegar, oil, and dill to make the mustard sauce. Cover and refrigerate the mustard sauce.
2. Place 1 fillet skin side down in a shallow bowl. Sprinkle half the sugar mixture over the fillet, followed by half the herb mixture, the rest of the sugar mixture, and the rest of the herb mixture. Place the second fillet on top of the first, flesh to flesh, and wrap with plastic wrap. Place the wrapped fillets in a shallow pan and weigh them down with something heavy, such as bricks covered in aluminum foil or a cast iron skillet. Refrigerate for 24 hours, then flip the fillets, weigh them down again, and refrigerate for another 24 hours. Serve with the mustard sauce.

Albondigas in Sherry Pepper Sauce

Yield: 40–50 meatballs   Heat Scale: Medium

These meatballs fall into a class of tapas called "cosas de picár." Named after the picks the picadors use during a bull fight, the term refers to those tapas that are served with toothpicks. In Spain, they would be made with minced meat, but since ground meats are more readily available, I use a combination of ground pork and beef. Traditionally these are made with paprika, but since I like my foods a little more spicy, I also add ground cayenne.

For the Sherry Pepper Sauce:
2 tablespoons (30 mL) olive oil (Spanish virgin olive oil preferred)
½ cup (118 mL) chopped onion
½ red bell pepper, thinly sliced
2 garlic cloves, peeled and minced
2 teaspoons (10 mL) ground paprika
½ teaspoon (2.5 mL) ground cayenne
2 tablespoons (30 mL) all-purpose flour
⅔ cup (158 mL) dry sherry
1 cup (236 mL) canned chicken broth

1. In a skillet, heat the oil over medium heat. Add the onion, bell pepper, and garlic and sauté until soft. Add the paprika, cayenne, and flour. Continue to cook for an additional minute. Whisk in the sherry and chicken broth, bring to a boil, and reduce the heat.

For the Meatballs:
2 slices stale bread, crusts removed
Water or milk as needed
½ pound (224 g) ground beef
½ pound (224 g) ground pork
½ cup (118 mL) finely chopped onion
¼ cup (59 mL) finely chopped bell pepper
2 cloves garlic, peeled and minced
2 tablespoons (30 mL) chopped fresh parsley
1 teaspoon (5 mL) ground paprika
1 teaspoon (5 mL) ground cayenne
½ teaspoon (2.5 mL) ground nutmeg
½ teaspoon (2.5 mL) ground cinnamon
1 egg, beaten
Salt, to taste
Freshly ground black pepper, to taste
All-purpose flour as needed
Olive oil for frying (Spanish virgin olive oil preferred)
Chopped fresh parsley for garnish

1. Cover the bread with water or milk in a bowl and soak until the bread is softened. Remove the bread and squeeze it to remove the liquid.

2. In a large bowl, combine the beef and pork. Add the bread, onion, bell pepper, garlic, parsley, spices, egg, salt, and pepper and mix well. Form the mixture into small (1 tablespoon [15 mL]) balls and roll them in the flour.
3. In a skillet, heat the oil over medium heat. Brown the meatballs in batches over medium heat, shaking the pan frequently so that the balls retain their round shape. Remove the meatballs from the skillet and drain them on paper towels.
4. Add the meatballs to the sauce and simmer, turning occasionally, for 20 to 25 minutes, until they are cooked and the sauce has thickened slightly. Serve the albondigas with the sauce, speared with a toothpick and garnished with the parsley.

Chiles and Garlic Fried in Oil

Yield: 6 servings   Heat Scale: Medium

This Greek dish is served as an appetizer with a loaf of French bread. The diners tear off pieces of the bread and spread the chiles and garlic over it. This dish has big, bold flavors, so it is not for timid diners.

2 red bell peppers, stems and seeds removed, sliced into ¼-inch (.5 cm) rings
3 yellow wax hot chiles, stems left on
3 jalapeños, sliced vertically, stems and seeds removed
6 small onions, peeled
10 cloves garlic, peeled
1 teaspoon (5 mL) crushed dill weed
2 cups (473 mL) olive oil

1. In a large skillet, arrange the bell peppers and chiles in a single layer. Add the rest of the ingredients and heat the skillet over medium-high heat so that the vegetables begin to fry. Turn once and fry for 2 minutes. Reduce the heat to the lowest possible level, cover the skillet, and allow the vegetables to cook until they are all very soft, 45 minutes to an hour. Transfer the vegetables to a bowl and mash them together, removing any stems and the skins of the chiles.

Spiced-Up Spanakopitas

Yield: 8 servings   Heat Scale: Medium

Here is the best version of this Greek appetizer I've had. This is a guaranteed crowd-pleaser—set a few aside for the cook or they'll disappear before you get a taste.

1 (10-ounce (280 g]) package frozen leaf spinach, thawed, squeezed dry, and chopped fine
4 green onions, white and green parts, minced
½ cup (118 mL) minced parsley
⅛ cup (30 mL) minced jalapeño or serrano chiles
½ teaspoon (2.5 mL) minced dill
½ cup (118 mL) crumbled feta cheese
¼ pound (113 g) low-fat cream cheese
2 tablespoons (30 mL) grated Parmesan cheese
2 eggs
½ pound (224 g) filo dough
¼ pound (113 g) butter, melted (or more if needed)

1. Preheat the oven to 350°F (180°C). Grease a baking sheet and line it with foil.
2. In a large bowl, combine the spinach, green onions, parsley, chiles, dill, feta, cream cheese, Parmesan, and eggs. Mix until the texture is smooth, then pour the mixture into a food processor and purée.
3. Unwrap the filo dough and cover it with a slightly dampened towel. Brush 1 sheet with melted butter and then cut it lengthwise into 5 strips. Fold the bottom of the strip over ⅓ of itself. Center ½ teaspoon (2.5 mL) of mixture on the folded end of the strip and fold at 45° angles (as if you were folding a flag) until you have formed a triangle shape. Repeat until all the spanakopitas are formed.
4. Arrange the triangles about 1 inch (2.5 cm) apart on the prepared baking sheet. Brush each triangle with melted butter and bake for 15 minutes or until they are golden brown.

Spanish Chorizo with Pimentón

Yield: About 2 pounds (1.1 kg)   Heat level: Medium

This is the classic Spanish sausage that was later transplanted to Mexico and fla-vored with different chiles. Traditionally, the links are air-dried in a cool place before being refrigerated. For a great breakfast treat, remove the sausage from the casings, crumble it, and fry it in a pan. Add beaten eggs and scramble them with the sausage. Serve with a chile sauce made from pimentón. To make this recipe, you will need a meat grinder with a sausage stuffer attachment. Some versions use other seasonings, such as cinnamon and coriander.

2 pounds (1.1 kg) lean pork, coarsely ground
3 cloves garlic, peeled and mashed in a press
¼ cup (59 mL) vinegar
1 teaspoon (5 mL) oregano
¼ cup (59 mL) hot pimentón (or substitute ⅛ cup [30 mL] red chile powder mixed with ⅛ cup [30 mL] chipotle powder)
1 teaspoon (5 mL) freshly ground black pepper
2 teaspoons (10 mL) salt
¼ teaspoon (1.25 mL) ground cumin
1 teaspoon (5 mL) dried oregano
1 yard (90 cm) sausage casing

1. In a large bowl, combine all the ingredients except the sausage casings. Using the sausage stuffer, force the mixture into the casings and twist off the links and tie them.

Seville-Style Olives
(Aceitunas a la Sevillana)

Yield: 8 servings   Heat Scale: Mild to Medium

Olives, whether whole or in the form of oil, are a very important part of Spanish cui-sine. Spain was occupied by the Moors for 800 years, and the Moorish influence on the architecture, culture, and food of the Iberian Peninsula is evident. The variety of herbs with which they are seasoned leave little doubt as to the Arabic origins of these typically Andalucian olives. (Note: This recipe requires advance preparation.)

1 (7-ounce [196 g]) jar large green Spanish olives
2 piquin chiles, crushed
½ teaspoon (2.5 mL) dried oregano
½ teaspoon (2.5 mL) dried thyme
2 bay leaves
4 cloves garlic, peeled and minced
¼ cup (59 mL) vinegar
1 cup (236 mL) dry sherry or white wine
1 anchovy fillet (optional)

1. Lightly crush the olives, put them in a glass jar, and add the remaining ingredients. Add just enough water to cover the olives. Stir well and marinate in the refrigerator.
2. Occasionally open the jar and stir the ingredients. The olives will take at least a week to marinate, but if you leave them longer, they will get hotter. The olives will keep for about a month in the refrigerator.
3. To serve, drain the olives and allow to warm to room temperature before serving, usually as part of a Spanish antipasto.

Pimientos de Padrón
Yield: 6 servings   Heat Scale: Varies

The heat level of these small, horn-shaped chiles is usually mild, but about 1 in 5 pods is spicy. Their nickname is "Spanish pepper roulette," because you never know how hot a given mouthful will be. You may substitute small, mild jalapeños or serrano chiles.

2 tablespoons (30 mL) olive oil
12 pimientos de Padrón, stems removed (or substitute mild serranos or jalapeños)
Sea or rock salt, to taste
Freshly ground black pepper, to taste

1. In a medium skillet, heat the olive oil over medium heat until hot. Add the chiles and fry, stirring, until they blister and start to turn brown.
2. Remove the chiles from the pan and scrape off their skins with a small knife. Return them to the pan and fry for 1 minute, stirring well.
3. Remove the chiles from the pan and drain them on paper towels. Transfer them to a bowl and add salt and pepper to taste. Stir or toss the chiles to coat.

Champinones al Ajillo (Spanish Garlic Mushrooms)

Yield: 12 servings   Heat Scale: Mild

Mushrooms—fried, grilled, marinated, or stuffed—are a popular tapa ingredient all over Spain. Another popular ingredient is Spanish garlic. Prized around the world for its flavor, it is used abundantly in Spanish cooking. There are many variations of mushrooms and garlic, but this version with chile is one of my favorites. White button mushrooms are traditionally used, but any mushrooms, such as sliced portobello or cremini mushroom, are a good substitute. If you have access to wild mushrooms, they are wonderful in this recipe.

1½ tablespoons (22.5 mL) olive oil (Spanish virgin oil preferred)
1 tablespoon (15 mL) chopped garlic
3 tablespoons (45 mL) finely chopped red bell pepper
½ pound (224 g) mushroom caps, rinsed and drained
3 tablespoons (45 mL) dry sherry
2 teaspoons (10 mL) lemon juice
1 teaspoon (5 mL) crushed red chile
1 tablespoon (15 mL) chopped fresh parsley
Salt, to taste
Freshly ground black pepper, to taste

1. In a heavy frying pan, heat the oil over high heat. Add the garlic and sauté until soft, about 2 minutes. Add the bell pepper and sauté for an additional minute.
2. Add the mushrooms, sherry, lemon juice, and chile. Lower the heat to medium-high and simmer, stirring occasionally. Remove from the heat and serve.

Mechouia

Yield: 4 servings   Heat Scale: Medium

In this traditional North African appetizer, the vegetables can be chopped or very briefly processed in a food processor or blender to make a chunky dip. Either way, serve it with warm, fresh pita bread.

2 large onions, peeled and sliced into thick rounds
2 red bell peppers
4 medium tomatoes
2 small, fresh hot peppers, such as serrano
1 (7-ounce [196 g]) can tuna, packed in water
2 ounces (56 g) crumbled feta cheese
2 hard boiled eggs, chopped
Salt, to taste
Freshly ground black pepper, to taste
3 tablespoons (45 mL) fresh lemon juice
3 tablespoons (45 mL) olive oil
1 teaspoon (5 mL) finely chopped fresh oregano

1. Over the highest flame of your gas range, under a broiler, or on a grill, cook the onions until they soften and the edges char slightly. Transfer them to a plate to cool.
2. Using the same cooking method, char the bell peppers, tomatoes, and hot peppers until they are dark and blistered. Place them in a bowl and cover with a dish towel for 10 minutes. When they are cool enough to handle, remove the stems, seeds, and charred skin, then dice. Dice the onion and combine it with the other vegetables.
3. Place the vegetables on a flat serving platter and top with the tuna, feta, and hard-boiled eggs. Sprinkle with salt and pepper.
4. In a small bowl, stir together the lemon juice, olive oil, and oregano and pour it over the platter.

Madagascar Pili-Pili Dip
Yield: 1½ cups (354 mL) Heat Scale: Extremely Hot

This hearty Madagascar recipe is a paté of sorts: a very hot mixture spread over toast or crackers and served as an appetizer. Pili-pili, like piri-piri, is the Swahili generic for small, hot peppers.

3 tablespoons (45 mL) vegetable oil
12 pili-pili chiles (or substitute other small, hot dried chiles, such as piquins or santakas) or fewer to taste
2 cups (473 mL) chicken livers
1 onion, peeled and minced
3 cloves garlic, peeled and minced
1 tablespoon (15 mL) fresh thyme leaves
2 tablespoons (30 mL) green peppercorns
2 tablespoons (30 mL) minced fresh parsley
1 hard boiled egg, chopped
Salt, to taste

1. In a skillet, heat the oil over medium heat. Add all the other ingredients and sauté until well cooked.
2. Transfer to a blender and blend until smooth.

White Cheese and Tomato "Salad"
Yield: ½ cup (118 mL) Heat Scale: Mild

World traveler Richard Sterling collected this recipe for me in Egypt. He notes, "The Egyptians call any dish of raw vegetables a 'salad' even though we would call this a dip or spread."

8 ounces (224 g) feta cheese
2 teaspoons (10 mL) olive oil
2 teaspoons (10 mL) lemon juice
½ teaspoon (2.5 mL) ground red New Mexican chile
2 tablespoons (30 mL) minced parsley
1 large tomato, finely diced

1. In a bowl, combine the cheese, oil, lemon juice, chile, and parsley and mash it together with a fork. Fold in the tomato. Spread the mixture out on a serving plate and serve with pita toast points, crackers, or other crisp bread.

South African Samosas

Yield: 8 servings   Heat Scale: Mild

A high tea treat in South Africa, this spicy meat pastry of sorts originated in India but was brought to South Africa by railway workers. Feel free to add more heat by increasing the amount of cayenne.

1 pound (454 g) ground beef
3 green bell peppers, stems and seeds removed, chopped
¼ teaspoon (1.25 mL) salt
6 cloves garlic, peeled and finely chopped
2 teaspoons (10 mL) caraway seeds
2 large onions, peeled and finely chopped
1 teaspoon (5 mL) ground cayenne
5 cardamom pods, crushed
1 teaspoon (5 mL) cinnamon
Juice of 2 lemons
1¾ pounds (784 g) all-purpose flour
Vegetable oil for frying

1. Place the ground beef in a large bowl. Add the green peppers, salt, garlic, caraway seeds, onions, cayenne pepper, cardamom, cinnamon, and lemon juice. Mix thoroughly with your hands.
2. Flour a surface suitable for rolling out dough. Place the meat mixture on the floured surface. Knead in the flour, 1 cup (236 mL) at a time, until all of the flour is kneaded in. Form meat-dough balls about the size of a walnut.
3. In a skillet, heat the oil over medium heat. Add the meatballs and fry them on all sides until browned, about 10 to 15 minutes per batch. Drain on paper towels and serve warm.

Smoky Hot Oyster Bites

Yield: 20 oyster bites   Heat Scale: Varies

These snacks from West Africa wrap canned oysters in crisp pastry for a quick and delicious taste sensation that may be served warm or cold.

2 (3.75-ounce [105 g]) cans smoked oysters, drained
1 (17.3-ounce [484 g]) package commercial puff pastry, such as Pepperidge Farms
L'Exotic Sauce Dynamite, to taste (page 90)

1. Preheat the oven to 375°F (190°C). Lightly oil a baking sheet.
2. Roll out the pastry thinly and cut out circles about 3 inches (7.5 cm) in diameter. Place a smoked oyster on each circle. Sprinkle some hot sauce over the oysters. Fold the pastry over and use a little water to seal the edges, crimping lightly with a fork.
3. Arrange the oyster bites on the prepared baking sheets and bake for 15 minutes, until golden brown.

Sesame Dipping Sauce

Yield: 6 servings   Heat Scale: Medium

This Middle Eastern dish is popular in Egypt and Sudan. It contains quite a lot of sesame seeds, which come from one of the oldest plants grown for oil. In eastern North Africa, sesame is called "been" or "simsim." Serve this dip with raw vegetables or crackers.

1 (16-ounce [454 g]) can chickpeas, drained
1 clove garlic, peeled
4 teaspoons (20 mL) sesame seeds
2 teaspoons (10 mL) lemon juice
½ teaspoon (2.5 mL) salt
1 teaspoon (5 mL) ground cayenne
½ teaspoon (2.5 mL) butter, softened

1. Combine the chickpeas and garlic in a blender and grind until smooth.
2. Scrape the mixture into a bowl, add the remaining ingredients, and mix well.

Powerful Plantains

Yield: 4 servings   Heat Scale: Medium

Plantains, those relatives of the banana that are eaten as a vegetable, are cultivated in many African countries. This melange of sweet and hot plantains makes a delicious crunchy appetizer. Serve it with Ugandan Groundnut Sauce (page 91).

2 green plantains
Vegetable oil as needed for frying
1 yellow plantain
½ onion
1 tablespoon (15 mL) garlic powder
¼ teaspoon (1.25 mL) salt, plus more as needed
2 teaspoons (10 mL) ground cayenne

1. Peel one of the green plantains with a vegetable peeler and cut it into very thin rounds.
2. Heat the oil in a large frying pan over medium heat. Fry the plantain rounds for about 3 minutes, turning once, until golden brown. Drain them on paper towels and keep them warm.

3. Coarsely grate the other green plantain and put it on a plate. Slice the onion wafer-thin and mix it with the grated plantain.
4. Heat a little more oil in the frying pan. Fry handfuls of the plaintain-onion mixture for 2 to 3 minutes, until golden, turning once. Drain on paper towels and keep warm with the green plantain rounds.
5. Peel the yellow plantain, cut it in half lengthwise, and dice it. Sprinkle it with the garlic powder, salt, and ground cayenne.
6. Heat more oil in the frying pan over medium heat. Fry the diced plantain in the hot oil until golden brown, turning to brown evenly. Drain on paper towels.
7. Arrange the three varieties of cooked plantains in shallow dishes. Sprinkle with salt and serve as an appetizer with your favorite hot sauce from Chapter 2.

Spicy Cape Kebabs

Yield: 6 servings   Heat Scale: Medium

In South Africa, these delicious kebabs are deliberately made small so that they fit the appetizer designation. Serve them with your favorite hot sauce from Chapter 2.

1 pound (454 g) ground beef
1 egg
3 garlic cloves, peeled and crushed
½ onion, finely chopped
½ teaspoon (2.5 mL) freshly ground black pepper
1½ teaspoons (7.5 mL) ground cumin
1½ teaspoons (7.5 mL) ground coriander
1 teaspoon (5 mL) ground ginger
2 teaspoons (10 mL) garam masala
1 tablespoon (15 mL) lemon juice
1–1½ cups (250–354 mL) fresh white bread crumbs
1 small green chile, such as jalapeño, stems and seeds removed, minced
Salt, to taste
Vegetable oil as needed for deep frying

1. Place the ground beef in a large bowl. Add the egg, garlic, onion, black pepper, cumin, coriander, ginger, garam masala, lemon juice, about 1 cup (236 mL) of the bread crumbs, the chile, and the salt.
2. Using your hands or a wooden spoon, mix the ingredients together until the mixture is firm. If it feels sticky, add more bread crumbs and mix again until firm.
3. In a large, heavy frying pan or deep fryer, heat the oil over high heat. Shape the mixture into balls or fingers and fry, a few at a time, for 5 minutes or until well browned all over.
4. Using a slotted spoon, drain the kebabs and then transfer them to a plate lined with paper towels. Cook the remaining kebabs in the same way and then serve, if you like, with a spicy dip from this chapter or a sauce from Chapter 2.

Mascarene "Hush Puppies"

Yield: 6–8 servings   Heat Scale: Medium

Okay, this is my name for this recipe because it sounds better than "chile balls." The channa dal used here is the common Indian dried yellow split peas that are available in Asian markets. The key to keeping the hush puppies from falling apart is to grind at least half of the soaked peas to a very fine consistency. Serve this as an accompaniment to any African meal. (Note: This recipe requires advance preparation.)

2 cups (473 mL) dried channa dal (dried yellow split peas)
2 red or green jalapeños, stems and seeds removed, minced
2 tablespoons (30 mL) chopped cilantro
2 tablespoons (30 mL) finely chopped green onions
½ teaspoon (2.5 mL) ground cumin
Vegetable oil as needed for frying

1. Wash the dal in a fine-mesh strainer, then transfer it to a bowl and cover with 6 cups (1.42 L) water. Soak for at least 4 hours and preferably overnight.
2. Drain the dal, place half of it in a blender, and process to a fine consistency. Transfer the dal from the blender to a bowl. Place the remaining dal in the blender and process to a medium consistency. Transfer it to the same bowl. Add the remaining jalapeños, cilantro, green onions, and cumin, and mix well.
3. Form the mixture into balls about 1½ inches (3.5 cm) in diameter.
4. In a frying pan or deep fryer, heat enough oil to deep fry the balls over high heat until hot. Fry the balls until they are golden brown. Transfer to paper towels to drain. Serve them hot.

San Jay's Jeera Chicken

Yield: 8 servings   Heat Scale: Varies

San Jay Anand, who owns Madhu's Brilliant Restaurant in Middlesex, England, gave Mary Jane and me a spirited demonstration of this incredibly simple—and amazingly tasty—dish when we stayed at the Shikarbadi Hunting Lodge near Udaipur in India. Jeera Chicken contains only chicken, salt, black pepper, cumin, and butter. He told us it was his father's favorite recipe. A high heat source is essential for this dish, which was cooked for us outdoors over a large gas flame and consequently took only a few minutes to prepare. It is usually served over plain white rice as an appetizer. San Jay notes that this chicken tastes better if the bones are left in. He also says that chileheads are permitted to add red chile powder, which I have done.

1 cup (236 mL) water
1 pound (454 g) butter
2 whole chickens, skin removed, chopped into 3-inch (7.5 cm) pieces
1 tablespoon (15 mL) salt
3 tablespoons (45 mL) ground jeera (cumin)
1 teaspoon (5 mL) cumin seeds
3 tablespoons (45 mL) freshly ground black pepper
1 tablespoon (15 mL) ground red New Mexican chile (optional)

1. In a large pot, heat the water to boiling, then add the butter. When the butter is melted and well mixed with the water, add the chicken and salt. Stir for 2 to 3 minutes over high heat. Then add the ground cumin, cumin seeds, black pepper, and ground red chile, if using, and continue cooking, stirring, for 20 to 25 minutes. The sauce should be almost a paste, and the chicken is usually done when the butter rises to the top of the paste. Cut a piece of chicken open to make sure all the pink is gone from the meat.

Molagi Bajii
(Madras Fried Chile Fritters)

Yield: 4 servings   Heat Scale: Medium

Bajii, the unstuffed Madras version of chiles rellenos, are popular teatime dishes in Madras and other cities of Tamil Nadu. They are often accompanied by a mango chutney, and the taste combination is delicious. Serve with fruit drinks or beer.

2 cups (473 mL) vegetable oil
½ cup (118 mL) corn flour
½ cup (118 mL) rice flour
1 teaspoon (5 mL) salt
½ cup (118 mL) water
2 teaspoons (10 mL) ground cumin
10 green New Mexican chiles, roasted and peeled, stems on, slit lengthwise on one side

1. Heat the oil in a skillet or wok over low heat.
2. Combine the flours and the salt in a bowl and add a teaspoon (5 mL) of the warm oil. Blend in the water and whisk to make a thick batter.
3. Turn the heat under the skillet or wok to high.
4. Rub the ground cumin inside the chiles and dip them in the batter. Reduce the heat to medium and fry the chiles for 2 minutes, turning once, or until they are golden brown all over.

Jungli Mans

Yield: 4–6 servings   Heat Scale: Hot

In the Mewari language of Rajasthan, jungli mans refers to a dish that would be prepared by a stranded hunter who only had the basics with him. It is amazingly tasty, considering the limited ingredients. It is also quite hot, so serve it with some plain white rice.

2 cups (473 mL) ghee (clarified butter; or substitute vegetable oil)
2 pounds (1.1 kg) lamb, cut into 1-inch (2.5 cm) cubes
10 lal mirch chiles (or substitute dried cayennes or mirasol), stems removed, left whole
2 teaspoons (10 mL) salt

1. In a pot, heat the ghee or oil over medium heat. Add the meat and cook, stirring constantly, for 10 minutes. Add the whole chiles and salt and continue cooking. Add water as necessary to make sure that the meat neither fries nor boils, but is essentially braised. Continue cooking until the meat is tender, stirring occasionally, about an hour more. Remove the chiles before serving.

Sina Aur Alu
(Fried Spare Ribs with Potatoes)

Yield: 6 servings   Heat Scale: Medium

This moderately spicy dish, which originated in the Punjab region, is traditionally cooked with lamb, but it is just as delicious with pork or beef. It is served as an appetizer, followed by a rice and meat curry.

1 pound (454 g) spare ribs (beef, pork, or lamb), cut into 1-inch (2.5 cm) long pieces
1 teaspoon (5 mL) ground cardamom
1 (1-inch [2.5 cm]) cinnamon stick, crushed
12 black peppercorns, crushed
2 onions, peeled and finely chopped
6 cloves garlic, peeled and finely minced
3 cups (708 mL) water, divided
4 large potatoes, chopped
Salt, to taste
1 teaspoon (5 mL) ground cayenne
1 teaspoon (5 mL) ground cumin
1 teaspoon (5 mL) ground coriander
1 teaspoon (5 mL) ground turmeric
4 green chiles, such as serranos, stems removed and finely minced
½ cup (118 mL) cilantro or mint leaves
4 eggs
1 cup (236 mL) dry bread crumbs
4 cups (.95 L) olive or vegetable oil

1. In a large, covered skillet, cook the spare ribs, cardamom, cinnamon, black peppercorns, onions, garlic, and 1 cup (236 mL) of the water over medium heat for 15 minutes or until all the water has evaporated.
2. Meanwhile, boil the potatoes in a pot with the remaining 2 cups (473 mL) water for about 12 minutes. Drain the potatoes and let them cool. When cool enough to handle, peel them and mash them well. Add a pinch of the salt, cayenne red pepper, cumin, coriander, turmeric, chiles, and cilantro or mint. Mix well.
3. Divide the potato mixture into portions equal to the number of spare ribs. Flatten each portion lightly. Coat each spare rib with the potato mixture.
4. Beat the eggs well with salt; add the breadcrumbs.

5. In a deep skillet, heat the oil over high heat for about 3 minutes, then lower the heat. Take a few spare ribs at a time, dip them into the egg batter, and fry them until they turn golden brown. Drain them on paper towels and serve.

Be Sipyan
(Spicy Duck Appetizer for Six)

Yield: 6 servings   Heat Scale: Mild

In parts of Burma, duck meat is a prized delicacy. This recipe combines the heat of jalapeño chiles with the sweetness of curry. For best results, serve this appetizer warm.

1 (4–5 pound [1.8–2.3 kg]) duck, with giblets
4 cloves garlic, peeled and thinly sliced
1 teaspoon (5 mL) curry powder
1 jalapeño chile, minced
½ teaspoon (2.5 mL) salt
1 teaspoon (5 mL) lemon juice
1 teaspoon (5 mL) lime juice
1 teaspoon (5 mL) shrimp paste
1 tablespoon (15 mL) peanut oil
1 (½-inch [1 cm]) piece fresh ginger, peeled and thinly sliced
1 cup (236 mL) sliced onions
1 tablespoon (15 mL) soy sauce
¼ teaspoon (1.25 mL) ground turmeric
2½ cups (591 mL) water

1. Cut the duck into 8 pieces, removing the loose skin and fat. Dry the duck pieces on paper towels and set aside.
2. In a large mixing bowl, combine the garlic, curry, jalapeño, salt, lemon juice, lime juice, shrimp paste, peanut oil, ginger, onions, soy sauce, and ground turmeric. Add the duck pieces to the mixture, coating each piece completely with the marinade. Place the bowl in the refrigerator and marinate the duck for 30 minutes.
3. Transfer the duck and marinade to a large pan and cook over medium heat for 5 minutes, then reduce the heat to low. Add 1 cup (236 mL) of the water and stir well. Cover the pan and cook the duck for 30 minutes.
4. Add the remaining 1½ cups (354 mL) water and continue to cook the duck over low heat for about 45 minutes. When the duck is done, the meat should be tender, and the water will have evaporated into a thick, spicy sauce. Pour off any excess oil, transfer the duck to a platter, and serve with white rice.

Indonesian Chicken, Shrimp, and Pineapple Satay
Yield: 4 servings   Heat Scale: Medium

My friends from the Golden Dragon Restaurant in Colorado Springs,
Colorado, sent me this excellent appetizer recipe.

For the Satay:
1 tablespoon (15 mL) soy sauce
1 tablespoon (15 mL) molasses
1 tablespoon (15 mL) curry powder
1 teaspoon (5 mL) ground cayenne
1 teaspoon (5 mL) commercial minced garlic
2 tablespoons (30 mL) lime juice
2 boneless, skinless chicken breasts, cubed
6 jumbo shrimp, shelled and deveined
1 cup (236 mL) cubed fresh pineapple
1 cup (236 mL) cubed red bell pepper

1. Combine all the ingredients in a bowl and marinate for 15 minutes in
the refrigerator.
2. Thread the chicken, shrimp, pineapple, and bell pepper on skewers and
grill or broil until browned and done.

For the Peanut Sauce:
1 cup (236 mL) chicken stock
½ cup (118 mL) peanut butter
¼ cup (59 mL) unsweetened shredded coconut
½ teaspoon (2.5 mL) ground cumin
½ teaspoon (2.5 mL) ground coriander
½ teaspoon (2.5 mL) minced garlic
½ teaspoon (2.5 mL) ground hot red chile

1. Combine all the ingredients in a bowl and mix well. Transfer to a sauce
pan and cook over medium heat until it thickens, stirring often.
2. Serve the satay with the peanut sauce for dipping.

Cha Gio
(Fried Crab and Pork Rolls)

Yield: 24 servings   Heat Scale: Medium

*This appetizer is very popular in Vietnam, especially with Westerners as tour-
ism increases in this part of Southeast Asia. Traditionally, the rolls are made with
Vietnamese rice paper. However, since I have found rice paper wrappers difficult to
locate, I have substituted Chinese spring roll wrappers.*

8 ounces (224 g) cellophane noodles
1 small onion, peeled and minced
6 green onions, minced
7 ounces (198 g) minced pork
7 ounces (198 g) flaky crab meat
½ teaspoon (2.5 mL) salt
1 tablespoon (15 mL) fish sauce (nam pla)
¼ teaspoon (1.25 mL) freshly ground black pepper
1 teaspoon (5 mL) ground cayenne
4 Chinese spring roll wrappers
Vegetable oil as needed for deep frying (peanut oil preferred)
Nuoc Cham (Vietnamese Dipping Sauce; page 96)

1. Soak the cellophane noodles in water for 10 minutes, then drain and
measure out ½ cup (118 mL) of the noodles. Cut the noodles into 1-inch
(2.5 cm) lengths. In a mixing bowl, combine the noodles, onions, green
onions, pork, crab, salt, fish sauce, pepper, and cayenne. Stir well and set
aside.
2. Cut each spring roll wrapper in half. Place 2 teaspoons (10 mL) of filling on one end and roll it up, turning in the sides so that the filling is
completely enclosed. Moisten the edge of the wrapper with a little water
to make it stick, and press the end down to seal the roll. Repeat with the
remaining wrappers and filling.
3. When all of the rolls are assembled, heat the oil in a wok over medium
heat until quite hot. Fry the rolls, a few at a time, until they are crisp and
light brown. Transfer the fried rolls to paper towels to drain. Place the
Nuoc Cham in small bowls and serve it with the spring rolls.

Bahn Mi Chien Tom
(Fiery Shrimp Toast)

Yield: 24 small servings   Heat Scale: Hot

No matter the country, just about everyone is glad to have a technique to turn not-so-fresh bread into something wonderful. This Vietnamese appetizer is best when made with two-day-old bread.

12 slices stale bread
½ cup (118 mL) shrimp paste
3 fresh piquin chiles, seeds removed, minced (or substitute any small, hot chile)
Vegetable oil as needed for deep frying (peanut oil preferred)
Fresh mint leaves for garnish
2 small cucumbers, peeled and sliced into small rounds
Nuoc Cham (Vietnamese Dipping Sauce; page 96)

1. Trim off the crusts and cut each piece of bread in half lengthwise. Place the shrimp paste in a small bowl and mix in the piquins. Spread each piece of bread with the shrimp-chile paste.
2. Fill a deep skillet with enough oil for deep frying. Heat the oil over high heat until it is barely bubbling, then put in the bread, shrimp-side down, a few pieces at a time. Fry the bread until it is light brown, transferring each piece to paper towels to drain after it is fried. Top each piece with a mint leaf and a cucumber slice and serve immediately.

Pazoon Lone-Jaun
(Fancy Burmese Shrimp Puffs)

Yield: 12 servings   Heat Scale: Medium

These Burmese shrimp balls may seem similar to the Chinese version, but they are much more delicate and moist, and thus I think they are better! A traditional fritter-type appetizer, these may be made with just about any kind of fish that you enjoy.

½ cup (118 mL) lightly salted butter, at room temperature
2 onions, peeled and quartered
2 pounds (1.1 kg) raw medium shrimp, shelled and deveined
¼ cup (59 mL) cornstarch
¼ cup (59 mL) chopped fresh cilantro
2 tablespoons (30 mL) dry vermouth
3 jalapeño chiles, stems and seeds removed, minced
2 tablespoons (30 mL) chopped red bell pepper
¼ teaspoon (1.25 mL) ground cayenne
¼ teaspoon (1.25 mL) kosher salt
4 egg whites, at room temperature
Peanut oil as needed for frying

1. Place the butter and onions in a food processor, and process until the onions are finely minced. Add the shrimp, a few at a time, and process until the mixture becomes a paste. Be careful not to over-process. Scrape the paste into a small mixing bowl and stir in the cornstarch, cilantro, vermouth, jalapeños, red bell peppers, cayenne, and salt, and mix well. Set the paste aside.

2. Place the egg whites in a small mixing bowl and beat them with an electric mixer until small peaks form. Gently fold the egg whites into the shrimp mixture. Place the mixture in the refrigerator, covered, until you are ready to use it. Place a platter in the refrigerator to chill at the same time.

3. In a large, heavy, saucepan, pour in enough oil to a depth of about 2½ inches (6 cm). Heat the oil to 350°F (180°C).

5. Preheat the oven to the lowest temperature. Loosely cover a baking sheet with foil.

4. Remove the shrimp mixture and the platter from the refrigerator. Fill a small bowl with cold water. Dip a teaspoon into the cold water, then scoop out a heaping spoonful of the shrimp mixture. Place the shrimp balls on the platter as you make them. Make sure to dip the teaspoon each time into the cold water between scoops.

5. Using a slotted spoon, gently place the balls in to the oil, making sure that they do not touch each other. Fry the puffs until they are golden brown, checking after 2 minutes and turning to make sure each side is browned. Carefully transfer each puff to a plate lined with paper towels to drain Transfer the drained puffs to the prepared baking sheet and place the baking sheet in the oven to keep them warm. Continue the frying and draining process until all of the shrimp mixture is used.

Ukoy
(Sweet Potato and Shrimp Squash Cakes)

Yield: About 10 cakes   Heat Scale: Medium

Fried cakes are a staple appetizer in the Philippines. For a veritable taste explosion, serve the cakes with Sambal Timun (Pineapple, Cucumber, and Chile Condiment; page 41).

½ cup (118 mL) hot water
12 medium raw shrimp in their shells
1 teaspoon (5 mL) annatto seeds
1 teaspoon (5 mL) salt
1 cup (236 mL) all-purpose flour
1 cup (236 mL) cornstarch
2 cloves garlic, peeled and minced
3 fresh piquin chiles, seeds removed, minced (or substitute any small, hot chile)
1 large sweet potato, peeled and grated
1 medium acorn squash, peeled, halved, seeded, and coarsely grated
2 cups (473 mL) vegetable oil
¼ cup (59 mL) finely chopped green onions
Sambal Timun (page 41)

1. Combine the water, shrimp, annatto seeds, and salt in a heavy sauce pan. Bring the mixture to a boil over high heat, stirring well. Reduce the heat to a low simmer and cook for 2 to 3 minutes, or until the shrimp turn pink. With a slotted spoon, transfer the shrimp to paper towels to drain, then pour the cooking liquid through a sieve into a bowl. Measure the liquid, and add enough water to make 1¼ cups (295 mL). Set aside. Shell and devein the shrimp.

2. In a deep mixing bowl, combine the flour and the cornstarch. Pour in the reserved cooking liquid and beat until it is absorbed. Add the garlic, chiles, sweet potato, and squash, and beat vigorously until the mixture is well combined.

3. Pour the oil into a heavy skillet. Heat the oil over high heat until it is very hot but not smoking. To make each cake, spoon about ⅓ cup (79 mL) of the vegetable mixture onto a saucer. Next, sprinkle a teaspoon or two (5–10 mL) of the green onion on top and lightly press a shrimp into the center. Then, holding the saucer close to the surface of the hot oil, use a spoon to slide the cake into it. Spoon hot oil over the cake. Fry the cakes, 3 to 4 at a time, for about 3 minutes, then turning them carefully with a spatula. Repeat the same process on the other side. Once the cakes are browned on both sides, transfer them to a paper towel to drain. Arrange the cakes shrimp-side up on a platter. Serve immediately with the sambal.

Lime Oysters with Garlic

Yield: 6–8 servings   Heat Scale: Medium

This Cambodian delicacy is one of many oyster-based recipes from Southeast Asia. The oysters are served in soups, simmered in miso and sake, and in a variety of other delicious ways. The meat of pearl oysters is said to be exceptionally tasty.

36 large fresh oysters, in their shells
1½ tablespoons (22.5 mL) vegetable oil
1 tablespoon (15 mL) minced garlic
1 teaspoon (5 mL) minced fresh piquin chiles (or substitute any small, hot chiles)
1 teaspoon (5 mL) minced fresh ginger
1 teaspoon (5 mL) ground turmeric
2 teaspoons (10 mL) minced lemongrass
¼ cup (59 mL) lime juice
¼ cup (59 mL) lemon juice
½ cup (118 mL) fish sauce (nam pla)
½ teaspoon (2.5 mL) salt
½ teaspoon (2.5 mL) freshly ground black pepper
1 teaspoon (5 mL) sugar
1 tablespoon (15 mL) finely minced mint leaves

1. Open the oysters over a dish to save their liquid. Remove and discard the top shells, loosening the oysters. Keep the bottom shells.

2. In a small pan, heat the oil over medium heat. Add the garlic, chile, ginger, turmeric, and lemongrass and fry gently for 3 minutes, stirring often. In a separate small pan, mix together the lime juice, lemon juice, fish sauce, salt, pepper, and sugar. Add the reserved oyster liquid and cook over medium heat until hot, stirring frequently. Poach the oysters in this mixture for 30 seconds. Return the oysters to their shells with some of the sauce and the fried mixture. Garnish each oyster with the chopped mint.

Ech Nau Ca-Ri
(Curried Frogs' Legs)

Yield: 4 servings   Heat Scale: Medium

This Vietnamese appetizer is sure to get any party hopping. All frog jokes aside, this dish is spicy and smooth, and doesn't taste like chicken! If you're watching your calories, substitute light coconut milk or half-and-half for the heavy cream. (Note: This recipe requires advance preparation.)

4 pairs of large frogs' legs, trimmed
1 stalk fresh lemongrass or 1 tablespoon (15 mL) dried lemongrass
2 fresh piquin chiles, seeded and chopped (or substitute any small, hot chiles)
3 shallots, peeled and sliced
3 cloves garlic, peeled and minced
1½ teaspoons (7.5 mL) sugar
1 teaspoon (5 mL) Gaeng Ped (Red Curry Paste; page 37; or substitute commercial curry paste)
2 teaspoons (10 mL) curry powder
¼ teaspoon (1.25 mL) salt
2 tablespoons (30 mL) Nuoc Cham (Vietnamese Dipping Sauce; page 96), divided
2 ounces (57 g) cellophane noodles
2 tablespoons (30 mL) peanut oil
1 small onion, peeled and chopped
1 cup (236 mL) chicken broth
½ cup (118 mL) coconut cream or heavy cream
1 teaspoon (5 mL) cornstarch
2 limes, quartered

1. Cut the frogs' legs into bite-sized pieces. Rinse them with cold water, pat dry with paper towels, and refrigerate. If you are using fresh lemongrass, peel away the outer leaves and cut away everything but the lower part of the stalk. Cut this part into thin slices, then mince. If you are using dried lemongrass, soak it in warm water for 1 hour, then drain and mince.
2. In a food processor, combine the lemongrass, chiles, shallots, garlic, sugar, curry paste, curry powder, salt, and 1 tablespoon (15 mL) of the Nuoc Cham. Process the ingredients to a very fine paste. Remove the frogs' legs from the refrigerator and rub the paste over them. Cover the legs and return them to the refrigerator for 30 minutes.
3. While the legs are marinating, soak the noodles in water for 30 minutes, then drain them and cut them into 2-inch (5 cm) lengths.

4. Heat the oil in a large skillet over medium heat. Add the onion and sauté it until it is translucent. Add the frogs' legs to the oil, and brown well on all sides, about 3 to 4 minutes. Add the chicken broth and bring to a boil. Reduce the heat, cover, and simmer for 15 minutes.
5. Add the coconut cream (or whatever variation you have chosen) and leave the lid off. In a bowl, add 1 tablespoon (15 mL) cold water and the remaining Nuoc Cham to the cornstarch and stir well. Add the cornstarch mixture to the skillet and cook, stirring, until the mixture thickens. Add the cellophane noodles and bring the mixture to a boil. Remove from the heat, transfer to a platter, and garnish with the lime wedges. This dish is also great over rice.

Miang Khum
(Spinach Leaf Wraps with Roasted Coconut)
Yield: 30 servings   Heat Scale: Varies

Foo Swasdee, a restaurant owner and sauce manufacturer in Austin, Texas, offers a unique and very flavorful Indonesian appetizer that should be made a few hours before your party or dinner.

30 fresh spinach leaves, cleaned and dried
¾ cup (177 mL) unsweetened coconut flakes, toasted
1 tablespoon (15 mL) diced fresh lime
1 tablespoon (15 mL) minced shallot
1 tablespoon (15 mL) minced garlic
1 tablespoon (15 mL) minced fresh ginger
½ cup (118 mL) roasted peanuts
1½ teaspoons (7.5 mL) minced fresh Thai chiles
½ cup (118 mL) prepared Asian coconut-based hot sauce

1. Arrange the spinach leaves flat on a serving platter. Place 2 to 3 peanuts, 1 teaspoon (5 mL) toasted coconut, and a few pieces each of the lime, shallot, garlic, ginger, peanuts, and chiles in the center of each spinach leaf.
2. To serve, add ½ teaspoon (2.5 mL) of the Asian hot sauce to each spinach leaf; wrap the leaf around the filling, and eat the whole topped leaf in one bite. This results in an explosion of delicious and varied flavors and textures.

Singapore Meat Dumplings

Yield: 24 dumplings   Heat Scale: Hot

These dumplings add a festive touch to any gathering. They are especially good served with a variety of the Asian dipping sauces in Chapter 2.

8 purple cabbage leaves, blanched
9 ounces (252 g) ground lean pork
1 tablespoon (15 mL) minced green onions
2 red jalapeño chiles, stems and seeds removed, minced
½ teaspoon (2.5 mL) minced garlic
1 tablespoon (15 mL) light soy sauce
1 tablespoon (15 mL) ginger juice (squeezed from fresh ginger)
⅛ teaspoon (.6 mL) minced ginger
1 tablespoon (15 mL) cornstarch
2 tablespoons (30 mL) sesame oil
1 teaspoon (5 mL) sugar
½ teaspoon (2.5 mL) freshly ground black pepper
8 commercial spring roll wrappers

1. Place four of the cabbage leaves in a steamer basket and set aside. Finely chop the other four leaves and put them in a medium-sized mixing bowl. Add the pork, green onions, chiles, garlic, soy sauce, ginger juice, ginger, cornstarch, sesame oil, sugar, and pepper. Mix well.

2. Place the spring roll wrappers on a plate and cut each wrapper in half. Place a heaping teaspoon (7.5 mL) of the filling in the center of each wrapper, then gather up the edges of the wrapper and twist them together to a point. Place the dumplings in the steamer on the cabbage leaves. Steam for about 18 minutes.

Tempa Tempa
(Fried Coconut Triangles)

Yield: 8 triangles   Heat Scale: Medium

Padang, Sumatra, is where you'll find these sweet and meaty treats. Make sure you use heavy-duty foil to prepare this recipe, as the triangles must be firmly packed.

5 shallots, peeled and sliced, divided
½ teaspoon (2.5 mL) ground turmeric
2 fresh piquin chiles, seeded and minced (or substitute any small, hot chiles)
1 teaspoon (5 mL) minced fresh ginger
1 clove garlic, peeled and sliced
1 teaspoon (5 mL) salt
¼ teaspoon (1.25 mL) freshly ground black pepper
1 tablespoon (15 mL) dried shrimp
2 cups (473 mL) grated coconut
1 tablespoon (15 mL) rice flour
Corn oil as needed for deep frying

1. In a food processor, blend 3 of the shallots, the turmeric, chiles, ginger, garlic, salt, pepper, and shrimp into a paste. Transfer the paste to a mixing bowl and mix in the remaining 2 shallots, the coconut, and the rice flour.
2. Cut out 8 (3½-inch [8.5 cm]) squares of aluminum foil, fold them in half diagonally into triangles, and fold over and pinch together the top and bottom edges along 2 of the open sides of each triangle, forming pockets with 1 open side. Fill each triangle with about ⅓ cup (79 mL) of the mixture and press them together firmly between your palms, so that the mix will stick together when removed from the foil pouch. Refrigerate until ready to use.
3. Heat the oil in a wok over medium heat. Carefully remove the coconut triangles from the foil and fry them in batches. Turn them over to brown on all sides, then transfer them to paper towels to drain.

Mendoan
(Tempeh Pancakes)

Yield: 12 servings   Heat Scale: Medium

This dish is a cocktail-hour appetizer in Indonesia. These fried squares offer an interesting texture as they are soft and not crispy. Tempeh is available in Asian markets and natural foods stores.

6 macadamia nuts
5 shallots, peeled and sliced
3 serrano or jalapeño chiles, seeded and minced
2 cloves garlic, peeled and sliced
⅛ teaspoon (.6 mL) ground turmeric
½ teaspoon (2.5 mL) salt
1 teaspoon (5 mL) ground coriander
2 cups (473 mL) rice flour
4 cups (.95 L) coconut milk
1 egg, beaten
5 green onion, dark green parts only, sliced thinly
2 pounds (1.1 kg) tempeh
Peanut oil as needed for deep frying

1. In a food processor, finely chop the nuts. Add the shallots, jalapeños, garlic, turmeric, salt, and coriander and blend to form a smooth paste.
2. In a large mixing bowl, mix together the rice flour, coconut milk, and egg until smooth. Add the paste and the green onions and mix well. The batter should be thin. Cut the tempeh into 2 × 3–inch (5 × 7.5 cm) slices ⅛-inch (.25 cm) thick. In a deep skillet, heat the oil over high heat. Dip the tempeh in the batter and fry it in batches until the tempeh is firm but not brown.

Spicy Mixed Satays

Yield: 8–10 servings   Heat Scale: Medium

Probably the most famous of all Indonesian dishes are the satays. They can be served as an appetizer or as an entrée. You will need to soak the wooden skewers overnight or for a couple of hours to prevent them from burning while grilling. This recipe comes from Bali.

For the Satay Sauce:
½ cup (118 mL) roasted and salted peanuts
1 onion, peeled and chopped
½ cup (118 mL) smooth peanut butter
2 cloves garlic, peeled and minced
⅓ cup (79 mL) chutney
¼ cup (59 mL) peanut oil
1 tablespoon (15 mL) light soy sauce
¼ cup (59 mL) lemon juice
6 dried birdseye chiles (chiltepins or piquins), stems removed, soaked in water, finely minced

1. In a blender or food processor, grind the peanuts until finely chopped, but not ground smooth. Add the onion and process for another 20 seconds. Add the peanut butter, garlic, chutney, oil, soy sauce, lemon juice, and chile and continue to process until smooth.

For the Satays:
1 pound (454 g) steak, cut in thin strips
6 large chicken breast fillets, cut in 1–1½ inch (2.5–3.5 cm) cubes
1 pound (454 g) pork fillet or boned pork loin, cut in 1–1½ inch (2.5–3.5 cm) cubes

1. Thread the meats onto wooden skewers. Don't combine the meats—use one type of meat on each skewer. Brush the meats well with the Satay Sauce and grill the satays until tender, brushing occasionally with the sauce while cooking.
2. Serve with the remaining Satay Sauce for dipping

Garlic Cheese

Yield: 3 cups (708 mL)   Heat Scale: Medium

Called pikantny syr ("spicy cheese") in Russian, this is a popular appetizer in Siberia and the Russian Far East. Russia expert and one of my longtime writers Sharon Hudgins contributed this recipe.

½ pound (224 g) medium-sharp white cheddar cheese, finely shredded
½ pound (224 g) Emmentaler cheese, finely shredded
¼ cup (59 mL) pure sour cream (containing no additives)
¼ cup (59 mL) full-fat mayonnaise
8–10 large cloves garlic, pressed
½ teaspoon (2.5 mL) ground cayenne or hot paprika, or more to taste
¼ teaspoon (1.25 mL) salt

1. Toss the shredded cheeses by hand in a large bowl.
2. In a small bowl, mix together the sour cream, mayonnaise, pressed garlic, cayenne or paprika, and salt in a small bowl. Add this mixture to the cheese, stirring to mix well. Cover and refrigerate at least 4 hours (and preferably overnight) to let the flavors meld.
3. Let the cheese mixture come to room temperature before serving. Use as a stuffing for small firm-ripe tomatoes or cherry tomatoes, as a topping for baked potatoes, or as a spread for dark bread.

SIX

Sizzling Salads

The wide range of spicy salad styles around the world is astonishing, and some of them are not even vegetarian. Just about any fruit, vegetable, and green you can think of will combine with the worldwide chile pepper selection to create these salads, usually expanding the conventional notion of what a salad is. These recipes are arranged region by region, west to east.

Nicaraguan Jalapeño Pork Salad

Yield: 6–8 servings   Heat Scale: Medium

In Latin America, pork is often treated with a generous squeeze of lime. The citrus flavors serve as a wake-up call to the flavors of the meat and work well with the heat of the jalapeño.

2 pounds (1.1 kg) boneless pork butt or shoulder, cut into 1-inch (2.5 cm) cubes
1½ quarts (1.42 L) plus ½ cup (118 mL) water, divided
Salt, to taste
Freshly ground black pepper, to taste
1 large tomato, cored
2 tablespoons (30 mL) vegetable oil
4 tablespoons (60 mL) lime juice, divided
3 cups (708 mL) finely shredded cabbage
½ cup (118 mL) finely chopped onion
3 or 4 fresh jalapeño chiles, stems and seeds removed, minced
1 pound (454 g) new potatoes, peeled and cut into ½-inch (1 cm) slices
Lime wedges for garnish

1. Preheat the oven to 400°F (200°C).
2. Place the pork in a 10 × 15–inch (25 × 37.5 cm) roasting pan. Add ½ cup (118 mL) of the water. Cover the pan tightly with aluminum foil and bake until the meat is very tender when pierced, about 1 hour. Uncover and continue roasting, stirring occasionally, until all the liquid has evaporated and the meat is well browned, about 15 minutes longer. Add salt and pepper to taste.
3. While the meat cooks, cut 2 wedges from the tomato and dice the remainder. In a large bowl, combine the diced tomato, oil, 3 tablespoons (45 mL) of the lime juice, the cabbage, and salt and pepper to taste. Cover and chill.
4. In a small bowl, mix together the remaining 1 tablespoon (15 mL) lime juice, the onion, and the chiles. Cover and chill.
5. About 25 minutes before the meat is finished cooking, bring the remaining 1½ quarts (1.42 L) water to a boil in a 3 to 4 quart (3 to 4 L) pan. Add the potatoes, cover, and simmer until the potatoes are tender when pierced (they may break apart slightly), about 10 to 15 minutes. Drain the potatoes.
6. When meat is well browned, use a slotted spoon to transfer it to a serving platter. Arrange the cabbage salad and hot potatoes next to it. Garnish with the tomato wedges. Serve the chile-onion salsa in a bowl with lime wedges for garnish.

Variation
Toss the pork with the cabbage salad and garnish with the potatoes.

Jicama and Orange Salad

Yield: 4–6 servings   Heat Scale: Medium

Jicama is a Central American root crop with a refreshing texture and a flavor reminiscent of apples. Here is Nancy Gerlach's recipe from a Nicaraguan friend.

Juice of 2 limes
¼ teaspoon (1.25 mL) ground habanero chile (or substitute ground cayenne)
2 small oranges, cut in segments
1 small jicama, julienned
3 green onions, thinly sliced
Chopped fresh cilantro for garnish

1. Combine the lime juice and habanero powder in a small bowl.
2. Arrange the orange segments on a platter and top with the jicama and onions. Pour the lime juice mixture over the salad, garnish with the cilantro, and serve.

Ensalada con Quinoa de Peru (Peruvian Quinoa Salad)

Yield: 6–8 servings.   Heat Scale: Medium

Quinoa is a very versatile grain. It can be added to soups, stews, and salads for additional nutrition and texture. It was a staple of the Incas, who called it "the mother grain." Quinoa grows successfully at high altitudes and was cultivated on the terraces of Machu Picchu. It is still an important food in Peru, Bolivia, and Ecuador. Its flavor has been compared to couscous or wild rice. In the United States, it is commonly available in natural food supermarkets and health food stores in several forms: the whole grain, flour, and pasta. Some nutritionists call it a complete protein because it contains all eight essential amino acids.

2 cups (473 mL) dried quinoa
8½ cups (2 L) cold water
⅓ cup (79 mL) fresh lime juice
2 fresh aji chiles, stems and seeds removed, finely chopped (or substitute yellow wax hot, jalapeño, or serrano)
⅔ cup (158 mL) olive oil
2 medium cucumbers, peeled, seeded, and cut into ½-inch (1 cm) cubes
1 large ripe tomato, seeded and cubed
8 green onions, white part only, thinly sliced
⅓ cup (79 mL) minced Italian parsley
⅓ cup (79 mL) minced fresh mint
Salt, to taste
Freshly ground black pepper, to taste
2 heads Bibb lettuce, shredded, for garnish (optional)
3 hard-boiled eggs, thinly sliced, for garnish (optional)
2 fresh ears of corn, cooked and cut into 2-inch (5 cm) rounds, for garnish (optional)
1 cup (236 mL) black olives, thickly sliced, for garnish (optional)

1. Rinse the quinoa thoroughly under cold running water. Keep rinsing until the water runs clear. In a large pan, combine the quinoa with the water. Bring the quinoa to a boil, then reduce the heat to a simmer and cook for 10 minutes, or until all the grains are translucent. Drain the quinoa, transfer it to a large bowl, and chill.

2. In a small bowl, whisk together the lime juice, chiles, and olive oil and set aside.

3. When the quinoa is cool, add the cucumbers, tomato, green onions, parsley, and mint and mix gently. Pour the lime juice mixture over the top of the quinoa-vegetable mixture and toss again. Add salt and pepper to taste.

4. To serve, mound the shredded Bibb lettuce on 6 or 8 individual plates and garnish with any or all of the suggested garnishes.

Ensalada de Flor de Calabaza con Vinagre Enchilado (Squash Blossom Salad with Chile Vinegar)

Yield: 1 cup (236 mL) vinegar; 4 servings of salad
Heat Scale: Medium

According to my friend Lula Bertrán in Mexico City, "We use squash blossoms very often in our recipes. We think they are very Mexican. What I wanted to do in this recipe was use my chile vinegar because everyone loves it so much. The vinegar will work in any kind of salad." (Note that the vinegar must sit for at least two days, so this recipe requires advance preparation.)

For the Chile Vinegar:
1 cup (236 mL) apple cider vinegar
2 cloves garlic, peeled
6 black peppercorns
6 white peppercorns
6 green peppercorns
1 chile de arbol (or substitute ½ New Mexican chile)
4 chiltepins (or substitute chile piquins)
1 serrano chile, seeds and stem removed, halved
1 sprig fresh basil
2 sprigs fresh rosemary
1 bay leaf

1. Combine all the ingredients in a bottle. Cover and let sit in a cool place for at least 2 days and preferably 1 month.

For the Squash Blossom Salad:
1½ cups (354 mL) julienned jicama
1 bunch watercress
5 ounces (140 g) mixed lettuce leaves
8 large squash blossoms, minced (or substitute other edible flowers)
½ cup (118 mL) sesame oil
½ teaspoon (2.5 mL) roasted sesame seeds
½ cup (118 mL) Chile Vinegar
Salt, to taste
Freshly ground black pepper, to taste
½ cup (118 mL) grated goat cheese

1. Place the julienned jicama in a cross-hatched pattern on the center of each of 4 salad plates. Cover partially with the watercress and lettuce leaves. Sprinkle on the minced squash blossoms.
2. In a jar, mix together the sesame oil, sesame seeds, Chile Vinegar, salt, and pepper. Lightly pour the dressing over the salads. Top with the goat cheese.

Ensalada de Garbanzos (Chickpea Salad)
Yield: 4 servings   Heat Scale: Mild

Serve this delicious Sonoran-style dish over shredded mixed greens to accompany one of the fish dishes in Chapter 11. I recommend using freshly cooked chickpeas, but the canned variety will also work if they are thoroughly rinsed. (Note: This recipe requires advance preparation.)

Juice of 1 lemon
Juice of 2 limes
¼ cup (59 mL) minced cilantro
¼ cup (59 mL) olive oil
¾ cup (177 mL) minced onion
2½ cups (591 mL) cooked chickpeas
6 ounces (168 g) cream cheese, softened
2 poblano chiles, roasted, peeled, stems and seeds removed, chopped fine
5 ounces (140 g) mixed greens

1. In a medium-sized glass bowl, mix together the citrus juices, cilantro, olive oil, and onion. Allow to stand at room temperature for 3 hours.
2. In a small bowl, combine the cooked chickpeas, softened cream cheese, and chiles and mix thoroughly. Add this mixture to the marinated citrus mixture and mix thoroughly.
3. Serve over shredded, mixed greens.

Solomon Gundy

Yield: 6–8 servings   Heat Scale: Medium

According to Caribbean food expert Cristine Mackie, Solomon Gundy was brought to the West Indies from England in the early 1600s. An old saying associated with the dish says, "you always make Solomon Gundy of such things that you have according to your fancy." No one seems to know who Solomon was or why a Caribbean salad was named after him. In the spirit of the dish, feel free to experiment with the ingredients. If salted herrings are not available, use a dozen or so anchovies. (Note: This recipe requires advanced preparation.)

1 pound (454 g) salted herring or other fish
1 pound (454 g) cold cooked potatoes, thinly sliced
1 mild red onion, peeled and chopped
2 carrots, grated
2 beets, peeled, cooked, and sliced
1 Scotch bonnet chile (or habanero), stems and seeds removed, chopped fine
¼ cup (59 mL) chopped Italian parsley
2 large hard-boiled eggs, cold, chopped
Olive oil, to taste
Wine vinegar, to taste
Freshly ground black pepper, to taste

1. Soak the herring overnight in a large bowl of water.
2. Remove the herring from the bowl and rinse it under running water. Peel off the skin, debone, and chop the herring. Combine it with the potatoes, onion, carrots, beets, chile, parsley, and eggs. Include any leftover cold beef, lamb, or roast chicken you have on hand.
3. Dress the salad with a vinaigrette of olive oil and wine vinegar to taste. Grind black pepper over it to taste. Chill before serving.

Hearts of Palm Jerk Salad

Yield: 2–4 servings   Heat Scale: Mild

I collected this recipe in Costa Rica with Nancy Gerlach when our families traveled there. Hearts of palm are literally the hearts of the tender shoots of the palm trees that are found throughout the Caribbean. Florida is the only place other than the Caribbean where these can be found fresh. However, locating canned hearts of palm is not a problem, and your guests will never know the difference.

For the Dry Jerk Seasoning:
½ teaspoon (2.5 mL) ground habanero chile
1 tablespoon (15 mL) onion powder
1½ teaspoons (7.5 mL) ground allspice
1½ teaspoons (7.5 mL) ground thyme
1 teaspoon (5 mL) ground cinnamon
1 teaspoon (5 mL) ground cloves
½ teaspoon (2.5 mL) ground black pepper
½ teaspoon (2.5 mL) garlic powder
¼ teaspoon (1.25 mL) ground nutmeg

1. Combine all the ingredients in a small bowl and mix well.

For the Salad:
2 tablespoons (30 mL) vegetable oil
Juice of 1 lime
1 (14-ounce [392 g]) can hearts of palm, drained and sliced
1 large tomato, sliced
Lettuce or spinach leaves as needed

1. In a bowl, whisk together the Jerk Seasoning, oil, and lime juice. Arrange the hearts of palm and tomato slices on the lettuce. Drizzle the dressing over the top and serve.

Mango Fandango

Yield: 4 servings   Heat Scale: Medium

Carmen Miranda would be jealous of this Caribbean fruit extravaganza! Who wouldn't enjoy a tropical salad, with its juicy pineapple, fresh coconut, tasty mangos, guavas, bananas, and, of course, a hint of heat? (Note: This recipe requires advance preparation.)

1 fresh pineapple, peeled, cored, and sliced
3 tablespoons (45 mL) rum
¼ cup (59 mL) brown sugar
Juice of 1 lime
2 bananas, sliced
2 mangos, sliced
2 ripe guavas, sliced
½ habanero, stems and seeds removed, minced
5 tablespoons (75 mL) grated fresh coconut meat
½ teaspoon (2.5 mL) freshly grated nutmeg

1. In a large, nonreactive bowl, combine the pineapple slices, rum, and sugar. Mix well, cover, and chill in the refrigerator for 1 hour.
2. Remove the pineapple mixture from the refrigerator and add the lime juice, the rest of the fruit, and the habanero. Garnish with the grated coconut and nutmeg and serve.

Cho-Cho Salad

Yield: 4–6 servings   Heat Scale: Medium

This pear-shaped fruit, a relative of the squash family, goes by many names: cho-cho, chayote, tropical squash, and christophene. It tastes very much like zucchini.

2 pounds (1.1 kg) christophenes (chayote squash)
1 dash salt
3 tablespoons (45 mL) corn or soy oil
1 tablespoon (15 mL) white wine vinegar or distilled white vinegar
1 clove garlic, peeled and crushed
2 green onions, chopped
2 shallots, peeled and chopped
½ teaspoon (2.5 mL) minced habanero chile
Freshly ground black pepper, to taste

1. Place the christophenes in a large saucepan, sprinkle them with the salt, add water to cover, and boil until tender, about 20 minutes. When the squash is tender, drain them and set aside.
2. When the squash is cool enough to handle, peel and halve the christophenes, discarding the seed and the skins. Cut it into cubes and transfer them to a large mixing bowl.
3. In a small bowl, combine the oil, vinegar, garlic, green onions, shallots, habanero, and pepper and mix well. Pour over the christophenes and chill before serving.

Chile-Conch Salad

Yield: 6–8 servings   Heat Scale: Hot

This recipe was collected by a friend of mine, photographer Chel Beeson, on one of his trips to the Bahamas. This very potent combination of conch, fresh vegetables, and habanero is usually served in a bowl. (Note: This recipe requires advance preparation.)

2 goat peppers (habaneros), stems and seeds removed, minced
Meat of 6 conchs, pounded with a mallet until tender, then minced
3 small onions, peeled and chopped fine
4 stalks celery, chopped fine
2 bell peppers, stems and seeds removed, chopped fine
8 small ripe tomatoes, chopped fine
Juice of 3 limes
Juice of 1 pomelo (or substitute grapefruit)
Salt, to taste

1. In a bowl, combine all the ingredients and allow to sit for at least 4 hours to blend the flavors. Divide the mixture into 6 tall glasses and garnish with lime.

Conch Salad Ceviche-Style

Yield: 6 servings   Heat Scale: Hot

This salad is great way to start off a seafood feast. If you simply can't get your hands on conch, substitute cooked chicken breast. (Note: This recipe requires advance preparation.)

Meat of 3 conchs, pounded with a mallet until soft, then minced
½ cup (118 mL) finely diced bell pepper
½ cup (118 mL) finely diced cucumber
¼ cup (59 mL) lime juice
¼ cup (59 mL) pomelo (grapefruit) juice
1 tablespoon (15 mL) minced habanero chile
½ cup (118 mL) finely diced celery
½ cup (118 mL) finely diced onion
2 fresh tomatoes, chopped
Salt, to taste

1. Mix all the ingredients together in a bowl and refrigerate for at least 1 hour. Serve over mixed greens and garnish with seashells for a beautiful display.

Curried Rice and Pigeon Pea Salad

Yield: 4 servings   Heat Scale: Medium-Hot

Pigeon peas, also called genteel and gung, are similar to black-eyed peas. This African native is very low in fat and full of protein, fiber, and iron. Black-eyed peas may be substituted for the pigeon peas. (Note: This recipe requires advance preparation.)

1 tablespoon (15 mL) butter
1 teaspoon (5 mL) West Indian Masala (page 5)
¾ cup (177 mL) vegetable or chicken broth
⅓ cup (79 mL) uncooked short-grain rice
¼ cup (59 mL) chopped celery
2 tablespoons (30 mL) minced green onions
2 tablespoons (30 mL) chopped pimiento or red bell pepper
1 tablespoon (15 mL) freshly squeezed lime juice
1 pound (454 g) frozen and thawed or freshly cooked pigeon peas, drained
¼ cup (59 mL) plain nonfat yogurt
2 tablespoons (30 mL) toasted slivered cashews
1 teaspoon (5 mL) minced habanero chile
Salt, to taste
Freshly ground black pepper, to taste
1 ripe tomato, cut into wedges
1 hard boiled egg, chopped
Minced fresh cilantro for garnish

1. Melt the butter in a large saucepan over medium-high heat. Stir in the masala, then the broth. Bring the mixture to a boil, then reduce the heat to medium. Add the rice, cover, and simmer 20 minutes until tender. Stir in the celery, onions, pimiento, and lime juice. Spoon the mixture into a storage container and refrigerate until thoroughly chilled, about 2 hours.
2. Once the mixture is chilled, stir in the pigeon peas, yogurt, cashews, chile, salt, and pepper. Spoon the salad into serving bowls, arrange the tomato wedges and egg over each serving, and garnish with the minced cilantro.

Julio's Salpicón
Yield: 12 servings   Heat Scale: Medium

It is generally believed that one of El Paso's most popular and unique dishes, the shredded meat salad called salpicón, crossed the border because of Julio Ramirez. Julio opened his first restaurant in 1944 in Juárez on Avenida 16 de Septiembre and a second location in El Paso in 1985. The recipe for salpicón has been imitated and begged for, and local restaurateurs have paid hundreds of dollars to professional recipe testers to attempt to approximate the recipe. Finally, the Ramirez family has released it. Here it is. (Note: This recipe requires advance preparation.)

1 (3-pound [1.36 kg]) beef brisket
2 cloves garlic, peeled and minced
Salt, to taste
1 cup (236 mL) diced white cheddar cheese
½ cup (118 mL) chopped cilantro
½ cup (118 mL) diced seeded tomatoes
½ cup (118 mL) vegetable oil
½ cup (118 mL) wine vinegar
4 chipotle chiles in adobo, minced
Lettuce or spinach leaves
Diced avocado for garnish

1. Put the brisket in a pot and add water to cover. Add the garlic and salt and bring to a boil. Reduce the heat and simmer for about 1½ hours, uncovered, until the meat is tender and can be shredded. Cool the meat in the broth, then shred it finely by hand. Save the broth to make a stew or soup.
2. Toss the shredded brisket with the cheddar, cilantro, tomatoes, oil, vinegar, and chiles. Chill the mixture and allow it to marinate for a couple of hours or, preferably, overnight.
3. Line a platter with lettuce or spinach leaves, place the salpicón on the leaves, and garnish with the avocado. Serve with hot, buttered flour tortillas.

Grilled Chicken Caesar Salad with Chile-Dusted Croutons

Yield: 4 servings   Heat Scale: Medium

The Caesar salad was invented in Tijuana, Mexico, so it has South of the Border roots. Here I give it a Southwestern twist by taking it outside to the grill to make a terrific summer entrée. Shaved Parmesan makes a better garnish than just grated. Use a vegetable peeler to make 1-inch (2.5 cm) wide shavings, then refrigerate them until ready to serve. (Note: This recipe requires advance preparation.)

For the Southwestern Chicken:
2 boneless, skinless chicken breasts
Olive oil as needed
2 tablespoons (30 mL) rub of your choice from Chapter 1

1. Brush the chicken with a little olive oil and sprinkle it with the rub.
2. Marinate at room temperature for 30 minutes to an hour.

For the Chile-Dusted Croutons:
3 cloves garlic, peeled and minced
⅓ cup (79 mL) olive oil
1 tablespoon (15 mL) ground red chile
½ teaspoon (2.5 mL) garlic salt
10 slices French or Italian bread, cut in ½-inch (1 cm) cubes

1. Preheat the oven to 350°F (180°C).
2. In a small bowl, mix together the garlic, olive oil, chile, and garlic salt. Toss this mixture with the bread cubes until thoroughly coated. Spread on a baking sheet and toast in the oven for 10 minutes.

For the Southwestern Caesar Dressing:
2 egg yolks
¼ cup (59 mL) grated Parmesan cheese
1 teaspoon (5 mL) anchovy paste
2 teaspoons (10 mL) Dijon mustard
1 tablespoon (15 mL) lemon juice
½ cup (118 mL) red wine vinegar
1½ cups (354 mL) olive oil
2 tablespoons (30 mL) ground red New Mexico chiles
¼ teaspoon (1.25 mL) cumin seeds
Freshly ground black pepper, to taste

1. In a bowl, whisk together the egg yolks, cheese, anchovy paste, and mustard. Add the lemon juice and blend well. While whisking, slowly add the vinegar and then the olive oil, a little at a time. Whisk in the chile, cumin, and black pepper. Refrigerate until ready to serve.
2. Just before serving time, taste the dressing and adjust as necessary, adding more vinegar if you like it more tart, more oil if you prefer it less tart, more chile for heat, or more anchovies for saltiness.

For the Salad:
Inner leaves of a head romaine lettuce, torn in 2-inch (5 cm) pieces
2 thin slices of red onion, separated into rings
⅓ cup (79 mL) shaved Parmesan cheese

1. Grill the chicken over a medium-hot fire until cooked through, about 20 minutes or until the internal temperature reaches 160°F (72°C). Remove the chicken breasts from the grill and cut them crosswise into thin slices.
2. To assemble the salad, toss the lettuce with some of the dressing until coated but not saturated. Divide the lettuce among individual chilled plates. Top with the onions, chicken, and croutons. Garnish with the shaved Parmesan and serve.

Chile Cactus Salad

Yield: 4 servings   Heat Scale: Medium

This interesting salad features nopalitos, the fleshy pads of the Opuntia, or prickly pear, cactus. Of course, the spines have been removed from the cactus pads.

For the Dressing:
⅔ cup (158 mL) olive oil
⅓ cup (79 mL) red wine vinegar
2 jalapeño chiles, stems and seeds removed, finely minced
1 clove garlic, peeled and finely minced
¼ teaspoon (1.25 mL) dried oregano
Freshly ground black pepper, to taste

1. Combine a small amount of the oil and vinegar in a bowl. Whisk in the chiles, garlic, oregano, and pepper and beat until smooth. Slowly add a little oil and beat well. Then add a little vinegar. Repeat the process until all the oil and vinegar have been added and the dressing is completely blended.

For the Salad:
1 large poblano chile, roasted, peeled, stems and seeds removed, cut in strips
1 (15-ounce [426 g]) jar nopalitos, drained and rinsed
4 small tomatoes, chopped
2 tablespoons (30 mL) chopped fresh cilantro
1 head red leaf lettuce
½ pound (224 g) goat cheese, crumbled (or substitute feta)

1. Combine all the ingredients in a bowl and toss with just enough dressing to coat and serve.

Variation

For a more elegant presentation, toss the lettuce with the tomatoes and divide it among individual plates. Arrange the chile and nopalito strips on the lettuce. Top with the cheese, garnish with the cilantro, and serve with the dressing on the side.

Sonoran-Style Taco Salad

Yield: 4–6 servings   Heat Scale: Mild

This popular salad is often served as an entrée in Arizona. It is quite dramatic when presented in a "bowl" fashioned from a deep-fried, oversized flour tortilla, which can be eaten along with the salad. Tortilla bowls can be made by deep frying flour tortillas in a "tortilla fryer," which is a double-cup tool made especially for this purpose.

For the Dressing:
¼ cup (59 mL) commercial taco sauce
¼ cup (59 mL) red wine vinegar
¼ cup (59 mL) salad oil
2 tablespoons (30 mL) lemon juice

1. Mix all the ingredients together and let sit for a few minutes to blend the flavors.

For the Salad:
1 teaspoon (5 mL) vegetable oil
1 pound (454 g) ground beef
1 medium onion, peeled and chopped
1 clove garlic, peeled and minced
2 teaspoons (10 mL) ground cayenne
1 tablespoon (15 mL) commercial chili powder
½ teaspoon (2.5 mL) ground cumin
½ cup (118 mL) tomato sauce
1 cup (236 mL) cooked pinto beans
Tortilla bowls or tortilla chips
1 head lettuce, chopped
1 medium tomato, chopped
1 cup (236 mL) grated cheddar cheese
¼ cup (59 mL) sliced black olives
1 small onion, sliced and separated into rings
1 avocado, peeled, pitted, and chopped, or 1 cup (236 mL) guacamole
(see Chapter 5)
Sour cream for garnish

1. In a large skillet, heat the oil over medium heat. Add the ground beef, chopped onion, garlic, cayenne, chili powder, and cumin and sauté until the beef is browned. Add the tomato sauce and the beans and continue to cook until heated through. Drain off any excess liquid and let cool slightly.
2. Place the lettuce in the tortilla bowl or on the chips. Top with the beef mixture. Arrange the tomatoes around the outside; top with the cheese, olives, onion rings, and avocado or guacamole; and garnish with the sour cream. Serve the dressing on the side.

Santa Fe Greens Dressed with Green Chile Mayonnaise
Yield: 4–6 servings   Heat Scale: Medium

If piñon nuts are not available, substitute sunflower seeds or chopped walnuts in this spicy tossed green salad. (Note: This recipe requires advance preparation.)

For the Dressing:
4–6 green New Mexican chiles, roasted, peeled, stems and seeds removed, chopped
¼ cup (59 mL) mayonnaise
2 tablespoons (30 mL) sour cream
1 tablespoon (15 mL) olive oil
1 tablespoon (15 mL) lime juice
1 clove garlic, peeled and minced
¼ teaspoon (1.25 mL) sugar
1 teaspoon (5 mL) chopped fresh cilantro
¼ teaspoon (1.25 mL) ground cumin

1. Combine all the ingredients in a bowl and allow the dressing to sit a few hours to blend the flavors.

For the Salad:
½ cup (118 mL) jicama, diced
4 green onions, chopped, including the green part
Mixed salad greens, such as radicchio, butter, and red leaf lettuce
¼ cup (59 mL) piñon nuts

1. Combine the jicama, onions, and salad greens in a bowl. Toss with the dressing, top with the nuts, and serve.

Texas "Caviar"
Yield: 4–6 servings   Heat Scale: Hot

No selection of dishes from the Southwest would be complete without a recipe for black-eyed peas or "Texas caviar," a major crop in eastern Texas. Black-eyed peas are traditionally served on New Year's Day for good luck, in Texas and throughout the South. (Note: This recipe requires advance preparation.)

4 jalapeño chiles, stems and seeds removed, minced
½ cup (118 mL) vegetable oil (olive oil preferred)
¼ cup (59 mL) vinegar
2 cloves garlic, peeled and minced
¼ teaspoon (1.25 mL) dry mustard
Freshly ground black pepper, to taste
3 cups (708 mL) cooked black-eyed peas
4 green onions, sliced, including the greens
1 stalk celery, chopped

1. In a bowl, combine the chiles, oil, vinegar, garlic, mustard, and black pepper. Toss the peas, onions, and celery with the dressing and marinate overnight in the refrigerator.

Tex-Mex Coleslaw for the Barbecue

Yield: 6–8 servings   Heat Scale: Medium

Texans love their barbecues, as do most people throughout the Southwest. This salad works well as a part of any outdoor extravaganza and makes a fine accompaniment to a more mundane meal, such as a pastrami sandwich. (Note: This recipe requires advance preparation.)

For the Dressing:
¼ teaspoon (1.25 mL) ground cayenne
½ cup (118 mL) mayonnaise
1 tablespoon (15 mL) sugar
1 tablespoon (15 mL) white vinegar
½ teaspoon (2.5 mL) celery seed
⅛ teaspoon (.5 mL) ground white pepper
Salt, to taste

1. Combine all the ingredients in a jar, stir, and let sit for 2 hours to blend the flavors.

For the Slaw:
4 jalapeño chiles, stems and seeds removed, chopped
½ head green cabbage, shredded
½ head red cabbage, shredded
1 small onion, peeled and chopped
2 tablespoons (30 mL) chopped fresh cilantro

1. Toss all the ingredients, except the cilantro, together in a bowl. To serve, combine the dressing with the salad and garnish with the cilantro.

Horn of Plenty Salad

Yield: 4 servings   Heat Scale: Mild

The "horn" in this salad is actually a roasted poblano chile. The stuffing is a zesty mixture that is rich and refreshing, with a contrast of textures. Serve it with one of the less rich main dishes from chapters 8 to 12.

4 poblano chiles, roasted, peeled, seeds removed, refrigerated
2 cups (473 mL) finely diced apples, such as Pippin
1 fresh lemon
1 cup (236 mL) crumbled blue cheese
¾ cup (177 mL) chopped walnuts
4 cups (.95 L) mixed salad greens
⅔ cup (158 mL) extra virgin olive oil
⅓ cup (79 mL) red wine vinegar

1. Place the apples in a ceramic bowl and squeeze just enough lemon juice over the apples to cover them. This will prevent the apples from turning brown and keep them attractive, especially if this dish is prepared an hour or two ahead of time.
2. Toss the cheese and walnuts with the apples. Stuff this mixture into the poblano chiles.
3. Arrange the stuffed chiles on a bed of greens.
4. Whisk the olive oil and vinegar together in a small bowl. Pour the dressing over the chiles and lettuce. Serve immediately.

Many Vegetables Salad

Yield: 6 servings   Heat Scale: Mild

This salad has a few basic ingredients, but it is ripe to receive odds and ends from your refrigerator. If you have a garden, the freshness of this salad will be further enhanced.

1 head romaine lettuce, washed and torn into pieces
1 cup (236 mL) broccoli florets
½ cup (118 mL) diced jicama or raw turnip
2 green onions, sliced
2 yellow Hungarian wax peppers, stems and seeds removed, cut into rings
5 radishes, sliced
1 cup (236 mL) cooked chickpeas
½ cup (118 mL) alfalfa sprouts (or substitute bean sprouts)+
2 tablespoons (30 mL) toasted sesame seeds
1½ cups (354 mL) diced tomatoes
2 pimientos, diced
⅔ cup (158 mL) olive oil
2 tablespoons (30 mL) Chile Oil (page 16)
3 tablespoons (45 mL) rice wine vinegar
1 clove garlic, peeled, minced, and crushed
½ teaspoon (2.5 mL) dry mustard
½ teaspoon (2.5 mL) soy sauce
¼ teaspoon (1.25 mL) salt
¼ teaspoon (1.25 mL) freshly ground white pepper

1. In a large salad bowl, lightly toss the lettuce, broccoli, jicama, green onions, wax peppers, radishes, chickpeas, sprouts, sesame seeds, tomatoes, and pimientos.
2. In a small glass jar, combine the olive oil, Chile Oil, vinegar, garlic, mustard, soy sauce, salt, and pepper, and shake thoroughly.
3. Pour the dressing over the tossed vegetables and lightly toss again. Serve immediately.

Zucchini Ensalada

Yield: 4 servings   Heat Scale: Mild

Since zucchini is such a prolific producer in home gardens, I felt I had to include at least one recipe to give you a jump on the crop. I suggest serving the zucchini raw, but if you don't like it raw, steam it for a minute or two. (Note: This recipe requires advance preparation.)

1 pound (454 g) zucchini
2 serrano chiles, stems and seeds removed, cut into rings
2 garlic cloves, peeled and minced
½ teaspoon (2.5 mL) paprika
¼ teaspoon (1.25 mL) freshly ground white pepper
¼ teaspoon (1.25 mL) sugar
½ teaspoon (2.5 mL) salt
3 tablespoons (45 mL) balsamic vinegar
⅓ cup (79 mL) virgin olive oil
3 tablespoons (45 mL) corn oil
4 large shallots, peeled and cut into ¼-inch (.5 cm) slices
1 large, ripe avocado
3 cups (708 mL) mixed baby salad greens
10 large pimiento-stuffed green olives, halved

1. Clean the zucchini, cut it into 1-inch (2.5 cm) thick slices, and place it in a ceramic bowl with the serrano chiles.
2. In a small glass jar with a cover, combine the garlic, paprika, pepper, sugar, salt, vinegar, and olive oil and shake thoroughly. Pour enough of the dressing over the zucchini and chiles to coat it, then toss the mixture. Cover and refrigerate for several hours. Just before serving, drain off the dressing and reserve it.
3. In a small sauté pan, heat the oil over medium heat. Add the shallots and sauté them until they are light brown and toasty, tossing frequently to avoid burning. Transfer them to paper towels to drain.
4. Peel, pit, and slice the avocado.
5. Place the salad greens on a serving dish and arrange the zucchini, avocado, and olives on top of the greens.
6. Shake the remaining dressing and pour it over the vegetables. Top the salad with the crisp shallots. Serve immediately.

Colorful Cauliflower Salad

Yield: 4 servings   Heat Scale: Mild

Raw cauliflower has great salad appeal, and many people would rather eat it raw than cooked. This colorful salad mix, served on a bed of Boston lettuce, would go well with a grilled portobello mushroom entrée or sandwich. (Note: This recipe requires advance preparation.)

1⅓ cups (315 mL) vegetable oil
⅔ cup (158 mL) rice wine vinegar
2 tablespoons (30 mL) sugar
½ teaspoon (2.5 mL) salt
½ teaspoon (2.5 mL) basil
¼ teaspoon (1.25 mL) oregano
1 clove garlic, peeled and minced
3 cups (708 mL) cauliflower florets
2 serrano or jalapeño chiles, stems and seeds removed, chopped
¾ cup (177 mL) pitted ripe olives, sliced
¾ cup (177 mL) chopped red bell pepper

1. Combine the oil, vinegar, sugar, salt, basil, oregano, and garlic in a glass jar with a lid. Shake the mixture until the sugar is dissolved and set aside.
2. Place the cauliflower and the serranos in a ceramic bowl. Shake the dressing again, pour it over the vegetables, toss lightly, cover, and refrigerate at least 2 hours or overnight.
3. Before serving, add the olives and bell pepper and toss the mixture.

Five-Bean Blaster Salad
Yield: 6 servings   Heat Scale: Medium

If you want to have a blast on May 5th, Cinco de Mayo, literally and figuratively, serve this unique salad. It has texture, color, and flavor. The dressing is deceptive: It starts out mild, and then goes wild on the tongue. Serve lots of margaritas with this salad.

1 cup (236 mL) sliced young green beans, steamed for 3 minutes
1 cup (236 mL) cooked chickpeas or canned chickpeas, drained and rinsed
1 cup (236 mL) cooked kidney beans or canned kidney beans, drained and rinsed
1 cup (236 mL) cooked lima beans or canned lima beans, drained and rinsed
1 cup (236 mL) cooked pinto beans or black beans or canned beans, drained and rinsed
1 medium onion, peeled and sliced into rings
3 serrano or jalapeño chiles, stems and seeds removed, cut into rings
2 tablespoons (30 mL) sugar
½ cup (118 mL) red wine vinegar
½ cup (118 mL) light olive oil
½ teaspoon (2.5 mL) salt
½ teaspoon (2.5 mL) dry mustard
½ teaspoon (2.5 mL) dried basil
1 tablespoon (15 mL) chopped Italian parsley
1 teaspoon (5 mL) finely minced habanero chile

1. Combine the green beans, chickpeas, kidney beans, lima beans, pinto or black beans, onion, and serrano chiles in a ceramic bowl. Cover and refrigerate.
2. In a glass jar with a lid, combine the sugar, vinegar, oil, salt, mustard, basil, parsley, and habanero chile. Shake the mixture until the sugar dissolves, then allow the dressing to sit at room temperature for 30 minutes.
3. Shake the dressing again, pour it over the bean mixture, cover, and allow the salad to marinate in the refrigerator for several hours or overnight.

Pungent Potato Salad with Lime Chipotle Dressing

Yield: 4   Heat Scale: Medium

This salad is filling and light all at the same time. I've kept the calories low and the satisfaction level high by including some of my favorite ingredients, including potatoes, mustard, and chipotles.

2 pounds (1.1 kg) small new potatoes, skins on, washed well, quartered
2 sprigs fresh mint
¼ teaspoon (1.25 mL) salt
2 cloves garlic, peeled
2 chipotle chiles in adobo, stems removed, chopped
1 teaspoon (5 mL) coarse salt
⅓ cup (79 mL) fresh lime juice
Grated zest of 1 lime
⅓ cup (79 mL) olive oil
2 teaspoons (10 mL) Dijon mustard
Lemon pepper, to taste
2 tablespoons (30 mL) chopped chives
¼ cup (59 mL) cilantro leaves

1. Fill a large pot ¾ full with water. Bring the water to a boil over high heat. Add the potatoes, mint, and salt. Reduce the heat and simmer the potatoes for about 20 minutes or until they are tender.
2. While the potatoes boil, place the garlic, chipotles, and salt in a mortar and crush into a paste. Transfer the paste to a bowl and whisk in the lime juice, lime zest, olive oil, mustard, and lemon pepper. Set aside.
3. When the potatoes are done, drain them in a colander and transfer them to a serving bowl. Pour the dressing over the potatoes while they are still hot, making sure that each potato is coated with the dressing. Garnish with the chopped chives and cilantro leaves.

Red, White, and Blue Potato Salad

Yield: 8–10 servings   Heat Scale: Mild

If you've never used "baby" vegetables, here's a great opportunity to experiment. Baby potatoes are incredibly delicious and tender, and they look great arranged on a serving plate.

¾ pound (336 g) baby blue or purple potatoes
¾ pound (336 g) baby red potatoes
¾ pound (336 g) baby white potatoes
¼ cup (59 mL) olive oil
1 teaspoon (5 mL) salt
½ teaspoon (2.5 mL) freshly ground white pepper
1¼ cup (295 mL) red wine vinegar, divided
1 cup (236 mL) diced sweet onion (Vidalia preferred)
½ cup (118 mL) chopped green onions
1 cup (236 mL) chopped celery
½ cup (118 mL) chopped yellow or red bell peppers
3 tablespoons (45 mL) chopped Italian parsley
3 green New Mexican chiles, roasted, peeled, stems and seeds removed, and chopped (or substitute 4 yellow wax hots)
¾ cup (177 mL) red wine vinegar
¼ cup (59 mL) olive oil
½ teaspoon (2.5 mL) sugar
1 teaspoon (5 mL) dried savory or basil

1. Preheat the oven to 400°F (200°C).
2. Clean the potatoes and put them in a large bowl. Add the olive oil and toss to coat. Place the potatoes on a large baking sheet and sprinkle with the salt and pepper. Spritz the potatoes with water. Cover the pan tightly with aluminum foil and roast for 30 to 35 minutes. Test for doneness by piercing a few test potatoes with a knife. The potatoes should be firm and not overly soft.
3. Remove the potatoes from the oven and allow them to cool for a few minutes. Cut them in half and place them in a large ceramic bowl.
4. Add ½ cup (118 mL) of the vinegar, the onion, the green onions, the celery, the bell peppers, the parsley, and the chiles and toss to combine.
5. Mix together the remaining ¾ cup (177 mL) vinegar, the oil, the sugar, and the savory or basil in a small covered jar. Shake the dressing and pour it over the potato-vegetable mixture. Toss the mixture and serve.

Red Hot Potato Salad

Yield: 3–4 servings   Heat Scale: Medium

*This simple potato salad is served warm and can be put together quickly after the po-
tatoes are boiled. The recipe can easily be doubled or tripled. It's a nice change from
ordinary potato salad, and the flavors will really charge your palate.*

10 small red potatoes, scrubbed thoroughly, skins left on
¼ cup (59 mL) rice wine vinegar or champagne vinegar
¼ cup (59 mL) Chile Oil (page 16)
2 tablespoons (30 mL) fresh dill or 1 tablespoon (15 mL) dill weed
¾ cup (177 mL) chopped shallots
2 serrano or jalapeño chiles, stems removed, sliced into thin rings
Salt, to taste
Freshly ground black pepper, to taste

1. Place the potatoes in a large Dutch oven and cover with water. Bring to
a full boil, then reduce the heat to a low boil. Cook the potatoes, uncovered, for 10 to 15 minutes. Test for doneness by inserting a sharp knife
through the center of a potato. The potato should just start to yield to
the knife. Do not overcook. Drain the potatoes and transfer them to a
large bowl.
2. Using a sharp knife, halve (if they are small) or quarter (if they are large)
the potatoes. Sprinkle the vinegar over the potatoes, then sprinkle them
with the chile oil. Toss gently. Add the dill, shallots, pepper rings, salt, and
pepper, and toss gently. Serve warm.

Vegetable Medley Potato Salad

Yield: 6 servings   Heat Scale: Mild

Here are a few recommendations to make this salad as tasty as possible: First, buy good white wine vinegar; second, make sure you use Italian parsley for its spark, and, if you can't find it, grow it or substitute watercress with its peppery overtones; and third, be prepared to run out of salad—it really is that good.

4 large russet potatoes
¼ cup (59 mL) white wine vinegar
1 clove garlic, peeled and minced
¾ cup (177 mL) chopped green onions
1 cup (236 mL) diced celery
2 hard-boiled eggs, whites only, chopped
¼ cup (59 mL) chopped Italian parsley
⅔ cup (158 mL) peeled, seeded, and diced cucumber
½ cup (118 mL) chopped green New Mexican chile
¾ cup (177 mL) low-fat mayonnaise
¼ cup (59 mL) plain yogurt
1 tablespoon (15 mL) prepared horseradish
2 tablespoons (30 mL) Dijon mustard
½ teaspoon (2.5 mL) salt
¼ teaspoon (1.25 mL) freshly ground black pepper

1. Place the potatoes in a large Dutch oven and add water to cover. Bring the water to a boil, then reduce the heat to a gentle boil. Cook for 15 to 20 minutes, until the potatoes are just tender. Do not overcook, or you will have mashed potato salad! Drain the potatoes and peel them quickly, while they are still hot. On a cutting board, slice the potatoes in half lengthwise, then slice the halves into ¼-inch (.5 cm) thick slices and transfer them to a large bowl. Sprinkle the potato slices with the vinegar.
2. Add the garlic, green onion, celery, eggs, parsley, cucumber, and chile to the potatoes and toss gently.
3. In a small bowl, whisk together the mayonnaise, yogurt, horseradish, mustard, salt, and black pepper. Pour this dressing over the potato-vegetable mixture and toss gently to coat. Serve slightly chilled.

Succulent Southwestern Potato Salad

Yield: 4–6 servings   Heat Scale: Medium

Here is the last of my potato salads. It calls for ground chile and hot sauce instead of fresh pods to elevate the heat level.

4 medium Russet potatoes
¼ cup (59 mL) olive oil
¼ cup (59 mL) white wine vinegar
2½ teaspoons (12.5 mL) ground red New Mexican chiles
1 tablespoon prepared hot sauce of your choice (we prefer Uno hot sauce)
½ cup (118 mL) chopped onion
1 (8-ounce [227 g]) can whole kernel corn, drained and rinsed
½ cup (118 mL) coarsely shredded carrot
⅓ cup (79 mL) chopped green bell pepper
½ cup (118 mL) sliced ripe olives

1. Place the potatoes in a large Dutch oven and add water to cover. Bring the water to a boil, then reduce the heat to a gentle boil. Cook for 15 to 20 minutes or until a knife pierces the potatoes easily. Drain, peel, and cube the potatoes while still warm. Transfer them to a large bowl.
2. In a small glass jar, combine the oil, vinegar, ground chile, and hot sauce and shake vigorously. Pour the dressing over the potatoes and toss gently. Add the remaining ingredients and toss gently.
3. Refrigerate for 1 hour before serving.

East Meets West Mushroom Butter Lettuce Salad

Yield: 4 servings   Heat Scale: Medium

The combination of shiitake mushrooms and piñons may sound a little strange, but it's amazing what wonderful things you can come up with when you are willing to work with what's in the cupboard! This salad has a bit of a kick, so don't serve it to friends who are faint of heart.

2 tablespoons (30 mL) soy sauce
2 tablespoons (30 mL) Chile Oil (page 16)
2 Thai chiles, stems and seeds removed, minced (or substitute serranos)
2 tablespoons (30 mL) olive oil
2 teaspoons (10 mL) sugar
1 head butter lettuce, cleaned
12 large shiitake mushrooms, cleaned and stemmed
½ cup (118 mL) chopped piñon nuts

1. In a small, non-reactive bowl, whisk together the soy sauce, Chile Oil, Thai chile, olive oil, and sugar and set aside.
2. Preheat the broiler.
3. Divide the butter lettuce leaves equally among 4 chilled salad plates.

4. Place the mushrooms stem-side down on a broiling rack. Brush the mushrooms with the sauce. Place the rack 4 to 6 inches from the heat and broil until the mushrooms are brown and crusty, about 2 minutes.
5. When the mushrooms are done, quickly arrange them on top of the butter lettuce, and pour any remaining sauce on top of the mushrooms. Sprinkle each plate with the piñons, and serve.

Chilied Cantaloupe, Cranberry, and Bean Salad

Yield: 6 servings   Heat Scale: Mild

So you're thinking, "What an odd combination of stuff." Actually, this is a gorgeous salad that is sweet and tart at the same time. It is also a time saver, as I happily suggest that you use one of the best inventions of the '90s—prewashed and chopped salad in a bag!

1 medium cantaloupe, halved, seeds removed
1 cup (236 mL) canned black beans, drained and rinsed
1 cup (236 mL) canned pinto beans, drained and rinsed
½ cup (118 mL) diced red bell pepper
1 jalapeño chile, stem and seeds removed, diced
¼ cup (59 mL) sliced green onions
2 tablespoons (30 mL) lime juice
2 tablespoons (30 mL) lemon juice
2 tablespoons (30 mL) honey
1 tablespoon (15 mL) safflower oil
¼ teaspoon (1.25 mL) ground allspice
⅛ teaspoon (.6 mL) salt
1 bag mixed baby lettuces
1 (15-ounce [420 g]) can cranberry sauce

1. Cut each cantaloupe half into 4 lengthwise slices. Cut the peel off of each slice. Dice half of the cantaloupe and place the pieces in a medium bowl. Cut each of the remaining slices into 3 thin slices, then cover them with plastic wrap and chill.
2. Add the beans, bell pepper, jalapeño, and green onions to the diced cantaloupe. In a separate small bowl, whisk together the lime juice, lemon juice, honey, safflower oil, allspice, and salt.
3. Distribute the baby lettuce equally among 6 salad plates. Place a dollop of cranberry sauce in the middle of the lettuce on each plate. Remove the chilled cantaloupe from the refrigerator and put 1 slice on each plate. Divide the bean mixture among the plates and dress each salad with the reserved dressing.

Spicy Spinach Salad with Fruits and Nuts

Yield: 4 servings   Heat Scale: Medium

Here's a spicy, skinny spinach salad that's sure to please.

¼ cup (59 mL) nonfat sour cream
¼ cup (59 mL) nonfat plain yogurt
2 kiwi fruit, peeled, each sliced into 8 rounds
2 teaspoons (10 mL) white wine vinegar
2 teaspoons (10 mL) Dijon mustard
1 tablespoon ground red New Mexican chile
1 tablespoon (15 mL) honey
1 tablespoon (15 mL) minced garlic
4 cups (.95 L) fresh spinach, cleaned and torn into bite-sized pieces
1 cup (236 mL) red seedless grapes, halved
¼ cup (59 mL) chopped walnuts
1 (11-ounce [308 g]) can mandarin oranges
½ cup (118 mL) diced tomatoes

1. In a blender, combine the sour cream, yogurt, kiwi, vinegar, mustard, ground chile, honey, and garlic and blend until smooth.
2. In a separate serving bowl, toss the spinach, grapes, walnuts, oranges, and tomatoes in a ½ cup (118 mL) of the dressing to start, adding more as desired. Keep the salad chilled until serving time.

Hot Habanero Mango Bulgur Salad

Yield: 6 servings   Heat Scale: Hot

Mango and habanero offer a tantalizing salad combination. As always, be judicious with your use of the world's hottest chile. Remember, you can always add more, but it's hard to take away the heat if you add too much.

1 cup (236 mL) bulgur wheat
1¾ cup (413 mL) boiling water
2 mangos, peeled, seeded, and diced
½ cup (118 mL) shredded carrot
½ cup (118 mL) red bell pepper strips
½ cup (118 mL) cucumber, peeled and sliced
½ cup (118 mL) thinly sliced celery
¼ cup (59 mL) thinly sliced green onion
¾ cup (177 mL) diced papaya
1 tablespoon (15 mL) fresh lime juice
¼ cup (59 mL) sweet rice vinegar
2 tablespoons (30 mL) Chile Oil (page 16)
¼ teaspoon (1.25 mL) grated fresh ginger
⅛ teaspoon (.6 mL) minced garlic
½ habanero chile, stem and seeds removed, minced

1. Place the bulgur and boiling water in a microwave-safe casserole dish. Cover the dish with a larger dish and microwave on high for 5 minutes to hydrate. Remove the bulgur from the microwave and set it aside to cool.
2. In a large bowl, combine the mangos, carrot, red bell pepper, cucumber, celery, and onion.
3. In a food processor, blend together the papaya, lime juice, rice vinegar, Chile Oil, ginger, garlic, and chile until smooth.
4. Add the cooled bulgur to the vegetables, then pour the dressing over the entire mixture. Stir gently to coat and serve immediately.

Peppered Pineapple Fruit Salad with Cayenne Turnips

Yield: 4 servings   Heat Scale: Medium

For some strange reason, I love the idea of combining naked root crops, vegetables, and fruit in a spicy salad. This recipe came to me in a nightma—uh, dream.

1 teaspoon (5 mL) grated lemon zest
1 tablespoon (15 mL) honey
1 shallot, peeled and minced
⅓ cup (79 mL) rice wine vinegar
1 teaspoon (5 mL) ground cayenne
1 dash salt
3 tablespoons (45 mL) lime juice
1 pound (454 g) turnips, peeled and cut into medium cubes
1 cucumber, peeled, seeded, and cut into small cubes
1 (11-ounce [308 g]) can mandarin oranges, drained
½ honeydew melon, peeled and seeded, cut into medium cubes
½ medium pineapple, peeled, cored, and cut into cubes
2 tablespoons (30 mL) minced fresh mint

1. In a medium saucepan, combine the lemon zest, honey, shallot, vinegar, cayenne, and salt. Bring the mixture to a boil, then remove it from the heat and let cool. When the mixture reaches room temperature, add the lime juice and set aside.
2. In a large ceramic bowl, mix together the turnips, cucumber, oranges, melon, and pineapple. Pour the dressing over the fruits and vegetables and toss gently to coat. Sprinkle the top of the salad with the mint. Chill the salad for at least 1 hour.

Key West Salad

Yield: 5 servings

Heat Scale: Medium to Hot, depending on the size and intensity of the habanero chile

The flavors of Margaritaville and Key West are all combined in this lively salad, which is replete with tequila and lime. If you're a Jimmy Buffet fan, you'll know what I mean. The salad is hot, spicy, and refreshing; serve it with one of the main dishes from chapters 8 to 12.

2 cups (473 mL) cubed fresh pineapple
1 small ripe papaya, peeled and diced (about 1–1½ cups [250–354 mL])
1 cup (236 mL) shredded cabbage
1 habanero chile, stem and seeds removed, minced
¼ cup (59 mL) chopped pistachios (chile-flavored preferred, or substitute pecans)
⅓ cup (79 mL) low-fat mayonnaise
⅓ cup (79 mL) low-fat sour cream
2 tablespoons (30 mL) tequila
2 tablespoons (30 mL) freshly squeezed lime juice
¼ teaspoon (1.25 mL) freshly ground white pepper
¼ teaspoon (1.25 mL) sugar

1. Mix together the pineapple, papaya, cabbage, chile, and pistachios in a medium bowl. Refrigerate the mixture for 1 hour.
2. In another bowl, whisk together the mayonnaise, sour cream, tequila, lime juice, white pepper, and sugar until the dressing is well blended. Pour it over the chilled mixture and toss lightly. Serve immediately.

Spinach with Horseradish-Cilantro Tomato Vinaigrette

Yield: 6 servings   Heat Scale: Medium

Horseradish is often overlooked as a viable hot and spicy ingredient. However, anyone who has ever eaten something prepared with a healthy helping of horserad-ish will attest to its potent powers. This recipe is an adaptation of a classic from the Horseradish Information Council.

½ cup (118 mL) chopped Roma tomatoes
1 tablespoon (15 mL) distilled white vinegar
2 teaspoons (10 mL) prepared horseradish
1 teaspoon (5 mL) honey
2 tablespoons (30 mL) tomato paste
1 tablespoon (15 mL) minced fresh cilantro
¼ teaspoon (1.25 mL) black pepper
1 teaspoon (5 mL) Dijon mustard
¼ teaspoon (1.25 mL) ground habanero chile
½ cup (118 mL) olive oil
Chopped spinach as needed

1. Combine all the ingredients except the olive oil and spinach in a blender. Blend until smooth. With the blender still running, slowly add the olive oil until the dressing is well combined and thick. Serve over the spinach leaves.

Hot Wilted Spinach Salad

Yield: 6 servings   Heat Scale: Medium

The dressing should be hot so the spinach wilts when the dressing is poured over it For a less hearty salad, omit the cheese and the nuts.

4 slices bacon, chopped
2 tablespoons (30 mL) crushed red New Mexican chile, seeds included
½ cup (118 mL) cider vinegar
1 tablespoon (15 mL) soy sauce
4 cups (.95 L) fresh spinach
1 medium red onion, peeled and thinly sliced
1 cup (236 mL) cauliflower florets
1 cup (236 mL) diced queso blanco or mozzarella cheese
¼ cup (59 mL) slivered almonds

1. In a skillet, sauté the bacon pieces over medium heat until crisp. Remove the bacon from the skillet, transfer it to paper towels to drain, then crumble it. Add the red chile to the bacon drippings and sauté for a couple of minutes.
2. In a bowl, mix together the vinegar and soy sauce.
3. In a separate bowl, combine the spinach, onion, cauliflower, and cheese. Add the vinegar mixture and toss to combine.
4. Reheat the bacon fat and chile mixture, pour it over the spinach, and toss well. Top with the nuts and bacon and serve.

Stir-Fry Pork and Avocado Salad

Yield: 4 servings   Heat Scale: Medium

Meat salads have been gaining popularity in the Southwest with the arrival of Southeast Asian immigrants.

2 tablespoons (30 mL) Chile Oil (page 16)
2 teaspoons (10 mL) ground chile de arbol (or substitute any ground hot chile)
½ teaspoon (2.5 mL) dried oregano
¼ teaspoon (1.25 mL) ground cumin
1 pinch garlic powder
1 pound (454 g) boneless pork, cut in strips 2 inches (5 cm) long and ¼-inch (.5 cm) wide and thick
5 ounces (140 g) mixed lettuce leaves, chopped
1 cup (236 mL) mung bean sprouts, or as needed
1 small onion, peeled, thinly sliced, and separated into rings
1 avocado, pitted, peeled, and sliced
1 small cucumber, sliced
½ cup (118 mL) prepared ranch salad dressing mixed with hot sauce of your choice, to taste
2 tablespoons (30 mL) sesame seeds

1. In a skillet, heat the oil over medium heat. Add the chile, oregano, cumin, and garlic powder. Add the pork and cook for a couple of minutes until the pork is done but still tender. Transfer the pork to paper towels to drain.
2. Divide the lettuce among 4 salad plates. Top the lettuce with the bean sprouts, onion, avocado, and cucumber slices. Arrange the warm pork strips over all, top with the spicy ranch dressing, garnish with the sesame seeds, and serve.

Marinated Vegetable Salad with Sun-Dried Tomatoes

Yield: 4–6 servings   Heat Scale: Mild

Try substituting cauliflower or broccoli for the mushrooms, or add your own combination of veggies. (Note: This recipe requires advance preparation.)

For the Vegetables:
1 cup (236 mL) water
½ cup (118 mL) apple cider vinegar
1 (9-ounce [252 g]) package frozen artichoke heart halves
½ pound (224 g) fresh button mushrooms, stems removed
4 oil-packed sun-dried tomatoes, drained, cut in thin strips
12 black olives

1. Bring the water and the cider vinegar to a boil in a pan, add the artichoke hearts, and immediately remove the pan from the heat. Let stand for 5 minutes, then remove the artichokes, reserving the liquid.

2. Add the mushrooms to the liquid and return the pan to the heat. Simmer for 5 minutes. Remove the pan from the heat and drain. In a bowl, combine the artichoke hearts, mushrooms, and the remaining ingredients. Stir well.

For the Dressing:
1 tablespoon (15 mL) crushed red chile
⅓ cup (79 mL) olive oil
¼ cup (59 mL) balsamic vinegar
Juice of 1 medium lemon
3 green onions, including some of the green, chopped
2 cloves garlic, peeled and minced
1 tablespoon (15 mL) dried oregano
½ teaspoon (2.5 mL) dried basil

1. In a bowl, mix together all the ingredients. Pour the dressing over the vegetables. Refrigerate them overnight to marinate.

Mixed Salad Greens with Santa Fe Serrano Dressing

Yield: 4 servings   Heat Scale: Mild

Make small batches of this dressing, because the avocado will discolor slightly by the second day; however, it is so good and so versatile that it probably won't last that long anyway. I have found that using champagne vinegar adds zest without the harshness associated with other vinegars. For a tasty and unusual touch, serve the dressing over cooked, chilled vegetables, such as asparagus or artichokes.

1 ripe avocado, peeled, pitted, and quartered
2 tablespoons (30 mL) champagne vinegar
¼ cup (59 mL) water
½ cup (118 mL) low-fat plain yogurt or sour cream
2 tablespoons (30 mL) chopped cilantro
¼ teaspoon (1.25 mL) salt
1 teaspoon (5 mL) sugar
1 clove garlic, peeled
1 fresh serrano chile, stem and seeds removed
5 ounces (140 g) mixed salad greens

1. Place all the ingredients except the greens in a blender or food processor and blend until thoroughly mixed. If the dressing seems too thick, add more water or yogurt. Use it to dress the salad greens as soon as possible or store, covered tightly in the refrigerator until ready to use.

Mangos and Peaches with Pungent Poppy Seed Dressing

Yield: 4 servings   Heat Scale: Mild

*My two favorite fruits combined with the seeds that will make me flunk a drug test!
The dry mustard and red chile flakes make this an unusual dressing for a fruit salad.
It can also be used for basting during the last 2 or 3 minutes of grilling vegetables, but
because of the sugar content, you don't want to use it too soon or the vegetables might
burn.*

¼ cup (59 mL) sugar
1½ teaspoons (7.5 mL) dry mustard
½ teaspoon (2.5 mL) salt
¼ teaspoon (1.25 mL) celery salt
1 teaspoon (5 mL) hot red chile flakes (such as piquin)
½ teaspoon (2.5 mL) paprika
⅓ cup (79 mL) apple cider vinegar
1½ tablespoons (22.5 mL) poppy seeds
1 cup (236 mL) vegetable oil
1 cup (236 mL) chopped fresh ripe mangos
1 cup (236 mL) chopped fresh peaches

1. In a small bowl, combine the sugar, mustard, salt, celery salt, chile
flakes, paprika, vinegar, poppy seeds, and vegetable oil. Beat with a small
electric beater until the dressing is thick.
2. Place the mangos and peaches together on 4 salad plates and drizzle the
dressing over them. Refrigerate any excess dressing.

Garden Fresh Tomatoes with Creamy Jalapeño Dressing

Yield: 4 servings   Heat Scale: Medium

*I usually have a huge harvest of heirloom tomatoes, and this is one way to use them
up. The watercress gives this dressing peppery overtones, and the jalapeños give it
some zing. It is good served over salad greens or poured over tender-crisp cooked vegetables, such as asparagus. You might even like it as a dip for carrots, jicama, turnip
spears, and celery.*

1 small bunch parsley, washed and drained
1 bunch watercress, washed and drained
½ cup (118 mL) canola oil
½ cup (118 mL) olive oil
1 clove garlic, peeled
⅓ cup (79 mL) tarragon vinegar
2 jalapeño or serrano chiles, stems and seeds removed
2 shallots, peeled and quartered
2 teaspoons (10 mL) dry mustard
1 tablespoon (15 mL) horseradish
1 teaspoon (5 mL) soy sauce
¼ cup (59 mL) plain yogurt
4 large fresh tomatoes, sliced

1. Combine all the ingredients except the tomatoes in a food processor or blender and purée. If the mixture seems too thick, add a few teaspoons (30–45 mL) yogurt or ice water.
2. Divide the tomato slices among 4 salad plates and drizzle the dressing over them. Store the remaining dressing in a jar in the refrigerator.

Grilled Bells with I Can't Believe It's Buttermilk Dressing

Yield: 4 servings   Heat Scale: Medium

This low-fat dressing should help get you over the fat hump, and, besides, buttermilk is good for you. I like to use red, yellow, and purple bell peppers for the nice mix of colors.

1 cup (236 mL) buttermilk
2 red jalapeño chiles, stems and seeds removed, minced
⅓ cup (79 mL) grated cucumber
3 green onions, chopped (with a little tender green included)
1 tablespoon (15 mL) Dijon mustard
2 tablespoons (30 mL) chopped fresh cilantro
2 teaspoons (10 mL) fresh lime juice
½ teaspoon (2.5 mL) dill
⅛ teaspoon (.6 mL) freshly ground black pepper
1 red bell pepper, grilled, peeled, and cut into strips
1 orange bell pepper, grilled, peeled, and cut into strips
1 purple bell pepper, grilled, peeled, and cut into strips

1. Place all the ingredients except the bell peppers in a large glass jar and shake briskly. Chill the dressing and shake again before using.
2. Divide the bell pepper strips among 4 salad plates and drizzle the dressing over them. Store the remaining dressing in the refrigerator.

Orange Gold Salad

Yield: 3–4 servings   Heat Scale: Mild

I love freshly grated ginger, but sometimes the stringiness of the root clogs up the mini-processor and drives me crazy. However, a suggestion from a fine Vietnamese chef, Binh Duong, solved the problem. Binh suggests placing the whole pieces of ginger over an electric burner on high or a gas burner on low and turning them every minute or so to char the ginger on all sides. Then rinse the charred ginger under water while scrubbing with a stiff vegetable brush. The ginger is then ready for chopping, grating, or processing. This salad can be served on Boston (Bibb) lettuce leaves or curly endive.

1 cup (236 mL) shredded carrot
2 oranges or 3 tangerines, peeled and sliced into thin rounds
¼ cup (59 mL) finely chopped shallots
½ teaspoon (2.5 mL) dried basil
2 tablespoons (30 mL) finely chopped fresh ginger
3 tablespoons (45 mL) rice vinegar
2 tablespoons (30 mL) Chile Oil (page 16)
¼ teaspoon (1.25 mL) freshly ground white pepper

1. In a medium glass bowl, toss together the carrot, oranges or tangerines, and shallots. Combine the remaining ingredients in a glass jar and shake thoroughly. Pour the dressing over the carrot mixture and toss gently. Chill for an hour or two before serving.

Spicy Sweet and Sour Coleslaw

Yield: 10–12 servings   Heat Scale: Medium

This excellent slaw is a far cry from the heavily mayonnaised coleslaws of childhood picnics. Because there is no mayo in this one, it is an excellent choice for a picnic or barbecue. The leftovers are great and will keep for 5 days in the refrigerator. (Note: This recipe requires advance preparation.)

3 pounds (1.36 kg) fresh green cabbage, thinly sliced
¼ cup (59 mL) chopped serrano chiles
1 green bell pepper, stem and seeds removed, finely chopped
1 red bell pepper, stem and seeds removed, finely chopped
1½ cups (354 mL) chopped onion
1 cup (236 mL) vegetable oil
1 cup (236 mL) white vinegar
¾ cup (177 mL) sugar
2 tablespoons (30 mL) celery seed
½ teaspoon (2.5 mL) freshly ground black pepper

1. In a very large glass bowl, combine the cabbage, serranos, bell pepper, and onion.
2. Combine the remaining ingredients in a saucepan and bring to a boil, stirring until the sugar dissolves. Boil gently for 1 minute, then pour the marinade over the vegetables and mix.
3. Refrigerate for several hours or, preferably, overnight before serving. The slaw will keep for 5 days.
4. Before serving, drain the slaw so the marinade doesn't drown everything else on the plate. Reserve the extra marinade to add to any leftover slaw.

Zippy Apple Coleslaw

Yield: 10–12 servings   Heat Scale: Medium

Apples and a little chimayo red chile make this hot and spicy coleslaw a memorable salad at any summer picnic.

1 small red cabbage, shredded
3 apples, peeled, cored, and shredded
2 cups (473 mL) diced red bell pepper
2 cups (473 mL) diced red onion
3 poblano chiles, roasted, peeled, stems and seeds removed, diced
1 chipotle chile in adobo sauce, puréed
½ cup (118 mL) lemon juice
½ cup (118 mL) plain nonfat yogurt
½ cup (118 mL) light mayonnaise
1 dash salt
1 tablespoon (15 mL) ground hot red New Mexican chile
(chimayo preferred)

1. Combine the cabbage, apples, bell pepper, red onion, and poblanos in a large bowl. Set aside.
2. In another bowl, mix together the puréed chipotle and lemon juice. Add the yogurt, mayonnaise, salt, and ground chile. Mix well. Pour the dressing over the cabbage mixture and toss to coat evenly. Refrigerate for at least 2 hours before serving.

Gingered and Grilled Shrimp Salad with Crispy Red Chile-Dusted Eggroll Strips

Yield: 4 servings   Heat Scale: Medium

The marinade in this recipe doubles as the dressing for the salad. I like to serve this salad with the shrimp hot off the grill, but it can also be prepared ahead and served chilled. This is a meal in itself, but why not treat yourself to a chilled gazpacho and a dry white wine? (Note: This recipe requires advance preparation.)

For the Gingered Shrimp Marinade and Dressing:
¼ cup (59 mL) vegetable oil
¼ cup (59 mL) peanut oil
6 tablespoons (90 mL) rice wine vinegar
6 small Thai chiles, stems removed, minced (or substitute serrano chiles)
2 tablespoons (30 mL) minced ginger
1 tablespoon (15 mL) chopped green onions, green part included
1 tablespoon (15 mL) dry sherry
1 teaspoon (5 mL) five-spice powder
1 teaspoon (5 mL) soy sauce
½ teaspoon (2.5 mL) sesame oil

1. Combine all the ingredients in a blender or food processor and purée until smooth. Transfer the marinade to a bowl and let sit at room temperature for an hour or two.

For the Grilled Shrimp Salad:
¼ cup (59 mL) peanut oil
24 medium shrimp, shelled and deveined, tails off
Vegetable oil for frying
4 eggroll wrappers, cut in ¼-inch (.5 cm) strips
Ground red New Mexico chile to taste
5 ounces (140 g) mixed baby greens
3 slices red onion

1. Remove the marinade from the refrigerator and strain it, saving the solids and the liquid. Combine the solids with the peanut oil and brush the mixture on the shrimp. Place the shrimp in a bowl and marinate in the refrigerator for a couple of hours.
2. Fill a deep-fat fryer or a wok with 2 inches (5 cm) of vegetable oil and heat to 375°F (190°C). Add the eggroll strips in batches and fry for 30 seconds to crisp. Transfer the strips to paper towels to drain and sprinkle them with the ground red chile.
3. Place the shrimp in a vegetable grill basket and grill over a medium-hot fire for about 6 minutes, shaking often so that they cook evenly.
4. Toss the greens with the reserved marinade and divide them among chilled salad plates. Arrange the sliced onion over the salads and top with the shrimp. Garnish the salads with the crispy egg roll strips and serve.

Green Chile Panzanella
(Southwestern-Style Tuscan Bread Salad)

Yield: 6 servings   Heat Scale: Medium

Use the very best quality red wine vinegar and olive oil in this recipe, because even the heat of the green chile will not mask the biting taste of inferior products. The vinegar and fresh vegetables make this salad surprisingly refreshing on a hot day. It is also a great way to use up leftover bread—but it has to be bread with substance. Soft, squishy, store-bought sandwich bread will make a salad akin to Elmer's Glue.

10 slices of good quality rustic bread, several days old
3 fresh tomatoes, peeled and coarsely chopped
2 cucumbers, peeled, seeded, and cubed
1 cup (236 mL) finely diced red onion
2 cloves garlic, peeled and minced very fine
1 cup (236 mL) chopped green New Mexican chile
½ cup (118 mL) chopped fresh basil
¼ cup (59 mL) red wine vinegar
¼ teaspoon (1.25 mL) salt
¼ teaspoon (1.25 mL) freshly ground black pepper
⅔ cup (158 mL) best-quality olive oil

1. In a large bowl, soak the bread in a little water, but not enough to get the bread totally soggy. Squeeze the bread dry with your hands and crumble it into a large bowl. Add the tomatoes, cucumbers, red onion, garlic, chile, and basil and toss with the bread.
2. Pour the vinegar into a small glass jar and add the salt and black pepper. Shake the jar until the salt is dissolved. Add the olive oil to the jar and shake until the mixture is blended.
3. Immediately pour the vinegar and oil mixture over the bread mixture and toss gently. Serve immediately.

Zesty French Bread Salad

Yield: 4 servings   Heat Scale: Medium

Here's another bread salad that makes use of crusty French or Italian bread that's hardened. The texture of the salad depends on the amount of time you allow it to sit. For a crunchy salad, serve it immediately. The longer it sits, the softer the salad will become as it soaks up the dressing and vegetable juices.

3 cups (708 mL) stale, crusty French bread, lightly toasted and cut in ½-inch (1 cm) cubes
½ cup (118 mL) finely chopped red onion
1 cucumber, peeled, quartered lengthwise, and cut crosswise into ½-inch (1 cm) pieces
2 large tomatoes, peeled, seeded, and chopped
1 cup (236 mL) firmly packed basil leaves
1 garlic clove, peeled and minced
2 serrano chiles, stems removed
¼ cup (59 mL) red wine vinegar
½ cup (118 mL) olive oil

1. In a large bowl, combine the bread, red onion, cucumber, and tomatoes. Toss the mixture well.
2. In a food processor, blend the basil, garlic, chiles, vinegar, and olive oil until the basil is puréed and the dressing is emulsified. Sprinkle the dressing over the bread mixture, tossing it well. Serve at once or allow to sit for a few minutes to soften. Serve at room temperature.

Curried Good Luck Fruit Salad

Yield: 12 servings   Heat Scale: Mild

A lucky dish to start the New Year out right, this lightly curried combination of peas and fruits is also infused with mustard and vinegar. What a combination! This recipe is designed to serve at a picnic or a family get-together.

4 (15-ounce [426 g]) cans black-eyed peas, rinsed and well drained
2 cups (473 mL) diced apples
2 cups (473 mL) diced fresh pineapple
1 small red onion, peeled and minced
2 tablespoons (30 mL) curry powder
½ cup (118 mL) yogurt
3 tablespoons (45 mL) Dijon mustard
2 tablespoons (30 mL) apple cider vinegar
½ cup (118 mL) olive oil
2 large purple cabbages

1. Combine the black-eyed peas, apples, pineapple, and onion in a large bowl and set aside.
2. Whisk together the curry powder, yogurt, mustard, and vinegar. Gradually whisk in the olive oil.

3. Add the dressing to the salad and toss gently to coat. Peel whole leaves off of the purple cabbage to line one large serving bowl or 12 individual salad bowls. Fill the bowl(s) with the fruit salad and serve.

Spicy Cold Cucumber Salad

Yield: 4 servings   Heat Scale: Mild

This salad has a bite, but the yogurt cools it down nicely. I like to make it in the summer when I can get the majority of the ingredients from the garden; sometimes cucumbers from the grocery store can be a little bitter. Taste the cucumber; if it seems bitter, slice it, put it in a colander, and salt it. Let it stand for 30 minutes, rinse thoroughly to remove the salt, and allow it to drain.

2 cucumbers, peeled and coarsely chopped
1 tomato, finely chopped
3 green onions, finely chopped, including some of the green parts
½ teaspoon (2.5 mL) cumin
2 tablespoons (30 mL) finely chopped fresh mint, or 1½ teaspoons (7.5 ml) dried mint
1 clove garlic, peeled and minced
1 teaspoon (5 mL) ground red New Mexican chile
½–¾ cup (125–177 mL) plain yogurt
1 dash sugar (optional)
Salt, to taste
Freshly ground black pepper, to taste

1. Combine the cucumbers, tomato, green onions, cumin, mint, garlic, and ground chile and mix gently. Spoon ½ cup (118 mL) yogurt over the top and mix again. If the yogurt doesn't completely coat the vegetables, add ¼ cup (59 mL) more. If it seems too sharp, add a dash of sugar; then add the salt and pepper to taste. Chill for 2 hours or more.

Chilly Chile Lentil Salad

Yield: 8–10 servings

Heat Scale: Medium to Hot, depending on the habanero

Lentils have been given short shrift by many people, but they are extremely versatile, nutritious, and cheap, cheap, cheap. In this spicy salad, there is a variety of textures, which adds interest to the dish, along with a nice blend of flavors. My preferred chile for this dish is the habanero; it delivers quite a pungent punch. (Note: This recipe requires advance preparation.)

1 pound (454 g) dried lentils, cleaned and washed
1 whole onion, peeled
6 whole cloves
2 carrots, each cut into 4 pieces
2 teaspoons (10 mL) chopped fresh oregano or 1 teaspoon (5 mL) dried oregano
2 cloves garlic, peeled and minced
1 whole bay leaf
⅓ cup (79 mL) balsamic vinegar
½ cup (118 mL) olive oil
½ cup (118 mL) cooked, chilled wild rice
2 cups (473 mL) cherry tomatoes, halved
⅔ cup (158 mL) toasted piñons
¼–½ cup chopped fresh cilantro, to taste
½ cup (118 mL) crumbled feta cheese
½ cup (118 mL) sliced green onions
1 habanero chile, stem and seeds removed, minced (or substitute 3 red serranos)
5 ounces (140 g) mixed greens

1. Put the lentils in a large, heavy saucepan and add water to cover. Stud the onion with the whole cloves, then add it to the pan along with the carrots, oregano, garlic, and bay leaf. Bring to a boil, then lower the heat to a simmer and cover. Simmer for 25 to 35 minutes, or until the lentils are done but still retain their shape and are not mushy. Drain thoroughly and discard the carrots, the onion with the cloves, and the bay leaf. Carefully transfer the cooked lentils to a large mixing bowl.
2. Whisk together the vinegar and olive oil. Pour it over the lentils and toss gently. Chill for at least 1 hour
3. Add the remaining ingredients and toss gently. Cover and chill until ready to serve. Serve on a bed of chilled greens.

Brown Rice and Snow Pea Salad with Rojo Vinaigrette

Yield: 6–8 servings   Heat Scale: Medium

Brown rice adds an interesting flair to this easy-to-make-and-serve salad. It relies on jalapeños for heat, but feel free to change to any fresh hot chile you happen to have in your garden.

3½ cups (826 mL) cooked long-grain brown rice
2 cups (473 mL) fresh snow peas, rinsed
1½ cups (354 mL) cooked fresh corn kernels
⅓ cup (79 mL) chopped green onions
2 jalapeño chiles, stems and seeds removed, minced
⅓ cup (79 mL) corn oil
2 tablespoons (30 mL) fresh lime juice
1 tablespoon (15 mL) red wine vinegar
1 tablespoon (15 mL) brown sugar, packed
1 teaspoon (5 mL) ground cayenne
1 teaspoon (5 mL) salt
½ teaspoon (2.5 mL) ground cumin

1. In a bowl, combine the rice, snow peas, corn, green onions, and jalapeños. Toss lightly.
2. In a small bowl, whisk together the corn oil, lime juice, vinegar, brown sugar, cayenne, salt, and cumin. Mix until the sugar is dissolved and the vinaigrette is well blended.
3. Sprinkle the dressing over the salad. Toss to coat the ingredients evenly. The salad should stand at room temperature for at least 1 hour before serving. It can be refrigerated for up to two days, covered.

Rougaille de Tomates

Yield: 4 servings   Heat Scale: Varies

This recipe comes from my writer Judith Ritter, who wrote about Madagascar cooking. She sampled this salad at the L'Exotic restaurant, in Montreal, Quebec.

2 fresh tomatoes, chopped
2 shallots, peeled and minced
½ onion, chopped
Juice of ½ lemon
1 tablespoon (15 mL) minced fresh ginger
1 tablespoon (15 mL) chopped fresh parsley
2 tablespoons (30 mL) olive oil
Salt, to taste
Freshly ground black pepper, to taste
L'Exotic Sauce Dynamite (page 90), to taste

1. Combine all the ingredients and serve over lettuce or spinach.

Salata Tomatim Bel Daqua
(Sudanese Tomato Salad)

Yield: 6 servings   Heat Scale: Mild

If you're lucky like David Karp, you have friends all over the world who prepare incredible, adventurous meals. David discovered this recipe while exploring hot and spicy London. There he met Yousif and Katie Mukhayer, who served this as part of a splendid Sudanese banquet in their home. And of course, he sent me the recipe.

5 tomatoes, seeds removed, diced
4 green onions, finely chopped
1–2 small green chiles, such as Thai, stems and seeds removed, minced
4 sprigs Italian parsley, finely chopped
½ cup (118 mL) vegetable oil
4 tablespoons (60 mL) smooth peanut butter
Juice of 2 limes
Salt, to taste

1. Combine the tomatoes, green onions, chiles, and parsley in a bowl and set aside.
2. In a separate bowl, whisk the oil into the peanut butter until smooth. Stir in the lime juice and season with salt. If the dressing is too thick, thin with 1–2 tablespoons (15–30 mL) water.
3. Gently toss the vegetable mixture with the dressing until lightly coated.

Green Mango Salad

Yield: 4–6 servings   Heat Scale: Hot

Here is another African salad from Judith Ritter. It is another unusual—and spicy—salad served at L'Exotic restaurant in Montreal.

3 jalapeño chiles, stems and seeds removed, minced
2 green mangos, peeled, pitted, and julienned
1 onion, peeled and minced
2 cloves garlic, peeled and minced
2–3 tablespoons (30–45 mL) minced fresh parsley
Juice of 2 limes
3 tablespoons (45 mL) olive oil
Salt, to taste

1. Combine all the ingredients and serve as a side dish to grilled or roasted meat or fish.

Tofu and Cucumber Salad with Spicy Peanut Sauce

Yield: 6 servings   Heat Scale: Medium

Mark Berlin collected this recipe while writing for me about Asian markets. He cre-ated this super spicy salad using a hybrid of Indonesian/Thai satay and Sichuan/ Hunan peanut sauces. This recipe transforms mild-mannered tofu and cukes into a memorable salad.

For the Spicy Peanut Sauce:
4 cloves garlic, peeled and minced
1 tablespoon (15 mL) sesame oil or sesame chili oil
¼ cup (59 mL) ground red New Mexican chile
½ cup (118 mL) mushroom soy sauce or regular soy sauce
½ cup (118 mL) hoisin sauce
¼ cup (59 mL) prepared Sambal Badjak (page 40) (or substitute ¼ cup [59 mL] sautéed onions)
¼ cup (59 mL) rice vinegar
1 cup (236 mL) dry roasted peanuts (or substitute ⅔ cup [158 mL] chunky peanut butter)

1. In a saucepan, heat the oil over medium heat. Add the garlic and sauté until golden. Stir in the ground chile, then stir in the soy sauce, hoisin, Sambal Badjak, vinegar, and peanuts. Bring the mixture to a simmer, re-move it from the heat, and let it cool slightly. Using a hand blender, food processor, or standard blender, process the mixture until it is very smooth. Let the sauce cool thoroughly.

For the Tofu and Cucumber Salad:
1 medium Napa cabbage, green or red cabbage, or iceberg lettuce, shredded
1 pound (454 g) firm tofu, cut in ¾-inch (1.5 cm) cubes
3 cucumbers, peeled, seeded, and cubed

1. Divide the cabbage among 6 salad plates and arrange the tofu and cucumber in an attractive pile on top. Drizzle with the peanut sauce and serve immediately.

Thai Beef Salad
(Yam Neua)

Yield: 4 servings   Heat Scale: Medium

This recipe comes from Gloria Zimmerman, one of the guest chefs and cookbook authors I met during the Hot and Spicy Asian Weekend at the Mohonk Mountain House. Gloria is the coauthor of The Classic Cuisine of Vietnam. *She and the kitchen staff prepared this recipe for at least 100 people at the event, but luckily she was able to scale it down to serve the more manageable number of 4. The salad is substantial, delicious, and spicy, and it makes a terrific luncheon entrée preceded by one of the lighter soups from Chapter 7.*

1½ pounds (681 g) sirloin steak, 1 inch (2.5 cm) thick
1 small head Boston (Bibb) lettuce
1 cucumber, peeled, seeded, and sliced
1 stalk lemongrass, bulb only, minced
2 tablespoons (30 mL) chopped fresh mint leaves
2 tablespoons (30 mL) chopped fresh cilantro
2 tablespoons (30 mL) fish sauce (nam pla)
4 tablespoons (60 mL) fresh lime juice
2–4 red serrano chiles, stems and seeds removed, finely chopped
1 teaspoon (5 mL) sugar
1 red onion, peeled and thinly sliced

1. Broil the steak in the oven or over charcoal until rare. Cut the steak into 1-inch (2.5 cm) slices and place it on a platter.
2. Arrange the lettuce on a serving platter or divide it among 4 individual plates. Sprinkle the cucumber over the lettuce, followed by the lemongrass, mint, and cilantro.
3. In a small glass jar, combine the fish sauce, lime juice, chiles, and sugar and shake.
4. Divide the steak among the 4 plates or arrange it on the platter. Arrange the sliced red onion over the steak and drizzle with the dressing.

Rujak
(Spicy Padang Fruit Salad)

Yield: 6–8 servings   Heat Scale: Medium

World traveler Jeff Corydon, who sent me this recipe from Indonesia, says that the secret of this spicy salad is in the sauce. The local taste is honored by the inclusion of crushed peanuts and additional chiles. Any firm, fleshy fruit, such as under-ripe bananas, carambolas, or Asian pears, can be used, as can some vegetables, such as jicama or cucumber.

4 serrano chiles, stems and seeds removed
2 tablespoons (30 mL) dried tamarind pulp
2 tablespoons (30 mL) hot water
¼ cup (59 mL) palm sugar or dark brown sugar
1 cup (236 mL) water
½ cup (118 mL) crushed roasted, unsalted peanuts (or substitute ¼ cup [59 mL] crunchy peanut butter)
1 pomelo or tart pink grapefruit, sectioned
1 slightly under-ripe mango, peeled, pitted, and cut into bite-size pieces
1 tart apple, peeled and cut into bite-size pieces
1 small pineapple, peeled and cut into bite-size pieces

1. Place the chiles in a blender with a little water and process until smooth.
2. In a bowl, mash the dried tamarind in the hot water until it softens and dissolves. Strain the mixture to remove any seeds or tissue.
3. Melt the brown sugar in a pan with 1 cup (236 mL) water over low heat until the sugar dissolves, about 5 minutes. Add the crushed peanuts, processed chiles, and tamarind water, and simmer for 5 minutes, stirring often, until a fairly thick, sticky syrup forms. Chill the syrup in the refrigerator.
4. When you're ready to serve, combine the fruits and divide them among salad plates. Pour the syrup over the fruit and serve at once.

Sichuan Cucumber Salad

Yield: 4 servings   Heat Scale: Mild

This unusual, simple salad comes from Martin Yan, who was profiled in one of the magazines I edited. It is easy to make and easy to eat!

1 large cucumber
1 teaspoon (5 mL) salt
3 tablespoons (45 mL) vegetable oil
3 tablespoons (45 mL) minced garlic
1½ teaspoons (7.5 mL) ground toasted Sichuan peppercorns
2 tablespoons (30 mL) rice vinegar
2 teaspoons (10 mL) sesame oil
2 teaspoons (10 mL) sugar
1 teaspoon (5 mL) prepared Asian chile garlic sauce (or substitute your favorite Asian chile paste from Chapter 1)

1. Cut the cucumber in half lengthwise, then cut each half crosswise into ¼-inch (.5 cm) slices. Combine the cucumber slices with the salt. Stir to coat and let stand for 30 minutes. Rinse and pat dry with paper towels.
2. Heat the oil in a saucepan over medium heat. Add the garlic and Sichuan peppercorns and cook until fragrant. Transfer the garlic and peppercorns to a bowl and let cool. Add the remaining ingredients to the bowl and mix until well blended. Pour the dressing over the cucumber slices and mix well. Serve at room temperature or refrigerate and serve cold.

La Phet
(Green Tea Salad)

Yield: 4 servings   Heat Scale: Mild

My friend Richard Sterling collected this recipe on his trip to Burma. It was graciously provided by Renatto Buhlman, executive chef of the Strand Hotel. Renatto says to use the best quality unscented tea available. At the Strand, they give you a fork, but everywhere else you eat this with your fingers. (Serving suggestion: La Phet makes an excellent appetizer with chips and a lager beer or a dry sparkling wine. At any rate, don't take it with iced tea!)

6 cloves garlic, peeled and sliced
¼ cup (59 mL) peanut oil, divided
⅓ cup (79 mL) loose green tea leaves
2 tablespoons (30 mL) coarsely chopped peanuts
1 tablespoon (15 mL) toasted sesame seeds
¼ teaspoon (1.25 mL) sugar
¾ cup (177 mL) finely shredded Napa cabbage or bok choy
Juice of ½ lime
½ teaspoon (2.5 mL) ground cayenne
Lime wedges for garnish
Whole dried red chiles for garnish

1. In a saucepan, heat 2 teaspoons (10 mL) of the oil over medium-high heat. Add the garlic and fry until it starts to brown.
2. In a bowl, combine the tea leaves with 1 tablespoon (15 mL) of the oil and, using your fingers, knead the oil into the leaves until it is well distributed. Let the mixture sit at least 1 hour or until the leaves soften. If your tea is extremely dry, you may want to add a few drops of water.
3. Add the remaining ingredients, including the remaining peanut oil, and mix well. Garnish with the lime wedges and chiles and serve.

Kula Greens with Ginger Chile Vinaigrette and Carmelized Macadamia Nuts

Yield: 4 servings   Heat Scale: Medium

Roger Dikon, former executive chef at the Maui Prince Hotel, attended the Chefs' Festival at the Kapalua Wine Symposium and demonstrated this exotic and terrific recipe. Stay sober and make it at your next party to really impress your guests with your good taste.

For the Dressing:
3 egg yolks
⅓ cup (79 mL) minced ginger
2 tablespoons (30 mL) soy sauce (Japanese shoyu preferred)
2 tablespoons (30 mL) rice wine vinegar
1 teaspoon (5 mL) dark sesame oil
2 tablespoons (30 mL) honey
¾ cup (177 mL) macadamia nut oil (or substitute peanut oil)
1 teaspoon (5 mL) salt
1 tablespoon (15 mL) Dijon mustard
2 fresh chile piquins, stems and seeds removed, diced (or substitute serranos)
1½ cups (354 mL) macadamia nut oil (or substitute peanut oil)
2 tablespoons (30 mL) water
Juice of 1 lemon

1. In a blender or food processor, blend the egg yolks, ginger, and soy sauce for 10 seconds. Add the vinegar, sesame oil, honey, salt, mustard, and chile and blend on low speed. With the machine still running, slowly add the oil. As the dressing thickens, slowly add the water and lemon juice. Chill before serving.

For the Carmelized Macadamia Nuts:
1 tablespoon (15 mL) dark brown sugar
2 tablespoons (30 mL) water
¾ cup (177 mL) diced Macadamia nuts

1. In a heavy skillet, heat the sugar over medium heat until it melts. Stir in the water, add the nuts, and cook, stirring constantly, until the nuts are sugar coated and the water has evaporated. Let cool to room temperature.

For the Salad:
1½ cups (354 mL) Kula greens (mixed baby lettuces)
1 cup (236 mL) dried papaya, mango, cherries, or raisins

1. Toss the dressing with the greens and dried fruit until well coated. Garnish with the macadamia nuts.

White Radish Salad

Yield: 4 servings   Heat Scale: Medium

Sharon Hudgins found this recipe when she was living in the Russian Far East, where it was made with large white Japanese daikon radishes. The same recipe would be made in European Russia with the large, bulbous white radishes that grow there.

2 large daikon radishes, peeled and shredded
1 teaspoon (5 mL) salt
1 teaspoon (5 mL) sugar
1–2 hard-boiled eggs, peeled and chopped
1 apple, peeled, cored, and shredded
4–6 tablespoons (60–90 mL) sour cream
1 teaspoon (5 mL) ground cayenne

1. Place the daikon in a bowl, sprinkle the salt and sugar over the top, and toss well. Let the radishes sit at room temperature for 30 minutes. Transfer the radishes to a large sieve and press firmly on the shredded pieces to get out as much moisture as possible. Discard the liquid.
2. Return the daikon to the bowl, toss with a fork to separate the pieces, and add the chopped hard-boiled eggs and shredded apple. Stir in the sour cream, mixing gently but thoroughly. Sprinkle with the cayenne and serve.

Bean Curd, Vegetable, and Peanut Salad with Hot Chile Dressing

Yield: 4 servings   Heat Scale: Medium

This salad is from West Java, and it is goes well with Indonesia curries like rendang.

For the Dressing:
¼ cup (59 mL) finely chopped fresh santaka chiles (or substitute serranos or jalapeños)
½ teaspoon (2.5 mL) finely grated fresh ginger root
1 teaspoon (5 mL) minced garlic
¼ cup (59 mL) distilled white vinegar
2 cups (473 mL) cold water
2 tablespoons (30 mL) sugar
½ teaspoon (2.5 mL) trassi (shrimp paste)
1 teaspoon (5 mL) salt

1. Combine the chiles, ginger, garlic, and vinegar in a food processor and blend for 30 seconds. Scrape down the sides of the processor bowl with a rubber spatula. Blend again until the mixture is smooth. Add the water, sugar, trassi, and salt to the chile mixture and blend for a few seconds longer. Taste for seasonings, adjust as needed, and set aside.

For the Salad:
1 cup (236 mL) fresh bean sprouts
20 ounces (560 g) tofu, cut into ½-inch (1 cm) cubes
1 cup (236 mL) thinly shredded purple cabbage
1 cup (236 mL) thinly sliced radishes
1 cup (236 mL) chopped prepared sauerkraut
1 cup (236 mL) shelled peanuts

1. Steam the bean sprouts for 12 to 15 minutes, then set them aside to cool. Next arrange the sprouts, tofu, cabbage, radishes, sauerkraut, and peanuts in layered mounds on a large platter. Pour the dressing evenly over the salad and serve immediately.

Som Tam
(Shrimp and Papaya Salad)
Yield: 6 servings   Heat Scale: Medium

This Thai recipe incorporates the highly aromatic flavors of lemongrass with robust, sweet papaya and succulent shrimp. Traditionally, an unripe papaya is used in this dish. However, since a green papaya may be difficult to find, a ripe papaya offers a slightly different, but tasty alternative.

1 bunch romaine lettuce, washed, leaves separated and gently dried
½ head purple cabbage, shredded
2 (1-inch [2.5 cm] stalks) lemongrass, minced
2 papayas, peeled, seeded, and thinly sliced
2 firm tomatoes, sliced into thin rounds
½ pound (224 g) cooked shrimp
2½ tablespoons (37.5 mL) roasted peanuts, crushed
2 serrano or jalapeño chiles, seeded and cut into slivers
Juice of 2 limes
Juice of 1 lemon
2 tablespoons (30 mL) fish sauce (nam pla)
1 tablespoon (15 mL) sugar
2 green onions, finely chopped

1. On a medium platter, arrange the lettuce leaves and set aside. In a bowl, combine the cabbage and lemongrass. Set a few slices of the papayas and tomatoes aside for garnish and add the rest to the bowl. Arrange the mixture on the platter, adding the shrimp and peanuts to cover. Garnish with the remaining papaya and tomatoes and the chiles.
2. In a separate bowl, mix the lime juice, lemon juice, fish sauce, sugar, and green onions together, stirring until the sugar dissolves. Pour the dressing evenly over the salad and refrigerate until serving time.

Spicy Coconut and Grapefruit Salad

Yield: 4 servings   Heat Scale: Medium

If you're feeling adventurous and have access to fresh, exotic fruits, substitute pomelos for the grapefruit, as they do in Thailand.

1 cup (236 mL) shredded fresh coconut
1 teaspoon (5 mL) sugar
2 teaspoons (10 mL) soy sauce
1 tablespoon (15 mL) lemon juice
1 tablespoon (15 mL) lime juice
2 tablespoons (30 mL) water
2 teaspoons (10 mL) vegetable oil
2 cloves garlic, crushed
1 serrano or jalapeño chile, stem and seeds removed, chopped
2 tablespoons (30 mL) finely diced onion
2 large grapefruit, peeled and sectioned

1. Place the coconut in a frying pan and roast it over medium heat until it just turns brown. Transfer the coconut to a mixing bowl. Add the sugar, soy sauce, lemon and lime juices, and water.
2. Pour the oil into the frying pan and add the garlic, chile, and onion. Sauté over medium heat until brown. Add this to the coconut mixture, stirring well.
3. Arrange equal amounts of the grapefruit segments on four plates, then pour some of the coconut dressing over each. Refrigerate for at least 15 minutes and before serving.

Nuom Trosot
(Cambodian Hot Cucumber Salad)

Yield: 4 servings   Heat Scale: Hot

This spicy dish features Cucumis sativus, *or the cucumber, along with fresh herbs and scallops. The addition of two types of chiles makes this Cambodian recipe twice as good!*

For the Dressing:
4 tablespoons (60 mL) sugar
1½ tablespoons (22.5 mL) salt
6 tablespoons (90 mL) water
4 tablespoons (60 mL) lime juice
1 tablespoon (15 mL) lemon juice
4 tablespoons (60 mL) fish sauce
3 cloves garlic, peeled and minced

1. Combine the sugar, salt, and water in a sauce pan. Cook, stirring, over low heat until the salt and sugar dissolve, then remove the pan from the heat and let cool. When the mixture is cool, add the juices, fish sauce, and garlic.

For the Salad:
8 medium cucumbers, peeled lengthwise and thinly sliced
7 ounces (196 g) boiled lean pork, cubed into ½-inch (1 cm) pieces
2 cups (473 mL) soaked bean thread noodles
½ cup (118 mL) green New Mexican chile, roasted, peeled, seeded, and chopped
2 pounds (1.1 kg) cooked scallops
¼ cup (59 mL) fresh mint leaves
¼ cup (59 mL) fresh basil leaves
3 shallots, peeled and minced
1 clove garlic, peeled and minced
1 tablespoon (15 mL) fresh Thai chiles, chopped (or substitute piquins)
1 large purple cabbage, washed, outer leaves removed
1 orange, peeled and quartered

1. Combine all the ingredients except the cabbage leaves and orange segments in a bowl. Add the salad dressing a little bit at a time, tossing the salad to cover evenly. Arrange each portion on a bed of cabbage leaves. Garnish each serving with an orange quarter.

Urab
(Vegetable Salad with Spiced Coconut Dressing)
Yield: 6 servings   Heat Scale: Medium

One of keys to authentic Indonesian cooking is to use the freshest ingredients possible. To find a "young" coconut, shake it and make sure it has lots of liquid. The more liquid, the fresher the fruit.

For the Dressing:
5 tablespoons (75 mL) prepared tamarind sauce
4 teaspoons (20 mL) prepared spicy coconut relish (sambal kelapa, available in Asian markets)
½ teaspoon (2.5 mL) crushed fresh ginger
2 teaspoons (10 mL) salt
1 cup (236 mL) fresh young coconut meat, coarsely grated

1. Combine the tamarind sauce, sambal kelapa, ginger, and salt in a bowl and mix well. Add the coconut last, gently tossing it in the dressing.

For the Salad:
½ pound (224 g) fresh bean sprouts, washed
2 cups (473 mL) shredded purple cabbage
½ pound (224 g) fresh spinach, coarsely chopped
½ pound (224 g) string beans, washed and broken into 1-inch (2.5 cm) strips
2 limes, sliced into rounds

1. Steam the bean sprouts, cabbage, spinach, and string beans separately, until they are al dente. When all of the vegetables have been steamed, combine them in a bowl and set them aside to cool to room temperature.
2. On individual salad plates, combine the vegetables with the dressing and serve immediately at room temperature. Garnish each plate with sliced limes.

Pla Talay
(Spiced-Out Seafood Salad)

Yield: 4 servings   Heat Scale: Hot

Fish is plentiful in Southeast Asia, especially in Bangkok, a city near the Gulf of Thailand. This recipe uses kaffir lime leaves, whose fragrance is thought to ward off evil spirits.

3 tablespoons (45 mL) lime juice
2 tablespoons (30 mL) fish sauce (nam pla)
5 dried Thai chiles, crushed (or substitute piquins)
1 tablespoon (15 mL) minced garlic
1 tablespoon (15 mL) minced ginger
2 tablespoons (30 mL) finely sliced lemongrass
2 tablespoons (30 mL) finely minced shallots
¼ cup (59 mL) prawns or shrimp, diced, boiled, and shelled
¼ cup (59 mL) fish, diced and boiled
¼ cup (59 mL) scallops, boiled
¼ cup (59 mL) baby squid, sliced
¼ cup (59 mL) clams, boiled and shelled
¼ cup (59 mL) fresh mint leaves
¼ cup (59 mL) cilantro
¼ cup (59 mL) shredded kaffir lime leaves
3 serrano or jalapeño chiles, stems and seeds removed, thinly sliced

1. In a large bowl, combine the lime juice, fish sauce, and crushed chiles. Gently mix in the garlic, ginger, lemongrass, and shallots, and set aside.
2. In a separate large bowl, combine the seafood. Pour the lime juice mixture on top of the seafood, tossing well. Garnish with the mint leaves, cilantro, kaffir lime leaves, and sliced chiles.

Hunan Strange Chicken Salad

Yield: 4 servings   Heat Scale: Mild

This cold chicken salad is not really strange—just delicious! It gets its name from the sauce, which is salty, sweet, sour, and hot, all in one dish. In the Chinese province of Hunan, where the summers are hot, a cool yet pungent entrée is always welcome. This is a great way to recycle leftover chicken. (Note: This recipe requires advance preparation.)

For the Dressing:
2 tablespoons (30 mL) rice vinegar
2 tablespoons (30 mL) light soy sauce
1½ tablespoons (22.5 mL) peanut oil
1 tablespoon (15 mL) sesame paste (available in Asian markets) or smooth peanut butter
1 tablespoon (15 mL) Chinese red chile oil (available in Asian markets)
1 tablespoon (15 mL) sugar
2 teaspoons (10 mL) ground Sichuan peppercorns
2 teaspoons (10 mL) sesame oil
1 teaspoon (5 mL) minced ginger
½ teaspoon (2.5 mL) crushed red chile flakes

1. In a bowl, combine all the ingredients and mix well. Allow the dressing to sit for a couple of hours to blend the flavors.

For the Salad:
8 ounces (224 g) cooked chicken, chopped
2 green onions, some of the green part included, chopped
1 cucumber, ½ cubed and ½ sliced
Shredded lettuce
¼ cup (59 mL) roasted peanuts
Crushed red chile flakes for garnish
Chopped fresh cilantro for garnish

1. Toss the chicken, green onions, and cubed cucumber in the dressing. Allow the mixture to sit at room temperature for 30 minutes.
2. Divide the lettuce among individual serving plates. Arrange the sliced cucumbers on the lettuce, top with the chicken salad, and garnish with the peanuts, chile flakes, and cilantro.

Japanese Cucumber Salsa Salad

Yield: 2 cups (473 mL)   Heat Scale: Medium

Sunomono is a Japanese salad made with sliced cucumbers in a tangy dressing; you may have seen it on the menu at your favorite sushi restaurant. If you dice the cucumbers, sunomono becomes a salsa that makes a lively accompaniment to fresh oysters, seared tuna steaks, or fried soft-shell crabs. Feel free to experiment with this simple recipe, adding shreds of dried seaweed or toasted sesame seeds.

2 small cucumbers, peeled, seeded, and diced (about 2 cups [473 mL])
3 tablespoons (45 mL) rice wine vinegar
1 tablespoon (15 mL) sugar
1 teaspoon (5 mL) crushed red chile flakes
Salt, to taste

1. In a bowl, toss the cucumbers with the rice wine vinegar and sugar. Add salt to taste. Marinate the salad for at least 20 minutes. Taste again, adjust the salt and sugar if necessary, and serve.

Korean Carrot Salad

Yield: 6 small servings as an appetizer or 4 servings as a side dish to accompany a main course
Heat Scale: Medium

This is a popular appetizer in Primorskii Krai (Russia's maritime territory), reflecting the Korean influence on the cuisine of that region. Korean vendors in the markets of Vladivostok and Ussuriisk sell this spicy salad ready made, in clear plastic tubes, and Russians who live in proximity to Koreans have incorporated this recipe into their own culinary repertoire.

1 pound carrots, peeled and grated lengthwise into long, thin strips
1½ teaspoons (7.5 mL) ground cayenne
½ teaspoon (2.5 mL) salt
3 tablespoons (45 mL) sunflower seed oil
2 large garlic cloves, peeled and put through a garlic press
1 green onion, white and tender green parts, finely chopped

1. Put the grated carrots in a medium heatproof bowl. Make a well in the center of the carrots, pushing them aside so you see the bottom of the bowl. Put the cayenne pepper and salt into this well.
2. In a small skillet, heat the oil over medium-high heat until it is very hot. Pour the hot oil over the spices in the bowl, stirring rapidly to mix them into the oil. Stir the pressed garlic into the oil. Then stir the seasoned oil into the grated carrots until well combined. Add the chopped green onion and toss to mix well.
3. Cover and refrigerate until needed. This salad tastes best if you make it a day in advance, so the flavors develop fully. Let the chilled carrot salad sit at room temperature for 30 minutes before serving.

Mongolian Asian Noodle Salad

Yield: 4 servings   Heat Scale: Medium

This salad makes an excellent first course or a spicy accompaniment to any Chinese meal, meatless or not. You can add whatever ingredients you desire to this very basic salad, such as blanched Chinese pea pods.

For the Dressing:
2 cups (473 mL) chicken broth, or more to dilute
¼ cup (59 mL) peanut butter
2 tablespoons (30 mL) peanut oil
2 tablespoons (30 mL) Asian garlic chile sauce or sambal oelek
2 tablespoons (30 mL) red wine vinegar
1 tablespoon (15 mL) Louisiana-style hot sauce
1 tablespoon (15 mL) soy sauce
1 teaspoon (5 mL) grated or minced fresh ginger
1 teaspoon (5 mL) sugar
1 teaspoon (5 mL) toasted sesame oil

1. Combine all the ingredients in a bowl and mix well. Add additional broth as needed to thin to the desired consistency. Allow the dressing to sit at room temperature for an hour to blend the flavors.

For the Salad:
2 cups (473 mL) cooked vermicelli or Chinese noodles
2 cups (473 mL) chopped green onions, some of the green parts included
1 cup (236 mL) sliced red bell peppers
2 cups (473 mL) shredded carrots
2 cups (473 mL) mung bean sprouts
¼ cup (59 mL) sliced cucumber
Chopped roasted peanuts for garnish
Chopped fresh cilantro for garnish

1. Place the noodles in a large bowl or on a serving platter and top them with the vegetables. Pour the dressing over the salad and gently toss to coat the noodles.
2. Garnish the salad with the peanuts and cilantro and serve.

Ramen Noodle Salad

Yield: 4–6 servings   Heat Scale: Medium

*Nancy Gerlach advises that you serve this salad as a first course or as an accompani-
ment to Asian dinners of all kinds. The ingredients can be prepared ahead of time,
but don't assemble the salad until just before serving, as the noodles tend to soak up
all the dressing. This salad is quick and easy to prepare with numerous variations.
Try substituting cooked shrimp, cooked chicken, shredded cabbage, cooked green
beans, or snow peas for some of the vegetables.*

For the Dressing:
3 tablespoons (45 mL) peanut oil
3 tablespoons (45 mL) peanut butter
3 tablespoons (45 mL) rice vinegar
2 tablespoons (30 mL) Asian garlic chile sauce or sambal oelek
1 tablespoon (15 mL) lime juice, fresh preferred
1 tablespoon (15 mL) dark soy sauce
2 teaspoons (10 mL) grated ginger
1 teaspoon (5 mL) sugar
1 teaspoon (5 mL) toasted sesame oil
1 clove garlic, peeled and minced

1. In a bowl, combine all the ingredients and mix well. Allow to sit at
room temperature for an hour to blend the flavors.

For the Salad:
2 cups (473 mL) cooked ramen noodles
½ cup (118 mL) shredded carrots
¼ cup (59 mL) green onions, chopped, green parts included
¼ cup (59 mL) bean sprouts
¼ cup (59 mL) sliced cucumber
4 radishes, sliced
Chopped peanuts for garnish
Chopped fresh cilantro for garnish

1. Place the noodles in a large bowl or on a serving platter and top with
the vegetables. Pour the dressing over the salad and gently toss.
2. Garnish the salad with the peanuts and cilantro and serve.

SEVEN

A Spicy Kettle of Soups, Stews, Chilis, and Gumbos

- - - - - - - - - - - - - -

Soups and stews are universally loved by every culture around the world. One soup expert described them as "comfort in a bowl, love on a spoon, satisfaction simmering on the stove." One major suggestion: Do not use canned or packaged broths or stocks to start your soup. Instead, go with one of the homemade stocks from Chapter 1. You won't regret it! This chapter is organized by types of soup rather than geographically, progressing from the simplest to the most complex. I start with broth-based soups, move on to cream soups and bisques, chill out on some cold soups, chomp on chowders, explore the world of stews, proceed to chilis, and finish with gumbos.

Sweet and Hot Pepper Consommé
Yield: 10–12 servings   Heat Scale: Medium

The flavor of peppers dominates this powerful, spiced-up broth. This recipe can also be used as a vegetarian stock for making other soups and stews. It is an elegant example of a first-course soup that can precede any entrée. For a more intensely flavored soup, substitute Super-Rich Vegetable Stock (page 48) for the water.

4 red bell peppers, seeds removed, quartered
4 green bell peppers, seeds removed, quartered
6 large ripe tomatoes, quartered
2 large onions, peeled and quartered
2 large hot green New Mexican chiles, split, stems and seeds removed
3 bay leaves
3 large jalapeño chiles, split, stems and seeds removed
½ cup (118 mL) chopped parsley
2 whole cloves
3 large cloves garlic, peeled
1½ tablespoons (22.5 mL) salt
6 quarts (5.7 L) boiling water

1. In a large stockpot, combine all the ingredients and boil for 10 minutes. Reduce the heat and simmer, covered, for 1½ hours.
2. Remove from the heat and let cool. Strain through a fine sieve. Serve hot or cold.

Tomato-Orange Ginger Soup
Yield: 8 servings   Heat Scale: Varies

This exciting blend of fresh, light flavors makes a great beginning-of-the-meal palate stimulator during the summer. It has beautiful color and a slight bite from the ginger. A thin lime wheel floated on the soup with a dollop of sour cream makes an excellent garnish.

2 medium onions, peeled and finely chopped
3 cloves garlic, peeled and finely chopped
4 tablespoons (60 mL) unsalted butter
Zest of ½ medium orange
6 cups (1.64 L) puréed fresh tomatoes
1 (5-ounce [140 g]) can tomato paste
6 cups (1.64 L) freshly squeezed orange juice
1 teaspoon (5 mL) ground ginger
1 tablespoon (15 mL) finely grated fresh ginger
¼ teaspoon (1.25 mL) white pepper
½ teaspoon (2.5 mL) salt
¾ tablespoon (11.25 mL) salt
Ground cayenne, to taste

1. In a large stockpot, melt the butter over medium heat. Add the onion and garlic and sauté lightly, but do not let them brown. Add the orange zest and stir well. Add the remaining ingredients, and stir well to combine. Bring almost to a boil, lower the heat, and simmer for 15 minutes. Serve hot or allow to cool before serving.

Sopa de Ajo
(Garlic Soup from Ecuador)
Yield: 4 servings   Heat Scale: Medium

A version of garlic soup is found in most Latin American countries, and this one is particularly tasty. Don't be put off by the idea of a whole soup being devoted to such a potent ingredient; when it is made well, garlic soup is smooth, mild, and never overpowering.

1 tablespoon (15 mL) olive oil
2 tablespoons (30 mL) butter
10 large cloves garlic, peeled and mashed
½ teaspoon (2.5 mL) all-purpose flour
2 aji chiles, stems and seeds removed, minced (or substitute yellow wax hot or jalapeños)
1 quart (.95 L) Classic Chicken Stock (page 46)
Salt, to taste
Freshly ground white or black pepper, to taste
4 large eggs, beaten
2 tablespoons (30 mL) finely grated romano cheese
1 tablespoon (15 mL) chopped fresh parsley

1. In a heavy pot, melt the oil and butter over medium heat. Add the garlic and sauté, quickly stirring in the flour. Stir until the garlic begins to brown. Add the chiles, stock, salt, pepper, eggs, and cheese and mix well. Bring to a boil, then reduce the heat to medium and cook, covered, for 15 minutes. If desired, strain the soup. Serve hot, garnished with the parsley.

Pimentón Garlic Soup
Yield: 4 servings   Heat Scale: Medium

The traditional, quick garlic soup of Madrid is transformed into a smoky-hot masterpiece with the addition of pimentón. What a perfect dish for a Sunday brunch!

¼ cup (59 mL) olive oil
2 ounces (56 g) diced bacon
6 cloves garlic, peeled and chopped
1½ tablespoons (22.5 mL) hot pimentón (or substitute ground chipotle)
¼ teaspoon (1.25 mL) ground cumin
6 cups (5.7 L) Classic Chicken Stock (page 46)
Salt, to taste
10 (½-inch [1 cm]) thick baguette slices, toasted
4 eggs

1. Heat the olive oil in a large soup pot over medium heat. Add the bacon and garlic and fry for about 3 minutes. Add the pimentón, cumin, stock, and salt. Bring the mixture to a boil, then reduce the heat. Add the baguette slices and simmer for 5 minutes. Break each egg into the soup so that it rests on top. Cover the pot and cook until the whites are set but the yolks are still liquid, about 4 minutes. Carefully ladle the soup and eggs into bowls and serve.

Sweet and Spicy Lobster Tail Soup

Yield: 6 servings   Heat Scale: Hot

This unusual seafood soup with an Asian flair owes its unique flavor to marinating the lobster tails for at least an hour before proceeding, so the recipe requires some advance preparation.

3 pounds (1.36 kg) lobster tails in the shell (approximately 6)
2 cups (473 mL) teriyaki sauce
2 cups (473 mL) rice vinegar
1 tablespoon (15 mL) freshly grated ginger
1½ tablespoons (22.5 mL) minced garlic
1¼ tablespoon (18.75 mL) five-spice powder, divided
1 tablespoon (15 mL) brown sugar
½ cup (118 mL) rice wine (or substitute any dry white wine)
1 cup (236 mL) prepared green gunpowder tea
6 cups (5.7 L) Classic Chicken Stock (page 46)
1 cup (236 mL) Traditional European Fish Stock (page 47)
12 Thai chiles, stems and seeds removed, minced (or substitute 6 serranos or jalapeños)
¼ cup (59 mL) soy sauce
2 tablespoons (30 mL) lemon juice
¼ cup (59 mL) honey
2 tablespoons (30 mL) minced garlic
1½ teaspoons (7.5 mL) ground ginger

1. In a bowl, combine the lobster tails, teriyaki sauce, rice vinegar, ginger, garlic, 1½ teaspoons (7.5 mL) five-spice powder, and brown sugar and marinate for at least 1 hour. Remove the lobster tails and discard the marinade.
2. In a wok, heat the wine and tea over high heat and add the lobster tails. Cover and cook 5 to 10 minutes. Remove the lobster tails and let cool. Remove the meat from the shells, coarsely chop it, and set it aside. Discard the shells.
3. In a large pot, combine the stocks, chiles, soy sauce, lemon juice, honey, garlic, ginger, and remaining five-spice powder and boil for 15 minutes. Add the lobster meat, turn off the heat, allow the soup to sit for 5 minutes, then serve.

Spicy Sweet Potato Soup

Yield: 4 servings   Heat Scale: Medium

Here is Nancy Gerlach's version of a soup from Arlene Lutz that we were served in Escazú, Costa Rica. We took the liberty of adding some habanero powder to spice it up. Arlene's secret is to add a little sugar if the potatoes are not sweet enough.

4 cups (.95 L) Classic Chicken Stock (page 46)
2 cups (473 mL) diced sweet potato
3 tablespoons (45 mL) orange juice
¼ teaspoon (1.25 mL) orange zest
3 tablespoons (45 mL) heavy cream
½ teaspoon (2.5 mL) ground habanero chile (or substitute cayenne)
1 pinch white pepper
Chopped parsley for garnish

1. In a soup pot, bring the broth to a boil, add the potatoes, and boil until the potatoes are soft, about 10 minutes. Transfer the potatoes and some of the broth to a food processor or blender and purée the mixture until smooth.
2. Return the puree to the pot and add the orange juice, zest, cream, ground chile, and pepper. Simmer for 20 minutes.
3. Garnish with the parsley and serve.

Grouper Soup in Puff Pastry

Yield: 4 servings   Heat Scale: Medium

The recipe for this soup, created by chef Philip Bethel at the Graycliff Hotel in the Bahamas, was given to Nancy Gerlach, who included it in her article "The Blistering Bahamas." "It is not only tasty," she wrote, "but makes a truly elegant presentation."

1 pound (454 g) fresh grouper fillet
Juice of 2 fresh limes or lemons, divided
Salt, to taste
4 slices bacon, diced
2 small potatoes, peeled and diced
1 stalk celery, diced
1 onion, peeled and diced
1 quart (.95 L) water
2 fresh cayenne chiles, stems and seeds removed, diced (or substitute 1 habanero)
2 tablespoons (30 mL) pimientos, diced
1 egg, beaten
4 (6-inch [15 cm]) circles of puff pastry

1. Preheat oven to 350°F (180°C).
2. Dice the grouper and season it with the juice of 1 lime and the salt. Divide equal portions of the fish among 4 small ovenproof cups and set aside.

3. In a large pot, fry the bacon for a couple of minutes. Add the potatoes, cover, and simmer over medium heat for 5 minutes. Add the celery and onion and continue to cook for another 5 minutes. Add the water and bring to a boil. Lower the heat, season with the remaining lime juice and chile, and simmer until the potatoes are done, about 10 minutes.
4. Divide the ingredients, including the broth, among the cups and add the pimientos.
5. Brush one side of each pastry circle with the egg and place the circles egg-side down over each cup. Brush the top side with the egg and place the cups in the oven. Bake for about 10 minutes, until the dough rises and turns golden. Serve the soup hot.

Sopa de Tortilla con Chiles Pasillas (Tortilla Soup with Pasilla Chiles)

Yield: 8 servings   Heat Scale: Medium

The broth in this recipe is about the only thing that stays the same from cook to cook. Basic to Mexican cuisine, this soup from Chihuahua is served with a multitude of ingredients, and even those vary widely from place to place. The garnishes vary too; it's all part of the fun of making or eating this soup!

4 pasilla chiles, stems and seeds removed
4 quarts (3.8 L) Classic Chicken Stock (page 46)
3 large tomatoes, peeled
2 onions, peeled and quartered
2 cloves garlic, peeled
1 teaspoon (5 mL) salt
¼ cup (59 mL) chopped cilantro
3 dozen corn tortillas, cut into ¼-inch (.5 cm) strips, fried in oil and drained (or substitute 4 cups [.95 L] broken tortilla chips)
2 tablespoons (30 mL) vegetable oil
2 pasilla chiles, stems and seeds removed, lightly fried and coarsely ground in a blender
1 cup (236 mL) chopped avocados
1 cup (236 mL) crumbled cheese such as panela, feta, or mozzarella

1. Tear the chiles into strips, cover them with hot water, and let sit for 15 minutes to rehydrate.
2. In a large pot, heat the chicken broth almost to the boiling point. Reduce the heat and let it simmer while you prepare the rest of the ingredients.
3. In a blender, combine the rehydrated chiles, tomatoes, onions, garlic, salt and cilantro and purée for 10 seconds.
4. In a small skillet, heat the oil over medium heat. Add the blended chile mixture and sauté for 5 minutes. Stir this mixture into the simmering chicken broth, cover, and simmer for 30 minutes.
5. Divide the fried tortilla strips among 8 bowls. Ladle the simmering chicken-chile stock over the strips and garnish with the crushed pasilla chiles, avocado, and cheese.

Sopa de Lima
(Lime Soup)

Yield: 8–10 servings   Heat Scale: Medium

Even though this style of soup, with its many variations, is served all over Mexico, it is believed to have originated in Yucatán because this area grows the small, tart Key limes in abundance. It is the limes that add the particularly good flavor to this soup.

1 (3-pound [1.36 kg]) chicken, cut into 6 pieces
3 quarts (2.85 L) water
2 teaspoons (10 mL) salt
3 cloves garlic, peeled and chopped
1 tablespoon (15 mL) Mexican oregano
3 tablespoons (45 mL) chopped cilantro
1½ cups (354 mL) chopped onion, divided
2 tablespoons (30 mL) vegetable oil
4 serrano or jalapeño chiles, stems and seeds removed, chopped
1½ cups (354 mL) chopped tomatoes
8 Key limes, thinly sliced
8 corn tortillas, cut into eighths, fried, and drained (or substitute tortilla chips)
½ cup (118 mL) minced cilantro

1. Wash the chicken pieces and place them in a large pot. Add the water, salt, garlic, oregano, cilantro, and 1 cup (236 mL) of the onion and bring the mixture to a boil, skimming the foam from the top. Reduce the heat to a simmer, cover, and simmer for 30 minutes.
2. Remove the chicken from the cooking liquid and set aside. Strain the broth through several thicknesses of cheesecloth into a clean pot. Bring the stock to a boil, reduce the heat to a light rolling boil, and cook uncovered for 20 minutes to reduce.
3. Remove the skin and bones from the chicken and discard. Coarsely shred the meat and set aside.
4. In a small, skillet heat the oil over medium heat. Add the remaining ½ cup (118 mL) onion, chiles, and tomatoes, and sauté for 3 minutes.
5. When the stock has reduced, stir in the shredded chicken and the sautéed tomato-chile mixture and simmer for 15 minutes.
6. Serve the soup in large, heated soup bowls, garnished with the tortilla chips and the minced cilantro.

Chipotle Tomato Soup with Cheese Toast
Yield: 8–10 servings   Heat Scale: Medium

Here's a different twist on tomato soup. If ground chipotle is not available, use
2 teaspoons (10 mL) canned chipotles in adobo, minced. Use a high-quality Swiss
cheese, not those cheap squares.

¼ cup (59 mL) olive oil
3 medium onions, peeled and chopped fine
2 tablespoons (30 mL) minced garlic
1 cup (236 mL) minced mushrooms
1 tablespoon (15 mL) minced parsley
2 cups (473 mL) minced celery, leaves included
8 cups (1.9 L) fresh Roma tomatoes, puréed, peeled, and seeded
1 cup (236 mL) tomato paste
2 cups (473 mL) tomato sauce
3 cups (708 mL) Super-Rich Vegetable Stock (page 48)
¼ cup (59 mL) sugar
2 tablespoons (30 mL) balsamic vinegar
¼ cup (59 mL) dry red wine
1 teaspoon (5 mL) ground chipotle
1 tablespoon (15 mL) ground red New Mexico chile (chimayó preferred)
1 tablespoon (15 mL) freshly ground white pepper
1 tablespoon (15 mL) ground thyme
1 tablespoon (15 mL) ground marjoram
1 teaspoon (5 mL) ground celery seed
1½ teaspoon (7.5 mL) ground coriander
2 teaspoons (10 mL) ground cinnamon
1 teaspoon (5 mL) ground ginger
Slices of toasted French bread for garnish
Grated Swiss cheese for garnish

1. In a large pot, heat the olive oil over medium heat. Add the onion,
garlic, mushrooms, parsley, and celery and sauté until the onions are soft,
about 7 minutes. Add the tomatoes, tomato paste, tomato sauce, stock,
sugar, balsamic vinegar, and wine and cook, stirring frequently until the
mixture boils.
2. Add the ground chipotle powder, ground red chile, white pepper,
thyme, marjoram, celery seed, coriander, cinnamon, and ginger and stir
well. Reduce the heat to medium and cook for 5 minutes, stirring often.
3. Divide the soup among soup bowls. Top each serving with a slice of
French bread and sprinkle them with the cheese. Place the bowls under a
broiler until the cheese melts, then serve.

Lemongrass-Gingered Chicken Wonton Soup

Yield: 8–10 servings   Heat Scale: Medium

This is my first of several wonton soups. You can buy ground chicken from your butcher, but be sure to specify that the skin should be removed before grinding. Or you can use a food processor with a sharp blade to chop your own chicken, but use the pulse mode to get the proper consistency. Serve this soup with a cold Tsingtao beer.

1 pound (454 g) ground chicken (dark meat)
½ cup (118 mL) finely chopped spinach leaves
1½ tablespoons (22.5 mL) sherry
1 tablespoon (15 mL) soy sauce
1 teaspoon (5 mL) ground ginger
¼ cup (59 mL) shredded fresh ginger
2 stalks lemongrass, minced
1½ tablespoons (22.5 mL) finely chopped fresh Asian chiles (or substitute serranos)
40 to 50 prepared wonton skins
2 quarts (1.9 L) Wonton Soup Broth (page 47)
Peanut oil as needed
Chopped parsley for garnish

1. In a bowl, combine the chicken, spinach, sherry, soy sauce, ground ginger, fresh ginger, lemongrass and chiles. Mix well and let sit for 30 minutes.
2. Spoon 1 teaspoon (5 mL) of the filling onto a won ton skin, fold the skin over, and press firmly to seal. Repeat until all the filling is used.
3. Heat the Wonton Soup Broth in a large pot.
4. Heat the peanut oil in a wok and fry the wontons in batches until they are golden brown, about 7 to 9 minutes. Transfer the wontons to paper towels to drain.
5. Place 4 or 5 wontons in each soup bowl, ladle the broth over them, and garnish with the parsley.

Duck and Asian Pear Wonton Soup

Yield: 8–10 servings   Heat Scale: Medium

Asian pears, which are found from Korea to Thailand, have less sugar and juice than other pears. If you're going to substitute, use an unripe pear. Garnish by floating sections of very thin starfruit that the diner can remove or eat.

1 pound (454 g) ground duck breast
1 teaspoon (5 mL) five-spice powder
1 tablespoon (15 mL) honey
1 tablespoon (15 mL) teriyaki sauce
3 fresh Thai chiles, stems and seeds removed, minced (or substitute serranos)
1 tablespoon (15 mL) dark brown sugar
1½ tablespoons (22.5 mL) freshly squeezed lemon juice
½ teaspoon (2.5 mL) salt
½ teaspoon (2.5 mL) finely ground white pepper
¼ teaspoon (1.25 mL) vanilla extract
2 Asian pears, peeled, cored, and grated
½ cup (118 mL) finely shredded red cabbage
1 tablespoon (15 mL) sherry
1 tablespoon (15 mL) soy sauce
40 to 50 wonton skins
2 quarts (1.9 L) Wonton Soup Broth (page 47)
Peanut oil as needed
Chopped cilantro for garnish

1. In a large bowl, combine the duck, five-spice powder, honey, teriyaki, chiles, brown sugar, lemon juice, salt, pepper, and vanilla. Mix well and let sit for 30 minutes. Add the pears, cabbage, sherry, and soy sauce, mix well, and let sit another 30 minutes. Drain and discard as much of the liquid from the filling as possible.
2. Spoon 1 teaspoon (5 mL) of the filling onto a wonton skin, fold the skin over, and press firmly to seal. Repeat until all the filling is used.
3. Heat the Wonton Soup Broth in a large pot.
4. Heat the peanut oil in a wok and fry the wontons in batches until they are golden brown, about 7 to 9 minutes. Transfer them to a paper towel to drain.
5. Place 4 or 5 wontons in each soup bowl, ladle the broth over them, and garnish with the cilantro.

Apricot, Crab, and Chile Wonton Soup

Yield: 8–10 servings   Heat Scale: Medium

If you want to wow your guests, this soup will do it! It's a nice blend of subtle flavors with a slight blast of heat from the ground chile. Serve this with a well-chilled Japanese plum wine.

½ cup (118 mL) apricot preserves
1 tablespoon (15 mL) brandy
½ teaspoon (2.5 mL) dry mustard
½ cup (118 mL) finely shredded white cabbage
¼ cup (59 mL) finely chopped bok choy, leaves included
4 green onions, minced
½ cup (118 mL) mung bean sprouts
¾ teaspoon (3.75 mL) ground ginger
2 tablespoons (30 mL) ground hot red chile
1 pound (454 g) blue crab meat, well cleaned
3 tablespoons (45 mL) oyster sauce
1¼ tablespoons (18.75 mL) minced garlic
2 tablespoons (30 mL) hot chile oil
40 to 50 wonton skins
2 quarts (1.9 L) Wonton Soup Broth (page 47)
Peanut oil as needed
Chopped parsley for garnish

1. In a bowl, combine the preserves, brandy, mustard, cabbage, bok choy, green onions, sprouts, ginger, chile, crab meat, oyster sauce, garlic, and chile oil. Mix well and let sit for 1 hour. Drain and discard as much of the liquid from the filling as possible.
2. Spoon 1 teaspoon (5 mL) of the filling onto a wonton skin, fold the skin over, and press firmly to seal. Repeat until all the filling is used.
3. Heat the Wonton Soup Broth in a large pot.
4. Heat the peanut oil in a wok and fry the wontons in batches until they are golden brown, about 7 to 9 minutes. Transfer them to a paper towel to drain.
5. Place 4 or 5 wontons in each soup bowl, ladle the broth over them, and garnish with the parsley.

Vietnamese Sweet and Sour Snapper Soup

Yield: 4 servings   Heat Scale: Varies, Medium to Hot

This soup, known as Canh Chua Ca, is representative of many of the soups of Vietnam. It is delicately seasoned, and one ingredient doesn't overwhelm the others; instead, all the ingredients present a balanced taste in this quick, easy-to-prepare recipe.

1 pound (454 g) snapper or other delicate white fish fillets
3 tablespoons (45 mL) frozen orange juice concentrate
1½ tablespoons (22.5 mL) apple cider vinegar
1 medium onion, peeled and thinly sliced
1 quart (.95 L) water
3 medium tomatoes, peeled and sliced
1½ cups (354 mL) mung bean sprouts
1⅓ cups (315 mL) thinly sliced celery
1 teaspoon (5 mL) soy sauce
Freshly ground black pepper, to taste
¼ teaspoon (1.25 mL) ground cayenne
2 tablespoons (30 mL) chopped fresh cilantro
Fresh red serrano or jalapeño slices, to taste

1. Rinse the fish fillets with cold water and dry them with paper towels. Cut the fish into 1-inch (2.5 cm) pieces and set aside.
2. In a large saucepan, combine the orange juice, vinegar, onion, and water and bring to a boil. Cover the pot and simmer gently for 15 minutes.
3. Add the tomatoes to the simmering water and continue to cook for 3 to 4 minutes, or until the tomatoes begin to soften.
4. Stir in the remaining ingredients and simmer for 2 minutes.

Bahamian Pumpkin Habanero Cream Soup

Yield: 4 servings   Heat Scale: Medium

This smooth bisque with island flavors has considerable heat because of the habanero. It also has great color. Garnished with fresh coconut shavings, it's perfect to serve before a seafood entrée or a dish of Jamaican jerk pork.

¼ pound (113 g) butter
1 large onion, peeled and minced
2 tablespoons (30 mL) all-purpose flour
2½ cups (591 mL) milk
½ cup (118 mL) heavy cream
3 cups (708 mL) Classic Chicken Stock (page 46)
3 cups (708 mL) cooked, mashed pumpkin
1 teaspoon (5 mL) salt
⅓ cup (79 mL) freshly squeezed lime juice
1 habanero chile, stem and seeds removed, minced
¼ cup (59 mL) dark brown sugar
½ teaspoon (2.5 mL) ground ginger
½ teaspoon (2.5 mL) ground cinnamon
½ teaspoon (2.5 mL) ground mace
Shaved or grated fresh coconut for garnish

1. In a large pot, melt the butter over medium heat. Add the onion and sauté until soft, about 5 minutes. Add the flour and stir until smooth, then add the milk and cream and stir well. Slowly mix in the chicken stock and pumpkin. Stir well and add the salt, lime juice, habanero, sugar, ginger, cinnamon, and mace. Reduce the heat and simmer for 10 minutes. Garnish with the coconut and serve.

Wild Mushroom Bisque with Grilled Chicken

Yield: 12 servings   Heat Scale: Mild

*Every year on the Saturday preceding the Super Bowl, Wild Oats Market in Albu-
querque sponsors the Chef's Invitational Souper Bowl Soup Contest. In 1995, my
friend W. C. Longacre defeated a dozen other Albuquerque chefs with this grand
prize winner. Use whatever wild mushrooms you have available—I have suggested a
mixture, below. W. C. gathered most of the mushrooms from the Sandia Mountains
near Albuquerque and urges aficionados to learn about wild mushrooms.*

1¾ pound (790 g) chicken breasts
½ cup (118 mL) teriyaki sauce
1½ tablespoons (22.5 mL) grated ginger
9 ounces (252 g) mixed wild mushrooms (suggested: 2½ ounces [71 g] bo-
letes, 2½ ounces [71 g] cepes, 2 ounces [57 g] morels, 1 ounce [28 g] golden
trumpets, and 1 ounce [28 g] black trumpets)
2 large shallots, peeled and minced
1 teaspoon (5 mL) minced garlic
1 teaspoon (5 mL) freshly ground black pepper
4 quarts (3.8 L) Classic Chicken Stock (page 46)
½ medium onion, chopped fine
¾ cup (177 mL) butter, divided in thirds
1 pound (454 g) domestic mushrooms, sliced
1 tablespoon (15 mL) minced garlic
¾ cup (177 mL) all-purpose flour
2 ounces (57 g) hard romano cheese, finely grated
1 quart (.95 L) cream
½ cup (118 mL) dry sherry
2 cups (473 mL) V-8 juice or other vegetable juice
Commercial hot sauce, to taste
Salt, to taste

1. Marinate the chicken in the teriyaki and ginger for 20 minutes. Grill the
chicken until done, chop fine, and set aside.
2. Soak the wild mushrooms in 3 cups (708 mL) warm water for 20
minutes. Rinse thoroughly. Soak the mushrooms again in 2 cups (473
mL) water. Remove the mushrooms, reserving the water, and finely chop
them. Place the mushrooms, reserved water, shallots, garlic, black pepper,
and chicken stock in a stock pot and boil for 30 minutes, adding water as
needed to maintain the original volume.
3. Sauté the onion in ¼ cup (59 mL) of the butter over medium heat and
set aside.
4. Sauté the domestic mushrooms and garlic in ¼ cup (59 mL) butter. Add
the sautéed onions, mushrooms, and garlic to the stock pot.
5. Melt the remaining ¼ cup (59 mL) butter in a pan, add the flour, and
stir until lightly browned to make a roux. Add the roux to the stock pot,
stirring well. Add the chopped chicken breast and romano cheese and stir
well. Add the cream, sherry, V-8 juice, and salt and heat for 10 minutes.

Southwest Cream of Corn Soup with Serranos

Yield: 8–10 servings   Heat Scale: Medium

This well-received classic is dramatically enhanced by floating large garlic croutons and a sprinkling of Parmesan cheese on top. It's great with any traditional Mexican or Southwestern fare, such as enchiladas or chiles rellenos.

1½ quarts (1.42 L) water
2 tablespoons (30 mL) salt
Kernels from 6 ears fresh sweet corn
8 serrano chiles, stems and seeds removed, minced
1 large green bell pepper, stem and seeds removed, finely chopped
1 large red bell pepper, stem and seeds removed, finely chopped
2 medium red onions, peeled and finely chopped, divided
½ cup (118 mL) red wine vinegar, divided
½ cup (118 mL) dry red wine, divided
3 ripe tomatoes, peeled, seeded, and finely chopped
½ bunch green onions, top 2 inches (5 cm) of greens removed, cut into ¼-inch (.5 cm) pieces
1½ teaspoons (7.5 mL) minced garlic
1 tablespoon (15 mL) minced parsley
2 tablespoons (30 mL) ground red New Mexican chile (chimayó preferred)
1½ tablespoons (22.5 mL) sugar
½ cup (118 mL) shredded carrots
5 cups Classic White Sauce (page 44)
Chopped cilantro for garnish

1. In a stock pot, combine the water, salt, corn, serranos, bell peppers, 1 onion, ¼ cup (79 mL) of the vinegar, ¼ cup (79 mL) of the wine, tomatoes, green onions, garlic, parsley, and ground chile and bring to a boil. Boil uncovered for 10 minutes, stirring occasionally. Reduce the heat to low and simmer for 5 minutes.
2. In a bowl, combine the remaining red onion, wine vinegar, and red wine and let stand for 20 minutes.
3. In a separate bowl, combine the sugar, carrots, and White Sauce. When the onions are finished marinating, add them, with 2 tablespoons (30 mL) of the marinade, to the White Sauce.
4. Add the White Sauce mixture to the simmering stock pot and cook for 5 minutes, blending with a whisk. Serve immediately or keep warm in a double boiler. Serve garnished with the cilantro.

Conch Bisque

Yield: 6–8 servings   Heat Scale: Medium to Hot

A very popular dish in the Turks and Caicos Islands, this conch bisque is devoid of the tomatoes so popular in most conch dishes. The flavor comes from heavily pounded conchs, good white wine, thyme, and hot peppers. Since the soup tends to be rather rich, I suggest serving it as a light lunch or dinner entrée. Squid may be substituted for the conch. Conch is a dish of great pride wherever it is served—the acclaim is due to the meat and the fine shell.

6 conchs, cleaned, pounded with a heavy mallet to flatten, and diced into ½-inch (1 cm) pieces
5 cups (1.18 L) water or Traditional European Fish Stock (page 47)
1 cup (236 mL) dry white wine, plus more as needed for cooking
2 tablespoons (30 mL) butter and 2 tablespoons (30 mL) vegetable oil (or use all vegetable oil)
1 cup (236 mL) chopped onions
½ cup (118 mL) chopped green bell pepper
1 cup (236 mL) chopped celery
2 cloves garlic, peeled and minced
2 teaspoons (10 mL) fresh thyme or 1 teaspoon (5 mL) dried thyme
1 cup (236 mL) diced carrots
2 medium potatoes, peeled and cut in ½-inch (1 cm) dice
1 large habanero chile, stem and seeds removed, minced
3 tablespoons (45 mL) chopped chives
1 cup (236 mL) half-and-half
Salt, to taste
Freshly ground black pepper, to taste

1. In a heavy soup pot, combine the pounded conch, water, and wine and bring the mixture to a hard boil. Lower the heat so the liquid is at a light rolling boil and boil for 45 minutes. Remove the mixture from the heat. Strain the liquid, reserving the conch meat. Measure the liquid and add enough more white wine to make 6 cups (1.42 L).
2. Wash out the soup pot. Pour the liquid back into the clean pot and bring to a boil.
3. Heat the butter and oil (or just oil, if you prefer) in a heavy skillet over low heat. Add the onions, green bell pepper, celery, and garlic and sauté for 1 minute. Stir in the thyme.
4. Add the sautéed mixture to the boiling conch liquid, then add the carrots, potatoes, habanero chile, chives, and reserved conch meat. Return the mixture to a boil, lower the heat, and simmer for 1 hour.
5. Remove the pot from the heat and let it cool slightly. Stir in the half-and-half and reheat the soup, taking care not to let it boil. Taste for seasoning and add salt and pepper as needed.

Colombian Coconut Soup

Yield: 4 servings   Heat Scale: Medium

This recipe hails from the tropical lowlands of the Republic of Colombia, where it is known, logically, as Sopa de Coco. Coconuts are frequently used in cooking there. Tortillas cut into strips and fried in vegetable oil are a nice accompaniment. To dress it up, serve the soup in coconut shell halves.

2 large, ripe coconuts, cracked, meat grated
2 cups (473 mL) milk, scalded
3 cups (708 mL) Traditional European Fish Stock (page 47) or Classic Chicken Stock (page 46)
2 egg yolks, well beaten
½ habanero chile, stem and seeds removed, minced (or substitute 1½ jalapeños)
Paprika, to taste
Salt, to taste

1. In a bowl, combine the grated coconut and the milk. Let the mixture cool, then squeeze it through cheesecloth or a linen napkin to extract all the liquid. Combine the coconut milk, stock, egg yolks, and chile in a saucepan and cook for 10 minutes, stirring constantly.
2. To serve, sprinkle with paprika and salt to taste, and accompany with strips of toast or fried tortillas.

Curried Coconut Soup

Yield: 4–6 servings   Heat Scale: Medium

From South America to Africa, I make a coconut culinary leap. The hot curry powder blends nicely with the coconut milk to create a tangy Nigerian soup. Curry has traveled around the world, and each country has its own variations on the spice blend.

3 cups (708 mL) coconut milk
3 cups (708 mL) Classic Chicken Stock (page 46), divided
2 teaspoons (10 mL) imported Indian curry powder
½ teaspoon (2.5 mL) salt
¼ teaspoon (1.25 mL) freshly ground white pepper
¼ cup (59 mL) prepared grated coconut
1 tablespoon (15 mL) freshly grated ginger
1 teaspoon (5 mL) cornstarch
½ cup (118 mL) plain yogurt
¼ cup (59 mL) toasted coconut
Minced parsley for garnish

1. Combine the coconut milk and 2¾ cups (629 mL) chicken stock in a large, heavy pot and bring it to a boil. Reduce the heat slightly and add the curry powder, salt, pepper, grated coconut, and ginger. Simmer for 10 minutes.

2. Mix the cornstarch with the remaining ¼ cup (59 mL) stock and add it in a steady stream to the simmering soup, stirring constantly until the soup thickens slightly.
3. Serve the soup hot, garnished with the yogurt, toasted coconut, and parsley.

Peanut-Piquin Cream Soup

Yield: 6 servings   Heat Scale: Medium

Each African country seems to have its own version of peanut, or groundnut, soup. It is common all over Africa, but it is especially popular in the western part. The soup can be made a day ahead to blend the flavors, then carefully reheated. Add some dried tropical fruits or a chutney for a nice variation when serving.

1 pound (454 g) shelled, roasted peanuts
1 tablespoon (15 mL) peanut oil
1 cup (236 mL) chopped onion
½ cup (118 mL) chopped carrots
3 dried, crushed piquin chiles, or 3 fresh jalapeños, stems and seeds removed, minced
8 cups (1.9 L) Basic Beef Stock (page 45) or Classic Chicken Stock (page 46)
¾ cup (177 mL) milk, divided
1 tablespoon (15 mL) cornstarch
¾ cup (177 mL) cream
½ teaspoon (2.5 mL) salt
Chopped parsley for garnish
Chopped chives for garnish

1. Rub the skins off the peanuts. Place the nuts in a food processor and grind them to a very fine meal. Set aside.
2. In a large pot, heat the oil over medium heat. Add the onion and carrots and sauté for 2 minutes. Add the chiles, the ground peanuts, and the stock and bring the mixture to a boil. Lower the heat and simmer, uncovered, for 1 hour, stirring occasionally.
3. Pour ½ cup (118 mL) of the milk into a small jar, add the cornstarch, and shake vigorously. Pour the mixture through a fine sieve into the soup and stir continuously for 1 minute. Add the remaining milk, the cream, and the salt. Simmer for 3 minutes, but do not allow the mixture to boil. Cover the soup and let it simmer for 30 minutes.
4. Serve the soup hot, garnished with the parsley and chives.

Cream of Roma Tomato Soup with Jalapeños

Yield: 4 servings   Heat Scale: Medium

This shocking pink soup is simply classic, and it is one of the best tomato soups I've ever tasted. Feel free to substitute habaneros for even a greater chile kick. This soup can precede any entrée, or it can accompany a sandwich for a light lunch.

2 cups (473 mL) Classic White Sauce (page 44)
2 cups (473 mL) chopped Roma tomatoes
⅓ cup (79 mL) tomato paste
1 large onion, peeled and minced
¾ tablespoon (11.25 mL) minced garlic
¼ cup (59 mL) Chianti (or any dry red wine)
¾ tablespoon (11.25 mL) sugar
1 teaspoon (5 mL) salt
½ teaspoon (2.5 mL) finely ground white pepper
½ tablespoon (7.5 mL) balsamic vinegar
2 jalapeños, stems and seeds removed, minced
⅔ cup (158 mL) heavy cream
1 tablespoon (15 mL) minced fresh basil

1. In a large pot, combine the White Sauce, tomatoes, tomato paste, onion, garlic, Chianti, sugar, salt, pepper, vinegar, and jalapeños. Heat to a simmer (do not boil) and simmer over low heat for 20 minutes. Blend in the cream and basil and serve.

Creamy Green Chile Chicken Soup

Yield: 8 servings   Heat Scale: Medium

Here's a Southwestern classic featuring green New Mexican chile. It was one of the favorites at W. C.'s Mountain Road Cafe in Albuquerque. If W. C. forgot to post it for a while on his specials board, his regulars would complain. Serve it before any Mexican or Southwestern entrées or with grilled meats.

6 cups (1.42 L) Classic New Mexico Green Chile Sauce (page 71)
2 cups (473 mL) Classic White Sauce (page 44)
1 cup (236 mL) Classic Chicken Stock (page 46)
1 (3½-pound [1.59 kg]) chicken, poached and deboned, meat chopped, skin and bones discarded
½ teaspoon (2.5 mL) salt
½ teaspoon (2.5 mL) finely ground white pepper
¼ teaspoon (1.25 mL) dried Mexican oregano
1 cup (236 mL) heavy cream

1. In a large pot, combine the Green Chile Sauce, White Sauce, and Classic Chicken Stock and heat, stirring well with a whisk. Add the remaining ingredients, stir well, and simmer, uncovered, for 10 minutes.

Callaloo and Crab Soup

Yield: 8–10 servings   Heat Scale: Medium to Hot

I collected this recipe from friends in Trinidad after eating this soup at every opportunity to sample its multiple variations. This version features crab meat, a common and tasty addition to this bright green soup. Callaloo, also called dasheen, is the top leaves of the taro plant. This soup is considered to be one of the national dishes of Trinidad and Tobago.

3 tablespoons (45 mL) butter, divided
1 medium onion, peeled and diced
½ cup (118 mL) chopped celery
1 clove garlic, peeled and minced
1 quart (.95 L) Classic Chicken Stock (page 46)
1 cup (236 mL) coconut milk
½ pound (224 g) smoked ham, diced, or 1 small ham hock
2½ cups (591 mL) washed, coarsely chopped, firmly packed callaloo (dasheen), or substitute spinach leaves
1 cup (236 mL) sliced okra
1 teaspoon (5 mL) dried thyme
¼ teaspoon (1.25 mL) freshly ground black pepper
1 Congo pepper (or habanero), stem and seeds removed, minced
1 pound (454 g) cooked crabmeat, chopped
Salt, to taste

1. In a large saucepan, melt 2 tablespoons (30 mL) of the butter over medium heat. Add the onion, celery, and garlic and sauté for 2 or 3 minutes. Add the chicken stock, coconut milk, and ham and bring to a boil. Add the callaloo or spinach, okra, thyme, black pepper, and Congo pepper.
2. Reduce the heat to a simmer and cook, covered, for about 50 minutes, stirring occasionally, until the callaloo is thoroughly cooked.
3. Whisk the soup until very smooth, or purée it in small batches in a blender. Add the crabmeat and heat through. Add the remaining 1 tablespoon (15 mL) butter, swizzled over the top. Taste for seasoning and add salt as needed.

Sweet Potato–Chipotle Chile Bisque

Yield: 8 servings   Heat Scale: Medium-Hot

This elegant soup is rich in color and taste. It allows the full color of the sweet pota-toes to show and retains the flavors that are so often lost in the canning process. The smoky accents complement the sweetness, and the silky texture of the soup encour-ages second helpings.

3 pounds (1.36 kg) sweet potatoes
1 tablespoon (15 mL) olive oil
4 large chipotle chiles
¼ cup (59 mL) dark rum
4 cups (.95 L) Classic White Sauce (page 44)
2 cups (473 mL) milk
⅔ cup (158 mL) Classic Chicken Stock (page 46)
3 tablespoons (45 mL) sour cream
2 tablespoons (30 mL) dark brown sugar
1 tablespoon (15 mL) raw honey (the darker the better)
1½ teaspoons (7.5 mL) molasses
1 teaspoon (5 mL) five-spice powder
½ teaspoon (2.5 mL) cinnamon
½ teaspoon (2.5 mL) salt
⅛ teaspoon (.6 mL) vanilla extract
Lemon zest for garnish

1. Preheat the oven to 375°F (190°C).
2. Scrub the sweet potatoes well with a vegetable brush and soak them in water for 5 minutes. Dry the sweet potatoes and rub them with the olive oil. Puncture them with the point of a knife about 5 times each. Place the sweet potatoes in a shallow baking dish and bake for about 1¼ hours, add-ing ¼ cup (59 mL) water to the baking dish after 15 minutes. Pierce them with a knife to test for softness, remove from the oven, and set them aside to cool. Scoop all the flesh out of the jackets and set aside.
2. While the sweet potatoes are baking, soak the chipotles in a bowl with the rum and ½ cup (118 mL) water. Place another bowl on top of the chiles to keep them submerged. When they are soft, after about 1 hour, purée the chipotles with the soaking mixture and set aside.
3. In a large pot, heat the White Sauce over medium heat, gradually add-ing the milk and stock and stirring with a whisk. Add the sour cream, brown sugar, honey, molasses, five-spice powder, cinnamon, salt, and vanilla and stir well, and simmer for 5 minutes. Add the reserved sweet potato, stir well, and simmer for 5 minutes. Just before serving, swirl in the reserved chipotle liquid. Serve garnished with the lemon zest.

Cream of Ginger Soup with Lemongrass

Yield: 8 servings   Heat Scale: Mild

I love this combination of flavors because of the distinctive lemongrass. Note that this soup is flavored only with herbs and has no meat, poultry, or fish in it. Serve it garnished with a little minced cilantro. If this soup is too mild, add ½ teaspoon (2.5 mL) ground habanero to the roux. If you're entertaining and don't know the palate preferences of all your guests, serve this soup!

3 tablespoons (45 mL) Sichuan Chile Sauce (page 101)
⅓ pound (303 g) butter
1 cup (236 mL) sifted all-purpose flour
1 teaspoon (5 mL) salt
1 teaspoon (5 mL) ground ginger
1 teaspoon (5 mL) minced shallots
½ teaspoon (2.5 mL) white pepper
2 stalks lemongrass, white parts only, cut into rings
2 cups (473 mL) Classic Chicken Stock (page 46)
2 tablespoons (30 mL) grated ginger
2 quarts (1.9 L) milk
2 cups (473 mL) heavy cream
3 tablespoons (45 mL) white wine
1½ tablespoons (22.5 mL) sugar

1. In a large pot, heat the oil and butter over medium heat. Whisk in the flour, salt, ginger, shallot, white pepper, and lemongrass to make a roux. Do not brown. Remove the pot from the heat and set aside.
2. In another pot, bring the chicken stock to a boil. Add the ginger, milk, and cream and return to a boil. Reduce the heat, add the wine and sugar, and stir well.
3. Reheat the roux over medium heat and whisk in the heated milk mixture until all is integrated and smooth. Adjust the consistency with milk if necessary and serve hot.

Caribbean Cold and Bold Gazpacho

Yield: 4–6 servings   Heat Scale: Medium

Traditionally, gazpacho is a Spanish-style cold soup. However, the cold, uncooked soup idea is taken one step further in this recipe by including some of the fruit available in the islands. The ultimate result is a soup that is cold, bold, and spicy—island style. (Note: This recipe requires advance preparation.)

2 cups (473 mL) pineapple or papaya juice
2 cups (473 mL) tomato juice
¾ cup (177 mL) almost-ripe papaya, peeled and chopped into large cubes
¾ cup (177 mL) coarsely chopped fresh pineapple
⅓ cup (79 mL) diced green bell pepper
⅓ cup (79 mL) diced red bell pepper
⅓ cup (79 mL) diced yellow bell pepper
½ fresh Scotch bonnet chile (or habanero), stem and seeds removed, minced
3 tablespoons (45 mL) fresh lime juice
2 tablespoons (30 mL) chopped fresh cilantro
½ teaspoon (2.5 mL) whole black peppercorns, crushed

1. Combine all the ingredients in batches in a blender and blend for 5 seconds. Refrigerate the mixture for 6 hours.
2. Serve the soup in icy cold bowls.

Chilled African Avocado Soup

Yield: 4–5 servings   Heat Scale: Medium

This pan-African soup is cold and hot at the same time. The chiles add the heat, and it is very refreshing in hot weather. The chiles help cool down the body through perspiration. Serve this soup as a first course with fresh bread. I love avocados, and their flavor shines through in this soup. (Note: This recipe requires advance preparation.)

4 ripe avocados, peeled and pitted
5 cups (1.8 L) Super-Rich Vegetable Stock (page 48)
1 tablespoon (15 mL) fresh lime juice
½ teaspoon (2.5 mL) salt
¼ teaspoon (1.25 mL) freshly ground white pepper
3 serrano or jalapeño chiles, stems and seeds removed, minced
1½ tablespoons (22.5 mL) minced green onions or chives

1. In a large bowl, mash the avocados. Add the stock, lime juice, salt, pepper, and chiles and mash until the mixture is semi-smooth. If you like a velvety texture, purée the mixture in a blender or food processor. Chill the soup for several hours.
2. Garnish the soup with the green onions or chives and serve.

Gulf of Mexico Seafood Tortilla Soup

Yield: 10–12 servings   Heat Scale: Medium

This soup was inspired by seafood available around Veracruz, Mexico, and its flavors are classic to the region. It's also visually appealing, especially when you use large shrimp. It's a rich but fresh-tasting soup that goes well with grilled entrées, so it's a great starting place for a barbecue.

1 tablespoon (15 mL) olive oil
4 medium tomatoes, peeled, seeded, and coarsely chopped
6 green onions, green and white parts, chopped
1 tablespoon (15 mL) minced garlic
⅛ teaspoon (.6 mL) ground bay leaf
4 cups (.95 L) Classic Chicken Stock (page 46)
2 cups (473 mL) Traditional European Fish Stock (page 47)
1 teaspoon (5 mL) ground cayenne
½ teaspoon (2.5 mL) ground white pepper
¾ teaspoon (3.75 mL) salt
½ teaspoon (2.5 mL) minced parsley
1 pound (454 g) Gulf crab meat
1 pound (454 g) Gulf medium shrimp, peeled, deveined, and sliced into quarters
1 pound (454 g) skinless red snapper fillets, cut into ½-inch (1 cm) pieces
¼ cup (59 mL) finely chopped red bell pepper
¼ cup (59 mL) finely chopped green bell pepper
¼ cup (59 mL) finely chopped yellow bell pepper
1 dozen yellow corn tortillas
2 tablespoons (30 mL) vegetable shortening
1¼ pound (568 g) mozzarella cheese, grated
2½ tablespoons (37.5 mL) sugar
2 tablespoons (30 mL) freshly squeezed lemon juice

1. In a skillet, heat the olive oil over medium heat. Add the tomatoes, green onions, garlic, and bay leaf and sauté for 10 minutes, stirring well. Remove from the heat and set aside.
2. In a large pot, combine the stocks, cayenne, white pepper, salt, and parsley. Bring to a boil, reduce the heat, and simmer, uncovered, for 5 minutes. Add the sautéed tomato mixture and mix well. Simmer for an additional 10 minutes. Add the crab meat, shrimp, red snapper, and bell peppers and simmer for 10 more minutes.
3. Cut the tortillas into strips ¼ inch (.5 cm) by 2 inches (5 cm). In a skillet, melt the shortening over high heat. Add the strips and fry them until crisp. Transfer them to paper towels to drain.
4. Line 10 to 12 soup bowls with the tortilla strips and divide the cheese, sugar, and lemon juice among the bowls. Ladle in the soup, taking care to distribute the seafood evenly.

Chilpachole Veracruzano
(Veracruz-Style Shrimp Chowder)
Yield: 4 servings   Heat Scale: Medium

Here's another soup from Veracruz. The use of dried shrimp here intensifies the flavor. Dried shrimp and epazote are available in Latin and Asian markets. There is no substitute for epazote's unique, pungent flavor. Serve the shrimp stew in bowls or over cooked rice, garnished with lemon or lime slices.

8 cloves garlic, unpeeled
2 chipotle chiles, stems and seeds removed
2 ancho chiles, stems and seeds removed
1 onion, peeled and cut into eighths
3 tomatoes, peeled and cut into quarters
3 tablespoons (45 mL) vegetable oil
3 cups (708 mL) water or Traditional European Fish Stock (page 47)
8 dried shrimps
¼ cup (59 mL) dried epazote
2 pounds (1.1 kg) fresh shrimp, shelled and deveined

1. Preheat the oven to 400°F (200°C).
2. Wrap the unpeeled garlic cloves in aluminum foil and roast them for 30 minutes. When they are cool enough to handle, squeeze the garlic out of the skins into a blender.
3. In a dry skillet, lightly roast the chiles over medium heat for 2 minutes, taking care not to burn them. Add the chiles to the blender, along with the onion and tomatoes, and purée the mixture.
4. Heat the oil in a medium skillet over medium-low heat. Add the puréed mixture and cook for 1 minute. Add the water, dried shrimp, and epazote and simmer for 3 minutes.
5. Add the fresh shrimp and simmer the mixture for an additional 5 minutes, or until the shrimp are cooked. Add more water if the mixture starts to get too thick. Serve immediately.

Bahamian Fish Chowder

Yield: 6 servings   Heat Scale: Medium

The unusual ingredients in this recipe all work together to produce a pungent, spicy chowder that delights the palate. The chowder is rich enough to serve as a main course for a luncheon or as a light dinner entrée, with crunchy garlic bread and a green salad.

2 tablespoons (30 mL) olive oil
4 cloves garlic, peeled and chopped
2½ teaspoons (12.5 mL) Puerto Rican Sofrito (page 63))
1 habanero chile, stem and seeds removed, chopped
1 cup (236 mL) chopped onion
½ cup (118 mL) chopped celery
¾ cup (177 mL) peeled and diced green plantains
1 cup (236 mL) diced potato, cut in a ½-inch (1 cm) dice
½ teaspoon (2.5 mL) freshly ground cinnamon
½ teaspoon (2.5 mL) ground annatto
2 pounds (1.1 kg) fish fillets (grouper, snapper, pompano), cut into large chunks
3 cups (708 mL) fish stock
2 cups (473 mL) water
1 cup (236 mL) milk
Salt, to taste
Freshly ground black pepper, to taste
Chopped green onions for garnish

1. Heat the olive oil in a large, heavy pot over medium heat. Add the garlic, Sofrito, habanero, onion, celery, plantains, and potato and sauté for 5 minutes, stirring, until the onions start to soften.
2. Add the cinnamon, annatto, fillets, stock, water, and milk and stir gently to mix. Bring the mixture to a light boil, reduce the heat to a simmer, and simmer for 15 minutes, or until the fish flakes easily with a fork. Add the salt and pepper.
3. Serve the soup in warmed bowls, garnished with the chopped green onions.

Sopapita
(Spicy Seafood Stew)

Yield: 4 servings   Heat Scale: Medium to Hot

This is one of my favorite stews because it contains so many interesting flavors: coconut milk, allspice, Old Bay, and celery. Serve this with a fruity white wine to bring out the spices.

1 quart (.95 L) Traditional European Fish Stock (page 47)
1 tablespoon (15 mL) butter
1 pound (454 g) sole or any light fish, chopped fine
12 large shrimps, coarsely chopped
12 medium-to-large whole scallops
1 medium onion, chopped
1 (15-ounce [420 g]) can Thai coconut milk
2 medium cloves garlic, peeled
4 hot chiles, such as chiltepins, Thai chiles, or piquins, stems and seeds removed
1 teaspoon (5 mL) Old Bay seasoning
¼ teaspoon (1.25 mL) chopped fresh thyme
1 tablespoon (15 mL) chopped celery leaves
¼ teaspoon (1.25 mL) freshly ground Jamaican allspice
1½ tablespoons (22.5 mL) sugar
Lime wedges for garnish

1. In a large pot, heat the fish stock.
2. In a sauté pan, melt the butter over medium heat. Add the fish, shrimp, and scallops and lightly sauté. Remove the seafood from the pan and set aside.
3. Combine the onion, coconut milk, garlic, chiles, Old Bay, thyme, celery leaves, allspice, and sugar in a food processor and purée. Add the purée to the sauté pan and cook over medium heat for 5 minutes.
4. Add the sautéed seafood and the purée to the fish stock in the large pot, stirring well. Cook over low heat for 15 minutes. Garnish with the lime wedges and serve hot.

Striped Bass Bouillabaisse with Rouille

Yield: 6–8 servings   Heat Scale: Varies

The French have so many contradictory rules and regulations regarding this dish that I have taken some liberties, such as substituting striped bass for scorpionfish. Many recipes included shellfish and lobster, but I have opted for just black mussels. Feel free to add scallops or other seafood to this soup.

For the Court Boullion:
¾ cup (177 mL) olive oil
2 cups (473 mL) thinly sliced onions
1 cup (236 mL) thinly sliced leeks
4 cups (.95 L) water
2 cups (473 mL) dry white wine
2 pounds (1.1 kg) fish heads, bones, and trimmings
3 pounds (1.36 kg) ripe tomatoes, coarsely chopped
½ teaspoon (2.5 mL) dried fennel seed, crushed
2 cloves garlic, peeled and minced
1 (3-inch [7.5 cm]) piece orange peel
1 teaspoon (5 mL) dried thyme
2 sprigs parsley
1 bay leaf
¼ teaspoon (1.25 mL) crushed saffron threads
Salt, to taste
Freshly ground black pepper, to taste

1. Heat the oil in a heavy 4 to 6 quart (4 to 6 L) saucepan over medium heat. Add the onions and leeks and cook until they are tender, but not brown, about 5 minutes. Add the remaining ingredients and cook, uncovered, over medium heat for 30 minutes.

For the Fish and Mussels:
4 pounds (1.82 kg) striped bass (or other firm white fish), cut into 2-inch (5 cm) cubes
2 pounds (1.1 kg) live black mussels (or substitute clams)
2 cups (473 mL) Rouille (page 79)

1. When the bouillon is done, strain it through a fine sieve into a soup pot, pressing the fish trimmings and vegetables to squeeze out all the juices. Bring the strained stock to a rapid boil and add the fish. Cook for 5 minutes, then add the mussels and boil for 5 minutes. Serve the soup with the Rouille and pieces of French bread.

Basque-Style Bonito-Tomato Chowder

Yield: 6–8 servings   Heat Scale: Medium

I recommend using bonito, a dark-meated tuna relative, in this hearty chowder, but any variety of tuna will work. Some people object to strongly flavored fish like bonito, but I love it. Serve this with a hard, crusty bread.

2 medium onions, peeled and chopped, divided
½ cup (118 mL) extra virgin olive oil
6 medium very ripe tomatoes, peeled, seeded, and finely chopped
1 teaspoon (5 mL) dried thyme
2 tablespoons (30 mL) minced parsley
1 tablespoon (15 mL) Spanish brandy or cognac
3 dried red New Mexico chiles, stems and seeds removed
2 tablespoons (30 mL) minced garlic
1 tablespoon (15 mL) freshly ground black pepper
1 tablespoon (15 mL) salt
2 medium green bell peppers, stems and seeds removed, chopped fine
¾ pound (336 g) red bliss potatoes, peeled and cut into ½-inch (1 cm) cubes
3 cups (708 mL) hot water or Traditional European Fish Stock (page 47)
1½ pounds (680 g) fresh bonito or tuna, cut into 1-inch (2.5 cm) cubes

1. In a pot, combine 2 tablespoons (30 mL) of the chopped onion with 2 tablespoons (30 mL) of the olive oil and sauté over medium heat until the onion is soft, about 3 minutes. Add the tomatoes, thyme, parsley, brandy, chile, pepper, and salt. Cover and cook over medium heat for 20 minutes.
2. Remove the pot from the heat and allow to cool. Transfer in batches to a food processor or blender and purée until smooth.
3. In another pot, combine the remaining olive oil, and onion and sauté over medium heat for about 7 minutes. Add the bell peppers and potatoes and cook for 2 minutes, stirring often. Add the hot water or stock and bring to a boil. Boil for 20 minutes. Add the reserved tomato purée and the bonito or tuna. Lower the heat, cover, and simmer until the fish is flaky, about 10 to 12 minutes. Serve as quickly as possible from the pot.

Creamy Green Chile and Bay Shrimp Chowder

Yield: 6 servings   Heat Scale: Mild to Medium

This soup started as a seafood sauce for enchiladas, but the staff at the Mountain Road Cafe couldn't keep their spoons out of it, so W. C. turned it into a soup. It's very rich and hearty and can also be garnished with fresh cilantro and a squeeze of lime.

1½ cups (354 mL) Classic New Mexico Green Chile Sauce (page 71)
3 cups (708 mL) Classic Chicken Stock (page 46)
1 cup (236 mL) Traditional European Fish Stock (page 47)
3 cups (708 mL) Classic White Sauce (page 44)
1 cup (236 mL) fresh or frozen peas
2 cups (473 mL) cubed potatoes, cut into ½-inch (1 cm) cubes
1 medium onion, peeled and chopped
2 tablespoons (30 mL) minced garlic
1 teaspoon (5 mL) dried thyme
¾ teaspoon (3.75 mL) dried basil
1 pound (454 g) bay shrimp, shelled but left whole
1 cup (236 mL) milk

1. In a large pot, combine the Green Chile Sauce and stocks and heat to a simmer. Blend in the White Sauce, whipping vigorously. Add the peas, potatoes, onion, garlic, thyme, basil, and shrimp and simmer for 15 minutes. Add the milk slowly, stirring constantly to avoid burning. Serve hot, garnished with croutons.

Thai Fish Chowder with Shrimp Wontons

Yield: 8 servings   Heat Scale: Medium

I love the Thai combination of lemongrass with the citrus flavor of lime leaves and the unique taste of fish sauce. Galangal (also known as laos) is a variety of Asian ginger that is available fresh in Asian markets.

1 egg
20 medium shrimp
1 teaspoon (5 mL) five-spice powder
½ teaspoon (2.5 mL) sesame oil
1 tablespoon (15 mL) dry bread crumbs
24 wonton skins
½ cup (118 mL) vegetable oil, divided
3 tablespoons (45 mL) crushed garlic
1 onion, peeled and chopped
2 quarts (1.9 L) Wonton Soup Broth (page 47)
1 tablespoon (15 mL) coarsely ground white pepper
2 lemongrass stalks, white part only, cut into rings
2 (1-inch [2.5 cm]) pieces galangal, peeled (or substitute ginger)
6 Thai chiles, stems and seeds removed, sliced (or substitute 3 serranos or jalapeños)
6 kaffir lime leaves (or zest of ½ lime)
¾ pound (336 g) rock shrimp, peeled and deveined
½ pound (224 g) crab meat or sole, coarsely chopped
½ cup (118 mL) straw mushrooms
½ cup (118 mL) chopped baby corn
6 tablespoons (90 mL) fish sauce (Tiparos brand preferred)
6 tablespoons (90 mL) freshly squeezed lime juice
1 teaspoon (5 mL) sugar
5–6 tablespoons (75–90 mL) coarsely chopped cilantro for garnish

1. Combine the egg, shrimp, five-spice powder, sesame oil, and bread crumbs in a food processor and coarsely purée. Spoon 1 teaspoon (5 mL) of the filling onto a wonton skin, fold the skin over, and press firmly to seal. Repeat until all the filling has been used.
2. Heat ¼ cup (59 mL) of the vegetable oil in a wok and fry the wontons in batches until they are golden brown. Transfer them to paper towels to drain.
3. In a large pot, heat the remaining oil over medium heat. Add the garlic and onion and sauté for 3 minutes. Add the Wonton Soup Broth and bring to a boil, stirring occasionally. Add the white pepper, lemongrass, galangal, chiles, kaffir lime leaves, shrimp, crab, straw mushrooms, and baby corn and boil for 3 minutes. Add the fish sauce, lime juice, and sugar and boil an additional 3 minutes. Remove the galangal pieces and kaffir lime leaves. Place 3 wontons in each bowl and ladle the chowder over them. Garnish with the cilantro.

Black Bean Chipotle Purée

Yield: 8–10 servings   Heat Scale: Medium

This exciting, thick soup marries the dark colors and flavors of the beans and chipotle chiles, but quite a few other ingredients are included as well. Serve this with a hearty bread and your favorite sharp cheese. (Note: This recipe requires advance preparation.)

2 quarts (1.9 L) water
1 tablespoon (15 mL) salt
3 cups (708 mL) black beans, rinsed and soaked overnight
½ stalk celery, chopped, leaves included
3 large dried chipotle chiles (approximately 3 ounces [84 g])
3 cups (708 mL) dry red wine
1 teaspoon (5 mL) freshly ground nutmeg
1 teaspoon (5 mL) freshly ground cinnamon
½ teaspoon (2.5 mL) ground ginger
1 tablespoon (15 mL) ground white pepper
2 tablespoons (30 mL) dried Mexican oregano
½ cup (118 mL) chopped fresh parsley
1 tablespoon (15 mL) Worcestershire sauce
1 medium onion, peeled and coarsely chopped
3 tablespoons (45 mL) chopped garlic
1 cup (236 mL) domestic mushrooms, chopped
¼ cup (59 mL) extra virgin olive oil
¼ cup (59 mL) peanut oil
⅓ cup (79 mL) tomato purée
2½ tablespoons (37.5 mL) red wine vinegar
¾ cup (177 mL) raw honey
Lime wedges for garnish
Coarsely chopped cilantro for garnish

1. In a large pot, combine the water, salt, black beans, celery, chipotles, wine, nutmeg, cinnamon, ginger, pepper, oregano, parsley, and Worcestershire sauce and bring to a boil.
2. In a skillet, combine the onion, garlic, mushrooms, olive oil, and peanut oil and sauté over medium heat until the onions are soft. Add this mixture to the pot and boil until the beans are soft, about 2 hours (this timing can vary greatly, so check them periodically). Add water as needed, but by the end there should be little water in the pot.
3. Allow the beans to cool. In a bowl, combine the tomato purée, vinegar, and honey. Add this mixture to the beans. Purée the soup in a food processor.
4. Reheat over very low heat (or use a double boiler), adding water as needed to achieve the desired consistency. Serve garnished with the lime wedges and chopped cilantro.

Southwestern Vegetarian Bean Goulash

Yield: 6–8 servings   Heat Scale: Mild

People constantly tell me that it's such a pain to cook beans that they would rather just buy them canned. I won't tell on you, but with canned beans you'll pay more money for an inferior product. Once the beans are cooked, however, this is an incredibly quick soup to make. Serve with sour cream on the side, if you wish.

1 tablespoon (15 mL) extra virgin olive oil
1 cup (236 mL) chopped onion
¾ cup (177 mL) chopped bell pepper
1 tablespoon (15 mL) minced jalapeño chile
2 tablespoons (30 mL) minced garlic
3 cups (708 mL) tomato sauce
½ cup (118 mL) Chianti or other red wine
6 Roma tomatoes, peeled and chopped
2 cups (473 mL) cooked long-grain brown rice
2 cups (473 mL) Super-Rich Vegetable Stock (page 48)
4 cups (.95 L) cooked black-eyed peas
4 cups (.95 L) cooked kidney beans
2 cups (473 mL) cooked pinto beans
1½ teaspoons (7.5 mL) salt
1 teaspoon (5 mL) ground oregano
½ teaspoon (2.5 mL) ground cumin
½ teaspoon (2.5 mL) ground bay leaf
2 tablespoons (30 mL) chopped fresh parsley
¼ cup (59 mL) teriyaki sauce

1. In a large pot, combine the oil, onion, bell pepper, jalapeño, garlic, and tomato sauce and bring to a full simmer. Add the Chianti, tomatoes, and rice and cook for 5 minutes. Add the remaining ingredients and simmer for 15 minutes. Adjust the consistency with water if necessary.

Ostras da Panela
(Brazilian-Style Oysters)

Yield: 4 servings.   Heat Scale: Medium

This recipe is rich, tasty, and reminiscent of a New England chowder—except that few New Englanders ever put malagueta chiles in their chowder! Until now, that is. The chiles heat up the oysters, but the creams act as neutralizers. Since this dish is rich, keep the accompaniments simple: sliced fresh tomatoes, excellent bread, and a cold white wine.

¼ cup (59 mL) plus 1 tablespoon (15 mL) butter, divided
1 tablespoon (15 mL) Worcestershire sauce
1 tablespoon (15 mL) fresh lemon juice
1 teaspoon (5 mL) crushed malagueta chile, or substitute piquin
3 tablespoons (45 mL) minced celery leaves
¼ teaspoon (1.25 mL) freshly ground black pepper
½ teaspoon (2.5 mL) salt
2 dozen shucked oysters, with their juice
1 cup (236 mL) heavy cream
1 (16 ounce [454 g]) can hearts of palm, drained, rinsed, and cut into ½-inch (1 cm) thick rounds
2 tablespoons (30 mL) chopped cilantro or Italian parsley

1. In a medium saucepan, melt ¼ cup (59 mL) of the butter over medium heat. Add the Worcestershire sauce, lemon juice, crushed chile, celery leaves, black pepper, and salt. Add the oysters and their juice and bring to a boil. Immediately lower the heat to a simmer and cook for 2 minutes.
2. Add the cream and heat through, but do not allow the mixture to boil.
3. Divide the hearts of palm among 4 bowls, add the oyster mixture, and top each bowl with a dab of the remaining butter and a sprinkling of cilantro or parsley.

Chilorio al Estilo Sinaloense
(Sinaloa-Style Chilorio)

Yield: 6 servings   Heat Scale: Mild

As with mole, chilorio can be two things at once—shredded pork with chile paste, or this rich pork stew from Sinaloa that is gently infused with the raisin flavor of pasilla chiles and laced with oregano, garlic, and coriander. Serve it with warm tortillas and a salad from Chapter 6.

3 pounds (1.36 g) pork, cut into ¾-inch (1.5 cm) cubes
1 onion, peeled and quartered
1 teaspoon (5 mL) salt
4 large pasilla chiles, stems and seeds removed
½ teaspoon (2.5 mL) coriander seeds
½ teaspoon (2.5 mL) cumin
1½ teaspoons (7.5 mL) Mexican oregano
¼ teaspoon (1.25 mL) salt
5 cloves garlic, peeled
1 tablespoon (15 mL) olive oil
3 tablespoons (45 mL) corn oil

1. Place the pork in a large pot and add just enough water to cover. Add the onion and salt and bring the mixture to a boil. Reduce the heat and simmer, covered, for 1 hour, occasionally skimming the foam from the top and discarding it. Transfer the meat to a colander to drain. Pour the broth into a heatproof bowl and place the bowl into the freezer for a few minutes to coagulate the fat. Remove and discard the fat, reserving the broth.
2. Cover the chiles with hot water and let sit for 15 minutes to rehydrate. Put the chiles and the water into a blender or a food processor along with the coriander seeds, cumin, oregano, salt, and garlic, and purée the mixture.
3. In a small skillet, heat the olive oil over low heat. Add the chile mixture and sauté for 3 minutes. Set aside.
4. In a large skillet, heat the corn oil over medium-high heat. Add the pork cubes and sauté until they are lightly browned. Add 1–2 tablespoons (15–30 mL) water if the cubes start to stick. Add the sautéed chile mixture and the remaining reserved broth and simmer for 10 minutes. Add more broth if the mixture gets too thick.
5. Serve in warmed soup bowls.

Caldillo Durangueño
(Durango Stew)

Yield: 5 servings   Heat Scale: Mild to Medium

A precursor to U.S. chili con carne, this recipe hails from beautiful, quaint Durango. Serve this caldillo or stew on football or soccer days—double the recipe, prepare it the day before, and reheat it. It can simmer for hours, and this only intensifies the flavor. Serve it with warm tortillas or fresh bread and plenty of cold Mexican beer. (Note: This recipe requires advance preparation.)

6 poblano chiles, roasted
2½ pounds (1.13 kg) beef roast
1½ teaspoons (7.5 mL) salt
½ pound (224 g) tomatillos, quartered
3 cloves garlic, peeled and minced
1 cup (236 mL) chopped onion
½ teaspoon (2.5 mL) Mexican oregano
½ teaspoon (2.5 mL) ground cumin
3 tablespoons (45 mL) chopped cilantro
3 tablespoons (45 mL) vegetable oil

1. Preheat the oven to 250°F (120°C).
2. Peel the chiles and remove the stems and seeds. Place the chiles on wire racks, put the racks on baking sheets, and bake them for 1 hour.
3. Place the beef in a shallow pan and sprinkle it with the salt. With a blunt edge, pound the salt into the meat. Let the meat dry out slightly at room temperature, about 2 hours.
4. In a pot, bring 3 cups (708 mL) water to a boil. Add the tomatillos, then reduce the heat to a simmer. Add the garlic, onion, oregano, cumin, and cilantro and simmer for 30 minutes, partially covered. Remove from the heat and set aside.
5. Place the oven-seasoned chiles in a heatproof bowl and cover with 1 cup (236 mL) of very hot water. Rehydrate for 10 minutes, then drain, reserving the water. Dice the chiles and add them with the reserved water to the tomatillo mixture.
6. Cut the beef into ½-inch (1 cm) cubes. In a large, heavy pot, heat the vegetable oil over medium heat. Add the beef and sauté for 5 minutes. Add 3 cups (708 mL) hot water and bring the mixture to a boil. Reduce the heat to a simmer, add half of the chile mixture, cover, and simmer for 1 hour. Add the remaining chile mixture, cover, and simmer for 1 hour more. Serve hot.

Posole with Red and Green Chile Sauces

Yield: 4 servings   Heat Scale: Varies

This is my version of a classic corn and chile dish from northern New Mexico. Serving the chile sauces as side dishes instead of mixing them with the posole allows guests to adjust the heat to their own liking. (Note that if you are using dried posole corn, this recipe requires advance preparation.)

2 dried red New Mexican chiles, stems and seeds removed
8 ounces (224 g) frozen posole corn or dried posole corn that has been soaked in water overnight
1 teaspoon (5 mL) garlic powder
1 medium onion, peeled and chopped
6 cups (1.42 L) Classic Chicken Stock (page 46)
1 pound (454 g) pork loin, cut in 1-inch (2.5 cm) cubes
Classic New Mexico Green Chile Sauce (page 71)
New Mexico Red Chile Sauce (page 71)
Chopped fresh cilantro for garnish
Chopped onion for garnish

1. Combine the chiles, posole corn, garlic powder, onion, and chicken stock in a pot. Bring to a boil over medium heat and boil for 3 hours or until the posole is tender, adding more water as needed.
2. Add the pork and continue cooking for 30 minutes, or until the pork is tender but not falling apart. The result should resemble a soup more than a stew. Remove the chile pods.
3. Warm the chile sauces separately and serve them in small bowls for each guest to add to the posole. Serve the posole garnished with the cilantro and onion.

Double-Chile Vegetable Stew

Yield: 6–8 servings   Heat Scale: Medium

Poblano chiles are used for their flavor and serranos for their serious bite in this hearty stew that's perfect for a crisp fall day. This is an understated fusion dish with vegetables from all over the globe. Serve it with cornbread or cornsticks.

2 pounds (1.1 kg) russet potatoes, peeled and chopped
2 large carrots, peeled and chopped
3 poblano chiles, roasted and peeled, stems and seeds removed, chopped
1 medium bunch bok choy, chopped
1 bunch green onions, chopped
1 leek, white part only, cut into ¼-inch (.5 cm) rings
1 large head cabbage, chopped
2 tablespoons (30 mL) red wine vinegar
2 tablespoons (30 mL) teriyaki sauce
¼ cup (59 mL) dry white wine
4 cups (.95 L) tomatoes, peeled, seeded, and chopped
1 (12-ounce [336 g]) can tomato purée
1 medium onion, peeled and finely chopped
6 serrano chiles, stems and seeds removed, finely chopped
1 red bell pepper, seeded and finely chopped
3 cups (708 mL) Basic Beef Stock (page 45) or Classic Chicken Stock (page 46)
⅛ teaspoon (.6 mL) freshly ground nutmeg
1 tablespoon (15 mL) salt
1¾ tablespoons (26.25 mL) sugar
1 teaspoon (5 mL) finely ground black pepper

1. Combine all the ingredients in a stock pot and boil, uncovered, for 30 minutes.

Texas Gunpowder Stew

Yield: 6 servings   Heat Scale: Medium

Here's some beef-and-bean cowboy food, campfire style. It's not for the faint at heart, featuring ranch beans, sirloin, and Texas gunpowder—better known as ground jalapeño. Serve this with a stout Mexican beer, such as Negra Modelo, and plenty of warmed tortillas.

2 tablespoons (30 mL) vegetable oil
1 tablespoon (15 mL) peanut oil
3 pounds(1.36 kg) beef sirloin, trimmed and cut into 1-inch (2.5 cm) cubes
3 medium onions, peeled and chopped
2 tablespoons (30 mL) minced garlic
2½ tablespoons (37.5 mL) minced parsley
5 very ripe medium tomatoes, coarsely chopped
¼ cup (59 mL) freshly squeezed lime juice
1½ teaspoons (7.5 mL) ground cumin
2 cups (473 mL) cooked pinto beans
3 pods okra, finely chopped
1 teaspoon (5 mL) ground cinnamon
½ teaspoon (2.5 mL) ground bay leaf
8 cups (1.9 L) Basic Beef Stock (page 45)
3 tablespoons (45 mL) ground green jalapeño
2 tablespoons (30 mL) apple cider vinegar
Chopped fresh cilantro for garnish

1. In a large pot, heat the oils over medium heat. Add the beef and sauté until browned. Add the onions, garlic, parsley, and tomatoes and sauté until the onions are softened, about 5 minutes. Add the lime juice, cumin, beans, okra, cinnamon, bay leaf, and beef stock and simmer for 1½ to 2 hours. Add water or more beef stock, if needed.
2. Add the ground jalapeño and simmer for 5 minutes, stirring occasionally. Just before serving, add the vinegar and stir well. Garnish with the cilantro and serve.

Border Chile Stew

Yield: 8–10 servings   Heat Scale: Medium

It's easy to pinpoint the origin of this recipe: northern Mexico. But I add a few touches of my own, such as zucchini and celery. Serve this with a hearty bread and your favorite microbrew beer.

2½ tablespoons (37.5 mL) extra virgin olive oil
1 cup (236 mL) green New Mexican chile, chopped, roasted, and peeled
1 cup (236 mL) red bell pepper, chopped
1 medium onion, peeled and chopped
2 tablespoons (30 mL) chopped garlic
3 cups (708 mL) Classic Chicken Stock (page 46)
2 ribs celery, sliced
2 cups (473 mL) cubed potatoes, cut in ½-inch (1 cm) cubes
1 teaspoon (5 mL) Mexican oregano
1 teaspoon (5 mL) thyme leaves
2 cups (473 mL) cooked pinto beans
6 cups (1.42 L) cooked corn kernels
2 cups (473 mL) cooked, chopped chicken
2 cups (473 mL) Classic White Sauce (page 44)
2 medium zucchinis, chopped
Fried tortilla strips for garnish

1. In a stock pot, heat the olive oil over medium heat. Add the chile, bell pepper, onion, and garlic and sauté for 5 to 7 minutes, stirring occasionally. Add the chicken stock, celery, and potatoes and bring to a boil. Reduce the heat, cover, and simmer for 20 minutes or until the potatoes are tender.
2. Add the oregano, thyme, beans, corn, chicken, White Sauce, zucchinis, and enough water to make a thick stew. Simmer over low heat for 15 to 20 minutes. Garnish with the tortilla strips and serve.

Carurú
(Bahian Shrimp Stew)

Yield: 4–6 servings   Heat Scale: Medium

The African influence is evident in this dish—the dende oil and the okra were brought to Brazil by African slaves. The chile of choice for the spice in this dish is the malagueta. Many of the ingredients can be found in Latin and Asian markets, such as the dende oil, manioc flour, and dried shrimp. Serve this dish with white rice or any of the rice dishes in Chapter 13.

1 pound (454 g) okra, chopped
3 cups (708 mL) water
½ teaspoon (2.5 mL) salt
¼ pound (113 g) dried shrimp, shelled
1 pound (454 g) fresh shrimp, shelled and deveined
3 tablespoons (45 mL) dende (palm) oil or peanut oil infused with 2 teaspoons (10 mL) paprika
1 cup (236 mL) chopped onion
1 teaspoon (5 mL) paprika
2 cloves garlic, peeled and minced
½ cup (118 mL) crushed cashews
¼ cup (59 mL) peanut butter
3 small dried malagueta chiles, stems removed, crushed (or substitute piquins)
½ teaspoon (2.5 mL) freshly grated ginger
¼ cup (59 mL) manioc flour or farina (optional)

1. Place the okra in a saucepan with the water and salt. Bring the water to a boil, turn the heat down to a simmer, and cook, uncovered, for 10 minutes.
2. In a food processor or blender, grind together the dried shrimp and half the fresh shrimp. Add this mixture to the simmering okra along with the oil, onion, paprika, garlic, and cashews, stirring for a minute.
3. Add the peanut butter, chiles, and ginger. Stir this mixture constantly for 2 to 3 minutes, until it starts to thicken a little. Add the remaining fresh shrimp and cook for 10 to 15 minutes, stirring gently. If the mixture seems too thick, add water, a little at a time. Conversely, if the mixture isn't thickening, stir in a little manioc flour.

New Mexican Green Chile Stew

Yield: 6 servings   Heat Scale: Medium

This is a staple dish with as many variations as there are cooks—and each one thinks his or hers is the finest. It is a basic in New Mexican cookery, and it is entered in its own category in Southwestern chili cook-offs. Serve corn or flour tortillas with this stew. Sometimes chopped raw onions and Mexican oregano are served as a garnish.

2 pounds (1.1 kg) lean pork, cubed
2 tablespoons (30 mL) vegetable oil
1 large onion, peeled and chopped
2 cloves garlic, peeled and minced
6–8 green New Mexican chiles, roasted, peeled, stems and seeds removed, chopped
1 large potato, peeled and diced (optional)
2 tomatoes, peeled and chopped
3 cups (708 mL) water or Basic Beef Stock (page 45)

1. In a skillet, brown the pork in the oil. Add the onion and garlic and sauté for a couple of minutes.
2. Transfer the pork, onion, garlic, and the remaining ingredients to a kettle or crockpot and simmer for 1½ to 2 hours or until the meat is very tender.

Axoa Lamb with Espelette Pepper

Yield: 4–6   Heat Scale: Mild to Medium

Lamb axoa is a recipe typical of the Basque region, prepared in the same fashion as a stew. In France, lamb tongue and hooves are used to further flavor the dish, but I have omitted them here. Serve with a crusty French bread and red wine. You may substitute hot paprika or ground red New Mexican chile for the Espelette. If you wish to make this more of a stew, add two potatoes, finely chopped, and double the beef stock.

¼ cup (59 mL) olive oil
2 onions, peeled and finely chopped
2 cloves garlic, peeled and finely chopped
4 green bell peppers, stems and seeds removed, finely chopped
2 red bell peppers, stems and seeds removed, finely chopped
1½ pounds (680 g) lamb, cut into ½-inch (1 cm) cubes
2 tablespoons (30 mL) ground Espelette pepper
1½ cups (354 mL) Basic Beef Stock (page 45)
2 bay leaves
Salt, to taste
Freshly ground black pepper, to taste

1. In a large pot, heat the olive oil over medium heat. Add the onions and garlic and sauté for 5 minutes, stirring occasionally. Add the bell peppers and sauté for 5 minutes, stirring occasionally. Add the lamb and sauté another 5 minutes. Add the ground Espelette, stock, and bay leaves, reduce the heat, and simmer, covered, for 25 minutes. If using potatoes, simmer until the potatoes are tender. Add salt and pepper to taste.

Sancoche de Gallina (Peruvian Spiced Chicken Stew with Vegetables)

Yield: 6 servings   Heat Scale: Medium

The combination of poultry and the sweet potatoes in this dish give it an extraordinary taste. This soup is hearty enough to work as a main meal, but feel free to accompany it with any spicy side dish.

8 cups (1.9 L) water
2 teaspoons (10 mL) salt
1 (2–3 pound [1.1–1.6 kg]) chicken, cut into serving pieces
1 pound (454 g) beef marrow bones
2 onions, peeled and sliced into rings
2 rocoto chiles, stems and seeds removed, chopped (or substitute jalapeños)
2 leeks, sliced into rings
Leaves from 8 stalks celery
3 potatoes, peeled and cubed
2 sweet potatoes, peeled and cubed
½ cup (118 mL) corn kernels
1 green bell pepper, stem and seeds removed, cubed
¾ pound (336 G) pumpkin, seeded, peeled, and cubed
Freshly ground black pepper, to taste

1. In a large saucepan, bring the water and salt to a boil. Add the chicken and beef bones. Lower the heat, cover, and simmer for 2 hours. Strain the broth into a clean saucepan. Discard the skin and bones of the chicken and the beef bones. Cut the chicken meat into small pieces and set aside.
2. Add the remaining ingredients to the broth, cover, and simmer for 30 minutes. Add the chicken meat and simmer 5 minutes more. Taste for seasoning, adjust as needed, and serve.

Mayan Turkey Stew

Yield: 6–8 servings   Heat Scale: Medium

The turkey represented the Mayan god of rain and fertility and was called tlaloc. A meal, to the Mayans, consisted of a stew, either with meat and vegetables, or vegetables alone in a broth base. This stew also uses mint, or native yerba buena, and cilantro for flavoring. Serve this Guatemalan stew with an avocado salad and corn tortillas.

4 pasilla chiles, stems and seeds removed (or substitute New Mexican)
4 jalapeño chiles, stems removed, chopped
3 tomatoes, peeled
1 onion, peeled and chopped
1 teaspoon (5 mL) achiote
¼ cup (59 mL) chopped cilantro
¼ cup (59 mL) chopped yerba buena or mint
1 small turkey, cut in serving pieces (or substitute duck [be sure to remove the fat if using])

1. Cover the pasilla chiles with hot water and let them sit for 15 minutes or until softened.
2. In a blender, combine the pasilla chiles with their soaking water, jalapeños, tomatoes, onion, and achiote and purée until smooth. Stir the cilantro and mint into the sauce.
3. Place the turkey pieces and 4 cups (.95 L) water in a pan. Add the sauce and bring to a boil. Reduce the heat, cover, and simmer until the turkey is tender, about 1 hour.

Black Bean Corned Beef Chile Stew

Yield: 8–10 servings   Heat Scale: Mild

Corned beef in a stew? Why not experiment? Cooks can either prepare their own corned beef or purchase it from a butcher. You'll find this dish a delightful mix of flavors and easy to make; just be sure to skim off any fat that comes to the surface. Serve it with an Irish soda bread (because of the corned beef), accompanied by a black and tan beer.

3 quarts (2.85 L) water
2½ pound (680 g) corned beef
2 carrots, chopped
1 large onion, peeled and chopped
½ bunch parsley, chopped
1 teaspoon (5 mL) salt
1 tablespoon (15 mL) freshly ground black pepper
1 tablespoon (15 mL) freshly ground white pepper
2 cups (473 mL) Classic New Mexico Green Chile Sauce (page 71)
2 cups (473 mL) cooked black beans

1. Combine all the ingredients except the beans in a stock pot and boil uncovered for 2 hours. Remove the corned beef, trim the fat, and set aside. Strain the soup and discard all solids, then skim the fat.

2. Shred the corned beef, cut it into 1½-inch (3.5 cm) lengths and return it to the soup. Add enough water to bring the volume of the soup to about 1 gallon (3.8 L) and add the beans. Heat to boiling, stir well, and serve.

Caribbean Pepper Pot Soup

Yield: 8 servings   Heat Scale: Medium to Hot

There are dozens of variations of this soup (actually a stew) throughout the Caribbean. If you talk to a dozen people, you'll get a dozen different recipes, with each person claiming that theirs is the way to create the perfect Pepper Pot Soup! I present to you a rather basic recipe, using the ingredients that most cooks will agree on. Please embellish it so that you have the best pepper pot.

2 cups (473 mL) chopped onion
½ pound (224 g) salt pork, rind removed, diced; or 1 salted pig's tail
2 garlic cloves, peeled and minced
1 teaspoon (5 mL) thyme
7 cups (1.65 L) water
1 pound callaloo (or substitute spinach), washed and chopped
½ pound (224 g) white potatoes, peeled and diced into ½-inch (1 cm) cubes
½ pound (224 g) yams, peeled and diced into ½-inch (1 cm) cubes
1 large fresh Scotch bonnet (or habanero), stem and seeds removed, minced
2 tablespoons (30 mL) vegetable oil
12 small pods okra, washed and sliced
1½ cups (354 mL) coconut milk
1 cup (236 mL) cooked, chopped shrimp
Salt, to taste
Freshly ground black pepper, to taste

1. Place the onion, salt pork, garlic, thyme, and water in a large, heavy soup pot or casserole. Bring the mixture to a boil and skim any froth that rises to the surface in the first 4 to 5 minutes of boiling. Reduce the heat to a simmer, cover, and cook for 1 hour.

2. Add the callaloo, potatoes, yams, and Scotch bonnet pepper to the soup. Return it to a boil, reduce the heat to a simmer, cover, and cook for another 45 minutes.

3. In a skillet, heat the oil over medium-high heat. Add the sliced okra and sauté until they are lightly browned, about 2 minutes. Add the okra to the soup and simmer for 5 more minutes, or until the okra is tender.

4. Stir in the coconut milk and shrimp and let the soup simmer for 5 minutes, stirring occasionally.

5. Serve the soup in heated bowls.

Rice, Beans, and Greens Stew with Cayenne

Yield: 8–10 servings   Heat Scale: Medium

Here's one of my favorite vegetarian stews that I imported from Valencia, Spain, and then fired up. It has a lot of great ingredients, especially the beans, greens, and turnips. I suggest serving this stew with corn bread or pan-fried corn cakes.

¾ pound (336 g) dried white beans
3 quarts (2.85 L) water
1 pound (454 g) well-trimmed collard greens, chopped
1 teaspoon (5 mL) Hungarian hot paprika
2 onions, peeled and finely chopped
2 tablespoons (30 mL) parsley, finely chopped
⅛ teaspoon (.6 mL) saffron
2 medium turnips, peeled and thinly sliced
2 quarts (1.9 L) Super-Rich Vegetable Stock (page 48)
1 teaspoon (5 mL) salt
½ teaspoon (2.5 mL) ground white pepper
2 teaspoons (10 mL) ground cayenne
1½ cups (354 mL) short-grain rice

1. Combine the beans and water in a large pot and bring to a boil. Reduce the heat and cook, uncovered, for 1 hour. Drain the beans and return them to the pot. Add all the other ingredients except the rice and cook, uncovered, for 30 minutes. Add the rice and and cook, covered, for 25 minutes. Adjust the consistency of the stew with water, if needed.

Caribbean Crab Gumbo

Yield: 4 servings   Heat Scale: Medium

Okra, of course, is a key ingredients of this rich gumbo, which is tasty and nutritious. Variations of this recipe can be found all over the West Indies. African slaves introduced okra to the islands, as along with callaloo and taro.

2 tablespoons (30 mL) butter
1 tablespoon (15 mL) vegetable oil
1 onion, peeled and chopped
1 pound (454 g) tomatoes, peeled, drained, and chopped
1 tablespoon (15 mL) chopped fresh basil
2 tablespoons (30 mL) chopped fresh parsley
½ pound (224 g) okra, trimmed and sliced
2 habanero chiles, left whole
2½ cups (591 mL) boiling water
2 cups (473 mL) cooked crab meat
Salt, to taste
Freshly ground black pepper, to taste

1. Heat the butter and oil in a large saucepan over medium heat. Add the onion and fry for 5 minutes. Stir in the tomatoes, basil, and parsley, and cook for 5 more minutes.

2. Add the okra and habanero, and pour in the boiling water. Add the crab meat, season with salt and pepper, then lower the heat and simmer for 45 minutes.

3. Discard the habaneros, spoon the gumbo into warmed soup bowls, and serve with fresh bread.

Chicken and Okra Stew, or African Gumbo

Yield: 4–6 servings   Heat Scale: Medium

Okra is frequently used in African stews as a thickening agent.

1 (3-pound [1.36 g]) chicken, cut into serving pieces
1 tablespoon (15 mL) all-purpose flour, plus more as needed for dredging
3 tablespoons (45 mL) peanut oil
2 cups (473 mL) chopped onion
1 teaspoon (5 mL) salt
2 teaspoons (10 mL) ground cayenne
4 cups (.95 L) chopped tomato
1 quart (.95 L) Classic Chicken Stock (page 46)
1 pound (454 g) okra, cut into rounds
¼ cup (59 mL) warm water

1. Wash the chicken and pat the pieces until they are dry. Place the flour for dredging in a paper or plastic bag and dredge the chicken, a few pieces at a time.

2. Heat the oil in a large, heavy pot. Add the chicken, a few pieces at a time, and brown them.

3. Add the onion, salt, cayenne, tomato, and stock and bring the mixture to a boil. Reduce the heat to a simmer, cover, and simmer until the chicken is tender, about 50 to 60 minutes.

4. When the chicken is tender, add the okra and simmer for 10 minutes. The okra should thicken the stew. If the stew is not thick enough, mix the 1 tablespoon (15 mL) flour and the water and stir the mixture into the stew.

Gulyasleves
(Goulash Soup)

Yield: 6 servings   Heat Scale: Medium

Best described as Hungarian goulash soup, this dish probably had its roots with the roving Magyar tribes of central Europe, who cooked their meat and vegetables over campfires in large kettles. If you can't find hot paprika, bring up the heat by adding small dried red chiles, rather than adding more paprika, which can make the soup too sweet.

5 tablespoons (75 mL) hot Hungarian paprika, divided
1 cup (236 mL) all-purpose flour
1 pound (454 g) cubed, boneless beef chuck
2 tablespoons (30 mL) bacon fat or oil
1 medium onion, peeled and cut in thin slices
6 small, dried red chiles, such as cayenne or piquin
1 large carrot, peeled and diced
4 cups (.95 L) Basic Beef Stock (page 45)
1 tablespoon (15 mL) coarsely ground black pepper
¾ teaspoon (3.75 mL) caraway seeds

1. In a bowl, mix 4 tablespoons (60 mL) of the paprika with the flour. Add the beef, toss to coat, and shake off the excess flour. In a skillet, brown the beef cubes in the bacon fat. Remove the beef from the skillet and drain.
2. Add the onions to the oil and sauté until they are browned.
3. Place the beef, onions, and remaining ingredients in a large pot or crock-pot, bring to a boil, reduce the heat, and simmer until the vegetables and meat are very tender and start to fall apart, about 1–1½ hours. Add more water if necessary to thin to the desired consistency.

Variation

Add diced potatoes and peeled, seeded tomatoes for a heartier stew.

Ethiopian Chicken Stew

Yield: 8 servings   Heat Scale: Medium

This recipe, known as doro we't, is considered the national dish of Ethiopia. Traditionally, it is served with native injera bread, which is difficult to make or find. I recommend any unleavened bread (such as pita or boboli) as a substitute.

1 (3–4 pound [1.36–1.82 kg]) chicken, quartered
¼ cup (59 mL) lemon juice
1 tablespoon (15 mL) salt
1½ cups (354 mL) minced onion
¼ cup (59 mL) Qibe (Ethiopian Curried Butter; page 36)
1½ cups (354 mL) minced garlic
1½ teaspoons (7.5 mL) freshly grated ginger
¼ teaspoon (1.25 mL) ground fenugreek seeds
¼ teaspoon (1.25 mL) ground nutmeg
¼ teaspoon (1.25 mL) ground cardamom
¼ cup (59 mL) Berbere (page 27)
1 tablespoon (15 mL) Hungarian paprika
¼ cup (59 mL) dry white wine
¾ cup (177 mL) water
8 hardboiled eggs
1 quart (.95 L) Classic Chicken Stock (page 46)
¾ teaspoon (3.75 mL) freshly ground black pepper

1. Rub the chicken quarters with lemon juice and sprinkle the salt over them. Set aside.
2. In a heavy pot, cook the onion over medium heat for 5 minutes, stirring constantly to avoid burning. Stir in the Qibe and continue cooking for 2 minutes, stirring constantly. Add the garlic, ginger, fenugreek, nutmeg, and cardamom and stir well. Add the Berbere and paprika and cook, stirring often, for 3 minutes. Stir in the wine and water and bring to a boil. Boil for 3 minutes or until thickened.
3. Add the chicken pieces and toss to coat. Reduce the heat to low, cover, and cook for 15 minutes. Peel the eggs and puncture their surfaces with a fork. Add them to the pot, cover, and cook 15 more minutes.
4. Remove the chicken, let it cool, and debone it. Return the chicken to the pot, add the stock, and heat, stirring often. Stir in the pepper.
5. To serve, place a whole egg in each bowl and spoon soup over it. Alternatively, the eggs can be chopped and sprinkled over the chicken stew.

Aji de Carne
(Bolivian Peppery Pork Stew)

Yield: 5–6 servings.   Heat Scale: Hot

The use of bananas in this pork dish is very typical of Latin American cooking. Bo-livians have a reputation for liking spicy foods, and this recipe contains enough chile pepper to satisfy even the most jaded palate. Because this is a rich, one-pot meal, I suggest serving it with a salad of greens and sliced tomatoes drizzled with olive oil.

3–4 tablespoons (45–60 mL) olive oil
3 cups (708 mL) chopped onion
3 cloves garlic, peeled and minced
2½ pounds (1.13 kg) boneless pork, cut into ½-inch (1 cm) cubes
3 cups (708 mL) chopped tomatoes
¼ teaspoon (1.25 mL) saffron
½ teaspoon (2.5 mL) salt
¼ teaspoon (1.25 mL) freshly ground black pepper
2 tablespoons (30 mL) ground aji chile (or substitute New Mexican, such as chimayó)
⅛ teaspoon (.6 mL) ground cloves
¼ teaspoon (1.25 mL) ground cinnamon
2 cups (473 mL) chicken stock or beef broth
4 medium potatoes, peeled and quartered
2 green bananas, peeled and quartered
½ cup (118 mL) heavy cream or coconut milk
1 tablespoon (15 mL) molasses
½ cup (118 mL) finely chopped raw cashews or unsalted peanuts

1. In a heavy Dutch oven, heat the oil over medium heat. Add the onion and garlic and sauté until the onion is soft. Add the pork, a few cubes at a time, and cook until browned. Add the tomatoes, saffron, salt, black pepper, ground chile, cloves, cinnamon, and stock. Bring this mixture to a boil, reduce the heat to a simmer, cover, and cook for 30 minutes.
2. Add the potatoes and bananas and simmer for 25 minutes.
3. Stir in the cream, molasses, and nuts and simmer until heated through, taking care that the cream does not boil. Serve immediately.

Feijoada Completa
(Brazilian Black Bean Stew)

Yield: 10–12 servings   Heat Scale: Medium

This recipe features smoked meats and the Brazilian favorite, black beans. To serve it without black beans would be sacrilege to a Brazilian! This stew is so popular that it is thought of as the national dish of Brazil. The smoked tongue and carne seca are available in Latin markets, but feel free to substitute other smoked meats. Serve the feijoada with rice, greens, and commercial Brazilian hot pepper sauce. (Note: This recipe requires advance preparation.)

1 smoked beef tongue
2 pounds (1.1 kg) black beans, soaked overnight and drained
2 pounds (1.1 kg) carne seca (dried beef), soaked overnight and drained
2 pounds (1.1 kg) linguica (seasoned Brazilian pork sausage) (or substitute Spanish Chorizo with Pimentón [page 182])
½ pound (224 g) bacon, in one piece
½ pound (224 g) smoked pork loin
½ pound (224 g) salt pork, cubed
2 tablespoons (30 mL) vegetable oil
2 onions, peeled and finely chopped
2 cloves garlic, peeled and crushed
2 tomatoes, peeled, seeded, and chopped
2 bay leaves
3 fresh a malgueta chiles, stems and seeds removed, minced (or substitute piquins or red serranos)
2 tablespoons (30 mL) finely chopped parsley
4 oranges, peeled and sliced, for garnish

1. Place the tongue in a large pot and add water to cover. Bring to a boil, lower the heat, and simmer, covered, 2½ hours or until tender. Remove from the heat and drain. When the tongue is cool enough to handle, remove the skin and any gristle. Place the beans, carne seca, linguica, bacon, pork loin, and salt pork in a very large stock pot. Add cold water to cover. Bring to a boil, lower the heat, and simmer, covered, for 1 hour. Check occasionally to see if the beans are absorbing the liquid too quickly and add boiling water as necessary to keep the ingredients barely covered. Add the tongue and continue cooking for another hour or until the beans are tender.

2. In a skillet, heat the oil over medium heat. Add the onions and garlic and sauté until the onion has softened. Add the tomatoes, bay leaves, chiles, and parsley and simmer for 5 minutes. Remove about 2 cups (473 mL) of the black beans from the casserole with a slotted spoon and mash them into the onion-tomato mixture. Cook, stirring constantly, about 2 minutes. Remove and slice the meats. Arrange them on a large platter with the tongue in the center. Garnish with the orange slices. Add the thick bean sauce to the remaining black beans in the casserole. Cook, stirring, about 2 minutes. Serve the beans alongside the meat.

Porotos Granados
(A Grand Chile Stew)

Yield: 6 servings   Heat Scale: Medium to Hot

This stew is the national dish of Chile. It should be served with Pebre (page 51). Porotos is the Indian word for fresh cranberry beans. They are available year-round in Chile, but I suggest substituting navy beans.

1½ cups (354 mL) dried cranberry beans (or substitute navy beans)
1 large onion, peeled and coarsely chopped
4 aji chiles, stems and seeds removed, chopped (or substitute yellow wax hot or jalapeño)
4 tablespoons (60 mL) olive oil
1 clove garlic, peeled and minced
6 tomatoes, peeled, seeded, and chopped
½ teaspoon (2.5 mL) dried basil
1½ teaspoons (7.5 mL) dried oregano
½ teaspoon (2.5 mL) dried thyme
Salt, to taste
Freshly ground black pepper, to taste
2 cups (473 mL) winter squash (about 1 pound [454 g]), peeled and cut into ½-inch (1 cm) cubes
⅓ cup (79 mL) corn kernels

1. Put the beans in a pot with cold water to cover. Bring to a boil, turn off the heat, and allow the beans to soak for 1 hour. Change the water, bring the beans to a boil again, reduce the heat, and simmer for 1 hour.
2. While the beans simmer, heat the oil in a large skillet over medium heat. Add the onion and chile and sauté until they are soft. Add the garlic, tomatoes, basil, oregano, thyme, salt, and pepper and cook, stirring, until a thick purée forms, 5 to 10 minutes.
3. When the beans have cooked for 1 hour and are almost tender, add the tomato purée and the squash and continue cooking until the beans are completely done and the squash is mushy. Stir in the corn and cook for an additional 5 minutes.

Peruvian Sopa de Lima

Yield: 6–8 servings   Heat Scale: Varies, but probably Medium

When is a stew not a stew? When it's cooked like a stew and served like a broth. This stew-soup is a favorite in Lima, the capital of Peru. It is different from the Yucatecan soup of the same name that features the Key lime. The rocoto, the favorite chile in this recipe, was a principal crop of the Inca society in Peru, and centuries later it is still the Peruvian chile of choice. Cooks will have to grow their own or substitute jalapeños; however, persons living near the Mexican border can often find the rocoto's close relatives, canarios, in markets in cities such as Ciudad Juárez.

4 quarts (3.8 L) water, or more if necessary
2 pounds (1.1 kg) beef brisket, flank, or short ribs
1 whole onion, peeled
1 whole tomato
½ cup (118 mL) canned chickpeas
1 bouquet garni: 2 sprigs parsley, 1 sprig fresh rosemary, 2 sprigs fresh thyme, 4 whole black peppercorns, tied in cheesecloth
1 whole rocoto or jalapeño chile
1 teaspoon (5 mL) salt, plus more to taste
6 carrots, cut into ½-inch (1 cm) pieces
3 turnips, peeled and cut into ½-inch (1 cm) cubes
2 ears corn, cut into 2-inch (5 cm) rounds
1 small yuca, peeled and cut into ½-inch (1 cm) cubes (optional)
3 potatoes, cut into ½-inch (1 cm) cubes
1 cabbage, cut into eighths
3 leeks, white part only, sliced into ½-inch (1 cm) pieces
1 celery stalk
1 tablespoon (15 mL) vegetable oil
1 cup (236 mL) sliced onion
½ cup (118 mL) sliced rocoto chiles (or substitute jalapeños)
Freshly ground black pepper, to taste

1. Heat the water in a large stock pot. When the water is warm, add the beef, onion, tomato, chickpeas, and the bouquet garni. Bring the water to a boil, reduce the heat, and simmer briskly for 30 minutes.
2. Transfer the onion and tomato to a blender and purée. Return the purée to the pot. Add the whole chile and cook for an additional 1½ hours.
3. Add the salt, carrots, turnips, corn, yuca (if using), potatoes, cabbage, leeks, and celery. Simmer until the vegetables are tender, 20 to 30 minutes.
4. Transfer the beef to a platter. Remove the vegetables from the pot with a slotted spoon and arrange them around the meat. Keep warm in the oven.
5. In a skillet, heat the oil over medium heat. Add the onions and sliced chiles and sauté until the onion is translucent. Add salt and pepper to taste.
6. Serve the broth first in soup bowls, followed by the meat and vegetables covered with the sauce.

Curried Chicken and Banana Stew

Yield: 6 servings   Heat Scale: Medium

This dish, also known as Supu Ya N Dizi, is from Tanzania, East Africa. Even though soups and stews are common throughout Africa, the addition of curry powder and coconut shows this recipe's Indian influence.

4 pounds (1.82 kg) chicken pieces
3 tablespoons (45 mL) peanut oil
3 cloves garlic, peeled and minced
1 cup (236 mL) chopped onion
2 cups (473 mL) chopped celery
2½ tablespoons (37.5 mL) hot Madras curry powder
1½ teaspoons (7.5 mL) salt
1 teaspoon (5 mL) freshly ground black pepper
1 tablespoon (15 mL) ground or crushed red chile
2 cups (473 mL) chopped tomato
1 cup (236 mL) shredded coconut
1½ quarts (1.42 L) Classic Chicken Stock (page 46)
2 slightly under-ripe bananas, peeled and sliced

1. In a large, heavy pot, brown the chicken in the oil over medium-high heat. Drain the chicken on paper towels and set aside.
2. Sauté the garlic, onion, and celery in the remaining oil for 1 minute. Add the curry powder, salt, black pepper, and red chile and sauté for 1 minute.
3. Add the chicken to the sautéed vegetables, along with the tomato, coconut, and chicken stock. Bring the mixture to a boil, reduce the heat to a simmer, cover, and simmer for 40 minutes or until the chicken is very tender.
4. Remove the chicken pieces from the pot. Remove the meat from the bones and add the meat back to the simmering stock mixture. Add the banana and simmer for 10 minutes.

Hot Tajine of Chicken with Lemons and Olives

Yield: 4 servings   Heat Scale: Mild

Rosemary Ann Ogilvie collected this tajine for me in Morocco. These stews are slowly simmered for long periods so that the meat literally falls off the bone. They are then placed in the center of the room, and everyone eats from the communal bowl, using small pieces of unleavened bread to pick up the stew.

1 (3-pound [1.36 kg]) chicken fryer, cut into serving pieces
3 tablespoons (45 mL) vegetable oil
1 teaspoon (5 mL) ground ginger
1 teaspoon (5 mL) ground red New Mexican chile
½ teaspoon (2.5 mL) ground turmeric
¼ teaspoon (1.25 mL) ground cumin
½ cup (118 mL) chopped fresh parsley
1 large onion, peeled and thinly sliced
1 tomato, peeled and diced
6 cloves garlic, peeled and minced
Juice of 1 lemon
2 cups (473 mL) water
2 lemons, quartered
1 (14-ounce [392 g]) jar pitted green olives, drained

1. In a large skillet, quickly brown the chicken in the oil over medium-high heat. Add the ginger, chile, turmeric, cumin, parsley, onion, tomato, garlic, lemon juice, and water. Bring to a boil, reduce the heat, and simmer, covered, until the chicken is tender, about 1½ hours, turning the chicken frequently.
2. Remove the chicken from the sauce and keep it warm. When ready to serve, return the chicken to the pan, add the lemon quarters and the olives, and simmer for 10 minutes.
3. Serve on a plate or in a traditionally made tajine with a pita-type flat bread.

Acorn Squash and Corn Stew with Chipotle

Yield: 8 servings   Heat Scale: Medium

There are a lot of rich, smoky flavors here for such a simple recipe. The chipotle can be either rehydrated dried pods that are then chopped fine or the canned chipotles in adobo. To prepare the acorn squash, cut them in half, remove the seeds, add 1 teaspoon (5 mL) bacon grease or butter to each half, and bake the squash at 350°F (180°C) for 1¼ hours.

1 tablespoon (15 mL) peanut oil
1 medium onion, peeled and chopped
1 tablespoon (15 mL) minced garlic
4 cups (.95 L) tomato sauce
2 tablespoons (30 mL) finely chopped chipotle chile
1 tablespoon (15 mL) salt
2 cups (473 mL) fresh corn kernels
3 cups (708 mL) baked, soft acorn squash (about 2 medium squashes)
½ cup (118 mL) teriyaki sauce
3 cups (708 mL) water
3 cups (708 mL) Classic Chicken Stock (page 46)
1 teaspoon (5 mL) ground cinnamon
½ teaspoon (2.5 mL) bay leaf
½ teaspoon (2.5 mL) vanilla
1 cup (236 mL) freshly squeezed orange juice
1 tablespoon (15 mL) sugar
1 tablespoon (15 mL) raw honey
1½ tablespoons (22.5 mL) freshly squeezed lime juice
Garlic croutons for garnish

1. Heat the oil in a large pot over medium heat. Add the onion and garlic and sauté until the onion is soft, about 5 minutes. Add the tomato sauce, chipotle chiles, salt, and corn and cook, uncovered, for 15 minutes.
2. Add the squash, teriyaki sauce, water, chicken stock, cinnamon, bay leaf, and vanilla and cook, uncovered, for 20 minutes.
3. In a bowl, combine the orange juice, sugar, honey, and lime juice. Add this mixture to the stew. Heat for 5 minutes.
4. Serve sprinkled with garlic croutons.

New Mexican Venison Cauldron

Yield: 8–10 servings   Heat Scale: Medium

Halfway between a stew and a chili, this recipe is one of the best uses I've found for venison, as it's marinated in both red and green chile. Since this is a variation on hunter's stew, I suggest serving it with biscuits. (Note: This recipe requires advance preparation.)

1 (3½–4 pound [1.6–2 kg]) venison roast, cut into 1½-inch (3.5 cm) cubes
1½ teaspoons (7.5 mL) salt
2 tablespoons (30 mL) ground red New Mexican chile (chimayó preferred)
2 cups (473 mL) Classic New Mexico Green Chile Sauce (page 71)
1½ teaspoons (7.5 mL) minced garlic
2 tablespoons (30 mL) red wine vinegar
2 medium onions, peeled and finely chopped
5 cups (1.18 L) Classic Chicken Stock (page 46)
2 medium stalks celery, chopped
2 medium carrots, cut in ½-inch (1 cm) rounds
6 medium potatoes, peeled and cut into 1-inch (2.5 cm) cubes
2 medium rutabagas, peeled and cut into ¾-inch (2 cm) cubes
1 teaspoon (5 mL) crushed black peppercorns

1. In a shallow baking dish, toss the venison cubes with the salt and ground red chile powder to cover.
2. In a bowl, combine the green chile sauce, garlic, and red wine vinegar. Pour this mixture over the venison. Marinate for at least 1 hour.
3. In a large pot, cook the onions over medium heat for 2 minutes, stirring constantly. Add the chicken stock, celery, carrots, potatoes, rutabagas, black pepper, and the venison with its marinade and simmer, uncovered, for 2 hours, adding water as needed to maintain the liquid.

Seum Sin Kuai
(Braised Water Buffalo Stew with Chiles)

Yield: 6 servings   Heat Scale: Medium

Don't let the use of water buffalo meat in this recipe from Laos prevent you from making it. Simply substitute buffalo meat that is available from specialty markets and through mail order. The use of eggplant is typical in Laotian cuisine; eggplant thickens and adds richness to stewed dishes.

2 pounds (1.1 kg) buffalo meat, cut into ¾-inch (2 cm) cubes (or substitute beef)
7 slices galangal (or substitute 3 tablespoons [45 mL] chopped fresh ginger)
1 onion, peeled and sliced
½ teaspoon (2.5 mL) salt
2 tablespoons (30 mL) fish sauce
1 eggplant, washed and sliced
1 small head garlic, roasted, peeled, and chopped
1 cup (236 mL) sliced green beans
3–4 fresh red serrano or jalapeño chiles, stems and seeds removed, cut into rings
Juice of 1 fresh lime
½ cup (118 mL) chopped green onions, white and light green parts only
¼ cup (59 mL) chopped fresh mint or basil
Chopped fresh cilantro for garnish
Freshly ground black pepper for garnish
Thin slices of cucumber for garnish

1. Put the meat, galangal, onion, and salt in a large, heavy soup pot and add water to cover. Bring to a boil and add the fish sauce and eggplant. Reduce the heat and cook at a rolling simmer for 10 minutes or until the eggplant is tender. Remove the eggplant from the pot, mash it, and set it aside. Cover the meat and continue to simmer until it is tender, about 1 hour.
2. When the meat is tender, add the mashed eggplants, garlic, green beans, chiles, and lime juice. Cook at a low boil, uncovered, for 10 minutes or until the beans are done and the sauce has thickened slightly.
3. Stir in the green onions and mint, and divide the stew among large soup bowls. Garnish with the cilantro, black pepper, and cucumber.

Cincinnati-Style Chili

Yield: 6 servings   Heat Scale: Mild

This chili is often served over spaghetti and is then called chili-mac or two-way chili. Cook the spaghetti al dente, cover it with chili, and top with grated Parmesan cheese.

2 pounds (1.1 kg) coarsely ground chuck steak, browned and drained of fat
1 quart (.95 L) water
1 cup (236 mL) chopped onions
2 (8-ounce [224 g]) cans tomato sauce
4 cloves garlic, peeled and minced
¼ teaspoon (1.25 mL) ground allspice
4 whole cloves, crushed
1 bay leaf, ground
½ ounce (14 g) unsweetened chocolate
3 tablespoons (45 mL) chili powder (or more to taste)
2 tablespoons (30 mL) apple cider vinegar
2 teaspoons (10 mL) Worcestershire sauce
½ teaspoon (2.5 mL) salt
1 teaspoon (5 mL) ground cumin
1 teaspoon (5 mL) ground cinnamon
1½ teaspoons (7.5 mL) sugar
2 tablespoons (30 mL) all-purpose flour mixed with ¼ cup (59 mL) water

1. Combine the chuck steak and the water in a large pot and simmer for 30 minutes. Add the remaining ingredients except the flour mixed with water and simmer, uncovered, for 3 hours.
2. Add the flour mixed with water, bring to a boil, and cook for 5 minutes. Remove from the heat and serve.

Buzzard's Breath Chili

Yield: 12 servings   Heat Scale: Varies, but usually Medium

Tom Griffin, a Houston stockbroker, was the Chili Appreciation Society International Terlingua champion in 1977 with this interestingly named chili. A small amount of additional cumin added during the last 10 minutes enhances the aroma.

8 pounds (3.63 kg) boneless beef chuck, cut into 3/8-inch (1 cm) cubes and trimmed of gristle and fat
¼ cup (59 mL) vegetable oil
2 (8-ounce [224 g]) cans tomato sauce
2 cups (473 mL) water
2 large onions, peeled and chopped
5 cloves garlic, peeled, chopped, and crushed
2 jalapeños, wrapped in cheese cloth
¼ cup (59 mL) chili powder
2 teaspoons (10 mL) ground cumin
¼–½ teaspoon (1.25–2.5 mL) dried oregano
Ground cayenne, to taste
Salt, to taste
1 quart (.95 L) Basic Beef Stock (page 45)
Masa harina as needed for thickening
1–2 teaspoons (5–10 mL) paprika

1. Brown the meat in the oil in an iron skillet, about 2 pounds (1.1 kg) at a time, until it turns gray. Transfer it to a large, cast-iron chili pot.
2. Add the tomato sauce and water. Add the onions, garlic, jalapeños, and chili powder. Simmer for 20 minutes, then add the cumin, oregano, cayenne, and salt. Add the beef stock and simmer, covered, until the meat is tender, about 2 hours, stirring occasionally.
3. Add masa to achieve the desired thickness, if needed.
4. Add the paprika for color and cook for 10 additional minutes. Correct the seasoning to taste, discard the jalapeños, and serve.

ICS-Style Chili

Yield: 6 servings   Heat Scale: Medium

The International Chili Society (ICS) forbids the publication of its winners'
recipes. Since this chili is my own creation and has never been entered in any ICS-
sanctioned cook-off, I am permitted to publish it here. However, it uses many of the
ingredients and techniques common to ICS-style chilis.

3 pounds sirloin steak, cut into ¼-inch (.5 cm) cubes
¼ cup (59 mL) vegetable oil
1 cup (236 mL) chorizo sausage
1 large onion, peeled and minced
3 cloves garlic, peeled and minced
1 stalk celery, minced
2 cups (473 mL) Basic Beef Stock (page 45)
2 cups (473 mL) tomato sauce
1 (12-ounce [350 mL]) bottle Corona beer
¼ cup (59 mL) ground red New Mexican chile (your choice, hot or mild)
3 tablespoons (45 mL) chili powder (your choice)
½ cup (118 mL) diced green New Mexican chiles
1 tablespoon (15 mL) ground cumin, plus more to taste
2 teaspoons (10 mL) Mexican oregano
Salt, to taste
Ground white pepper, to taste
Ground cayenne, to taste
Ground cumin, to taste
Brown sugar, to taste

1. In a skillet, heat the oil over medium-high heat. Add the steak and
sauté until lightly browned. With a slotted spoon, remove the steak and
set it aside. Add the sausage to the same skillet and fry for 5 minutes,
then remove it with the slotted spoon and reserve with the steak. Add the
onion, garlic, and celery to the oil and sauté until the onions are softened.
Remove them with the slotted spoon and reserve them with the meat.
2. Transfer the steak, sausage, and onion mixture to a chili pot or Dutch
oven. Add the beef broth, tomato sauce, and beer and bring to a simmer.
Cook for 30 minutes.
3. Add the ground chile, chili powder, green chiles, cumin, and oregano
and simmer, uncovered, for 1 hour, stirring occasionally.
4. Taste the chile and add just enough salt, white pepper, cayenne,
cumin, and brown sugar to make the chili perfect. Simmer an additional
15 minutes.

Chili Cook's Hints
Experiment with other spices to make your chili unique. Some suggestions
are ¼–½ teaspoon (1.25–2.5 mL) paprika, coriander, cilantro, sage, or basil.
You also might want to draw attention to your chili by floating an habanero chile on top, but if you do this, omit the cayenne and take care that
the habanero does not burst!

Short Rib Chili

Yield: 8 servings   Heat Scale: Medium

This chili recipe, one of my favorites, was invented by my wife, Mary Jane. It is easy to make, cooks in 2½ hours, and combines the best of both red and green chiles. Serve it with fresh bread or corn bread and a big green salad.

4 pounds (1.82 kg) beef short ribs
2 tablespoons (30 mL) corn oil
1 onion, peeled and chopped
1 green bell pepper, stem and seeds removed, chopped
2 cloves garlic, peeled and chopped
2 cups (473 mL) Basic Beef Stock (page 45)
2 tablespoons (30 mL) ground red New Mexican chile
1 (12-ounce [336 g]) can stewed tomatoes, crushed
1 cup (236 mL) chopped, roasted, and peeled green New Mexican chile
2 cups (473 mL) cooked fresh corn kernels
3½ cups (826 mL) cooked black beans, drained

1. Trim the excess fat from the short ribs. In a large Dutch oven, heat the oil over medium-high heat. Add the ribs, and fry them until they are browned. Add the onion, bell pepper, and garlic and sauté for 1 minute. Add the Beef Stock.
2. Add the—ground chile, tomatoes, and green chile and bring to a boil. Reduce the heat to a simmer. Cover and cook for 2½ hours, stirring occasionally.
3. Just before serving, add the drained corn and beans and heat through. For convenience, you may want to cut the meat off the bones while it is in the pot.

U.B. Alarmed Five-Chile Chili

Yield: 10–12 servings   Heat Scale: Extremely Hot

This unusual chili could also be termed a stew. It is not for beginning chileheads but for the serious aficionado. The name was inspired by the pantywaist heat scales of most other chilis. I have taken some grief over the turnips and potatoes here, but do I care? In case it's too hot, serve this with milk or beer.

7 cups (1.65 L) Basic Beef Stock (page 45)
1 tablespoon (15 mL) minced garlic
4 small carrots, sliced into ¼-inch (.5 cm) rounds
1½ tablespoons (22.5 mL) minced parsley
½ teaspoon (2.5 mL) ground cumin
1½ teaspoons (7.5 mL) dried Mexican oregano
½ teaspoon (2.5 mL) cinnamon
1 pound (454 g) turnips, peeled and coarsely shredded
2 pounds (1.1 kg) potatoes, peeled and cut into ½-inch (1 cm) cubes
2 tablespoons (30 mL) vegetable shortening
1 medium onion, peeled and chopped
1 pound (454 g) ground beef
1½ cups (354 mL) canned crushed tomatoes
½ cup (118 mL) apple cider
3 tablespoons (45 mL) tomato paste
½ cup (118 mL) browned butter roux (½ cup [118 mL] all-purpose flour browned in ¼ cup [59 mL] butter)
3 large chipotle chiles
½ cup (118 mL) Jack Daniels Bourbon (Black Label)
1 teaspoon (5 mL) salt
6 chiles de arbol, stems and seeds removed, crushed (or substitute any small, hot, dried red chiles)
¾ teaspoon (3.75 mL) ground habanero
1 large mirasol chile, stem and seeds removed, crushed (or substitute New Mexican)
8 chiltepins, crushed (or substitute piquins)
3 tablespoons (45 mL) olive oil
3 tablespoons (45 mL) red wine vinegar
6 tablespoons (90 mL) raw or dark honey
Sour cream for garnish
Chopped green onions for garnish

1. In a pot, combine the stock, garlic, carrots, parsley, cumin, oregano, cinnamon, turnips, and potatoes and bring to a boil. Boil, uncovered, for 20 minutes, adding water as needed. Remove and set aside.
2. In a large skillet, heat the shortening over medium heat. Add the onion and sauté for 5 minutes. Add the beef and cooked until browned. Add the tomatoes, apple cider, tomato paste, and roux and simmer, uncovered, stirring occasionally, for 10 minutes. Remove from the heat and set aside.

3. Soak the chipotles in the bourbon for 45 minutes to rehydrate, using a bowl to weigh them down and keep them submerged. In a food processor, combine the chipotles and bourbon with the remaining ingredients and purée. Add this purée to the meat mixture and stir well. Add the meat mixture to the soup, bring to a boil, and mix well. Reduce the heat and simmer for 10 minutes before serving. Garnish with the sour cream and green onions.

Rock Shrimp Gumbo with Tabasco and Cayenne

Yield: 6–8 servings   Heat Scale: Medium

Be sure and buy the shrimp in their rock-hard shells because they'll be fresher tasting. Rock shrimp have more flavor than other shrimp, so it is worth the effort to open the shell. Serve this over some dirty rice with a side of cornbread for a Louisiana treat.

¼ cup (59 mL) olive oil
1½ pound (680 g) okra, stems removed, thinly sliced
¼ pound (113 g) butter
1 large green bell pepper, stem and seeds removed, chopped
1½ medium onions, peeled and chopped
2 tablespoons (30 mL) minced garlic
2 tablespoons (30 mL) all-purpose flour
4 cups (.95 L) Classic Chicken Stock (page 46)
3 medium tomatoes, peeled and chopped
½ teaspoon (2.5 mL) ground white pepper
½ teaspoon (2.5 mL) dried thyme
1 teaspoon (5 mL) salt
2 tablespoons (30 mL) tomato paste
2 pounds (1.1 kg) rock shrimp, peeled and deveined
¾ pound (336 g) blue crab meat
1 tablespoon (15 mL) Tabasco sauce
1½ tablespoons (22.5 mL) Worcestershire sauce
½ teaspoon (2.5 mL) ground cayenne

1. In a skillet, heat the olive oil over medium heat. Add the okra and cook, stirring constantly, for 5 minutes. Set aside.
2. In a large pot, melt the butter over medium heat. Add the bell pepper, onion, and garlic and cook until the onions are soft, about 4 minutes. Add the flour and stir until it is integrated. Add the stock and stir briskly with a whisk until everything is well blended. Add the reserved okra, tomatoes, pepper, thyme, salt, tomato paste, rock shrimp, and crab meat and simmer over low heat, covered, for 20 minutes. Add the remaining ingredients, stir well, and cook for 10 more minutes, then serve.

Poor Man's Lobster Gumbo

Yield: 8–10 servings   Heat Scale: Medium

Monkfish is called "poor man's lobster" because of its flavor and its inexpensiveness relative to lobster. It is a firm fish that does well in a gumbo such as this, and it is a real bargain to buy. When making the roux, heat the shortening until it smokes a bit, and the resulting roux will be browned.

7 tablespoons (105 mL) vegetable shortening, divided
1 pound (454 g) okra, cut into ½-inch (1 cm) rounds
2 cups (473 mL) chopped tomatoes
2 tablespoons (30 mL) tomato paste
¼ cup (59 mL) all-purpose flour
3 medium onions, peeled and chopped
3 stalks celery, cut into ½ inch (1 cm) pieces
1½ tablespoons (22.5 mL) minced garlic
1 medium red bell pepper, diced
1 medium green bell pepper, diced
4 cups (.95 L) Classic Chicken Stock (page 46)
2 cups (473 mL) Traditional European Fish Stock (page 47)
2½ pounds (680 g) monkfish, cut into 1-inch (2.5 cm) cubes
1½ tablespoons (22.5 mL) ground cayenne
1½ tablespoons (22.5 mL) Tabasco sauce
Salt, to taste

1. In a pot melt 4 tablespoons (60 mL) of the shortening over medium heat. Add the okra, tomato, and tomato paste. Cook, stirring occasionally, for 15 minutes.
2. In a separate pot, melt the remaining 3 tablespoons (45 mL) shortening over medium heat. Add the flour and cook, stirring well, until a roux forms. Add the onions, celery, garlic, and bell peppers, and remove the pot from the heat for 5 minutes. Add this mixture to the tomato mixture, stir well, and add the remaining ingredients.
3. Cook, uncovered, over medium heat for 20 minutes, stirring occasionally and adding water as needed if the gumbo is too thick.

Wild Mushroom and Vegetable Gumbo with Jalapeños

Yield: 8–10 servings   Heat Scale: Medium

This gumbo is unusual because it is vegetarian, but the flavors of the mushrooms and vegetables are so intense that no one will miss the seafood or sausage. Use your choice of three separate garnishes for this gumbo.

4 tablespoons (60 mL) vegetable shortening
4 tablespoons (60 mL) all-purpose flour
4 cups (.95 L) Super-Rich Vegetable Stock (page 48)
2 tablespoons (30 mL) butter
½ pound (224 g) morels, chopped
½ pound (224 g) chanterelles, chopped
1 medium onion, peeled and chopped
Kernels from 3 ears of corn
3 medium yellow tomatoes, chopped
3 medium red tomatoes, chopped
1 cup (236 mL) freshly shelled peas
1 medium red bell pepper, chopped
1 medium green bell pepper, chopped
2 jalapeños, stems and seeds removed, minced
1 tablespoon (15 mL) minced garlic
Salsa for garnish
Strips of lemon rind for garnish
Carmelized red onions for garnish

1. In a large pot, melt the shortening over medium heat. Whisk in the flour. Add the vegetable stock, whisk well, and cook, uncovered, at a very low simmer.
2. In a separate pot, melt the butter over medium heat. Add the mushrooms and onion and sauté for 3 minutes. Add the corn, tomatoes, peas, bell peppers, jalapeños, and garlic and cook over low heat, uncovered, for 10 minutes, stirring occasionally to prevent sticking. Add the stock and cook, covered, over low heat for 20 minutes, stirring occasionally. If the gumbo is too thick, add water as needed . Garnish with your favorite salsa, strips of lemon rind, or some caramelized red onions.

EIGHT

Molten Meaty Main Dishes

- - - - - - - - - - - - - - - - - -

This chapter is heaven for all chilehead carnivores! It focuses on beef, pork, and lamb dishes with chiles, but occasionally some kind of game hops into the picture. I have organized the recipes regionally from west to east, the same route that chile peppers traveled after their "discovery" by Columbus and his men in the Bahamas.

Rocotos Rellenos (Stuffed Rocoto Chiles)

Yield: 20 stuffed chiles   Heat Scale: Hot

Rocoto chiles grow very large in Peru, almost as large as bell peppers, so they are easy to stuff. The heat factor in this dish can be very high, but the other ingredients will temper it somewhat. Serve these with hot slices of fresh corn on the cob and rounds of sweet potatoes.

20 red rocoto chiles (or substitute the largest jalapeños available)
1 pound (454 g) ground pork
3 cups (708 mL) water
2 tablespoons (30 mL) vegetable oil
2 onions, peeled and chopped
2 cloves garlic, peeled and minced
1 cup (236 mL) peanuts, toasted and ground
1 pound (454 g) cooked green peas
½ teaspoon (2.5 mL) salt
¼ teaspoon (1.25 mL) freshly ground black pepper
2 hardboiled eggs, diced
4 eggs, separated
Vegetable oil for frying

1. Wash the chiles and, leaving the stems intact, cut them half open, and carefully remove the seeds. Place the peppers in a large pot with water to cover, and bring to a low boil. Boil the chiles for 3 minutes. Drain them carefully, keeping them intact, and set them aside.
2. Put the pork in a medium saucepan, add the 3 cups of water, and bring to a boil. Lower the heat to a simmer and cook for 1 hour or until the pork is tender. Drain the pork and reserve the cooking liquid. With a meat grinder on a coarse setting, grind the pork. Set it aside.
3. In a medium skillet, heat the oil over medium heat. Add the onions and garlic and sauté until soft. Add the ground pork, peanuts, peas, salt, pepper, and enough of the reserved pork stock to keep the mixture moist. Mix in the chopped eggs. Remove the pot from the heat and let the mixture cool for a few minutes.
4. Stuff the chiles with this mixture and close them as tightly as possible.
5. Beat the egg whites until they are quite stiff. Beat the yolks well and fold them into the whites.
6. In a separate skillet, heat the oil over high heat. Dip each pepper into the egg mixture and deep fry for 30 to 60 seconds, until the outside is golden brown.

Cara Pulcra
(Pork with Dried Potatoes)

Yield: 5–6 servings   Heat Scale: Medium

This simple, spicy, and exotic Peruvian pork main dish probably dates back to ancient Incan times, with the Incan penchant for drying and freeze-drying food. Papa seca is available in Latin American markets; it is dried, ground potatoes. If you cannot find papa seca, it is easy to prepare your own. Clean 2 pounds (1.1 kg) small potatoes and boil them in their skins until they are done. Peel the potatoes, slice them, put them on a raised screen, and dry them in the sun, turning often (or use a food dehydrator). When they are thoroughly dry, grind them in a spice mill and store them in a jar to use as needed. (Note: This recipe requires advance preparation.)

1 pound (454 g) papa seca
4 tablespoons (60 mL) olive oil
1 cup (236 mL) finely chopped onion
1 clove garlic, peeled and minced
2 pounds (1.1 kg) boneless pork, cut into ½-inch (1 cm) cubes
½ cup (118 mL) ground peanuts
¼ cup (59 mL) grated aji chiles (or substitute yellow wax hot or jalapeño)
¼ teaspoon (1.25 mL) cumin
½ teaspoon (2.5 mL) salt
½ teaspoon (2.5 mL) annatto seeds
¼ teaspoon (1.25 mL) freshly ground black pepper
1–2 cups (250–473 mL) chicken stock

1. Roast the papa seca in a large, dry skillet over medium-high heat, taking care not to burn it. Transfer the roasted papa seca to a large bowl, add water to cover, and refrigerate overnight. Transfer the papa seca to a colander and drain thoroughly, pressing down on the mixture.
2. In a large skillet, heat the oil over medium heat. Add the onion and the garlic and sauté briefly. Add the cubed pork and brown it; then add the remaining ingredients and the drained papa seca and simmer for 45 to 60 minutes, stirring occasionally, adding more stock or water if the mixture seems too thick.

Chicharrones con Camotes
(Pork Ribs and Sweet Potatoes)

Yield: 4 servings   Heat Scale: Medium

This easy, tasty recipe comes from Creole Cookery *by Na Conce, published in Peru in 1951 and now quite rare. This cookbook is the repository of some classic household recipes that were prepared by the lady of the house or her cook. The recipes are simple and use basic ingredients available in the area and at that time. The word "chicharrón" refers both to fried pork skins and fried ribs.*

4 sweet potatoes, scrubbed
2 pounds (1.1 kg) pork ribs, cut into individual ribs
¼ teaspoon (1.25 mL) salt
¼ teaspoon (1.25 mL) freshly ground black pepper
1 cup (236 mL) cold water
1 clove garlic, peeled and mashed
1 large onion, peeled and thinly sliced
1 cup (236 mL) boiling water
2 fresh aji chiles, stems and seeds removed, puréed in a blender (or substitute yellow wax hot or jalapeño)
Juice of 1 lemon
1 teaspoon (5 mL) vinegar
Melted butter

1. Preheat the oven to 350°F (180°C).
2. Place the sweet potatoes in the oven and bake until they are easily pierced with a fork, about 1 hour.
3. Wash the ribs and pat them dry. Sprinkle them with the salt and pepper.
4. Pour the cold water into a large, heavy skillet. Add the ribs and the garlic and bring the mixture to a low boil. Boil the ribs until the water has evaporated and the ribs start to fry in their own fat. Stir the ribs to make sure they don't burn, and keep frying until they start to crisp up.
5. Place the onion slices in a colander and pour the hot water over them. Let stand for 5 minutes, then transfer the onion slices to a ceramic bowl. Add the puréed chile peppers, lemon juice, and vinegar. Allow the mixture to marinate for 15 minutes.
6. Push the ribs to one side of the skillet, add the onions, and bring the mixture to a quick boil. Serve immediately, accompanied by slices of hot baked sweet potatoes drizzled with melted butter.

Chancho Picante
(Spicy Pork with an Asian Touch)

Yield: 4 servings   Heat Scale: Medium

The Spanish conquistadors brought pigs to Peru, and the Indians soon incorporated pork into their cuisine. This pork dish in a hot sauce spiced with green onion, peanuts, ginger, and soy sauce also shows the influence Asian immigrants have had on local foods. Serve this dish with white rice or one of the spicier rice dishes from South America.

1½ pounds (680 g) pork shoulder
2 tablespoons (30 mL) soy sauce, divided
1½ tablespoons (22.5 mL) cornstarch, dissolved in ¼ cup (59 mL) cold water
2 teaspoons (10 mL) sugar, divided
4 dried aji chiles (or substitute New Mexican or pasilla), soaked in water until soft
1 tablespoon (15 mL) white vinegar
2 tablespoons (30 mL) grated fresh ginger
3 tablespoons (45 mL) water
¼ cup (59 mL) peanut oil
½ cup (118 mL) peanuts, chopped

1. Cut the pork into thin strips and place them in a large bowl. Add 1 tablespoon (15 mL) of the soy sauce, ⅔ of the cornstarch mixture, and 1 teaspoon (5 mL) of the sugar and stir well to coat the meat. Set aside for 15 minutes.
2. Remove the stems and seeds from the chiles and purée them in a blender with 2 tablespoons (30 mL) of their soaking water. In a small bowl, combine the remaining soy sauce, sugar, and cornstarch. Add the vinegar, ginger, and water.
3. In a bowl, combine the pork strips with the puréed chiles. Heat a wok, add the peanut oil, and stir-fry the pork until done, about 5 minutes. Remove the pork from the wok. Put the soy-sugar-ginger mixture and the peanuts in the wok and cook, stirring well, until hot. Add water if the mixture thickens too much. Mix in the meat and serve immediately.

Cerdo con Limón
(Pork with Lime)

Yield: 4–5 servings   Heat Scale: Medium

I thank Winifred Galarza for this Ecuadorean recipe. I know that there are many variations on this dish because pork is frequently cooked with citrus juices, and, of course, each cook has a favorite recipe. Serve slices of cooked sweet potatoes with this dish, along with a South American rice or potato side dish.

2 pounds (1.1 kg) boneless lean pork, cut into 1-inch (2.5 cm) cubes
2–4 tablespoons (30–60 mL) all-purpose flour
¼ cup (59 mL) vegetable oil
1 tablespoon (15 mL) grated fresh ginger
2 onions, peeled and sliced
½ cup (118 mL) peeled and chopped tomatoes
2 tablespoons (30 mL) chopped parsley
½ cup (118 mL) fresh lime juice
2 cups (473 mL) Classic Chicken Stock (page 46)
2 teaspoons (10 mL) habanero-based hot sauce
2 tablespoons (30 mL) mayonnaise (optional)
Lemon wedges for garnish
Chopped parsley for garnish

1. In a large bowl, sprinkle the cubes of meat with the flour and toss well. Heat the oil in a large, heavy casserole over medium heat. Add the pork and the ginger. Cook for 3 minutes, turning the cubes to brown them slightly.
2. Add the onions, tomatoes, and parsley and cook for a few minutes until the onions start to soften. Add the lime juice, stock, and hot sauce. Bring the mixture to a boil, then reduce the heat and simmer, uncovered, for about 1 hour, until the pork is tender and the stock is reduced to a gravy, stirring several times to prevent burning. Just before serving, stir in the mayonnaise, if using. Garnish with the lemon wedges and parsley.

Porco Moda Amazonas
(Amazon-Style Pork)

Yield: 6–7 servings   Heat Scale: Hot

The isolated area of the Amazon, Amazonas, yields this updated recipe including pork coconut milk, and the traditional heavy use of herbs and chiles for seasoning. This rich dish could be served with a salad of hearts of palm, Bibb lettuce, and fresh tomatoes. (Note: This recipe requires advance preparation.)

For the Marinade:
1 cup (236 mL) dry white wine
½ cup (118 mL) fresh lemon juice
2 cloves garlic, peeled and minced
1 teaspoon (5 mL) sugar
½ teaspoon (2.5 mL) salt
¼ teaspoon (1.25 mL) freshly ground black pepper
⅓ cup (79 mL) olive oil
1 teaspoon (5 mL) chopped fresh rosemary
1 bay leaf
1 teaspoon (5 mL) crushed, dried malagueta chile (or substitute piquin or cayenne)
2½ pounds (1.13 kg) boneless, lean pork, cut into ½-inch (1 cm) cubes

1. In a large ceramic bowl or pan, combine all the ingredients except the pork. Add the cubed pork and toss the cubes to coat them with the marinade. Cover and refrigerate the pork for 4 to 6 hours to marinate.
2. Drain the pork in a colander and reserve the marinade.

For the Breading:
¾ cup (177 mL) ground Brazil nuts
2 cups (473 mL) dry breadcrumbs
2 teaspoons (10 mL) lemon zest

1. Mix all the ingredients together. Toss the pork cubes in the mixture to coat.

For the Pork:
1 cup (236 mL) vegetable oil
2 tablespoons (30 mL) olive oil
1 onion, peeled and sliced
3 tablespoons (45 mL) heavy cream
3 tablespoons (45 mL) coconut milk
½ teaspoon (2.5 mL) dried, crushed tarragon
¾ teaspoon (3.75 mL) dill weed
½ teaspoon (2.5 mL) crushed, dried malagueta chile (or substitute piquin or cayenne)

1. In a large, heavy skillet, heat the vegetable oil over medium-high heat. Add the breaded pork cubes, a few at a time, tossing them in the pan to brown and taking care not to burn them. As the pork cubes brown, transfer them to paper towels to drain, then arrange them on a platter and keep them warm.

2. In a medium skillet, heat the olive oil over medium heat. Add the onion and sauté until it is softened. Pour in the reserved marinade and bring the mixture to a boil. Lower the heat to a simmer, and simmer the mixture for 12 minutes. Add the remaining ingredients and heat through, but do not boil.

3. Pour the warmed sauce over the heated pork cubes and serve immediately.

Chorizo Criollo
(Chorizo Sausage from Argentina)

Yield: 12–14 patties   Heat Scale: Medium

These delicious sausages have counterparts all over Latin America. They can vary widely—some recipes call for saltpeter, some use all pork, some include spices such as cloves and cinnamon, and still others prefer vinegar or wine. I have included this rather traditional recipe from Argentina that uses the famed aji p-p, the "bad word" chile. For a substitute, use pure ground hot red chile, such as New Mexican chimayó. In Argentina, these sausages are almost always included at an asado—a barbecue. The uncooked patties freeze well for future use; after forming the patties, layer them between layers of plastic wrap, then wrap securely for the freezer. That way, you can pull off one or several patties to thaw and fry. (Note: This recipe requires advance preparation.)

2 pounds (1.1 kg) boneless pork
1 pound (454 g) round steak
½ pound (224 g) fresh bacon (available at natural supermarkets)
½ teaspoon (2.5 mL) salt
1 clove garlic, peeled
1½ teaspoons (7.5 mL) oregano
½ teaspoon (2.5 mL) cumin
6 peppercorns, crushed
2 teaspoons (10 mL) ground aji p-p chile (or substitute another ground hot red chile, such as cayenne or New Mexican chimayó)
¾ cup (177 mL) dry white wine

1. In a meat grinder or food processor, coarsely grind together the pork, round steak, bacon, salt, and garlic. If you use a food processor, take care not to grind the meat too finely; you want the mixture to have some texture.

2. Transfer the ground meats to a large ceramic bowl. Add the remaining ingredients and mix thoroughly. Cover and refrigerate for 24 hours.

3. Form the meat into 12 to 14 patties and fry them in a skillet over a medium heat for 3 to 4 minutes per side, or until no pink remains on the inside. Drain the patties on paper towels and serve hot.

Matambre
(Hunger-Killer Steak)

Yield: 6–8 servings   Heat Scale: Medium

From the Spanish words "matar," to kill, and "hambre," hunger, comes the name for this filling dish. There are many variations on it in Chile and Argentina. It is said to have originated as an easy-to-carry meal on long stagecoach rides across the pampas. This recipe comes from Nancy Gerlach. Serve it with any potato dish from South America. (Note: This recipe requires advance preparation.)

½ cup (118 mL) beer
½ cup (118 mL) vinegar
¼ cup (59 mL) vegetable oil
2 cloves garlic, peeled and minced
1 bay leaf
1 (2-pound [1.1 kg]) flank steak
6 fresh aji chiles, stems and seeds removed, chopped (or substitute yellow wax hot or jalapeño)
1 cup (236 mL) chopped fresh spinach
2 carrots, peeled and julienned
1 medium onion, peeled, thinly sliced, and separated into rings
4 slices bacon
1 tablespoon (15 mL) dried oregano
¼ cup (59 mL) chopped fresh parsley
1 quart (.95 L) beef broth

1. Combine the beer, vinegar, oil, garlic, and bay leaf. Marinate the steak in this mixture for 4 hours.
2. Remove the steak from the marinade, reserving the marinade. Flatten the steak with a rolling pin. Spread the chiles over the meat, followed by the spinach, carrots, onions, bacon, oregano, and parsley. Roll up the steak, turning the edges in so the stuffing does not fall out. Tie the roll with string to hold it together.
3. Place the rolled steak in a large pan with the marinade and enough beef broth to cover the meat. Simmer for 2½ hours or until the meat is very tender. Slice into rounds and serve.

Biftec al Horno
(Uruguayan Baked Beef)

Yield: 4–6 servings   Heat Scale: Medium

Some Latin cooks say that the beef of Uruguay can give some competition to the beef of neighboring Argentina, which only makes sense, since the two countries share the plains of the pampas. This simple, easy dish is baked slowly and spiced up with aji chiles. It is a staple menu item in restaurants all over the country, with subtle changes from place to place.

3 tablespoons (45 mL) vegetable oil, divided
4 onions, peeled and sliced, divided
2 cloves garlic, peeled and minced
1 dried aji chile, stem and seeds removed, crushed (or substitute New Mexican)
1 teaspoon (5 mL) salt
¼ teaspoon (1.25 mL) freshly ground black pepper
½ teaspoon (2.5 mL) ground cayenne
3 tablespoons (45 mL) all-purpose flour, divided
2½ pounds (1.13 kg) round steak
1 cup (236 mL) beef broth, divided
2 tomatoes, sliced ¼-inch (.5 cm) thick

1. Preheat the oven to 350°F (180°C).
2. In a Dutch oven, heat 1 tablespoon (15 mL) of the oil over medium heat. Add 1 of the sliced onions, the garlic, and the crushed chile and sauté until the onion is softened. Using a slotted spoon, transfer the sautéed mixture to a small bowl and set aside.
3. Mix together the salt, pepper, cayenne, and 2 tablespoons (30 mL) of the flour and press the mixture into both sides of the round steak. Heat the remaining 2 tablespoons (30 mL) oil in the Dutch oven and brown the steak on both sides. Cover the steak with the remaining sliced onions and ¼ cup (59 mL) of the broth and cover tightly. Bake for 1 hour or until the meat is tender.
4. Layer the tomatoes on top of the onions and bake for 15 to 20 minutes more. Transfer the meat to a heated platter, allow it to sit for a few minutes, and then slice it thinly and keep it warm.
5. Bring the juices in the casserole to a slow boil on top of the stove. In a jar, combine the remaining 1 tablespoon (15 mL) flour and ¾ cup (177 mL) broth and shake thoroughly. Slowly strain this mixture into the simmering pan juices and whisk until the mixture is smooth. Add the reserved sautéed onion mixture and heat through. Pour this sauce over the sliced meat and serve immediately.

Carne Picadinho
(Minced Meat, Brazilian-Style)

Yield: 4–5 servings   Heat Scale: Medium

This recipe has many permutations and many names. In Portuguese, it is carne picadinho; in Spanish, it is picadillo; and in slang, it is referred to as Hangover Hash because it is reputed to cure hangovers. The variations in the recipes are mind-boggling—the simplest recipe I heard about had only seven ingredients, several had twelve to fourteen, and the most ingredients in a recipe of the same name was twenty-five. I think it depends on the budget and the creativity of the person making the dish. Try this version for breakfast with a fried egg on top.

3 tablespoons (45 mL) vegetable oil, plus more if needed
1 cup (236 mL) finely chopped onion
1 bell pepper, stem and seeds removed, minced
2 cloves garlic, peeled and minced
1 pound (454 g) sirloin, cut into ¼-inch (.5 cm) cubes
¼ pound (113 g) lean pork loin, cut into ¼-inch (.5 cm) cubes
¼ pound (113 g) spicy smoked sausage, such as chorizo, cut into ¼-inch (.5 cm) cubes
¼ teaspoon (1.25 mL) salt
1 habanero chile, stem and seeds removed, minced, or substitute 3 jalapeños
2 tomatoes, peeled, seeded, and chopped
½ teaspoon (2.5 mL) cumin
½ teaspoon (2.5 mL) oregano
1 tablespoon (15 mL) red wine vinegar
½ teaspoon (2.5 mL) sugar
1 cup (236 mL) beef stock

1. In a heavy skillet, heat the oil over medium heat. Add the onion, bell pepper, and garlic and sauté until the onion is softened. Push this mixture to one side of the skillet and sauté the sirloin, pork loin, sausage, salt, and hot peppers, stirring until the meat is lightly browned, then mix the meat and the onion mixture together.
2. Add the remaining ingredients and bring the mixture to a boil. Reduce the heat to a simmer, half cover the skillet, and cook for 30 to 45 minutes to blend the flavors and cook off most of the liquid. The resulting mixture will be what is called a "dry" picadinho.

Variations

Heat 1 cup (236 mL) of additional beef stock to a slow boil. Make a roux of 1 tablespoon (15 mL) butter and 1 tablespoon (15 mL) all-purpose flour, add it to the hot beef stock, and whisk until the mixture is smooth. Add this gravy to the cooking meat and simmer for an additional 15 to 20 minutes, with the skillet covered. Or, add cooked, diced potatoes to either the dry or gravy version. For another "dry" version, top it with chopped, hard-boiled eggs and halved green olives or ripe olives. Or, serve the dry version topped with cooked, diced potatoes and a fried egg.

Bifes
(Bahian Beef Steaks)

Yield: 4 servings   Heat Scale: Medium

A food of the Bahian gods (Orixa), the bifes are actually an English contribution to the great range of Bahian cooking. The English helped the Portuguese defend Salvador, the capital of Bahia, from pirates. This dish is the food of Exu, who is considered to be the middle man between the gods and the people; the Christian counterpart is the devil. This recipe for bifes includes farofa, which is made from manioc flour and is used extensively in Brazil.

4 thin beef steaks
2 cloves garlic, peeled and chopped
1 teaspoon (5 mL) salt
Freshly ground black pepper, to taste
2 –3 tablespoons (30–45 mL) palm oil (or substitute vegetable oil with
1 tablespoon [15 mL] paprika added)
1 small onion, peeled, sliced, and separated into rings
1 habanero chile, stem and seeds removed, minced (or substitute 2 jalapeños)
1 tablespoon (15 mL) lemon juice (fresh preferred)
Farofa de Malagueta (page 3), to taste

1. Rub the steaks with the garlic and season them with the salt and pepper.
2. In a skillet, heat the oil over medium-high heat. Add the steaks and pan-fry until they are almost done. Add the onions and chile and sauté until the onions are softened.
3. To serve, place the steaks on a plate, sprinkle them with the lemon juice, and top them with the onion mixture. Sprinkle the farofa over the top and serve with rice.

Pastel de Choclo
(Chilean Meat Pie)

Yield: 6 servings   Heat Scale: Mild

This delicious, spicy, one-dish meal only needs a large green salad, sliced tomatoes, a South America potato dish, and a Chilean wine to create a feast. I have used lean, ground beef in this recipe, but coarsely ground chicken, rabbit, or pork could also be used.

1½ pounds (680 g) coarsely ground lean beef
1–2 tablespoons (15–30 mL), plus 1 tablespoon (15 mL) vegetable oil, divided
1 cup (236 mL) chopped onion
1 large dried aji chile, crushed (or substitute New Mexican)
½ teaspoon (2.5 mL) ground cumin
1 teaspoon (5 mL) paprika
½ teaspoon (2.5 mL) salt
¼ teaspoon (1.25 mL) freshly ground black pepper
½ teaspoon (2.5 mL) dried oregano
10 black olives, halved
2 cups (473 mL) fresh corn
1 tablespoon (15 mL) milk
1½ teaspoons (7.5 mL) sugar, divided

1. Preheat the oven to 350°F (180°C).
2. In a heavy skillet over medium-high heat, brown the meat. Drain the meat and transfer it to a bowl. Add 1–2 tablespoons (15–30 mL) of the oil to the skillet. Add the onion and sauté it until soft. Add the chile, cumin, paprika, salt, pepper, and oregano. Add the sautéed mixture to the meat and mix. Pack the meat mixture into a shallow 3 to 4 quart (3 to 4 L) ovenproof casserole, and arrange the olives over the top.
3. Put the corn in a blender with the milk and ½ teaspoon (2.5 mL) of the sugar and purée. In a skillet, heat the remaining oil over medium heat. Add the puréed corn and simmer, stirring, until the purée thickens. Pour this mixture over the meat mixture and sprinkle with the remaining 1 teaspoon (5 mL) sugar.
4. Bake for 45 to 60 minutes, or until the top is golden.

Lomo a la Huancaina
(Steaks with Cheese and Chile Sauce)

Yield: 6 servings   Heat Scale: Medium

In Peru, "Huancaina" style usually refers to potatoes sauced with cheese, chile, and onions. But this recipe has an interesting twist—the sauce is used over broiled beef-steaks. To complete this dinner, I suggest baked potatoes and a tomato and cucumber salad drizzled with olive oil and fresh lime juice.

1 (3-ounce [84 g]) package cream cheese
3 hard-boiled egg yolks
½ teaspoon (2.5 mL) salt
¼ teaspoon (1.25 mL) freshly ground black pepper
2 teaspoons (10 mL) dried, crushed aji chile (or substitute hot New Mexican)
¼ cup (59 mL) olive oil
¾ cup (177 mL) heavy cream
1 tablespoon (15 mL) fresh lemon juice
¼ cup (59 mL) finely chopped onion
6 steaks
18 ripe olives, halved
3 hard-boiled eggs, quartered
6 tablespoons (90 mL) minced Italian parsley

1. Preheat the broiler.
2. Beat the cream cheese until it is smooth. Press the egg yolks through a sieve into the cream cheese. Add the salt, pepper, and dried chile and beat them into the cheese.
3. Add the olive oil, a few drops at a time, beating thoroughly. Mix in the cream, lemon juice, and onion.
4. Pour this mixture into a small saucepan and heat slowly, stirring constantly. Do not allow the mixture to boil. Keep the cheese mixture warm while the steaks are broiling.
5. Broil the steaks and transfer them to a heated platter. Top each steak with some of the warm cheese mixture and garnish with the olives, hard-boiled eggs, and parsley.

La Junta Jalapeño Steaks

Yield: 4 servings   Heat Scale: Medium

This recipe comes from Nancy Gerlach, who, with her husband, Jeff, accompanied Mary Jane and me to Costa Rica. She wrote, "On the way back to San Jose from the habanero fields in Los Chiles, we stopped at the restaurant La Junta to sample some of the local beef. After enjoying an appetizer of black bean purée, flour tortillas, and cilantro salsa, we were served thick, tender steaks topped with a mild jalapeño sauce."

1 tablespoon (15 mL) olive oil
4 tablespoons (60 mL) butter, divided
4 boneless steaks, cut 1-inch (2.5 cm) thick
¼ cup (59 mL) minced onions
3 jalapeño chiles, stems and seeds removed, minced
½ cup (118 mL) red wine
1 tablespoon (15 mL) freshly ground black pepper
1½ cups (354 mL) Basic Beef Stock (page 45)
⅓ cup (79 mL) heavy cream
3 jalapeño chiles, stems and seeds removed, cut in thin strips
2 tablespoons (30 mL) chopped fresh cilantro

1. In a heavy skillet, heat the olive oil and 2 tablespoons (30 mL) of the butter over medium-high heat. Brown the steaks on both sides. Reduce the heat and cook gently until they are medium rare or cooked to the desired doneness. Remove the steak from the pan and keep warm.
2. Pour off the fat. Add the remaining butter to the juices in the skillet. Add the onion and minced jalapeños and simmer, stirring constantly, until softened.
3. Add the red wine, bring to a boil, and deglaze the pan, being sure to scrape up any bits that may have stuck to the bottom or sides of the pan. Add the black pepper, stock, and cream and bring to a boil. Reduce the heat and simmer until the sauce is smooth and thick.
4. Place the steaks on a plate, pour the sauce over the top, garnish with the jalapeño slices and cilantro, and serve.

Carne en Jocon
(Beef in Tomato and Chile Sauce)

Yield: 6–7 servings   Heat Scale: Medium

This spicy beef dish is found throughout Guatemala; it is a traditional favorite that is usually served with hot cooked rice. Mexican green tomatoes, or tomatillos, are available at Latin American markets and even in some chain grocery stores. The tomatillos add an interesting taste dimension with a hint of lemon and herbs.

3–4 tablespoons (45–60 mL) vegetable oil
1 cup (236 mL) chopped onion
2 cloves garlic, peeled and minced
1 bell pepper, stem and seeds removed, chopped
2 fresh serrano chiles, stems and seeds removed, chopped (or substitute jalapeños)
3 pounds (1.36 kg) boneless beef, cut into 1-inch (2.5 cm) cubes
½ teaspoon (2.5 mL) salt
¼ teaspoon (1.25 mL) freshly ground black pepper
10 ounces (280 g) fresh tomatillos, husks removed, diced (or substitute 1 [10-ounce (280 g)] can tomatillos)
3 tomatoes, peeled and chopped
1 bay leaf
¼ teaspoon (1.25 mL) ground cloves
1 teaspoon (5 mL) dried oregano
¾ cup (177 mL) beef stock
2 tortillas

1. In a heavy casserole, heat the oil over medium heat. Add the onion, garlic, bell peppers, and chiles and sauté until soft. Push the mixture to one side of the casserole. Add the beef and brown it lightly. Mix the meat with the onion sauté. Add the salt, pepper, tomatillos, tomatoes, bay leaf, cloves, oregano, and stock.
2. Bring the mixture to a boil. Reduce the heat and gently simmer, covered, for 2 hours.
3. Soak the tortillas in cold water for a few minutes. Squeeze out the water and finely crumble the tortillas into the beef. Stir and simmer for a few minutes until the meat mixture thickens.

Panamanian Picante Tomato Beef

Yield: 2–3 servings   Heat Scale: Medium

I thank Alois Dogue for this recipe. Alois is a native Panamanian who certainly knows his way around a kitchen, and he is also the manufacturer of an habanero-based, Panamanian-style hot sauce. Alois recommends serving this dish with hot rice and some crusty French or Italian bread.

1 pound (454 g) sirloin steak
1 tablespoon (15 mL) soy sauce
½ teaspoon (2.5 mL) seasoning salt
1 teaspoon (5 mL) habanero hot sauce
2 tablespoons (30 mL) vegetable oil
2 tomatoes, sliced
1 large onion, peeled and sliced
¼ teaspoon (1.25 mL) oregano

1. Pound the sirloin and rinse it under running water. Pat the sirloin dry and place it in a large ceramic bowl.
2. Pour the soy sauce, seasoning salt, and hot sauce over the steak and marinate for 20 minutes.
3. In a medium skillet, heat the oil over medium-high heat and brown the steak on both sides. Add the tomatoes, onions, and oregano and simmer for 15 minutes.

Conejo en Mole Picante
(Rabbit in Venezuelan Spicy Sauce)

Yield: 6–8 servings   Heat Scale: Medium

Rabbit is readily available from many U.S. markets. It is a mild, tasty white meat—and no, it doesn't taste exactly like chicken! Rabbit is extremely versatile: It can be fried, deep-fried, sautéed, and sauced. This spicy sauce can also be used with pork, veal, and poultry.

4 pounds (1.82 kg) rabbit, washed, dried, and cut into 6–8 pieces
½ teaspoon (2.5 mL) salt
¼ teaspoon (1.25 mL) freshly ground black pepper
2 teaspoons (10 mL) freshly grated ginger root
3 tablespoons (45 mL) vegetable oil
1 cup (236 mL) chopped onions
2 cloves garlic, peeled and minced
½ teaspoon (2.5 mL) ground habanero or 1 teaspoon (5 mL) ground cayenne
1 small green apple, peeled, cored, and grated
½ teaspoon (2.5 mL) dried tarragon
2 bay leaves
1 teaspoon (5 mL) dried thyme
2 tablespoons (30 mL) chopped Italian parsley
½ cup (118 mL) milk
¾ cup (177 mL) chicken stock

1. Season the rabbit with the salt, pepper, and ginger.

2. In a large, heavy skillet, heat the oil over medium-high heat. Add the rabbit pieces and sauté them until they are browned, turning frequently, about 10 minutes. Transfer the rabbit to a heated platter.

3. Add the onion to the skillet and sauté it until it browns. Add the garlic and sauté for 30 seconds. Add the ground chile, grated apple, tarragon, bay leaves, thyme, and parsley and stir to mix.

4. Return the browned rabbit to the skillet. Add the milk and stock, cover, and simmer for 45 to 60 minutes or until tender. Remove the bay leaves before serving.

Seco de Chivo
(Ecuadorian Braised Goat)

Yield: 8 servings   Heat Scale: Mild

Winifred Galarza gave me this recipe for a dish she said is easy to make and is quite tender and delicious. It is served with cooked rice and sometimes a side dish of a hot chile sauce or salsa. However, as Winifred reminded me, Ecuadorians, as a rule, don't eat their food as hot as their Peruvian neighbors and will often serve the hot stuff on the side, rather than cooking it into the food. Chicha is a pale yellow, milky beverage available in Latin markets.

2 tablespoons (30 mL) olive oil
4 pounds (1.82 kg) goat or lamb, cut into ¾-inch (2 cm) cubes
1 cup (236 mL) chicha (or substitute raspberry juice)
4 tomatoes, peeled and diced
1 large onion, peeled and diced
1 clove garlic, peeled and minced
½ teaspoon (2.5 mL) salt
1 fresh aji chile, stems and seeds removed, chopped (or substitute yellow wax hot or jalapeño)

1. In a heavy casserole, heat the oil over medium-high heat. Add the meat and fry it until brown. Add the remaining ingredients and bring the pot to a boil. Cover the pot and reduce the heat to a simmer. Cook for 2 to 3 hours, until the meat is tender and the water is consumed. Serve over hot rice.

Chorizo con Chiltepines
(Chiltepin Chorizo)

Yield: 4 servings   Heat Scale: Hot to Extremely Hot

There are as many versions of chorizo in Mexico and the Southwest as there are of enchiladas. Essentially, it is a hot and spicy sausage that is served with eggs for breakfast, as a filling for tostadas or tacos, or mixed with refried beans. This Sonoran version is spicier than most and is served crumbled rather than formed into patties. Use fewer chiltepins to reduce the heat level.

1 pound (454 g) ground lean pork
15–20 chiltepins, crushed
1 cup (236 mL) ground red New Mexican chile
¼ teaspoon (1.25 mL) salt
¼ teaspoon (1.25 mL) freshly ground black pepper
½ teaspoon (2.5 mL) dried Mexican oregano
3 tablespoons (45 mL) distilled white vinegar
4 cloves garlic, peeled and minced
1 teaspoon (5 mL) ground cloves

1. Combine all the ingredients, mix well, and let it sit at room temperature for 1 or 2 hours or in the refrigerator overnight. (It keeps well in the refrigerator for up to a week. Or, freeze the chorizo in small portions and use as needed.)
2. Fry the chorizo until it is well-browned.

Longaniza con Chiles Guajillos
(Pork Sausage with Guajillo Chiles)

Yield: 50 small sausages   Heat Scale: Medium

The art of sausage making is alive and well in Jalisco, where one would be lucky to be offered a sampling of a señora's homemade sausage. While making sausage is not too difficult, please be careful to keep it refrigerated and to clean all working areas well, to avoid cross-contamination. (Note: This recipe requires advance preparation.)

8 guajillo chiles, toasted, stems and seeds removed, crushed (or substitute New Mexican)
1 cup (236 mL) distilled white vinegar
6 cloves garlic, peeled and minced
5 whole cloves, crushed
20 black peppercorns, crushed
½ teaspoon (2.5 mL) ground cumin
½ teaspoon (2.5 mL) ground cinnamon
½ teaspoon (2.5 mL) ground ginger
1 teaspoon (5 mL) dried Mexican oregano
2 tablespoons (30 mL) lemon juice
2 tablespoons (30 mL) orange juice
Salt, to taste
2½ pounds (1.13 kg) ground or minced pork
Sausage casings for stuffing

1. In a large mixing bowl, place the chiles in the vinegar along with the garlic, cloves, peppercorns, cumin, cinnamon, ginger, oregano, lemon juice, orange juice, and salt. Mix well. Add the meat and stir well to combine. Cover and refrigerate the mixture for 24 hours.
2. Clean the sausage casings well, then use a funnel to stuff them with the meat mixture. Refrigerate just the amount you plan to use in the next day or two, then freeze the rest.

Chilorio Sorpresa
(Pork Surprise)

Yield: 6–8 servings   Heat Scale: Medium

You will be surprised how tender the pork comes out in this excellent recipe from Playa del Carmen. The Maya used wild boar for this dish until the Spanish introduced domesticated pigs.

2 pounds (1.1 kg) pork, cubed
1 tablespoon (15 mL) salt
1 cup (236 mL) orange juice
6 ancho chiles, stems and seeds removed
1 pasilla chile, stem and seeds removed
5 cloves garlic, peeled
1 small onion, peeled and chopped
1 teaspoon (5 mL) ground oregano
¼ teaspoon (1.25 mL) ground cumin
1 teaspoon (5 mL) freshly ground black pepper
¼ cup (59 mL) distilled white vinegar
½ cup (118 mL) beef broth
2 tablespoons (30 mL) pork lard (or substitute vegetable shortening)
1 small onion, peeled and sliced
2 yellow squash, sliced and lightly boiled

1. Place the meat in a skillet with a little water, the salt, and the orange juice. Cook over medium heat, covered, until the meat is tender, about 45 minutes. Shred the meat and set it aside.
2. Combine the chiles, garlic, onion, oregano, cumin, pepper, vinegar, and beef broth in a blender. Blend until smooth and set aside.
3. In a separate skillet, heat the lard over medium-high heat. Fry the meat and chile mixture together until blended. Serve with the onion and squash.

Cochinita Pibil
(Pork Cooked in the Pibil Method)

Yield: 4–6 servings   Heat Scale: Mild

This pre-Columbian dish is probably the best known food of the Maya, according to Jeff and Nancy Gerlach, who collected this recipe on one of their many trips to Yucatán. It is one of the most popular entrées of the area and is on virtually every menu. The dish is traditionally served with warmed corn tortillas, black beans, cebollas encuridas (marinated onions), and a habanero salsa. (Note: This recipe requires advance preparation.)

10 whole black peppercorns
¼ teaspoon (1.25 mL) cumin seeds
5 cloves garlic, peeled
3 tablespoons (45 mL) commercial achiote paste
1 teaspoon (5 mL) dried Mexican oregano
2 bay leaves
⅓ cup (79 mL) bitter orange juice (or substitute ⅓ cup [79 mL] lime juice, fresh preferred)
2 pounds (1.1 kg) lean pork, cut in 1½- or 2-inch (4 or 5 cm) cubes
Banana leaves or aluminum foil
3 xcatic chiles, stems and seeds removed, cut in strips (or substitute banana or yellow wax hot)
1 large purple onion, peeled and sliced

1. Place the peppercorns and cumin seeds in a spice mill or coffee grinder and process to a fine powder. Add the garlic and continue to grind.
2. Combine the spice mixture, achiote paste, oregano, bay leaves, and orange juice. Pour this marinade over the pork and marinate for 3 hours at room temperature or overnight in the refrigerator.
3. Preheat the oven to 325°F (165°C).
4. If using banana leaves, cut them to fit a roasting pan. Soften the leaves by passing them over a gas flame or holding them over an electric burner for several seconds until they begin to turn light green. Remove the center ribs from the leaves and use them for tying. Lay a couple of strings (long enough to tie around the pork) along the bottom of the pan. Line the pan with the banana leaves or foil.
5. Place the pork, including its marinade, on the leaves or foil. Top with the chiles and onions. Fold the banana leaves over and tie with the strings, or fold the foil over and press to seal. Cover the pan and bake for 1½ hours.

Soufflé de Chilorio
(Pork Soufflé)

Yield: 4–6 servings   Heat Scale: Medium

This dish is served for lunch or dinner in Sinaloa, but I see no reason it wouldn't make a great breakfast when served with fruits such as mangos, bananas, and pineapples on the side.

3 tablespoons (45 mL) butter
3 tablespoons (45 mL) all-purpose flour
1 cup (236 mL) milk
1 cup (236 mL) chilorio (stewed and shredded pork, as prepared in Chilorio Sorpresa, page 349)
½ cup (118 mL) grated gruyere cheese
¼ cup (59 mL) grated Parmesan cheese
4 chipotle chiles in adobo sauce, seeded and minced
Salt and pepper, to taste
4 eggs, separated
1 egg white

1. Preheat the oven to 300°F (150°C). Grease a soufflé pan.
2. Melt the butter in a saucepan over low heat and mix in the flour. Once the flour is dissolved, remove the pan from the burner. Add the milk little by little until the mixture thickens. Return the pan to low heat and add the chilorio, cheese, chiles, salt, and pepper.
3. Beat the egg yolks until they become foamy and pale yellow, then add them to the mixture in the saucepan.
3. In a separate bowl, beat the egg whites until they form stiff peaks, then add them to the mixture.
4. Transfer the mixture to the prepared soufflé pan and bake for about 20 minutes, or until the soufflé has risen and is firm and golden brown. Serve immediately.

Mango de Puerco
(Pork with Mango)

Yield: 6–8 servings   Heat Scale: Medium

This recipe was collected in Colima, where artists from around the world go to paint the surrounding mountains and the nearby ocean. Colima is the home of Mexico's second highest active volcano. Serve this dish with one of the rice dishes in Chapter 13.

8 guajillo chiles, toasted, stems and seeds removed (or substitute New Mexican)
1 pinch coriander seeds, roasted
2 cloves garlic, peeled
1 tablespoon (15 mL) chopped cilantro
1 pinch ground cumin
2 whole cloves, ground
1 cinnamon stick
½ teaspoon (2.5 mL) grated fresh ginger
¼ cup (59 mL) vinegar
Salt, to taste
Freshly ground black pepper, to taste
4 pounds (1.82 kg) pork meat, cut into 1½-inch (2 cm) cubes
4 ripe mangos, peeled, pitted, and cubed
1 onion, sliced
6 radishes, sliced
Pineapple slices for garnish
Shredded lettuce for garnish

1. Preheat the oven to 275°F (140°C).
2. In a blender, combine the chiles, coriander, garlic, cilantro, cumin, cloves, cinnamon, ginger, and vinegar. Season with salt and pepper to taste and purée.
3. Place the pork in a baking dish and pour the chile mixture over it. Scatter the mango cubes over the mixture. Bake for about 1 hour or until done. Garnish with the onion, radishes, pineapple, and lettuce.

Bisteces de Cerdo con Chiles Pasillas
(Pork Steaks with Pasilla Chiles)

Yield: 4–8 servings   Heat Scale: Medium

This recipe comes from Zacatecas, which is also known as the "pink city." The sloping town, which is 8,200 feet (2,500 m) above sea level, received this name because of the cumulative results of the pink sandstone used on most of the homes in the area. Parts of the town are so steep that steps cut into the sides of the canyon, instead of streets, are the only way to get around. Serve these steaks with guacamole. (Note: This recipe requires advanced preparation.)

4 pasilla chiles, toasted, stems and seeds removed, soaked in hot water
1 large clove garlic, peeled
1 teaspoon (5 mL) oregano
1 tablespoon (15 mL) distilled white vinegar, or to taste
1 teaspoon (5 mL) salt
8 pork steaks (about 5–6 pounds [2.27–2.72 kg] total)
Oil as needed for frying

1. Place the chiles, garlic, oregano, vinegar, and salt in a blender and blend until smooth.
2. Pound the steaks, cover them with the chile sauce, and let them sit for about 2 hours.
3. In a skillet, heat a little oil over medium-high heat and fry the steaks.

Machaca Estilo Norteño
(Northern-Style Shredded Beef)

Yield: 6–8 servings   Heat Scale: Medium

The word "machaca" derives from the verb machacar, to pound or crush, and that description of this meat dish is apt. The shredded meat is often used as a filling for burritos or chimichangas and is sometimes dried. Serve the meat wrapped in a flour tortilla with shredded lettuce, chopped tomatoes, grated cheese, and sour cream, which will reduce the heat scale.

1 (3-pound [1.36 kg]) arm roast
5 chiltepins, crushed
1½ cups (354 mL) chopped roasted green New Mexican chile
1 cup (236 mL) chopped, peeled tomatoes
½ cup (118 mL) chopped onions
2 cloves garlic, peeled and minced

1. Place the roast in a large pan and add water to cover. Bring to a boil. Reduce the heat, cover, and simmer until the meat starts to fall apart, about 3 or 4 hours. Check it periodically to make sure it doesn't burn, adding more water if necessary.

2. Remove the roast from the pan and remove the fat from the roast. Remove the broth from the pan, chill it, and remove the fat. Shred the roast with a fork.

3. Return the shredded meat and the defatted broth to the pan, add the remaining ingredients, and simmer until the meat has absorbed all the broth.

Chichillo Oaxaqueño (Oaxacan Chicillo)

Yield: 4–6 servings   Heat Scale: Medium

Susana Trilling, of the Seasons of My Heart cooking school in Oaxaca, notes, "Here is the legendary seventh mole from Oaxaca, my friend Celia's famous mole chichilo."

1½ pounds (680 g) beef bones with meat; meat cut off the bones in 1-inch (2.5 cm) cubes
2 quarts (1.9 L) water
1 onion, peeled and chopped
9 cloves garlic, peeled, divided
1 bay leaf
1 chile de arbol (or substitute 1 large piquin or santaka chile)
5 whole black peppercorns
2 carrots, chopped
2 stalks celery, chopped
3 whole allspice berries, divided
2 whole cloves, divided
½ pound (224 g) pork butt, cut in 1-inch (2.5 cm) cubes
5 chilhuacle negro chiles, stems and seeds removed, seeds reserved (or substitute anchos)
6 guajillo chiles, stems and seeds removed, seeds reserved (or substitute dried red New Mexican chiles)
1 corn tortilla, torn into strips
Leaves of 1 sprig fresh oregano
Leaves of 1 sprig fresh thyme
1 teaspoon (5 mL) cumin seeds
1 (2-inch [5 cm]) cinnamon stick (Mexican preferred)
4 large tomatoes, quartered
3 fresh tomatillos, husks removed, halved
1 small onion
2 chayotes, thinly sliced (or substitute zucchini)
½ pound (224 g) green beans, chopped
5 small potatoes, peeled and quartered
3 tablespoons (45 mL) lard or vegetable oil
2 to 3 avocado leaves, or substitute bay leaves
Salt, to taste
Sliced onion for garnish
Lime slices for garnish

1. In a large stock pot, cover the beef bones with cold water and bring to a boil. Boil for 20 minutes, skimming off any foam that forms. Lower the heat and add the onion, 8 cloves of the garlic, the bay leaf, the chile de arbol, the peppercorns, the carrots, the celery, 1 of the cloves, and 1 of the allspice berries, and cook for 5 minutes. Add the beef and pork cubes, lower the heat, and simmer, covered, for 1 hour. Strain the stock and cool it in the refrigerator. Skim off any fat that rises to the top.

2. In a large frying pan or comal (a smooth, flat griddle traditionally used in Mexican cooking), toast the chiles over high heat, turning once until darkened but not burned. Place the chiles in a bowl and cover them with hot water. Soak for 30 minutes to soften.

3. Toast the tortilla strips on the comal until they blacken, remove. Toast the reserved chile seeds on the comal until they are blackened. Remove the seeds and place them in water to soak. Change the water after 5 minutes, and soak again for another 5 minutes. Drain.

4. Drain the chiles and transfer them to a blender or food processor with the tortillas, blackened seeds, oregano, thyme, the remaining 2 allspice berries, the remaining whole clove, the cumin, the cinnamon, and a little water. Purée to a paste.

5. Roast the tomatoes and tomatillos on the comal until soft, then remove them. Roast the onion and the remaining garlic. Place them all in the blender and purée.

6. Bring 3 cups (708 mL) of the chilled stock to a boil. Add the chayote, green beans, and potatoes. Reduce the heat and simmer until the potato is easily pierced with a fork, about 10 minutes. Drain the vegetables and set them aside.

7. Heat the lard or oil in a heavy pot or cazuela (clay pan) over medium heat. Add the chile purée and fry about 2 minutes. Add the tomato mixture and fry for a couple of minutes. Stir in just enough of the beef stock to thin the mixture and add salt to taste. Toast the avocado leaves and add them.

8. Add the meat and vegetables to the mole and heat through.

9. Garnish the mole with the onion and lime slices and serve.

Carnero Asado con Jitomate y Chile
(Roasted Beef with Tomatoes and Chile)

Yield: 20 servings   Heat Scale: Medium

This is the perfect fiesta food, in quantities large enough to offer a nice-size helping for 20 or so guests. Add a few tamales, as well as some flan for dessert, and you'll have an authentic party straight from Mexico City. (Note: This recipe require advance preparation.)

2 (5-pound [2.3 kg]) rump roasts
4 cups (.95 L) vinegar
3 ancho chiles, stems and seeds removed, toasted, rehydrated, and minced
3 poblano chiles, stems and seeds removed, roasted, peeled, and chopped
5 ripe tomatoes, chopped
1 head garlic, peeled, crushed, and chopped
1 cup (236 mL) white wine
Ground cloves, to taste
Ground cumin, to taste
Dried thyme, to taste
Dried marjoram, to taste
1 bay leaf
Dried oregano, to taste
Salt, to taste
4 ounces (112 g) ham, sliced
4 ounces (112 g) bacon or salt pork, chopped
Lemon juice, to taste
1 large onion, peeled and sliced
40 corn tortillas

1. Place the beef in a large stock pot. Add the vinegar and water as needed to cover. Add the chiles, tomatoes, garlic, wine, and spices and let it marinate for a few hours, covered, in the refrigerator.
2. Preheat the oven to 350°F (180°C).
3. Transfer the meat from the pot to a roasting dish, along with the strained ingredients from the pot. Ladle the chiles over the roast. Place the ham and bacon on top of the roast and insert a meat thermometer in the thickest part of the meat. Cook for 1 hour 45 minutes, or until the meat thermometer reads 180°F (90°C). Remove the roast from the oven and sprinkle lemon juice over the top.
4. Place the roast beef on a platter and cut it into slices. Serve with the onion slices and tortillas and the salsa of your choice from Chapter 2.

Puntas de Filete Estilo Norteño
(Northern-Style Points of Beef)

Yield: 6 servings   Heat Scale: Medium

This recipe is a northern Mexico specialty. I love this style of cuisine and am lucky enough have several authentic northern Mexican restaurants to choose from here in Albuquerque.

¼ cup (59 mL) corn oil
½ cup (118 mL) olive oil
1 large onion, peeled and sliced
2 cloves garlic, peeled
2 green bell peppers, sliced
2 red bell peppers, sliced
4 serrano chiles, stems and seeds removed, sliced into rings
6 beef fillets, cut into 1½-inch (2 cm) cubes
Salt, to taste
Freshly ground black pepper, to taste

1. In a skillet, heat the oils over medium heat. Add the onion and fry until soft. Add the garlic, bell peppers, and chiles and fry for another 5 minutes. Add the meat and salt and pepper to taste. Cook until done, stirring constantly. Serve with a bean dish from Chapter 13.

Filete en Salsa de Oregano
(Fillet in Oregano Sauce)

Yield: 6 servings   Heat Scale: Mild

This recipe from Sinaloa features oregano, a member of the mint family. Mexican oregano offers a much stronger flavor than Italian or Mediterranean oregano, so remember that a little goes a long way!

2 tablespoons (30 mL) butter, divided
3 tablespoons (45 mL) oil
2 pounds (1.1 kg) beef medallions
2 cups (473 mL) fresh Mexican oregano leaves, ground
1 cup (236 mL) chicken broth
1 poblano chile, roasted, peeled, stem and seeds removed
1 cup (236 mL) heavy cream
2 tablespoons (30 mL) minced onion
Salt, to taste
Freshly ground black pepper, to taste
Fresh Mexican oregano leaves for garnish

1. In a skillet, heat 1 tablespoon (15 mL) of the butter and the oil over medium-high heat. Add the beef and cook to your preferred doneness. Set aside and keep warm.

2. In a blender, combine the oregano leaves with the broth, chile, cream, and onion and purée. Strain the mixture. Heat the remaining butter over medium heat. Add the sauce and cook for about 25 minutes, adding salt and pepper to taste and stirring constantly.

3. Serve the sauce over the medallions and decorate with oregano leaves.

Carnitas con Chile Negro (Steak Bits with Black Chile)

Yield: 4–6 servings   Heat Scale: Medium

This recipe features a variety of poblano that is grown exclusively in Queréndaro, Michoacán. When dried, these Morelian pods dry to a dark black color and are called the chile negro. If they are unavailable, substitute the darkest poblano chiles available. Serve this with a rice dish from Chapter 13.

6 green tomatoes, roasted
10 chiles negros, roasted, peeled, stems and seeds removed (seeds reserved)
2 cloves garlic, peeled
¼ cup (59 mL) olive oil
2 pounds (1.1 kg) flank steak, cut into ½-inch (1 cm) cubes
½ cup (118 mL) chopped cilantro
1 pinch cumin
Salt, to taste

1. In a blender, combine the tomatoes, chiles, and garlic and process until coarsely chopped.

2. In a skillet, heat the olive oil over medium heat. Add the tomato mixture and fry for about 10 minutes, stirring constantly. Add the meat, cilantro, cumin, and salt and simmer for 30 minutes. Serve with tortillas on the side.

Chiles Anchos Encaramelados con Picadillo en Salsa de Aguacate
(Caramelized Ancho Chiles with Picadillo in Avocado Sauce)

Yield: 6 servings   Heat Scale: Medium

"This is one of my top creations regarding chiles," says Lula Bertrán. The key to this recipe is the absorption of the orange juice into the skin of the ancho, making the chile soft enough to eat. Make sure you choose anchos that are still pliable; if they are hard as a brick, they will need to be steamed first. The presentation of the chiles is elegant on the light green sauce.

For the Chiles:
6 medium ancho chiles, stems left on
1½ cups (354 mL) orange juice
½ cup (118 mL) grated piloncillo (or substitute molasses)
½ cup (118 mL) vinegar
1 teaspoon (5 mL) salt

1. Take each ancho by the stem and, using scissors, cut a T-shaped incision that extends across the shoulders of the chile and about ⅔ of the way down the pod. Carefully remove the seeds and membrane.
2. In a saucepan, combine the remaining ingredients and bring to a boil. Add the cleaned anchos and cook at a low boil for 15 minutes, carefully turning once. Remove the pan from the heat and let the mixture cool. Remove the anchos, clean off any remaining seeds, and transfer them to paper towels to drain.

For the Picadillo:
3 tablespoons (45 mL) vegetable oil
1 clove garlic, peeled and minced
1 small onion, peeled and chopped fine
½ pound (224 g) ground beef
½ pound (224 g) ground pork
¼ cup (59 mL) raisins
1 medium tomato, chopped
2 teaspoons (10 mL) minced cilantro
5 serrano chiles, stems and seeds removed, minced
½ teaspoon (2.5 mL) dried Mexican oregano
Salt, to taste

1. In a sauté pan, heat the oil over medium heat. Add the onion and garlic and sauté until soft. Add the beef and pork, turn the heat to high, and brown thoroughly, stirring often. Drain nearly all the fat and liquid from the pan. Add the remaining ingredients and cook over medium heat, uncovered, for about 15 to 20 minutes.

For the Avocado Sauce:
3 tomatillos, husks removed
2 tablespoons (30 mL) chopped onion
2 serrano chiles, stems and seeds removed, halved
1 clove garlic, peeled
1 tablespoon (15 mL) chopped cilantro
1 avocado, peeled and pitted
1 teaspoon (5 mL) lime juice
⅛ teaspoon (.6 mL) sugar
½ teaspoon (2.5 mL) salt
½ cup (118 mL) half-and-half

1. In a food processor, combine all the ingredients and purée. Add more half-and-half if necessary; the sauce should be just thin enough to pour. Strain the sauce. Transfer it to a saucepan and heat it, but do not let it boil.
2. To assemble the dish, carefully stuff the anchos with the picadillo and place each one on a plate. Heat the plates in the oven or the microwave. Drizzle the sauce over each ancho and serve.

Hongos y Costillas Estilo Mexicano (Mexican-Style Mushrooms and Ribs)

Yield: 4–6 servings   Heat Scale: Medium

Mushrooms have been gathered in the wild since ancient times, but they have only been cultivated since the eighteenth century. They are very popular in Mexican cuisine; several Mexican cookbooks are devoted to them.

¾ cup (177 mL) button mushrooms
2 tablespoons (30 mL) vegetable oil
8 cloves garlic, peeled
3 onions, peeled and chopped
1½ pounds (680 g) pork ribs
3 poblano chiles, roasted, stems and seeds removed, sliced
1 bunch fresh epazote
1 pound tomatoes, roasted and puréed
Salt, to taste
Freshly ground black pepper, to taste

1. Clean the mushrooms well with a mushroom brush.
2. In a large skillet, heat the oil over medium heat. Add the garlic, onions, and mushrooms and fry them together for about 10 minutes.
3. Add the ribs, chiles, epazote, tomatoes, salt, and pepper. Cook over low heat for about 1 hour, until done.

Chiles Rellenos con Res y Pasa
(Beef-and-Raisin-Stuffed Chiles)

Yield: 6 servings   Heat Scale: Mild

This recipe is from Aguascalientes, which translates as "hot water." The town received this name because it is close to thermal springs. This stuffed chile recipe is unusual in that the chiles are not battered and fried, thus the pure taste of roasted chiles shines through.

1 pound (454 g) beef roast
1 clove garlic, peeled and chopped
½ teaspoon (2.5 mL) salt, plus more to taste
1 tablespoon (15 mL) vegetable oil
½ onion, chopped
1 cup (236 mL) chopped tomato
1 tablespoon (15 mL) distilled white vinegar
10 green olives, chopped
20 raisins, chopped
10 almonds, peeled and chopped
6 poblano chiles, roasted, peeled, seeds removed
½ cup (118 mL) heavy cream
½ cup (118 mL) grated Mexican cheese of your choice
Cilantro leaves for garnish

1. Preheat the oven to 350°F (180°C). Grease a baking sheet.
2. Put the meat in a large pot with water to cover. Add the garlic and salt and simmer for about 1 hour. Once the meat is cooked, remove it from the pot and chop it into small pieces.
3. In a skillet, heat the oil over medium heat. Add the onion and sauté until soft. Add the tomato and vinegar and fry about 3 minutes longer. Add the meat and stir. Add the olives, raisins, almonds, and salt to taste. Stuff the chiles with this mixture and arrange them on the prepared baking sheet. Bake for 10 minutes. Heat the cream and cheese in a saucepan and drizzle this mixture evenly over each chile. Garnish with the cilantro leaves and serve.

Cabrito y Res con Chiles Anchos
(Braised Goat and Beef with Ancho Chiles)

Yield: 8–10 servings   Heat Scale: Mild to Medium

Goat is often saved for celebrations in Mexico, such as a baptism or a wedding.
The baby goats offer the most tender, succulent meat imaginable. This recipe from
Nayar't includes beef and is flavored with ancho chiles. Serve it with the side dish of
your choice from Chapter 13.

5 ancho chiles, toasted, stems and seeds removed, rehydrated
2 pounds (1.1 kg) tomatoes, chopped
1 pinch ground ginger
8 black peppercorns
5 cloves garlic, peeled
½ teaspoon (2.5 mL) ground cumin
2 whole cloves
½ cup (118 mL) distilled white vinegar
½ cup (118 mL) dry red wine
2 bay leaves
2 pounds (1.1 kg) goat or lamb meat, cut into 1-inch (2.5 cm) cubes
2 pounds (1.1 kg) beef, cut into 1-inch (2.5 cm) cubes

1. Preheat the oven to 250°F (120°C).
2. In a food processor or blender, purée the chiles, tomatoes, ginger, pep-percorns, garlic, cumin, cloves, and vinegar in batches. Transfer the purée to a bowl. Add the wine and bay leaves. Place the goat and beef in a large baking pan, and pour the chile mixture over it. Bake, covered, for 2 hours, or until the meat is falling apart. Serve with tortillas and the salsa of your choice from Chapter 2.

Trinidadian Coconut-Curried Goat

Yield: 4 servings   Heat Scale: Medium-Hot

Goat meat, which is not commonly eaten in the United States (except in the South-west), appears in many West Indian recipes. The Trinis sometimes eat curried goat Jamaican-style (see the recipe that follows this one), but this version with coconut is more customary in the eastern Caribbean.

2 tablespoons (30 mL) ghee (clarified butter) or vegetable oil
1 onion, peeled and finely chopped
2 cloves garlic, peeled and minced
1 Congo pepper or habanero, stem and seeds removed, chopped fine
1 tablespoon (15 mL) freshly grated ginger
2 teaspoons (10 mL) ground coriander
1 teaspoon (5 mL) ground turmeric
½ teaspoon (2.5 mL) freshly ground black pepper
2 teaspoons (10 mL) ground red chile
1 teaspoon (5 mL) ground cumin
1½ pounds (680 g) lean goat meat (or substitute lamb), cut into ½-inch (1 cm) cubes
1½ cups (354 mL) water
2 tablespoons (30 mL) coconut cream, or more to taste
Salt, to taste

1. In a skillet, heat the ghee or oil over medium heat. Add the onion, garlic, chile, and ginger and sauté for 5 minutes, stirring occasionally.
2. Add the coriander, turmeric, black pepper, ground chile, and cumin and sauté for another 3 minutes, stirring constantly.
3. Add the meat and brown it, stirring occasionally. Add the water, cover, and simmer the meat until it is tender, about 1 hour. Add more water if the mixture becomes too dry. Stir in the coconut cream and cook for 5 minutes.
4. Add salt to taste and serve hot with a chutney from Chapter 1 and a side dish from Chapter 13.

Jamaican Curry Goat

Yield: 6 servings   Heat Scale: Hot

Here is a classic, much-beloved Jamaican dish. As usual, lamb may be substituted for the goat. Note the West Indian trait of using a masala without ground chile and then adding chiles to the curry. The dish is traditionally served with white rice, mango chutney, and grated coconut.

2 pounds (1.1 kg) goat meat, cut into ½-inch (1 cm) cubes
3 tablespoons (45 mL) West Indian Masala (page 5)
½ teaspoon (2.5 mL) salt
½ teaspoon (2.5 mL) ground cardamom
½ teaspoon (2.5 mL) freshly ground black pepper
2 cloves garlic, peeled and minced
2 onions, peeled and sliced
2 tomatoes, chopped
2 green onions, chopped
2 Scotch bonnet or habanero chiles, stems and seeds removed, chopped
2 tablespoons (30 mL) butter
¼ cup (59 mL) vegetable oil
3 cups (708 mL) water

1. In a large bowl, combine the goat meat, masala, salt, cardamom, pepper, garlic, onions, tomatoes, green onions, and chiles and mix well. Allow the meat to marinate for 1 hour.
2. Remove the meat from the seasonings and reserve the seasonings. In a large skillet, heat the butter and oil over medium heat. Add the meat and sauté until lightly browned. Add the water, cover, and simmer until the goat is very tender, about 1 hour, adding more water if necessary as the meat cooks.
3. Return the reserved seasonings to the meat mixture, cover, and simmer for 15 minutes.

Pork Colombo from Martinique

Yield: 4 servings   Heat Scale: Hot

This recipe, curried with colombo paste, illustrates the Bengal influence in Marti-nique, particularly in the northern part of the island. Why the Bengalis named their curry after Colombo, Sri Lanka—so far from Calcutta—is not known. Cooks can choose between wine or coconut milk for cooking this curry. This rather spicy dish is traditionally served with fried plantains.

2 pounds (1.1 kg) lean pork, diced
¼ cup (59 mL) butter
1 cup (236 mL) chopped cabbage
2 onions, peeled and chopped
1 green (or slightly ripe) mango, sliced
1 cup (236 mL) white wine or coconut milk
2 tablespoons (30 mL) Colombo Curry Paste (page 6)
2 teaspoons (10 mL) tamarind sauce
3 cloves garlic, peeled and crushed
1 Scotch bonnet or habanero chile, seeds and stem removed, minced
2 medium eggplants, peeled and chopped
2 chayotes, peeled and chopped (or substitute yellow squash)
1 cup (236 mL) cooked navy beans

1. In a large skillet, brown the pork in the butter over medium heat for 4 minutes. Add the cabbage, onions, and mango and stir-fry for 3 more minutes. Add the wine or coconut milk and enough water to cover the meat mixture and bring it to a boil. Immediately reduce the heat and stir in the curry paste, tamarind, garlic, and chile. Cook, covered, over low heat for 1 hour, stirring occasionally.
2. Remove the lid and add the eggplants, chayote, and navy beans. Cook, uncovered, over low heat for 1 hour, stirring occasionally. The curry sauce should be fairly thick.

Aruba Lamb Barbecue

Yield: 4–6 servings   Heat Scale: Medium

This recipe is as upbeat and exciting as Aruba itself, with its casinos, nightlife, and more than a hundred international restaurants within its tiny 70 square miles. The presentation of this particular dish is enticing and unusual with its delicious flavors of curry and ginger, along with the zing of hot sauce and peppers. The lamb can be grilled in an oven broiler or on an outdoor grill. If you use an outdoor grill, I recommend using a hot burning wood, such as oak, and very little charcoal. (Note: This recipe requires advance preparation.)

1 cup (236 mL) chopped onion
3 cloves garlic, peeled and minced
2 tablespoons (30 mL) freshly grated ginger
2 teaspoons (10 mL) curry powder
1 tablespoon (15 mL) hot Hungarian paprika
½ teaspoon (2.5 mL) salt
½ cup (118 mL) dry white wine
2 tablespoons (30 mL) fresh lemon juice
2 tablespoons (30 mL) vegetable or peanut oil
3 Scotch bonnet (or habanero) chiles, stems and seeds removed, minced
2½ pounds (680 g) lamb, fat removed, cut into 1-inch (2.5 cm) cubes
3 bell peppers, cut into 1½-inch (3.5 cm) squares and parboiled for 1 minute
20 pearl onions, precooked for 4 minutes, skins removed
20 cherry tomatoes, pierced once with a knife
16 mild, pickled cherry peppers
1 small pineapple, cleaned and cut into cubes
6 yard-long beans left whole, parboiled (optional)

1. Combine the onion, garlic, ginger, curry powder, paprika, salt, wine, lemon juice, oil, chiles, and lamb in a large, shallow glass baking pan and mix thoroughly. Pierce the meat cubes several times with the tines of a fork so the marinade can penetrate them. Cover the pan with plastic wrap and refrigerate the meat overnight.
2. Remove the meat mixture from the refrigerator and let it stand until it reaches room temperature, about 20 minutes. Drain the meat in a colander, discarding the marinade.
3. On metal skewers, alternate pieces of the meat with the green peppers, pearl onions, tomatoes, pickled cherry peppers, and pineapple. Be careful not to pack them too tightly on the skewer, or it will not broil evenly. Wrap the beans around the skewer at an angle, and make sure to leave enough room at either end of the skewer to securely tie the ends of the beans with several thicknesses of aluminum foil, so they beans won't fall off while grilling.
4. Grill the skewers under the broiler or on an outdoor grill for 10 to 14 minutes, turning every 2 minutes to ensure even cooking.
5. For a spectacular presentation, bring the skewers to the table on a warm platter, and remove the meat and vegetables in front of your guests.

Curaçao-Style Roast Lamb or Kid

Yield: 8–10 servings   Heat Scale: Medium

This recipe was originally created for a big cookout (for 30 to 40 people), but I have modified the recipe to serve 8 to 10. The spicy sauce permeates the meat as it cooks very slowly over a grill, fueled with fragrant wood (such as pecan or apple), with just enough charcoal to keep the heat up. Alternatively, you can slowly roast the meat in an oven at 300°F (150°C) for 3 to 4 hours. The sauce should be made at least 2 to 3 days before the actual cooking. (Note: This recipe requires advance preparation.)

For the Lamb:
4–5 pounds (1.8–2.3 kg) lamb or kid (cabrito), cut into large pieces
½ cup (118 mL) olive oil
½ cup (118 mL) gin or dry white wine
2 teaspoons (10 mL) rosemary
1 tablespoon (15 mL) oregano
1 tablespoon (15 mL) thyme
2 teaspoons (10 mL) dried basil

1. Place the lamb in a large, shallow glass pan. Combine the remaining ingredients and sprinkle the marinade over the meat, turning the meat to coat it. Cover and refrigerate the meat for 24 hours.

For the Sauce:
1 cup (236 mL) tomato sauce
½ cup (118 mL) white wine vinegar
2 cloves garlic, peeled and minced
2 whole cloves
1 teaspoon (5 mL) salt
½ teaspoon (2.5 mL) freshly ground black pepper
2 Scotch bonnet or habanero chiles, stems and seeds removed, chopped
2 cups (473 mL) chopped onion
½ cup (118 mL) olive oil
½ cup (118 mL) water

1. Combine the tomato sauce, vinegar, garlic, cloves, salt, and pepper in a saucepan. Bring the mixture to a boil, reduce the heat to a simmer, and simmer for 2 minutes. Remove the pan from the heat and allow the sauce to cool for 10 minutes. Pour the sauce into a large, glass heatproof jar with a lid. Add the hot peppers, onion, olive oil, and water. Refrigerate the sauce for 2 to 3 days before bringing it to room temperature and using it to baste the meat, shaking the jar several times to blend the ingredients.
2. Drain some of the marinade off the meat and place the meat on the grill. Baste the meat with the sauce about every 5 minutes while the meat is cooking. Grill for about 10 minutes per side over a medium fire.
3. Cut the hot meat into serving-size pieces (removing the bones, if any), and serve it hot.

Chilindrón de Cordero
(Cuban Lamb with Peppers)

Yield: 4–6 servings   Heat Scale: Medium

Rudolfo de Garay and Thomas Brown, two experts on Cuban cuisine, uncovered this unique recipe. Although primarily made with kid, chilindrón also lends itself to lamb, rabbit, veal, and lechón (suckling pig). Serve with white rice, fried plantains (ripe or green), and a salad. Chilindrón is almost always served with beer, but sometimes with a young red wine. (Note: This recipe requires advance preparation.)

For the Adobo:
¼ cup (59 mL) olive oil
2 cloves garlic, peeled and minced
1 tablespoon (15 mL) salt
1 tablespoon (15 mL) freshly ground black pepper
¼ cup (59 mL) dry sherry
½ cup (118 mL) sour orange juice
3 pounds (1.36 kg) boned and trimmed lamb or kid (baby goat) leg, neck, or shoulder, cut into 1½-inch (3.5 cm) chunks

1. In a bowl, combine all the ingredients and mix well. Add the meat and marinate overnight.

For the Stock:
Bones and trimmings of the meat
6 cups (1.42 L) water
1 large onion, unpeeled, quartered
1 green bell pepper, stem and seed removed, roughly chopped
2 cloves garlic, unpeeled, crushed
1 bay leaf
2 allspice berries

1. Brown the bones under the broiler. Put the bones in a stock pot with the water and bring to a simmer. Simmer until the liquid reduces to about 1 cup (236 mL), about 2 to 3 hours. Strain and refrigerate the stock until a layer of fat hardens on top. Remove and discard the fat.

For the Chilindrón:
¼ cup (59 mL) olive oil
2 cups (473 mL) chopped, seeded cubanelle or green bell pepper
1 tablespoon (15 mL) minced garlic
2 cups (473 mL) chopped onion
½ cup (118 mL) tomato sauce
2 teaspoons (10 mL) salt
¼ teaspoon (1.25 mL) ground cinnamon
¼ teaspoon (1.25 mL) ground allspice
5 or more rocotillo chiles or 1 or more habanero chiles, stems and seeds removed, minced
1 tablespoon (15 mL) distilled or white wine vinegar

1. When the meat is finished marinating, drain it and reserve the adobo. Heat the olive oil in a casserole over medium heat. Add the meat and brown it. Turn the heat to high. Add the peppers, garlic, and onions, and sauté until onions are translucent. Add the tomato sauce and cook for 3 minutes. Add the salt, cinnamon, allspice, rocotillo or habanero chiles, the reserved stock, and the reserved adobo.
2. Cover and simmer for 45 minutes. The sauce should thicken and turn a deep, rich, reddish color. If the sauce is too watery, uncover the casserole, increase the heat, and reduce it. Test the sauce for seasonings and the meat for tenderness. Just before serving, stir in the vinegar.

Garlic Pork

Yield: 6–8 servings   Heat Scale: Medium

This traditional Portuguese dish probably originated in Guyana. Our main culinary guide in Trinidad, Michael Coelho, told me that years ago his father would slaughter a pig, cut it up, and marinate it in a huge mass of garlic, malt vinegar, and fresh thyme. After a week, the meat was cooked in a large pot, creating its own garlic oil. Nowadays, most Trinis forego the slaughtering and buy their pork at the Hi-Lo Supermarkets, but the taste is still strong and memorable. (Note: This recipe requires advance preparation.)

30 cloves garlic, peeled
2 tablespoons (30 mL) minced fresh thyme or 4 tablespoons (60 mL) dried thyme
2 onions, peeled and chopped
1 Congo pepper or habanero, seeds and stem removed, chopped
2 teaspoons (10 mL) salt
Juice of 1 lime
2 cups (473 mL) distilled white vinegar
4 pounds (1.82 kg) boneless pork leg or shoulder, cut into 1-inch (2.5 cm) cubes
Vegetable oil as needed for frying

1. Combine all the ingredients except the pork and oil and purée in a blender in batches until smooth. Pour this mixture over the pork and marinate, covered, in a nonmetallic bowl in the refrigerator for at least 2 days.
2. Drain the pork and pat it dry. Heat the oil in a frying pan and fry the pork cubes, a few at a time, turning often, until they are browned on all sides, about 5 to 7 minutes.
3. Drain the pork on paper towels, and keep it warm in the oven.

Variations

Some cooks lightly brown the pork and then finish the cooking in a 350°F (180°C) oven for about 30 minutes in a covered casserole, adding some water or marinade. Garlic lovers should simmer the marinade until thick and serve it over the pork cubes.

North Coast Jerk Pork

Yield: 6–8   Heat Scale: Hot

Jamaican jerk cooks use a cooking technique best described as "smoke-grilling." It combines the direct heat of grilling with smoke produced by fresh pimiento leaves and branches. While it grills, the meat is often covered with a piece of corrugated aluminum to keep the heat and smoke contained. This method can be approximated by using a Weber-type barbecue with a round drip pan filled with water in the center of the coals to catch drippings and prevent flare-ups. Although marinated pork can be smoked with cooler smoke in an indirect-heat smoker, the texture will not be the same as with smoke-grilling, and the traditional crust will not form. I prefer to smoke-grill over wood rather than charcoal, as the flavor is far superior. (Note: This recipe requires advance preparation.)

5–6 pounds (2.3–2.7 kg) pork (roasts or chops; if using ribs, use more), coarsely cut into pieces about 2–3 inches (5–7.5 cm) wide and 4–5 inches (10–12.5 cm) long, fat left on
2 cups (473 mL) North Coast Jerk Marinade (page 7)
Hardwood for the fire, such as apple, hickory, pecan, or oak
Hardwood chips, soaked in water, for the smoke, or substitute fresh branches and leaves

1. Combine the pork and the marinade, toss well, and marinate the meat, covered, overnight in the refrigerator.
2. Using the hardwood chips, build a fire in the barbecue. It is permissible to start the fire with charcoal—just don't cook over it, unless it is natural chunks of mesquite or oak charcoal rather than briquets. When the wood has burned to coals, spread them apart and place a metal drip pan, half-filled with water, in the center of the fire. Place the marinated pork on the grill, directly over the pan, as far from the fire as possible. Next, either use the barbecue cover to cover the meat, leaving a small vent for fresh air, or make a tent with aluminum foil to cover the meat and keep in the smoke.
3. The trick for the next few hours is to add sufficient wood to keep the fire going while avoiding making it too hot. Every half-hour or so, add some soaked hardwood chips to the coals to produce smoke. Feel free to drink some Red Stripe beer while tending the fire.
4. Cook the pork for 2 to 3 hours, depending on the heat of the fire, turning the meat occasionally. If you like, baste it with more marinade. The pork should be crispy on the outside and tender almost to the point of falling apart on the inside.

Tamal en Cazuela
(Tamal in a Pot)

Yield: 4–6 servings   Heat Scale: Medium

Rudolfo de Garay and Thomas Brown sent me this recipe for Cuban "polenta" made with pork. If you want to make a vegetarian tamal, eliminate the pork and add the garlic after you add the onions and add the lime juice with the tomato sauce. Serve this with a salad of avocado, watercress, and raw onions. (Note: This recipe requires advance preparation.)

1 small habanero chile or 5 piquins (or more, to taste), stems and seeds removed, chopped
5 cloves garlic, peeled
½ teaspoon (2.5 mL) freshly ground black pepper, divided
2 tablespoons (30 mL) lime juice
1 pound (454 g) diced pork
2 cups (473 mL) fresh corn kernels, divided
½ cup (118 mL) fine corn meal
⅓ cup (79 mL) sherry
2 teaspoons (10 mL) salt
3 tablespoons (45 mL) corn or vegetable oil
1½ cups (354 mL) chopped and seeded cubanelle or green bell pepper
½ cup (118 mL) chopped and seeded red bell pepper
1½ cups (354 mL) chopped onion
¼ cup (59 mL) tomato sauce
1 tablespoon (15 mL) distilled or white wine vinegar
Chopped parsley for garnish

1. In a mortar, mash the habanero chile and garlic with ¼ teaspoon (1.25 mL) of the black pepper. Add the lime juice and stir to make the adobo. Marinate the diced pork in the adobo for at least an hour, but overnight is better.
2. Purée 1½ cups (354 mL) of the corn kernels with the corn meal, sherry, 1 cup (236 mL) water, salt, and the remaining black pepper.
3. Heat the corn oil in a saucepan over medium heat. Add the pork and sauté until it begins to brown. Add the cubanelle and red bell peppers and onion, increase the heat, and sauté for about 5 minutes. Add the adobo and stir, scraping up any coagulated juices from the bottom of the pan.
4. Add the tomato sauce and chiles and cook for a minute and a half. Add the puréed corn mixture, 2 cups (473 mL) water, and the remaining ½ cup (118 mL) corn kernels and cook, stirring, for 5 minutes. Lower the heat and cook, stirring constantly, for 20 minutes. Stir in the vinegar. Pour the tamal onto a greased platter and garnish with chopped parsley.

Griot
(Hot Haitian Fried Pork)

Yield: 5–6 servings   Heat Scale: Hot

This traditional Haitian dish of marinated, fried pork remains very popular in Haiti. It can be served as a snack or as the main meat dish for a spectacular dinner. Accompany it with beans and rice and/or fried plantains and a salad of sliced cucumbers, and enjoy. (Note: This recipe requires advance preparation.)

2 pounds (1.1 kg) pork loin, trimmed of all fat, cut into ½-inch (1 cm) cubes
2 cups (473 mL) chopped onion
3 Scotch bonnet or habanero chiles, stems and seeds removed, minced
3 cloves garlic, peeled and minced
4 green onions, chopped (white part with a little of the green)
Juice of 2 limes (about ⅓ cup [79 mL])
½ cup (118 mL) juice from Seville oranges (or substitute underripe Valencia oranges)
½ teaspoon (2.5 mL) salt
¼ teaspoon (1.25 mL) freshly ground black pepper
⅔ cup (158 mL) vegetable oil

1. Combine the pork, onion, chile, garlic, green onions, lime juice, orange juice, salt, and pepper in a large, shallow glass baking dish and marinate for 3 hours in the refrigerator.
2. Put the marinated meat in a large, heavy saucepan and add just enough water to cover. Bring the mixture to a boil, then reduce the heat to a simmer. Cover and simmer for 45 to 60 minutes or until almost all of the liquid has evaporated.
3. Spread the cooked meat over several layers of paper towels to remove the excess moisture.
4. In a large skillet, heat the oil over medium-high heat. Add the pork cubes and fry until they are quite browned. Drain the fried meat on additional paper towels. Serve this dish hot.

Jug Jug

Yield: 4–6 servings   Heat Scale: Medium

This transplanted dish from Scotland is very popular in Barbados at Christmastime, and variations of it have been handed down through many generations. It is usually served with roast chicken or ham. Fresh, dried, and canned pigeon peas are available in Latin American and Caribbean markets. Try this combination for your next Christmas dinner to give it a delightful Caribbean theme.

½ pound (224 g) lean pork, cut into ½-inch (1 cm) cubes
½ cup (118 mL) lean corned beef, cut into ½-inch (1 cm) cubes
1 chicken leg, skin removed
1 pound (454 g) fresh or canned pigeon peas
3 tablespoons (45 mL) vegetable oil
3 onions, peeled and chopped
3 cloves garlic, peeled and minced
2 teaspoons (10 mL) dried thyme or 3 sprigs fresh thyme
2 Bonney Bajan or habanero chiles, stems and seeds removed, minced
2 tablespoons (30 mL) minced parsley
¼ cup (59 mL) minced celery
2 green onions, chopped, some of the green parts included
¼ teaspoon (1.25 mL) salt, or more to taste
¼ teaspoon (1.25 mL) freshly ground black pepper
½ cup (118 mL) corn meal or ground millet
1 cup (236 mL) coconut milk
2 tablespoons (30 mL) butter, divided

1. Wash the meats and place them in a large, heavy casserole with the pigeon peas. Add cold water to cover. Bring the mixture to a boil, reduce the heat to medium, cover, and cook for 45 minutes. Cool and strain the mixture, reserving the stock.
2. When the strained meat is cool enough to handle, remove the meat from the chicken leg. Shred the chicken and chop the meat and pea mixture.
3. In a large skillet, heat the oil over medium heat. Add the onions, garlic, thyme, chiles, parsley, celery, green onions, salt, and pepper and sauté until the vegetables are wilted, about 2 minutes.
4. Reduce the heat to a simmer. Stir in the chopped meats and the peas, and let the mixture simmer, covered, for a few minutes.
5. In a saucepan, blend the cornmeal with the coconut milk and gently heat the mixture over medium heat, stirring constantly. As the mixture starts to thicken, add 2 tablespoons (30 mL) of the reserved stock and stir it in thoroughly. Add 2 to 4 more tablespoons (30 to 60 mL) of the stock and continue stirring until the mixture doesn't stick to the pan. The entire process should take about 15 minutes.
6. Grease a medium bowl. Add the cooked cornmeal to the sautéed meat and vegetables and mix thoroughly. Spoon the mixture into the prepared bowl and press down to eliminate any air bubbles. Let the mixture sit for 15 minutes, turn the mold out onto a serving plate, slice, and serve.

Ropa Vieja

Yield: 6 servings   Heat Scale: Medium

This spicy, shredded flank steak recipe originated in Cuba and has become popular on many of the Spanish-speaking islands of the Caribbean. The final result of the shredded meat should resemble ragged, old clothes; hence, its name, which means "old clothes." The addition of annatto is very traditional in many Spanish and Cuban dishes, and it adds a slightly musky flavor to the dish. It should be used judiciously.

2½ pounds (1.13 kg) flank steak
2 bay leaves
1 teaspoon (5 mL) salt
¼ teaspoon (1.25 mL) freshly ground black pepper
1 onion, peeled and cut into eighths
1 carrot, sliced
1 turnip, peeled and quartered
2 tablespoons (30 mL) olive oil
½ teaspoon (2.5 mL) annatto oil
2 leeks, chopped (white part only)
2 cloves garlic, peeled and minced
1 green pepper, stems and seeds removed, chopped
2 habanero chiles, stem and seeds removed, chopped
3 large tomatoes, peeled, seeded, and chopped
⅛ teaspoon (.6 mL) ground cinnamon
⅛ teaspoon (.6 mL) ground cloves
2 canned pimientos, drained and chopped
1 tablespoon (15 mL) capers

1. Wash the flank steak and place it in a large casserole. Add the bay leaves, salt, pepper, onion, carrot, and turnip, then add water to cover. Bring the mixture to a boil,. Reduce the heat to a simmer, cover, and cook for 1½ hours, or until everything is tender. Check the water level occasionally and add more if necessary.
2. Transfer the steak to a plate to cool. Strain the cooking liquid into a bowl and set it aside.
3. When the steak is cool enough to handle, use 2 forks to shred the meat apart and set aside.
4. In a large, heavy skillet, heat the oils over medium heat. Add the leeks, garlic, green pepper, and chiles and sauté until the vegetables are tender but not browned.
5. Add the tomatoes, cinnamon, and cloves and simmer the sauce, stirring, until it starts to thicken. Mix in 2 cups (473 mL) of the reserved stock, the reserved shredded meat, the pimientos, and the capers and simmer for 5 minutes longer. Serve with hot cooked rice and/or fried plantains.

Stuffed Haitian Fillet of Beef

Yield: 4–6 servings   Heat Scale: Hot

This recipe is a new twist on the usual baked fillet. When it is cut diagonally, the inside stuffing reveals the smells and sights of Haitian peppers, garlic, and cashews. (Note: This recipe requires advance preparation.)

1 (3-pound [1.36 kg]) beef fillet (tenderloin preferred)
½ fresh lime
2 cloves garlic, peeled and minced
1 onion, peeled and thinly sliced
2 habanero chiles, stems and seeds removed, julienned
6 strips bacon
¾ cup (177 mL) chopped cashews
Salt, to taste
Freshly ground black pepper, to taste

1. Rub the outside of the fillet with the fresh lime half. Split the fillet open lengthwise, taking care not to cut all the way through. Rub the inside of the fillet with the lime.
2. Spread one side of the butterflied fillet with the garlic. Arrange the onion on top of the garlic and follow with the habanero chiles, 3 slices of the bacon, and the cashews. Add salt and pepper to taste.
3. Put the fillet back together and carefully wrap it in the remaining 3 strips of bacon. Secure the fillet and bacon with toothpicks so the filling doesn't fall out. (An alternative to the toothpicks is to wrap the fillet every few inches [about every 5 cm] with cotton kitchen string.) Refrigerate the fillet for 2 hours.
4. Preheat the oven to 450°F (240°C). Lightly oil a shallow glass pan.
5. Remove the fillet and let it sit until it reaches room temperature, about 20 minutes. Place the fillet in the prepared pan, place the pan into the oven, and immediately turn the temperature down to 350°F (180°C). Bake the fillet for 35 to 45 minutes, until brown and tender. To check for doneness, carefully separate the meat to check the interior.
6. Arrange the fillet on a heated serving dish and remove the toothpicks or string. Carefully slice the meat into 1-inch (2.5 cm) pieces and serve immediately.

Trinidadian-Style Oxtail

Yield: 6–8 servings   Heat Scale: Medium

The first time I ever tasted this dish, I was in Trinidad. I found that this cut of meat, though bony, is tasty, rich, and quite succulent. It was served with dumplings and a side of green vegetables and lentils. It can also be served with yams or potatoes drizzled with butter and sprinkled with chopped parsley. In Jamaica, this dish is considered a special meal—with its own island variations, of course.

3 pounds (1.36 kg) oxtails (beef tails), washed, dried, and cut into 2-inch (5 cm) sections
2 tablespoons (30 mL) vegetable oil
2 onions, peeled and coarsely chopped
3 cloves garlic, peeled and finely chopped
1 teaspoon (5 mL) dried thyme
3 carrots, cut into 1-inch (2.5 cm) pieces
2 tablespoons (30 mL) habanero hot sauce or ½ fresh Congo pepper or habanero, stems and seeds removed, minced
½ teaspoon (2.5 mL) freshly ground black pepper
3 cups (708 mL) Basic Beef Stock (page 45)
3 cups (708 mL) water
1 cup (236 mL) dried split peas or beans
Salt, to taste
1 tablespoon (15 mL) rum or 2 tablespoons (30 mL) sherry (optional)

1. In a large pot, brown the oxtails in the oil over medium-high heat. Add the onions and garlic and sauté for a minute. Add the thyme, carrots, hot sauce, and black pepper and sauté for 2 minutes. Add the beef stock and water and bring to a boil. Add the split peas or beans and reduce the heat. Cover the pot and simmer for 2½ hours, stirring occasionally and adding water if necessary to prevent burning.
2. The meat should be falling off the bones, but if it isn't, simmer for another 30 minutes. Just before serving, skim any fat off the top and add the rum or sherry and salt to taste. This dish can be served in a bowl if is a little thin, or on a plate if you allow it to thicken more.

Variation
The Creole version of this dish calls for caramelizing sugar with vegetable oil until it is almost burned, then adding the oxtails and proceeding with the recipe.

Beef Kebabs Tropicale

Yield: 6–8 servings   Heat Scale: Medium

These spicy kebabs can be found on the island of St. Croix and on many other islands where fruits abound. Because of the abundance of tropical fruits, combining them with meat is not that unusual—especially with the addition of a Caribbean habanero hot sauce or the peppers themselves. Serve the kebabs with a rice dish and a cool-down salad. (Note: This recipe requires advance preparation.)

1 ripe mango, peeled and pitted
1 clove garlic, peeled
3 green onions, peeled, white parts only
2 tablespoons (30 mL) brown sugar
2 Scotch bonnet or habanero chiles, stems and seeds removed
2 tablespoons (30 mL) fresh lemon juice
2 tablespoons (30 mL) fresh lime juice
¼ cup (59 mL) dry white wine
¼ cup (59 mL) passion flower fruit juice (available in most Latin American and Caribbean markets)
3 tablespoons (45 mL) vegetable oil
3 pounds (1.36 kg) sirloin steak, trimmed of fat and cut into 1-inch (2.5 cm) cubes
1 large pineapple, peeled, cored, and cut into 1½-inch (3.5 cm) cubes
3 small, partially ripe papayas, peeled, seeded, and cut into 1½-inch (3.5 cm) cubes
3 white onions, peeled, quartered, and separated

1. In a food processor or blender, purée the mango, garlic, green onions, brown sugar, chiles, lemon juice, lime juice, white wine, passion flower juice, and oil to make a marinade. Spread the cubed meat out evenly in a large glass or Pyrex shallow baking dish and pour the marinade over the meat. Pierce the meat cubes with a fork, then cover the dish and refrigerate the mixture for 4 to 6 hours.
2. Remove the dish from the refrigerator and allow the meat to sit at room temperature for 10 minutes.
3. On skewers, alternate the meat, pineapple, papaya, and onion pieces. Broil the skewers in an oven broiler or on an outdoor grill for 8 to 10 minutes (depending on how well you want the meat done). Serve hot off of the grill.

Carne Riplada
(Spicy Flank Steak)

Yield: 6 servings   Heat Scale: Medium-Hot

This dish is popular on the Spanish-speaking islands of the Caribbean, especially in the Dominican Republic. Flank used to be considered an inexpensive cut of meat in the United States, but with the popularity of fajitas, its price has risen. In the islands, Spicy Flank Steak is served shredded, accompanied by rice or mashed potatoes.

2½ pounds (1.13 kg) flank or skirt steak
1 onion, peeled and quartered
2 cloves garlic, peeled and sliced
2 tablespoons (30 mL) olive oil
2 Scotch bonnet or habanero chiles, stems and seeds removed, coarsely chopped, divided
½ cup (118 mL) olive oil
¾ cup (177 mL) chopped green bell pepper
1 cup (236 mL) chopped onion
2 cloves garlic, peeled and minced
½ teaspoon (2.5 mL) salt
¼ teaspoon (1.25 mL) freshly ground black pepper
2 fresh tomatoes, peeled, seeded, and coarsely chopped

1. Wash the steak and put it in a large, heavy casserole. Add the onion, garlic, olive oil, 1 of the chopped chiles, and water to cover by 2 inches (5 cm). Bring the mixture to a boil, turn the heat down to a simmer, cover, and simmer for at least 2 hours. Check the water level occasionally and add more water if necessary.

2. When the meat is tender, remove it from the casserole and drain it. Let the meat cool, then shred it or chop it very finely and set it aside. Strain and reserve 1 cup (236 mL) of the cooking water.

3. In a large skillet, heat the olive oil over medium heat. Add the bell pepper, onion, and garlic and sauté until the onion softens, about 2 minutes. Add the salt, pepper, the remaining chile, and the tomatoes and simmer for 1 minute. Stir in the shredded meat and simmer the mixture until the meat is heated through, about 15 minutes. The meat should be a little moist (not dry). If the meat mixture starts to dry out, add several tablespoons (30 to 45 mL) of the reserved cooking liquid. Serve hot.

Cuban-Style Spicy Picadillo

Yield: 6 servings   Heat Scale: Medium-Hot

You can use either beef or pork for this spicy dish. There is a minor debate about which meat makes a superior picadillo. Picadillo is traditionally served with Cristianos y Moros (Black Beans and Rice), fried plantains, and a cucumber salad.

2 tablespoons (30 mL) vegetable oil
1 bell pepper, seeded and chopped
1 cup (236 mL) chopped onions
2 cloves garlic, peeled and minced
2 habanero chiles, stems and seeds removed, minced
4 tomatoes, peeled, seeded, and chopped
¼ teaspoon (1.25 mL) ground cloves
1 cup (236 mL) chopped green olives
¼ cup (59 mL) raisins
1 tablespoon (15 mL) distilled white vinegar
Salt, to taste
Freshly ground pepper, to taste
2 pounds (1.1 kg) boiled lean, boneless beef (chuck or brisket) or pork, coarsely chopped

1. In a large skillet, heat the oil over medium heat. Add the bell pepper, onions, garlic, and chiles and sauté for 3 minutes or until the mixture is soft.
2. Add the tomatoes and the ground cloves and cook, stirring, until most of the liquid has been cooked off, about 8 minutes. Stir in the olives, raisins, vinegar, salt, and pepper and simmer for 1 minute.
3. Add the chopped meat and heat thoroughly.

Chile-Roasted Rosemary Leg of Lamb

Yield: 8–10 servings   Heat Scale: Mild

Here is a Southwestern entrée that is dramatic and elegant. The lamb is carved at the table and served with twice-baked potatoes and a colorful vegetable, such as dilled whole baby carrots.

8–10 green New Mexican chiles, roasted, peeled, stems removed, chopped
2 cups (473 mL) chopped leeks
½ cup (118 mL) chopped fresh rosemary
8 cloves garlic, peeled and coarsely chopped
4 tablespoons (60 mL) butter
1 (4-pound [1.82 kg]) leg of lamb, boned and butterflied
Flour as needed for dredging
Ground red New Mexican chiles, to taste
Salt, to taste
Freshly ground black pepper, to taste
1 large carrot, chopped
1 large onion, peeled and chopped
1 large potato, peeled and chopped
2 cups (473 mL) dry red wine
3 tablespoons (45 mL) all-purpose flour
½ cup (118 mL) milk

1. Preheat the oven to 450°F (240°C).
2. In a large skillet, melt the butter over medium heat. Add the chile, leeks, rosemary, and garlic and sauté until the leeks are soft. Spread the mixture on the lamb. Roll the roast up and tie it in 4 to 6 places to hold it together. Mix the flour with ground chile to taste. Lightly dust the roast with the flour mixture and salt and pepper to taste.
3. Place the carrot, onion, and potato in a roasting pan with 1½ cups (354 mL) water.
4. Place the roast on a rack in a roasting pan above the vegetables and put the pan in the preheated oven. Immediately reduce the heat to 350°F (180°C) and roast the lamb to your desired doneness—usually 20 minutes per pound for rare.
5. Remove the lamb from the pan and keep it warm. Deglaze the pan with the wine, stirring constantly. Strain the drippings and vegetables into a saucepan, and bring the liquid to a boil. Combine the flour and milk and slowly stir this mixture into the drippings to form a thick sauce.
6. To serve, carve the lamb and serve the slices with the wine sauce over them.

Grilled Piñon Lamb Chops

Yield: 4 servings   Heat Scale: Mild

Here is a delicious combination of ingredients from the Southwest—pine nuts, chile, and lamb. For an authentic, smoky flavor, grill the lamb chops over mesquite wood or charcoal covered with mesquite chips soaked in water.

1 tablespoon (15 mL) ground red New Mexican chile
¾ cup (177 mL) olive oil
5 tablespoons (75 mL) toasted piñons (pine nuts)
½ cup (118 mL) tomato paste
¼ cup (59 mL) distilled white vinegar
3 cloves garlic, peeled
4 lamb chops, cut 1–1½-inches (2.5–3.5 cm) thick

1. Combine all the ingredients, except the lamb, in a blender and purée until smooth. Paint the chops with the mixture and allow them to marinate for at least an hour.
2. Grill the chops, turning them occasionally, until done, about 7 to 10 minutes per side.

Sautéed Lamb Chops with Chimayó Red Wine Sauce

Yield: 4 servings   Heat Scale: Medium

This recipe combines wine with chile to produce a spicy sauce. Many aficionados say that chimayó chile is the most flavorful of the New Mexican red chiles, but if it is not available, substitute any ground red chile.

4 teaspoons (20 mL) ground red New Mexican chile (chimayó preferred), divided
2 teaspoons (10 mL) finely chopped fresh cilantro
2 teaspoons (10 mL) ground oregano
1 teaspoon (5 mL) ground cumin
1 teaspoon (5 mL) garlic powder
4 large, thick lamb chops (2–3 pounds [1.1–1.3 kg] total)
3 tablespoons (45 mL) vegetable oil, divided
4 tablespoons (60 mL) chopped onion
1 clove garlic, peeled and minced
½ cup (118 mL) beef broth
1 cup (236 mL) dry red wine
2 tablespoons (30 mL) butter

1. Combine 1 teaspoon (5 mL) of the chile, cilantro, oregano, cumin, and garlic powder and rub this mixture into the lamb chops. Marinate the meat for an hour or longer.
2. In a heavy skillet, heat 2 tablespoons (30 mL) of the oil over medium-high heat until very hot. Sauté the lamb for a few minutes on each side or until medium rare. Remove the chops and keep them warm.

3. Add the remaining oil, the remaining ground chile, the onion, and the garlic. Quickly sauté until the onions start to brown.

4. Increase the heat to high and add the broth. Bring the broth to a boil and deglaze the pan. Add the wine, reduce the heat, and simmer for 15 to 20 minutes or until the sauce is reduced by half. Remove the pan from the heat, strain the sauce, and stir in the butter.

5. To serve, place the lamb chops on a plate and top them with the sauce. Serve any remaining sauce on the side.

New Mexico Carne Adovada

Yield: 6 servings   Heat Scale: Hot

This variation of an ancient recipe evolved from the need to preserve meat before refrigeration. The red chile acts as an antioxidant and prevents the meat from spoiling. Such technical details should not detract from the fact that this simple dish is incredibly tasty, and once you eat it, you never forget it. (Note: This recipe requires advance preparation.)

1½ cups (354 mL) crushed red New Mexican chiles, stems removed, seeds included
4 cloves garlic, peeled and minced
1 teaspoon (5 mL) dried oregano
3 cups (708 mL) water
2 pounds (1.1 kg) pork, cut into strips
2 medium potatoes, peeled and chopped
2 onions, peeled and chopped

1. Combine the chile, garlic, and oregano in a sauce pan. Add the water and heat for 5 minutes to make a coarse chile sauce.

2. Place the pork in a glass pan and cover it with the chile sauce. Marinate the pork for 12 to 24 hours in the refrigerator, turning it once or twice.

3. Preheat the oven to 300°F (150°C).

4. Add the potatoes and onions to the pork and chile and bake for 2 hours or until the pork is very tender and starts to fall apart.

Serving Suggestions:
Place the adovada mixture in a flour tortilla, top with grated cheese, and eat as a burrito.
Use it as a stuffing for sopaipillas or as a filling for enchiladas.

Smoked Pork Mole Enchiladas

Yield: 6–8 servings   Heat Scale: Medium

Serve these unusual enchiladas with a chilled citrus salad, a rice pilaf, and a seasoned green vegetable dish from Chapter 13.

2 ancho chiles, stems and seeds removed
2 pasilla chiles, stems and seeds removed
3 dried red New Mexican chiles, stems and seeds removed
3 cups (708 mL) water
1 large onion, peeled and chopped
2 cups (473 mL) chicken broth
1 (4–6 pound [1.82–2.72 kg]) pork roast
1 dozen corn tortillas
2 tablespoons (30 mL) vegetable oil
8 ounces (224 g) sour cream
Mole Sauce (page 57)
¼ cup (59 mL) sesame seeds (1 tablespoon [15 mL] reserved for garnish)

1. Simmer the chiles in the water for 15 minutes to soften. Drain the chiles and transfer them to a blender. Add the onion and chicken broth and purée until smooth. Strain the sauce if desired.
2. Make diagonal slits about 1-inch (2.5 cm) deep in the pork roast. Rub the chile mixture over the roast, taking care that it goes deeply into the cuts.
3. Smoke the roast in a smoker with indirect heat, following the manufacturer's directions. When the roast has smoked to an internal temperature of 160°F (75°C), carve it into thin strips.
4. Preheat the oven to 325°F (165°C).
5. Soften the tortillas by frying them in oil in a small skillet over medium-high heat for a few seconds on each side, then drain them on paper towels. Place the pork strips in the tortillas, top them with sour cream and sesame seeds, and roll up. Place them in a baking dish, cover with mole sauce, and bake for about 20 minutes. Sprinkle the reserved sesame seeds on top and serve.

Tamales y Mas Tamales

Yield: 2 dozen   Heat Scale: Medium

Tamales can be filled with almost anything, from meat or poultry to fruits and nuts. To create variations on this traditional recipe, simply replace the pork with the ingredient of your choice. For example, many of the meat and poultry entrées in this cookbook could be used.

2 pounds (1.1 kg) boneless pork
1 recipe Classic New Mexico Green Chile Sauce (page 71)
About 30 dried corn husks
4 cups (.95 L) masa harina
1 teaspoon (5 mL) salt
2½–3 cups (591–708 mL) broth or water
⅔ cup (158 mL) lard or vegetable shortening

1. In a large pot, cover the pork with water, bring it to a boil, reduce the heat, and simmer for 1 hour or until the pork is very tender and starts to fall apart. Remove the roast from the pan and save the broth. With 2 forks or your fingers, finely shred the meat.

2. Combine the pork with 1 cup (236 mL) of the chile sauce and simmer for 15 minutes, adding more sauce if the meat becomes too dry.

3. Soak the corn husks in water to soften.

4. Mix together the masa and salt. Slowly add the reserved pork broth, stirring with a fork until the mixture holds together. Whip the lard or shortening until fluffy. Add the masa to the shortening and continue to beat. Drop 1 teaspoon (5 mL) of the dough into a glass of cold water. If the dough floats, it is ready. If it sinks, continue to beat it until it floats.

5. Select corn husks that measure about 5 × 8 inches (12.5 × 20 cm) or overlap smaller husks together. Place 2 tablespoons (30 mL) of the masa mixture in the center of the husk, and pat or spread the dough evenly into a 2 × 3–inch (5 × 7.5 cm) rectangle. Place about 1 tablespoon (15 mL) of the pork and 1 tablespoon (15 mL) of the sauce down the center and fold the husk around the masa and filling, being careful not to squeeze the tamale.

6. There are two basic ways to fold the husks. The first is to take two corn husk strips and use them to firmly tie each end of the tamale. This method works well with smaller corn husks.

The second method is to fold the tapered end over the filled husk, and then fold the remaining end over it. Tie the tamale around the middle with a strip of the corn husk to keep the ends folded down. Fold all the tamales using either method.

7. Place a rack in the bottom of a steamer or large pot. Make sure that the rack is high enough to keep the tamales above the water. Place the tamales on the rack, folded-side down or, if the pot is large enough, stand them up. Do not pack them tightly, as they will expand as they cook. Cover with additional husks or a clean towel to absorb the moisture. Bring the water to a boil, reduce to a gentle boil, and steam for an hour for each dozen tamales or until done. To test for doneness, open one end of the husk. If the masa pulls away from the wrapper, the tamale is done.

Serving Suggestion:
Serve with additional Classic New Mexico Green Chile Sauce on the side for pouring over the opened tamales.

Pork Chops Rancheros

Yield: 4 servings   Heat Scale: Medium

The addition of cumin and chiles gives these pork chops a wonderful Southwestern flavor. Serve with a jicama and tomato salad and Mexican rice pilaf. The remaining marinade can be heated and served on the side as a sauce. (Note: This recipe requires advance preparation.)

6 green New Mexican chiles, roasted, peeled, stems and seeds removed, chopped
¼ cup (59 mL) lime juice
2 tablespoons (30 mL) vegetable oil
¼ cup (59 mL) chopped onions
2 cloves garlic, peeled and minced
2 teaspoons (10 mL) ground cumin
1 teaspoon (5 mL) dried oregano
½ teaspoon (2.5 mL) ground coriander
½ teaspoon (2.5 mL) salt
4 thick-cut pork chops

1. Combine all the ingredients, except the pork, in a large bowl. Add the pork, and marinate it in the mixture for 4 hours or overnight.
2. Remove the chops from the marinade and grill them until done.

Southwestern Spicy Pork Paella with Artichokes

Yield: 6 servings   Heat Scale: Mild

Paella, one of the most famous one-dish meals, was born in Valencia, Spain. Traditionally made with seafood and/or chicken, there are also countless variations using a wide variety of ingredients, such as this recipe.

¾ pound (336 g) boneless pork, cut in 1-inch (2.5 cm) cubes
3 tablespoons (45 mL) olive oil
2 chorizo sausages, cut in thin slices or crumbled
1 medium onion, peeled and chopped fine
4 cloves garlic, peeled and chopped fine
1 tablespoon (15 mL) crushed red New Mexican chile, including the seeds
¼ teaspoon (1.25 mL) saffron
¼ cup (59 mL) chicken stock
1 large tomato, peeled and chopped fine
2 cups (473 mL) uncooked long-grain rice
4 cups (.95 L) Classic Chicken Stock (page 46)
1 (14-ounce [392 g]) can artichoke hearts, drained and quartered
½ cup (118 mL) cooked green peas

1. Preheat the oven to 400°F (200°C).
2. In a large pot, brown the pork in the oil over medium heat. Add the chorizo, onions, garlic, and chile and sauté until the onion is soft. Remove the pork and chorizo and set them aside. Add the rice and continue to sauté until the rice starts to turn golden.
3. Mix the saffron with the chicken stock. Stir this mixture, along with the tomato, into the sautéed mixture and remove the pan from the heat. Transfer the contents of the pan to a baking dish and arrange the pork, chorizo, artichoke hearts, and peas over the top. Bake, covered, for 30 to 45 minutes or until the rice is done.
4. Remove the dish from the oven, remove the lid, and drape a kitchen towel loosely over the top. Let it sit for 5 to 8 minutes before serving.

Brisket of Beef, Austin-Style

Yield: 6 servings   Heat Scale: Medium

Brisket, one of the tastiest cuts of beef, needs marinating and slow cooking to achieve perfect flavor. The key to cooking the brisket is to keep the moisture in by sealing the pan and holding the cooking temperature below the boiling point of water. Leftover brisket makes great sandwiches. Brisket is great with coleslaw and a baked potato or Texas Jalapeño Onion Rings (page 787). (Note: This recipe requires advance preparation.)

6 jalapeño chiles, stems and seeds removed, chopped
½ cup (118 mL) vegetable oil
¼ cup (59 mL) dry red wine
¼ cup (59 mL) soy sauce
1 large onion, peeled and finely chopped
4 cloves garlic, peeled and minced
2 tablespoons (30 mL) lime juice
2 tablespoons (30 mL) tequila
1 tablespoon (15 mL) coarsely ground black pepper
1 teaspoon (5 mL) ground cumin
1 (3-pound [1.36 kg]) beef brisket
1 cup (236 mL) water

1. In a bowl, combine all the ingredients except the beef and water. Put the brisket in a nonmetallic pan, cover it with the marinade, and refrigerate for 12 to 24 hours, turning two or three times.
2. Preheat the oven to 200°F (100°C).
3. Place the brisket, the marinade, and the water in a baking dish. Cover and bake for 3 hours or longer, until the brisket starts to fall apart.
4. Remove the brisket from the baking dish. Transfer the marinade and juices to a saucepan, and reduce over medium-low heat until thick.
5. Slice the brisket against the grain into thin slices. Serve the sauce over the carved brisket.

Jalapeño-Stuffed Steaks

Yield: 6 servings   Heat Scale: Medium-Hot

Grilled steaks no longer have to be just a piece of plain meat. Any fresh chile or combinations of chiles can be substituted for the jalapeños in this recipe. The stuffing can be prepared a day in advance and refrigerated. An hour before cooking, slice the steaks and fill them with the chile mixture.

10 jalapeños, stems removed, chopped
1 medium onion, chopped
4 cloves garlic, peeled and chopped
1 tablespoon (15 mL) vegetable oil
½ cup (118 mL) grated Monterey Jack cheese
3 pounds (1.36 kg) trimmed fillet of beef, cut into 6 thick steaks
Freshly ground black pepper, to taste

1. In a skillet, heat the oil over medium heat. Add the chiles, onion, and garlic and sauté for a couple of minutes, until just soft but still a little crisp. Remove the skillet from the heat and let the mixture cool. Mix in the cheese.
2. Slice into the steaks from the edge, creating a pocket for the stuffing. Stuff with the jalapeño mixture and fasten the opening with a toothpick, if necessary. Season the outside of each steak with the black pepper.
3. Grill the steaks over hot charcoal or gas to the desired doneness.

Soft Machaca Avocado Tacos

Yield: 4 servings   Heat Scale: Medium

The use of shredded beef instead of ground beef in these tacos reflects their more tradi-tional Mexican influences. Besides, shredded beef is much more tasty.

8 piquins or chiltepins, crushed
1 pound (454 g) boneless beef roast, cut up
2 small onions, peeled and chopped, divided
2 cloves garlic, peeled and sliced
8 corn tortillas
1 tablespoon (15 mL) vegetable oil
2 poblano chiles, roasted, peeled, stems and seeds removed, chopped
2 medium tomatoes, chopped
2 teaspoons (10 mL) dried oregano
¼ teaspoon (1.25 mL) ground cumin
Diced avocados or guacamole (page 170) for garnish
Chopped cilantro for garnish
Pico de Gallo Salsa (page 69) for serving

1. Preheat the oven to 300°F (150°C).
2. Place the piquins, beef, half of the onion, and the garlic in a pan with enough water to cover. Bring to a boil, reduce the heat, and simmer, cov-ered, for 1 to 2 hours or until the meat starts to fall apart.

3. Remove the meat from the pan and let it cool. Using 2 forks, shred the meat.

4. Wrap the tortillas in a damp towel and warm them in the preheated oven for about 5 minutes.

5. In a sauté pan, heat the oil over medium heat. Add the remaining onions and sauté them until softened. Add the chopped poblanos, tomatoes, oregano, and cumin, and sauté for 5 minutes. Add the meat and cook until it is thoroughly heated.

6. To each warmed tortilla, add some of the meat, avocados or guacamole, and chopped cilantro. Serve the salsa on the side.

Barbecued Ribs, Texas-Style

Yield: 4–6 servings   Heat Scale: Medium-Hot

The Texas Panhandle is beef country; cattle were once driven through such cities as Amarillo and Abilene. Texans love to barbecue beef, which can take hours or even days, but the results are worth it. The following recipe doesn't take 24 hours, but the ribs should be cooked slowly over charcoal while you take care that the sauce doesn't burn.

2 tablespoons (30 mL) vegetable oil
6 jalapeño chiles, stems and seeds removed, chopped
1 medium onion, peeled and chopped
3 cloves garlic, peeled and chopped
1 cup (236 mL) tomato sauce
2 cups (473 mL) Basic Beef Stock (page 45)
¼ cup (59 mL) cider vinegar
Juice of 1 lemon
1 tablespoon (15 mL) prepared mustard
1 tablespoon (15 mL) brown sugar
½ teaspoon (2.5 mL) dried oregano
⅛ teaspoon (.6 mL) ground habanero chile
Freshly ground black pepper, to taste
3 pounds (1.36 kg) pork spareribs

1. In a skillet, heat the oil over medium heat. Add the jalapeños, onion, and garlic and sauté them until softened. Transfer the mixture to a blender and purée until smooth. Transfer the purée to a saucepan.

2. Add the remaining ingredients, except the ribs, and bring to a boil. Reduce the heat and simmer until the sauce thickens.

3. Grill the ribs about 6 inches (15 cm) from the coals until browned, about 30 to 45 minutes. Baste the ribs with the sauce and continue to baste every 10 minutes for an additional 30 minutes, being careful that they do not burn.

Tournedos Chipotle

Yield: 4   Heat Scale: Hot

I confess to smuggling Mexican recipes into the Southwest. Here is the preferred way to prepare steaks in Puerto Vallarta, a method I fell completely in love with during my visits there.

4 (1–2 inch [2.5–5 cm] thick) beef fillets
Olive oil as needed
2 tablespoons (30 mL) vegetable oil
1 onion, peeled and chopped
3 cloves garlic, peeled and minced
3 canned chipotle chiles in adobo
1 medium tomato, peeled, seeded, and chopped
½ teaspoon (2.5 mL) oregano
½ teaspoon (2.5 mL) sugar
½ teaspoon (2.5 mL) freshly ground black pepper
2 cups (473 mL) Basic Beef Stock (page 45)
1 cup (236 mL) dry red wine

1. Brush the steaks with olive oil and set them aside.
2. In a skillet, heat the oil over medium heat. Add the onion and garlic and sauté until browned. Add the chipotles, tomato, oregano, sugar, and pepper. Sauté for an additional couple of minutes. Stir in the broth and wine and simmer for 20 to 30 minutes or until reduced by half.
3. Remove the pan from the heat. Transfer the mixture to a blender, purée until smooth, and strain. Return the sauce to the pan and keep warm until serving time.
4. Broil or grill the steaks to desired doneness.
5. To serve, spoon some sauce onto a plate, place the steak on the sauce, and top with additional sauce.

Fajita Feast

Yield: 8 servings   Heat Scale: Medium

Typically Texan, these strips of skirt steak make a great outdoor barbecue party. They are easy to prepare—simply marinate them the night before and grill them when the guests arrive. Serve with flour tortillas, chopped onions, grated cheese, sour cream, diced avocados, and a variety of sauces and salsas from Chapter 2. The idea is for each guest to custom-make his or her own fajita sandwiches. A crisp salad from Chapter 6 and cornbread from Chapter 4 are perfect accompaniments. (Note: This recipe requires advance preparation.)

½ cup (118 mL) chopped serranos, stems removed
⅓ cup (79 mL) lime juice
⅓ cup (79 mL) soy sauce
⅓ cup (79 mL) red wine
2 tablespoons (30 mL) vegetable oil
2 cloves garlic, peeled and minced
2 pounds (1.1 kg) skirt or flank steak

1. In a large bowl, combine all the ingredients except the beef. Add the beef and marinate in the refrigerator for 12 to 24 hours.
2. Grill the meat over mesquite wood or charcoal and mesquite chips to the desired doneness. Carve the steak diagonally against the grain in thin strips, as for London broil.

Sliced Veal with Espelette Peppers

Yield: 4–6 servings   Heat Scale: Mild to Medium

This classic veal dish from southwest France used the famed Espelette pepper. If you cannot find Espelette purée, use fresh red New Mexican chiles, puréed in a blender with a little water. Another substitute is fresh red bell peppers with ground red New Mexico chile. Serve this dish with garlic mashed potatoes and yellow squash.

¼ cup (59 mL) olive oil
1 onion, peeled and sliced
1 clove garlic, peeled and chopped
4 green bell peppers, stems and seeds removed, finely chopped
2 red bell peppers, stems and seeds removed, finely chopped
1½ pounds (680 g) veal, thinly sliced and then cut into 1-inch (2.5 cm) pieces
¼–½ cup (60–118 mL) Espelette purée
2 teaspoons (10 mL) freshly chopped thyme
2 bay leaves
1 cup (236 mL) Basic Beef Stock (page 45)
Salt, to taste
Freshly ground black pepper, to taste

1. In a large sauté pan, heat the olive oil over medium heat. Add the onion and garlic and sauté for 5 minutes, then add the bell peppers and sauté for 5 more minutes, stirring occasionally. Add the veal, Espelette purée, thyme, and bay leaves, and sauté for 5 more minutes. Add the stock, cover, reduce the heat, and simmer for about 30 minutes. Remove the cover and continue cooking for 10 more minutes until the mixture thickens. Add salt and pepper to taste.

Lamb Couscous with Onions and Raisins

Yield: 6–8 servings   Heat Scale: Mild

Thanks to Rosemary Ann Ogilvie for giving me this recipe. She says, "This recipe by the manager of the Salaam Hotel in Morocco, like most of the recipes that I gathered, feeds a number of people. You can, however, reduce it by cutting the ingredients in half. Serve with side of Harissa Sauce (page 23) to increase the heat."

2 tablespoons (30 mL) olive oil
2 pounds (1.1 kg) boneless lamb, cubed
2 medium onions, peeled and sliced, divided
2 quarts (1.9 L) water
1 bunch cilantro, tied together with string
¼ teaspoon (1.25 mL) crushed saffron threads
1 teaspoon (5 mL) ground turmeric, divided
4 cups (.95 L) cubed, unpeeled pumpkin or squash
4 tablespoons (60 mL) butter, divided
2 teaspoons (10 mL) ground cinnamon
2 teaspoons (10 mL) ground ginger
2 tablespoons (30 mL) slivered almonds
2 tablespoons (30 mL) sugar or 3 tablespoons (45 mL) honey
1½ cups (354 mL) raisins, soaked in warm water and drained
2 teaspoons (10 mL) ground red New Mexican chile
3 cups (708 mL) Basic Beef Stock (page 45)
1 pound (454 g) couscous
Salt, to taste
Freshly ground black pepper, to taste

1. In a skillet, heat the oil over medium-high heat. Add the lamb and half the onion and sauté until browned. Transfer the lamb and onion to a large pot. Add the water, cilantro, saffron, ½ teaspoon (2.5 mL) of the turmeric, and the pumpkin cubes. Bring to a boil, reduce the heat, cover, and cook until the pumpkin is tender, about 1 hour and 15 minutes. Remove the pumpkin from the pot and set it aside. When it is cool enough to handle, peel the skin off and set the vegetable aside. Remove the cilantro, replace the cover on the pot, and continue cooking until the meat is tender. Set aside.
2. In a skillet, melt 3 tablespoons (45 mL) of the butter over medium heat. Add the remaining onions, the remaining turmeric, cinnamon, ginger, almonds, sugar, raisins, and ground chile. Cover and cook over a very low heat for 30 minutes. Set aside.

3. In a saucepan, bring the broth to a boil. Place the couscous in a large bowl and pour the broth over it. Cover the bowl and allow the couscous to stand until all the liquid is absorbed. Mix in the remaining butter. Use a fork to fluff up the grains. Cover and keep warm until serving time.
4. Pile the couscous on a large plate. Make a well in the center of the mound, place the pumpkin and lamb inside the well, top with the onion and raisin mixture, salt and pepper to taste, and serve.

Spiced Lamb with Apricots

Yield: 5–6 servings

Heat Scale: Medium to Hot, depending on how much Harissa you add at the table

When shopping in a North African spice souk, you can find as many as 200 different spices and herbs from all over the world, including some of the hottest chile peppers around. I recommend that you buy your apricots at a natural foods store. (Note: This recipe requires advance preparation.)

⅓ cup (79 mL) freshly squeezed orange juice
¼ cup (59 mL) olive oil, divided
3 cloves garlic, peeled and minced
2 tablespoons (30 mL) minced fresh cilantro
2 tablespoons (30 mL) Harissa Sauce, plus more for serving (page 23)
2 tablespoons (30 mL) minced fresh mint
½ teaspoon (2.5 mL) ground cumin
⅛ teaspoon (.6 mL) freshly grated nutmeg
1½ pounds (680 mL) cubed lamb
1 cup (236 mL) chopped onion
8 dried apricots, soaked in water overnight in the refrigerator
¼ cup (59 mL) chopped dried dates
2 cups (473 mL) chicken stock
3 tablespoons (45 mL) toasted sesame seeds for garnish

1. In a shallow glass baking dish, mix together the orange juice, 2 table-spoons (30 mL) of the oil, the garlic, the cilantro, the Harissa, the mint, the cumin, the nutmeg, and the lamb. Cover and refrigerate overnight.
2. The next day, uncover the mixture, and allow it to sit outside the refrigerator for 30 minutes. Drain the lamb in a colander, reserving the marinade.
3. Drain the apricots, reserving the water, and set them aside.
4. Heat the remaining 2 tablespoons (30 mL) oil in a large, heavy casse-role. Add the onion and sauté for 2 minutes. Add the drained lamb and sauté for 4 minutes or until the lamb is browned. Add the reserved mari-nade, apricots, apricot soaking liquid, dates, and chicken stock and bring the mixture to a boil. Allow it to boil for 1 minute.

5. Reduce the heat to a simmer, cover, and simmer gently for 1 hour and 15 minutes, until the lamb is tender. Remove the cover and continue simmering the lamb until the mixture has thickened slightly.
6. Serve the lamb over hot, saffron-infused rice and sprinkle the toasted sesame seeds over the top. Serve a small bowl of additional Harissa on the side.

Lamb and Cayenne Kefta

Yield: 4 servings   Heat Scale: Medium

Keftas are meatballs prepared with ground lamb or beef and a number of different herbs and spices. They can be served in a variety of ways. You can add them to stews or serve them as brochettes hot off the charcoal grill in flat Arab or pita bread. Although there are many recipes for this dish, the one Moroccan ingredient that seems to remain a constant is fresh mint.

2 teaspoons (10 mL) ground cayenne
1 pound (454 g) ground lamb
1 medium onion, peeled and finely chopped
2 tablespoons (30 mL) chopped fresh mint
1 teaspoon (5 mL) ground cloves
1 teaspoon (5 mL) ground allspice
1 teaspoon (5 mL) ground ginger
1 teaspoon (5 mL) ground cardamom
½ teaspoon (2.5 mL) ground nutmeg
½ teaspoon (2.5 mL) ground cinnamon
½ teaspoon (2.5 mL) ground cumin
Freshly ground black pepper, to taste

1. Combine all the ingredients and allow the mixture to sit at room temperature for an hour to blend the flavors.
2. Shape the mixture into 1-inch (2.5 cm) meatballs and thread them onto skewers. Either slightly flatten them into a sausage shape or leave them as balls. Grill the meat over charcoal or under the broiler to desired doneness.

Lamb Tajine with Cayenne and Herbs (T'Dlla)

Yield: 5–6 servings   Heat Scale: Medium

The use of multiple spices is characteristic of this dish. True to the cooking traditions of the North African desert, the lamb is roasted in an oven. You can eat the hot, roasted lamb by taking a small piece of bread and using it to remove some meat, or, you may use forks and knives.

1 cup (236 mL) minced onion
3 garlic cloves, peeled and minced
1 teaspoon (5 mL) freshly grated ginger
½ teaspoon (2.5 mL) ground cumin
¾ teaspoon (3.75 mL) ground cinnamon
⅛ teaspoon (.6 mL) crushed saffron threads
1 teaspoon (5 mL) salt
2 teaspoons (10 mL) ground cayenne
⅓ cup (79 mL) water
6 tablespoons (90 mL) olive oil
1 (4-pound [1.82 kg]) lamb leg or shoulder
⅓ cup (79 mL) butter, melted, divided
¼ cup (59 mL) chopped cilantro

1. Preheat the oven to 400°F (200°C).
2. In a small bowl, mix together the onion, garlic, ginger, cumin, cinnamon, saffron, salt, cayenne, water, and olive.
3. Place the lamb in a heavy, ovenproof casserole. Deeply pierce the lamb several times, and stuff the onion and spice mixture into as many of the pockets as you can. Pour the remaining mixture over the lamb. Drizzle 3 tablespoons (45 mL) of the butter over the lamb. Add enough water to cover ¼ of the way up the roast. On the stovetop, bring the pan to a boil. Cover the pan, transfer it to the oven, and roast for 15 minutes.
4. Reduce the oven heat to 350°F (180°C). Cook the lamb for 2 hours, occasionally checking to make sure some water remains at the bottom of the pan, and drizzle the remaining butter over the top. The lamb should be so tender that it is falling away from the bone. As an optional finishing touch, cook the lamb under a hot broiler until the top is golden and crisped.
5. Before serving, sprinkle the cilantro over the top of the lamb.

Middle Eastern Meatball Sandwich

Yield: 4 sandwiches   Heat Scale: Varies

This recipe, from my wife, Mary Jane, makes an incredibly tasty lunch. Serve it with sliced tomatoes drizzled with fine olive oil and balsamic vinegar.

For the Sauce:
1 cucumber, seeded and finely diced
3 green onions, white part only, minced
1 medium tomato, seeded and diced
¼ cup (59 mL) crumbled feta cheese
Plain yogurt to bind the sauce (thick Greek yogurt preferred)
¼ cup (59 mL) minced Italian parsley

1. In a bowl, combine all the ingredients and mix well. Set the sauce aside while you make the meatballs.

For the Meatballs:
⅓ cup (79 mL) chopped golden raisins
½ pound (224 g) ground lamb (or substitute lean hamburger)
¼ cup (59 mL) minced onion
1 teaspoon (5 mL) fresh lime juice
1 teaspoon (5 mL) ground cinnamon
¼ teaspoon (1.25 mL) ground nutmeg
2 teaspoons (10 mL) hot sauce of your choice, or to taste
Plain breadcrumbs as needed
4 pita bread pockets

1. In a bowl, mix together the raisins, lamb, onion, lime juice, cinnamon, nutmeg, and hot sauce. If the mixture seems too loose, add a few teaspoons (30–45 mL) bread crumbs to hold it together. Form into meatballs (large enough so that 2 of them will fit into a pita pocket) and thread 2 skewers through each meatball to add stability when grilling or broiling. Broil or grill the meatballs to medium doneness.
2. Toast the pita pockets. Place 2 meatballs in each pocket and top with sauce.

Sosaties

Yield: 4 servings   Heat Scale: Medium

In this South African recipe, the meat is marinated and then grilled. Many think that the recipe has its origins in Malaysia, where Malay sate, or spiced, grilled meat with hot sauce, is so popular. It is traditionally grilled over charcoal, and vendors skewer the meat and grill it right in front of you. Serve the sosaties with hot, cooked rice. (Note: This recipe requires advance preparation.)

8 dried apricots
3 tablespoons (45 mL) vegetable oil
1 clove garlic, peeled and minced
3 cups (708 mL) sliced onions
1 teaspoon (5 mL) ground cayenne
5 grape leaves, fresh or jarred
½ teaspoon (2.5 mL) salt
3 tablespoons (45 mL) red wine vinegar
2 pounds (1.1 kg) lamb chops or sirloin
12–14 slices bacon
3 tablespoons (45 mL) sour cream

1. Wash the dried apricots and place them in a small saucepan with water to cover. Let them soak for 2½ hours. Make sure the apricots are still covered with water, then simmer them for 15 to 20 minutes, until they are tender. Allow them to cool slightly. Place the apricots and some of the cooking water in a blender or food processor and purée, adding a little more water if the mixture gets too thick. Set aside.
2. In a medium skillet, heat the oil over medium heat. Add the garlic and onions and sauté for 5 minutes. Add the cayenne, grape leaves, salt, and vinegar. Sauté this mixture for 4 minutes, remove it from the heat, and let it cool slightly.
3. In a large ceramic bowl, alternately layer the meat, the bacon, and the apricot mixture. Cover the bowl and marinate overnight in the refrigerator.
4. Allow the meat to reach room temperature. Cut it into 1½-inch (3.5 cm) cubes. Wrap each cube with half a bacon slice and thread them on a skewer. Reserve the extra marinade. Grill the cubes to your liking.
5. While the meat is grilling, scrape the extra marinade into a small sauce-pan, add 2 tablespoons (30 mL) water and the sour cream, and simmer the mixture, taking care not to let it boil.
6. Serve the meat over hot rice and top it with some of the sauce.

Boer Lamb Chops Marinated in a Spicy Sambal

Yield: 4 servings   Heat Scale: Mild

This recipe was influenced by the Cape Malay cuisine, which was—and is—so prevalent in South Africa. "Boer" is the Dutch word for farmer. Historically, a Boer in South Africa (in the early years) was part of the elite society. Serve this dish with a big bowl of steaming, hot rice and a hearty red wine.

1 cup (236 mL) tomato sauce
¼ cup (59 mL) apple cider vinegar
1½ tablespoons (22.5 mL) Worcestershire sauce
2 tablespoons (30 mL) Sambal Matah (page 40)
2 cups (473 mL) grated onion
1 tablespoon (15 mL) dry mustard
½ teaspoon (2.5 mL) salt
¼ teaspoon (1.25 mL) freshly ground black pepper
8 (1-inch [2.5 cm] thick) lamb chops
2 tablespoons (30 mL) butter
½ cup (118 mL) beef stock
½ cup (118 mL) half-and-half
3 tablespoons (45 mL) finely minced celery
½ cup (118 mL) minced leek, white part only
3 tablespoons (45 mL) minced carrot

1. In a shallow ceramic baking dish, stir together the tomato sauce, vinegar, Worcestershire sauce, sambal, onion, mustard, salt, and pepper. Add the lamb chops and turn them to coat. Marinate the chops for 1 hour in the refrigerator.
2. Remove the chops from the marinade (reserving the remaining marinade) and pat them dry between paper towels. In a large, heavy skillet, heat the butter over medium heat and brown the chops quickly to maintain a rare interior. Transfer the chops to a warmed plate lined with paper towels. Cover the plate with aluminum foil to keep the meat warm.
3. Pour the reserved marinade into a small saucepan. Add the stock, half-and-half, celery, leek, and carrot and simmer over a low heat for 10 to 15 minutes, until the vegetables are tender.
4. Serve the sauce over the rare chops.

Bobotie

Yield: 4–6 servings   Heat Scale: Mild

Bobotie was brought to South Africa by Malaysian slaves in the eighteenth century. There are many variations of this recipe, but the constant ingredient seems to be curry powder. It is traditionally served with plain boiled rice and accompanied by chutney and various condiments, including chopped bananas, sliced green onions, and coconut.

2 (1-inch [2.5 cm]) thick slices white bread
2 cups (473 mL) milk
2 tablespoons (30 mL) vegetable oil
1½ medium onions, peeled and coarsely chopped
2 garlic cloves, peeled and minced
1½ tablespoons (22.5 mL) curry powder
1 tablespoon (15 mL) ground turmeric
1 teaspoon (5 mL) ground ginger
1 teaspoon (5 mL) salt
1 teaspoon (5 mL) freshly ground black pepper
2 tablespoons (30 mL) water
1½ pounds (680 g) ground lamb
1 large tomato, peeled, seeded, and finely chopped
1 large pippin apple, peeled, cored, and chopped
⅓ cup (79 mL) raisins
¼ cup (59 mL) chopped blanched almonds
3 tablespoons (45 mL) mango chutney
1 tablespoon (15 mL) fresh lemon juice
1 tablespoon (15 mL) Worcestershire sauce
1 tablespoon (15 mL) apricot preserves
4 eggs
2–3 cups (473–708 mL) cooked rice

1. Soak the bread in the milk and set it aside.
2. Heat the oil in a large, heavy skillet over low heat. Add the onions and garlic and cook until golden brown, stirring occasionally, about 10 minutes. Mix in the curry, turmeric, ginger, salt, pepper, and water. Simmer the mixture until it thickens slightly, about 2 minutes. Transfer the mixture to a bowl.
3. Preheat the oven to 325°F (165°C).
4. Add the lamb to the skillet that the onions were sautéed in and cook it over medium heat until it is no longer pink. Line a bowl with several layers of paper towels and transfer the cooked lamb to the bowl to drain. Add the lamb to the onion mixture, along with the tomato, apple, raisins, almonds, chutney, lemon juice, Worcestershire sauce, and preserves.
5. Squeeze the milk from the bread and reserve the milk. Mix the bread into the lamb mixture. Transfer the mixture to a 3-quart (3 L) soufflé dish.
6. Beat the reserved milk with the eggs. Pour this over the lamb mixture. Bake until the custard is set and light brown, about 1 hour. Serve with the rice.

Pinang-Kerrie

Yield: 4–5 servings   Heat Scale: Mild

This curry is very popular in South Africa. It is traditionally served dry, which means that the sauce needs to cook until it is very, very thick. Serve it with a rice dish from Chapter 13.

1 tablespoon (15 mL) curry powder
1 teaspoon (5 mL) ground turmeric
4 cloves garlic, peeled and minced
½ teaspoon (2.5 mL) salt
2 tablespoons (30 mL) cider vinegar
1 tablespoon (15 mL) freshly grated ginger
1 teaspoon (5 mL) sugar
1 teaspoon (5 mL) fresh lemon juice or tamarind paste
2 bay leaves
1 pound (454 g) lamb, cut into 1-inch (2.5 cm) cubes
2 tablespoons (30 mL) vegetable oil
2 onions, peeled and finely
1½ cups (354 mL) chicken stock or water

1. In a ceramic bowl, combine the curry powder, turmeric, garlic, salt, vinegar, ginger, sugar, lemon juice, and bay leaves. Add the lamb and toss it gently to cover it with the marinade. Cover the lamb, refrigerate, and allow the mixture to marinate for 2 hours.

2. Heat the oil in a large, heavy skillet over low heat. Add the onions and sauté them for 5 minutes. Add the lamb cubes and sauté for 1 minute. Add the stock or water and bring the mixture to a simmer. Simmer for 40 to 50 minutes, uncovered, or until the meat is tender. The sauce should be very thick, but be careful to keep enough moisture in the skillet to keep it from burning. Remove the bay leaves before serving.

Lamb and Mchicha, a One-Dish Meal

Yield: 4 servings   Heat Scale: Medium

Thanks to Richard Sterling for this recipe he collected while touring Kenya. Mchicha is a ground-crawling, small-leaf vegetable resembling spinach that is used frequently in local cooking; however, Richard suggests fresh spinach as a good substitute.

1 pound mchicha, chopped (or substitute fresh spinach)
1 (14-ounce [392 g]) can coconut milk
1 teaspoon (5 mL) ground turmeric
½ teaspoon (2.5 mL) ground cloves
½ teaspoon (2.5 mL) ground cinnamon
1 teaspoon (5 mL) freshly ground cayenne
1 teaspoon (5 mL) freshly ground black pepper
1 teaspoon (5 mL) salt
Vegetable oil for frying
1 onion, peeled and chopped fine
1 (16-ounce [454 g]) can chopped tomatoes, with their juice
1 bell pepper, stem and seeds removed, finely chopped
3 medium potatoes, peeled and diced
½ pound (224 g) coarsely ground lamb

1. Combine the mchicha or spinach, coconut, milk, turmeric, cloves, cinnamon, cayenne, pepper, and salt in a large pan. Bring to a simmer and cook for 5 minutes. Set aside.
2. In a skillet, heat the vegetable oil over medium heat. Add the onion, tomatoes, and bell pepper and sauté until the onion is translucent. Remove this mixture from the pan. Add more oil to the pan. Add the potatoes and fry them for 5 to 7 minutes. Drain the potatoes and set them aside.
3. Place the meat in a large pot with water to cover and simmer until the meat is tender. Add all the other ingredients to the pot and simmer for an additional 20 minutes.

Marinated and Grilled Round Steak
(Tsitsinga)

Yield: 4–5 servings   Heat Scale: Medium

Tsitsinga requires some marinating, which helps to flavor and tenderize the meat. The original version of this dish calls for roasted corn flour, or ablemanu. Since it is difficult to find, I suggest you substitute oven -toasted corn meal. Serve this dish with hot, cooked rice; a salad; and a African hot sauce from Chapter 2.

1 cup (236 mL) vegetable oil, divided
2 tablespoons (30 mL) red wine vinegar
1 teaspoon (5 mL) salt
1 (1-pound [454 g]) round steak, cut into 1-inch (2.5 cm) cubes
½ cup (118 mL) chopped onion
1 (2-inch [5 cm]) piece fresh ginger, peeled
3 jalapeño chiles, stems and seeds removed
1 tomato, peeled
½ cup (118 mL) corn meal, roasted in a 350°F (180°C) oven for 10 minutes

1. In a flat, ceramic dish, mix together ½ cup (118 mL) of the oil, the vinegar, and the salt. Add the meat and toss to coat. Marinate in the refrigerator for at least 1 hour.
2. In a blender, purée the onion, ginger, chiles, and tomato. Transfer the purée to a small bowl and set it aside.
3. Thread the meat onto skewers and grill it until it is half done. Remove the meat from the skewers and toss it with the vegetable purée to thoroughly coat it. Re-skewer the meat, sprinkle it with the corn meal, drizzle it with the remaining oil, and grill it until it is done. Serve immediately.

Yesiga T'ibs
(Beef Berbere)

Yield: 4–6 servings   Heat Scale: Medium-Hot

This dish is very common in Ethiopia. I've included the ingredients used most frequently, but an individual cook will often add a little of this and a little of that. Part of the rich flavor of this dish comes from caramelizing the onions.

1½ cups (354 mL) chopped onion
1 tablespoon (15 mL) vegetable oil
⅔ cup (158 mL) Qibe (Ethiopian Curried Butter; page 36)
1 cup (236 mL) Berbere (Ethiopian Chile Paste; page 27)
¾ cup (177 mL) dry red wine
1½ pounds (680 g) beef, cut into 1-inch (2.5 cm) cubes
¼ teaspoon (1.25 mL) ground cardamom
½ teaspoon (2.5 mL) salt
1 clove garlic, peeled and minced
¼ teaspoon (1.25 mL) freshly ground black pepper

1. Heat a medium, heavy skillet over low heat. Add the onions and oil and sauté them slowly until they are brownish in color, about 10 minutes. Stir occasionally to keep them from burning.

2. Add the Qibe, Berbere, and wine and simmer the mixture for 2 minutes. Add the beef, cardamom, salt, garlic, and pepper. Cover and simmer for 20 to 30 minutes, until the meat is tender.

Pepper-Peanut Beef Kebabs

Yield: 4–6 servings   Heat Scale: Medium-Hot

The combination of two ingredients native to the tropics, peppers and peanuts, is a natural in these kebabs. This recipe comes from my good friend, Jeff Gerlach, who was in Nigeria with the Peace Corps. In Nigeria, these kebabs are served hot off the grill, and Jeff says they can be found on every street corner. Warning: These are extremely addictive. (Note: This recipe requires advance preparation.)

1½ pounds (680 g) beef, cut in 1½–2 inch (3.5–5 cm) cubes
12 ounces (350 mL) beer
⅔ cup (158 mL) crushed dried red New Mexican chile, seeds included
1½ cups (354 mL) crushed peanuts
⅔ cup (158 mL) crushed dried red New Mexican chile, seeds included

1. Marinate the beef in the beer for 3 to 4 hours.

2. Combine the chiles and peanuts in a shallow dish. Roll the beef cubes in this mixture until they are completely covered. Thread the beef onto skewers and grill over charcoal until done.

Papaya Ginger Beef with Piri-Piris

Yield: 4 servings   Heat Scale: Medium

Thanks to Michelle Cox of Malindi, Kenya, for this terrific recipe. She likes this recipe in particular because papaya is one of her favorite fruits. It is always eaten with lime juice sprinkled over it. Papaya is also a natural meat tenderizer—just place slices on both sides of the piece of meat you wish to tenderize, and let it sit at room temperature for an hour. Kenyan local wisdom also says papaya is good for digestion. Medicinally, it's applied to jellyfish stings to draw out the toxins.

1 pound (454 g) sirloin
1 barely ripe papaya
2 cups (473 mL) ice water mixed with 1 tablespoon (15 mL) salt
2 tablespoons (30 mL) vegetable oil
1 onion, peeled and thinly sliced
2 tablespoons (30 mL) crushed fresh ginger
3 green piri-piri chiles, or substitute jalapeños, stems and seeds removed, sliced very thin
2 cups (473 mL) Basic Beef Stock (page 45)
½ teaspoon (2.5 mL) salt
¼ teaspoon (1.25 mL) freshly ground black pepper
1 tablespoon (15 mL) cornstarch
½ cup (118 mL) water
1 teaspoon (5 mL) soy sauce

1. Place the beef in the freezer for 30 minutes to facilitate slicing.
2. Remove the seeds from the papaya, peel it, and cut the flesh into 1-inch (2.5 cm) cubes. Add the papaya cubes to the salted ice water and let them soak for 1 hour. Rinse the cubes well in cold water and drain.
3. Remove the beef from the freezer. Slice it as thinly as possible and set it aside.
4. In a large, heavy skillet, heat the oil over medium heat. Add the onions and sauté until they are golden. Add the beef, ginger, chiles, and papaya. Stir-fry for a few minutes, taking care not to break the papaya pieces. Add the stock, salt, and pepper, and bring to a boil.
5. Combine the cornstarch with the water and soy sauce. Add this mixture to the meat, and simmer until the dish has thickened. Serve hot with freshly cooked rice.

Romazava

Yield: 4 servings　　　　　　　　　　　　　　　　　　Heat Scale: Varies

According to one of my writers, Judith Ritter, this is the "national dish" of Mada-gascar. Serve it over hot cooked rice or a simple pilaf, topped with L'Exotic Sauce Dynamite (page 90) to taste. For a salad, serve cucumbers marinated in vinegar.

2 teaspoons (10 mL) vegetable oil
1 (1-pound [454 g]) beef shank, cut into small cubes
½ medium onion, chopped
2 cloves garlic, peeled and minced
1 teaspoon (5 mL) minced fresh ginger
2 ripe tomatoes, chopped
1 cup (236 mL) Basic Beef Stock (page 45)
1 bunch watercress, chopped
½ pound (224 g) fresh spinach, chopped
½ pound (224 g) Chinese cabbage, chopped
Salt, to taste
Freshly ground black pepper, to taste

1. In a large skillet, heat the oil over medium-high heat. Add the beef, onion, garlic, and ginger and sauté until the beef is browned. Add the tomatoes and broth, cover, and reduce the heat to low. Cook for 45 minutes to 1 hour. Add the watercress, spinach, and cabbage and cook for 10 minutes.
2. Serve the Romazava over rice, accompanied by the Madagascar Sauce Dynamite.

Black Lamb Curry

Yield: 4 servings　　　　　　　　　　　　　　　　　　Heat Scale: Hot

Sri Lanka is famous for its fiery cuisine, and this is one of the hottest of all Sri Lankan dishes.

3 tablespoons (45 mL) Hot Madras Curry Paste (page 29), or less for a milder curry
2½ cups (591 mL) water
1 pound (454 g) lamb, cut into 1-inch (2.5 cm) cubes
2 tablespoons (30 mL) vegetable oil
4 yellow wax hot chiles, stems and seeds removed, finely chopped
1 onion, peeled and chopped

1. In a blender, purée the curry powder and ½ cup (118 mL) of the water to a smooth, thin paste. Transfer the purée to a bowl. Toss the lamb cubes in the mixture and marinate for an hour at room temperature.
2. In a sauté pan, heat the oil over medium heat. Add the chiles and onion and sauté until soft. Add the lamb with the marinade and the remaining 2 cups (473 mL) water. Bring to a boil, reduce the heat, and simmer, cov-ered, until the lamb is tender, about 1 hour, or until the lamb starts to fall apart. Add more water if necessary.

Raan Shahnshahi
(Curried Lamb Shanks)

Yield: 6 servings   Heat Scale: Medium-Hot

Traditionally, an entire leg of lamb is marinated in the masala overnight and cooked over low heat for two or three hours. A simplified version follows.

1 tablespoon (15 mL) saffron strands
4 tablespoons (60 mL) warm milk
1 tablespoon (15 mL) almonds
1 tablespoon (15 mL) walnuts
1 tablespoon (15 mL) cashews
1 tablespoon (15 mL) peanuts
1 tablespoon (15 mL) raisins
1 teaspoon (5 mL) poppy seeds
1 cup (236 mL) coconut milk
1 (1-inch [2.5 cm]) piece ginger, peeled and minced
10 cloves garlic, peeled
1 small green papaya, peeled, seeds removed, diced
½ teaspoon (2.5 mL) ground nutmeg
½ teaspoon (2.5 mL) ground mace
1 tablespoon (15 mL) ground coriander
1 tablespoon (15 mL) ground cumin
6 fresh red chiles, such as serranos, stems removed
2 cups (473 mL) plain yogurt
Salt, to taste
4 pounds (1.82 kg) lamb shanks, chopped with a cleaver into 1-inch (2.5 cm) long sections
4 teaspoons (20 mL) ghee or vegetable oil
2 large onions, peeled and finely chopped

1. In a blender, combine the saffron and milk and purée into a smooth paste. Set aside.
2. In a food processor or blender, grind together the almonds, walnuts, cashews, peanuts, raisins, poppy seeds, and coconut milk into a smooth paste. Set aside.
3. In a food processor or blender, grind together the ginger, garlic, papaya, nutmeg, mace, coriander, cumin, and chiles into a paste. Combine this paste with the yogurt, add the salt, and set the mixture aside.
4. In a large saucepan, combine the nut paste, the yogurt paste, and the lamb shanks and marinate for 30 minutes.
5. Heat the ghee or oil in a skillet over medium heat for about 1 minute. Add the onions and cook for 1 minute. Add the shanks with the marinade and reduce the heat to low. Cook, covered, for 45 to 50 minutes, stirring occasionally and adding cold water if the mixture is too thick. Add the saffron mixture and continue cooking, covered, for another 10 minutes.

Keema Bafat
(Minced Meat Curry)

Yield: 4 servings   Heat Scale: Medium

This popular dish from the coastal region of Karnataka uses the basic Hurry Curry powder. It is traditionally prepared with beef or lamb, but chicken may be substituted (reduce the cooking time by 7 minutes). Serve this with any of the rice recipes in Chapter 13.

2 tablespoons (30 mL) vegetable oil
1 tablespoon (15 mL) ghee
1 large onion, peeled and chopped
6 cloves garlic, peeled and minced
1 (1-inch [2.5 cm]) piece ginger, minced
1 tablespoon (15 mL) Hurry Curry (page 29)
1 pound (454 g) minced beef or lamb
Salt, to taste
¼ cup (59 mL) chopped cilantro or mint leaves

1. In a skillet, heat the oil over medium heat for 1 minute. Add the ghee and the onion and cook until the onion wilts, about 1 minute. Add the garlic and ginger and sauté for 1 minute. Add the Hurry Curry, lower the heat, and cook for 1 minute.
2. Add the minced meat, mix well, and cook for 20 minutes. Sprinkle with cold water from time to time. Add the salt and stir. Serve garnished with the cilantro or mint leaves.

Lamb Sukuti
(Nepal-Style Smoked Lamb)

Yield: 4–6 servings   Heat Scale: Medium

Mike Stines writes, "My youngest daughter recently visited Tibet and Nepal. She came back with this recipe that I've modified a bit. Traditionally, Sukuti is prepared with a dried meat, almost like a jerky. This recipe could also be prepared with beef or buffalo, although beef is never eaten in Nepal. This recipe requires advance preparation to allow the meat to marinate."

½ cup (118 mL) chopped yellow onion
2 tablespoons (30 mL) dark molasses
2 tablespoons (30 mL) clover honey
2 tablespoons (30 mL) olive oil
2 tablespoons (30 mL) minced ginger
1 tablespoon (15 mL) ground cumin
1 tablespoon (15 mL) chili paste
1 teaspoon (5 mL) ground Szechuan peppercorns
1 teaspoon (5 mL) ground turmeric
½ teaspoon (2.5 mL) grated nutmeg
¼ teaspoon (1.25 mL) fennel seed
Coarse kosher salt, to taste
Freshly ground black pepper, to taste
2 pounds (1.1 kg) boneless lamb shoulder, cut into thin 3-inch (7.5 cm) long slices

1. In a food processor, combine all the ingredients except the lamb and process into a smooth paste.
2. Transfer the paste to a large bowl. Add the lamb pieces and mix to coat. Cover and marinate for at least 2 hours.
3. Prepare a grill for indirect cooking, using wood chips for the smoke, and place the lamb pieces on the cooler side of the grill. Smoke for about 1 hour or until the slices are slightly crisp.

Sindhi Gohst
(Nutty Curried Lamb from Sind)

Yield: 6 servings   Heat Scale: Medium

The region of Sind in Pakistan is well-known for its many lamb and beef dishes. This dish is marinated for at least six hours in a fragrant paste of onion, garlic, ginger, and dried spices, so it takes advance preparation.

3 large onions, peeled and chopped
2 large ripe tomatoes, chopped
8 cloves garlic, peeled
2 green chiles, such as serranos, stems removed, halved
1 (2-inch [5 cm]) piece ginger, peeled
1 tablespoon (15 mL) ground cumin
2 teaspoons (10 mL) ground coriander
1 teaspoon (5 mL) ground turmeric
1 teaspoon (5 mL) ground cayenne
2 tablespoons (30 mL) distilled white vinegar
3 pounds (1.36 kg) boneless lamb or beef, cut into 1-inch (2.5 cm) cubes
2 teaspoons (10 mL) fennel seeds
¼ cup (59 mL) raw cashews
¼ cup (59 mL) raw almonds
Salt, to taste
6 tablespoons (90 mL) vegetable oil

1. In a food processor or blender, grind the onions, tomatoes, garlic, chiles, ginger, cumin, coriander, turmeric, cayenne, and vinegar. Transfer this paste to a large bowl.
2. Puncture the lamb cubes with a sharp knife in many places. Add the lamb to the paste and marinate at room temperature for 6 hours.
3. In a skillet over low heat, cook the lamb and fennel seeds, covered, for about 1 hour or until the lamb is tender. Sprinkle water occasionally.
4. Remove the lid and add the cashews, almonds, and salt. Raise the heat and cook until all the liquid evaporates.
5. Add the oil to the lamb, reduce the heat, and simmer for about 5 minutes before serving.

Ghurka Pork Curry

Yield: 4–6 servings   Heat Scale: Medium-Hot

Gurkhas, the sturdy soldiers from Nepal, took this curry formula wherever they went, be it Malaya or the Falkland Islands. The yogurt in this curry tempers the chiles. (Note: This recipe requires advance preparation.)

1 teaspoon (5 mL) distilled white vinegar
1 tablespoon (15 mL) ground cayenne
2 pounds (1.1 kg) lean and boneless pork, cut into 1-inch (2.5 cm) cubes
2 cups (473 mL) plain yogurt
1 (2-inch [5 cm]) piece ginger, peeled and minced
1 teaspoon (5 mL) vegetable oil
¼ cup (59 mL) ghee
1 teaspoon (5 mL) freshly ground black pepper
1 teaspoon (5 mL) ground turmeric
1 cup (236 mL) water
Salt, to taste
½ cup (118 mL) cilantro leaves
1 teaspoon (5 mL) ground cumin
1 teaspoon (5 mL) ground nutmeg
½ teaspoon (2.5 mL) ground cloves
½ teaspoon (2.5 mL) ground cardamom

1. In a bowl, combine the vinegar and cayenne. Add the meat and toss to coat. Add the yogurt and ginger and marinate the meat for about 3 hours at room temperature.
2. Heat the oil in a skillet over low heat for 1 minute. Add the ghee, the pork with its marinade, the black pepper, the turmeric, the water, and the salt and bring to a rapid boil. Lower the heat, cover the skillet, and simmer for 40 minutes.
3. Add the cilantro, cumin, nutmeg, cloves, and cardamom and stir well. Serve hot.

Pungent Pork Vindaloo

Yield: 6 servings   Heat Scale: Hot

Vindaloo describes a style of Indian cooking where the meat or fish is marinated in a vinegar-based sauce and then cooked in that marinade. This recipe can also be used for beef or lamb and, like a pasta sauce, is best if prepared a day in advance and reheated. Add ground cayenne if more heat is desired. (Note: This recipe requires advance preparation.)

½ cup (118 mL) apple cider vinegar
4–5 tablespoons (60–75 mL) vegetable oil, divided
2 teaspoons (10 mL) crushed red chile
2 teaspoons (10 mL) minced ginger
1 teaspoon (5 mL) ground cardamom
1 teaspoon (5 mL) ground cinnamon
½ teaspoon (2.5 mL) ground cloves
½ teaspoon (2.5 mL) ground turmeric
Freshly ground black pepper, to taste
1½ pounds (680 g) pork, cut in 1-inch (2.5 cm) cubes
1 medium onion, peeled and chopped
1 medium potato, peeled and cubed
2 cups (473 mL) Classic Chicken Stock (page 46)
2 cups (473 mL) cooked rice

1. In a nonreactive bowl, combine the vinegar, 3 tablespoons (45 mL) of the oil, the chile, the ginger, the cardamom, the cinnamon, the cloves, the turmeric, and the black pepper. Add the pork and toss until well coated. Cover and marinate for 2 to 3 hours at room temperature or overnight in the refrigerator. Remove the pork, drain, and reserve the marinade.
2. In a heavy skillet, heat a little of the remaining oil over medium-high heat. Add the pork and sauté until browned. Add more oil if needed to keep the meat from burning. Add the onions and potato and continue to sauté until the onions are softened and the potatoes are browned.
3. Add the reserved marinade and the broth. Bring to a boil, reduce the heat, and simmer until the meat is very tender and the sauce is thickened, about 30 minutes. Add more broth if needed.
4. Serve the vindaloo over the hot rice.

Moo Pad Bai Kra Pow
(Spicy Sautéed Pork with Chiles and Basil)

Yield: 4–6 servings   Heat Scale: Medium

From Thailand comes this hot and spicy, delicious, easy-to-prepare dish. The bai kra pow or holy basil (also called purple basil, Thai basil, or Oriental basil) used in this recipe is often available in Asian markets; if you can't find it, substitute fresh mint. Serve this dish with cooked rice noodles.

2 tablespoons (30 mL) vegetable oil
6 garlic cloves, peeled and finely minced
5 fresh green serrano or jalapeño chiles, stems and seeds removed, finely chopped
2 pounds (1.1 kg) ground pork
3 tablespoons (45 mL) fish sauce
2 tablespoons (30 mL) dark soy sauce
¼ cup (59 mL) sugar
½ cup (118 mL) chopped, fresh bai kra pow (holy basil)

1. Heat the oil in a large wok or skillet over medium heat. Add the garlic and sauté it carefully, taking care not to burn it. Add the chiles and stir-fry for 30 seconds. Add the pork and continue cooking, breaking up the meat, until all the pink is gone.
2. Stir in the remaining ingredients and cook until the mixture is well-blended and hot, about 1 minute.

Ma Ho or Mah Haw
(Thai Minced Pork or Galloping Horses)

Yield: 4 servings   Heat Scale: Medium

"Galloping Horses" is literally translated as "horses of the Haw people," a tribal group who migrated to northern Thailand from Yunan, China. The combination of pork, fish sauce, sugar, peanuts, and cilantro creates a unique taste sensation. Serve this over hot cooked rice. It is also sometimes served as an appetizer over fruit.

2 tablespoons (30 mL) vegetable oil
5 cloves garlic, peeled and minced
4 fresh cilantro roots, crushed (or substitute 2 tablespoons [30 mL] chopped fresh cilantro leaves and stems)
1 pound (454 g) coarsely ground or finely minced lean pork
4 tablespoons (60 mL) coarsely ground roasted peanuts
3 tablespoons (45 mL) fish sauce
Freshly ground black pepper, to taste
3 tablespoons (45 mL) palm sugar or brown sugar
3 fresh jalapeño or serrano chiles, stems and seeds removed, finely chopped
3 tablespoons (45 mL) chopped fresh cilantro

1. Heat the vegetable oil in a wok or skillet over low heat. Add the garlic and cilantro roots and fry for a few seconds. Add the pork, peanuts, fish sauce, pepper, sugar, chiles, and cilantro. Cook until the mixture is dark brown in color and the liquid starts to thicken.

Variation
Serve fresh, sliced mandarin oranges and fresh, cubed pineapple with this dish.

Neua Pad Prik
(Stir-Fried Mushroom Chile Beef)
Yield: 4–6 servings   Heat Scale: Medium

This stir-fry dish from Thailand contains some interesting ingredients that all complement each other in taste and textures. It also contains bell peppers and hot and spicy chile peppers, known as prik in Thailand. Because the flavors are so intense, I suggest serving it with hot, cooked rice.

1 (2-inch [5 cm]) piece fresh ginger
1 tablespoon (15 mL) soy sauce
3 cloves garlic, peeled
1 tablespoon (15 mL) palm sugar (or substitute dark brown sugar)
1½ pounds (680 g) tender beef fillet, thinly sliced
2 tablespoons (30 mL) vegetable oil
1 green bell pepper, seeded, cored, and cut into ½-inch (1 cm) pieces
3 dried Chinese or shiitake mushrooms, rehydrated in hot water, rinsed, and sliced, soaking liquid reserved
1 (12.5-ounce [350 g]) jar miniature (baby) corn, drained and rinsed
3 serrano or jalapeño chiles, stems and seeds removed, cut into rings
4 green onions, white and light green parts, sliced
⅔ cup (158 mL) Basic Beef Stock (page 45)
1 tablespoon (15 mL) fish sauce
2 tablespoons (30 mL) oyster sauce

1. In a mini-blender, purée the ginger, soy sauce, garlic, and sugar until smooth. If it becomes too thick to mix, add 1 teaspoon (5 mL) or more of the soy sauce. Place the meat slices in a large bowl, add the puréed mixture, and toss to coat. Allow the beef to marinate for 30 minutes at room temperature.
2. Heat the oil over high heat in a wok or large skillet. Add the beef strips and stir-fry until the pink is gone. Lower the heat slightly and push the meat to one side of the pan. Add the bell pepper and mushrooms and sauté them for 30 seconds. Add the corn, chiles, and green onions and combine with the beef strips. Add the beef stock and the mushroom liquid and cook over medium-low for 1 minute.
3. Stir in the fish sauce and oyster sauce and serve hot.

Gaeng Mussamun
(Thai Muslim Curry)

Yield: 6–8 servings   Heat Scale: Medium to Hot

The spices in this curry, similar to those used in garam masala, indicate its Indian origins. This very festive curry is usually served at special occasions, such as weddings. The final result should have a taste that balances the sweet, the sour, and the salty; if it seems too sweet, add a little more lime juice.

4 cups (.95 L) coconut milk
2 pounds (1.1 kg) chuck roast or another inexpensive cut of beef, trimmed of all fat and cut into 1½-inch (3.5 cm) chunks
1 cup (236 mL) dry roasted peanuts
½–¾ cup (118–177 mL) Gaeng Mussamun (Muslim Curry Paste, page 39)
½ cup (118 mL) coconut milk (optional)
4 (2–3 inch [5–7.5 cm]) cinnamon sticks
6 whole cardamom seeds
3 tablespoons (45 mL) fish sauce
2 tablespoons (30 mL) palm sugar (or substitute dark brown sugar)
3 tablespoons (45 mL) tamarind sauce
2 tablespoons (30 mL) lime juice

1. In a large, heavy skillet, bring the coconut milk to a slow boil. Add the beef chunks and peanuts and simmer for 45 minutes to 1 hour, until the meat is tender. With a slotted spoon, transfer the beef to another pan and keep warm.
2. Continue to boil the coconut milk until it is reduced by about half. Stir in the curry paste and the coconut cream, if desired. Simmer the mixture for 1 minute, and then return the meat to the pan. Stir in the remaining ingredients and simmer for 5 more minutes.

Gaeng Ped Korat
(Hot Beef Curry with Lemongrass and Citrus)

Yield: 4 servings   Heat Scale: Hot

This spicy curry comes from Korat, northeast of Bangkok, and it is infused with freshly ground spices, chiles, and lemongrass. Remember, freshly ground spices add more flavor and freshness to the dish than spices that are kept in bottles in your cupboard. Serve this dish with hot, cooked rice.

6 dried red cayenne or Thai chiles, seeded, soaked in water until soft, and chopped
Zest of 1 lime
1 tablespoon (15 mL) whole black peppercorns
1 tablespoon (15 mL) coarsely chopped fresh ginger
1 teaspoon (5 mL) shrimp paste
2 stalks lemongrass, white bulb lightly mashed
5 shallots, peeled and coarsely chopped
1 tablespoon (15 mL) chopped fresh cilantro
½ teaspoon (2.5 mL) cumin seeds
2 tablespoons (30 mL) vegetable oil, divided
1 pound (454 g) lean ground beef, or 1 pound (454 g) lean boneless beef cut into paper-thin strips
1 cup (236 mL) Classic Chicken stock (page 46)
3 tablespoons (45 mL) fish sauce

1. In a food processor or blender, purée the chiles, lime zest, black pepper-corns, ginger, shrimp paste, lemongrass, shallots, cilantro, and cumin, add-ing 1 or 2 teaspoons (10 mL) of the oil to make a paste. Scrape this mixture into a large bowl, add the beef, and mix until the beef is well coated.
2. Heat 1 tablespoon (15 mL) of the remaining oil over medium heat in a wok or large skillet. Add the beef-curry mixture and stir-fry for 1 minute, or until the beef loses its pink tinge. Add the chicken stock and bring the mixture to a boil. Cover and simmer for 30 minutes, or until the beef is cooked (or the strips are tender). Stir in the fish sauce and serve.

Gaeng Nuea
(Beef in Red Curry Sauce)

Yield: 6 servings   Heat Scale: Hot

This is a classic, hot and spicy Thai curry dish that is often prepared at home. Traditionally, one of the many kinds of Thai eggplants, makeua poh or makeua peuang, are used, but these are sometimes difficult to find. The flavor won't be the same, but feel free to substitute cubes of Japanese eggplant or, for the look of a traditional Thai curry, add some green peas.

3 cups (708 mL) coconut milk, divided
5 tablespoons (75 mL) Gaeng Ped (Red Curry Paste, page 37)
1½ pounds (680 g) prepared chuck steak, thinly sliced
1 teaspoon (5 mL) lemon zest or 2 crushed kaffir lime leaves
½ teaspoon (2.5 mL) salt
¾ cup (177 mL) bamboo shoots
3 tablespoons (45 mL) fish sauce
2 teaspoons (10 mL) palm sugar or brown sugar
1 cup (236 mL) eggplant, zucchini, or yellow squash, cut into ¾-inch (1.5 cm) cubes
2 green serrano or jalapeño chiles, stems and seeds removed, sliced into rings
½ cup (118 mL) coarsely chopped fresh basil leaves

1. In a large, heavy Dutch oven, heat 1 cup (236 mL) of the coconut milk. When it is hot, stir in the curry paste and cook until little drops of oil appear on the surface, about 5 minutes. Continue to cook, stirring, for 1 minute.
2. Add the meat and simmer the mixture for 5 minutes, making sure some liquid remains in the pan. If it starts to disappear before the meat is cooked, add a little more coconut milk. At the end of the 5 minutes, add the remaining coconut milk, lemon zest or lime leaves, salt, bamboo shoots, fish sauce, sugar, and eggplant and simmer for 10 minutes, or until the beef is tender.
3. Stir in the chiles and the basil and simmer for 2 minutes. Serve with steamed rice.

Singapore Noodles in Spiced Sauce

Yield: 2–4 servings

Heat Scale: Mild to Medium, depending on how much sauce you use

---

This recipe comes from the owners of the Golden Dragon Restaurant in Colorado Springs, Colorado, who have traveled extensively. Donald Louie, his sister Sue Louie, and the third sibling, Linda Gant, collected this recipe on their travels and have adopted it to use in their restaurant. As Sue says of this recipe, "The first bite is a bit mild, but as you keep eating, the dish seems to get hotter and hotter."

For the Spiced Sauce:
1 teaspoon (5 mL) soy sauce
½ teaspoon (2.5 mL) Asian chile paste
½ teaspoon (2.5 mL) hoisin sauce
½ teaspoon (2.5 mL) cooking sherry
½ teaspoon (2.5 mL) rice vinegar
½ teaspoon (2.5 mL) ground ginger
½ teaspoon (2.5 mL) minced garlic
½ teaspoon (2.5 mL) ground hot red chile
1 teaspoon (5 mL) Major Grey's Mango Chutney

1. In a saucepan, combine all the sauce ingredients and cook over medium heat for 5 minutes, stirring constantly.

For the Noodles:
1 cup (236 mL) rice stick noodles, broken into pieces
3–4 tablespoons vegetable oil
1 pound (454 g) cooked or raw pork
1 cup (236 mL) bean sprouts
1 cup (236 mL) sliced bok choy
1 cup (236 mL) chopped red and green bell peppers
1 cup (236 mL) Classic Chicken Stock (page 46)
12 small shrimp, cleaned, cooked, and peeled
¼ teaspoon (1.25 mL) curry powder
1 pinch salt
1 pinch sugar

1. Place the rice noodles in a bowl, add enough hot water to cover, and soak for 5 minutes. Drain the noodles and set them aside.
2. In a wok or a large skillet, heat the oil over medium-high heat. Add the pork and cook until browned. Add the bean sprouts, bok choy, bell pepper, and chicken stock and bring to a boil. Add the drained rice noodles, Spiced Sauce, shrimp, curry powder, salt, and sugar. Toss well in the wok until all of the ingredients are hot, and serve immediately.

Babi Assam
(Sautéed Pork in Tamarind Sauce)

Yield: 4–6 servings   Heat Scale: Hot

This dish is one hot and spicy Nonya specialty from Singapore. If you ever go to Singapore, make sure you get the taste buds tuned up—hot and spicy is a way of life, just as it is here in the Southwest. Serve this intense dish with hot, cooked white rice and a cool cucumber salad. And forget to count the fat calories on this one.

2 tablespoons (30 mL) vegetable oil
4 candlenuts or macadamia nuts, ground
1 tablespoon (15 mL) shrimp paste
2 shallots, peeled and minced
2 tablespoons (30 mL) preserved, salted soybeans, pounded into a paste
1¼ pounds (568 g) pork belly, cut into thick strips, lightly sautéed and drained (or substitute thick-cut bacon)
1 cup (236 mL) tamarind sauce
4 fresh green serrano or jalapeño chiles, stems and seeds removed, thinly sliced
1 cup (236 mL) Classic Chicken Stock (page 46), divided
2 tablespoons (30 mL) sugar, divided

1. Heat the oil in a wok or large skillet over low heat. Add the candlenuts, shrimp paste, and shallots and sauté until the mixture is lightly browned. Add the soybean paste and cook, stirring, for 1 minute.
2. Add the pork, tamarind sauce, chiles, ½ cup (118 mL) of the chicken stock, and 1 tablespoon (15 mL) of the sugar and bring to a boil. Reduce the heat to a simmer, half cover the wok, and simmer for 30 minutes, stirring once. If the mixture seems too thick, add a little more stock. Taste the mixture, and if it seems too tart, sprinkle in more of the sugar and simmer a few more minutes.

Spicy Mixed Satays

Yield: 4 servings   Heat Scale: Medium

When food writer Rosemary Ann Ogilvie was in Bali, she collected this classic recipe for me. She says, "Probably the most well-known of all the Indonesian dishes are the satays. They can be served as an appetizer as well as an entrée. Soak the bamboo skewers overnight or for a couple of hours to prevent them from burning while grilling."

For the Satay Sauce:
½ cup (118 mL) peanuts, roasted and salted
1 onion, peeled and chopped
½ cup (118 mL) creamy peanut butter
2 cloves garlic, peeled and minced
⅓ cup (79 mL) chutney, as hot as you prefer
¼ cup (59 mL) peanut oil
1 tablespoon (15 mL) light soy sauce
¼ cup (59 mL) lemon juice
6 dried birdseye chiles (chiltepins), stems removed, soaked in water, minced fine (or substitute piquin chiles)

1. In a food processor or blender, blend or process the peanuts until finely chopped, but not ground smooth. Add the onion and process for another 20 seconds. Add the peanut butter, garlic, chutney, oil, soy sauce, lemon juice, and chiles and continue to process until smooth.

For the Satays:
1 pound (454 g) rump steak, cut in thin strips
6 large chicken breast fillets, cut in 1–1½-inch (2.5–3.5 cm) cubes
1 (1-pound [454 g]) pork fillet or boned pork loin, cut in 1–1½-inch (2.5–3.5 cm) cubes

1. Thread the meats onto skewers. (Don't combine the meats—use one type of meat per skewer.) Brush the meats well with the Satay Sauce, and grill or barbecue the satays until tender, brushing occasionally with the sauce while cooking.
2. Serve with the remaining Satay Sauce for dipping.

Daging Masak Bali
(Balinese-Style Beef Strips)

Yield: 6 servings   Heat Scale: Hot

Although a majority of the island population are Balinese Hindu, there are still some hot and tasty beef dishes to be found. These could be found at a snack food stall or a large feast. This Balinese dish is usually served with hot rice, cooked vegetables, and a selection of the sambals in Chapter 2.

4 cloves garlic, peeled and minced
2 tablespoons (30 mL) chopped fresh ginger
6 red or green serrano or jalapeño chiles, seeded and chopped
½ teaspoon (2.5 mL) shrimp paste
1½ cups (354 mL) chopped onion
3 tablespoons (45 mL) vegetable oil
1½ pounds (680 g) beef, thinly sliced
1 cup (236 mL) water
3 tablespoons (45 mL) tamarind sauce
1½ tablespoons (22.5 mL) soy sauce
2 teaspoons (10 mL) palm sugar (or substitute brown sugar)
Salt, to taste

1. In a blender or food processor, blend the garlic, ginger, chiles, shrimp paste, and onions until smooth.
2. In a large, heavy skillet or wok, heat the oil over high heat. Add the blended mixture and fry, stirring constantly, for 4 to 5 minutes until the mixture no longer sticks to the pan. Add the beef strips and stir-fry them until there is no pink showing. Add the remaining ingredients and simmer until the beef is tender and most of the liquid has evaporated, about 10 minutes.

Rendang
(West Sumatran Rendang)

Yield: 6 servings   Heat Scale: Medium

Here is the traditional way the Sumatrans cook the often-tough meat of the water buffalo—by slowly simmering it in coconut milk. This recipe takes some time to make, but it's worth it. It keeps for months in the freezer, so make a lot. Serve the rendang with any of the rice dishes in Chapter 13.

6 shallots, peeled
3 cloves garlic, peeled
5 fresh red serrano or jalapeño chiles, seeded
1 tablespoon (15 mL) freshly grated ginger
1 teaspoon (5 mL) ground turmeric
1 pinch salt
8 cups (1.9 L) coconut milk
3½ pounds (1.59 kg) chuck roast, cut into 1-inch (2.5 cm) cubes

1. In a blender or food processor, grind the shallots, garlic, chiles, ginger, turmeric, and salt to a coarse paste.
2. Heat the coconut milk in a large pot. Add the paste and the meat. Cook over low heat, uncovered, for 1½ to 2 hours, or until the meat is quite tender. Stir the mixture every 15 minutes or so. The sauce will become very thick.
3. Raise the heat and, stirring continuously, cook the mixture until all the sauce is incorporated into the meat and the meat turns golden brown, about 30 minutes.

Abon Daging
(Hot and Spicy Fried Shredded Beef)

Yield: 6 servings   Heat Scale: Medium

This dish is also known as dendeng pedas in Indonesia and be sampi mesitsit in Bali. In the most basic recipe, beef is boiled, shredded, and then fried with chiles and various spices. In Bali, this dish is served fresh over rice or deep fried to serve as a finger food appetizer. Research leads me to believe that, in times past, this cooking method was used on cuts of old, tough beef to make something interesting and palatable.

2 pounds (1.1 kg) beef arm roast
1 teaspoon (5 mL) salt
4 cloves garlic, peeled
2 teaspoons (10 mL) dried shrimp paste
1 tablespoon (15 mL) fresh lime juice
1 teaspoon (5 mL) whole black peppercorns
1 teaspoon (5 mL) coriander seeds
¼ teaspoon (1.25 mL) ground coriander
2 teaspoons (10 mL) palm sugar (or substitute brown sugar)
2 tablespoons (30 mL) sliced galangal (or substitute 1 teaspoon [5 mL] powdered galangal)
4 fresh serrano or jalapeño chiles, stems and seeds removed
3 tablespoons (45 mL) oil (peanut preferred)

1. Wash the beef, place it in a heavy pot with enough water to cover it, and add the salt. Bring the water to a boil, then reduce the heat to a simmer and cover the pot. Cook for 1½ to 2 hours, or until the meat is very tender. Transfer the meat to a colander and let it drain until it is cool enough to handle. Shred the meat using 2 forks and discard the fat.
2. In a blender, blend the garlic, shrimp paste, lime juice, peppercorns, coriander seeds, ground coriander, sugar, galangal, and chiles until smooth.
3. Heat the oil in a large, heavy skillet over low heat. Add the blended mixture and sauté for 1 to 2 minutes.
4. Add the shredded beef and stir well to coat. Serve over hot, cooked rice with vegetables from Chapter 13 and sambals from Chapter 2.

Bakso Terong
(Spicy Pork in Eggplant)

Yield: 4 servings   Heat Scale: Mild

This Indonesian recipe illustrates the use of vegetables with meat to make the meat go further. Since the eggplant has such a mild flavor, the hot sauce and garlic spices up an otherwise bland dish. Serve the eggplant with one of the side dishes from Chapter 13.

1 pound (454 g) ground pork
½ teaspoon (2.5 mL) salt
¼ teaspoon (1.25 mL) freshly ground black pepper
1 cup (236 mL) chopped onions
2 cloves garlic, peeled and minced
1 egg, beaten
2 teaspoons (10 mL) any sambal from Chapter 2 (or substitute a hot sauce such as Tabasco)
2 medium eggplants
2 tablespoons (30 mL) vegetable oil

1. Quickly sauté the pork in a skillet, drain off the excess fat, and mix the pork with the salt, pepper, onions, garlic, egg, and sambal.
2. Remove about 2 inches off the stem end of the eggplant and carefully core out the interior, leaving about a ¾-inch (1.5 cm) thick shell. Cube the cored-out eggplant flesh. In a skillet, heat the vegetable oil over medium heat. Add the chopped eggplant and sauté for about 5 minutes. Add the eggplant to the pork mixture and toss lightly to mix.
4. Stuff the pork and eggplant mixture into the cored-out eggplants.
5. Place the stuffed eggplants in a deep saucepan and add enough water to come about 3 inches (7.5 cm) up the sides of the eggplants. Bring the water to a boil, reduce the heat to a rolling simmer, and cook, covered, for 30 to 45 minutes, until the eggplants can be easily pierced with a knife. Carefully remove the eggplants from the saucepan and let them rest for 5 minutes. Then cut the eggplants into 1-inch slices, taking care that the filling doesn't fall out.
6. Arrange 2 slices on each plate and serve with additional sambal.

Indonesian Beef, Prawn, and Noodle Curry

Yield: 6–8 servings   Heat Scale: Medium

This is a great dish for a party. Food writer Rosemary Ann Ogelvie commented, "I was given this recipe twenty-five years ago when I was a teenager just discovering the delights of cooking, and I believe it still takes some beating for sheer taste!"

1 pound (454 g) tender beef, sliced into thin strips
½ pound (224 g) prawns or shrimp, shelled and deveined
1 cup (236 mL) cooked chicken, sliced into thin strips
2 tablespoons (30 mL) curry powder (freshly made or imported preferred)
2 tablespoons (30 mL) vegetable oil
1 tablespoon (15 mL) chopped celery
1 large onion, peeled and chopped
2 cups (473 mL) finely sliced carrots
1 cup (236 mL) shredded cabbage
4–6 birdseye chiles (chiltepins), stems removed, soaked in water until soft, finely minced (or substitute piquin or cayenne chiles)
½ teaspoon (2.5 mL) freshly ground black pepper
2 cloves garlic, peeled and crushed
½ pound (224 g) thin egg noodles, cooked and rinsed well
1 cup (236 mL) Classic Chicken Stock (page 46)

1. In a bowl, combine the beef, prawns, chicken, and curry powder.
2. In a skillet, heat the oil over high heat. Add the curried mixture and stir-fry for a couple minutes, or until the beef is almost done. Add the celery, onion, carrots, cabbage, chiles, pepper, and garlic and stir-fry for another 3 minutes.
3. Add the noodles and chicken stock and simmer for 7 to 10 minutes, stirring occasionally.

Satay Padang
(West Sumatra Barbecue)

Yield 10–12 servings   Heat Scale: Medium

This satay recipe is from Padang in West Sumatra. The different kinds of meats add a contrast in textures; I have listed the meats that are traditionally used, but feel free to experiment with your own combinations. The liberal use of chiles contrasts nicely with the spices and the lemongrass. Serve the barbecued meats with cubes of fresh cucumber.

For the Satay:
2 tablespoons (30 mL) peanut or corn oil
¾ cup (177 mL) chopped onion
6 garlic cloves, peeled and minced
2 beef hearts, cut into 1-inch (2.5 cm) cubes
2 pounds (1.1 kg) beef chuck, cut into 1-inch (2.5 cm) cubes
1½ pounds (680 g) veal or beef tongue, cut into 1-inch (2.5 cm) cubes
1 pound (454 g) beef tripe, cut into 1-inch (2.5 cm) cubes
4 fresh serrano or jalapeño chiles, stems and seeds removed, puréed into a paste
2 tablespoons (30 mL) chopped fresh cilantro
1 teaspoon (5 mL) ground cumin
1 teaspoon (5 mL) salt
1 tablespoon (15 mL) ground turmeric
1 tablespoon (15 mL) finely chopped fresh ginger
1 (2-inch [5 cm]) piece galangal (or double the amount of fresh ginger)
1 (3–inch [7.5 cm]) square lemon peel or bitter orange
2 salam leaves (or substitute 2 bay leaves)
1 (2-inch [5 cm]) stick cinnamon
1 cup (236 mL) water
2 stalks lemongrass, bulbs only, mashed lightly
3½ cups (826 mL) coconut milk

1. In a large, heavy skillet, heat the oil over medium heat. Add the onion and sauté for 30 seconds, then add the garlic and sauté lightly, taking care not to burn it.
2. Add the cubed meats and toss until they are coated with the onion-garlic mixture, adding more oil if necessary. Add the chiles, cilantro, cumin, salt, turmeric, ginger, galangal, lemon peel, salam leaves, cinnamon, water, and lemongrass. Cover the skillet, turn the heat to low heat, and cook for 45 minutes to 1 hour, or until the meats are tender. Stir in the coconut milk and simmer for an additional 30 minutes.
3. Using a slotted spoon, transfer the meats to a bowl.
4. Pour the meat sauce into a saucepan and measure 2½ cups (591 mL) of the sauce back into the skillet. Bring the sauce to a slow, rolling boil

For the Sauce:
1 cup (236 mL) coconut milk
½ cup (118 mL) rice flour
Reserved sauce from the meat
1 large tomato, peeled, seeded, and coarsely chopped

1. Pour the coconut milk and the rice flour into a small glass jar and shake vigorously to blend them into a thin mixture. Slowly pour the mixture into the boiling meat sauce and cook, stirring constantly until the mixture thickens slightly. Add the chopped tomato and reduce the heat to a simmer. The mixture should resemble a thick white sauce.

2. Thread the different cuts of meat onto soaked bamboo skewers, so that there is variation of textures on each skewer. Broil in the oven or charcoal-broil the skewers until the meat starts to crisp a little, 2 to 3 minutes on each side. Dip the skewers into the hot meat sauce and arrange them on a heated platter. Serve the sauce in a warmed bowl for extra dipping pleasure.

Satay Padang #2
(Beef Satay with Spicy Sauce)

Yield: 3–4 servings   Heat Scale: Medium

Anyone who has ever visited Malaysia or Indonesia will find it hard to forget the multitude of satays that are served everywhere. Practically a national food of the country, satay is served as part of a meal or sold by a vendor as a snack food on the street. Almost every kind of meat and shellfish is used, and, in Bali, turtle meat is the favorite choice.

1 clove garlic, peeled
1 small onion, peeled and quartered
1 cup (236 mL) roasted peanuts
3 fresh serrano or jalapeño chiles, stems and seeds removed
1 teaspoon (5 mL) sugar
1 (1-inch [2.5 cm]) piece fresh ginger, peeled
3 tablespoons (45 mL) tamarind sauce
1 tablespoon (15 mL) fresh lime juice
2 tablespoons (30 mL) water
¼ cup (59 mL) coconut milk
1 tablespoon (15 mL) soybean sauce
Salt, to taste
Freshly ground black pepper, to taste
1 pound beef fillet, cut into 1-inch (2.5 cm) cubes
½ cup (118 mL) thick coconut milk

1. Soak some bamboo skewers in water for 30 minutes.

2. In a blender, blend the garlic, onion, peanuts, chiles, sugar, ginger, and tamarind sauce until the mixture is smooth.

3. Fry the blended mixture in a small, heavy skillet over medium-high heat for 1 minute. Add the lime juice, water, coconut milk, and soybean sauce and bring the mixture to a quick boil. Reduce the heat to a simmer and cook the mixture for 1 minute. Remove the mixture from the heat and set it aside.

4. Lightly salt and pepper the beef cubes and toss them to coat. Thread 5 to 6 cubes of beef on each skewer, brush the meat with the coconut milk, and brush on the chile mixture.

5. Broil or barbecue the meat, about 3 minutes per side. Place the grilled meat on a heated platter and serve it with the remaining dipping sauce in a small bowl.

Wettha Thayet Thi Chet
(Spiced Burmese Pork with Green Mango)

Yield: 5–6 servings   Heat Scale: Medium

In Burma or Myanmar, pork is the most popular meat for a number of reasons. Upper Burma is heavily populated by Chinese, who are traditionally big pork consumers; pork is cheaper than lamb or beef; and pork combines well with a number of diverse ingredients, including the green mango.

1 (2-inch [5 cm]) piece fresh ginger, peeled and sliced
3 cloves garlic, peeled
1 large onion, peeled and cut into eighths
3 tablespoons (45 mL) vegetable oil
½ teaspoon (2.5 mL) ground turmeric
1 tablespoon (15 mL) crushed chile piquin or other small, hot dried chiles
½ teaspoon (2.5 mL) fish sauce
1 teaspoon (5 mL) shrimp paste
1 teaspoon (5 mL) shrimp sauce
2 pounds (1.1 kg) boneless, lean pork, cut into pieces 2 inches (5 cm) long and 1 inch (2.5 cm) wide
½ teaspoon (2.5 mL) salt
¾ cup (177 mL) grated unripe (green) mango
1 teaspoon (5 mL) paprika
3 cups (708 mL) water

1. In a blender or small food processor, purée the ginger, garlic, and onion. Heat the oil in a large, heavy skillet over low heat. Add the purée, the turmeric, and the chile until the mixture becomes red-brown, about 3 to 5 minutes. Stir in the fish sauce, shrimp paste, and shrimp sauce and fry for 1 minute.
2. Add the pork, salt, green mango, and paprika and continue to stir-fry until the pork starts to brown, about 8 to 10 minutes.
3. Stir the water into the simmering pork mixture and bring it to a boil. Reduce the heat to a simmer, cover, and simmer until the liquid is reduced to 1 cup (236 mL), about 1 hour and 15 minutes. Check the meat and stir occasionally to prevent sticking and burning. At the end of the cooking period, the sauce should be thick, about the consistency of a thick white sauce.
4. Serve with steamed rice and stir-fried vegetables.

Cambogee Beef

Yield: 8 skewers   Heat Scale: Medium

When the aroma of this dish rises up from the cooking fire, it tantalizes the nostrils. For the best results, use a mortar and pestle to combine the aromatic ingredients, or, if you don't have one, use a blender. Thanks to Richard Sterling for this Cambodian recipe, gathered on one of his extensive Southeast Asian trips. Serving suggestion: Before cooking, thread a chunk of fresh pineapple onto the end of each skewer. Serve with a salad from Chapter 6 and steamed rice.

2 red serrano or jalapeño chiles, stems removed
¼ cup (59 mL) thinly sliced lemongrass
6 kaffir lime leaves or the peel of 1 lime
4 cloves garlic, peeled
1 slice or 1 teaspoon (5 mL) galangal (or substitute ginger)
½ cup (118 mL) oyster sauce
2 tablespoons (30 mL) sugar
1 pinch salt
½ cup (118 mL) water
1 pound (454 g) beef, cut into thin slices and threaded onto skewers

1. Mash or blend together the chiles, lemongrass, lime leaves, garlic, and galangal. Add the oyster sauce, salt, sugar, and water. Place the mixture in a saucepan, bring it to a boil, and boil for 1 minute. Remove the pan from the heat and let the mixture cool. Taste for sweetness—the sugar should be present but not dominant.
2. Marinate the beef on skewers in the refrigerator for at least 1 hour.
3. Grill the skewers over hot coals, keeping the beef at least 4 inches (10 cm) from the heat lest the sugar burn, until it reaches your desired doneness.

Adobong Baboy
(Pork in Adobo)

Yield: 8 servings   Heat Scale: Medium

Adobo is considered the national dish of the Philippines. But it is more than just a dish; it is a style of cooking that has numerous variations and can be made with pork, chicken, fish, or vegetables. The one common factor, however, is that a subtle sourness be present. The sourness is imparted by the vinegar, which also helps to preserve the dish for several days without refrigeration. (Note: This recipe requires advance preparation.)

3 serrano or jalapeño chiles, roasted and peeled, stems and seeds removed
4 poblano or New Mexican green chiles, roasted and peeled, stems and seeds removed
¼ cup (59 mL) soy sauce
1 onion, peeled and cut into eighths
10 cloves garlic, peeled
1 cup (236 mL) orange juice
½ cup (118 mL) apple cider vinegar
1 teaspoon (5 mL) whole black peppercorns, ground
1 (1-inch [2.5 cm]) cinnamon stick, ground
½ teaspoon (2.5 mL) cumin seed, ground
1 teaspoon (5 mL) whole coriander, ground
3 pounds (1.36 kg) pork loin
3 tablespoons (45 mL) vegetable oil

1. In a blender, purée both chiles, the soy sauce, the onion, the garlic, the orange juice, and the vinegar. Transfer the mixture to a bowl and stir in the ground peppercorns, cinnamon, cumin, and coriander.
2. Place the meat in a glass baking pan. Pour the puréed mixture over the meat, cover the pan with plastic wrap, and refrigerate overnight.
3. Preheat the oven to 350°F (180°C). Remove the meat from the refrigerator and let it sit at room temperature for about an hour. With a butter knife, scrape the sauce off the roast and back into the pan. Drizzle the pork with the vegetable oil.
4. Roast the pork for 1½ hours, basting every 20 minutes with the sauce in the pan.
5. Transfer the roast to a heated platter. Remove as much fat as possible. Pour the sauce into a saucepan and boil it until it is thick and rich.
6. Slice the meat and serve the sauce on the side.

Hoisin Beef Ribs

Yield: 4 servings   Heat Scale: Medium Hot

This is my version of a Korean rib dish. If these ribs were going to be smoked, I would not boil them first, but since they tend to be fatty, I do boil them before grilling. Serve the ribs with fried rice, stir-fried vegetables, and cucumber slices sprinkled with ground hot red chile.

3 pounds (1.36 kg) beef ribs
3 tablespoons (45 mL) hoisin sauce
3 tablespoons (45 mL) chopped green onion, green parts included
2 tablespoons (30 mL) rice vinegar
2 tablespoons (30 mL) orange juice
2 tablespoons (30 mL) Asian chile sauce with ginger
2 tablespoons (30 mL) chopped ginger
1 tablespoon (15 mL) crushed chile piquin or other small, red chiles
1 tablespoon (15 mL) brown sugar
1 tablespoon (15 mL) orange zest
2 cloves garlic, peeled and minced

1. Cut the ribs into individual pieces. Place them in a pot, add water to cover, and bring to a boil. Reduce the heat and simmer, uncovered, for 30 minutes. Remove the ribs from the heat and drain them.
2. Combine all the remaining ingredients and allow the mixture to sit at room temperature while the ribs simmer.
3. Grill the ribs over a medium fire for about 10 minutes without basting. Move the ribs away from direct flames and cook about 10 minutes longer, basting with the sauce, until crisp.

Sichuan Beef with Hot Sauce

Yield: 2–4 servings   Heat Scale: Varies, but usually Medium

The most important thing to remember in preparing this classic Sichuanese recipe is that the beef should be stir-fried until it is dry and crispy, but not burned. Use the shredding blade of a food processor to cut the celery and carrot. Serve over steamed rice.

For the Marinade:
½ teaspoon (2.5 mL) cornstarch
2 tablespoons (30 mL) soy sauce
1 tablespoon (15 mL) dry vermouth or white wine
8 ounces (224 g) flank steak, cut with the grain into 2-inch (5 cm) julienne

1. In a bowl, combine the ingredients for the marinade and stir well. Add the beef and toss to coat. Let sit, covered, for 30 minutes.

For the Sauce:
2 tablespoons (30 mL) soy sauce
2 tablespoons (30 mL) dry vermouth or white wine
1½ teaspoons (7.5 mL) sugar
3 tablespoons (45 mL) hot bean sauce
1½ teaspoons (7.5 mL) sweet bean sauce
½ teaspoon (2.5 mL) sesame oil
1 tablespoon (15 mL) Asian chile paste

1. In a bowl, combine all the sauce ingredients and mix well.

For the Stir-Fry:
¼ cup (59 mL) peanut oil, divided
1 tablespoon (15 mL) minced ginger
1 tablespoon (15 mL) minced garlic
1 green onion, white part only, minced
1 large celery rib, shredded
1 carrot, shredded
2 green New Mexico or poblano chiles, roasted, peeled, stems and seeds removed, julienned
Asian chile paste to taste

1. Heat a wok over high heat and add 3 tablespoons (45 mL) of the peanut oil. Just when it begins to smoke, add the beef and stir-fry until the beef is browned to the point of being crispy. Remove the beef with a slotted spoon and set it on paper towels to drain.
2. Heat the remaining peanut oil. Add the ginger, garlic, and green onion and stir for 15 seconds. Add the celery, carrot, and chile. Stir-fry for 30 seconds, then add the beef. Stir briefly to mix the beef with the vegetables, add the sauce, and stir-fry for 30 seconds to 1 minute. Adjust the heat with more Asian chile paste.

Mongolian Beef

Yield: 4 servings   Heat Scale: Medium

This Mandarin recipe also goes by the name of Beijing Beef. The crispy noodles add texture to this simple stir-fry. Some recipes call for soaking the noodles before frying as the only way to get really crisp noodles, but putting wet noodles in hot oil will cause the oil to spatter and may cause burns, so I don't recommend frying them this way. Just be sure they are crisp before removing and remember that they puff up quickly, so don't put too many in the wok at any one time.

For the Marinade:
2 tablespoons (30 mL) dark soy sauce
1 tablespoon (15 mL) vegetable oil
1 tablespoon (15 mL) rice wine or dry sherry
2 teaspoons (10 mL) cornstarch
1 teaspoon (5 mL) sesame oil
½ teaspoon (2.5 mL) sugar

1. In a bowl, combine all the ingredients and mix well.

For the Beef:
1 pound (454 g) flank or round steak, thinly sliced in 1½ × ¾–inch (3.5 × 1.5 cm) pieces
2 cups (473 mL) vegetable oil
2–3 ounces (56–84 mL) rice vermicelli noodles
4 small dried red chiles, such as piquin or Thai
2 cloves garlic, peeled and minced
1 tablespoon (15 mL) hoisin sauce
1 tablespoon (15 mL) hot bean sauce
½ teaspoon (2.5 mL) cornstarch
8 green onions, cut in 1½-inch (3.5 cm) lengths

1. Slice the beef across grain and at an angle into thin strips. Add the beef to the marinade. Marinate at room temperature for 1 hour or in the refrigerator for up to 4 hours.
2. Heat a wok until hot. Add the oil and heat to 375°F (190°C). Gently loosen the roll of noodles with your fingers and break it into 3 portions. Carefully lower one of the noodle portions into the oil with a slotted spoon and press the noodles under the oil for 2 seconds until they are puffed and crisp. Immediately remove the noodles from the wok and drain them. Repeat with the remaining noodles.
3. Pour off all but 1 to 2 tablespoons (15 to 30 mL) of the oil and reheat it over medium heat. Add the chiles and garlic and stir-fry for 1 minute. Add the beef and stir-fry until it is lightly browned.
4. Add the hoisin sauce, hot bean sauce, cornstarch, and ½ cup (118 mL) water to the wok. Bring to a boil over medium heat and add the green onions. Simmer for a couple of minutes to thicken the sauce so it clings to the meat.
5. To serve, place the noodles on a platter and top with the meat.

Smokin' Chilli Mullumbimby

Yield: 4 servings   Heat Scale: Medium Hot

My friend John Boland is Australia's number one hot sauce manufacturer. He lives in Byron Bay, New South Wales, and he writes, "Mullumbimby is our nearest town. It is hot and tropical, like our Mango Chilli Sauce with Smoked Jalapeños."

2 teaspoons (10 mL) vegetable oil
2 pounds (1.1 kg) lean pork or beef, cubed
1 onion, peeled and diced
1 teaspoon (5 mL) salt
1 clove garlic, peeled and crushed
1 (8.5-ounce [238 g]) bottle Byron Bay Chilli Co. Smokin' Mango Chilli Sauce with Chipotles (or substitute your favorite mango-based medium hot sauce)

1. Heat the oil in a large skillet over medium-high heat. Add the meat and cook until it is browned on all sides.
2. Add the onion and cook an additional 2 to 3 minutes.
3. Stir in the remaining ingredients, cover, and simmer for 30 to 45 minutes. Check the pot occasionally. If the sauce gets too thick, add water as needed.
4. Serve this dish over cooked rice or use it as a filling for warm tortillas.

NINE

Bodacious Barbecue

I use the word "barbecue" in three ways. First, in the most general sense, it is a gathering of people where food—especially meat—is cooked outdoors rather that inside or on a stove. At most family barbecues, the meat is grilled—that is, cooked on a grate directly over the heat source. The second definition of barbecue, in the technical culinary sense, is meat cooked indirectly by the heat source and flavored with smoke. Finally, the grilling apparatus, no matter how modest or sophisticated, is called a barbecue. The apparatus for producing true barbecue is not called a barbecue but rather a smoker or a pit. Go figure.

Part 1 of this chapter is my take, with the help of Nancy Gerlach, on international combo barbecues. Part 2, fired-up American barbecue classics, requires a little explanation. In the midst of all the wars that exist among regions of the United States famous for their barbecue, a few food historians have noticed that there tends to be a common denominator in regional barbecue: the overwhelming tendency to use chile peppers to spice up the smoked meats. So, traditional American regional barbecue is true fiery food, with chile peppers appearing in rubs, sops, marinades, and barbecue sauces from all over the country.

Despite the tradition of chiles in barbecue, purist critics might complain that I have altered hallowed, sacred, and traditional regional recipes by spicing them up too much. To counter that charge, I reply that home cooks are not stupid. By reading the recipe first and noting the heat scale, you can easily adjust the amount of chile in the recipe to taste.

So, grab some chile pods from the garden, fire up the smoker, and turn on the gas grill. Oh, and better grab a beer before you go, 'cause it's gonna get hot.

Grilled Green Chile-Stuffed Pepper Steaks Wrapped in Bacon

Yield: 4 servings   Heat Scale: Medium

This is one of my favorite ways of grilling steaks. I find myself using the basic recipe and altering it again and again. Leftovers can be turned into a fabulous Southwest Steak Sandwich by thinly slicing it and layering it on sourdough bread with Muenster cheese and more chile. (Note: This recipe requires advance preparation.)

4 boneless rib eye steaks (or substitute fillet mignon or sirloin steaks, 1–2 inches [2.5–5 cm] thick)
4 roasted and peeled green New Mexican chiles, stems and seeds removed
4 strips raw bacon
2 tablespoons (30 mL) red peppercorns
2 tablespoons (30 mL) white peppercorns
2 tablespoons (30 mL) black peppercorns
2 tablespoons (30 mL) Caribbean habanero sauce
2 tablespoons (30 mL) Worcestershire sauce
2 tablespoons (30 mL) soy sauce
2 tablespoons (30 mL) rice wine vinegar
½ teaspoon (2.5 mL) garlic powder

1. Slice the steaks horizontally to create a pocket in each. Do not cut all the way through the steak. Place a green chile in each pocket. Wrap a strip of bacon around each steak horizontally and secure with a toothpick.
2. Place the peppercorns in a towel and pound them with a hammer or a mortar until roughly crushed. Press the crushed pepper into each side of the steak.
3. Combine the habanero sauce, Worcestershire sauce, soy sauce, vinegar, and garlic powder. Place the steaks in a nonmetallic pan, pour the marinade over the meat, and marinate in the refrigerator for a couple hours. Bring the steaks to room temperature before grilling.
4. Grill the steaks over a medium-hot fire. For medium-rare steaks, the internal temperature should be 150°F (75°C). Feel free to slice a steak to check for doneness.

Variation
For those not enamored of peppercorns, omit and wrap the steaks in peppered bacon.

Chimayó Chile Steaks with Chipotle Potatoes

Yield: 4 servings   Heat Scale: Mild

*From the little village of Chimayó, New Mexico, comes what many chileheads con-
sider to be the finest tasting red chile. I use it in my enchilada sauces and for making
rubs such as this one. The smoky taste of the chipotle potatoes is a nice complement
to the grilled steak. Serve the steak and potatoes with mixed green and yellow snap
beans and Jalapeño-Cheddar Blue Cornbread (page 143).*

For the Chimayó Rub:
2 tablespoons (30 mL) ground red New Mexican chile (Chimayó preferred)
1 tablespoon (15 mL) sugar
1 tablespoon (15 mL) ground cinnamon
2 teaspoons (10 mL) ground coriander
1 teaspoon (5 mL) ground cumin
1 teaspoon (5 mL) salt
½ teaspoon (2.5 mL) ground cumin
¼ teaspoon (1.25 mL) ground thyme

1. Combine all the ingredients in a bowl and set aside.

For the Chipotle Potatoes:
2 large baking potatoes
2 tablespoons (30–45 mL) milk, plus more as needed
1 tablespoon (15 mL) chipotles in adobo, chopped
¼ teaspoon (1.25 mL) garlic powder
Chopped chives for garnish
Salt, to taste
Freshly ground black pepper, to taste

1. Bake the potatoes until just done. Scoop out the potatoes into a bowl
and set the skins aside. Whip the potato flesh with the milk, chipotles,
garlic, and just enough additional milk to hold them together.
2. Spoon the potatoes back into the skins. Place the potatoes on the grill,
away from the direct flame, and heat the grill.

For the Steaks:
Olive oil as needed for brushing
4 New York Strip steaks

1. When the grill is hot, brush the steaks with the olive oil and liberally
coat them with the dry rub. Grill the steaks for about 12 to 16 minutes,
turning often, for rare, or 15 to 20 minutes for medium rare (the internal
temperature should reach 150°F [75°C]). You can slice the steaks open to
check for doneness, too. Serve with the potatoes.

Chipotle Barbecued Ribs with Chile-Grilled Potato Wedges

Yield: 4 servings   Heat Scale: Medium-Hot

There's something magical about chipotle chiles and grilling—maybe it's the fact that these chiles were created with smoke. Serve with spicy black bean and corn salad and buttermilk biscuits. And pick a dessert from Chapter 14 to finish off the meal.

For the Chipotle Barbecue Sauce:
4 dried chipotle chiles, stems removed
3 dried red New Mexican chiles, stems and seeds removed
2 teaspoons (10 mL) vegetable oil
1 medium onion, peeled and chopped
4 cloves garlic, peeled and chopped
1 (12-ounce [336 mL]) can beer
3 cups (708 mL) catsup
½ cup (118 mL) strongly brewed coffee
1½ tablespoons (22.5 mL) apple cider vinegar
¼ cup (59 mL) molasses
3 tablespoons (45 mL) Dijon mustard
2 teaspoons (10 mL) Worcestershire sauce
½ teaspoon (2.5 mL) freshly ground black pepper

1. Cover the dried chiles with hot water and let sit for 30 minutes to soften. Drain the chiles and discard the water.
2. In a saucepan, heat the oil over medium heat. Add the onions and sauté until softened. Add the garlic and sauté for an additional 2 to 3 minutes. Add the remaining sauce ingredients, including the chiles, and bring the mixture to a boil. Reduce the heat and simmer for 20 to 30 minutes. Remove from the heat, transfer to a blender or food processor, and purée until smooth. Strain if desired.

For the Ribs and Chile-Grilled Potato Wedges:
2 cloves garlic, peeled and minced
1 teaspoon (5 mL) ground red New Mexican chile
2 tablespoons (30 mL) olive oil
Salt, to taste
Freshly ground black pepper, to taste
4 pounds (1.82 kg) pork ribs
2 medium potatoes, cut in wedges
2 green onions, finely chopped

1. In a bowl, combine the garlic, chile, and olive oil. Set aside.
2. Liberally salt and pepper the ribs. Grill over a medium-hot grill for 10 minutes. Move the ribs away from the direct flame and continue to grill for an hour. Brush with the sauce during the last 10 minutes of grilling.
3. While the ribs are cooking, toss the potatoes in the seasoned oil until well-coated. Place in a grill basket and grill for 15 minutes over a direct flame until browned, shaking the basket often.
4. Cut the ribs apart. Toss the potatoes with the green onions. Serve with the remaining sauce.

Argentinian Parrilla with Chimichurri Sauce

Yield: 4–6 servings   Heat Scale: Medium

A parrilla is a simple grill in Argentina, but the wonders it can create! As barbecue expert Steven Raichlen noted, "Argentina can be a forbidding place for a vegetarian." Chimichurri is the sauce most commonly served with beef straight from the parrilla, and there are dozens—if not hundreds—of variations of it and a debate about whether it should contain chiles. You know which side I favor, and my version of chimichurri contains green aji chiles. Since cattle are so prevalent in Argentina, why not use a huge steak? Serve with grilled sweet potato and poblano chile kabobs and black beans and rice. (Note: This recipe requires advance preparation.)

For the Steak Rub:
2 tablespoons (30 mL) ground red aji chile (or substitute ground red New Mexican chile)
1 teaspoon (5 mL) dried oregano
1 teaspoon (5 mL) sugar
¼ teaspoon (1.25 mL) ground cumin
½ teaspoon (2.5 mL) salt
1 (3-pound [1.36 kg]) sirloin steak, 2 inches (5 cm) thick

1. In a bowl, combine the ground chile, oregano, sugar, cumin, and salt. Rub this mixture well into the steak. Place the steak in a large freezer bag and marinate it in the refrigerator for a couple of hours or preferably overnight.

For the Chimichurri Sauce:
¼ cup (59 mL) red wine vinegar
4 cloves garlic, peeled and chopped
3 green aji amarillo chiles, seeds removed, chopped (or substitute jalapeños)
1 bay leaf, center rib removed
1 small onion, peeled and finely chopped
¾ cup (177 mL) chopped fresh parsley
¼ cup (59 mL) chopped fresh oregano (or 2 tablespoons [30 mL] dried)
½ teaspoon (2.5 mL) salt
1 teaspoon (5 mL) freshly ground black pepper
¼–⅓ cup (59–79 mL) olive oil

1. In a food processor or blender, combine the vinegar, garlic, chiles, and bay leaf and process until smooth. Add the onion, parsley, oregano, salt, and pepper and pulse until blended but not puréed. Whisk in the oil and allow to sit for a couple hours to blend the flavors.
2. Before grilling, remove the meat from the refrigerator and bring it to room temperature.
3. Grill the steak over a medium-hot fire for about 20 minutes, turning often for medium-rare (the internal temperature should reach 150°F [75°C]). Remove the steak from the grill and let it sit for 5 minutes. Slice the meat against the grain and arrange it on a serving platter. Ladle some of the chimichurri sauce over the meat and serve the remainder on the side.

Brazilian Churrasco with Molho Campanha

Yield: 6–8 servings   Heat Scale: Medium

Restaurants in Brazil called churrascarias sell spit-roasted meats to order, and the skewers the meat is grilled on are actually swords. A churrasco is simply a Brazilian mixed barbecue featuring beef and pork, but feel free to throw in a few sausages, as that's the way it's done in Brazil. Molho Campanha is the Brazilian version of the Mexican pico de gallo salsa. It's best to prepare it fresh, as it doesn't keep well. This is a lot of food, great for a small party, but if you're not serving the starving masses, just grill one of the meats. The malagueta chile used in the first basting sauce is a relative of the tabasco chile and is a favorite in Brazil. As for the chile in the pork basting sauce, many habanero relatives grow in the Amazon Basin, where the species was domesticated. Serve this with achiote-spiced rice, sautéed greens and onions, and a tropical fruit salad. (Note: This recipe requires advance preparation.)

For the Malagueta Basting Sauce and Steak:
½ cup (118 mL) vinegar
½ cup (118 mL) lime juice
½ cup (118 mL) red wine
6 fresh malagueta chiles, chopped (or substitute tabascos or serranos)
1 small onion, peeled and finely chopped
2 cloves garlic, peeled and minced
1 tablespoon (15 mL) sugar
1 tablespoon (15 mL) chopped fresh oregano (or 1 teaspoon [5 mL] dried)
1 teaspoon (5 mL) dried thyme
1 teaspoon (5 mL) salt
Freshly ground black pepper, to taste
1 (2-pound [1.1 kg]) T-bone steak, 1 inch (2.5 cm) thick

1. In a blender or food processor, combine the vinegar, lime juice, wine, chiles, onion, garlic, sugar, oregano, thyme, salt, and pepper and purée. Transfer the mixture to a nonreactive bowl and let it sit for a couple hours to blend the flavors. Add the steak to the mixture and marinate for 1 to 2 hours.

For the Habanero Basting Sauce and Pork Chops:
4 boneless loin pork chops
1 cup (236 mL) water
2 tablespoons (30 mL) salt
½ cup (118 mL) sugar
6 juniper berries, bruised (lightly bashed all over with a spoon)
2 fresh habanero chiles, stems and seeds removed, chopped
1 teaspoon (5 mL) freshly ground white peppercorns
1 teaspoon (5 mL) freshly ground black peppercorns
1 teaspoon (5 mL) freshly ground coriander seeds
3 bay leaves, crushed
4 whole cloves
1 teaspoon (5 mL) dried thyme

1. Place the pork in a nonreactive bowl. In a separate bowl, combine the water, salt, and sugar and stir until dissolved. Add the remaining ingredients and mix well. Pour the marinade over the pork and add additional water to cover, if necessary. Cover the bowl and marinate in the refrigerator overnight.

For the Molho Campanha
2 tomatoes, coarsely chopped
1 large onion, peeled and finely chopped
1 small bell pepper, stem and seeds removed, coarsely chopped
½ cup (118 mL) red wine vinegar
3–4 dried malagueta peppers, crushed (or substitute piquin)
1 teaspoon (5 mL) chopped fresh cilantro

1. Combine all the ingredients and transfer the salsa to a serving bowl.
2. Bring all the meats to room temperature.
3. Drain the beef and transfer the marinade to a saucepan. Bring the marinade to a boil, reduce the heat, and simmer for 20 minutes.
4. Remove the pork from the marinade and transfer it to a plate. Discard the marinade.
5. If adding sausages to the churrasco, pierce them lightly with a fork and grill them away from direct flames for about 10 minutes before adding the rest of the meat. Grill the beef over a medium-hot fire, basting frequently with the marinade and turning often, for about 10 to 12 minutes for medium-rare (the internal temperature should reach 150°F [75°C]).
6. Grill the pork for about 10 to 12 minutes, turning occasionally, until done (the internal temperature should reach 160°F [80°C]).
7. Remove the meats from the grill and let them sit for 5 minutes. Slice the steaks against the grain in thin strips and arrange them on a large serving platter. Arrange the pork and sausages on the platter and serve with the Molho Campanha.

Carnita-Filled Tortillas with Chile de Arbol Salsa

Yield: 4 servings   Heat Scale: Medium

Carnita is the Spanish diminutive for carne and refers to a little piece of meat, usually pork, that is cooked in many different ways throughout Mexico. Fried and topped with chile sauce, carnitas make a great breakfast side dish. Grilled and wrapped in a warmed corn tortilla with a grilled onion plus salsa, as here, they can be a delicious entrée. I prefer the large Mexican bulb onion, a type of spring onion, but if you can't find any, use large green onions with the green tops left on. This recipe makes great hands-on luncheon soft tacos, or burritos if you use flour tortillas. Serve with seasoned pinto beans or frijoles borracho. (Note: This recipe requires advance preparation.)

For the Carnitas:
⅓ cup (79 mL) vegetable oil
3 tablespoons (45 mL) lime juice (fresh preferred)
3 tablespoons (45 mL) ground ancho chile
1 tablespoon (15 mL) ground chipotle chile
2 tablespoons (30 mL) chopped fresh cilantro
1 tablespoon (15 mL) garlic powder
1 tablespoon (15 mL) ground cumin
1½ teaspoons (7.5 mL) salt
1 teaspoon (5 mL) freshly ground black pepper
1½ pounds (680 g) boneless pork, trimmed and cut into 1-inch (2.5 cm) cubes

1. In a bowl, combine the oil, lime juice, ground chiles, cilantro, garlic powder, cumin, salt, and pepper and mix well. Rub the pork cubes with the paste until well-coated. Marinate, covered, in the refrigerator for 2 hours.

For the Chile de Arbol and Tomatillo Salsa:
6–8 dried chiles de arbol, stems removed
1 tablespoon (15 mL) vegetable oil
4 cloves garlic, peeled
2 tablespoons (30 mL) chopped onion
1 (8-ounce [224 g]) can tomatillos, drained
1 tablespoon (15 mL) distilled vinegar

1. Rinse the chiles and slit them open lengthwise. Sauté the chiles in the oil over medium heat until lightly browned. Add the garlic and onion and continue to sauté until the onions are lightly browned. Place all the ingredients in a blender or food processor and purée until smooth, adding a little water if necessary.

To Prepare the Carnitas:
1 bunch large green onions
2 tablespoons (30 mL) vegetable oil
2 teaspoons (10 mL) ground ancho chile
8 large corn tortillas

1. Thread the pork cubes onto skewers. Brush the onions with oil and sprinkle them with the ground chile. Grill the pork cubes over a medium fire until well-done and crisp, about 10 to 15 minutes. Cut open a test cube to see if it is done. Place the onions on the grill and cook until they are browned but not burned, turning often, about 4 minutes. Meanwhile, warm the tortillas in aluminum foil on the grill, away from direct flames. **2.** Remove everything from the grill. Remove the pork from the skewers. Place the carnitas in tortillas, top each with an onion, and cover with some of the salsa. Wrap up each tortilla and serve.

Thai Ginger Pork Steaks
Yield: 4 servings   Heat Scale: Medium

Pork is a preferred meat in China and Southeast Asia, so it is not surprising to find it combined with chiles and traditional Asian seasonings. The marinade is also excellent with chicken and fish. Serve the grilled pork steaks with jasmine rice, sweet and sour vegetables, and a green papaya salad. (Note: This recipe requires advance preparation.)

2 tablespoons (30 mL) rice wine vinegar or dry sherry
2 tablespoons (30 mL) tomato sauce
2 tablespoons (30 mL) soy sauce
1 tablespoon (15 mL) brown sugar
2 tablespoons (30 mL) minced ginger
1 tablespoon (15 mL) vegetable oil (peanut preferred)
6 small prik kee nu Thai chiles, stems removed, minced (or substitute 3 serrano or jalapeño chiles)
1 clove garlic, peeled and minced
1 teaspoon (5 mL) fish sauce
4 pork steaks

1. In a blender or food processor, combine all the ingredients except the pork and purée until smooth. Transfer the mixture to a bowl and let it sit for an hour to blend the flavors. Cover the pork steaks completely with the marinade and let them sit in a glass bowl for 3 hours, covered, in the refrigerator.
2. Bring the steaks to room temperature and grill over a medium fire for 10 to 15 minutes, turning often, until the internal temperature reaches 160°F (80°C), which is medium. Cut a steak open to test for doneness, if you prefer. You can use any leftover marinade as a basting sauce, but be sure to simmer it in a saucepan for 20 minutes first.

Vietnamese Chile and Garlic-Grilled Pork with Bun Cha Salad

Yield: 4 servings   Heat Scale: Medium

This northern Vietnamese specialty is traditionally prepared on small charcoal grills that don't require too much fuel. Bun cha is rice vermicelli, thin, brittle white rice noodles that are used in soups and salads and, as here, can be served cold as an accompaniment to a grilled dish. The bun cha noodles are best when made an hour or two ahead, covered, and set aside in the refrigerator or at room temperature. This recipe can also be prepared with beef. (Note: This recipe requires advance preparation.)

For the Thai Chile Accent Sauce or Dressing:
¼ cup (59 mL) lime juice (fresh preferred)
3 tablespoons (45 mL) fish sauce
3 tablespoons (45 mL) sugar
2 teaspoons (10 mL) peanut oil
2 cloves garlic, peeled and minced
3 green prik chee fa Thai chiles, stems removed, sliced thinly into rounds (or substitute jalapeños)
¼ cup (59 mL) water

1. In a bowl, combine all the ingredients and mix until the sugar dissolves. Allow to sit, covered, for a couple of hours to blend the flavors.

For the Chile and Garlic-Grilled Pork:
2 tablespoons (30 mL) fish sauce
1 tablespoon (15 mL) lime juice
1 tablespoon (15 mL) Asian chile garlic sauce
2 shallots, peeled and finely chopped
¾ teaspoon (3.75 mL) sugar
Freshly ground black pepper, to taste
1 pound (454 g) boneless pork butt, trimmed of fat, thinly sliced, and cut into 2 × 1–inch (5 × 2.5 cm) pieces

1. In a bowl, combine the fish sauce, lime juice, chile garlic sauce, shallots, sugar, and black pepper and mix well. Add the pork and marinate for an hour at room temperature.

For the Bun Cha Salad:
¼ pound (113 g) dried rice vermicelli
2 cups (473 mL) shredded lettuce or spinach
¼ cup (59 mL) diced peeled cucumber
¼ cup (59 mL) shredded carrots
¼ cup (59 mL) coarsely chopped fresh cilantro
¼ cup (59 mL) chopped fresh mint
¼ cup (59 mL) toasted unsalted peanuts

1. In a large bowl, soak the noodles in warm water for 20 minutes, then drain. Bring a large pot of water to a boil and add the noodles. Using chopsticks or a wooden spoon, gently lift and separate the noodles to prevent them from clumping and cook for no more than 3 minutes. They should be al dente. Drain the noodles and rinse them well with cold water.

2. Grill the pork slices over a medium-hot fire for 1 to 2 minutes per side, turning often, until the meat is slightly charred. Remove the pork from the grill and transfer it to a plate.

3. To serve, divide the noodles among 4 shallow bowls or plates. Arrange the lettuce, cucumber, and carrots over the noodles. Top with the pork slices and spoon some of the accent sauce over the meat. Serve the remaining sauce, cilantro, mint, and peanuts in separate bowls for sprinkling over the top.

Barbecued Pork Adobo Sandwiches with Puerto Rican Mojo Sauce

Yield: 4–6 servings   Heat Scale: Medium-Hot

Because of the Spanish control of various parts of the world, adobos show up from the Philippines all the way to Puerto Rico. There are almost an infinite number of variations, but most have a vinegar base. Be sure to inject the marinade or cut slits in the pork so that the marinade penetrates into the meat. Serve with fried plantain chips and an avocado and grapefruit salad. Mojo is an oil- and citrus-based hot sauce used primarily with pork. (Note: This recipe requires advance preparation.)

For the Adobo:
1 ½ cup orange juice (fresh preferred)
⅓ cup (79 mL) apple cider vinegar
¼ cup (59 mL) lime juice (fresh preferred)
¼ cup (59 mL) dry sherry
¼ cup (59 mL) vegetable oil
¼ cup (59 mL) chopped fresh parsley
1 small onion, peeled and chopped
4 cloves garlic, peeled and chopped
2–3 habanero chiles, stems removed, chopped
3 tablespoons (45 mL) brown sugar
2 teaspoons (10 mL) soy sauce
1 bay leaf
½ teaspoon (2.5 mL) salt
Freshly ground black pepper, to taste
1 (3-pound [1.36 kg]) pork roast

1. In a blender or food processor, combine the orange juice, vinegar, lime juice, sherry, oil, parsley, onion, garlic, chiles, brown sugar, soy sauce, bay leaf, salt, and pepper and purée until smooth. If you don't have an injector, make shallow slits about 2 inches (5 cm) apart all over the roast. Rub the marinade over the meat, and if you made slits in the meat, make sure to rub the marinade into the slits . Place the pork, along with the remaining marinade, in a bowl, cover, and marinate in the refrigerator overnight.

2. Remove the pork from the marinade. Transfer the marinade to a saucepan and simmer it for 20 minutes.

3. Secure the roast on a spit and grill it over a medium-hot grill, basting with the marinade, for about 2 hours or until it reaches an internal temperature of 155°F (78°C). Allow the roast to sit for 10 minutes before carving and the temperature will increase to 160°F (80°C).

For the Mojo Sauce
¼ cup (59 mL) vegetable oil (peanut preferred)
½ cup (118 mL) chopped green onion
6 cloves garlic, peeled
2 habanero chiles, stems removed, chopped
⅓ cup (79 mL) orange juice (fresh preferred)
2 tablespoons (30 mL) lime juice (fresh preferred)
Salt, to taste
Freshly ground black pepper, to taste
Bolillo or hard rolls for serving

1. In a saucepan, heat the oil over medium heat. Add the onions and garlic and sauté until soft. Add the chiles, orange juice, lime juice, salt, and pepper and simmer for a couple of minutes. Transfer the sauce to a blender or food processor and purée until smooth.
2. Carve the roast and serve it on the hard rolls covered with the sauce.

Seared Chipotle and Garlic Venison
Yield: 4 servings   Heat Scale: Medium

Game is turning up more and more in many fancy restaurants because, like venison, most of it is low in fat and has about half the calories of most cuts of beef, pork, and lamb. All game available from butchers is farm raised and less gamey than wild meat. Because venison is so low in fat, the cook often needs to add additional oil or fat during the cooking. It is best cooked rare or medium-rare. If you can find it, you can substitute elk for the venison. Serve this with steak fries, steamed broccoli, and an elegant semi-rilled dessert from Chapter 14. (Note: This recipe requires advance preparation.)

4 dried chipotle chiles
1 cup (236 mL) hot water
⅓ cup (79 mL) olive oil
8 cloves garlic, peeled
½ cup (118 mL) chopped onion
½ cup (118 mL) dry red wine
2 tablespoons (30 mL) red wine vinegar
2 teaspoons (10 mL) Dijon mustard
2 teaspoons (10 mL) brown sugar
2 teaspoons (10 mL) ground chile de arbol or other small, hot red chiles
1 teaspoon (5 mL) Worcestershire sauce
4 venison steaks (or substitute beef steaks), 1 inch (2.5 cm) thick

1. In a bowl, cover the chipotle chiles with the hot water and soak for 30 minutes to soften. Drain and remove the stems and seeds from the chiles.
2. In a skillet, heat the oil over medium heat. Add the garlic and onion and sauté until softened. Allow the garlic and onion to cool.
3. In a blender or food processor, combine the drained chiles, the sautéed garlic and onion, the wine, the vinegar, the mustard, the brown sugar, the ground chile, and the Worcestershire sauce and purée until smooth.
4. Place the meat in a nonreactive pan, cover it with the marinade, and marinate, covered, for 2 hours in the refrigerator.
5. Grill the meat over a medium fire, basting frequently with the marinade and turning often, for about 16 minutes, until rare or medium-rare (the internal temperature should reach 150°F [75°C]). Slice one of the steaks open to check for doneness, if you wish.

Mayan Achiote-Marinated Pork Cooked in Banana Leaves and Served with Habanero-Spiced Black Beans

Yield: 4–6 servings   Heat Scale: Medium-Hot

This Pre-Columbian dish, probably the best known of all Yucatán foods, is known as cochinita pibil. It was cooked in the pibil method—in a pit. The center of the Mayan community was the cooking hole called the pib, in which charcoal with flat stones over it was used for the cooking. This easier variation can be done on the grill, which does not require digging a hole in your backyard. Achiote is annatto, which is both a spice and an orange coloring agent, and the paste can be found in Latin and sometimes Asian markets. Banana leaves can be found in Asian markets, but you can also use aluminum foil. Epazote is an herb that is always used to flavor beans in Yucatán. Because of its distinctive flavor, there is really no substitute. So, if you don't have any epazote, just omit it from the recipe. Serve this dish with pickled red onions and yellow rice. (Note: This recipe requires advance preparation.)

For the Achiote-Marinated Pork:
10 whole black peppercorns
¼ teaspoon (1.25 mL) cumin seeds
5 cloves garlic, peeled
2 habanero chiles, stems and seeds removed
3 tablespoons (45 mL) achiote paste
1 teaspoon (5 mL) dried oregano (Mexican preferred)
2 bay leaves
⅓ cup (79 mL) lime juice (fresh preferred)
2 pounds (1.1 kg) lean pork, cut in 1½–2 inch (3.5–5 inch) cubes
3 fresh banana or guero chiles, stems and seeds removed, cut in strips
1 small purple onion, peeled, sliced, and separated into rings
Banana leaves for grilling

1. Place the peppercorns and cumin seeds in a spice or coffee grinder and process to a fine powder. Transfer the powder to a blender or food processor, add the garlic and habanero chile, and purée.

2. Transfer the mixture to a bowl. Add the achiote, oregano, bay leaves, and lime juice. Pour the marinade over the pork and marinate overnight or for 24 hours.

3. Cut 2 pieces of string, each about 6 inches (15 cm) long. Lay the strings down on a flat surface and place banana leaves on top of the strings. Place the marinated pork on the leaves and top with the chiles and onions. Fold the banana leaves over the meat and tie with the strings. Make two or three banana packets.

4. Cook the packets on the grill over indirect heat for 1½ hours.

For the Habanero-Spiced Black Beans:
1 pound (454 g) dried black beans
2 small onions, peeled and quartered
4 large cloves garlic, peeled
1 tablespoon (15 mL) dried epazote
1 fresh habanero chile, stems and seeds removed, chopped

1. Place the beans in a large pot and add water to cover. Let the beans soak overnight.

2. Bring the pot with the beans to a boil, reduce the heat slightly, and cook for an hour. Add the onions, garlic, epazote, and chiles. Simmer for an additional hour or until the beans are done.

Remove the onion, if possible, and mash the beans along with some of the water to a smooth consistency.

3. Serve the pork with warmed corn tortillas and the spiced black beans.

Genghis Khan Mixed Barbecue

Yield: 4–6 servings   Heat Scale: Medium

No, this is not barbecued camel, but you could use camel if American supermarkets would only wise up and stock it. ("Special: Bactrian Hump, Just $12.95 a Pound!") This Mongol specialty is my take on a nomadic campfire feast. So if you would like to camp in your backyard, this would work fine over a hardwood fire. You could also use your Weber. (Note: This recipe requires advance preparation.)

For the Khan Marinade:
2 tablespoons (30 mL) rice wine
1 tablespoon (15 mL) soy sauce
2 tablespoons (30 mL) minced leeks
1 teaspoon (5 mL) sugar
2 teaspoons (10 mL) sesame oil
2 teaspoons (10 mL) minced garlic
3 jalapeño chiles, stems and seeds removed, minced
¼ teaspoon (1.25 mL) ground white pepper
1½ pounds (680 g) lamb, sliced 1½ inches (3.5 cm) thick

1. In a blender or food processor, combine the rice wine, soy sauce, leeks, sugar, sesame oil, garlic, and chiles and purée until smooth. Place the lamb in a glass dish and pour the marinade over it, coating it thoroughly. Marinate the meat for 3 to 4 hours, covered, in the refrigerator.

2. Drain the lamb and transfer the leftover marinade in a saucepan. Simmer the marinade for 20 minutes.

For the Red Wine–Chile Dipping Sauce:
⅓ cup (79 mL) dry red wine
1 green onion, minced, green part included
1 jalapeño chile, stem and seeds removed, minced
2 teaspoons (10 mL) chile oil
1 clove garlic, peeled and minced

1. In a bowl, combine all the ingredients and let sit for at least an hour to blend the flavors. Transfer the sauce to a blender or food processor and process until smooth.

For the Chile-Garlic Dipping Sauce:
1 tablespoon (15 mL) rice wine vinegar (or substitute 2 tablespoons [30 mL] rice wine)
4 red serrano or jalapeño chiles, stems and seeds removed, minced
4 cloves garlic, peeled and chopped
1 teaspoon (5 mL) sugar
1 teaspoon (5 mL) peanut oil

1. In a bowl, combine all the ingredients and let sit at for at least an hour to blend the flavors. Transfer the sauce to a blender or food processor and process until smooth.

For the Vegetable Barbecue:
12 cremini or button mushrooms
1 leek, cut in 3-inch (7.5 cm) lengths, then cut in strips
4 green onions, cut in 3-inch (7.5 cm) lengths
1 small bell pepper, stem and seeds removed, thickly sliced
¼ pound (113 g) edible pea pods
2 jalapeño chiles, stems and seeds removed, cut in strips

1. Toss the vegetables in the simmered marinade and transfer them to a vegetable grilling basket.

2. Over a medium fire, grill the lamb and the vegetables. The lamb should be cooked until medium rare (the internal temperature should reach 150°F [75°C]), about 10 to 12 minutes. You may cut open a sample to check for doneness. The vegetables should be shaken often and cooked until they can be easily pierced with a knife, about 15 minutes.

3. Serve the lamb and vegetables with rice and the dipping sauces on the side. Of course, you can pour the dipping sauces over the entire meal.

Variation

Thread the meat and vegetables on skewers to grill.

Armenian Spiced Lamb Brochettes on Nutty Rice Pilaf

Yield: 4–6 servings   Heat Scale: Medium

This robust specialty features skewered chunks of meat and onions marinated in oil and spices and then grilled over an open flame. The technique apparently originated in the Caucasus and spread southward to Mediterranean countries. The traditional meat has always been leg of lamb, a meat that seems to be permitted by most major religions. To make a perfect kebab, remove any tough membrane from the meat, cut the meat across the grain, and don't forget that the meat must be marinated before grilling. Serve this with a salad of tossed greens, ripe olives, and feta cheese and, for dessert, baklava and Turkish coffee. (Note: This recipe requires advance preparation.)

For the Cayenne-Infused Meat Marinade:
1 teaspoon (5 mL) cumin seeds
⅓ cup (79 mL) olive oil
2 tablespoons (30 mL) lemon juice (fresh preferred)
1 tablespoon (15 mL) soy sauce
2 tablespoons (30 mL) dry sherry
1 cup (236 mL) finely chopped onion
3 tablespoons (45 mL) finely chopped parsley
1 tablespoon (15 mL) finely chopped ginger
2 cloves garlic, peeled and minced
2 teaspoons (10 mL) ground cayenne
1 teaspoon (5 mL) ground paprika
2 teaspoons (10 mL) chopped fresh oregano
½ teaspoon (2.5 mL) ground cinnamon
Salt, to taste
Freshly ground black pepper, to taste

1. Toast the cumin seeds on a dry skillet over high heat until fragrant, about 2 minutes, taking care that they don't burn. Remove the seeds from the heat, let them cool, and crush them. In a blender or food processor, combine the cumin with the olive oil, lemon juice, soy sauce, sherry, onion, parsley, ginger, garlic, cayenne, paprika, oregano, and cinnamon and purée until smooth. Season with salt and pepper. Reserve 2 teaspoons (10 mL) of the marinade for the rice.

For the Brochettes:
1½ pounds (680 g) boneless lamb, cut into 1-inch (2.5 cm) cubes
1 large bell pepper, stem and seeds removed, cut in 1½-inch (3.5 cm) squares
1 small onion, peeled and cut in 1½-inch (3.5 cm) cubes
12 cherry tomatoes
12 cremini mushrooms, stems removed

1. Transfer the marinade to a bowl. Add the lamb, toss well to coat, cover, and marinate overnight in the refrigerator, turning occasionally.
2. Blanch the bell pepper and onions in boiling water for 2 minutes. Remove them from the water, run them under cold water, and drain them. Remove the lamb from the marinade. Transfer the marinade to a sauce pan and simmer for 20 minutes. Thread the meat onto skewers, alternating with the pepper, onion, tomatoes, and mushrooms. Brush with the reserved marinade.
3. Grill the kebabs over a medium-hot fire until medium-rare, about 15 minutes. Baste occasionally with the marinade. Cut a sample of the meat to check for doneness, and remove when it is a little underdone.

For the Nutty Rice Pilaf:
2 tablespoons (30 mL) boiling water
2 tablespoons (30 mL) olive oil
3 tablespoons (45 mL) blanched almonds
3 tablespoons (45 mL) shelled unsalted pistachios
½ cup (118 mL) vermicelli, broken into 1-inch (2.5 cm) pieces
1 cup (236 mL) uncooked long-grain rice
2½ cups (591 mL) Basic Beef Stock (page 45)
⅛ teaspoon (.6 mL) saffron
½ teaspoon (2.5 mL) ground cayenne

1. Place the saffron in a cup and add the water. Let sit for 20 minutes.
2. In a skillet, heat the oil over medium heat. Add the nuts and lightly fry them, stirring constantly, for 2 minutes. Remove them with a slotted spoon and set them aside. Turn heat to low, add the vermicelli to the pan, and cook, stirring constantly, until lightly browned, about 2 minutes. Add the rice, stir to coat, and sauté until the kernels are opaque, about 3 minutes.
3. Bring the beef stock, saffron, and cayenne to a boil and pour it over the rice mixture. Bring to a boil while stirring. Reduce the heat to low, and simmer, covered, until the rice is done, about 20 minutes. Fluff with a fork and add the nuts. (The rice also can be baked, covered, in a 325°F [165°C] oven for 40 minutes.
4. Serve the meat over the rice, accompanied by a sauce from Chapter 2, or make an additional half batch of the marinade and thicken it slightly with cornstarch.

Smokehouse Habanero Rum-Glazed Ham

Yield: 6–8 servings   Heat Scale: Medium

Here is a daring way to transform bland ham into something hot and sensational. The key here is not to spare the smoke or the habaneros, which appear in two forms in this recipe. For a double smoke effect, substitute chipotles for the habaneros, doubling the amount. It's okay to brush the ham with glaze every 20 minutes, as the meat is already cooked and the drop in temperature won't matter. Serve with cinnamon-baked pumpkin, steamed fresh peas and onions, and Georgia peach muffins. (Note: This recipe requires advance preparation.)

For the Habanero Marinated Ham:
2 tablespoons (30 mL) brown sugar
1 tablespoon (15 mL) Dijon mustard
2 tablespoons (30 mL) vegetable oil
1 tablespoon (15 mL) red wine vinegar
2 habanero chiles, stems and seeds removed, minced
2 teaspoons (10 mL) onion salt
¼ teaspoon (1.25 mL) ground turmeric
1 pinch ground cloves
1 (4-pound [1.82 kg]) fully cooked ham

1. In a bowl, combine the brown sugar, mustard, oil, vinegar, chiles, onion salt, turmeric, and cloves and mix well. Score the ham through the fat side about ½-inch (1 cm) deep. Rub the marinade all over the ham, making sure it penetrates into the scoring. Marinate the ham in a plastic bag in the refrigerator overnight.
2. Allow the meat to come to room temperature. Smoke the ham for 3 hours at 200 to 220°F (100 to 110°C). Remember, the ham is already cooked and you are just adding heat and flavor.

For the Rum Glaze:
¼ cup (59 mL) brown sugar
2 tablespoons (30 mL) dark rum
1½ tablespoons (22.5 mL) butter
1 tablespoon (15 mL) pineapple juice
2 teaspoons (10 mL) Dijon mustard
1 teaspoon (5 mL) ground habanero chile

1. In a saucepan, combine the brown sugar, rum, butter, pineapple juice, mustard, and chile and bring to a simmer. Simmer for 15 minutes. During the last hour of smoking, brush the ham with the glaze every 20 minutes.

Pita Pockets Stuffed with Harissa-Spiced Moroccan Lamb Brochettes

Yield: 4 servings   Heat Scale: Medium-Hot

Nancy Gerlach learned how to make these brochettes while traveling through Morocco in a VW bus in the 1970s. She and Jeff would find small, homemade charcoal braziers by the side of the road, and a smiling vendor would sell them the brochettes by the skewer and served in flat Arab bread. After hanging around enough vendors, Nancy witnessed the entire spicing and grilling process. Harissa is a fiery pepper paste that is used as an ingredient in couscous and grilled dishes or as a condiment served on the side of a Moroccan meal. Serve this dish with cold artichokes with cilantro mayonnaise. (Note: This recipe requires advance preparation.)

1 cup (236 mL) Harissa
1½ pounds (680 g) boneless lamb, cut into 1-inch (2.5 cm) cubes
4 pocket pita breads
Chopped cucumber for garnish
Chopped onion for garnish
Chopped tomatoes for garnish
Shredded lettuce for garnish

1. Reserve some of the Harissa to serve with the meat and place the remaining Harissa in a plastic bag. Add the lamb, mix them together with your hands, and marinate in the refrigerator for 3 hours or overnight. Save some of the Harissa to serve on the side.
2. Bring the meat to room temperature, thread the cubes onto skewers, and grill over a medium-hot fire for about 15 minutes, turning often.
3. Serve the lamb cubes in the pita bread with a little reserved Harissa, cucumber, onion, tomato, and lettuce.

Texas Beef Brisket, New Mexico–Style

Yield: About 20 servings, depending on the individual brisket and the size of the appetites of the guests

Heat Scale: Medium

Okay, okay, I borrowed a Texas technique and changed the rub to reflect my chilehead tastes. For years I have been perfecting recipes using a smoker known as an Oklahoma Joe's. It is a horizontal, cylindrical smoker about 3½ feet (1 m) long and about 14 inches (35 cm) in diameter. It has an attached, dropped fire box that allows smoking with fairly cool smoke because the fire is separated a bit from the smoking area. Because smoking is so time consuming, it makes sense to smoke several things at once. Some cooks use the basting sauce as a mop during the smoking process and eliminate the long marinade at the end of smoking. Leftovers, if there are any, make the best barbecue sandwiches when served on a crusty hard roll with your choice of sauce from Chapter 2.

1 (9–10-pound [4.1–4.5 kg) brisket ("packer trimmed" preferred)
½ cup (118 mL) lemon juice
2 cups (473 mL) ground mild red New Mexican chile
1 tablespoon (15 mL) ground cayenne
2 tablespoons (30 mL) freshly ground black pepper
¼ cup (59 mL) garlic powder
Deep, Way Deep in the Heart of Texas Barbecue Sauce (page 74)

1. Thoroughly coat all surfaces of the brisket with lemon juice, and rub it in well. Combine the ground chile, cayenne, black pepper, and garlic powder in a bowl, and sprinkle this mixture generously all over the brisket, rubbing it in well. Make sure that the brisket is entirely covered. Marinate for at least an hour before smoking.
2. To smoke the brisket, build a hardwood fire in the fire box using pecan, oak, or any fruit wood. When the fire is smoking nicely, place the brisket on the rack fat-side up, to let gravity and nature do the basting. Place the breast as far from the heat source as possible and close the smoker. During the smoking, do nothing to the brisket. The smoking will take approximately 8 hours at 200°F (100°C) smoke temperature. This means a lot of beer will be consumed while you wait and tend the fire.
3. After the brisket has finished smoking, remove it from the smoker, slather it generously with the barbecue sauce, wrap it tightly in aluminum foil, and return it to the smoker. Close off all of the air supplies to the fire, and allow the meat to "set" in the pit for about 2 hours.

Texas Fajitas

Yield: 6–8 servings   Heat Scale: Mild to Medium

There is no such thing as a chicken or tofu fajita because the word refers specifically to marinated and grilled skirt steak. This is actually a simple recipe to prepare, and it works best when the steak is grilled over mesquite wood or natural charcoal with mesquite chips. The technique known as smoke-grilling is perfect for this meat, and flank steak can be substituted for the skirt steak. Tradition holds that fajitas were first perfected in South Texas in the 1960s and quickly became a staple for Mexican restaurants—and others—north of the border. It is a classic example of combining several methods to make tough meat more palatable: marinate it, grill it, and slice it thinly against the grain. (Note: This recipe requires advance preparation.)

2 cloves garlic, peeled and minced
2 tablespoons (30 mL) vegetable oil
3 jalapeño chiles, stems and seeds removed, minced
⅓ cup (79 mL) lime juice
⅓ cup (79 mL) soy sauce
⅓ cup (79 mL) red wine
2 pounds (1.1 kg) skirt steak
8 flour tortillas
Grated Monterey Jack cheese for serving
Cheddar cheese for serving
Sour cream for serving
Guacamole for serving
Grilled onions for serving
Deep, Way Deep in the Heart of Texas Barbecue Sauce (page 74) for serving
Pico de Gallo Salsa (page 69) for serving
Commercial hot sauce to taste

1. In a bowl, combine the garlic, oil chiles, lime juice, soy sauce, and red wine and mix well. Place the steak in a glass dish and pour the marinade over it. Cover and marinate in the refrigerator overnight.
2. Remove the steak from the marinade. Grill the steak over a hot fire until medium-rare, about 10 to 15 minutes (the internal temperature should reach 150°F (75°C). You can also check for doneness by cutting into the steak. Remove the steak from the grill and slice thinly against the grain.
3. Quickly heat each tortilla on the grill. Serve the sliced steak wrapped in a tortilla and topped with your choice of the toppings.

Variation
Sauté onions, bell peppers, chiles, and tomato wedges in hot oil as a topping for fajitas.

Memphis Baby Back Ribs

Yield: 4 servings   Heat Scale: Medium

This particular specialty can be smoked or smoke-grilled, and it typifies the Memphis approach to cooking ribs—a double whammy of spices and sauce. As usual, watch for burning as the finishing sauce gets a bit of sugar from the tomato. Why not serve these delicious ribs with traditional potato salad, coleslaw, and pickled peppers? Remember that the meat on smoked ribs looks pink, but that's a chemical reaction with the smoke, and the ribs are really done. Really. It is difficult to take the temperature of the ribs because of the bones, so some cooking instinct is required here. (Note: This recipe requires advance preparation.)

1 cup (236 mL) Memphis Rib Rub (page 10)
3 slabs baby back ribs, about 4 pounds (1.82 kg) total
1 cup (236 mL) Memphis-Style Finishing Sauce (page 77)

1. In a large, shallow pan, pour the rub over the ribs and massage it into the meat on both sides. Cover and refrigerate for 4 hours. Remove the ribs from the refrigerator and bring them to room temperature.
2. If smoke-grilling the ribs, build a fire that is 300 to 350°F (150 to 190°C). Cook the ribs, covered, for 1 hour, turning often. Smoke-grill, basting the finishing sauce on the ribs with a brush, for another 30 minutes.
3. If smoking the ribs, maintain the smoke at 200 to 220°F (100 to 160°C) and smoke for 2 hours. Brush the finishing sauce over the ribs several times during the last hour of smoking, and turn the ribs occasionally.
4. Remove the ribs from the grill or smoker. Serve with additional finishing sauce on the side.

Kansas City Long Ends

Yield: 4–6 servings   Heat Scale: Medium

Long ends are the lean, thin bones of spareribs, while short ends are the shorter, fatter, meatier hind sections. The combination of the rub and finishing sauce is traditional in Kansas City–style barbecue. The sauce is sometimes slathered over the ribs during the last half hour of smoking and is always served on the side. Why not serve these ribs with french fries, corn on the cob, spicy baked beans, and hot peach cobbler for dessert? (Note: This recipe requires advance preparation.)

Kansas City Dry Rub (page 11)
6–8 pounds (2.72–3.63 kg) pork spare ribs, long ends only
Kansas City–Style Barbecue Sauce (page 75)

1. Place the rub in a shaker. Sprinkle it evenly over the ribs and let them marinate for 2 hours at room temperature or overnight in the refrigerator.
2. Prepare a fire and place the ribs on racks in the smoker. Smoke at approximately 200°F (100°C) for 4 hours. If desired, baste with the sauce during the last half hour of smoking. Serve with the sauce on the side.

Smoked Prime Ribs of Beef

Yield: 4 servings   Heat Scale: Medium

We cannot eliminate beef from the rib race. It is smoked everywhere in the United States, but the only area claiming it as the main barbecue meat is Texas—and that's mostly brisket and skirt steak. Buy a large prime rib roast, cut away the center, and use it for rib eye steaks. Then slice the ribs apart so that more smoke will reach them. Serve these ribs with a roasted corn salad and buttermilk biscuits.

8 large prime ribs
⅔ cup (158 mL) Genuine, Authentic, South-of-the-Border Chile Rub (page 11)
Any barbecue sauce from Chapter 2

1. Trim the excess fat from the ribs. Massage the rub into the meat. Cover and let stand at room temperature for 1 hour.
2. Build a fire in the smoker and bring the smoke to 200 to 220°F (100 to 110°C). Place the ribs on the grill or on racks and smoke for 4½ hours, turning occasionally. Thirty minutes before you remove the ribs from the smoker, brush them all over with the barbecue sauce.

Carolina Pulled Pork Sandwiches with Coleslaw

Yield: 6–8 servings   Heat Scale: Mild

Notice that I have not limited this recipe to the "southeastern corner of western North Carolina," but rather have made a universal Carolina recipe that you can sauce up with two or three styles of the Carolina BBQ sauces in Chapter 2. Even the coleslaw can go north or south. There is a minor debate about whether or not to use a rub, with purists generally preferring to simply salt the pork roast—a practice of which most smoking chefs don't approve. If you wish to use a rub, use the Memphis Rib Rub (page 10), which is quite similar to Carolina rubs. (Note: This recipe requires advance preparation.)

For the Pulled Pork Sandwiches:
1 (3–4 pound [1.36–1.82 kg]) Boston Butt pork roast
6–8 Kaiser rolls
North Carolina Barbecue Sauce (page 76) or South Carolina Mustard Barbecue Sauce (page 76) for serving

1. If using a rub, sprinkle it thickly over the roast and allow it to sit, covered, at room temperature, for 3 hours. Start a fire and place the roast in the smoker on a rack. Place a drip pan beneath the grill, as this roast will drip a lot of fat. Smoke the roast with 200°F (100°C) smoke for 4 hours, until it is falling off the bone or until the internal temperature reaches 170°F (85°C).
2. Remove the roast from the smoker, transfer it to a cutting board, and allow it to sit for 20 minutes. With your fingers, remove any skin and fat from the roast. Pull the pork into thin pieces about 1½ inches (3.5 cm) long. This is slippery and tedious work, so if you get frustrated, take out a knife and chop the pork into ½-inch (1 cm) pieces. Then change the name of this recipe to Carolina Chopped Pork Sandwiches.
3. To serve, place the pork on the buns and spread the sauce of your choice over the pork.

For the Carolina Cole Slaw:
3 cups (708 mL) shredded cabbage
1 small green bell pepper, stem and seeds removed, thinly sliced
¼ cup (59 mL) thinly sliced onion
4 teaspoons (20 mL) sugar
1 tablespoon (15 mL) vegetable oil
3 tablespoons (45 mL) apple cider vinegar
1 teaspoon (5 mL) Dijon mustard
½ teaspoon (2.5 mL) celery seeds
Salt, to taste
Freshly ground black pepper, to taste

1. In a bowl, mix together the cabbage, bell pepper, and onion. In a separate bowl, combine the sugar, oil, vinegar, mustard, celery seeds, salt and pepper. Pour the dressing over the salad and mix well. Cover and refrigerate for 2 hours. Serve with the sandwiches.

Kentucky Barbecued Lamb

Yield: 8–10 servings   Heat Scale: Mild

To my knowledge, there are only two places in the States where lamb or goat are really popular: Kentucky and the true Southwest, meaning West and South Texas, New Mexico, Arizona, and sometimes Colorado. In the Southwest, the cabrito or young goat is barbecued pit-style, with limited smoke and no flame. In Kentucky, lamb and mutton are celebrated barbecue meats, with a festival tradition that dates back to 1834. They still reign supreme today at the Owensboro Bar-B-Q Championship. This barbecue is unusual in that the lamb is first marinated in what's locally called a "dip," then rubbed with a spice mixture. Serve with grilled green tomatoes, a black-eyed pea salad, and of course, a cool mint julep. (Note: This recipe requires advance preparation.)

1 cup (236 mL) Worcestershire sauce
1 cup (236 mL) distilled white vinegar
¾ cup (177 mL) brown sugar, divided
1 quart (.95 L) water
4 tablespoons (60 mL) freshly ground black pepper, divided
2 tablespoons (30 mL) minced garlic
¼ cup (59 mL) minced onion
2 teaspoons (10 mL) ground allspice, divided
1 teaspoon (5 mL) salt
¼ cup (59 mL) lime juice (fresh preferred)
1 4- to 5-pound leg of lamb
2 teaspoons (10 mL) commercial chili powder
1 tablespoon (15 mL) garlic powder
2 tablespoons (30 mL) dried onion

1. In a large pot, combine the Worcestershire sauce, vinegar, ½ cup (118 mL) of the brown sugar, the water, 2 tablespoons (30 mL) of the pepper, the garlic, the onion, 2 teaspoons (10 mL) of the allspice, the salt, and the lime juice and bring to a boil. Reduce the heat and simmer for 45 minutes. Remove the marinade from the heat and allow it to cool. Place the lamb in a large plastic bag or nonreactive container, add the marinade, and refrigerate for 12 to 24 hours.

2. Remove the lamb from the marinade and bring it to room temperature. Heat the remaining marinade in a saucepan and simmer for 20 minutes. Start a fire in the smoker and bring the smoke to 200 to 220°F (100 to 110°C). In a bowl, mix together the chili powder, the remaining 2 teaspoons (10 mL) allspice, the garlic powder, the remaining 2 tablespoons (30 mL) black pepper, the remaining ¼ cup (59 mL) brown sugar, and the dried onion. Spread the rub evenly over the lamb. Place the lamb on a rack in the smoker and smoke for 6 to 7 hours, until the internal temperature is 170°F (85°C) for well done. Serve the lamb pulled or sliced, with some of the remaining marinade poured over it.

Barbecued Kid, Shepherd-Style

Yield: 20 or more servings   Heat Scale: Varies

Known in the Southwest as cabrito al pastor, barbecued young goat is a spring tradition that can be duplicated in a grill with a spit or in a smoker. The biggest problem is going to be finding a young, tender 12- to 15-pound (5.5 to 7 kg) young goat. You may have to search out butchers, farmers, or Latin markets. You can substitute a large leg of lamb if you can't find the young goat, and adjust the smoking time downward.

Genuine, Authentic, South-of-the-Border Chile Rub (page 11)
1 (12-pound [5.5 kg]) young goat, cleaned
Barbecue sauce of your choice from Chapter 2 for serving
Flour or corn tortillas for serving
Guacamole for serving
Salsa of your choice from Chapter 2 for serving

1. Sprinkle the rub all over the goat and rub it in thoroughly. If grilling the goat, build a mesquite wood fire in a large barbecue with a spit, or use natural charcoal and mesquite chips. Arrange the goat on a spit about 1 foot (30 cm) above the coals. You can use a motor to turn the spit, or turn it manually every 10 or 15 minutes. Cook until the internal temperature reaches 170°F (80°C), for well done.

2. If smoking the goat, place the goat on a rack in the smoker with the smoke from pecan, oak, or fruitwood at 200 to 220°F (100 to 110°C). Smoke for about 1 hour per pound, or until the internal temperature reaches 180°F (85°C).

3. To serve, slice the cabrito thinly and top it with barbecue sauce. Serve with the tortillas, guacamole, and salsa on the side, or make tacos topped with the salsa.

Southern Hot Links
Yield: 10 servings   Heat Scale: Medium

Here is my recipe for a typically Southern sausage made with ground pork and lamb. For this recipe, you will need a meat grinder with a sausage funnel, a tube that fits over the end of the grinder for filling sausage casings. You can also use a stand mixer, such as a KitchenAid, with a sausage stuffer attachment. When stuffing, fill the casings until the sausage segments are about 4 inches (10 cm) long, then twist the casing and tie the sausages off with string. Then cut the casing off with scissors. Serve the links on buns with raw onions and barbecue sauce accompanied by a macaroni salad and baked beans.

2 pounds (1.1 kg) ground pork, shoulder cut preferred
2 pounds (1.1 kg) ground beef, round steak preferred
2 teaspoons (10 mL) crushed red chile (piquin for hot, New Mexican for mild)
2 teaspoons (10 mL) paprika
2 teaspoons (10 mL) dried sage
1 teaspoon (5 mL) ground cumin
2 teaspoons (10 mL) dried basil
1 teaspoon (5 mL) anise seed
2 teaspoons (10 mL) dried oregano
Sausage casings
Barbecue sauce of your choice, (such as North Carolina Barbecue Sauce; page 76)

1. In a bowl, combine the ground meats, chiles, and spices and mix well. Using a meat grinder with a stuffing attachment, stuff the sausage casings and tie them off. Build a fire in the smoker, place the sausages on the grill in the smoker, and smoke at 200 to 220°F (100 to 110°C) for about 3 hours, or until the internal temperature reaches 170°F (80°C). Remove from the smoker and serve with the barbecue sauce.

Honey- and Chile-Glazed Smoked Ham
Yield: 20 servings   Heat Scale: Medium

Some specialty hams, like those from around Smithfield, Virginia, take months and months to cure and smoke, which is way too long to approximate in the home smoker. Most commercial hams found in supermarkets are cured and cooked, but not smoked. However, you can prepare a mighty tasty smoked ham in just a few hours in the smoker. How? By purchasing a cooked ham and smoking it yourself. Serve this with herb-scalloped potatoes, fresh peas, and hot cornbread. (Note: This recipe requires advance preparation.)

1 (10-pound [4.5 kg]) cooked ham
1 recipe Ragin' Cajun Rub (page 12)
1 cup (236 mL) honey
½ cup (118 mL) soy sauce
¼ cup (59 mL) ground red New Mexican chile
South Carolina Mustard Barbecue Sauce (page 76) for serving

1. Wash the ham in cold water and pat dry. Spread the rub thoroughly over the ham, place the ham in a plastic bag, and refrigerate for 12 hours or preferably overnight.
2. Prepare a fire in the smoker with a hardwood such as oak and bring the smoke to 200 to 220°F (100 to 110°C). Smoke the ham for 4 hours.
3. In a bowl, combine the honey, soy sauce, and chile and mix well. Brush the glaze over the ham and smoke for another hour, applying the glaze three more times. Remove the ham from the smoker and let it sit for 15 minutes. Carve the ham and serve it with the South Carolina Mustard Barbecue Sauce.

Southwestern Chicken Barbecue

Yield: 8–10 servings   Heat Scale: Medium

Some regions specialize in certain barbecued meats—beef brisket in Texas, pork in the Carolinas, and lamb and mutton in Kentucky. But around every cook-off where you find these specialty meats, people are smoking chickens as well. This is because people love barbecued chicken so much that it's a specialty everywhere, with no particular regional claim for it. This is the way I prepare it in New Mexico, but feel free to vary the rub and finishing sauce. It doesn't make any sense to fire up the smoker to do just one chicken, so smoke three because it freezes so well. (Note: This recipe requires advance preparation.)

3 whole chickens, split down the back to make 6 chicken halves, tails removed
1 recipe Genuine, Authentic, South-of-the-Border Chile Rub (page 11)
1 recipe Chipotle BBQ Sauce (page 73)

1. Wash the chicken halves and pat them dry. Cover the halves with the rub and marinate them in plastic bags in the refrigerator for 12 to 24 hours.
2. Remove the chicken from the refrigerator and bring it to room temperature. Prepare a fruitwood fire in the smoker and bring the smoke to 200 to 220°F (100 to 110°C). Place the chicken halves on the grill, cut-side down, and smoke for about 3 hours or until the internal temperature reaches 175°F (80°C).
3. Remove the chicken from the smoker and cut it into serving pieces, discarding the backs. Slather it with the Chipotle BBQ Sauce and serve.

Grilled Split Thai Chicken with Fiery Red Chile Sauce

Yield: 4–6 servings   Heat Scale: Hot

Chickens grilled in this manner are very popular throughout Thailand, where they're sold in village bus depots, portable food stations, at the beach—everywhere. The Thai would use bamboo skewers, but metal ones work fine. The skewers keep the chicken flat as it cooks on the grill. You will notice that the chicken is doubly spiced, like American barbecue, but much hotter. The Thai like their food very pungent! The chiles traditionally used are prik chee fa, with medium-hot, cayenne-like, bright red pods.

For the Thai Seasoning Paste:
12 large cloves garlic, peeled and chopped
½ cup (118 mL) chopped shallots
¼ cup (59 mL) chopped ginger
¼ cup (59 mL) fish sauce (or substitute soy sauce)
4 stalks lemongrass, peeled to reveal the soft inner root and lower stem, chopped
8–10 red Thai chiles (prik kee nu), stems and seeds removed, chopped (or substitute 4 red jalapeños)

1. In a food processor or blender, combine all the ingredients and process to a thick paste.

For the Chicken:
1 (3–3½-pound [1.36–1.59 kg) chicken

1. Using poultry shears or a heavy knife, cut down both sides of the backbone to cut the chicken in half. Remove the backbone and place the chicken on a cutting board, skin-side up. Press hard on the breastbone to break it and flatten the bird.
2. Loosen the skin and rub the paste all over the chicken, over and under the skin.
3. Force a skewer through one thigh perpendicular to bone and just above drumstick, into the breast, and out through the middle joint of the wing. Repeat on the other side of the chicken.
4. Place the skewers on the grill over a medium-hot fire. Grill slowly, turning as needed to brown evenly, for about 30 minutes, or until the internal temperature of the chicken is 160°F (75°C) for medium.

For the Fiery Red Chile Sauce:
3 dried red New Mexican chiles, stems and seeds removed
4 red Thai chiles, stems and seeds removed, chopped (or substitute red jalapeños)
1 tablespoon (15 mL) chopped ginger
4 cloves garlic, peeled
½ cup (118 mL) distilled white vinegar
2 tablespoons (30 mL) sugar
2 tablespoons (30 mL) chopped fresh basil (Thai preferred)
Salt, to taste

1. Soak the dried chiles in hot water to soften for about 20 minutes. Remove the chiles from the water, drain them, and chop them. In a blender or food processor, combine the chiles, ginger, garlic, and ¾ cup (177 mL) water and process until almost puréed, but still coarse. Transfer this mixture to a saucepan and add the vinegar and sugar. Cook until the sauce reduced is by about half. Transfer it to a bowl and add basil and salt to taste. Stir well.
2. Serve the chicken with the sauce on the side.

Mexican Chile-Rubbed Rotisserie Chicken with Frijoles Borrachos and Pico de Gallo

Yield: 4–6 servings   Heat Scale: Medium

Nancy Gerlach made dozens of attempts to extract the recipe for this classic Mexican chicken from vendors all over Mexico, but they stonewalled her. When she asked what rub was used, they would answer only, "chile and herbs." But she persisted, and with some careful spying, she deduced this recipe. This is the chicken sold in little stalls in the marketplaces, in small restaurants on the streets, and even in grocery stores. The meat is placed in tortillas and topped with Pico de Gallo Salsa. The drunken beans are usually served on the side, but if you want to put them in your taco, I won't call the food police. (Note: This recipe requires advance preparation.)

For the Frijoles Borrachos:
2 cups (473 mL) dried pinto beans, sorted and rinsed clean
4 jalapeño chiles, stems and seeds removed, cut in strips
1 small onion, peeled and cut in wedges
1 strip of bacon, cut in pieces
1 (12-ounce [336 mL]) can beer (Mexican preferred)
Salt, to taste

1. Combine the beans, chile, onion, bacon, and beer in a large pot. Cover with water and let sit overnight.
2. Drain the beans, reserving the water. Place the beans, chiles, onion, and bacon in a large pot. Add 2 cups (473 mL) of the bean water, bring to a boil, reduce the heat, and simmer for 45 minutes or until the beans are tender, adding more of the bean water if necessary. When the beans are done, either mash them until smooth or serve whole. Add the salt.

For the Chicken:
1 (3½–4 pound [1.59–1.82 kg]) chicken
4 large guajillo chiles, stems and seeds removed (or substitute New Mexican chiles)
4 chiles de arbol, stems and seeds removed
1 teaspoon (5 mL) dried oregano (Mexican preferred)
2–3 teaspoons (10–15 mL) garlic salt
2 limes (Mexican preferred), cut in half
6 cloves garlic, peeled and cut in large pieces or slices

1. Clean the chicken and pat it dry. Combine the dried chiles and oregano in a spice grinder and process to a fine powder. Sprinkle the inside of the chicken with the garlic salt. Rub the outside of the chicken with the lime juice and then the garlic. Coat the chicken with the chile mixture and put the chicken on a spit. Place the spit on the rotisserie over a medium fire and grill for about 1 hour, or until the internal temperature in the thigh of the chicken is 165°F (75°C) for medium. Remove the chicken from the spit and allow it to sit for 10 minutes before carving.

For the Pico de Gallo Salsa:
6 jalapeño or serrano chiles, stems and seeds removed, finely chopped
2 tomatoes, finely chopped
1 small onion, peeled and finely chopped
2 tablespoons (30 mL) finely chopped fresh cilantro
3 tablespoons (45 mL) vegetable oil
2–3 tablespoons (30–45 mL) red wine vinegar
Salt, to taste

1. Combine all the ingredients in a bowl and let stand for at least an hour to allow the flavors to blend.

To Finish:
12 corn tortillas

1. To serve, cut the chicken into pieces and pile the pieces on a serving platter. Serve with the hot beans, hot steamed corn tortillas, and the salsa on the side. Guests can assemble their own grilled chicken tacos topped with the salsa.

Tikka Chicken and Cauliflower Kebabs

Yield: 4 servings   Heat Scale: Mild

Thanks to Pat Chapman, England's King of Curries, for this recipe from one of his best-selling curry cookbooks. Tikka refers to food cut into small pieces and marinated. In this case, the marinade is the same used for high-heat tandoori cooking, so it works very well with grilled foods. These low-fat kebabs are usually served over rice with a spicy cucumber and yogurt salad on the side. Serve as Pat does on a bed of greens—shredded radicchio, white cabbage, and strips of red and green bell peppers, along with an onion chutney and a yogurt-tomato-cucumber raita. (Note: This recipe requires advance preparation.)

¼ cup (59 mL) plain yogurt
1 tablespoon (15 mL) vegetable oil
1 tablespoon (15 mL) lemon juice
2 cloves garlic, peeled and chopped
3 green New Mexican chiles, roasted and peeled, stems and seeds removed, chopped
1½ tablespoons (22.5 mL) chopped fresh mint
1½ tablespoons (22.5 mL) chopped fresh cilantro
1½ tablespoons (22.5 mL) green masala paste (available in Asian markets)
½ teaspoon (2.5 mL) cumin seeds, toasted and ground
1 pinch salt
2 tablespoons (30 mL) milk, or more as needed
2 boneless, skinless, chicken breasts, cut in 1½-inch (1 cm) cubes
1 small head cauliflower, cut in florets

1. In a blender or food processor, combine the yogurt, oil, lemon juice, garlic, chiles, mint, cilantro, and masala paste and purée to a smooth paste. Add the cumin and salt and continue processing. While the machine is running, add just enough milk to form a pourable purée.
2. Reserve a little of the marinade for the cauliflower. Toss the chicken in the remaining marinade and marinate for 24 hours in the refrigerator.
3. Cook the cauliflower in pot of boiling, salted water until just tender, about 2 minutes, then drain. Rinse under cold water to stop the cooking. Toss the cauliflower in the marinade.
4. Thread the chicken and cauliflower onto skewers and grill over a medium fire for 10 to 14 minutes, turning occasionally. Cut open a piece of chicken to check for doneness.

Double-Spiced Barbecued Pineapple Chicken

Yield: 4 servings   Heat Scale: Hot

This method can be used for whole chicken or pieces such as legs and thighs. When the paste is rubbed under the skin, the juices emanating from both the skin and the meat infuse the flavor of the paste into the chicken—and the evil, fatty, crispy, heavenly tasting skin. Serve this dish with hearts of palm salad, pumpkin rice, and a coconut milk sorbet for dessert.

¼ cup (59 mL) chopped fresh cilantro leaves
1 (5-ounce [140 g]) can pineapple chunks, drained, divided, juice reserved
2 tablespoons (30 mL) lime juice, divided (fresh preferred)
3 tablespoons (45 mL) chopped red onion, divided
½ habanero chile, stems and seeds removed, minced (or substitute
¼ teaspoon [1.25 mL] ground habanero chile)
¼ teaspoon (1.25 mL) grated ginger
2 teaspoons (10 mL) olive oil
12 tablespoons (30 mL) catsup
1 tablespoon (15 mL) apple cider vinegar
1 tablespoon (15 mL) brown sugar
1 teaspoon (5 mL) soy sauce
½ to 1 habanero chile, stem and seeds removed
¼ cup (59 mL) fresh cilantro leaves
4 chicken legs and thighs

1. In a blender or food processor, combine the chopped cilantro, half the drained pineapple chunks, 1 tablespoon (15 mL) of the lime juice, 1 tablespoon (5 mL) of the red onion, the minced chile, and the ginger and purée until smooth. Run your finger between the skin and meat of the chicken to loosen the skin and make a pocket. Be sure to leave some of the skin attached. Gently stuff the paste into the pockets and pull the skin back over the chicken pieces. Set the chicken aside while you make the sauce.
2. In a sauté pan, heat the oil over medium heat. Add the remaining red onion and sauté until softened, about 5 minutes. Add 6 tablespoons (90 mL) of the reserved pineapple juice, the remaining pineapple chunks, the catsup, the remaining lime juice, the vinegar, the brown sugar, the soy sauce, and the chile and bring to a boil. Reduce the heat and simmer for 30 minutes. Transfer the sauce to a blender or food processor. Add the cilantro leaves and purée until smooth. Keep the sauce warm while cooking the chicken.
3. Place the chicken on the grill, skin-side up, and grill for 20 to 30 minutes over medium heat. Liberally baste the chicken with the sauce. Continue to cook until the chicken reaches an internal temperature of 160°F (75°C).

Belizean Rubbed and Grilled Fish Burger

Yield: 4 servings   Heat Scale: Medium

This particular burger is a fired-up re-creation of a fish sandwich I devoured in the tiny town of San Pedro on Ambergris Caye, Belize, in 1985. The restaurant was called Elvie's Burger Isle, and the diners sat outside on picnic benches under a tamarind tree. If ever there was a simple-to-prepare, quick and easy fish recipe with significant heat, this is it. Serve with french fries, crisp coleslaw, and, to toast Elvie, a frosty tamarind cooler.

1 teaspoon (5 mL) ground habanero chile
1 teaspoon (5 mL) garlic salt
1 teaspoon (5 mL) ground thyme
½ teaspoon (2.5 mL) ground allspice
¼ teaspoon (1.25 mL) ground nutmeg
1 tablespoon (15 mL) olive oil, plus more for brushing the fish
4 small white fish fillets, such as snapper, trigger fish, or grouper
4 burger rolls
Your choice of a Belizean habanero hot sauce, such as Marie Sharp's, or any salsa from Chapter 2

1. In a bowl, combine the chile, garlic salt, thyme, allspice, and nutmeg. Brush the fillets with oil and dust them with the spice mixture. Let them sit at room temperature while you prepare the grill.
2. Cut the rolls in half length-wise and brush with 1 tablespoon (15 mL) oil.
3. Grill the fish in a grill basket over medium heat, about 5 minutes per side, or until the fillets flake.
4. Grill the rolls to slightly warm. Place the fish on the rolls and top with the sauce of your choice.

Chile-Infused Red Snapper, Veracruz-Style

Yield: 4–6 servings   Heat Scale: Mild

This is one of the most delicious Mexican coastal fish recipes. It is served in Veracruz, the area of Mexico most influenced by Spanish cooking, but it is popular all over the country. Often the snapper is dusted with flour and pan-fried, then covered with a sauce, but I prefer mine beach-style. I grill it over wood or natural charcoal (gas is acceptable, too) and then serve it with the sauce on the side. Charring the tomatoes on the grill adds a smoky dimension to the sauce. This elegant and colorful fish is served with white rice, additional pickled jalapeños, and an equally elegant dessert from Chapter 14.

For the Snapper:
1 (3–4 pound [1.36–1.82 kg]) whole dressed red snapper
1 lime, halved
¼ cup (59 mL) ground chile de arbol, or substitute ground red New Mexican chile
1 teaspoon (5 mL) salt
Olive oil for basting
Chopped parsley for garnish

1. With a knife, lightly score the fish on both sides. Squeeze lime juice all over the fish, inside and out. In a small bowl, combine the chile and salt and mix well. Sprinkle the fish with this mixture inside and out.
2. Place the fish on the grill indirectly over a medium fire, baste it with olive oil, and cook about 1 hour per side, turning twice and basting with the oil. The fish should flake easily, and the internal temperature of the fish at its thickest part should be 135°F (60°C) for medium.

For the Veracruz Sauce:
6 small tomatoes
1 small onion, peeled
1 tablespoon (15 mL) olive oil
3 cloves garlic, peeled
1 tablespoon (15 mL) lemon juice
2 bay leaves
4 canned pickled jalapeño chiles (jalapeños en escabeche), seeds removed, cut in thin strips
1 tablespoon (15 mL) juice from the pickled jalapeños
½ cup (118 mL) sliced pimiento-stuffed olives
1 tablespoon (15 mL) capers
½ teaspoon (2.5 mL) sugar
¼ teaspoon (1.25 mL) ground cinnamon
¼ teaspoon (1.25 mL) ground cloves
Salt, to taste
Freshly ground black pepper, to taste

1. Roast the tomatoes and onions on the grill until charred evenly. Remove them from the grill and chop them. In a small pan, heat the oil over medium heat. Add the garlic and sauté until lightly browned. Add the tomatoes and bring to a boil. Reduce the heat, add the lemon juice, bay leaves, pickled chiles, juice, olives, capers, sugar, cinnamon, and cloves and simmer until thickened. Season with salt and pepper and remove the bay leaves.
2. Place the fish on a serving platter and pour most of the sauce over it. At the table, carve the fish and serve it with some sauce spooned over each portion. Garnish with the parsley. Serve with heated corn tortillas and the additional sauce on the table.

Cuban Two-Chile Stuffed Grouper with Creole Sofrito
Yield: 4 servings   Heat Scale: Medium

The stuffing is mild, but watch out for the Creole Sofrito. Yes, there is a debate about the presence of chiles in traditional Cuban food, but since I spice up everything as a matter of course, this recipe is how I would prepare Cuban seafood if I owned a restaurant (shudder) in, say, Santa Fe or Austin. Serve with avocado and mango salad, black beans and rice, and coconut flan.

For the Two-Chile Stuffing:
1 tablespoon (15 mL) olive oil
3 cloves garlic, peeled and minced
1 small onion, peeled, cut in slivers, and separated
4 cubanelle chiles, stems and seeds removed, cut into strips (or substitute yellow wax hot peppers)
2 rocotillo chiles, stems and seeds removed, minced (or substitute ½ habanero chile)
½ cup (118 mL) fresh bread crumbs
2 tablespoons (30 mL) lemon juice
1 tablespoon (15 mL) distilled white vinegar
½ cup (118 mL) chopped green olives
1 teaspoon (5 mL) dried thyme
¼ teaspoon (1.25 mL) grated nutmeg
Salt, to taste
Freshly ground black pepper, to taste

1. In a small pan, heat the oil over medium heat. Add the garlic, onion, and chiles and sauté until softened. Transfer the sautéed mixture to a bowl, add the remaining ingredients, and mix well.

For the Grouper:
1 (3-pound [1.36 kg]) grouper, snapper, or other favorite fish, even large-mouth bass, cleaned
Olive oil for basting
Fresh parsley for garnish

1. Stuff the cavity of the fish loosely with the stuffing, and secure the fish shut with toothpicks. Brush the fish with olive oil, place in a hinged grill basket, and grill over a medium fire for about 15 minutes, turning occasionally. The fish is done when it flakes easily or reaches 135°F (60°C) in its thickest part.

For the Creole Sofrito:
1 small onion, peeled, cut in rings, and separated
½ small green bell pepper, cut in strips
½ small red bell pepper, cut in strips
1 teaspoon (5 mL) minced habanero chiles
2 tablespoons (30 mL) olive oil
1 tomato, peeled and chopped
3 tablespoons (45 mL) dry sherry
½ teaspoon (2.5 mL) dried thyme
Salt, to taste

1. In a saucepan, heat the oil over medium heat. Add the onion, peppers, and chile and sauté until the onion is soft, about 3 minutes. Add the remaining ingredients and simmer until it forms a sauce, about 10 to 15 minutes.
2. Serve the fish with the stuffing on the side, topped with the sofrito and garnished with the fresh parsley.

Spicy Grilled Coconut Shrimp Kebabs with Jalapeño-Cilantro Couscous

Yield: 4 servings   Heat Scale: Medium

A staple in North Africa, couscous is wheat in granular form that is usually steamed. It is often combined with meats or vegetables, and of course we've added chiles to it. The marinade is quite sweet, but it works well with the shrimp. This is a re-creation of a dish Nancy Gerlach was served in the British Virgin Islands. Serve with a salad of star fruit, avocado, and grapefruit and a cooling Key lime sorbet for dessert.

For the Sweet-Hot Coconut Marinade:
¼ cup (59 mL) brown sugar
1 teaspoon (5 mL) ground habanero chile
2 cloves garlic, peeled and minced
2 teaspoons (10 mL) chopped fresh thyme (or substitute ½ teaspoon [2.5 mL] dried)
2 tablespoons (30 mL) honey
¼ cup (59 mL) coconut milk
3 tablespoons (45 mL) vegetable oil
1 tablespoon (15 mL) lime juice (fresh preferred)
2 dozen medium shrimp, shelled and deveined, tails on

1. In a bowl, combine the brown sugar, chile, garlic, thyme, honey, and coconut milk and mix well. Slowly whisk the oil into the marinade. Place the shrimp in a separate bowl and pour the lime juice and the marinade over them, coating them well. Cover and marinate the shrimp for 1 hour at room temperature.

For the Jalapeño-Cilantro Couscous:
1 tablespoon (15 mL) vegetable oil
2 cloves garlic, peeled and minced
2 shallots, peeled and chopped
1 jalapeño chile, stem and seeds removed, minced
1 teaspoon (5 mL) dried thyme
2 cups (473 mL) chicken broth
1 cup (236 mL) couscous
2 tablespoons (30 mL) chopped fresh cilantro
1 tablespoon (15 mL) chopped chives
Salt, to taste
Freshly ground black pepper, to taste

1. In a sauté pan, heat the oil over medium heat. Add the garlic, shallots, and jalapeño and sauté until soft. Stir in the thyme and remove the pan from the heat. In a saucepan, bring the chicken broth to a boil. Put the couscous in a bowl and pour the chicken broth over it. Cover the bowl and let sit for 15 minutes. Drain off any excess liquid and fluff the couscous with a fork. Add the shallot mixture, cilantro, and chives and toss to mix well. Season with salt and pepper and keep warm.

For the Kebabs:
1 green or red bell pepper, stem and seeds removed, cut in wedges
1 small onion, peeled, cut into wedges and separated
3–4 jalapeño chiles, stems and seeds removed, cut in slivers
8 cherry tomatoes

1. Remove the shrimp from the marinade. Thread the shrimp onto skewers alternating with the vegetables. Grill the kebabs over a medium fire, basting frequently with the marinade and turning occasionally, until done, about 6 to 8 minutes.
2. Spoon the couscous onto a warm serving platter. Lay the kebabs over the couscous and serve.

Smoked Oysters with Ancho Chile Sauce

Yield: 2 dozen   Heat Scale: Medium

This recipe requires hot smoke, and a lot of it, for a short period of time. Instead of 200°F (100°C) smoke from your smoker or grill, try for about 400°F (200°C). Oysters can also be grilled by placing them on the grill over high heat until the shells open, about 6 to 10 minutes.

24 large oysters
½ cup (118 mL) clam juice
3 tablespoons (45 mL) vegetable oil, divided
Juice of 1 lime plus 1 tablespoon (15 mL), divided
1 ancho chile, stems and seeds removed
1 chipotle chile in adobo sauce
3 tablespoons tomato sauce
2 tablespoons (30 mL) chopped onions
2 cloves garlic, peeled and chopped
2 tablespoons (30 mL) vinegar
⅛ teaspoon (.6 mL) ground allspice
1 pinch ground cloves
1 tablespoon (15 mL) vegetable oil
Chopped cilantro for garnish

1. Shuck the oysters, reserving the liquid. In a bowl, combine ½ cup (118 mL) of the reserved oyster liquid, the clam juice, 2 tablespoons (30 mL) of the vegetable oil, and the juice of 1 lime. Place the oysters in a shallow pan and pour the marinade over them. Marinate the oysters for 30 minutes in the refrigerator. Drain the oysters and return them to the refrigerator until ready to use.

2. Soak the ancho chile in hot water for 20 to 30 minutes until soft, then drain. In a blender or food processor, combine the soaked ancho chile, chipotle in adobo, tomato sauce, onions, garlic, and vinegar purée until smooth. Add a little water if necessary. Add the allspice and cloves and purée until smooth. In a saucepan, heat the remaining oil over medium heat. Add the sauce and sauté until almost dry, about 15 minutes. Remove the sauce from the heat and stir in the lime juice and cilantro.

3. Build a hot fire in the smoker or grill and add hickory or other hardwood chips or chunks, as you will need a lot of smoke.

4. Put ½ to 1 teaspoon (2.5 to 5 mL) sauce on each oyster. Set the oysters on the grill, close the cover, and smoke for 10 minutes

5. Serve immediately with any remaining sauce on the side. Oysters remaining on the grill too long will overcook.

TEN

Powerful Poultry

- - - - - - - - - - - - - - -

If any mass-produced food needs chiles, it's chicken. Certain meats, like an aged fillet mignon, can be grilled as is with no rub, marinade, or finishing sauce, and they will be superb. But bland chicken and other poultry need some help. It needs to be marinated, spiced up, combined with other ingredients, and otherwise altered. Duck is perhaps the most flavorful bird for the poultry consumer, but for some reason it is rarely used.

Please note that the recipes in this chapter work well with all types of birds, so you can interchange all the poultry, but take into consideration the size of birds or pieces of birds that you are working with. Obviously, a 20-pound (9 kg) turkey will take longer to cook than a 3-pound (1.5 kg) chicken.

Some birds have more fat than others, so it is important to grill poultry slowly and watch it carefully so that the fatty skin doesn't flare up and burn. The food police will order you to remove all the skin from poultry before cooking it, but I buck that trend because of one simple reason: As bland as chicken is, once it's treated with the right marinade and sauces and cooked correctly, few things in the world taste better than a perfect, crispy piece of chicken skin. My mom, Barbara, used to insist on eating only the skin of grilled chicken—provided that my father didn't burn it.

There has been a lot of interest lately in specialty birds such as ostrich, emu, and guinea hen. They are very lean and need marinades and sauces to make them palatable. They are also rather expensive when you can find them. I like them, but I doubt that they will become overwhelmingly popular for the home kitchen or for smoking and grilling outdoors.

Pollo al Ajo Estilo Peruano
(Peruvian Garlic Chicken)

Yield: 6 servings   Heat Scale: Hot

Garlic, a member of the onion family, is one of the oldest vegetables used by mankind. There are records of garlic being consumed by the workers who built the pyramids. When this allium was transferred to the New World, it was eagerly added to dishes such as this one. Serve this garlic chicken garnished with boiled potatoes and topped with a dollop of yogurt.

½ cup (118 mL) vegetable oil
3 onions, peeled and chopped
6 cloves garlic, peeled and minced
4 rocoto chiles, stems and seeds removed, minced (or substitute jalapeños)
½ teaspoon (2.5 mL) ground cinnamon
1 tablespoon (15 mL) cumin seeds, crushed
1 teaspoon (5 mL) dried basil
2 cups (473 mL) unsalted roasted peanuts, coarsely chopped
½ cup (118 mL) freshly grated Parmesan cheese
1 (3½–4 pound [1.6–1.8 kg]) chicken, poached, meat removed from the bones and chopped
¾ cup (177 mL) low-fat plain yogurt, at room temperature
Salt, to taste
Freshly ground black pepper, to taste
Boiled potatoes for garnish

1. In a large saucepan, heat the oil over medium heat. Add the onion and garlic and sauté until the onion is soft. Add the chiles, cinnamon, cumin, basil, peanuts, cheese, and chicken meat to the saucepan and fold gently. Cook to heat through.
2. Two or three minutes before serving, stir in the yogurt and correct the seasonings. Serve with the boiled potatoes.

Aji de Gallina
(Piquant Creamed Hen)

Yield: 6 servings   Heat Scale: Hot

Here's another version of Peruvian chicken, in a cheese sauce spiced with hot aji chiles. It is served over sliced boiled potatoes and garnished with hard-boiled eggs.

1 carrot, peeled and sliced
2 onions, peeled; one sliced, one minced
1 (4-pound [1.82 kg]) chicken, quartered
½ loaf white bread, crust removed
1 (12-ounce [336 mL]) can evaporated milk
¼ cup (59 mL) vegetable oil
8 fresh aji chiles, stems and seeds removed, puréed in a blender (or substitute yellow wax hot or red jalapeños)
2 cloves garlic, peeled and minced
1 cup (236 mL) grated Parmesan cheese
¼ cup (59 mL) chopped walnuts
6 to 8 potatoes, boiled in their skins until tender, peeled, and sliced
3 hard-boiled eggs, peeled and halved
Freshly ground black pepper, to taste

1. Bring 1 quart (.95 L) salted water to a boil in a large pot. Add the carrot, sliced onion, and chicken. When the chicken is poached (about 45 minutes), remove it from the water, let it cool, and shred it into small strips. Strain the broth into a bowl. Reserve the carrot and onion. Reserve 3 cups (708 mL) of the broth.
2. Break the bread into pieces and soak them in the milk. In a large pot, heat the oil over medium heat. Add the minced onion, puréed chiles, and garlic and sauté for a few minutes. Add the reserved broth, soggy bread, chicken, cheese, walnuts, and the reserved carrot and onion. Add pepper to taste. Cook, stirring, over medium heat for about 20 minutes, until thick. Place the potatoes on serving plates and pour the chicken sauce over them. Garnish with the hard-boiled egg halves.

Chicken Cazuela

Yield: 10–12 servings   Heat Scale: Mild

This Andean chicken recipe features Capsicum pubescens, *the hairy-leafed chile pepper, better known as the rocoto. Rocotos are typically apple shaped, and they are said to be hot enough to wake the dead. Substitute jalapeños, as they have a similar thick wall.*

1 (3–4 pound [1.36–1.82 kg]) chicken
1 tomato, chopped
1 onion, peeled and chopped
1 teaspoon (5 mL) dried basil
1 teaspoon (5 mL) dried marjoram
½ teaspoon (2.5 mL) dried oregano
10 cups (2.36 L) water
1 cup (236 mL) vegetable oil
1 clove garlic, peeled
½ cup (118 mL) chopped onions
½ cup (118 mL) diced carrots
½ cup (118 mL) diced leeks
½ cup (118 mL) thinly sliced fresh string beans
½ cup (118 mL) fresh peas
½ cup (118 mL) diced celery
½ cup (118 mL) shredded cabbage
2 bay leaves
½ teaspoon (2.5 mL) freshly ground black pepper
1 rocoto chile, stem and seeds removed, grated (or substitute jalapeño)
Salt, to taste
Sliced oranges for garnish

1. Cut the chicken into small pieces. In a large pan, place the gizzard, legs, and carcass of the chicken. Add the tomato, onion, basil, marjoram, oregano, and water and bring to a boil. Boil gently for about 30 minutes. Strain the stock and reserve the chicken and the stock separately.
2. In a skillet, heat the oil over medium heat. Add the garlic and onion and fry them. When the garlic is brown, remove it from the pan and add the chicken. Fry the chicken until brown, then add the carrots, leeks, string beans, peas, celery, cabbage, bay leaves, pepper, chile, and salt and cook gently for about 10 minutes. Add 2 cups (473 mL) of the reserved stock and simmer until the vegetables and chicken are done, about 15 minutes. Serve very hot, with sliced oranges in each soup bowl.

Xin-Xin
(Spicy Chicken with Pumpkin Seeds)

Yield: 4–6 servings   Heat Scale: Medium

This Afro-Brazilian recipe has roots deep in the voodoo religion, and it is known to be served at black magic rituals. The use of ground prawns and malaguetas reflects its African roots. Serve the xin-xin with a South American rice dish.

1 (3-pound [1.36 kg]) chicken, cut into serving pieces
3 cups (708 mL) water
¼ cup (59 mL) ground dried prawns or shrimp
½ cup (118 mL) chopped fresh pineapple
¼ cup (59 mL) grated coconut
1½ teaspoons (7.5 mL) salt
½ cup (118 mL) chopped parsley
2 onions, peeled and sliced
1 teaspoon (5 mL) dried crushed malagueta chile (or substitute piquin or cayenne)
¾ cup (177 mL) pumpkin seeds, shelled and roasted
1 teaspoon (5 mL) ground coriander
¼ cup (59 mL) vegetable oil
Parsley for garnish

1. Place the chicken in a large pan with the water, ground prawns, pineapple, coconut, salt, parsley, onions, and chile. Cover and braise until the chicken is tender (about 30 minutes). Remove the lid and cook until the liquid is reduced by half.

2. Set aside 10 whole pumpkin seeds for garnish. Grind the remaining seeds in a spice mill. Add the ground pumpkin seeds, coriander, and oil to the chicken. Heat through and serve garnished with parsley and the whole pumpkin seeds.

Gallina en Salsa de Manis
(Chicken in Nut Sauce)

Yield: 6–8 servings   Heat Scale: Medium

Peanuts play a large role in the foods of Latin America. They are a hardy legume that provides an excellent source of protein and a cooking oil. This easy Argentinian recipe mates peanuts and chiles, a common theme in the region.

1 (5–6 pound [2.27–2.72 kg]) chicken, cut up, fat removed
4 cups (.95 L) water
1 teaspoon (5 mL) salt
2 tablespoons (30 mL) butter
½ cup (118 mL) chopped onions
1 tablespoon (15 mL) cornstarch
2 tablespoons (30 mL) cold water
1 cup (236 mL) ground peanuts
2 malagueta chiles, crushed (or substitute piquin or Japanese)
2 pimientos, stems and seeds removed, julienned (or substitute red bell peppers)
2 tablespoons (30 mL) minced parsley

1. Combine the chicken and water in a saucepan and bring to a boil. Add the salt, cover, reduce the heat, and simmer for 30 minutes. Remove the chicken, drain it on paper towels, and keep it warm. Continue cooking the broth until it is reduced to 2 cups (473 mL). Strain and reserve the broth.
2. In a skillet, melt the butter over medium heat. Add the onions and sauté until browned, about 10 minutes. Add the reserved broth and heat. Mix the cornstarch with the cold water and stir it into the broth until thickened. Mix in the peanuts, chile, pimientos, and parsley. Cook, uncovered, over low heat for 5 minutes. Taste for seasoning and adjust as needed. Arrange the chicken on a platter and pour the sauce over it.

Peruvian Walnut Chicken

Yield: 12–14 servings   Heat Scale: Medium

*Here is another chicken and nut recipe, this time with walnuts. Walnuts were intro-
duced by the Spanish and today are popular through Latin America.*

3 (4–5 pound [1.82–2.27 kg]) chickens, cut up
1 loaf white bread, crust removed
1 (6-ounce [168 g]) can evaporated milk
2 tablespoons (30 mL) ground aji chile (or substitute New Mexican)
1 onion, peeled and minced
½ cup (118 mL) vegetable oil
1 teaspoon (5 mL) salt
1 teaspoon (5 mL) cumin
½ teaspoon (2.5 mL) coriander
Freshly ground black pepper, to taste
1 cup (236 mL) grated Parmesan cheese
½ cup (118 mL) walnuts, peeled and finely ground
4 hard-boiled eggs, peeled and sliced

1. Cook the chickens in a large pot of boiling water until tender, about 25
minutes. Remove the chicken from the water, shred it, and set it aside.
2. In a bowl, soak the bread in the evaporated milk. Add the ground chile
and mix.
3. Place the onion in a skillet with the oil and sauté over medium heat.
When the oil comes to a boil, add the salt, cumin, coriander, and pepper to taste. Cook the mixture for about 7 minutes. Remove the bread
from the milk, squeeze out the excess milk, and mash the bread. Add the
mashed bread to the pan. Add the shredded chicken and the grated cheese.
Simmer for 20 minutes, covered, checking frequently to make sure that
the mixture does not burn. Add the walnuts, stirring to blend. Serve hot,
garnished with the hard-boiled eggs.

Pollo en Salsa de Pipian Rojo
(Chicken in Red Pipian Sauce)

Yield: 4 servings   Heat Scale: Medium

The squash seeds make this a very New World dish, as squash has been a staple of the Central American diet since it was domesticated millennia ago. Serve this dish with coconut rice. To add an elegant touch to the end of this meal, you might serve your guests champurrado, or Guatemalan chocolate coffee.

1 (3½-pound [1.59 kg]) chicken, cut into serving pieces, trimmed of loose skin and fat
4 cups (.95 L) water
1 teaspoon (5 mL) salt, or to taste
1½ cups (354 mL) chopped ripe tomatoes
½ cup (118 mL) chopped tomatillos
1 pasilla chile, stem and seeds removed
1 guajillo chile, stem and seeds removed (or substitute New Mexican)
¼ cup (59 mL) lime juice
½ cup (118 mL) sesame seeds, plus more for garnish
1 tablespoon (15 mL) squash seeds (pepitas), plus more for garnish
1 (1-inch [2.5 cm]) cinnamon stick, broken up
2 teaspoons (10 mL) crushed hot red New Mexican chile
½ cup (118 mL) cubed French bread, moistened with broth
¼ teaspoon (1.25 mL) achiote (annatto seed)
1 tablespoon (15 mL) all-purpose flour

1. In a skillet, cook the chicken in 3 cups (708 mL) of the water and the salt over medium heat for 30 minutes. Remove the chicken, keep it warm, and reserve the broth for the sauce.
2. In a saucepan, combine the tomatoes, tomatillos, and chiles in ¾ cup (177 mL) of the remaining water and the lime juice and cook over medium heat for 10 minutes.
3. In a dry skillet, toast the sesame seeds, squash seeds, cinnamon stick, and crushed chile over low heat for about 10 minutes.
4. In a food processor or blender, process the toasted ingredients. Add the cooked tomato mixture and stir to create a smooth paste. Add the bread, achiote, 2 cups (473 mL) of the reserved chicken broth, and the flour, and process everything until smooth. Return the sauce to the stove and heat through.
5. Place the cooked chicken on a platter and cover it with the red sauce. Sprinkle the remaining squash and sesame seeds over the top.

Jocón
(Chicken in Green Sauce with Smoked Chiles)

Yield: 4 servings   Heat Scale: Hot

This Mayan chicken in green sauce was originally made with turkey or duck. After the Spanish introduced chickens, onions, and cilantro to Guatemala, this recipe evolved. Cobán chiles are used in this dish, but since they are difficult to find outside of Guatemala, you may substitute another smoked chile—the chipotle. Serve the Jocón with black beans, corn tortillas, and sliced mango.

1 (3-pound [1.36 kg]) chicken, cut in serving pieces
1 onion, peeled and chopped
2 cloves garlic, peeled and chopped
1 quart (.95 L) water
4 dried cobán chiles, stems removed (or substitute 2 dried chipotle chiles)
1 tablespoon (15 mL) pumpkin seeds
½ cup (118 mL) chopped fresh cilantro
1 cup (236 mL) sliced green onions, green parts included
½ cup (118 mL) canned tomatillos, drained and chopped
1 tablespoon (15 mL) vegetable oil

1. In a large pot, combine the chicken, onion, garlic, and water. Bring it to a boil, reduce the heat, and simmer until done, about 30 minutes, skimming off any foam that forms. Remove the chicken and set it aside. Strain and reserve the broth.
2. Cover the chiles with boiling water and let them sit for 15 minutes to soften.
3. Toast the pumpkin seeds in a hot skillet over high heat until they start to brown, taking care not to let them burn. Let the seeds cool, then grind them in a blender or spice mill.
4. Combine the chile, toasted seeds, cilantro, green onions, tomatillos, and 2 cups (473 mL) of the chicken broth and purée until smooth.
5. Remove the skin from the chicken. In a large skillet, heat the oil over medium heat. Add the chicken and fry it until browned.
6. Combine the sauce with 1 cup (236 mL) of the reserved broth and pour it over the chicken. Simmer for 15 minutes before serving.

Smoked Pineapple Chicken

Yield: 4–5 servings   Heat Scale: Medium

The pineapple plant, or Ananas comosus, is a native of Central America. Pineapples were first discovered by Christopher Columbus on his second voyage to the West Indies. This Guatemalan recipe combines the delicious fruit with chicken and smoked chiles.

1 (3–4 pound [1.36–1.82 kg]) chicken, cut up
3 cups (708 mL) water
½ teaspoon (2.5 mL) salt, plus more to taste
½ teaspoon (2.5 mL) freshly ground pepper, plus more to taste
3 tablespoons (45 mL) vegetable oil
1 onion, peeled and chopped
2 teaspoons (10 mL) finely chopped parsley
1 red bell pepper, stem and seeds removed, finely sliced
1 green bell pepper, stem and seeds removed, chopped
3 cobán chiles, soaked in water and then puréed (or substitute 2 chipotles)
2 garlic cloves, peeled and minced
3 carrots, sliced
½ pound (224 g) sugar snap peas or snow peas
1 cup (236 mL) chopped fresh pineapple
2 teaspoons (10 mL) dried oregano
½ teaspoon (2.5 mL) ground turmeric or saffron
½ teaspoon (2.5 mL) ground cumin
1½ cups (354 mL) canned diced tomatoes with liquid
2 cups (473 mL) uncooked long-grain rice
¼ cup (59 mL) raisins

1. In a large pot, combine the chicken with 3 cups (708 mL) of water and salt and pepper to taste. Cook until tender, about 25 minutes. Remove the chicken, reserving the broth, and cut it into bite-size pieces.
2. In a separate large pot, heat the oil over low heat. Add the onion and parsley and sauté until the onion is translucent, but not brown. Stir in the bell peppers, chiles, garlic, carrots, peas, pineapple, oregano, turmeric, the ½ teaspoon (2.5 mL) salt, the ½ teaspoon (2.5 mL) pepper, and the cumin. Simmer for 5 minutes. Add the tomatoes with their liquid, the rice, the chicken, 3 cups (708 mL) of the reserved broth, and the raisins. Mix well and bring to a boil. Reduce the heat, cover, and simmer for 20 to 25 minutes or until the liquid is absorbed.

Escabeche de Pollo
(Bolivian Hot Pickled Chicken)

Yield: 4 servings   Heat Scale: Hot

Most Latin Americans know that escabeche de pescado (fish) is often wickedly hot. Here's fair warning that the chicken equivalent of this recipe also offers a suitable amount of heat through the use of habaneros. Serve this in large soup bowls accompanied by warm corn tortillas.

1 (4–5 pound [1.82–2.27 kg]) chicken, cut into pieces
2 large onions, peeled and thinly sliced
2 fresh habaneros, stems and seeds removed, minced (or substitute 6 jalapeños)
3 carrots, peeled and quartered
1 red bell pepper, stem and seeds removed, sliced
½ cup (118 mL) olive oil
1 cup (236 mL) red wine vinegar
1 large bay leaf, crumbled
¼ teaspoon (1.25 mL) ground nutmeg
Salt, to taste
Freshly ground black pepper, to taste

1. Combine all ingredients in a pot and cook, covered, over low heat for about 40 minutes. Taste for seasoning, add salt and pepper as needed, and let it cool before serving.

Pato con Arroz Picante
(Duck with Spicy Rice)

Yield: 4 servings   Heat Scale: Medium

The Incas were said to have kept domesticated ducks as well as jungle fowl. This Peruvian duck dish combines citrus and the hot aji chile to create a flavorful entrée. For a tasty accompaniment, serve this duck with an avocado salad.

2 tablespoons (30 mL) vegetable oil
1 (5–6 pound [2.27–2.72 kg]) duck, cut up
1 large onion, peeled and chopped
1½ cups (354 mL) chopped tomatoes
2 cloves garlic, peeled and minced
Salt, to taste
1 tablespoon (15 mL) finely chopped parsley
1 tablespoon (15 mL) ground aji chile (or substitute New Mexican)
5 cups (1.18 L) water
2½ cups (591 mL) uncooked long-grain rice, washed
1½ cups (354 mL) fresh green peas
4 tablespoons (60 mL) brandy
1 mango, peeled, seeded, and puréed

1. In a saucepan, heat the oil over medium heat. Add the pieces of duck and fry them to a golden brown. Add the onion, tomatoes, garlic, salt, parsley, and ground chile. Sauté for a minute, stirring well. Add the water and simmer the duck until it is tender, about 20 minutes. Add the rice and peas, cover, reduce the heat, and cook for about 25 minutes, or until the rice is done. Stir in the brandy and the puréed mango.

Pato Asado
(Orange Chile Duck)

Yield: 4 servings   Heat Scale: Medium

Brazil was first discovered in 1500 by Portuguese navigator Pedro Cabrál, who didn't have to bring ducks with him. This dish is hot and sweet at the same time, which makes it reminiscent of Chinese duck dishes. Serve this with any spicy bean dish from Chapter 13. (Note: This recipe requires advance preparation.)

1 (4-pound [1.82 kg]) duck
¼ cup (59 mL) orange juice
¼ cup (59 mL) pineapple juice
Salt, to taste
Freshly ground black pepper, to taste
1 (1–2 inch [2.5–5 cm]) strip lime peel
1 onion, peeled and chopped
1 green onion, chopped
1 clove garlic, peeled and crushed
½ cup (118 mL) dry white wine
1 teaspoon (5 mL) ground malagueta chile (or substitute cayenne)
2 tablespoons (30 mL) blackberry jelly
1 tablespoon (15 mL) vegetable oil
2 tablespoons (30 mL) raisins
10 whole jalapeño chiles
2 oranges, sliced in thin rounds

1. Split the duck in half and place it in a shallow glass bowl. In a separate bowl, mix together the orange juice, pineapple juice, salt, pepper, lime peel, onion, green onion, garlic, wine, and chile. Pour the sauce over the duck and marinate for 1 to 3 hours, turning occasionally.
2. Preheat the oven to 350°F (180°C).
3. Remove the duck, reserving the marinade, and place it skin-side up in a roasting pan. Mix the blackberry jelly with the reserved marinade. Brush the duck with the oil and bake it for 1 hour, basting with the marinade and jelly mixture.
4. When the duck is cooked, transfer it to a heated platter. Pour off any fat and add the raisins and any remaining marinade to the pan drippings. Bring this mixture to a boil on the stovetop and cook for a few minutes, scraping the bottom of the pan as it cooks. If you do not have enough liquid, add stock or water. Pour the sauce around the duck and garnish with the jalapeños and orange slices.

Pato al Vino Picante
(Duckling with Spicy Wine Sauce)

Yield: 4 servings   Heat Scale: Medium

*The secret to this succulent dish is the combination of wine and fruity habaneros—
they flavor the duck to perfection. The heavy use of peppers and spices in this recipe is
highly representative of the evolution of Spanish cuisine into Colombian. Serve this
dish with rice with coconut and raisins and a green salad.*

1 (4½–5 pound [2–2.3 kg]) duckling
Salt, to taste
Freshly ground black pepper, to taste
2 tablespoons (30 mL) butter
2 large onions, peeled and finely chopped
1 bay leaf
2 whole cloves
1 (1-inch [2.5 cm]) cinnamon stick
2 teaspoons (10 mL) ground cardamom
1 whole habanero chile (or substitute 3 jalapeños)
1 cup (236 mL) dry red wine
1 cup (236 mL) Classic Chicken Stock (page 46)

1. Preheat the oven to 350°F (180°C).
2. Remove the loose fat from inside the duckling and prick the bird all
over with a fork to help release the excess fat. Season it inside and out with
salt and pepper. In a heavy casserole, melt the butter over medium-high
heat. Add the duckling and sauté until it is golden brown all over. Lift it
out of the pan and set it aside.
3. Spoon off all but 4 tablespoons (60 mL) fat from the casserole. Add
the onions and sauté until soft. Return the duckling to the casserole. Tie
the bay leaf, cloves, cinnamon, cardamom, and habanero in a square of
cheesecloth and add it to the casserole with the red wine and chicken
stock. Season to taste with more salt and pepper if necessary, and bring to
a boil on top of the stove. Cover with aluminum foil, then with the casserole lid, and bake for 1½ hours, or until the duckling is tender.
4. Transfer the duckling to a serving platter and keep it warm. Remove
and discard the cheesecloth bag. Skim the excess fat from the sauce. If
the amount of sauce seems excessive, put the casserole over high heat to
quickly reduce it. Spoon a little sauce over the duckling and serve with the
remaining sauce.

Pato com Molho de Limao
(Duck with Lime Sauce)

Yield: 4 servings   Heat Scale: Hot

No collection of Latin American recipes would be complete without a Brazilian recipe calling for limes and Brazil nuts. The nuts make this a delicious entrée. It may appear that the duck is overcooked, but trust me on this one.

1 (4-pound [1.82 kg]) duck
2 cups (473 mL) lime juice
2 cups (473 mL) orange juice
1 bay leaf
2 teaspoons (10 mL) salt
½ teaspoon (2.5 mL) freshly ground black pepper
2 habanero chiles, stems and seeds removed, minced (or substitute 6 jalapeños)
¼ cup (59 mL) cognac
3 bananas, cut in 2-inch (5 cm) pieces
1 tablespoon (15 mL) cornstarch
¼ cup (59 mL) slivered Brazil nuts
¼ cup (59 mL) Cointreau

1. Preheat the oven to 450°F (240°C).
2. Wash and dry the duck. In a large pot, bring the citrus juices and the bay leaf to a boil. Add the duck, reduce the heat to low, and cook, covered, for 1 hour, turning the duck several times. Drain, skim the fat, and reserve 3 cups (708 mL) the stock. Season the duck with the salt, pepper, and minced chiles. Transfer it to a shallow roasting pan. Roast it in the oven for 20 minutes. Add 1½ cups (354 mL) of the reserved stock, the cognac, and the bananas. Reduce the heat to 350°F (180°C) and roast for 30 minutes longer, basting frequently. Transfer the duck and bananas to a serving platter and keep warm.
3. Skim the fat from the pan gravy, and pour the gravy and the remaining stock into a saucepan. Heat the gravy over low heat. Mix the cornstarch with a little water to form a smooth paste and stir it into the gravy until it thickens. Add the Brazil nuts and Cointreau and cook for 5 minutes.
4. Carve the duck and pour some of the sauce over it.

Pato Asado con Tequila y Salsa Chipotle
(Roasted Duck with Tequila and Honey Chipotle Sauce)

Yield: 4–6 servings   Heat Scale: Medium

This recipe was contributed by John Gray, former chef at the Ritz-Carlton Hotel in Cancún. This dish is an excellent example of the sophisticated flavors that can be created with seemingly simple ingredients and one pan. Serve the duck with rice or polenta and julienned vegetables or asparagus.

2 tablespoons (30 mL) olive oil
6 shallots, peeled and roughly sliced
½ cup (118 mL) seeded raisins
1 tablespoon (15 mL) sugar
¼ cup (59 mL) balsamic vinegar
1 cup (236 mL) port wine
¾ cup (177 mL) Classic Chicken Stock (page 46)
2 chipotle chiles, rehydrated in warm water, stems and seeds removed, chopped
¼ cup (59 mL) tequila
¼ cup (59 mL) honey
1 (5½-pound [2.5 kg]) duck

1. Preheat the oven to 300°F (150°C).
2. Heat a saucepan over high heat until very hot. Add the olive oil and shallots and sauté until golden, stirring constantly, then add the raisins and sugar. Allow the sugar to dissolve and lightly caramelize; do not let it burn. Add the balsamic vinegar and port wine and reduce to about ¼ cup (59 mL).
3. Add the chicken stock to the reduced sauce and mix well. Add the chipotles. Remove the sauce from the heat and let stand for 10 to 15 minutes, then strain. The less time the peppers are in the sauce, the lighter the chipotle flavor. Add the tequila and honey to the sauce, return it to the heat, and keep it just warm, stirring occasionally.
4. Put the duck in a roasting pan and roast it, uncovered, for 45 minutes. Debone, the duck, including the skin, and cover the meat with the sauce.

Pato Mulato con Piñones
(Roasted Duck with Piñons and Mulato Chiles)

Yield: 4–6 servings   Heat Scale: Medium

In Mexico, nuts are often used as a thickening agent for sauces. The pine nuts in this recipe from Chihuahua help coat the duck and keep in the juices that make the meat tender. Serve this with a rice or bean dish from Chapter 13.

1½ cup (354 mL) water, divided
1 sprig fresh rosemary
4 cloves garlic, peeled
2 black peppercorns
2 cups (473 mL) piñones (pine nuts)
4 mulato chiles, stems and seeds removed (or substitute anchos)
½ cup (118 mL) water
3 tablespoons (45 mL) honey
½ teaspoon (2.5 mL) soy sauce
1 teaspoon (5 mL) corn oil
1 (6-pound [2.7 kg]) duck

1. Preheat the oven to 350°F (180°C).
2. In a saucepan, heat 1 cup (236 mL) of the water to a simmer. Add the rosemary, garlic, peppercorns, and pine nuts and cook for about 10 minutes. Remove the rosemary sprig, transfer the mixture to a blender, and purée. Set aside.
3. In a blender, combine the chiles and the remaining ½ cup (118 mL) water and purée. Transfer the purée to a saucepan. Add the honey, soy sauce, and oil and cook over low heat for about 5 minutes, stirring constantly. Add the nut purée and adjust the consistency by adding water if necessary. Cook the sauce until it is thick enough to cling to the duck.
4. Place the duck in a roasting pan and cover it with the sauce. Baste the duck with the sauce and roast, uncovered, for 1½ hours, or until done. Continue basting while roasting.

Pato con Chiles Habaneros
(Duck with Habanero Chiles)

Yield: 6–8 servings   Heat Scale: Hot

You may never have tasted anything as quite snappy as this specialty from Yucatán. The habanero actually brings out the flavor of the duck, especially when combined with five strong spices. Serve this dish over rice, with fried plantains on the side.

2 (5½-pound [2.5 kg]) ducks, cut up in pieces
1 medium onion, peeled and sliced
2 cloves garlic, peeled, divided
6 pounds (2.72 kg) tomatoes, roasted
2 habanero chiles, stems and seeds removed, minced
2 whole cloves
2 bay leaves
1 sprig fresh thyme
1 sprig fresh oregano
1 heaping tablespoon (20 mL) butter
Salt, to taste

1. Place the duck, onion, and 1 clove garlic in a large pot and add water to just cover. Bring to a boil over high heat and boil for about 1 hour, or until the duck is tender.
2. In a blender, combine the tomatoes, chiles, cloves, bay leaves, thyme, oregano, and the remaining clove garlic and purée. In a large saucepan, melt the butter over low heat. Add the puréed mixture and sauté for about 20 minutes, stirring constantly. Add the duck and continue to cook for about 30 minutes. Add salt to taste and serve.

Mole Poblano con Pollo
(Mole Poblano with Chicken)

Yield: 4 servings   Heat Scale: Mild

This recipe comes from a friend of mine, author Jim Peyton, who has written several books on the foods of the border country. He says that as with most Mexican dishes, there are probably as many recipes for mole poblano as there are cooks who have pre-pared it. According to Jim, the mole recipe presented here is an amalgamation that is about as elaborate as this recipe gets in terms of the number of different ingredients.

For the Chile Paste:
1 dried mulato chile, stem and seeds removed
1 dried ancho chile, stem and seeds removed
2 pasilla chiles, stems and seeds removed
1 tablespoon (15 mL) vegetable oil (optional)
1 chipotle chile, stem removed

1. Either fry the chiles, except the chipotle, in the oil or toast them in a 250°F (120°C) oven until they just begin to brown and become fragrant, taking care that they do not burn. Place the toasted chiles and the chipotle in 2 cups (473 mL) hot water and soak for 15 minutes or until soft. Transfer the chiles and a little of the soaking water in a blender and purée to a paste.

For the Spice Mixture:
4 fresh tomatillos, husks removed
3 tablespoons (45 mL) vegetable oil, divided, plus more if needed
1 tomato, roasted and peeled
½ teaspoon (2.5 mL) coriander seeds
½ teaspoon (2.5 mL) red chile seeds
3 tablespoons (45 mL) sesame seeds
¼ teaspoon (1.25 mL) ground anise
2 whole cloves
1 (½-inch [1 cm]) stick cinnamon
¼ teaspoon (1.25 mL) whole black peppercorns
3 tablespoons (45 mL) pumpkin seeds
2 tablespoons (30 mL) peanuts
2 tablespoons (30 mL) almonds
2 tablespoons (30 mL) raisins
3 tablespoons (45 mL) chopped dried prunes
1 (3-inch [7.5 cm]) piece plantain (or substitute a banana)
½ corn tortilla
½ slice white sandwich bread
1–2 cups (250–473 mL) Classic Chicken Stock (page 46)

1. In a skillet, heat 1 tablespoon (15 mL) of the oil over medium heat. Add the tomatillo and fry until just soft, about 5 minutes. Drain the tomatillo and transfer it to a blender. Add the tomato. Toast the coriander, chile seeds, sesame seeds, anise, cloves, cinnamon, and peppercorns in a heavy skillet over low heat, stirring constantly, until the sesame seeds just begin to brown, 3 to 5 minutes. Allow the seeds to cool, transfer them to a coffee or spice grinder, and grind them to a fine powder. Add the powder to the blender. Fry the pumpkin seeds in 1 tablespoon (15 mL) oil over high heat until they puff up. Be careful, as they will pop and spatter as they brown. Drain the seeds and add them to the blender.
2. Fry the nuts, raisins, and prunes in the remaining oil over medium heat for about 2 minutes or until the raisins are puffed. Drain this mixture and add them to the blender.
3. Fry the plantain over medium-high heat until it begins to brown. Add it to the blender. Finally, fry the tortilla and bread until the tortilla is softened, adding more oil if necessary. Remove, drain, and coarsely chop the tortilla and bread. Add them to the blender. Blend the mixture, adding just enough chicken broth to make a thick paste. Transfer the paste to a bowl.

To Finish:
2–3 tablespoons (30–45 mL) vegetable oil
4 boneless, skinless chicken breasts, cut in half
1–2 cups (250–473 mL) chicken broth
1 tablespoon (15 mL) sugar
1 ounce (28 g) Mexican or bittersweet chocolate
2–3 tablespoons (30–45 mL) sesame seeds

1. In a skillet, heat the oil over high heat and quickly brown the chicken breasts. Remove the chicken from the pan and keep it warm. Add the chile paste to the skillet and simmer for 5 minutes. Add the spice mixture and continue simmering for an additional 5 minutes. Stir in enough broth to produce a sauce that just coats a spoon or is about as thick as a thin milkshake. Add the sugar and chocolate to the sauce and stir to dissolve. Add the chicken breasts and simmer, uncovered, for 5 to 10 minutes or until just cooked through.
2. Garnish with the sesame seeds and serve.

Variation
To prepare mole enchiladas, simply wrap the shredded chicken in corn tortillas that have been softened in hot oil, top with the sauce and garnish, and heat at 350°F (180°C) for 10 minutes.

Rice Mole
Yield: 6 servings   Heat Scale: Medium

This recipe comes from Jalisco, where cooks combine pasillas, cascabels, and pickled jalapeños to form their trilogy of chiles. This is certainly one of the more simple mole recipes I've come across. It's also very good.

1 (5–6 pound [2.27–2.72 kg]) chicken, sectioned
2 medium onions, peeled and sliced
Salt, to taste
1½ cups (354 mL) uncooked rice, washed and soaked
4 tablespoons (60 mL) vegetable oil
4 pasilla chiles, stems and seeds removed
3 cascabel chiles, stems and seeds removed
1 teaspoon (5 mL) ground cumin
6 black peppercorns
4 cloves garlic, peeled and crushed
4 green tomatoes, chopped
½–1 head lettuce, shredded
Pickled jalapeños, to taste

1. Place the chicken parts in a large pan and add water to cover. Add the onions and salt to taste. Cook the chicken until it is tender, 45 minutes to 1 hour. Once cooked, remove the chicken from the broth, keep it warm, and set the broth aside.

2. Measure 3 cups (708 mL) broth, adding more water if necessary. Add the rice to the broth and cook over medium-low heat until done, stirring occasionally to make sure it doesn't stick, about 20 minutes.
3. In a separate pan, heat the oil over medium heat. Add the chiles and fry them for 5 to 7 minutes, then add the cumin, peppercorns, garlic, and green tomatoes and sauté until the chiles become soft. Transfer this mixture to a blender and purée, then return it to the pan. Add the rice and cook for a few minutes.
4. Serve the rice with the chicken, garnished with the lettuce and jalapeños.

Smoked Mexican Turkey with Orange Chile Oil Marinade

Yield: 4–6 servings   Heat Scale: Mild

Here's a double Mexican influence—turkeys and chiles are native to the Americas. This recipe will work with a breast or the legs. If using a whole turkey or breast, increase the amount of the marinade and inject it into the bird as well as basting it while it smokes. Use any Mexican chiles, such as ancho, pasilla, cascabel, or guajillo. Serve this with avocado slices, beans, and grilled corn on the cob. (Note: This recipe requires advance preparation.)

6 cascabel chiles, stems and seeds removed (or substitute 2 of the chiles listed in the headnote)
¼ cup (59 mL) chopped onions
½ cup (118 mL) vegetable oil
2 cloves garlic, peeled and minced
1 teaspoon (5 mL) cumin seeds
1 cup (236 mL) orange juice
1 tablespoon (15 mL) lime juice
2 teaspoons (10 mL) achiote paste
1 teaspoon (5 mL) dried oregano (Mexican preferred)
1 pinch ground cloves
Salt, to taste
Freshly ground black pepper, to taste
4 turkey legs

1. In a pan, heat the oil over medium heat. Add the chiles and onion and sauté until softened. Add the garlic and cumin and continue to sauté for an additional minute. Remove the pan from the heat.
2. In a food processor or blender, combine the chile mixture (with the oil), orange juice, lime juice, achiote paste, oregano, cloves, salt, and pepper and purée until a smooth sauce.
3. Make slits in the turkey to allow the chile oil marinade to penetrate. Place the turkey and marinade in a large plastic bag and marinate overnight.

4. Prepare the smoker using hickory or pecan wood and smoke the legs in 200°F (100°C) smoke for 3 to 3½ hours or until the turkey reaches an internal temperature of 160°F (75°C). If you wish to continue marinating, simmer the marinade in a pan for 20 minutes and brush it over the legs occasionally. When the turkey is done, remove it from the smoker and brush it with the marinade.

5. To serve, slice the smoked turkey off the legs and serve it with a selection of sauces from Chapter 2.

Pollo en Escabeche Estilo Yucateca (Shredded Chicken Yucatan-Style)

Yield: 4 servings   Heat Scale: Hot

Marta Figel wrote for me about Isla Mujeres, where she discovered this fiery, fantastic chicken recipe. Your guests will enjoy it even more if you serve it with a round of margaritas. The drinks won't cut the heat, but they may help you forget how hot it is!

10 black peppercorns
¼ teaspoon (1.25 mL) ground oregano
1½ teaspoon (7.5 mL) salt, divided
2 cloves garlic, peeled and crushed
1 tablespoon (15 mL) distilled white vinegar
2 large red onions
2 heads garlic
Juice of 3 bitter oranges (or mix 1 cup [236 mL] lime juice with ½ cup [118 mL] orange juice)
3 pounds (1.36 kg) chicken legs and thighs
1 teaspoon (5 mL) salt
½ teaspoon (2.5 mL) ground oregano
1 xcatic chile, stem and seeds removed (or substitute yellow wax hot)
1 habanero chile, stem and seeds removed
2 serrano chiles, stems and seeds removed

1. Preheat the oven to 350°F (180°C).
2. Place the peppercorns, oregano, and ½ teaspoon (2.5 mL) of the salt in a spice or coffee grinder and grind to a powder. Transfer this powder to a bowl and combine it with the garlic and vinegar to make a paste. Set aside.
3. Roast one of the onions and both heads of garlic in the preheated oven for 20 minutes. Remove them from the oven, but leave the oven on. Let the onion and garlic cool.
4. Measure 2 tablespoons (30 mL) of the bitter orange juice and set it aside. Peel the remaining onion, slice it into rings, and marinate the rings in the remaining juice.
5. Place the chicken in a stockpot with water to cover, the remaining salt, and the ground oregano and simmer until the chicken is tender, about 30 minutes.
6. Drain the chicken, reserving the broth, and transfer it to an ovenproof dish. Add the peppercorn paste and the reserved 2 tablespoons (30 mL) bitter orange juice, and bake uncovered until golden brown, about 30 minutes.

7. Peel the roasted onions and garlic and combine them with the reserved chicken stock. Add the chiles and simmer for 5 minutes. Add the marinated onion, bring to a boil, and remove from the heat immediately.
8. Drain the stock and reserve it. Reserve the chiles and onions separately. Separate the chiles from the onion and coarsely chop the chiles.
9. Skin the chicken and shred the meat from the bones. Add the chopped chiles and the onion to the chicken and mix well. Boil 1½ cups (354 mL) of the stock and add it to the chicken mixture so that the mixture is moist but not soupy.
10. Serve the chicken with your favorite salsa from Chapter 2.

Pollo Pibil
(Pibil-Style Chicken)

Yield: 4 servings   Heat Scale: Mild

This recipe was contributed by Nancy and Jeff Gerlach, who now have retired to Yucatán, where this dish is available in nearly every restaurant. In Cancún, there are even pollo pibil take-out stands! Pibil refers to the method of cooking marinated meats wrapped in banana leaves in a rock-lined pit. Banana leaves are hard to find, so use aluminum foil instead. Bitter or Seville oranges are also hard to find, but mixing orange, grapefruit, and lime juices makes an acceptable substitute. (Note: This recipe requires advance preparation.)

¼ cup (59 mL) Recado Rojo (page 5)
2 tablespoons (30 mL) lime juice
1 tablespoon (15 mL) orange juice
1 tablespoon (15 mL) grapefruit juice
4 chicken breasts
2 tablespoons (30 mL) vegetable oil, divided
1 medium onion, peeled and sliced
3 xcatic or banana chiles, chopped (or substitute yellow wax hot)
4 large banana leaves or aluminum foil

1. Preheat the oven to 350°F (180°C).
2. Mix the recado with the fruit juices. Marinate the chicken in the mixture for 4 hours or overnight in the refrigerator.
3. In a skillet, heat 1 tablespoon (15 mL) of the oil over medium heat. Add the onion and chiles and sauté until soft.
4. Brush the banana leaf or foil with the remaining oil. Place one chicken breast in the center, pour ¼ of the marinade over the chicken, and top with the onion mixture. Fold the foil over and tightly secure the seams. Repeat with the remaining chicken breasts.
5. Place the packages on a pan, and bake them for 1 hour.
6. Remove the leaves or foil and drain off any excess liquid. Serve with onion salsa, refried black beans, and a habanero salsa from Chapter 2.

Pollo con Salchichas en Chile Chipotle
(Chicken and Sausage with Chipotle Chiles)

Yield: 4–6 servings   Heat Scale: Hot

This hearty dish offers a smoky taste that comes from the sausages and the chipotles. You might like to start this dish with a guacamole salad from Chapter 6. If you can't find canned chipotles in adobo, rehydrate dried chipotles in hot water.

1 (2-pound [1.1 kg]) chicken, sectioned
1½ cloves garlic, peeled, divided
1 small onion, peeled
1 pound (454 g) tomatoes, chopped
4 chipotle chiles in adobo, chopped
2 tablespoons (30 mL) vegetable oil
1 medium onion, peeled and sliced
5 slices sausage
Salt, to taste

1. Put the chicken in a large pan and add water to cover. Add 1 clove of the garlic and the whole onion and cook over high heat until the chicken is tender, about 45 minutes.
2. In a separate pan, cook the tomatoes over medium heat for 5 minutes. Add the chiles and the remaining ½ clove garlic.
3. In a large skillet, heat the oil over high heat. Add the sliced onion and fry until browned. Add the tomato mixture. Cook over a low heat for about 10 minutes. Add the chicken, sausage, and salt to taste. Cook for another 10 minutes. Serve with rice.

Gallina en Nogada
(Hen in Walnut Sauce)

Yield: 6–8 servings   Heat Scale: Medium

This recipe requires you to grind spices in a coffee grinder or spice mill. If you have a coffee grinder, don't worry about removing the leftover spices after you're done. Simply grind white rice in the grinder and then wipe it out with a wet paper towel. The rice will remove all spices, ensuring you won't have chile coffee!

6 tablespoons (90 mL) butter
1 slice white bread
¼ cup (59 mL) peanuts, peeled
¼ cup (59 mL) walnuts
1 stick cinnamon
2 whole cloves
3 piquin chiles, stems removed
2 cloves garlic, peeled
2 onions, peeled
4 ancho chiles, stems and seeds removed, rehydrated in hot water
¾ cup (177 mL) Classic Chicken Stock (page 46)
1 (5–6 pound [2.27–2.72 kg]) chicken, separated and cooked in 3 cups (708 mL) water with salt and pepper to taste for 45 minutes

1. In a skillet, melt the butter over medium heat. Add the bread, peanuts and walnuts and fry for 5 minutes. Transfer them to a food processor or blender and purée. Set aside.

2. In a spice mill, combine the cinnamon stick, cloves, and piquin chiles and grind them to a powder. Transfer this powder to a food processor or blender. Add the garlic, onions, ancho chiles, and chicken broth and purée.

3. Transfer this mixture to a saucepan, and add the puréed nuts and cooked chicken parts. Cook over medium heat until the flavors blend, 10 to 15 minutes. Serve over white rice.

Almendrado Oaxaqueño
(Almond Chicken Oaxacan-Style)

Yield: 4–6 servings   Heat Scale: Medium

The Oaxaca marketplace is famous for its incredible selection of chiles and other lo-cally grown produce. This recipe features the chile ancho, which is the dried version of the poblano. Serve with a Mexican side dish from Chapter 13.

1 (4–5 pound [1.82–2.27 kg]) chicken, sectioned
Salt, to taste
Freshly ground black pepper, to taste
Corn oil as needed for frying
3 ancho chiles, stems and seeds removed
½ cup (118 mL) almonds, divided
4 tomatoes, roasted, peeled, and seeded
2 cloves garlic, peeled
1 medium onion, peeled
6 black peppercorns
3 whole cloves
1 cinnamon stick
½ bolillo (or small French roll), ground into crumbs
2 tablespoons (30 mL) sugar
4 cups (.95 L) Classic Chicken Stock (page 46)

1. Salt and pepper the chicken and fry it in the oil in a large skillet over medium-high heat, making sure it doesn't burn or stick. Remove the chicken from the pan and drain it.

2. In the same oil, fry the chiles, all but 2 tablespoons (30 mL) of the almonds, the tomatoes, the garlic, the onion, the peppercorns, the cloves, the cinnamon, and the bread crumbs over medium heat. Pour this mixture into a blender and blend until smooth. If necessary, add a little broth. Return the mixture to the pan and cook it over low heat. Add the chicken, sugar, and chicken broth. Cover and cook until the chicken is tender, about 45 minutes. Before serving, add the remaining whole almonds.

Mexican Chicken, Barbacoa-Style

Yield: 4 servings   Heat Scale: Medium

The word "barbecue" comes from the Spanish barbacoa, but the two words no longer mean the same thing because barbacoa is cooked in a rock-lined pit. It is difficult to duplicate the flavor of wrapping meat or poultry in banana leaves and cooking it in a pit, but I make a noble effort by grilling the chicken while it's covered with a chile paste. Serve with jicama-lime sticks, potatoes with green chile, grilled zucchini and corn, and warm corn or flour tortillas. (Note: This recipe requires advance preparation.)

8 guajillo chiles, stems and seeds removed (or substitute dried red New Mexican chiles)
4 chiles de arbol, stems and seeds removed
2 tablespoons (30 mL) sesame seeds
1 (1-inch [2.5 cm]) cinnamon stick (or 1 teaspoon [5 mL] ground cinnamon)
8 whole allspice berries
6 whole cloves
2 teaspoons (10 mL) dried oregano (Mexican preferred)
½ cup (118 mL) chopped onions
4 cloves garlic, chopped
2 tablespoons (30 mL) apple cider vinegar
1 cup (236 mL) Classic Chicken Stock (page 46)
1 tablespoon (15 mL) vegetable oil
1 (3-pound [1.36 kg]) chicken, cut in serving-size pieces

1. On a hot, dry griddle or skillet, toast the chiles over high heat until they turn slightly dark, taking care that they don't burn. Transfer them to a bowl, cover them with very hot water, and allow them to steep for 20 minutes until softened. Drain the chiles.
2. Toast the sesame seeds on the hot skillet until browned, taking care that they don't burn. Allow them to cool.
3. Combine the sesame seeds, cinnamon, allspice, and cloves in a spice grinder or coffee mill and process to a fine powder. Transfer the ground spices to a blender or food processor. Add the chiles, oregano, onions, garlic, vinegar, and stock and purée until smooth. Strain if desired.
4. In a frying pan, heat the oil over medium heat. Add the sauce and sauté for 5 minutes, stirring occasionally, until thickened. Allow to cool.
5. Spread the paste all over the chicken pieces (including under the skin), place them in a plastic bag, and refrigerate overnight.
6. Remove the chicken from the refrigerator. Make sure the pieces are thickly coated with the paste. Grill them slowly over a medium or low fire so the paste doesn't burn. Cook for about 40 minutes, turning occasionally, or until the internal temperature reaches 160°F (70°C).

Ajo-Comino de Gallina
(Garlic and Cumin Chicken)

Yield: 4–6 servings   Heat Scale: Medium

This recipe from Hidalgo calls for nine cloves of garlic. I know what you're thinking—that's a lot of garlic! But in Mexico, garlic is reputed to fight infections, stimulate the immune system, reduce high blood pressure, and cleanse the system of harmful substances. All that, and it tastes good, too.

1 (5–6 pound [2.27–2.72 kg]) chicken, sectioned
Salt, to taste
1 onion, peeled and chopped
9 cloves garlic, peeled, divided
5 ancho chiles, stems and seeds removed, rehydrated in hot water
2 pasilla chiles, stems and seeds removed, rehydrated in hot water
½ teaspoon (2.5 mL) ground cumin
¼ cup (59 mL) butter

1. In a large pot, cook the chicken with the salt, onion, 1 clove of the garlic, and water to cover over medium heat for 1 hour
2. In a mortar and pestle, grind the chiles with the remaining garlic and the cumin. In a separate frying pan, fry this mixture over medium-high heat with the butter for about 5 minutes, stirring constantly.
3. Add the chicken and some of the broth and let it cook until the flavors marry, about 45 minutes. Serve with white rice.

Chileajo de Pollo
(Chicken with Chile and Garlic)

Yield: 4 servings   Heat Scale: Medium

This pungent sautéed chicken will make your kitchen smell heavenly—that is, if you love chiles and garlic the way I do! If you're feeling really adventurous, substitute 1 dried habanero for the guajillos.

1 loaf white bread, sliced
1 (4–5 pound [1.82–2.27 kg]) chicken, separated into pieces
4 cloves garlic, peeled, divided
½ onion
Salt, to taste
7 ancho chiles, stems and seeds removed
6 guajillo chiles, stems and seeds removed (or substitute New Mexican)
10 black peppercorns
1 whole clove
1½ teaspoons (1.5 mL) dried oregano
1 stick cinnamon
¼ cup (59 mL) vegetable oil

1. Preheat the oven to 300°F (150°C). Put the loaf of bread on a baking sheet and bake it for 15 minutes or until completely dried.
2. In a large pot, combine the chicken, 2 cloves of the garlic, and the onion. Add water to cover and cook in a large pan for about 45 minutes, then set aside.
3. Cover the chiles in hot water and soak them until soft.
4. In a mortar and pestle, food processor, or blender, grind together the softened chiles, bread, peppercorns, clove, oregano, cinnamon, and the remaining garlic. In a large sauté pan, heat a little oil over medium heat. Add the bread mixture and fry until cooked, about 5 minutes.
5. Add the chicken and a little of the broth to the chile mixture, making a thick sauce, then cover the pan and simmer the ingredients over low heat long enough for the flavors to blend.

Pechugas en Salsa de Chipotle con Piña (Chicken Breasts in Chipotle-Pineapple Sauce)

Yield: 4–6 servings   Heat Scale: Medium

Pineapples thrive in the tropical parts of Mexico. This fruity-hot dish is from Mazatlán, which, while full of college students and tourists, is still home to fine traditional Mexican cooking.

1½ pounds (680 g) tomatoes, cooked and peeled
1 medium onion, peeled
2 cloves garlic, peeled
4 chipotle chiles in adobo
Salt, to taste
Freshly ground black pepper, to taste
2 tablespoons (30 mL) vegetable oil
3 chicken breasts, boned and pounded
1 (8-ounce [224 g]) can pineapple in heavy syrup, drained and chopped
1 cup (236 mL) Classic Chicken Stock (page 46)

1. In a food processor, combine the tomatoes, onion, garlic, chiles, salt, and pepper and pulse until just blended.
2. In a large pan, heat the oil over medium heat. Add the tomato mixture and sauté for 5 to 7 minutes. Add the chicken, pineapple, and broth.
3. Cook uncovered until done, about 40 minutes, stirring occasionally. Serve with white rice or a spiced rice from Chapter 13.

Pollo en Frutas
(Chicken with Mixed Fruits)

Yield: 4–6 servings   Heat Scale: Mild

Mango is the featured fruit in this mild but wild dish, which is especially popular in Chiapas, where the Mayan city of Palenque now lies in ruins. Serve this with a bean dish from Chapter 13.

1 (4–5 pound [1.82–2.27 kg]) chicken, cut in sections
Salt, to taste
1 bay leaf
Fresh or dried thyme, to taste
Mexican oregano, to taste
2 tablespoons (30 mL) vinegar
1 chayote, peeled and cubed (or substitute zucchini)
3 carrots, peeled and cubed
1 small onion, peeled and chopped
½ cup (118 mL) chopped tomatoes
½ cup (118 mL) cubed potatoes
1 ripe mango, peeled, pitted, and cubed
8 prunes
2 tablespoons (30 mL) raisins
8 green olives
1 ancho chile, stem and seeds removed, rehydrated in hot water and chopped

1. Clean the chicken and season it with the salt, pepper, thyme, oregano, and vinegar. Let it marinate in a large pot in the refrigerator for 15 minutes.
2. Remove the pot from the refrigerator. Add the remaining ingredients and cook over medium heat, stirring occasionally, for 45 minutes to 1 hour or until done.

Pollo con Limón Cascabella
(Chicken with Lemon and Cascabel Chiles)

Yield: 4–6 servings   Heat Scale: Medium

This tart dinner treat from the city of Culiacán makes a wonderful luncheon item or early evening supper. The addition of cascabels provides heat and a nutty depth of flavor. This dish is excellent served hot or cold. (Note: This recipe requires advance preparation.)

1 (2-pound [1.1 kg]) chicken, cut in sections
Juice of 8 lemons
Salt, to taste
4 tablespoons (60 mL) olive oil
2 (8-ounce [224 g]) cans stewed tomatoes
4 cloves garlic, peeled and chopped
1 onion, peeled and chopped
3 cascabel chiles, stems and seeds removed, crushed (or substitute pasillas)
1 pinch cumin
6 avocado leaves (or substitute bay leaves)

1. In a bowl, marinate the chicken with the lemon juice and salt for about 2 hours in the refrigerator. Remove the chicken from the refrigerator. In a large skillet, heat the oil over medium heat. Add the chicken and fry until golden brown and somewhat crispy, about 20 minutes. Transfer the chicken to paper towels to drain.
2. In a separate pan, combine the tomatoes, garlic, onion, chiles, and cumin and cook over medium heat for about 10 minutes. Add the chicken to the chile mixture. Add enough water to half-cover the chicken. Cover the top of the chicken with the avocado leaves and cook over low heat for 20 minutes or until all the flavors have combined. Remove the leaves and serve with white rice or fried plantains.

Pollo en Chile Verde
(Green Chile Chicken)

Yield: 4–5   Heat Scale: Medium

It's easy to see how this traditional Mexican recipe from the state of Chihuahua received its name—more than half of the ingredients are green, including poblanos and serranos, which offer high heat when combined.

14 tomatillos, husks removed, chopped
4 serrano chiles, stems and seeds removed, coarsely chopped
2 poblano chiles, stems and seeds removed, coarsely chopped
2 cloves garlic, peeled
½ medium onion
1 small bunch cilantro
1 (4–5 pound [1.82–2.27 kg]) chicken, sectioned
Salt, to taste
Freshly ground black pepper, to taste
½ cup (118 mL) hot water

1. In a large sauté pan, cook the tomatillos over medium heat for 5 to 7 minutes. Set aside.
2. In a blender, grind together the chiles, garlic, onion, and cilantro. Add the chile mixture to the tomatillos, then add the chicken, salt, and pepper. Add the hot water to the skillet and cook over medium heat for 1 hour 15 minutes, or until the chicken is done. Serve with white rice.

Gallina Rellena con Chiles Chipotles (Stuffed Chicken with Chipotles)

Yield: 6–8   Heat Scale: Medium

The Spaniards first brought chickens to Mexico, where they were enthusiastically received by the turkey-eating natives. I'm sure this stuffed recipe will rival any turkey dish around. Although it requires a bit of work, it is well worth it.

6 tablespoons (90 mL) vegetable oil, divided
2 cloves garlic, peeled
½ onion, chopped
7 ounces (196 g) ground pork
4 ounces (96 g) ground ham
2 medium tomatoes, chopped
3 cloves garlic, peeled and chopped
4 bunches parsley, chopped
8 green olives, chopped
6 capers, chopped
2½ cups (591 mL) raisins, chopped
6 chipotle chiles in adobo, chopped, divided
Salt, to taste
1 (4–5 pound [1.82–2.27 kg]) chicken
Freshly ground black pepper, to taste

1. Preheat the oven to 350°F (180°C).
2. In a large skillet, heat 3 tablespoons (45 mL) of the oil over medium heat. Add the garlic and onion and fry until soft. Add the pork and ham and cook over high heat for about 10 minutes, stirring frequently. Add the tomatoes, chopped garlic, parsley, olives, capers, raisins, 3 of the chopped chipotles, and salt and continue to cook for about 20 minutes, stirring often.
3. Place the chicken in a large baking dish and sprinkle it with salt and pepper. In a skillet, combine the remaining chipotles, a few teaspoons of adobo sauce, and the oil and sauté over medium heat. Remove the pan from the heat and pour the mixture over the chicken. Bake for 45 minutes.

Pollo Enchilado
(Grilled Chile-Chicken)

Yield: 4–6 servings   Heat Scale: Medium

This recipe comes from Querétaro, where I was happy to find a Mexican dish that is low in fat and high in flavor. This chicken is also wonderful cubed and served in tortillas, fajita-style, with a sauce from Chapter 2. (Note: This recipe requires advance preparation.)

2 cloves garlic, peeled
6 ancho chiles, toasted, stems and seeds removed, chopped
3 chiles de arbol, toasted, stems and seeds removed (or substitute 1 red New Mexican chile)
3 cascabel chiles, toasted, stems and seeds removed (or substitute 1 pasilla chile)
¾ cup (177 mL) apple cider vinegar
2 tablespoons (30 mL) vegetable oil
Juice of 1 sour orange (or substitute 1 orange and 1 lime)
1 teaspoon (5 mL) Mexican oregano
2 whole cloves
½ teaspoon (2.5 mL) ground cumin
Salt, to taste
Freshly ground black pepper, to taste
1 (4–5 pound [1.82–2.27 kg]) chicken, sectioned
Lettuce leaves for serving
Avocado slices for serving
Tortillas for serving

1. In a blender, combine the garlic, chiles, vinegar, oil, orange juice, oregano, cloves, cumin, salt, and pepper and process until it is thoroughly blended. Marinate the chicken in this mixture in the refrigerator overnight.
2. Grill the chicken over gas or hot coals until done. Or, bake uncovered in a 400°F (200°C) oven for 40 minutes. Serve with lettuce, avocados, and warmed tortillas.

Caribbean Smoked Chicken with Habanero Marinade

Yield: 4–6 servings   Heat Scale: Medium

This is an ideal way to prepare chicken because it doesn't need to be turned and the fat and marinade baste the bird as it smokes. Smoke with a delicate wood, such as apple, so that it doesn't mask the taste of the chicken. Serve this with an avocado salad, Jamaican rice and peas, and warm banana bread. (Note: This recipe requires advance preparation.)

½ cup (118 mL) orange juice
⅓ cup (79 mL) rum
½ cup (118 mL) chopped red onion
½ cup (118 mL) chopped green onions, green parts included
2 habanero chiles, stems removed, chopped
2 large cloves garlic, peeled and chopped
2 shallots, peeled and chopped
1 tablespoon (15 mL) chopped fresh thyme (or substitute 1 teaspoon [5 mL] dried thyme)
2 bay leaves, crumbled
1 teaspoon (5 mL) salt
Freshly ground black pepper, to taste
⅓ cup (79 mL) vegetable oil
1 (3½–4 pound [1.6–1.8 kg]) chicken

1. In a blender or food processor, combine the juice, rum, red onions, green onions, chiles, garlic, shallots, thyme, bay leaves, salt, and pepper and purée until smooth. With the machine running, slowly pour in the oil until the mixture thickens.
2. Place the chicken in a deep, nonreactive bowl. Loosen the skin on the chicken and rub the marinade under the skin. Fill the cavities with the marinade, rubbing it into the flesh. Pour the remaining marinade over the chicken and marinate, covered, in the refrigerator for 24 hours. Remove the chicken from the marinade. Transfer the remaining marinade to a pot and simmer it for 20 minutes.
3. Place the chicken on a rack in the smoker. Smoke at 200°F (100°C) for 4 hours (the internal temperature should reach at least 160°F [75°C]), basting occasionally with the marinade. Remove the chicken from the smoker and let it sit for 20 minutes before slicing.

St. Kitts Jerk Chicken

Yield: 4–6 servings   Heat Scale: Medium-Hot

Nearly every island in the Caribbean has its version of this Jamaican specialty. This recipe comes from my friends Neil and Sandy Mann, who perfected it when they were in the Peace Corps on the island. The marinade can also be used with pork. Serve this chicken with black beans and rice, johnny cakes, and grilled tropical fruits, such as pineapple, mangos, and plantains.

2 bunches green onions, chopped, some of the greens included
2 habanero chiles, stems and seeds removed, minced
2 tablespoons (30 mL) soy sauce
2 tablespoons (30 mL) lime juice (fresh preferred)
5 teaspoons (25 mL) ground allspice
2 teaspoons (10 mL) dry mustard
2 bay leaves, center rib removed, crumbled
2 cloves garlic, peeled and chopped
1 teaspoon (5 mL) sugar (straw or raw sugar preferred)
1½ teaspoons (7.5 mL) dried thyme, crumbled
1 teaspoon (5 mL) ground cinnamon
4–6 skinless chicken breasts

1. In a blender or food processor, combine the green onions, chiles, soy sauce, lime juice, allspice, mustard, bay leaves, garlic, sugar, thyme, and cinnamon and purée until smooth.
2. Pierce the chicken pieces with a fork so that the marinade will penetrate the meat. Put the chicken in sealable plastic bags along with the marinade. Marinate in the refrigerator for at least 24 hours and up to 2 days.
3. Grill the chicken over a medium-hot fire, turning occasionally, until the chicken reaches an internal temperature of 160°F (75°C).

Spice-Infused Barbecued Chicken Kebabs

Yield: 4 servings   Heat Scale: Medium

Direct from St. Lucia, this dish is a tribute to the lush and fertile soils of the island. For over 150 years, the English and French battled for control of St. Lucia. Fortunately, they now coexist nicely and have blended the heritage of their cuisines. The spices, chicken, and vegetables in this dish all combine well with the heat of the habanero. (Note: This recipe requires advance preparation.)

8 large garlic cloves, peeled and minced
2 teaspoons (10 mL) ground coriander
2 teaspoons (10 mL) ground turmeric
2 teaspoons (10 mL) dry mustard
2 teaspoons (10 mL) ground cloves
2 teaspoons (10 mL) ground habanero
1 teaspoon (5 mL) anise seed
2 pounds (1.1 kg) boneless, skinless chicken breasts, cut into 1-inch (2.5 cm) pieces
1⅓ pounds (600 mL) boneless, skinless chicken thighs, cut into 1-inch (2.5 cm) pieces
6 yellow summer squash, cut into ½-inch (1 cm) thick rounds
4 chayote squash, halved lengthwise, cut into ¼-inch (.5 cm) thick slices (or substitute 4 zucchini, cut into ½-inch [1 cm] thick rounds)
1½ cups (354 mL) olive oil
⅓ cup (79 mL) fresh lime juice
Salt, to taste
Freshly ground black pepper, to taste

1. Soak 12 bamboo skewers in water.
2. In a small bowl, combine the garlic, coriander, turmeric, mustard, cloves, habanero, and anise seed. Place the chicken in a glass baking dish and both squash in a similar dish. Sprinkle each with half of spice mixture. Add half the olive oil and half the fresh lime juice to each and mix to coat well. Cover and refrigerate for 6 to 8 hours.
3. Thread each skewer, alternating the chicken and vegetables.
4. Prepare the barbecue or preheat the broiler to a medium heat. Season the kebabs with salt and pepper. Grill until chicken is cooked through, about 5 minutes per side. Transfer the kebabs to a platter. Serve with a fruit salsa from Chapter 2.

Tart and Hot Grilled Chicken

Yield: 6 servings   Heat Scale: Medium

According to Arnold Krochmal, who wrote for me, this dish is sold in the suburbs in Puerto Rico and the Dominican Republic, where it is the local equivalent of fast food. The street vendors do a great job, and the aroma is enticing. (Note: This recipe requires advance preparation.)

¾ cup (177 mL) vegetable oil
Juice of 3 limes
6 cloves garlic, peeled and minced
1½ teaspoons (7.5 mL) freshly ground black pepper
2 tablespoons (30 mL) commercial habanero hot sauce, or one from Chapter 2
2 teaspoons (10 mL) oregano
1½ tablespoons (22.5 mL) minced cilantro
3 pounds (1.36 kg) boneless chicken breasts

1. In a glass bowl, combine the oil, lime juice, garlic, pepper, hot sauce, oregano, and cilantro and mix well. Add the chicken, toss well, and marinate it in the refrigerator for 2 to 3 hours.
2. Grill the breasts for about 12 minutes on each side, basting with the marinade. Serve with any of the rice dishes in Chapter 8.

Grenadian Grilled Chicken

Yield: 4–6 servings   Heat Scale: Medium

Shirley Jordan, who wrote for me, reported that Islanders love to cook outdoors and that most cooks in the Caribbean take pride in developing their own spicy marinades. Here is a tangy one that works for pork or chicken. (Note: This recipe requires advance preparation.)

1 Scotch bonnet chile (or habanero), seeds and stem removed, minced
1 green bell pepper, stem and seeds removed, finely chopped
1 teaspoon (5 mL) dried thyme
1 teaspoon (5 mL) Worcestershire sauce
2 tablespoons (30 mL) butter
2 cloves garlic, peeled and minced
2 shallots, peeled and minced
3 tablespoons (45 mL) tomato paste
½ cup (118 mL) dry white wine
¼ cup (59 mL) white wine vinegar
1 (4–5 pound [1.82–2.27 kg]) chicken, cut in serving-size pieces

1. In a bowl, combine the chile, bell pepper, thyme, and Worcestershire sauce and mix well.

2. In a saucepan, melt the butter over medium heat. Add the garlic and shallots and sauté until lightly browned. Stir in the tomato paste, wine, and vinegar. Add the chile mixture and bring to a boil. Reduce the heat and simmer for 5 minutes. Allow to cool.

3. Put the chicken in a bowl and cover it with the sauce. Marinate it for 3 to 4 hours in the refrigerator.

4. Preheat the barbecue. Arrange the chicken on the hot grill and cook, turning often and basting with sauce, until done, about 10 to 15 minutes.

Goat Pepper Coconut Chicken

Yield: 4 servings   Heat Scale: Medium

Coconut is combined with almost everything in the Bahamas. Its water is used in drinks, the flesh is made into milk and cream, and it is grated and dried to use in various dishes. Purchase the freshest coconut possible when preparing this dish. Choose one that's heavy for its size and sounds full when shaken. One fruit will yield 3 to 4 cups (708 to 950 mL) grated coconut.

½ cup (118 mL) butter
1 onion, peeled and finely chopped
1 (4–5 pound [1.82–2.27 kg]) chicken, cut into 8 pieces
1 goat pepper, seeds and stem removed, minced (or substitute 1 habanero)
Salt, to taste
Freshly ground black pepper, to taste
2 teaspoons (10 mL) West Indian Masala (page 5)
1 tablespoon (15 mL) sugar
½ teaspoon (2.5 mL) saffron
2 cups (473 mL) chicken stock
1 cup (236 mL) freshly grated coconut

1. In a large frying pan, melt the butter over medium heat. Add the onion and sauté until softened. Add the chicken pieces and sauté until browned. Add the chile, salt, pepper, masala, sugar, and saffron and cook, stirring, until the chicken is golden. Remove the chicken from the pan and keep it warm.

2. Add the stock to the pan and heat it over low heat for 15 minutes. Return the chicken pieces to the pan and simmer, uncovered, over low heat for 25 minutes.

3. Add the coconut and simmer for another 10 minutes. If possible, serve each portion separately in half a coconut shell.

Patito con Piña
(Duckling with Pineapple)
Yield: 6 servings   Heat Scale: Medium

The pineapple that Columbus saw for the first time in the West Indies has spread all over the world, and he would be amazed at how it is being used now. It can be found in everything from meat dishes, to drinks, to salads. It flourishes in the Caribbean and is Puerto Rico's largest export crop. Serve this with a rice dish from Chapter 13.

1 (4½-pound [2 kg]) duckling
Salt, to taste
Freshly ground black pepper, to taste
2 tablespoons (30 mL) unsalted butter
¾ cup (177 mL) dark rum, divided
1 cup (236 mL) unsweetened pineapple juice (fresh preferred), divided
1 habanero chile, stem and seeds removed, minced
1 cup (236 mL) Classic Chicken Stock (page 46)
2 cups (473 mL) chopped fresh pineapple or unsweetened canned pineapple
2 teaspoons (10 mL) arrowroot
¼ cup (59 mL) cold water

1. Preheat the oven to 325°F (165°C).
2. Pull any loose fat from the cavity of the duckling and prick the fatty parts all over with a fork. Season with salt and pepper. Heat the butter in a heavy casserole large enough to hold the duckling comfortably. Add the bird and brown it all over. Remove the duck from the casserole and discard all the fat left behind.
3. Return the duckling to the casserole with ½ cup (118 mL) of the rum and ½ cup (118 mL) pineapple juice. Cover and bake for 1 hour and 15 minutes. Transfer the duckling to a serving platter, carve it, and keep it warm.
4. Discard all the fat from the casserole. Add the remaining ¼ cup (59 mL) of rum to the casserole and stir to scrape up all the brown bits. Transfer the run to a saucepan. Add the remaining pineapple juice, habanero, and chicken stock, and cook over a high heat until the liquid is reduced to 2 cups (473 mL). Adjust the seasoning as needed, add the chopped pineapple, reduce the heat to very low, and cook for 5 minutes.
5. Mix the arrowroot with the cold water and stir this mixture into the sauce. Cook just long enough to slightly thicken the sauce. Serve separately to accompany the duckling and rice.

Twice-Cooked Spicy Chicken

Yield: 4 Servings   Heat Scale: Mild

This is a great dish for those who can't handle a lot of heat. Chicken dishes are very popular all over the Caribbean. They are especially popular in Trinidad and Tobago, as evidenced by the number of fast-food shops that sell them. The best "fast food" chicken I ever had was at one of Marie Permenter's Royal Castle restaurants in Trinidad. In this recipe, the chicken is prepared home style, and the phrase "twice-cooked" refers to the browning and then the baking. (Note: This recipe requires advance preparation.)

½ cup (118 mL) plus 1 tablespoon (15 mL) Trinidad Herb Seasoning Paste (page 8), divided
1 cup (236 mL) water
1 (4–5 pound [1.82–2.27 kg]) chicken, cut up
3 tablespoons (45 mL) vegetable oil
2 tablespoons (30 mL) butter
1 tablespoon (15 mL) brown sugar
2 cloves garlic, peeled and crushed
1 tablespoon (15 mL) Worcestershire sauce
2 tablespoons (30 mL) tomato paste
2 seasoning peppers (or substitute yellow wax hot), stems and seeds removed, chopped
2 onions, peeled and sliced into rings
½ cup (118 mL) dry sherry

1. Combine ½ cup (118 mL) of the seasoning paste with the water to make a marinade. Pierce the chicken pieces with a fork and toss them in the marinade. Allow the chicken to marinate for at least 4 hours.
2. Preheat the oven to 350°F (180°C).
3. Remove the chicken from the marinade and pat it dry. In a frying pan, heat the oil and butter over medium heat and add the brown sugar. Cook, stirring constantly, for 1 minute. Add the chicken and sauté until brown, about 5 to 7 minutes.
4. Add the remaining seasoning paste, garlic, Worcestershire sauce, tomato paste, peppers, onions, and sherry, stir well, and cook over medium heat for about 5 minutes.
5. Transfer the mixture to a casserole dish and bake, uncovered, until well-browned, about 30 to 40 minutes.

Spicy Plantation Chicken

Yield: 4 servings   Heat Scale: Medium

When I was in Jamaica shooting a video documentary, I ate a great meal prepared by Chef André Niederhauser of the Harmony Hall Restaurant in Ocho Rios. He recommends cooking this chicken on a rotisserie, but roasting it in the oven will also work. The key to success with this dish is basting the chicken as many as 20 times during the cooking. (Note: This recipe requires advance preparation.)

½ cup (118 mL) chopped green onions
3 whole cloves
1 (4½-pound [2 kg]) chicken, left whole
Salt, to taste
1 tablespoon (15 mL) ground allspice
¼ cup (59 mL) honey
¼ cup (59 mL) lime or lemon juice
1 Scotch bonnet chile, seeds and stem removed, minced very fine (or substitute 1 habanero)
½ cup (118 mL) butter, melted
2 cloves garlic, peeled and minced
1 tablespoon (15 mL) commercial demi-glace

1. Combine the green onions and cloves and spread them over the chicken, inside and out. Cover the chicken and marinate it in this mixture overnight in the refrigerator. Remove the chicken and season it lightly with salt.
2. Preheat the oven to 350°F (180°C).
3. In a bowl, combine the allspice, honey, lime juice, and chile in a bowl and mix well to make a basting sauce. Brush some of the sauce on the chicken and skewer it on a rotisserie or place it in a roasting pan. Cook the chicken for about 40 minutes, basting often.
4. Remove the chicken and cut it up into serving pieces.
5. In a small saucepan, heat the butter over medium heat. Add the garlic and sauté for 1 minute. Add the remaining basting sauce and the demi-glace and cook until slightly thickened. Serve this sauce over the chicken.

Pelau
(Caramelized Guyanan Chicken)

Yield: 4–6 servings   Heat Scale: Mild

Caramelizing the meat is an African influence that became part of the Caribbean Creole culinary tradition. The process gives the pelau its dark brown coloró—a sure sign of a good pelau. The brown layer that forms on the bottom of the pot is called "bun-bun," and some people consider it their favorite part of this meal. This recipe comes from Johnny's Food Haven in Port of Spain, Trinidad. (Note: This recipe requires advance preparation.)

3 tablespoons (45 mL) vegetable oil
¾ cup (177 mL) white or brown sugar
1 (2½–3 pound [1.13–1.36 kg]) chicken, cut up
1 onion, peeled and chopped
1 clove garlic, peeled and minced
1 Congo pepper, seeds and stem removed, minced (or substitute 1 habanero)
1½ cups (354 mL) dried pigeon peas, soaked overnight (or substitute black-eyed peas)
2 cups (473 mL) long-grain rice (do not use instant rice)
3 cups (708 mL) water
1 cup (236 mL) coconut milk
2 cups (473 mL) cubed fresh Hubbard squash
2 carrots, chopped
¼ cup (59 mL) chopped parsley
1 teaspoon (5 mL) dried thyme
1 bunch green onions, greens included, chopped
¼ cup (59 mL) catsup
3 tablespoons (45 mL) butter

1. Heat the oil in a heavy pot or skillet over high heat. Add the sugar and let it caramelize until it is almost burned, stirring constantly. Add the chicken and stir until all the pieces are covered with the sugar. Reduce the heat to medium. Add the onion, garlic, and Congo pepper and cook, stirring constantly, for 1 minute.
2. Drain the pigeon peas and add them to the pot along with the rice, water, and coconut milk. Reduce the heat and simmer, covered, for 30 minutes.
3. Add the remaining ingredients and stir until well mixed. Cover and cook until the vegetables are tender, about 20 to 30 minutes. The pelau should be moist at the end of the cooking time.

Montego Bay Chicken

Yield: 6 servings   Heat Scale: Medium

Here is a classic fricasseed chicken recipe from Montego Bay, Jamaica. The people who live in the shanty-town area of Montego Bay cook this "yardie" dish often. One of the secrets, they say, is to use the freshest chicken possible. (Note: This recipe requires advance preparation.)

1 red bell pepper, stem and seeds removed, chopped
1 yellow bell pepper, stem and seeds removed, chopped
1 large onion, peeled and chopped
8 green onions, greens included, chopped
2 carrots, peeled and sliced ¼-inch (.5 cm) thick
¾ cup (177 mL) finely chopped celery tops
8 fresh okra, sliced ½-inch (1 cm) thick
1 cho-cho (chayote squash), peeled and chopped (or substitute 2 small zucchini)
1 Scotch bonnet chile, stem and seeds removed, minced (or substitute 1 habanero)
2 cloves garlic, peeled and minced
1½ tablespoons (22.5 mL) fresh thyme
4 chicken legs with thighs attached
Vegetable oil for frying
1½ cups (354 mL) milk
All-purpose flour for dredging
2 tomatoes, chopped
2 (4-ounce [112 g]) jars sliced pimientos, drained

1. In a bowl, combine the bell peppers, onions, green onions, carrots, celery, okra, chayote, chile, garlic, and thyme. Place the chicken legs in a glass dish, cover them with the mixture, and marinate for 3 hours.
2. Remove the chicken and scrape off any vegetables. Reserve the vegetable mixture. Fill a large sauté pan with 1 inch (2.5 cm) oil and heat it. Dip the chicken in the milk and then the flour, shaking off any excess. Pan-fry the chicken until golden brown, about 20 minutes. Reserve the remaining milk. Remove and drain off all but 1 tablespoon (15 mL) of the oil.
3. Reduce the heat and pour ½ cup (118 mL) of the reserved milk in the pan to deglaze it. Add the vegetable mixture and braise for 2 minutes. Push the vegetables aside and return the chicken to the pan. Add enough of the reserved milk to half cover the chicken.
4. Simmer the mixture for 25 minutes, stirring occasionally and taking care not to knock the breading off the chicken. Turn the chicken pieces, add the tomatoes and pimientos, and continue to simmer, stirring occasionally, for 20 minutes or until the chicken is done.
If the gravy is too thick, thin it with additional milk. If it is too thin, raise the heat and reduce until thickened.

Fancy Fricasseed Chicken
Yield: 4 servings   Heat Scale: Medium

This is one of the most delicious ways to cook Caribbean chicken, as it is marinated before it is cooked, then cooked twice. The marinade is rich and spicy, and the finished dish ends up that way as well. This dish tastes great with rice and peas and twice-fried plantains. (Note: This recipe requires advance preparation.)

1 (4-pound [1.82 kg]) chicken
Juice of 1 lime
Salt, to taste
Freshly ground black pepper, to taste
1 clove garlic, peeled and crushed
1 sprig fresh thyme
2 onions, peeled and chopped
2 tomatoes, chopped
2 Scotch bonnet chiles, stems and seeds removed, minced (or substitute habaneros)
¼ cup (59 mL) vegetable oil
2–3 cups (473–708 mL) water
1 whole green Scotch bonnet chile (or habanero)

1. Wash and dry the chicken. Rub it all over with the lime juice. Cut it into pieces and place the pieces in a bowl. Season the chicken with salt and plenty of black pepper.
2. In a separate bowl, combine the garlic, thyme, onions, tomatoes, and minced chiles. Mix well, then coat each piece of chicken well with the spice mixture. Let the chicken marinate, covered, for 1 hour in the refrigerator.
3. Remove the chicken pieces from the bowl, reserving the marinade, and pat them dry. In a sauté pan, heat the oil over medium heat. Add as many pieces of chicken as the pan will hold without overlapping and fry them until very brown. Repeat with the remaining chicken. Remove the browned chicken from the pan.
4. Take the pan off the heat for a minute or so, let it cool a little, lower the heat, put the pan back, and add the reserved marinade. Cook, stirring, for a minute or so. Add the water and bring it to a boil. Add the chicken pieces and the whole chile. Reduce the heat, cover the pan, and simmer for 45 minutes to 1 hour or until the chicken is tender but not falling apart. Be careful not to break the whole Scotch bonnet.
5. Taste the juices for salt and adjust as needed. If the gravy is too thin, increase the heat and simmer, uncovered, until the excess liquid evaporates. Carefully remove the whole chile before serving.

Jamaican Jerk Chicken Wings

Yield: 4–6 servings   Heat Scale: Medium

Jamaican jerk huts are everywhere in Jamaica, especially in Kingston, where many a steel drum has been converted to a grill. There is also an ongoing controversy as to what part of Jamaica (and what particular place) has the best jerk. So far, the unofficial taste troop has designated Boston Beach. Use the marinade in the recipe or substitute North Coast Jerk Marinade (page 7) if you have some prepared. (Note: This recipe requires advance preparation.)

1 onion, peeled and chopped
⅔ cup (158 mL) finely chopped green onions
2 garlic cloves, peeled
½ teaspoon (2.5 mL) dried thyme, crumbled
1½ teaspoons (7.5 mL) salt
1½ teaspoons (7.5 mL) ground allspice
¼ teaspoon (1.25 mL) freshly grated nutmeg
½ teaspoon (2.5 mL) ground cinnamon
½ teaspoon (2.5 mL) minced habanero chile
1 teaspoon (5 mL) freshly ground black pepper
10 drops commercial habanero hot sauce, or to taste
2 tablespoons (30 mL) soy sauce
¼ cup (59 mL) vegetable oil
18 chicken wings (about 3¼ pounds [1.48 kg]), wing tips cut off

1. In a food processor or blender, purée the onion, green onions, garlic, thyme, salt, allspice, nutmeg, cinnamon, habanero, black pepper, hot sauce, soy sauce, and oil.
2. In a large, shallow dish, arrange the wings in a single layer and spoon the marinade over them, rubbing it in. Let the wings marinate, covered, in the refrigerator, turning them once, for at least 1 hour or, preferably, overnight.
3. Preheat the oven to 450°F (240°C). Oil a roasting rack and line a roasting pan with foil.
4. Arrange the wings in a single layer on the prepared rack set over the prepared pan. Spoon the marinade over them and bake the wings in the upper third of the oven for 30 to 35 minutes or until they are cooked through.

Pollo Glazeado con Salsa de Habanero
(Glazed Chicken with Habanero Sauce)

Yield: 4–8 servings   Heat Scale: Medium

This chicken dish comes from Rodolfo de Garay and Thomas Brown, who wrote for me about spicy Cuban dishes. They noted, "This recipe also works well as a barbecue. Make sure the chicken is half-cooked over the coals before beginning to brush on the habanero sauce." Sour orange juice can be approximated by mixing equal parts orange juice and lime juice. (Note: This recipe requires advance preparation.)

½ cup (118 mL) sour orange juice
½ teaspoon (2.5 mL) freshly ground black pepper
1 teaspoon (5 mL) minced garlic
1¼ teaspoon (6.25 mL) salt, divided
8 pieces chicken (about 5–6 pounds [2.27–2.72 kg] total)
1 habanero chile, stem and seeds removed, quartered (or substitute a commercial habanero hot sauce, to taste)
1 teaspoon (5 mL) lemon juice
1 teaspoon (5 mL) distilled white vinegar
2 tablespoons (30 mL) tomato sauce
2 tablespoons (30 mL) grated onion
Vegetable oil for sautéing

1. Combine the orange juice, black pepper, garlic, and 1 teaspoon (5 mL) of the salt to make an adobo. Add the chicken and marinate it for at least 2 hours or, preferably, overnight.
2. When the chicken has finished marinating, preheat the oven to 400°F (200°C).
3. In a blender or food processor, combine the habanero, lemon juice, vinegar, the remaining salt, and the grated onion and blend to make a sauce. Add a little water if necessary.
4. Remove the chicken from the adobo and reserve the liquid. Heat about ⅛ inch of oil in a frying pan over medium-high heat. Brown the chicken until golden on both sides.
5. Mix the remaining adobo with the habanero sauce. Place the chicken pieces in a baking pan and brush with the sauce. Bake for about 6 minutes, then turn the chicken over, brush the other side with sauce, and continue baking for another 6 minutes. Repeat until the sauce has been used up and the chicken is finished cooking, about 30 minutes. This dish may be served hot or cold.

Caribbean Chicken with Black Ginger Sauce

Yield: 4 servings   Heat Scale: Medium

Peggy Barnes collected this Antiguan recipe for me on location. In this dish, im-ported pickled ginger and soy sauce combine with local rum to turn chicken into black magic. Peggy wrote, "Local cooks choose a sweet soy sauce, like Kikkoman, to balance the heat generated by the habanero peppers. Serve with steamed white rice topped with the ginger sauce and a quick stir-fry of snow peas or zucchini slices." (Note: This recipe requires advance preparation.)

2½ pounds (1.14 kg) bone-in, skinless chicken breasts
1 cup (236 mL) white rum
¼ cup (59 mL) vegetable oil
1 large onion, peeled and coarsely chopped
1 habanero chile, stem and seeds removed, minced
4 garlic cloves, peeled and finely chopped
2 tablespoons (30 mL) grated fresh ginger
1 teaspoon (5 mL) freshly ground black pepper
2 teaspoons (10 mL) cornstarch
1 cup (236 mL) soy sauce
½ cup (118 mL) Japanese pickled ginger
2 tablespoons (30 mL) slivered green onions, green part only

1. Marinate the chicken in the rum for several hours or overnight.
2. Remove the chicken and reserve the rum.
3. Preheat the oven to 350°F (180°C).
4. In a large skillet, heat the oil over medium heat. Add the chicken and cook until golden brown. Remove the chicken from the pan and keep it warm. Add the onions and cook for 1 minute. Add the habanero, garlic, fresh ginger, and pepper. Cook for 2 minutes.
5. In a bowl, dissolve the cornstarch in the soy sauce, then add the reserved rum and the onion-garlic mixture and combine well to make a sauce.
6. Place the chicken in a baking pan, pour the sauce over the chicken, and bake for 1 hour. Turn the chicken several times during baking to coat with the sauce. Five minutes before serving, top the chicken pieces with the pickled ginger, turn off the oven, and let the dish stand in the oven for 10 minutes. Garnish with the green onion before serving.

Colombo de Poulet
(Chicken Colombo)

Yield: 4 servings   Heat Scale: Medium

This recipe hails from Guadeloupe, where they are not afraid of peppers. Shaped like a butterfly, the two islands of Basse-Terre and Grande-Terre are separated by the Riviere Salee. The island sports a 74,000-acre Parc National that is full of waterfalls, lakes, rainforests, and even a volcano. This curry is as lush as the landscape and should be served over white rice. (Note: This recipe requires advance preparation.)

¼ cup (59 mL) peanut oil
2 pounds (1.1 kg) chicken pieces
1 medium onion, peeled and finely chopped
2 green onions, finely chopped
2 cloves garlic, peeled and minced
2 tablespoons (30 mL) Colombo Curry Paste (page 6)
½ teaspoon (2.5 mL) ground allspice
2 cups (473 mL) water
1 tablespoon (15 mL) white wine vinegar
3 sprigs thyme, finely chopped (or substitute 1 teaspoon [5 mL] dried thyme)
1 tablespoon (15 mL) minced fresh parsley
¼ cup (59 mL) dried chickpeas, soaked overnight and drained
1 large carrot, diced
2 chayotes or zucchini, peeled and sliced
1 habanero chile, stem and seeds removed, minced

1. Heat the oil in a large, deep saucepan over high heat and brown the chicken. Reduce the heat to medium-high, add the onions, green onions, and garlic, and cook until soft. Add the curry paste, allspice, water, vinegar, thyme, parsley, and chickpeas. Reduce the heat to low, cover, and cook for 40 minutes. Add the carrot, chayote or zucchini, and habanero and cook until the vegetables are tender, about 10 to 15 minutes. Serve hot.

Calypso Ginger Chicken Breasts

Yield: 6 servings Heat Scale: Medium

True to its name, this recipe will make you sing. With key ingredients such as liqueurs and paw-paw (better known as papaya), this recipe is truly a combination of the rich flavors of the islands.

4 tablespoons (60 mL) butter, divided
6 large chicken breasts (4–5 pounds [1.82–2.27 kg] total)
Juice of 1 lemon
Salt, to taste
Freshly ground black pepper, to taste
2 callaloo leaves (or substitute 6 spinach leaves)
6–8 (1-inch [2.5 cm]) slices papaya
½ teaspoon (2.5 mL) minced Scotch bonnet chile (or substitute habanero)
3 chives, chopped
2 tablespoons (30 mL) grated fresh ginger
1 onion, peeled and chopped
½ cup (118 mL) Classic Chicken Stock (page 46)
½ cup (118 mL) La Grenade liqueur
1 teaspoon (5 mL) Worcestershire sauce
1 teaspoon (5 mL) cornstarch
1 teaspoon (5 mL) rum
4 teaspoons (20 mL) soy sauce
½ teaspoon (2.5 mL) grated nutmeg

1. Preheat the oven to 350°F (180°C). Grease a baking dish with 2 tablespoons (30 mL) of the butter.
2. Remove the skin from the chicken breasts and wash the breasts with the lemon juice. Flatten them with a mallet and season them with salt and pepper.
3. Spread the callaloo leaves on the bottom of the prepared baking dish. Spread the chicken breasts over the leaves. Add the papaya slices, chile, chives, ginger, and onion. Cover the dish with aluminum foil and bake for 30 minutes.
4. In a saucepan, combine the chicken stock, liqueur, Worcestershire sauce, the remaining 2 tablespoons (30 mL) butter, the cornstarch, the rum, the soy sauce, and the nutmeg. Cook over medium heat for 5 minutes.
5. Remove the chicken breasts from the baking dish and arrange them on a platter over a bed of rice. Pour the sauce over them and serve hot.

Bajan Fried Chicken

Yield: 4–6 servings   Heat Scale: Medium

This chicken dish from Barbados is famous because of its tasty seasonings. But be-
ware if you're a tourist in Barbados. What may be pitched to you as authentic "Ba-
jan" seasoning may actually be only dried green onions! (Note: This recipe requires
advance preparation.)

1 cup (236 mL) Bonney Bajan Seasoning (page 9)
2 pounds (1.1 kg) chicken parts, poked all over with a fork
2 cups (473 mL) vegetable or corn oil
1 cup (236 mL) all-purpose flour
½ teaspoon (2.5 mL) baking powder
Salt, to taste
½ teaspoon (2.5 mL) freshly ground black pepper

1. In a bowl, combine the seasoning and the chicken. Marinate it in the
refrigerator for 1 hour or longer.
2. Heat the oil in a frying pan over medium heat. In a bowl, combine the
flour, baking powder, salt, and pepper. Remove the chicken pieces from the
refrigerator and pat them dry with paper towels. Separate some of the skin
from the chicken pieces and place some of the marinade between the skin
and meat. Coat the chicken with the flour mixture.
3. Fry the chicken until cooked through and golden brown on both sides,
15 to 20 minutes. Serve hot.

Stir-Fried Cashew Chicken

Yield: 4 serves   Heat Scale: Medium

Cashews are a cash crop of the Caribbean. The cashew tree produces a nut and a
fruit, and, strangely enough, it is related botanically to mangos and poison ivy. This
recipe illustrates the Asian influence on the Caribbean.

¼ cup (59 mL) peanut oil
3 boned chicken breasts, thinly sliced (1–2 pounds [454 g–1.1 kg])
½ cup (118 mL) chopped onion
3 green onions, chopped, white and green parts included
1 cup (236 mL) peeled and coarsely chopped cucumber
1 cup (236 mL) coarsely chopped carrots
1 (8-ounce [224 g]) can water chestnuts, drained and sliced
1 cup (236 mL) sliced mushrooms
1 (8-ounce [224 g]) can bamboo shoots, drained and chopped
2 teaspoons (10 mL) salt
2 tablespoons (30 mL) commercial habanero hot sauce (or a habanero hot
sauce from Chapter 2)
¾ cup (177 mL) whole roasted cashews
2 tablespoons (30 mL) butter or vegetable oil

1. Heat the peanut oil in a heavy frying pan or wok over high heat. Add the chicken and stir-fry for 3 minutes. Add the onion, green onions, cucumber, carrots, water chestnuts, mushrooms, bamboo shoots, and salt and cook, stirring constantly, for about 5 minutes longer. Pour the hot sauce over the mixture and cook without stirring for 1 more minute.
2. Meanwhile, sauté the cashews in a little butter or oil until golden brown.
3. Pile the chicken-vegetable mixture into a warmed serving dish and top it with the cashews. Serve with rice.

Chicken Victoria

Yield: 6 servings   Heat Scale: Medium

In 1838, Jamaica was emancipated from England. This recipe is in honor of Queen Victoria, who is remembered as "Missus Queen who set us free." This dish is great to make ahead for a dinner party, especially a buffet. (Note: This recipe requires advance preparation.)

2 tablespoons (30 mL) lime juice, divided
1 (4-pound [1.82 kg]) chicken, cut into serving pieces
1 teaspoon (5 mL) salt
½ teaspoon (2.5 mL) freshly ground black pepper
1 medium onion, peeled and thinly sliced
1 clove garlic, peeled, crushed, and chopped
1 green bell pepper, stem and seeds removed, chopped
1 tablespoon (15 mL) commercial habanero hot sauce (or a habanero hot sauce from Chapter 2)
3 tablespoons (45 mL) vegetable oil
½ teaspoon (2.5 mL) annatto seeds
2 cups (473 mL) uncooked long-grain rice
1 cup (236 mL) sliced mushrooms, sautéed in butter
1 tablespoon (15 mL) tomato sauce
1 (2–3 inch [5–7.5 cm]) piece lemon peel
1 teaspoon (5 mL) sherry
4 cups (.95 L) Classic Chicken Stock (page 46)
3 tablespoons (45 mL) gold Jamaican rum

1. In a shallow baking dish, squeeze 1 tablespoon (15 mL) of the fresh lime juice over the chicken pieces, then sprinkle them well with the salt and pepper. Add the onion, garlic, green bell pepper, and hot sauce. Cover and refrigerate for up to 24 hours.
2. Shake the seasoning off the chicken and reserve it. Pat the chicken pieces dry with paper towels.
3. In a heavy-bottomed casserole, heat the oil and annatto seeds over high heat until the oil turns red. Discard the seeds. Add the chicken pieces to the oil and sauté until browned. Remove the chicken from the pan and set it aside.

4. To the casserole, add the uncooked rice and the reserved seasoning and sauté, stirring, until the oil is absorbed. (Be careful that the rice does not burn.) Add the mushrooms and return the chicken pieces to the casserole. Add the tomato sauce, the lemon peel, the remaining lime juice, the sherry, and the chicken stock. Taste for seasoning and make any necessary corrections. Cover and simmer gently until the rice is cooked, the chicken is tender, and the liquid has been absorbed,, about 40 minutes. Add the rum and cook, uncovered, for about 5 minutes longer.

Habanero-Marinated and Pecan-Smoked Quail
Yield: 6 servings   Heat Scale: Medium-Hot

The wild quail most commonly eaten are those that have white meat, such as the bobwhite and the crested, or Gambel's quail of the west. The Courternix, a domesticated variety, is raised on farms in South Carolina and Georgia. Its taste can be mild to strong, depending on the age of the bird. Quail are small and lean, so they must be marinated before cooking. The lengthy marinating time is countered by the short time it takes to smoke these birds. Serve this dish with a wild and white rice pilaf and sautéed carrots and pearl onions. (Note: This recipe requires advance preparation.)

¼ cup (59 mL) golden raisins
¼ cup (59 mL) soy sauce
2 habanero chiles, stems and seeds removed, chopped
4 cloves garlic, peeled and chopped
2 tablespoons (30 mL) minced ginger
2 teaspoons (10 mL) ground coriander
1 teaspoon (5 mL) ground turmeric
1 teaspoon (5 mL) ground cinnamon
½ teaspoon (2.5 mL) ground cloves
Juice of 2 limes
⅓ cup (79 mL) vegetable oil
6 whole quails

1. In a bowl, soak the raisins in the soy sauce for 15 minutes to soften. In a blender or food processor, combine the raisins and soy sauce with the chiles, garlic, ginger, coriander, turmeric, cinnamon, cloves, and lime juice and purée until smooth. With the machine running, add the oil a little at a time.
2. Place the quail in a nonreactive pan or a large plastic bag. Add the marinade and marinate for 24 hours, or just overnight if you are strapped for time.
3. Build a fire with pecan or fruitwood in the smoker and bring the smoke to 200 to 220°F (100 to 110°C). Place the quail on a rack in the smoker and smoke until the leg bones move easily, about 1 to 2 hours. Alternatively, smoke-grill the quail over a hot fire for about 15 minutes, turning often. In either case, the internal temperature should reach 160°F (75°C).

Roasted Saguaro Jam–Glazed Cornish Hens Stuffed with Cornbread, Piñons, and Green Chiles

Yield: 4 servings   Heat Scale: Mild

Here is a good example of some of the substitutions that can be made in these poultry recipes. In place of saguaro cactus fruit jam, try prickly pear jam or even jalapeño jelly. The stuffing can be used in roasted chicken or turkey, and the Cornish hens can be replaced with a duck or chicken.

2 tablespoons (30 mL) butter
1 small onion, peeled and chopped
4 green New Mexican chiles, roasted, peeled, stems and seeds removed, chopped
½ cup (118 mL) chopped celery
3 cups (708 mL) coarsely crumbled corn bread
½ cup (118 mL) roasted pine nuts
1 teaspoon (5 mL) fresh thyme, chopped
1 teaspoon (5 mL) fresh sage, chopped
½ cup (118 mL) chicken broth
1 cup (236 mL) saguaro cactus jam
4 Cornish hens

1. Preheat the oven to 350°F (180°C).
2. In a saucepan, melt the butter over medium heat. Add the onion and sauté until soft. Transfer the onion to a bowl. Add the chiles, celery, cornbread, pine nuts, thyme, and sage and mix thoroughly. Add enough broth to moisten but not saturate the mixture and mix well.
3. Stuff the hens with the mixture and close the openings. Spread the jam over the hens and roast them for 1 hour, basting with additional jam.
4. To serve, carefully cut each hen in half to expose the stuffing. Serve additional jam warm on the side, along with a sauce or salsa or two selected from Chapter 2.

Mesquite-Grilled Turkey Legs with Jalapeño-Cilantro Lime Basting Sauce

Yield: 4 servings   Heat Scale: Medium

This is one of the simpler and quicker ways to prepare turkey. You can add mesquite chips soaked in water to the fire to give the turkey legs a little smoke flavor. And go ahead, be daring and add a couple of tablespoons (30 mL) of tequila to the sauce. Serve with hot German potato salad, ranch-style baked beans, and a spicy dessert from Chapter 14.

¼ cup (59 mL) lime juice
6 jalapeño chiles, stems and seeds removed, chopped
2 fresh tomatillos
1½ teaspoons (7.5 mL) sugar
2 cloves garlic, peeled and chopped
¾ cup (177 mL) chopped fresh cilantro
2 tablespoons (30 mL) vegetable oil
½ teaspoon (2.5 mL) ground coriander
¼ teaspoon (1.25 mL) ground white pepper
4 small turkey legs

1. In a blender or food processor, combine all the ingredients except the turkey and purée until smooth, adding some water if necessary, to make a sauce.

2. Bring the turkey to room temperature and gently loosen the skin without tearing it. Brush the sauce over the legs and under the skin, reserving any remaining sauce. Allow the turkey to sit at room temperature for an hour.

3. Grill the turkey legs over a medium fire, basting regularly with the sauce. Cook for 30 minutes, turning often, or until the internal temperature of the legs reaches 160°F (75°C) for medium.

Chicken, Chile, and Cheese Chimichangas

Yield: 6 servings   Heat Scale: Mild

These sweet chicken chimichangas with fruit are lighter than the more traditional beef and bean recipe popular in Arizona.

1 medium onion, peeled and chopped fine
1 tablespoon (15 mL) vegetable oil, plus more for deep frying
4 green New Mexican chiles, roasted, peeled, stems and seeds removed, chopped
3 cups (708 mL) diced cooked chicken
½ teaspoon (2.5 mL) ground cinnamon
¼ teaspoon (1.25 mL) ground cloves
1 small orange, peeled, seeded, and chopped
6 flour tortillas
1 cup (236 mL) grated Monterey Jack cheese
Chopped lettuce for garnish
Chopped tomatoes for garnish

1. Preheat the oven to the lowest setting.
2. In a large skillet, heat 1 tablespoon (15 mL) of the oil over medium heat. Add the onion and sauté it until soft. Add the chiles, chicken, cinnamon, and cloves and sauté for an additional 5 minutes. Add the chopped orange and mix well.
3. Wrap the tortillas in a moist towel and place them in the oven to soften. Place approximately ½ cup (118 mL) of the chicken mixture in the center of each tortilla and top with cheese. Fold each tortilla like an envelope and secure them with toothpicks.
4. Heat the oil for deep frying to 375°F (190°C). Deep-fry the chimichangas, one at a time, until well browned. Drain on paper towels and remove the toothpicks.
5. Serve topped with shredded lettuce, chopped tomatoes, and a salsa selected from Chapter 2.

Margarita-Marinated Game Hens

Yield: 4 servings   Heat Scale: Medium

This is the recipe for people who would like to eat their margarita rather than drink it. The hens can be either baked or split and cooked on a grill with the marinade used as a basting sauce. (Note: This recipe requires advance preparation.)

4–5 serrano chiles, stems and seeds removed
½ cup (118 mL) lime juice
¼ cup (59 mL) vegetable oil
2 tablespoons (30 mL) tequila
2 teaspoons (10 mL) sugar
1 teaspoon (5 mL) chopped fresh cilantro
4 Cornish game hens

1. Preheat the oven to 400°F.
2. In a blender, combine all the ingredients except the hens and purée. Put the hens in a ceramic bowl and pour the marinade over them. Marinate for 2 hours at room temperature or overnight in the refrigerator.
3. Place the hens in the oven and immediately reduce the heat to 350°F (180°C). Roast for 30 to 45 minutes or until done, basting often with the marinade.

Tomatillo-Chicken Enchiladas with Two Kinds of Green Chile

Yield: 6 servings   Heat Scale: Medium

Southwestern cooks are forever improvising on traditional recipes. This interesting variation on green chile and chicken enchiladas has been tested so many times in my kitchens that I now consider it a New Southwest classic. The enchiladas go well with the traditional dishes of rice, refried beans, and a crisp garden salad.

4 chicken breasts (1½–2½ pounds [681 g–1.14 kg] total)
8 ounces (224 g) cream cheese
1 cup (236 mL) finely chopped onions
1 cup (236 mL) heavy cream or half-and-half, divided
3 green serrano chiles, stems and seeds removed, chopped fine
5 green New Mexican chiles, roasted, peeled, stems and seeds removed, chopped
1 cup (236 mL) tomatillos, husks removed, washed, chopped fine
¼ cup (59 mL) chopped fresh cilantro
½ teaspoon (2.5 mL) freshly ground black pepper
1 egg
Vegetable oil for frying tortillas
12 corn tortillas

1. Preheat the oven to 350°F (180°C).
2. Put the chicken in a pot and add water to cover. Bring to a boil, reduce the heat, and simmer 30 minutes. Remove the chicken and reserve the stock. When the chicken has cooled, remove the skin and bones. Shred the meat using two forks.
3. In a bowl, combine the cream cheese, onions, and ¼ cup (59 mL) of the cream. Add the chicken and mix well.
4. In a blender or food processor, combine the serranos, green chile, tomatillos, cilantro, pepper, egg, remaining cream, and ⅓ cup (79 mL) of the reserved chicken stock and purée to make a smooth sauce.
5. In a frying pan, heat a couple inches (5 cm) of oil until hot. Fry each tortilla for a few seconds on each side until soft, taking care that they do not become crisp. Remove the tortillas and transfer them to paper towels to drain.

6. To assemble the enchiladas, dip a tortilla into the green sauce and place it in a shallow casserole dish. Spread about ¼ cup (59 mL) of the chicken mixture in the center of the tortilla, roll it up, and place it at the end of the dish with the seam side down. Repeat the process until the enchiladas form a single layer in the dish. Pour the remaining sauce over the enchiladas.
7. Bake the enchiladas, uncovered, for 20 minutes. Serve immediately.

Smoked Turkey Basted with Cascabel Oil

Yield: 8 or more servings   Heat Scale: Mild

This simple dish yields a complex taste. Serve the turkey hot with the chile oil and a salsa on the side, or cold on a bolillo roll. (Note: This recipe requires advance preparation.)

½ cup (118 mL) vegetable oil
6 cascabel chiles, stems and seeds removed, crushed (or substitute 3 pasillas)
4 cloves garlic, peeled and chopped
2 teaspoons (10 mL) dried oregano
Salt, to taste
Freshly ground black pepper, to taste
1 (10-pound [4.5 kg]) turkey

1. In a sauté pan, heat the oil over medium heat. Add the chiles and garlic and sauté until softened. Remove the pan from the heat and add the oregano, salt, and pepper.
2. Split the turkey in half by cutting through the breast and backbone. Brush the chile oil over the turkey and marinate for a couple of hours at room temperature.
3. Place the turkey sections, breast side up, on a grill in a smoker. Smoke with indirect heat over an aromatic wood such as pecan, apple, or hickory. Baste the turkey with the oil every half hour until done, about 4 hours.

Stuffed Chicken Breasts with Walnut Pipian Sauce

Yield: 4–6 servings   Heat Scale: Mild

*The Maya are credited with creating pipians, or sauces that are flavored and thick-
ened with seeds and/or nuts. In this dish, the pipian also adds color.*

3 chicken breasts, skinned, bones removed, halved
6 green New Mexican chiles, roasted, peeled, stems and seeds removed
6 thin slices ham
6 slices asadero or Monterey Jack cheese
1 large avocado, peeled, pitted, and sliced
¼ cup (59 mL) plus 3 tablespoons (45 mL) chopped fresh cilantro
¼ cup (59 mL) melted butter
4 tablespoons (60 mL) butter or vegetable oil
1 medium onion, peeled and chopped
1 clove garlic, peeled and chopped
1 poblano, roasted, peeled, stem and seeds removed, chopped
½ cup (118 mL) chopped walnuts
2 cups (473 mL) Classic Chicken Stock (page 46)

1. Preheat the oven to 325°F (165°C).
2. Pound the chicken breasts until thin. Top each piece of chicken with
the green New Mexican chiles, ham, cheese, avocado, and 3 tablespoons
(45 mL) of the cilantro. Roll each breast tightly and arrange them, seam-
side down, in a shallow baking dish, and brush them with the melted
butter. Cover and bake for 45 minutes. Remove the cover and continue to
bake until the top is golden brown, about 10 minutes.
3. To make the sauce, heat the butter or oil in a saucepan over medium
heat. Add the onion, garlic, and poblano and sauté until the onion starts
to brown. Transfer the mixture to a blender. Add the walnuts and purée
until smooth, using a little broth to thin the sauce if necessary.
4. Return the sauce to the pan, stir in the broth, and simmer for 20 to 30
minutes or until thickened.
5. To serve, arrange the chicken on a plate, pour the sauce over the top,
and garnish with a few chopped walnut pieces.

Mesquite-Grilled Chicken with Apple Pistachio Chutney

Yield: 4 servings   Heat Scale: Medium

The chutney is best made the day before so that the flavors have time to blend. Here I serve it with chicken, but it also is good with fish.

3 green New Mexican chiles, roasted, peeled, stems and seeds removed, chopped
3 tablespoons (45 mL) distilled white vinegar
2 tablespoons (30 mL) orange juice
3 tablespoons (45 mL) brown sugar
3 tart apples, such as Granny Smith or Jonathan, peeled, cored, and chopped
2 tablespoons (30 mL) raisins
3 tablespoons (45 mL) shelled pistachios, coarsely chopped
4 boneless chicken breasts

1. Soak some mesquite chips in water.
2. In a saucepan, combine the chile, vinegar, orange juice, and brown sugar. Bring to boil, stirring constantly, to dissolve the sugar. Add the apples and raisins and simmer for 30 minutes or until the apples are tender.
3. Stir in the pistachios and simmer for 2 more minutes.
4. Prepare a fire of mesquite wood or charcoal. When the coals have burned down to a medium heat, add the water-soaked mesquite chips. Place the chicken breasts on the grill, skin-side down, and grill for 10 to 12 minutes on the skin side. Turn them and cook for an additional 5 to 6 minutes or until done.
5. Serve the chicken topped with the chutney.

El Pollo al Carbón
(Grilled Fruity Chicken)

Yield: 4 servings   Heat Scale: Medium-Hot

The concept of marinating chicken in a spicy fruit juice and then char-broiling it originated in Mexico and is becoming quite popular throughout the Southwest. This chicken is served with warm corn tortillas, fresh salsa, and a side of pinto beans. Guests remove the chicken from the bones, place it in a tortilla, top it with salsa, and enjoy. (Note: This recipe requires advance preparation.)

2 tablespoons (30 mL) butter or vegetable oil
1 small onion, peeled and chopped
2 cloves garlic, peeled and minced
2 tomatillos, husks removed, chopped
½ cup (118 mL) orange juice
2 tablespoons (30 mL) lime juice
1 tablespoon (15 mL) lemon juice
¼ teaspoon (1.25 mL) ground cinnamon
¼ teaspoon (1.25 mL) ground cloves
½ teaspoon (2.5 mL) ground habanero chile
2 small chickens, cut in half lengthwise (6–8 pounds [2.72–3.63 kg])
Pico de Gallo Salsa (page 69) for serving
Corn tortillas for serving

1. In a saucepan, heat the butter or oil over medium heat. Add the onion, garlic, and tomatillos and sauté them until softened. Add the orange juice, lime juice, lemon juice, cinnamon, cloves, and chile and simmer for 10 minutes. Transfer this mixture to a blender and purée to form a sauce.
2. Marinate the chicken in the sauce for at least 3 hours.
3. Grill the chicken until done, basting frequently with the sauce.

Chicken and Jicama Pita Pockets

Yield: 4 Servings   Heat Scale: Mild

Pita bread makes great pockets for holding a wide variety of fillings, such as the one in this recipe. These sandwiches are great for any outing, as everything can be prepared the day before, with the exception of the avocado, which should be sliced just before serving so that it doesn't turn brown. (Note: This recipe requires advance preparation.)

4 green New Mexican chiles, roasted, peeled, stems and seeds removed, chopped
¼ cup (59 mL) sour cream or plain yogurt
¼ cup (59 mL) mayonnaise
1 tablespoon (15 mL) lime juice
⅓ cup (79 mL) minced onion
1 clove garlic, peeled and minced
¼ teaspoon (1.25 mL) ground cumin
2 cups (473 mL) cooked, diced chicken
1 cup (236 mL) shredded jicama
2 small tomatoes, diced
Shredded lettuce for serving
4 pocket pita bread rounds
1 avocado, sliced

1. In a bowl, combine the chiles, sour cream or yogurt, mayonnaise, lime juice, onion, garlic, and cumin. Add the chicken and toss it until well coated. Marinate the chicken in the refrigerator for at least 4 hours or overnight.

To serve:
Cut the pita rounds in half and gently open the pockets with a fork. To the chicken, add the jicama and tomatoes. Place the lettuce and chicken mixture in the pitas, add the sliced avocado, and serve.

Tamale Pie with Cheese and Chicken

Yield: 6 servings   Heat Scale: Medium

This recipe is a delicious alternative to traditional tamales. A green salad is all you need to complete the meal.

1 (4-pound [1.82 kg]) chicken, cut in pieces
2 large onions, peeled and chopped, divided
2 cloves garlic, peeled and minced
4 green New Mexican chiles, roasted, peeled, stems and seeds removed, chopped
3 jalapeño chiles, stems and seeds removed, chopped
1 teaspoon (5 mL) ground red New Mexican chile
1 cup (236 mL) ripe black olives, chopped
1 cup (236 mL) whole kernel corn
2 cups (473 mL) sour cream
2 cups (473 mL) Classic Chicken Stock (page 46)
1 cup (236 mL) masa harina
2 eggs, separated
2 cups (473 mL) grated Monterey Jack cheese

1. Preheat the oven to 375°F (190°C).
2. In a large pot, combine the chicken, half the onions, and the garlic. Add water to cover and simmer until the chicken is done and starts to fall away from the bones. Remove the chicken. Strain and reserve the broth.
3. Remove the meat from the bones and chop the chicken. In a bowl, combine the chicken, remaining onions, jalapeños, ground chile, olives, corn, and sour cream. Transfer the mixture to a casserole dish.
4. In a pot, bring the stock to a boil. Gradually add the masa, stirring constantly. Reduce the heat and cook until the mixture thickens, about 10 minutes. Remove the pot from the heat and stir in the egg yolks. Whip the egg whites until stiff and fold them in. Spread this batter over the casserole and top with the grated cheese.
5. Bake, uncovered, for 35 minutes.

Grape-Grilled Quail with Goat Cheese Rounds

Yield: 6 servings   Heat Scale: Mild

Although many Southwestern barbecuers and grillers use mesquite, it is not the only aromatic wood. Experiment with pecan, apple, peach, and grape clippings. If you use charcoal for the main fire, be sure to soak the wood in water for an hour before grilling.

12 quails
2 ancho chiles, stems and seeds removed
⅔ cup (158 mL) plus 2 tablespoons (30 mL) olive oil, divided
¼ cup (59 mL) orange juice
2 tablespoons (30 mL) lime juice
1 clove garlic, peeled
6 (2-ounce [56 g]) goat cheese rounds
¼ cup (59 mL) dried cornbread crumbs
Serrano Salsa with Mangos and Tomatillos (page 69) for serving

1. Soak 6 (6-inch [15 cm]) pieces of thick grape vine clippings in water.
2. Cut the wing tips off the quails, then split the birds down the backs and remove theirs backbones. With a knife tip, remove the rib bones from each quail, then slice open the thighs to remove the bones and joints, taking care to keep the skin intact. Open up each quail and press the legs together, securing them with toothpicks.
3. Simmer the chiles in water for 15 minutes. Drain the chiles and transfer them to a blender. Add ⅔ cup (158 mL) of the olive oil, the orange and lime juices, and the garlic and purée. Pour this sauce over the quail and marinate for an hour.
4. While the quail are marinating, prepare a medium-hot charcoal fire and preheat the oven to 350°F (180°C). Brush the goat cheese rounds with the remaining olive oil, coat them with the cornbread crumbs, arrange them on a baking sheet, and bake for 5 minutes. If you start the baking just when the quail are being grilled, both should be done at the same time.
5. Add the grape clippings to the coals. Arrange the quail skin-side down on the rack and grill for 2 minutes, taking care not to burn them. Turn the quail and grill for an additional 2 minutes. If the skin is not yet crisp, turn once more and grill for an additional minute.
6. Serve 2 quail on each plate, topped with the salsa and a goat cheese round.

Chicken Basquaise with Espelette Piperade

Yield 4–6 servings   Heat Scale: Mild to Medium

Piperade is a colorful pepper sauce that is only spicy when made in the Basque region. This simple but delicious dish is often served at the Celebration of the Peppers in Espelette, France. Serve it with boiled potatoes and green beans.

½ cup (118 mL) olive oil, divided
4 medium onions, peeled and chopped
3 cloves garlic, peeled
4 green bell peppers, stems and seeds removed, chopped
2 red bell peppers, stems and seeds removed, chopped
4 large tomatoes, peeled and chopped
3 tablespoons (45 mL) ground Espelette pepper, or more to taste (or substitute hot paprika or ground red New Mexico chile)
1 pinch dried thyme
Salt, to taste
Freshly ground black pepper, to taste
1 (4–5 pound [1.82–2.27 kg]) chicken, cut up

1. In a large sauté pan, heat ¼ cup (59 mL) of the olive oil over medium heat. Add the onions and garlic and sauté for 5 minutes, stirring occasionally. Add the bell peppers and cook for 10 minutes. Add the tomatoes and ground Espelette and cook for 20 minutes, stirring occasionally. Add the thyme, salt, and pepper and transfer the mixture to a bowl.
2. Wipe out the sauté pan and heat the remaining ¼ cup (59 mL) oil. Brown the chicken in the oil until golden, turning often. Pour the piperade over the chicken, reduce the heat, cover, and simmer until tender, about 30 to 40 minutes. Add salt and pepper to taste.

Pollo alla Cacciatora
(Chicken Cacciatore)

Yield: 4 servings   Heat Scale: Medium

Believe it or not, my mother (who was not Italian) would prepare this dish for the family in the 1950s, way before Italian food became popular in the United States. This particular recipe comes from the province of Cosenza in Calabria. Serve it over the pasta of your choice.

¼ cup (59 mL) olive oil
1 (3½–4 pound [1.59–2.27 kg]) roasting chicken, cut into serving pieces
1 small onion, peeled and chopped
1 green bell pepper, seeds and ribs removed, thinly sliced
1 tablespoon (15 mL) minced celery
1 clove garlic, peeled and minced
1 pinch rosemary
1 cup (236 mL) red wine
3 large tomatoes, peeled and chopped
1 tablespoon (15 mL) minced Italian parsley
2 teaspoons (10 mL) crushed red chile, or more to taste
1 cup (236 mL) sliced mushrooms
Salt, to taste
Freshly ground black pepper, to taste

1. In a large pan, heat the olive oil over medium heat. Add the chicken pieces and fry for about 10 minutes, until they are browned on all sides. Add the onion, bell pepper, celery, garlic, and rosemary. Sauté for 10 more minutes.
2. Add the wine, tomatoes, parsley, and crushed red chile. Stir well, cover, and cook over low heat for 30 minutes. Add the mushrooms, salt, and pepper, and cook for 15 more minutes.

Pollo alla Diavolo
(Tuscan Devil Chicken)

Yield: 4 servings   Heat Scale: Medium

In Italian, this chicken is called pollo alla diavolo because of the addition of crushed red peperoncini chiles, the same kind that are sprinkled on pizzas to liven them up. Traditionally, the chickens are split before grilling, but you can use a rotisserie if you wish—it just takes longer to cook. Adding rosemary branches to the fire creates a very aromatic smoke. Make this a true meal off the grill and serve the devil chicken with a salad and polenta. (Note: This recipe requires advance preparation.)

1 (4-pound [1.82 kg]) chicken
⅔ cup (158 mL) dry red wine, such as Chianti
⅓ cup (79 mL) olive oil
2 tablespoons (30 mL) lemon juice (fresh preferred)
1½ tablespoons (22.5 mL) finely chopped fresh rosemary (or substitute 1½ teaspoons [7.5 mL] dried)
1½ tablespoons (22.5 mL) finely chopped fresh sage (or substitute 1½ teaspoons [7.5 mL] dried)
2 teaspoons (10 mL) crushed red chile (piquin for hot, New Mexican for mild)
2 cloves garlic, peeled
¼ teaspoon (1.25 mL) salt

1. Using poultry shears or a heavy knife, cut down both sides of the backbone to cut the chicken in half. Remove the backbone and place the chicken on a cutting board, skin-side up. Press hard on the breastbone to break it and flatten the bird.
2. In a bowl, whisk together the wine, olive oil, lemon juice, rosemary, sage, crushed chile, garlic, and salt. Coat the chicken with the marinade, transfer it to a freezer bag, and marinate it for 2 hours in the refrigerator.
3. Lightly oil a clean grill surface. Remove the chicken from the marinade and set it aside. Transfer the remaining marinade to a small saucepan and simmer it for 20 minutes. Place the chicken on the grill, skin-side down, and weigh it down with a cast-iron skillet so the chicken remains flat. Grill for 15 to 20 minutes per side, basting frequently with the marinade, until the juices run clear when pierced with a fork or the internal temperature reaches 160°F (75°C).
4. Using a cleaver, chop the split chicken halves into quarters.

Greek-Grilled Chicken Oregano
Yield: 4 servings   Heat Scale: Mild

Sure, I added some nontraditional chiles to this recipe, something the Greeks have needed since 1500 BC but didn't get until 3,000 years later. This marinade can also be used on lamb kebabs for an appetizer to a Greek feast. Retsina is a wine flavored with pine resin—an acquired taste for sipping, but one that works very well in a marinade. Serve this with a traditional Greek salad, a rice pilaf, and dilled green beans. (Note: This recipe requires advance preparation.)

¼ cup (59 mL) retsina or dry white wine
⅓ cup (79 mL) lemon juice (fresh preferred)
2 tablespoons (30 mL) olive oil
1 tablespoon (15 mL) chopped fresh oregano (or substitute 1 teaspoon [5 mL] dried)
2 teaspoons (10 mL) chopped fresh thyme (or substitute ¾ teaspoon [6.25 mL] dried)
1 teaspoon (5 mL) ground cinnamon
2 jalapeño chiles, stems and seeds removed, chopped
Salt, to taste
Freshly ground black pepper, to taste
4 boneless, skinless chicken breasts

1. In a blender or food processor, combine all the ingredients except the chicken and purée until smooth. Place the chicken breasts in a freezer bag, coat them with the marinade, and marinate for 2 hours in the refrigerator.
2. Remove the chicken from the marinade and set it aside. Transfer the marinade to a small saucepan and simmer it for 20 minutes. Grill the breasts over a medium fire, basting with the marinade, for about 20 minutes or until the internal temperature reaches 160°F (75°C).

Sidi's Tamarind and Coconut Chicken
Yield: 4 servings   Heat Scale: Medium-Hot

This is an authentic home recipe shared by the wife of the food and beverage manager of the Driftwood Beach Club in Malindi, Kenya. Recipe collector Michelle Cox says, "although Sidi spends his whole life around food, he never tires of being served this one when he gets away from the hotel kitchen."

8 pieces of chicken (legs and thighs are good)
Vegetable oil for browning
1 medium onion, peeled and chopped
1 medium tomato, chopped
2 cloves garlic, peeled and chopped
2–3 Kenya chiles, stems and seeds removed, chopped fine (or substitute fresh red jalapeños)
1 heaping teaspoon (7.5 mL) ground turmeric
Salt, to taste
Freshly ground black pepper, to taste
2 cups (473 mL) coconut milk
1 cup (236 mL) lime juice

1. In a frying pan, heat the oil. Add the chicken and brown it on all sides. Remove the chicken and set it aside. To the pan, add the onion, tomato, garlic, chiles, and turmeric and fry until the onion is browned. Return the chicken to the pan. Pour the coconut milk and lime juice over the chicken. Simmer over low heat for 30 minutes, until the chicken is cooked through. Serve with rice.

Hyderabad Chicken Curry

Yield: 4 servings   Heat Scale: Medium

From Kenya comes this curry imported from India, which is the way things work in immigrant-happy Africa. To spice it up even further, substitute jalapeños for the New Mexican chiles. This recipe is best served with freshly cooked basmati rice. (Note: This recipe requires advance preparation.)

1 cup (236 mL) plain yogurt
3 medium cloves garlic, peeled and minced
2 teaspoons (10 mL) chopped fresh ginger
¼ teaspoon (1.25 mL) saffron threads, crushed and mixed in 1 tablespoon (15 mL) water
1 (3½-pound [1.59 kg]) chicken, cut into 6 pieces and patted dry
3 New Mexican chiles, roasted, peeled, stems and seeds removed, chopped (about 6 ounces [168 g] total)
10 cardamom pods, skinned, seeds removed and reserved
6 black peppercorns
4 whole cloves
1 tablespoon (15 mL) caraway seed
1 (¾-inch [1.5 cm]) cinnamon stick, broken into small pieces
1¼ teaspoons (8.75 mL) ground turmeric
1 teaspoon (5 mL) salt
3 tablespoons (45 mL) ghee or vegetable oil
2 medium onions, peeled and thinly sliced
3 tablespoons (45 mL) grated coconut
1 cup (236 mL) Classic Chicken Stock (page 46)
1 tablespoon (15 mL) fresh lemon juice
Cilantro leaves for garnish

1. In a large bowl, combine the yogurt, garlic, ginger, and dissolved saffron. Add the chicken and marinate at room temperature for 2 hours, turning occasionally.
2. In a food processor or blender, purée the chiles.
3. Heat a heavy medium skillet over medium heat. Add the cardamom pods and seeds, peppercorns, cloves, caraway seed, and cinnamon and cook until aromatic, 6 to 7 minutes. Transfer to a small bowl and let cool. In a spice grinder or blender, blend the mixture to a powder. Return the mixture to a small bowl and stir in the chile purée, turmeric, and salt.
4. Melt the ghee or heat the oil in a large heavy skillet over medium-low heat. Add the onions and sauté until golden, 5 to 7 minutes. Blend in

the spice mixture and stir for 2 minutes. Add the chicken pieces with the marinade and the coconut. Increase the heat to medium-high and bring to a boil. Stir in the stock and return to a boil. Reduce the heat to low and simmer until the chicken is tender, about 20 minutes for white meat and 30 minutes for dark, turning the pieces once. Transfer the chicken to a platter. Add the lemon juice to the sauce and pour it over the chicken. Garnish with cilantro and serve.

Berber Chicken Stuffed with Fruited Rice

Yield: 4–6 servings   Heat Scale: Mild

Here is a delicious chicken dish for special occasions. It based on a recipe from the Berbers, a formerly nomadic people of Morocco. It has the flavor of the famous tajines but is cooked on a spit rather than as a stew. The ubiquitous mint appears in the marinade and as a garnish, and you can serve mint tea, or "Berber whiskey," with this dish as well. For more flavor, rub the marinade under the skin of the chicken. (Note: This recipe requires advance preparation.)

2 tablespoons (30 mL) Harissa Sauce (page 23; or substitute ground red New Mexican chile)
¼ cup (59 mL) vegetable oil
¼ cup (59 mL) lemon juice (fresh preferred)
¼ cup (59 mL) water
1 tablespoon (15 mL) ground ginger, divided
1 teaspoon (5 mL) ground cayenne
¾ teaspoon (3.75 mL) ground turmeric, divided
¼ teaspoon (1.25 mL) ground cumin
¼ cup (59 mL) finely chopped fresh mint (or substitute 2 tablespoons [30 mL] dried mint)
1 (3–4-pound [1.36–1.82 kg]) chicken
6 dried apricots
4 dried prunes
1 heaping teaspoon (7.5 mL) golden raisins
¼ cup (59 mL) chopped onions
1 tablespoon (15 mL) olive oil
¼ cup (59 mL) blanched almonds
2 cups (473 mL) cooked rice
2 tablespoons (30 mL) chopped fresh mint, plus more for garnish
1 tablespoon (15 mL) Harissa Sauce (page 23; or substitute ½–1 teaspoon [2.5–5 ml] ground cayenne)
1 teaspoon (5 mL) ground coriander
½ teaspoon (2.5 mL) ground cinnamon
2 pinches pulverized saffron
Sliced toasted almonds for garnish

1. In a bowl, combine the 2 tablespoons (30 mL) Harissa, vegetable oil, lemon juice, water, 2 teaspoons (10 mL) of the ginger, the cayenne, ½ teaspoon (2.5 mL) of the turmeric, the cumin, and the finely chopped mint and mix well. Place the chicken in a freezer bag, add the marinade, and marinate for 4 hours or overnight. Remove the chicken from the bag and set it aside. Transfer the marinade to a small saucepan and simmer for 20 minutes, adding water as needed to get a good consistency for a basting sauce.

2. In a bowl, cover the dried apricots, prunes, and raisins with hot water and soak for about 15 to 20 minutes or until plump. Chop the fruit into large pieces.

3. In a saucepan, heat the olive oil over medium heat. Add the onions and sauté until softened. Transfer the onions to a bowl. Add the chopped fruit, almonds, rice, 2 tablespoons (30 mL) chopped mint, 1 tablespoon (15 mL) Harissa, the remaining ginger, the coriander, the cinnamon, the remaining turmeric, and the saffron. Stuff the chicken with this mixture. Any extra rice can be reheated and served with the bird. Place the chicken on a spit and seal the opening with string or toothpicks.

4. Place the chicken on a rotisserie above a medium fire and cook, uncovered, for about 1½ hours or until done, basting with the marinade. If you are cooking it in a covered grill, it will only take about an hour. The internal temperature of the chicken should reach 160°F (75°C).

5. To serve, remove the rice from chicken cavity and cut the chicken into serving pieces. Arrange the chicken on a platter, mound rice in the center, and garnish with the chopped mint and almonds.

Variation
Just about any dried fruits will work for this dish, including peaches, cherries, or pears.

Poulet au Gnemboue (Chicken with Spiced Almonds)

Yield: 4–6 servings   Heat Scale: Hot

This recipe is a simple North African tajine intensely flavored with almonds and cayenne. Serve it over couscous.

1 cup (236 mL) almonds
1¾ cups (413 mL) water
2 teaspoons (10 mL) ground cayenne
¼ teaspoon (1.25 mL) freshly ground black pepper
1 teaspoon (5 mL) salt
1 clove garlic, peeled
3 green onions, thinly sliced
1 (3-pound [1.36 kg]) chicken, cut for frying

1. Pulverize the almonds with a mortar and pestle and combine them with the water. Pour the mixture into a 12-inch (30 cm) skillet or saucepan. Add the cayenne, black pepper, salt, garlic, and onions and mix well.

2. Add the chicken pieces, cover, and cook over a very low heat for 1½ hours. Check often, stirring and adding water if needed. It should be very thick, more of a sauce than a stew.

Tajine Tafarout

Yield: 4 servings   Heat Scale: Hot

This tajine honors the flowering of the almond trees and comes from Tafarout, Morocco. This dish is often served at a wedding feast. Serve it with a carrot salad, couscous, and pita bread.

1 (3–4 pound [1.36–1.82 kg] chicken, cut in serving pieces
4 tablespoons (60 mL) extra virgin olive oil
1 large onion, peeled and finely sliced
4 teaspoons (20 mL) ground cayenne
1 teaspoon (5 mL) ground ginger
1 teaspoon (5 mL) ground coriander
½ teaspoon (2.5 mL) ground cumin
½ teaspoon (2.5 mL) ground cinnamon
¼ teaspoon (1.25 mL) ground turmeric
2 cups (473 mL) water
1 cup (236 mL) dried apricot halves, soaked in water until soft
1 cup (236 mL) whole, blanched almonds
2 tablespoons (30 mL) butter

1. In a large skillet, brown the chicken in the olive oil. Remove the chicken from the skillet and pour off all but 1 tablespoon (15 mL) of the oil.
2. Add the onion and sauté until browned. Add the spices and sauté for 2 minutes. Add the water and bring to a boil.
3. Reduce the heat. Return the chicken pieces to the skillet. Add the apricots and simmer for 30 minutes, turning the chicken frequently, until the chicken is very tender and starts to fall from the bone. Add more water if necessary. It should be very thick, more of a sauce than a stew.
4. Brown the almonds in the butter.
5. To serve, arrange the chicken on a platter, top it with the sauce, and garnish with the almonds.

Tagine Mderbel
(Cayenne Chicken Tagine Smothered in a Spicy Eggplant Purée)

Yield: 4–6 servings   Heat Scale: Medium

Here, chicken simmers in a sauce of garlic, ginger, saffron, and black pepper until it is tender. Then the chicken is piled in the center of a dish and topped with a thick, intensely flavored topping of fried eggplant, tomatoes, and spices. (Note: This recipe requires advance preparation.)

2 pounds (1.1 kg) eggplant
2 tablespoons (30 mL) plus 2 teaspoons (10 mL) coarse (kosher) salt, divided
Olive or corn oil for shallow frying
3 medium cloves garlic, peeled and crushed, divided
¼ cup (59 mL) chopped Italian parsley, divided
¼ cup (59 mL) chopped cilantro, divided
1 teaspoon (5 mL) sweet paprika
¼ teaspoon (1.25 mL) ground cumin
1 teaspoon (5 mL) ground cayenne
2 large tomatoes, peeled, seeded, and chopped (about 2 cups [473 mL])
1 pinch sugar
2 tablespoons (30 mL) lemon juice
1 tablespoon (15 mL) apple cider vinegar
1 (4-pound [1.82 kg]) chicken, cut into 8 pieces
1¼ teaspoons (6.25 mL) ground ginger
1 pinch ground saffron
¼ teaspoon (1.25 mL) freshly ground black pepper
½ cup (118 mL) grated onion (about 2 small onions)
Sprigs of fresh cilantro for garnish
Thin slices of lemon for garnish

1. Trim the top and bottom from each eggplant. With a vegetable peeler, remove 3 to 4 thin vertical strips of skin from each vegetable, leaving the eggplants striped. Slice the eggplants crosswise into ½-inch (1 cm) slices. Sprinkle the eggplant slices with 2 tablespoons (30 mL) of the salt and let them drain in a non-aluminum colander for at least 2 hours or preferably overnight. Rinse and drain the eggplant; pat dry with paper towels.
2. Heat ¼ inch (.5 cm) of oil in a large heavy skillet over high heat. Add the eggplant slices in batches and fry them until golden brown on both sides, about 4 minutes. Drain them on paper towels and transfer them to a cutting board. Strain the oil and reserve it. With a potato masher, crush the eggplant with 1 of the garlic cloves, 2 tablespoons (30 mL) each of the parsley and cilantro, the paprika, the cumin, and the cayenne.
3. Return 3 tablespoons (45 mL) of the reserved oil to the skillet and reheat it. Add the tomatoes, 1 teaspoon (5 mL) of the remaining salt, and the sugar. Cook over medium-high heat, stirring frequently, until most of the moisture evaporates, about 5 minutes.

4. Add the mashed eggplant to the skillet and reduce the heat to very low. Cook, stirring frequently, until most of the moisture evaporates and the mixture is very thick, about 20 minutes. Remove the skillet from the heat and stir in the lemon juice and vinegar. (The recipe can be prepared to this point up to 3 days in advance.)

5. Preheat the oven to 400°F (200°C).

6. Wash the chicken and pat it dry. In a mortar, pound the remaining 2 cloves garlic with the remaining 1 teaspoon (5 mL) salt. Blend in the ginger, saffron, and black pepper. Gradually stir in 2 tablespoons (30 mL) of the reserved oil and ½ cup (118 mL) of hot water.

7. In a large flameproof casserole or deep skillet, toss the chicken with the garlic-spice mixture to coat each piece. Cover and cook over low heat for 5 minutes. Add the onion, the remaining parsley and cilantro, and water to just cover (about 2½ cups [591 mL]). Bring to a boil, reduce the heat to medium, cover, and simmer for 1 hour, or until the chicken begins to fall off the bone. Transfer the chicken to a serving dish and cover it to keep it moist. Skim most of the fat from the pan, then continue cooking juices until they are reduced to 1½ cups (354 mL), about 15 minutes.

8. Mix half the pan juices with the eggplant purée and adjust the seasoning with additional salt, black pepper, and lemon juice as needed. Place the chicken in a small heatproof serving bowl. Pile the eggplant on top, forming a pyramid. Surround it with the remaining sauce. Cover loosely with foil and reheat for 10 minutes in the oven just before serving. Garnish the purée with the sprigs of cilantro and lemon slices.

Chicken Doro Weit

Yield: 4 servings   Heat Scale: Hot

Also spelled wait, doro weit or chicken stew is the most well-known of the "national dishes" of Ethiopia. This dish is served with any sourdough bread—injera is traditional. The serving dish is a brightly colored woven straw basket three feet high that is placed in the center of the room. Everyone sits around it and eats the weit with their fingers.

1 (3-pound [1.36 kg]) chicken, cut into small pieces
3 tablespoons (45 mL) lemon juice
2 tablespoons (30 mL) butter
1 large onion, peeled and chopped
2 cloves garlic, peeled and chopped
2 teaspoons (10 mL) ground ginger
1 teaspoon (5 mL) freshly ground black pepper
¼ teaspoon (1.25 mL) ground cardamom
¼ teaspoon (1.25 mL) ground nutmeg
¼ cup (59 mL) Berbere (page 27)
2 tablespoons (30 mL) paprika
4 hard-boiled eggs, peeled

1. Remove the chicken skin and score it all over so that sauce will penetrate the meat. Rub the chicken with the lemon juice and let it marinate for 30 minutes at room temperature.
2. In a sauté pan, melt the butter over medium heat. Add the onion and garlic and sauté until browned. Add the spices, Berbere, and paprika and cook for 2 to 3 minutes.
3. Add the chicken to the pan and toss to coat. Stir in enough water to form a thick sauce. Bring to a boil, reduce the heat, cover, and simmer for 45 minutes or until the meat starts to fall off the bone.
4. Using a fork, poke holes all over the eggs, then add them to the stew. Replace the cover and simmer for an additional 15 minutes.

Five-Chile Chicken

Yield: 4 servings   Heat Scale: Hot

This West African dish is popular in Nigeria, and it is very hot. However, feel free to adjust the heat level up or down to your taste. Traditionally, this is served over bland Imoya Eba, a porridge-like mixture of cassava and green banana, but you can use the closest equivalent: dumplings, stiff cornmeal mush such as polenta, or rice.

1 (3-pound [1.36 kg]) fryer chicken, skin and fat removed, cut up
½ cup (118 mL) lemon juice
½ cup (118 mL) water
2 tablespoons (30 mL) vegetable oil, divided
2 tomatoes, skinned and sieved or crushed
5 green chiles, such as jalapeños, stems and seeds removed, minced
1 (½-inch [1 cm]) piece ginger root, peeled and grated
½ pound (224 g) okra, trimmed and cut into thin rounds
2 cups (473 mL) Classic Chicken Stock (page 46)
Salt, to taste
Freshly ground black pepper, to taste

1. Remove skin and fat from chicken. In a large bowl, combine the lemon juice and water. Add the chicken..
2. Heat 1 tablespoon (15 mL) of the oil in a skillet over medium heat. Add the tomatoes, chiles, ginger, and okra and sauté for about 8 minutes. Remove the sautéed ingredients from the skillet and set them aside.
3. Drain the chicken and dry it with paper towels. Heat the remaining oil in the skillet. Add the chicken and fry it until browned. Add the stock and sautéed ingredients, cover, and simmer for 40 to 60 minutes.
4. Taste for seasoning, adjust as needed, and serve.

Palaver Chicken

Yield: 4–6 servings   Heat Scale: Medium

This is a variation of the popular "sauce" from Ghana (see Palaver Sauce, page 89) which was originally made from fish. In Africa, a sauce is sometimes a stew. This version is from Sierra Leone, where peanut butter is often added. Serve this dish with boiled yams or rice.

1½ pounds (680 g) skinless, boneless chicken breasts
2 garlic cloves, peeled and crushed
Salt, to taste
Freshly ground black pepper, to taste
2 tablespoons (30 mL) butter
2 tablespoons (30 mL) vegetable oil (palm oil is traditional)
1 onion, peeled and finely chopped
4 tomatoes, peeled and chopped
2 tablespoons (30 mL) peanut butter
2½ cups (591 mL) Classic Chicken Stock (page 46)
1 sprig thyme (or substitute 1 teaspoon [5 mL] dried thyme)
8 ounces (224 g) frozen spinach, defrosted and chopped
2 green chiles, such as jalapeños, stems and seeds removed, chopped

1. Thinly slice the chicken breasts. Put them in a bowl and stir in the garlic and a little salt and pepper. In a large frying pan, melt the butter over medium heat. Add the chicken and fry it, turning once or twice to brown evenly. Transfer it to a plate with a slotted spoon and set aside.
2. In a large saucepan, heat the oil over high heat. Add the onion and tomatoes and fry them for 5 minutes, until softened.
3. Reduce the heat to medium. Add the peanut butter and half the stock and blend well.
4. Cook for 4 to 5 minutes, stirring constantly to prevent the peanut butter from burning. Add the remaining stock, the thyme, the spinach, the chiles, and salt and pepper to taste. Stir in the chicken slices and cook for 10 to 15 minutes or until the chicken is cooked through.
5. Pour into a warmed serving dish and serve.

Bombay Grilled Chicken

Yield: 4 servings   Heat Scale: Medium

This recipe has a long list of ingredients, but it is easy to prepare and produces a complex flavor. It is also low in fat. It is typical of Indian dishes in that a spice paste is used first, followed by a marinade. The spiced yogurt marinade keeps the chicken moist when grilling, even without the skin. Serve the chicken as they do in India, on a bed of salad—slivers of onion, tomato wedges, radishes, and green chile garnished with lemon wedges, accompanied by curried potatoes and peas and a chutney from Chapter 1. (Note: This recipe requires advance preparation.)

6 tablespoons (90 mL) lemon juice, divided
4 tablespoons (60 mL) vegetable oil, divided
4 teaspoons (20 mL) ground cayenne, divided
1 teaspoon (5 mL) salt
½ teaspoon (2.5 mL) freshly ground black pepper, plus more to taste
4–6 skinless chicken breasts
1½ cups (354 mL) plain yogurt
½ cup (118 mL) minced onion
2 tablespoons (30 mL) minced ginger
1 teaspoon (5 mL) ground cumin
1 teaspoon (5 mL) ground turmeric
1 teaspoon (5 mL) ground coriander
½ teaspoon (2.5 mL) ground cardamom
½ teaspoon (2.5 mL) ground cinnamon
¼ teaspoon (1.25 mL) ground nutmeg
⅛ teaspoon (.6 mL) ground allspice

1. In a bowl, combine 3 tablespoons (45 mL) of the lemon juice, 2 tablespoons (30 mL) of the vegetable oil, 2 teaspoons (10 mL) of the cayenne, the salt, and ½ teaspoon (2.5 mL) of the pepper. Allow this paste to sit at room temperature for 30 minutes to blend the flavors.
2. If the chicken pieces aren't skinless, remove the skin. Make slits in the pieces and rub the paste over the chicken, making sure the paste gets in the slits. Let the chicken sit at room temperature for 30 minutes, then drain it.
3. In a food processor or blender, combine the yogurt, onion, remaining lemon juice, remaining vegetable oil, ginger, remaining cayenne, cumin, turmeric, coriander, cardamom, cinnamon, nutmeg, allspice, and black pepper to taste and process until smooth. Place the chicken in a nonreactive bowl and cover it with the marinade. Marinate, covered, in the refrigerator for 4 hours or overnight.
4. Remove the chicken from the marinade, reserving the marinade, and place the chicken on the grill. Transfer the marinade to a saucepan and simmer it for 20 minutes. Cover the grill and grill the chicken for 5 minutes. Turn the pieces, cover and cook for an additional 5 minutes. Uncover the grill, turn the chicken pieces, and baste them with any remaining marinade. Continue cooking, uncovered, until the chicken is done, about 12 minutes or the internal temperature reaches 160°F (75°C).

Chicken Biryani

Yield: 6 servings   Heat Scale: Medium

One of the richest, tastiest, most aromatic, and most colorful of Indian dishes, biryani is prepared across India. But the best biryani—whether made from beef, lamb, chicken, fish, or vegetables—is found in the regions around Delhi. These regions were ruled by Muslims for several centuries, and their hearty love for rich food has left behind a culinary legacy. Biryani is a time-consuming culinary exercise, but it has rich rewards. (Note: This recipe requires advance preparation.)

1 tablespoon (15 mL) saffron strands
4 teaspoons (20 mL) warm milk
2 fresh green chiles, such as serranos, stems removed
2 fresh red chiles, such as serranos, stems removed
2 large onions, peeled and chopped
8 cloves garlic, peeled
1 (2-inch [5 cm]) piece ginger, peeled
3 whole cloves
8 black peppercorns
½ teaspoon (2.5 mL) cardamom seeds
1 (1-inch [2.5 cm]) stick cinnamon, crushed
1 teaspoon (5 mL) coriander seeds
1 teaspoon (5 mL) cumin seeds
½ teaspoon (2.5 mL) poppy seeds
¼ teaspoon (1.25 mL) ground nutmeg
¼ teaspoon (1.25 mL) ground mace
½ cup (118 mL) mint or cilantro leaves
¼ cup (59 mL) lemon juice
2 cups (473 mL) plain yogurt
3 pounds (1.36 kg) boneless chicken, cut into 1-inch (2.5 cm) cubes
Salt, to taste
2 tablespoons (30 mL) olive or vegetable oil
1 tablespoon (15 mL) ghee
1 onion, peeled and finely chopped
8 large tomatoes, chopped
2 cups (473 mL) uncooked basmati or other long-grain rice
⅓ cup (79 mL) raisins
⅓ cup (79 mL) raw cashews
⅓ cup (79 mL) raw almonds
6 hard-boiled eggs, halved

1. In a bowl, soak the saffron in the warm milk in a bowl for 5 minutes. Transfer the mixture to a blender and purée it. Add the chiles, onions, garlic, ginger, cloves, peppercorns, cardamom, cinnamon, coriander, cumin, poppy seeds, nutmeg, mace, mint or cilantro leaves, and lemon juice. Blend into a smooth paste. Transfer the paste to a large bowl, add the yogurt, and mix well.
2. Add the chicken to the yogurt mixture and add salt to taste. Marinate for at least 2 hours. For the best results, marinate for 6 hours.

3. In a large skillet, heat the oil over medium heat for 1 minute. Add the ghee and, 15 seconds later, add the onions, and fry them for about 8 minutes. Reserve the fried onions for garnishing.

4. In the same skillet, combine the marinated chicken and the tomatoes and cook for about 10 minutes, uncovered. Remove the chicken pieces from the sauce and set them aside.

5. Add the rice to the sauce, bring to a boil, and cook, covered, over low heat for 15 minutes. Return the chicken to the sauce, along with any remaining saffron paste, the raisins, the cashews, and the almonds and mix well. Simmer, covered, for 5 minutes.

6. Arrange the chicken, eggs, and rice so that the yellow of the eggs, the saffron colored rice, the nuts, and the chicken make a colorful display. Add the reserved onions as a garnish.

Nimbu Masala Murgh (Moghlai Chicken Curry)

Yield: 4 servings   Heat Scale: Medium

Moghlai dishes, popular across India but particularly in Delhi and the neighboring Uttar Pradesh, owe their ancestry to sixteenth- and seventeenth-century Moghul rulers, Akbar and Shehjehan, who were connoisseurs of music, literature, architecture, and food. Unlike their immediate ancestors, who invaded India and were too busy consolidating their empire to pay much attention to cuisine, Akbar and Shehjehan recruited the best chefs in northern India and encouraged them to create dishes that carried the influence of the ingredients of Central Asia and India. (Note: This recipe requires advance preparation.)

2 large onions, peeled and chopped
1 (2-inch [5 cm]) piece ginger, peeled
10 cloves garlic, peeled
2 cups (473 mL) plain yogurt
Salt, to taste
1 teaspoon (5 mL) ground cayenne
1 tablespoon (15 mL) ground cumin, divided
1 tablespoon (15 mL) ground coriander, divided
1 tablespoon (15 mL) commercial garam masala, divided
1 (3–4 pound [1.36–1.82 kg]) chicken, cut into serving pieces
¼ cup (59 mL) ghee or vegetable oil
1 teaspoon (5 mL) yellow mustard seeds
4 green chiles, such as serranos, stems removed, finely minced
¼ cup (59 mL) lime juice
1 lime, cut into small pieces
½ cup (118 mL) raw cashews
1 large tomato, diced
1 large onion, cut into rings
¼ cup (59 mL) cilantro or mint leaves

1. In a food processor or blender, grind the onion, ginger, and garlic to a smooth paste. Transfer the paste to a bowl and add the yogurt, salt, cayenne, half the cumin, half the coriander, and half the garam masala. Add the chicken pieces, mix well, and marinate at room temperature for 6 hours.

2. Transfer the chicken and marinade to a large skillet, and cook, covered, for about 12 minutes over low heat.

3. In a separate skillet, heat the ghee or oil over medium heat for 2 minutes. Add the mustard seeds and, when they begin to pop, add the chiles. Pour this mixture over the chicken and continue cooking for 8 to 10 minutes or until the moisture evaporates.

4. Transfer the chicken to a serving dish. Squeeze the lime juice over the meat, and sprinkle it with the remaining cumin, coriander, and garam masala. Garnish with the lime pieces, cashews, tomato, onion rings, and cilantro or mint leaves.

Moghul Chicken Dilruba

Yield: 4 servings   Heat Scale: Medium

This rich, spicy-sweet chicken dish from northwestern India has distinct Moghul influences. "Dilruba" means sweetheart. The Moghuls controlled most of India from 1526 until 1839, leaving behind some of India's most famous architecture, including the Taj Mahal. The Moghul emperors loved to eat, and twenty-course meals were common in the royal courts. Not surprisingly, Moghul rule had a greater influence on Punjabi cuisine than that of any other conqueror.

2 medium onions, peeled
2 tablespoons (30 mL) chopped fresh ginger
6 tablespoons (90 mL) butter or vegetable oil
1 (3–4 pound [1.36–1.82 kg]) chicken, skin removed, cut into small serving pieces
1 cup (236 mL) plain yogurt
¼ cup (59 mL) raw almonds
¼ cup (59 mL) raw walnuts
¼ cup (59 mL) melon, pumpkin, or squash seeds (optional)
1 cup (236 mL) milk
2 tablespoons (30 mL) garam masala
1 teaspoon (5 mL) ground turmeric
2 or 3 fresh green cayenne peppers, minced (or substitute any small, hot chiles such as serranos or jalapeños)
Salt, to taste
Ground cayenne, to taste
A few strands whole saffron, soaked in 2 tablespoons (30 mL) warm milk
Minced cilantro for garnish
Whole almonds for garnish
Whole cashews for garnish

1. In a blender or food processor, combine the onions and ginger and process to a smooth paste (about the consistency of applesauce). In a heavy, deep skillet heat the butter or oil over medium heat. Add the onion mixture and gently brown, stirring often.

2. Add the chicken and yogurt. Mix well and cook until the mixture becomes rather dry and the chicken begins to brown, about 10 minutes.
3. Grind the almonds, walnuts, and melon seeds, if using, until quite fine. Stir them into the milk. Add this mixture to the chicken along with the garam masala, turmeric, chiles, salt, and cayenne.
4. Cook, stirring often, until the chicken is very tender and the sauce is very thick (about 10 to 15 minutes). Stir in the saffron and milk mixture and cook for 1 to 2 minutes longer.
5. Garnish with the cilantro and nuts and serve hot.

Tandoori Murg
(Chicken Tandoori-Style)

Yield: 4–6 servings   Heat Scale: Medium

Tandoori chicken, a famous Indian dish, is also one of the tastiest. The word "tandoori" refers to any food cooked in a tandoor, which is a giant, unglazed clay oven. The chicken in this recipe is marinated twice: first with the lemon juice, then with the yogurt mixture. You can approximate a tandoor by using a charcoal grill or gas broiler, but the food won't achieve quite the same flavor. The taste is hard to duplicate since the tandoor reaches temperatures up to 800°F (425°C), but even if the chicken is not strictly traditional, it's still flavorful. Those who are watching their fat intake will like cooking chicken in the tandoori style, since the skin is removed from the chicken before it is cooked. And, by using a low-fat yogurt in the marinade, you reduce the fat even further. This chicken is traditionally served with a cooling mint chutney. (Note: This recipe requires advance preparation.)

1 cup (236 mL) plain yogurt
4 chicken breasts, skin removed
2–3 teaspoons (10–15 mL) ground cayenne chile
1 tablespoon (15 mL) ground paprika
1 teaspoon (5 mL) freshly ground black pepper, divided
½ cup (118 mL) lemon juice
¼ teaspoon (1.25 mL) crushed saffron threads dissolved in ¼ cup (59 mL) hot water
1 tablespoon (15 mL) grated ginger
1 tablespoon (15 mL) chopped garlic
1 tablespoon ground red chile, such as New Mexican or piquin
2 teaspoons (10 mL) garam masala
1 teaspoon (5 mL) ground coriander
½ teaspoon (2.5 mL) ground turmeric
½ teaspoon (2.5 mL) ground nutmeg
½ teaspoon (2.5 mL) ground cinnamon
¼ teaspoon (1.25 mL) ground cumin
¼ teaspoon (1.25 mL) ground cloves
½ teaspoon (2.5 mL) salt
3 tablespoons (45 mL) melted butter
Lemon slices for garnish

1. Line a strainer with a dampened cheesecloth. Add the yogurt and place the strainer over a bowl. Put the bowl and strainer in the refrigerator and let the yogurt drain for 4 hours to thicken.
2. Make slashes in the chicken about 2 inches (5 cm) deep. In a bowl, combine the cayenne, paprika, and ½ teaspoon (2.5 mL) of the black pepper. Rub this mixture into the slashes and coat the chicken with the lemon juice. Marinate the chicken for 30 minutes at room temperature, then drain.
3. In a food processor or blender, combine the drained yogurt, dissolved saffron, ginger, garlic, ground chile, garam masala, coriander, nutmeg, cinnamon, cumin, cloves, salt, and the remaining black pepper and purée until smooth. Pour the marinade over the chicken and, using your fingers, rub it into the meat. Cover the chicken and refrigerate for 24 hours, turning at least once.
4. Start a charcoal or hardwood fire in your barbecue. Place the grill 2 inches (5 cm) above the coals and grill the chicken for 10 minutes, turning once. Use the marinade to baste the chicken as it cooks. Raise the grill to 5 inches (12.5 cm) and cook for another 5 minutes, turning once.
5. Remove the chicken from the grill and brush it with the melted butter. Return the chicken to the grill and cook for another 5 minutes, turning once, until the chicken is done and the juices run clear.
6. Serve the chicken garnished with lemon slices, with the mint chutney on the side.

Vietnamese-Style Beijing Duck

Yield: 8 servings   Heat Scale: Mild

Duck is quite a delicacy in Southeast Asia. Beijing ducks are specially bred to grow extra plump in the breast area, with a layer of fat between the skin and the meat. Serve this dish with Nuoc Cham dipping sauce from Chapter 2, an assortment of vegetables, and vermicelli rice.

2¼ cups (532 mL) water
1 (5-pound [2.3 kg]) fresh duck
1 tablespoon (15 mL) annatto seeds
½ cup (118 mL) soy sauce
3 jalapeño chiles, stems and seeds removed, minced
2 cloves garlic, peeled and minced
1 teaspoon (5 mL) finely grated ginger
¼ cup (59 mL) sugar
½ cup (118 mL) sliced green onions
1 recipe Vietnamese Dipping Sauce (Nuoc Cham; page 96)

1. Preheat the oven to 350°F (180°C).
2. Pour the water in a pan and bring it to a boil. Place the duck in a deep dish. Pour 2 cups (473 mL) of the boiling water over the duck. Drain the water out of the dish and pat the duck dry. In a small bowl, crush the annatto seeds and mix them with the remaining ¼ cup (59 mL) boiling water. Let this mixture sit for 15 minutes. Strain the liquid into another small

bowl and add the soy sauce, jalapeños, garlic, ginger, and sugar. Place the duck on a rack over a roasting pan.

3. Pour some of the marinade, along with the green onion, into the cavity of the duck. Close the duck with a skewer and brush the marinade over the skin of the duck. Roast the duck for 45 minutes. Reduce the oven temperature to 300°F (150°C), brush more of the marinade over the duck, and roast for another 45 minutes. Brush the remaining marinade over the duck and check for doneness (a meat thermometer inserted into the thigh should read 160°F [75°C], cooking it longer if needed. Slice and serve with the Nuoc Cham and a rice dish from Chapter 13.

Com Tay Cam
(Chicken and Rice in a Clay Pot)

Yield: 4 servings   Heat Scale: Medium

Poultry cooked in a clay pot always seems to turn out wonderfully tender and juicy. This Vietnamese recipe is no exception. The pot helps the spicy marinade really penetrate the chicken and creates a well-spiced, succulent treat.

2 shallots, peeled and minced
2 tablespoons (30 mL) minced garlic
1 tablespoon (15 mL) minced ginger
2 pounds (1.1 kg) chicken parts
1 tablespoon (15 mL) fish sauce
1 tablespoon (15 mL) soy sauce
2 tablespoons (30 mL) vegetable oil
¼ teaspoon (1.25 mL) freshly ground black pepper
3 cups (708 mL) water
3 fresh Thai chiles, stems and seeds removed, chopped (or substitute other small, hot chiles)
8 black mushroom caps, soaked, drained and halved (soaking liquid reserved)
2 cups (473 mL) uncooked long-grain rice
1 recipe Vietnamese Dipping Sauce (Nuoc Cham; page 96)

1. In a mortar, pound the shallots, garlic, and ginger into a paste. Disjoint the chicken and place it in a large bowl. Add the paste, the fish sauce, and the soy sauce to the chicken, mix well to coat, and marinate it in the refrigerator for 1 hour.

2. In a large skillet, heat the oil over medium heat. Scrape the excess marinade from the chicken and reserve it. Cook the chicken, a few pieces at a time, until it is browned on all sides, removing the pieces from the pan as they finish cooking.

3. To the skillet, add the reserved marinade, pepper, water, chiles, and reserved mushroom liquid. Bring this mixture to a boil. Arrange the chicken pieces in a braising pot and pour the mushroom/chile mixture over it. Cover the pot and simmer until the chicken is tender, about 20 minutes. Remove the chicken from the pot and let it cool. When it is cool enough to handle, remove the skin, cut the meat from the bones, and tear it into thick shreds. Set it aside.

4. Skim the excess fat from the liquid and add the rice and mushrooms to the pot. Bring the mixture to a boil, reduce the heat to low, and cook until the liquid is nearly absorbed. Stir in the chicken, cover, and cook for another 10 minutes. Turn off the heat and let stand for another 15 minutes. Serve the chicken and rice with Nuoc Cham sauce.

Four Cs Chicken Curry

Yield: 4 servings   Heat Scale: Hot

Here's an interesting chicken curry from Vietnam. This recipe combines cinnamon, coriander, cumin, and cayenne for a four-spice treat. Serve this with a rice dish from Chapter 13 and a dessert from Chapter 14 for a perfect meal.

1 teaspoon (5 mL) corn oil
4 chicken breasts, halved, skin removed
2 tablespoons (30 mL) crushed garlic
1 tablespoon (15 mL) fresh turmeric (available at Indian markets)
1 teaspoon (5 mL) ground cinnamon
1½ teaspoons (7.5 mL) ground cumin
1 teaspoon (5 mL) ground coriander
1 tablespoon (15 mL) minced fresh lemongrass
2 teaspoons (10 mL) ground cayenne
¼ teaspoon (1.25 mL) freshly ground black pepper
⅓ cup (79 mL) plain yogurt
1 cup (236 mL) water
1 teaspoon (5 mL) fish sauce

1. In a large skillet, heat the oil over medium heat until very hot but not smoking. Add the chicken breasts and sauté, turning, until the breasts are golden. Add the garlic, turmeric, cinnamon, cumin, coriander, lemongrass, cayenne, and pepper. Continue to sauté until the spices are fragrant, then add the yogurt, water, and fish sauce. Cover the skillet and simmer for 10 to 20 minutes or until the chicken is cooked through.

Ga Xao Sa Ot
(Lemongrass Chicken)

Yield: 4 servings   Heat Scale: Medium

Vietnamese cuisine blends the foods of many cultures, as Vietnam has been invaded by the French, the Chinese, and the Portuguese. All three of these cultures have left a mark on this recipe, making it truly representative of the best of Southeast Asian cuisine.

2 stalks lemongrass
2 pounds (1.1 kg) chicken, cut up into serving pieces
2 tablespoons (30 mL) fish sauce
1 teaspoon (5 mL) sugar
½ teaspoon (2.5 mL) kosher salt
¼ teaspoon (1.25 mL) freshly ground black pepper
3 green onions, green parts included, chopped
1½ tablespoons (22.5 mL) minced garlic
1 teaspoon (5 mL) ground ginger
Vegetable oil for stir-frying
2 fresh santaka chiles, stems and seeds removed, julienned (or substitute any small, hot chile)
4–5 fresh basil leaves

1. Remove the tops and tough outer layers of the lemongrass. Slice the tender inner parts as thinly as possible. In a large bowl, combine the chicken, lemongrass, fish sauce, sugar, salt, pepper, green onions, garlic, and ginger. Toss the chicken to evenly coat it, then marinate it in the refrigerator for 45 minutes.
2. Heat the oil in a large sauté pan. Add the chiles and stir-fry for 2 to 4 minutes, then add the chicken mixture and stir-fry it until the chicken is completely cooked and shows no sign of pinkness. Add a little water if the chicken begins to scorch. When the chicken is thoroughly cooked, sprinkle it with any remaining fish sauce, toss it with the basil leaves, and transfer it to a serving platter.

Fried Chicken with Green Chile

Yield: 4 servings   Heat Scale: Hot

This quick and easy fried chicken also comes from Vietnam. Feel free to increase the onions, garlic, and coconut for this meal. Serve it with a salad from Chapter 6 for a healthy touch.

1 tablespoon (15 mL) peanut oil
½ onion, sliced
1 (3½–4½ pound [1.59–2 kg]) chicken, cut into large pieces
2 teaspoons (10 mL) salt
2 teaspoons (10 mL) freshly ground black pepper
1 tablespoon (15 mL) fish sauce
2 cups (473 mL) coconut milk
5 shallots, peeled and sliced
14 green onions, white part only, chopped
4 serrano or jalapeño chiles, stems and seeds removed, chopped
Chopped cilantro for garnish

1. In a wok, heat the oil over high heat. Rub the chicken with the salt and pepper. When the oil is hot, add the sliced onion and chicken. Fry until the chicken is golden brown, then add the fish sauce and enough of the coconut milk to cover. Reduce the heat to low and cook until the chicken parts are well done.
2. In a separate pan, heat the oil over medium heat. Add the shallots and chiles and sauté until they are fragrant. Add the green onions. Arrange the chicken on a platter and garnish it with the cilantro.

Not The Colonel's Fried Chicken

Yield: 4 servings   Heat Scale: Hot

The folks at KFC wouldn't dream of preparing their chicken this way. Perhaps this Indonesian recipe will inspire them to new spicy heights.

1 onion, peeled and chopped
2 cloves garlic, peeled
1 teaspoon (5 mL) fresh ginger
3 fresh cayenne chiles, stems and seeds removed, chopped (or substitute
5 serranos or jalapeños)
4 macadamia nuts
1 tablespoon (15 mL) dark soy sauce
1 (3-pound [1.36 kg]) frying chicken
¾ cup (177 mL) peanut oil, divided
2 teaspoons (10 mL) brown sugar
2 tablespoons (30 mL) lime juice
½ teaspoon (2.5 mL) salt
1 cup (236 mL) coconut milk
Cilantro leaves for garnish

1. In a food processor, combine the onion, garlic, ginger, chiles, macadamia nuts, and soy sauce and blend to a paste. Cut the chicken into quarters, rinse the pieces, and pat them dry with paper towels.

2. In a frying pan, heat ½ cup (118 mL) of the peanut oil over medium-high heat. Add the chicken and fry it quickly until browned. Transfer the chicken to paper towels to drain. Pour off the oil, leaving only 1 tablespoon (15 mL). Add the paste and fry it for a few minutes, stirring constantly. Add the sugar, lime juice, salt, and coconut milk and bring the mixture to a boil, stirring constantly. Return the chicken to the pan and simmer, uncovered, for 30 minutes. Serve with plain white rice, garnished with the cilantro.

Santaka Chicken in Lime and Coconut Milk Sauce

Yield: 6 servings   Heat Scale: Medium

In Indonesia, fine cooks are said to add a bit of this and a bit of that from their gardens. So, often, a dish may not turn out the same twice. Experiment with your own favorite Asian spices to make this your own signature dish.

1 (3-pound [1.36 kg]) chicken, cut into pieces, loose skin and fat removed
2 cups (473 mL) coconut milk
½ teaspoon (2.5 mL) turmeric
4 shallots, peeled and chopped
1 clove garlic, peeled minced
1 teaspoon (5 mL) salt
1 stalk lemongrass, chopped
½ lime, sliced in rounds
2 dried santaka chiles, stems and seeds removed, crushed (or substitute other hot, dried red chiles)

1. Combine all the ingredients in a large pan. Cook, covered, over medium heat for 30 minutes, stirring occasionally, until the chicken is tender and the sauce thickens. Serve with white rice and a salad from Chapter 6.

Ayam Masabulu
(Spicy Galangal Chicken)

Yield: 4 servings   Heat Scale: Medium

This Indonesian poultry dish features galangal, which is also (confusingly) known as laos. This plant, which is a relative of ginger, grows very well all over Southeast Asia and should be available in Asian markets. However, if you have trouble locating galangal, you may substitute double the amount of ginger.

1 tablespoon (15 mL) chopped ripe tomatoes
1 teaspoon (5 mL) salt
4 fresh piquin chiles, stems and seeds removed, chopped (or substitute other small, hot chiles)
5 shallots, peeled and chopped
2 garlic cloves, peeled and minced
1 cup (236 mL) plus 1 tablespoon (15 mL) water, divided
1 tablespoon (15 mL) peanut oil
3 salam leaves (or substitute bay leaves)
3 slices galangal
2 stalks lemongrass
1 (3-pound [1.36 kg]) chicken, cut into 8 to 10 pieces, giblets included
2 tablespoons (30 mL) fresh lemon juice

1. In a food processor, blend the tomatoes, salt, chiles, shallots, garlic, and 1 tablespoon (15 mL) of the water until the mixture forms a paste. In a wok, heat the oil over medium heat. Add the paste, salam leaves, galangal, and lemongrass and stir-fry for 2 minutes. Add the chicken parts and fry for 5 minutes. Add the lemon juice and the remaining water. Cover and cook for 30 minutes or until the chicken is done and the sauce is thickened.

Ayam Taliwang
(Grilled Hot Hen)

Yield: 4 servings   Heat Scale: Medium

The small island of Lombok, which is next to Bali, is the home of this recipe. The word "Lombok" translates to "spicy chiles" and is the perfect descriptor of the food on this island.

1 (2-pound [1.1 kg]) Cornish hen, butterflied and flattened
1 teaspoon (5 mL) salt
1 tablespoon (15 mL) corn oil
5 shallots, peeled and sliced
3 cloves garlic, peeled and sliced
1 teaspoon (5 mL) shrimp paste
½ teaspoon (2.5 mL) sugar
1 tablespoon (15 mL) fresh birdseye chiles (chiltepins) or substitute piquins
2 teaspoons (10 mL) pineapple juice
2 cups (473 mL) chopped fresh pineapple

1. Rub the hen all over with the salt and oil. In a food processor, blend the shallots, garlic, shrimp paste, sugar, peppers, pineapple juice, and pineapple into a paste.
2. Grill the hen slowly over hot coals or under a preheated gas or electric broiler for 5 minutes. Baste the hen well with the paste on both sides, and grill for 3 more minutes.
3. Spread all the remaining paste on the skin side and grill for 10 minutes or until done.

Bebek Bumbu Bali (Balinese Duck)

Yield: 6 servings   Heat Scale: Medium

This Asian duck recipe features the tastes of Bali. Prepare this dish when you're in the mood for a rich and filling meal. A nice fruit salad from Chapter 6 would make an excellent accompaniment.

1 (5-pound [2.3 kg]) duck
10 macadamia nuts, crushed
½ teaspoon (2.5 mL) shrimp paste
1 tablespoon (15 mL) chopped hot chiles, such as Thai or piquin
¼ cup (59 mL) sliced onion
5 cloves garlic, peeled and chopped
2 tablespoons (30 mL) soy sauce
½ teaspoon (2.5 mL) turmeric
2 teaspoons (10 mL) salt
2 cups (473 mL) water, divided
4 bay leaves
2 tablespoons (30 mL) galangal or ginger, peeled and grated
2 stalks lemongrass, white part only, minced

1. Disjoint the duck and cut it into about 10 pieces. Trim and remove the loose skin and fat. In a processor, blend the nuts, shrimp paste, chiles, onion, garlic, soy sauce, turmeric, salt, and ½ cup (118 mL) of the water. Transfer the sauce to a saucepan large enough to accomodate the duck and cook for 3 minutes over medium-high heat.
2. Add the duck, bay leaves, galangal, lemongrass, and the remaining water. Stir well, and cook over medium heat for about 1½ hours, or until the duck is soft and about half the sauce has evaporated. Should the duck seem too dry, add ½ cup (118 mL) water during the cooking process.

Chicken Satay with Spicy Peanut Sauce

Yield: 4 servings   Heat Scale: Medium

This recipe is courtesy of the Equatorial Penang hotel in Penang, Malaysia. It is a classic Indonesian dish that combines the heat of chiles with the exotic fragrances of the Spice Islands. (Note: This recipe requires advance preparation.)

4 (2-inch [5 cm]) pieces ginger, peeled
4 piquins, chopped
5 cloves garlic, peeled
3 shallots, peeled
1 teaspoon (5 mL) cumin seed
1 teaspoon (5 mL) anise seed
1 tablespoon (15 mL) ground turmeric
3 stalks lemongrass
2 teaspoons (10 mL) sugar
1 (1-pound [454 g]) boneless chicken, cut into strips
1 recipe Indonesian Peanut-Chile Sauce (Katjang Saos; page 99)
Diced cucumbers for garnish
Diced onions for garnish

1. Soak some bamboo skewers in water.
2. In a food processor, combine the ginger, chiles, garlic, shallots, cumin, anise, turmeric, lemongrass, and sugar and purée, adding water if necessary to make a thick sauce. Marinate the chicken strips in this mixture for 12 hours in the refrigerator.
3. Thread the chicken strips onto the soaked skewers. Grill the satay sticks over coals until the meat is done, turning often, about 12 minutes. Serve the satays with the sauce on the side and garnished with the diced cucumbers and onions.

Ayam Di Batok Kelapa
(Chicken-Stuffed Coconut)

Yield: 4 servings   Heat Scale: Medium

This unusual Indonesian recipe is a specialty on the island of Sulawesi. Covering the coconut with foil allows it to retain all of its hot and sweet flavoring.

1 large, young, green coconut
1 pound (454 g) boneless chicken, cut into 1-inch (2.5 cm) cubes
1 stalk lemongrass, minced
2 green onions, cut into ½-inch (1 cm) slices
2 shallots, peeled and sliced
1 teaspoon (5 mL) salt
3 Thai chiles, stems and seeds removed, minced (or substitute any small, hot chiles)
1 (1-inch [2.5 cm]) piece fresh ginger, peeled and minced

1. Preheat the oven to 325°F (165°C).
2. With a sharp knife or a saw, cut a 2-inch (5 cm) wide plug from the eye end of the coconut, set the plug aside, and drain and discard the coconut water.
3. In a bowl, mix together the remaining ingredients. Fill the coconut with the mixture and replace the reserved plug. Wrap the coconut in aluminum foil to seal it further.
4. Bake the stuffed coconut for 2 hours. Unseal and unplug the coconut and turn it on its side. Spoon out the chicken stuffing and serve it warm.

His Majesty's Chicken

Yield: 6 servings   Heat Scale: Medium-Hot

Some of Southeast Asia's most exotic spices are the stars of this Indonesian dish. Ginger, coriander, cardamom, and cloves give it a distinctly rich taste. If you enjoy this recipe, try it next time using lamb. Serve this with a salad from Chapter 6.

4 shallots, peeled and sliced
4 serrano or jalapeño chiles, stems and seeds removed, chopped
2 tablespoons (30 mL) freshly grated ginger
2 cloves garlic, peeled
2 teaspoons (10 mL) ground coriander
1 teaspoon (5 mL) ground cumin
2½ cups (591 mL) coconut milk, divided
2 tablespoons (30 mL) corn oil
1 (2-inch [5 cm]) piece cinnamon stick
¼ teaspoon (1.25 mL) freshly ground black pepper
1 teaspoon (5 mL) lemon juice
4 whole cloves
4 cardamom pods
1 teaspoon (5 mL) ground anise
1 (3-pound [1.36 kg]) chicken, cut into 8 pieces, loose skin and fat removed
1 teaspoon (5 mL) salt
2 ripe tomatoes, sliced
Cilantro leaves for garnish

1. In a food processor, combine the shallots, chiles, ginger, garlic, coriander, cumin, pepper, and ¼ cup (59 mL) of the coconut milk and blend to form a paste.
2. In a skillet, heat the oil over medium heat. Add the paste, cinnamon stick, lemon juice, cloves, and cardamom, and stir-fry for a couple of minutes. Add the chicken and fry it for 5 minutes, until browned.
3. Add the remaining coconut milk, salt, and tomatoes, and cook over medium heat for about 40 minutes, basting the chicken frequently with the sauce. Serve warm, garnished with the cilantro.

Marinated Thai Chicken

Yield: 6 servings   Heat Scale: Medium

This interesting main dish mixes elements from the Thai and Chinese cultures. I added the yellow rice wine for an authentic "drunken" touch. The ginger and jalapeños give it spice and zip. (Note: This recipe requires advance preparation.)

2 pounds (1.1 kg) chicken pieces
1¼ cups (295 mL) yellow rice wine
1 teaspoon (5 mL) salt
2½ teaspoons (7.5 mL) sugar
1 clove garlic, peeled and minced
2 teaspoons (10 mL) freshly grated ginger
3 fresh serrano or jalapeño chiles, stems and seeds removed, minced
Fresh mint leaves for garnish

1. Rinse the chicken parts well, then place them in a large pan and add water to cover. Bring the water to a boil. Cover the pan tightly, reduce the heat, and simmer for 20 minutes. Drain the chicken and transfer it to a deep dish.
2. In a separate bowl, mix together the wine, salt, sugar, garlic, ginger, and chiles. Pour this mixture over the chicken. Cover the chicken with plastic wrap and marinate it overnight in the refrigerator. When you are ready to serve, drain the liquid from the dish, garnish it with mint leaves, and serve cold.

Stir-Fried Minced Chicken with Balsam Leaves

Yield: 4   Heat Scale: Hot

This recipe comes from the Thai Cooking School at the Oriental in Bangkok, Thailand. Balsam is another name for holy basil, and since the balsam leaves can be difficult to locate, feel free to substitute basil, mint, or a combination of the two.

10 fresh Thai chiles, chopped (or substitute piquins or other small, hot chiles)
1 heaping teaspoon (7.5 mL) shrimp paste
1 tablespoon (15 mL) salt
1 tablespoon (15 mL) plus 1 teaspoon (5 mL) vegetable oil, divided
2 cups (473 mL) chopped chicken breast
1 cup (236 mL) fresh straw mushrooms, halved
½ cup (118 mL) ripe tomatoes, blanched, peeled, and roughly chopped
8 cloves garlic, peeled and sliced
6 shallots, peeled and sliced
1 cup (236 mL) balsam leaves (or substitute basil and/or mint)

1. In a food processor, combine the chiles, shrimp paste, and salt and purée. In a sauté pan, heat 1 tablespoon (15 mL) of the vegetable oil over medium heat. Add the paste and fry, stirring well, until fragrant. Add the chicken meat and mix well. Mix in the mushrooms and tomatoes and turn well. Cook until the chicken is done, about 10 minutes. In a separate sauté pan, heat the remaining oil. Add the garlic, shallots, and balsam leaves and fry, stirring quickly. Transfer the chicken to a platter and sprinkle half of the fried shallots and garlic on top of the dish. Arrange the rest of the fried vegetables on the platter.

Gai Yang
(Eight-Hour Chicken)

Yield: 4 servings   Heat Scale: Medium

This Thai recipe must be started early in the day, but the extra work is well worth it. Red curry paste, which is readily available in Asian markets, is the perfect combination of chiles and spices. Please keep in mind that the chicken should marinate for at least 8 hours for the best results.

1 tablespoon (15 mL) Red Curry Paste (Gaeng Ped; page 37) or commercial red curry paste
1 cup (236 mL) light soy sauce
2 Thai chiles, stems and seeds removed, chopped (or substitute piquins or other small, hot chiles)
4 cilantro stems with roots, finely chopped
8 garlic cloves, peeled and finely chopped
1 carrot, chopped
2 celery stalks, chopped
1 teaspoon (5 mL) lime juice
1 small onion, peeled and chopped
¼ cup (59 mL) vegetable oil
¼ cup (59 mL) cracked black peppercorns
2 (3-pound [1.36 kg]) broiler chickens, halved lengthwise
1 recipe Thai Pepper Water Sauce (Nam Prik; page 95)

1. In a large mixing bowl, combine the curry paste, soy sauce, chiles, cilantro, garlic, carrot, celery, lime juice, onion, oil, and peppercorns and blend well. Place the chicken, skin-side down, in a shallow baking dish. Pour the marinade over the chicken. Cover the chicken with plastic wrap and refrigerate for at least 8 hours (overnight is preferable).
2. Preheat the oven to 350°F (180°C). Bake the chicken, uncovered, in the marinade for 40 to 50 minutes. Just before serving, place the chicken under the broiler for 5 minutes to crisp it up. Cut the chicken in half and serve it with the Thai Pepper Water Sauce.

Gai Gup Kao Lad
(Chicken with Water Chestnuts)

Yield: 4–6 servings   Heat Scale: Medium

Water chestnuts come from an aquatic bulb that has long been a staple in Chinese, Vietnamese, and Thai cuisines. This quick and easy stir-fry dish should be served over a rice pilaf and accompanied by an Asian salad from Chapter 6.

4 cloves garlic, peeled and chopped
2 tablespoons (30 mL) chopped cilantro roots
1 teaspoon (5 mL) black peppercorns
1 jalapeño chile, stems and seeds removed, chopped
2 tablespoons (30 mL) vegetable oil
1 pound (454 g) boned chicken meat, cut into bite-sized pieces
1½ cups (354 mL) Classic Chicken Stock (page 46)
4 chicken livers, diced
16 canned water chestnuts, drained and halved
1 teaspoon (5 mL) salt
1 teaspoon (5 mL) palm sugar

1. In a food processor, purée the garlic, cilantro roots, black peppercorns, and jalapeños into a paste. In a wok, heat the oil over high heat. Add the paste and fry, stirring, for 2 to 3 minutes. Add the chicken pieces (not the livers) and stir-fry until they are just brown. Pour in the chicken stock and add the livers. Reduce the heat and simmer for 5 minutes. Stir in the water chestnuts, season with salt, and sprinkle with the palm sugar. Cover and simmer until the chicken is tender, about 5 minutes.

Panaeng Kruang Don
(Chile Chicken)

Yield: 4 servings   Heat Scale: Hot

Thailand is known for the beauty and flavors of its cuisine. Allow a little extra time to arrange this dish on the platter, and prepare carved chile "flowers" for garnish. Your efforts will be much admired by your guests, and they might offer to pay you for dinner. Decline their offer or next you'll be opening a restaurant!

4 dried cayenne chiles, stems and seeds removed, soaked in warm water, finely chopped
2 cloves garlic, peeled and chopped
2 shallots, peeled and chopped
1 stalk lemongrass, minced
1 teaspoon (5 mL) minced cilantro roots (or substitute stems)
1 teaspoon (5 mL) shrimp paste
3 (2-inch [5 cm]) pieces galangal, peeled and chopped (or substitute ginger)
1 teaspoon (5 mL) black peppercorns
1 cup (236 mL) coconut milk
1 teaspoon (5 mL) sugar
2 tablespoons (30 mL) fish sauce
1 pound (454 g) chicken meat, cooked and cut into bite-sized pieces, kept warm in the oven
4 fresh red serranos or jalapeños, cut into flowers
2 tablespoons (30 mL) cilantro leaves

1. In a food processor, combine the cayenne chiles, garlic, shallots, lemongrass, cilantro roots, shrimp paste, galangal, and peppercorns and process to a coarse paste.
2. Pour the coconut milk into a wok and bring it to a boil. Stir in the paste and cook over medium heat until the mixture is almost dry. Stir in the sugar and fish sauce and remove the pan from the heat. Arrange the chicken pieces on a large, heated platter. Top the chicken with the curry paste. Decorate with red chile flowers and sprinkle with cilantro leaves. Serve warm.

Guay Tiew Gai Amanpuri
(Chicken Sautéed with Holy Basil)

Yield: 2 servings   Heat Scale: Hot

This recipe from the Amanpuri Resort on Phuket Island, Thailand, comes courtesy of chef Daniel Lentz. It was collected by Jennifer Basye Sander. The basil in this dish, called graprao or sometimes krapau, is holy basil (Ocimum sanctum) and is revered by Hindus. It has a more pungent flavor than sweet basil, and that is why mint is sometimes substituted.

4 large lettuce leaves, cut in thin strips with scissors
5 tablespoons (75 mL) vegetable oil, divided
½ pound (224 g) guay tiew noodles (thick, flat rice noodles, available in Asian markets)
2 tablespoons (30 mL) minced garlic
4 red serranos or jalapeños, stems and seeds removed, chopped fine
1 cup (236 mL) ground chicken
2 tablespoons (30 mL) oyster sauce
3 tablespoons (45 mL) fish sauce
⅓ cup (79 mL) Classic Chicken Stock (page 46)
20 bi graprao or holy basil leaves (or substitute fresh basil, mint, or a mixture of the two)

1. Divide the lettuce strips between two plates. Heat 2 tablespoons (30 mL) of oil the in a wok until medium-hot, then add the noodles and stir-fry until heated through but not browned. Drain the noodles and place them on top of the lettuce.
2. In the wok, heat the remaining oil over medium heat. Add the garlic and chiles and stir-fry for 15 seconds. Add the chicken and stir-fry for another 15 seconds. Add the oyster and fish sauces and stock and stir-fry until the chicken is done, about 5 minutes. The mixture should have a sauce-like consistency, so thin it by adding more stock, if necessary. Add the basil and stir-fry for 15 seconds. Serve the chicken on top of the noodles.

Kyet Tha Sipyan
(Burmese Chicken Curry)

Yield: 4 servings   Heat Scale: Medium-Hot

This curry is a favorite all over the world. The use of fish sauce, tomatoes, and two types of chiles add to the heat level and enjoyment of this dish. Serve with fresh orange slices for a nice, light meal.

1 (3½-pound [1.6 kg]) chicken, cut into 8 pieces, loose skin and fat removed
1 teaspoon (5 mL) salt
½ teaspoon (2.5 mL) ground turmeric
4 tablespoons (60 mL) fish sauce
2 small onions, peeled and sliced
4 garlic cloves, peeled and minced
2 tablespoons (30 mL) fresh ginger, sliced
1 teaspoon (5 mL) paprika
1 teaspoon (5 mL) dried red chile flakes
½ cup (118 mL) plus 2 tablespoons (30 mL) water, divided
1 jalapeño, stems and seeds removed, minced
3 tablespoons (45 mL) corn oil
¼ cup (59 mL) chopped ripe tomatoes

1. Wash the chicken well and pat it dry with paper towels. Place the chicken in a deep dish. In a separate bowl, mix together the salt, turmeric, and fish sauce. Pour this mixture over the chicken. Marinate the chicken in the refrigerator for 15 minutes. In a food processor, blend the onions, garlic, ginger, paprika, chile flakes, 2 tablespoons (30 mL) of the water, and the jalapeño to a coarse paste.
2. In a large, deep frying pan, heat over medium heat. Add the paste and stir-fry for 2 minutes. Add the chicken and tomatoes and stir-fry for about 15 minutes. The oil will separate and rise to the top of the mixture. Add the remaining water, cover the pan, and cook over medium-low heat for about 25 minutes, until the chicken is done and the sauce is nice and thick. Serve with white rice, or over noodles if you prefer.

Cashew-Orange Spiced Chicken

Yield: 4 servings   Heat Scale: Hot

This hot and sweet dish from China can be made even hotter by using chile-spiked soy sauce. Sichuan peppercorns are readily available in Asian markets and in large grocery stores. (Note: This recipe requires advance preparation.)

½ cup (118 mL) orange juice (fresh preferred)
2 tablespoons (30 mL) rice wine
1 tablespoon (15 mL) soy sauce
2 teaspoons (10 mL) orange zest
1 teaspoon (5 mL) crushed Sichuan peppercorns
1 teaspoon (5 mL) peanut oil
1 pound (454 g) boneless chicken breasts, cubed
2 tablespoons (30 mL) chile oil, either Asian or habanero
6 small dried red chiles, such as Japanese or piquin
2 teaspoons (10 mL) grated ginger
2 tablespoons (30 mL) cornstarch mixed with 3 tablespoons (45 mL) water
2 cups (473 mL) cooked white rice
1 cup (236 mL) cashew pieces or halves
3 green onions, green parts included, chopped

1. In a nonreactive bowl, combine the orange juice, rice wine, soy sauce, orange zest, Sichuan peppercorns, and peanut oil. Toss the chicken in this mixture and marinate for 1 hour. Drain the chicken and reserve the marinade.
2. In a wok or heavy pan, heat the chile oil to about 350°F (180°C). Add the chiles and sauté for a minute. Add the ginger and stir-fry for an additional minute. Add the chicken and stir-fry until done. Remove the chicken from the wok and keep it warm.
3. Add the marinade to the wok or pan and heat until boiling. Slowly stir in enough of the cornstarch mixture to thicken the sauce. Return the chicken to the wok and heat thoroughly.
4. Pour the chicken over the rice, garnish with the cashews and onions, and serve.

Chile Chicken Yakatori

Yield: 4–6 servings   Heat Scale: Medium

Yakatori got its name from the Japanese words "yaki" for grilled and "tori" for chicken. I have already taken some liberties with traditional recipes in making this spicy version, so if you prefer, you can also make it with pork. Plain white rice and a crisp cucumber salad are all you need to complete a light and tasty meal. Mirin is sweet sake and is available in Oriental markets.

3 chicken breasts
6 green onions, cut in 1-inch (2.5 cm) pieces
8 water chestnuts
2 teaspoons (10 mL) crushed chile piquin
1 tablespoon (15 mL) chile oil
1 teaspoon (5 mL) sesame oil
1¼ cup (295 mL) rice wine or dry sherry
⅔ cup (158 mL) mirin
2 teaspoons (10 mL) soy sauce
2 tablespoons (30 mL) sugar
2 teaspoons (10 mL) minced ginger

1. Cut the chicken into 1-inch (2.5 cm) cubes or crosswise into pieces 2 inches (5 cm) long and ½ inch (1 cm) thick and wide. Thread the chicken on skewers, alternating with the green onion and water chestnuts.
2. In a saucepan, combine the chile, oils, rice wine, mirin, soy sauce, sugar, and ginger. Cook over medium heat until just boiling. Reduce the heat and simmer, uncovered, until the sauce is reduced by half and forms a glaze.
3. Grill the yakatori over medium heat for 2 minutes per side or until lightly browned. Brush liberally with the glaze and continue cooking for a couple more minutes per side, until the chicken is done. Remove, brush again with the glaze, and serve.

Chongqing La Zi Ji
(Chile-Chicken Stir-Fry)

Yield: 4 servings   Heat Scale: Hot

This Chinese recipe is hot and slightly sweet. Serve it with plain white rice and warn your guest not to eat the red chile pod pieces.

1 tablespoon (15 mL) dark soy sauce
½ teaspoon (2.5 mL) salt
1 tablespoon (15 mL) sugar
2 tablespoons (30 mL) rice cooking wine
2 teaspoons (10 mL) fresh ginger, peeled and chopped
2 teaspoons (10 mL) green onions, chopped
3 cups (708 mL) ½-inch (1 cm) chicken cubes
¼ cup (59 mL) plus 2 tablespoons (30 mL) Chile Oil (page 16), divided
⅔ cup (158 mL) dried hot red chile pods, coarsely chopped
2 tablespoons (30 mL) Sichuan peppercorns, crushed
2 tablespoons (30 mL) unsalted peanuts, chopped
1 tablespoon (15 mL) white sesame seeds
Cilantro sprigs for garnish

1. In a bowl, combine the dark soy sauce, salt, sugar, cooking wine, ginger, and green onions. Mix in the cubed chicken and marinate in the refrigerator for 20 minutes.
2. In a wok or skillet, heat ¼ cup (59 mL) of the red chile oil over high heat. Add the chicken and cook it quickly, stirring constantly. As the chicken cooks, add the chile pods and Sichuan peppercorns. Cook until the chicken is done. Remove the pan from the heat and transfer the chicken to a serving dish.
3. In a small skillet or heavy saucepan, heat the remaining 2 tablespoons (30 mL) chile oil over medium heat. Add the chopped peanuts and the sesame seeds and lightly fry them. Remove them from the heat and sprinkle them over the chicken before serving. Garnish with fresh cilantro.

Sweet and Hot Gingered Plum Smoked Duck
Yield: 4–6 servings   Heat Scale: Medium

For some reason, smoked poultry benefits from a marinade that is somewhat sweet.
The duck can also be grilled over indirect heat, if you don't want such a smoky flavor.
Use a fruitwood such as apple or apricot for the smoking. Serve this Chinese duck
with jasmine rice, stir-fried snow peas and black mushrooms, and a Mandarin
orange ice for dessert. (Note: This recipe requires advance preparation.)

1 (16-ounce [454 g]) can purple plums, pitted and drained, syrup reserved
2 tablespoons (30 mL) grated ginger
2 cloves garlic, peeled and chopped
2 tablespoons (30 mL) crushed chiltepins (or substitute another hot red chile)
1 tablespoon (15 mL) hoisin sauce
2 tablespoons (30 mL) brown sugar or honey
2 tablespoons (30 mL) dry sherry
1 tablespoon (15 mL) soy sauce
1 tablespoon (15 mL) Asian plum sauce (available in Asian markets)
4 whole star anise
2 tablespoons (30 mL) distilled white vinegar
1 (4–5-pound [1.8–2.3 kg]) duck
Salt, to taste
Freshly ground black pepper, to taste
2 green onions
2 cloves garlic, peeled
2 (1-inch [2.5 cm]) pieces peeled ginger

1. In a blender or food processor, combine the plums, ginger, and garlic
and purée until smooth, thinning with some of the reserved syrup if necessary.
2. Transfer the purée to a saucepan. Add the remaining reserved plum
syrup, chiles, hoisin sauce, brown sugar or honey, sherry, soy sauce, plum
sauce, and star anise and simmer for 30 minutes to thicken. Add the vinegar and simmer for 10 more minutes. Remove and discard the star anise.
3. Spread the sauce inside and outside the duck and under the skin. Place
it in a freezer bag and marinate it in the refrigerator overnight. Remove the
duck from the marinade, reserve the marinade, and let the duck come to
room temperature before smoking. Season the cavity with salt and pepper
and put the green onions, garlic, and ginger inside. Inject the duck with
more marinade if desired.
4. Build a fire in the smoker and bring the smoke to 200–220°F (100–
110°C). Smoke the duck for 4 hours, basting occasionally with the marinade. The internal temperature should reach 160°F.
5. Heat the remaining marinade and simmer it for 20 minutes, thinning
with a little water if necessary. Remove the duck from the smoker, brush it
with the sauce, and serve with some additional sauce on the side.

Tea-Smoked Sichuan Chicken

Yield: 4 servings   Heat Scale: Medium-Hot

This is a another version of the famous smoked duck. You can make this in a stove-top smoker. The tea turns the skin an appealing color, and any loose black tea will work, even the orange pekoe found in most tea bags. If using chicken pieces, cut the marinade recipe in half. Serve with fresh spring rolls, pickled radish and carrot relish, and Sichuan noodles with vegetables. (Note: This recipe requires advance preparation.)

1 (3½–4-pound [1.6–1.8 kg]) whole chicken or 4 legs and thighs
10 green onions, green parts included, chopped
¼ cup (59 mL) Sichuan peppercorns, roasted and crushed
¼ cup (59 mL) chopped ginger
2 tablespoons (30 mL) sugar
⅓ cup (79 mL) rice wine or cooking sherry
2 tablespoons (30 mL) orange zest
2 tablespoons (30 mL) crushed chile piquin (or substitute another hot red chile)
2 teaspoons (10 mL) plus 3 tablespoons (45 mL) sesame oil
½ cup (118 mL) peanut oil
1 cup (236 mL) uncooked rice
⅔ cup (158 mL) brown sugar
½ cup (118 mL) dry tea leaves
½ cup (118 mL) Sichuan peppercorns
14 whole star anise, broken in pieces
12 whole cloves
4 (2-inch [5 cm]) sticks cinnamon
2 teaspoons (10 mL) ground cayenne

1. If you are using a whole chicken, tie the legs together. In a bowl, combine the green onions, crushed Sichuan peppercorns, ginger, sugar, rice wine, orange zest, crushed chile, 2 teaspoons (10 mL) of the sesame oil, and the peanut oil. Place the chicken in a nonreactive pan or large freezer bag, add the marinade, and marinate for 24 hours.
2. If you are using legs and thighs, combine the rice, brown sugar, tea leaves, peppercorns, star anise, cloves, and cinnamon in the pan of a stovetop smoker. If you are using a whole chicken and a smoker or grill, wrap the mixture in aluminum foil and poke holes in the foil. Smoke the chicken in 200°F (100°C) smoke for 3 to 4 hours or to an internal temperature of 160°F (75°C).
3. In a small bowl, combine the remaining 3 tablespoons (45 mL) sesame oil and the ground cayenne. Let the mixture sit while the chicken is smoking.
4. Preheat the oven to 450°F (240°C). Remove the chicken from the smoker, brush it with the finishing oil, and place it in the oven for 5 minutes to crisp the skin.

Kung Po Chicken

Yield: 4 servings   Heat Scale: Medium-Hot

This classic Sichuan stir-fry dish can be made with shrimp, pork, beef, or even tofu as well as chicken. It's a simple dish with just a few ingredients combined with crunchy peanuts for texture. The complex flavors come from the marinating and seasoning sauces.

1 tablespoon (15 mL) rice wine or dry sherry
1 tablespoon (15 mL) plus 2 teaspoons (10 mL) light soy sauce, divided
1 tablespoon (15 mL) sugar, divided
1 tablespoon (15 mL) water
2 boneless, skinless chicken breasts, cut in bite-sized pieces
¼ cup (59 mL) Classic Chicken Stock (page 46)
2 tablespoons (30 mL) Asian chile sauce
2 tablespoons (30 mL) hoisin sauce
1 tablespoon (15 mL) plus 1 teaspoon (5 mL) Asian hot bean sauce
2 teaspoons (10 mL) rice vinegar
2 teaspoons (10 mL) ground Sichuan peppercorns
1 teaspoon (5 mL) distilled white vinegar
2–3 tablespoons (30–45 mL) vegetable oil (peanut preferred)
4–6 whole dried red chiles, such as piquin or cayenne
1 tablespoon (15 mL) chopped garlic
2 teaspoons (10 mL) grated ginger
½ green bell pepper, cubed
1 small onion, peeled and cubed
2 teaspoons (10 mL) sesame oil
½ cup (118 mL) roasted peanuts
1 green onion, some of the green part included, chopped

1. In a large bowl, combine the rice wine, 1 tablespoon (15 mL) of the soy sauce, 1 teaspoon (5 mL) of the sugar, and the water and stir to mix. Toss the chicken in the sauce to coat and marinate at room temperature for 30 minutes.
2. In another bowl, combine the chicken stock, chile sauce, hoisin sauce, hot bean sauce, remaining 2 teaspoons (10 mL) soy sauce, rice vinegar, ground peppercorns, remaining 2 teaspoons (10 mL) sugar, and white vinegar, stir to mix, and set aside.
3. Heat a wok or heavy skillet over medium-high heat until hot and add the oil. Add the chiles and stir-fry for a couple of minutes or until they start to blacken. Push them to one side of the wok, add the garlic and ginger, and stir-fry until fragrant.
4. Drain the chicken and add it to the wok. Stir-fry the chicken for a couple of minutes, until the chicken changes color. Remove the chicken from the wok, drain it, and keep it warm. Add the onion and bell pepper and stir-fry until they just soften.

5. Add the seasoning sauce to the wok and cook until the sauce thickens. Return the chicken to the wok and toss to coat. Heat until the sauce forms a glaze over the chicken. Add the sesame oil and peanuts and toss until coated.
6. To serve, mound the chicken on a serving platter and garnish with the chopped green onions. Serve with plain white rice.

Lemon and Soy Barbecued Chicken

Yield: 4–6 servings   Heat Scale: Medium

Filipinos love grilled chicken, and this recipe is an interesting twist on it. Serve this with any of the Asian hot sauces in Chapter 2. (Note: This recipe requires advance preparation.)

⅓ cup (79 mL) fresh lemon juice
⅓ cup (79 mL) soy sauce
6 cloves garlic, peeled and crushed
⅓ cup (79 mL) vegetable oil
2 tablespoons (30 mL) Asian hot sauce (any kind)
½ teaspoon (2.5 mL) sugar
4 large chicken breasts, boned and slightly flattened

1. In a bowl, combine the lemon juice, soy sauce, garlic, vegetable oil, hot sauce, and sugar and mix well. Place the chicken breasts in a large, square baking dish and pour some of the marinade over them, reserving some for basting. Cover the dish with plastic wrap and refrigerate overnight.
2. Remove the chicken from the refrigerator and allow it to reach room temperature. Grill the breasts over hot coals for 10 to 12 minutes, turning them often and basting them with the reserved marinade. Remove from the heat and serve with rice and an Asian hot sauce.

Orange Chicken with Red Chiles

Yield 2–4 servings   Heat Scale: Medium-Hot

This chicken and chile dish is a standard in western China, where the flavors of poultry and citrus are often combined. Dried orange peel is available in Asian markets. Any small, dried red chiles may be used in this recipe. Serve it over steamed rice or a rice pilaf.

1½ teaspoons (7.5 mL) cornstarch
2 tablespoons (30 mL) dry vermouth or white wine, divided
½ pound (224 g) boneless chicken breast, cut into ½-inch (1 cm) pieces
1½ teaspoons (7.5 mL) minced ginger
1½ teaspoons (7.5 mL) minced garlic
1 green onion, minced
½ teaspoon (2.5 mL) ground Sichuan peppercorns
2 tablespoons (30 mL) soy sauce
1 tablespoon (15 mL) hot bean sauce
2 tablespoons (30 mL) dried orange peel, soaked in hot water for 30 minutes and shredded
2 teaspoons (10 mL) sugar or honey
½ teaspoon (2.5 mL) sesame oil
2 tablespoons (30 mL) peanut oil
6 small dried hot red chiles, such as Japones or de Arbol

1. In a bowl, combine the cornstarch and 1 tablespoon (15 mL) of the vermouth, stir well, and add the chicken. Let sit for 30 minutes.
2. In a separate bowl, combine the ginger, garlic, green onion, peppercorns, remaining 1 tablespoon (15 mL) vermouth, soy sauce, bean sauce, shredded orange peel, sugar, and sesame oil. Stir well and set aside.
3. Heat a wok over high heat. Add the peanut oil and, when it begins to smoke, add the chiles and the marinated chicken. Stir-fry for about 1 minute. Add the sauce and stir-fry for an additional 30 seconds. Remove the chiles before serving.

Panamanian Style Chicken and Vegetables

Yield: 6 servings   Heat Scale: Hot

Thanks to Alois Dogue for this wonderful recipe that incorporates the peppery, hot flavors of Latin America. Alois told me that much of the food of Panama (his home) combines the best of Latin America with the best of the Caribbean. He would like the cook to use his Habanero Hot! Hot! Hot! Panamanian-Style Sauce for this dish, as it is a family recipe. However, feel free to use any bottled habanero sauce.

1 (3-pound [1.36 kg]) chicken, cut into 6 pieces
1 teaspoon (5 mL) salt
1 teaspoon (5 mL) dried oregano, divided
¼ cup (59 mL) vegetable oil
2 teaspoons (10 mL) achiote (annatto) powder
1 cup (236 mL) water
3 tablespoons (45 mL) tomato paste
1 medium onion, peeled and chopped
1 medium tomato, coarsely chopped
1 teaspoon (5 mL) chopped cilantro
2 green bell peppers, stems and seeds removed, coarsely chopped
⅛ cup (30 mL) bottled habanero sauce
2 carrots, sliced
1 chayote squash, peeled and diced (or substitute zucchini)
1 potato, peeled and diced
1 (12-ounce [336 g]) can kidney beans, drained

1. Wash the chicken pieces and pat them dry. Season the chicken with the salt and ½ teaspoon (2.5 mL) of the oregano.
2. In a large, heavy skillet, heat the oil over medium heat. Add the achiote powder and simmer for 3 minutes.
3. Add the chicken to the oil and sauté until it is golden brown. Add the water, tomato paste, onion, tomato, cilantro, bell peppers, and the remaining ½ teaspoon (2.5 mL) oregano, cover, and simmer for 25 minutes.
4. Add the habanero sauce, carrots, chayote, potato, and beans and simmer until the vegetables are tender, about 15 to 20 minutes. Serve over hot, cooked white rice.

ELEVEN

Searing Seafood

- - - - - - - - - - - - - - - - - - -

The first really hot and spicy dish I ever ate was a conch salad aboard the Flying Cloud in the Bahamas. It was a shocking experience for a Southern guy, but it was so good I went to the schooner's galley and asked the cook what was in it besides conch. He replied, "goat pepper," but I had no idea what that was at the time. I ate a second helping of the salad despite the burn, and my food would never be the same.

The world of seafood is incredibly diverse, as humans have been known to eat just about everything that swims, crawls, or wiggles. There are some absolutely, unbelievably delicious seafood dishes, like the hamachi sushi or fried flying fish I ate in Trinidad and Barbados, and then there are sea slugs—yuck. In this tour of hot and spicy seafood, I promise you that I have collected only the most delicious recipes and have ignored the borderline or outrageous concoctions like fugu, that Japanese puffer fish that's so loaded with tetrodotoxin that 176 people died from eating it in Japan in 1958!

From eating it raw to blackening it, every possible technique is used to prepare seafood, but perhaps the best—yet most difficult method—uses the outdoor grill. You think chicken is difficult to cook on the grill? Try grilling fish. At least chicken breasts don't fall apart and crumble into the fire. But fish can and does, especially if it sticks to the grill and you're trying to turn it with a spatula. Another possible disaster is a tendency for fatty fish or fish saturated with oils in the marinade to burn intensely during a flare-up. I lost a mackerel fillet that way on a charcoal grill on the beach in Islamorada, Florida. The fatty fish ignited like a flare, and before I could run for water, the fillet resembled a stick of charcoal. Even a minor flare-up that catches the fish on fire can spoil its flavor, so have a squirt gun or spray bottle nearby when you grill fish or other seafood.

Another thing that can go wrong with grilled fish is the dreaded overmarination. Fish—especially delicate white fish—has a tendency to absorb the marinade so much that the intense flavors can overwhelm the fish. Stick to the suggested marinade times in the individual recipes in this chapter.

It is especially important to have a clean, well-oiled grill surface when working with fish, and a fish basket is recommended not only for the fillets in this chapter, but also for the steaks. You can also buy special fish turners. They have tongs like a fork that fit into the spaces in the grill so that you can get under the piece of fish without scraping.

Smoking fish is less confrontational. A light smoke can be applied during the grilling process, but the most intense smoke is usually reserved for thick hunks of salmon that have been treated with a liquid spice cure first. It is very difficult to take the temperature of fish with an instant-read thermometer, so you'll need to "eyeball" the fish to see when it is done. The rule of thumb for seafood is that fish is done when the outside flakes easily with a fork, and shrimp and scallops are done when they lose their translucency and become opaque.

Because of their enormous popularity, I am starting this chapter with a collection of Latin American ceviches (also "seviche" or "cerviche"), those seafood dishes that include citric acid from fruits. The acid causes the proteins in the seafood to become denatured, which pickles or "cooks" the fish without heat.

Ceviche de Camarones
(Ecuadorian Marinated Shrimp)

Yield: 4–5 servings   Heat Scale: Mild

This recipe comes from a friend, Loretta Salazar, who lived in Ecuador while she attended the university on an exchange program. The popcorn served on top of the ceviche is an American approximation of the toasted corn, or cancha, that is served over Peruvian ceviches. This ceviche is a quick one if you use precooked, frozen mini-shrimp. Serve the ceviche on a bed of Bibb lettuce, garnished with black olives, sliced hard-boiled egg, feta cheese, a slice of cooked corn on the cob, and maybe some crusty bread for a very appetizing luncheon or light dinner. (Note: This recipe requires advance preparation.)

2 pounds (1.1 kg) frozen cooked shrimp
1 medium red onion, peeled and very thinly sliced
1–2 tablespoons (15–30 mL) chopped fresh aji chiles (or substitute yellow wax hot or jalapeño)
2 tablespoons (30 mL) chopped cilantro
3 medium tomatoes, finely chopped
3 tablespoons (45 mL) white wine vinegar
¾ cup (177 mL) fresh lemon juice
¾ cup (177 mL) fresh lime juice
½ cup (118 mL) good-quality olive oil
½ teaspoon (2.5 mL) salt
Shredded lettuce for serving
2½ cups (591 mL) freshly popped popcorn

1. Pour the frozen shrimp into a colander and run cold water over them for a minute or two. Drain the shrimp thoroughly and transfer them to paper towels to drain off the excess. Place the shrimp in a nonreactive bowl (such as Pyrex). Add the red onion, chiles, cilantro, tomatoes, vinegar, lemon juice, lime juice, olive oil, and salt and mix lightly. Marinate the mixture in the refrigerator for 2 to 4 hours.
2. Drain the ceviche in a colander and serve it on individual plates on beds of shredded lettuce, garnished with the warm popcorn.

Ceviche with Bitter Orange

Yield: 4–5 servings   Heat Scale: Medium

This recipe is a second version of the Ecuadorian specialty. The fish can be served as an appetizer or as a main dish for a refreshing summer meal. It is traditionally served with maiz tostada (toasted corn) or popcorn on the side. (Note: This recipe requires advance preparation.)

1½ pounds (680 g) any firm white fish fillets (snapper or catfish recommended)
1 cup (236 mL) bitter (Seville) orange juice (or substitute ½ cup [118 mL] lemon juice mixed with ½ cup [118 mL] orange juice)
1 cup (236 mL) fresh lime juice
1 onion, peeled and thinly sliced
1 cup (236 mL) chopped green bell pepper
1 cup (236 mL) chopped red bell pepper
1 habanero chile, stem and seeds removed, minced (or substitute 3 jalapeños)
½ cup (118 mL) olive oil
1 clove garlic, peeled and minced
½ teaspoon (2.5 mL) salt
¼ teaspoon (1.25 mL) freshly ground black pepper
Popped popcorn for garnish
Red bell pepper rings for garnish
Green bell pepper rings for garnish

1. Cut the cleaned fillets into thin, diagonal slices and place them in a large ceramic bowl. Pour the citrus juices over the fish. Add the onion, chopped bell peppers, habanero, olive oil, garlic, salt, and pepper and mix gently to coat the fish. Cover the bowl tightly and refrigerate for at least 6 hours to "cook" the fish.
2. Drain the fish and arrange the slices on individual plates, garnishing with the popcorn and pepper rings.

Marinated Halibut Chilean-Style

Yield: 4 servings   Heat Scale: Medium

Since Chile has a 2,600-mile coastline, I would be remiss if I didn't include some fish recipes from that country. There is minimal grazing land in Chile, so instead of beef being the major source of protein, it is fish and shellfish. The wines of Chile are quite good, so be sure to include a nice chilled Chilean white wine when you serve this ceviche. (Note: This recipe requires advance preparation.)

2 pounds (1.1 kg) halibut fillets (or substitute sole or flounder)
1 cup (236 mL) fresh lemon juice
½ cup (118 mL) fresh orange juice
1 cup (236 mL) chopped onions
2 teaspoons (10 mL) Caribbean-style habanero sauce
1 fresh aji chile, stem and seeds removed, sliced into rings, or substitute yellow wax hot or jalapeño
1 teaspoon (5 mL) salt
2 tomatoes, peeled, seeded, and diced
Lettuce leaves for serving
Tomato wedges for garnish
Cilantro sprigs for garnish

1. Cut the fillets into 1-inch (2.5 cm) pieces and place them in a ceramic bowl. Add the fruit juices and toss lightly to coat.
2. Add the onions, habanero sauce, chiles, salt, and tomatoes and mix gently. Cover the bowl tightly and refrigerate overnight. Drain off some of the juice. Line 4 individual plates with lettuce leaves and arrange the fillets on top. Garnish with the tomatoes and cilantro and serve.

Ceviche de Ostras
(Guatemalan Marinated Oysters)

Yield: 6 servings   Heat Scale: Medium

Although the triad of corn, beans, and rice reigns supreme in Guatemala, a myriad of exotic dishes, perhaps the traces of Mayan foraging, is also present. This dish intrigues because the habaneros add the heat and the mint provides an interesting twist on the more traditional cilantro. (Note: This recipe requires advance preparation.)

48 oysters, shucked
½ cup (118 mL) fresh lime juice
½ cup (118 mL) fresh lemon juice
3 tomatoes, peeled, seeded, and chopped
1 cup (236 mL) chopped onion
1 fresh habanero chile, stem and seeds removed, minced (or substitute
3 jalapeños)
3 tablespoons (45 mL) finely chopped fresh mint leaves
½ teaspoon (2.5 mL) salt
¼ teaspoon (1.25 mL) freshly ground black pepper
Lettuce leaves for garnish
Fresh mint sprigs for garnish
Tomato wedges for garnish

1. Place the oysters in a large ceramic bowl and cover them with the lime and lemon juices. Cover the bowl tightly and refrigerate overnight.
2. Drain the oysters, reserving ¼ cup (59 mL) of the juice. Add the chopped tomatoes, onion, chile, chopped mint, salt, pepper, and ¼ cup (59 mL) of the reserved juice and toss the mixture gently.
3. Line 6 plates with the lettuce leaves. Arrange 8 oysters with their marinade on the lettuce on each plate, and serve garnished with the fresh mint and the tomato wedges.

Ceviche de Corvina
(Peruvian Sea Bass Ceviche)

Yield: 4 servings   Heat Scale: Medium

I am including several ceviches from Peru because some travelers claim that they are superior to those of Ecuador. The most popular fish used in Peru is sea bass, or grouper, but every type of seafood and shellfish is used. The Peruvian ceviches include a few rounds of cooked corn on the cob and cooked slices of sweet potatoes. (Note: This recipe requires advance preparation.)

1½ pounds (680 g) sea bass fillets, cut into 1-inch (2.5 cm) pieces (or substitute swordfish)
1 teaspoon (5 mL) salt
¼ teaspoon (1.25 mL) freshly ground black pepper
2 rocoto chiles, stems and seeds removed, thinly sliced into rings (or substitute 1 habanero or 3 jalapeños)
1 teaspoon (5 mL) paprika
1 large onion, peeled and thinly sliced
1 cup (236 mL) fresh lemon juice
1 cup (236 mL) fresh lime juice
1 clove garlic, peeled and minced
1 pound (454 g) sweet potatoes, peeled and sliced 1 inch (2.5 cm) thick
3 ears fresh corn, cleaned and sliced 2 inches (5 cm) thick
Bibb lettuce leaves for serving

1. Place the cut and cleaned fish into a large glass or ceramic bowl and sprinkle it with the salt and pepper. Add half the chile rings, the paprika, the onion, the lemon juice, the lime juice, and the garlic and mix lightly. Cover the mixture and refrigerate for 3 to 5 hours, until the flesh is opaque.
2. About 30 minutes before serving the fish, cook the sweet potatoes in a large pot of boiling salted water for 12 minutes, then add the corn to the pot and cook for 10 minutes more, or until tender. Drain the vegetables and let them cool to room temperature.
3. Drain the fish thoroughly in a colander. Arrange the Bibb lettuce leaves on 4 dinner plates. Arrange the fish on the lettuce leaves and garnish with the remaining chile rings. Surround the fish with the cooked sweet potatoes and corn.

Marinated Snapper, Peruvian-Style

Yield: 4 servings   Heat Scale: Medium

This ceviche is different from the others because the spicy chile-vegetable mixture is spread on the fish after it has finished "cooking." Add more chiles to pack more punch into your ceviche. Speaking of packing a punch, South American legend holds that ceviches are aphrodisiacs and will give a woman many sons. (Note: This recipe requires advance preparation.)

2 pounds (1.1 kg) snapper or sole fillets, washed and cut into 1-inch (2.5 cm) strips
½ cup (118 mL) fresh lime juice
½ cup (118 mL) fresh lemon juice
½ cup (118 mL) finely chopped red bell peppers
1 large tomato, peeled, seeded, and chopped
2 fresh pimientos, stems and seeds removed, finely chopped (or substitute 1 red bell pepper, chopped)
½ cup (118 mL) finely chopped onions
2 cloves garlic, peeled and minced
2 tablespoons (30 mL) minced cilantro or Italian parsley
1 teaspoon (5 mL) salt
2 fresh aji chiles, stems and seeds removed, minced (or substitute yellow wax hot or jalapeños)
½ teaspoon (2.5 mL) sugar
½ cup (118 mL) white wine vinegar
Lettuce leaves for serving

1. Place the fillet strips in a ceramic bowl. Pour the lemon and lime juice over them and mix gently to coat the fish with the juices. Cover the bowl tightly and refrigerate for 8 hours or, preferably, overnight.
2. In a separate bowl, mix together the bell peppers, tomato, pimientos, onions, garlic, cilantro or parsley, salt, aji chiles, sugar, and vinegar. Let the mixture stand at room temperature for 1 hour.
3. Drain the fish. Arrange the lettuce leaves on 4 individual plates and arrange the fish on top. Spread the chile mixture over the fish, dividing it evenly among the plates.

Peruvian Mixed Seafood Ceviche

Yield: 4 servings   Heat Scale: Medium

This particular ceviche is spicy thanks to the addition of a fair amount of crushed ajis or whatever dried chiles you have available. The use of corn and sweet potatoes identifies this dish as very typically Peruvian. Serve it as a lunch or dinner entrée on those hot and sweltering days of summer. (Note: This recipe requires advance preparation.)

¾ cup (177 mL) fresh lime juice
¾ cup (177 mL) fresh lemon juice
3 dried aji chiles, stems and seeds removed, crushed in a mortar (or substitute 2 New Mexican chiles [mild] or 6 piquins]hot])
1 clove garlic, peeled and minced
1 large red onion, peeled and sliced paper thin
1 teaspoon (5 mL) salt
¼ teaspoon (1.25 mL) freshly ground black pepper
½ pound (224 g) white fish fillets, such as catfish, cut into 1-inch (2.5 cm) pieces
1 pound (454 g) cleaned shellfish (clams, oysters, mussels, or a mix)
1 teaspoon (5 mL) paprika (optional)
1 tablespoon (15 mL) chopped fresh parsley, Italian preferred
3 sweet potatoes, peeled and cut into 1-inch (2.5 cm) thick slices
3 ears of fresh corn, cleaned and cut into 2-inch (5 cm) thick slices
4 Bibb lettuce leaves

1. In a ceramic bowl, combine all the ingredients except the potatoes, corn, and lettuce and mix well. Cover tightly and refrigerate for 3 to 5 hours. If the citrus juice doesn't cover the fish, add more in the same proportion.

2. Just before serving, bring a large pot of salted water to a boil. Drop in the sweet potatoes and boil for 10 minutes. Add the rounds of corn to the pot and boil for another 10 minutes. Drain the vegetables thoroughly.

3. Drain the fish in a colander. Place a lettuce leaf on each of 4 dinner plates and arrange the fish on the lettuce. Garnish with the sweet potatoes and the rounds of corn.

Escabeche de Pescado
(Peruvian Fish in Aji Sauce)

Yield: 6 servings   Heat Scale: Hot

As befitting a nation with miles of Pacific coastline, many dishes in Peru use seafood. Escabeche is cold fried fish in a marinade of onions and hot peppers. Serve it with boiled sweet potatoes, corn on the cob, and a crisp salad.

6 fillets white fish, such as catfish
All-purpose flour for dredging
2 tablespoons (30 mL) vegetable oil
Ground cumin, to taste
Salt, to taste
Freshly ground black pepper, to taste
4 fresh aji chiles, stems and seeds removed (or substitute red serranos or jalapeños)
2 cloves garlic, peeled
2 onions, peeled and cut into thin wedges
2 fresh aji chiles, seeds and stems removed, cut into thin strips (or substitute yellow wax hot or red serranos or jalapeños)
⅓ cup (79 mL) vinegar
Lettuce for serving

1. Roll the fish fillets in flour and fry them in the oil until golden brown, about 10 minutes, turning occasionally. Transfer the fish to paper towels to drain. Season with cumin, salt, and pepper. Set aside to cool.
2. In a blender, grind together the whole ajis and the garlic. In the same pan you used for the fish, fry the puréed chile-garlic mixture over medium heat until golden, then add the onions, chile strips, and vinegar, adding more oil if necessary. Sauté for 5 minutes.
3. Place the fried fish fillets on a bed of lettuce and cover it with the escabeche sauce. Serve warm or at room temperature.

Red Snapper Escabeche

Yield: 6–8 servings   Heat Scale: Medium

This Peruvian dish is popular throughout South America, probably because of the great availability of fresh fish. Even the Inca nobility, high up in the Andes, had access to fresh fish, thanks to the intricate system of runners that was set up. (When the royalty wanted it, the runners even brought snow.) The technique of cooking this dish is Spanish , although New World cooks have added their own special touches and ingredients. The use of achiote seed adds a slight musky taste and colors the dish yellow.

3 pounds (1.36 kg) red snapper fillets (or substitute any firm white fish)
1 teaspoon (5 mL) salt
¼ teaspoon (1.25 mL) freshly ground black pepper
1 cup (236 mL) all-purpose flour
2 teaspoons (10 mL) paprika
3 tablespoons (45 mL) butter or vegetable oil
½ cup (118 mL) olive oil
2 cloves garlic, peeled and minced
½ teaspoon (2.5 mL) achiote (annatto seeds)
3 onions, peeled and sliced into ¼-inch (.5 cm) thick rings
2 fresh aji or rocoto chiles, stems and seeds removed, chopped fine (or substitute yellow wax hot or jalapeño)
¼ teaspoon (1.25 mL) dried oregano or thyme
¾ cup (177 mL) white wine vinegar
Muenster or Monterey jack cheese for garnish
Black olives for garnish
Cooked corn on the cob, cut into 2-inch (5 cm) rounds for garnish
Sliced hard-boiled eggs for garnish
Lettuce leaves for garnish

1. Sprinkle the fish with the salt and pepper. Combine the flour and the paprika in a large freezer bag and dredge the fillets, shaking off any excess flour.
2. In a skillet, melt the butter over medium heat. Add the fish and sauté until it is lightly browned on both sides. Transfer the fish to a warm platter and keep it warm.
3. In another large skillet, heat the olive oil over medium heat. Add the garlic, achiote, onions, and chiles and sauté until the onions are softened. Sprinkle in the oregano and vinegar and stir until the mixture is hot. Pour the mixture over the fish and serve. Garnish with some or all of the suggested garnishes.

Eja
(Bahian Snapper with Malagueta Shrimp Sauce)

Yield: 4 servings   Heat Scale: Hot

This recipe comes from Tita Lib'n, who has spent much time studying the foods, the gods, and the lore of Bahia. Bahia is the homeland of the Orixas, the Brazilian gods. In Bahia, the African religions blended with Catholicism, and each Orixa has a favorite food and specific characteristics. Ye Manja is the Queen of the Sea; her Catholic counterpart is Our Lady of the Sailors, her colors are blue and white, her special day is Saturday, and her favorite food is Eja, or Bahian Snapper. (Note: This recipe requires advance preparation.)

¼ cup (59 mL) dried shrimp (available in Latin or Asian markets)
8 dried malagueta chiles, stems and seeds removed, crushed, divided (or substitute piquins)
1 cup (236 mL) lemon juice
4 (½-inch [1 cm]) thick red snapper fillets (or substitute any firm white fish)
3 tablespoons (45 mL) olive oil
1 cup (236 mL) chopped onions
¼ teaspoon (1.25 mL) freshly ground black pepper
Salt, to taste

1. In a glass or ceramic bowl, combine the shrimp, half the chiles, and the lemon juice. Add the fish and marinate it for 1 hour. Remove the fish, pat it dry, and reserve the marinade.
2. Preheat the oven to its lowest setting.
3. In a frying pan, heat the oil over medium-high heat. Add the fish and fry it on both sides until cooked, about 5 minutes per side. Remove the fish from the pan and transfer it to the oven to keep warm.
4. Add the onions to the frying pan and sauté them until softened. Stir in the reserved marinade, the marinated shrimp, the remaining chiles, and the black pepper. Simmer for a couple of minutes to thicken and add salt to taste.
5. Place the fish fillets on a serving platter, top them with the shrimp sauce, and serve.

Bobó de Camarao
(Bahian Spicy Shrimp)
Yield: 6–8 servings　　　　　　　　　　　Heat Scale: Medium

This recipe is the food of another Bahian Orixa, Nana, the oldest and kindest of all sacred women. Tita Lib'n found that Nana's Catholic counterpart is Saint Ann, her colors are blue and white, her sacred day is Tuesday, her element is sweet water, and her food is Bobó de Camarao.

6 dried malagueta chiles, stems and seeds removed (or substitute piquins)
3 tablespoons (45 mL) olive oil
½ cup (118 mL) chopped onions
¼ cup (59 mL) finely chopped celery
6 cloves garlic, peeled and chopped
1 cup (236 mL) chopped pimiento, stems and seeds removed (or substitute red bell pepper)
4 cups (.95 L) shrimp, peeled and deveined
2 cups (473 mL) chopped tomatoes
1 cup (236 mL) coconut milk
1 tablespoon (15 mL) palm oil (or substitute vegetable oil mixed with 1 teaspoon [5 mL] ground paprika)
½ teaspoon (2.5 mL) ground cinnamon
¼ teaspoon (1.25 mL) ground cloves
¼ teaspoon (1.25 mL) ground ginger
3 tablespoons (45 mL) lemon juice
Salt, to taste
Freshly ground black pepper, to taste
¼ cup (59 mL) finely chopped cilantro
6 cups cooked rice

1. In a bowl, cover the chiles with hot water and soak them for 15 minutes or until soft. Remove the chiles from the water and chop them.
2. In a frying pan, heat the oil over medium heat. Add the onions and sauté until soft. Add the celery, garlic, chiles, and pimiento and sauté for an additional 5 minutes. Stir in the shrimp, sauté until they turn pink, and remove them from the pan and set them aside.
3. Add the tomatoes, coconut milk, palm oil, cinnamon, cloves, and ginger. Bring to a boil, reduce the heat, and simmer until the mixture thickens, about 10 minutes.
4. Return the shrimp to the pan, stir in the lemon juice, and season with salt and pepper. Garnish with the cilantro and serve immediately on top of the rice.

Vatapá
(Fish and Shrimp in Ginger-Peanut Sauce)

Yield: 4 servings   Heat Scale: Medium

This recipe is typical of Bahia. It has the African influences of palm oil, red chiles (usually malaguetas), bananas, and coconuts. The food of Salvador, the capital, also plays a central role in Jorge Amado's novels, including Doña Flor and Her Two Husbands. *Vatapá is the food of Ogun, the Bahian Orixa of iron and war. His Catholic counterpart is Saint Anthony, and his color is navy blue.*

2–3 tablespoons (30–45 mL) olive oil
1 pound (454 g) white fish fillets, cut in 2-inch (5 cm) cubes
½ cup (118 mL) dried shrimp, finely chopped
¼ cup (59 mL) chopped green onions
1 small onion, peeled and finely chopped
1 teaspoon (5 mL) minced fresh ginger
2 cups (473 mL) chopped tomatoes
2 teaspoons (10 mL) crushed malagueta chile (or substitute piquin)
1 cup (236 mL) coconut milk
½ cup (118 mL) cashews, chopped
1 cup (236 mL) chunky peanut butter
2 slices bread, soaked in water
½ teaspoon (2.5 mL) freshly ground black pepper
½ teaspoon (2.5 mL) ground cloves
1 tablespoon (15 mL) palm oil (or substitute vegetable oil with 1 teaspoon [5 mL] ground paprika)
2 cups (473 mL) water
¼ cup (59 mL) chopped fresh cilantro

1. In a Dutch oven, heat the oil over medium heat. Add the fish and shrimp and sauté until just done, about 5 to 6 minutes. Remove the seafood from the pan and keep it warm.
2. Add the green onions, onions, and ginger and sauté until soft. Stir in the tomatoes and simmer for 5 minutes. Add the chiles, coconut milk, cashews, peanut butter, soaked bread, pepper, cloves, oil, and water. Bring to a boil, reduce the heat, and simmer, uncovered, for 15 minutes or until the sauce has thickened.
3. Return the fish and shrimp to the pan. Add the cilantro and heat through. Serve with rice and beans.

Seafood in Hot Peanut Sauce

Yield: 4–6 servings   Heat Scale: Medium

Nancy Gerlach collected this recipe in Rio de Janeiro. Serve it with Camotes Fritos (page 752), fried sweet potatoes, and any rice dish from Chapter 13.

3–4 tablespoons (45–60 mL) olive oil
1 pound (454 g) white fish fillets, cut in 3-inch (7.5 cm) pieces
1 pound (454 g) raw shrimp, shelled and deveined
1 small onion, peeled and finely chopped
1 small green bell pepper, stem and seeds removed, chopped
1 tablespoon (15 mL) grated ginger
1 habanero chile, stem and seeds removed, minced (or substitute
3 jalapeños)
2 teaspoons (10 mL) coriander seeds
2 large tomatoes, peeled and chopped
1 cup (236 mL) chicken broth
1 cup (236 mL) coconut milk
½ cup (118 mL) chopped peanuts
1 cup (236 mL) grated coconut
Chopped fresh cilantro

1. In a sauté pan, heat the oil over medium heat. Add the fish and heat for about 2 minutes per side. Remove it from the pan and keep it warm. Add the shrimp and sauté until just pink. Remove it from the pan and keep it warm.
2. Add the onion, pepper, ginger, and habanero and sauté until the onions are soft. Stir in the coriander, tomatoes, broth, and coconut milk. Simmer the sauce for 15 to 20 minutes. Transfer it to a blender or food processor and purée until smooth.
3. Return the sauce to the pan, add the peanuts and coconut, and simmer until the sauce is slightly thickened. Return the fish and shrimp to the sauce and heat through.
4. Garnish with the cilantro and serve.

Huachinango con Coco
(Red Snapper Fillets in Coconut Milk)

Yield: 6 servings   Heat Scale: Medium

Seafood reigns supreme on the Caribbean coast of Colombia, and when it is cooked with coconut milk, it yields a delicate, flavorful dish. To avoid overpowering the delicacy of this dish, I suggest serving it with cooked rice and a lightly dressed green salad. (Note: To make thick coconut milk, grate about 1 cup [236 mL] fresh coconut meat into a small bowl and pour 1¼ cups [295 mL] hot water over it. Allow the mixture to sit for 15 minutes. Press this mixture through a fine sieve, removing as much liquid as possible, and discard the coconut meat. The result should be about 1 cup [236 mL] thick coconut milk.)

3 pounds (1.36 kg) red snapper fillets, cut into 6 pieces (or substitute grouper or any firm, white fish)
1 teaspoon (5 mL) salt
Freshly ground black pepper, to taste
3 tomatoes, peeled, seeded, and diced
1 cup (236 mL) finely chopped onion
2 fresh habanero chiles, stems and seeds removed, minced (or substitute 3 jalapeños)
3 cups (708 mL) coconut milk
1 cup (236 mL) thick coconut milk (see Note)

1. In a large skillet, arrange the fillets and sprinkle them with the salt and pepper. Spread the tomatoes, onions, and habanero chiles evenly over the fish. Pour in the coconut milk and simmer for 10 minutes. Transfer the fish to a warm platter and keep the fish warm. Reserve the remaining coconut milk in the skillet.
2. Bring the reserved milk to a slow boil and cook it down, stirring, until about 1 cup (236 mL) remains. Add the thick coconut milk and heat through. Pour the mixture through a sieve, onto the fish on the platter. Serve immediately.

Guyanese Curried Fish

Yield: 4 servings   Heat Scale: Medium

The Guyanese often use canned salmon in this dish, but I suggest any other flavorful fish, cooked and flaked. The addition of hot sauce and curry powder suggests that this dish has its roots with the East Indian laborers who were brought to the Caribbean. In keeping with a curry dinner, I suggest serving it with white rice and condiments such as chopped salted peanuts, pickle relish, chopped hard-boiled eggs, mango chutney, and finely diced cucumber. (Note: If you are using fresh fish, cook it briefly in a little water and use the cooking water as part of the liquid measurement.)

4 whole fresh coconuts
2 tablespoons (30 mL) butter
1 cup (236 mL) onion, finely diced
2 cloves garlic, peeled and minced
¼ teaspoon (1.25 mL) freshly ground black pepper
2 teaspoons (10 mL) habanero hot sauce
1 tablespoon (15 mL) curry powder (Indian preferred)
5–6 tablespoons (75–90 mL) plus ¼ cup (59 mL) all-purpose flour, divided, plus more as needed
1 pound (454 g) cooked white fish, such as flounder or catfish, flaked
¼ cup (59 mL) mango chutney
¼ teaspoon (1.25 mL) salt
2 tablespoons (30 mL) fresh lime juice
¾ cup (177 mL) diced partially ripe papaya
2–3 tablespoons (30–45 mL) water

1. Preheat the oven to 200°F (100°C).
2. Saw the tops off the coconuts and reserve the coconut water. Remove the coconut meat from the tops, grate it, and toast it on a baking sheet in the oven, stirring often, until lightly toasted. Set aside. Increase the oven temperature to 350°F (180°C).
3. In a large skillet, melt the butter over medium heat. Add the onion and garlic and sauté until they are softened. Add the black pepper, hot sauce, and curry powder and cook for 5 minutes over low heat, stirring constantly so the mixture doesn't burn. Sprinkle in 5–6 tablespoons (75–90 mL) of the flour and blend thoroughly.
4. Add 2½ cups (591 mL) of the reserved coconut water and cook, stirring constantly, until the sauce is thick and smooth.
5. Add the flaked fish, chutney, salt, lime juice, and diced papaya and mix thoroughly but gently. Spoon this mixture into the coconut shells and replace the tops.
5. Combine the remaining ¼ cup (59 mL) flour and water to make a thick paste. Use this paste to seal the coconuts.
6. Place the filled coconuts in a large baking dish. Stabilize them by placing them in metal rings (such as tuna fish cans with the tops and bottoms cut out). Bake for 1 hour. Crack open the coconut tops and serve with the reserved toasted coconut and suggested accompaniments.

Camarones Picantes
(Spicy Shrimp Salad)

Yield: 4 servings   Heat Scale: Medium

While visiting friends in Costa Rica, I was served a version of this as a luncheon en-
trée. Since Costa Ricans generally don't eat their food very spicy, I think this dish may
have been an invention of my hosts, using the best of the local vegetables and shrimp.

20 large shrimp, cooked, peeled, deveined, and chilled
1⅓ cups (315 mL) hearts of palm, cut into chunks
2 fresh tomatoes, sliced
½ cup (118 mL) sliced green onions
1 fresh habanero chile, stems and seeds removed, minced (or substitute 3
jalapeños)
Bibb lettuce leaves for serving
Juice of 2 fresh limes
¼ cup (59 mL) olive oil
Salt, to taste
Freshly ground black pepper, to taste

1. In a large bowl, toss together the shrimp, hearts of palm, tomatoes,
green onions, and habanero.
2. Arrange the lettuce leaves on 4 plates and mound the shrimp mixture
on top. Combine the lime juice and olive oil and drizzle this mixture over
the salads. Season with the salt and pepper.

Mariscos con Frutas
(Argentine Citrus Seafood)

Yield: 8 servings　　　　　　　　　　　　　　　Heat Scale: Medium

Many of the stews in Argentina are made with fresh and even dried fruit. This spicy, creamed seafood dish is very elegant and makes a gorgeous presentation dish. Accompany the dish with a simple green salad and a chilled Argentine white wine.

2 cups (473 mL) uncooked long-grain white rice
½ cup (118 mL) butter, divided
1 (2-inch [5 cm]) thread saffron
½ teaspoon (2.5 mL) salt
4 cups (.95 L) Classic Chicken Stock, boiling (page 46)
¼ cup (59 mL) chopped pimientos (or substitute red bell pepper)
½ cup (118 mL) cooked tiny green peas
2 tablespoons (30 mL) all-purpose flour
1½ cups (354 mL) milk
1 tablespoon (15 mL) Louisiana-style hot sauce
¼ cup (59 mL) minced onion
2 cloves garlic, peeled and minced
3 tablespoons (45 mL) finely chopped green bell pepper
3 pounds (1.36 kg) lobster, cooked and cubed
1 pound (454 g) medium shrimp, cooked, peeled, and deveined
½ pound (224 g) crabmeat, cooked and flaked
3 oranges, peeled and thinly sliced into circles
2 ripe avocados, peeled, pitted, and sliced
2 grapefruits, peeled and sectioned
16 lime wedges

1. In a saucepan, combine the rice, 3 tablespoons (45 mL) of the butter, the saffron, the salt, and the boiling chicken stock. Bring to a boil, reduce the heat to a simmer, cover, and simmer for 20 minutes. When the rice is tender, stir in the pimientos and the peas and keep the rice warm.
2. In a large, heavy saucepan, melt 2 tablespoons (30 mL) of the remaining butter over medium heat. Sprinkle in the flour and stir for 30 seconds until it is well blended with the butter, taking care not to burn the mixture. Add the milk and hot sauce and cook, stirring constantly, until the mixture starts to thicken. If the mixture is not smooth, beat it with a whisk. Remove the cream sauce from the heat and set it aside.
3. In a large skillet, melt the remaining 3 tablespoons (45 mL) butter. Add the onion, garlic, and bell pepper and sauté for 30 seconds.
4. Add the lobster, shrimp, and crabmeat and toss lightly. Add the cream sauce and heat slowly until the mixture is hot. Serve the creamed seafood over the cooked rice, garnished with the oranges, avocados, grapefruit, and lime wedges.

Camarones con Salsa de Almendras
(Ecuadorian Shrimp in Almond Sauce)

Yield: 6 servings   Heat Scale: Medium

This recipe appears in many different forms in Ecuador and Chile. Each country claims it as its own, which is not unlikely as both countries have an abundance of seafood in general and shrimp in particular. The almonds and cream make this a very rich dish. For accompaniments, I suggest cooked quinoa, a simply dressed green salad, and a good, chilled Chilean white wine.

1½ cups (354 mL) water
2 celery stalks, cut into 3-inch (7.5 cm) pieces
½ teaspoon (2.5 mL) pickling spice
½ cup (118 mL) dry white wine
½ teaspoon (2.5 mL) salt
2 pounds (1.1 kg) shrimp, shelled and deveined
1¼ cups (295 mL) diced day-old, good white bread
1¼ cups (295 mL) milk
¼ cup (59 mL) butter
2 cups (473 mL) diced onion
2 cloves garlic, peeled and minced
¼ teaspoon (1.25 mL) freshly ground black pepper
1 teaspoon (5 mL) dried, crushed aji chiles (or substitute New Mexican)
1 teaspoon (5 mL) paprika
½ cup (118 mL) cream
2 tablespoons (30 mL) olive oil
1 cup (236 mL) ground almonds
Hard-boiled egg slices for garnish
Grated Parmesan cheese for garnish

1. In a large pot, bring the water to a boil. Add the celery, pickling spice, white wine, salt, and shrimp, and cook over a medium heat for 3 minutes. Drain the shrimp and reserve 1 cup (236 mL) of the cooking liquid. Pick off any large pieces of the pickling spice that remain on the shrimp.
2. Soak the bread in the milk for 10 to 12 minutes, then mash the bread until it is smooth.
3. In a skillet, melt the butter over medium heat. Add the onions and garlic and sauté until the onions are softened. Add the black pepper, crushed chiles, and paprika and mix.
4. Squeeze some of the milk out of the bread and add the bread and the cream to the onion mixture. Cook for 3 to 5 minutes, stirring constantly, until the mixture is thickened. Mix in the olive oil and the ground almonds and cook for 2 minutes, stirring. If the mixture seems too thick, add some of the reserved shrimp stock to thin it. Add the shrimp and heat through.
5. Serve the shrimp on warmed plates, garnished with the hard-boiled egg slices and grated Parmesan cheese.

Arroz con Mariscos
(Rice with Shrimp, Scallops, and Clams)

Yield: 6–8 servings   Heat Scale: Medium

Even though Peru claims this recipe, variations are found throughout coastal areas of Ecuador and Chile, where fish and shellfish abound. In a salute to Chile, serve a chilled Chilean white wine with this dish. A bean dish, a fresh green salad, and some sliced tomatoes should make this meal a feast.

4 tablespoons (60 mL) olive oil, divided
18 medium shrimp, cleaned, shells reserved
1 sprig parsley
2 onion slices
¼ teaspoon (1.25 mL) thyme
4 whole black peppercorns
4 cups (.95 L) water
½–1 cup (118–236 mL) clam broth
½ teaspoon (2.5 mL) salt
1 cup (236 mL) chopped onion
2 cloves garlic, peeled and minced
2 fresh aji or rocoto chiles, stems and seeds removed, minced (or substitute yellow wax hot or jalapeños)
2 cups (473 mL) uncooked long-grain white rice
2 tablespoons (30 mL) chopped cilantro or Italian parsley
½ pound (224 g) fresh scallops
14 cherrystone clams, shelled and washed
14 oysters, shucked and washed

1. In a small, heavy saucepan, heat 1 tablespoon (15 mL) of the olive oil over medium heat. Add the shrimp shells and stir them until they turn pink. Add the parsley, onion, thyme, peppercorns, and water. Bring this mixture to a boil. Lower the heat to a simmer, cover, and cook for 30 minutes. Strain the liquid and measure it. Add enough of the clam broth to make 4 cups (.95 L) total. Season with the salt and set aside.
2. In a heavy skillet, heat the remaining 3 tablespoons (45 mL) olive oil over medium heat. Add the onion, garlic, and chiles and sauté until the onion is softened. Transfer the sautéed mixture to a casserole, leaving as much oil as possible in the skillet; if there isn't 2 to 3 tablespoons (30 to 45 mL), add more oil. Add the rice and sauté over low heat for 1 minute, stirring frequently. Transfer the rice to the casserole, add the reserved shrimp stock, and bring the mixture to a boil. Reduce the heat to low, cover the casserole, and simmer for 20 minutes, until the rice is tender and the liquid is absorbed. Stir the cilantro, reserved shrimp, scallops, and clams into the rice, cover, and cook for 3 to 5 minutes, until the shrimp is pink. Add the oysters and cook for 1 minute.

Ocopa with Potatoes
(Shrimp Sauce and Potatoes)

Yield: 4 servings   Heat Scale: Hot

This Peruvian dish has everything: shrimp, potatoes, and chile. However, the amount of chiles used means it is a very hot and spicy dish, very typical of Peru, where people consume vast quantities of chiles. Try serving this dish on a hot summer night, along with a fresh green salad, and watch your guests perspire their way to coolness.

6 dried aji chile pods, stems and seeds removed, torn into small pieces (or substitute New Mexican)
½ teaspoon (2.5 mL) salt
18 medium shrimp, washed
½ cup (118 mL) plus 2 tablespoons (30 mL) olive oil, divided
½ cup (118 mL) chopped onion
2 cloves garlic, peeled and chopped
½ teaspoon (2.5 mL) marjoram
3 tablespoons (45 mL) fresh parsley
2–4 tablespoons (30–60 mL) cottage cheese
¼ cup (59 mL) walnuts, chopped
4 potatoes, boiled, peeled, and sliced
2 hard-boiled eggs, sliced for garnish
Minced cilantro for garnish

1. Soak the chiles in the warm water with the salt for 1 hour. Rinse the chiles, drain them in a colander, and set them aside.
2. In a medium saucepan, cover the shrimp with water and boil them for 5 to 6 minutes. Reserve the cooking water and clean the shrimp. Transfer the cleaned shrimp to a food processor.
3. In a small skillet, heat 2 tablespoons (30 mL) of the olive oil over medium heat. Add the onion and the garlic and sauté for 1 minute. Add the sautéed mixture to the shrimp in the food processor, along with the chiles, marjoram, parsley, cottage cheese, and walnuts.
4. Purée the shrimp mixture, adding the remaining oil and shrimp water to thin the sauce a little. The mixture should be a thick and creamy but pourable sauce.
5. Arrange the sliced potatoes on a platter or on individual plates and pour the shrimp sauce over the potatoes. Garnish with the hard-boiled egg slices and sprinkle the minced cilantro over the top.

Mero Estilo Tik en Xic
(Whole Grouper "Tik in Xic")

Yield: 4 servings   Heat Scale: Medium-Hot

I thank Chef John Gray of the Ritz-Carlton Hotel in Cancún for this recipe. The habanero chile adds just a little heat to the fish dish. As in many Cancún resorts, the guests are "gently" introduced to the flaming chiles of the area; many of these tourists have probably never eaten chiles before, so the chefs tend to use a light and judicious hand with them. Serve this with a rice dish from Chapter 13 and a salad from Chapter 6.

1 cup (236 mL) Recado Rojo (Red Seasoning Paste; page 5)
1 cup (236 mL) orange juice
½ cup (118 mL) water
¼ cup plus 2 tablespoons (148 mL) fresh lemon juice
¼ cup plus 2 tablespoons (148 mL) vinegar
2 cloves garlic, peeled and chopped
1 (2-pound [1.1 kg]) whole grouper, butterflied
1 medium onion, sliced
1 medium tomato, sliced
2 tablespoons (30 mL) finely minced habanero chiles
Salt, to taste

1. In a large, shallow bowl, combine the Recado Rojo, orange juice, water, lemon juice, vinegar, and garlic. Add the whole butterflied grouper and marinate for 1 hour. Cover the fish with the slices of onion and tomato, sprinkle the chiles on top, and lightly salt the fish.
2. Heat up a gas or charcoal grill. Wrap the fish in aluminum foil and place it on the grill over low heat. "Bake" the fish for about an hour and then check it. When it flakes immediately with a fork, it is done.

Salmon Estilo Ritz-Carlton Cancún
(Salmon with Roasted Tomato-Pasilla Chile Vinaigrette)

Yield: 4 servings   Heat Scale: Mild

John Gray presents another one of his terrific fish recipes. The pasilla chiles and the balsamic vinegar add a spicy and herbal edge to the grilled salmon. Chef Gray suggests serving this dish with mashed potatoes with serrano chiles and roasted onions.

½ cup (118 mL) finely chopped shallots
½ cup (118 mL) dried pasilla chiles, stems and seeds removed, julienned
1 medium tomato, peeled
Salt, to taste
Freshly ground black pepper, to taste
1 pinch dried basil
1 cup (236 mL) plus 2 tablespoons (30 mL) balsamic vinegar
2 cups (473 mL) olive oil, divided
4 salmon steaks

1. In a dry skillet, roast the shallots and pasilla chiles over medium heat until the shallots are golden. Transfer them to a bowl. Peel the tomato and roast it on the grill or in a griddle for 5 minutes. Seed and dice the tomato. Add the tomato to the chiles and shallots. Add salt and pepper to taste. Allow the mixture to sit for 5 minutes, then add the basil, balsamic vinegar, 1¾ cups (413 mL) of the olive oil, and additional salt and pepper to taste.
2. Brush the salmon with the remaining olive oil and grill the steaks for 3 to 5 minutes per side. Arrange the finished salmon on a heated platter and cover with the reserved vinaigrette.

Pescado Empapelado (Fish Baked in Foil)

Yield: 4–5 servings   Heat Scale: Hot

This recipe from Tabasco, Mexico, is deceptively easy to make, and it only takes a few minutes. The garlic and salsa infuse the fish and give it a wonderful flavor. Serve the fish with warm tortillas and a salad from Chapter 6.

6 cichlid or sunfish fillets (or substitute a freshwater fish such as perch, panfish, or bass)
5 cloves garlic, peeled and minced
½ teaspoon (2.5 mL) salt
¼ teaspoon (1.25 mL) freshly ground black pepper
3 tablespoons (45 mL) oil
5 green serrano or jalapeño chiles, roasted, peeled, stems and seeds removed, coarsely chopped
1 large onion, peeled and thinly sliced
2 cloves garlic, peeled and minced
6 large spinach leaves

1. Preheat the oven to 325°F (165°C)
2. Wash the fillets and blot them dry with paper towels. Spread the garlic over the fillets and sprinkle them with the salt and pepper.
3. In a sauté pan, heat the oil over medium heat. Add the chiles, onion, and garlic and sauté until the onion softens and wilts, 1 or 2 minutes. Stir in ¼ cup (59 mL) water and remove the pan from the heat.
4. Place a fillet on a spinach leaf, spoon some cooked salsa on top, wrap the spinach (envelope style) around the fillet, and then wrap the fillet in a piece of aluminum foil. Repeat with the remaining fillets.
5. Place the wrapped fillets in a large, glass baking dish and bake for 20 minutes or until the fish flakes.

Makum
(Baked Chile-Spiced Snapper)

Yield: 4 servings   Heat Scale: Medium

For fish and garlic lovers, this recipe from Campeche is the one to cook. The roasted garlic and onion, along with the cumin, vinegar, and chiles add a burst of flavor.

2 medium onions, halved
8 cloves garlic, unpeeled
1 teaspoon (5 mL) butter
2 tablespoons (30 mL) dry white wine
½ teaspoon (2.5 mL) ground achiote
1 teaspoon (5 mL) Mexican oregano
1½ teaspoons (7.5 mL) ground cumin
5 whole cloves, ground
1 teaspoon (5 mL) whole black peppercorns, ground
3 large jalapeño chiles, roasted, peeled, stems and seeds removed
½ cup (118 mL) olive oil
¼ cup (59 mL) fresh lemon juice or lime juice
½ cup (118 mL) vinegar
½ teaspoon (2.5 mL) salt
1 large banana leaf
4 (8-ounce [224 mL]) snapper or grouper fillets
3 tomatoes, sliced
4 güero chiles, stems and seeds removed, chopped (or substitute yellow wax hots)

1. Preheat the oven to 400°F (200°C). Lightly oil a shallow baking pan.
2. Place the onions and garlic in a small, covered glass casserole dish (or use a terra cotta garlic roaster). Dot them with the butter and pour in the wine. Roast for 30 to 40 minutes or until the garlic is soft. Carefully squeeze the cloves out of the peels and place them in a blender, along with the onion. Decrease the oven heat to 350°F (180°C).
3. To the blender, add the achiote, oregano, cumin, ground cloves, ground black peppercorns, chiles, oil, lemon juice, vinegar, and salt and purée until the mixture is smooth.
4. Spread the banana leaf in the prepared baking pan and pour half of the puréed mixture over the banana leaf. Place the fish in a single layer toward the middle of the leaf, and pour the remaining purée over the fish.
5. Arrange the tomatoes and the chiles over the purée, wrap the leaf over the mixture, and secure the leaf with a toothpick.
6. Bake the fish for 25 minutes or until the fish is tender.

Escabeche de Marlin
(Pickled Marlin)

Yield: 6 servings   Heat Scale: Medium to Hot

The pickling in this recipe from Baja California comes from the pickled jalapeños and the vinegar. Serve the fish hot and accompany it with a salad from Chapter 6, a rice dish from Chapter 13 and a tamale appetizer from Chapter 5.

2 pounds (1.1 kg) fresh marlin, cleaned and cut into 6 fillets
(or substitute tuna)
1 cup (236 mL) chopped onion
2 cloves garlic, peeled and sliced
2 bay leaves
1 teaspoon (5 mL) Mexican oregano
1 tablespoon (15 mL) whole black peppercorns
¼ teaspoon (1.25 mL) freshly ground black pepper
1 teaspoon (5 mL) salt
3 tablespoons (45 mL) oil
2 cloves garlic, peeled and minced
1 cup (236 mL) chopped onion
1 cup (236 mL) sliced red bell peppers
2 cups (473 mL) sliced carrots
1 cup (236 mL) frozen peas, thawed
4 pickled jalapeño chiles, sliced
¾ cup (177 mL) white wine vinegar

1. Put the fish in a large pot and add water to cover. Add the onion, sliced garlic, bay leaves, oregano, peppercorns, pepper, and salt and bring the mixture to a light boil. Reduce the heat to a simmer, cover, and simmer for 15 minutes or until done. Remove the fish from the pot and keep it warm. Reserve the cooking broth.
2. In a medium skillet, heat the oil over medium heat. Add the minced garlic, onion, red peppers, and carrots and sauté for 4 minutes. Add the peas, jalapeños, vinegar, and 3 tablespoons (45 mL) of the reserved fish broth and simmer for 2 minutes.
3. Arrange the fish on heated dinner plates and spoon the vegetable mixture over the fish.

Ceviche de Mojarra
(Sunfish Ceviche)

Yield: 4 to 5 servings   Heat Scale: Hot

This spicy ceviche from the southern state of Chiapas can be served on fresh greens for lunch or for a light dinner, accompanied by warm tortillas. Any of the fish substitutions will work equally as well in this dish. Serve this with a salad from Chapter 6.

2 pounds (1.1 kg) cichlid or sunfish fillets (or substitute a freshwater fish: bass, perch, or pan fish)
1½ cups (354 mL) fresh lemon juice
4 jalapeño chiles, stems and seeds removed, minced
1 cup (236 mL) chopped red onion or sweet onion
2 cups (473 mL) peeled, seeded, and chopped tomatoes
1 teaspoon (5 mL) salt
¼ teaspoon (1.25 mL) freshly ground black pepper
½ cup (118 mL) chopped cilantro
3 tablespoons (45 mL) olive oil
2 cloves garlic, peeled and minced
½ cup (118 mL) chopped green olives
3 tablespoons (45 mL) mayonnaise

1. Cut the fish into 1-inch (2.5cm) pieces and place them in a shallow glass baking dish. Pour the lemon juice over the fish and sprinkle it with half the minced jalapeños. Marinate the fish for 1 hour in the refrigerator.
2. Pour the fish and the marinade into a colander and let it drain for a few minutes. Carefully transfer the fish to a glass bowl and set it aside.
3. In a small bowl, mix together the onion, tomatoes, salt, pepper, cilantro, olive oil, garlic, and the remaining jalapeños. Pour this mixture over the fish and mix gently.
4. In a small bowl, mix together the green olives and mayonnaise.
5. Serve the marinated fish on fresh greens with a dollop of the olive-mayonnaise mixture.

Ceviche de Palapa Adriana—Estilo Acapulquito (Acalpulco-Style Ceviche from Palapa Adriana)

Yield: 3–4 servings   Heat Scale: Medium

This recipe comes from Kathy Gallantine, who wrote about her search for the best ceviche. "If you wish to try Acapulquito-Style Ceviche at Palapa Adriana," she wrote, "a restaurant on the Malecón in La Paz, Baja California Sur, you must specially request it. The ceviche listed on the menu is served without the peas, carrots, and serrano chiles. Serve this dish for a light lunch or a light dinner on hot nights when you don't even want to turn on an oven!" (Note: This recipe requires advance preparation.)

1½ pounds (680 g) any white fish fillet, chopped
8 Key limes, juiced
2 serrano chiles, stems and seeds removed, minced
1 tomato, finely chopped
½ onion, finely chopped
¼ cup (59 mL) canned peas
¼ cup (59 mL) finely diced cooked carrots
2 teaspoons (10 mL) minced fresh cilantro
Salt, to taste
Freshly ground black pepper, to taste
8–10 corn tortillas, fried flat and very crisp

1. Place the chopped fish in a shallow container. Pour the lime juice over the fish. Cover and refrigerate for about 2 hours, stirring occasionally, until the fish is opaque.
2. Just before serving, stir in the tomato, onion, peas, carrots, and cilantro. Add the salt and pepper to taste. With a slotted spoon, heap the ceviche onto the crisp tortillas and serve.

Variation
Use tiny cocktail shrimp or sliced bay scallops in place of the white fish. Reduce the marinating time to 30 minutes or less.

Ceviche de Almejas Estilo Baja
(Clam Ceviche from Baja)

Yield: 4–6 servings

Heat Scale: Varies depending on the type and amount of hot sauce used

This recipe also comes from Kathy Gallantine. She collected it from Antonio Seja Torrez, a clam-picker in Baja. Every day at low tide, Antonio crawls through the mangroves and collects 500 pata de mula "clams" that are really mussels. He carries them several miles to the dock at Magdalena Bay, where he sells them for ten pesos apiece. His daily earnings come to about $2 U.S. "About enough to buy a kilo of beans," he says cheerfully. Try this recipe with true clams, but be prepared to pay a much higher price for them! (Note: This recipe requires advance preparation.)

Bottled Mexican hot sauce or a hot sauce from Chapter 2, to taste
24 whole clams, removed from their shells
1 onion, peeled and chopped
1 tomato, chopped
Juice of 6–8 Key limes
Salt, to taste
Freshly ground black pepper, to taste
¼ bunch fresh cilantro (optional)
2 pounds (1.1 kg) crushed ice (optional)

1. In a container with a cover, combine all the ingredients except the cilantro and ice. Refrigerate the ceviche until it's well-chilled. Serve it immediately or let the flavors marry and serve it up to 3 days later.
2. To serve the ceviche Guaymas-style, save the clam shells and scrub them well. Fill 4 to 6 shallow bowls or plates with crushed ice. Nest the half shells into the ice and heap them with the ceviche. Garnish each plate with a sprig of cilantro.

Variation
Use fresh shucked oysters in place of the clams. Omit the tomato and add an 8-ounce (224 g) can of sliced water chestnuts and half a red bell pepper, seeds removed and chopped.

Ostiónes Frescos en Escabeche (Pickled Fresh Oysters)

Yield: 4 servings   Heat Scale: Hot

If you are fond of oysters, you will love this dish from Jalisco—just make sure the oysters are fresh. There are many myths surrounding oysters, including their supposed aphrodisiac qualities. Some oystermen claim that they can tell the gender of oysters and say that females should be fried and males should be stewed! In Spanish, ostra means oyster, and ostión means large oyster. (Note: This recipe requires advance preparation.)

30 fresh oysters, shucked and washed
½ cup (118 mL) white wine
¼ cup (59 mL) fresh lemon juice
½ teaspoon (2.5 mL) salt
1 cup (236 mL) chopped onion
3 cloves garlic, peeled and minced
¼ cup (59 mL) vinegar
¼ teaspoon (1.25 mL) freshly ground black pepper
4 jalapeño chiles, stems and seeds removed, thinly sliced
⅓ cup (79 mL) olive oil
Shredded mixed greens for serving

1. Place the oysters in a medium saucepan. Add the wine, lemon juice, salt, and enough water to just cover. Bring the mixture to a light boil, reduce the heat to a simmer, and cook for 3 minutes. Drain the oysters, transfer them to a ceramic bowl, and set them aside.
2. Bring 2 cups (473 mL) water to a boil. Turn off the heat, add the onion, and let it sit in the hot water for 2 minutes. Drain the onion and add it to the oysters, along with the garlic, vinegar, pepper, chiles, and olive oil. Toss the mixture lightly to distribute the ingredients. Chill for 4 hours and serve on shredded greens with slices of avocado and warm tortillas or toasted garlic bread.

Ceviche de Caracol del Mar (Conch Ceviche)

Yield: 3–4 servings   Heat Scale: Hot

This dish is one where you get to beat the heck out of the conch with a meat tenderizing mallet! If you don't, you'll still be chewing it three years from now. It is tough, but it is also extremely tasty, much like abalone. Serve this dish from Yucatán on chopped mixed greens, and include some grated radish. Garnish with warm corn chips and lime slices. (Note: This recipe requires advance preparation.)

1 pound (454 g) fresh conch, pounded to tenderize and cut into bite-sized pieces
¼ cup (59 mL) fresh lime juice
¾ cup (177 mL) fresh lemon juice
1 habanero chile, stem and seeds removed, minced
1 cup (236 mL) finely chopped onion
¼ cup (59 mL) chopped cilantro
1 cup (236 mL) peeled and chopped tomato
¼ cup (59 mL) olive oil
1 teaspoon (5 mL) salt
¼ teaspoon (1.25 mL) freshly ground black pepper

1. Put the cut-up conch in a shallow, glass pan and cover it with the lime and lemon juices. Marinate in the refrigerator for 5 hours. Drain the conch and transfer it to a mixing bowl.
2. Add the chile, onion, cilantro, tomato, olive oil, salt, and pepper, mix, and serve.

Chiles Rellenos de Jaiba
(Crab-Stuffed Chiles)

Yield: 4 servings   Heat Scale: Medium

The chipotle chiles in this recipe from Sinaloa add a smoky taste to the crab. I recommend the meat from freshly cooked crab legs, but if they are unavailable, good-quality canned crab meat can be substituted.

4 tomatoes, roasted, peeled, and chopped
1 cup (236 mL) chopped onion
½ cup (118 mL) chicken broth
½ cup (118 mL) water
3 chipotle chiles in adobo sauce, diced
½ teaspoon (2.5 mL) salt
¼ teaspoon (1.25 mL) freshly ground black pepper
8 green chiles (poblanos or New Mexican), roasted, peeled, stem and seeds removed
2 cups (473 mL) cooked, shredded crab
½ cup (118 mL) minced onion
1 teaspoon (5 mL) dried Mexican oregano or 2 teaspoons (10 mL) fresh, minced
2 tomatoes, peeled, seeded, and chopped
2–3 tablespoons (30–45 mL) chicken broth
1½ cups (354 mL) corn oil
½ cup (118 mL) all-purpose flour
3 egg whites, stiffly beaten

1. In a small saucepan, combine the tomatoes, 1 cup (236 mL) chopped onion, chicken broth, water, chipotle chiles, salt, and pepper. Bring the mixture to a boil, lower the heat to a simmer, and simmer while you stuff the chiles.
2. In a small bowl, mix together the crab, onion, oregano, and tomatoes. If the mixture seems dry, add the chicken stock 1 tablespoon (15 mL) at a time. Stuff the chiles with this mixture.
3. In a frying pan, heat the oil over high heat. Dredge the stuffed chiles in the flour, dip them into the egg whites, and deep fry them in the oil for 2 minutes per side or until golden brown. Drain them on paper towels. Arrange the rellenos on a warm dinner plate and top them with warm salsa.

Jaiba a la Veracruzana (Veracruz-Style Crab)

Yield: 6–8 servings   Heat Scale: Medium

This is another delicious recipe from beautiful Veracruz. If fresh, whole crabs are not available, cook crab legs, remove the meat, and serve the finished dish in small, ovenproof, shell-shaped, individual serving dishes. This entrée is easy to prepare and makes an elegant presentation.

12 fresh whole crabs, cooked, meat removed and shells reserved (or substitute 3 pounds [1.36 kg] freshly cooked crab legs)
¼ cup (59 mL) olive oil, plus more as needed
1 cup (236 mL) minced onions
3 cloves garlic, peeled and minced
1½ cups (354 mL) peeled, chopped tomatoes
4 serrano chiles, stems and seeds removed, minced
2 tablespoons (30 mL) minced parsley
½ teaspoon (2.5 mL) salt
¼ teaspoon (1.25 mL) freshly ground black pepper
¾ cup (177 mL) coarsely chopped green olives
⅔ cup (158 mL) dry bread crumbs
1 egg, beaten well
Thinly sliced lemons or limes for garnish
Minced parsley for garnish

1. Preheat the oven to 350°F (180°C). Lightly oil the reserved crab shells or ovenproof shell ramekins.
2. Coarsely chop the crab meat and set it aside.
3. In a medium sauté pan, heat the oil over medium heat. Add the onions and garlic and sauté for 1 minute. Add the tomatoes, chiles, parsley, salt, and black pepper and sauté for another minute, stirring and tossing the mixture.
4. Mix in the reserved crab, olives, and bread crumbs. Mound this mixture lightly into the prepared crab shells or ramekins.
5. Pour about 1 teaspoon (5 mL) of the beaten egg and a few drops of olive oil over each portion. Place the shells or ramekins on a baking sheet and bake for 20 minutes or until golden. Garnish with the sliced lemons or limes and the parsley and serve immediately.

Tacos Rellenos de Camarón (Shrimp Tacos)

Yield: 6 servings   Heat Scale: Medium to Hot

Since fresh shrimp is abundant, shrimp tacos are popular with locals and tourists alike on all coasts of Mexico. They are sold as street food and appear on menus at the finest restaurants. Here is a particularly tasty taco treat from Campeche.

5 ancho chiles, stems and seeds removed
2 tomatoes, peeled and seeded
1 onion, peeled and chopped
¼ teaspoon (1.25 mL) salt
Corn oil as needed to fry tortillas
18 tortillas
2 tablespoons (30 mL) olive oil
2 cups (473 mL) finely chopped shrimp
2 tomatoes, crushed
1 onion, peeled and finely chopped
1 habanero chile, stem and seeds removed, minced
1½ cups (354 mL) finely chopped cooked potatoes
½ teaspoon (2.5 mL) salt
Freshly ground black pepper, to taste
2 cups (473 mL) thinly sliced onion, soaked in ½ cup (118 mL) vinegar
5 cups (1.2 L) finely shredded lettuce

1. In a food processor, combine the ancho chiles, tomatoes, onion, and salt to a smooth purée. Set the mixture aside.
2. In a deep skillet, heat the corn oil over high heat. Dip each tortilla in the ancho chile mixture, then fry them for a few seconds on each side and transfer them to paper towels to drain. Place the tortillas on a platter.
2. In a medium skillet, heat the 2 tablespoons (30 mL) olive oil over medium heat. Add the shrimp, tomatoes, onion, chile, and potatoes. Lightly fry the mixture for 2 minutes, until the shrimp is cooked. Add the salt and pepper to taste. Divide this mixture among the tortillas and roll up each tortilla.
3. Drain the onion-vinegar mixture thoroughly and sprinkle it over the tortillas, along with the shredded lettuce.

Camarón en Chile Rojo
(Shrimp in Red Chile)

Yield: 3–4 servings   Heat Scale: Mild

The ancho chiles in this recipe from the México D.F. do not overpower the delicate flavor of the shrimp. Instead, they add just a bit of heat and color. Serve this dish with warm tortillas, a chopped lettuce and tomato salad, and minted fresh fruit for dessert.

6 ancho chiles, stems and seeds removed
2 cloves garlic, peeled
1 medium onion, peeled and coarsely chopped
3 medium tomatoes
2 tablespoons (30 mL) vegetable oil
1 pound (454 g) fresh whole shrimp
½ teaspoon (2.5 mL) salt
¼ teaspoon (1.25 mL) freshly ground black pepper
¼ cup (59 mL) coarsely chopped epazote
2 potatoes, peeled and cut in small cubes

1. In a hot, dry skillet, toast the chiles for 1 minute, tossing constantly so they do not burn. Transfer the chiles to a heat-resistant bowl, add water to cover, and soak for 15 minutes. Drain the chiles and reserve the water.
2. Put the drained chiles in a small blender with the garlic and onion. Purée the ingredients, adding more of the soaking water if necessary. Set this mixture aside.
3. Roast the tomatoes by holding them over a gas flame until they blister or gently rolling them in a small, dry sauté pan over high heat until they start to blister. Remove the skins, crush them between your fingers, and set them aside. In a sauté pan, heat the vegetable oil over medium heat. Add the crumbled tomato skins and the tomatoes and sauté for 30 seconds. Add the reserved chile mixture and sauté for 30 seconds. Remove the pan from the heat and set aside.
4. Wash the shrimp and place them in a small saucepan with water to cover. Add the salt, pepper, and epazote. Bring the water to a boil, reduce the heat to a simmer, and cook for 2 minutes. Remove the shrimp from the water and let them cool slightly. When they are cool to enough to handle, clean them and cut them in half lengthwise. Reserve the cooking water.
5. Cook the potatoes in the shrimp water for 10 minutes, or until they are tender. Drain the potatoes, reserving 1 cup (236 mL) of the water. Add the sliced shrimp and the potatoes to the chile mixture and toss to blend. Heat the mixture and serve.

Camarones Adobados Estilo de Baja
(Adobo Shrimp Baja-Style)

Yield: 4 servings   Heat Scale: Medium

If you can't find mulato chiles, substitute an extra ancho or pasilla chile. Serve this chile shrimp from Baja California with hot, cooked rice and complement the dish with sautéed baby vegetables.

2 dozen large, fresh shrimp
1 mulato chile, stem and seeds removed
1 ancho chile, stem and seeds removed
1 pasilla chile, stem and seeds removed
1 onion, peeled and cut into eighths
2 cloves garlic, peeled
½ teaspoon (2.5 mL) salt
2 teaspoons (10 mL) Mexican oregano
2 tablespoons (30 mL) white wine vinegar
2 tablespoons (30 mL) olive oil

1. Preheat the oven to 350°F (180°C). Lightly oil a small casserole dish.
2. Bring a small pot of water to a boil, rinse the shrimp in cold water, and add the shrimp to the pot. Boil for 3 minutes or until the shrimp turns pink. Drain the shrimp and let them cool. When they are cool enough to handle, peel them and set them aside.
3. In a skillet over low heat, toast the chiles for 1 minute, tossing them and taking care that they don't burn. Remove the pan from the heat and add hot water to cover the chiles. Let them soak for 10 minutes, then drain them.
4. Transfer the chiles and the soaking water to a blender. Add the onion, garlic, salt, oregano, and white wine vinegar and purée until smooth.
5. In a small skillet, heat the oil over medium heat. Pour in the puréed chile mixture and simmer for 5 minutes, adding more water if the mixture gets too thick. Add the shrimp, mix it with the chile sauce, and simmer for 30 seconds.
6. Pour the shrimp mixture into the prepared casserole dish and bake for 5 minutes. Serve the shrimp hot from the oven.

Camarones Adobados Estilo Veracruz
(Adobo Shrimp Veracruz-Style)

Yield: 2–3 servings   Heat Scale: Medium

This Veracruz-style dish calls for sautéing the shrimp rather than boiling it, as in the Baja-style. The chiles and the cider vinegar add the spark to this recipe. Serve with warm tortillas and a shredded lettuce, tomato, and jicama salad with an oil and vinegar dressing.

4 tablespoons (60 mL) corn or canola oil, divided
1 pound (454 g) fresh shrimp, peeled
5 pasilla chiles, stems and seeds removed, roasted
1 onion, peeled and cut into eighths
2 cloves garlic, peeled
1 teaspoon (5 mL) freshly ground black pepper
⅓ cup (79 mL) apple cider vinegar
½ teaspoon (2.5 mL) whole cumin seeds, crushed

1. In a medium skillet, heat 2 tablespoons (30 mL) of the oil over medium heat. Add the shrimp and sauté for 2 minutes. Using a slotted spoon, transfer the shrimp to a small bowl and set aside.
2. Add 1 tablespoon (15 mL) of the oil to the same skillet. Add the onion and garlic and sauté for 1 minute. Remove the pan from the heat and stir in the chiles, black pepper, vinegar, and cumin. Allow the mixture to cool for a few minutes, then transfer it to a blender and purée until smooth.
3. Heat the remaining 1 tablespoon (15 mL) oil in the sauté pan. Add the puréed chile mixture and bring it to a simmer. Cook for 15 minutes, stirring frequently and adding enough water to keep the mixture thick and heavy and to avoid burning.
4. Add the reserved shrimp to the sauce and simmer for 2 minutes or just long enough to heat the mixture and to allow the chile flavor to infuse the shrimp. Serve hot.

Chiles Rellenos de Mariscos
(Seafood-Stuffed Poblano Chiles)

Yield: 3 servings   Heat Scale: Medium-Hot

The state of Quintana Roo has become popular, along with the rest of the Yucatán Peninsula, for its Mayan ruins and its delicious seafood. The use of habanero chiles in this recipe is also very typical of this area.

3 tablespoons (45 mL) corn oil
1 pound (454 g) mixed seafood, cleaned and chopped
2 cloves garlic, peeled and finely chopped
½ teaspoon (2.5 mL) salt
¼ teaspoon (1.25 mL) freshly ground black pepper
½ teaspoon (2.5 mL) Mexican oregano
3 tablespoons (45 mL) finely chopped cilantro
3 tablespoons (45 mL) white sauce, plus more if needed
6 poblano chiles, roasted and peeled, seeds removed
¾ cup (177 mL) all-purpose flour
1 whole egg plus one egg white, beaten
Vegetable oil for frying
2 tablespoons (30 mL) vegetable oil
1 cup (236 mL) chopped onion
1 habanero chile, stems and seeds removed, minced
1 xcatic chile (or substitute yellow wax hot), stem and seeds removed, minced
4 cups (.95 L) peeled, seeded and chopped tomatoes

1. In a skillet, heat the oil over medium heat. Add the seafood and sauté until done, about 5 minutes. Add the garlic, salt, pepper, oregano, and cilantro and simmer until the seafood is cooked. Remove the skillet from the heat and stir in the white sauce to bind the ingredients. Add more white sauce, if necessary.
2. Using a small spoon, stuff the seafood mixture into the chiles. Dredge the chiles in the flour, dip them into the beaten egg mixture, and fry them in the hot oil for 2 minutes on each side. Drain them on paper towels and transfer them to a heated platter.
3. In a medium skillet, heat the 2 tablespoons (30 mL) oil over medium heat. Add the onion, habanero, and xcatic chile and sauté for 1 minute. Add the tomatoes, reduce the heat to low, and cook for 2 minutes.
4. Spoon the sauce over the rellenos and serve.

Barbacoa de Langostinos (Barbecued Langostinos)

Yield: 3–4 servings   Heat Scale: Mild

This is a beautifully spiced way to serve langostinos. Because these large prawns with a lobster flavor are so rich, serve the dish with simple but elegant side dishes, such as a tomato salad with balsamic vinegar dressing and maybe some good pasta. A citrus dessert would be the perfect finish. The authentic touch in this recipe is to serve the langostinos and chile sauce as they do in Veracruz—on banana leaves.

4 ancho chiles, stems and seeds removed
3 pasilla chiles, stems and seeds removed
1 cup (236 mL) boiling water
6 tablespoons (90 mL) corn or canola oil, divided
½ teaspoon (2.5 mL) salt
3 cups (708 mL) peeled, coarsely chopped tomatoes
10 cloves garlic, peeled and minced, divided
1 cup (236 mL) chopped onion
½ teaspoon (2.5 mL) freshly ground black pepper, divided
2 whole cloves, ground, divided
¼ teaspoon (1.25 mL) ground cinnamon
½ teaspoon (2.5 mL) ground cumin
2 tablespoons (30 mL) white wine vinegar
2 pounds (1.1 kg) cleaned langostinos, split lengthwise (or substitute lobster tails)

1. Tear the chile into strips, put them in a bowl, and cover them with the boiling water. Let the chiles soak for 10 minutes. Transfer the chiles and soaking water to a blender, purée, and set aside.
2. In a medium skillet, heat 3 tablespoons (45 mL) of the oil over medium heat. Add the tomatoes, salt, half the garlic, the onion, half the ground black pepper, half the ground cloves, the cinnamon, the cumin, and the puréed chile mixture. Simmer, covered, for 15 minutes. Remove the skillet from the heat and set it aside.
3. In a small bowl, mix together the remaining garlic, cloves, and black pepper, and the vinegar. Set aside.
4. Bring a large pot of water to a boil. Add the langostinos and cook for 8 minutes. Drain the langostinos and plunge them into cold water to cool them quickly. Drain them again. Remove the meat and cut it into cubes. Toss the meat in the garlic-vinegar mixture.
5. In a sauté pan, heat the remaining 3 tablespoons (45 mL) oil over medium heat. Add the langostino mixture and sauté for 30 seconds. Add the reserved chile mixture and bring it to a boil. Quickly reduce the heat to a simmer, cover, and simmer for 5 minutes, or until it is hot. Serve immediately.

Camarones Enchilado
(Shrimp Enchilado)

Yield: 4 servings   Heat Scale: Medium

This recipe is from Rodolfo de Garay and Thomas Brown, who noted: "The word enchilado as used in Cuba refers to chiles, not to the Mexican dish of a rolled and stuffed tortilla. This dish is a sauté of seafood and peppers; lobster is often substituted for shrimp."

¼ cup (59 mL) extra virgin olive oil
¾ cup (177 mL) canola oil
1½ pound (680 g) large fresh shrimp, peeled and deveined (shells reserved)
1 cup (236 mL) chopped cubanelle pepper (or substitute green bell pepper)
1 cup (236 mL) chopped red bell pepper
1 cup (236 mL) chopped yellow bell pepper
1½ cups (354 mL) chopped onion
1 habanero chile, stem and seeds removed, thinly sliced
2 tablespoons (30 mL) minced garlic
½ teaspoon (2.5 mL) dried oregano
2 bay leaves
1 teaspoon (5 mL) salt
1 teaspoon (5 mL) freshly ground black pepper
½ cup (118 mL) tomato purée
½ cup (118 mL) fine dry sherry
4 tablespoons (60 mL) distilled white vinegar
1 cup (236 mL) Spanish olives stuffed with anchovies (optional)

1. In a skillet, heat the olive and canola oils over medium-high heat. Add the shrimp shells and heads (if available) and sauté for about 15 minutes, taking care that they don't burn. They will turn color as they cook. With a wooden spoon, crush them as much as possible as they become crisp. This will extract as much shrimp flavor as possible. The oil mixture will darken into a rich, dark amber. Strain the oil mixture through a fine sieve, pressing the shells to extract as much of the flavored oil as possible.
2. Transfer ¼ cup (59 mL) of the shrimp-flavored oil to a large sauté pan and heat it over medium heat. Add half the cubanelle and bell peppers and the onions and sauté until the onions are translucent. Add the remaining peppers and onions. Add the habanero, garlic, oregano, bay leaves, salt, and pepper and sauté until the onions are soft and the pan is almost dry.
3. Add the tomato purée and the sherry. Increase the heat and cook until the liquid is reduced by half. Add the peeled shrimp and cook just until they turn pink, no more than 3 to 5 minutes. Add the vinegar and, if using, the stuffed olives, and cook for an additional minute to heat through.
4. Serve with white rice and beer and, if desired, fried ripe plantains and shrimp toast (made with the remainder of the shrimp-flavored oil).

Pescado Sobre Uso
(Sofrito for "Reused" Fish)

Yield: 6 servings   Heat Scale: Hot

The name of this Cuban dish may not sound too appetizing, as Rodolpho de Garay and Thomas Brown explain, but it actually refers to the poorer households where lack of refrigeration required that an entire catch of fish be cooked immediately. Later that day or the next, the leftover fish is eaten with a sofrito. This sofrito, of course, can be spooned over fish you've just cooked and is delicious with most kinds of fish.

1 cup (236 mL) olive oil
6 firm white fish fillets
1½ cups (354 mL) sliced onions
½ cup (118 mL) chopped and seeded green bell peppers
5 cloves garlic, peeled and minced
1 teaspoon (5 mL) salt
¼ teaspoon (1.25 mL) freshly ground black pepper
2 habanero chiles or 6 rocotillo chiles, stems and seeds removed, halved
1 tablespoon (15 mL) distilled white vinegar (hot chile vinegar may be used for extra heat)

1. In a skillet, heat the oil over medium-high heat. Add the fillets and fry them until they are done and slightly brown. Remove the fillets from the pan and keep them warm. Strain the olive oil.
2. In a sauté pan, heat the reused oil over medium heat. Add the onions and sauté until they begin to wilt. Add the bell pepper, garlic, salt, and pepper and cook for about 2 minutes. Add the chiles and cook for 2 minutes. Stir in the vinegar and remove the pan from the heat.
3. With a slotted spoon, ladle the sofrito over the fillets.

Flash-in-the-Pan Snapper

Yield: 4 servings   Heat Scale: Hot

The Bahamas is the home of this quick-fried dish. An interesting ingredient in the recipe is lime salt, which is simply minced bird peppers or piquins mixed with salt, sprinkled with lime juice, and set out to dry. (Note: This recipe requires advance preparation.)

2 whole small red snappers, cleaned, scaled, heads and tails left on
1 teaspoon (5 mL) crushed black peppercorns
Juice of 1 lime
Juice of 1 lemon
2 teaspoons (10 mL) minced fresh goat peppers (or substitute habaneros)
Lime salt, to taste
½ cup (118 mL) vegetable oil
1 cup (236 mL) water
2 teaspoons (10 mL) minced fresh serrano chiles
1 small white onion, peeled and minced
2 teaspoons (10 mL) ground allspice

1. Score the skin of the snappers in a checkerboard shape and put them in a shallow dish. Sprinkle them with the lime and lemon juice, crushed black peppercorns, and goat peppers. Marinate the fish overnight. Remove the fish from the marinade and rub it with the lime salt.

2. In a deep skillet, heat the oil over high heat. Add the fish and fry it until the skin turns brown, about 5 minutes per side. Turn the fish only once while frying.

3. Remove the fish from the pan and keep it warm. Reserve the pan juices. Add the water, serranos, onion, and allspice, and boil the mixture until it's thick. Serve the gravy over the fish.

Kingfish for a Day

Yield: 4 servings   Heat Scale: Hot

This fish dish is another Bahamian treat. I had a wonderful lunch of fresh mangos, kingfish, and Red Stripe beer on one of the beautiful beaches of that country of many islands. Try this as a lazy-day luncheon or dinner. And don't forget the beer!

1 goat pepper, seeds and stem removed, minced (or substitute 1 habanero)
1 cup (236 mL) all-purpose flour
2 eggs, beaten
½ cup (118 mL) milk
4 chives, minced
½ teaspoon (2.5 mL) dried thyme
3 cloves garlic, peeled and minced
1 pound (454 g) kingfish fillets, boiled and flaked
Vegetable oil for frying

1. In a mixing bowl, mix together the minced goat pepper, flour, eggs, milk, chives, thyme, garlic, and minced fish. Form this batter into fingers.

2. In a frying pan, heat the oil over medium-high heat. Add the fingers and fry them until golden brown, about 10 minutes.

Trinidadian Wood-Grilled Shark Steaks

Yield: 4 servings   Heat Scale: Medium

Here is a tasty option for cooking shark—or, for that matter, any firm fish that is big enough to have steaks cut from it, such as swordfish. I prefer to grill over hardwood rather than charcoal briquets, and two of the best woods to use are pecan and hickory. Mesquite can be substituted, but it imparts a strong flavor to the fish. I collected this recipe in Trinidad, where a dish called Shark and Bake is a specialty. Serve with conch chowder, curried cauliflower, potatoes, peas, and a fruit chutney. (Note: This recipe requires advance preparation.)

4 shark steaks
1 cup (236 mL) freshly squeezed lime juice
½ teaspoon (2.5 mL) crushed black pepper
⅛ cup (30 mL) sherry
1 habanero chile, stem and seeds removed, minced
¼ cup (59 mL) olive oil
1 teaspoon (5 mL) salt

1. In a nonreactive bowl, combine the shark steaks, lime juice, black pepper, sherry, and habanero. Marinate for 2 hours in the refrigerator.
2. Remove the steaks from the marinade and pat them dry. Combine the olive oil and salt and spread this mixture over the steaks. Place the steaks in a hinged wire basket (for easy turning) and grill them over hot hardwood coals, taking care that the dripping olive oil does not cause flames to burn the steak. Grill for about 15 minutes, depending on the thickness of the steaks, or until the fish flakes easily.

Coconut–Hot Sauce Shrimp

Yield: 4 servings   Heat Scale: Varies, but make it hot

Photographer Chel Beeson collected this easy recipe while he was in the Bahamas. You can serve it with the commercial hot sauces of your choice. Better yet, have each guest bring a different hot sauce to share!

2 cups (473 mL) all-purpose flour
4 eggs, beaten
1 cup (236 mL) coconut milk
2 pounds (1.1 kg) jumbo shrimp, shelled and deveined
2 cups (473 mL) flaked coconut
Vegetable oil for frying
Commercial habanero hot sauce or a hot sauce from Chapter 2 for serving

1. In a bowl, combine the flour, eggs, and milk to form a batter. Dip the shrimp in the batter, then roll them in the coconut flakes. In a skillet, fry the shrimp in the vegetable oil until they are brown, about 5 minutes. Serve with a hot sauce (preferably habanero) of your choice.

Bahamian Curried Conch

Yield: 4 servings   Heat Scale: Medium-Hot

Conch has been described as the escargot of the West Indies. It has been a mainstay of the Bahamian diet, as well as the economy, for many years. Conch just needs to be pounded forever to make it tender. Prepare a conch dinner to release all of your pent-up frustrations!

2–3 tablespoons (30–45 mL) butter
3 stalks celery, chopped
2 large onions, peeled and chopped
1 clove garlic, peeled and minced
4 tablespoons (60 mL) curry paste of your choice from Chapter 1
1 teaspoon (5 mL) ground allspice
1 goat pepper (or habanero), stem and seeds removed, minced
3 bay leaves
2 pinches dried thyme
1 pound (454 g) conch meat, pounded until tender, minced

1. In a medium frying pan, melt the butter over medium heat. Add the celery, onions, and garlic and sauté until soft. Add the curry paste and allspice and sauté another 3 minutes. Add the remaining ingredients and water to barely cover them and cook, uncovered, for about 15 minutes over low heat. Serve over white rice.

French Caribbean Crabs

Yield: 6 to 8 servings   Heat Scale: Medium

This delectable crab dish is served on the island of Martinique. Since it offers wonderful French flavors, I suggest you complement your meal with a nice bottle of Sauvignon blanc and a loaf of French bread. If you can't find land crabs, sea crabs will do nicely. Bon appétit!

10 land crabs
⅓ cup (79 mL) olive oil
1 Scotch bonnet chile, seeds and stem removed, minced (or substitute 1 habanero)
2 cloves garlic, peeled and finely chopped
1 red onion, peeled and finely chopped
½ teaspoon (2.5 mL) dried thyme
1 sprig parsley, chopped
½ cup (118 mL) boiling water
1 bay leaf
Juice of 1 lime
Salt, to taste
Freshly ground black pepper, to taste
6 cups (1.4 L) cooked white rice
2 chives, chopped

1. Bring a large pot of water to a boil. Brush the crabs, add them to the boiling water, and boil them for 10 minutes. Remove and clean the crabs, reserving the meat. Cut the crab meat into small pieces. Break off the claws and remove as much of the meat as possible. In a skillet, heat the oil until very hot. Add the crab pieces, chile, garlic, onion, thyme, and parsley and sauté until the crab is browned. Add the boiling water, bay leaf, lime juice, salt, and pepper.

2. Simmer the mixture for 10 minutes. Mix the crab and the sauce with cooked white rice and garnish it with the chopped chives.

Blue Crab Backs

Yield: 4 servings   Heat Scale: Medium

This entrée is known by many names, but one of the most popular renditions of the dish comes from Trinidad, where it is called Crab Backs. In the West Indies, Crab Backs are made with the small blue-backed land crabs that live in the swamps and sugar cane fields. However, if you can't get to a sugar cane field right away, blue crabs from the market will work just fine.

4 cooked blue crabs, about ¾ pounds (336 g) each, split open
2 tablespoons (30 mL) butter
1 onion, peeled and minced
3 green onions, trimmed and minced
1 habanero chile, stem and seeds removed, minced
2 tablespoons (30 mL) minced fresh chives
2 teaspoons (10 mL) Worcestershire sauce
1 tablespoon (15 mL) fresh pineapple juice
2 tablespoons (30 mL) rum
1 pinch grated nutmeg
1 teaspoon (5 mL) salt
Freshly ground black pepper, to taste
2 cups (473 mL) soft white bread crumbs, divided

1. Preheat the oven to 350°F (180°C).

2. Clean the crabs, removing and discarding the stomach, digestive tract, and gills ("dead man's fingers"). Pick out all the crab meat from the shell, discarding any skin or cartilage. Reserve the shells. Crack open the claws and remove as much meat as you can. Combine all the meat together in a large mixing bowl.

3. In a skillet, melt the butter over medium heat. Add the onion and green onions and sauté, stirring constantly, for 5 minutes, until soft and golden.

4. Remove the pan from the heat and stir the onion and green onions into the crab meat. Add the habanero, chives, Worcestershire, pineapple juice, rum, nutmeg, salt, and pepper. Stir in 1¾ cups (413 mL) of the bread crumbs and mix thoroughly.

5. Spoon the filling into the reserved shells and place the shells on a baking sheet. Cook in the center of the oven for 15 minutes.

6. Remove the crabs from the oven and sprinkle them with the remaining bread crumbs. Return to the oven and bake for 15 to 20 minutes, until the crumbs are a golden brown. Serve hot.

Resurrection Crab Supper

Yield: 6 servings   Heat Scale: Hot

Surprise your family this year and substitute the traditional ham or lamb with this traditional Easter feast from "down de islands." Team it with the Hearts of Palm Jerk Salad (page 211) to make a memorable party.

1 cup (236 mL) cooked crab meat
Juice of ½ lime
1 tablespoon (15 mL) pineapple juice
2 tablespoons (30 mL) butter
1 small onion, peeled and minced
2 green onions, finely chopped
2 habanero chiles, stems and seeds removed, minced
6 cloves garlic, peeled and crushed
2 sprigs thyme, finely chopped
2 sprigs parsley, finely chopped
2 medium tomatoes, quartered
3 cups (708 mL) uncooked rice, rinsed until the water runs almost clear
4 cups (.95 L) water
1 teaspoon (5 mL) grated nutmeg
2 bay leaves
Salt, to taste
Freshly ground black pepper, to taste

1. Put the crab meat in a bowl and sprinkle it with the lime and pineapple juices.
2. In a saucepan, melt the butter over medium-high heat. Add the onions, green onions, habaneros, garlic, thyme, parsley, and crab meat, and sauté for 4 minutes.
3. Add the tomatoes, rice, water, nutmeg, bay leaves, salt, and pepper. Bring to a boil, lower the heat, and cook, covered, until the rice is tender and has absorbed all the liquid, about 25 minutes. Serve hot.

Black River Swimp

Yield: 4–6 servings   Heat Scale: Hot

Michael Baim collected this recipe for me while he was traveling in Jamaica. "Swimp are fresh water crayfish," he wrote, "cooked in a fiery concoction that would have blistered our lips if it weren't for the fact that they were in bite-sized portions." Baim re-created the recipe from the prepared swimp he bought from roadside vendors in plastic baggies. This is a peel-and-eat delight!

2 Scotch bonnet chiles, stems and seeds removed, coarsely chopped (or substitute habaneros)
2 cloves garlic, peeled and crushed
3 green onions, coarsely chopped
⅛ teaspoon (.6 mL) ground thyme
10 black peppercorns
½ teaspoon (2.5 mL) salt
2 quarts (1.9 L) water
2 pounds (1.1 kg) unshelled shrimp or freshwater crayfish

1. In a large pot, combine the chiles, garlic, green onions, thyme, peppercorns, salt, and water and bring to a boil. Boil for 5 minutes. Add the shrimp or crayfish and cook until they just turn pink, about 3 to 5 minutes. Rinse under cold water to stop the cooking.

Spiny Lobster in Sizzling Sauce

Yield: 2 servings   Heat Scale: Medium

One could definitely taste the night away with this incredible dish. This recipe does take a little extra effort, but it's worth it. I suggest using the spiny lobster found in Caribbean waters, the ones also known as langosta in the Spanish Caribbean. They are available in U.S. fish markets.

2 (1½–2 pound [681 g–1.1 kg]) lobsters, uncooked and split in half lengthwise
2½ tablespoons (37.5 mL) vegetable oil mixed with 1 teaspoon (5 mL) liquid annatto
½ cup (118 mL) dry white wine
1¾ cups (413 ml) Sofrito (page 63)
2 tablespoons (30 mL) finely chopped habanero chiles
1 teaspoon (5 mL) salt
1 teaspoon (5 mL) minced fresh basil
Lemon slices for garnish
Lime slices for garnish

1. Remove and discard the gelatinous sac in the head of each lobster and the long intestinal vein attached to it. Cut off the tail section of each lobster directly at the point where it joins the body. Twist off the claws (if any) and cut the flat underside of each large claw with a sturdy, sharp knife. Cut off and discard the small claws and the antennae.

2. In a large, heavy frying pan, heat the oil over a high heat until a light haze forms above it. Add the lobster bodies, tails, and large claws and, turning constantly, fry them for 3 to 4 minutes, until the shells begin to turn pink. Transfer the lobsters to a large platter.
3. Pour off all but a thin layer of oil from the pan. Add the wine and bring it to a boil over high heat. Stir in the Sofrito, chiles, salt, and basil. Add the lobsters and any juices that have collected around them to the wine mixture. Turn the pieces over in the sauce to coat them evenly, then reduce the heat to medium. Cover the pan tightly and cook the lobsters for 8 to 10 minutes, basting them from time to time with the sauce.
4. To serve, place the lobsters on a large platter, garnished with lemon and lime slices. Offer the sauce on the side.

Escoveitched Fish

Yield: 4 servings   Heat Scale: Hot

This recipe is definitely in a pickle! This tasty preservation technique was brought to the Caribbean by the Spanish. While this method is popular on most of the islands, this dish is one of the highlights of visiting Old Harbor and Port Royal in Jamaica, where the "fish ladies" compete for business.

1 Scotch bonnet chile, seeds and stem removed, minced (or substitute 1 habanero)
3 green bell peppers, seeded and sliced
2 medium onions, peeled and thinly sliced
3 carrots, peeled and thinly sliced
1 bay leaf
1 (½-inch [1 cm]) slice fresh ginger, finely chopped
6 black peppercorns
Salt, to taste
2 cups (473 mL) water
5 tablespoons (75 mL) olive oil, divided
6 tablespoons (90 mL) vinegar
2 pounds (1.1 kg) kingfish, skinned and filleted (or substitute snapper)
Stuffed olives for garnish

1. In a medium saucepan, combine the chile, bell peppers, onions, carrots, bay leaf, ginger, peppercorns, salt, and water. Cover the pan and simmer for about 30 minutes.
2. Add 2 tablespoons (30 mL) of the olive oil and the vinegar and simmer for a minute or two longer. Turn off the heat and set the pan aside.
3. In a large, heavy frying pan, heat the remaining olive oil over medium-high heat. Add the fish fillets and sauté until they are lightly browned on both sides; be careful not to overcook. Drain the fish and arrange it in a warmed shallow serving dish. Pour the hot sauce over the fish and serve warm, garnished with stuffed olives.

Chinese-Style Swordfish with Crispy Slaw and Soy Vinaigrette

Yield: 4 servings   Heat Scale: Medium

This recipe celebrates the Asian influences that abound in Caribbean cooking. The Chinese were introduced to the islands through the practice of indentured servitude after slavery was abolished. Happily, the only practices that survived that era are the wonderful culinary contributions of all cultures. (Note: This recipe requires advance preparation.)

¼ cup (59 mL) low-sodium soy sauce
2 tablespoons (30 mL) vegetable oil
2 tablespoons (30 mL) rice vinegar
2 tablespoons (30 mL) sweet rice cooking wine
4 teaspoons (20 mL) fresh lime juice
4 teaspoons (20 mL) fresh lemon juice
1 tablespoon (15 mL) sugar
2 teaspoons (10 mL) grated fresh ginger
2 teaspoons (10 mL) sesame oil
2 cloves garlic, peeled and minced
1 cup (236 mL) finely shredded cabbage
½ cup (118 mL) julienned snow peas
½ cup (118 mL) julienned carrots
4 (2-inch [5 cm]) thick swordfish, tuna, or halibut steaks (6 ounces [168 g] each)
2 teaspoons (10 mL) coarsely ground black pepper
1 habanero chile, stem and seeds removed, minced
3 tablespoons (45 mL) peanut oil
2 tablespoons (30 mL) chopped fresh ginger
2 wonton wrappers, cut into thin strips
Tomato wedges for garnish
Bean sprouts for garnish

1. In a small bowl, combine the soy sauce, vegetable oil, rice vinegar, rice wine, lime juice, lemon juice, sugar, grated ginger, sesame oil, and garlic. (This vinaigrette can be prepared up to 2 days ahead.)
2. In a separate small bowl, combine the shredded cabbage, snow peas, and carrots. Cover and refrigerate.
3. Sprinkle both sides of the fish with the pepper and habanero, cover, and refrigerate for 1 to 4 hours.
4. In a heavy skillet, heat the peanut oil over medium-high heat. Add the ginger and fry until it is a golden brown, about 30 seconds. Remove the ginger and set it aside.
5. Add the fish to the skillet and fry it until it is brown and cooked through, about 3 minutes per side. Transfer the fish to a plate. Add half of the vinaigrette to the refrigerated vegetables. Toss well. Divide the slaw among the plates. Sprinkle the chopped ginger and the wonton strips over the slaw. Spoon the remaining vinaigrette over the fish. Garnish with the tomato wedges and sprouts.

Pucker Up and Snap

Yield: 2 servings   Heat Scale: Medium

This tangy, marinated dish from Curaçao marries the land and the sea with its per-fect use of citrus and the plentiful and mild red snapper. Snapper is given great culi-nary respect on the island, where it is served everywhere—from the fanciest resorts to the humblest homes. (Note: This recipe requires advance preparation.)

2½ cups (591 mL) water, divided
¼ cup (59 mL) grapefruit juice, divided
2½ teaspoons (12.5 mL) salt, divided
2 (1-pound [454 g]) red snappers, cleaned, heads and tails left on
½ cup (118 mL) finely chopped onions
3 cloves garlic, peeled and finely chopped
1 teaspoon (5 mL) minced habanero chile
4 parsley sprigs
½ teaspoon (2.5 mL) dried thyme
Sliced mangos for garnish
Sliced papaya for garnish

1. In a large, shallow baking dish, combine 1½ cups (354 mL) of the water, all but 1 tablespoon (15 mL) of the grapefruit juice, and 1 teaspoon (5 mL) of the salt and stir until the salt dissolves completely.
2. Wash the fish under cold running water and add them to the juice mix-ture. The liquid should cover the fish completely; add more water if neces-sary. Let the fish marinate for about 1½ hours in the refrigerator. Drain the fish and discard the marinade.
3. Pour the remaining 1 cup (236 mL) water into a heavy, medium-sized frying pan. Add the onions, garlic, habaneros, parsley, and thyme. Bring the mixture to a boil over high heat, then reduce the heat to low, cover tightly, and simmer for 5 minutes.
4. Add the fish to the pan and return it to a boil. Reduce the heat to the lowest possible setting, cover, and simmer for 8 to 10 minutes, turning once or twice.
5. Using a slotted spoon, transfer the fish to a deep, heated dish. Add the remaining 1 tablespoon (15 mL) grapefruit juice and the remaining 1½ teaspoons (7.5 mL) salt to the cooking liquid and taste for seasoning. Pour the broth over the fish and serve at once. Garnish with sliced mangos and papayas.

"Poisson" Catch of the Day

Yield: 4 servings   Heat Scale: Medium-Hot

I promise there is not any poison in this dish! Poisson is the French word for fish, and this fish dish from Martinique and Guadeloupe delivers quite a punch. Bring a fire extinguisher (or at least a dairy product or two) to this meal to put out the delicious flames. (Note: This recipe requires advance preparation.)

1 medium onion, peeled and sliced
2 cloves garlic, peeled and crushed
¼ teaspoon (1.25 mL) plus ⅛ teaspoons (.6 mL) ground allspice, divided
2 habanero chiles, stems and seeds removed, crushed
Juice of 2 limes
¼ cup (59 mL) plus 2 tablespoons (30 mL) water, divided
Salt, to taste
Freshly ground black pepper, to taste
1½–2 pounds (681 g–1.1 kg) monk fish fillets (or substitute another firm, white fish)
2 tablespoons (30 mL) distilled white vinegar
½ teaspoon (2.5 mL) dried thyme
1 teaspoon (5 mL) minced habanero chile
Starfruit for garnish
Parsley sprigs for garnish

1. In a bowl, combine the onion, garlic, ¼ teaspoon (1.25 mL) of the allspice, the crushed habanero, the lime juice, 2 tablespoons (30 mL) of the water, the salt, and the pepper. Add the fish and coat it with the marinade. Cover and refrigerate the fish for 1 to 2 hours.
2. Prepare the barbecue or preheat the broiler or grill. Remove the fish from the marinade, allow it stand at room temperature for 10 minutes, and broil it at a moderate heat until golden brown and cooked on both sides, about 10 minutes.
3. While the fish grills, combine the vinegar, the remaining ¼ cup (59 mL) water, the remaining ⅛ teaspoon (.6 mL) allspice, the thyme, the mince habanero, and salt to taste in a small nonreactive saucepan and simmer over low heat for 1 minute. Pour the basting sauce over the fish just before serving. Garnish the platter with the starfruit and parsley sprigs.

Hot Prawns with Curry Cream Sauce

Yield: 4 servings   Heat Scale: Medium

Prawns, also known as the Caribbean lobsterette, are considered quite a delicacy. This recipe is a seafood lover's delight created on the island of Anguilla, where cooks have mixed a bit of habanero, fresh herbs, and tropical fruits to make a most succulent entrée.

3 tablespoons (45 mL) olive oil
2 shallots, peeled and chopped
2 cloves garlic, peeled and chopped
2 Scotch bonnet chiles, stems and seeds removed, minced (or substitute habaneros)
½ teaspoon (2.5 mL) West Indian Masala (page 5)
1 pinch ground turmeric
1 pinch saffron threads
½ cup (118 mL) dry white wine
1 tablespoon (15 mL) fresh lemon juice
2 pounds (1.1 kg) medium uncooked prawns, peeled and deveined (or substitute jumbo shrimp)
½ cup (118 mL) half-and-half
1 ripe mango, peeled, pitted, and chopped fine
4 cups (.95 L) cooked rice
Minced fresh dill for garnish

1. In a large, heavy skillet, heat the oil over medium heat. Add the shallots, garlic, chiles, masala, turmeric, and saffron and sauté for 2 minutes. Add the wine, lemon juice, and prawns. Simmer until the prawns are just cooked through, about 4 minutes. Using a slotted spoon, transfer the seafood to large bowl, and cover with foil to keep warm.
2. Transfer the sauce to a skillet and bring it to a boil. Cook the sauce until it is reduced to ¼ cup (59 mL), about 3 minutes. Add the half-and-half and simmer until the mixture has thickened to a sauce consistency, about 5 minutes, stirring occasionally. Do not allow the mixture to boil. Turn off the heat, add the mango, and stir well.
3. Scoop the cooked rice onto 4 warmed plates, divide the shellfish among the plates, and pour the sauce over the rice and prawns. Garnish with the dill.

Drunken Seafood, Creole-Style

Yield: 4 servings   Heat Scale: Medium

Red Stripe beer is the magical ingredient in this ship-shape dish from Antigua. Make sure you buy extra beer for the cook; that way, you may be served the largest part of the lobster during dinner!

2 tablespoons (30 mL) butter
1 clove garlic, peeled and minced
¼ cup (59 mL) chopped onion
¼ cup (59 mL) diced green bell pepper
1 habanero chile, stem and seeds removed, minced
1 cup (236 mL) uncooked rice
2 cups (473 mL) Red Stripe beer
½ pound (224 g) raw medium shrimp, shelled and deveined
2 (1-pound [454 g]) lobster tails, shelled, meat chopped
3 tablespoons (45 mL) tomato paste
½ cup (118 mL) diced celery
1 beef boullion cube
½ pound (224 g) freshly cooked crab meat, drained and picked over for pieces of shell (or substitute canned crab meat)

1. In a medium frying pan, melt the butter over medium heat. Add the garlic, onion, bell pepper, and habanero and sauté until softened. Add the rice, beer, shrimp, lobster, tomato paste, celery, and boullion. Bring the mixture to a boil, stirring occasionally. Cover the pan and cook over medium heat until the rice is done, about 15 minutes.
2. Stir in the crab meat, heat for a minute or two, and serve on a heated platter.

Bridgetown Flying Fish

Yield: 6 servings   Heat Scale: Varies

This is a famous dish in Barbados that is served with a hot chile oil from Chapter 1, but be careful not to use too much, or you may end up drowning your overheated mouth in a Mount Gay punch, made with the famous Bajan rum. Try saying "fried flying fish" three times in a row after you've had some of that punch. It can't be done. (Note: This recipe requires advance preparation.)

6 small, boned flying fish fillets (or substitute another small white fish)
1 tablespoon (15 mL) lime juice
1 garlic clove, peeled and crushed
¼ teaspoon (1.25 mL) salt
¾ teaspoon (3.75 mL) freshly ground black pepper, divided
1 teaspoon (5 mL) chopped fresh thyme
2 whole cloves
2 teaspoons (10 mL) all-purpose flour
Vegetable oil for frying

1. In a shallow glass baking dish, marinate the fish in the lime juice, garlic, salt, ¼ teaspoon (1.25 mL) of the black pepper, the thyme, and the cloves for at least 1 hour in the refrigerator.

2. Remove the fillets from the marinade and dry them well with paper towels.

3. In a separate bowl, mix the flour with the remaining ½ teaspoon (2.5 mL) freshly ground black pepper and dredge the fish this mixture, shaking off any excess.

4. In a large frying pan, heat enough oil to cover the fish over medium-high heat. Fry the fish until it is golden brown, then serve immediately. This dish can be served with hot rice, chile oil, and lots of rum punch.

Rum-Cured Hawaiian Salmon with Thai Pepper Mint-Mango Chutney

Yield: 4 servings   Heat Scale: Medium-Hot

Before smoking, some fish are treated with a liquid cure, a mixture of various ingredients that helps in the preservation process. This cure is both sweet and hot. Fresh Thai chiles are available in Asian markets. Serve this dish on a bed of white rice with the chutney on the side, along with grilled pineapple and mango slices. (Note: This recipe requires advance preparation.)

¼ cup (59 mL) dark rum
1 tablespoon (15 mL) brown sugar
1 teaspoon (5 mL) vegetable oil
2 teaspoons (10 mL) chopped fresh mint
2 teaspoons (10 mL) chopped fresh ginger
½ teaspoon (2.5 mL) ground habanero chile
4 salmon steaks
2½ cups (591 mL) diced mango
1 small red bell pepper, stem and seeds removed, diced
½ cup (118 mL) thinly sliced red onion
¼ cup (59 mL) golden raisins
4 Thai chiles (prik kee nu), stems removed, chopped (or substitute 2 serrano chiles)
1 cup (236 mL) dry white wine
¼ cup (59 mL) red wine vinegar
2 teaspoons (10 mL) honey
6 whole black peppercorns
2 tablespoons (30 mL) coarsely chopped fresh mint

1. In a bowl, combine the rum, sugar, oil, mint, ginger, and chile. Allow this mixture to sit for 30 minutes to blend the flavors. Place the steaks in a shallow glass dish and brush both sides of them with the cure. Cover and marinate for 4 hours in the refrigerator.

2. To make the chutney, combine the mango, red bell pepper, red onion, raisins, Thai chiles, wine, vinegar, honey, and peppercorns in a saucepan and bring to a boil. Reduce the heat and simmer until the fruits and vegetables are soft, about 10 minutes. Remove the mango, bell pepper, onion, and chiles and simmer the sauce until the liquid is reduced to a syrup. Return the fruit and vegetables and simmer for an additional 5 minutes. Allow the chutney to cool and add the mint.

3. Place the salmon steaks in a grill basket with handles. Grill the salmon over a medium fire until it flakes, about 15 minutes, turning occasionally. Serve the salmon with the chutney on the side.

Drunken Gulf Coast Shrimp Sautéed with Jalapeños

Yield: 6 servings   Heat Scale: Hot

Serve this tasty shrimp entrée over white rice accompanied by a green vegetable and a cold beer.

2 tablespoons (30 mL) olive oil
6 red jalapeño chiles, stems and seeds removed, minced
1 small onion, peeled and chopped fine
1 clove garlic, peeled and minced
2 small tomatoes, peeled and chopped
⅓ cup (79 mL) tequila
1 teaspoon (5 mL) minced fresh basil
1 tablespoon (15 mL) minced fresh cilantro
36 large Gulf Coast shrimp, peeled and deveined
All-purpose flour for dredging
3 tablespoons (45 mL) vegetable oil, or more if needed
2 teaspoons (10 mL) cornstarch mixed with ¼ cup (59 mL) water

1. In a skillet, heat the olive oil over medium heat. Add the chiles, onion, and garlic and sauté until soft. Add the tomatoes, tequila, basil, and cilantro and simmer for 30 minutes, covered, to make a sauce.

2. Dredge the shrimp in the flour and shake off any excess. In a separate skillet, heat the vegetable oil over medium heat. Add the shrimp and sauté until golden brown. Remove the shrimp from the heat and keep them warm.

3. Stir the cornstarch mixture into the sauce and heat until it becomes slightly thickened. Simmer for 5 minutes. Add the shrimp and cook for another couple of minutes or until the shrimp is hot.

Blue Corn Pan-Fried Trout Stuffed with Arbol Chiles

Yield: 2   Heat Scale: Medium

This recipe combines a couple of ingredients common to northern New Mexico: blue corn and fresh trout. Using the blue cornmeal in place of yellow imparts a nutty flavor to the fish.

2 small whole trout, split open and cleaned
8 chiles de arbol, stems and seeds removed, crushed (or substitute other small, dried red chiles)
1 small onion, peeled, thinly sliced, and separated into rings
1 lemon, sliced in thin rings
2 sprigs fresh dill (or substitute 1 teaspoon [5 mL] dried dill weed)
Blue cornmeal for dredging
Vegetable oil for frying

1. Stuff the fish with the chiles, onion rings, lemon slices, and dill. Roll the fish in the cornmeal and pan fry in the oil until browned and done, turning once.

Mesquite-Grilled Snapper with Ancho Sauce

Yield: 4 servings   Heat Scale: Mild

The fish absorbs the mesquite wood smoke as it grills, which gives it a distinctly Southwestern flavor. Take care not to overcook—or burn—the fish.

1 tablespoon (15 mL) vegetable oil
2 ancho chiles, stems and seeds removed, chopped
1 small onion, peeled and chopped
2 small tomatoes, peeled and chopped
¼ cup (59 mL) raisins
2 cups (473 mL) Classic Chicken Stock (page 46)
4 snapper fillets
Olive oil as needed

1. Soak in water enough mesquite chips for grilling.
2. In a sauté pan, heat the vegetable oil over medium heat. Add the chile and onion and sauté them until soft. Add the tomatoes, raisins, and chicken stock and simmer for an additional 10 minutes. Transfer the mixture to a blender and purée until smooth. Keep the sauce warm.
3. Prepare a fire of mesquite wood, or a charcoal fire with the soaked mesquite chips added. When the coals have burned down to a medium heat, rub the fillets with olive oil and grill them for 4 or 5 minutes per side, turning once. (Turning more often could cause the fillets to fall apart.)
4. Place the fish on individual plates, pour the sauce over the top, and serve.

Camarones al Mojo de Ajo
(Garlic Shrimp)

Yield: 4 servings   Heat Scale: Medium

This garlic shrimp dish hails from Guerrero, Mexico, but it is commonly served in Mexican seafood restaurants in the Southwest. The shrimp are messy to peel and eat, but they are delicious. (Note: This recipe requires advance preparation.)

1 tablespoon (15 mL) ground red New Mexican chile
10 cloves garlic, peeled and minced
Salt, to taste
Freshly ground black pepper, to taste
1 teaspoon (5 mL) distilled white vinegar
24 large shrimp, unpeeled
2 tablespoons (30 mL) olive oil
4 tablespoons (60 mL) butter
2 tablespoons (30 mL) lime juice

1. In a molcaljete or mortar, crush together the chile, garlic, salt, pepper, and vinegar. Marinate the shrimp in this mixture for 1 hour.
2. In a skillet, heat the oil and butter over medium heat. Add the garlic marinade and sauté for 3 minutes. Add the shrimp and sauté another 3 minutes, turning often. Sprinkle the shrimp with the lime juice and serve.

Gorditos con Langostos
(Lobster "Tamales")

Yield: 6 servings   Heat Scale: Medium

These "little fat ones" are served along the Texas-Mexico border, where they are traditionally filled with beans or shredded meat. This recipe features seafood—either lobster or crab—stuffed in a corn masa pastry.

1 cup (236 mL) masa harina
2 cups (473 mL) all-purpose flour
1½ teaspoons (7.5 mL) baking powder
½ teaspoon (2.5 mL) salt
1⅓ cup (315 mL) warm water
Vegetable oil for frying
2 tablespoons (30 mL) butter
3 green New Mexican chiles, roasted, peeled, stems and seeds removed, chopped
¼ cup (59 mL) chopped bell peppers
1 small onion, peeled and chopped
2 tomatoes, peeled and chopped
½ pound (224 g) lobster meat or lump crab meat

1. In a bowl, combine the masa, flour, baking powder, and salt. Add the water slowly and knead to form a stiff dough. Cover the dough with plastic wrap and allow it to sit for 15 minutes.

2. Divide the dough into 6 portions and roll each portion into a ball. Roll out each ball to a circle about ¼-inch (.5 cm) thick. In a frying pan, heat the oil to 350°F (180°C). Add the gorditos and fry them until they are puffed and browned. Transfer them to paper towels to drain; they will be hollow inside.

3. In a skillet, melt the butter over medium heat. Add the chiles, bell peppers, and onion and sauté until softened. Add the tomatoes and simmer for 10 minutes. Stir in the lobster meat and cook until heated. The mixture should be thick.

4. To serve, cut off the end of each gordito, stuff them with the lobster mixture, and keep them warm in the oven. These gorditos are eaten like sandwiches.

Seafood Flautas

Yield: 12 "flutes"   Heat Scale: Medium

Here's a quick and tasty supper dish that works just as easily as an appetizer. For a heartier flauta, use tuna or salmon. Flauta means "flute," so these should be fairly thin.

2 tablespoons (30 mL) olive oil
1 pound (454 g) firm white fish, such as snapper or halibut
1 onion, peeled and chopped
2 cloves garlic, peeled and minced
3 jalapeños en escabeche, stems removed, chopped
1 small tomato, peeled, seeded, and chopped
1 teaspoon (5 mL) dried oregano
¼ teaspoon (1.25 mL) ground cinnamon
12 corn tortillas
1 cup (236 mL) grated asadaro cheese
Vegetable oil for frying

1. In a skillet, heat the olive oil over medium heat. Add the fish and sauté until done. Remove it from the pan and, using two forks, flake the fish.

2. Add the onion and garlic to the skillet and sauté until soft. Add the jalapeños, tomato, oregano, and cinnamon and simmer until the liquid has evaporated. Stir the fish into the sauce.

3. Heat the tortillas briefly on a hot griddle to soften. Put 2 tablespoons (30 mL) of the mixture on a tortilla. Add some cheese and roll it up tightly. Secure the flauta with a toothpick to hold it together. Repeat with the remaining flautas.

4. In a skillet, heat 2 inches (5 cm) of oil. Fry the flautas until golden brown. Remove them from the skillet and let them drain.

Texas Crab Cakes with Jalapeño Cream

Yield: 4–6 servings   Heat Scale: Medium

Crab is a favorite around the Texas Gulf Coast, where it is plentiful and available almost all year round. This recipe combines that favorite with another—jalapeños— to create a spicy entrée. (Note: This recipe requires advance preparation.)

For the Jalapeño Cream:
2 tablespoons (30 mL) butter
2 tablespoons (30 mL) minced onion
1 clove garlic, peeled and minced
3 jalapeño chiles, stems and seeds removed, chopped
2 tablespoons (30 mL) sour cream
2 cups (473 mL) heavy cream or half-and-half

1. In a saucepan, heat the butter over medium heat. Add the onion and garlic and sauté until softened. Add the chiles and sauté for an additional 2 minutes. Stir in the sour cream and cream and bring the mixture to a boil. Reduce the heat and simmer until the sauce has thickened.

For the Crab Cakes:
1 tablespoon (15 mL) olive oil
2 jalapeño chiles, stems and seeds removed, finely chopped
½ cup (118 mL) finely chopped onions
¼ cup (59 mL) finely chopped celery
¼ cup (59 mL) finely chopped bell pepper
1 pound (454 g) crabmeat
2 cups (473 mL) dry bread crumbs, divided
1 tablespoon (15 mL) chopped parsley
1 tablespoon (15 mL) lemon juice
2 teaspoons (10 mL) Worcestershire sauce
½ teaspoon (2.5 mL) ground cayenne
2 eggs, divided
½ cup (118 mL) milk
All-purpose flour for dredging
Vegetable oil for frying

1. In a large skillet, heat the olive oil over medium heat. Add the jalapeños, onions, celery, and bell pepper and sauté until softened. Transfer the mixture to a bowl and add the crab, 1 cup (236 mL) of the bread crumbs, the parsley, the lemon juice, the Worcestershire sauce, and the cayenne. Beat 1 of the eggs and add it to the crab mixture. Refrigerate for 1 hour. Shape the crab mixture into 6 patties or cakes.
2. Beat the remaining egg with the milk. Dip each cake in the flour, then the egg, and finally the remaining bread crumbs. Refrigerate for an additional hour.
3. In a frying pan, heat the vegetable oil to 350°F (180°C). Fry each cake on both sides until browned. Top with the Jalapeño Cream and serve.

Bayou-Grilled Catfish with Creole Mustard Sauce

Yield: 4 servings   Heat Scale: Mild

Creole and Cajun cuisines are not considered bastions of barbecue and grilling, but the people of Louisiana certainly know how to cook fish. Although this sauce is not for those counting calories, you can substitute a plain, low-fat yogurt for the sour cream. The sauce goes well with other seafood dishes and replaces a red tomato-based sauce. Serve this with dirty rice and a tomato and basil salad. You'd better put the rest of the hot sauce on the table, too. (Note: This recipe requires advance preparation.)

1 teaspoon (5 mL) distilled white vinegar
1 tablespoon (15 mL) olive oil
2 cloves garlic, peeled and pressed
2 teaspoons (10 mL) cracked black pepper
1 tablespoon (15 mL) Louisiana-style hot sauce, divided
4 catfish fillets
½ cup (118 mL) heavy cream
3 tablespoons (45 mL) sour cream
3 tablespoons (45 mL) Creole mustard or other coarse-grained mustard
2 teaspoons (10 mL) Worcestershire sauce
2 teaspoons (10 mL) prepared horseradish
1 teaspoon (5 mL) prepared yellow mustard
¼ teaspoon (1.25 mL) salt
¼ teaspoon (1.25 mL) ground white pepper
½ teaspoon (2.5 mL) dried basil
1 teaspoon (5 mL) honey

1. In a bowl, combine the vinegar, olive, garlic, black pepper, and 2 teaspoons (10 mL) of the hot sauce. Stir well and let sit for 20 minutes to blend the flavors. Spread this marinade over the fillets and let them sit at room temperature, covered, for 1 hour.
2. In a saucepan, combine the remaining 1 teaspoon (5 mL) hot sauce with all the remaining ingredients and simmer for 10 minutes. Remove the pan from the heat and cool to room temperature.
3. Place the fillets in a grill basket with handles and grill over a medium fire until the fish flakes easily, about 6 minutes, turning occasionally.
4. To serve, place the fillets on individual plates and pour 1 tablespoon (15 mL) of the sauce over each, with extra sauce on the side.

Blackened Red Snapper

Yield: 4 servings   Heat Scale: Medium

Chef Paul Prudhomme made blackened fish popular. Although it is very tasty, trying to prepare this dish in a home kitchen can set off all smoke alarms in a 2-mile (3.2 km) radius. It is much easier to do on the backyard grill, where only your immediate neighbors will think your house is on fire. A variety of fish fillets works well in this recipe, including redfish, sea bass, or grouper.

4 (6-ounce [168 g]) red snapper fillets
2 tablespoons (30 mL) melted butter
4 tablespoons (60 mL) barbecue dry rub or Cajun dry rub
Chopped fresh parsley for garnish
Sliced lemons for garnish

1. Brush the fish with the butter and rub it with the dry rub so that it is evenly coated. Cover and let sit for an hour at room temperature to allow the seasonings to penetrate.
2. Oil the barbecue grill so that the fish will not stick. When the fire is hot, place the fish skin-side down and grill for 3 to 5 minutes or until the rub starts to blacken.
3. Turn the fish and sprinkle a little lemon juice on the cooked side to keep it moistened. Cook for another 3 to 5 minutes.
4. Garnish the fish with the chopped parsley and serve with the sliced lemon.

Crazy Cajun Salmon

Yield: 4 servings   Heat Scale: Medium

Everyone loves salmon. It is such a flavorful fish, especially with all the great herbs and spices included here. Give this recipe a try and it will be Mardi Gras in your mouth.

4 salmon fillets
2 teaspoons (10 mL) salt
1 teaspoon (5 mL) ground cayenne
1 teaspoon (5 mL) paprika
½ teaspoon (2.5 mL) ground white pepper
¼ teaspoon (1.25 mL) garlic powder
½ teaspoon (2.5 mL) freshly ground black pepper
¼ teaspoon (1.25 mL) dried thyme
¼ teaspoon (1.25 mL) dried basil
1 teaspoon (5 mL) crushed red pepper flakes
8 ounces (224 g) unsalted butter, softened
2 fresh green jalapeño chiles, stems and seeds removed, very finely minced
4 sprigs cilantro, leaves only, finely chopped
2 sprigs parsley, leaves only, finely chopped
Canola oil for grilling
Salsa of your choice from Chapter 2 for serving

1. Preheat the grill to medium-high. Rinse the fillets and make sure that all of the bones have been removed and no skin is left on the edges. Pat the fillets dry and set them aside.

2. In a sauté pan, combine the salt, cayenne, paprika, white pepper, garlic powder, black pepper, thyme, basil, and red pepper flakes. Lightly toast the spices over very low heat, stirring constantly, until they are light brown and aromatic. Transfer the spices to a shallow dish or plate.

3. In a small bowl, combine the butter, chiles, cilantro, and parsley and blend with a wooden spoon until smooth and well mixed. Place the herb butter on a piece of wax paper or plastic wrap and rolling it into a tube shape. Refrigerate briefly while the fillets grill.

4. Lightly oil each fillet with canola oil, then roll the fillet in the spice blend until it is uniformly covered. Grill the fillets over medium heat until browned on each side and cooked through to the middle, about 3 minutes per side.

5. Unroll the tube of butter and allow it to soften briefly. Cut the butter crosswise into ½-inch (1 cm) thick rounds. Serve the fillets hot from the grill, topped with the chile-herb butter and Insanity Seafood Sauce or your favorite salsa.

Grilled Salmon Steaks with Green Chile Lime Sauce

Yield: 4 servings   Heat Scale: Medium

Here is a simple salmon recipe that's quick to prepare but tastes great. You can literally whip it up while you are starting the grill. Feel free to flavor this with a little light smoke—say, apple or another fruitwood. Serve this with a creamy risotto, an arugula and tomato salad, and a chilled white wine.

4 salmon steaks
Olive oil for grilling
Salt, to taste
Freshly ground black pepper, to taste
½ cup (118 mL) chopped fresh cilantro leaves
3 green New Mexican chiles, roasted and peeled, stems and seeds removed
2 cloves garlic, peeled and chopped
Juice of 1 lime
1 tablespoon (15 mL) vegetable oil
1 teaspoon (5 mL) lime zest

1. Brush the steaks with the oil and season them with the salt and pepper. In a blender or food processor, combine all the remaining ingredients and purée until smooth.

2. Grill the steaks over a medium fire for about 8 minutes or until the fish flakes on the outside, turning several times.

3. To serve, pour some of the sauce on individual plates, place the steaks on top of the sauce, and top with additional sauce.

Coconut-Smoked Mahi-Mahi with Curried Pineapple Serrano Salsa

Yield: 4 servings   Heat Scale: Medium

Mahi-mahi is the Hawaiian term for the fish also called dorado in Spanish and dolphin in English. This recipe also works well with "fishier" fish, such as kingfish, bluefish, and mackerel. Yes, you can substitute steaks for the fillets, but be sure to adjust the cooking time. Smoking with coconut gives the fish a sweet flavor with tropical overtones. This recipe is designed for a water smoker or a charcoal grill with indirect heat, a water-filled pan beneath the fish, and the coconut placed on the coals. Use a fish grill basket with handles for easy turning. Serve with lemon cashew rice, spring asparagus spears, and Key lime pie.

¼ cup (59 mL) vegetable oil
2 tablespoons (30 mL) rice wine
Juice of 1 lime
2 teaspoons (10 mL) ground habanero chile
1 teaspoon (5 mL) minced ginger
1 fresh coconut, broken in pieces, milk reserved
4 mahi-mahi fillets (or substitute snapper or grouper)
1 ripe pineapple, peeled, cored, and cut in ¼-inch (.5 cm) slices
3 serrano chiles, stems removed, chopped
2 tablespoons (30 mL) rice wine vinegar
1 tablespoon (15 mL) orange juice
2 teaspoons (10 mL) curry powder
2 teaspoons (10 mL) brown sugar
1 tablespoon (15 mL) chopped fresh cilantro

1. In a bowl, combine the oil, rice wine, lime juice, chile, and ginger to make a marinade. Place the fish in a nonreactive dish, pour the marinade over the top, and marinate, covered, at room temperature for 30 to 45 minutes.
2. Prepare a fire in a water smoker or a charcoal grill. When it's hot, place the coconut pieces on the coals. Pour the reserved coconut milk into the pan with the water. Smoke the fish for 1 to 2 hours or until the fish flakes, keeping the heat very low. You may quickly baste the fish a couple of times with the marinade, if desired, to keep it from drying out.
3. To make the salsa, grill the pineapple slices or heat them in a pan for 5 to 10 minutes, until the pineapple is browned. Dice the pineapple and transfer it to a bowl. Add the serrano chiles, vinegar, orange juice, curry powder, and brown sugar and allow it to sit at room temperature for an hour to blend the flavors. Toss with the cilantro.
4. Place the fish on individual plates, top each fillet with a little salsa, and serve the remaining salsa on the side.

Shrimp Jambalaya

Yield: 4–6 servings   Heat Scale: Medium

Jambalaya is one of the most popular foods in the bayous of Louisiana. It was originally created by cooks cleaning out their iceboxes and using what foods were left over; the term "jambalaya" even means a mix of food or events, so any mix of meats and seafood you like is appropriate. The word got its name from the French word "jambon," for ham, which the dish traditionally contains. The following recipe doesn't contain any, but if you have some cooked ham in the refrigerator, dice it and add it to the pot.

3 tablespoons (45 mL) vegetable oil, divided
1 large bell pepper, stem and seeds removed, chopped
1 onion, peeled and chopped
1 cup (236 mL) chopped celery
½ cup (118 mL) diced carrots
2 cloves garlic, peeled and minced
1 teaspoon (5 mL) ground cayenne
1 teaspoon (5 mL) dried thyme
1 teaspoon (5 mL) dried oregano
2 bay leaves
1 quart (.95 L) Classic Chicken Stock (page 46) or Traditional European
Fish Stock (page 47)
1½ cups (354 mL) tomato sauce
½ cup (118 mL) dry white wine, optional
1 cup (236 mL) long-grain rice
1½ pounds (680 g) shrimp, shelled and deveined
Salt and freshly ground black pepper
Garnishes: Chopped green onions, chopped fresh parsley

1. In a large stockpot, heat 2 tablespoons (30 mL) of the oil over medium-high heat. Add the bell pepper, onions, celery, carrots, and garlic and sauté until softened, about 5 minutes. . Add the cayenne, thyme, oregano, and bay leaves and sauté for an additional 3 minutes, stirring constantly.
2. Add the stock, tomato sauce, and wine, if using, bring the mixture to a boil, reduce the heat, and simmer for 30 minutes.
3. In a small frying pan, heat the remaining 1 tablespoon (15 mL) oil until hot. Add the rice and fry, stirring constantly, until it becomes opaque. Transfer the rice to the stock pot and simmer for 30 to 45 minutes or until the rice is tender.
4. Stir in the shrimp and simmer for 5 minutes or until the shrimp is done.
5. Ladle the jambalaya into bowls, garnish with the green onions and parsley, and serve with a bottle of Louisiana hot sauce on the side.

Spaghetti with Spicy Seafood

Yield: 4 servings   Heat Scale: Mild

When preparing this recipe, the cook has several options with the mussels and clams. He or she can add them, shells and all, to the tomato sauce; serve them on the side in the shells; or remove the meat from the shells and add it to the sauce.

½ pound (224 g) mussels, beards removed, scrubbed
½ pound (224 g) clams
1 tablespoon (15 mL) salt
½ cup (118 mL) extra virgin olive oil, divided
2 garlic cloves, peeled and minced
2 dried peperoncino chiles, crushed (or substitute 1 New Mexican)
2 cups (473 mL) canned Italian plum tomatoes, chopped
1 pound (454 g) spaghetti
12 basil leaves, torn
2 tablespoons (30 mL) minced Italian parsley

1. Place the mussels and clams in a bowl. Add the salt and cool water to cover. Set aside to purge for 30 minutes, then drain and rinse.

2. Place the mussels and clams in a 12-inch (30 cm) sauté pan with the 1 cup (236 mL) water and bring to a boil, uncovered, over medium heat. As they open, transfer the mussels and clams to a plate. Discard any that do not open. Strain the cooking juices into a small bowl through a cheese-cloth-lined sieve. Remove the meat from the shells, if desired.

3. In a skillet large enough to hold the spaghetti, heat ¼ cup (59 mL) of the olive oil over medium heat. Add the garlic and crushed peperoncino. Cook for 1 minute, stirring well. Stir in the tomatoes and the reserved cooking juices from the mussels and clams, bring to a boil over medium heat, and cook until the sauce has reduced, about 5 minutes, stirring occasionally. Fold in the mussels and clams and keep warm.

4. Bring 5 quarts (4.75 L) salted water to a boil. Add the spaghetti and cook until al dente. Drain the spaghetti, reserving ⅓ cup (79 mL) of the cooking water. Fold the spaghetti, reserved cooking water, basil, and parsley into the tomato sauce, and cook, stirring, for 1 minute. Serve immediately, drizzled with the remaining olive oil.

Tonno Alla Marinara
(Tuna with Marinara Sauce)

Yield: 4 servings   Heat Scale: Medium

This Calabrian dish is a specialty of the Gulf of Sant'Eufemia and is another classic combination of seafood, tomatoes, and peperoncino.

Olive oil for greasing the pan
2¼ pounds (1.2 kg) fresh tuna, cut into ¾-inch (1.5 cm) slices
Dry bread crumbs for dredging
1 pound (454 g) fresh, ripe tomatoes, blanched, peeled, and chopped (or substitute canned tomatoes)
8 ounces (224 g) pitted black olives
2 ounces (54 g) salted capers, rinsed
Chopped fresh basil, to taste
2 small dried peperoncinos, crushed
Salt, to taste

1. Preheat the oven to 360°F (185°C). Grease an ovenproof dish with the oil.
2. Lay the slices of tuna in the prepared pan and dust them with bread crumbs. Add the tomatoes, olives, capers, basil, peppers, and salt. Sprinkle with more olive oil and bake until the fish is done, about 20 minutes (it will flake when pressed).

Pescado en Escabeche
"Pickled" Halibut

Yield: 4 servings   Heat Scale: Mild

The Portuguese, who can take most of the credit for spreading chiles around the world, do not appear to have incorporated them very much into their cuisine. The following recipe is an exception. Escabeche is a method of preserving fish in a spicy vinegar-based sauce. In Portugal, sardines are most commonly used, but any firm white fish will produce good results. (Note: This recipe requires advance preparation.)

3 tablespoons (45 mL) olive oil, divided
1 pound (454 g) halibut or other firm fish, cut in 1½-inch (3.5 cm) cubes
6 cloves garlic, peeled
1 small carrot, peeled and sliced in rings
1 medium onion, peeled, sliced, and separated into rings
1 tablespoon (15 mL) dried red New Mexican chile, crushed, seeds included
¾ cup (177 mL) red wine vinegar
¾ cup (177 mL) white wine
10 whole black peppercorns

1. In a skillet, heat 2 tablespoons (30 mL) of the olive oil over medium heat. Add the fish and sauté until browned, then remove and drain. Add the garlic, carrot, and onion and sauté until softened. Remove and drain.

2. In a saucepan, combine the remaining oil, chiles, vinegar, wine, and peppercorns. Simmer for 10 minutes to blend the flavors and reduce the sauce.

3. Transfer the fish to a ceramic or glass pan. Arrange the chiles, garlic, carrots and onions on the fish. Pour the sauce over the top and marinate in the refrigerator for at least 2 days.

4. Drain the fish and bring it to room temperature before serving.

Marinated and Grilled Fish Middle Eastern–Style

Yield: 4 servings   Heat Scale: Medium

Since, technically, fourteen or more countries can be classified as Middle Eastern, you're probably wondering if this recipe came from Oman or Egypt. No, this reflects a style rather than a single country, and it is designed so that the spice flavors don't overwhelm the fish. Use a fish grill basket with handles to protect the fillets. Serve with a tabouleh salad, orzo or rice, and sautéed zucchini, eggplant, and tomatoes.

½ cup (118 mL) chopped onion
2 jalapeño chiles, stems and seeds removed, chopped
1 large clove garlic, peeled and chopped
2 tablespoons (30 mL) lemon juice (fresh preferred)
1 tablespoon (15 mL) olive oil
½ teaspoon (2.5 mL) ground paprika
½ teaspoon (2.5 mL) ground cinnamon
¼ teaspoon (1.25 mL) ground cumin
Freshly ground black pepper, to taste
4 white fish fillets, such as snapper

1. In a blender or food processor, combine all the ingredients except the fish and purée until smooth. Place the fillets in a glass dish and pour the marinade over them. Marinate the fish for an hour at room temperature, covered.

2. Remove the fish from the marinade and grill it over a medium grill until the fish flakes easily.

Grilled Tuna with Ras El Hanout Spice Rub and Yogurt-Cilantro Sauce

Yield: 4 servings   Heat Scale: Medium

The key to the unique flavor of this recipe is the versatile Moroccan spice rub that can also be used with grilled chicken and lamb. Ras el hanout literally means "top of the shop," and is a mixture of many spices. Some extreme recipes are reputed to have about a hundred ingredients, but I've included an abbreviated recipe. This mixture also spices up rice and couscous. It is best to toast the seeds first to release their aroma. Serve this dish with fresh figs or pears, a Moroccan carrot salad, and couscous. (Note: This recipe requires advance preparation.)

1 teaspoon (5 mL) cumin seeds
1 teaspoon (5 mL) caraway seeds
¼ teaspoon (1.25 mL) cardamom seeds
1 (2-inch [5 cm]) stick cinnamon
6 allspice berries
4 whole cloves
½ cup (118 mL) chopped onion
2 teaspoons (10 mL) grated ginger
1½ teaspoons (2.5 mL) freshly ground black pepper
1 teaspoon (5 mL) ground cayenne
1 teaspoon (5 mL) ground coriander
¼ teaspoon (1.25 mL) ground nutmeg
¼ teaspoon (1.25 mL) ground turmeric
2 tablespoons (30 mL) vegetable oil
4 (1-inch [2.5 cm]) thick tuna steaks
½ cup (118 mL) plain yogurt
2 tablespoons (30 mL) finely chopped fresh cilantro
1 clove garlic, peeled and minced
2 teaspoons (10 mL) lemon zest

1. To make the spice rub, combine the cumin, caraway, and cardamom seeds on a hot, dry skillet and toast over high heat until the seeds start to pop and are very fragrant. Remove the seeds from the pan and let them cool. Transfer them to a spice grinder along with the cinnamon, allspice, and cloves and process to a fine powder. Sift the powder if desired.
2. Transfer the spices to a blender or food processor and add the onion, ginger, black pepper, cayenne, coriander, nutmeg, turmeric, and oil. Process this mixture to a paste, adding a little water if more liquid is needed.
3. Rub the paste on the fish and marinate it in a bowl, covered, at room temperature, for an hour.
4. In a bowl, combine the remaining ingredients and allow the sauce to sit at room temperature to blend the flavors.
5. Grill the fish over a medium-low heat until it flakes on the outside, about 8 to 10 minutes, taking care that the paste doesn't burn.
6. Spread some sauce on the plates and place the fish on top of it. Swizzle the remaining sauce artistically over the grilled steaks.

Crab Claws Piri-Piri

Yield: 2 servings   Heat Scale: Medium

Michelle Cox collected this recipe from the Driftwood Beach Club, in Malindi, Kenya. According to Michelle, there's only one variety of ground chile available there, with medium to low heat. She suggests you choose any variety that you like, calling red New Mexican chile a perfect pick.

1 pound (454 g) cooked crab claws
2 tablespoons (30 mL) butter
1 teaspoon (5 mL) minced garlic
1 tablespoon (15 mL) ground red chile, such as New Mexican
1 tablespoon (15 mL) tomato paste
1 cup (236 mL) white wine
Juice of ½ lime
1 tablespoon (15 mL) finely chopped parsley or cilantro

1. Partially crack the crab claws so that the sauce will be able to soak in. In a deep-sided frying pan, melt the butter over low heat. Add the garlic, ground chile, tomato paste, wine, and lime juice. Cook slowly until the wine is cooked off and the flavors have blended, about 15 minutes. Add the crab claws and increase the heat. Carefully toss the claws in the sauce until they are warmed through. Sprinkle with parsley and serve with rice and lime wedges.

Shrimp Piri-Piri

Yield: 4 servings   Heat Scale: Medium

Shellfish is abundant off the coast of West Africa, and the prawns are so large that a couple will make a meal. This Mozambique marinade goes well not only with shrimp or prawns, but also with fish and chicken. (Note: This recipe requires advance preparation.)

¼ cup (59 mL) butter
¼ cup (59 mL) peanut oil
2 tablespoons (30 mL) crushed dried piri-piri chile, seeds included (or substitute piquins)
4 cloves garlic, peeled and minced
3 tablespoons (45 mL) lime or lemon juice (fresh preferred)
1 pound (454 g) shrimp or prawns, shelled and deveined

1. In a skillet, melt the butter over medium heat. Add the oil, chiles, garlic, and lime or lemon juice. Simmer for a couple of minutes to blend the flavors.
2. Toss the shrimp in the marinade and marinate for a couple of hours.
3. Thread the shrimp on skewers and grill them over charcoal or broil, basting with the marinade, until done.
4. Heat the marinade and serve it on the side.

Kenyan Baked Fish, Swahili-Style

Yield: 3 servings   Heat Scale: Medium

"Swahili cooking," as the cuisine is called, involves heavy use of local ingredients, such as coconut milk, tomatoes, and chiles, says Michelle Cox, who collected this recipe from Kenya. She says tamarind pulp would normally be used as a tangy ingredient to cut the heaviness of coconut milk, but lime is commonly substituted. As a variation, make the sauce ahead and serve it with a grilled whole fish.

2 tablespoons (30 mL) ghee or cooking oil
3 small green bell peppers, chopped
3 medium tomatoes, chopped
1 small onion, peeled and chopped
3 Kenya chiles, stems and seeds removed, chopped fine (or substitute red jalapeños)
2 tablespoons (30 mL) cornstarch
2¼ cups (532 mL) coconut milk
2¼ cups (532 mL) Traditional European Fish Stock (page 47)
1 tablespoon (15 mL) ground turmeric or mild curry powder
Salt, to taste
Freshly ground black pepper, to taste
3 (7-ounce [196 g]) fish fillets
Juice of 3 limes

1. Preheat the oven to 350°F (180°C).
2. In a frying pan, heat the ghee or cooking oil over medium heat. Add the green peppers, tomatoes, onions, and chiles and sauté until they are just cooked, then lower the heat. Add the cornstarch, coconut milk, fish stock, and turmeric. Cook slowly until the mixture thickens. Season to taste with salt and pepper. Place the fish fillets in a large, ovenproof frying pan, cover them with the sauce, and sprinkle them with the lime juice. Bake for 15 to 20 minutes, until the fish is cooked. Serve with your favorite rice dish from Chapter 13.

Curried Prawns in Pineapple

Yield: 4 servings   Heat Scale: Mild

This Ethiopian dish offers a very unusual and beautiful presentation, as well as a taste of India through the use of curry. While Red Sea prawns are customary, any large shrimp or prawns from your local fish market will work.

1½ pounds (680 g) fresh prawns
Juice of 1 lemon
2 tablespoons (30 mL) vegetable oil
1 onion, peeled and chopped
1 tablespoon (15 mL) chopped chives or green onions, plus more for garnish
2 tomatoes, chopped
2 teaspoons (10 mL) curry powder
½ teaspoon (2.5 mL) ground cayenne
1 ounce (28 g) butter, melted
1 ounce (28 g) all-purpose flour
1 large or 2 small pineapples (for individual dishes, use small pineapples)

1. Boil the prawns in salted water for 10 minutes. Reserve 1 cup (236 mL) of the cooking water. Peel off the shells and remove the black vein running down the back. Sprinkle the prawns with lemon juice.
2. In a frying pan, heat the oil over medium-high heat. Add the onion, chives, tomatoes, curry powder, and cayenne. Cook for 5 minutes, then add the reserved stock and prawns and simmer over a low heat for 5 minutes. Mix together the butter and flour and add it, a little at a time, to the prawns, stirring after each addition until smooth. Cook 3 to 5 minutes longer. Halve the pineapples lengthwise and cut out some of the flesh. Fill the pineapple hollows with the prawn mixture and sprinkle with more chopped chives.

Pastel com Diabo Dentro (Pastry with the Devil Inside)

Yield: 14–16 pastries   Heat Scale: Medium

This recipe comes from the Cape Verde Islands, which are located just off the western tip of Africa. This former Portuguese colony offers this unusual dish, which should be prepared with very fresh tuna. For corn flour, check natural foods groceries, or make your own by grinding corn meal in a spice mill until it is extremely fine.

2 large sweet potatoes, unpeeled
1–2 cups (236–473 mL) corn flour
2 tablespoons (30 mL) olive oil
1 medium onion, peeled and finely chopped
1 pound (454 g) fresh tuna, cooked
1 medium tomato, chopped
2 red jalapeño chiles, stems and seeds removed, finely chopped (or substitute 1 teaspoon [5 mL] ground cayenne)
1 teaspoon (5 mL) salt
Vegetable oil for deep frying

1. Wash the sweet potatoes well and boil them until they are very tender, about 15 minutes. Reserve a little of the cooking water. Let the potatoes cool slightly, then remove their skins. Transfer the potatoes to a food processor and blend them to a smooth paste, or mash them thoroughly in a large bowl, making sure to get out all the lumps. Slowly add the corn flour, blending it in with your hands or a wooden spoon to make a stiff dough. The moisture in your potatoes will determine how much flour you need, but the dough should resemble biscuit dough or a coarse pie pastry. If it becomes too dry, add a few teaspoons (10–15 mL) of the water in which the potatoes were cooked. Roll the dough into a ball, wrap it in a damp, lint-free cloth, and refrigerate it while you make the filling.

2. In a sauté pan, heat the olive oil over medium heat. Add the onions and sauté until they become transparent. Flake the tuna into a bowl and add the sautéed onions, tomato, jalapeños, and salt. Unwrap the dough and spread the damp towel on a flat surface. Working on top of the towel, tear off golf-ball-sized pieces of the dough and roll them into circles about ⅛-inch (.25 cm) thick and 4–5 inches (10–12.5 cm) in diameter. Put a tablespoonful (15 mL) of the tuna filling on half of a dough circle; fold the other half over it and pinch the edges to seal. Repeat with the remaining dough and filling.

3. In a deep, heavy pot, heat the oil for frying until a test piece of dough sputters vigorously. You may either deep-fry the turnovers or fry them in a couple of inches (5 cm) of oil, turning them once to allow both sides to cook. Fry 2 or 3 at a time. The oil is the right temperature when a test turnover becomes golden brown after frying about 3 minutes on each side. Drain the pastries on paper towels and serve immediately.

Mozambican Peite Lumbo (Red Chile–Stewed Sea Bass)

Yield: 4–6 servings   Heat Scale: Medium

Mozambicans have been known to throw whole handfuls of chiles into dishes all at once. I certainly like their thinking, and I really like this particularly spicy dish. If you have extra sauce, you might want to save it and serve with cassava dumplings or rice.

4–5 dried red New Mexican chiles, stems and seeds removed
1 pound (454 g) shrimp, shelled and deveined, shells reserved
2 cups (473 mL) water
1 cup (236 mL) lemon juice
3 pounds (1.36 kg) sea bass, grouper, or snapper
Salt, to taste
Freshly ground black pepper, to taste
3 tablespoons (45 mL) peanut oil
2 bell peppers, stems and seeds removed, finely chopped
2 medium tomatoes, peeled and sieved
2 red onions, peeled and finely chopped
½ teaspoon (2.5 mL) ground nutmeg
2¼ teaspoons (11.25 mL) ground dried shrimp
½ cup (118 mL) coconut milk
½ cup (118 mL) grated coconut
¼ teaspoon (1.25 mL) ground coriander

1. Rehydrate the chile pods in a bowl of water. Purée them in a blender with about 2 tablespoons (30 mL) of the soaking water and set the purée aside.

2. In a large bowl, combine the water and lemon juice. Clean and eviscerate the fish, leaving the head on and the eyes out. Wash the fish and acidulate it in the lemon water for a few minutes. Season the fish inside and out with salt and pepper and refrigerate until ready to cook.

3. In a skillet, heat the oil over medium heat. Add the bell peppers, tomatoes, chile purée, onions, nutmeg, and ground dried shrimp and sauté for 7 minutes. Add the coconut milk, grated coconut, and coriander and simmer, covered, for 15 minutes, stirring occasionally.

4. Place the marinated fish and shrimp in a pan large enough to hold it intact, and pour the sauce over it. Add a little water at this point if necessary. Cover the pan with foil and simmer for 15 minutes. Stir only once, without breaking the fish, then simmer, covered, for another 10 minutes or so. Add small amounts of water as needed.

Green Masala Fish

Yield: 4 servings   Heat Scale: Hot

This East African recipe by way of India gives some options for preparation. First, prawns may be substituted for the fish fillets. Second, New Mexican chile can be used as part of the chile requirement, if less heat is desired. And third, non-garlic lovers can substitute onion.

2 pounds (1.1 kg) fish fillets
2 tablespoons (30 mL) chopped fresh cilantro
2 tablespoons (30 mL) chopped fresh mint or basil
6 Kenya chiles, stems and seeds removed, chopped (or substitute red jalapeños)
5 tablespoons (75 mL) ground cumin
5 tablespoons (75 mL) grated coconut
1 teaspoon (5 mL) salt
1 tablespoon (15 mL) chopped garlic or onion
2 tablespoons (30 mL) chopped fresh ginger
2 tablespoons (30 mL) oil, divided
½ cup (118 mL) lime juice, divided

1. Place the fish in a shallow dish. In a blender or food processor, combine the cilantro, mint, chiles, cumin, coconut, salt, garlic, and ginger. Blend to a fine paste. Mix in 1 tablespoon (15 mL) each of the oil and lime juice. Coat the fish with this mixture and leave to marinate for 30 minutes.

2. Preheat the broiler pan on high. Brush the pan with the remaining oil to prevent sticking. Put the fish under the broiler for 2 minutes, then reduce the heat or lower the pan and broil, basting with the remaining lime juice, until the fish is cooked but not dry, 7 to 10 minutes.

Wali Na Samaki
(Tanzanian Fiery Fried Fish and Rice)

Yield: 8 servings   Heat Scale: Medium

Tanzania, formerly called Tanganyika, is on the east coast of Africa and is home to Mount Kilimanjaro, as well as many tropical beaches and great lakes that provide an abundance of tasty fish, perfect for fiery recipes such as this.

1 cup (236 mL) vegetable oil, divided
4 large tomatoes, sliced
2 bell peppers, stems and seeds removed, sliced in rings
2 jalapeño chiles, stems and seeds removed, chopped
2 onions, peeled and chopped
Zest of 1 lemon
1 teaspoon (5 mL) salt, plus more to taste
1 teaspoon (5 mL) freshly ground black pepper, plus more to taste
2 bay leaves
2 cups (473 mL) water
Juice of 1 lemon
2 pounds (1.1 kg) red snapper or halibut, cut into 6 sections
1 cup (236 mL) all-purpose flour
4 cups (.95 L) cooked rice

1. In a large saucepan, heat ½ cup (118 mL) of the oil over medium heat. Add the tomatoes, bell pepper, jalapeños, onions, lemon peel, salt, and pepper and sauté for about 10 minutes, stirring occasionally. Add the water, lemon juice, and bay leaves and simmer for 15 minutes or until the sauce is moderately thick.
2. In a large skillet, heat the remaining oil. Rub the fish with salt and pepper and dip it in the flour. Add the fish to the pan and fry it until it is brown and tender. To serve, place the cooked rice on a large platter. Put the fish on top of the rice and pour the sauce over everything.

Hut Benoua
(Almond-Coated Baked Fish)

Yield: 6 servings   Heat Scale: Mild to Medium

This unusual, sweet-heat entrée is made beautiful and hot with startling red paprika. With origins in the Moroccan fishing port of Safi, this is quite a delicious fish dish, with its crisp, sweet, spiced coating.

1½ cups (354 mL) blanched almonds, toasted and ground
½ cup (118 mL) confectioner's sugar
1 tablespoon (15 mL) orange-flower water
1 tablespoon (15 mL) ground cinnamon
2 teaspoons (10 mL) hot paprika
½ cup (118 mL) water, divided, plus more if needed
¼ cup (59 mL) butter, softened, divided, plus more for buttering the baking dish
Salt, to taste
Freshly ground black pepper, to taste
1 (3–4 pound [1.36–1.82 kg]) whole white fish, such as snapper or grouper, cleaned
1 onion, peeled and finely chopped
1 pinch saffron threads, crushed

1. Preheat the oven to 375°F (190°C). Butter a large baking dish.
2. In a bowl, combine the almonds, sugar, orange-flower water, cinnamon, paprika, 3 tablespoons (45 mL) of the water, half the butter, the salt, and the pepper and mix to a smooth paste. Salt and pepper the fish inside and out, then fill it with half the almond mixture.
3. In a bowl, mix together the onion, saffron, and the remaining water. Pour this mixture into the prepared baking dish. Place the fish on the onion mixture and spread the remaining almond mixture over the fish. Melt the remaining butter and trickle it over the almond mixture.
4. Bake for about 45 minutes, until the fish is cooked and the almond topping has a crust on it yet is still soft underneath.

Poisson En Tajine Mqualli
(Marinated Fish Cooked in Spiced Oil)

Yield: 4–6 servings   Heat Scale: Mild to Medium

This Tunisian dish is a classic. Feel free to substitute a fish that's more to your liking; halibut can be replaced by hake, cod, or snapper in this recipe. Serve this dish with your favorite salad from Chapter 6. (Note: This recipe requires advance preparation.)

3 cloves garlic, peeled
Salt, to taste
1 teaspoon (5 mL) ground cayenne
1 teaspoon (5 mL) ground coriander
1 teaspoon (5 mL) ground cumin
2 pounds (1.1 kg) halibut steaks
¾ cup (177 mL) olive oil
1 teaspoon (5 mL) ground ginger
1 pinch saffron threads, crushed
Black olives for garnish
Lemon quarters for garnish

1. In a mortar, crush the garlic with a large pinch of salt. Transfer the mixture to a bowl and mix in the cayenne, coriander, and cumin. Rub each halibut with the marinade, then arrange the steaks in a single layer in a heavy baking dish and marinate in a cool place for 6 hours.
2. Preheat the oven to 375°F (190°C).
3. In a small bowl, mix the oil with the ginger and saffron. Pour this mixture over the fish, cover the dish, and bake for 20 to 25 minutes, until the fish flakes easily. Serve garnished with the olives and lemons.

Curried Lobster with Rice

Yield: 4–6 servings   Heat Scale: Medium

This West African recipe features lobsters, which are scarce in the area and difficult to catch, making this a very special and expensive meal. Crab meat is often substituted, as it is much more affordable and accessible.

2 (2-pound [1.1 kg]) live lobsters
1 cup (236 mL) fresh shrimp
2 cups (473 mL) chopped onions, divided
2 tablespoons (30 mL) lemon juice
⅔ cup (158 mL) melted butter
1 cup (236 mL) cubed eggplant
Salt, to taste
Garlic powder, to taste
1 cup (236 mL) tomato sauce
½ teaspoon (2.5 mL) ground nutmeg
2 tablespoons (30 mL) curry powder of your choice from Chapter 1
1 teaspoon (5 mL) ground ginger
2 teaspoons (10 mL) ground cayenne
2 cups (473 mL) coconut milk (optional)
4 cups (.95 L) cooked rice

1. Wash lobsters and shrimp and boil them for 7 to 10 minutes in a large pot of salted water with 1 tablespoon (15 mL) of the chopped onions. Remove the lobster meat from the shell and cut it into pieces. Reserve the stock and the shells.
2. Peel, devein, and wash the shrimp, then combine the lobster meat and the shrimp in a bowl and sprinkle them with the lemon juice.
3. In a large skillet, heat the butter over medium heat. Add the remaining onion and sauté for 5 minutes. Add the eggplant, lobster meat, shrimp, salt, and garlic powder. Cook for another 10 minutes. Pour the tomato sauce over the mixture, then stir in the nutmeg, curry powder, ginger, and cayenne. Add 2 cups of the reserved stock or the coconut milk. Simmer, stirring occasionally, for 20 minutes.
4. Serve the dish hot. For a festive touch, fill the lobster or crab shells halfway with hot boiled rice and spoon sauce over the rice.

Paprika-Grilled Fish

Yield: 4 servings   Heat Scale: Medium

Hot paprika adds the extra zing to this South African recipe. Many fish in South African waters have charming names such as geelbek, kob, kingklip, and steenbras, but I suggest using yellowtail snapper for a superb meal. Please note that the sauce may be made a couple of days ahead and reheated. Also, you can use your outdoor grill rather than the broiler if you wish.

4 large, thick fish steaks
Salt, to taste
Freshly ground black pepper, to taste
3½ tablespoons (52.5 mL) butter
2 tablespoons (30 mL) chopped parsley
1 tablespoon (15 mL) chopped basil leaves
1 squeeze fresh lemon juice
2 teaspoons (10 mL) hot paprika
⅔ cups (158 mL) heavy cream

1. Preheat the broiler.
2. Arrange the fish on an oiled grilling tray and season it with salt and pepper.
3. In a small saucepan, melt the butter over medium heat. Mix in the parsley, basil, lemon juice, and paprika and remove the pan from the heat. Brush half of this mixture over the fish and broil for 3 to 4 minutes. Turn the fish, brush it with the remaining buttery mixture, and broil for 2 to 4 minutes, until cooked. Transfer the fish to a heated serving platter.
4. Pour the cream into the grilling pan and cook on the stovetop over medium-high heat, stirring in all the buttery fish juices. Pour this sauce over the fish and garnish with an extra sprinkling of paprika. Serve with your favorite side dish from Chapter 13 and a green salad from Chapter 6.

Tunisian Broiled Shrimp

Yield: 4 servings   Heat Scale: Medium

I love unusually spiced, broiled shrimp so this Tunisian specialty is perfect: cloves, cumin, ginger, and cayenne combine for a fragrant and feisty delight. Serve this with couscous or a rice dish from Chapter 13. (Note: This recipe requires advance preparation.)

4 pounds (1.82 kg) raw shrimp in the shell
2 cloves garlic, peeled and crushed
4 tablespoons (60 mL) olive oil
1 teaspoon (5 mL) ground cumin
½ teaspoon (2.5 mL) ground ginger
1 teaspoon (5 mL) paprika
1 teaspoon (5 mL) ground cayenne
1 bunch cilantro leaves, finely chopped
Salt, to taste
Lemon wedges for garnish
Lime wedges for garnish

1. Remove the heads and legs from the shrimp. Using kitchen scissors, cut the shrimp in half lengthwise, leaving the tails intact. Lay the shrimp in a single layer in a large, shallow dish.

2. In a small bowl, combine the garlic, olive oil, cumin, ginger, paprika, cayenne, cilantro, and salt, then pour the spice mixture over the shrimp and leave it in a cool place for 1 to 2 hours, turning the shrimp occasionally.

3. Preheat the broiler. Broil the shrimp for 3–4 minutes until they turn pink, brushing them with any remaining marinade as they cook. Serve with the lime and lemon wedges.

Monkfish Curry with Fresh Fruit

Yield: 4–6 servings   Heat Scale: Mild

Here's another tasty and unusual South African seafood dish, featuring—of course—curry. Seafood curries are extremely popular in the country, and I was served several on my visit there. If you think the curry is too mild, add some ground cayenne. Serve with saffron rice and garnish with slices of whatever fresh fruit is available.

½ cup (118 mL) dry white wine
1 cup (236 mL) Traditional European Fish Stock (page 47)
1 cup (236 mL) heavy cream
3 ounces (84 g) butter
1 small onion, peeled and finely diced
4 cloves fresh garlic, peeled and crushed
2 teaspoons (10 mL) South African Cape Curry Powder (page 23)
2 pounds (1.1 kg) monkfish fillets, cut into large dice and dredged in all-purpose flour
Salt, to taste
Freshly ground white pepper, to taste
4 tablespoons (60 mL) cold butter
1 squeeze lemon juice
Fresh sliced fruit in season, such as peaches, nectarines, plums, pineapple, or apples, for garnish

1. Combine the white wine and fish stock in a saucepan over high heat and cook until reduced by two-thirds. Add the cream and simmer for 5 minutes. In a skillet, melt the butter over medium heat. Add the onion, ginger, and curry powder and sauté for 7–10 minutes. Add the diced monkfish and cook until heated through. Season with the salt and white pepper.

2. Just before serving, whisk the cold butter into the white wine, fish stock, and cream sauce, to thicken it. Add the squeeze of lemon to sharpen the flavor. Pour the sauce into the pan with the monkfish and combine gently. Serve with your choice of the suggested garnishes.

Laksa Lemak Melaka
(Malaysian Seafood with Noodles and Coconut Sauce)

Yield: 6–8 servings   Heat Scale: Medium

The Malaysian people hold chile peppers in the highest esteem, picking them out
carefully at the market and using them to incorporate a bit of heat into most recipes.
This dish features serranos, but you may substitute piquins if you would like a little
more heat.

1 pound (454 g) shrimp, peeled and deveined
1 pound (454 g) halibut or other white fish, cut into ¾-inch (1.5 cm)
chunks
1 cup (236 mL) water
8 candlenuts (or substitute Brazil nuts)
3 serranos or jalapeños, stems and seeds removed, chopped
1½ teaspoons (7.5 mL) ground turmeric
¾ teaspoon (3.75 mL) ground ginger
1 pinch ground cinnamon
2 large cloves garlic, peeled
1 teaspoon (5 mL) grated lemon zest
¼ cup (59 mL) vegetable oil
½ cup (118 mL) minced onion
1½ cups (354 mL) coconut milk
1½ cups (354 mL) water
2 tablespoons (30 mL) lime juice
1 pound (454 g) bean sprouts
1 pound (454 g) vermicelli or spaghetti
1 cucumber, peeled, seeded, and cut into strips
Fresh or dried mint for garnish (optional)

1. Place the shrimp and fish in a pan, add the water, and simmer for about
5 minutes. Remove the pan from the heat and let cool. Reserve the broth.
2. In a food processor, combine the nuts, chiles, turmeric, ginger, cinnamon, garlic, and lemon zest and process to a paste. In a skillet, heat the
vegetable oil over medium heat. Add the onions and the paste and stir-fry
until the onions are soft. Add the coconut milk, water, and lime juice and
simmer, uncovered, for 8 minutes, stirring occasionally.
3. Add the cooked shrimp, the fish, and the reserved fish broth. Simmer
over low heat for 10 minutes. In a pot of rapidly boiling water, blanch the
bean sprouts for 1 minute. Cook the noodles according to the package
directions and drain them. Divide the noodles and bean sprouts equally
among individual bowls. Pour the shrimp, fish, and sauce over each serving and garnish with cucumber and mint.

Acar Ikan
(Hot and Sour Flounder)

Yield: 4–6 servings   Heat Scale: Hot

Jeff Corydon collected this recipe in Indonesia. He found the area endowed with coastal waters, lakes, and rivers. "Acar" refers to the pungent sweet and sour vegetables or relish typical of the region.

1 (2-pound [1.1 kg]) whole flounder
1 teaspoon (5 mL) salt
1 teaspoon (5 mL) ground cayenne
4 dried cayenne chiles, stems and seeds removed, soaked in water until soft, and chopped
3 cloves garlic, peeled and chopped
1 large onion, peeled and chopped
3 macadamia nuts
1 teaspoon (5 mL) ground ginger
1 teaspoon (5 mL) ground cumin
½ cup (118 mL) vegetable oil, divided
½ cup (118 mL) apple cider vinegar
1 teaspoon (5 mL) dry mustard
1 teaspoon (5 mL) sugar
1 cup (236 mL) water

1. Clean the fish and remove the head, but leave the skin on. Firmly rub the salt and cayenne into both sides of the fish.
2. In a blender or food processor, process the chiles, garlic, onion, nuts, ginger, and cumin.
3. In a large skillet or wok, heat 2 tablespoons (30 mL) of the oil over low heat. Add the chile paste and fry for 2 to 3 minutes, stirring constantly. Add the vinegar, mustard, sugar, and water and simmer, uncovered, for 15 minutes.
4. In a separate skillet, heat the remaining oil over medium heat. Add the fish and fry until both sides are golden brown.
5. Add the fish to the sauce in the other skillet and simmer 2 to 3 minutes over low heat, basting frequently with the sauce. Serve immediately.

Tauco Ikan
(Tuna in Brown Bean Sauce with Stir-Fried Vegetables)
Yield: 6 servings   Heat Scale: Medium

Indonesian cuisine often combines fish with vegetables and herbs for spectacular results. I highly recommend experimenting with various chiles in this dish to experience different heat levels and flavors. Serve this with a salad from Chapter 6 and a side dish from Chapter 13.

1½ pounds (680 g) tuna steaks
Salt, to taste
1 small onion, peeled, cut into ⅛-inch (.25 cm) thick rings, the rings cut in half
1 fresh cayenne chile, stem and seeds removed, cut into strips (or substitute 2 serranos or jalapeños)
1 cup (236 mL) thinly sliced fresh green beans
1 cup (236 mL) sliced bamboo shoots
1 small onion, peeled and chopped
2 cloves garlic, peeled and finely chopped
1½ teaspoons (7.5 mL) finely grated fresh ginger
2 tablespoons (30 mL) brown bean sauce
4 tablespoons (60 mL) peanut oil
1 teaspoon (5 mL) shrimp paste
1 tablespoon (15 mL) soy sauce
⅔ cup (158 mL) water

1. Cut the fish into serving pieces, sprinkle the pieces with salt, and set them aside.
2. Place the onion rings, chiles, green beans, and bamboo shoots on separate plates. In a bowl, combine the chopped onion, garlic, ginger, and bean sauce.
3. Wipe the fish with paper towels to remove the excess moisture. In a wok or frying pan, heat the peanut oil over high heat. Add the fish pieces and fry until the pieces are browned on all sides. Remove them from the pan.
4. Pour off all but 2 tablespoons (30 mL) of the oil. Add the onion-bean sauce mixture and fry, stirring constantly, over medium heat until the onions are soft. Add the shrimp paste and green beans and stir-fry for 2 minutes. Add the chiles and sliced onion and stir-fry for 1 minute. Add the bamboo shoots, soy sauce, and water, stir well, cover, and simmer for 3 minutes. Add the fish to the mixture and heat through. Serve with white rice.

Thai Crab-Fried Rice

Yield: 4–6 servings   Heat Scale: Varies according sauce added

My correspondent Peter Aiken paddled a kayak to the floating markets of Bangkok. There, he discovered that while white rice in the region is eaten with meals, fried rice is a meal in itself. It is often made from leftover rice and other ingredients and cooked and served with Nam Prik sauce, which is quite salty, high in vitamins, and takes some getting used to.

2 tablespoons (30 mL) peanut oil
1 medium onion, peeled and minced
1 jalapeño chile, stem and seeds removed, minced
2 cloves garlic, peeled and minced
3 cups (708 mL) cooked white rice
1 cup (236 mL) crabmeat
2 eggs
3 green onions, sliced
Lime wedges for garnish
Nam Prik (Thai Pepper Water Sauce; page 95), for serving

1. In a wok, heat the oil over high heat. Add the onion, chile, and garlic, and stir-fry for a minute. Add the rice and crabmeat and heat through. Push the rice mixture to the side. Add the eggs to the center of the wok and, stirring continuously, cook until the eggs are half done. Stir the rice into the eggs. Add the green onions just before you remove the wok from the heat. The entire cooking process should take about 5 minutes.
2. Squeeze fresh lime over the finished dish and add Nam Prik as desired to individual plates.

Thod Mun Pla
(Deep-Fried Curried Fish Patties)

Yield: 4 servings   Heat Scale: Hot

It is easy to understand why, next to rice, fish is the main food consumed in Thailand. More than 60 percent of Thai people who live in the country catch their own fish for their meals. And although I do not use it in this recipe, one of their favorite fresh fish is carp, a true delicacy in much of Asia. What an exciting combination of ingredients this recipe has! The delicacy of the trout and the complexity of the red curry offer an aromatic and pungent Thai delight.

2 cups (473 mL) minced sea trout or other white fish
2 tablespoons (30 mL) Gaeng Ped (Red Curry Paste; paste 37)
1 tablespoon (15 mL) finely shredded kaffir lime leaves
5 fresh Thai chiles, stems and seeds removed, chopped (or substitute piquins or other small, hot chiles)
3 tablespoons (45 mL) fish sauce
1 teaspoon (5 mL) brown sugar
¼ teaspoon (1.25 mL) freshly ground black pepper
1 egg, beaten
1 cup (236 mL) sliced string beans
1 cup (236 mL) basil leaves
Vegetable oil for frying

1. In a large bowl, mix together all the ingredients except the oil. Form the mixture into small, flat, patties.
2. In a frying pan, heat the oil over medium heat. Fry the patties until they turn golden brown. Transfer them to paper towels to drain. Serve hot with a sampling of Asian hot sauces from Chapter 2.

Prik Chee Sy Moo
(Thai Baked Stuffed Chile Peppers)

Yield: 4 servings   Heat Scale: Medium

This low-calorie dish comes from Thailand, and it reminds one of chiles rellenos, the stuffed green chile dish of the American Southwest. Serve it with fried rice and an Asian salad from Chapter 6.

¾ pound (336 g) fresh or frozen snapper fillets, minced
⅓ cup (79 mL) water chestnuts, finely chopped
1 egg white, lightly beaten
2 green onions, minced
2 teaspoons (10 mL) peanut oil, divided
2 teaspoons (10 mL) soy sauce
8 green New Mexican chiles, stems left on, roasted, peeled, and seeded

1. Preheat the oven to 350°F (180°C). Spray a baking dish with nonstick vegetable oil spray.
2. In a bowl, combine the fish, water chestnuts, egg white, green onions, 1 teaspoon (5 mL) of the oil, and the soy sauce. Mix well.
3. Cut a slit in the side of each roasted chile. Carefully spoon the fish filling into the slits to avoid splitting. Place the stuffed chiles in the prepared baking dish. Brush the chiles lightly with the remaining oil.
4. Bake for 30 minutes or until the chiles are tender and the filling is cooked.

Haw Mog Hoy
(Spicy Steamed Mussels with Coconut)
Yield: 4 servings   Heat Scale: Medium

The coconut plays an important part in Thai cuisine. The tradition in upper-class households in this region says that coconut should be the first solid food to pass through the lips of any Thai baby. This is accomplished at the age of 1 month, when the infant is bathed in water containing coconut and fed three spoonfuls of soft, young coconut by a priest.

2 pounds (1.1 kg) fresh mussels
2 tablespoons (30 mL) vegetable oil
1 shallot, peeled and chopped
1 clove garlic, peeled and chopped
4 fresh serrano or jalapeño chiles, stems and seeds removed, chopped
1 teaspoon (5 mL) chopped cilantro root (or stems)
1 teaspoon (5 mL) chopped fresh ginger
1 teaspoon (5 mL) chopped lemongrass
½ teaspoon (2.5 mL) minced lemon peel
2 teaspoons (10 mL) shrimp paste
¾ cup (177 mL) thick coconut milk
1 large egg, lightly whisked
2 tablespoons (30 mL) rice flour
Salt, to taste
Freshly ground black pepper, to taste
¼ cup (59 mL) basil leaves

1. Scrub the mussels with a stiff wire brush and rinse them in cold salted water. Cook them in a steamer until they open, discarding any that fail to do so. Remove the mussels from the shells and reserve the larger shells.
2. In a sauté pan, heat the oil over medium heat. Add the shallot and garlic and sauté for 3 to 4 minutes. Add the chiles, cilantro, ginger, lemongrass, lemon peel, and shrimp paste. Continue to cook, stirring frequently, until the mixture gives off a fragrant aroma, then remove the pan from the heat and transfer the contents to a mixing bowl. Add the coconut milk, egg, flour, salt, and pepper and stir to combine thoroughly.
3. Blanch the basil leaves in boiling water and arrange on the bottom of the reserved shells. Place 3 mussels in each shell and spoon a little sauce over the top of each. Place the mussels in a steamer and cook until heated through, about 5 minutes. Serve immediately.

Singapore Chile Crab

Yield: 4 servings   Heat Scale: Medium

Here is a classic hot and spicy dish from this island nation that I ate twice during my visit. There are a seemingly endless supply of chiles in Singapore and a huge assortment of chile pastes and hot sauces of every heat level. If you can't make it to Singapore right away, this dish will give you the inspiration you need to buy your tickets!

2 tablespoons (30 mL) sugar
1 tablespoon (15 mL) salt
2 tablespoons (30 mL) tomato paste
1½ teaspoons (7.5 mL) chopped fresh ginger
2 garlic cloves, peeled and chopped
4 serrano or jalapeño chiles, stems and seeds removed, chopped
2 pounds (1.1 kg) live hard-shelled crabs
½ cup (118 mL) vegetable oil
2 large eggs, beaten lightly

1. In a small bowl, stir together the sugar, salt, and tomato paste. In a mortar, use a pestle and mash to a paste the ginger, garlic, and chile peppers.
2. In a pot, blanch the crabs in boiling water for 2 minutes, drain them, and let them cool until they can be handled. Discard the top shells, aprons, gills, sacs, mouths, and mandibles, and break the bodies in half, reserving the claws for another use.
3. In a large, heavy skillet heat the oil over medium-high heat until it is hot but not smoking. Add the crabs and fry them in the oil, turning them, for 4 minutes. With a slotted spoon, transfer the crabs to a platter. In the oil remaining in the skillet, fry the ginger mixture, stirring, for 2 minutes. Stir in the tomato paste mixture until well combined. Add the crabs and cook, stirring, until they are coated. Stir in the eggs and cook, stirring, about 1 minute or until the eggs are just set. Serve with a spicy rice dish from Chapter 13.

Singapore Fried Prawns with Dried Chile

Yield: 3–4 servings   Heat Scale: Extremely Hot

Here is another Singapore classic, this time featuring prawns. Prawns are used extensively in Asian cooking. They are often dried, ground, and processed into various types of pungent pastes. The use of 12 cayenne chiles in this sauce will definitely give your guests a thrill! You can tone it down by replacing the cayennes with 6 dried red New Mexican chiles.

For the Sauce:
12 dried cayenne peppers, stems and seeds removed, crushed
¼ cup (59 mL) rice wine
1 tablespoon (15 mL) vegetable oil
2 teaspoons (10 mL) sugar
1 teaspoon (5 mL) soy sauce
4 thin slices fresh ginger
4 thin diagonal slices green onion
1 clove garlic, peeled and minced
¼ teaspoon (1.25 mL) cornstarch mixed with ½ teaspoon (2.5 mL) cold water
1 dash dark soy sauce

1. In a small saucepan, combine all the ingredients over high heat and cook, stirring, until the mixture thickens slightly.

For the Prawns:
1 tablespoon (15 mL) cornstarch
1 teaspoon (5 mL) light soy sauce
2 eggs, beaten
2 tablespoons (30 mL) all-purpose flour
½ teaspoon (2.5 mL) salt
3 piquin chiles, stems and seeds removed, crushed, or substitute other small, hot dried chiles
Freshly ground black pepper, to taste
Vegetable oil for deep frying
1 pound (454 g) large prawns or shrimp, shelled and deveined

1. In a small bowl, combine the cornstarch, and soy sauce and blend until smooth. Add the eggs, flour, salt, piquins, and pepper and blend thoroughly.
2. In a large saucepan or deep fryer, heat the oil to 400°F (200°C). Meanwhile, pat the prawns dry with paper towels. Dip the shrimp into the batter, then drop them gently into the oil and fry for 15 to 20 seconds. Remove the shrimp with a slotted spoon and drain them well on paper towels.
3. Add the prawns to the sauce in batches, stirring just enough to coat. Transfer them to a platter and serve immediately with rice.

Udang Goreng Chilli
(Prawns in Chile-Garlic Sauce)

Yield: 2 servings   Heat Scale: Hot

This simple recipe is a Nonya favorite. The garlic combined with the chile makes for a spicy Singapore extravaganza. Serve with a collection of Asian appetizers from Chapter 5 for sampling.

½ pound (224 g) large prawns, peeled and deveined (or substitute large shrimp)
5 serrano or jalapeño chiles, stems and seeds removed
10 cloves garlic, peeled
1 teaspoon (5 mL) minced ginger
¼ cup (59 mL) vegetable oil
2 tablespoons (30 mL) soy sauce

1. Trim the heads of the prawns by removing the feelers, but leave the heads on. Wash the prawns and pat them dry with paper towels.
2. In a blender or food processor, purée together the chiles, garlic, and ginger to make a rough paste.
3. In a wok, heat the oil over high heat. When it smokes, add the chile-garlic paste and stir-fry until fragrant. Add the prawns and stir-fry for about 5 minutes. Add the soy sauce and stir fry until well-mixed, about 1 minute. Serve with hot steamed rice.

Lemongrass-Enrobed Catfish Fillets
(Trey Trung Kroeung)

Yield: 4 servings   Heat Scale: Medium

This Cambodian recipe was collected by David Karp from the Elephant Walk restaurant in Somerville, Massachusetts. The chef features catfish in this recipe, as it is close in flavor and texture to some of the freshwater fishes found in Cambodia.

3 dried New Mexican chiles, stems and seeds removed
1 tablespoon (15 mL) minced lemongrass
3 cloves garlic, peeled
2 medium shallots, peeled
4 dried piquin chiles, stems and seeds removed (or substitute other small hot chiles)
4 kaffir lime leaves
3 thin slices peeled galangal (or substitute ginger)
1 pinch ground turmeric
½ cup (118 mL) water
2 tablespoons (30 mL) vegetable oil
4 (8-ounce [224 g]) catfish fillets
1 cup (236 mL) coconut milk
1 teaspoon (5 mL) salt
2 teaspoons (10 mL) sugar
4 very finely julienned kaffir lime leaves for garnish

1. Soak the New Mexican chiles for 10 minutes in lukewarm water to soften. Remove the chiles from the water and drain them.

2. In a blender or food processor, combine the lemongrass, garlic, shallots, piquin chiles, lime leaves, galangal, turmeric, and water and purée until smooth.

3. In a frying pan, heat the oil over high heat. Add the catfish and pan-fry them until they are firm, but not browned, turning once.

4. In a separate pan, cook the paste over medium heat for about 2 minutes, stirring constantly, until the aroma is released. Add the coconut milk, salt, and sugar. Add the fish to the sauce and cook for 5 more minutes. If the paste is too thick, add more water until you achieve the desired consistency.

5. Serve with jasmine rice, garnished with the kaffir lime leaves.

Amok
(Tantalizing Catfish)

Yield: 4 servings   Heat Scale: Medium

Cambodian cooking is similar to Thai cooking because both countries share the influence of Vietnam, China, and Indonesia. It can be characterized by the use of lemongrass, galangal, ginger, garlic, and many freshwater fish, most of which are not available in the United States. I have used catfish in this recipe, as it bears a close resemblance to its Vietnamese counterparts. (Note: This recipe requires advance preparation.)

1 teaspoon (5 mL) thin slices peeled galangal
1 clove garlic, peeled
1½ tablespoons (22.5 mL) very finely julienned kaffir lime leaves, divided
¼ teaspoon (1.25 mL) ground turmeric
4 tablespoons (60 mL) fresh minced lemongrass
5 dried santaka or piquin chiles, stems and seeds removed, soaked 10 minutes in lukewarm water, chopped fine
2 tablespoons (30 mL) fish sauce
1 egg, well beaten
2 tablespoons (30 mL) sugar
2 cups (473 mL) coconut milk
1½ pounds (680 g) catfish fillets, sliced into ¼-inch (.5 cm) thick strips
8 (14 × 10–inch [35 × 25 cm]) pieces banana leaves
½ pound (224 g) fresh spinach leaves

1. In a blender or food processor, combine the galangal, garlic, 1 teaspoon (5 mL) of the kaffir lime leaves, the turmeric, the lemongrass, the chiles, the fish sauce, the egg, the sugar, and the coconut milk. Process, scraping the sides of the container occasionally, until the ingredients are puréed.

2. Transfer the contents of the blender to a glass bowl. Add the fish and coat thoroughly with mix. Cover and refrigerate overnight or at least 5 hours.

3. Layer one piece of banana leaf on top of another, to make a double thickness. Place one-quarter of the spinach leaves into the center and top with one-quarter of the fish mixture (about 1 cup [236 mL]). Garnish with a pinch of the remaining julienned kaffir lime leaves. Fold the two layers of banana leaves lengthwise in thirds, then fold the ends up to the top and secure with toothpicks. Keep the sides up to prevent leaking. Repeat the procedure, making four packages.

4. Place the bottom rack of a 9- or 10-inch (22.5 or 25 cm) bamboo steamer in a wok and pour in enough water to come to about an inch (2.5 cm) below the steamer. Put two fish packages on the bottom rack. Fit a second rack above it and put on the remaining two packages. Cover and cook over high heat for about 5 minutes to bring to a boil. Reduce the heat to medium-low and cook for 45 minutes. To serve, remove the toothpicks and open the packages.

Fish with Ginger Salsa

Yield: 4 servings   Heat Scale: Varies

This recipe comes from my good friend Richard Sterling. Richard, who now lives in Vietnam, has spent many years in Southeast Asia, and he collected this recipe for me from his foodie friends in Saigon.

¼ teaspoon (1.25 mL) salt
½ teaspoon (2.5 mL) freshly ground black pepper
1 teaspoon (5 mL) sugar
4 teaspoons (20 mL) fish sauce
12 large basil leaves
1 (2-pound [1.1 kg]) whole fish, cleaned, head and tail left on (snapper recommended)
4 cloves garlic, peeled and minced
1 tablespoon (15 mL) grated ginger
1 serrano or jalapeño chile, stem and seeds removed, minced
Juice of 1 lime
1 recipe Nuoc Cham (Vietnamese Dipping Sauce; page 96)

1. In a bowl, combine the salt, pepper, sugar, and fish sauce. Spread a plate with basil leaves and place the fish on the plate. Sprinkle the fish sauce mixture over the fish. Marinate for 30 minutes.

2. In a separate bowl, combine the garlic, ginger, chile, and lime juice and spread this mixture evenly on the top of the fish. Transfer the fish and the plate to a steamer and cook for 30 minutes.

3. Serve with the Nuoc Cham.

Pla Nuang
(Steamed Spicy Fish)

Yield: 4 servings   Heat Scale: Medium

Vietnam is also the origin of this steamed fish recipe. The pickled plums, which can be found in Asian markets, offer a tart taste. Pickled mangos can also be used, if you would like a sweeter flavor.

1 (3-pound [1.36 kg]) whole grouper or snapper, cleaned and scaled, head and tail left on
3 pickled plums, coarsely chopped
¼ cup (59 mL) juice from the pickled plum jar
½ cup (118 mL) Traditional European Fish Stock (page 47)
¼ teaspoon (1.25 mL) freshly ground black pepper
¼ cup (59 mL) celery leaves
2 green onions, chopped
3 fresh serrano or jalapeño chiles, stems and seeds removed, coarsely chopped

1. Make two slits in the skin across the width of the fish on both sides, to prevent curling. Place the fish in a fish poacher or in a shallow pan with a lid.
2. In a bowl, combine the chopped pickled plums, plum juice, fish stock, and black pepper. Pour this mixture over the fish. Cover and steam over low heat for 15 minutes.
3. In a separate bowl, combine the celery leaves, green onions, and chopped chiles. Pour this mixture over the fish, cover, and steam for another 5 to 7 minutes or until the fish is completely cooked. Serve with a rice dish from Chapter 13.

Nga Wetma
(Pigfish Curry)

Yield: 4   Heat Scale: Medium

The Burmese call the grouper the "pig of the sea," referring to its meaty texture and large size. A grouper may grow to more than 700 pounds (315 kg), but you won't need one that big for this recipe. This curry is sweet, hot, and smooth all at the same time.

1 pound (454 g) grouper fillets, cut into 1-inch (2.5 cm) cubes
1 teaspoon (5 mL) paprika, divided
¼ teaspoon (1.25 mL) turmeric, divided
½ teaspoon (2.5 mL) salt
1 tablespoon (15 mL) fish sauce, divided
2 tablespoons (30 mL) corn oil
2 tablespoons (30 mL) finely chopped onion
1 tablespoon (15 mL) minced fresh ginger
2 cloves garlic, peeled and minced
1 cup (236 mL) diced tomatoes, fresh or canned
⅔ cup (158 mL) water
2 tablespoons (30 mL) chopped cilantro
2 serrano or jalapeño chiles, stems and seeds removed, sliced thin

1. In a large dish, marinate the fish with ½ teaspoon (2.5 mL) of the paprika, ⅛ teaspoon (.6 mL) of the turmeric, the salt, and 1 teaspoon (5 mL) of the fish sauce for 15 minutes.
2. In a frying pan, heat the oil over medium heat. Add the onion, ginger, garlic, and the remaining turmeric and paprika and fry for 2 minutes. Add the tomatoes and the remaining fish sauce and stir-fry for 3 minutes to reduce the mixture to a thick sauce.
3. Add the fish and stir-fry it for 5 minutes. Add the water, stir for a moment, cover the pan, and reduce the heat to low. Cook for 20 minutes to evaporate the liquid and create a thick sauce.
4. Sprinkle the curry with the cilantro and chile and serve it with rice or noodles.

Umai
(Tangy Marinated Fish)
Yield: 3–4 servings   Heat Scale: Medium

The key to this recipe from Borneo is to use the freshest fish possible. The Latin American version of this dish would be ceviche, which also cooks the meat of fish with lime juice. Fresh scallops or shrimp can be substituted for an interesting change.

½ cup (118 mL) freshly squeezed lime juice, or more if needed
1 pound (454 g) very fresh fish fillets, cut into thin slices (Spanish mackerel preferred)
3 serrano or jalapeño chiles, stems and seeds removed, chopped
1 teaspoon (5 mL) salt
8 shallots, peeled and thinly sliced
1 (2-inch [5 cm]) piece ginger, peeled and grated
2 sprigs cilantro, chopped
2 sprigs celery leaves, chopped

1. In a shallow dish, marinate the fish in all but 2 tablespoons (30 mL) of the lime juice for at least 30 minutes, stirring once or twice, until the fish turns white. Drain and discard the lime juice.
2. While the fish is marinating, pound the chiles and salt to a paste. When the fish is ready, transfer it to a bowl and add the chile paste, shallots, ginger, fresh cilantro, celery, and the remaining 2 tablespoons (30 mL) lime juice. Taste for seasonings and add more salt if desired. Serve immediately with any fried rice from Chapter 13.

Ikan Bandeng
(Fiery Party Snapper)

Yield: 6 servings   Heat Scale: Mild

This fish makes a truly elegant entrée for a dinner party when unwrapped at the table, says Rosemary Ogilvie, who collected this fine recipe in Bali for me.

1 (3–4 pound [1.36–1.82 kg]) whole snapper or grouper, cleaned, head and tail left on
1 medium onion, peeled and chopped
2 cloves garlic, peeled and minced
1 teaspoon (5 mL) minced ginger
¼ cup (59 mL) tamarind sauce
1 tablespoon (15 mL) dark soy sauce
1 tablespoon (15 mL) vegetable oil
1 teaspoon (5 mL) ground turmeric
2 teaspoons (10 mL) commercial Asian chile paste, or more to taste
1 teaspoon (5 mL) salt
3 tablespoons (45 mL) finely chopped cilantro

1. Preheat the oven to 350°F (180°C). Line a baking dish with foil.
2. Wash the fish, dry it well with paper towels, and score the flesh diagonally on each side.
3. In a blender, combine the onion, garlic, ginger, tamarind, soy sauce, oil, turmeric, sambalan, and salt and purée until smooth. Rub this mixture well into both sides of the fish and put the remaining mixture inside the body cavity.
4. Place fish in the prepared baking dish. Sprinkle it with the cilantro and fold the foil over to enclose the fish.
5. Bake for 35 to 40 minutes. When it's done, the flesh of the fish will appear milky white and be easy to flake with a fork. Transfer the fish to a serving platter and open the foil at the table.

Byron Bay Chilli Fish Tacos

Yield: 4–6 servings   Heat Scale: Varies

My friend and Australian hot sauce maker John Boland is promoting a fusion cuisine he calls "OxMex," and this is one of his signature recipes. Fish tacos are almost always good, but with John's sweet chile sauces, they shine. Use either Byron Bay Chilli Co. Fiery Coconut Chilli Sauce or Byron Bay Chilli Co. Spicy Sweet Chilli Sauce, available from various online hot sauce shops.

2 pounds (1.1 kg) boneless fish fillets
¼ cup (59 mL) olive oil
Juice of 1 lime
2 green onions, chopped, white and green parts included
¼ cup (59 mL) chopped cilantro
2 cups (473 mL) shredded cabbage
¼ cup (59 mL) mayonnaise
1 cup (236 mL) plain yogurt or sour cream
Ground red chile of your choice, to taste
Salt, to taste
12 flour tortillas
1 (8.5-ounce [238 g]) bottle Byron Bay Chilli Co. sauce of your choice (or substitute an Asian hot sauce from Chapter 2)

1. Place the fish in a large, shallow dish. Sprinkle it with the olive oil and lime juice and allow it to marinate for 30 minutes.
2. In a large bowl, combine the green onion, cilantro, and cabbage.
3. In a small bowl, whisk together the mayonnaise, yogurt or sour cream, ground chile, and salt.
4. Preheat a grill to medium-low heat.
5. Wrap the tortillas in foil and place them on a not-too-hot part of the grill to slowly warm them.
6. On a very clean, thoroughly oiled grate, grill the fish until it is just cooked through, about 10 minutes per inch (2.5 cm) of thickness of the fish. Remove the fish to a clean platter, allow it to rest for10 minutes, then slice it into thick strips.
7. For each taco, place a warm tortilla on a plate, add a few chunks of fish, and drizzle with the chile sauce, a spoonful of the salad, some of the creamy sauce, and more chile sauce. Make a small fold along the bottom edge of the tortilla, then fold it closed from both the sides, creating a little parcel that won't drip out the bottom.

Grilled Garlic Fish

Yield: 4 servings   Heat Scale: Medium

This is a simple but classic method of preparing any firm, white-fleshed fish in the Philippines. To make the coconut vinegar, soak 2 tablespoons (30 mL) grated coconut in ¼ cup (59 mL) distilled white vinegar for 30 minutes. You can use a fish basket on the grill so the fillets don't stick. Serve with an Asian hot sauce from Chapter 2. (Note: This recipe requires advance preparation.)

4 cloves garlic, peeled and minced
¼ cup (59 mL) coconut vinegar
1 small chile, such as serrano, stem and seeds removed, minced
Salt, to taste
Freshly ground black pepper, to taste
1 pound (454 g) white fish fillets
Vegetable oil for the grill

1. In a bowl, combine the garlic, coconut vinegar, chile, salt, and pepper and mix well. Reserve some of this marinade for basting. Place the fish fillets in a shallow bowl and pour the marinade over them. Marinate for 30 minutes.
2. Brush the grill with vegetable oil and grill the fillets over medium-hot flames for 4 to 5 minutes, turning once and basting with the marinade. Remove the fish from the grill, top with the reserved marinade, and serve immediately.

Sichuan Shrimp and Snow Peas

Yield: 4 servings   Heat Scale: Medium

I've substituted shrimp for the traditional prawns in this dish, as they are more widely available and less expensive. After all, prawns are just really big shrimp. Since they signify good fortune and happiness, they are usually included in a traditional New Year's feast. If you want to increase the heat, use either small dried red chiles or crushed chiles, as increasing the chile paste will change the flavor of the dish.

2 teaspoons (10 mL) vegetable oil (peanut preferred)
2 teaspoons (10 mL) dark sesame oil, divided
1 cup (236 mL) snow peas
3 jalapeño chiles, stems and seeds removed, sliced
2 teaspoons (10 mL) minced garlic
1 pound (454 g) large shrimp, shelled and deveined
½ cup (118 mL) rice vinegar
¼ cup (59 mL) catsup
1 tablespoon (15 mL) Asian garlic chile-based sauce
1 tablespoon (15 mL) sugar
2 tablespoons (30 mL) cornstarch
¼ cup (59 mL) sliced mushrooms
2 cups (473 mL) cooked white rice

1. In a wok or heavy skillet, heat the vegetable oil and half the sesame oil over high heat until very hot. Add the snow peas and stir-fry for 1 minute. Remove the peas and pour off all but 1 teaspoon (5 mL) of the oil.
2. Add the remaining sesame oil and heat it. Add the jalapeños and garlic and stir-fry for 30 seconds. Add the shrimp and fry until the shrimp turns pink, about 3 minutes. Remove the shrimp and keep it warm.
3. In a bowl, blend together the vinegar, catsup, chile paste, sugar, and cornstarch.
4. Raise the heat under the wok and pour in the vinegar blend. Heat the sauce, stirring constantly, until it thickens. Lower the heat, add the mushrooms, return the shrimp and peas to the wok, and heat through.
5. Serve the shrimp in a bowl accompanied by the white rice.

Sichuan-Marinated Grilled Tilapia
Yield : 4 servings   Heat Scale: Medium-Hot

Tilapia, a farm-raised fish originally from Asia, is mild and sweet-tasting with a delicate flesh. You can substitute catfish or flounder fillets if you can't find tilapia. These are the fish fillets most enjoyed by people who don't like "fishy" fish. They work particularly well for chile-infused recipes because they are soft and absorb the marinade quickly. Use a fish basket to turn the fillets without destroying them. Sichuan peppercorns and Asian garlic chile paste are available at Asian markets and online. Serve this dish with a Chinese peanut and noodle salad and garlic broccoli. (Note: This recipe requires advance preparation.)

For the Sichuan Marinade:
1 teaspoon (5 mL) Sichuan peppercorns
¼ cup (59 mL) dry sherry
1 tablespoon (15 mL) finely chopped ginger
1 green onion, finely chopped, green part included
1 teaspoon (5 mL) minced garlic
1 teaspoon (5 mL) sesame oil
4 tilapia fillets
½ teaspoon (2.5 mL) crushed santaka chile or other small, hot red chile

1. In a hot, dry frying pan toast the Sichuan peppercorns until fragrant. Remove them from the pan, let them cool, and crush them. In a bowl, combine the crushed peppercorns with the remaining ingredients and allow to sit for 30 minutes to blend the flavors.
2. Place the fish in a nonreactive dish, pour the marinade over the fish, and marinate, covered, for 1 hour at room temperature.

¾ cup (177 mL) Classic Chicken Stock (page 46)
¼ cup (59 mL) rice wine vinegar
2 tablespoons (30 mL) Asian plum sauce (available in Asian markets)
1 tablespoon (15 mL) sugar
1 tablespoon (15 mL) cornstarch
½ teaspoon (2.5 mL) sesame oil
1 tablespoon (15 mL) vegetable oil, peanut preferred
1 green onion, chopped
1 teaspoon (5 mL) minced ginger
4 whole santaka chiles, chile piquins, or other small hot, red chiles
2 tablespoons (30 mL) Asian garlic chile-based sauce
1 tablespoon (15 mL) ground red New Mexican chile
Minced green onion for garnish

1. In a bowl, whisk together the broth, vinegar, plum sauce, sugar, cornstarch, and sesame oil.
2. Heat a wok over high heat until hot and add the vegetable oil. Add the green onion, ginger, and santaka chiles and stir-fry for a couple of minutes. Add the chile paste and stir-fry for 1 minute. Add the broth mixture and the ground red chile and stir well. Increase the heat and bring the sauce to a boil, then reduce the heat and simmer it until thickened. Remove the whole chiles.
3. Place the fillets in a grill basket with handles and grill them over a medium fire until they flake with a fork, turning occasionally, about 8 to 10 minutes. Take care that the fillets don't burn.
4. To serve, pour a little of the sauce on a plate, place the fish on top, and garnish with the green onion.

Wasabi-Marinated Ahi Tuna with Asian Chile Slaw
Yield: 4 servings   Heat Scale: Mild

Wasabi is an extremely powerful Japanese horseradish that can be found as a powder or as a paste in easy-to-use tubes. If using it as a powder, reconstitute it in rice wine vinegar. This tuna should be served medium-rare. (Note: This recipe requires advance preparation.)

¼ cup (118 mL) plus 5 tablespoons (75 mL) rice wine vinegar, divided
2 tablespoons (30 mL) soy sauce
1½ tablespoons (22.5 mL) wasabi paste
1½ tablespoons (22.5 mL) grated fresh ginger
1 tablespoon (15 mL) vegetable oil
1 tablespoon (15 mL) minced shallots
1 tablespoon (15 mL) hot mustard
2 cloves garlic, peeled and minced
1 serrano or jalapeño chile, stem and seeds removed, minced
4 ahi tuna steaks (or substitute swordfish)
⅓ cup (79 mL) vegetable oil, peanut preferred
1 tablespoon (15 mL) apple cider vinegar
2 teaspoons (10 mL) Thai fish sauce
2 teaspoons (10 mL) sesame oil
2 teaspoons (10 mL) sugar
4 small fresh Thai chiles), stems removed, minced, or substitute 2 serrano chiles
¼ cup (59 mL) plus 2 teaspoons (10 mL) finely sliced green onions, divided
Salt, to taste
Freshly ground white pepper, to taste
2 cups (473 mL) finely shredded Napa or regular cabbage
¼ cup (59 mL) shredded carrots
¼ cup (59 mL) sliced edible pea pods, sliced lengthwise
¼ cup (59 mL) chopped peanuts
Chopped fresh cilantro for garnish

1. In a bowl, combine 5 tablespoons (75 mL) of the rice wine vinegar with the soy sauce, wasabi paste, ginger, vegetable oil, shallots, hot mustard, garlic, and serrano or jalapeño. Allow the marinade to sit at room temperature for 20 minutes to blend the flavors.
2. Place the fish in a single layer in a nonreactive bowl, pour the marinade over the fish, and turn to coat. Cover and marinate for an hour at room temperature.
3. Whisk together the peanut oil, apple cider vinegar, remaining ¼ cup (118 mL) rice wine vinegar, fish sauce, sesame oil, sugar, Thai chiles, the 2 teaspoons (10 mL) green onions, the salt, and the white pepper. Allow the dressing to sit, covered, at room temperature for 30 minutes to blend the flavors.
4. Grill the fish over a medium fire for about 10 minutes, turning occasionally, until medium-rare. Cut one of the steaks open to check for doneness.
5. In a bowl, toss together the cabbage, carrots, remaining ¼ cup (59 mL) green onions, and pea pods. Toss with just enough of the dressing to coat. Garnish with the peanuts and cilantro.
6. To serve, place the fish on a plate and serve with the slaw on the side.

TWELVE

Mighty Meatless
Main Dishes

- - - - - - - - - - - - - - -

I am not a vegetarian, merely a cook who enjoys a wide variety of foods. Hot and spicy food lends itself to the absence of meat because of the intense flavors and sensations produced by the chiles. This regimen also works perfectly with low-salt, low-cholesterol, and low-fat diets, so the recipes in this chapter reflect those health considerations. Meats and meat products eliminated here include red meats, poultry, fish, shellfish, and all stocks and gravies made from them, but this chapter is not vegan. I have included dairy products such as milk and cheese, but cooks should note the many varieties of nondairy substitutes available.

If you are a practicing vegetarian, there are many more vegetarian recipes in this book—hundreds in all. Check out chapters 1, 2, 3, 4, 6, 13, and 14 for more meatless dishes.

The organization of this chapter is somewhat eclectic because of the enormous number of possible meatless styles of cooking. So I decided to start with pungent pasta dishes, move on to meatless Mexican, then recipes using meat substitutes, and ending with a wide assortment of other meatless entrées.

Red Chile Noodles

Yield: 2–3 servings   Heat Scale: Mild

This homemade pasta is excellent and can be served with any pasta topping you like, spicy or not. To make other chile pastas, simply change the size of the noodles. If you are making them a day ahead of time, store them in the refrigerator until ready to use.

3 tablespoons (45 mL) ground hot red New Mexican chile
3 cups (708 mL) semolina flour (available in gourmet shops and health food stores)
2 large eggs, beaten lightly
1 tablespoon (15 mL) olive oil

1. In a bowl, mix together the ground chile and semolina. Make a well in the middle and place the eggs and olive oil in it.
2. Mix with your hands, then knead for 10 minutes. Cover the dough, and let it sit for 30 minutes.
3. Bring a large pot of salted water to a boil.
4. Using a rolling pin (or a pasta machine), roll the dough very thin (⅟₃₂ inch [.8 mm] or thinner). Cut the dough into 1½-inch (3.5 cm) wide strips.
5. Cook the noodles in the boiling salted water for 1 to 2 minutes, no more. Drain them, place them on a kitchen towel, and cover them with plastic wrap until you are ready to use them in your recipe.

Jalapeño Pasta

Yield: 3 servings   Heat Scale: Medium

From an article Nanette Blanchard wrote for me on pepper pastas comes this additional chile pasta. It has a great fresh chile aroma and a golden color with green flecks.

3 large eggs, at room temperature
6 jalapeño chiles, stems and seeds removed, coarsely chopped
2 teaspoons (10 mL) olive oil
2 cups (473 mL) unbleached all-purpose flour, plus more as needed
2 tablespoons (30 mL) water, plus more as needed

1. In a food processor, combine the eggs, jalapeños, and olive oil and purée. Add the flour and continue to process until the dough forms a ball.
2. If the mixture remains crumbly, add the water 1 teaspoon (5 mL) at a time until the dough forms a ball. Knead by hand for 10 minutes to increase the dough's elasticity. Cover the dough and let it sit for 30 minutes.
3. Using a pasta machine or a rolling pin and a well-floured work area, roll the dough out as thinly as possible (about a 4 on the Atlas hand-cranked pasta machine). Drape the sheets of rolled dough over the back of chairs and let them dry for about 10 minutes before cutting the pasta.
4. With a sharp knife or a pasta machine, cut the sheets into thin strips to the desired width and hang them on a wooden rack to dry overnight. To cook, gently immerse the pasta in boiling salted water and cook for several minutes or until tender.

Green Chile Pasta

Yield: 3–4 servings   Heat Scale: Mild

Green chile pasta has been popular in the Southwest for many years. It is surprisingly easy to make and even easier to eat. Just remember that if you are using green chiles, it is necessary to remove all of the liquid, or the excess will interfere with the water measurement.

3 tablespoons (45 mL) ground green chile (or substitute ¼ cup [59 mL] drained green chile finely minced or processed in a food processor to a paste consistency)
2 cups (473 mL) all-purpose flour
1 teaspoon (5 mL) salt
2 eggs, lightly beaten
2 tablespoons (30 mL) vegetable oil

1. In a small, heavy skillet, sauté the green chile over low heat until the moisture has evaporated. Allow the chile to cool.
2. Mix together all the ingredients to make a dough. If you are using an electric pasta machine and the dough still seems too dry, you may need to add some water, a tablespoon (15 mL) at a time, until the dough reaches the desired consistency.
3. Cut or extrude the dough into the desired shape. Separate the dough, allow it to dry, and cook it in boiling, salted water for 2 to 3 minutes. Drain the pasta and serve it with your favorite sauce from Chapter 2.

Red Chile Peanut Pasta

Yield: 3–4 servings   Heat Scale: Mild

This combination of flavors harkens back to Thai cooking, as well as to some popular Nigerian recipes. The pasta tastes great with many different sauce combinations; it is also terrific deep-fried and served as a snack. Or, try it deep-fried, shaped into nests, and filled with sautéed vegetables and seafood.

¼ cup (59 mL) smooth peanut butter, at room temperature
2–3 tablespoons red chile flakes
2 cups (473 mL) all-purpose flour
½ teaspoon (2.5 mL) salt
1 egg
Enough water to bring the egg to 1 cup (236 mL)

1. In a bowl, combine all the ingredients and mix well. Using a rolling pin (or a pasta machine), roll the dough very thin (¹⁄₃₂ inch [.8 mm] or thinner). Cut it into 1½-inch (3.5 cm) wide strips.

Cajun Cayenne Pasta
Yield: 1 pound (454 g) pasta   Heat Scale: Medium

Use this spicy pasta to accompany any favorite Cajun dish. Try it with seafood or deep-fry it for an unusual snack.

3 cups (708 mL) all-purpose flour
2 tablespoons (30 mL) ground cayenne
½ teaspoon (2.5 mL) paprika
½ teaspoon (2.5 mL) garlic salt
½ teaspoon (2.5 mL) onion salt
1 tablespoon (15 mL) vegetable oil
3 eggs, lightly beaten
Enough water to bring the liquid measurement to 1 cup (236 mL)

1. In a bowl, combine the flour, cayenne, paprika, garlic salt, and onion salt and mix well. Combine the oil, eggs, and water and add this mixture to the dry ingredients. Using a rolling pin (or a pasta machine), roll the dough very thin (½2 inch [.8 mm] or thinner). Cut it into 1½-inch (3.5 cm) wide strips.

Chipotle and Cilantro Pasta
Yield: 1 pound (454 g) pasta   Heat Scale: Medium

This beautiful, red-flecked pasta is great in pasta salads. It also works well as a filled pasta, such as ravioli or tortellini. Be sure the chipotle is very finely minced so it does not clog the machine, or use this as a flat noodle rather than a shaped noodle.

3 tablespoons (45 mL) canned or bottled chipotle in adobo, finely minced
1 tablespoon (15 mL) vegetable oil
3 eggs, lightly beaten
Enough water to bring the liquid measurement to 1 cup (236 mL)
3 cups (708 mL) all-purpose flour
1 teaspoon (5 mL) salt
1 tablespoon (15 mL) minced fresh cilantro

1. In a bowl combine the minced chipotle in adobo with the liquid ingredients. Add the flour, salt, and cilantro and mix together. Using a rolling pin (or a pasta machine), roll the dough very thin (½2 inch [.8 mm] or thinner). Cut the dough into 1½-inch (3.5 cm) wide strips.

Pasta alle Melanzane
(Roasted Eggplant and Garlic Pasta)

Yield: 4 servings   Heat Scale: Mild to Medium

There are many variations on a combination of tomatoes and eggplants all over the Mediterranean, but I like this one from Abulia in southern Italy, where they prefer their food spicy. This region of Italy also grows a dazzling variety of vegetables and holds the title to the most vegetable-based pasta sauces in the country. The residents of Abulia air-dry cherry tomatoes like chiles and then use the half-dried tomatoes in dishes such as this, but I have substituted canned tomatoes so you can prepare this pasta year-round. I like to roast the eggplant rather than sauté it, which retains more of its texture and flavor, giving the dish an almost meaty flavor. And since cheese is not used in many versions of this pasta, vegans can just omit the Parmesan.

1 medium eggplant, ends trimmed, cut into 1-inch (2.5 cm) chunks
4 cloves garlic, peeled and minced
3 tablespoons (45 mL) extra virgin olive oil, divided
Salt, to taste
Freshly ground black pepper, to taste
1½ cups (354 mL) chopped onion
2 (14-ounce [392 g]) cans chopped tomatoes, liquid included
2 tablespoons (30 mL) chopped Italian parsley
3 tablespoons (45 mL) coarsely chopped cured black olives
1 tablespoon (15 mL) dry red wine (optional)
1 tablespoon (15 mL) chopped fresh basil
2 teaspoons (10 mL) dried oregano
2–4 dried peperoncinos, crushed (or substitute 1–2 teaspoons [5–10 mL]) crushed red chile, such as piquin
8 ounces (224 g) penne
Grated Parmesan cheese (optional)

1. Preheat the oven to 350°F (180°C).
2. Place the eggplant and garlic in a bowl. Add 2 tablespoons (30 mL) of the olive oil, season with salt and pepper, and toss to coat. Transfer to a baking sheet and arrange in a single layer.
3. Place the pan on the center rack of the oven and roast for 10 minutes. Stir and turn the eggplant, and continue to roast for an additional 10 to 15 minutes or until the eggplant is browned.
4. In a saucepan, heat the remaining oil over medium heat. Add the onion and sauté until soft and golden, about 5 minutes; do not brown.
5. Add the tomatoes, parsley, olives, wine (if using), basil, oregano, and chiles. Bring to a boil, reduce the heat, and simmer, stirring occasionally, until the mixture has thickened, about 20 to 30 minutes. Add the eggplant and heat through.
6. Bring a large stockpot of cold water to a boil, add salt, then add the pasta. Cook the pasta until al dente. Drain the pasta, but don't rinse it, and transfer it to a large, warmed bowl.
7. Toss the pasta with the sauce and serve with the cheese on the side.

Blazin' High Noon Pasta

Yield: 2 servings   Heat Scale: Medium to Medium-Hot

Thanks to Tim Fex for this recipe. The hot nuts really make a difference when you are preparing this pasta. Not only do they add texture, they also provide a different flavor experience with their heat. Add the chiltepins for additional heat.

½ pound (224 g) linguine (red pepper linguine is a great substitute)
1½ teaspoons (7.5 mL) canola oil
½ cup (118 mL) diced red onion
1 cup (236 mL) wild mushrooms, coarsely chopped
2 cloves garlic, peeled and finely minced
3–4 Roma tomatoes, peeled, seeded and chopped
3–4 tomatillos, blackened and chopped
1–2 jalapeño peppers, stems and seeds removed, diced
½ teaspoon (2.5 mL) ground cumin
¼ teaspoon (1.25 mL) Mexican oregano
2–3 chiltepins, crushed (optional)
½ cup (118 mL) finely chopped hot hazelnuts, pecans, pistachios, or pea-nuts, divided
½ cup (118 mL) Super Rich Vegetable Stock (page 48), divided
Salt, to taste
Freshly ground black pepper, to taste
¼ cup (59 mL) finely grated Parmesan cheese

1. Bring a large pot of water to a boil. Add the linguine and cook until al dente. Drain the pasta, transfer it to a bowl, and keep it warm.
2. In a large skillet, heat the canola oil over medium heat. Add the onions and sauté until they are limp. Add the mushrooms and cook until they are halfway done, about 1 minute.
3. Add the garlic and stir briefly. Add the tomatoes, tomatillos, jalapeños, cumin, oregano, and chiltepins (if using). Cook until the tomatoes begin to collapse, approximately 2 minutes. Add three-quarters of the hot nuts (use the finer parts, reserving the larger parts for a garnish) and half the stock. Cook to a medium consistency, thinning the mixture with more stock if necessary. Season with the salt and pepper.
4. Pour the sauce over the pasta and top it with the grated cheese. Garnish with the larger pieces of the hazelnuts.

Pasta with Creamy Habanero Sauce

Yield: 4–6 servings   Heat Scale: Medium-Hot

This simple and quick pasta dish has the distinctive habanero flavor and heat, which is tempered somewhat by the tomatoes and cream.

6 medium tomatoes (or 2 cups [473 mL] stewed tomatoes)
3 tablespoons (45 mL) butter, divided
3 tablespoons (45 mL) habanero hot sauce from Chapter 2
1½ tablespoons (22.5 mL) all-purpose flour
1 cup (236 mL) light cream
Salt, to taste
1 pound (454 g) fusilli or rigatoni, cooked

1. If you are using fresh tomatoes, peel them and purée them in a blender.
2. Melt 1 tablespoon (15 mL) of the butter in a saucepan over medium heat. Add the hot sauce and sauté for 1 minute. Add the tomatoes and simmer for 15 minutes.
3. In a separate saucepan, melt the remaining 2 tablespoons (30 mL) butter over medium heat. Add the flour and cook until it is golden, stirring constantly with a whisk. In a separate saucepan or in the microwave, heat the cream but do not let it boil. Add the hot cream to the flour mixture and stir over a low heat until the mixture thickens.
4. Combine the cream and tomato mixtures. Add salt to taste. Spoon the sauce over the pasta and serve immediately.

Southwestern Pasta with Tabasco Sauce

Yield: 4 servings   Heat Scale: Medium

Thanks to Hunter-McKenzie PR firm and the McIlhenny Company for this recipe. The punch of the Tabasco Sauce contrasts nicely with the cilantro, and this dish is a winner. Serve it with a big green salad, dressed with a creamy dressing, or a salad from Chapter 6.

¼ cup (59 mL) olive oil
2 medium onions, peeled and sliced
1 clove garlic, peeled and minced
3½ cups (826 mL) stewed tomatoes, crushed
¾ teaspoon (3.75 mL) Tabasco Sauce
¼ teaspoon (1.25 mL) salt
2–3 tablespoons minced fresh cilantro
¼ teaspoon (1.25 mL) sugar
12 ounces (336 g) angel hair pasta, cooked
Grated Parmesan cheese for serving (optional)

1. In a large, heavy, non-aluminum saucepan, heat the oil over medium heat. Add the onions and garlic and sauté for 10 to 12 minutes, stirring occasionally, until tender. Add the tomatoes, Tabasco Sauce, salt, cilantro, and sugar and bring to a boil. Reduce the heat to low and simmer, uncovered, for 30 minutes, until the mixture is slightly thickened.

2. Place the hot, cooked pasta on a heated serving platter and top it with the sauce. Sprinkle with Parmesan cheese if desired.

Angel Hair Pasta with Spicy Chile Pickled Garlic Sauce

Yield: 2–3 servings   Heat Scale: Medium

Judy Knapp gave me this quick recipe for serious garlic lovers. If you have never tasted spiced-up chile garlic, treat yourself to this addictive delight! Several companies now make pickled garlic infused with crushed chiles.

½ pound (224 g) angel hair pasta
1 tablespoon (15 mL) olive oil
3 cloves commercial chile-pickled garlic, or more to taste, chopped
2 fresh medium tomatoes, cut in half, squeezed to remove excess liquid and seeds, and roughly chopped
6 tablespoons (90 mL) garlic-flavored hot sauce or salsa from Chapter 2

1. Cook the pasta according to the package directions, set it aside, and keep it warm.

2. In a skillet, heat the olive oil over low heat. Add the garlic and sauté for 1 minute. Add the tomato and cook for 5 minutes. Add the salsa or hot sauce and heat through. In a bowl, toss the pasta and sauce together.

Penne Pasta with Chile and Sun-Dried Tomatoes

Yield: 6 servings   Heat Scale: Medium

This flavorful and spicy pasta with uncooked sauce comes from my wife, Mary Jane. Serve it with a simple green salad, crisp garlic toast, and a chilled dry Italian red wine. (Note: This recipe requires advance preparation.)

4 tablespoons (60 mL) crushed red New Mexican chile
½ cup (118 mL) oil-packed sun-dried tomatoes, slivered
1 cup (236 mL) black olives, cured in oil, pitted, and halved
½ cup (118 mL) fresh basil, chopped
½ cup (118 mL) fresh Italian parsley, chopped
1 tablespoon (15 mL) grated lemon peel
3 cloves garlic, peeled and minced
½ cup (118 mL) olive oil
2 tablespoons (30 mL) oil from the tomatoes (or substitute olive oil)
2 teaspoons (10 mL) freshly ground black pepper
4 quarts (3.8 L) salted water
1 pound (454 g) penne pasta
12 ounces (336 g) Parmesan cheese, grated

1. In a bowl, combine the chile, tomatoes, olives, basil, parsley, lemon peel, garlic, olive oil, tomato oil, and pepper and let the mixture sit at room temperature for a couple of hours to blend the flavors.
2. Bring the salted water to a boil, add the pasta, and cook it until al dente. Drain the pasta.
3. Toss the pasta with the sauce and cheese until well coated and serve.

Classic Tomato-Chile Spaghetti

Yield: 4 servings   Heat Scale: Medium

Unlike the heavy, rich tomato sauces for pasta, this one is simple, light, and spicy—perfect for the warmer months. It can be served as an appetizer or a light entrée. Serve it with herbed crostini (crunchy herbed toasts).

1 pound (454 g) fresh cherry tomatoes (or ¼ pound [113 g] sun-dried cherry tomatoes)
½ cup (118 mL) olive oil
3 cloves garlic, peeled and minced
2 teaspoons (10 mL) hot red chile flakes (such as crushed piquins)
Salt, to taste
Freshly ground black pepper, to taste
1 pound (454 g) spaghetti
Italian parsley leaves for garnish
Grated pecorino, romano, or Parmesan cheese for garnish

1. Preheat the oven to 375°F (190°C).
2. Place cherry tomatoes on a baking sheet and bake for 5 minutes. Remove them from the oven and allow them to cool for 15 minutes. Cut the tomatoes in half, keeping the seeds and skin.
3. In a sauté pan, heat the olive oil over medium heat. Add the garlic and sauté for 2 minutes. Increase the heat to high, add the tomatoes, and sauté for 5 minutes. Sprinkle with the pepper flakes and the salt and pepper.
4. Bring a large pot of salted water to a boil. Add the spaghetti and cook until it is al dente. Drain the pasta and toss it with the tomato mixture. Sprinkle the Italian parsley and the cheese on top.

Spaghetti a Cacio e Pepe
(Spaghetti with Black Pepper and Pecorino)

Yield: 2 servings   Heat Scale: Varies

Simple, rustic, and popular, spaghetti with black pepper is one of the tastiest dishes found in the Roman trattorias that offer traditional foods. The dish originated in the province of Romano Lazio, where pecorino romano cheese is made from the flocks of sheep that graze the hills around Rome. Pecorino romano is a sharp, hard cheese that is used in sauces and eaten at the end of a meal. This ultra-rich pasta is so quick to prepare, you'll be amazed that a dish so easy tastes so good. There are a couple of tricks to making the perfect spaghetti a cacio e pepe. First, use the ragged-edged holes of a box grater, not the small holes, for cheese that will melt easily and not clump. The second tip is to use a technique called mantecare, "to mix and meld," diluting the cheese and pepper with some of the starchy cooking water before tossing it with the spaghetti.

½ pound (224 g) dried spaghetti
2 tablespoons (30 mL) extra virgin olive oil
2 cloves garlic, peeled and sliced
2 tablespoons (30 mL) butter
1 tablespoon (15 mL) freshly ground black pepper
1–2 cups (250–473 mL) grated pecorino romano cheese, divided
Salt, to taste
Hot sauce of your choice from Chapter 2, to taste

1. In a large saucepan or stockpot, bring 4 quarts (3.8 L) salted water to a boil. Add the spaghetti and cook the pasta until al dente. Reserve at least 1 cup (236 mL) of the cooking liquid, then drain the pasta, but do not rinse it.
2. Heat a small skillet over medium heat and add the olive oil. When the oil is hot, add the garlic and sauté until golden, but not brown. Remove the garlic, as it will continue to cook and burn. Add the butter and pepper to the pan.
3. Return ½ to 1 cup (118 to 236 mL) of the cooking water to the saucepan, add the olive oil mixture and 1 cup (236 mL) of the cheese, stir, and heat over medium. Add the pasta and toss for about 3 minutes, until the cheese melts and the sauce coats the pasta, adding more reserved cooking liquid if it seems too dry. Taste and season with the salt and hot sauce.
4. Place the pasta in a large bowl, top it with the reserved garlic, and serve it with the remaining cheese on the side.

Ravioli with Green Chile–Tofu Filling

Yield: 48 1½-inch (3.5 cm) square raviolis   Heat Scale: Medium

Ravioli has always been one of my favorite pasta dishes because it presents so many possibilities! One can fill the ravioli with just about anything and create a superb taste that can be savored all at once, or the ravioli can be frozen and served at another meal. This rascally ravioli is a shoe-in for a main dish, but I also like to serve it as an appetizer. Serve them with the spicy dipping sauce of your choice or, better yet, serve different sauces from Chapter 2 with the ravioli to provide the perfect spicy soiree.

¼ cup (59 mL) chopped New Mexican green chile
3 cloves garlic, peeled and minced
1 (4½-ounce [126 g]) can chopped black olives
¾ cup (177 mL) firm tofu, shredded
¼ cup (59 mL) minced onion
¼ cup (59 mL) grated Parmesan cheese
1 tablespoon (15 mL) chopped cilantro
Cornstarch for dusting
1 (10-ounce [280 g]) package potsticker wrappers
1 egg white, beaten
Vegetable oil for frying

1. In a bowl, combine the chiles, garlic, olives, tofu, onion, Parmesan, and cilantro. Chill until ready to use.
2. Dust a baking sheet with cornstarch. Arrange as many wrappers as will fit on the baking sheet. Brush the wrappers with the egg white. Fill each wrapper with 1 rounded teaspoon (7.5 mL) of the filling. Fold each wrapper in half and seal all edges. Place the filled ravioli on a pan in a single layer. Continue the process until all the raviolis are filled and sealed.
3. In a large, deep pot, heat the vegetable oil to 375°F (190°C). Fry the ravioli in batches until they are golden brown (about 30 to 45 seconds). Transfer the ravioli to paper towels with a slotted spoon to drain off excess oil. Freeze or serve immediately with your favorite sauces.

Linguine with Pasilla, Cilantro, and Parsley Pesto

Yield: 4 to 6 servings   Heat Scale: Medium

I think it is impossible not to love pesto—especially since I've lowered the fat content in this hot adaptation with a peppery twist. Consider serving it with one of the hot fruit salads from Chapter 6 and your favorite Chardonnay.

24 ounces (672 g) linguine
½ cup (118 mL) chopped basil leaves
½ cup (118 mL) chopped cilantro leaves
2 cups (473 mL) chopped Italian parsley
1 cup (236 mL) vegetable stock
4 tablespoons (60 mL) olive oil
4 tablespoons (60 mL) toasted pine nuts
4 tablespoons (60 mL) grated Parmesan cheese
1 tablespoon (15 mL) crushed garlic
2 pasilla chiles, rehydrated, stems and seeds removed, chopped

1. In a large pot, cook the pasta according to the package directions until it is al dente. Drain the pasta in a colander and transfer it to a serving bowl.

2. In a food processor, blend the basil leaves, cilantro leaves, parsley, stock, olive oil, pine nuts, cheese, garlic, and chiles. Pour the pesto over the pasta and toss well. Serve immediately.

Spicy, Urbane Mac and Cheese

Yield: 8 servings   Heat Scale: Medium

The variety of cheeses in this upscale and tasty dish makes it dangerously delicious! The chiles in the dish and in the flavored pasta add a subtle punch and contrast nicely with the cheeses and herbs.

1 teaspoon (5 mL) salt
¼ cup (118 mL) plus 4 tablespoons (60 mL) olive oil, divided
1 pound (454 g) flavored pasta, such as green or red chile or habanero
½ pound (224 g) mascarpone cheese, softened
1 teaspoon (5 mL) coarsely ground white pepper
½ teaspoon (2.5 mL) coarsely ground black pepper
4 ounces (112 g) gorgonzola cheese, crumbled
8 ounces (224 g) fontina cheese, cut into ¼-inch (.5 cm) cubes
¾ cup (177 mL) grated Parmesan cheese
1 habanero chile, stem and seeds removed, minced (or substitute 3 serrano chiles)
¼ cup (59 mL) minced Italian parsley
2 teaspoons (10 mL) chopped fresh thyme (or substitute 1 teaspoon [5 mL] dried thyme)
¾ teaspoon (3.75 mL) dried oregano
1 teaspoon (5 mL) dried savory
½ teaspoon (2.5 mL) salt
4–5 cups (.95–1.18 L) mixed greens, such as Boston Bibb lettuce, endive, escarole, and mizuna

1. Bring a large pot of water to a boil. Add the salt and 2 tablespoons (30 mL) of the olive oil. Add the dry pasta and cook according to the package directions. Drain thoroughly and place the pasta in a large bowl lined with paper towels.

2. In a small bowl, mix together the mascarpone, the remaining olive oil, and the ground peppers. Remove the towels from the pasta and mix in the mascarpone mixture. Add the gorgonzola, fontina, Parmesan, chile, parsley, thyme, oregano, savory, and salt and toss the mixture lightly.

3. Arrange a bed of mixed greens on each plate and mound the pasta mixture on top. Serve immediately.

Habanero Lasagne

Yield: 8–10 servings   Heat Scale: Hot

Give me your bland, give me your vegetarian—I will help! Mine is not a lasagne to be taken lightly; it is filled with the robust flavor of habaneros and black olives—a real taste combination. As you bite into this luscious, layered delight, you are temporarily lulled into the garlic-infused sauce when all of a sudden, the habanero layer hits your mouth like a cannonball from heaven, and then it melds with the taste of the tomato and the vegetables. (Note: This recipe requires 3 days of advance preparation—marinating the olives and peppers—and then some steaming and shuffling on the day of serving. But, making good lasagne has never been easy, or neat.)

1 (16-ounce [454 g]) can whole black olives, drained, rinsed, and thinly sliced
3 habanero chiles, stems and seeds removed, minced
½ cup (118 mL) white wine
2 tablespoons (30 mL) olive oil
1 cup (236 mL) chopped onion
¼ cup (59 mL) grated carrots
½ cup (118 mL) finely diced celery
3 cloves garlic, peeled and minced
8 ripe tomatoes (about 2 pounds [1.1 kg]) peeled, seeded, and chopped (or substitute 1 [28-ounce (784 g)] can whole tomatoes, crushed)
¼ cup (59 mL) sun-dried tomatoes, rehydrated in white wine then finely chopped
1 (8-ounce [224 g]) can tomato paste (I recommend using the best quality you can find)
2 tablespoons (30 mL) dried basil (or substitute 4 tablespoons [60 mL] fresh, chopped)
2 teaspoons (10 mL) dried oregano (or substitute 4 tablespoons [60 mL] fresh, chopped)
1 bay leaf
¼ cup (59 mL) chopped Italian parsley
½ teaspoon (2.5 mL) rosemary, crushed
1 teaspoon (5 mL) sugar
1 tablespoon (15 mL) balsamic vinegar
2 cups (473 mL) Super-Rich Vegetable Stock (page 48), divided
1 pound (454 g) cooked lasagne noodles
1 or 2 (9-ounce [252 g]) packages frozen artichoke hearts (depending on how big a fan you are), cooked (or substitute 4 fresh zucchini, peeled, sliced horizontally, and steamed for 1 minute)
1 bunch fresh spinach, cleaned and steamed for 1 minute
1 pound (454 g) low-fat ricotta cheese
½ cup (118 mL) grated Parmesan cheese
1 cup (236 mL) shredded low-fat mozzarella cheese

1. In a glass jar, combine the black olives, habaneros, and white wine. Place the jar in the refrigerator for 3 days, and, once a day, turn the jar upside down and shake it gently.
2. In a large, heavy Dutch oven, heat the olive oil over medium heat. Add the onion, carrots, celery, and garlic and sauté for 2 minutes. Add the tomatoes, sun-dried tomatoes, and tomato paste and mix thoroughly.

3. Bring the tomato mixture to a low boil and add the basil, oregano, bay leaf, parsley, rosemary, sugar, balsamic vinegar, and 1 cup (236 mL) of the stock. Cover and simmer the mixture for at least 1 hour, stirring occasionally. If the mixture becomes too thick, thin with the reserved stock.
4. Preheat the oven to 350°F (180°C).
5. Remove and discard the bay leaf. Spread ½ cup (118 mL) of the tomato sauce in a 9 × 13-inch (22.5 × 32.5 cm) baking dish. Place a layer of cooked lasagne noodles on top of the sauce. Thoroughly drain the olive-habanero mixture and spread one-third of it over the noodles. Top the olive mixture with one-third of the sliced artichokes (or zucchinis), and one-third of the steamed spinach leaves. Mix the three cheeses together and spread one-third of this mixture over the spinach. Pour 1 cup (236 mL) of the tomato sauce over this mixture, and then cover with more lasagne noodles. Repeat the whole process for two more layers, ending with the noodles and topping off with the tomato sauce.
6. Bake for 45 minutes. (Or, cover and refrigerate and bake later; just allow the dish to reach room temperature before baking.)

Absolut-ly the Best Pasta

Yield: 4 servings   Heat Scale: Mild without the cayenne, Medium with

This sauce made with Absolut Peppar vodka contains a hint of heat and tastes so rich your friends will think you're Italian!

2 tablespoons (30 mL) butter
3 cloves garlic, peeled and minced
1 teaspoon (5 mL) dried oregano
1 teaspoon (5 mL) dried thyme
1 teaspoon (5 mL) dried rosemary
1 small onion, peeled and chopped
1 (16-ounce [454 g]) can Italian plum tomatoes, chopped, with their juices
½ cup (118 mL) Absolute Peppar vodka
½ teaspoon (2.5 mL) ground cayenne
¾ cup (177 mL) half-and-half
1 cup (236 mL) freshly grated Parmesan cheese
12 ounces (336 g) fresh linguine (or substitute 8 ounces [224 g] dried linguine, cooked according to the package instructions)
Finely chopped Italian parsley for garnish

1. In a large skillet, melt the butter over medium heat. Add the garlic, oregano, thyme, rosemary, and onion and sauté for about 5 minutes. Add the tomatoes and their juices and simmer for about 10 minutes, stirring 3 to 4 times. Add the vodka and the cayenne, if using, and simmer for about 5 minutes. Add the cream and half the Parmesan. Simmer for about 4 minutes, or until the sauce thickens lightly. Add the linguine and stir until the sauce coats the pasta. Garnish with the parsley and sprinkle with the remaining Parmesan.

Grilled Portobello Mushrooms with Chipotle Chile Sauce, Served on Peppered Fettuccine

Yield: 4 servings   Heat Scale: Mild

Somehow, a wonderful grilled portobello mushroom seems to satisfy even the most carnivorous diner. Eating this mushroom is akin to eating a steak, and it can take on a multitude of seasonings and flavors. In this recipe, the sauce has more ingredients than the main course! Serve this elegant dish with a light, crunchy salad from Chapter 6. (Note: This recipe requires advance preparation.)

4 large, fresh portobello mushrooms
¼ cup (59 mL) red wine vinegar
2 cloves garlic, peeled and minced
3 tablespoons (45 mL) olive oil, divided
1 cup (236 mL) safflower oil
⅓ cup (79 mL) fresh lemon juice
¼ cup (59 mL) tahini (sesame seed paste)
2 teaspoons (10 mL) soy sauce
1 tablespoon (15 mL) Worcestershire sauce
1 tablespoon (15 mL) strong whole-grain mustard
¼ cup (59 mL) freshly grated pecorino or Parmesan cheese
½ teaspoon (2.5 mL) imported curry powder (or substitute a curry powder from Chapter 1)
¾ teaspoon (3.75 mL) freshly ground black pepper
2 chipotle chiles in adobo
¼ teaspoon (1.25 mL) salt
12 ounces (336 g) fettuccine

1. Clean the mushrooms and place them in a shallow glass pan. In a bowl, mix together the vinegar, garlic, and 2 tablespoons (30 mL) of the olive oil. Pour this mixture over the mushrooms and then turn the mushrooms to coat. Cover tightly and marinate for 1 hour at room temperature.

2. While the mushrooms are marinating, make the sauce. In a blender, combine the safflower oil, lemon juice, tahini, soy sauce, Worcestershire sauce, mustard, cheese, curry powder, ¼ teaspoon (1.25 mL) of the black pepper, the chiles, and salt and blend until smooth, about 30 seconds. Allow the mixture to sit at room temperature.

3. Cook the pasta according to the package instructions. When it is done, drain it thoroughly, return it to the cooking pot, add the remaining olive oil and black pepper, and toss. Keep the pasta warm. Remove the mushrooms from the marinade and grill them for 2 to 3 minutes on each side or, sauté them in a heavy skillet over medium heat for 4 to 5 minutes on each side.

4. Divide the pasta among 4 warmed dinner plates, place a grilled mushroom on each serving of pasta, and top each mushroom with the sauce. Serve immediately.

Green and White Spicy Pasta

Yield: 6 servings   Heat Scale: Mild

The unusual combination of ingredients in this recipe makes a great explosion on the tongue. Other vegetables can be substituted in the sauté—try some zucchini or green beans.

3 tablespoons (55 mL) olive oil
¼ cup (59 mL) minced shallots
3 jalapeño chiles, stems and seeds removed, chopped fine
2 cloves garlic, peeled and minced
1–1½ cups (236–354 mL) Super-Rich Vegetable Stock (page 48)
¾ cup (177 mL) cream or milk
¾ cup (177 mL) dry white wine
¼ teaspoon (1.25 mL) freshly grated nutmeg
1 teaspoon (5 mL) chopped fresh ginger
2 teaspoons (10 mL) ground red New Mexican chile
8 ounces (224 g) brie, rind removed, diced
8 ounces (224 g) snow peas
1 red bell pepper, stem and seeds removed, cut into ⅛-inch (.25 cm) strips
1 yellow bell pepper, stem and seeds removed, cut into ⅛-inch (.25 cm) strips
2 yellow summer squash, peeled and cut into ¼-inch (.5 cm) strips
4 ounces (113 g) mushrooms, cleaned and sliced
1 pound (454 g) spinach fettuccine

1. In a large, heavy skillet, heat 1 tablespoon (15 mL) of the olive oil over low heat. Add the shallots, chiles, and garlic and sauté for 3 minutes, taking care not to burn the garlic. Add the stock, cream or milk, wine, nutmeg, ginger, and ground chile and bring the mixture to a boil. Lower the heat to a simmer and cook for 20 minutes, stirring occasionally, until the mixture is thickened and reduced by one-third.
2. Add the brie, a few pieces at a time, stirring until the cheese melts. Remove the skillet from the heat and cover it to keep everything warm.
3. In a separate large skillet, heat the remaining 2 tablespoons (30 mL) olive oil over medium heat. Add the snow peas, bell peppers, squash, and mushrooms and sauté for 3 minutes.
4. Cook the fettuccine according to the package directions until al dente, drain it, and pour into a heated bowl. Add the sautéed vegetables and the chile-wine sauce and gently toss them with the pasta. Serve immediately.

Pasta from Hell

Yield: 4 servings   Heat Scale: Hot, verging on Extremely Hot

"This dish is on the outer limits," says Chris Schlesinger, owner of the East Coast Grill in Cambridge, Massachusetts. He featured this pasta in an article he wrote for me entitled "Equatorial Cuisine." The East Coast Grill's Inner Beauty Hot Sauce is available at gourmet shops and by mail order.

2 tablespoons (30 mL) olive oil
1 yellow onion, peeled and cut in small dice
1 red bell pepper, stem and seeds removed, cut in small dice
2 bananas, sliced
¼ cup (59 mL) pineapple juice
Juice of 3 oranges
Juice of 2 limes
¼ cup (59 mL) chopped fresh cilantro
3–4 tablespoons (45–60 mL) minced habanero chiles (or substitute ⅓ cup [79 mL] Inner Beauty Hot Sauce or other habanero-based sauce)
2 teaspoons (10 mL) butter
¼ cup (59 mL) grated Parmesan cheese, divided
1 pound (454 g) dried fettuccine
Salt, to taste
Freshly cracked black pepper, to taste

1. In a large saucepan, heat the oil over medium heat. Add the onion and red bell pepper and sauté for about 4 minutes. Add the bananas, pineapple juice, and orange juice. Simmer over medium heat for 5 minutes, until the bananas are soft. Remove the pan from the heat. Add the lime juice, cilantro, habaneros or hot sauce, and 3 tablespoons (45 mL) of the Parmesan cheese and mix well.
2. In a large pot of boiling salted water, cook the fettuccine until al dente, about 8 to 10 minutes. Drain the pasta and transfer it to a large bowl.
3. Add the chile mixture and mix well. Season with salt and pepper and garnish with the remaining grated Parmesan.

Orzo from Hades

Yield: 8 servings   Heat Scale: Hot

*Edward Janos, an executive chef, sent me this recipe with the comment that chile
peppers and sauces make ordinary foods exciting. Sometimes, as in this orzo recipe,
chiles make them dynamite. Orzo is a small, rice-shaped pasta slightly smaller than
a pine nut that is often used as a substitute for rice. This dish, which is a signature
menu item at whatever restaurant Edward is toiling, is so hot and is served in such
quantities that the restaurant advertises that if guests can eat it all, it's free.*

½ cup (118 mL) olive oil
1 habanero chile, stem removed, minced
1 serrano chile, stem removed, minced
1 large poblano chile, stem removed, julienned
2 cloves garlic, peeled and minced
10 medium shiitake mushrooms, julienned
¾ cup (177 mL) green onions, minced
8 cups (1.9 L) cooked orzo pasta, al dente
2 cups (473 mL) spinach, roughly chopped
1½ cups (354 mL) broccoli, blanched and chopped
6 tablespoons (90 mL) fresh basil, chopped fine
Salt, to taste
1 tablespoon (15 mL) habanero hot sauce of your choice from Chapter 2
1 cup (236 mL) reduced Classic Chicken Stock (page 46)
1 cup (236 mL) grated parmigiano-reggiano cheese

1. In a sauté pan, heat the olive oil over medium heat. Add the habanero,
serrano, poblano, garlic, mushroom, and green onions and sauté for about
2 minutes, stirring constantly.
2. Add the orzo, spinach, broccoli, and basil and cook until heated
through, stirring. Add the salt, hot sauce, and chicken stock, and cook
until heated through, stirring constantly.
3. Serve the pasta topped with the cheese.

Sonoran Enchiladas

Yield: 4–6 servings

Heat Scale: Medium to Hot, depending on the amount of sauce

From Antonio Heras-Duran and Cindy Castillo, who took Mary Jane and I on a chiltepin tour of Sonora, comes this regional specialty. These enchiladas are not the same as those served north of the border. The main differences are the use of freshly made, thick corn tortillas and the fact that the enchiladas are not baked. I dined on these enchiladas one night in Tucson as they were prepared by Cindy, who is well-versed in Sonoran cookery.

15–20 chiltepins (or piquins), crushed
15 dried red New Mexican chiles, stems and seeds removed
2 teaspoons (10 mL) salt, divided
3 cloves garlic, peeled
1 teaspoon (5 mL) vegetable oil, plus more for deep frying
1 teaspoon (5 mL) all-purpose flour
2 cups (473 mL) masa harina
1 egg
1 teaspoon (5 mL) baking powder
2 cups (473 mL) grated queso blanco or Monterey Jack cheese
Shredded lettuce for serving
3–4 green onions, white part only, minced

1. In a saucepan, combine the two kinds of chiles with 1 teaspoon (5 mL) of the salt. Add enough water to cover. Boil for 10 or 15 minutes or until the chiles are quite soft. Remove the pan from the heat and allow the chiles to cool.

2. Transfer the chiles and their water to a blender. Add the garlic and purée. Strain the mixture, mash the pulp through the strainer, and discard the skins.

3. In a separate saucepan, heat 1 teaspoon (5 mL) of the oil over medium heat. Add the flour and brown, taking care that it does not burn. Add the chile purée and boil for 5 or 10 minutes, until the sauce has thickened slightly. Remove the pan from the heat and keep the mixture warm.

4. To make the tortillas, thoroughly mix together the masa, egg, baking powder, and remaining 1 teaspoon (5 mL) salt. Add just enough water to make a dough. Using a tortilla press, make the tortillas. In a skillet, heat enough oil to deep-fry the tortillas. Add the tortillas one at a time and fry until they puff up and turn slightly brown. Transfer them to paper towels to drain and keep them warm.

5. Place a tortilla on each plate and spoon a generous amount of sauce over it. Top with the cheese, lettuce, and green onions.

Enchiladas Very Verde

Yield: 6 servings (2 filled tortillas per person)   Heat Scale: Medium

To illustrate the contrasting styles of Mexican enchiladas that I serve, here is a recipe I found in Mexico many years ago. About twenty years ago, I used to make enchiladas with sour cream and then bake them, with mixed results. In Mexico at that time, there was no sour cream as we know it, so cooks used a cream-cheese type cream with excellent results. The beans and the corn add some crunch to the creamy onion filling, all adding up to a "rave" entrée. Serve these enchiladas with a rice dish from Chapter 13 and sliced tomatoes drizzled with olive oil and sprinkled with ground red chile. (Note: I prefer La Victoria Brand Green Taco Sauce because it has a lot of the tomatillo taste that I like. However, other brands may be just as good—just check the ingredients to make sure that a fair amount of tomatillos are included.

8 ounces (224 g) low-fat cream cheese, softened
½ cup (118 mL) Super-Rich Vegetable Stock (page 48), divided
1 cup (236 mL) low-fat milk, divided
1 cup (236 mL) finely chopped onions
1½ cups (354 mL) chopped green New Mexico chile, roasted, peeled, stems and seeds removed, chopped (or substitute 6 poblano chiles)
1 (10-ounce [280 g]) jar green taco sauce (see Note)
2 fresh serrano chiles, stems and seeds removed
½ cup (118 mL) fresh cilantro
1 egg (or an equivalent amount egg substitute)
½ teaspoon (2.5 mL) salt (optional)
¼ teaspoon (1.25 mL) freshly ground black pepper
1 cup (236 mL) half-and-half (or substitute more low-fat milk)
¼ cup (59 mL) vegetable oil, divided
12 corn tortillas
1½ cups (354 mL) cooked pinto beans or black beans
1¼ cups (295 mL) lightly cooked whole kernel corn

1. Preheat the oven to 350°F (180°C).
2. In a large mixing bowl, beat the cream cheese until it is smooth. Add ¼ cup (59 mL) of the stock and ¼ cup (59 mL) of the milk and beat until the mixture is thoroughly blended. Mix in the chopped onions. Set aside.
3. In a blender, combine the green chile, the green taco sauce, the serrano chiles, the cilantro, the egg, the salt and black pepper, the remaining stock, the remaining milk, and the half-and-half. Blend on high speed for 15 seconds. Transfer the purée to a bowl.
4. In a small, heavy skillet, heat 2 tablespoons (30 mL) of the oil. When the oil is hot enough to sizzle when you flick a drop of water into it, quickly fry the tortillas, one at a time, about 5 seconds per side. Drain the fried tortillas on layers of paper towels.
5. Dip a tortilla into the purée, drain it for a second, and place it in a 9 × 13–inch (22.5 × 32.5 cm) baking dish. (This procedure is messy.) Spread the tortilla with some of the cream cheese–onion mix and add 2 tablespoons (30 mL) of the beans and 1 tablespoon (15 mL) of the corn. Tightly roll up the tortilla and place it at one end of the glass casserole, seam-side

down. Fill the remaining tortillas and place in the pan. Pour the remaining sauce over the filled tortillas.

6. Bake for 15 to 20 minutes.

Vegetable Enchiladas with Chipotle Cream Sauce

Yield: 4 servings   Heat Scale: Mild

These enchiladas from Nancy Gerlach are about the tastiest meatless enchiladas imaginable. Rice can be substituted for or combined with the pinto beans, or you could use black beans and corn.

2 chipotle chiles in adobo, stems removed
4 canned tomatillos, drained
1¼ cups (295 mL) heavy cream
1½ teaspoons (7.5 mL) sugar
¼ teaspoon (1.25 mL) ground cinnamon
1–2 tablespoons (15–30 mL) vegetable oil
1 cup (236 mL) chopped onion
2 cloves garlic, peeled and chopped
1 medium potato, diced, boiled, and drained
1 zucchini, diced
1 cup (236 mL) chopped mushrooms
4 green New Mexican chiles, roasted, peeled, stems and seeds removed, diced
1½ teaspoons (7.5 ml) dried oregano
¼ teaspoon (1.25 mL) ground cumin
½ cup (118 mL) cooked pinto beans
1 cup (236 mL) grated longhorn cheese
8 corn tortillas

1. Preheat the oven to 350°F (180°C).

2. To make the sauce, combine the chiles and tomatillos in a blender or food processor and purée until smooth. Transfer the purée to a saucepan and add the cream, sugar, and cinnamon. Simmer until thickened, about 10 minutes.

3. To make the filling, heat the oil in a sauté pan over medium heat. Add the onion and garlic and sauté until soft. Add the potato and zucchini and cook until the potato is browned and the zucchini is done but still crisp, 3 to 5 minutes. Add the mushrooms, green chile, oregano, and cumin and sauté until the mushrooms are soft, about 5 minutes. Remove the pan from the heat and stir in the beans and cheese.

4. Soften the tortillas in a microwave by individually wrapping them in plastic and zapping each tortilla on high for 10 seconds. Fill the tortillas with the vegetables and roll them up. Arrange the enchiladas seam-side down in a baking dish. Bake until the cheese melts, about 10 minutes. Top them with the sauce, garnish them with the cheese, and serve.

Grilled Brie Quesadillas with Caribbean Salsa

Yield: 4 servings   Heat Scale: Hot

These South-of-the-Border grilled cheese sandwiches can be made with either corn or flour tortillas. According to Nancy Gerlach, in Mexico, they are often made with un-cooked corn tortillas that are filled and then fried, but it is easier to use cooked ones. Cheese is the traditional filling, but almost anything will work. Instead of folding them over as in this recipe, you can layer the tortillas with the filling, cook the stack, and then cut it like a pie.

1½ cups (295 mL) finely diced pineapple
3 tomatillos, husks removed, finely diced
½–1 habanero chile, stem and seeds removed, finely diced (or substitute ground habanero)
2 tablespoons (30 mL) chopped fresh cilantro
1 teaspoon (5 mL) grated ginger
2 tablespoons (30 mL) vegetable oil, divided
8 ounces (224 g) brie, rinds removed, cut in wide strips (or substitute 8 ounces [224 g] goat cheese, crumbled)
4 (8-inch [20 cm]) flour tortillas

1. In a bowl, combine the pineapple, tomatillos, chile, cilantro, and gin-ger, and 2 teaspoons (10 mL) of the oil.
2. Prepare the grill.
3. Soften the tortillas, if necessary. Place one-fourth of the cheese on half of each tortilla. Top the cheese with the salsa mixture and fold the tortilla in half. Repeat with the remaining tortillas.
4. Brush the top of the quesadillas with a little of the remaining oil and place them on the grill, oiled side down. Cook for 1 minute, brush the top with oil, turn, and cook for an additional minute.
5. Cut each quesadilla in thirds, arrange them on a plate, and serve.

Variation
Quesadillas can be heated on an ungreased heavy skillet. Heat until brown spots appear, turn, and heat on the other side until the cheese has melted.

Goat Cheese Poblanos Rellenos with Chipotle Cream

Yield: 6 servings   Heat Scale: Varies, but usually mild

Rosa Rajkovic, formerly head chef of the Monte Vista Fire Station restaurant in Albuquerque, created these cheese-infused stuffed peppers, on which I have dined many times. She says that because of the varying heat of poblanos (they are usually quite mild), preparing this recipe is "culinary roulette." However, the cheese does cut the heat of any renegade poblanos.

½ cup (118 mL) sour cream
¼ cup (59 mL) chevre (goat cheese)
1 small chipotle chile (if dry, soak it in water first to soften)
Half-and-half or heavy cream as needed
1 tablespoon (15 mL) finely chopped cilantro
6 large poblano chiles
½ pound (224 g) chevre (goat cheese)
⅓ pound (151 g) low-fat cream cheese
¼ pound (113 g) cambozola or sago bleu cheese
2 eggs, beaten
1 cup (236 mL) blue cornmeal
½ cup (118 mL) canola or vegetable oil

1. In a food processor or blender, blend together the sour cream, the ¼ cup (59 mL) goat cheese, and the chipotle until very smooth. Add enough half-and-half or cream to achieve a pourable consistency. Add the cilantro and process for a few seconds longer. Pour the cream into a squeeze bottle, but make sure the cilantro is fine enough that it doesn't clog the opening.
2. Roast the poblanos on a grill, over gas burners, or under a broiler until the skins blister and blacken. Remove the peppers from the heat, place them in a bowl, and cover tightly with plastic wrap. Allow the peppers to cool completely. Peel the peppers, carefully slit them along one side, and remove the seeds. Leave the stems intact.
3. Mix or process the three cheeses together and, using a pastry bag with a plain tip or a coupler, pipe the mixture into the cavities of the peppers, or spoon it in. Refrigerate until ready to assemble the final dish. (Chilling the rellenos until they are very cold will help keep the blue-corn coating crispy after the rellenos are sautéed.)
4. Right before serving the chile, place the eggs and the blue corn in two separate, shallow bowls. Heat the oil in a large skillet over medium-low heat. Dip the rellenos in the egg mixture first and then into the blue corn. Sauté the rellenos until they are lightly browned, turning each one three times in the hot oil to ensure even crisping. Drain on a double thickness of paper towels.
5. Place the rellenos in shallow bowls and artistically drizzle the Chipotle Cream over them.

Tofu-Stuffed Poblanos

Yield: 4 servings   Heat Scale: Medium

This superb recipe, another variation on stuffed chiles, was given to me by Chef Todd Sanson, formerly the day chef at the El Nido Restaurant in Santa Fe. Back in the day, Todd spent his days creating fine dishes at the restaurant and his weekends as a caterer to various movie stars who now live in "the City Different."

8 large poblano chiles, roasted and peeled
1 cup (236 mL) golden raisins (or substitute regular raisins or currants)
½ cup (118 mL) toasted pine nuts, pumpkin seeds, or sunflower seeds
1 cup (236 mL) cooked yellow corn kernels
1 cup (236 mL) cubed tofu, drained and sautéed for 5 minutes in a robust oil (such as peanut or sesame) in a frying pan
1 cup (236 mL) shredded Monterey Jack cheese
2 cups (473 mL) soft goat cheese or feta

1. Preheat the oven to 375°F (190°C). Grease a baking sheet.
2. Cut a slit in the side of each poblano and remove the seeds. In a large bowl, mix together the raisins, pine nuts or seeds, corn, tofu, and cheeses. Stuff this mixture into the poblano chiles.
3. Place the stuffed chiles on the prepared baking sheet. At the slit in the poblanos, place a teaspoon (5 mL) or so of shredded cheese. This cheese will melt and allow to chile to hold together better in the oven.
4. Bake the poblanos for 15 to 20 minutes or until the cheese is bubbling. Serve the chiles on heated plates, covered with a mole sauce from Chapter 2.

Tempting Tempeh "Fajitas"

Yield: 4 servings   Heat Scale: Medium

This spicy recipe comes from my friend Jeanette DeAnda, who is an excellent creative chef and caterer. If you don't know what to make for dinner some night, call Jeanette—she'll give you twenty ideas off the top of her head! This recipe also makes a great stuffing for burritos. Serve this tempeh dish with flour tortillas and garnishes such as salsa, fresh lime slices, guacamole, tomatoes, and green onions. The ingredients can be wrapped up in the tortilla and eaten like a sandwich.

2 teaspoons (10 mL) brown sugar
¼ cup (59 mL) water
¼ cup (59 mL) tamari
4 jalapeño chiles, stems and seeds removed, thinly sliced
2 cloves garlic, peeled and minced
Juice of 2 limes
1 pound (454 g) tempeh, sliced into thin strips (available at natural foods stores)
½ green bell pepper, stem and seeds removed, cut lengthwise into thin strips
½ red bell pepper, stem and seeds removed, cut lengthwise into thin strips
½ yellow onion, peeled and sliced
4 flour tortillas

1. Preheat the oven to 350°F (180°C).
2. In an ovenproof casserole, mix together the brown sugar, water, tamari, chiles, garlic, and lime juice. Mix in the sliced tempeh. Marinate the mixture for at least 45 minutes.
3. Add the bell pepper and onion to the tempeh mixture and mix gently. Bake the tempeh for 15 minutes, covered. Remove the cover and broil for 3 to 5 minutes. Spoon the tempeh into the tortillas and serve sizzling hot.

Chiles en Nogada
(Fruit-Stuffed Poblanos without Walnuts)

Yield: 6 servings   Heat Scale: Mild

Here is another variation on stuffed chiles, this one courtesy of Zarela Martinez of Zarela Restaurant in New York City, who says that her version is based on the classic recipe served on national holidays in Mexico. She, however, bakes the chiles instead of deep-frying them and eliminates the walnuts that give the dish its name and the chicken. No matter—Zarela says the dish is "one of our most beloved at Zarela."

For the Salsa de Tomate Asado:
1½ cups (354 mL) heavy cream
6 medium garlic cloves, unpeeled
1 medium onion, unpeeled and halved crosswise
3 –4 large tomatoes (2 ¾ pounds [1250 g])
Salt, to taste

1. In a small saucepan, simmer the cream until reduced to about 1 cup (236 mL).
2. In a large skillet or griddle, roast the garlic and onion over high heat, turning several times, until the garlic is dark on all sides and somewhat softened and the onion is partly charred. Add the tomatoes and roast until the skins start to come off.
3. Peel the garlic, onions, and tomatoes and put them in a blender. (It's okay if a few charred bits get into the mixture.) Purée on medium speed until smooth. Add the cream and purée until smooth. Season with salt to taste and keep warm.

For the Stuffed Poblanos:
½ cup (118 mL) unsalted butter
1 medium onion, peeled and chopped
2 medium garlic cloves, peeled and minced
½ cup (118 mL) pimiento-stuffed green olives, sliced
¾ cup (177 mL) pitted prunes, diced
¾ cup (177 mL) dried apricots, diced
¾ cup (177 mL) dried peaches, diced
1½ teaspoons (7.5 mL) cumin seed, ground
1½ teaspoons (7.5 mL) ground cinnamon (Ceylon preferred)
¼ teaspoon (1.25 mL) ground cloves
6 large green poblano chiles, roasted, peeled, and seeded
Salt, to taste

1. Preheat the oven to 350°F (180°C). Grease a baking sheet.
2. In a saucepan, melt the butter over medium heat. Add the onion and garlic and sauté until the onion is soft. Add the olives and the dried fruits and continue to sauté until the fruits are soft, 1 to 2 minutes. Add the spices and cook for 1 more minute. Taste for seasoning and add salt as needed.
3. Carefully fill the chiles with the mixture and bake them for 7 minutes.
4. To serve, spoon the Salsa de Tomate Asado on individual plates and place one chile on each plate, over the salsa.

Todd's Terrific Tofu Adovada

Yield: 6–8 servings   Heat Scale: Hot

This is a tasty tofu recipe from Chef Todd Sanson. He says, "This is a great way to still have a traditionally flavored New Mexican dish with the heat, but without the meat." This dish can be dressed with red chile sauce, served in a bowl, or folded in flour tortillas for burritos. Serve it with a bowl of pinto beans or black beans and a big green salad. (Note: This recipe requires advance preparation.)

4 pounds (1.82 L) firm tofu
6 tablespoons (90 mL) flavored oil (such as peanut, sesame, or avocado)
2 cups (473 mL) Super-Rich Vegetable Stock (page 48)
2 medium onions, peeled and chopped
3 cloves garlic, peeled and minced
1 teaspoon (5 mL) dried oregano
2 teaspoons (10 mL) crushed coriander seed
2 tablespoons (30 mL) honey
⅓ cup (79 mL) ground red New Mexican chile
¼ cup (59 mL) ground ancho chile
1 tablespoon (15 mL) chile caribe (crushed hot red chiles, such as piquin or santaka)
3 tablespoons (45 mL) sherry vinegar or rice wine
¼ cup (59 mL) toasted pumpkin seeds
1 tablespoon (15 mL) ground cinnamon
Salt, to taste

1. Place several layers of paper towels on a cookie sheet. Slice each cake of tofu in half lengthwise and place the slices on the towels. Cover the tofu with several more layers of paper towels and another cookie sheet. Then put some heavy objects on the sheet to weight down the tofu; heavy canned goods will work (and Todd suggests using your thick French cookbooks). Allow the tofu to sit for 20 minutes. Cut the tofu into ½-inch (1 cm) cubes.
2. In a large skillet, heat the oil over medium heat. Add the cubed tofu and sauté it until golden brown. Set aside.
3. In a blender, combine 1 cup (236 mL) of the stock with the onions, garlic, oregano, coriander, honey, ground chiles, chile caribe, sherry vinegar, pumpkin seeds, cinnamon, and salt. Purée for a few seconds, add the

remaining stock, and blend again. Transfer the mixture to a large bowl and gently mix in the sautéed tofu.

4. Refrigerate for 1 to 2 hours. Remove the mixture from the refrigerator and allow it to stand for 10 minutes.

5. Pour the mixture into a deep saucepan and bring to a boil. Turn the heat down and simmer for 1 hour. Adjust the seasonings and serve.

Eggplant El Paso

Yield: 8–10 servings   Heat Scale: Medium

This recipe appears courtesy of Bud Spillar, who does the cooking at his restaurant and admits (tongue in cheek) that his wife, Ruth, helps "some." Bud says his business has "maxed out," but he refuses to expand because he doesn't want to lose personal contact with his customers. This eggplant recipe is one of his creations that utilizes traditional ingredients in an innovative manner. This recipe is a party dish, hence the large yield.

For the Sauce:
½ cup (118 mL) chopped canned New Mexican green chiles
2 quarts (1.9 L) vegetable stock
6 bay leaves
2 tablespoons (30 mL) Mexican oregano
½ cup (118 mL) diced onions
½ cup (118 mL) diced fresh tomato
Salt, to taste
2 tablespoons (30 mL) masa harina
2 tablespoons (30 mL) all-purpose flour
1 cup (236 mL) water

1. In a pot, combine the chiles, broth, bay leaves, oregano, onions, tomato, and salt. Bring to a boil, reduce the heat, and simmer for 15 minutes. Mix the masa and flour with the water, add the mixture to the sauce, and simmer, stirring constantly, until the sauce has reduced and thickened to the consistency of cream gravy.

For the Casserole:
3½ cups (826 mL) chopped green New Mexican chiles
1 dozen eggs
2 tablespoons (30 mL) minced garlic
1 tablespoon (15 mL) ground cumin
1 teaspoon (5 mL) salt
1 teaspoon (5 mL) freshly ground black pepper
4 large eggplants, unpeeled, sliced into ¼-inch (.5 cm) thick slices
Cracker crumbs for dredging
Peanut oil for frying
12 ounces (336 g) grated cheddar cheese
12 ounces (336 g) grated Monterey Jack cheese

1. Preheat the oven to 350°F (180°C).
2. In a large bowl, beat the eggs with a wire whisk. Add the garlic, cumin, salt, and pepper. In a large frying pan, heat the peanut oil to 350°F (180°C). Dip the eggplant slices into the egg mixture, coat them with the cracker crumbs, and fry them in the peanut oil until golden brown. Transfer the slices to paper towels to drain.
3. Pour a small amount of the sauce into the bottom of a 3-inch (7.5 cm) deep, 8 × 13–inch (20 × 32.5 cm) casserole. Add one-fourth of the eggplant slices, one-fourth of the remaining sauce, one-fourth of the green chiles, and one-fourth of the cheeses. Repeat this process until there are 4 layers, the last topped with cheese. Bake for 45 minutes.

The Produce Guy's Favorite Burgers

Yield: 6 servings   Heat Scale: Medium

Okay, prepare yourself for these totally vegetarian burgers. Sure they're good for you, but they taste good, too. And just think—none of these vegetables was given any hormones!

1½ cups (354 mL) finely chopped walnuts
¼ cup (59 mL) chopped green bell pepper
¼ cup (59 mL) chopped red bell pepper
½ cup (118 mL) chopped green New Mexican chile
3 cloves garlic, peeled and minced
4 green onions, peeled and chopped
¼ cup (59 mL) chopped carrots
1¼ cups (295 mL) thawed frozen spinach, finely chopped
1½ cups (354 mL) whole wheat bread crumbs
1 tablespoon (15 mL) chopped tarragon
2 tablespoons (30 mL) chopped celery
¼ cup (59 mL) mayonnaise
¼ teaspoon (1.25 mL) freshly ground black pepper
2 tablespoons (30 mL) butter

1. In a large bowl, combine all the ingredients except the butter. Shape the mixture into 6 patties. In a large skillet, melt the butter over medium heat. Add the patties and sauté, browning on both sides, until cooked, about 8 to 10 minutes total.

Spicy To(o)fu(n) Burgers

Yield: 6 servings   Heat Scale: Mild

The next burger step is to try tofu. Tofu burgers are great fun to cook because it is such a surprise to see how much people enjoy them—especially meat eaters who occasionally start out a bit skeptical but are quickly converted.

1 pound (454 g) firm tofu
2 teaspoons (10 mL) ground red New Mexican chile
½ teaspoon (2.5 mL) dill weed
⅓ cup (79 mL) grated Monterey Jack cheese
2 cups (473 mL) mashed potatoes
6 shallots, peeled and chopped
½ cup (118 mL) bread crumbs
2 tablespoons (30 mL) butter

1. Place the tofu in a colander and drain thoroughly. When it has completely drained, pat it dry with paper towels, chop it into small pieces, and place it in a bowl.
2. To the tofu, add the ground chile, dill weed, cheese, potatoes, and shallots. Mix well and shape the mixture into 6 patties. Gently coat each burger with the bread crumbs.
3. In a large skillet, melt the butter over medium heat. Add the patties and cook for about 5 minute on each side.

Tofu Patties with Spicy Chile Sauce

Yield: 4 servings   Heat Scale: Medium

Even though the list of ingredients seems to go on forever, this dish is very easy to make and will bring great reviews from your diners. Jeanette DeAnda is the creator of this tongue-tingling entrée. (Note: This recipe requires advance preparation.)

For the Tofu:
¼ cup (59 mL) tamari
½ cup (118 mL) water
1 tablespoon (15 mL) brown sugar
½ teaspoon (2.5 mL) grated fresh ginger
2 cloves garlic, peeled and minced
1 pound (454 g) firm tofu, rinsed, drained, carefully squeezed dry in a clean towel, and sliced ½-inch (1 cm) thick
1 cup (236 mL) unbleached all-purpose flour
1 tablespoon (15 mL) ground red New Mexican chile
½ cup (118 mL) peanut oil
1 tablespoon (15 mL) Chile Oil (page 16)

1. In a shallow dish, mix together the tamari, water, brown sugar, ginger, and garlic. Add the sliced tofu. Marinate for 1 hour.
2. In a small bowl, mix together the flour and ground chile In a skillet, heat the peanut and chile oils over medium heat. Lightly flour the tofu patties and fry them until lightly browned. Reserve 2 tablespoons (30 mL) of the oil.

For the Spicy Chile Sauce:
2 tablespoons (30 mL) peanut-chile oil reserved from frying the tofu
2 cloves garlic, peeled and minced
2 green onions, chopped
3 serrano chiles, stems and seeds removed, minced
1 tablespoon (15 mL) freshly squeezed lemon juice
1 teaspoon (5 mL) freshly grated ginger
3 tablespoons (45 mL) tamari
¼ cup (59 mL) water
¼ cup (59 mL) dry sherry
1 tablespoon (15 mL) chopped fresh cilantro

1. In a skillet, heat the peanut-chile oil over medium heat. Add the garlic, onions, and chiles and fry for 2 to 3 minutes. Add the remaining lemon juice, ginger, tamari, water, and sherry and simmer for 5 minutes. Add the cilantro and stir. Serve the sauce with the patties over mung bean noodles or rice.

Savory Seitan Simmer with Green Chile

Yield: 4 servings   Heat Scale: Mild

I first tasted seitan at a Thai restaurant in Des Moines, Iowa, during a chile pepper celebration. I asked the chef, "What kind of meat is this?" He grinned and replied, "Wheat meat!" (Seitan is wheat protein.) This dish really tastes like beef! And, of course, I added a bit of heat to make it complete! Serve this with a rice pilaf.

1 tablespoon (15 mL) vegetable oil
2 medium onions, peeled and thinly sliced
¼ cup (59 mL) chopped green New Mexican chile
2 cups (473 mL) mushrooms, thinly sliced
8 ounces (224 g) seitan, cut into thin rectangles
¼ cup (59 mL) white wine
½ cup (118 mL) fresh thyme, chopped
¼ cup (59 mL) tahini
1 teaspoon (5 mL) prepared Dijon mustard

1. In a sauté pan, heat the oil over low heat. Add the onions, chile, and mushrooms and sauté for 20 minutes. Add the seitan and white wine and simmer until the seitan is heated through, about 3 minutes. Remove the mixture from the heat and gently stir in the thyme, tahini, and Dijon mustard. Serve immediately over rice.

Explosive Tofu-Veggie Stir-Fry

Yield: 4 servings   Heat Scale: Medium

Because of its absorbent nature, tofu tends to hold a lot of flavors well. In this stir-fry dish, the tofu combines with fresh vegetables and three kinds of peppers for the perfect one-two-three punch!

8 ounces (224 g) firm, water-packed tofu, drained and cut into ½-inch (1 cm) cubes
¼ cup (59 mL) Super-Rich Vegetable Stock (page 48)
1 teaspoon (5 mL) cornstarch
2 teaspoons (10 mL) red chile paste (available at Asian markets)
2 teaspoons (10 mL) brown sugar
1 tablespoon (15 mL) soy sauce
1 teaspoon (5 mL) peanut oil
4 tablespoons (60 mL) safflower oil, divided
3 cups (708 mL) mushrooms, stemmed and sliced
1 tablespoon (15 mL) minced fresh ginger
2 cloves garlic, peeled and minced
2 tablespoons (30 mL) minced jalapeño chile
½ cup (118 mL) sliced red bell pepper
½ cup (118 mL) sliced green onions
Freshly cooked rice for serving

1. Place a double layer of paper towels in a colander. Place the tofu cubes on the towels and let them drain for at least 25 minutes.
2. In a bowl, combine the vegetable broth and cornstarch and stir until the cornstarch is dissolved. Whisk in the chile paste, brown sugar, soy sauce, and peanut oil. Set the mixture aside.
3. In a wok or large sauté pan, heat 2 tablespoons (30 mL) of the safflower oil over high heat. Add the tofu and stir-fry until it is light brown. Using a slotted spoon, transfer the tofu to a plate. Add the remaining safflower oil to the wok. Add the mushrooms and stir-fry for about 5 minutes. Add the ginger, garlic, chile, bell pepper, and green onions. Add the tofu and stir-fry for about for 1 minute. Stir the broth-cornstarch mixture into the wok and bring to a boil. Divide rice among plates and top it with the tofu-vegetable mix.

New-Mex Stroganoff

Yield: 4–5 servings   Heat Scale: Mild

I like to serve this entrée during the cooler months. It is rich, filling, and mouth-watering. The two types of mushrooms add body and flavor to the sauce. Serve over hot, wide noodles with a chilled marinated salad of garlic, vinegar, and cucumbers or a hot salad of spicy sweet-and-sour red cabbage. Crusty rolls would be nice to sop up all of the sauce.

3 tablespoons (45 mL) fine-quality olive oil
1 onion, peeled and diced
1 pound (454 g) button mushrooms, washed and sliced
⅛ ounce (3.5 g) dried porcini mushrooms, rehydrated, rinsed, and diced
3 tablespoons (45 mL) all-purpose flour
¼ cup (59 mL) dry white wine
¾ cup (177 mL) Super-Rich Vegetable Stock (page 48)
1 clove garlic, peeled and minced
½ teaspoon (2.5 mL) dried thyme
½ teaspoon (2.5 mL) dried basil
2 tablespoons (30 mL) hot Hungarian paprika (Szeged brand preferred)
2 teaspoons (10 mL) ground red New Mexican chile
3 tablespoons (45 mL) minced fresh parsley
2 tablespoons (30 mL) minced fresh chives
2 cups (473 mL) low-fat sour cream (or use a mix of sour cream and plain yogurt)
Salt, to taste
Freshly ground black pepper, to taste
12–16 ounces (336–454 g) wide noodles, cooked

1. In a large skillet with a lid, heat the olive oil over medium heat. Add the onions and sauté for 1 minute. Add all the mushrooms and sauté for a minute or two, until only some of the mushroom juice is left. Sprinkle the mixture with the flour and toss lightly, until the vegetables are evenly coated.
2. Add the wine and stock and stir until the mixture starts to thicken. Reduce the heat to a simmer and add the garlic, thyme, basil, paprika, and ground chile. Cover the pan and let the mixture simmer for about 15 minutes to blend the flavors. Check to see that there is enough liquid in the skillet; if more is needed, add stock or wine.
3. Add the parsley, chives, and sour cream and stir thoroughly. Do not let the mixture boil. Add salt and pepper to taste.
4. Serve over the wide boiled noodles and garnish with more parsley if desired. If you have enough of the vegetable stock on hand, try boiling the noodles (either white or spinach) in it for a richer flavor.

Green Chile Polenta with Three Cheeses

Yield: 4 servings   Heat Scale: Medium

I think this recipe is especially wonderful—but then, it's hard to go wrong when you combine fresh green chile and three cheeses.

4 cups (.95 L) Super-Rich Vegetable Stock (page 48), divided
1½ cups (354 mL) cornmeal
3 green New Mexican chiles, roasted, peeled, stems and seeds removed,
chopped (or substitute ½ cup [118 mL] chopped New Mexican green chile)
1 cup (236 mL) shredded jalapeño cheese
1 cup (236 mL) shredded fontina cheese
½ cup (118 mL) grated Parmesan cheese
½ cup (118 mL) half-and-half

1. Preheat the oven to 350°F (180°C). Lightly grease a shallow, 6-cup (1.5 L) casserole.
2. In a saucepan, bring 2 cups (473 mL) of the stock to a boil. In a mixing bowl, combine the remaining broth and the cornmeal and stir until smooth. Pour the cornmeal mixture into the boiling broth. Cook over medium heat for about 10 minutes, or until the polenta clings to the side of the pan.
3. Pour half the polenta into the casserole. Smooth out the batter with a spatula, then sprinkle half of the green chile and half of the cheeses evenly over the mixture. Pour the half-and-half over the batter. Spoon the remaining polenta over the top of the prepared casserole. Sprinkle with the rest of the chile and top with the remaining cheeses. Bake until the polenta is bubbly, about 25 minutes. Let cool for 10 to 15 minutes before serving.

T.A.P. Sandwich

Yield: 8 sandwiches   Heat Scale: Medium

Dagwood would definitely make a beeline for this sandwich that incorporates tomatoes, avocados, and pita—T.A.P.

1 cup (236 mL) plain nonfat yogurt
2 tablespoons (30 mL) tahini
2 teaspoons (10 mL) lime juice
2 teaspoons (10 mL) paprika
1 shallot, peeled and minced
4 pocket pita breads, sliced in half
8 ounces (224 g) tofu, drained and cut into pita-size slices
2 tomatoes, chopped fine
1 avocado, peeled, pitted, and sliced into crescents
½ cup (118 mL) chopped New Mexican chile
¼ cup (59 mL) chopped mint
8 sprigs parsley

1. In a small bowl, combine the yogurt, tahini, lime juice, paprika, and shallots. Mix well and set aside.
2. Open each pita pocket. Separate the tofu into 8 equal portions. Insert 1 portion of tofu in each pocket, along with equal parts tomatoes, avocado, chile, and mint. Spoon 2 teaspoons (10 mL) of the yogurt-tahini sauce into each pocket. Garnish with parsley.

Red Hot Lover's Vegetarian Lo Mein

Yield: 4 servings   Heat Scale: Medium

Recipe contributor Daryl Malloy wrote that every time he makes this dish, his wife is putty in his hands for several days. Needless to say, they eat it often! The heat level can be adjusted by increasing or decreasing the amount of chiles. Daryl recommends it very hot.

¼ cup (59 mL) Super-Rich Vegetable Stock (page 48)
1 tablespoon (15 mL) soy sauce
4 cloves garlic, peeled and minced, divided
1 tablespoon (15 mL) dry sherry
1 tablespoon (15 mL) hoisin sauce
2 teaspoons (10 mL) sesame oil
1 teaspoon (5 mL) chile paste or hot bean sauce
1 teaspoon (5 mL) minced ginger
¼ teaspoon (1.25 mL) ground white pepper
1 pound (454 g) thin Chinese egg noodles
1 tablespoon (15 mL) peanut oil
3 or 4 Thai chiles (or other small, dried Asian chiles)
1 medium onion, peeled and julienned
¼ cup (59 mL) dry sherry
1 red bell pepper, stem and seeds removed, julienned
1 cup (236 mL) sliced mushrooms
2 carrots, julienned
¼ pound (113 g) pea pods
1½ tablespoons (22.5 mL) cornstarch mixed with 1½ tablespoons [22.5 mL] water
2 cups (473 mL) julienned Napa cabbage
½ cup (118 mL) chopped green onions

1. In a bowl, combine the vegetable stock, the soy sauce, half the garlic, the sherry, the hoisin sauce, the sesame oil, the chile paste, the ginger, and the white pepper.
2. Cook the noodles according to the package directions. Drain the noodles and toss them lightly with oil to prevent sticking.
3. Heat a skillet or wok until very hot and add the peanut oil. Stir-fry the remaining garlic, chiles, and onions until translucent. Add the sherry and reduce for 1 minute.
4. Add the bell pepper, mushrooms, carrots, and pea pods and stir to coat. Cover and cook for 1 minute. Add the sauce, cover, and cook for 4 minutes.

The vegetables should still be crisp. Raise the heat and slowly stir in the cornstarch mixture until the sauce thickens.

5. Add the noodles and toss to coat. Stir in the cabbage and green onions and serve.

Dan Dan Mein
(Dan Dan Noodles)

Yield: 4 servings   Heat Scale: Medium-Hot

Mary Kinnunen, writing for me about Sichuan cuisine, says this dish is simply delicious. Sidewalk snack vendors used to carry pots of these noodles on shoulder poles. (Dan means "shoulder pole.") Dan Dan Noodles became so popular that they began to appear at first-class banquets. Dan Dan Mein, with its strong spice flavors, is one of Sichuan's most popular foods.

2 cups (473 mL) Super-Rich Vegetable Stock (page 48)
3 tablespoons (45 mL) hot Chile Oil (page 16)
1 tablespoon (15 mL) minced garlic
1 tablespoon (15 mL) minced ginger
1 tablespoon (15 mL) vegetable oil
1 tablespoon (15 mL) sesame paste
2 teaspoons (10 mL) sesame oil
1 green onion, chopped
½ pound (224 g) cooked spaghetti noodles
¼ cup (59 mL) chopped leafy green vegetable, such as spinach or Chinese cabbage

1. In a large pot, combine the stock, chile oil, garlic, ginger, vegetable oil, sesame paste, sesame oil, and green onion and heat through. Add the noodles and green vegetable to the sauce and heat through.

2. Divide the noodles among serving bowls.

Ballistic Baby Bok Choy and Fried Tofu

Yield: 4 servings   Heat Scale: Medium to Hot

Because tofu soaks up so many flavors and seasonings, it is ideal to use in dishes that have a strong flavor base. If you have been eating tofu, consider yourself lucky—it is now touted as reducing some risks of cancer and lowering cholesterol levels. If it is used and cooked properly, even your most carnivorous friends can be persuaded to try it. Seduce them with this recipe. (Note: If you are using santaka or Thai chile, the heat scale will be considerable; if you are using New Mexican crushed red chile, the heat scale will be lower, unless you add more of the crushed chiles.)

16 ounces (454 g) firm tofu
3 tablespoons (45 mL) Chile Oil (page 16; or substitute 3 tablespoons [45 mL] corn oil and 1 teaspoon [5 mL] crushed, dried santaka, Thai, or 2 teaspoons [10 mL] New Mexican red chile [see Note])
1½ pounds (680 g) baby bok choy, washed and coarsely chopped
4 cloves garlic, peeled and minced
6 green onions, sliced
1 red bell pepper, stem and seeds removed, julienned
4 tablespoons (60 mL) water
4 tablespoons (60 mL) soy sauce
2 dried shiitake mushrooms, rehydrated and sliced
¾ cup (177 mL) coarsely chopped water chestnuts or jicama
2 teaspoons (10 mL) sugar
2 teaspoons (10 mL) crushed, dried santaka, Thai, or New Mexican red chile
1½ teaspoons (7.5 mL) cornstarch or arrowroot mixed with 2 tablespoons (30 mL) water
4 cups (.95 L) cooked rice

1. Cut the tofu into 1-inch (2.5 cm) slices and place them on paper or linen towels. Cover them with more towels. Place a cookie sheet on top of the tofu and place several weights (such as canned goods) on top to help squeeze the excess liquid out of the tofu. Press for 15 to 20 minutes. Cut the tofu into 1-inch (2.5 cm) cubes.
2. In a large sauté pan or a wok, heat the oil over medium-high heat. Add the tofu cubes and sauté, turning them when necessary, to achieve a golden brown color. Transfer the cubes to paper towels to drain.
3. In a large skillet with a lid, combine the bok choy, garlic, green onions, bell pepper, and water. Cover and steam over medium heat until the bok choy is tender, about 5 minutes.
4. Uncover the skillet and add the tofu, mushrooms, water chestnuts, sugar, crushed red chile, and cornstarch mixture and toss to mix. Cook, stirring lightly, until the sauce boils. Reduce the heat and simmer for 1 minute.
5. Serve immediately over the hot, cooked rice.

Spicy Sweet and Sour Tempeh

Yield: 4 servings   Heat Scale: Medium-Hot

Tempeh is available in health food and whole food stores. Not long ago, it was hard to find because it wasn't as mainstream as tofu. Tempeh, which is fermented cooked soybeans, was originally eaten in Indonesia, and few people in this country knew about it. The intense flavors of this dish make for a very satisfying entrée. This dish can be served over cooked rice or it can be served with a crisp salad and some warm pita bread.

1 small pineapple, peeled and cored
3 tablespoons (45 mL) Chile Oil (page 16), divided
1 tablespoon (15 mL) minced fresh ginger
3 cloves garlic, peeled and minced
2 tablespoons (30 mL) minced onion
2 tablespoons (30 mL) rice vinegar
½ cup (118 mL) water
¾ cup (177 mL) brown rice syrup
3 tablespoons (45 mL) miso
1 teaspoon (5 mL) shoyu soy sauce
8 ounces (224 g) 5-grain tempeh, cubed
1 teaspoon (5 mL) sesame oil
2 dried Thai chiles
¼ cup (59 mL) cubed red bell pepper
½ cup (118 mL) coarsely chopped onion
1 cup (236 mL) sliced bok choy
½ cup (118 mL) chopped jicama
¾ cup (177 mL) bean sprouts
¼ cup (59 mL) sliced mushrooms

1. Cut the fresh pineapple into ½-inch (1 cm) cubes and set aside 1½ cups (354 mL) of it. Purée some of the remaining pineapple in a food processor, drain, measure out 2 tablespoons (30 mL), and set the pulp aside. Refrigerate the remaining fruit.
2. In a small wok or heavy skillet, heat 1 teaspoon (5 mL) of the oil over high heat. Add the ginger, garlic, and onion and sauté for 30 seconds, stirring so the garlic doesn't burn.
3. Add 5 teaspoons (25 mL) of the remaining oil, the vinegar, and the water and stir. Add the 2 tablespoons (30 mL) puréed pineapple, rice syrup, miso, and shoyu and stir until the miso is dissolved. Stir in the cubed pineapple, remove the mixture from the heat, and set it aside.
4. In a wok or large skillet, heat the remaining 1 tablespoon (15 mL) chile oil over high heat. Add the cubed tempeh and sauté it until it is crisp. Transfer the tempeh to paper towels to drain.
5. Wipe out the wok with a paper towel. Heat the sesame oil in the wok over high heat and quickly sauté the Thai chiles, bell pepper, onion, bok choy, jicama, bean sprouts, and mushrooms until they are heated through but still crisp. Remove the chiles, stir in the reserved tempeh and pineapple sauce, and heat through. Serve immediately over a rice pilaf.

Terrific Tongue-Tingling Tofu Sloppy Joes

Yield: 5–6 servings   Heat Scale: Medium

I think of this recipe as a Saturday or Sunday night special. It's fast, easy, and deli-cious, with very little cleanup. Besides, tofu is good for you. Serve the mixture on good-quality buns.

2 cups (473 mL) chopped firm tofu
2 tablespoons (30 mL) canola oil
¾ cup (177 mL) chopped onion
¼ cup (59 mL) chopped green bell pepper
¼ cup (59 mL) chopped celery
1 (8-ounce [224 g]) can tomato sauce
1½ teaspoons (7.5 mL) vegetarian Worcestershire sauce or tamari
½ teaspoon (2.5 mL) salt
⅛ teaspoon (.6 mL) freshly ground black pepper
1 tablespoon (15 mL) vinegar
¼ cup (59 mL) commercial habanero catsup (or substitute ¼ cup [59 mL] tomato catsup plus ¼ cup [59 mL] chopped green chile, 1 chopped ser-rano, or 1 chopped jalapeño)
1 teaspoon (5 mL) sugar

1. Drain the tofu and weight it down on paper towels to drain off any excess liquid. Crumble it into a bowl and set it aside.
2. In a medium skillet, heat the oil over medium heat. Add the onion, bell pepper, and celery and sauté for about 3 minutes. Add the crumbled tofu and toss lightly.
3. Stir in the tomato sauce, Worcestershire, salt, pepper, vinegar, catsup, and sugar. Add a little water if the mixture looks too thick. Reduce the heat to a simmer, cover, and simmer for 20 minutes.
4. Serve the mixture on toasted buns.

Veggie Tacos with Spicy Curry Sauce

Yield: 6 servings   Heat Scale: Medium

I've cut a bunch of the fat out of this tasty recipe by substituting corn tortillas for the flour tortillas and nonfat yogurt for the sour cream. These meatless tacos are so delicious you'll want to make them a standard item on your dinner menu.

1 tablespoon (15 mL) plus 1 teaspoon (5 mL) safflower oil, divided
1 small onion, peeled and chopped
1 shallot, peeled and chopped
2 cloves garlic, peeled and minced
1 tablespoon (15 mL) curry powder of your choice from Chapter 1
½ teaspoon (2.5 mL) ground cayenne
1 teaspoon (5 mL) ground cumin
¼ cup (59 mL) plain nonfat yogurt
1 tablespoon (15 mL) prepared mango chutney
1 red bell pepper, stem and seeds removed, julienned
1 yellow bell pepper, stem and seeds removed, julienned
1 green bell pepper, stem and seeds removed, chopped
1 red onion, peeled and chopped
12 (4-inch [10 cm]) corn tortillas

1. In a small skillet, heat 1 teaspoon (5 mL) of the oil over medium heat. Add the onions and sauté until golden brown. Add the shallot, garlic, curry powder, cayenne, and cumin and sauté for another minute, then remove the skillet from the heat.
2. In a bowl, mix together the yogurt, the chutney, and the sautéed mixture, and refrigerate this mixture. In a medium skillet, heat the remaining oil over medium heat. Add the bell peppers and red onion and sauté until they are soft, but still slightly crisp.
3. Place the tortillas in a tortilla warmer (or between two cloths), and microwave for 25 seconds. Remove the tortillas from the microwave and the curry mixture from the refrigerator and place the sautéed vegetables on a platter. Allow each person to construct his or her own tacos, or make them all up ahead of time.

Koshary

Yield: 6–8 servings   Heat Scale: Varies

A friend of mine, world traveler Richard Sterling, collected this recipe for me in Egypt. He wrote on the back of a risque postcard, "Koshary is the most common Egyptian street food. It is ubiquitous, and the streets of Cairo are alive with its savor. The best example is to be found at Koshary Khadewi, a small restaurant immediately around the corner from the Stella Bar. An authentic Egyptian recipe for this dish would take up pages. Therefore I have taken liberties with Chef Gabriel Khalid's version so that busy people can enjoy this wonderful dish at home. Leftovers keep very well in a sealed container and make a good lunch or snack."

Layer 1: 2 cups (473 mL) cooked rice or rice with vermicelli (Rice-a-Roni works well)
Layer 2: 2 cups (473 mL) cooked elbow macaroni
Layer 3: 1 cup (236 mL) cooked lentils
Layer 4: 1 cup (236 mL) spicy tomato sauce, meatless spaghetti sauce, or salsa picante of your choice
Layer 5: 3 large yellow onions, sliced thin and fried in oil until very brown and toasty (very important)
Layer 6: 1 cup (236 mL) cooked chickpeas

Sauces:
Garlic-Vinegar Sauce:
6 cloves garlic, mashed
4 tablespoons (60 mL) distilled white vinegar
½ cup (118 mL) water
2 tablespoons (30 mL) lemon juice
1 teaspoon (5 mL) ground cumin
1 pinch salt

1. Combine all the ingredients in a jar and shake well.
2. On a serving platter or large plate, pile on each layer successively, in proportion with the volume in the recipe. Sprinkle with the garlic-vinegar sauce and the hot sauce. Garnish with parsley.

Stuffed Roti with Potato Curry

Yield: 4 servings   Heat Scale: Medium

When Nancy Gerlach was visiting the British Virgin Islands, she enjoyed eating this dish at Foxy's Tamarind Bar. Rotis are traditional fare throughout the Caribbean and have been called a West Indian version of a burrito. The bread wrapper is East Indian in origin and always contains something curried.

4 cups (.95 L) all-purpose flour
2 teaspoons (10 mL) baking powder
1¼ teaspoon (6.25 mL) salt, divided
¼ cup (59 mL) plus 4 tablespoons (60 mL) vegetable oil, divided
3 cups (708 mL) water, divided
2 cloves garlic, minced
1 tablespoon (15 mL) minced ginger
1 Scotch bonnet chile, stem and seeds removed, minced (or substitute habanero or 2 fresh cayenne chiles)
1 onion, peeled and diced
3 tablespoons (45 mL) imported curry powder (or substitute a curry powder from Chapter 1)
1 teaspoon (5 mL) dried thyme
½ teaspoon (2.5 mL) ground cloves
½ teaspoon (2.5 mL) freshly ground black pepper
3 cups (708 mL) cooked, peeled, and diced potato
2 tablespoons (30 mL) tamarind paste dissolved in ¼ cup (59 mL) water (optional)
1 (15-ounce [420 g]) can chickpeas, drained
Vegetable oil for frying

1. To make the dough, sift together the flour, baking powder, and 1 teaspoon (5 mL) of the salt in a bowl. Gradually stir in ¼ cup (59 mL) of the oil and enough water to form a ball with the dough (about 1 cup [236 mL]). Knead for 5 minutes or until soft. Form the dough into a ball, cover, and let rise for 15 minutes.
2. In a skillet, heat 1–2 tablespoons (15–30 mL) of the remaining oil over medium heat. Add the garlic, ginger, and chile and sauté for a couple of minutes. Add the onions, curry powder, thyme, cloves, pepper, and the remaining salt and sauté until the onions are soft. Add the potatoes, 2 cups (473 mL) water, tamarind, and chickpeas and simmer for 15 minutes, until soft but not mushy.
3. Divide the dough into 4 equal balls. Flatten each and roll it out into a circle 8 to 9 inches (20 to 22.5 cm) in diameter. Heat the remaining 2 tablespoons (30 mL) oil in a skillet until very hot (a drop of water will sizzle). Reduce the heat and place the rotis in the skillet. Cook for 2 to 3 minutes, until browned, then turn and brown the other side. Remove the rotis from the oil and cover them with a towel until ready to serve.
4. To serve, place about a cup (236 mL) of the filling in the center of a roti. Fold over the sides and fold up the ends, as you would with a burrito. Serve accompanied by a chutney from Chapter 1 and a Caribbean hot sauce from Chapter 2.

Snappy Sautéed Portobello Chipotle Sandwich
Yield: 4 servings   Heat Scale: Medium-Hot

This is the perfect meatless alternative for game day—it offers interesting textures, lots of heat, and, best of all, it is served on a toasted spicy bread from Chapter 4.

2 tablespoons (30 mL) butter
2 pounds (1.1 kg) portobello mushrooms, brushed and sliced
1 large onion, peeled and cut into thin rings
3 chipotles in adobo, stems removed, chopped
8 slices spicy bread of your choice from Chapter 4
4 splashes balsamic vinegar

1. In a large sauté pan, melt the butter over medium-high heat. Add the mushrooms, onions, and chipotles and sauté until the onions are caramelized, about 10 minutes. Remove the mixture from the heat and divide equally among four thick slices of bread, then give each a splash of the balsamic vinegar. Top each half with another slice of the bread and serve.

Hot Stuffed Pita Pockets with Harissa
Yield: 4 servings   Heat Scale: Mild

From Ellen Burr of Truro, Massachusetts, comes this great main dish. She confesses: "In the '60s I became an addicted chilehead after sniffing a vat of Tabasco Sauce in Louisiana. Ever since, I've brought home the perfect, and eminently edible, memento: hot peppers, canned, bottled, dried and powdered, including harissa, which I discovered not in a souk but in a Santa Fe market! Here is a family favorite, my healthy version of falafel, low in fat and high in flavor." (Note: Harissa is a North African chile paste. If none is available, substitute 5 dried red New Mexican chiles, rehydrated and puréed with a clove of garlic, ½ teaspoon [2.5 mL] each ground cumin, cinnamon, coriander, and caraway.)

1 tablespoon (15 mL) olive oil
1 small onion, peeled and sliced
1 small red bell pepper, stem and seeds removed, sliced
1 large clove garlic, peeled and minced
¼ teaspoon (1.25 mL) ground cumin
¼ teaspoon (1.25 mL) ground coriander
1 (15.5-ounce [434 g]) can cannellini (white kidney) beans, rinsed and drained
1 teaspoon (5 mL) Harissa (page 23)
¼ cup (59 mL) tahini or prepared hummus
Salt, to taste
4 whole wheat pocket pita rounds, halved and warmed
8 lettuce leaves
1 tomato, sliced
1 small cucumber, peeled and thinly sliced
8 sprigs cilantro or parsley

1. In a saucepan, heat the oil over medium heat. Add the onions, bell peppers, and garlic and sauté for a couple of minutes. Add the cumin and coriander and cook for an additional 5 minutes.
2. Stir in the beans, Harissa, and tahini. Mash the beans slightly and heat them over a low heat until hot. Add salt to taste
3. Line the pita pockets with the lettuce, tomato, and cucumber. Stuff with the hot bean mixture and cilantro sprigs. Serve warm or cold, with extra Harissa on the side.

Marvelous Meatless Spicy Paella

Yield: 4 servings   Heat Scale: Medium

There's no reason anyone should miss out on the Spanish treat of paella just because he or she doesn't eat meat. I admit that this colorful recipe has a lot of ingredients, but it's really worth the trouble.

3¼ cups (767 mL) Super-Rich Vegetable Stock (page 48)
¼ teaspoon (1.25 mL) saffron threads
1 head garlic, broken into cloves, unpeeled
2 yellow bell peppers, stems and seeds removed, cut into bite-size strips
1 red bell pepper, stem and seeds removed, cut into bite-size strips
1 orange bell pepper, stem and seeds removed, cut into bite-size pieces
2 small zucchini, trimmed and cut into rounds
2 tablespoons (30 mL) extra virgin olive oil, divided
2 shallots, peeled and minced
1 small onion, peeled and minced
2 serrano or jalapeño chiles, stems and seeds removed, minced
3 Roma tomatoes, diced
1 tablespoon (15 mL) minced fresh oregano
1 tablespoon (15 mL) minced fresh thyme
1½ cups (354 mL) uncooked medium-grain white rice
2 lemons, quartered
2 tablespoons (30 mL) chopped fresh parsley

1. In a saucepan, combine the vegetable stock and saffron. Bring the mixture to a rapid boil. Reduce the heat and simmer, covered, for 25 minutes. Set aside.
2. In another saucepan, combine the garlic with just enough water to cover, then boil for 5 minutes or until tender. Drain the garlic and let it cool. When the garlic is cool enough to handle, peel the cloves and set them aside.
3. Preheat the oven to 400°F (200°C).
4. Place the garlic, bell peppers and zucchini in a rectangular baking dish. Pour 3 tablespoons (45 mL) of the vegetable stock and 1 tablespoon (15 mL) of the olive oil over the vegetables. Bake for 28 minutes or until the vegetables are tender, stirring twice. Set aside.
5. In a deep skillet, heat the remaining olive oil over medium heat. Add the shallots, onion, and serranos and sauté until the onions are brown.

Add the tomatoes, oregano, and thyme and cook for about 4 minutes, or until the liquid has evaporated. Add the rice and the remaining vegetable stock and bring to a boil. Simmer, covered, for 20 to 30 minutes or until the rice is tender. Gently fold in the roasted vegetables and simmer, covered, for 5 more minutes. Transfer the paella to a colorful serving dish and garnish with the lemon wedges and parsley. Serve with crusty rolls.

Summer Smart Tart

Yield: 6 servings   Heat Scale: Medium

While I like to make this tart for brunches in the summertime, it is just as nice in the winter or fall. Simply couple the tart with the applicable seasonal side dishes from Chapter 13 and a little apple cider, and you're ready to go.

1 prepared pie crust
2 cups (473 mL) reduced-fat mozzarella cheese
6 Roma tomatoes, sliced
4 cloves garlic, peeled and minced
½ cup (118 mL) black olives, rinsed
2 green New Mexican chiles, roasted, peeled, stems and seeds removed, chopped
1 tablespoon (15 mL) capers, rinsed and drained
1 tablespoon (15 mL) olive oil
1 tablespoon (15 mL) minced fresh basil

1. Bake the pie crust according to the package directions until it is barely done, not browned. Remove it from the oven and let it cool to room temperature. Set the oven temperature to 350°F (180°C).
2. Spread the cheese evenly over the bottom of the crust. Place the sliced tomatoes on top of the cheese, overlapping each slice over the next in a concentric circle. In a bowl, combine the garlic, black olives, green chiles, capers, olive oil, and basil. Spread this mixture over the tomatoes. Bake the tart for about 15 minutes, or until the cheese is melted, the tomatoes have softened, and the crust has browned. Cool the tart to room temperature.

Grilled Corn Potato Cakes with Poblano Chile Lime Vinaigrette

Yield: 4 servings   Heat Scale: Mild

From chefs Charles Wiley and Jeff Gustie of the Boulders Resort in Scottsdale, Arizona, this recipe is delicious enough to grace any chilehead's table.

1 tablespoon (15 mL) butter
1 small red onion, peeled and diced
3 russet potatoes, skin left on
1 ear sweet corn, grilled until slightly blackened, kernels removed from the cob
¼ cup (59 mL) plain nonfat yogurt
2 teaspoons (10 mL) ground ancho chile (or substitute ground New Mexican or other pure chile powder)
Kosher salt, to taste
Freshly ground black pepper, to taste
6 poblano chiles, roasted, peeled, stems and seeds removed
½ cup (118 mL) white wine
¼ cup (59 mL) vegetable oil
2 tablespoons (30 mL) chopped fresh cilantro
4 cloves garlic, peeled
2 shallots, peeled
2 teaspoons (10 mL) Dijon mustard
Juice of 2 limes
Cilantro sprigs for garnish

1. In a skillet, melt the butter over medium heat. Add the onion and sauté until the onions have browned slightly.
2. Steam or boil the potatoes for 25 to 30 minutes. While the potatoes are still warm, mash them coarsely in a mixing bowl. Add the sautéed onion, corn kernels, yogurt, ground chile, and salt and pepper to taste and mix well. In the bottom of an 8-inch (20 cm) square baking dish, spread a ¾-inch (1.5 cm) thick layer of the mixture. Refrigerate until firm, at least 2 hours. Using a 2-inch (5 cm) circular cutter, cut out 12 cakes. Grill or broil the cakes until browned.
3. In a blender, combine the poblanos, wine, oil, chopped cilantro, garlic, shallots, mustard, lime, and salt and pepper to taste and process until smooth.
4. Divide the vinaigrette equally among 4 plates so that it covers the bottom of each plate. Stand three corn cakes on edge on each plate and garnish with cilantro sprigs.

Vegetable Pad Thai
(Stir-Fried Rice Noodles, Thai-Style)

Yield: 2 to 4 servings   Heat Scale: Medium to Hot

Pad Thai is a popular, healthy, noodle dish served in restaurants, by street vendors, and in homes in Thailand. There are many variations of this one-dish meal; it can include seafood, chicken, meat, or just vegetables (as this one does), or any combination thereof. Thailand was settled in the twelfth century by refugees from southern China, and the Chinese influence is reflected in this dish, the name of which means "Thai stir-fry." The cuisine of Thailand reflects a number of influences— not just Chinese, but also those of its other neighbors, Burma, India, Vietnam, and Laos. Their food is known for its freshness and the way it balances a variety of flavors, as in this dish. Nam pla, fermented fish sauce, which is thin, salty, and not terribly fishy, is used here instead of soy sauce, but you may substitute soy sauce for a strictly vegetarian dish.

8 ounces (224 g) firm tofu
2–3 tablespoons (30–45 mL) vegetable oil (peanut preferred), divided
2 eggs, lightly beaten
4–6 Thai chiles, stems removed, chopped
3–4 cloves garlic, peeled and minced
3 shallots, peeled and thinly sliced
1 tablespoon (15 mL) distilled white vinegar
2 teaspoons (10 mL) sugar
½ pound (224 g) dried rice stick noodles (ban pho noodles), available in Asian markets
1 tablespoon (15 mL) Thai fish sauce
1 cup (236 mL) bean sprouts
¼ cup (59 mL) chopped fresh Thai basil, optional
¼ cup (59 mL) chopped peanuts
4 green onions, thinly sliced
Chopped cilantro for garnish
Lime wedges for garnish

1. Place 3 to 4 paper towels on a plate. Set the tofu on the towels, top with additional towels, place another plate on top, and weight the top plate down with a heavy skillet for about 15 minutes to extract the excess moisture. Rinse the tofu with cold water and drain. Cut the tofu into strips about 1½ inches (3.5 cm) long, ½ inch (1 cm) wide and thick.
2. Heat a wok over high heat. Add 1 tablespoon (15 mL) of the oil and swirl to coat the pan. When the oil is hot, add the tofu and stir-fry until golden, about 20 seconds. Transfer the tofu to paper towels to drain.
3. Heat a little more oil, if necessary, in the wok, and add the eggs. Allow the eggs to set, turning as needed, until cooked—don't scramble. Remove the egg from the pan and cut it into chunks.
4. Add more oil, if necessary, then add the chiles, garlic, and shallots. Stir-fry for 15 to 20 seconds or until fragrant. Stir in the vinegar and sugar.
5. Add another tablespoon (15 mL) of the oil. When it's very hot, add the noodles and toss to stir-fry, adding a little water if the mixture starts to dry.

To stir-fry, spread and pull the noodles into a thin layer, scrape, and gently turn them over. Repeat this process several times until the stiff, white noodles soften and curl.

6. Season the noodles with the fish sauce and turn them until coated. Add the bean sprouts, basil, peanuts, and onions and toss. Return the tofu and eggs to the pan and toss to mix. Taste for seasonings and adjust as needed.

7. To serve: place the pad thai on a serving platter and garnish it with the cilantro. Arrange the limes around the platter; guests can squeeze the lime over the top before eating.

Dijon-Sauced Portobello Mushrooms with Blue Cheese

Yield: 4 servings   Heat Scale: Mild

There is no reason those of you who are either giving up or cutting back on red meat can't enjoy a dish with a "beefy" flavor. Portobello mushrooms have a steak-like texture and flavor, so why not serve them with a sauce that goes equally well with meat? This simple, creamy sauce doesn't overpower the flavor of the mushroom. I suggest you serve these mushrooms with a wild rice pilaf.

2 tablespoons (30 mL) butter
3 tablespoons (45 mL) chopped shallots
½ cup (118 mL) dry white wine
1 cup (236 mL) heavy cream
3–4 tablespoons (45–60 mL) Dijon mustard, store-bought or homemade (page 18)
1 teaspoon (5 mL) minced fresh thyme
Salt, to taste
Freshly ground black pepper, to taste
2 large portobello mushrooms
Extra virgin olive oil as needed
Crumbled blue cheese for garnish

1. Preheat the broiler and set the broiler pan as far as possible from the heat source. Lightly oil a baking sheet.

2. In a saucepan over medium heat, melt the butter. Add the shallots and sauté until soft. Add the wine and simmer until the liquid has reduced by half. Stir in the cream, mustard, and thyme and simmer until the sauce has thickened.

3. Place the mushrooms on the prepared baking sheet, gill-side up, and brush them with the olive oil. Broil for 5 minutes. Turn the mushrooms and brush them with more oil.

4. Turn the oven to 425°F (225°C). Bake the mushrooms for 15 minutes, or until they are done.

5. To serve, slice the mushrooms at an angle. Spoon some of the mustard sauce on individual plates; top with the mushroom slices, garnish with the blue cheese, and serve.

Missayeko Dal Haru
(Nepalese Mixed Lentils)

Yield: 4 servings   Heat Scale: Medium to Hot

Pat Chapman, the "King of Curries" in England, collected this recipe on one of his many trips to the subcontinent, where they grow over sixty types of lentils, or dals. According to Pat, "In Nepal, these lentils are either eaten freshly picked, when they are lovely and soft, or in the more familiar dried form." Since it is impossible to obtain these legumes fresh outside the subcontinent, he uses dried lentils. There is a difference, of course, but who is to say which is better? (Note: This recipe requires advance preparation.)

2 ounces (56 g) whole black urad dal (a black-skinned white lentil available in Asian markets)
2 ounces (56 g) whole red masoor dal (an orange-red lentil with green skin available in Asian markets)
2 ounces (56 g) whole green moong dal (available in Asian markets)
2 ounces (56 g) split yellow chana dal (yellow split peas available in Asian markets)
3–4 tablespoons (45–60 mL) ghee (or substitute vegetable oil)
½ cup (118 mL) finely chopped onion
4 cloves garlic, peeled and finely chopped
1 tablespoon (15 mL) grated ginger
1 teaspoon (5 mL) ground cumin
1 teaspoon (5 mL) ground coriander
1 teaspoon (5 mL) garam masala, store-bought or homemade
1 teaspoon (5 mL) ground turmeric
1 teaspoon (5 mL) ground red chile, such as New Mexican
Salt, to taste
Chopped fresh cilantro for garnish

1. Pick over the lentils and remove any grit or impurities. Combine them in a bowl, cover them with water, and soak for at least 4 hours, adding more water if necessary. Drain, rinse several times, and drain again.
2. Measure twice the lentils' volume of water into a large saucepan and bring it to a boil over high heat. Add the lentils, reduce the heat, and simmer for 30 minutes, stirring occasionally as the water is absorbed.
3. Heat a wok over medium-high heat and add the ghee. When the ghee is hot, add the onions, garlic, and ginger. Stir-fry the mixture until fragrant, about 2 minutes. Add the spices and stir-fry for about 5 more minutes, adding a little water if needed to prevent sticking.
4. Add the stir-fry mixture to the lentils and stir to mix well. Taste for seasonings and add salt as needed.
5. To serve, place the lentils in a large bowl and garnish with the cilantro.

THIRTEEN

Vegetables
and Other
Accompaniments

If you think the international hot and spicy recipes so far are rather eclectic, this chapter will amaze you. The worldwide diversity of chile peppers are combined here with nearly everything you can imagine to make side dishes. I start with all the combinations and permutations of rice and other grains, such as like quinoa; proceed to legumes, such as beans, peas, and chickpeas; move on to potatoes of all kinds, including sweet potatoes and yams; explore garden vegetables from around the world, plus fruits that are served as vegetables, such as chiles themselves and avocados; examine fruits such as bananas, mangos, and breadfruit and their relationships to the hot pods; and finally settle on some miscellaneous side dishes. Enjoy the ride—it's really fun.

Arroz de Huaca
(Oxala's Rice)
Yield: 4 servings   Heat Scale: Medium

Oxala is the highest Orixa of the Bahian gods of Brazil, the king of the universe. The Catholic counterpart is Jesus. His day is Friday, his color is white, his greeting is exe e baba, and his element is the whole universe. This is his favorite dish, and the recipe comes from Tita Libin.

2 tablespoons (30 mL) olive oil
½ cup (118 mL) minced onion
1 dried malagueta chile, stems and seeds removed, crushed (or substitute piquin, Thai, or Japanese)
1 cup (236 mL) uncooked white rice
½ cup (118 mL) boiling water
1½ cups (354 mL) coconut milk

1. In a saucepan with a lid, heat the oil over medium heat. Add the onion and chiles and sauté until the onions are soft. Add the rice and continue to sauté until the rice turns opaque.
2. Combine the water and coconut milk, add it to the pot, and bring it to a boil. Lower the heat, cover, and simmer for 30 minutes or until the rice is tender.
3. Fluff the rice with a fork before serving.

Coconut-Chile Rice
Yield: 4–6 servings   Heat Scale: Hot

Coconuts are plentiful in Belize and all along the Caribbean coast of Central and South America. This Belizean recipe comes from Nancy Gerlach, who was almost beaned on the head by one while sitting on the porch of our temporary family residence on Ambergris Caye.

2 tablespoons (30 mL) butter
1 cup (236 mL) grated fresh coconut
1 small onion, peeled and chopped fine
1 habanero chile, stem and seeds removed, minced (or substitute 3 jalapeños)
1 cup (236 mL) uncooked white rice
1 cup (236 mL) coconut milk
1½ cups (354 mL) Classic Chicken Stock (page 46)
Minced cilantro for garnish

1. In a saucepan with a lid, melt the butter over medium heat. Add the grated coconut and sauté for a couple of minutes or until it starts to brown. Add the onion and habanero and sauté until the onion is soft.
2. Add the rice and sauté until it turns light brown.
3. In separate pot, bring the coconut milk and chicken stock to a boil. Add the rice mixture, reduce the heat, and simmer, covered, until the rice is done, about 25 to 30 minutes. Serve the rice garnished with the minced cilantro.

Arroz con Coco y Pasas
(Colombian Coconut Rice with Raisins)

Yield: 6 servings   Heat Scale: Medium

Rice cooked with coconut milk has a unique flavor and is part of the Spanish-Indian cuisine of Colombia. The Colombians on the coasts prefer rice, just as those in the interior depend on corn and potatoes. As a side dish, this delicious rice can be served with grilled meats or fish. (Note: This recipe requires advance preparation.)

2 cups (473 mL) shredded coconut
4 cups (.95 L) water
½ teaspoon (2.5 mL) salt
3 tablespoons (45 mL) butter, divided
1 teaspoon (5 mL) sugar
½ cup (118 mL) raisins
½ habanero chile, seeds and stem removed, minced (or substitute 1½ jalapeños)
¼ cup (59 mL) finely chopped onion
1½ cups (354 mL) uncooked rice

1. In a bowl, soak the coconut in the water for at least 3 hours. Drain the coconut milk through a strainer into a separate bowl, squeezing out as much juice as possible. Reserve the coconut milk and discard the meat.
2. In a saucepan, combine 3 cups (708 mL) of the coconut milk, the salt, 2 tablespoons (30 mL) of the butter, the sugar, the raisins, and the habanero. Bring the mixture to a boil, then lower the heat and simmer gently for 3 minutes.
3. In a small skillet, melt the remaining 1 tablespoon (15 mL) butter over medium heat. Add the onion and sauté until it is soft. Add the onion to the simmering mixture and stir in the rice. Cook, covered, for 20 to 25 minutes, stirring once or twice to check for sticking. If the mixture starts to stick, add some of the remaining coconut liquid and stir thoroughly.

Arroz con Chiles Poblanos Rojos (Rice with Red Poblano Chiles)

Yield: 4–6 servings   Heat Scale: Medium

The addition of green tomatoes (or tomatillos) and sliced hard-boiled eggs makes this rice recipe from Nuevo León in Mexico unusual. The roasted red poblano chile adds color and a dash of heat. Serve the rice with a chicken dish from Chapter 10.

3 tablespoons (45 mL) olive oil
2 cups (473 mL) uncooked rice
1 cup (236 mL) minced onion
2 cloves garlic, peeled and minced
2 jalapeño chiles, stems and seeds removed, cut into thin rings
1 cup (236 mL) chopped tomatillos (or substitute green tomatoes)
½ teaspoon (2.5 mL) ground cumin
½ teaspoon (2.5 mL) salt
¼ teaspoon (1.25 mL) freshly ground black pepper
4 cups (.95 L) Basic Beef Stock (page 46)
2 red poblano chiles, roasted, peeled, stems and seeds removed, chopped fine
2 hard-boiled eggs, sliced

1. In a medium saucepan, heat the oil over medium heat. Add the rice, onion, garlic, jalapeños, tomatillos, cumin, salt, and pepper and sauté for 2 minutes, or until the rice turns golden. Stir in the broth, bring the mixture to a boil, cover, and reduce the heat. Cook the rice for 20 to 30 minutes.
2. Stir in the red poblano chiles and the eggs and serve.

Arroz Con Rajas y Elotes (Rice with Sliced Chiles and Corn)

Yield: 4 servings   Heat Scale: Mild

Rice, chiles, and corn combine together in this delicious side dish from Veracruz. Serve it with a Mexican fish recipe from Chapter 11, befitting Veracruz's seaside location.

4 tablespoons (60 mL) vegetable oil, divided
1 cup (236 mL) uncooked rice
1 cup (236 mL) chopped onion
2 cloves garlic, peeled and minced
2 cups (473 mL) water
½ teaspoon (2.5 mL) salt
4 poblano chiles, roasted, peeled, stems and seeds removed, cut into thin strips
¾ cup (177 mL) canned or frozen whole kernel corn
¼ cup (59 mL) heavy cream
¾ cup (177 mL) grated gruyere cheese

1. Preheat the oven to 350°F (180°C).

2. In a saucepan, heat 3 tablespoons (45 mL) of the oil over low heat. Add the rice and sauté, stirring, until it turns golden, about 1 minute. Add half of the chopped onion and all of the garlic and sauté for 1 more minute. Add the water and salt, bring the mixture to a boil, reduce the heat to a simmer, cover, and cook for 20 minutes.

3. In a small skillet, heat the remaining 1 tablespoon (15 mL) oil over medium heat. Add the remaining chopped onion and sauté for 1 minute. Add the chopped chiles and sauté for 30 seconds. Add the corn and the cream and heat the mixture over a low heat. Do not boil.

4. Spoon the cooked rice into a small, ovenproof, glass baking dish (such as a Pyrex dish) and mix in the sautéed chile-corn-cream sauté. Cover the mixture with the grated cheese and bake for 10 to 15 minutes or until the cheese has melted and the mixture is heated through.

Spiced Indian Fried Rice

Yield: 6–8 servings   Heat Scale: Medium

This side dish from Trinidad resembles a pilaf, and, in fact, it can be baked rather than cooked on the stove. The key to the taste is the mixture of spices, which reflects the East Indian influence in the cookery of the West Indies. Serve this with any Caribbean meat, poultry, or seafood entrée in this book.

¼ cup (59 mL) vegetable oil or ghee
1 large onion, peeled and minced
2 cups (473 mL) uncooked long-grain white rice
½ teaspoon (2.5 mL) ground cayenne
½ teaspoon (2.5 mL) ground cloves
½ teaspoon (2.5 mL) ground cardamom
½ teaspoon (2.5 mL) ground cinnamon
½ teaspoon (2.5 mL) ground cumin
4 cups (.95 L) water

1. In a saucepan with a lid, heat the oil over medium heat. Add the onion and sauté until soft. Add the rice and sauté until it is golden brown. Stir in the spices, add the water, and stir again.

2. Cover the pan and cook over low heat for about 20 minutes. Remove the pan from the heat, stir the rice, and let it sit for 5 or 10 minutes before serving.

Variations

Transfer the rice mixture to a ceramic baking dish and bake, covered, in a 350°F (180°C) oven for about 40 minutes. Remove the top during the last 10 minutes for a crispier rice. Chicken or beef stock may be substituted for the water to match the rice to a main dish. Substitute a curry paste for the spices.

Reggae Rice
Yield: 6 servings   Heat Scale: Medium-Hot

Similar rice recipes are found all over the Caribbean—just like reggae music, even though Jamaica claims the genre. Serve this spicy side dish with jerk-style meat or grilled fish.

2 tablespoons (30 mL) vegetable oil
½ cup (118 mL) chopped onion
2 cloves garlic, peeled and minced
½ cup (118 mL) grated carrot
¼ cup (59 mL) chopped bell pepper
1 Scotch bonnet chile, stem and seeds removed, minced (or substitute
1 habanero)
2 cups (473 mL) uncooked rice
4 cups (.95 L) boiling water
1 teaspoon (5 mL) salt
¼ teaspoon (1.25 mL) freshly ground white pepper

1. In a large, heavy skillet, heat the oil over medium heat. Add the onion, garlic, carrot, bell pepper, and chile and sauté for 2 minutes.
2. Add the rice and toss and stir for 1 minute.
3. Transfer the sautéed mixture to a large saucepan. Add the boiling water, salt, and pepper, and bring to a boil. Reduce the heat to a simmer, cover, and cook for 20 minutes. or until all the water is absorbed.

Island-Style Okra and Rice
Yield: 4–6 servings   Heat Scale: Medium

This traditional Barbadian dish, with salt beef and salt fish (or salted codfish) harkens back to the days when salting was used to preserve food. Salted meats and fish are still a part of the food tradition on many of the Caribbean islands. Just boil and rinse, boil and rinse, to remove the excess salt. You can substitute minced beef and fresh grouper or snapper, but the dish will not taste like the traditional Barbadian recipe. (Note: This recipe requires advance preparation.)

4 ounces (112 g) salt beef, cut into ½-inch (1 cm) pieces
½ pound (224 g) salted codfish, soaked overnight in the refrigerator
2 tablespoons (30 mL) vegetable oil
2 cups (473 mL) chopped onion
2 cloves garlic, peeled and chopped
6 cups (1.4 L) boiling water
6 okra pods, cut crosswise into 4 pieces
1 habanero chile, seeds and stem removed, minced
2 cups (473 mL) uncooked rice

1. Bring 2 separate pots of water to a boil. Add the beef to one and the soaked codfish to the other. Reduce the heat to a simmer and cook for 15 minutes. Drain the pots and remove the bones from the cod. Reserve the beef and the fish.

2. In a large, heavy pot, heat the oil over medium heat. Add the onion and garlic and sauté for 1 minute. Add the boiling water, okras, and reserved salt beef. Cover and simmer for 15 minutes.

Add the chile, rice, and reserved codfish; cover the pot, and simmer for 20 minutes, until the rice is cooked.

Jamaican Rice and Peas

Yield: 6 servings   Heat Scale: Medium

This dish is sometimes referred to as the "Jamaican Coat of Arms" because it is cooked everywhere by everyone. The "peas" are actually red kidney beans. The coconut milk is a traditional ingredient, and the dish simply wouldn't be Jamaican without it. If you do not want to make your own coconut milk, it can be purchased in Latin or Asian markets or your favorite supermarket, but do not buy the sweetened coconut cream used for piña coladas.

1 cup (236 mL) dried red kidney beans
2 ounces (56 g) salt pork, minced, or 2 slices bacon, chopped
2 cloves garlic, peeled and minced
2 green onions or 1 leek, white part only, chopped
½ teaspoon (2.5 mL) dried thyme (or substitute 1 sprig fresh thyme)
¼ teaspoon (1.25 mL) freshly ground black pepper
1 Scotch bonnet chile, stem and seeds removed, minced (or substitute 1 habanero)
2 cups (473 mL) coconut milk, commercial or homemade
2½ cups (591 mL) water
2½ cups (591 mL) uncooked white rice
Salt, to taste

1. Wash and clean the kidney beans, then put them in a heavy pot and add water to cover. Bring the beans to a boil, reduce the heat to a simmer, and cover. Simmer the beans for about 2 hours or until they are almost tender.

2. Stir in the salt pork, garlic, leek, thyme, pepper, chile, coconut milk, and water and bring the mixture to a light boil. Reduce the heat to a simmer, cover, and cook for 20 to 25 minutes, until all of the liquid has been absorbed. If the mixture seems too dry, add a little water; if it seems too wet, remove the cover and allow the liquids to slowly evaporate. Add salt to taste.

Spiced-Up Vegetarian Jollof Rice

Yield: 6–8 servings Heat Scale: Medium

This version of Jollof Rice from Sierra Leone differs from others because it is a veg-etarian side dish rather than a meaty main course. Traditionally, this recipe calls for palm oil, but I have substituted canola oil because the palm oil is high in saturated fat. (Note: This recipe requires advance preparation.)

½ cup (118 mL) dried black-eyed peas (or substitute 1 [16-ounce (454 g)] can, drained)
1 pound (454 g) eggplant, peeled and cubed
½ teaspoon (2.5 mL) salt
1½ tablespoons (22.5 mL) canola oil
1 cup (236 mL) chopped onion
2 jalapeño chiles, stems and seeds removed, chopped
2 cloves garlic, peeled and minced
⅛ cup (30 mL) chopped fresh ginger
½ cup (118 mL) chopped green bell pepper
2 cups (473 mL) chopped tomatoes
1 tablespoon (15 mL) tomato paste
1 tablespoon (15 mL) ground cayenne
1 teaspoon (5 mL) curry powder of your choice from Chapter 1
2 teaspoons (10 mL) hot pepper sauce of your choice (or use one from Chapter 2)
¼ pound (112 g) fresh green beans, cleaned and cut into 1-inch (2.5 cm) pieces
1 cup (236 mL) cooked long-grain rice

1. If you are using dry dried peas, wash them, cover them with cold water, and soak them in the refrigerator overnight. The following day, drain them, add new water, and boil them for 30 minutes. If you are using canned beans, put them in a large, heavy pot, cover them with water, and bring the mixture to a boil. Reduce the heat and simmer for 30 to 40 minutes, until they are tender.
2. Preheat the oven to 350°F (180°C).
3. Place the cubed eggplant in a colander, sprinkle it with the salt, and let it drain for 30 minutes. Rinse off the salt, place the cubes on paper towels, and blot dry.
4. In a large casserole, heat the oil over medium heat. Add the eggplant and sauté for 2 minutes. Add the onion, chiles, garlic, ginger, bell pepper, tomatoes, tomato paste, cayenne, curry powder, and hot sauce and simmer for 8 minutes, stirring occasionally.
5. Stir in the black-eyed peas and green beans, cover, and simmer for 10 minutes. Stir in the rice, cover, and bake for 30 to 40 minutes, checking occasionally to make sure there is enough liquid to prevent burning.

African Chile-Coconut Rice

Yield: 4 servings   Heat Scale: Medium

This popular and delicious side dish from Kenya and Tanzania is easy to make and easy to eat. It complements the flavor of chicken, any kind of fish or seafood, and curry dishes. Just make sure that you buy unsweetened coconut milk, rather than the sweetened variety that is used for bar drinks.

2 cups (473 mL) unsweetened coconut milk
1 cup (236 mL) uncooked white rice
1 teaspoon (5 mL) salt
¼ teaspoon (1.25 mL) freshly ground white pepper
½ cup (118 mL) chopped green New Mexican chile, stems and seeds removed, excess moisture blotted out

1. Bring the coconut milk to a rolling boil. Add the remaining ingredients. Stir the mixture to blend, cover, reduce the heat to a simmer, and cook for 20 minutes.

Nasi Kerabu
(Spicy Rice Medley with Roasted Fish)

Yield: 5–6 servings   Heat Scale: Medium

This Malaysian rice dish has just a touch of roasted fish added to give it a different flavor dimension, and it contrasts nicely with the coconut and chiles. Serve this rice at room temperature with one of the meat recipes from Chapter 8 or one of the poultry recipes from Chapter 10.

2 cups (473 mL) cooked white rice, slightly chilled
1 teaspoon (5 mL) crushed black pepper
¼ cup (59 mL) roasted and chopped fish (grouper preferred)
1 cup (236 mL) chopped red onion
¼ cup (59 mL) shredded coconut
¼ cup (59 mL) sliced and cooked long beans (or substitute green beans)
¾ cup (177 mL) sliced cucumber
¼ cup (59 mL) bean sprouts
⅛ cup (30 mL) grated fresh ginger
3 fresh serrano or jalapeño chiles, stems and seeds removed, minced
2 tablespoons (30 mL) chopped fresh mint leaves

1. In a large bowl, toss all the ingredients together. Place the rice in a serving bowl and decorate it with sliced green onions and fresh mint leaves.

Khow Pat Prik Sapbhalot
(Piquant Pineapple Fried Rice)

Yield: 4 servings   Heat Scale: Medium

This rice dish makes a spectacular showpiece at a buffet or a special dinner. The decoratively cut pineapple is one of those lovely Thai touches, as the Thais create the most gorgeous designs for fruit and vegetables. At the Royal Sheraton in Bangkok, I watched a master carver create some memorable flowers out of fresh vegetables. However, this dish also tastes wonderful with just the pineapple, chiles, and rice.

1 large, ripe pineapple

2–3 tablespoons (30–45 mL) vegetable oil
3 fresh prawns, shelled, cleaned, and finely chopped
¼ pound (113 g) Chinese sausage, chopped, or browned ground pork
1 shallot, peeled and finely chopped
1 clove garlic, peeled and minced
2 fresh red serrano or jalapeño chiles, stems and seeds removed, sliced into rings
2 cups (473 mL) cooked and cooled rice
¼ teaspoon (1.25 mL) freshly ground black pepper
1 tablespoon (15 mL) fish sauce
1 tablespoon (15 mL) soy sauce
½ teaspoon (2.5 mL) lemon zest
1 teaspoon (5 mL) sugar

1. Cut the pineapple in half lengthwise, using a decorative zigzag cut. Carefully cut out the flesh and measure out ¾ cup (177 mL). Place the pineapple pulp in a colander to drain. Cut a very small slice from the bottom of each pineapple half so it will lay flat without tipping.
2. In a wok or large skillet, heat the oil over high heat. Add the prawns, sausage, shallot, garlic, and chile rings and sauté for 2 minutes.
3. Add the remaining ingredients and toss until blended and heated through. Serve immediately or keep warm in a 350°F (180°C) oven for a few minutes until serving.

Kao Pad Prik
(Chile Fried Rice)

Yield: 4 servings   Heat Scale: Hot

This spicy Thai side dish is not for the faint hearted! It is rich in chiles and makes a great accompaniment to hearty meat dishes. The preferred rice to use is jasmine, but ordinary white rice is transformed when it is cooked in this manner. Chilling the rice first helps keep the grains separated when it is mixed with the other ingredients.

2 tablespoons (30 mL) vegetable oil
½ cup (118 mL) finely chopped onion
3 fresh serrano of jalapeño chiles, stems and seeds removed, minced
1 tablespoon (15 mL) Red Curry Paste (page 37)
2 cloves garlic, peeled and minced
¼ cup (59 mL) finely minced pork or ham
4 cups (.95 L) cooked rice, chilled
2 eggs, beaten
1 tablespoon (15 mL) fish sauce
2 teaspoons (10 mL) sweet soy sauce
Salt, to taste
Freshly ground white pepper, to taste
¼ cup (59 mL) finely chopped green onions
⅓ cup (79 mL) thinly sliced cucumber
3 tablespoons (45 mL) minced cilantro

1. In a wok or large skillet, heat the oil over medium heat. Add the onion and chiles and fry until the onion starts to wilt. Add the curry paste and fry for 2 minutes, until the oil starts to separate.
2. Add the garlic and pork and stir-fry for 2 minutes.
3. Stir in the rice and toss until it is coated with the chile paste mixture.
4. Make a deep well in the center of the rice mixture. Add the beaten eggs and allow them to cook, undisturbed, for about 20 seconds, then mix them throughout the rice.
5. Add the fish sauce, sweet soy sauce, salt, pepper, and green onions and toss with the rice.
6. Place the rice on a heated platter and garnish with the cucumber and cilantro.

Nasi Kunyit
(Yellow Festive Rice)

Yield: 6 servings   Heat Scale: Mild

Thanks to Devagi Shanmugan, who runs the Thomson Cooking School in Singapore and taught me how to prepare this rice recipe. It makes a very colorful, fragrant dish that goes well with meat dishes. If you ever get to Singapore, be sure to take some of Devagi's classes. Be sure to use coconut milk, not canned coconut cream, which is too sweet.

4 teaspoons (20 mL) ground coriander
2 teaspoons (10 mL) ground cumin
1 teaspoon (5 mL) ground turmeric
½ teaspoon (2.5 mL) ground cayenne
1 (5-inch [12.5]) piece ginger, peeled
3 cloves garlic, peeled
20 shallots, peeled
1 cup (236 mL) water
6 tablespoons (90 mL) vegetable oil
6 cups (1.4 L) coconut milk
3 cups (708 mL) rice, washed and drained
4 bulbs lemongrass, minced
Salt, to taste
Fried green onion rings for garnish

1. In a blender or food processor, combine the coriander, cumin, turmeric, cayenne, ginger, garlic, shallots, and water and purée. In a heavy skillet, heat the oil over medium heat. When it is almost sizzling, add the puréed ingredients and cook, stirring, until they are fragrant, about 1 minute.
2. Add the coconut milk and bring to a slow boil. Reduce the heat to a simmer, add the rice and lemongrass, cover, and cook until the rice is done, about 30 to 40 minutes.
3. Add the salt to taste and garnish with the fried green onion rings.

Nasi Goreng
(Indonesian Spicy Fried Rice)

Yield: 6–8 servings   Heat Scale: Mild

Rosemary Ann Ogilvie provided this Balinese specialty. She comments, "Nasi goreng is the Indonesian term for fried rice. Recipes will vary, as no two dishes are ever quite the same—it depends on what combinations of seemingly endless ingredients are used. Sambal oelek is a paste made of ground chiles and salt and can be found in Asian markets."

Cooking spray
3 eggs, lightly beaten
2 medium onions, peeled and coarsely chopped
2 cloves garlic, peeled
½ teaspoon (2.5 mL) dried shrimp paste
2 tablespoons (30 mL) vegetable oil
1 pound (454 g) boneless pork or lean beef, cut in thin strips
1 pound (454 g) medium prawns or shrimp, shelled and deveined
6 cups (1.4 L) cold cooked rice
2 cups (473 mL) firmly packed mung bean sprouts
2 tablespoons (30 mL) light soy sauce
1 tablespoon (15 mL) prepared sambal oelek
1 cucumber, thinly sliced

1. Spray a large frying pan with cooking spray. Pour the eggs into the pan and cook over medium heat until the omelette is set. Remove the omelette and cut it into strips.
2. In a blender, combine the onions, garlic, and shrimp paste and blend to a paste. If no blender is available, finely chop the onions, crush the garlic, dissolve the shrimp paste in a little hot water, and combine the three ingredients together.
3. In a frying pan, heat the oil over medium-high heat. Add the paste and fry for a minute. Add the meat and stir-fry for a couple of minutes until cooked. Add the shrimp and cook until they begin to curl up and turn light pink, about 2 minutes. Stir in the rice, bean sprouts, soy sauce, and sambal oelek. Toss until everything is well mixed and heated through.
4. Decorate with the cucumber and the strips of omelette and serve.

Nasi Goreng #2
(Indonesian Savory Rice)

Yield: 8–10 servings   Heat Scale: Mild

The owners of the Golden Dragon Restaurant in Colorado Springs, Colorado, collected this recipe on one of their Southeast Asian trips and currently serve it in their restaurant. This easy-to-make dish is an attractive, tasty side dish for a party.

4 tablespoons (60 mL) vegetable oil, divided
1 cup (236 mL) chopped onions
1 tablespoon (15 mL) chopped garlic
1 teaspoon (5 mL) ground coriander
1 teaspoon (5 mL) ground turmeric
1 tablespoon (15 mL) ground cumin
½ teaspoon (2.5 mL) ground hot red chile
½ teaspoon (2.5 mL) ground ginger
2 quarts (1.9 L) cooked rice
4 eggs
2 tablespoons (30 mL) water
¾ pound (336 g) shrimp, cooked and peeled
½ pound (224 g) ham, cut into strips

1. In a heavy skillet, heat 2 tablespoons (30 mL) of the oil over medium heat. Add the onion and garlic and sauté until the onion is wilted. Stir in the coriander, turmeric, cumin, chile, and ginger, reduce the heat, and cook, stirring, for about 20 seconds. Stir in the rice, mix well, and keep warm.
2. In a bowl, combine the eggs and water in a bowl and whisk until frothy. In a skillet, heat the remaining 2 tablespoons (30 mL) oil over medium heat. Pour in the eggs and cook. When the bottom begins to set, carefully pull the edges away from the side of the skillet and allow the uncooked eggs to slide down to the bottom, as with an omelette. Slide the eggs from the pan, roll them up, and, slice them into pinwheels.
3. To serve, heap the rice in a large bowl. Garnish the top with the shrimp and create runners down the rice with the ham. Place the egg pinwheels around the edge.

Mee Grob
(Herbed Crispy Vermicelli)

Yield: 6–8 servings   Heat Scale: Mild

This recipe was given to me at the Thai Cooking School at the Oriental Hotel in Bangkok, where I visited, watched, inhaled the delightful aromas, and interviewed the chef. Serve this with meat, chicken, or fish with the addition of bean sprouts on the side. You could also add meat to the noodles to make a one-dish meal.

1 pound (454 g) rice vermicelli
Vegetable oil for deep frying
4 tablespoons (60 mL) vegetable oil
½ cup (118 mL) chopped shallots
4 cloves garlic, peeled
1 cup (236 mL) yellow tofu (available at Asian markets), cut into ¾-inch (1.5 cm) cubes
1 teaspoon (5 mL) salt
5 eggs, beaten
¼ cup (59 mL) distilled white vinegar
¼ cup (59 mL) fish sauce
5 tablespoons (75 mL) sugar
1 teaspoon (5 mL) ground hot red chile
Sliced pickled garlic for garnish
Minced fresh serrano or Thai chiles for garnish
Chopped cilantro for garnish

1. In a bowl, sprinkle the noodles with cold water and allow them to soften for a few minutes. If they are not uniformly soft or are too dry, sprinkle more water on them. Keep them moist.

2. In a deep fat fryer, heat the oil to 350°F (180°C). Add the noodles and deep fry until they are golden. Remove them from the oil and keep them warm and crisp by wrapping them in paper towels.

3. In a large skillet, heat several tablespoons (30–45 mL) of the oil over medium heat. Add the shallots and garlic and fry until soft. Push the mixture to one side of the pan and add the cubed bean curd. Fry the curd until it is crisp, turning it carefully in the pan.

4. Add the salt and add more oil if necessary. Add the eggs and turn continuously until they are almost done.

5. Sprinkle the eggs with the vinegar, fish sauce, sugar, and ground chile and stir until the ingredients are blended. Mix in the crisp fried noodles and the egg mixture and heat gently.

6. Serve the finished dish with any or all of the garnishes.

Happy Pancakes with Nuoc Cham Dipping Sauce

Yield: 10 side-dish servings   Heat Scale: Mild

This interesting Vietnamese dish was presented to Mary Jane and me by cookbook author Binh Duong at the Mohonk Mountain House's hot and spicy weekend. When we asked Binh why they are called "happy pancakes," he replied, logically: "Because they make people happy when they eat them!" Both the dipping sauce and the batter will keep in the refrigerator for up to three days. Serve the pancakes with Nuoc Cham (page 96).

1¼ cups (295 mL) rice flour
2 cups (473 mL) water
¼ teaspoon (1.25 mL) ground turmeric
1 green onion, thinly sliced
¼ cup (59 mL) plus 2 tablespoons (30 mL) vegetable oil, divided
1 pound (454 g) lean pork shoulder or loin, cut into ¼-inch (.5 cm) slices, divided
1 pound (454 g) medium shrimp, peeled and deveined, divided
2 small onions, peeled and thinly sliced, divided
10 medium mushrooms, sliced, divided
1¼ teaspoons (6.25 mL) freshly ground black pepper
2½ cups (591 mL) mung bean sprouts, divided
1 recipe Nuoc Cham (Vietnamese Dipping Sauce; page 96)

1. In a bowl, whisk together the rice flour and water. Add the turmeric and green onion and mix well. Set the batter aside.
2. In a large, nonstick skillet, heat 1½ tablespoons (22.5 mL) of the oil over high heat. Add 3 slices of pork, 3 shrimps, a few slices of onion, and 1 sliced mushroom. Lightly sprinkle with black pepper and cook until the onion starts to brown slightly, about 1 minute. Ladle ⅓ cup (79 mL) of the batter into the skillet and tilt the pan to distribute the batter evenly. Keep the heat on high, cover the skillet, and cook until the sides of the pancake turn deep brown and curl up, about 3 to 4 minutes. Scatter ¼ cup (59 mL) bean sprouts over the pancake, fold it in half, and slide it onto a warm platter. Keep the pancake warm in the oven while you make more pancakes with the remaining ingredients.
3. Sprinkle the pancakes with the dipping sauce before serving, or serve it on the side.

Frijoles Negros
(Brazilian Black Beans)

Yield: 6–8 servings   Heat Scale: Mild

Just as corn and potatoes have been a staple in the diet of many Latin countries, beans also rank high on the staple list because of their high protein content. Since many of the poorer people eat very little meat, their diet includes many different kinds of beans. In Brazil, the black bean is so favored that the national dish, feijoada completa, centers around black beans. This dish is also popular in Colombia and Venezuela. Serve the beans with cooked rice. (Note: This recipe requires advance preparation.)

1 pound (454 g) dried black beans, rinsed
14 cups (3.3 L) hot water, divided
1 habanero chile, left whole (or substitute 3 whole jalapeños)
3 tablespoons (45 mL) lard or vegetable oil
1 cup (236 mL) chopped onion
2 cloves garlic, minced
Salt, to taste
Freshly ground black pepper, to taste
4–5 cups (.95–1.18 L) cooked white rice

1. Place the beans in a heavy Dutch oven and cover them with 8 cups (1.9 L) of the hot water. Bring the beans to a boil and boil, uncovered, for 2 minutes. Remove the pot from the heat, cover, and set aside to soak for 1 hour.
2. Drain the soaked beans. Clean out the Dutch oven, return the beans to it, and cover with the remaining 6 cups (1.4 L) hot water. Add the whole habanero. Bring the beans to a boil, lower the heat to a simmer, cover, and simmer for 1 hour or until the beans are tender. Remove the habanero. Using a small strainer, remove about one-third of the beans from the pot, letting the cooking liquid drain back into the pot. Set the drained beans aside.
3. In a large skillet, heat the lard or oil over medium heat. Add the onion and sauté for 30 seconds. Add the garlic and toss for a few seconds. Add the drained beans and mash them with a potato masher until they are smooth. Return this mixture to the pot of cooked beans and stir thoroughly. Reheat for 20 minutes, or until the beans are hot and bubbling. Add salt and pepper to taste. Serve the beans with hot rice.

Frijoles Negros en Salsa de Nueces (Black Beans in Walnut Sauce)

Yield: 6–8 servings   Heat Scale: Hot

This recipe is an elegant variation on the simply cooked black beans. It comes from Peru, and, true to tradition, it is hot and spicy with the addition of rocoto or aji chiles. When sautéing the garlic, be very careful not to burn it, or it will give an "off" taste to this dish.

¼ pound (113 g) bacon, cut into ¼-inch (.5 cm) pieces
3 cloves garlic, peeled and mashed
1 cup (236 mL) chopped onions
¾ cup (177 mL) coarsely chopped walnuts
4 rocoto chiles, stems and seeds removed, minced (or substitute 6 jalapeños)
¼ teaspoon (1.25 mL) salt
¼ teaspoon (1.25 mL) freshly ground black pepper
1 pound (454 g) dried black beans, boiled according to the Brazilian Black Beans recipe (page 737) and pressed through a sieve to remove the skins
¾ cup (177 mL) evaporated milk or half-and-half
3 hard-boiled eggs, thinly sliced for garnish

1. Preheat the oven to 350°F (180°C).
2. In a small skillet, fry the bacon until it is crisp. Drain the bacon and return the fat to the skillet.
3. Add the garlic and onions and sauté until the onions are soft. Add the walnuts, chiles, salt, pepper, and beans and mix well. Cook, adding the milk a little at a time, until the beans are creamy.
4. Transfer the mixture to a baking dish and bake for 15 to 20 minutes.
5. Garnish with the reserved cooked bacon and the egg slices.

Lima Beans with Aji Chiles

Yield: 3–4 servings   Heat Scale: Medium

Lima beans were possibly one of the first crops cultivated by early South American farmers. They have been found in excavations dated 5,000 to 6,000 BCE in the coastal regions. The many varieties of limas range from the very tiny, or baby, limas, to some limas that are 11/2 inches (3.5 cm) long. This easy and delicious Peruvian recipe makes a good side dish for any of the meat recipes in this book because its taste is not overwhelming and it will complement any dish nicely.

2 tablespoons (30 mL) butter, divided
1 tablespoon (15 mL) olive oil
1 leek, white part only, finely diced
2 fresh aji chiles, stems and seeds removed, minced (or substitute yellow wax hot or jalapeño)
16 ounces (about 4 cups [.95 L]) fresh lima beans or 1 (16-ounce [454 g]) package frozen baby lima beans, thawed (do not use dried beans)
½–1 cup (118–236 mL) water
1 tablespoon (15 mL) fresh lemon or lime juice
1 teaspoon (5 mL) lemon or lime zest
¼ teaspoon (1.25 mL) salt
¼ teaspoon (1.25 mL) freshly ground black pepper

1. In a small, heavy skillet, melt 1 tablespoon (15 mL) of the butter with the olive oil. Add the leek and aji chiles and sauté for 30 seconds. Add the lima beans, water, and citrus juice and bring the mixture to a boil. Lower the heat to a simmer, cover, and simmer for 8 to 10 minutes.
2. In a bowl, combine the remaining 1 tablespoon (15 mL) butter with the citrus zest and the salt and pepper. When the beans are tender, drain them and add the butter mixture. Simmer for 1 minute and stir to coat the beans.

Gallo Pinto
(Costa Rican Beans and Rice)

Yield: 4 servings   Heat Scale: Varies, but usually mild

Gallo Pinto can be called the national dish of Costa Rica, and it is served at break-
fast, lunch, and dinner. As with any dish this popular, everyone has his or her own
version. David Tucker of the Hotel La Mariposa in Quepos was kind enough to share
this recipe with me. Cooks are invited to spice up Gallo Pinto by simply adding some
ground chile or more hot sauce to the recipe. (Note: This recipe requires advance
preparation.)

1 cup (236 mL) black beans
1 bay leaf
4 tablespoons (60 mL) vegetable oil, divided
¼ teaspoon (1.25 mL) ground cumin, or to taste
¼ teaspoon (1.25 mL) dried oregano, or to taste
1 clove garlic, peeled
1 pinch curry powder
Salt, to taste
Freshly ground black pepper, to taste
½ cup (118 mL) chopped onion
⅓ cup (79 mL) chopped red bell pepper
1 tablespoon (15 mL) Worcestershire sauce
1 teaspoon (5 mL) Lea & Perrins steak sauce
Louisiana hot sauce, to taste
1½ cups (354 mL) cooked rice

1. In a large pot, cover the beans with water and soak for at least 4 hours.
Bring the water to a boil. Add the bay leaf, 3 tablespoons (45 mL) of the oil,
the cumin, the oregano, the garlic, and the curry powder. Reduce the heat
and simmer for an hour or until the beans are soft. Season with the salt
and pepper. Drain the beans and reserve the liquid.
2. In a large skillet, heat the remaining oil over medium heat. Add the onion and bell pepper and sauté until soft. Add the remaining ingredients.
3. Combine the beans with the rice mixture. If the mixture is too stiff,
add a little of the bean water or some chicken stock to achieve the desired
consistency.

Variation
Gallo Pinto on the Caribbean side of the country is flavored with local coconuts. Cook the beans in coconut milk with a couple of small, hot, fresh
chiles until the beans are soft. Drain and add sautéed onion and garlic.
Combine with cooked rice, garnish with chopped cilantro, and serve.

Frijoles Charros Numero Uno
(Cowboy Beans #1)

Yield: 10–12 servings   Heat Scale: Medium to Hot

Beans, or frijoles, are an integral part of Mexican cuisine, from border to border and coast to coast. Many kinds of dried beans are available, and they are cooked in every possible method and manner, sometimes by adding a bit of this and a bit of that. A rich bean pot in Mexico is akin to a multi-ingredient omelette or casserole in the states. My first version of Cowboy or Ranch-Style Beans comes from Coahuila. (Note: This recipe requires advance preparation.)

2 pounds (1.1 kg) flor de mayo beans (or substitute pink or pinto beans)
5 serrano chiles, stems and seeds removed, cut into slices
1 cup (236 mL) coarsely chopped onion
1 cup (236 mL) chopped tomato
½ cup (118 mL) chopped cilantro
4 cloves garlic, peeled and chopped
¼ teaspoon (1.25 mL) freshly ground black pepper
¼ pound (113 g) chopped bacon or salt pork
¼ pound (113 g) pork sausage
½ pound (224 g) pork meat, cut into ¼-inch (.5 cm) cubes
¼ pound (113 g) chorizo
¼ pound (113 g) chopped ham

1. Wash and pick over the beans. Place them in a very large, heavy pot and cover them with cold water. Bring them to a boil, boil for 2 minutes, then turn off the heat. Allow the beans to sit, covered, for 1 hour. Drain the beans, return them to the pot, and cover them with hot water. Bring them to a boil and add the chiles, onion, tomato, cilantro, garlic, and black pepper. Reduce the heat to a simmer and cover.

2. In a large skillet over medium heat, sauté all the meats together for 3 minutes. Drain off all of the fat and blot the meat with paper towels. Add the meats to the simmering beans, cover, and simmer for 3½ hours. Stir the beans several times during the cooking. If more water is needed, add hot water only. The bean mixture should have a slightly soupy consistency.

3. Serve hot with any entrée or with warmed tortillas.

Frijoles Charros Numero Dos
(Cowboy Beans #2)

Yield: 6 servings   Heat Scale: Medium

Here is my second version of Cowboy Beans, this one from Sonora. The chicharrón in this recipe is fried pork cracklings, which can be seasoned with different sauces and seasonings, depending on the region. In the United States, they can be purchased in many grocery stores, since former president George Bush made them famous as his favorite snack. (Note: This recipe requires advance preparation.)

1 pound (454 g) cleaned pinto beans
2 cups (473 mL) beer (not dark)
3 tablespoons (45 mL) vegetable oil
1 pound (454 g) cooked pork, shredded
¼ cup (59 mL) ground ancho chiles
2 cups (473 mL) Salsa Chile de Arbol (page 59)
¾ cup (177 mL) chicharrón

1. Place the beans in a large, heavy casserole pot. Cover them with cold water and bring to a boil. Boil for 2 minutes, then turn off the heat and allow the beans to sit for 1 hour. Drain the beans and return them to the cleaned casserole. Add the beer and enough hot water to cover the beans by about 2 inches (5 cm). Bring the mixture to a boil, reduce the heat to a simmer, and partially cover.
2. Heat the oil in a skillet over medium heat. Add the shredded pork, ancho chiles, and salsa and simmer for 1 minute. Stir this mixture into the cooking beans, cover, and simmer for 3 to 3½ hours, stirring occasionally and adding more water if the beans get too dry. You want a semi-soupy consistency.
3. Just before serving, stir the chicharron into the beans.

Frijoles Zacatecanos
(Zacatecas-Style Beans)

Yield: 5 servings   Heat Scale: Mild

This side dish is very substantial and should be served with a light entrée, such as one of the chicken recipes in Chapter 10 or one of the fish recipes in Chapter 11. Layering the different colors of mashed beans gives this dish an artistic look that will most certainly please the eye as much as this dish's flavor pleases the taste buds. (Note: This recipe requires advance preparation.)

½ pound (224 g) canary beans, washed and picked over (or substitute pinto beans)
½ pound (224 g) black beans, washed and picked over
½ pound (224 g) pork ribs, excess fat removed
6 tablespoons (90 mL) oil, divided
1½ cups (354 mL) chopped onion
4 poblano chiles, roasted, peeled, stems and seeds removed, cut into strips
2 cups (473 mL) roasted, peeled, chopped tomatoes
¾ cup (177 mL) heavy cream
½ cup (118 mL) grated aged cotija cheese (or substitute mild cheddar)
4 corn tortillas, quartered and fried (or substitute purchased tortillas chips)

1. Place the 2 different types of beans into separate large sauce pans, cover each with cold water, and bring them to a boil. Cover each pot and boil for 1 minute. Turn off the heat and allow the beans to soak for 1 hour. Drain the beans and return them to the separate pans. Cover each with hot water and bring them to a boil. Cover each pot and simmer for 1 to 1½ hours or until tender.

2. While the beans are cooking, wash the pork ribs and place them in a small saucepan. Add cold water to cover and bring to a boil. Reduce the heat to a simmer and cook for 20 minutes. Remove the ribs from the water and drain. Reserve the cooking broth. Remove the bones and coarsely shred the pork, discarding any fat that remains. Set the pork aside.

3. When the beans are done, drain them and set them aside, keeping the 2 types separated. In 2 separate small skillets, heat 2 tablespoons (30 mL) of the oil over medium heat. Add one type of beans to each skillet and mash them with a potato masher. Add ½ cup (118 mL) of the onion to each skillet and simmer for a minute or two. If the beans start to get too thick, add a few tablespoons (30–45 mL) of the reserved pork cooking broth to thin slightly.

4. In a third skillet, heat the remaining 2 tablespoons (30 mL) oil over medium heat. Add the remaining ½ cup (118 mL) onion and the shredded pork and sauté for 3 minutes. Add the chiles and tomatoes and simmer for 1 minute. Stir in the cream, remove the skillet from the heat, and let it sit for 3 minutes.

5. On a small, decorative, heated platter, spread a thin layer of the canary beans. Top them with some of the pork mixture, then spread a thin layer of black beans, and repeat the layers until all the beans and pork are used up. Sprinkle the top with the grated cheese and arrange the corn chips around the platter.

Ensalada de Garbanzos (Chickpea Salad)

Yield: 4 servings   Heat Scale: Mild

Serve this delicious Sonoran-style dish over shredded mixed greens to accompany one of the fish dishes from Chapter 11. I recommend using freshly cooked chickpeas, but the canned variety will also work if the peas are thoroughly rinsed. (Note: This recipe requires advance preparation.)

Juice of 1 lemon
Juice of 2 limes
¼ cup (59 mL) minced cilantro
¼ cup (59 mL) olive oil
¾ cup (177 mL) minced onion
2½ cups (591 mL) cooked chickpeas
6 ounces (168 g) cream cheese, softened
2 poblano chiles, roasted and peeled, stems and seeds removed, chopped fine
Mixed greens for serving

1. In a medium glass bowl, mix together the citrus juices, cilantro, olive oil, and onion. Let stand at room temperature for 3 hours.
2. In a small bowl, combine the cooked chickpeas, softened cream cheese, and chiles and mix thoroughly. Add this mixture to the marinated citrus mixture and mix thoroughly.
3. Serve over shredded, mixed greens.

Frijoles Negros Estilo Cubana
(Black Beans, Cuban-Style)

Yield: 8 servings   Heat Scale: Medium-Hot

This recipe comes from Rudolpho de Garay and Thomas Brown, who noted, "Black beans are the classic Cuban dish and are eaten nearly every day. Most versions are not spicy with chiles, but some cooks like a little heat. This recipe calls for rocotillo chiles, but habanero and your favorite chiles can be substituted, as there are enough black bean recipes to fill a book. This version may also be puréed and served cold with pepper fritters as a garnish." (Note: This recipe requires advance preparation.)

1 pound (454 g) dried black beans
2 bay leaves
1 teaspoon (5 mL) ground cumin
¼ teaspoon (1.25 mL) dried oregano
¼ teaspoon (1.25 mL) dried thyme
2 teaspoons (10 mL) salt
½ teaspoon (2.5 mL) freshly ground black pepper
1 teaspoon (5 mL) sugar
1 cup (236 mL) chopped onion
2 tablespoons (30 mL) chopped garlic
1 cup (236 mL) chopped seeded cubanelle (or green bell) pepper
1 cup (236 mL) chopped seeded red bell pepper
10 rocotillo chiles, stems removed, seeded, and chopped (or substitute
1 habanero chile and 3 yellow wax hot chiles)
¼ cup (59 mL) dry sherry
¼ cup (59 mL) olive oil
¼ cup (59 mL) distilled white vinegar
Freshly chopped parsley for garnish

1. Inspect the beans, removing all stones and other foreign particles and broken or discolored beans. Wash them thoroughly in cold water.
2. In a large pot, bring 3 cups (708 mL) water to a boil. Add the beans, return the water to a boil, and boil, uncovered, for 3 minutes. Turn the heat off and let sit, partially covered, for 1 hour.
3. To the beans, add 6 cups (1.4 L) water, the bay leaves, cumin, oregano, thyme, salt, pepper, sugar, onion, garlic, and the chopped green and red peppers. Bring to a boil again, lower the heat, and simmer for about 2 hours. Add the rocotillos and simmer for another 30 minutes or until done.
4. Add the sherry, olive oil, and vinegar. Sprinkle parsley over each serving. Finely chopped raw onion may also be sprinkled over each serving. When serving with rice, use only white rice, never yellow.

Moros y Cristianos
(Black Beans and White Rice)

Yield: 6 servings   Heat Scale: Medium

This recipe translates as "Moors and Christians," and refers back to Spain, when the Moors fought the Spanish over the acquisition of Grenada. The Spanish were entrenched in Cuba at the time, and the loyalists named this dish after the struggle going on in Spain. This Cuban dish is still popular today, and the name has not changed. The dish is a tasty, healthy addition to grilled meats or fish. (Note: This recipe requires advance preparation.)

1 cup (236 mL) dried black beans
3 cups (708 mL) water
2 tablespoons (30 mL) olive oil
1 habanero chile, stem and seeds removed, minced
3 cloves garlic, peeled and minced
1 large onion, peeled and chopped
2 cups (473 mL) partially cooked white rice
1 teaspoon (5 mL) salt
Freshly ground black pepper, to taste

1. Wash the beans and pick out any extraneous material. Put the beans in a large bowl, add cold water to cover, and refrigerate overnight. Alternatively, clean the beans, put them in a large, heavy pot, and cover them with cold water. Bring the beans to a boil, cover, and boil for 2 minutes. Remove the pot from the heat and let it stand for 1 hour.
2. Drain the beans, rinse them, and place them in a large, heavy saucepan. Add the water and bring the mixture to a boil. Reduce the heat to a simmer, cover, and cook over a low heat for 40 to 50 minutes. The beans should be tender but not mushy.
3. In a large, heavy skillet, heat the oil over medium heat. Add the chile, garlic, and onion and sauté until the onion is tender. Add this mixture to the beans, along with the rice, salt, and pepper. Stir to mix all the ingredients.
4. Increase the heat to medium and cook until most of the water is absorbed. Reduce the heat to low and cook until most of the liquid has been absorbed, stirring frequently to avoid burning.

Spicy Caribbean Black Beans

Yield: 6–8 servings   Heat Scale: Mild

This recipe is another variation on preparing black beans to be served with white rice; however, this is my personal favorite. It is not very spicy, but it is traditional and truly delicious. Feel free to add more peppers to suit your taste. Add the salt at the end of the cooking time; adding it sooner will make the beans tough. (Note: This recipe requires advance preparation.)

1 pound (454 g) dried black beans
10 cups (2.36 L) hot water
2 green bell peppers, stems and seeds removed, diced
5 tablespoons (75 mL) olive oil, divided
1 cup (236 mL) diced onion
4 cloves garlic, peeled and minced
½ teaspoon (2.5 mL) freshly ground black pepper
1½ teaspoons (7.5 mL) oregano
1 bay leaf
1 habanero chile, stem and seeds removed, minced
1 tablespoon (15 mL) sugar
2 tablespoons (30 mL) distilled white vinegar
2 tablespoons (30 mL) white wine
1 teaspoon (5 mL) salt

1. Wash the beans and put them in a large pot. Add cold water to cover and bring the beans to a boil. Boil them for 2 minutes, uncovered. Remove the pan from the heat, cover, and allow the beans to sit for 1 hour. Drain and rinse the beans and return them to the pot. Add the hot water and half the diced bell peppers, and bring the beans to a full boil. Turn the heat down to a simmer.
2. In a skillet, heat 3 tablespoons (45 mL) of the olive oil over medium heat. Add the onion, garlic, and remaining bell pepper and sauté until soft. Add this mixture to the simmering beans, along with the black pepper, oregano, bay leaf, habanero, and sugar. Cover the pot and simmer for 45 minutes.
3. Stir the simmering beans and add the vinegar and wine. Simmer, covered, for an additional 45 minutes. At the end of the cooking time, stir in the remaining olive oil and the salt.

Mbaazi za Nazi
(Swahili Beans)

Yield: 4 servings   Heat Scale: Mild

This recipe was given to me by Michelle Cox of Malindi, Kenya. She says, "Beans are an inexpensive and nutritious way to get the family fed. While this is a traditional recipe, it is uncommonly popular with overseas guests at Saturday night poolside barbecues." The coconut milk produces a very subtle richness, which completely changes the character of the beans. Any green chile can be used, and the minced garlic and chopped green bell pepper add interest to this dish. (Note: This recipe requires advance preparation.)

1 pound (454 g) dried pigeon peas or light red kidney beans
1 cup (236 mL) light coconut milk
1 onion, peeled and sliced
1–2 teaspoons (5–10 mL) curry powder
2 green chiles, such as jalapeños, stems and seeds removed, chopped
1 teaspoon (5 mL) salt
1 cup (236 mL) thick coconut milk

1. Clean and wash the beans. Put them in a large pot with water to cover and soak them for at least 6 hours. Drain the beans and return them to the pot. Cover them with cold water and boil them until they are soft and the water has been absorbed, 30 to 40 minutes. Add more water if necessary during cooking.
2. Add the light coconut milk, onion, curry powder, chiles, and salt. Cook over medium heat until the mixture is almost dry. Add the thick coconut milk, reduce the heat to low, and cook for 5 minutes.

Sugar Bean Curry with Jalapeños

Yield: 6 servings   Heat Scale: Medium

In this recipe, you may substitute any dry bean for the South African sugar beans. The flavors in this dish are unusual and exotic. It goes particularly well with lamb. (Note: This recipe requires advance preparation.)

¾ pound (336 g) dried beans
2 tablespoons (30 mL) vegetable oil
1 cup (236 mL) coarsely chopped onion
3 cloves garlic, peeled and minced
3 jalapeños, stems and seeds removed, chopped
1 tablespoon (15 mL) chopped fresh ginger
2 (3-inch [7.5 cm]) sticks cinnamon
1 teaspoon (5 mL) turmeric
2 cardamom seeds
1 tablespoon (15 mL) Hurry Curry (page 29)
1 cup (236 mL) chopped tomato
½ teaspoon (2.5 mL) salt
½ teaspoon (2.5 mL) sugar
½ cup (118 mL) water

1. In a large pot, cover the beans with water and soak them overnight in the refrigerator. Drain and wash the beans, return them to the pot, and cover them with fresh water. Bring the beans to a boil, then reduce the heat to a simmer. Cook the beans until they are soft, about 1 to 1½ hours. Drain the beans.

2. In a large, heavy skillet, heat the oil. Add the onion and sauté for 3 minutes. Add the garlic and reduce the heat to a simmer. Add the chiles, ginger, cinnamon, turmeric, cardamom, curry powder, tomato, salt, sugar, and water, cover, and simmer for 20 to 30 minutes.

3. Add the drained beans and simmer for an additional 20 minutes.

Tagine Bil Hummus
(Aromatic Chickpea Tagine)

Yield: 6 servings   Heat Scale: Mild

Moroccan vegetable dishes are so good that they are sometimes served with rice or couscous for a light vegetarian meal. This particular recipe is aromatic with spices and smells wonderful cooking. You could also serve it with roasted lamb. Another interesting way to serve this dish is as a filling for toasted pita bread—a Moroccan sandwich. (Note: This recipe requires advance preparation.)

1½ pounds (680 g) dried chickpeas
3 tablespoons (45 mL) olive oil
¾ cup (177 mL) grated onion (red onion preferred)
2 fresh green chiles, such as jalapeños, stems and seeds removed, sliced
½ teaspoon (2.5 mL) ground cumin
¾ teaspoon (3.75 mL) hot paprika
1 teaspoon (5 mL) freshly grated ginger
½ teaspoon (2.5 mL) ground cinnamon
1 (½-inch [1 cm]) saffron thread, crushed
2½ cups (591 mL) peeled, chopped tomatoes
1 teaspoon (5 mL) salt
¼ teaspoon (1.25 mL) freshly ground black pepper
3 tablespoons (45 mL) chopped parsley
2 teaspoons (10 mL) chopped fresh cilantro

1. Put the chickpeas in a pot, add water to cover, and soak them overnight in the refrigerator. Drain the chickpeas, rinse them, and place them in a large, heavy casserole. Add fresh water to cover by 2 inches (5 cm). Bring the water to a boil, reduce the heat to a simmer, and simmer for at least 1 hour, until they are tender. Drain well and set aside.

2. In a large skillet, heat the oil over medium heat. Add the onion and chile and sauté for 1 minute. Add the cumin, paprika, ginger, cinnamon, and saffron, and sauté for 1 minute. Stir in the tomatoes, salt, pepper, parsley, cilantro, and the drained chickpeas.

3. Cover the skillet and simmer gently for 15 to 20 minutes, stirring once or twice.

Mixed Vegetable Tagine

Yield: 4–6 servings   Heat Scale: Mild

Tagine is a North African word for stew or casserole and also refers to the peaked pot in which they are cooked. The meat chapter includes several recipes for tagines containing meat; however, this recipe is a vegetable stew that can be served with rice or couscous. (Note: This recipe requires advance preparation.)

1 cup (236 mL) dried chickpeas
2 tablespoons (30 mL) olive oil
2 cups (473 mL) chopped onions
2 garlic cloves, peeled and minced
1 cup (236 mL) sliced carrots
2 fresh green chiles, such as jalapeños, stems and seeds removed, sliced
1 cup (236 mL) sliced zucchini
2 cups (473 mL) chopped tomatoes
1 teaspoon (5 mL) ground cumin
1 teaspoon (5 mL) salt
¼ teaspoon (1.25 mL) freshly ground black pepper
2½ cups (591 mL) Super-Rich Vegetable Stock (page 48)
½ cup (118 mL) raisins
Juice of 1 fresh lemon
¼ cup (59 mL) chopped green onions, white part only
2 tablespoons (30 mL) chopped fresh cilantro

1. Put the chickpeas in a large bowl or pot, add water to cover, and soak them overnight in the refrigerator. Drain and rinse the chickpeas and place them in a large, heavy casserole. Add cold water to cover, bring to a boil, and cook the chickpeas until tender, about 1 hour. (The cooking time depends on the age of the chickpeas and your altitude.) Drain the chickpeas, chop them coarsely, and set them aside.
2. In a large, heavy skillet, heat the oil over medium heat. Add the onion, garlic, carrots, chiles, and zucchini and sauté for 3 minutes. Add the tomatoes, cumin, salt, and pepper, and simmer for 2 minutes.
3. Add the stock and raisins and bring the mixture to a boil. Add the chopped chickpeas, reduce the heat to a simmer, cover, and simmer for 25 minutes.
4. Stir in the lemon juice, green onions, and cilantro and serve.

Dal Curry

Yield: 6 servings   Heat Scale: Medium

Dal is the Hindi word for several of the legumes or beans that resemble lentils or split peas. In India, they can be found both fresh and dried, but in the United States they are usually only available dried. The bean used in this curry is called toovar dal and resembles a yellow split pea. Pulses or dried lentils are sometimes hard to digest, so cooks in India suggest preparing them with ginger or turmeric to make them more digestible. This recipe contains both.

½ teaspoon (2.5 mL) ground cayenne
1 cup (236 mL) dried yellow split peas, cleaned and rinsed
¼ teaspoon (1.25 mL) ground turmeric
3 cups (708 mL) water
1 tablespoon (15 mL) vegetable oil
4 serrano chiles, stems and seeds removed, chopped
1 tablespoon (15 mL) minced fresh ginger
½ cup (118 mL) chopped onions
1 clove garlic, peeled and chopped
1 teaspoon (5 mL) ground coriander
½ teaspoon (2.5 mL) ground cumin
1 medium tomato, peeled and chopped
2 cups (473 mL) cooked white rice (optional)
Flaked coconut for garnish
Chopped fresh cilantro for garnish

1. In a large saucepan, combine the cayenne, split peas, turmeric, and water. Bring the mixture to a boil, reduce the heat, and simmer, partially covered, for 45 minutes or until the peas are tender and the mixture is the consistency of a thick soup.
2. In a heavy skillet, heat the oil over medium heat. Add the serrano chiles, ginger, onions, and garlic and sauté until soft. Add the coriander, cumin, and tomato and cook for 5 more minutes. Add the tomato mixture to the bean mixture and simmer until heated through.
3. To serve, place some rice in the bottom of a bowl and ladle the dal over the top. Garnish with the coconut and cilantro.

Camotes Fritos
(Hot Fried Sweet Potatoes)
Yield: 4–6 servings.   Heat Scale: Varies

Another mainstay of South American cooking is the sweet potato, which comes in several varieties, and some of these relatives can be found in Hispanic markets in the United States. In fact, a variation of this Brazilian recipe, sweet potato chips, accompanied a sandwich that I enjoyed in a bistro in Albuquerque.

Vegetable oil for frying
3 sweet potatoes, peeled and cut lengthwise into strips slightly thicker than ¼ inch (.5 cm)
Salt, to taste
Ground habanero, to taste (or substitute piquin or cayenne)

1. In a fryer or a deep saucepan, heat the oil. When the oil is hot enough that a drop of water bounces on it, add a few of the sweet potato strips and fry them until they are lightly browned, 2 to 3 minutes. Drain the strips on paper towels and salt them lightly. Repeat this process with the remaining strips, adjusting the frying time if necessary. Keep the finished fries hot in the oven. Sprinkle the fries with salt and ground habanero and toss to coat.

Variation
After draining the strips, refry them for extra crispness before spicing them.

Llapingachos
(Ecuadorian Spiced Potato Cakes)
Yield: 5–6 servings   Heat Scale: Medium to Hot

Loretta Salazar, who lived in Ecuador for several years, collected this recipe. The llapingachos (no one seems to know what the exact English translation is) can accompany other entrées or can be served as an entrée when accompanied by a salad of lettuce, tomatoes, and avocado slices. You can also serve each potato cake topped with a fried egg or accompanied with a hot sauce of your choice.

4 cups (.95 L) diced, peeled raw potatoes
½ teaspoon (2.5 mL) salt
1 egg yolk
2 tablespoons (30 mL) cornstarch
2 tablespoons (30 mL) butter
1½ cups (354 mL) chopped onion
½ cup (118 mL) freshly grated Parmesan cheese
½ cup (118 mL) small-curd, low-fat creamed cottage cheese
¼ cup (59 mL) chopped fresh aji chiles (or substitute yellow wax hot or jalapeño)
¼ cup (59 mL) vegetable oil

1. Put the potatoes in a large saucepan with water to cover. Add the salt. Bring to a boil and cook until tender, 10 to 15 minutes. Drain and mash. Add the egg yolk and cornstarch and mix well.

2. In a sauté pan, melt the butter over medium heat. Add the onions and sauté until golden. Add the cheeses and the chile and mix well.

3. Shape the mashed potato mixture into 10 balls, stuffing some of the cheese-chile mixture in the center of each. Refrigerate for 30 minutes.

4. In a skillet, heat the oil over medium heat. Flatten the balls slightly and sauté them until well browned on both sides.

Papas Arequipeña
(Fiery Potatoes in Peanut and Cheese Sauce)

Yield: 6 servings   Heat Scale: Medium

Here is a sauce-infused Peruvian potato recipe. The city of Arequipa is known for its fondness for very hot and spicy foods, so the addition of rocoto chiles in this recipe is a natural. The potatoes may be served as a vegetarian entrée or as a separate course.

¾ cup (177 mL) salted, roasted peanuts
½–¾ cup (118–177 mL) half-and-half
Salt, to taste
Freshly ground black pepper, to taste
2–3 fresh rocoto chiles, stems and seeds removed (or substitute 5 jalapeños)
½ cup (118 mL) grated Monterey Jack cheese (or substitute Meunster)
3 green onions, some of the green parts included
6 medium boiling potatoes, peeled
6 Bibb (Boston) lettuce leaves
6 hard-boiled eggs, halved lengthwise
12 ripe olives, halved lengthwise
Chopped cilantro for garnish

1. In a blender, purée the peanuts, ½ cup (118 mL) half-and-half, the salt, the pepper, the chiles, the cheese, and the green onions. The mixture should resemble mayonnaise. If it seems too thick, add more half-and-half, a little at a time.

2. Boil the potatoes until they are tender enough to pierce with the tip of a sharp knife. Do not overcook. Drain the potatoes, cool them slightly, and then halve them lengthwise.

3. On each of six individual plates, place a lettuce leaf and 2 potato halves (cut-side down). Drizzle with the sauce and garnish with the hard-boiled egg, olives, and cilantro.

Papas Huancaino, Numero Uno
(Potatoes Huancayo-Style, #1)

Yield: 8 servings   Heat Scale: Medium

This dish is one version of a popular, traditional potato dish from the highlands of Peru. Many recipes call for a local herb, palillo, which colors the dish a bright yellow. However, turmeric can be substituted. Originally, this dish is from the Andes mountain town of Huancayo—the final stop on the world's highest single-gauge rail line. It is one of Peru's most popular plates and can be found throughout the country. This dish is typically served with small pieces of corn on the cob. (Note: This recipe requires advance preparation.)

Juice of 1 small lemon
1 teaspoon (5 mL) ground aji chile (or substitute New Mexican)
½ teaspoon (2.5 mL) salt
¼ teaspoon (1.25 mL) freshly ground black pepper
1 medium onion, peeled, thinly sliced, and separated into rings
1½ cups (354 mL) grated cheese (Monterey Jack or Meunster preferred)
2 fresh rocoto chiles, halved, seeds and stems removed (or substitute yellow wax hot or jalapeños)
½ teaspoon (2.5 mL) turmeric
1–1½ cups (236–354 mL) half-and-half
⅓ cup (79 mL) olive oil
8 Bibb (Boston) lettuce leaves
8 medium potatoes, boiled, peeled, and halved lengthwise
4 hard-boiled eggs, halved lengthwise
2–3 ears cooked corn on the cob, each cut into 8 (2-inch [5 cm]) sections
½ cup (118 mL) sliced black olives

1. In a ceramic bowl, combine the lemon juice, ground chile, salt, black pepper, and onion slices. Marinate at room temperature for 1 to 2 hours.
2. In a blender purée the cheese, fresh chiles, turmeric, and 1 cup (236 mL) of the half-and-half. If the mixture seems too thick, add more half-and-half, a little at a time.
3. In a skillet, heat the oil over medium heat. Pour in the cheese-cream mixture and reduce the heat to very low. Cook for a few minutes, stirring constantly, until the sauce is smooth, thick, and creamy.
4. Arrange the lettuce leaves on a platter or on individual plates. Top the leaves with the potatoes, cut-side down, and pour the sauce over the potatoes. Garnish with the eggs, corn slices, and olives.
5. Drain the onion rings and mop up any excess oil with paper towels. Arrange the onion rings over the potatoes.

Papas Huancaino, Numero Dos
(Potatoes Huancayo-Style #2)

Yield: 6–8 servings   Heat Scale: Medium

This version of the spicy Peruvian potato recipe calls for cream cheese and cottage cheese instead of the queso blanco in the other recipe. It also calls for ajis instead of rocotos, but that won't make much difference unless you grow your own, as I do in my Albuquerque garden.

8 ounces (224 g) cream cheese
12 ounces (336 g) small curd cottage cheese
½–¾ cup (118–177 mL) half-and-half cream
¼–½ cup (59–118 mL) olive oil
¾ teaspoon (3.75 mL) palillo or turmeric
2 cloves garlic, peeled and minced
½ cup (118 mL) minced onion
3 fresh aji chiles, stems and seeds removed, finely minced (or substitute yellow wax hot or jalapeño)
12 black olives, coarsely chopped
1 head lettuce, shredded
8 large potatoes, cooked, cooled, and quartered
3 hard-boiled eggs, sliced, for garnish
¼ cup (59 mL) diced green and red sweet peppers for garnish
4 sprigs cilantro or parsley, chopped, for garnish
8 black olives for garnish

1. In a large mixing bowl, combine the cheeses and beat them together with a hand mixer until they are well blended. Gradually add the half-and-half and the oil, beating continuously. Add the palillo or turmeric, garlic, onion, and chiles and beat thoroughly, adding more half-and-half if the mixture seems too thick to pour. Stir in the chopped black olives.
2. Arrange the shredded lettuce on a platter, arrange the potatoes on top, and cover with the sauce. Garnish with the hard-boiled eggs and the remaining garnishes. Serve at room temperature.

Papitas con Chile
(Little Potatoes with Chile)

Yield: 4 servings   Heat Scale: Extremely Hot

This recipe is extremely hot and very typical of Sonora, where people make Salsa Casera (page 58) with 2 to 3 cups (500 to 708 mL) of chiltepins! To reduce the heat, add fewer chiltepins. Serve this with a mild Mexican fish entrée from Chapter 11.

3 tablespoons (45 mL) butter
3 tablespoons (45 mL) olive oil
2 pounds (1.1 kg) potatoes, peeled and cut in a ½-inch (1 cm) dice
1 cup (236 mL) water, divided
5 cloves garlic, peeled
1 teaspoon (5 mL) whole chiltepin chiles
½ teaspoon (2.5 mL) salt

1. In a large skillet, heat the butter and olive oil over medium heat. Add the diced potatoes. Toss and turn the potatoes with a spatula for 1 minute. Reduce the heat to low, add 3 tablespoons (45 mL) of the water, and let the potatoes cook while you make the chile sauce.
2. In a blender, combine the garlic, chiles, remaining water, and salt and purée thoroughly. Pour this mixture over the potatoes and simmer for 10 to 15 minutes, or until the potatoes are tender.

Barbacoa de Papas (Barbecued Potatoes)

Yield: 4–5 servings   Heat Scale: Medium

Potatoes, one of the New World crops, stars in this recipe from Tlaxcala. It's a new twist to warm potato salad, redolent of chile, herbs, and spices. Serve it at your next hot and spicy Mexican barbecue.

4 guajillo chiles, stems and seeds removed (or substitute dried red New Mexico chiles)
3 tablespoons (45 mL) vegetable oil
1 cup (236 mL) chopped onions
3 cloves garlic, peeled and minced
¼ teaspoon (1.25 mL) cinnamon
2 whole cloves, ground
½ teaspoon (2.5 mL) ground cumin
1 teaspoon (5 mL) dried thyme
1 teaspoon (5 mL) Mexican oregano
½ teaspoon (2.5 mL) salt
2 whole bay leaves
½ cup (118 mL) chopped mint
4 cups (.95 L) cubed potatoes, cut in ½-inch (1 cm) cubes

1. Tear the chiles into strips and place them in a small saucepan with boiling water to cover. Rehydrate for 20 minutes. Pour the mixture into a blender and purée until smooth. Set aside.
2. In a medium skillet, heat the oil over medium heat. Add the onion and garlic and sauté for 1 minute. Pour in the chile purée and add the cinnamon, ground cloves, cumin, thyme, oregano, salt, bay leaves, and mint and simmer for 2 minutes. If the mixture gets too thick, add a few tablespoons (30–45 mL) water.
3. Add the cubed potatoes and stir to coat them with the chile mixture. Cover and simmer the potatoes for 15 to 20 minutes, or until they are tender. Remove the bay leaves and serve.

Aloo Curry
(Curried Potatoes)

Yield: 4 servings   Heat Scale: Medium

This curry is found all over Trinidad, with the usual variations from cook to cook. The best I ever ate was at an out-of-the-way East Indian restaurant outside of Port of Spain that served this as one of their many roti fillings. Aloo is the Hindi word for potato. The curry shows the great melding of the East Indian flavors with the flavors of Trinidad. Serve this potato curry as a side dish or use it as a roti filling.

1 tablespoon (15 mL) West Indian Masala (page 5)
2 tablespoons (30 mL) olive oil
¼ teaspoon (1.25 mL) cumin seeds
3 cloves garlic, peeled and minced
½ cup (118 mL) minced onion
2 green onions, chopped
3 tablespoons (45 mL) chopped celery leaves
1 Congo pepper, seeds and stem removed, minced (or substitute habanero)
4 potatoes, peeled and cut into 1-inch (2.5 cm) cubes
2 cups (473 mL) hot water
Salt, to taste

1. In a small bowl, mix the curry powder with 3 tablespoons (45 mL) water and set aside.
2. In a heavy, medium skillet, heat the olive oil over medium heat. Add the cumin seeds and stir-fry for 30 seconds. Add the garlic, onions, green onions, celery leaves, and the Congo pepper and sauté for 1 minute.
3. Add the reserved curry paste to the skillet, reduce the heat to low, and sauté for 2 minutes. Add the potatoes and toss them with the sautéed mixture. Add the hot water, stir gently, and cook over a medium heat for 10 minutes or until the potatoes are tender. Add salt to taste.

Sizzling Shrimp and Potato Fritters

Yield: 4 servings (about 16 patties)   Heat Scale: Medium

Different versions of this dish can be found all over the Caribbean. Start with this basic recipe and add your own taste preferences, as many cooks in the islands do. This side dish is a tasty addition to a grilled fish or chicken dinner. Even though the list of ingredients may look long, these fritters are very easy to prepare, and they can be made a few hours ahead of time, refrigerated, and fried just before serving. (Note: This recipe requires advance preparation.)

2 large potatoes, washed and quartered
1½ teaspoons (7.5 mL) salt, divided
1 cup (236 mL) minced onion
3 tablespoons (45 mL) minced fresh cilantro
2 tablespoons (30 mL) minced fresh parsley
¾ cup (177 mL) grated cheddar cheese
4 tablespoons (60 mL) butter, cut into small pieces
½ habanero chile, stem and seeds removed, minced
1 teaspoon (5 mL) salt
½ teaspoon (2.5 mL) freshly grated black pepper
1 egg yolk
3 tablespoons (45 mL) olive oil
¾ pound (336 g) unshelled shrimp
¾ cup (177 mL) all-purpose flour
2 eggs, beaten
½ cup (118 mL) bread crumbs
Vegetable oil for frying

1. Put the potatoes in a pot, cover them with cold water, and add ½ teaspoon (2.5 mL) of the salt. Bring the mixture to a boil, reduce to a rolling simmer, and cook for 15 to 20 minutes. Drain the potatoes, peel them, and mash them in a bowl.
2. Add the onion, cilantro, parsley, cheese, butter, habanero, remaining salt, black pepper, and egg yolk, mix thoroughly, and set aside.
3. In a large skillet, heat the olive oil over medium heat. Add the shrimp and sauté for 3 minutes. Remove the skillet from the heat. Cool, peel, and devein the shrimp; cut the shrimp into ¼-inch (.5 cm) pieces, and mix them into the potato mixture.
4. Put the flour in a shallow bowl and the egg yolk and bread crumbs in separate additional bowls. Flour your hands (to avoid the mixture sticking to them), scoop up about 2 tablespoons (30 mL) of the potato mixture, and shape it into a patty. Repeat with the remaining potato mixture.
5. Dip the patties into the flour and pat off the excess, dip them into the beaten eggs, and coat them with the bread crumbs. Place the patties on a cookie sheet and refrigerate them for 30 minutes to 3 hours.
6. In a deep-fryer or a large, heavy pot, heat the vegetable oil. The oil is hot enough when a drop of water sizzles in it. Add the patties to the oil, but do not crowd them; fry them in two or three batches, if necessary. Fry the patties until they are golden, about 4 minutes, and drain them on paper towels.

Jamaica Jammin' Sweet Potatoes

Yield: 4 servings   Heat Scale: Mild

Since Jamaicans prefer sweet potatoes to normal potatoes, this recipe incorporates the best of the country. Serve this with jerk pork or chicken and a zesty salad for a real taste combo that will leave your guests asking for "more, mon." (Note: To substitute Jamaican allspice, use ½ teaspoon [2.5 mL] ground cinnamon, ½ teaspoon [2.5 mL] ground nutmeg, and ⅛ teaspoon [.6 mL] ground cloves. However, be forewarned, nothing is as good as Jamaican allspice!)

3 large sweet potatoes, scrubbed
1 tablespoon (15 mL) vegetable oil
2 tablespoons (30 mL) melted butter
½ teaspoon (2.5 mL) ground habanero
¼ cup (59 mL) dark brown sugar
3 tablespoons (45 mL) freshly grated ginger
⅔ cup (158 mL) fresh orange juice
2 tablespoons (30 mL) fresh lime juice
1 tablespoon (15 mL) dark rum
½ teaspoon (2.5 mL) freshly ground Jamaican allspice (see Note)

1. Preheat the oven to 350°F (180°C) for 20 minutes. Coat a 9 × 13–inch (22.5 × 32.5 cm) glass baking dish with the vegetable oil. Wrap the sweet potatoes in foil and bake them for 30 minutes. Leaving the oven on, remove the foil, allow the potatoes to cool enough to be handled, and then slice them into ½-inch (1 cm) slices. Layer the potato slices in the prepared pan.
2. In a small bowl, mix together the remaining ingredients and drizzle the mixture over the potatoes.
3. Cover the dish with foil and bake for 15 to 20 minutes, until the potatoes are barely tender. Remove the foil and bake for an additional 10 to 15 minutes, until the coating starts to crisp up.

Homestyle Fries with Red Chile Salt and Cilantro Catsup

Yield: 2–4 servings   Heat Scale: Mild

Here's the perfect addition to any casual meal, such as grilled meats or vegetables. Feel free to add some chile to the catsup, or replace the bland catsup with one of the habanero or jalapeño catsups on the market.

½ cup (118 mL) catsup
1 teaspoon (5 mL) finely minced cilantro
1 teaspoon (5 mL) balsamic vinegar
2 teaspoons (10 mL) salt
2 teaspoons (10 mL) ground red New Mexican chile
3 large white potatoes, peeled, dried, and cut into ¼-inch (.5 cm) thick sticks
Vegetable oil for deep frying

1. In a small bowl, combine the catsup, cilantro, and vinegar. In a separate small bowl, mix together the salt and ground chile powder. Set both bowls aside.

2. Arrange the potato sticks in a row on paper towels. Completely cover the strips with the towels and let them stand for at least 45 minutes or until potatoes are dry to the touch. Pour the oil into a large skillet and heat it to 350°F (180°C). Separate the potato sticks into four equal batches. Fry each batch until just slightly brown. Remove the potatoes from the oil with a slotted spoon and place them on paper towels to drain. Continue until all the sticks are fried, then cool the fries.

3. Heat the oil to 400°F (200°C) and fry the sticks again in batches until they turn a deep golden brown. Using a slotted spoon, transfer the fries to a basket lined with paper towels. Sprinkle the sticks with the red chile salt. Serve with the cilantro catsup.

Papas Canary Island–Style

Yield: 4 servings   Heat Scale: Medium

In the Canary Island, these potatoes would be boiled in sea water, but since sea water is not readily available, you can substitute heavily salted water. These are reminiscent of twice-baked potatoes, but with a spicy bite from the sauce.

2 medium potatoes
4 dried chile piquins, stems and seeds removed
4 cloves garlic, peeled and chopped
2 tablespoons (30 mL) red wine vinegar
1 tablespoon (15 mL) olive oil
½ teaspoon (2.5 mL) ground cumin
4 tablespoons (60 mL) Parmesan cheese

1. Preheat the oven to 400°F (200°C).

2. In a pot, boil the potatoes with their skins on in heavily salted water for 15 to 20 minutes, until done. Cut the potatoes in half lengthwise, scoop out the flesh, and reserve the skins.

3. Put the chiles in a bowl, cover them with hot water, and let them sit for 15 minutes, until softened. Drain the chiles

4. In a blender, purée the chiles, garlic, vinegar, oil, and cumin until smooth.

5. Mash the potatoes with the sauce and spoon them back into the potato skins. Top with the cheese and bake for 5 minutes or until hot.

Amuyale
(Spiced and Steamed Yams)

Yield: 4 servings   Heat Scale: Medium

This Nigerian yam recipe is rather unusual because the yams end up having the consistency of a dumpling. It is a delicious addition to any meal. For a light dinner, serve it with an African or Indonesian salad from Chapter 6.

4 pounds (1.82 kg) yams
1 teaspoon (5 mL) salt
½ teaspoon (2.5 mL) freshly ground white pepper
¾ cup (177 mL) minced onion, excess moisture drained out
¼ teaspoon (1.25 mL) thyme
2 teaspoons (10 mL) ground cayenne

1. Peel the yams and grate them into a sieve, so that any excess moisture can drain off.
2. Place the grated yams in a ceramic bowl, add the salt, pepper, onion, thyme, and cayenne, and toss.
3. Place 3 tablespoons (45 mL) of the mixture in the center of a 6-inch (15 cm) square of aluminum foil. Wrap the foil around the mixture to form a ball. Repeat with the remaining mixture.
4. Place the mixture in a steamer and steam for 25 minutes.

Isu
(Spiced Boiled Yams)

Yield: 4 servings   Heat Scale: Medium

In Nigeria, yams are often used instead of potatoes. Yams can be prepared and served any way potatoes can be. Yams are also added to soups and stews. Nigerians, with their love of hot and spicy flavors, would probably serve boiled yams just sprinkled with ground hot red chiles, but this recipe is slightly more elaborate.

4 pounds (1.82 kg) yams
1 teaspoon (5 mL) salt
2 cloves garlic, peeled
1 stick cinnamon
¼ cup (59 mL) melted butter
1 tablespoon (15 mL) ground red piri-piri chile (or substitute cayenne)

1. Peel the yams and slice them ½-inch thick. Place them in a casserole and add water to cover. Add the salt, garlic, and cinnamon. Bring the water to a boil, reduce the heat, and simmer until tender, about 15 to 20 minutes.
2. Drain the yams and arrange them on a heated platter. Drizzle the butter over the top, sprinkle the yams with the ground chile, and serve.

Perkadels
(Spiced Mashed Potatoes)

Yield: 6–8 servings   Heat Scale: Medium

This Balinese recipe comes from Rosemary Ann Ogilvie, who says, "What an unusual way to rework leftover mashed potatoes! Serve them as an accompaniment to both meats and poultry."

2 tablespoons (30 mL) butter
1 small onion, peeled and chopped
2 cloves garlic, peeled and minced
¼ pound (113 g) ground beef
3 small, fresh, hot red chiles, such as serranos or jalapeños, stems removed, minced
½ teaspoon (2.5 mL) ground nutmeg
6 shallots, peeled and chopped, or 6 green onions, chopped
3 cups (708 mL) cooked, mashed potatoes
2 eggs, separated
Vegetable oil for frying

1. In a sauté pan, melt the butter over medium heat. Add the onion and garlic and sauté until golden brown. Add the beef, chiles, and nutmeg and toss until the meat browns well. Stir in the shallots or green onions and cook for three more minutes.
2. Combine the meat mixture with the potatoes and add the egg yolks. Beat until well combined. Let the mixture cool, then refrigerate for 30 minutes.
3. Remove the mixture from the refrigerator and roll it into balls the size and shape of an egg.
4. In a deep fryer, heat the oil to 350 to 375°F (180 to 190°C). Beat the egg whites until just frothy and dip the balls in the egg whites. Deep-fry until the balls are golden brown. Drain the fried balls on paper towels.

Sambal Ubi Kentang
(Potato Sambal)

Yield: 4 servings   Heat Scale: Medium

Although many people think of sambal as a spicy condiment or sauce that is added to other dishes, sambals also include side dishes that range in heat from mild to wild, particularly in Indonesia and Malaysia. This Indonesian recipe is a good example of a spicy side dish that is labeled a "sambal." Serve these spicy, chilled potatoes with an Asian meat dish from Chapter 8.

½ pound (224 g) small potatoes (all approximately the same size)
¼ teaspoon (1.25 mL) salt
2 serrano or jalapeño chiles, stems and seeds removed, minced
¼ cup (59 mL) finely chopped green onions
2 teaspoons (10 mL) fresh lime juice
2 tablespoons (30 mL) thick coconut milk
¼ teaspoon (1.25 mL) freshly grated nutmeg
2 tablespoons (30 mL) chopped cilantro

1. Put the scrubbed potatoes in a large pot and cover them with water. Bring the water to a boil and boil the potatoes for 15 to 20 minutes or until a fork can easily pierce them. Drain the potatoes, let them cool, and peel them.

2. Place the potatoes in a bowl. Add the salt, chiles, green onion, lime juice, coconut milk, and nutmeg and mash very coarsely.

3. Mound the potato mixture in a serving bowl, sprinkle it with the cilantro, and chill it in the refrigerator until serving time.

Hongos con Chile y Queso (Mushrooms with Chile and Cheese)

Yield: 4–6 servings   Heat Scale: Medium

This is a rich and satisfying side dish from Chile. I suggest serving it with grilled or braised chicken, fish, or meat. The mushrooms can be wild or the grocery store button variety.

2 tablespoons (30 mL) butter
4 green onions, chopped
1 clove garlic, peeled and minced
1 pound (454 g) mushrooms, cleaned and sliced
2 fresh tomatoes, peeled, seeded, and diced
2 fresh aji chiles, stems and seeds removed, minced (or substitute yellow wax hot or jalapeño)
1 tablespoon (15 mL) minced fresh cilantro
½ cup (118 mL) shredded Münster or cheddar cheese

1. In a medium skillet, melt the butter over medium heat. Add the green onions and garlic and sauté for 1 minute, then add the mushrooms and toss to coat them with the sautéed mixture. Sauté for a minute or two. Add the tomatoes and chiles and stir them into the mushrooms. Simmer, covered, for 5 minutes.

2. Drain off any excess liquid from the sautéed mixture and add the cilantro and cheese. Simmer until the cheese just melts.

Hongos con Chile Pasilla
(Mushrooms with Pasilla Chiles)
Yield: 6 servings   Heat Scale: Mild

Mushrooms are very plentiful in Morelos and throughout most of central Mexico. The following recipe is easy to prepare and is a great favorite with cooks throughout the region. If wild mushrooms are not available, I suggest a mixture of button, oyster, shiitake, and maybe even a small portobello for interest. Serve this with a meat dish from Chapter 8.

3 pasilla chiles, toasted, stems and seeds removed
4 cloves garlic, peeled
3 tablespoons (45 mL) butter
1–2 tablespoons (15–30 mL) oil
¾ cup (177 mL) thinly sliced onion
4 cloves garlic, peeled and minced
1 pound (454 g) wild mushrooms, left whole if small, thickly sliced if large
¼ cup (59 mL) chopped epazote

1. Soak the toasted chiles in hot water for 15 minutes. Drain them and reserve the water. Place the chiles in a blender with the 4 whole garlic cloves and purée, adding a few tablespoons (30–45 mL) of the reserved water to make a thick sauce.
2. In a large sauté pan, heat the butter and oil over low heat. Add the onions and minced garlic and sauté for 1 minute, stirring constantly, so the garlic doesn't burn.
3. Add the mushrooms and toss them with the onion mixture for 2 minutes. Add the chile purée and epazote and simmer for 5 minutes. Serve hot.

Setas à la Vinagreta
(Mushrooms Vinaigrette)

Yield: 5 servings   Heat Scale: Medium

Since a wide variety of mushrooms are found in Mexico, it is no wonder that they are used extensively in many different kinds of dishes. This spicy side dish comes from Veracruz, and I suggest serving it with one of the fish dishes from Chapter 11 or one of the meat entrées from Chapter 8.

3 tablespoons (45 mL) olive oil
1½ cups (354 mL) thinly sliced carrots
2 cups (473 mL) thinly sliced onion
3 jalapeño chiles, stems and seeds removed, sliced into rings
5 cups (1.2 L) cleaned, sliced mushrooms
2 bay leaves
½ teaspoon (2.5 mL) salt
1 tablespoon (15 mL) Mexican oregano
1 tablespoon (15 mL) dried thyme
¼ teaspoon (1.25 mL) ground cumin
1 tablespoon (15 mL) whole black peppercorns, coarsely ground in a food processor
5 cloves garlic, peeled and minced
¼ cup (59 mL) apple cider vinegar

1. In a sauté pan, heat the oil over medium heat. Add the carrots, onion, chiles, and mushrooms, and sauté for 1 minute, tossing and stirring. Add the bay leaves, salt, oregano, thyme, cumin, ground peppercorns, garlic, and vinegar. Cover and simmer for 15 minutes.
2. Remove the bay leaves. Serve the mushrooms hot, or chill the mixture for several hours and serve cold.

Humitas con Achiote
(Puréed Corn with Annatto)

Yield: 20–22 husks   Heat Scale: Mild

This dish is especially popular in Argentina and Chile, but it is served throughout all of South America, with each cook or chef adding his or her particular trademark. The best versions are made from very young corn, although frozen corn kernels make an adequate substitute. These humitas are wrapped in dried cornhusks and steamed like tamales. They can be served as a snack or as an accompaniment to meat or chicken dishes.

2 dried aji chiles, stems and seeds removed, soaked in hot water for
20 minutes (or substitute ancho, pasilla, or New Mexican)
4 cups (.95 L) fresh young corn kernels, or substitute 4 cups (.95 L) defrosted
frozen corn kernels
⅓ cup (79 mL) milk
2 eggs
¼ teaspoon (1.25 mL) freshly ground black pepper
½ teaspoon (2.5 mL) salt
4 tablespoons achiote oil (or substitute 2 tablespoons [30 mL] butter,
2 tablespoons [30 mL] olive oil, and ½ teaspoon [2.5 mL] paprika)
¾ cup (177 mL) minced onions
1 clove garlic, peeled and minced
¼ cup (59 mL) grated Parmesan cheese
20–22 dried corn husks

1. In a blender, combine the chiles, corn, and milk in a blender and purée on high for 20 seconds. Add the eggs, black pepper, and salt and blend for 15 seconds or until the mixture is thick.
2. In a large, heavy skillet, heat the achiote oil over medium heat. When the oil is hot, add the onions and sauté until they are almost softened. Add the garlic and sauté for 30 seconds, taking care that it does not burn.
3. Pour the puréed corn mixture into the skillet and reduce the heat to low. Simmer, uncovered, for 5 to 7 minutes, stirring frequently, until the mixture thickens. Stir in the grated cheese and keep stirring until it melts. Remove the skillet from the heat.
4. Place 2 tablespoons (30 mL) of the seasoned corn in each cornhusk and roll the husk around the mixture, tucking in the ends. Tie each individual husk with kitchen string.
5. Stack the husks on a steamer rack and steam them in a large pot for 2 hours.

Guiso de Repollo
(Bolivian Cabbage in Tomato Sauce)

Yield: 4 servings   Heat Scale: Medium

Cabbage dishes are found all over Latin America, probably because cabbage itself is so easy to grow. This versatile vegetable is served cooked, raw in salads (as a cole-slaw), and as sauerkraut. The latter dish shows the European influence in Latin America. Generally, cabbage is available in green, white, and red varieties.

¾ teaspoon (3.75 mL) salt, divided
1 small white or green cabbage, finely shredded
2 tablespoons (30 mL) olive oil
1 cup (236 mL) chopped onion
2 medium tomatoes, peeled and chopped
2 fresh rocoto chiles, stems and seeds removed, chopped (or substitute
jalapeños)
¼ teaspoon (1.25 mL) freshly ground black pepper
3 tablespoons (45 mL) chopped cilantro
4 medium potatoes, cooked, peeled, and quartered

1. Bring a large pot of water to a boil, add ½ teaspoon (2.5 mL) of the salt and the cabbage and simmer for 4 to 5 minutes. Drain thoroughly and set aside.
2. In a large skillet, heat the oil over medium heat. Add the onion and sauté until it is soft. Add the tomatoes, chile, remaining salt, pepper, and cilantro and simmer for 1 minute, until the mixture is well blended.
3. Add the drained cabbage and the potatoes and heat thoroughly.

Repolho com Vinho
(Chile-Spiced Cabbage with Wine)

Yield: 4 servings   Heat Scale: Medium

This dish is the Brazilian version of the Guiso de Repollo of Bolivia. I suggest serving it with grilled or fried meat to add a crunch to the dinner plate. Another interesting addition would be llapingachos or camotes fritos.

½ teaspoon (2.5 mL) salt
1 small green cabbage, finely shredded
2 tablespoons (30 mL) olive oil
1 cup (236 mL) diced onion
1 fresh habanero chile, seeds and stem removed, minced (or substitute
3 jalapeños)
1 bell pepper, stem and seeds removed, chopped
2 tablespoons (30 mL) chopped cilantro
2 tomatoes, peeled, seeded, and chopped
½ cup (118 mL) dry white wine

1. Bring a large pot of water to a boil. Add the salt and the cabbage. Bring the water back to a boil and simmer the cabbage for 3 to 4 minutes. Drain the cabbage and set it aside.
2. In a large skillet, heat the oil over medium heat. Add the onion, chile, bell pepper, cilantro, and tomatoes and sauté until the onion is soft.
3. Add the drained cabbage and pour the wine over the top. Cover the skillet and simmer the mixture for 4 to 5 minutes, until it is hot.

Paltas Rellenas
(Peruvian Stuffed Avocados)

Yield: 3 servings   Heat Scale: Mild

The yellow potatoes of Peru are preferred for this dish. White potatoes will change the color and the taste, but it will still be good. The potato is king in Peru, as it can grow even at altitudes where maize won't. Food scholars think the potato has been grown in the Andean region for 8,000 years; the first Europeans to see the potato were probably Pizarro and his men. A few of the 200 or so varieties of Andean potato are beginning to show up in North American markets, but they are grown by local farmers.

1 pound (454 g) yellow potatoes, cooked, peeled, and pressed through a fine sieve
1 rocoto chile, stem and seeds removed, ground or finely grated (or substitute jalapeño)
3 tablespoons (45 mL) grated onion
1 tablespoon (15 mL) fresh lime juice
3–5 tablespoons (45–75 mL) olive oil
Bibb lettuce leaves for serving
3 large, ripe avocados
2 ears fresh corn, cooked and cut into rounds
12 prawns or shrimp, cooked, peeled, deveined, drizzled with olive oil, and sprinkled with ground red chile
12 black olives
Salt, to taste
Freshly ground black pepper, to taste

1. In a bowl, combine the sieved potatoes, rocoto chile, onion, lime juice, and enough olive oil to make a thick purée.
2. Arrange the lettuce leaves on 3 plates.
3. Cut the avocados in half, discard the pits, and place 2 halves on each plate. Stuff them with the potato mixture.
4. Garnish each plate with the corn, shrimp, and olives and season with the salt and pepper.

Picante de Aguacates
(Spicy Chilean Avocado)

Yield: 8 side dish servings   Heat Scale: Medium

The Aztec name for avocado translates into "testicle tree," referring to the shape and the fact that they grow in pairs. The avocado made its way south into Peru, Ecuador, and Chile and was in Peru at the time Pizarro arrived. This spicy, stuffed avocado is a good side dish for grilled meat or some of that fine Chilean fish.

3 hard-boiled egg yolks
2 fresh aji chiles, stems and seeds removed, minced (or substitute yellow wax hot or jalapeño)
1 clove garlic, peeled and minced
1 cup (236 mL) chopped onions
3 tablespoons (45 mL) chopped cilantro
3 tablespoons (45 mL) champagne vinegar
½ teaspoon (2.5 mL) salt
¼ teaspoon (1.25 mL) freshly ground black pepper
6 large, ripe avocados

1. In a bowl, mash the egg yolks. Add the chiles, garlic, cilantro, vinegar, salt, and pepper and mix thoroughly.
2. Peel 2 of the avocados, discard the pits, and chop them coarsely. Add them to the egg yolk mixture and mix in gently.
3. Peel the remaining 4 avocados, halve them, and discard the pits. Mound the stuffing into the 8 avocado halves.

Chayote con Ajis
(Chayote Squash Sautéed with Chiles)

Yield: 6–8 servings   Heat Scale: Medium

Chayote has many names—chocho and christophene, to name two. This squash is common to many countries in Latin America and the Caribbean, and variations on this recipe appear from Brazil to Chile. It is a versatile vegetable—it can be stuffed, sautéed, baked, or added to soups and stews. It shares many traits with the zucchini.

3 chayote squash, peeled and cubed
2 tablespoons (30 mL) olive oil
1 cup (236 mL) chopped onion
2 cloves garlic, peeled and minced
2 fresh aji chiles, stems and seeds removed, minced (or substitute yellow wax hot or jalapeño)
1½ cups (354 mL) fresh or frozen corn kernels
1 tablespoon (15 mL) minced cilantro
¼ cup (59 mL) grated Parmesan cheese

1. In a pot of salted water, boil the cubed chayotes for 5 minutes or until barely done. Drain the squash in a sieve and set it aside.
2. In a large skillet, heat the olive oil over medium heat. Add the onion, garlic, and chile and sauté until the onion wilts.
3. Add the chayote and corn to the skillet and sauté for a minute or two, tossing the ingredients to coat the squash.
4. Sprinkle the sautéed mixture with the cilantro and cheese and heat just until the cheese starts to melt and coat the mixture. Serve immediately.

Chayotes Exquisitos (Exquisite Chayotes)

Yield: 6 servings   Heat Scale: Mild

Squash is one of the staples of the New World foods, and in this recipe from Hidalgo, chayote squash plays the starring role. Chayote has a delicate flavor and takes well to any type of seasoning. Serve this side dish with a spicy pork recipe from Chapter 8.

1 tablespoon (15 mL) vegetable oil
2 tablespoons (30 mL) butter
1 cup (236 mL) chopped onion
5 chayotes, washed and cut into eighths
1½ cups (354 mL) whole corn kernels (fresh preferred)
4 poblano chiles, roasted, peeled, stems and seeds removed, cut into 1-inch (2.5 cm) squares
½ cup (118 mL) milk
½ teaspoon (2.5 mL) salt
¼ teaspoon (1.25 mL) freshly grated black pepper
1 cup (236 mL) grated Monterey Jack cheese

1. Preheat the oven to 350°F (180°C).
2. In a skillet, heat the oil and butter over low heat. Add the onion and sauté for 1 minute. Add the chayote squash and corn and sauté for 2 minutes. If the mixture starts to dry out, add a few tablespoons (30–45 mL) water.
3. Stir in the cubed chile, milk, salt, and pepper and simmer until the chayote has softened.
4. Transfer the mixture to a small glass baking dish, cover the mixture with the cheese, and bake for 10 minutes, or until the cheese has melted.

Calabacitas en Adobillo
(Squash in Adobo Sauce)

Yield: 5–6 servings   Heat Scale: Mild

When you eat chayote squash, you are eating a part of history, starting with the Aztecs and the Mayas. Chayote was one of the mainstays of their diet. The squash has a delicate taste and takes well to high seasoning. This side dish from Sinaloa goes well with any meat, poultry, or seafood dish.

2 ancho chiles, stems and seeds removed
3 cloves garlic
1 teaspoon (5 mL) dried thyme
¼ teaspoon (1.25 mL) ground cumin
½ teaspoon (2.5 mL) salt
2 teaspoons (10 mL) butter or vegetable oil
¼ cup (59 mL) chopped onion
3 tablespoons (45 mL) dried bread crumbs
2 tablespoons (30 mL) apple cider vinegar
1 pound (454 g) chayote squash, peeled and sliced ¼-inch (.5 cm) thick

1. Tear the ancho chile into strips, put them into a small dish, add 1 cup (236 mL) hot water, and let the chile rehydrate for 20 minutes.
2. Transfer the chiles and water to a blender and add the garlic, thyme, cumin, and salt. Purée until smooth. Set aside.
3. In a skillet, heat the butter over medium heat. Add the onion and sauté for 1 minute. Add the chile purée, bread crumbs, and vinegar, cover, and simmer for 10 minutes. Stir the mixture and add more water or stock if it gets too thick.
4. While the sauce is simmering, steam the chayote squash in ½ cup (118 mL) water for 8 minutes. Drain the squash and add it to the simmering sauce. Serve immediately.

Rajas con Crema
(Sliced Chiles with Cream)

Yield: 4–5 servings   Heat Scale: Mild

This accompaniment comes from Jalisco, an area rich in food and traditions. The region includes Guadalajara, which is one of the most famous cities in Mexico. Mary Jane ate in a large restaurant there that specialized in cabrito (goat), and the waiters wore roller skates! Serve this classy dish over hot, cooked rice with a simple, spicy grilled fish recipe from Chapter 11.

8 poblano chiles, roasted, peeled, and stems and seeds removed
3 tablespoons (45 mL) butter
3 tablespoons (45 mL) oil
3 cups (708 mL) thinly sliced onion
½ teaspoon (2.5 mL) salt
¼ teaspoon (1.25 mL) freshly ground black or white pepper
2–2½ cups (473–591 mL) Classic Chicken Stock (page 46)
¾ cup (177 mL) cream
¼ pound (113 g) grated asadero cheese, or substitute queso blanco or Monterey Jack cheese

1. Slice the poblano chiles into strips and set them aside.
2. In a medium sauté pan, heat the butter and oil over medium heat. Add the onions, sprinkle them with the salt and pepper, and sauté the onions for 3 minutes, or until they are just beginning to brown.
3. Stir in the reserved chile strips and toss the mixture over a low heat for 1 minute.
4. Add 2 cups (473 mL) of the chicken stock and the cream. Bring the mixture to a light boil and reduce the heat immediately to a simmer. Cook, stirring frequently, until the mixture starts to thicken slightly, about 1 minute. If it thickens too much, add a few tablespoons (30–45 mL) of the chicken stock.
5. Sprinkle the cheese over the mixture and gently mix it in. Serve immediately over hot, cooked rice.

Elote con Crema y Chiles Serranos
(Spicy Creamed Corn and Serrano Chiles)
Yield: 4 servings   Heat Scale: Medium

The state of Morelos is beautiful and diverse. Mary Jane lived in Cuernavaca for three months while going to summer school language classes and ate herself silly the entire time! This rich side dish is very typical of the area. I suggest serving it with a simple, spicy grilled meat from Chapter 8.

5 ears fresh corn, steamed for 3 minutes
2 tablespoons (30 mL) butter or vegetable oil
¼ cup (59 mL) minced onion
4 serrano chiles, stems and seeds removed, minced
1 tablespoon (15 mL) epazote
2 tablespoons (30 mL) water
¼ cup (59 mL) milk
½ teaspoon (2.5 mL) salt
¼ teaspoon (1.25 mL) freshly ground black pepper
¾ cup (177 mL) cream, warmed
½ cup (118 mL) grated white cheese, such as Mexican queso blanco

1. When the corn has cooled enough to handle, cut the kernels from the ears and set them aside.
2. In a small sauté pan, heat the butter over medium heat. Add the onion, chile, and epazote and sauté for 30 seconds. Add the water, milk, salt, black pepper, and reserved corn and bring the mixture to a light boil. Reduce the heat to a simmer and add the cream and the cheese. Simmer just until everything is heated through and the cheese is melted. Do not let the mixture boil.

Chiles Rellenos de Aguacate
(Avocado Rellenos)
Yield: 6 servings   Heat Scale: Mild

Mary Jane first saw some of Zacatecas from a train in 1970. She bought some beautiful wool ponchos, negotiating the whole deal from the train window. She also ate some great food from the vendors; the train system had forgotten to attach the dining car! These tasty rellenos can be served at room temperature or slightly chilled. The entrée could be a spicy Mexican meat or chicken dish.

3 large, ripe avocados, peeled and pitted
2 teaspoons (10 mL) fresh lemon juice
1 teaspoon (5 mL) fresh lime juice
½ teaspoon (2.5 mL) salt
¼ teaspoon (1.25 mL) freshly ground black pepper
¼ cup (59 mL) minced onion
¾ cup (177 mL) grated queso blanco cheese (or substitute Monterey Jack)
3 tablespoons (45 mL) olive oil
6 poblano chiles, roasted, peeled, stems and seeds removed, left whole
6 tablespoons (90 mL) sour cream

1. Coarsely chop the avocados and put them in a ceramic or glass bowl. Add the citrus juices, salt, pepper, onion, cheese, and olive oil and mix well.
2. Stuff the avocado mixture into the chiles; arrange the stuffed chiles on a platter, and cover each chile with the sour cream. Serve at room temperature, or warm the chiles a little in an oven set to 200°F (100°C).

Chiles Rellenos de Verdura (Vegetable Rellenos)

Yield: 10 servings   Heat Scale: Mild

Squash blossoms are a common ingredient in many Mexican recipes. Look for them in a Latin American market in your area; if they don't have them, they can probably get them for you. The taste of the blossoms is exquisite. The heat on this recipe is mild, so serve it with one of the spicier fish or meat entrées.

2 tablespoons (30 mL) butter
2 tablespoons (30 mL) vegetable oil
1 cup (236 mL) coarsely chopped carrots
1 cup (236 mL) chopped onion
3 cups (708 mL) chopped chayote squash (or substitute zucchini)
½ cup (118 mL) fresh corn kernels
1 cup (236 mL) chopped squash blossoms
½ teaspoon (2.5 mL) salt
¼ teaspoon (1.25 mL) freshly ground black pepper
1 cup (236 mL) milk
½ cup (118 mL) grated queso blanco cheese (or substitute Monterey Jack)
10 poblano chiles, roasted, peeled, stems and seeds removed
⅔ cup (158 mL) heavy cream

1. Preheat the oven to 200°F (180°C).
2. In a sauté pan, heat the butter and oil over medium heat. Add the carrots, onion, squash, and corn, and sauté for 2 minutes. Add the squash blossoms, salt, and black pepper and sauté until the pan is almost dry.
3. Add the milk, bring the mixture to a boil, and reduce the heat to a simmer. Simmer until the mixture has thickened, about 4 to 5 minutes. Stir in the cheese and remove the pan from the heat.
4. Using a teaspoon, stuff the chiles with the cooked squash mixture. Arrange the stuffed chiles on a warmed serving platter and drizzle 1 tablespoon (15 mL) cream over each chile. Warm the chiles in the oven for several minutes before serving.

Chiles Pasilla Tlaxcaltecas
(Pasilla Chiles in Sweet Sauce)

Yield: 6 servings   Heat Scale: Mild

Here's a dish from Tlaxcala that Norteamericanos will find very unusual! It is delicious, especially if you serve it with a spicy seafood dish from Chapter 11. The sweet taste will complement the hot and spicy flavoring of the seafood. Piloncillo is unrefined brown sugar, and dark brown sugar makes a good substitute.

5 tablespoons (45 mL) olive oil
1 tablespoon (15 mL) butter
3 cups (708 mL) thinly sliced onion
5 cloves garlic, peeled and minced
2 cups (473 mL) water
2 cups (473 mL) piloncillo (or substitute dark brown sugar)
12 pasilla chiles, stems and seeds removed
½ pound (224 g) manchego cheese, cut into 12 thick strips (or substitute Parmesan)

1. In a large sauté pan, heat the oil and butter over medium heat. Add the onions and sauté for 1 minute. Add the garlic and sauté for 2 minutes more.
2. Add the water and piloncillo. Bring the mixture to a boil, reduce the heat, and simmer the mixture until it thickens to the consistency of honey.
3. Stuff each chile with a piece of the cheese, taking care not to break the chile. Place the stuffed chiles in the simmering skillet and sauté over a low heat until the cheese starts to soften.
4. Place 2 chiles on each plate and drizzle some sauce over them.

Callaloo–Scotch Bonnet Strudel

Yield: 6 servings   Heat Scale: Medium

This was the most unusual recipe I tasted during my videotaping sojourn to Jamaica. It is not surprising that it is chef Norma Shirley's creation; after all, she received her culinary training in New York State. Norma notes that this side dish can be served with bechamel sauce.

3 ounces (84 g) butter, divided
1 medium onion, peeled and diced
¼–½ teaspoon (1.25–2.5 mL) finely chopped Scotch bonnet chile (or habanero)
8–10 cups (1.9–2.3 L) callaloo or spinach leaves (washed)
Salt, to taste
Freshly ground black pepper, to taste
4 ounces (112 g) cream cheese
2 ounces (56 g) montrachet cheese, softened (or substitute goat cheese)
1 tablespoon (15 mL) chopped fresh chives
6–8 sheets phyllo dough

1. Preheat the oven to 350°F (180°C).

2. In a skillet, melt 2 ounces (56 g) of the butter over medium heat. Add the onions and sauté until transparent. Add the Scotch bonnet and callaloo or spinach and sauté until the greens wilt (do not overcook). Add salt and pepper to taste. Set aside to cool.

3. In a bowl, mix together the cream cheese, montrachet, and chives, and set the mixture aside. In a small bowl, melt the remaining butter.

4. Place a sheet of phyllo dough on a cool pastry board. Brush it lightly with the melted butter. Lay another sheet directly over the first and brush it with butter. Repeat until all the sheets are used. Place the callaloo mixture in the middle of the phyllo dough and top it with the cheese mixture. Fold the edges of dough to form a log. Brush the outside with the melted butter. Place the log on a baking sheet and bake for 15 to 20 minutes, until golden brown.

Spicy Chayote Gratin

Yield: 4 servings   Heat Scale: Medium

This gratin dish, with its many variations, is served frequently in Guadeloupe, and it exemplifies the French influence on the island. Since the flavor of the chayote is delicate, I suggest serving this dish hot with grilled fish.

4 medium chayotes (about 1 pound [454 g]), seeds removed
3 slices bacon, chopped
1–2 tablespoons (15–30 mL) olive oil (if needed)
1 cup (236 mL) minced onion
2 cloves garlic, peeled and minced
6 green onions, chopped
2 Scotch bonnet chiles (or habaneros), stems and seeds removed, minced
½ teaspoon (2.5 mL) salt
½ cup (118 mL) coconut milk
2 teaspoons (10 mL) chopped parsley
½ pound (224 g) grated gruyere cheese
¼ cup (59 mL) dry bread crumbs
2 teaspoons (10 mL) butter, softened

1. Preheat the oven to 350°F (180°C).

2. Bring a large pot of salted water to a boil. Add the cleaned chayotes and boil them gently until they are easily pierced with a knife, 10 to 15 minutes. Remove them from the water and allow them to cool.

3. When the chayotes are cool enough to handle, carefully remove the pulp, mash it, and set it aside. Reserve the skins.

4. In a large skillet, sauté the bacon for 5 to 7 minutes. Add the onion, garlic, green onions, chiles, and salt and sauté for 1 minute. If there isn't enough bacon grease, add the olive oil.

5. Add the coconut milk and the reserved mashed chayote and simmer for 5 minutes. Remove the skillet from the heat and stir in the parsley and cheese.

6. Carefully fill the reserved chayote skins with this mixture. Sprinkle with the bread crumbs and top with the butter. Arrange the stuffed skins in a shallow baking dish and bake for 15 to 20 minutes, until the tops are browned.

French Caribbean Ratatouille

Yield: 6–8 servings   Heat Scale: Medium-Hot

Even if you eat ratatouille two nights in a row at the same restaurant in the French Caribbean, the second meal may be slightly different from the one you had the night before. It depends on what vegetables are available. This particular recipe is delicious and easy to prepare (especially ahead of time), despite the long list of ingredients. Serve it hot or chilled with spicy grilled fish or meat, and add a salad and some crusty bread, to sop up all those good juices.

¼ pound (113 g) bacon, diced
2–3 tablespoons (30–45 mL) vegetable oil
3 onions, peeled and chopped
3 cloves garlic, peeled and minced
2 bell peppers, stems and seeds removed, sliced
½ pound (224 g) pumpkin, peeled and cut into 1-inch (2.5 cm) cubes
¼ pound (113 g) green papaya, peeled and cut into 1-inch (2.5 cm) cubes
½ pound (224 g) eggplant, peeled and cut into ½-inch (2.5 cm) slices
¼ pound (112 g) peeled and sliced cucumbers
2 Scotch bonnet peppers or habaneros, stems and seeds removed, minced
½ pound (224 g) tomatoes, peeled, seeded, and chopped
1 teaspoon (5 mL) dried thyme (or substitute 2 sprigs fresh thyme)
½ teaspoon (2.5 mL) dried rosemary (or substitute 1 sprig fresh rosemary)
2 teaspoons (10 mL) dried basil (or substitute 3 sprigs fresh basil)
2 teaspoons (10 mL) chopped fresh parsley
Salt, to taste
Freshly ground black pepper, to taste

1. In a large, heavy skillet, sauté the bacon. Remove the bacon from the pan, leaving the fat behind. If there isn't enough fat to sauté the vegetables, add some vegetable oil. Or, you could drain off the fat and substitute vegetable oil.
2. Add the onions, garlic, and bell peppers to the skillet. Reduce the heat and sauté the mixture for 2 minutes.
3. Add the pumpkin, papaya, eggplant, cucumber, chiles, tomatoes, thyme, rosemary, and basil. Cover and simmer the mixture slowly for 1½ to 2 hours, until all the flavors have melded. Add the parsley and salt and pepper to taste.

Caribbean Cabbage and Green Peas

Yield: 4 servings   Heat Scale: Medium

The ingredients in this recipe are simple, reflecting the small garden patches that are seen throughout the Caribbean. Most everyone living outside the cities has a vegetable garden; given the climate and good growing conditions, vegetables flourish without much care or tending. If callaloo is not available, substitute fresh spinach.

1 tablespoon (15 mL) olive oil
4 cups (.95 L) coarsely chopped cabbage
1 clove garlic, peeled and minced
1½ cups (354 mL) chopped callaloo (or substitute fresh spinach)
1 medium tomato, peeled and diced, juice reserved
1 tablespoon (15 mL) minced habanero chile
1½ cups (354 mL) frozen petite peas, or blanched fresh petite peas
2 teaspoons (10 mL) minced fresh basil (or substitute ½ teaspoon [2.5 mL] dried)
Salt, to taste
Freshly ground black pepper, to taste

1. In a large, nonstick skillet, heat the olive oil over medium heat. Add the cabbage and garlic and sauté for 4 minutes, stirring constantly, until the cabbage starts to wilt.
2. Add the callaloo, tomato, reserved tomato juice, chile, peas, and basil and sauté for 2 minutes, stirring constantly. Cover the skillet, reduce the heat to medium-low, and steam for 2 minutes, until the peas are tender. Add salt and pepper to taste.

Trinidadian Curried Cauliflower, Potatoes, and Peas

Yield: 5 servings   Heat Scale: Mild

This dish can be served hot as a side dish, or it can be chilled and served over fresh greens as a salad. The fresh ginger adds a nice tang to some otherwise ordinary vegetables. Do not use the packaged yellow curry powder; the taste will overpower the vegetables and be too cloying.

1 tablespoon (15 mL) olive oil
1 large onion, peeled and chopped
4 garlic cloves, peeled and minced
2 tablespoons (30 mL) chopped fresh ginger root
2 teaspoons (10 mL) minced Congo pepper (or substitute habanero)
⅓ cup (79 mL) plus 2–3 tablespoons (30–45 mL) water
⅔ cup (158 mL) tomato purée
½ cup (118 mL) chopped dates or raisins
1 teaspoon (5 mL) ground coriander
1 teaspoon (5 mL) ground cumin
¼ teaspoon (1.25 mL) ground turmeric
¼ cup (59 mL) chopped fresh cilantro
1 tablespoon (15 mL) soy sauce
4 cups (.95 L) potatoes cut into 1-inch (2.5 cm) cubes
2½ cups (591 mL) cauliflower florets, broken into bite-size pieces
2 cups green peas, fresh or frozen

1. In a large, nonstick skillet, heat the olive oil over medium heat. Add the onion, garlic, ginger, and Congo pepper and sauté, stirring, until the onion begins to stick and turn light brown. Stir in the 2–3 tablespoons (30–45 mL) water and cook, stirring, until the onion softens.
2. Stir in the tomato purée, dates or raisins, coriander, cumin, turmeric, cilantro, soy sauce, remaining water, and potatoes, reduce the heat to low, and cook, uncovered, for 15 minutes.
3. Add the cauliflower and toss it with the mixture. Cover and simmer for 15 to 20 minutes or until the potatoes are almost tender. Add the peas and cook for an additional 5 minutes.

Orange-Glazed Fiery Green Beans

Yield: 4 servings   Heat Scale: Medium

These sweet and spicy green beans are an excellent accompaniment for roast pork, beef, lamb, poultry, or fish dishes. (Note: This recipe requires advance preparation.)

4 serrano chiles, stems and seeds removed, cut in thin strips
1 pound (454 g) French-cut green beans
2 tablespoons (30 mL) orange juice
2 teaspoons (10 mL) orange zest or grated orange peel
¼ cup (59 mL) butter
¼ cup (59 mL) light brown sugar

1. In a bowl, combine the chiles, green beans, orange juice, and orange zest. Allow the mixture to marinate for an hour.
2. In a sauté pan, melt the butter over medium heat. Add the sugar and heat until dissolved.
3. Add the green bean mixture and simmer until the beans are glazed and cooked.

Grilled Spicy Onions

Yield: 6 servings   Heat Scale: Mild

These onions go well with a variety of foods, such as steaks, fajitas, and hamburgers. Marinate the onions overnight and throw them on the grill while cooking the entrée. (Note: This recipe requires advance preparation.)

1 tablespoon (15 mL) ground red New Mexican chile
1 cup (236 mL) olive oil
3 cloves garlic, peeled and minced
18–24 large green onions, 3–4 inches (7.5–10 cm) of the greens included

1. In a bowl, combine all the ingredients. Marinate for at least 4 hours.
2. Grill the onions over hot coals until all sides are browned.

Calabacitas con Chile Verde
(Squash with Green Chile)

Yield: 6 servings   Heat Scale: Medium

Squash and corn are familiar accompaniments throughout the Southwest. This recipe is particularly good with traditional entrées, such as enchiladas, tamales, and burritos.

1 tablespoon (15 mL) bacon drippings or vegetable oil
1 cup (236 mL) chopped onions
2 cloves garlic, peeled and minced
4 green New Mexican chiles, roasted, peeled, stems and seeds removed, chopped
2 medium zucchini, sliced
1 cup (236 mL) whole kernel corn
⅓ cup (79 mL) cream or half-and-half

1. In a skillet, heat the bacon drippings or oil over medium heat. Add the onions and garlic and sauté them until softened.
2. Add the chiles, zucchini, and corn. Simmer for 15 or 20 minutes or until the squash is almost done.
3. Add the cream, increase the heat until the cream starts to boil, and cook until the vegetables are done and the sauce has thickened.

Chile-Grilled Caponata

Yield: 12 servings   Heat Scale: Mild

This recipe has gone through several incarnations to reach its present delicious state. Chef Rosa Rajkovic suggested the inclusion of dill, basil, oregano, and marjoram to add an herbal punch. In addition, she uses fine-quality balsamic vinegar and fresh lemon juice, which I find work well with the smoky, spicy flavor of the grilled eggplant and onions. Use a vegetable grilling screen so the vegetables don't fall through the wide spaces on the grill. The caponata can be served any number of ways: on leaves of Bibb lettuce, as an antipasto with toasted baguettes or focaccia bread, or as a sandwich filling on good rolls. (Note: This recipe requires advance preparation.)

2½ pounds (1.13 kg) eggplant, peeled and sliced ¾-inch (1.5 cm) thick (Japanese or white eggplant preferred)
2 shallots, peeled and sliced ½-inch (1 cm) thick
4 onions, peeled and sliced ½-inch (1 cm) thick
¾ cup (177 mL) Chile Oil (page 16)
1½ pounds (680 g) Italian plum tomatoes
⅔ cup (158 mL) balsamic vinegar
3 tablespoons (45 mL) fresh lemon juice
2 teaspoons (10 mL) sugar
¾ teaspoon (3.75 mL) dill weed
1½ teaspoons (7.5 mL) dried basil
1 teaspoon (5 mL) dried oregano (Greek or Italian preferred)
1 teaspoon (5 mL) dried marjoram
¾ cup (177 mL) pitted green olives, sliced
½–¾ cup (118–177 mL) olives, pitted and quartered
2 tablespoons (30 mL) capers, drained
3 tablespoons (45 mL) pine nuts

1. On an outside grill, start a hot fire using a good hardwood, such as oak, pecan, or apple. (Use charcoal only as a last resort.) When the fire is ready, position the rack about 4 to 5 inches (10 to 12.5 cm) from the wood. (If you do not have access to a grill, use the broiler in your oven; just remember that the vegetables will not have the same slightly smoky flavor.)
2. Brush both sides of the eggplant, shallots, and onion with the chile oil. Grill the eggplant 5 to 6 minutes per side until it is browned and soft inside. Grill the shallots 3 to 4 minutes per side. Grill the onion slices 7 to 8 minutes per side, or until they are slightly charred. Remove the vegetables from the fire and allow them to cool. When the vegetables are cool, chop them coarsely and set them aside.
3. In a large skillet, heat the remaining chile oil (at least 3 tablespoons [45 mL]) over medium heat. Add the tomatoes. Sauté, stirring frequently, until the liquid from the tomatoes starts to evaporate, about 10 to 15 minutes. Add the balsamic vinegar, lemon juice, sugar, dill weed, basil, oregano, and marjoram. Cover and simmer slowly for 10 minutes, checking to make sure the mixture doesn't get too dry. (If the mixture starts to dry out, add a little water and remove the mixture from the heat.)
4. Add the reserved grilled vegetables and mix gently. Add the olives, capers, and pine nuts and mix again. Chill this mixture for 24 hours.

Sweet and Hot Glazed Carrots

Yield: 6 servings   Heat Scale: Medium

The sweet spiciness of the glaze complements the heat of the chile to produce a vegetable treat that goes great with any grilled or roasted meats.

1 pound (454 g) carrots, julienned
4 teaspoons (20 mL) ground dried red New Mexican chile
2 tablespoons (30 mL) butter
1 tablespoon (15 mL) honey
½ teaspoon (2.5 mL) cinnamon

1. Steam the carrots until tender but still slightly crisp.
2. In a separate saucepan, combine the remaining ingredients and bring to a simmer. Simmer for 10 minutes.
3. Add the carrots, toss them in the glaze until coated, and serve.

Corn and Jalapeño Custard

Yield: 4–6 servings   Heat Scale: Mild

This unusual creation can be served either as a vegetarian entrée or as a vegetable second course. Double the amount of jalapeños for a more daring dish.

2 tablespoons (30 mL) chopped jalapeño chiles
½ cup (118 mL) cream corn
½ cup (118 mL) cooked rice
½ cup (118 mL) grated cheddar cheese
¼ cup (59 mL) yellow cornmeal
¼ cup (59 mL) whole milk
¼ cup (59 mL) minced onion
¼ cup (59 mL) chopped black olives
1 egg, beaten
½ teaspoon (2.5 mL) ground cumin
½ teaspoon (2.5 mL) salt
⅛ teaspoon (.6 mL) baking powder

1. Preheat the oven to 350°F (180°C). Grease an 8-inch (20 cm) square baking dish.
2. In a bowl, combine all the ingredients. Transfer the mixture to the prepared baking dish. Bake for 30 minutes or until set and lightly browned.

Marinated Chipotle Zucchini

Yield: 8 servings   Heat Scale: Medium

One of the chiles of choice when preparing Southwestern food, the chipotle imparts a wonderful smoky-hot flavor to the squash.

3–4 tablespoons (45–60 mL) olive oil
1 medium onion, peeled and sliced ¼-inch (.5 cm) thick
4 small zucchini, halved lengthwise
1 tablespoon (15 mL) wine vinegar
1 canned chipotle in adobo, chopped
Chopped fresh cilantro or parsley for garnish

1. In a sauté pan, heat the oil over medium heat. Add the onion and sauté until soft. Place the zucchini halves, cut-side down, on top of the onion. Reduce the heat, cover the pan, and cook for 20 minutes or until tender. Remove the vegetables and keep warm.
2. Stir in the vinegar and chile. Add more oil if the mixture is dry. Simmer the marinade for a couple of minutes to blend the flavors.
3. Place the zucchinis on a plate and top them with the onions. Pour the marinade over the top and allow to marinate for 15 to 20 minutes.
4. Top with the chopped cilantro or parsley and serve either warm or at room temperature.

Chile-Cheese Broccoli Casserole

Yield: 6 servings   Heat Scale: Medium

Although broccoli—a close relative of cabbage and cauliflower—was grown in Williamsburg, Virginia, as early as 1775, it disappeared from American recipes until the mid-20th century. This combination of the vegetable with chile peppers and cheese is a good example of the adoption of "foreign" elements into Southwest cuisines.

4 green New Mexican chiles, roasted, peeled, stems and seeds removed, chopped
1½ pounds (680 g) fresh broccoli, steamed but still firm, drained, and chopped
½ pound (224 g) mushrooms, sliced and sautéed briefly in butter
4 tablespoons (60 mL) butter or margarine
4 tablespoons (60 mL) all-purpose flour
2 cups (473 mL) milk
2 tablespoons (30 mL) grated onion
1¾ cups (413 mL) grated sharp cheddar cheese
½ teaspoon (2.5 mL) salt
½ teaspoon (2.5 mL) ground cayenne
½ teaspoon (2.5 mL) freshly ground black pepper

1. Preheat the oven to 325°F (165°C).
2. In a bowl, mix together the chiles, broccoli, and mushrooms. Transfer the mixture to a casserole dish.
3. In a small saucepan, melt the butter over medium heat. Add the flour and simmer for 2 minutes. Reduce the heat, add the milk, and stir constantly until the mixture thickens. Add the onion, cheese, salt, cayenne, and black pepper and cook for 2 minutes, stirring constantly.
4. Pour the cheese sauce over the vegetables. Cover and bake for 30 minutes.

Southwest Summer Vegetables
Yield: 4–6 servings   Heat Scale: Mild

This recipe combines a variety of summer vegetables—use whatever you have available. Serve in a flour tortilla for an unusual meatless burrito.

¼ cup (59 mL) olive oil
2 tablespoons (30 mL) red wine vinegar
1 tablespoon (15 mL) crushed red New Mexican chile, seeds included
1 tablespoon (15 mL) chopped fresh cilantro
¼ teaspoon (1.25 mL) crushed cumin seeds
4 ears of corn, cut into 2-inch (5 cm) lengths
1 bell pepper, stem and seeds removed, cut in wedges
2 large onions, cut into 1½-inch (3.5 cm) pieces
2 zucchini, cut in 1-inch (2.5 cm) rounds
1 cup (236 mL) cherry tomatoes

1. In a saucepan, combine the oil, vinegar, chile, cilantro, and cumin. Simmer for a couple of minutes to blend the flavors.
2. Thread the vegetables on skewers and grill for 7 to 10 minutes or until done, basting frequently with the marinade.

Blue Corn Vegetable Tamales
Yield: 24 tamales   Heat Scale: Mild

Blue corn, native to the Southwest, gives these tamales a distinctive, nutty taste. Make them smaller than an entrée tamale and serve them as a side dish instead of a vegetable.

6 green New Mexico chiles, roasted, peeled, stems and seeds removed, chopped
2 cups (473 mL) whole kernel corn
¾ cup (177 mL) shredded cheddar cheese
24 corn husks
2 cups (473 mL) coarse blue corn meal
1 teaspoon (5 mL) salt
⅓ cup (79 mL) lard or shortening
2 cups (473 mL) Classic Chicken Stock (page 46)

1. In a bowl, combine the chiles, corn, and cheese.

2. Soak the corn husks in water to soften them.

3. In a separate bowl, mix together the corn meal and salt. Slowly add the broth, stirring with a fork, until the mixture holds together. In a third bowl, whip the lard or shortening until fluffy. Add the masa to the shortening and continue to beat. Drop a teaspoonful (5 mL) of the dough into a glass of cold water. If the dough floats, it is ready. If it sinks, continue to beat it until it floats.

4. To assemble, select corn husks that measure about 5 × 8 inches (12.5 × 20 cm) or overlap smaller ones together. Place 2 tablespoons (30 mL) of the masa in the center of one husk and pat or spread the dough evenly into a 2 × 3–inch (5 × 7.5 cm) rectangle. Place about 2 to 3 tablespoons (30 to 45 mL) of the filling down the center and top with some cheese. Fold the husk around the masa and filling, being careful not to squeeze the tamale. There are two basic ways of folding the husks. The first is to take two strips of the corn husks and firmly tie each end of the tamale. This method works well with smaller corn husks. The second method is to fold the tapered end over the filled husk, and then fold the remaining end over it. Tie the tamale around the middle with a strip of the corn husk to keep the ends folded down. Assemble and fold all the tamales.

5. Place a rack in the bottom of a steamer or large pot. Make sure the rack is high enough to keep the tamales above the water. Place the tamales on the rack, folded side down, or, if the pot is large enough, stand them up. Do not pack them tightly, as they need room to expand as they cook. Cover the tamales with additional husks or a towel to absorb the moisture. Bring the water to a boil, reduce to a gentle boil, and steam for an hour for each dozen tamales or until done. To test for doneness, open one end of the husk. If the masa pulls away from the wrapper, it is done.

Texas Jalapeño Onion Rings

Yield: 4–6 servings   Heat Scale: Medium

These fiery onion rings go with any barbecued or grilled dish from Chapter 10, or you can serve them in place of french fries to spice up a hamburger plate.

5 jalapeño chiles, stems and seeds removed, chopped
12 ounces (336 mL) beer, at room temperature
3 large onions, peeled and sliced in ¼-inch (.5 cm) thick rings, separated
1⅓ cups (315 mL) all-purpose flour
1 egg, beaten
Vegetable oil for frying

1. In a blender, combine the chiles with a little of the beer and purée.

2. In a bowl, combine the puréed chiles, remaining beer, onions, flour, and egg.

3. Pour about 1 to 1½ inches (2.5 to 3.5 cm) of oil in a skillet and heat it to 350°F (180°C).

4. Dip the rings in the batter and drain the excess. Fry them in the oil until golden brown and transfer to paper towels to drain.

Double-Whammy Onion Rings

Yield: 8 servings   Heat Scale: Medium

Most onion rings from fast food restaurants feature "reformed" onions that are molded back into a ring. This recipe features actual rings of real onion, and I promise twice the heat with this tasty treat.

⅔ cup (158 mL) buttermilk
6 green New Mexican chiles, roasted, peeled, stems and seeds removed, chopped
2 large white onions, peeled and cut into ¼-inch (.5 cm) thick rings
6 cups (1.42 L) vegetable oil
4 cups (.95 L) all-purpose flour
Salt, to taste
Ground hot red New Mexican chile, such as chimayo, to taste

1. In a blender, blend the buttermilk and chile until only small bits of chile are still visible. Pour this mixture into a large bowl. Add the onions, completely coating each one. Cover the onion-buttermilk mixture and let it stand at room temperature for at least 4 hours, but not more than 5 hours.
2. Preheat the oven to 200°F (100°C).
3. Line a baking sheet with paper towels. In a deep pan, heat the oil to 325°F (165°C). Transfer the onion rings to a colander and let any excess liquid drain off. Thoroughly dredge one-fourth of the onion rings in flour. The more flour that sticks, the better.
4. Fry the onion rings in the oil until golden brown, 3 to 4 minutes. Using tongs, transfer the onion rings to the paper towels. Repeat until all the rings are fried. Keep the rings warm in the oven while you fry the other batches. Sprinkle with salt and dust lightly with ground red chile.

Calabrian Peppers

Yield: 4 servings   Heat Scale: Varies

This dish can be prepared with any Italian peppers of a decent size. Even bell peppers can be used, but be sure to add some crushed hot peperoncino to obtain that classic Calabrian heat level.

3 tablespoons (45 mL) extra virgin olive oil
4 medium to large fresh red Italian peppers, washed, quartered, stems and seeds removed (or substitute red jalapeños)
1 ounce (28 g) grated pecorino cheese
1 ounce (28 g) grated white bread crumbs
1 tablespoon (15 mL) fresh capers
1 pinch dried oregano
Crushed red chile, to taste
Salt, to taste

1. In a large pan, heat the olive oil over medium heat. Cut the peppers in vertical slices and sauté them for about 5 minutes. Remove the peppers set them aside. Remove half of the olive oil from the pan and discard it. Add the cheese, bread crumbs, capers, oregano, crushed red chile, and salt. Stir to mix well, return the pepper strips to the pan, and cook for 2 minutes. Remove from the heat and let sit for about 10 minutes to blend the flavors.

Peperonata

Yield: 4 servings   Heat Scale: Medium

Although the peppers are prepared the same way here as in the previous recipe, the addition of tomatoes transforms this into a vegetable side dish that doubles as a pasta sauce. It is made all over Italy, but in the south the cooks add crushed hot peperoncino.

5 tablespoons (75 mL) olive oil
2 onions, peeled and chopped
4 red and yellow bell peppers; quartered; stems, seeds, and ribs removed; thinly sliced
1 clove garlic, peeled and minced
Salt, to taste
1 pound (454 g) ripe tomatoes, peeled and chopped
2 teaspoons (10 mL) crushed red chile, or more to taste
Freshly ground black pepper, to taste
1 tablespoon (15 mL) chopped Italian parsley

1. In a large pan, heat the olive oil over medium heat. Add the onions and sauté for 5 minutes, stirring well. Add the pepper strips, garlic, and salt and sauté for 10 minutes, stirring well. Add the tomatoes and crushed red chile, cover, and cook over low heat for about 30 minutes, stirring occasionally and making sure the mixture doesn't burn. Add pepper to taste and stir in the parsley.

Hot Zucchini with Sour Cream and Dill

Yield: 4–6 servings   Heat Scale: Mild

Vegetables from the regions of the Hungarian Plain are rarely served plain. Instead, herbs and various seeds, such as dill or caraway, are added, or they are cooked in a creamy sauce as in this recipe. These vegetables go well with veal or roast pork.

1 medium zucchini, julienned
½ teaspoon (2.5 mL) salt
2 tablespoons (30 mL) distilled white vinegar
2 tablespoons (30 mL) butter or vegetable oil
1 small onion, peeled and chopped
2 teaspoons (10 mL) hot Hungarian paprika
2 tablespoons (30 mL) finely chopped fresh dill (or substitute 2 teaspoons [10 mL] dried dill)
2 tablespoons (30 mL) all-purpose flour
⅓ cup (79 mL) sour cream

1. In a bowl, sprinkle the zucchini with the salt and vinegar and toss to coat. Let the mixture stand for 15 minutes. Drain off and reserve the liquid that accumulates.
2. In a skillet, heat the oil over medium heat. Add the onion and sauté until softened. Add the zucchini, paprika, and dill. Cover the pan and cook until the squash is done but still crisp, about 10 minutes.
3. In a bowl, mix together the flour and 3 tablespoons (45 mL) of the reserved zucchini liquid. Add this mixture to the zucchini and heat for a couple of minutes to cook the flour. Stir in the sour cream and cook, stirring gently, until the sauce has thickened.

Spiced Glazed Carrots with Dill

Yield: 6 servings   Heat Scale: Medium

The spice in this South African vegetable side dish comes from a big dollop of fresh ginger. It is particularly good with any type of roasted fowl. Watch it carefully toward the end of the cooking time, so the carrots don't burn; you may have to sprinkle in a few drops of water.

4 cups (.95 L) chopped carrots
2 tablespoons (30 mL) honey
1 tablespoon (15 mL) freshly grated ginger
1 jalapeño chile, stem and seeds removed, minced
⅓ cup (79 mL) butter
2 teaspoons (10 mL) grated orange zest
3 tablespoons (45 mL) fresh orange juice
2 teaspoons (10 mL) dill weed
1 teaspoon (5 mL) salt
¼ teaspoon (1.25 mL) freshly ground white pepper

1. Combine all the ingredients in a heavy, nonstick saucepan and add just enough water to barely cover. Bring the mixture to a boil, reduce the heat to a simmer, and simmer for 10 to 12 minutes, until the carrots are just tender and the water has evaporated.

Vegetables in Peanut Sauce

Yield: 4 servings   Heat Scale: Mild

This West African side dish can be served over rice as a vegetarian meal or as an accompaniment to a meat dish. Palm oil is a reddish oil extracted from the pulp of the fruit of the African palm. It has a distinct color and flavor, but because it is high in saturated fat, I suggest substituting a vegetable oil.

1 tablespoon (15 mL) palm or vegetable oil
1 cup (236 mL) chopped onion
3 garlic cloves, peeled and minced
¼ cup (59 mL) unsalted smooth peanut butter
2 pounds (1.1 kg) tomatoes, peeled, seeded, and puréed
1 teaspoon (5 mL) thyme
3½ cups (826 mL) water
2 hot green chiles, such as jalapeños, stems and seeds removed, chopped
½ cup (118 mL) Super-Rich Vegetable Stock (page 48), boiled and reduced to ¼ cup (59 mL)
¼ teaspoon (1.25 mL) ground allspice
1 teaspoon (5 mL) salt
⅔ cup (158 mL) Super-Rich Vegetable Stock (page 48)
2 carrots, sliced
2 cups (473 mL) shredded white cabbage
1 cup (236 mL) fresh okra, washed and trimmed
½ cup (118 mL) chopped red bell pepper

1. In a large, heavy skillet, heat the oil over medium heat. Add the onion and garlic and sauté for 3 minutes, stirring to prevent the garlic from burning. Stir in the peanut butter and tomatoes and simmer for 1 minute.
2. Add the thyme, water, chiles, reduced vegetable stock, allspice, and salt and bring the mixture to a boil. Reduce the heat to a simmer and simmer for 30 minutes, uncovered, stirring occasionally to make sure it doesn't burn. This is the sauce for the vegetables, and it should be just slightly thick.
3. In a medium saucepan, bring the ⅔ cup (158 mL) stock to a boil; add the carrots, cabbage, okra, and bell pepper and reduce the heat to a simmer. Cook the vegetables until they are just barely tender. Drain the vegetables and transfer them to a warm serving dish. Pour the sauce over the vegetables and serve immediately.

Timun Mesanten
(Chile- and Coconut-Braised Cucumbers)
Yield: 4–6 servings   Heat Scale: Medium

Serve this tasty recipe from Bali with spicy grilled fish or satay. The spices jazz up the bland cucumber, and the coconut milk adds a touch of richness. Because the dish tends to be rather soupy, serve a rice dish to help soak up some of the delicious sauce. Shallots are used frequently in Bali instead of the sharper yellow onions that are so prevalent in North America.

3 tablespoons (45 mL) vegetable oil
3 shallots, peeled and chopped
3 cloves garlic, peeled and minced
3 red serrano or jalapeño chiles, stems and seeds removed, minced
½ teaspoon (2.5 mL) shrimp paste
2 cups (473 mL) coconut milk
½ teaspoon (2.5 mL) white peppercorns, crushed
3 cucumbers, peeled, seeded, and cut into ½-inch (.5 cm) slices
Fried shallots for garnish (optional)

1. In a heavy skillet, heat the oil over medium heat. Add the shallots, garlic, and chiles. Reduce the heat to low and sauté for 2 minutes. Mix in the shrimp paste and simmer for 1 minute.
2. Pour in the coconut milk and bring the mixture to a boil. Reduce the heat and simmer for 3 minutes.
3. Add the white pepper and cucumbers and simmer, uncovered, until the cucumbers are tender and the sauce starts to thicken slightly, 5 to 7 minutes.

Smoky Eggplant, Country Style
Yield: 6 servings   Heat Scale: Medium

My favorite traveling culinary adventurer and recipe collector, Richard Sterling, discovered this unique dish in Cambodia. As he says, "This is a very typical Cambodian dish. People who roast their own chiles will appreciate its distinctive, smoky flavor. When I tasted it near the town of Udong, I was unable to get the recipe, but Sidney and Bopah Ke were kind enough to provide it."

1 large eggplant
½ pound (224 g) lean ground pork
1 green onions, peeled and chopped
1 clove garlic, peeled and minced
1 tablespoon (15 mL) fish sauce
1 tablespoon (15 mL) oyster sauce
1 tablespoon (15 mL) soy sauce
4 large shrimp, cooked, peeled, and chopped
Salt, to taste
Freshly ground black pepper, to taste
1 green onion, sliced
3 serrano or jalapeño chiles, stems and seeds removed, coarsely chopped

1. Pierce the eggplant several times with a fork. Holding the stem with tongs or a long fork, stand it up over hot coals (or a gas flame) until the skin on the bottom is thoroughly charred. Lay it down on its side and continue cooking in this manner, turning when necessary, to char the entire eggplant on the outside and cook it through on the inside. Wash off the black crust under cool running water. Tear the eggplant into manageable pieces, place them on a warm platter, and set aside.

2. In a large sauté pan or wok, combine the pork, chopped green onions, and garlic. Quickly brown the pork. Stir in the fish sauce, oyster sauce, and soy sauce and bring the mixture to a quick boil. Add the shrimp and heat through. Add salt and pepper to taste. Pour this mixture over the eggplant. Garnish with the sliced green onions and the chopped chiles.

Asparagus Sheaves Kambu

Yield: About 8 sheaves   Heat Scale: Mild

Richard Sterling collected this recipe when he was in Cambodia. Richard says, "Use slender, tender spears, with the lower third removed. If you don't want to make your own fish paste, you can buy it from any Chinese supermarket or fish monger. It is important that the chile paste have enough sugar content to taste. Thai style is good."

For the Fish Paste:
1 pound (454 g) firm white fish
1 tablespoon (15 mL) light soy sauce
1 tablespoon (15 mL) dry sherry
1 teaspoon (5 mL) ground fresh ginger
½ cup (118 mL) sliced green onions
2 egg whites
4 tablespoons (60 mL) cornstarch

1. In a blender or food processor, combine all the ingredients and blend to a paste. The paste should have the consistency of cookie dough. If it is not dry enough, add more cornstarch.

For the Asparagus:
1 pound (454 g) asparagus
2 cups (473 mL) vegetable oil
1 cup (236 mL) fish paste
4 teaspoons (20 mL) spicy catsup
Asian chile paste to taste

1. In a wok or other deep, heavy vessel, heat the oil over medium heat. Take 3 or 4 asparagus spears in one hand and about 2 or 3 tablespoons (30 or 45 mL) fish paste in the other. Wrap the fish paste around the middle of the sheave to bind it together. Drop it into the hot oil and deep-fry for about 3 minutes, or until the fish paste is set and just beginning to brown. Remove and drain the sheaves. Repeat, cooking three or four sheaves at a time. Combine the remaining fish sauce with chile paste and drizzle it over the cooked sheaves.

Mawk Mak Phet
(Stuffed Chile Peppers)

Yield: 4 servings   Heat Scale: Mild

These stuffed chiles are steamed in banana leaves in Laos, but sometimes the leaves are hard to find in the United States. I have found them in Asian and Latin American markets, even here in Albuquerque. If you can't find them in your area, steam the chiles in foil. Experiment with a variety of fillings, such as ground pork, ground beef, and rice.

8 poblano or fresh green New Mexican chiles
¾ pound (336 g) flounder, snapper, or any white fish fillets, flaked
½ cup (118 mL) cooked rice
4 green onions, chopped, green parts included
2 cloves garlic, peeled and minced
1 tablespoon (15 mL) fish sauce
1 teaspoon (5 mL) minced fresh ginger
Juice of 1 lemon
Banana leaves or aluminum foil

1. Slit each chile from the stem to the tip, being careful not to cut completely through the chile to the other side. Remove the membrane and the seeds.
2. In a bowl, combine the fish, rice, green onions, garlic, fish sauce, ginger, and lemon juice and toss until thoroughly mixed.
3. Stuff each chile with the mixture and wrap the chiles, two to a packet, tightly in the banana leaves or aluminum foil.
4. Place the packets in a bamboo steamer or colander over boiling water. Cover and steam for 20 to 25 minutes.
5. Serve the chiles with any juices from the packet poured over the top.

Pickled Mixed Vegetables

Yield: 4 servings   Heat Scale: Hot

This recipe hails from Thailand, where pickled vegetables are often served warm. This dish works well served with meat, poultry, or fish dishes.

2 cups (473 mL) rice vinegar
1 tablespoon (15 mL) white sugar
1 teaspoon (5 mL) salt
¼ cup (59 mL) cucumber slices
¼ cup (59 mL) cauliflower florets
¼ cup (59 mL) bite-size pieces red bell pepper
¼ cup (59 mL) bite-size pieces green bell pepper
¼ cup (59 mL) bite-size pieces carrots
¼ cup (59 mL) broccoli florets
¼ cup (59 mL) bite-size pieces celery
¼ cup (59 mL) bite-size pieces jicama
6 cloves garlic, peeled and finely chopped
6 fresh santaka chiles, stems and seeds removed, finely chopped (or substitute piquins or 10 serranos)
3 shallots, peeled and finely chopped
½ white onion, finely chopped
¾ cup (177 mL) peanut oil
⅓ cup (79 mL) sesame seeds, roasted in a dry skillet

1. In a large saucepan, bring the vinegar, sugar, and salt to a boil. Cook each vegetable separately in the mixture, until they are slightly cooked but still crunchy. Set the vegetables aside after they are cooked.

2. In a food processor, combine the garlic, chiles, and shallots and blend them to a paste. If the paste seems too thick, blend in a tablespoon (15 mL) of oil.

3. In a wok, heat the oil over high heat. Add the paste and fry for 2 to 3 minutes. Add the vegetables, and stir-fry for 30 seconds. Place the vegetables on a platter and sprinkle them with the toasted sesame seeds. Serve immediately or store them in airtight jars in the refrigerator.

Chile de Mango
(Mango Chile)

Yield: 4 servings   Heat Scale: Medium

This recipe is an unusual fruity and slightly spicy dish from Guerrero. Mango and chile have a natural affinity, as their flavors blend and meld to create a most delicious taste. Serve this dish with a chicken or fish entrée from Chapters 10 or 11.

7 guajillo chiles, toasted, stems and seeds removed
3 cloves garlic, peeled
½ teaspoon (2.5 mL) salt
3 tablespoons (45 mL) butter
6 ripe mangos, peeled and cut into small cubes

1. Place the toasted chiles in a small bowl and cover them with hot water. Soak them for 15 minutes. Drain the chiles and reserve the soaking water. Transfer the chiles to a blender. Add the garlic and salt and purée, adding a few tablespoons of the reserved soaking water if the chile mixture gets too thick.
2. In a small sauté pan, heat the butter over medium heat. Add the puréed chile mixture and simmer for 10 minutes. Remove the purée from the heat and allow it to cool.
3. When the mixture has cooled to room temperature, stir in the cubed mangos and serve.

Breadfruit Creole

Yield: 6 servings   Heat Scale: Medium

In this traditional recipe from "de islands," the addition of tomatoes earns it the appellation of Creole. This easily prepared, tasty recipe is a good accompaniment to any kind of grilled meat or fish. It will add a touch of the Caribbean to your next dinner party.

1 large or 2 medium fresh, ripe breadfruits, peeled, seeds removed, cut into 1-inch (2.5 cm) cubes
3 tablespoons (45 mL) vegetable oil
3 cloves garlic, peeled and minced
1 cup (236 mL) chopped onion
1 habanero chile, stem and seeds removed, minced
2 medium tomatoes, peeled and chopped
1 teaspoon (5 mL) dried thyme
½ teaspoon (2.5 mL) salt
¼ teaspoon (1.25 mL) freshly ground black pepper

1. Place the cubed breadfruit in a large saucepan, add enough water to cover, and bring to a boil. Reduce the heat to a low rolling boil, cover, and cook until the breadfruit is tender, 30 to 40 minutes. Transfer the breadfruit to a sieve and allow it to drain for 5 minutes.

2. In a large, heavy skillet, heat the oil over medium heat. Add the garlic, onion, and chile and sauté for 2 minutes.

3. Add breadfruit and the remaining ingredients and stir to blend. Partially cover the skillet and simmer for 15 to 20 minutes, until the breadfruit is tender.

Breadfruit Oil-Down

Yield: 6 servings   Heat Scale: Medium

This recipe hails from Barbados, although breadfruit is cooked this way on other islands as well. You should be able to find fresh breadfruit at Latin and West Indian markets; if not, buy the canned variety and rinse it before using. The Barbadian (as well as many other islands) method is to cook it in a manner called "oil-down." This method means the breadfruit has been cooked with coconut milk until all the liquid has been absorbed, leaving a small amount of coconut oil in the pan.

½ pound (224 g) salt pork or smoked ham, cubed
4 cups (.95 L) cold water, divided
1 tablespoon (15 mL) vegetable oil
1 cup (236 mL) chopped onion
1 leek or 5 green onions, white parts only, chopped
1 Scotch bonnet chile, seeds and stem removed, minced (or substitute habanero)
2 sprigs fresh thyme (or substitute 1 teaspoon [5 mL] dried)
4 cups (.95 L) coconut milk
3 pounds (1.36 kg) fresh breadfruit, peeled and cut into 3-inch (7.5 cm) cubes
Salt, to taste
Freshly ground black pepper, to taste

1. In a small saucepan, combine the salt pork and 2 cups (473 mL) of the water. Bring to a boil. Lower the heat to a simmer and cook the meat for 10 minutes. Drain the meat, rinse it, and set it aside.

2. In a large, heavy skillet, heat the oil over medium heat. Add the onion, leek, chiles, and thyme and sauté for 4 minutes. Pour the coconut milk into the saucepan and bring the mixture to a boil, then lower the heat and add the reserved salt pork and the breadfruit. Simmer the mixture, covered, for 25 to 30 minutes, or until the breadfruit is tender and the milk has been absorbed. There should only be a small amount of coconut oil left in the pan. Add salt and pepper to taste.

West Indies Plantains with Cheese

Yield: 4 servings   Heat Scale: Medium

Plantains can be broiled, boiled, mashed, or fried, and the incredible diversity of this fruit is only limited by your imagination. Joe Brown, a chef in Trinidad, even gave me a recipe for Island Lasagne in which the pasta was sliced plantains! This recipe, with a Continental flair, involves pouring a light cream sauce laced with cheese over the fried plantains. Another, simpler island variation would be to grate some Parmesan cheese over the lightly frying plantains. Try this rich recipe with grilled meat or fish.

2 tablespoons (30 mL) vegetable oil
1 tablespoon (15 mL) butter
3 ripe plantains, peeled and sliced lengthwise into uniform slices
2 tablespoons (30 mL) butter
1 tablespoon (15 mL) minced fresh Scotch bonnet chiles (or substitute habaneros or ½ teaspoon [2.5 mL] ground dried habanero) 2 tablespoons (30 mL) all-purpose flour
2 cups (473 mL) milk
⅛ teaspoon (.6 mL) freshly grated nutmeg
½ teaspoon (2.5 mL) salt
⅛ teaspoon (.6 mL) freshly ground white pepper
¾ cup (177 mL) grated sharp cheddar cheese
1 tablespoon (15 mL) grated Parmesan or romano cheese

1. Preheat the oven to 325°F (165°C).
2. In a large, heavy skillet, heat the oil and butter over medium heat. In several batches, add the sliced plantains and sauté them until they are golden brown, 1 to 1½ minutes. Do not crowd the plantains in the skillet.
3. Transfer the sautéed plantains to paper towels to drain.
4. In a small saucepan, melt the of butter over medium heat. Add the peppers and sprinkle in the flour. Stir the mixture for 30 seconds. Pour in the milk all at once, and stir constantly with a wire whisk until the mixture starts to thicken, 1 or 2 minutes.
5. Whisk in the nutmeg, salt, white pepper, and cheeses and simmer for 30 seconds or until the cheeses are blended into the mixture. Remove the mixture from the heat.
6. Arrange the sautéed plantains in a shallow 8-inch (20 cm) square ovenproof dish and pour the sauce evenly over the top of the plantains.
7. Bake, uncovered, for 20 to 25 minutes and serve hot.

Dried Fruit Curry

Yield: 4 servings   Heat Scale: Medium

This South African recipe shows the influence the East had on African cooking. Many recipes use dried fruits, rice, and spices from the East brought to Africa by the traders. Serve this dish with lamb.

¼ cup (59 mL) chopped dates
¼ cup (59 mL) chopped prunes
½ cup (118 mL) raisins
1 cup (236 mL) chopped dried apples
2 cups (473 mL) water
2 tablespoons (30 mL) vegetable oil
1 cup (236 mL) chopped onion
3 tablespoons (45 mL) Hurry Curry (page 29)
2 tablespoons (30 mL) lemon juice
2 tablespoons (30 mL) red wine vinegar
2 bananas, sliced
¼ cup (59 mL) chopped, salted peanuts

1. In a small, heavy saucepan, combine the dates, prunes, raisins, apples, and water. Bring the mixture to a boil, reduce the heat to a simmer, and simmer for 45 minutes. Stir the mixture occasionally to prevent burning.
2. In a skillet, heat the oil over medium heat. Add the onions and sauté for three minutes, until the onion starts to soften. Add the curry powder, cooked fruit, lemon juice, and vinegar and simmer for 2 minutes for the flavors to blend. If the mixture looks too dry, add a few tablespoons (30–45 mL) of water.
3. Place the fruit on a small platter, surround it with the bananas, and sprinkle it with the chopped nuts.

Pisang Kari
(Malaysian Banana Curry)

Yield: 4–6 servings   Heat Scale: Medium

Malaysia is believed to be the original home of the banana, or pisang, cultivated there for more than 4,000 years. Banana leaves are often used as plates for curry— at the Banana Leaf Apollo Restaurant in Singapore, for example. Do not use ripe bananas in this recipe.

4 large, unripe bananas
1 teaspoon (5 mL) salt
½ teaspoon (2.5 mL) ground turmeric
3 tablespoons (45 mL) ghee or vegetable oil
2 cups (473 mL) coconut milk
2 small, fresh, hot green chiles, such as serranos or jalapeño, stems and seeds removed, chopped
2 teaspoons (10 mL) pounded Bombay duck (optional)
½ teaspoon (2.5 mL) ground fenugreek
½ teaspoon (2.5 mL) crushed fennel seed
1 (1-inch [2.5 cm]) stick cinnamon
3 curry leaves, crushed (or substitute 1 bay leaf)
½ cup (118 mL) minced onion

1. Peel the bananas, halve them lengthwise, and sprinkle them with the salt and turmeric. In a skillet, heat the oil over medium-high heat. Add the bananas and sauté for 2 minutes on each side.
2. In another pan, combine the coconut milk, chiles, Bombay duck (if using), fenugreek, fennel, cinnamon, curry leaves, and onion. Cook over medium heat for 30 minutes, then add the bananas, decrease the heat to low, and cook, uncovered, for 10 minutes.

Pad Thai
Spicy Thai Noodles

Yield: 4–6 servings   Heat Scale: Mild

When I was a speaker at the famous Mohonk Mountain House in New Paltz, New York, enjoying a hot and spicy Asian weekend, Gloria Zimmerman was one of the guest chefs, and she prepared her recipe for Pad Thai. Gloria has studied Thai cuisine extensively and is a true master at preparing almost any dish. I thank Gloria for truly tingling my taste buds at the Mohonk.

½ cup (118 mL) vegetable oil
6 cloves garlic, peeled and finely chopped
1 cup (236 mL) small cooked shrimp
1 tablespoon (15 mL) sugar
3 tablespoons (45 mL) fish sauce
1½ tablespoons (22.5 mL) catsup
2 eggs, beaten
½ pound (224 g) rice vermicelli, soaked in hot water for 15 minutes and drained
1 cup (236 mL) bean sprouts, plus ½ cup (118 mL) for garnish
2 green onions, cut into 1-inch (2.5 cm) lengths
½ cup (118 mL) bean sprouts
1 tablespoon (15 mL) ground dried shrimp
2 tablespoons (30 mL) roasted peanuts, coarsely chopped
1 teaspoon (5 mL) dried red chile flakes
2 green onions, chopped
2 tablespoons (30 mL) chopped cilantro leaves
2 limes, sliced into ⅛-inch (.25 cm) circles

1. In a wok, heat the oil over high heat. Add the garlic and sauté until it is golden. Add the shrimp and stir-fry until it is heated through.
2. Quickly add the sugar, fish sauce, and catsup and stir until the sugar dissolves.
3. Add the beaten eggs, let them set slightly, then stir to scramble them.
4. Add the rice vermicelli, toss, and stir for 2 minutes. Toss in 1 cup (236 mL) of the bean sprouts and lengths of green onion, and stir until the sprouts are heated through. Turn the mixture onto a heated platter.
5. Place the remaining ½ cup (118 mL) bean sprouts along one side of the vermicelli mixture and sprinkle the noodles with the ground dried shrimp, peanuts, chile flakes, chopped green onions, and cilantro, in that order. Ring the platter with the rounds of sliced lime and serve.

Vegetarian Fried Noodles
(Sayur Mee Goreng)

Yield: 6 servings   Heat Scale: Medium

Serve this unusual and delicious dish from Malaysia with any Asian curry. The turmeric gives the noodles a lovely yellow hue that contrasts nicely with the red chiles.

2 teaspoons (10 mL) plus ½ teaspoon (2.5 mL) ground cayenne or piquin chiles, divided
1 teaspoon (5 mL) plus ¼ teaspoon (1.25 mL) ground turmeric, divided
2 potatoes, peeled, boiled, and chopped into ⅛-inch (.25 cm) cubes
4 tablespoons (60 mL) vegetable oil, divided
1 cup (236 mL) finely sliced onion
½ teaspoon (2.5 mL) fish sauce
2 fresh red serrano or jalapeño chiles, stems and seeds removed, sliced into rings
1 tablespoon (15 mL) soy sauce
½ pound (224 g) bean sprouts, washed and drained
4 pieces bean curd, fried and sliced
12 ounces (336 g) egg noodles, cooked and drained
2 eggs, beaten

1. In a small bowl, mix together 2 teaspoons (2 mL) of the ground chile, 1 teaspoon (5 mL) of the turmeric, and a little water to make a thick paste and set aside.
2. Mix the chopped potatoes with the remaining ground chile and the turmeric. Set aside.
3. In a wok or large skillet, heat 3 tablespoons (45 mL) of the oil over high heat. Add the onion and sauté until it is soft. Add the fish paste, reserved chile paste, fresh chiles, and soy sauce and stir-fry for 2 minutes.
4. Add the reserved potatoes and toss them in the pan for 1 minute. Add the bean sprouts, bean curd slices, and cooked noodles and gently toss until the noodles are coated with the stir-fry mixture.
5. Make a well in the center of the noodles, add the remaining oil (if necessary), and pour in the beaten eggs. Allow the eggs to cook undisturbed for a few seconds, and when they start to set, mix them in with the noodle mixture, gently tossing and stirring until the eggs are cooked.

FOURTEEN

Sweet Heat and Devilish Desserts

In 1996, Melissa Stock and I published a cookbook entitled *Sweet Heat*. We thought it was on the cutting edge of the hot and spicy movement in the United States, but we were years ahead of our time, and the cookbook tanked. Since then, sweet heat products have dominated the Scovie Awards Competition my company produces, winning two-thirds of the grand prizes over the past decade. These commercial products have included sweet hot sauces, spicy chocolate candies, chile-pistachio brittle (twice!), and a sweet-hot fruit jam. So maybe we predicted a food trend. Melissa assisted in the development and testing of the recipes in this chapter.

Included in my last chapter are tangy temptations such as fiery fruits, cookies caliente, candies of all kinds, mousses, flans, custards, puddings, cakes, pies, tarts, sorbets, and ice creams. It's not quite a cool-down finale, but it's certainly a spicy, sweet, and spectacular one!

Habanero-Infused Tropical Fruits with Rum

Yield: 6 servings   Heat Scale: Medium-Hot

This is my favorite combination of tropical fruits, but considering all the options, cooks should feel free to make substitutions based on seasonal availability. Guavas and exotic citrus fruits such as Jamaican ortaniques come to mind as possible additions to this mélange. Add just a little bit of sugar if this is not sweet enough.

1 habanero chile, stem and seeds removed, minced
1 ripe mango, peeled, pitted, and diced
2 ripe bananas, peeled and diced
1 ripe papaya, peeled, seeded, and diced
½ pineapple, peeled, cored, and diced
Juice of 3 limes
¼ cup (59 mL) dark rum

1. In a bowl, combine all the ingredients and mix well. Marinate in the refrigerator for at least 30 minutes.

Balsamic Strawbaneros with Minted Chantilly Cream

Yield: 4   Heat Scale: Medium

Forget peaches and cream! Here's a summer dessert you'll want to serve over and over again. The tartness of the strawberries works well with the sweet cream and habanero heat.

1 pint (946 g) ripened sweet strawberries, washed, hulled, and quartered
½ cup (118 mL) balsamic vinegar, plus more to taste
½ cup (118 mL) brown sugar, plus more to taste
3 tablespoons (45 mL) freshly chopped mint leaves, divided
¼ fresh habanero chile, minced
½ cup (118 mL) heavy whipping cream
2 tablespoons (30 mL) sugar

1. Put the prepared strawberries in a bowl and refrigerate them. In a medium mixing bowl, combine the balsamic vinegar with the brown sugar. Taste the mixture and add more vinegar or sugar until the balance of sweet and sour is to your liking. Add 2 tablespoons (30 mL) of the chopped mint leaves and the habanero, stir, and pour the mixture over the strawberries. Allow the strawberries to marinate for at least 30 minutes.
2. While the berries are marinating, whip the heavy cream with a wire whisk in a medium bowl. As the cream starts to form peaks, add the granulated sugar and the remaining chopped mint. To serve, spoon the strawberries into a bowl with a little of the marinade, and top with a dollop of the hot chantilly cream.

Strawberries with Tex-Mex Tequila and Black Pepper

Yield: 6 servings   Heat Scale: Mild

This is a shocking dessert if there ever was one, with the sharp flavors of the pepper tequila and black pepper strangely complementing the sweetness of the strawberries. Only a truly daring chilehead would serve this over one of our chile ice creams in this chapter. (Note: This recipe requires advance preparation.)

6 cups (1.42 L) halved strawberries
½ cup (118 mL) orange juice
¼ cup (59 mL) Tequila Enchilado (page 104)
2 teaspoons (10 mL) freshly ground black pepper
2 teaspoons (10 mL) balsamic vinegar
Mint sprigs for garnish

1. In a bowl, combine the strawberries, orange juice, tequila, black pepper, and balsamic vinegar and toss well. Cover and chill for 3 hours, stirring occasionally. Spoon the mixture into 6 small glass bowls and garnish with the mint sprigs.

Segmented Tangerines in Fiery Syrup Topped with Toasted Coconut

Yield: 4–6 servings   Heat Scale: Medium

Please remember to remove the habanero; since they are often colored orange, there could be serious consequences to mistaken identity. Toasting the coconut is optional, but it gives this dish an added, nutty flavor. Serve this dessert accompanied by cognac. (Note: This recipe requires advance preparation.)

1 cup (236 mL) freshly squeezed orange juice
¼ cup (59 mL) freshly squeezed lemon juice
½ cup (118 mL) sugar
1/16 teaspoon (.3 mL) salt
½ fresh habanero chile, stem and seeds removed, halved
2 cups (473 mL) fresh tangerine sections, cleaned well
½ cup (118 mL) grated fresh coconut

1. In a saucepan, combine the orange juice, lemon juice, sugar, salt, and habanero. Stir well and bring to a boil. Boil for 5 minutes. Add the tangerine sections and boil for 1 minute longer. Remove the pan from heat and place it in a cold water bath to chill the mixture. Remove the habanero at this point. Transfer the tangerines and syrup to a serving bowl, cover, and chill for at least 1 hour.
2. If desired, toast the coconut in a dry skillet, stirring with a wooden spoon, until the coconut is lightly browned. Serve the tangerine sections in glass bowls with the toasted coconut sprinkled on top.

Pears Quemado

Yield: 6 servings   Heat Scale: Medium

I have updated this 1975 recipe from the legendary John Philips Cranwell, the hilarious author of the very first collection of hot and spicy recipes, The Hellfire Cookbook. *Alas, it is long out of print, but we can still enjoy John's dessert. He wrote of this dish, "Frankly it is too good to leave out of any cookbook and far too appropriate to this specific one to be omitted. It is eaten with a small spoon from gold or silver saucers, if you have gold or silver saucers. China will serve. Quemado, which means a kind of burned drink, is literally fiery in every sense of the word. I suggest you serve it before or with the coffee. According to a legend, quemado is a lovers' potion. The fire in and on it reflects the fire in their eyes, souls, and bodies. Mayhap 'tis true. Mayhap if after two bowls each they are not stone cold drunk on the floor, they pass the remainder of the night in an ethereal, if fuzzy, lovers' paradise. I can't vouch for the legend, but this is a most unusual dish both in appearance and taste."*

2 lemons
1 fresh habanero chile, stem and seeds removed, halved
2 teaspoons (10 mL) sugar
4 whole cloves
1 (4-inch [10 cm]) stick cinnamon
⅔ cup (158 mL) light Barbados rum
⅔ cup (158 mL) cognac
6 tablespoons (90 mL) 151-proof Jamaica rum
3 ripe but firm pears
½ cup (118 mL) blanched almonds

1. Zest both lemons into a large bowl. Add the habanero halves and the juice of the lemons. Add the sugar, cloves, and cinnamon, and stir. Pour in the Barbados rum, the cognac, and the Jamaica rum. Allow this mixture to steep for 20 minutes at room temperature, occasionally gently stirring.
2. Meanwhile, peel and core the pears and cut them into 1-inch (2.5 cm) sections. About 15 minutes before you are ready to serve, remove the habanero halves and transfer the mixture to a saucepan. Cover the pan and bring the mixture to a simmer. Divide the pears among 6 very warm saucers and sprinkle the blanched almonds over them.
3. After the contents of the saucepan have simmered about 1 minute, remove the cover and ignite the mixture with a thrown match. ("The flames will rise so high you'll think you have opened Hell's front door," warns Cranwell.) Let the flames die down a little and ladle the blazing mixture over the pears and almonds. Serve while flames still rise from each dish.

Bananas in Rum Flambé

Yield: 8–10 servings   Heat Scale: Mild

The very name of this banana dessert conjures up memories for me. My parents, Dick and Barbara, regularly prepared it—without the chile—in the late 1950s. As kids, my brother Rick and I were entranced with the idea of setting food on fire! Sometimes if they were out of rum, Dick would substitute brandy or even blended whiskey. The bananas were always served with vanilla ice cream.

¼ cup (59 mL) melted butter
¾ cup (177 mL) brown sugar
1 teaspoon (5 mL) finely ground red New Mexican chile, such as chimayó
5 firm bananas, peeled and sliced lengthwise
¾ cup (177 mL) dark rum
Ground allspice to taste

1. In a large skillet, combine the butter, sugar, and chile over low heat. Add the bananas and cook gently until they are just soft, turning once.
2. Add the dark rum and allow it to heat up for a minute or two. Throw a lighted match into the skillet and set the bananas aflame. When the flame dies out, transfer the bananas to serving plates, remove the match, spoon some of the sauce over them, and sprinkle with the allspice.

Variation
Sprinkle the bananas with toasted coconut, too.

Grand Cayenne Good-Goods

Yield: 32 candies   Heat Scale: Medium

Bon bons, the official name of this confection, translates to "doubly good." You'll find this is the tastiest treat by any name and a perfect gift for your sweetheart on Valentine's Day or any other occasion. (Note: This recipe requires advance preparation.)

2 cups (473 mL) creme-filled chocolate cookie (such as Oreo) crumbs
½ cup (118 mL) confectioners' sugar
2 teaspoons (10 mL) ground cayenne
2 tablespoons (30 mL) unsweetened cocoa
2 tablespoons (30 mL) light corn syrup
⅓ cup (79 mL) Grand Marnier
1 cup (236 mL) chopped walnuts
3 tablespoons (45 mL) sugar
6 ounces (168 g) semisweet or white chocolate, melted

1. In a medium bowl, combine the cookie crumbs, confectioners' sugar, ground cayenne, cocoa, corn syrup, Grand Marnier, and walnuts. Blend the mixture well, then cover with plastic wrap and refrigerate for 1 hour or longer. Remove the dough from the refrigerator and shape it into 1-inch

(2.5 cm) balls. Put the sugar in a shallow bowl and roll the dough balls in it until they are well-coated . Store the balls in an airtight container for at least 1 day.

2. Line a baking sheet with waxed paper. Dip half of each ball in melted chocolate and place the balls ½ inch (1 cm) apart on the prepared baking sheet. Refrigerate until firm. Store in a tin in the refrigerator.

Devilish Divinity

Yield: 40 pieces   Heat Scale: Medium

This candy is light as air, but don't be fooled—it packs a powerful punch! This recipe is a tribute to all the chilehead grandmas out there—you know who you are! The cook will need a candy thermometer for this recipe.

2½ cups (591 mL) sugar
½ cup (118 mL) water
½ cup (118 mL) light corn syrup
2 large egg whites, at room temperature
1 pinch cream of tartar
¼ teaspoon (1.25 mL) ground habanero
1 cup (236 mL) finely chopped pine nuts
1½ teaspoon (2.5 mL) vanilla extract

1. In a medium heavy saucepan, combine the sugar, water, and corn syrup and cook over medium heat, stirring constantly with a wooden spoon, until the sugar is dissolved. Raise the heat to medium-high, place a candy thermometer inside the pan, and cook without stirring until the temperature of the candy reaches 265°F (130°C). This should take about 10 minutes.

2. Meanwhile, place the two egg whites in a mixing bowl and whip them with an electric mixer until they are frothy. Add the cream of tartar and habanero powder, and increase the speed of the mixer to beat the egg whites until they form firm peaks.

3. When the sugar mixture reaches 265°F (130°C), remove it from the heat. Slowly pour the sugar mixture into the center of the egg whites, continuing to mix on a slow speed. When all of the sugar mixture is in the bowl, increase the mixer speed and beat until the candy is firm, about 12 minutes. Stir in the pine nuts and the vanilla extract.

4. Line 2 baking sheets with waxed paper. Drop 2-inch (5 cm) wide spoonfuls of the candy onto the paper, leaving ample space between them. Let the candy set at room temperature until firm, then store it in an airtight container between sheets of waxed paper.

Picante Pirate Truffles

Yield: About 3 dozen truffles   Heat Scale: Medium-Hot

From the Caribbean island of Antigua comes this unique rum candy. You may roll these truffles in the minced nuts of your choice if you are not a coconut fan.

2 cups (473 mL) milk chocolate chips
⅓ cup (79 mL) butter
½ teaspoon (2.5 mL) ground habanero
¼ cup (59 mL) half-and-half
1 tablespoon (15 mL) rum
¼ cup (59 mL) minced mango
2 cups (473 mL) flaked coconut

1. In a microwave-safe bowl, combine the chocolate chips, butter, ground habanero, and half-and-half. Microwave at 50 percent power for 1 minute. Remove the bowl from the microwave and stir it. Continue to cook at 50 percent power in 30-second increments until the chocolate is smooth and well-blended. Stir in the rum and mango. Refrigerate the mixture for about 15 minutes.
2. When the mixture is almost hard, drop the candy by the teaspoonful into the coconut. Shape the candies into 1-inch (2.5 cm) balls with your fingers.

Cascabel Caramel Turtles

Yield: 24 turtles   Heat Scale: Medium

The word "cascabel" means rattle in Spanish. This full-flavored dried chile probably received its name because of its shape and the fact that its seeds rattle around when you shake it! These turtles are like no others you've tasted before. They offer a bit of sweet and a bit of heat to round out this most beloved candy.

24 soft caramels
2 tablespoons (30 mL) frozen whipped topping
Butter-flavored vegetable cooking spray
120 pecan halves, 24 remaining whole and the rest halved
4 ounces (112 g) semisweet chocolate chips
6 cascabel chiles, stems and seeds removed, ground in a spice mill until fine (or substitute 2 pasillas)

1. In a microwave-safe mixing bowl, combine the caramels and whipped topping and microwave at 50 percent power for 45 seconds. Remove the bowl from the microwave and stir. Repeat this process, cooking in 10-second increments until the mixture has melted and is smooth and well-blended. Let it cool slightly.
2. Spray a baking sheet lightly with the cooking spray. Place the pecan halves on the sheet and arrange the pecan quarters around them to form the turtles' heads and legs.

3. Carefully spoon the caramel mixture over each turtle, leaving the ends of the pecans showing. Set the baking sheet aside until the caramel is hard.
4. Put the chocolate chips in a microwave-safe bowl. Microwave at 50 percent power for 45 seconds., Remove the bowl from the microwave and stir. Repeat the process, cooking in 10-second increments, until the chocolate is melted and smooth. Stir in the ground cascabel, then let the chocolate mixture cool slightly.
5. Spoon the melted chocolate over the caramel, being careful not to cover the exposed ends of the pecans. Set aside until hard, then store the turtles in a covered container in a cool place.

Cashew Chile Brittle

Yield: About 50 or more pieces, depending on their size
Heat Scale: Medium

This crunchy treat puts a new bite into a traditional candy. It keeps for up to 2 weeks in an airtight container, although I doubt you'll be able to keep your friends and family from eating it all within a day or two!

2 tablespoons (30 mL) safflower oil
2 cups (473 mL) sugar
½ cup (118 mL) water
½ teaspoon (2.5 mL) cream of tartar
½ teaspoon (2.5 mL) ground green New Mexican chile
1 tablespoon (15 mL) ground red New Mexican chile
2 cups (473 mL) cashew nuts, shelled and toasted

1. Coat a rimmed baking sheet with the safflower oil.
2. In a medium saucepan, combine the sugar, water, cream of tartar, and ground chile. Cook the mixture over high heat, stirring constantly, until it turns a light golden color. Brush down the sides of the pan twice with a pastry brush dipped in water to prevent the mixture from crystallizing.
3. While stirring the mixture, add the cashews. When the cashews are completely coated, remove the caramel from the heat and pour it onto the oiled baking sheet, spreading it out with the wooden spoon. Do this as quickly as possible, as the candy sets fast! Relax for the next 30 minutes while the brittle cools. Break the brittle into pieces with your hands. Store the candy in airtight containers.

Not So English Toffee

Yield: About 36 pieces   Heat Scale: Medium-Hot

Preparing this candy is a snap! It's a delectable delight that would most definitely shock the queen. The best part of this treat is the slow afterburn from the candy that gets stuck in your back teeth. You'll need a candy thermometer for this recipe.

¾ cup (177 mL) finely chopped pecans or walnuts
1 cup (236 mL) unsalted butter
1 cup (236 mL) sugar
1 teaspoon (5 mL) ground habanero
2 tablespoons (30 mL) water
1 tablespoon (15 mL) light corn syrup
¼ pound (113 g) semisweet chocolate, coarsely chopped

1. Butter a 9 × 13–inch (27 × 32.5 cm) glass baking dish. Sprinkle half the nuts over the bottom.
2. In a medium heavy saucepan fitted with a candy thermometer, melt the butter over low heat. Whisk in the sugar; reduce the heat to low, and cook, stirring constantly, until the mixture comes to a rolling boil. Stir in the ground habanero, water, and corn syrup, mixing well. Continue to cook, stirring often, until the mixture reaches 290°F (145°C).
3. Pour the candy into the prepared pan, spreading it evenly with the back of a spoon. While the toffee is cooling, place the chocolate pieces in a small mixing bowl, and microwave on 50 percent power for 25 seconds, then remove and stir with a plastic spatula. Continue to microwave in 10-second increments until the chocolate is melted. Be careful not to burn the chocolate. Spread the chocolate over the top of the toffee and sprinkle on the remaining nuts. Refrigerate the candy until it sets. When the toffee is hard, cut it into squares and store it in a covered container.

Fast and Fierce Fudge

Yield: 4 dozen pieces   Heat Scale: Medium

There's no need for a messy double boiler with this easy recipe, which is perfect to give to your friends over the holidays.

3 cups (708 mL) semisweet chocolate chips
1 (14-ounce [392 g]) can sweetened condensed milk
1 tablespoon ground red New Mexican chile (chimayo preferred)
¼ cup (59 mL) butter, cut into pieces
1 cup (236 mL) chopped walnuts

1. Butter an 8-inch (20 cm) square baking dish.
2. In a 2-quart (1.9 L) glass bowl, combine the chocolate chips, condensed milk, ground chile, and butter. Microwave the mixture at 50 percent power for 4 to 5 minutes, stirring at 1½-minute intervals. Once the chocolate is

completely melted, remove the bowl from the microwave and stir in the walnuts. Pour this mixture into the prepared baking dish. Chill for at least 2 hours. Cut into squares and store in an airtight container.

Hot Hula Squares

Yield: About 16 pieces   Heat Scale: Hot

This candy combines two of the best products from Hawaii: coconut and macadamia nuts. It is especially wonderful with the addition of Scotch bonnets, which give each piece extra zip. Remember to be very careful when mincing these ferocious chiles. You may want use a food processor to chop them in the easiest and safest manner possible.

1 cup (236 mL) semisweet chocolate chips
2 tablespoons (30 mL) shortening
1 Scotch bonnet chile, stem and seeds removed, finely minced (or substitute habanero)
1 (14-ounce [392 g]) can light sweetened condensed milk
¼ ounce (7 g) unflavored gelatin
6 cups (1.42 L) flaked coconut
½ cup (118 mL) chopped macadamia nuts

1. Butter an 8-inch (20 cm) square glass baking pan, making sure to coat the sides and the bottom. In a microwave-safe mixing bowl, combine the chocolate chips, shortening, and habanero and cook at 50 percent power for 30 seconds. Remove the bowl from the microwave and stir. Repeat this process, cooking in 10-second increments, until the mixture is melted, smooth, and well-blended. Quickly spread half the chocolate mixture in the pan. Chill the pan in the refrigerator until it is hard. Set the other half of the chocolate mixture aside.
2. In a heavy saucepan, combine the milk and gelatin and bring it to a boil, stirring constantly to help the gelatin dissolve. When the gelatin is completely dissolved, remove the mixture from the heat and stir in the coconut and macadamia nuts. Let the mixture cook to a slightly warm temperature.
3. Remove the pan from the refrigerator. Spread the milk mixture over the chocolate in the pan, then spread the remaining chocolate mixture over the milk mixture. Set aside to cool. Cut the candy into 2-inch (5 cm) squares, then wrap each candy individually in colored foil.

The Honorable Biscochito from the Land of Enchantment

Yield: 4 to 5 dozen cookies   Heat Scale: Mild

These cookies are so distinctly New Mexican that despite the fact that they were copied directly from Old Mexican bizcochitos, they were named the New Mexico State Cookie in 1998. By the way, they are at their delicious best when spiced up just a little with native ground New Mexican chimayó chile. You can buy cookie cutters in Southwestern shapes online.

1 pound (454 g) butter, softened
1¾ cups (413 mL) sugar, divided
2 teaspoons (10 mL) anise seeds
2 eggs, beaten
6 cups (1.42 L) all-purpose flour
1 tablespoon (15 mL) baking powder
1 teaspoon (5 mL) salt
½ cup (118 mL) brandy
1 tablespoon (15 mL) ground cinnamon
1 teaspoon (5 mL) ground chimayó chile

1. Preheat the oven to 350°F (180°C).
2. In a bowl, cream together the butter, 1½ cups (354 g) of the sugar, and the anise seeds. Add the eggs and beat well.
3. In a separate bowl, sift together the flour, baking powder, and salt 3 times.
4. Add the flour mixture 1 cup (236 mL) at a time to the creamed butter, mixing well after each addition, until all the flour is used.
5. Pour the brandy over the dough and mix well. Lightly knead the dough until it holds together.
6. In a third bowl, combine the remaining sugar, the cinnamon, and the ground chile.
7. Roll out the dough ¼-inch (.5 cm) thick and cut it into fancy shapes, such as chiles, coyotes, or saguaro cacti (even if they don't grow in New Mexico). Dip each cookie in the cinnamon sugar and then bake on a baking sheet for 10 to 12 minutes or until golden brown.

Nuclear Macaroons

Yield: 2 dozen cookies   Heat Scale: Hot

The habanero raises the heat level of these cookies and makes them catch fire in the back of your throat. But don't worry, they're not too hot to enjoy, especially when followed by a milk chaser.

3 cups (708 mL) sweetened flaked coconut
1 cup (236 mL) macadamia nuts, chopped
1 cup (236 mL) light sweetened condensed milk
1 teaspoon (5 mL) vanilla extract
1 teaspoon (5 mL) ground habanero
2 egg whites
1 pinch salt

1. Preheat the oven to 350°F (180°C). Grease 2 large cookie sheets.
2. Place the coconut and macadamia nuts on a large baking sheet. Bake them until lightly toasted, stirring frequently, for about 10 minutes. Remove the pan from the oven and set aside.
3. In a large mixing bowl, combine the condensed milk, vanilla, and ground habanero. Add the coconut and macadamia nuts and combine well. Using an electric mixer, beat the egg whites and salt until stiff but not dry. Carefully fold the whites into the coconut mixture.
4. Drop the batter by rounded tablespoonfuls onto the prepared baking sheets. Bake for about 13 minutes, until the cookies are just barely golden brown. Cool completely on the baking sheet.

Habanero Mango-Walnut Cookies

Yield: 6 dozen cookies   Heat Scale: Hot

Another highly heated treat, these cookies are especially good since they combine my favorite fruit, the mango, with the equally fruity but fierce heat of the habanero. Substitute pine nuts for the walnuts for a nice change of pace.

4 cups (.95 L) all-purpose flour
2 cups (473 mL) sifted confectioners' sugar
1 cup (236 mL) cornstarch
2 cups (473 mL) butter
2 cups (473 mL) walnuts, chopped
2 egg yolks
½ teaspoon (2.5 mL) fresh minced habanero chile
1 tablespoon (15 mL) grated orange peel
5 tablespoons (75 mL) mango juice, divided
Sugar for dipping
1 (16-ounce [454 g]) tub vanilla cream cheese frosting

1. Preheat the oven to 350°F (180°C).
2. In a large mixing bowl, stir together the flour, confectioners' sugar, and cornstarch. Using two blunt-edged knives, cut in the butter until the

mixture resembles coarse crumbs. Stir in the nuts. In a separate bowl, combine the egg yolks, habanero, orange peel, and 4 tablespoons (60 mL) of the mango juice and mix well. Add the flour mixture, stirring until moistened. If necessary, add the remaining juice to moisten.

3. On a lightly floured surface, knead the dough until it forms a ball. Divide the dough into 1¼-inch (3 cm) balls. Arrange the balls on an ungreased baking sheet and flatten them by pressing each with the bottom of a glass to ¼-inch (.5 mL) thick, dipping the glass into sugar for each round.

4. Bake for 12 to 15 minutes or until the edges begin to brown. Remove the cookies from the baking sheet and cool them on a wire rack. Frost with the cream cheese vanilla frosting. If desired, garnish with finely grated orange peel.

Green Chile Chocolate Chunk Pecan Cookies

Yield: 3 dozen cookies   Heat Scale: Hot

Mrs. Fields, move over! There's a new chocolate chunk cookie in town, and it's hot! These cookies are a perfect addition to a Hot Luck party.

½ pound (224 g) unsalted butter
1 cup (236 mL) light brown sugar
¾ cup (177 mL) sugar
2 eggs, beaten
1 tablespoon (15 mL) vanilla extract
2½ cups (591 mL) all-purpose flour
½ teaspoon (2.5 mL) salt
½ teaspoon (2.5 mL) baking powder
½ teaspoon (2.5 mL) baking soda
4 tablespoons (60 mL) ground green chile
3 cups (708 mL) chocolate chunks
1 cup (236 mL) pecans

1. Preheat the oven to 375°F (190°C). Grease a baking sheet.

2. In a large mixing bowl, cream together the butter, brown sugar, sugar, eggs, and vanilla with an electric mixer. In a separate bowl, sift together the flour, salt, baking powder, baking soda, and ground green chile. Gradually add the flour mixture to the batter and beat until just combined and smooth. Add the chocolate chunks and nuts. Scoop the cookies onto the prepared baking sheet and bake until light golden-brown, about 10 minutes. Remove the cookies from the baking sheet while hot. Serve with milk—lots of milk.

Ancho-Chocolate Mousse with Grand Marnier

Yield: 6 servings   Heat Scale: Mild

Ah, there's nothing like a mousse to complete a dinner, and this one is spiked with the raisiny flavor of ancho chile. You can use other chiles, but only ground pasilla has a flavor similar to ancho.

4 ounces (112 g) sweet baking chocolate
4 (1-ounce [28 g]) squares semisweet chocolate
¼ cup (59 mL) Grand Marnier or other orange-flavored liqueur
1 teaspoon (5 mL) ground ancho chile (freshly ground preferred)
2 cups (473 mL) heavy cream
½ cup (118 mL) sifted confectioners' sugar
Semisweet chocolate curls for garnish

1. In a heavy saucepan, combine the chocolates, Grand Marnier, and ground ancho. Cook over low heat until the chocolate melts, stirring constantly. Remove from the heat and cool to lukewarm.
2. Beat the heavy cream, gradually adding the confectioners' sugar, until soft peaks form. Gently fold about one-fourth of the whipped cream into the chocolate, then fold in the remaining whipped cream. Spoon the mousse into individual serving dishes and chill until ready to serve. Garnish with semisweet chocolate curls.

Dark Chocolate, Red Chile Mousse with Lemon Liqueur

Yield: 4 servings   Heat Scale: Medium

Dare I mix the flavors of chocolate, lemon, and red chile? You bet! Here is a mousse that is extremely simple to make yet has a very complex taste. (Note: This recipe requires advance preparation.)

4 ounces (112 g) sweet, dark chocolate
2 ounces (56 g) unsweetened chocolate
7 tablespoons (105 mL) lemon liqueur, divided
1 teaspoon (5 mL) ground red New Mexican chile
5 eggs, separated
Lemon slices for garnish

1. Lightly butter a saucepan, place it over low heat, and add the 2 chocolates. As the chocolate starts to melt, add 5 tablespoons (75 mL) of the lemon liqueur and the ground chile. When the chocolate is completely melted, add the egg yolks, one at a time, mixing well after each addition. Remove the pan from heat and add the remaining 2 tablespoons (30 mL) lemon liqueur. Mix gently.
2. Beat the egg whites until they form soft peaks and fold them thoroughly into the chocolate mixture. Pour the mousse into a 2-quart (2 L) soufflé dish and refrigerate for at least 2 hours. Serve garnished with the lemon slices.

Powerful Pear and Chocolate Mousse

Yield: 6–8 servings   Heat Scale: Hot

Further exploring the range of chocolate in mousses, I combine it with pears and habaneros in this dessert. (Note: This recipe requires advance preparation.)

2 large, fresh California Bartlett pears, peeled, cored, and chopped
½ habanero chile, stem and seeds removed
1 (¼-ounce [7 g]) envelope unflavored gelatin
6 tablespoons (90 mL) sugar, divided
¼ teaspoon (1.25 mL) salt
3 large eggs, separated
1 ounce (28 g) semisweet chocolate, chopped
1 teaspoon (5 mL) vanilla
½ teaspoon (2.5 mL) unsweetened chocolate extract
⅛ teaspoon (.6 mL) ground cinnamon
½ cup (118 mL) heavy cream
Whipped cream and chocolate curls for garnish

1. In a food processor or blender, purée the pears and the habanero. Measure out 1¼ cups (295 mL). In the top part of a double boiler, combine the gelatin, 2 tablespoons (30 mL) of the sugar, and the salt. In a bowl, beat the egg yolks lightly and add them to the gelatin mixture, along with the puréed pears. Mix well. Add water to the bottom part of the double boiler and bring it to a boil.
2. Set the top part of the double boiler over the bottom part and cook, stirring constantly, for about 5 minutes, until the mixture is slightly thickened. Add the chocolate and stir until it melts. Remove the double boiler from the heat and stir in the vanilla, chocolate extract, and cinnamon. Let the mixture cool until it thickens slightly.
3. In a bowl, beat the egg whites until they form soft peaks. Gradually beat in the remaining 4 tablespoons (60 mL) sugar, beating to a soft meringue. In a separate bowl, use the same beater to beat the cream to soft peaks. Fold the meringue and cream into the thickened gelatin mixture. Turn the mousse into a soufflé dish about 6 inches (15 cm) in diameter and 3 inches (7.5 cm) deep or into a greased 1-quart (1 L) mold and chill until firm, at least 3 hours. Shortly before serving, garnish with the whipped cream and chocolate curls.

Pungent Plum and Peach Ambrosia

Yield: 6–8 servings   Heat Scale: Medium

Here's a fruit-dominated mousse if ever there was one. Also dominating is the soft burn of the ground chile as it's blended into the whipped cream. This recipe is extremely simple to make. (Note: This recipe requires advance preparation.)

2 cups (473 mL) heavy cream
⅓ cup (79 mL) confectioners' sugar
2 teaspoons (10 mL) vanilla
½ teaspoon (2.5 mL) ground habanero
2 cups (473 mL) pitted and diced ripe plums
2 bananas, peeled and sliced
1 cup (236 mL) peeled, pitted, and diced ripe peaches
⅓ cup (79 mL) pecan or walnut halves
2 navel oranges, peeled and sectioned
Plum slices for garnish
Peach slices for garnish

1. In a large bowl, whip the cream with the sugar, vanilla, and ground chile until stiff peaks form. Fold in the diced plums, bananas, diced peaches, nuts, and orange sections.
2. Spoon the mixture into a serving bowl and chill for at least 3 hours. Serve garnished with plum and peach slices.

Piñon Flan with Red Chile Caramel Sauce

Yield: 6 servings   Heat Scale: Mild

Flan is a traditional Mexican custard dessert that has been adopted by all parts of the Southwest. This version is flavored with two other native Southwestern ingredients: pine nuts and red chile.

2 cups (473 mL) sugar, divided
3½ cups (826 mL) whole milk
1 vanilla bean
6 eggs
1 teaspoon (5 mL) ground cinnamon
1 teaspoon (5 mL) ground nutmeg
1 teaspoon (5 mL) ground ginger
1 teaspoon (5 mL) ground red New Mexican chile
1 tablespoon (15 mL) dark rum
1 cup (236 mL) whole shelled pine nuts

1. Preheat the oven to 350°F (180°C).
2. In a heavy saucepan, combine 1 cup (236 mL) of the sugar and ⅔ cup (158 mL) water. Cook, stirring, over a low heat, until the sugar is dissolved. Increase the heat and boil until the mixture turns light brown. Reduce the heat and simmer until the syrup is an amber color, swirling the pan

occasionally to push any crystals back in the syrup. Allow the syrup to cool slightly and pour it evenly into six warmed custard cups so that this caramel sauce coats them.

3. In a separate saucepan, scald the milk and vanilla bean in a pan. Remove the pan from the heat and allow the milk to cool. Remove the vanilla bean.

4. In a bowl, beat together the eggs, cinnamon, nutmeg, ginger, ground chile, and rum until foamy. Whisk in the remaining sugar and the pine nuts. Gradually add the milk, stirring until the sugar is dissolved.

5. Pour the mixture into the custard cups. Place the cups in a pan with enough hot water to come halfway up the sides of the cups.

6. Bake for 60 to 70 minutes or until a thin knife inserted halfway between the center and the edge of the custard comes out clean.

7. To serve, run a thin knife around the outside of a cup and invert the custard onto a dish. The pine nuts should be on top. Let the custard sit at room temperature for 10 minutes to set before serving.

Coconut Ginger Flan with Ancho

Yield: 6 servings   Heat Scale: Mild

This recipe is adapted from Susana Trilling, who owns the Seasons of My Heart Cooking School at Rancho Aurora in Oaxaca, Mexico. She writes: "This is one of the favorite desserts of my students at Rancho Aurora. It's much better to make it a day ahead and chill it icy cold."

¼ cup (59 mL) plus 3 tablespoons (45 mL) sugar, divided
½ cup (118 mL) sliced almonds
2 (12-ounce [336 g]) cans coconut milk (not sweetened coconut syrup)
½ cup (118 mL) milk
6 eggs
5 egg yolks
¼ teaspoon (1.25 mL) vanilla extract
1 teaspoon (5 mL) ground ancho chile (freshly ground preferred)
1 tablespoon (15 mL) minced crystallized ginger

1. Preheat the oven to 350°F (180°C).

2. In a sauté pan, melt 3 tablespoons (45 mL) of the sugar over medium heat until it turns brown and bubbly; do not stir. Remove the pan from the heat and pour the melted sugar into a flan pan (a round, 9-inch [22.5 cm] pan) and rotate the pan so the sugar syrup completely covers the bottom. Place the almonds on the syrup and set the pan aside.

3. In a bowl, combine the coconut milk, remaining ¼ cup (59 mL) sugar, milk, eggs, egg yolks, vanilla, and ground ancho and whisk well. Add the ginger, stir well, and pour the mixture into the pan.

4. Place the pan in a water bath, cover it with aluminum foil, and bake for 1 hour. Remove the pan from the oven and chill the flan completely.

5. To serve, flip the pan over on a platter, garnish it with more ginger, and slice it thinly.

Raspberry Creme Brûlée with Jalapeño Vodka

Yield: 6 servings   Heat Scale: Mild

Cooking the custard on the stove rather than baking it produces a very soft and creamy texture. (Note: This recipe requires advance preparation.)

1 (12-ounce [336 g]) package frozen unsweetened raspberries, thawed and drained
¾ cup (177 mL) sugar, divided
2 teaspoons (10 mL) Chile-Flavored Vodka (page 105–106)
5 egg yolks
2 cups (473 mL) heavy cream
¼ teaspoon (1.25 mL) vanilla extract
5 teaspoons (25 mL) unsalted butter
⅓ cup (79 mL) firmly packed brown sugar

1. In a bowl, combine the berries with ¼ cup (59 mL) of the sugar and the vodka. Divide the mixture among six ¾-cup (177 mL) broiler-proof ramekins or custard cups.
2. In a heavy medium saucepan, whisk the egg yolks and the remaining ½ cup (118 mL) sugar until pale and thick, about 3 minutes. Add the cream and vanilla and mix well. Set the saucepan over medium heat and stir until the custard thickens, about 7 minutes. Do not boil. Add the butter and stir until it melts. Spoon this mixture over the berries. Cover and refrigerate at least 4 hours or overnight.
3. Preheat the broiler. Press the brown sugar through a sieve over the custards. Broil until the sugar begins to melt and caramelize, about 2 minutes. Chill 3 for hours.

Bread Pudding with Chocolate and Chile Powder

Yield: 6–8 servings   Heat Scale: Medium

Jasmine DeLuisa of Las Vegas graciously contributed this recipe. She suggests serving this dessert with espresso. Use ground chiltepn in this recipe for heat but little or no change in flavor.

1 (8-ounce [224 g]) baguette, cut into ¼-inch (.5 cm) thick rounds
½ cup (118 mL) unsalted butter, melted
3 cups (708 mL) heavy cream
1 cup (236 mL) milk
8 large egg yolks
2 large eggs
½ cup (118 mL) sugar
1 tablespoon (15 mL) vanilla extract
1 pinch salt
½ teaspoon (2.5 mL) ground habanero or chiltepn
8 ounces (224 g) bittersweet or semisweet chocolate, chopped and melted in a double boiler
Whipped cream for garnish
Ground allspice for garnish

1. Preheat the oven to 350°F (180°C).
2. Arrange the bread slices on a large baking sheet. Brush them with the melted butter. Bake until crisp, about 15 minutes. Remove the bread from the oven, leaving the oven on, and let it cool.
3. In a medium saucepan, heat the cream and milk over medium heat until it is just warm to the touch. In a bowl, whisk together the yolks, eggs, sugar, vanilla, salt, and ground chile. Gradually whisk in the warm cream mixture.
4. Place the melted chocolate in large bowl. Gradually whisk in the cream mixture until well blended. Stand the bread slices on their sides in a 9-inch (22.5 cm) round cake pan with 2-inch (5 cm) high sides. Pour the chocolate custard over the bread and let it stand until the bread softens and absorbs some of the custard, pressing the bread down occasionally, about 40 minutes.
5. Place the cake pan in large baking pan. Add enough hot water to the baking pan to come halfway up the sides of the cake pan. Bake until a knife inserted in the center of the pudding comes out clean, about 1 hour. Let cool slightly. To serve, spoon the pudding into dishes, top each serving with a dollop of whipped cream, and sprinkle a little allspice on top.

New Mexico Bread Pudding with Chimayó Chile

Yield: 10–12 servings   Heat Scale: Medium

Here's a Southwestern twist on bread pudding. The tequila, bolillo rolls, red chile, pine nuts, and pecans are familiar flavors of New Mexico. I prefer chimayó red chile, a hot chile from the northern part of the state. Why not serve it with hot chocolate? (Note: This recipe requires advance preparation.)

1 cup (236 mL) raisins
¼ cup (59 mL) tequila
11 ounces (308 g) day-old bolillo rolls, cut into ½ inch (1 cm) pieces (about 8 cups [1.9 L])
2½ cups (591 mL) heavy cream
2½ cups (591 mL) applesauce
1⅓ cups (315 mL) sugar
6 tablespoons (90 mL) unsalted butter, melted
3 large eggs
1 teaspoon (5 mL) ground cinnamon
½ teaspoon (2.5 mL) ground nutmeg
2 teaspoons (10 mL) ground New Mexican chimayó red chile
1⅓ cups (315 mL) chopped pecans
1 cup (236 mL) pine nuts
Vanilla ice cream for serving

1. In a small bowl, combine the raisins and tequila. Marinate for 1 hour. Drain the raisins.
2. Preheat the oven to 350°F (180°C). Generously butter a 12 × 12 × 2–inch (30 × 30 × 5 cm) baking pan. Place the bread in the pan.
3. In a large bowl, combine the cream, applesauce, sugar, butter, eggs, cinnamon, nutmeg, and ground chile and whisk to blend. Add the marinated raisins, pecans, and pine nuts. Pour this mixture over the bread in the pan. Cover the pan with aluminum foil. Bake until the center of the pudding is firm, about 1 hour. Let cool slightly. Spoon the pudding into bowls and top each serving with ice cream.

Rice Pudding with Coconut-Habanero-Mango Topping

Yield: 8–10 servings   Heat Scale: Medium

This tropical dessert should be served with brandy Alexanders. Non-imbibers can have a cappuccino.

6 eggs, beaten
1½ cups (354 mL) cooked white rice
¼ teaspoon (1.25 mL) salt
½ cup (118 mL) sugar
2 teaspoons (10 mL) vanilla extract
1½ teaspoons (7.5 mL) grated lemon zest
3½ cups (826 mL) milk
2 cups (473 mL) sliced fresh mango
1 tablespoon (15 mL) freshly squeezed lemon juice
2 tablespoons (30 mL) brandy
¼ habanero chile, puréed in a little water
1 cup (236 mL) sweetened shredded coconut

1. Preheat the oven to 350°F (180°C). Lightly butter a 2-quart (2 L) baking dish.
2. In a bowl, combine the eggs, rice, salt, sugar, vanilla, lemon zest, and milk and mix well. Pour this mixture into the prepared baking dish. Set the dish in a larger pan partially filled with hot water. Bake for 1 hour, or until the pudding is set. Remove the pan from the oven and let the pudding cool.
3. Meanwhile, combine the mangos, lemon juice, brandy, habanero, and coconut in a bowl. Cover and chill for 2 hours.
4. To serve, spoon the chilled mangos on top of the cooled pudding.

Serious Shortbread With Habanero-Infused Tropical Fruits with Rum

Yield: 12 servings   Heat Scale: Hot

Have you ever met a kiwi or mango that you haven't liked? I hope not, as they make up the bulk of this fantastic fruit topping that I've combined with our simple shortbread.

¾ cup (177 mL) butter
1½ cups (354 mL) all-purpose flour
⅓ cup (79 mL) confectioners' sugar
1 recipe Habanero-Infused Tropical Fruit with Rum (page 804)

1. Preheat the oven to 350°F (180°C).
2. In a large bowl, blend together the butter, flour, and sugar to make a soft dough. Pat the dough into a 10-inch (25 cm) quiche pan. Prick the loaf well. Bake for 15 to 20 minutes. Remove from the oven and cool on a wire rack.
3. Slice the bread and top each piece with some of the fruit sauce.

Not Your Aunt Edna's Fruitcake

Yield: 12 servings   Heat Scale: Medium

Before you turn the page and go on to another recipe, stop and give this a try! This is not the famed traveling fruitcake recipe. Nope, this is a green chile fruit cake, new and improved and spunkier than ever. The chile mangos are made in Thailand, where they are dried but still bend and are dusted with sugar and ground chile. In the United States, they can be found in Albertsons stores or Asian markets.

3 cups (708 mL) chopped pecans (about 12 ounces [336 g])
2 cups (473 mL) chopped candied pineapple (about 10 ounces [280 g])
¾ cup (177 mL) chopped dried chile mangos
⅓ cup (79 mL) chopped candied orange peel (about 1½ ounces [42 g])
1¾ cups (413 mL) plus 3 tablespoons (45 mL) all-purpose flour
1 cup (236 mL) butter, at room temperature
1 cup (236 mL) sugar
5 eggs
½ cup (118 mL) green chile, roasted, peeled, stems and seeds removed, chopped
1 tablespoon (15 mL) vanilla extract
1 tablespoon (15 mL) lemon extract
1 teaspoon (5 mL) banana extract
½ teaspoon (2.5 mL) baking powder
1 pinch salt
Confectioners' sugar for dusting

1. Position an oven rack in the lowest third of the oven, and preheat to 250°F (120°C). Grease and flour a 12-cup (2.8 L) bundt pan.
2. In a large bowl, combine the pecans, pineapple, mangos, orange peel, and 3 tablespoons (45 mL) of the flour. In another large bowl, cream together the butter and sugar with an electric mixer until light and fluffy. Beat in the eggs one at a time. Stir in the green chile and vanilla, lemon, and banana extracts. In a separate bowl, sift the remaining 1¾ cups (413 mL) flour with the baking powder and salt. Add the dry ingredients to the batter and stir until blended. Mix the fruit mixture into the batter.
3. Pour the batter into the prepared pan. Bake the cake until it turns golden brown and a toothpick inserted into the center comes out clean, about 2½ hours. Cool the cake in the pan on a rack for about 15 minutes, then turn it out onto the rack to cool completely. Dust with confectioners' sugar.

Hawaii Five O-So-Hot-Upside Down Cake

Yield: 8 servings   Heat Scale: Medium

Melissa collected this recipe on a trip to Maui. If possible, she suggests that you substitute fresh pineapple for the canned stuff. After tasting pineapple taken right off of the plant, she discovered there's almost nothing better than this fresh tropical treat.

¼ cup (59 mL) butter
¾ cup (177 mL) packed light brown sugar
1 (20-ounce [560 g]) can pineapple slices, drained
1 jalapeño chile, stem and seeds removed, chopped
10 maraschino cherries
10 pecan halves
1¼ cups (295 mL) sifted all-purpose flour
1¾ teaspoons (8.75 mL) baking powder
½ teaspoon (2.5 mL) salt
1 cup (236 mL) shortening
1 cup (236 mL) sugar
1 egg
½ cup (118 mL) plus 1 teaspoon (5 mL) milk
1¼ teaspoons (6.25 mL) vanilla extract
¼ teaspoon (1.25 mL) lemon extract
¾ teaspoon (3.75 mL) grated orange peel
¾ teaspoon (3.75 mL) grated lemon peel
½ cup (118 mL) shredded coconut

1. Preheat the oven to 350°F (180°C).
2. In a small saucepan, melt the butter. Pour the melted butter into a 9-inch (22.5 cm) cake pan. Mix in the brown sugar. Arrange the pineapple slices and jalapeño pieces close together in the mixture in a single layer.
3. Halve the remaining pineapple slices and stand them up around the sides of the pan. Place a cherry and a pecan half in the center of each slice. Set aside.
4. In a large mixing bowl, sift together the flour, baking powder, and salt. In a separate bowl, beat together the shortening and sugar with an electric mixer until light and fluffy. Beat in the egg. Add the flour mixture alternately with the milk, mixing well. Stir in the flavoring and peels and fold in the coconut. Spread the batter over the pineapple in the prepared pan. Bake for 55 to 65 minutes or until a toothpick inserted in the center of the cake comes out clean. Remove the cake from the oven and let it stand in the pan for 15 minutes. Loosen the edges carefully and invert the cake onto a serving plate.

Grand Marnier Cake with a Kick

Yield: 16 servings   Heat Scale: Mild

This three-level-high tower of heat is not only hot and tasty, it's smooth and sweet. You might want to substitute Kahlua for the Grand Marnier for a nice change.

For the Cake:
¾ cup (177 mL) butter, softened
2¼ cups (531 mL) sugar
4 eggs
2 (1-ounce [28 g]) envelopes premelted unsweetened chocolate
⅓ cup (79 mL) Grand Marnier
2¼ cups (531 mL) sifted cake flour
4 teaspoons (20 mL) ground green chile
1 teaspoon (5 mL) cream of tartar
½ teaspoon (2.5 mL) baking soda
¼ teaspoon (1.25 mL) salt
¾ cup (177 mL) milk

1. Preheat the oven to 350°F (180°C). Grease and flour 3 (9-inch [22.5 cm]) round cake pans.
2. In a bowl, whip the butter with an electric mixer at medium speed. Gradually add the sugar, beating well. Add the eggs, one at a time, beating well after each addition. Add the chocolate and Grand Marnier and beat until blended.
3. In a separate bowl, combine the flour, ground chile, cream of tartar, baking soda, and salt. Add the dry mixture to the creamed mixture in small amounts alternately with the milk, beginning and ending with the flour mixture. Mix well after each addition.
4. Pour the batter into the prepared cake pans. Bake for 18 to 23 minutes or until a wooden toothpick inserted in the cake center comes out clean. Cool the cakes in the pans for 10 minutes, remove them from the pans, and cool them completely on wire racks.

For the Chocolate Grand Marnier Frosting:
¼ cup (59 mL) butter, softened
1 (8-ounce [224 g]) package cream cheese, softened
1 (16-ounce [454 g]) package confectioners' sugar, sifted, divided
3 (1-ounce [28 g]) envelopes pre-melted unsweetened chocolate
¼ cup (59 mL) Grand Marnier
¾ cup (177 mL) chopped hazelnuts

1. In a large bowl, beat together the butter and cream cheese with an electric mixer at medium speed. Add 1 cup (236 mL) of the confectioners' sugar and the chocolate and beat at low speed until smooth. Gradually add the remaining confectioners' sugar and Grand Marnier, beating at low speed until the frosting is smooth enough to spread.
2. Stir ½ cup (118 mL) of the hazelnuts into 1 cup (236 mL) of the frosting and spread this mixture between the layers. Spread the remaining frosting on the top and sides of the cake. Sprinkle the remaining hazelnuts on top.

Tart, Hot Apple Pie

Yield: 8 servings   Heat Scale: Medium

Here's a dramatic transformation of a classic American dessert. A spicy apple pie may make your great-great-great grandmother turn over in her grave, but for me it's just a natural evolution in cuisine.

For the Crust:
2½ cups (591 mL) all-purpose flour
1 teaspoon (5 mL) salt
1 teaspoon (5 mL) sugar
½ cup (118 mL) chilled unsalted butter, cut into pieces
½ cup (118 mL) chilled solid vegetable shortening
1½ teaspoons (7.5 mL) apple cider vinegar
5 tablespoons (75 mL) ice water

1. In a food processor, combine the flour, salt, and sugar. Add the butter and shortening and process until the mixture resembles a coarse meal. In a small bowl, combine the vinegar and 2 tablespoons (30 mL) of the ice water. Add this mixture to the food processor. With the processor running, gradually add enough of the remaining water, 1 tablespoon (15 mL) at a time, to form moist clumps of dough. Divide the dough into two equal portions and form each into a ball. Flatten each ball into a disk. Wrap each disk in plastic wrap. Chill for 30 minutes.

For the Filling:
2⅔ cups (628 mL) apple cider
8 Granny Smith apples, peeled, cored, and sliced
2 Golden Delicious apples, peeled, cored, and sliced
½ cup (118 mL) chopped roasted green chile
1 cup (236 mL) sugar
¼ cup (59 mL) all-purpose flour
½ teaspoon (2.5 mL) ground cinnamon
¼ teaspoon (1.25 mL) ground mace
¼ teaspoon (1.25 mL) salt
4 teaspoons (20 mL) fresh lemon juice
3 tablespoons (45 mL) unsalted butter, cut into small pieces

1. Position an oven rack in the lowest third of the oven and preheat the oven to 425°F (220°C).
2. In a heavy saucepan, boil the cider until it's reduced to ⅔ cup (158 mL), about 25 minutes. Let the cider cool. In a large mixing bowl, combine the apples, chile, sugar, flour, cinnamon, mace, and salt. Add the reduced the cider and lemon juice and toss well. Set aside. Remove the dough from the refrigerator and, on a lightly floured surface, roll out 1 pie crust to a 14-inch (35 cm) round. Roll the dough over the rolling pin and transfer it to a 10-inch (25 cm) pie plate. Gently press the crust into place. Trim the edges, leaving a ½ inch (1 cm) overhang. Spoon the apple mixture into the

crust-lined pan, mounding the apples in the center. Dot the apples with the butter. Roll out the second crust to a 13-inch (32.5 cm) round. Roll the dough over the rolling pin and unroll it over the pie. Trim edges, leaving a ¾ inch (1.5 cm) overhang. Fold the overhang of the top crust under the edge of the bottom crust. Pinch the upper and bottom crust to seal. Crimp the edges to make a decorative border. Cut several slashes in the top crust to allow steam to escape. Cover the edges with foil so that they do not brown too quickly.

3. Bake the pie for 25 minutes. Reduce the oven temperature to 350°F (180°C). Continue baking until the filling bubbles, about 50 minutes longer. Remove the pie from the oven and let it cool. Serve the pie slightly warm.

Warm Chocolate Pecan Pie

Yield: 8–10 servings   Heat Scale: Medium

This recipe by Stella Fong was a winner in Chile Pepper *magazine's 14-recipe contest. The pie was even featured on the cover! I have added additional heat to the crust to make it a little more pungent.*

For the Warm Chocolate Pie Pastry:
1 cup (236 mL) unbleached all-purpose flour
2 tablespoons (30 mL) unsweetened cocoa
4 tablespoons (60 mL) sugar, divided
3 tablespoons (45 mL) ground red New Mexican chimayó chile
½ cup (118 mL) vegetable shortening
¼ cup (59 mL) unsalted butter
3 tablespoons (45 mL) cold water

1. In a food processor, combine the flour, cocoa, 2 tablespoons (30 mL) of the sugar, and the ground chile. Add the shortening. Cut the butter into chunks, add it to the food processor, and process it until it is cut into very tiny pieces, about 1 minute.

2. Add the water and continue to mix until the dough wraps itself around the blade and forms a ball.

3. Wrap the dough in plastic wrap and refrigerate it for at least 30 minutes. The pastry can be kept in the refrigerator for about a week, or it can be frozen for several months. If you freeze it, defrost it slowly in the refrigerator before using.

For the Pie Filling:
4 tablespoons (90 mL) butter
¼ cup (59 mL) commercial fudge sauce
3 eggs, beaten
¾ cup (177 mL) dark corn syrup
½ cup (118 mL) dark brown sugar
2 teaspoons (10 mL) ground red New Mexican chimayó chile
1 teaspoon (5 mL) vanilla extract
1¼ cups (295 mL) pecan halves

1. Preheat the oven to 425°F (220°C). Line a 9-inch (22.5 cm) pie pan with the chocolate pie pastry and set it aside.
2. In a microwave-safe bowl, combine the butter and hot fudge and microwave on high for about a minute. Set aside.
3. In a large mixing bowl, combine the eggs, corn syrup, sugar, fudge mixture, and vanilla. Stir in the pecans and pour the mixture into the pie shell. Bake the pie for 15 minutes, then reduce the heat to 350°F (180°C) and continue baking for an additional 30 minutes, or until the edges are set.

Pumpkin Pie with a Kiss of Cayenne

Yield: 6–8 servings   Heat Scale: Medium

Many people are flabbergasted when they read a recipe that contains lard. Contrary popular belief, a little indulgence with lard will not seriously harm you. It is my opinion that for a truly flaky pie crust, lard is almost always in the ingredient list.

For the Crust:
½ cup (118 mL) unsalted butter, cut into bits
3 tablespoons (45 mL) lard, cut into bits
1¾ cups (413 mL) all-purpose flour
⅓ cup (79 mL) cold water
¼ teaspoon (1.25 mL) salt
½ teaspoon (2.5 mL) sugar

1. Lightly butter a 9-inch (22.5 cm) pie plate.
2. In a deep bowl, cut the butter and lard pieces into the flour with a with a knife and fork until the mixture resembles a coarse meal. In a small bowl, dissolve the salt and sugar in the cold water. Stir the liquids into the flour to form a loose ball of dough.
3. On a lightly floured surface, knead the chunks of dough, distributing the butter and lard through the mixture with the heel of your palm. Re-form the dough into a ball, dust it lightly with flour, and chill for 30 minutes.
4. On a lightly floured surface, roll out the chilled dough into a rough 12-inch (30 cm) square about ¼-inch (.5 cm) thick. Fold the square down to one quarter diagonally, like a handkerchief. Place the dough in the center of the prepared pie plate. Unfold the dough, gently easing it into the bottom and along the sides of the plate.
5. Trim the dough hanging over the edge of the pie plate, leaving a ½-inch (1 cm) overlap. Fold this overlap back over the edge of the plate and pinch all around to make a decorative edge. Prick the bottom and sides of the dough with a fork and refrigerate it until the filling is complete.

For the Filling:
2 eggs
1 cup (236 mL) canned pumpkin purée
½ cup (118 mL) light brown sugar, firmly packed
½ teaspoon (2.5 mL) ground allspice
½ teaspoon (2.5 mL) ground cinnamon
¼ teaspoon (1.25 mL) ground ginger
2 teaspoons (10 mL) ground cayenne
¼ teaspoon (1.25 mL) salt
¾ cup (177 mL) light cream

1. Preheat the oven to 400°F (200°C).
2. In a bowl, beat the eggs with an electric mixer until they are frothy. Add the pumpkin and brown sugar and stir well. Add the spices and salt, then stir in the cream, blending thoroughly.
3. Four the filling into the pie shell. Place a sheet pan under the oven rack to catch drips and bake the pie for 45 to 50 minutes. Let the pie cool to set the filling.

For the Topping:
1 cup (236 mL) coarsely chopped pecans
2 tablespoons (30 mL) melted butter
1 teaspoon (5 mL) ground cayenne
¼ cup (59 mL) loosely packed light brown sugar
1 cup (236 mL) heavy cream, chilled
1 teaspoon (5 mL) sugar
1 tablespoon (15 mL) vanilla extract

1. In a small mixing bowl, toss together the pecans, butter, cayenne, and brown sugar. Spread this mixture evenly over the top of the cooled pumpkin pie.
2. In a separate bowl, whip the cream until it forms peaks. Stir in the sugar and vanilla. Place the pie under the broiler, approximately 4 inches (10 cm) from the heat, and broil for 2 minutes or less, until the top is bubbly. Do not let the crust brown too quickly. Top the pie with the whipped cream and serve.

Secret Habanero Lemon Meringue Pie

Yield: 8 servings   Heat Scale: Hot

The fruity heat of the habanero combined with the lemon forms the perfect tart and hot taste explosion! I call this a "secret" pie recipe because it can be made very quickly, but it tastes like it took all day.

For the Pie:
1 prepared, baked graham cracker pie crust
4 tablespoons (60 mL) cornstarch
4 tablespoons (60 mL) all-purpose flour
¼ teaspoon (1.25 mL) salt
1¼ cups (295 mL) sugar
1½ cups (354 mL) water
Grated zest of 1 lemon
¼ teaspoon (1.25 mL) ground habanero
2 tablespoons (30 mL) butter
4 egg yolks, lightly beaten

1. Preheat the oven to 425°F (220°C).
2. In a saucepan, mix together the cornstarch, flour, salt, sugar, and water. Cook over medium-high heat, stirring constantly, until thickened, 2 to 3 minutes. Remove the pan from the heat and stir in the lemon zest, ground habanero, and butter. Stir ½ cup (118 mL) of this mixture into the egg yolks, then stir the yolks into the remaining mixture. Return the pan to the heat and cook, stirring constantly, for another 3 minutes. Remove the lemon mixture from the heat and let it cool for a few minutes. Spread the pie filling in the crust and set it aside.

For the Meringue:
5 egg whites at room temperature
½ cup (118 mL) sugar
¼ teaspoon (1.25 mL) salt

1. In a mixing bowl, combine the egg whites and sugar. Place the bowl in a pan of hot water. Stir constantly, until the eggs feel warm, then add the salt. Remove the bowl from the hot water and beat the egg white mixture with an electric beater until the eggs are stiff and shiny. Spread the meringue over the filled pie shell, making sure the meringue touches the inner shell of the crust. Place the pie under the broiler for a minute or two. Remove and serve.

Cherrano Turnovers

Yield: 6 servings   Heat Scale: Medium

I've combined cherries and serranos to create cherrano turnovers. These little personal pies are great to bring along on picnics or to eat with some of the hot fruit-filled sorbets in this chapter. This is also one of the lower-fat selections; there's no guilt with this recipe.

Butter-flavored low-calorie cooking spray
1 (16-ounce [454 g]) can sour pitted cherries, undrained
2 tablespoons (30 mL) cornstarch
¼ cup (59 mL) frozen apple juice concentrate
2 serrano chiles, stems and seeds removed, minced (or substitute jalapeños)
2 tablespoons (30 mL) sugar, divided
1 teaspoon (5 mL) vanilla extract
6 sheets phyllo pastry
¾ teaspoon (3.75 mL) ground nutmeg

1. Preheat the oven to 400°F (200°C). Spray a baking sheet with the cooking spray.
2. In a small saucepan, combine the cherries, cornstarch, apple juice concentrate, and 1½ tablespoons (22.5 mL) of the sugar. Stir until the cornstarch is dissolved. Bring the mixture to a boil and cook, stirring constantly, for 1 minute. Remove the pan from the heat and add the vanilla extract. Let the mixture cool for 10 minutes.
3. Working with 1 phyllo sheet at a time, (keeping the others covered with a moistened cloth), spray the sheet with the cooking spray. Fold the phyllo sheet in half crosswise, then coat it again with the spray. Spoon ⅓ cup (79 mL) of the cherry mixture near one end of the sheet. Fold the edges inward and carefully roll up the phyllo, making about a 3 × 4–inch (7.5 × 10 cm) turnover. Place the turnover on the cookie sheet and repeat this process until all 6 of the turnovers are prepared.
4. In a separate bowl, combine the remaining sugar and the nutmeg. Spray the top of each turnover with cooking spray and sprinkle the sugar mixture evenly over each one. Bake the turnovers for 20 minutes, then remove them from the oven and cool them on a wire rack.

German Chocolate Piñon Pie with Pizzazz

Yield: 8 servings   Heat Scale: Medium

It's hard to beat the combination of chocolate, nuts, and coconut. Add some ground jalapeño, and you've got a powerfully wonderful dessert! I use a prepared crust in this recipe, but feel free to borrow any of the other crust recipes in this chapter if you feel like making your own.

4 ounces (112 g) sweet baking chocolate
¼ cup (59 mL) butter
1 (14-ounce [392 g]) can light sweetened condensed milk
2 eggs, lightly beaten
½ cup (118 mL) hot water
1 teaspoon (5 mL) vanilla extract
2 teaspoons (10 mL) ground jalapeño
⅛ teaspoon (.6 mL) salt
1 prepared 9-inch pie shell, unbaked
½ cup (118 mL) chopped pine nuts
1 cup (236 mL) unsweetened flaked coconut
1 jalapeño, stem and seeds removed, cut into rings

1. Preheat the oven to 350°F (180°C).
2. In a heavy sauce pan, melt the chocolate and butter over low heat. When the chocolate is melted, remove the pan from the heat transfer the chocolate mixture to a large mixing bowl. Add the condensed milk. Stir in the eggs, hot water, vanilla, ground jalapeño, and salt. Mix well until all of the ingredients are combined. Pour the mixture into the prepared crust, and top with the pine nuts and coconut. Bake for 35 to 45 minutes, or until the coconut is lightly browned. Garnish with the jalapeño rings and whipped cream, if desired.

Dangerous Daiquiri Pie

Yield: 8 servings   Heat Scale: Medium

This refreshing pie is great on a hot summer's night, although the red chiles within may heat things up even more! This pie is also wonderful when made with frozen lemonade and a shot of tequila. Bottoms up!

8 ounces (224 g) light cream cheese, softened
1 (14-ounce [392 g]) can light sweetened condensed milk
2 teaspoons (10 mL) ground red New Mexican chile
1 (6-ounce [168 g]) can frozen limeade concentrate
⅓ cup (79 mL) light rum
1 cup (236 mL) frozen whipped topping
1 9-inch prepared pie shell, baked according to the package instructions
Lime twists for garnish

1. In a medium-sized mixing bowl, beat the cream cheese with an electric mixer until it is fluffy. Mix in the condensed milk, ground chile, and lime-ade until the mixture is smooth. Mix in the rum and fold in the frozen whipped topping. Pour the pie filling into the crust, cover, and chill in the refrigerator for at least 2 hours. Garnish with the lime twists and serve.

Serrano Lime Tart
Yield: 8 servings   Heat Scale: Medium

This is a tropical tart of sorts, full of limes and pineapple juice and enough chile to "sweeten and heat" things up a bit. (Note: This recipe requires advance preparation.)

For the Crust:
1¼ cups (295 mL) unbleached all-purpose flour
2 tablespoons (30 mL) sugar
¼ teaspoon (1.25 mL) salt
½ cup (118 mL) chilled unsalted butter, cut into pieces
1 egg yolk
1 tablespoon (15 mL) cold water

1. In a food processor, combine the flour, sugar, and salt. Add the butter and pulse until the mixture resembles a coarse meal. Add the yolk and water and blend until the dough begins to clump together. Gather the dough into ball, then flatten it into a disk. Wrap the dough in plastic wrap and refrigerate for 30 minutes.
2. On a lightly floured surface, roll the dough out into a 13-inch (32.5 cm) round. Roll the dough over the rolling pin and transfer it to a 9-inch (22.5 cm) tart pan with a removable bottom. Press the dough into the pan and trim the edges. Freeze until firm, about 1 hour.
3. Preheat the oven to 400°F (200°C). Line the crust with foil, then fill it with dried beans or pie weights. Bake until the crust is set around its edges, about 12 minutes. Remove the beans and foil from the crust. Continue baking until the crust is golden in the center, about 14 minutes. Transfer the crust to a wire rack and cool completely.

For the Filling:
½ cup (118 mL) heavy cream
2 tablespoons (30 mL) cornstarch
2 large eggs
6 large egg yolks
¾ cup (177 mL) sugar
2 serrano chiles, stems and seeds removed, minced (or substitute jalapeños)
¾ cup (177 mL) fresh lime juice
½ cup (118 mL) pineapple juice
¼ cup (59 mL) unsalted butter
Lime peel strips rolled in sugar

1. In a bowl, whisk together the cream and cornstarch in bowl. Whisk in the eggs and yolks.
2. In a medium saucepan, combine the sugar, serranos, lime juice, pineapple juice, and butter over medium heat. Stir until the sugar dissolves and the butter melts. Bring to a boil and boil for 1 minute, whisking constantly. Strain the mixture into a bowl and let it cool slightly.
3. Spoon the filling into the tart shell. Chill overnight, and garnish with the lime peel before serving.

Piquin-Lemon Granita with Biscochitos

Yield: 6 serving   Heat Scale: Hot

Scoops of these icy-spicy lemon crystals with the hot red flecks can be served in wine glasses, to be savored slowly with the anise-scented, spiced-up biscochitos from New Mexico. The granita can also be served between the courses of an elaborate dinner. Either way, it should be accompanied by a chilled, crisp Riesling.

2 cups (473 mL) sugar
2 cups (473 mL) water
1 cup (236 mL) freshly squeezed lemon juice
3 small, fresh red piqun or chiltepn chiles, stems and seeds removed, minced extremely fine or puréed (or substitute rehydrated dried piquns or Asian chiles)
1 recipe The Honorable Biscochito from the Land of Enchantment (page 813)

1. In a saucepan, combine the sugar and water. Bring the mixture to a boil, then lower the heat and simmer for 5 to 6 minutes, or until the sugar has melted. Cool to room temperature. Add the lemon juice and chiles and mix until well blended.
2. Pour the mixture into ice cube trays or a shallow pan, cover with aluminum foil, and place it in the freezer. After 1 hour, check to see if the mixture has started to freeze. When it has, remove it from the freezer and break it up into ice crystals, using a dull knife or a metal spoon. Return the granita to the freezer. Check again in 30 minutes, and when the mixture has begun to freeze, repeat the chopping process. Do this at least once more to ensure that the mixture forms into tiny pellets of lemon ice. At serving time you may need to chop the mixture gently once more if the granita is frozen too solid.
3. Spoon the granita into parfait or wine glasses and serve it with the Biscochitos.

Blood Orange-Yellow Hot Sorbet

Yield: 6 servings   Heat Scale: Medium

Most blood oranges in the markets are imported from the Mediterranean, but there are California varieties with bright red pulp. Use fresh yellow wax hot chiles or substitute a combination of one banana chile and one jalapeño chile. You will need an ice cream maker for this recipe.

4 cups (.95 L) blood orange juice from 12 to 16 oranges, divided
2 yellow wax hot chiles, stems and seeds removed, chopped
1 cup (236 mL) sugar
Zest of 2 blood oranges
¼ cup (59 mL) toasted grated coconut

1. Strain the orange juice through a sieve into a bowl.
2. In a blender, combine 1 cup (236 mL) of the juice with the chiles and purée. Return the purée to the rest of the juice. Add the sugar and zest and stir until the sugar is entirely dissolved. Chill the mixture in the freezer for 30 minutes.
3. Freeze the mixture in an ice cream maker following the manufacturer's instructions. Serve the ice cream garnished with the coconut.

Key Lime Sorbet with a Heap of Heat

Yield: 6 servings   Heat Scale: Medium

I love Key limes, but they are sometimes hard to find. Check your local Latin market. This recipe works best with an ice cream maker, but you can also pour the sherbet mixture into a metal cake pan and freeze it until almost solid, about 6 hours. Then purée it in a blender and serve.

1¼ cups (295 mL) sugar
2½ cups (591 mL) water
1 cup (236 mL) freshly squeezed Key lime juice
¼ cup (59 mL) freshly squeezed orange juice
½ teaspoon (2.5 mL) ground habanero
½ teaspoon (2.5 mL) powdered gelatin
2 tablespoons (30 mL) cold water
Lime zest for garnish

1. In a saucepan, combine the sugar and water. Bring the mixture to a boil and boil for 5 minutes without stirring.
2. Remove the pan from the heat and stir in the lime juice, orange juice, and ground habanero.
3. In a separate small saucepan, sprinkle the gelatin over the cold water. Let the mixture stand for 1 minute to soften. Heat it over medium heat until the gelatin is dissolved. Stir the gelatin mixture into the lime juice mixture. Transfer the mixture to a bowl and chill in the freezer for 30 minutes. Freeze in an ice cream maker following the manufacturer's instructions. Serve with a sprinkle of lime zest.

Mango-Scotch Bonnet Sorbet

Yield: 6–8 servings   Heat Scale: Hot

There's just something about mangos and Scotch bonnets that makes them fit together. They're usually combined in chutneys and hot sauces, but here they are married in a hot sorbet that is made without an ice cream maker. (Note: This recipe requires advance preparation.)

2 large mangos, peeled and chopped
⅓ cup (79 mL) honey dissolved in 1½ cups (354 mL) warm water
1 Scotch bonnet chile, stem and seeds removed, minced (or substitute habanero)
2 tablespoons (30 mL) dark rum
¼ cup (59 mL) freshly squeezed lemon juice
Thin slices of mango for garnish

1. In a food processor or blender, purée the mangos. Add the honey water and blend the mixture until it is smooth. Pour all but ½ cup (118 mL) of the mixture into a bowl. Add the Scotch bonnet chile to the reserved mixture, and blend until puréed fine. Stir the chile mixture into the mango mixture with the rum and the lemon juice and pour the mixture into 2 ice cube trays without dividers or a wide, shallow bowl. Freeze the sorbet for 1 to 2 hours or until it is almost firm. Scoop the sorbet into the food processor, purée it, and return it to the trays or bowl. Freeze the sorbet for 2 to 4 hours, or until it is firm but not hard. Scoop it into dessert glasses and serve it garnished with the mango slices.

Mole-Tequila Sorbet

Yield: 4 servings   Heat Scale: Medium

The flavors of Mexican mole sauces infuse this chocolate-based sorbet. Of course, I couldn't use all the chiles and spices of mole, but this dessert will finish off any Mexican meal containing moles or other chile sauces. You will need an ice cream maker for this recipe.

¾ cup (177 mL) sugar
1½ cups (354 mL) room temperature water
1½ ounces (42 g) semisweet chocolate, melted
½ cup (118 mL) unsweetened cocoa
1½ tablespoons (22.5 mL) ground ancho or pasilla chile
½ teaspoon (2.5 mL) ground cinnamon
2 tablespoons (30 mL) Tequila Enchilado (page 104)
2 tablespoons (30 mL) chopped pine nuts

1. In a bowl, combine the sugar and water and whisk well. Pour half the sugar-water into a separate bowl. Whisk the melted chocolate, cocoa, ground chile, cinnamon, tequila, and salt into one of the sugar-water bowls. Add the remaining sugar-water and whisk until smooth. Freeze for 15 minutes.
2. Process the mixture in an ice cream maker according to the manufacturer's instructions. Serve immediately, garnished with the pine nuts.

Arizona Chiltepn Ice Cream

Yield: 20 or more servings   Heat Scale: Hot

This was quite a novelty when it was first served in 1988 for the symposium on wild chiles at the Desert Botanical Garden in Phoenix and at the Fiesta de Los Chiles at the Tucson Botanical Gardens. It is quite hot in the proportions given (despite the tendency of ice cream to cut the heat), so cooks may wish to reduce the quantity of chiltepns.

¼ cup (59 mL) fresh green chiltepns, thoroughly puréed (or substitute chiltepnes en escabeche or dried red chiltepns that have been rehydrated and puréed)
1 gallon (3.8 L) vanilla ice cream (French preferred—just kidding)

1. Combine both ingredients and mix thoroughly until green (or red) flecks appear throughout the ice cream. Serve in small portions and warn people about what they're eating.

Peach Sundaes with Cayenne Bourbon Sauce

Yield: 4 servings   Heat Scale: Medium

Here's a dessert with definite New Orleans overtones—bourbon, pecans, and cayenne. Only a daring host or hostess would serve one of the spicy ice creams in this chapter with the sauce.

1 tablespoon (15 mL) fresh lemon juice
3 large, firm, ripe peaches, peeled, pitted, and thinly sliced
6 tablespoons (90 mL) unsalted butter
½ cup (118 mL) firmly packed light brown sugar
½ teaspoon (2.5 mL) ground cayenne
3 tablespoons (45 mL) whipping cream
½ cup (118 mL) chopped toasted pecan pieces
1 tablespoon (15 mL) bourbon
1 pint (473 mL) vanilla ice cream

1. Place the lemon juice in a medium bowl. Add the peach slices and toss to coat with the juice.
2. In a medium heavy saucepan, melt the butter over medium heat. Add the brown sugar and cayenne and stir until the mixture thickens and bubbles. Add the cream 1 tablespoon (15 mL) at a time and stir until the sugar dissolves and the sauce becomes thick and smooth, about 3 minutes. Stir in the peaches, pecans, and bourbon. Cook until the sauce is heated through, stirring constantly, about 1 minute longer.
3. Scoop the ice cream into bowls. Spoon the sauce over it and serve.

Hawaiian Mango-Habanero-Macadamia Ice Cream
Yield: 6 servings   Heat Scale: Hot

Extra-ripe mangos are recommended when preparing this rich, creamy dessert. You will also need an ice cream maker.

2 cups (473 mL) heavy cream
1 cup (236 mL) whole milk
6 egg yolks
1 cup (236 mL) sugar
2 large, ripe mangos, peeled, pitted, and diced
½ habanero chile, stem and seeds removed, minced
2 teaspoons (10 mL) fresh lime juice
½ teaspoon (2.5 mL) lime zest
1 cup (236 mL) toasted and coarsely chopped unsalted macadamia nuts

1. In a saucepan, combine the cream and milk and bring to a boil. Turn off the heat. In a bowl, whisk together the yolks and sugar. Gradually whisk the hot cream into the yolk mixture and return it to the same saucepan. Cook, stirring, over low heat until the custard thickens and will coat the spoon lightly, about 5 minutes. Immediately transfer the custard to a blender. Add the mangos and habanero and blend until smooth. Chill the custard for 1 hour in the freezer, then stir in the remaining ingredients.
2. Process the custard in an ice cream maker according to the manufacturer's instructions. Serve immediately or freeze the ice cream in a covered container.

White Chocolate Ancho Chile Ice Cream

Yield: 1 quart (.95 L)   Heat Scale: Mild

This stunning ice cream comes from Suzy Dayton, former pastry chef at the Coyote Café, who served it at the Santa Fe Wine and Chile Festival.

3 ancho chiles, stems removed
½ teaspoon (2.5 mL) ground cinnamon
¼ teaspoon (1.25 mL) ground cloves
6 ounces (168 g) good quality white chocolate, such as Tobler or Lindt
2 cups (473 mL) milk
2 cups (473 mL) heavy cream
¾ cup (177 mL) sugar
1 vanilla bean
6 egg yolks
Cinnamon stick for garnish
Shaved semisweet chocolate for garnish

1. Cover the chiles with hot water and let them soak until pliable, about 15 minutes. Remove and discard the seeds. Place the chiles in a blender or food processor and purée them with a little of the soaking water. Stir in the cinnamon and cloves.
2. In a double boiler, melt the chocolate over hot water.
3. In a medium saucepan, combine the milk, cream, and sugar. Split the vanilla bean and scrape some of the seeds into the mixture. Bring the mixture to a boil.
4. Whisk the egg yolks, pouring in about one-third of the hot milk mixture as you do so. Reheat the remaining milk and add the egg yolks. Heat for 1 minute, whisking constantly.
5. Strain the mixture into a bowl. Stir in the chiles and chocolate and freeze for 15 minutes.
6. Freeze in an ice cream maker according to the manufacturer's instructions. Serve garnished with a cinnamon stick and the shaved chocolate.

Index

METRIC GUIDELINES

With the tables below and a little common sense, you'll have no trouble making these recipes using metric measuring instruments. We have rounded off the liters, milliliters, centimeters, and kilos to make conversion as simple as possible.

SOME BENCHMARKS—ALL YOU REALLY NEED TO KNOW

Water boils at 212°F
Water freezes at 32°F
325°F is the oven temperature for roasting
Your 15 mL measure replaces one tablespoon
Your 5 mL measure replaces one teaspoon
A 20 cm x 20 cm baking pan replaces a U.S. 8" x 8"
A 22.5 cm x 22.5 cm baking pan replaces a U.S. 9" x 9"
A 30 cm x 20 cm baking pan replaces a U.S. 12" x 8"
A 22.5 cm pie pan replaces a 9" pie pan
A 21.25 cm x 11.25 cm loaf pan replaces an 8" x 4" loaf pan
A 1.5 liter casserole, sauce pan, or soufflé dish replaces a 1½ qt dish
A 3 liter casserole, sauce pan, or soufflé dish replaces a 3 qt dish
5 cm is about 2 inches
1 pound is a little less than 500 gm
2 pounds is a little less than 1 kg

OVEN TEMPERATURES

175°F............80°C	350°F..........180°C
200°F..........100°C	375°F..........190°C
225°F..........110°C	400°F..........200°C
250°F..........120°C	425°F..........220°C
275°F..........140°C	450°F..........240°C
300°F..........150°C	500°F..........260°C

FAHRENHEIT TO U.K. GAS STOVE MARKS

275°F.........mark 1	425°F.........mark 7
300°F.........mark 2	450°F.........mark 8
325°F.........mark 3	475°F.........mark 9
350°F.........mark 4	
375°F.........mark 5	
400°F.........mark 6	

VOLUME

¼ cup...59 mL	4 cups (1 quart)..........................0.95 L
½ cup..118 mL	1.06 quarts..1 L
⅓ cup...79 mL	4 quarts (1 gallon).......................3.8 L
¾ cup..177 mL	
1 cup...236 mL	¼ teaspoon ....1.25 mL
1¼ cups ....295 mL	½ teaspoon ....2.5 mL
1½ cups ....354 mL	1 teaspoon ....5 mL
2 cups ....473 mL	1 tablespoon ....15 mL
2½ cups ....591 mL	2 tablespoons ....30 mL
3 cups ....708 mL	3 tablespoons ....45 mL

WEIGHT

1 oz...28 gm
2 oz...56 gm
¼ pound ....112 gm (4 oz)
1 pound ....454 gm
2 pounds.....................................1.1 kg
5 pounds.....................................2.3 kg

LENGTH

½ inch...1 cm
1 inch...2.5 cm
4 inches.......................................10 cm